SELECTED ILLUSTRATIONS  ...CATIONS

Starred (*) examples involve Canadian ... s.

THIRD CANADIAN EDITION

Microeconomics & Behaviour

ROBERT H. FRANK

IAN C. PARKER

McGraw-Hill Ryerson

Toronto   Montréal   Boston   Burr Ridge, IL   Dubuque, IA   Madison, WI
New York   San Francisco   St. Louis   Bangkok   Bogotá   Caracas
Kuala Lumpur   Lisbon   London   Madrid   Mexico City   Milan
New Delhi   Santiago   Seoul   Singapore   Sydney   Taipei

The McGraw·Hill Companies

McGraw-Hill Ryerson

Microeconomics and Behaviour
Third Canadian Edition

ISBN-13: 978-0-07-095166-2
ISBN-10: 0-07-095166-7

1 2 3 4 5 6 7 8 9 10   TCP   0 9 8 7

Printed and bound in Canada

EDITORIAL DIRECTOR: Joanna Cotton
PUBLISHER: Lynn Fisher
SPONSORING EDITOR: Bruce McIntosh
MARKETING MANAGER: Joy Armitage Taylor
SENIOR DEVELOPMENTAL EDITOR: Maria Chu
EDITORIAL ASSOCIATE: Stephanie Hess
SUPERVISING EDITOR: Graeme Powell
COPY EDITOR: Karen Rolfe
SENIOR PRODUCTION COORDINATOR: Madeleine Harrington
COVER DESIGN: ArtPlus Limited
COVER IMAGE: Getty Images/Photonica Collection
INTERIOR DESIGN: ArtPlus Limited
PAGE LAYOUT: ArtPlus Limited
PRINTER: Transcontinental Printing Group

Library and Archives Canada Cataloguing in Publication

Frank, Robert H.
   Microeconomics and behaviour / Robert H. Frank, Ian C. Parker. — 3rd Canadian ed.

Includes index.
ISBN-13: 978-0-07-095166-2
ISBN-10: 0-07-095166-7

   1. Microeconomics—Textbooks.   2. Economic man—Textbooks.
3. Self-interest—Textbooks.   4. Consumer behavior—Textbooks.
I. Parker, Ian C.   II. Title.

HB171.5.F72 2007   338.5   C2006-904976-9

For David, Jason, Christopher, and Hayden
R.F.

For Jacquie, Jackie, Josh, and Jamie
I.P.

ABOUT THE AUTHORS

Robert H. Frank received his B.S. in mathematics from Georgia Tech in 1966, then taught math and science for two years as a Peace Corps Volunteer in rural Nepal. He received his M.A. in statistics from the University of California at Berkeley in 1971, and his Ph.D. in economics in 1972, also from U.C. Berkeley. He is the Goldwin Smith Professor of Economics at Cornell University, where he has taught since 1972 and where he currently holds a joint appointment in the department of economics and the Johnson Graduate School of Management. During leaves of absence from Cornell, he served as chief economist for the Civil Aeronautics Board from 1978 to 1980 and was a Fellow at the Center for Advanced Study in the Behavioral Sciences in 1992–93. He has published on a variety of subjects, including price and wage discrimination, public utility pricing, the measurement of unemployment spell lengths, and the distributional consequences of direct foreign investment. For the past several years, his research has focused on rivalry and cooperation in economic and social behaviour. His books on these themes include *Choosing the Right Pond: Human Behavior and the Quest for Status* (Oxford University Press, 1985) and *Passions Within Reason: The Strategic Role of the Emotions* (W. W. Norton, 1988). He and Philip Cook are co-authors of *The Winner-Take-All Society* (The Free Press, 1995), which received a Critic's Choice Award and appeared on both the *New York Times* Notable Books list and *Business Week* Ten Best list for 1995. His most recent general interest publication is *Luxury Fever* (The Free Press, 1999). Professor Frank's books have been translated into eight languages. He has been awarded an Andrew W. Mellon Professorship (1987–1990), a Kenan Enterprise Award (1993), and a Merrill Scholars Program Outstanding Educator Citation (1991).

Ian C. Parker received his B.A.(Hons.) in economics and English from the University of Manitoba in 1966, and completed Masters programs in economics and in English at the University of Toronto in 1968. As a volunteer with Canadian University Service Overseas (CUSO), he then worked for three years as an economist with the National Development Corporation of Tanzania. He subsequently received his doctorate in economics from Yale University. Since 1975, he has taught at the University of Toronto. He has conducted economic research in East and West Africa and in Europe, and has served as an economic consultant in the area of media economics. Apart from his teaching in core economic theory courses, he has designed and taught courses on the economics of media, international economics, development economics, comparative economic systems, North American and European economic history, and the history of economic thought. He has published journal articles, book chapters and encyclopedia articles in these fields, as well as full-length studies of Canadian cigarette advertising and post-secondary education, and has edited or co-edited several books. His principal current research preoccupations include the economics of the Internet, the contributions of Keynes's theory of probability to the economics of information and uncertainty, and the theoretical and practical implications of fixed capital for the economics of communications systems.

CONTENTS

$U = X^\alpha Y^\beta$

PREFACE

In this third Canadian edition of *Microeconomics and Behaviour*, we have continued to build on the strengths of preceding editions of the work. We have also made a number of changes that we believe will make it even more useful and accessible. In its present form, we feel that *Microeconomics and Behaviour* offers at least ten significant advantages to Canadian students and instructors of intermediate microeconomics:

1. The largest number of Canadian examples and illustrations of any intermediate microeconomics text.
2. Unique Web-based resources, including the online *Basic Math Review*.
3. The "Economic Naturalist" approach to learning microeconomics.
4. The unobtrusive integration of basic elements of a strategic, game-theoretical approach *throughout* the text.
5. The most extensive and systematic treatment of behavioural, experimental, and evolutionary models of economic decision making.
6. A strong emphasis on "core" topics, combined with the most extensive treatment at the intermediate level of externalities, property rights, and the Coase Theorem; the economics of altruism, envy, and positional goods; search theory; and auctions and the "winner's curse."
7. The widest range and the greatest potential number of exercises and problems, and the most systematic use of "reinforcement" to support a problem-solving approach to learning the material.
8. Flexibility with regard to the level of mathematical difficulty of the course.
9. Flexibility in relation to course structure.
10. The most extensive and detailed appendices of any intermediate microeconomics text.

Microeconomics and Behaviour was the first, and remains the only, intermediate microeconomics text designed specifically for Canadian students. At a basic but important level, in every chapter students will encounter Canadian spelling, units of measurement, people, companies, places, historical examples, and, of course, applications of micro-economic principles to Canadian economic policy issues.

As previous editions have demonstrated, moreover, our purpose has not been to produce a narrow, insular text. Quite the contrary. In preparing all editions, we have included additional examples of a North American and global *comparative* nature, so that students can gain a clearer sense of how microeconomic principles work themselves out in different political, economic, and institutional contexts. For similar reasons, we have in this edition added further examples drawn from the new media and institutions that will condition the development of the global economy in the early decades of the 21st century.

We have constantly kept in mind that the primary objective in virtually all inter-mediate microeconomics courses is to enable students to acquire a mastery of the *core* of microeconomics. Microeconomics is an evolving discipline. This fact is reflected in the text, where students will encounter a number of topics that we regard as *durable* contributions on the frontiers of microeconomics. Yet, like any evolving field, micro-economics also has its share of "flavour of the month" analyses. We have made a conscious decision to eschew fad chasing in order to provide more thorough coverage of the *core* tools students will require in upper-level economics courses.

Microeconomic theory is the *lingua franca* of economists, and hence mastering microeconomics is to a considerable extent a process of language learning. As with learning any language, becoming fluent in economics requires not only mastery of the *basic tools and concepts*, but also acquisition of that intangible quality, *economic intuition*, regarding precisely where and how these tools should be applied.

In our experience, three elements are vital in developing students' economic intuition. The first is that the *examples* through which they learn the concepts are familiar ones, so that students can build on what they already know in grounding the concepts in their own experience. The second is *reinforcement*: repetition with variations of the *same* concept in different contexts. Students thus acquire not merely abstract knowledge, but rather a working knowledge of how the models function in different contexts and under varying assumptions. The third is *enjoyment*. Learning economics is hard work, but it does not have to be boring.

In preparing previous editions and this third edition, we have been mindful of some continuing trends in Canadian university finance that have had a direct impact on the teaching of upper-level economics courses. Many instructors and students confront high and rising course and lecture section enrolments, reduced classroom lecture hours per course, and a high proportion of one-term rather than year-long courses. Among the consequences have been an increased reliance on teaching assistants and growing pressure to download more of the tasks involved in learning the material onto the students themselves. If students are increasingly being asked to "teach themselves," however, then they need to be provided—in their text and in the so-called "ancillary" materials—with the means to do so. In the next two sections, "Continuing Strengths" and "New Features in this Edition," we outline our strategies to respond to these challenges.

CONTINUING STRENGTHS

1. Use of Canadian and Comparative Illustrations

It has been argued that "microeconomics is microeconomics," and that the origin of the examples used to illustrate microeconomic principles is unimportant. This text is evidence that we do not accept this view. Students who read an entire text with only a few (if any) Canadian illustrations may tend to assume that "microeconomics doesn't happen in Canada," or that if it does happen here it's probably not very important or interesting. Canadian illustrations have the dual advantage of drawing on situations that are (or should be) familiar and correcting the misperceptions induced by a dearth of Canadian applications of the principles.

There is a further, and in our view even more compelling, reason for using Canadian illustrations. Students who are presented with a wealth of institutional detail from, say, the United States can come to treat such detail as an accurate depiction of the Canadian economic system. Yet with regard to competition policy (as distinct from U.S. antitrust policy), legal environments, unions, agriculture, and the balance between public and private sectors, there are significant differences between the Canadian and U.S. systems. These differences matter. The use of Canadian illustrations ensures that students will be informed about Canadian institutions and policies, rather than being actively misinformed, if they assume that conclusions drawn from U. S. examples apply in the Canadian context. Moreover, our use of *comparative* examples highlights the implications of institutional differences across countries, both in North America and globally, for economic behaviour.

2. Combination of Rigour and Accessibility

Previous editions of the text have been praised for their combination of rigorous development of the theory and an engaging, readable style. We have used puzzles, humour, and arresting examples to involve students in the process of acquiring the concepts. Yet in our experience, one of the best ways of ensuring accessibility and "user-friendliness" is a rigorous approach to the theory. Rigour and accessibility are complements, not substitutes.

We have not equated rigour with a flood of inadequately motivated mathematical symbolism. Rather, we interpret rigour as "playing fair" with the student: carefully specifying the assumptions of the models; indicating clearly how mathematical formulas and diagrams mirror the economic realities they are intended to capture; developing the logic of the argument in explicit, step-by-step fashion; and showing what happens to our conclusions when we relax certain assumptions. We have found that rigour in this sense actually increases access to that elusive capacity known as "thinking like an economist," by developing students' "curiosity bump" and their capacity to solve new puzzles.

3. The Problem-Solving Approach

Before the growth of e-commerce, the three keys to retailing success used to be described as "location, location and location." In our view, three keys to mastering microeconomics are "practise, practise and practise." Every chapter contains an integrated set of *worked-out examples*; *in-chapter exercises* (with answers at the end of the chapter) that allow students to test their understanding of the material as they go; and *end-of-chapter questions and problems*, graduated in difficulty from simple to challenging. So do the eight substantial *chapter Appendices*. In addition, the *iStudy* Guide found on the Online Learning Centre, provides for each chapter a multipart *"Case to Consider," multiple-choice questions*, and *problems*, while the *Instructor's Manual* includes an extended "Homework Assignment," which can be assigned during the term or reserved for examination purposes. Similarly, the online *Basic Math Review*, described in more detail below in the "New Features" section, contains in each of its 11 modules a number of problems with fully worked-out solutions. No other text currently available provides this range of opportunities for students to practise and refine their skills and understanding.

4. Flexibility

The text package is designed for flexibility, in three respects:

- **Course Structure:** The text enables maximum flexibility in tailoring the course material to time constraints, desired degree of difficulty, and instructors' priorities. The core of a short one-term course is contained in 6 to 8 chapters (Chapters 3–5 and 9–11, to cover consumption and production theory and competitive market equilibrium; or Chapters 3–5 and 9–13, to cover imperfect competition models as well). Chapters 1 and 2 can be treated as the start of the course (if a quick but illuminating review of introductory microeconomics is required), *or* assigned as "Required Refresher" reading. Since they are incorporated into the text, the instructor has the option of teaching with them or assigning them as background reading, depending on the level of preparedness of the students. Similarly, *a thorough two-term core course* (including the above topics plus factor markets, general equilibrium, externalities and transaction costs, public goods and redistribution) requires only 12 (or fewer) chapters. It is common not to finish any text completely, but this text provides some realistic ways of making the course reading load manageable.

- **Suitability for a Range of Mathematical Levels:** The text is designed so that it can be used readily in a number of ways: for a course that requires calculus, for one that requires only basic high school mathematics, or for a course where some but not all students have calculus. Challenging end-of-chapter problems are indicated with a single asterisk (*), and problems requiring calculus are indicated with double asterisks (**). The calculus in the text, however, has been confined to footnotes and to the Chapter Appendices. Hence it is available for students who prefer or require it, but it does not present an obstacle for students who will not use it in the course.

- **The Role of the Appendices, the Web Supplements, and Basic Math Review:** The eight Appendices and the online Web Supplements and Basic Math Review play a crucial role in increasing the flexibility of the teaching package. The Appendices (at about 90 pages in length) are the most extensive in any intermediate microeconomics text. They develop the calculus basis of some of the central topics in careful, step-by-step fashion, with numerous examples and exercises. For courses using calculus, they will be an integral part of the course. For non-calculus courses, they can serve as background for the more ambitious students, while not breaking the flow of the course proper for the majority. The Appendices and Web Supplements also include some *less* mathematical topics (such as the optimal degree of product variety in Appendix 13, renewable and exhaustible resources in Appendix 15, and workplace health and safety in Web Supplement 14). These latter topics are important, but are often casualties of time pressures in core microeconomics courses. Their inclusion in the Appendices and Web Supplements increases flexibility of coverage.

The 90-page, 11-module online *Basic Math Review*, discussed in detail below under "New Features," provides a means for students to verify—and if necessary, to upgrade—their degree of preparedness for the mathematical requirements of the course.

5. Integration of a Strategic, Game-Theoretic Focus throughout the Text

The approach to game theory in virtually all current intermediate economics texts is to treat it as a special topic in the theory of the firm. The game theory discussion typically occurs either within the chapters on oligopoly and monopolistic competition or in a separate chapter adjacent to the imperfect competition chapters. Students tend to finish such a text with the notion that the strategic behaviour modelled by game theory is relevant only to the economics of the firm under conditions of imperfect competition.

We have adopted a different approach. The text is designed to illustrate that strategic behaviour pervades *all* economic activities, those of consumers as well as of firms. Concepts, theoretical components, and models reflective of a game-theoretic and strategic approach are developed not only in Chapter 13 ("Oligopoly and Monopolistic Competition") but also in Chapters 5, 6, 7, 8, 17, and 18; in Appendices 6 and 13; and in Web Supplement 14. In these chapters, students will learn how basic game-theoretic concepts can illuminate not only the strategic behaviour of the imperfectly competitive firm, but also such topics as positional goods; problems of credibility, commitment, and trust; workplace safety and relative wages; *self*-control; cooperator–defector interactions; bounded rationality; and the strategic value of being or appearing *non*rational.

The foregoing is not a complete list, but it should give a flavour of the ways in which the text unpacks game-theoretic elements from their imperfect-competition box and applies them to a wider range of economic strategic behaviour. Students are intended to come away from the text with an understanding that strategic behaviour is at the core (pun semi-intended) of economic activity, and that game-theoretical tools can be widely applied in understanding economic behaviour.

6. Extensive Analysis of "Frontier" Topics

Apart from its thorough coverage of the core of microeconomics, the text contains a thorough discussion of a number of frontier research areas in economics:

- The Coase Theorem, externalities, and property rights: what the theorem implies, and what it *doesn't* imply when there are costs of negotiation (Chapter 17).
- Basic results in experimental and behavioural economics (Chapters 1 and 8).
- Evolutionary economics (Chapter 7).
- The economics of altruism, envy, and positional goods (Chapters 5, 7, 17, and 18 and Web Supplement 14).
- Search theory, auctions, and the "winner's curse" (Appendix 6).

NEW FEATURES IN THIS EDITION

1. Reorganization, Streamlining, and the Web Supplements

In this edition, we have reorganized the text to increase its accessibility. Both Chapter 6, "The Economics of Information and Choice under Uncertainty," and Chapter 13, "Oligopoly and Monopolistic Competition," have been significantly reorganized. In Chapter 6, adverse selection, moral hazard, and statistical discrimination are now more closely linked to the theory of insurance. In Chapter 13, the discussion of the Chamberlinian model of monopolistic competition has been shifted from Appendix 13 into Chapter 13. In addition, we have integrated all Appendices directly into the text, immediately following the appropriate chapters, for ease of reference. We have also added new subheadings throughout the text, to provide more guideposts to the structure of the analysis. A number of the diagrams have been enlarged, to increase their impact and make them easier to absorb.

The Demand Curve

To do this, we begin with the basic *demand curve*, a simple mathematical relationship that tells how many lobsters buyers wish to purchase at various possible prices (holding all else constant). The curve *DD* depicted in Figure 2-1, for example, tells us that 4000 lobsters will be demanded at a price of $4 each, 1000 at a price of $10, and so on.

If a visitor from Mars were told only that lobsters sell for $4 each, he would have no way of knowing whether they were cheap or expensive. In 1900, a $4 lobster would have been out of reach of all but the wealthiest consumers. In 2020, in contrast, lobsters would be an incredible bargain at that price. Unless otherwise stated, the price on the vertical axis of the demand curve diagram will refer to the *real price* of the good, which means its price relative to the prices of all other goods and services. Thus, the prices on the

Real price of a product Its price relative to the prices of other goods and services.

To make space within the text for these changes *and* for the new material introduced in this edition, we have created a Web Supplement, accessible at the Online Learning Centre (OLC). The Web Supplement contains material, linked to the relevant text chapters, on price indices; the spatial model of monopolistic competition; the internal wage structure of firms; and occupational health and safety. A survey indicated that time pressures had squeezed these topics out of most courses, but their presence in the Web Supplement ensures that they are available for teachers and students when time permits. The Web Supplement will also provide a means of introducing new material between editions.

2. Expanded "Economic Naturalist" Features

Previous editions have stressed the importance of developing students' intuition and "curiosity bump." Once students come to appreciate that microeconomics is not just a set of theorems and results to be memorized and regurgitated at exam time, but rather a method of seeing and understanding how the world operates, they are well on their way to acquiring genuine economic intuition. What we have called the "economic naturalist" approach is one of the more effective ways we have found of developing this capacity. The approach is described in some detail in Section 1.7 of Chapter 1. In this edition, we have added a number of new Economic Naturalist cases. We now have 30 Economic Naturalist puzzles, using humorous or apparently paradoxical examples from common experience to highlight the working out of economic principles in practice. The Economic Naturalist examples are listed on the inside back cover.

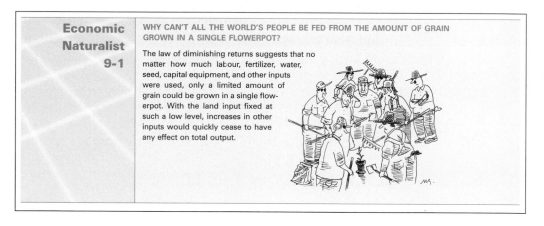

Economic Naturalist 9-1

WHY CAN'T ALL THE WORLD'S PEOPLE BE FED FROM THE AMOUNT OF GRAIN GROWN IN A SINGLE FLOWERPOT?

The law of diminishing returns suggests that no matter how much labour, fertilizer, water, seed, capital equipment, and other inputs were used, only a limited amount of grain could be grown in a single flowerpot. With the land input fixed at such a low level, increases in other inputs would quickly cease to have any effect on total output.

We have provided explanations for the puzzles in the Economic Naturalist examples, but we have not provided definitive answers. Indeed, we believe that readers may be able to provide better explanations, and that they can develop new Economic Naturalist examples that could appear in subsequent editions of *Microeconomics and Behaviour*. This is the basis for our **Challenge to the Reader**, which is open to both students and instructors. Send in your "new and improved" interpretations or your ideas for completely new Economic Naturalist questions (with a suggested explanation) to Ian Parker at parker@utsc.utoronto.ca. If your idea is the first received and is used in a subsequent edition, your contribution will be acknowledged in print. In addition, you will receive a package of economics books from MHR as a token of our thanks. We hope that in some courses entire classes may take up the challenge, either as a class assignment or for course bonus marks. In any event, we do expect that the puzzles will assist in grounding the concepts they illustrate.

3. New and Updated Canadian Examples

Microeconomics and Behaviour has more Canadian and comparative illustrations than any other intermediate microeconomics text. In this edition, we have added further Canadian examples and updated existing ones. The inside front cover provides a list of illustrations, and examples with significant Canadian content are marked with an asterisk (*) for ease of reference.

6.2 THE COSTLY-TO-FAKE PRINCIPLE

Costly-to-fake principle
For a signal to an adversary to be credible, it must be costly to fake.

For a signal between adversaries to be credible, it must be costly (or, more generally, difficult) to fake. If small toads could costlessly imitate the deep croak that is characteristic of big toads, a deep croak would no longer *be* characteristic of big toads. But they cannot. Big toads have a natural advantage, and it is that fact alone that enables deepness of croak to emerge as a reliable signal.

This *costly-to-fake principle* has clear application to signals between people. On April 12, 1980, Terry Fox, a 21-year-old cancer patient whose right leg had been amputated above the knee, set out from St. John's, Newfoundland, on his Marathon of Hope, a cross-Canada run to raise money for cancer research. The run had to be ended on September 1, 1980, just outside Thunder Bay, after 143 days and 5373 kilometres, because the cancer had spread. Terry died in hospital in New Westminster, B.C. on June 28, 1981. Since then, however, the total of money raised in his name for cancer research has reached over $360 million. Between 1985 and 1987, Rick Hansen's 40,000-kilometre around-the-world "Man in Motion" wheelchair tour raised public awareness of spinal cord injury paralysis and millions of dollars for research and rehabilitation.

---

4. Expanded Online *Basic Math Review*

The online *Basic Math Review* is unique among intermediate microeconomics text packages. We have devoted considerable effort and attention to ensuring that the mathematical underpinnings of the text assist students in comprehending the economics, rather than constituting a "barrier to entry." Yet even when calculus is a prerequisite or a co-requisite for admission, and especially when it is not, students come into intermediate microeconomics courses with widely varying skill levels, prior training in mathematics, and degrees of rustiness. Moreover, in our experience the most serious problems of comprehension at this level are not with topics such as the use of Lagrangeans to solve constrained maximization problems, but rather with the most elementary mathematical concepts, such as interpreting the economic significance of the slope of a line in the context of different models.

The *Basic Math Review* (available online in downloadable form at **www.mcgrawhill.ca/olc/frank**) has been designed to address this situation. It can be assigned (in part or in its entirety) at the beginning of the course, and referred to by students when the need arises as the course progresses. It thus provides both an "early warning system" and diagnostic basis for students from the outset of the course regarding areas where they need to upgrade their *basic* mathematical skills, *and* a self-contained reference centre for study and exam preparation.

In this edition, we have expanded the *Basic Math Review* so that it now includes over 90 pages in 11 modules: functions, graphs, and the coordinate system; linear equations; solving linear equation systems; using economic units; total, average, and marginal functions; elasticities; proportions, weights, and percentages; some special functions and formulas; interest and growth rates; "Calculus Results for the Non-Calculus Speaker"; and "Maximizing Total *Net* Benefit." Concepts in the *Basic Math Review* are cross-referenced to the text, so that students know where the concepts apply. The exposition and the practice problems are not narrowly mathematical, but include significant economic content. Among the topics dealt with are the following:

- Why, if quantity demanded is a function of price, do economists put quantity on the *horizontal* axis?
- Stock and flow variables.
- Why the slope of the budget line is $\Delta Y/\Delta X = -P_X/P_Y$.
- Why total revenue is sometimes measured as an area, and sometimes as the height of a line.
- Using economic units to relate profit maximization in input and output markets.
- The segment-ratio and "eyeballing" methods for calculating supply elasticity.

The *Basic Math Review* helps solve one of the major problems instructors confront in a time of larger class and section sizes, and restricted teaching contact hours: how to ensure that *all* students have the *basic minimum* of required mathematical competence, *without* losing class time.

5. New Text and Appendix Material

In addition to the expanded Economic Naturalist feature and the new and updated Canadian material, we have undertaken a thorough revision and updating of all chapters. We have added many new chapter-end questions and problems. We have also added a number of new passages, sections, tables, cartoons, and diagrams. They include the following:

- "The Budget Constraint and Expenditure Shares" (Chapter 3).
- The opportunity cost of goods in the interior of the affordable set (Chapter 3).
- "Goods and 'Bads,' Bliss, and 'Optimal' Pollution" (Appendix 3).
- "The Price-Consumption Curve and the Demand Curve: Some Extensions" (Appendix 4).
- Gross and net complements and substitutes (Appendix 4).
- The economics of dating (Chapter 6).
- "Moral Hazard" (Chapter 6).
- "From Production Functions to Cost Functions" (Appendix 10).
- Updates on Canadian merger policy and regulation (Chapter 12), tax treatment of capital gains and dividends (Chapter 15), and renewable and exhaustible resources (Appendix 15).

SUPPLEMENTS AND WEB-BASED RESOURCES

Instructor's Online Learning Centre (OLC)
The OLC at **www.mcgrawhill.ca/olc/frank** includes a password-protected website for instructors. The site offers downloadable supplements and access to PageOut, the McGraw-Hill Ryerson website development centre.

Instructor's CD-ROM
The Instructor's CD-ROM contains the Instructor's Manual, Computerized Test Bank, and PowerPoint Presentation:

- **Instructor's Manual:** Each chapter contains a Chapter Summary, a Chapter Outline, Teaching Suggestions, a list of Stumbling Blocks for Students, Answers to Text Questions for Review and Problems, and Homework Assignments.

- **Computerized Test Bank:** Contains multiple-choice questions, problems, and essay questions.

- **PowerPoint Presentation:** Offers a visual presentation of all the figures and tables from the text.

Student Supplements:

Student Online Learning Centre (OLC)
The OLC at **www.mcgrawhill.ca/olc/frank** offers study aids for each chapter, including Web Supplements, *Globe and Mail* Headline Links, Link to E-STAT and CANSIM II database, Key Terms, and Searchable Glossary.

In addition, an extensive online **Basic Math Review** is included. This online review can be used as an "early warning system" and diagnostic basis for students from the outset of the course regarding areas where they need to upgrade their basic math skills, and a self-contained reference centre for study and exam preparation.

www.mcgrawhill.ca/olc/frankparker_

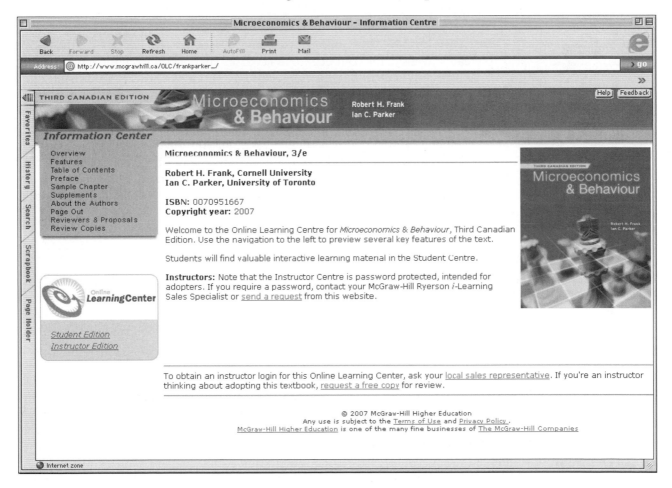

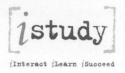

iStudy, prepared by Patrick Martin of University of Guelph

Many students find study guide materials to be indispensable in helping to understand the course material being learned. *iStudy* (the interactive study guide) will help students meet their goals by testing their cumulative understanding of the material they are studying; this will help students assess their mastery of the concepts they are learning.

Each chapter in *iStudy* contains an introductory section that provides a chapter overview titled Boiling Down the Chapter. This is followed by a Chapter Outline, Important Terms, a Case to Consider, Multiple-Choice Questions, and a section with Problems. The answers and grading are provided automatically when the student clicks the submit button. *iStudy* also contains "Interactive Graphs" which depict major graphs and instruct students to shift the curves, observe the outcomes, and derive relevant generalizations.

iStudy comprises a superb "tutor" for students. To see a free sample chapter, go to the OLC at **www.mcgrawhill.ca/olc/frank**. Full access can be purchased at the OLC or by purchasing a PIN code card through your campus bookstore.

Please contact your iLearning Sales Specialist for additional information regarding packaging access to **iStudy** with the student text.

Course Management

PageOut   McGraw-Hill Ryerson's course management system, PageOut, is the easiest way to create a website for your economics course. There is no need for HTML coding, graphic design, or a thick how-to book. Just fill in a series of boxes in plain English and click on one of our professional designs. In no time, your course is online!

For the integrated instructor, we offer *Microeconomics and Behaviour* content for complete online courses. Whatever your needs, you can customize the *Microeconomics and Behaviour* Online Learning Centre content and author your own online course materials. It is entirely up to you. You can offer online discussion and message boards that will complement your office hours, and reduce the lines outside your door. Content cartridges are also available for course management systems, such as **WebCT** and **Blackboard**. Ask your *i*Learning Sales Specialist for details.

Superior Service

Service takes on a whole new meaning with McGraw-Hill Ryerson and *Microeconomics and Behaviour*. More than just bringing you to the textbook, we have consistently raised the bar in terms of innovation and educational research—both in economics and in education in general. These investments in learning and the education community have helped us to understand the needs of students and educators across the country, and allowed us to foster the growth of truly innovative, integrated learning.

Integrated Learning   Your integrated Learning Sales Specialist is a McGraw-Hill Ryerson representative who has the experience, product knowledge, training, and support to help you assess and integrate any of our products, technology, and services into your course for optimum teaching and learning performance. Whether it's helping your students improve their grades, or putting your entire course online, your *i*Learning Sales Specialist is there to help you do it. Contact your *i*Learning Sales Specialist today to learn how to maximize all of McGraw-Hill Ryerson's resources!

_i_Learning Services   McGraw-Hill Ryerson offers a unique _i_Service package designed for Canadian faculty. Our mission is to equip providers of higher education with superior tools and resources required for excellence in teaching. For additional information, visit www.mcgrawhill.ca/highereducation/iservices or contact your local _i_Learning Sales Specialist.

Teaching, Learning & Technology Conference Series   The educational environment has changed tremendously in recent years, and McGraw-Hill Ryerson continues to be committed to helping you acquire the skills you need to succeed in this new milieu. Our innovative Teaching, Learning & Technology Conference Series brings faculty together from across Canada with 3M Teaching Excellence award winners to share teaching and learning best practices in a collaborative and stimulating environment. Preconference workshops on general topics, such as teaching large classes and technology integration, will also be offered. We will also work with you at your own institution to customize workshops that best suit the needs of your faculty.

ACKNOWLEDGEMENTS

In preparing the three Canadian editions of *Microeconomics and Behaviour*, we have benefitted considerably from the insights, constructive criticisms, and positive comments of the reviewers who became involved in the project. Their thoughtful suggestions have led to many improvements in the book, and we hope they are as pleased as we are with their influence on the final product.

Tikaram Adhikari	*University of Manitoba*
Nancy Carson	*Thompson Rivers University*
Ajit Dayanandan	*University of Northern British Columbia*
Ida Ferrara	*York University*
Veronique Flambard	*Grant MacEwan College*
Neill Fortune	*University of Windsor*
Michael Hoy	*University of Guelph*
Mobinul Huq	*University of Saskatchewan*
Hasan Imam	*Brock University*
Nural Islam	*Concordia University*
Irwin Lipnowski	*University of Manitoba*
Leigh MacDonald	*University of Western Ontario*
Varghese Manaloor	*University of Alberta*
Peter McCabe	*McMaster University*
Ted Mcdonald	*University of New Brunswick*
Rob Moir	*University of New Brunswick*
Garrett Milam	*Ryerson University*
Tomson Ogwang	*Brock University*
Abigail Payne	*McMaster University*
Charles Plourde	*York University*
Lance Shandler	*Kwantlen College University*
Ratna Shrestha	*University of British Columbia*
Paul Schure	*University of Victoria*
Khaled Soufani	*Concordia University*
Gary Tompkins	*University of Regina*
Linda Welling	*University of Victoria*

In the text, Figure 9-2 provides an image of a production function, with inputs being poured in at the top and outputs magically pouring out at the bottom. That abstract image is useful for some purposes, but it certainly does not fully capture all of the process of producing a book such as this one. It gives little sense of the teamwork that is involved from the outset, and particularly once the authors' golden prose is initially committed to CD-ROM, in producing the book you are now holding. We count ourselves as fortunate to have worked with the competent and very human team of editors assembled by McGraw-Hill Ryerson: Lynn Fisher, Publisher; Bruce McIntosh, Sponsoring Editor; Graeme Powell, Supervising Editor; and particularly Maria Chu, Senior Developmental Editor; Ron Doleman, Economics Editor; and Karen Rolfe, Copy Editor. All of them brought their special areas of expertise to bear on producing the best book possible, and so you as well as we owe them a debt of gratitude.

Robert H. Frank
Ian C. Parker

Part 1

In these first two chapters we review material from the introductory microeconomics course. Chapter 1 applies the principles of cost-benefit analysis to a variety of choices familiar from experience. Its goal is to give you an intuitive feel for what it means to "think like an economist."

Chapter 2 develops basic supply and demand analysis, our analytical tool for explaining the prices and quantities of goods traded in markets. We shall see that although unregulated markets may not always yield outcomes we like, under the right conditions they can often produce the best results attainable under the circumstances. In contrast, governmental efforts to help the poor by regulating prices and quantities can produce undesired side effects. Often, a better way to assist the poor is with programs that directly enlarge their incomes or earning capacity.

Chapter 1

THINKING LIKE AN ECONOMIST

Microeconomics
The study of how people choose under conditions of scarcity.

Microeconomics is the study of how people choose under conditions of scarcity. Hearing this definition for the first time, many people react by saying that the subject is of little real relevance to most citizens of developed countries, for whom, after all, material scarcity is largely a thing of the past.

This reaction, however, takes too narrow a view of scarcity. Even when material resources are abundant, other important resources are certain not to be. At his death, Aristotle Onassis was worth several billion dollars. He had more money than he could possibly spend and used it for such things as finely crafted whale ivory footrests for the barstools on his yacht. And yet, in an important sense, he confronted the problem of scarcity much more than many of us will ever have to. Onassis was the victim of *myasthenia gravis*, a debilitating and progressive neurological disease. For him, the scarcity that mattered was not money but time, energy, and the physical skill needed to carry out ordinary activities.

Time is a scarce resource for everyone, not just the terminally ill. In deciding which movies to see, for example, it is time, not the price of admission, that constrains many of us. With only a few free nights available each month, seeing one movie means not being able to see another, or not being able to have dinner with friends.

Time and money are not the only important scarce resources. Consider the economic choice you confront when a friend brings you along as his guest to a buffet brunch. It is an all-you-can-eat affair, and you must decide how to fill your plate. Even if you are not rich, money would be no object, since you can eat as much as you want for free. Nor is time an obstacle, since you have all afternoon and would rather spend it in the company of your friend than be anywhere else. The important scarce resource here is the capacity of your stomach. A smorgasbord of your favourite foods lies before you, and you must decide which to eat and in what quantities. Eating another waffle necessarily means having less room for more scrambled eggs. The fact that no money changes hands here does not make your choice any less an economic one.

Every choice involves important elements of scarcity. Sometimes the most relevant scarcity will be of monetary resources, but in many of our most pressing decisions it

"Oh, it's great here, all right, but I sort of feel uncomfortable in a place with no budget at all."

Drawing by D. Reilly; © 1976 The New Yorker Magazine, Inc.

will not. Coping with scarcity in one form or another is the essence of the human condition. Indeed, were it not for the problem of scarcity, life would be stripped of much of its intensity. For someone with an infinite lifetime and limitless material resources, hardly a single decision would ever matter.

In this chapter we examine some basic principles of microeconomic theory and see how an economist might apply them to a wide variety of choices involving scarcity. Later chapters more formally develop the theory. For now, our only goal is to get an intuitive feel for that distinctive mindset known as "thinking like an economist." And the best way to do that is to work through a series of problems familiar from actual experience.

1.1 THE COST-BENEFIT APPROACH TO DECISIONS

Many of the choices economists study can be posed in the form of the following question:

Should I do activity x?

For the choice confronting a moviegoer, ". . . do activity x?" might be, for example, ". . . see *Casablanca* tonight?" For the person attending the buffet brunch, it might be ". . . eat another waffle?" Economists answer such questions by comparing the costs and benefits of doing the activity in question. The decision rule we use is disarmingly simple. If $C(x)$ denotes the costs of doing x and $B(x)$ the benefits, it is:

If $B(x) > C(x)$, do x; otherwise don't.

To apply this rule, we need some way to define and measure costs and benefits. Monetary values are a useful common denominator for this purpose, even when the activity has nothing directly to do with money. We define $B(x)$ as the maximum dollar amount you would be willing to pay to do x. Often $B(x)$ will be a hypothetical magnitude, the amount of money you would be willing to pay if you had to, even though no money will actually change hands. $C(x)$, in turn, is the value of all the resources you must give up in order to do x. Here too $C(x)$ need not involve an explicit transfer of money to anyone.

For most decisions, at least some of the benefits or costs will not be readily available in monetary terms. To see how we proceed in such cases, consider the following simple decision.

Should I reprogram my stereo?

You have settled into a comfortable chair and are listening to a CD when you realize that the next two tracks on the CD are ones you dislike. If you had remembered, you would have programmed the CD player not to play them. But you didn't, and so you must decide whether to get up and skip the tracks or to stay put and wait it out.

The benefit of skipping the tracks is not having the songs you don't like blare at you. The cost, in turn, is the inconvenience of getting out of your chair. If you are extremely comfortable and the music is only mildly annoying, you will probably stay put. But if you haven't been settled for long or if the music is really bothersome, you are more likely to get up.

Even for simple decisions like this one, it is possible to translate the relevant costs and benefits into a monetary framework. Consider first the cost of getting out of your chair. If someone offered you one cent to get up out of a comfortable chair and there were no reason other than the penny to do it, would you take the offer? If you are like most people, you would not. But if someone offered you $1000, you would be on your feet in an instant. Somewhere between one cent and $1000 lies your reservation price, the minimum amount it would take to get you out of the chair.

To see where the threshold lies, imagine a mental auction with yourself in which you keep boosting the offer by small increments from one cent until you reach the point where it is barely worthwhile to get up. Where this point occurs will obviously depend on circumstance. If you are rich, it will tend to be higher than if you are poor, because a given amount of money will seem less important; if you feel energetic, it will be lower than if you feel tired; and so on. For the sake of discussion, suppose your *reservation price* for getting out of the chair turns out to be $1. You can conduct a similar mental auction to determine the maximum sum you would be willing to pay someone to skip the tracks. This reservation price measures the benefits of skipping the tracks; let us suppose it turns out to be 75 cents.

In terms of our formal decision rule, we then have x = "skip the tracks," with $B(x)$ = $\$.75 < C(x) = \$1$, which means that you should remain in your chair. Listening to the next two songs will be unpleasant, but less so than getting up would be. A reversal of these cost and benefit figures would imply a decision to get up and skip the tracks. If $B(x)$ and $C(x)$ happened to be equal, you would be indifferent between the two alternatives.

Reservation price of activity x
The price at which a person would be indifferent between doing x and not doing x.

1.2 A NOTE ON THE ROLE OF ECONOMIC THEORY

The idea that anyone might actually calculate the costs and benefits of skipping a few songs may sound a little strange, not to say absurd. Economists have come under heavy criticism for making unrealistic assumptions about how people behave, and outsiders are quick to wonder what purpose is served by the image of a person trying to decide how much he would pay to avoid getting up out of his chair.

There are two responses to this criticism. The first is that economists don't assume that people make explicit calculations of this sort at all. Rather, many economists argue, we can make useful predictions if we assume that people act as if they made such calculations. This view is forcefully expressed by Nobel Laureate Milton Friedman, who illustrates his point by looking at the techniques expert pool players use. He argues that the shots they choose, and the specific ways they attempt to make them, can be predicted extremely well by someone who assumes that the players take careful account of all the relevant laws of Newtonian physics. Of course, very few expert pool players have had formal training in physics, and hardly any can recite such laws as "the angle of incidence equals the angle of reflection." Nor are they likely to know the definitions of "elastic collisions" and "angular momentum." Even so, Friedman argues, they would never have become expert players in the first place unless they played as dictated by the laws of physics. Our theory of pool player behaviour assumes, unrealistically, that pool players know the laws of physics. Friedman urges us to judge this theory not by how accurate its central assumption is but by how well it predicts behaviour. And on this score, it often performs very well indeed.

Like pool players, the rest of us too must develop skills for coping with our environments. Many economists, Friedman among them, believe that useful insights into our behaviour can be gained by assuming that we act as if governed by the rules of rational decision making. He feels that by trial and error we eventually absorb these rules, just as pool players absorb the laws of physics.

A second response to the charge that economists make unrealistic assumptions is to concede that actual behaviour does often differ from the predictions of economic models. Thus, as economist Richard Thaler puts it, we often behave more like novice than like expert pool players—ignoring bank shots and having no idea about putting the proper spin on the cue ball to position it for the next shot. We will see considerable evidence in support of this second view.

But even where economic models fail on descriptive grounds, they often provide very useful guidance for making better decisions. That is, even if they don't always predict how we do behave, they may often give useful insights into how to achieve our goals more efficiently. If novice pool players have not yet internalized the relevant physical laws, they may nonetheless consult them for guidance about how to improve. Economic models often play an analogous role with respect to ordinary consumer and business decisions. Indeed, this role alone provides a compelling reason for learning economics.

1.3 COMMON PITFALLS IN DECISION MAKING

Some economists are embarrassed if an outsider points out that much of what they do boils down to an application of the principle that we should perform an action if and only if its benefits exceed its costs. That just doesn't sound like enough to keep a person with a Ph.D. busy all day! There is more to it, however, than meets the eye. People who study economics quickly discover that measuring costs and benefits is a tricky business. Indeed, it is as much an art as a science. Some costs seem almost deliberately hidden from view. Others may seem relevant but, on a closer look, turn out not to be.

Economics teaches us how to identify the costs and benefits that really matter. The principles we use are simple and commonsensical, but they are ones that many people ignore in everyday life. An important goal of this book is to teach you how to become a better decision maker. One of the best ways to do this is to examine the kinds of decisions that many people make *incorrectly*.

Pitfall 1. Ignoring Implicit Costs

Opportunity cost
The cost of taking an action, as measured by the benefit forgone by not taking the best alternative action.

One pitfall is to overlook costs that are not explicit. If doing activity x means not being able to do activity y, then the value to you of doing y is an ***opportunity cost*** of doing x. Many people make bad decisions because they tend to ignore the value of such forgone opportunities. This insight suggests that it will almost always be instructive to translate questions such as "Should I do x?" into ones such as "Should I do x or y?" In the latter question, y is simply the most highly valued alternative to doing x. The following example helps drive this important point home.

EXAMPLE 1-2

Should I go skiing today or work as a research assistant?

There is a ski area near your campus, and you often go skiing there. From experience you can confidently say that a day on the slopes is worth $60 to you. The charge for the day is $40 (which includes bus fare, lift ticket, and equipment). But this is not the only cost of going skiing. You must also take into account the value of the most attractive alternative you will forgo by heading for the slopes. Suppose that if you don't go skiing, you will work at your new job as a research assistant for one of your professors. The job pays $45 per day, and you like it just well enough to have been willing to do it for free. So the question you face is, "Should I go skiing or stay and work as a research assistant?"

Here the cost of skiing is not only the explicit cost of the ski package ($40) but also the opportunity cost of the lost earnings ($45). The total costs are therefore $85, which exceeds the benefits of $60. Since $C(x) > B(x)$, you should stay on campus and work for your professor. Someone who ignored the opportunity cost of the forgone earnings, however, would have decided incorrectly to go skiing.

Note in Example 1-2 the role of your feelings about the job. The fact that you liked it just well enough to have been willing to do it for free is another way of saying that there are no psychic costs associated with doing it. This is important because it means that by not doing the job you would not be escaping something unpleasant. Of course, not all jobs fall into this category. Suppose instead that your job had been to scrape plates in the cafeteria for the same pay, $45 per day, and that the job was so unpleasant that you would be unwilling to do it for less than $30 per day. Assuming your manager at the cafeteria permits you to take a day off whenever you want, let us now reconsider your decision about whether to go skiing.

EXAMPLE 1-3

Should I go skiing today or scrape plates (same as Example 1-2 except for the alternative)?

There are two equivalent ways to look at this decision. One is to say that one benefit of going skiing is not having to scrape plates. Since you would never be willing to scrape plates for less than $30 per day, avoiding that task is worth that amount to you. Going skiing thus carries with it the indirect benefit of not scraping plates. When we add that indirect benefit to the $60 direct benefit of the skiing, we get $B(x) = \$90$. In this view of the problem, $C(x)$ is the same as before, namely, the $40 ski charge plus the $45 opportunity cost of the lost earnings, or $85. So now $B(x) > C(x)$, which means you should go skiing.

Alternatively, we could have viewed the unpleasantness of the plate-scraping job as an offset against its salary. Using this approach, we would subtract the $30 per day of unpleasantness of the job from its $45 per day earnings and say that the opportunity cost of not working in the dining hall is only $15 per day. Then $C(x) = \$40 + \$15 = \$55 < B(x) = \$60$, and again the conclusion is that you should go skiing.

It makes no difference which of these two ways you handle the valuation of the unpleasantness of scraping plates. It is critically important, however, that you do it either one way or the other. Don't count it twice!

Example 1-3 makes it clear that there is a reciprocal relationship between costs and benefits. Not incurring a cost is the same as getting a benefit. By the same token, not getting a benefit is the same as incurring a cost.

EXAMPLE 1-4

Should I work first or go to university first?

The costs of going to university are not limited to tuition, fees, housing, food, books, supplies, and the like. They also include the opportunity cost of the earnings forgone while studying. The amount you earn increases with the amount of experience you have. The more experience you have, the greater the earnings you must forgo to attend university. This opportunity cost of attending university is therefore lowest when you are right out of high school.

On the benefit side, one big gain of a higher education is that it leads to sharply higher earnings. The sooner you go to university, the longer you will be able to take advantage of this benefit. Another benefit is the pleasantness of going to university as opposed to working. In general, the kinds of jobs people hold tend to be less unpleasant (or more pleasant) the more education and experience they have. By going to university right away, you thus minimize the time you spend working at the least pleasant jobs. For most people, then, it makes sense to go to university first and work afterward. Certainly it makes more sense to attend university at age 20 than at age 50.

A common exception to this general rule involves people who are not ready right out of high school to reap the benefits of university work. For them, it will often be sensible to work for a year or two and then go to university.

Why do most students start university right after finishing high school?

No one would pretend that high school students make their decisions about when to attend university on the basis of sophisticated calculations involving opportunity costs. On the contrary, most students go to university right out of high school simply because that is what most of their peers do. It is the thing to do.

But this begs the question of how it got to *be* the thing to do. Customs such as going to university right out of high school do not originate out of thin air. A host of different societies have had centuries to experiment with this issue. If there were a significantly better way of arranging the learning and working periods of life, some society ought to have long since discovered it. Our current custom has probably survived because it is so efficient. People may not make explicit calculations about the opportunity cost of forgone earnings, but they often behave *as if* they do.[1]

Many university students, of course, work part-time, often at fairly unpleasant, low-paying jobs, to reduce the size of the student loan debt they will accumulate during their post-secondary education. Here again, there is a tradeoff. Working 20 hours a week and trying at the same time to manage a full courseload, a student who could be pulling down B+ grades can find he is barely scraping by with a C− average. This sort of transcript is not the best way of impressing a prospective employer. It can result in a longer delay after graduation before finding a job, and a lower starting salary. A failure to calculate the *full* opportunity cost of the time spent on the job instead of studying can be very costly.

---

[1] This does not mean that all customs necessarily promote efficiency. For example, circumstances may have changed in such a way that a custom that promoted efficiency in the past no longer does so. In time, such a custom might change. Yet many habits and customs, once firmly entrenched, are very slow to change.

A number of Canadian universities have developed cooperative (or "co-op") programs, where students include as an integral part of their degree requirements several work terms at challenging jobs for "real" money (as opposed to burger-flipping wages). Co-op programs are a response to some of the limits of the straight-through-university path. They convert an "either-or" decision (either work or university) to a "both-and" option. They reduce the size of the student loan burden, and at the same time increase the practical work experience of graduates *before* graduation, thereby enhancing their credentials for prospective employers. For the employers who participate, co-op programs provide a relatively low-cost source of bright, motivated, short-term employees and a method of prescreening potential future recruitment prospects. Well-designed co-op programs work because they both lower the opportunity cost and increase the benefits of a university education.

As the following example makes clear, failure to take opportunity costs into account often causes people to misjudge what fairness requires of certain transactions.

EXAMPLE 1-5	**Is it fair to charge *interest* when lending a friend or relative some money?**

Interest The sum paid by a borrower to a lender in addition to repayment of the principal amount of a loan, to compensate the lender for the opportunity cost of not having the use of the principal during the loan period.

Suppose a friend lends you $10,000, and her primary concern in deciding whether to charge interest is to decide if it would be "fair" to do so. She could have put that same money in the bank, where it would have earned, say, 5 percent interest, or $500, each year. If she charges you $500 interest for each year the loan is out, she is merely recovering the opportunity cost of her money. If she didn't charge you any interest, it would be the same as making you a gift of $500 a year. Now, she might well wish to make you a yearly gift of that amount, or indeed even a much larger amount. But no one would say it was unfair if she didn't give you a large cash gift each year. And it makes no more sense to say that her recovery of the opportunity cost of lending you money is unfair.

Should a *parent* charge her children interest if she loans them money? There is no absolutely "right" answer to this question. Suppose that she has four sons, and one makes a loan request that is for a "good" purpose (it will not be used to purchase illicit drugs) and arises out of genuine need (the banks will not lend the son the money). One possible (and defensible) answer is, "Never charge your children interest!" If the family operates on the principle that (wherever possible) they help one another in case of genuine need, and that all a family member has to do is ask, then the "No interest" rule makes sense. Notice, however, that if the mother plans to bequeath her estate to all four children equally on her death, the value of her estate will be lower by the compounded value of the forgone loan interest. Not charging interest thus means, in effect, providing the son with a gift, three-quarters of which will be financed out of the future inheritances of the other children. This is not necessarily a bad thing, if the loans to *all* of the children tend to even out over time, *or* if the family *all* agree on the principle of responding to situations of genuine need *and* on how "need" is defined. Yet if this failure to account for the opportunity cost of the interest-free loan causes resentment, then the mother might do better by charging interest, or alternatively by bestowing a gift on each of the other three children at the same time, equal in value to the interest forgone. This last alternative might even have the added benefit for all the children of reducing the estate taxes after her death! We have still, however, not directly addressed the question asked in the next example.

EXAMPLE 1-6

Why do banks pay interest in the first place?

The main reason is that banks receive *more* interest than they pay to depositors, when they loan out the money that has been deposited. Suppose you owned a bank and someone deposited $10,000 in it on January 1 without your having to pay him interest. You could then take the money and buy a productive asset, such as a stand of trees (see Figure 1-1). Suppose that each year trees grow at the rate of 6 percent and that the price of a tree is proportional to the amount of lumber in it. At the end of the year, you could then sell the trees for $10,600 and have $600 more than before.

If you pay him 4 percent interest, he gets an additional $400 without the trouble of tending the trees. You loan the $10,000 to a tree-tending investor at a 4.75 percent interest rate. At the end of the year, the tree tender returns $10,475 to you, keeping $10,600 - 10,475 = $125 for her tree tending. You return $10,400 to the depositor, keeping $75 as your return for arranging the transactions.

FIGURE 1-1

Interest Reflects the Opportunity Cost of Money
Money can be used to buy a productive asset, like a tree, that grows more valuable with the passage of time. To lend someone money is to forgo the opportunity to reap the gain from such an investment. The interest paid on loans merely reflects this opportunity cost.

January 1   December 31

Everyone is better off as a result of the above set of transactions. But if this is so, and interest can be explained as a reimbursement for the opportunity cost of money, then why has moneylending historically had such a bad reputation? Aristotle, Roman law, the *Qur'an*, and medieval Christian scholastic thought all opposed usury, the taking of interest in exchange for the use of money for a period. Even today in Canada, there are usury laws on the books, and "loansharking" (charging exorbitant rates of interest) is illegal.

There were several reasons for the opposition to usury in a world where the price system was not fully developed and many loans were for consumption purposes rather than for productive investment. Pure interest was a payment to the lender that involved no labour or risk bearing on the part of the lender. If the opportunity cost to the lender of loaning the money was zero, because the best alternative use was simply to leave the money sitting in a strongbox, then the lender seemed to be getting something for nothing at the expense of his fellows. A consumption loan enabled the borrower to consume at a higher rate than otherwise over the term of the loan, but did not add to productive capacity. If the borrower could not repay the loan plus interest, then a spiral of increasing indebtedness could result, with serious consequences for social stability. Yet even among the scholastics, 13th-century writers like Peter Olivi treated interest, essentially in opportunity cost terms, as legitimate if it was a payment for the use of productive capital.[2]

As simple as the opportunity cost concept is, it is one of the most important in microeconomics. The art in applying the concept correctly lies in being able to recognize the most valuable alternative that is sacrificed by the pursuit of a given activity.

Pitfall 2. Failing to Ignore Sunk Costs

Sunk costs Past expenditures that can no longer be recovered at the time of making a decision.

An opportunity cost will often not seem like a relevant cost when in reality it is. Sometimes, however, an expenditure will seem like a relevant cost when in reality it is not. Such is often the case with *sunk costs*, costs that are beyond recovery at the moment a decision is made. Unlike opportunity costs, these costs should be ignored. The principle of ignoring sunk costs emerges clearly in the following example.

EXAMPLE 1-7

Should I drive to Halifax or take the bus?

You are planning a 500-km trip to Halifax. Except for the cost, you are completely indifferent between driving and taking the bus. Bus fare is $100. You don't know how much it would cost to drive your car, so you check the Internet for an estimate. On one website, you find that for your make of car the costs of a typical 20,000-km driving year are as follows:

Insurance	$1000
Interest	2000
Fuel & oil	1000
Maintenance	1000
Total	$5000

You calculate that these costs come to $.25 per kilometre and use this figure to compute that the 500-km trip will cost you $125 by car. And since this is more than the $100 bus fare, you decide to take the bus.

If you decide in this fashion, you commit the error of counting sunk costs. Your interest payments and, to a significant extent, your insurance payments do not vary with the number of kilometres you drive each year. Both are sunk costs and will be the same whether or not you drive to Halifax. Of the costs listed, fuel and oil and maintenance are the only ones that vary with kilometres driven. These come to $2000 for each 20,000 km you drive, or $.10 per km. At $.10 per km, it costs you only $50 to drive to Halifax, and since this is much less than the bus fare, you should drive.

In Example 1-7, note the role of the assumption that, costs aside, you are indifferent between the two modes of transport. This lets us say that the only comparison that matters is the actual cost of the two modes. If you had preferred one mode to the other, however, we would also have had to weigh that preference. For example, if you were willing to pay $60 to avoid the hassle of driving, the real cost of driving would be $110, not $50, and you should take the bus.

Exercises such as the one below are sprinkled throughout the text to help you make sure that you understand important analytical concepts. You will master microeconomics more effectively if you do these exercises as you go along.

---

[2]Raymond de Roover, *Business, Banking, and Economic Thought*, Chicago: University of Chicago Press, 1974.

How, if at all, would your answer to the question in Example 1-7 be different if the hassle of driving is $20 and you average one $28 ticket for every 400 kilometres you drive?

As a check, the answers to the in-chapter exercises are at the end of each chapter. Naturally, the exercises will be much more useful if you work through them before consulting the answers.

EXAMPLE 1-8

The pizza experiment.

A pizza parlour offers an all-you-can-eat lunch for $3. You pay at the door, and then the waiter brings you as many slices of pizza as you like. One economist performed this experiment: he had an assistant serve as the waiter for one group of tables.[3] The "waiter" selected half of the tables at random and gave everyone at those tables a $3 refund before taking orders. The remaining half of his tables received no refund. He then kept careful count of the number of slices of pizza each diner ate. What difference, if any, do you predict in the amounts eaten by these two groups?

Diners in each group confront the question "Should I eat another slice of pizza?" Here, the activity x consists of eating one more slice. For both groups, $C(x)$ is exactly zero: even members of the group that did not get a refund can get as many additional slices as they want at no extra charge. Because the refund group was chosen at random, there is no reason to suppose that its members like pizza any more or less than the others. For everyone, the decision rule says keep eating until there is no longer any extra pleasure in eating another slice. Thus, $B(x)$ should be the same for each group, and people from both groups should keep eating until $B(x)$ falls to zero.

By this reasoning, the two groups should eat the same amount of pizza, on the average. The $3 admission fee is a sunk cost and should have no influence on the amount of pizza one eats. *In fact, however, the group that did not get the refund consumed substantially more pizza.*

Although our cost-benefit decision rule fails the test of prediction in this experiment, its message for the rational decision maker stands unchallenged. The two groups logically *should* have behaved the same. The only difference between them, after all, is that patrons in the refund group have lifetime incomes that are $3 higher than the others'. Surely no one believes that such a trivial difference should have any effect on pizza consumption. Members of the no-refund group seemed to want to make sure they "got their money's worth." In all likelihood, however, this motive merely led them to overeat.[4]

What's wrong with being motivated to "get your money's worth"? Absolutely nothing, as long as the force of this motive operates *before* you enter into transactions. Thus it makes perfectly good sense to be led by this motive to choose one restaurant

---

[3]See Richard Thaler, "Toward a Positive Theory of Consumer Choice," *Journal of Economic Behavior and Organization*, 1, 1980.

[4]An alternative to the "get-your-money's-worth" explanation is that $3 is a significant fraction of the amount of cash many diners have available to spend *in the short run*. Thus members of the refund group might have held back in order to save room for the dessert they could now afford to buy. To test this alternative explanation, the experimenter could give members of the no-refund group a $3 cash gift earlier in the day and then see if the amount of pizza consumed by the two groups still differed.

over an otherwise identical competitor that happens to cost more. Once the price of your lunch has been determined, however, the get-your-money's-worth motive should be abandoned. The satisfaction you get from eating another slice of pizza should then depend only on how hungry you are and on how much you like pizza, not on how much you paid for the privilege of eating all you can eat. Yet people often seem not to behave in this fashion. The difficulty may be that we are not creatures of complete flexibility. Perhaps motives it makes sense to be influenced by in one context are not easily abandoned in another.

EXERCISE 1-2

Jim wins a ticket from a radio station to see a jazz band perform at an outdoor concert. Mike has paid $18 for a ticket to the same concert. On the evening of the concert there is a tremendous thunderstorm. If Jim and Mike have the same tastes, which of them will be more likely to attend the concert, assuming that each decides whether to attend the concert on the basis of a standard benefit-cost comparison?

Pitfall 3. Measuring Costs and Benefits as Proportions Rather than Absolute Dollar Amounts

When a boy asks his mother "Are we almost there yet?" how will she answer if they are 10 km from their destination? Without some knowledge of the context of their journey, we cannot say. If they are near the end of a 300-km journey, her answer will almost surely be yes. But if they have just left on a 12-km journey, she will undoubtedly answer no.

Contextual clues are important for a variety of ordinary judgments. Thinking about distance as a percentage of the total amount to be travelled is natural and informative. Many also find it natural to think in percentage terms when comparing costs and benefits. But as the following pair of simple examples illustrates, this tendency often causes trouble.

EXAMPLE 1-9A | **Should you drive to BigBox Mall to save $10 on a $20 clock radio?**

You are about to buy a clock radio at a nearby store for $20 when a friend tells you that the very same radio is on sale at BigBox Mall for only $10. If the Mall is a 15-minute drive away, where would you buy the radio?

EXAMPLE 1-9B | **Should you drive to BigBox Mall to save $10 on a $1000 television set?**

You are about to buy a new television set at a nearby store for $1010 when a friend tells you that the very same set is on sale at BigBox Mall for only $1000. If the Mall is a 15-minute drive away, where would you buy the television?

There is no uniquely correct answer to either of these questions, both of which ask whether the benefit of driving to the Mall is worth the cost. Most people say that the trip would definitely be worth making in the case of the clock radio, but definitely not worth making in the case of the television set. When pressed to explain why, they explain that driving yields a 50 percent savings on the clock radio, but less than a 1 percent savings on the television.

These percentages, however, are irrelevant. In each case the benefit of driving to the Mall is exactly the $10 savings from the lower purchase price. What is the cost of driving to the Mall? Some people might be willing to make the drive for as little as $5, while others might not be willing to do it for less than $50. But whatever the number, it should be the same in both cases. And that means that your answers to the questions just posed should be the same. For example, if you would be willing to make the drive for, say, $8, then you should buy both the clock radio and the television at the Mall. But if your reservation price for making the drive is, say, $12, then you should buy both appliances at the nearby store.

When using the cost-benefit test, you should express costs and benefits in absolute dollar terms. Comparing percentages is not a fruitful way to think about decisions like these.

EXERCISE 1-3

You are holding a discount coupon that will entitle you to a fare reduction on one of the two trips you are scheduled to take during the coming month. You can either get 50% off the normal $200 airfare to Montreal, or you can get 5% off the normal $2400 airfare to New Delhi. On which trip should you use your coupon?

Pitfall 4. Failure to Understand the Average-Marginal Distinction

So far we have looked at decisions about whether to perform a given action. Often, however, the choice we face is not whether to perform the action but rather the extent to which it should be performed. But even in this more complex case, we can still apply the cost–benefit principle by reformulating the question. Instead of asking "Should I do activity *x*?," we repeatedly pose the question "Should I increase the level by which I am currently engaging in activity *x*?"

To answer this question, we must focus on the benefit and cost of an *additional* unit of activity. The cost of an additional unit of activity is called the **marginal cost** of the activity, and the benefit of an additional unit is called its **marginal benefit**.

The cost–benefit rule tells us to keep increasing the level of an activity as long as its marginal benefit exceeds its marginal cost. But as the following example illustrates, people often fail to apply this rule correctly.

> **Marginal cost** The increase in total cost that results from carrying out one additional unit of an activity.

> **Marginal benefit** The increase in total benefit that results from carrying out one additional unit of an activity.

EXAMPLE 1-10 | Should Tom launch another boat?

Tom manages a small fishing fleet of three boats. His current daily costs of operations, including boat rentals and fishermen's wages, are $300, or an average of $100 per boat launched. His daily total revenue, or benefit, from the sale of fish is currently $600, or an average of $200 per boat launched. Tom decides that since his costs per boat are less than his revenues per boat, he should launch another boat. Is this a sound decision?

To answer this question, we must compare the marginal cost of launching a boat with the marginal benefit of launching a boat. The information given, however, tells us only the **average cost** and **average benefit** of launching a boat—which are, respectively, one-third of the total cost of three boats and one-third of the total revenue from three boats. Knowing the average benefit and average cost per boat launched does not enable us to decide whether launching another boat makes economic sense. For although the average benefit of the three boats launched thus far *might* be the same as the marginal benefit of launching another boat, it might also be either higher or lower. The same statement holds true regarding average and marginal costs.

> **Average cost** The average cost of undertaking *n* units of an activity is the total cost of the activity divided by *n*.

> **Average benefit** The average benefit of undertaking *n* units of an activity is the total benefit of the activity divided by *n*.

To illustrate the nature of the problem, suppose that marginal cost of launching a boat and crew is constant at $100 per boat per day. Then Tom should launch a fourth boat only if doing so will add at least $100 in daily revenue from his total fish catch. The mere fact that the current average revenue is $200 per boat simply doesn't tell us what the marginal benefit of launching the fourth boat will be.

Suppose, for example, that the relationship between the number of boats launched and the daily total revenue from the catch is as described in Table 1-1. With three boats per day, the average benefit per boat would then be $200, just as indicated above. If Tom launched a fourth boat, the *average* daily revenue would fall to $160 per boat, which is still more than the assumed marginal cost of $100. Note, however, that in the second column the total revenue from four boats is only $40 per day more than the total revenue from three boats. That means that the marginal revenue from launching the fourth boat is only $40. And since that is less than its marginal cost ($100), launching the fourth boat makes no sense.

TABLE 1-1		
How Total Cost Varies with the Number of Boats Launched		

Number of boats	Daily total benefit ($)	Daily average benefit ($/boat)
0	0	0
1	300	300
2	480	240
3	600	200
4	640	160

The following example illustrates how to apply the cost-benefit principle correctly in this case.

EXAMPLE 1-11   How many boats should Tom launch?

The marginal cost of launching a boat and crew is again constant at $100 each day. If total daily revenue from the catch again varies with the number of boats launched as shown in Table 1-1, how many boats should Tom launch?

Tom should keep launching boats as long as the marginal benefit of doing so is at least as great as the marginal cost. With marginal cost constant at $100 per launch, Tom should thus keep launching boats as long as the marginal benefit is at least $100.

Applying the definition of marginal benefit to the total benefit entries in the second column of Table 1-1 yields the marginal benefit values in the third column of Table 1–2. (Because marginal benefit is the *change* in total benefit that results when we change the number of boats by one, we place each marginal cost entry midway between the rows showing the corresponding total benefit entries.) For example, the marginal benefit of increasing the number of boats from one to two is $180, the difference between the $480 total revenue that results with two boats and the $300 that results with one.

Comparing the $100 marginal cost per boat with the marginal benefit entries in the third column of Table 1-2, we see that the first three launches satisfy the cost-benefit test, but the fourth does not. Tom should therefore launch three boats.

TABLE 1-2	Number of boats	Daily total benefit ($)	Daily marginal benefit ($/boat)
How Marginal Benefit Varies with the Number of Boats Launched	0	0	
			300
	1	300	
			180
	2	480	
			120
	3	600	
			40
	4	640	

EXERCISE 1-4

If the marginal cost of launching each boat had not been $100 but $150, how many boats should Tom have launched?

The cost-benefit principle tells us that *marginal* costs and benefits—measures that correspond to the *increment* of an activity under consideration—are the relevant ones for choosing the level at which to pursue the activity. Yet many people compare the *average* cost and benefit of the activity when making such decisions. As Examples 1-10 and 1-11 should have made clear, however, increasing the level of an activity may not be justified, even though its average benefit at the current level is significantly greater than its average cost.

1.4 USING MARGINAL BENEFIT AND MARGINAL COST GRAPHICALLY

The examples just discussed involve decisions about an activity that could take place only on discrete levels—no boats, one boat, two boats, and so on. The levels of many other activities, however, can vary continuously. One can buy gasoline, for example, in any quantity one wishes. For activities that are continuously variable, it is often convenient to display the comparison of marginal benefit and marginal cost graphically.

EXAMPLE 1-12 | **How much should Susan talk to Hal each month?**

Susan has a telephone plan for which the charge is 4 cents per minute for a long-distance call to her boyfriend Hal. (Fractional minutes are billed at the same rate, so a 30-second call would cost her 2 cents.) The value to Susan, measured in terms of her willingness to pay, of an additional minute of conversation with Hal is as shown on curve *MB* in Figure 1-2. How many minutes should she spend on the phone with Hal each month?

The downward slope of curve *MB* reflects the fact that the value of an additional minute of conversation declines with the total amount of conversation that has occurred thus far. (As we will see in Chapter 3, it is a common pattern that the more someone has of a good, the less value he assigns to having additional units of it.)

FIGURE 1–2

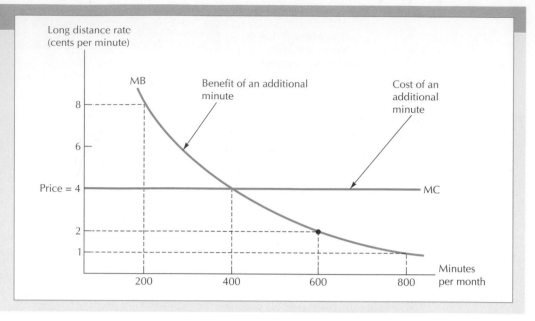

Curve *MC* in the diagram measures the cost of each additional minute, assumed to be constant at $0.04. The optimal quantity of conversation is the quantity for which these two curves cross—namely, 400 minutes per month. If Susan speaks with Hal for less than that amount, the marginal benefit from adding another minute would exceed the marginal cost, so she should talk longer. But if they speak for more than 400 minutes per month, the amount she would save by speaking less would exceed the benefit she would sacrifice, which means they should speak less.[5]

EXERCISE 1-5

If her marginal benefit curve is again as given in Figure 1–2, how many minutes should Susan speak with Hal each month if the long-distance rate falls to 2 cents per minute?

1.5 THE INVISIBLE HAND AND ITS LIMITS: EXTERNALITIES

One of the most important insights of economic analysis is that the individual pursuit of self-interest is often not only consistent with broader social objectives, but also actually even *required* by them. Wholly unaware of the effects of their actions, self-interested consumers often act as if driven by what Adam Smith called an invisible hand to produce the greatest social good. In perhaps the most widely quoted passage from *The Wealth of Nations*, Smith wrote:

---

[5]Module 11 of the online *Basic Math Review*, "Maximizing Total *Net* Benefit," provides a more general and more detailed analysis of the "marginal benefit–marginal cost" criterion, using diagrams and some basic calculus.

It is not from the benevolence of the butcher, the brewer, or the baker, that we expect our dinner, but from their regard to their own interest. We address ourselves, not to their humanity but to their self-love, and never talk to them of our own necessities but of their advantages.[6]

Modern economists sometimes lose sight of the fact that Smith did not believe that *only* selfish motives are important. In his earlier treatise, *The Theory of Moral Sentiments*, for example, he wrote movingly about the compassion we feel for others:

How selfish soever man may be supposed, there are evidently some principles in his nature, which interest him in the fortune of others, and render their happiness necessary to him, though he derives nothing from it except the pleasure of seeing it. Of this kind is pity or compassion, the emotion which we feel for the misery of others, when we either see it, or are made to conceive it in a very lively manner. That we often derive sorrow from the sorrow of others, is a matter of fact too obvious to require any instances to prove it; for this sentiment, like all the other original passions of human nature, is by no means confined to the virtuous and humane, though they perhaps may feel it with the most exquisite sensibility. The greatest ruffian, the most hardened violator of the laws of society, is not altogether without it.[7]

Smith was well aware, moreover, that the pure pursuit of self-interest is sometimes far from socially benign. As the following example illustrates, the invisible hand mechanism breaks down when important costs or benefits accrue to people other than the decision makers themselves.

EXAMPLE 1-13	**Should I burn my leaves or haul them into the woods?**

External cost of an activity A cost that is generated by an activity and that falls on people who are not directly involved in the activity.

Suppose the cost of hauling the leaves is $20 and the cost to the homeowner of burning them is only $1. If the homeowner cares only about costs that accrue directly to herself, she will burn her leaves. The difficulty is that burning leaves entails an important **externality** or **external cost**, which means a cost borne by people who are not directly involved in the decision. This external cost is the damage done by the smoke from the fire. That cost accrues not to the homeowner who makes the decision about burning the leaves but to the people who live downwind. Suppose the smoke damage amounts to $25. The good of the community then requires that the leaves be hauled, not burned. From the perspective of the self-interested homeowner, however, it seems best to burn them.[8]

Market failure Situation in which the unaided operation of the market mechanism results in an inefficient allocation of resources.

When externalities are present, the private costs or benefits of an activity as valued by the market can diverge significantly from the overall costs or benefits of the activity to society as a whole. Externalities thus often lead to what economists call **market failure**: the failure of the unaided market to provide an efficient allocation of resources. We shall explore such cases at many points in the text, particularly in Chapters 16, 17, and 18. External costs and benefits are often the underlying reason for laws that limit individual discretion. Most communities, for example, now have laws prohibiting the burning of leaves within city limits. Such laws may be viewed as a way of making the

---

[6]Adam Smith, *An Inquiry into the Nature and Causes of the Wealth of Nations*, ed. Edwin Cannan, University of Chicago Press, 1976. p. 18.

[7]Adam Smith, *The Theory of Moral Sentiments*, ed. D. D. Raphael and A. L. Macfie, Indianapolis: Liberty Fund, 1984, p. 9.

[8]Of course, if the homeowner interacts frequently with the people downwind, self-interest may still dictate hauling the leaves, to preserve goodwill for future interactions. But where the people downwind are anonymous strangers, this motive will operate with much less force.

costs and benefits as seen by individuals more nearly resemble the costs and benefits experienced by the community as a whole. With a law against burning leaves in effect, the potential leaf burner weighs the penalty of breaking the law against the cost of hauling the leaves. Most people conclude it is cheaper to haul them.

1.6 RATIONALITY AND SELF-INTEREST

Self-interest standard of rationality A theory that says rational people consider only costs and benefits that accrue directly to themselves.

Present-aim standard of rationality A theory that says rational people act efficiently in pursuit of whatever objectives they hold at the moment of choice.

To be rational in the economist's sense means to make decisions according to the cost-benefit criterion—that is, to take an action if and only if its benefits exceed its costs. There are two important refinements of this definition of rationality. One is the ***self-interest standard of rationality***, which says that rational persons assign significant weight to only those costs and benefits that accrue directly to themselves. This standard explicitly sets aside such motives as trying to make others happy, trying to do the right thing, envy of others' good fortune, and so on.

The alternative definition is the so-called ***present-aim standard of rationality***. Its only requirement is that persons act efficiently in the pursuit of whatever aims or objectives they happen to hold at the moment of action. The attraction of this broader standard is that it encompasses such common human motives as charity, duty, envy, jealousy, and the like. We know, after all, that many people hold such motives, and our theory becomes more descriptively accurate if it incorporates them explicitly.

Neither the self-interest nor the present-aim standard of rationality, however, is completely airtight and problem free. The self-interest standard assumes that people are basically selfish egoists, unmoved by love or envy, whose behaviour is governed solely by their desire to maximize their own personal net benefit. Yet what exactly does this assumption mean? It must mean that rationally self-interested individuals have perfect knowledge of what their own "self-interest" actually is. They must be able to calculate costlessly the tradeoffs between present costs and expected future benefits and between present benefits and expected future costs, when these benefits and costs are causally linked. They must know not only the *immediate* consequences of their actions but also how the responses of *others* to their selfish actions will affect *future* opportunities.

Without any feeling of guilt, they must be prepared to cheat and lie to others, provided that their net gains from cheating and lying exceed the costs of being caught, weighted by the probability of their being caught. But of course if everyone behaves in this way, then all individuals must devote substantial resources to protecting themselves against the predatory self-interested behaviour of others, rather than to productive activities. Unbridled self-interest is thus socially and individually highly wasteful. A major challenge for *all* societies is therefore how to design socially efficient mechanisms that ensure that it will be in the rational self-interest of even an *egoistic* person to behave cooperatively, at least to some degree.

The "individual self-interest" standard is not wholly satisfying. Yet the present-interest standard also has its limits. Unless we actually know what the "present interests" are, we are thrown back on the "anything goes" assumption: however bizarre a person's behaviour, that person *must* have had *some* "present aim" that warranted it. Suppose, for example, that we see someone drink a large can of crankcase oil and keel over dead. The present-aim approach can "explain" this behaviour by saying that the person must have *really* liked crankcase oil!

Could such an act ever occur within the "rational self-interest" model? Consider an individual suffering from an incurable terminal disease, in agonizing pain that not even costly medication can alleviate. The crankcase oil is the only means at hand of ending the expected long-term suffering. We are not concerned here with the *morality* of suicide, but merely with whether suicide by crankcase oil could fit the rational self-interest model. The answer is that under certain circumstances it can.

This example suggests a larger question. As outside observers, can we always distinguish between two people, one behaving with egoistic self-interest rationality and one behaving with altruistic present-aim rationality? Not necessarily. If cooperative behaviour benefits *both* cooperators more than competition does, the self-interested individual should choose to cooperate, at least for the moment, so that her own net benefit is maximized. Furthermore, generous actions are often rewarded by society with respect, status, and trust. If such status increases one's subsequent chances of doing well, it could be in the egoist's interest to cooperate, or even to "invest" in some short-term *sacrifice*, for the sake of larger long-term gains.

Both standards of rationality, despite their limits, find widespread application in economic analysis. Chapter 7 discusses how to impose reasonable restrictions on the use of the present-aim standard. For now, however, let us focus on the self-interest standard in a fairly basic form, and see what sorts of behaviour it predicts.

| EXAMPLE 1-14 | Should I vote in the next federal election? |

"Don't vote. It only encourages them." "If voting made any difference, we wouldn't be *allowed* to vote." These cynical views of voting reflect two different perspectives. The first views politics as a second-rate play, poorly performed by a cast of bad actors, with voting as a form of applause. The second views government as an elaborate shell game, providing citizens with the *forms* but not the *substance* of democracy: popular control of social decision making. In this view, which party forms the government matters little; the real political-economic power rests elsewhere.

Let us suppose, however, that it *does* matter which party wins the election and forms the government. A purely self-interested person is still almost certain not to vote, even if she believes that one party will serve her interests much better than the others. Out of the thousands of votes cast in her riding, her vote will not matter unless it tips the outcome of the election. The likelihood of casting the decisive ballot in her riding is virtually nil. Even if her party's candidate wins in her riding, the party that actually forms the government will be determined by the outcomes in 300 *other* ridings, in which her vote has no effect. Only if her vote is the decisive vote in a decisive riding will it matter. Against this negligible chance of receiving any benefit from voting, the costs of getting to the polling station, in terms of time, energy, and stress are real and significant. The cost-benefit model hence predicts that a purely self-interested person will not vote.

Several points must be made about Example 1-14. First, the standard rejoinder—"What would happen if *everyone* who favoured your candidate stayed home?"—fails to acknowledge the fundamental incentive problem. The higher the voter turnout, the less any one person's vote matters. The irony is that the converse is also true. If *everyone* followed the "self-interest prescription," no one would vote, in which case it *would* pay a self-interested person to vote.

Yet we cannot explain the millions of voters who do vote by assuming that *all* of them expected everyone else to stay home. Critics of the self-interest model point to these voters as evidence of its limited predictive power. Supporters of the model, however, would emphasize that although large numbers do vote, many do not. They would also insist, correctly, that the self-interest model helps us understand *why* they don't. Some nonvoters may not care about the outcome of the election, but others may care deeply and yet not vote because of the virtual certainty that their votes will make no difference. The self-interest model thus gives mixed results. It seems to explain some people's behaviour, but not others'.

In emphasizing the *material* determinants of voting behaviour, however, the self-interest model helps explain why in Canada and in other countries with democratic forms of government, scarce resources are devoted to teaching that voting is not only a right, but also a citizen's *duty*. A person who accepts this teaching will not behave in strict accordance with the self-interest model, as narrowly defined. Instead, she will also take into account her feelings of guilt and shame should she *fail* to vote. The costs of voting will still be as before. Now, however, the benefits will not be zero, but rather the amount she would be willing to pay to avoid feeling guilty at not voting. This amended model does not guarantee that she will *always* vote. Certain individuals will value "fulfilling their duty" more highly than others, and in any given election, the costs of voting could be increased by a violent storm or by pressing alternative demands on a person's time. Yet recognizing the effect on the cost-benefit calculus of social mechanisms for inculcating a sense of duty increases our capacity to explain voter behaviour.

1.7 WOULD PARENTS WANT THEIR DAUGHTER OR SON TO MARRY *HOMO ECONOMICUS*?

Many economists remain skeptical about the importance of duty and other unselfish motives. They feel that the material payoffs associated with selfish behaviour so strongly dominate other motives that, as a first approximation, we may safely ignore nonegoistic motives.

The stereotypical decision maker in the self-interest model is often given the label *Homo economicus*, or "economic man." *Homo economicus* does not experience the sorts of sentiments that motivate people to vote, or to return lost wallets to their owners with the cash intact. On the contrary, personal material costs and benefits are the only things he cares about.

Obviously, many people do not fit the me-first caricature of the self-interest model. They donate bone marrow to strangers with leukemia. They endure great trouble and expense to see justice done, even when it will not undo the original injury. At great risk to themselves, they pull people from burning buildings and jump into icy rivers to rescue people who are about to drown. Soldiers throw their bodies atop live grenades to save their comrades.

Selfish motives *are* important. They obviously account for a great deal. When a detective investigates a murder, for example, her first question is, "Who stood to benefit from the victim's death?" When an economist studies a government regulation, he wants to know whose incomes it enhances. When government proposes a new spending project, the political scientist tries to discover which constituencies will be its primary beneficiaries.

Our goal in much of this text is to understand the kinds of behaviours to which selfish motives give rise in specific situations. But throughout this process, it is critical to remember that the self-interest model is not intended as a prescription for how to conduct your own affairs. On the contrary, we will see in later chapters that *Homo economicus* is woefully ill suited to the demands of social existence as we know it. Each of us probably knows people who more or less fit the *Homo economicus* caricature. Our first priority, most of the time, is to steer clear of them.

Ironically, a purely self-interested person embraces a degree of social isolation that is not only bad for the soul but also harmful to the wallet. To succeed in life, even in purely material terms, people must be able to work together, to form alliances and relationships of trust. But what sensible person would be willing to trust *Homo economicus*? Later chapters present specific examples of how unselfish motives can confer material rewards on the people who hold them. For now, however, bear in mind that the self-interest model is intended only to capture one part of human behaviour, albeit an important one.

1.8 THE ECONOMIC NATURALIST

Studying biology enables people to observe and marvel at many details of life that would otherwise escape them. For the naturalist, a walk in a quiet wood becomes an adventure. Similarly, studying microeconomics enables someone to become an "economic naturalist," a person who sees the mundane details of ordinary existence in a sharp new light. Each feature of the manmade landscape is no longer an amorphous mass but the result of an implicit cost-benefit calculation. Using economic tools to make sense of the world, discovering the *hidden* logic underlying economic phenomena, is a good part of the excitement of the economic naturalist approach. Despite appearances to the contrary (especially around exam time), microeconomics is not an unchanging, settled body of theorems and "truths" about the world. It is an evolving discipline, a tool kit, a way of seeing, a method of inquiry, and an aid to creative thought.

A creative economic naturalist insight will often begin with a simple "Why" question about an apparent anomaly, something that doesn't square with common sense. "Why do people use liquid laundry detergent, when it's more expensive than the powdered varieties and can't clean as well?" "Why are maximum retail prices for Beanie Babies fixed by the manufacturer, when many Beanie Babies command much higher prices in the collectibles market?" "If the Internet costs massive resources to maintain, then why have some Internet service providers (ISPs) been so generous that they have provided free e-mail service? And why have some Internet users been *paid* just to use the Internet? And why are the ISPs starting to charge for services that used to be free?" As these examples show, the questions can be about very large issues, like the Internet, or about apparently trivial ones, like laundry detergent and Beanie Babies. And it's not always the size of the question that matters. Michael Spence, one of the Canadian Nobel Laureates in economics, wondered why there was so much competition to get into "elite" universities. Was it really because they increased students' productivity more than other schools did? His reflections led him to the economic theory of screening and signalling under asymmetric information, which you will meet in Chapters 6 and 14.

In this and the following chapters, you will encounter some "Why" questions, high-lighted by the "Economic Naturalist" symbol. These questions are designed to stimulate your creative juices and develop your economic intuition. We have provided interpretations for each case, but the interpretations are intended to be suggestive, not definitive. In fact, we are convinced that for some of the "Economic Naturalist" questions, *you* can provide *better* explanations than those in the text. We also believe that you can create *new* "Economic Naturalist" questions and answers, which could appear in future editions of *Microeconomics and Behaviour*.[9] As you read the "Economic Naturalist" examples, don't simply take the explanations for granted. Instead, read them critically, and try to come up with your own alternative explanations.

---

[9]The details of our "Challenge to the Reader" are contained in the Preface and online at www.mcgrawhill.ca/college/frank.

WHY IS AIRLINE FOOD SO BAD?

Everyone complains about airline food. Indeed, if any serious restaurant dared to serve such food, it would go bankrupt in short order. Our complaints seem to take for granted that airline meals should be as good as the ones we eat in restaurants. But why should they?

The cost-benefit perspective makes clear that airlines should increase the quality of their meals if and only if the benefits would outweigh the costs of doing so. The benefits of better food can be measured by what passengers would be willing to pay for it, in the form of higher ticket prices. If a restaurant-quality meal could be had for, say, a mere $5 increase in costs, most people would probably be delighted to pay it. The difficulty, however, is that it would be much more costly than that to prepare significantly better meals at 39,000 feet in a tiny galley with virtually no time. It could be done, of course. But the extra cost would be more like $50 per passenger than $5. Few of us would be willing to bear this extra burden. The sad result is that airline food is destined to remain relatively unpalatable because the costs of improving it outweigh the benefits.

Many of us respond warmly to the maxim "Anything worth doing is worth doing well." It encourages a certain pride of workmanship that is often sadly lacking. Economic Naturalist 1-1 makes clear, however, that if the maxim is interpreted literally, it makes no sense. It ignores the need to weigh costs against benefits. To do something well means to devote time, effort, and resources to it. But time, effort, and resources are scarce. To devote them to one activity makes them unavailable for another. Increasing the quality of one of the things we do thus necessarily means to reduce the quality of others—yet another application of the concept of opportunity cost. Every intelligent decision must take account of this tradeoff.

Everything we see in life is the result of some such compromise. For Mats Sundin to play hockey as well as he does means that he cannot become a concert pianist. He could still play piano, but he should hold himself to a lower standard there than in the hockey arena.

WHY DO SPAMMERS SPAM?

Most of us have been "spammed"—subjected to unsolicited and unwanted bulk electronic junk mail. And as spammees, our response is usually the same every time: hit the "Delete" button before even reading the message the spam e-mail contains. A recent European Union study estimated the cost of spam, in terms of wasted workplace time and bandwidth requirements, at about $12 billion annually. To these costs we should add the cost of anti-spamming filtering technologies, the shutting down of legitimate addresses, and the accidental loss or deletion of *real* messages in the process of deleting junk e-mail.

So why do spammers bother spamming? A simple comparison suggests why. Broadcasting a single 30-second TV commercial on a top-rated prime time show in a major Canadian market area can cost an advertiser well over $50,000. Creating and producing the commercial can cost over $1 million, although that cost is spread over many (sometimes many many) repetitions. In contrast, spamming software plus e-mail lists containing tens of millions of e-mail addresses can be purchased for under $1000, and the cost per transmission is negligible. If only one person in a hundred actually reads the spammed message, and one person in fifty who have read it responds, then the benefits to the spammer swamp the negligible cost. Not only that, but ordering a product from the spammer is usually only a click away, whereas there is often a significant separation between getting a TV commercial message and the next opportunity to make a purchase. The social costs of spamming are substantial, but the private cost-benefit calculation of the spammer suggests that we can expect more spam, not less, in the foreseeable future.

Economic Naturalist 1-3

WHY PAPER TOWELS VERSUS HOT-AIR HAND DRYERS IN PUBLIC RESTROOMS?

In the 1950s and 1960s, paper towel dispensers were replaced by electric hot-air hand dryers in many public washrooms. Nowadays, part of the excitement of going into a public washroom (if you're *really* short on excitement in your life) is checking whether the washroom has paper towels or hot-air dryers. Which system is used naturally has to do with the costs and benefits of the different methods of drying hands. For customers, paper towels are quicker and more convenient, and involve shorter queues. For the washroom owners, there are *three* main types of cost: *initial set-up costs* (where hot-air dryers cost more than towel dispensers); *operating input costs* (which depend on the relative costs of energy and paper and the extent of paper towel theft); and *maintenance labour costs* (where durable hot-air dryers tend to be cheaper, because towel dispensers need to be filled, used towel receptacles need to be emptied, and towels strewn on the floor need to be cleaned up). If a system is already in place, the "set-up" costs are now *sunk* costs. Yet significant increases in paper prices *or* hourly wages *or* public sloppiness will tend to increase the proportion of hot-air dryers, while sharp energy price hikes mean you'll likely see more paper towels.

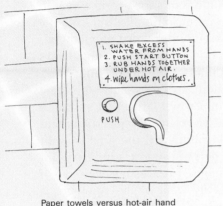

Paper towels versus hot-air hand dryers: part of the cost-benefit story.

Some economic naturalists may also be interested in speculating about the comparative economics of different types of paper towel dispensers. Some dispense a standardized individual sheet. Others feature a large roll, with a continuous hand crank. The longer you turn the crank, the longer the sheet of paper towel you get. Still others have the roll, but release only a limited amount of paper with each pull. To get more, you have to reset the release mechanism by pushing a button on the front of the dispenser.

This last design induces people to use less paper. Indeed, if your hands are wet enough, it's difficult to get any paper at all: when you pull, the wet paper simply tears away in your hands. But if this design saves paper, why don't all establishments with paper towel systems adopt it? The answer is that saving on paper is not their only objective. They also want satisfied customers, and customers seem prepared to pay slightly more for their meals or gasoline in order to cover the cost of the added convenience of alternative systems.

Yet from a conservationist standpoint, isn't a design that economizes on paper towels a "good thing," even if it is frustrating to operate? By extension, can we justify the sacrifice of thousands of trees to print the weekend editions of Canadian newspapers, most of the pages of which will go unread? There are several answers to this question. After over a century and a half of short-sighted, wasteful, and destructive use of Canada's forest resources, the last 30 years have witnessed an increase in awareness of the potential value of scientific "integrated forest management." There is now a more widespread understanding that forests are ecosystems; that trees are a "renewable" resource only if extensive replantation programs are undertaken; and that there are alternatives to such practices as the clear-cutting of large tracts of forest land that are ecologically less risky and equally profitable. "Sustainable forestry" has the potential to be not just ecologically sensible but also good business. Moreover, over the last thirty years, in Canada as well as elsewhere in the world, the proportion of recycled paper used in newsprint production has risen dramatically. Thus the share of total newsprint tonnage that must be supplied from the forest industries has fallen.

Yet this is not the whole story. Trees are not the only input into pulp and paper; paper production requires substantial *energy* inputs. In Canada, hydroelectricity (which is in the "*in*exhaustible resource" category) and energy generated from waste biomass within the pulp and paper mills themselves are the two most important *direct* sources of energy in paper production. The high energy demands of pulp and paper production, however, indirectly increase the need for *thermal* energy, and the coal, petroleum, and natural gas used in thermal energy production are *non*renewable resources. The conservationist concern is a real one, but it may be that the weekend newspaper is more of a long-term threat to *coal, oil, and gas reserves* than to forests! Part of being an economic naturalist is tracing the indirect and hidden economic connections between apparently unrelated phenomena.

One further observation should be made at this point. Private markets do not always provide the correct incentives to conserve the resources that society deems important. When the invisible hand fumbles the ball, it is government's responsibility to protect these resources. Provincial government ownership of the Crown lands that sustain a large proportion of the Canadian forest industry has made it possible to put the brakes on unrestricted exploitation of the forests, and has contributed to the gradual shift toward a "sustainable development" orientation on the part of the forest industry. Yet the moratorium on cod fishing on the Grand Banks in response to excessive depletion of cod stocks is a reminder that even in the case of supposedly "renewable" resources, a failure to institute adequate conservation measures can have drastic economic consequences.

1.9 POSITIVE QUESTIONS AND NORMATIVE QUESTIONS

Normative question
A question regarding the action that *should* be taken in a particular situation, in relation to given ethical criteria.

Positive question
A question regarding the probable consequences of taking a specific action in a particular situation.

Whether British Columbia should preserve some or all of its old-growth forest is a **normative question**—a question involving our values. A normative question is a question about what *ought* to be or *should* be. By itself, economic analysis cannot answer such questions. A society that reveres nature and antiquity may well decide the fate of this effectively irreplaceable resource differently from one holding other values, even though members of both societies are in complete agreement about all the relevant economic facts and theories. Economic analysis is on firmer ground when it comes to answering **positive questions**—questions about what the consequences of specific policies or institutional arrangements will be. If we convert logging forests into parks, what will happen to the price of lumber? What substitute building materials are likely to be developed, and at what cost? How will employment in the logging and housing industries be affected? If we permit unrestricted clear-cutting of Canadian forests, how do we calculate the environmental costs in terms of increased pollution, accelerated erosion, and loss of biodiversity? These are all positive economic questions, and the answers to them are clearly relevant to our thinking about the underlying normative question.

1.10 MICROECONOMICS AND MACROECONOMICS

Our focus in this chapter is on issues confronting the individual decision maker. As we proceed, we'll also consider economic models of groups of individuals—for example, the group of all buyers or all sellers in a market. The study of individual choices and the study of group behaviour in individual markets both come under the rubric of microeconomics. Macroeconomics, in contrast, is the study of broader aggregations of markets. For example, it tries to explain the national unemployment rate, the overall price level, and the total value of national output.

Economists are much better at predicting and explaining what goes on in individual markets than what happens in the economy as a whole. When prominent economists disagree in the press or on television, the subject is much more likely to be one from macroeconomics than from microeconomics. But even though economists are still not very good at answering macroeconomic questions, there is no denying the importance of macroeconomic analysis. After all, recessions and inflation disrupt the lives of millions of people.

Modern economists increasingly believe that the key to progress in macroeconomics lies in more careful analysis of the individual markets that make up broader aggregates. As a result, the distinction between micro and macro has become less clear in recent years. The graduate training of all economists, micro and macro alike, is increasingly focused on microeconomic analysis.

SUMMARY

www.mcgrawhill.ca/olc/frank

- Microeconomics is the science of choice under scarcity. Scarcity is ever present, even when material resources are abundant. There are always important limitations on time, energy, and the other things we need to pursue our goals.

- Much of the economist's task is to try to answer questions of the form "Should I do activity x?" The approach to answering them is disarmingly simple. It is to do x if and only if its costs are smaller than its benefits. Not incurring a cost is the same as getting a benefit.

- We saw that the cost-benefit model sometimes fails to predict how people behave when confronted with everyday choices. The art of cost-benefit analysis lies in being able to specify and measure the relevant costs and benefits, a skill that many decision makers conspicuously lack. Some costs, like sunk costs, will often seem relevant but turn out not to be. Others, like implicit costs, are sometimes ignored, even

though they are of central importance. Benefits too are often difficult to conceptualize and measure. Experience has taught that becoming aware of the most common pitfalls helps most people become better decision makers.

- When the question is not whether to perform an activity but rather at what level to perform it, marginal analysis draws our attention to the importance of marginal benefits and marginal costs. We should increase the level of an activity whenever its marginal benefit exceeds its marginal cost.

- The principles of rational choice are by no means limited to formal markets for goods and services. Indeed, some form of implicit or explicit cost-benefit calculation lies behind almost every human action, object, and behaviour. Knowledge of the underlying principles casts our world in a sharp new light, not always flattering, but ever a source of stimulating insight.

QUESTIONS FOR REVIEW

1. What is the opportunity cost of your reading a novel this evening?
2. Distinguish between the present-aim and self-interest standards of rationality.
3. Give three examples of activities that are accompanied by external costs *or* benefits.
4. How does the self-interest model help us understand

why children in most democratic countries are brought up to believe that it is their duty to vote?
5. Why should sunk costs be irrelevant for current decisions?
6. How can the cost-benefit model be useful for studying the behaviour of people who do not think explicitly in terms of costs and benefits?

1. Jamal has a very flexible summer job. He works every day but is allowed to take a day off anytime he wants. His friend Don suggests they take off work on Tuesday and go to the amusement park. The admission charge for the amusement park is $15 per person, and it will cost them $5 each for gasoline and parking. Jamal loves amusement parks and a day at the park is worth $45 to him. However, Jamal also enjoys his job so much that he would actually be willing to pay $10 per day to do it.

   a. If Jamal earns $10 if he works, should he go to the amusement park?
   b. If Jamal earns $15 . . . ?
   c. If Jamal earns $20 . . . ?

2. Tom is a Muskoka mushroom farmer. He invests all his spare cash in additional mushrooms, which grow on otherwise useless land behind his barn. The mushrooms double in size during their first year, after which time they are harvested by the buyers and sold at a constant price per kilogram. Tom's friend Dick asks Tom for a loan of $200, which he promises to repay after one year. How much interest will Dick have to pay Tom in order for Tom to be no worse off than if he had not made the loan?

3. The meal plan at University A lets students eat as much as they like for a fixed fee of $500 per term. The average student there eats 100 kg of food per term. University B charges students $500 for a book of meal tickets that entitles the student to eat 100 kg of food per term. If the student eats more than 100 kg, he or she pays extra; if the student eats less, he or she gets a refund. If students are rational and have the same appetites at A and B, where will average food consumption be higher?

4. You are planning a 2000-km trip to Banff. Except for the matter of cost, you are completely indifferent between driving and taking the bus. Bus fare is $260. The costs of operating your car during a typical 20,000-km driving year are as follows:

Insurance	$1000
Interest	2000
Fuel & oil	1200
Tires	200
Licence & registration	50
Maintenance	1100
Total	$5550

Should you drive or take the bus?

5. Al and Jane have rented a banquet hall with a 100-person capacity to host a party in celebration of their wedding anniversary. Forty-eight people have already accepted their invitation. Given 50 people, the caterers will charge $400 for food and $100 for drinks. The band will cost $300 for the evening, and the hall costs $200. Now Al and Jane are considering inviting 10 more people. By how much will these extra guests increase the cost of their party?

*6. You drive 8000 km a year and buy gasoline at the price of $.70 per litre. Except for differences in annual costs, you are indifferent between driving a 10-year-old Buick ($600 annual rental, 10 L/100 km) or a 10-year-old Toyota ($1000 annual rental, 4 L/100 km). Which one should you drive? At what price of gas would you be indifferent between the two cars?

7. Bill and Joe live in Barrie. At 2 p.m., Bill goes online and buys a $30 ticket to a Raptors game to be played that night in Toronto (100 km south). Joe plans to attend the same game, but doesn't purchase his ticket in advance because he knows from experience that it is always possible to buy just as good a seat at the arena. At 4 p.m., a heavy, unexpected snowstorm begins, making the drive to Toronto much less attractive than before. If both Bill and Joe have the same tastes and are rational, is one of them more likely to attend the game than the other? If so, say who and explain why. If not, explain why not.

8. Two types of radar weather-detection devices are available for commercial passenger aircraft: the "state-of-the-art" machine and another that is significantly less costly, but also less effective.

The federal government has hired you for advice on whether all passenger planes should be required to use the state-of-the-art machine. After careful study, your recommendation is to require the more expensive machine only in passenger aircraft with more than 200 seats. How would you justify such a recommendation to a civil servant who complains that all passengers have a right to the best weather-detecting radar currently available?

9. A group has chartered a bus to Niagara Falls. The driver costs $100, the bus costs $500, and trip insurance (purchased the day of the trip) will cost $75. The driver's fee is nonrefundable, but the bus may be cancelled a week in advance at a charge of only $50. At $18 per ticket, how many people must buy tickets so that the trip need not be cancelled?

10. Residents of Tracheville are charged a fixed weekly fee of $6 for refuse collection. They are allowed to put out as many garbage bags as they wish. The average household disposes of three bags per week in this way. Now, suppose that Tracheville changes to a "tag" system. Each bag of refuse to be collected must have a tag affixed to it. The tags cost $2 each. What effect do you think the introduction of the tag system will have on the total quantity of trash collected in Tracheville?

11. Susan (from Example 1-12) has a *new* long-distance boyfriend, Stan Jevons, but the same telephone plan, which costs her 4 cents per minute. Her marginal benefit of talking to Stan is given by the equation $MB = 40 - .025M$, where the marginal benefit or value of an additional minute (MB) is in cents per minute and M is in minutes per month. Draw a graph of Susan's marginal cost and marginal benefit curves. How many minutes per month will she talk with Stan? If the long-distance rate fell to 2 cents per minute, how many minutes per month would she talk to Stan?

12. Suppose that Susan from Problem 11 meets someone new, Alfie Marshall, in her microeconomics class, and that as a result the marginal benefit of talking long-distance with Stan becomes $MB = 20 - .025M$, with the cost still at 4 cents per minute. Draw Susan's new graph. Now how many minutes per month will she talk with Stan? If the long-distance rate fell to 2 cents per minute, how many minutes per month would she talk to Stan?

*13. Dana has purchased a $40 ticket to a rock concert. On the day of the concert she is invited to a welcome-home party for a friend returning from abroad. She cannot attend both the concert and the party. If she had known about the party before buying the ticket, she would have chosen the party over the concert. True or false: It follows that if she is rational, she will go to the party anyway. Explain.

*14. Yesterday you were unexpectedly given a free ticket to a Def Zeppelin concert scheduled for April 1. The price printed on the ticket is $75, but the most you could sell it for is only $50. Today you discover that U-Who will be giving a concert that same evening. Tickets for the U-Who concert are still available at $75. Had you known before receiving your Zeppelin ticket yesterday that U-Who would be coming, you definitely would have bought a ticket to see them, not Def Zeppelin. True or false: From what we are told of your preferences, it follows that if you are a rational utility maximizer, you should attend the U-Who concert. Explain.

15. You loan a friend $1000, and at the end of 1 year she writes you a cheque for $1000 to pay off this loan. If the annual interest rate on your savings account is 6 percent, what was your opportunity cost of making this loan?

*16. You have just purchased a new Ford Taurus for $30,000, but the most you could get for it if you sold it privately is $25,000. Now you learn that Toyota is offering its Camry, which normally sells for $35,000, at a special sale price of $30,000. If you had known before buying the Taurus that you could buy a Camry at the same price, you would have definitely chosen the Camry. *True or false*: From what we are told of your preferences, it follows that if you are a rational utility maximizer, you should definitely not sell the Taurus and buy the Camry. Explain.

---

*Problems marked with an asterisk are more difficult.

1-1. Someone who gets a $28 ticket every 400 km driven will pay $35 in fines, on the average, for every 500 km driven. Adding that figure to the $20 hassle cost of driving, and then adding the $50 fuel, oil, and maintenance cost, we have $105. This is more than the $100 bus fare, which means taking the bus is best.

1-2. The $18 Mike paid for his ticket is a sunk cost at the moment he must decide whether to attend the concert. For both Jim and Mike, therefore, the costs and benefits should be the same. If the benefit of seeing the concert outweighs the cost of sitting in the rain, they should go. Otherwise they should stay home.

1-3. You should use your coupon for the New Delhi trip, because it is better to save $120 than to save $100.

1-4. Two boats. Referring to Table 1-2, note that if marginal cost is $150, it now pays to launch the second boat (marginal benefit = $180) but not the third (marginal benefit = $120).

1-5. At 2 cents per minute, Susan should talk for 600 minutes per month.

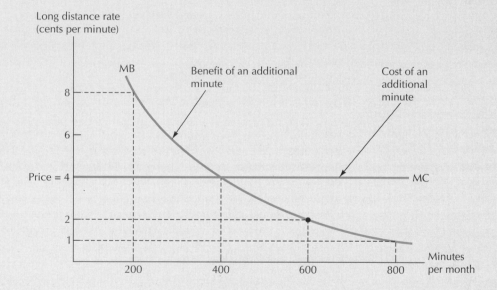

Chapter 2

SUPPLY AND DEMAND

During the Second World War, the Canadian government instituted a complex and extensive system of price controls and rationing. Ration coupons were issued to families, and to buy one of the rationed goods a person had to surrender one of the coupons in paying for the good. The rationing system was part of a full-scale mobilization of the Canadian economy. Its objectives were to restrain inflationary pressures; to increase the security of supply of the materials being redirected toward the war effort; and to ensure that the sacrifices the war required were shared more or less equally among all Canadians. To a considerable extent, it was successful in achieving these objectives.

Yet almost inevitably, despite the growth of a bureaucracy to administer and enforce the system, illegal **black markets** emerged. In these markets, rationed goods were sold at higher than controlled price levels. The rationing system involved three types of cost. First, resources were consumed both in maintaining the administrative apparatus and in evading the controls. Second, since individuals received more ration coupons than they wanted for certain commodities and fewer than they wanted for others, and there were restrictions on selling or swapping coupons, there were inefficiencies in their choices as consumers. Third, insofar as prices were fixed for extended periods, prices could not change in relation to changes in relative scarcity of particular goods. The "rationing" function of higher prices for the goods in shortest supply was constrained, and queuing for such goods consumed the time of those in line.

Seventeenth-century Holland fell prey to an epidemic of speculative fever now known as the Tulip Mania. At the height of the craze, from 1633 to 1637, rapidly rising prices for rare varieties of tulip bulb led people to expect that tulip prices would keep rising indefinitely. Otherwise sensible middle-class individuals mortgaged all their property to purchase even a few bulbs, which they hoped to resell at a profit. In 1637, when the inevitable crash came, many ordinary families were ruined.

Twenty-first-century North America has witnessed dramatic increases in high-tech and dot-com stock prices, high volumes of trading, and equally dramatic and precipitous drops in the prices of these same stocks. Is this volatility a sign of the rapidity with

Black market An illegal market, set up to facilitate transactions prohibited by law.

which the market enables informed investors to respond to new information that alters the long-term growth potential of the companies concerned? Or, particularly with the growth of e-trading, does the stock market function for at least some of the players as a form of legalized gambling, driven by mob psychology, the herd instinct, bluffing, ignorance, and greed?

When markets function properly, they are a remarkably economical and effective medium of communication, providing a means for mutually beneficial exchange with a minimum of central direction and control. But in certain circumstances, markets as a medium can also transmit and amplify pathological behaviour that is individually and socially destructive. Centralized coordination and control of production, consumption, and distribution is sometimes resorted to in situations of perceived social crisis or of market failure. Indeed, *inside* firms, as in the military, some type of centralized command structure is essential. Yet such centralized systems can generate inefficiencies of their own, as well as attempts at evasion of control, because they cannot perform certain functions as flexibly or as effectively as the market can.

CHAPTER PREVIEW

In this chapter we explore why markets function so smoothly much of the time and why attempts at direct allocation are often problematic. The early part of the chapter looks at basic supply and demand analysis. First, we review the usual descriptive features of supply and demand analysis covered in the introductory course. Next, we'll see that, under certain assumptions, the unregulated competitive market can yield the best attainable outcome, in the sense that any other combination of price and quantity would be worse for at least some buyers or sellers.

Despite this attractive feature, market outcomes do not always command society's approval. Concern for the well-being of the poor, for example, has motivated governments to intervene in a variety of ways—for instance, by adopting laws that peg prices above or below their equilibrium levels. Such laws, we will see, can generate harmful, if unintended, consequences.

We shall also see that often a more efficient solution to the problems of the poor is to boost their incomes directly. The laws of supply and demand cannot be repealed by legislators. But legislatures can alter the underlying forces that govern the shape and position of supply and demand schedules.

Finally, we explore supply and demand analysis as a useful device for understanding how taxes affect equilibrium prices and quantities. Such analysis helps dispel the myth that a tax is paid primarily by the party on whom it is directly levied; rather, the burden of a tax falls on whichever side of the market is least able to avoid it.

2.1 SUPPLY AND DEMAND ANALYSIS

Our basic tool for analyzing market outcomes is supply and demand analysis, already familiar to most of you from your introductory course. Let us begin with the following working definition of a market.

Definition: A market consists of the buyers and sellers of a good or service.

Some markets are confined to a single specific time and location. For example, at many antiques auctions, all the participating buyers and sellers (or at least their designated representatives) gather together in the same place. Other markets span vast geographic territory, and most participants in them never meet or even see one another.

The world's major stock exchanges are such markets, and the growth of Internet securities trading has intensified the "virtual" nature of these markets. The Internet has also become a major alternative to traditional marketing channels for thousands of products, ranging from antiques, books, CDs, and downloadable music to home-delivered groceries.

Sometimes the choice of market definition will depend on the bias of the observer. In competition cases, for example, current policy restricts mergers between companies whose combined share of the market exceeds a given threshold. Accordingly, in opposing a merger the Commissioner of Competition will tend to define markets as narrowly as possible, thereby making the combined market share as large as possible. The merging companies, in contrast, prefer to view their markets in much broader terms, which naturally makes their combined market share smaller. In the Superior Propane-ICG Propane merger proposed in 1998, the companies argued to the Canadian Competition Tribunal that they were in the "fuel" business, where their market share was about 2 percent. The Commissioner of Competition argued, in a position accepted by the Tribunal, that the relevant markets were the propane delivery market and the national accounts coordination services market. The merger would create a monopoly in the latter market, and restrict competition in 65 local markets for propane delivery. In general, as in this particular instance, the best market definition will depend on the purpose at hand.

Over the years, economists have increasingly recognized that even subtle product differences matter a great deal to some consumers. The trend in analysis has been toward ever narrower definitions of goods and markets. Two otherwise identical products are often classified as separate if they differ only with respect to the times or places they are available. An umbrella on a sunny day is in this sense a very different product from an umbrella during a downpour. And the markets for these two products can behave quite differently.

To make our discussion concrete, let us consider the workings of a hypothetical perfectly competitive market—say, the one for 1-kg lobsters in Shediac, New Brunswick, on July 20, 2020. The concept of a perfectly competitive market is developed in detail in Chapters 4, 10, and 11. For present purposes, we can think of the market as being made up of a large number of buyers and sellers. None of them has enough market power to be able to affect the equilibrium price in the market by his or her actions. All of them have full information regarding the price and quality of the lobsters (the good being exchanged), and all of them have perfect freedom of entry into and exit from the market. For this market, the task of analysis is to explain both the price of lobsters and the quantity traded.

The Demand Curve

To do this, we begin with the basic *demand curve,* a simple mathematical relationship that tells how many lobsters buyers wish to purchase at various possible prices (holding all else constant). The curve *DD* depicted in Figure 2-1, for example, tells us that 4000 lobsters will be demanded at a price of $4 each, 1000 at a price of $10, and so on.

If a visitor from Mars were told only that lobsters sell for $4 each, he would have no way of knowing whether they were cheap or expensive. In 1900, a $4 lobster would have been out of reach of all but the wealthiest consumers. In 2020, in contrast, lobsters would be an incredible bargain at that price. Unless otherwise stated, the price on the vertical axis of the demand curve diagram will refer to the ***real price*** of the good, which means its price relative to the prices of all other goods and services. Thus, the prices on the

Real price of a product Its price relative to the prices of other goods and services.

FIGURE 2-1

The Demand Curve for Lobsters in Shediac, N.B., July 20, 2020
The demand curve tells the quantities buyers will wish to purchase at various prices. Its key property is its downward slope; when price falls, the quantity demanded increases. This property is called the law of demand.

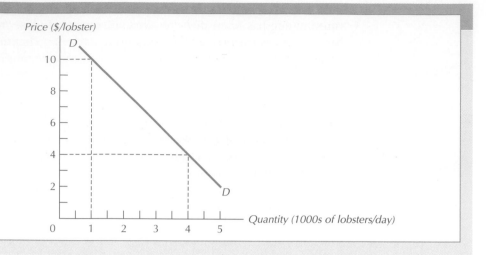

vertical axis of Figure 2-1 represent lobster prices on July 20, 2020, and the context within which those prices are interpreted by buyers is the set of prices of all other goods on that same date.

The discussion above describes the demand curve as a schedule telling how much of a product consumers wish to purchase at various prices. This is called the *horizontal interpretation* of the demand curve. Under this interpretation, we start with price on the vertical axis and read the corresponding quantity demanded on the horizontal axis. For instance, at a price of $10 per lobster, the demand curve in Figure 2-1 tells us that the quantity demanded will be 1000 lobsters per day.

A second interpretation of the demand curve is to start with quantity on the horizontal axis and then read the marginal buyer's reservation price on the vertical axis. Thus when the quantity of lobsters sold is 4000 per day, the demand curve in Figure 2-1 tells us that the marginal buyer's reservation price is $4 per lobster. This second way of reading the demand curve is called the *vertical interpretation*.

The demand curve shown in Figure 2-1 happens to be linear, but demand curves in general need not be. The key property assumed of them is that they are downward sloping: the quantity demanded rises as the price of the product falls. This property is often called the **law of demand**. Although we will see in Chapter 4 that it is possible for a demand curve to slope upward, such exceptions are rarely encountered in practice. The negative slope of the demand curve accords in every way with our intuitions about how people respond to rising prices.

As we will see in more detail in Chapter 4, there are normally two independent reasons for the quantity demanded to fall when the price rises. One is that many people will switch to a close substitute. When lobster gets more expensive, consumers may switch to crab, meat, or poultry. A second reason people buy less when the price rises is that they are not *able* to buy as much as before. Incomes, after all, go only so far. When the price of a product goes up, we can't buy as much as before unless we at the same time purchase less of something else.

The demand curve for a good is a summary of the various cost-benefit calculations that buyers make with respect to the good, as we shall see in greater detail in the next chapter. The question each person faces is, "Should I buy the product?" (and usually, "If so, how much of it?"). The cost side of the calculation is simply the price of the

Law of demand The empirical observation that when the price of a product falls, people demand larger quantities of it.

product (and implicitly, the other goods or services that could be bought with the same money). The benefit side is the satisfaction provided by the product. The negative slope of the demand schedule tells us that the cost-benefit criterion will be met for fewer and fewer potential buyers as the price of the product rises.

The Supply Curve

On the seller's side of the market, the corresponding analytical tool is the *supply schedule*. A hypothetical schedule for our lobster market is shown as line *SS* in Figure 2-2. Again, the linear form of this particular schedule is not a characteristic feature of supply schedules generally. What these schedules do tend to have in common is their upward slope: the quantity supplied rises as the price of a product rises. This property can be called the **law of supply**. For a supplier to be willing to sell a product, its price must cover the cost of producing or acquiring it. As we shall see in detail in Chapter 9, the cost of producing additional units often tends to rise as more units are produced, especially in the short run. When this is the case, increased production is profitable only at higher prices. In our stylized lobster market, the reasons for this are clear. The larger the catch, the farther the lobster boats have to travel per lobster, and the higher the cost per lobster. Another factor contributing to the upward slope of the supply curve is substitution on the part of fishermen. As the price of lobsters increases, more producers switch to lobsters, rather than continue to fish for, say, cod.

Like demand curves, supply curves can be interpreted either horizontally or vertically. Under the horizontal interpretation, we begin with a price, then go over to the supply curve to read the quantity that sellers wish to sell at that price on the horizontal axis. For instance, at a price of $4 per lobster, sellers in Figure 2-2 wish to sell 2000 lobsters per day.

Under the vertical interpretation, we begin with a quantity, then go up to the supply curve to read the corresponding marginal cost on the vertical axis. For example, if sellers in Figure 2-2 are currently supplying 5000 lobsters per day, the opportunity cost of the last lobster supplied by the marginal seller would be $10. In other words, the supply curve tells us that the marginal cost of delivering the 5000th lobster is $10. If someone could deliver a 5001st lobster for less than $10, she would have had an incentive to do so, in which case the quantity of lobster supplied at a price of $10 would not have been

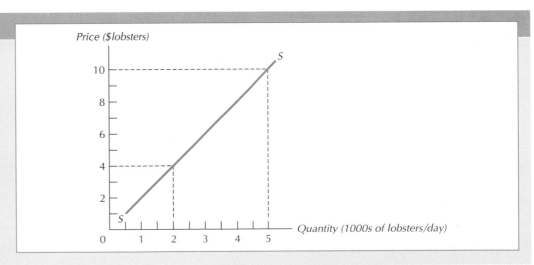

FIGURE 2-2

A Supply Schedule for Lobsters in Shediac, N.B., July 20, 2020
The upward slope of the supply schedule reflects the fact that costs tend to rise when producers expand production in the short run.

5000 per day to begin with. By similar reasoning, when the quantity of lobster supplied is 2000 per day, the marginal cost of delivering another lobster must be $4.

An alternative way of describing the supply schedule is to call it the set of price-quantity pairs for which suppliers are satisfied. The term "satisfied" has a technical meaning here, which is that any point on the supply schedule represents the quantity that suppliers want to sell, *given the price they face*. They would obviously be happy to get even higher prices for their offerings. But for any given price, suppliers would consider themselves worse off if forced to sell either more or less than the corresponding quantity on the supply schedule. If, for example, the price of lobsters in Figure 2-2 were $4, suppliers would not be satisfied selling either more or fewer than 2000 lobsters a day.

The demand schedule may be given a parallel description. It is the set of price-quantity pairs for which buyers are satisfied in precisely the same sense. At any given price, they would consider themselves worse off if forced to purchase either more or less than the corresponding quantity on the demand schedule.

2.2 EQUILIBRIUM QUANTITY AND PRICE

With both the supply and demand schedules in hand, we can describe the *equilibrium quantity and price* of lobsters. It is the price-quantity pair at which both buyers and sellers are satisfied. Put another way, it is the price-quantity pair at which the supply and demand schedules intersect. Figure 2-3 depicts the equilibrium in our lobster market, at which a total of 3000 lobsters is traded at a price of $6 each.

If we were at any price-quantity pair other than the one in Figure 2-3, either buyers or sellers, or both, would be dissatisfied in the sense described above. If the price happened for some reason to lie above the $6 equilibrium level, sellers would tend to be the ones who are frustrated. At a price of $8, for example, buyers would purchase only 2000 lobsters, whereas sellers would offer 4000. (See Figure 2-4.) Buyers would be satisfied at a price of $8, but sellers would not. A situation in which price exceeds its equilibrium value is called one of **excess supply**, or *surplus*. At $8, there is an excess supply of 2000 lobsters.

Excess supply The amount by which quantity supplied exceeds quantity demanded at a given price.

FIGURE 2-3

Equilibrium in the Lobster Market
The intersection of the supply and demand curves represents the price-quantity pair at which all participants in the market are "satisfied": buyers are buying the amount they want to buy at that price, and sellers are selling the amount they want to sell.

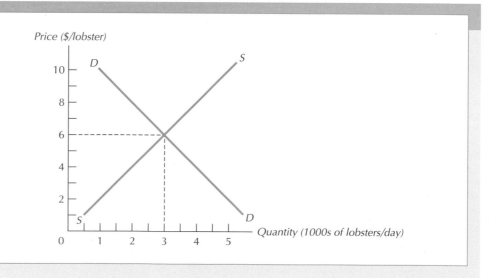

FIGURE 2-4

Excess Supply and Excess Demand
When price exceeds the equilibrium level, there is excess supply, or surplus. When price is below the equilibrium level, there is excess demand, or shortage.

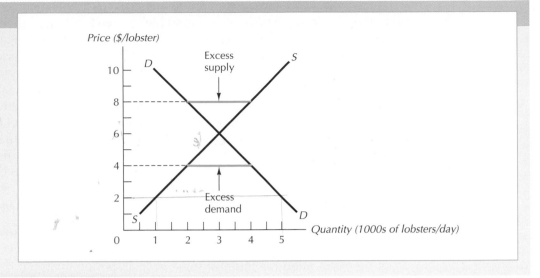

If, in contrast, the price happened to lie below the equilibrium price of $6, then buyers would be the ones dissatisfied. At a price of $4, for example, they would want to purchase 4000 lobsters, whereas suppliers would be willing to sell only 2000. A situation in which price lies below its equilibrium value is referred to as one of ***excess demand***, or *shortage*. At a price of $4 in this lobster market, there is an excess demand of 2000 lobsters. At the market equilibrium price of $6, both excess demand and excess supply are exactly zero.

Excess demand
The amount by which quantity demanded exceeds quantity supplied at a given price.

EXERCISE 2-1

4.

At a price of $2 in this hypothetical lobster market, how much excess demand for lobsters will there be? How much excess supply will there be at a price of $10?

2.3 ADJUSTMENT TO EQUILIBRIUM

When price differs from the equilibrium price, trading in the marketplace will be constrained—by the behaviour of buyers if the price lies above equilibrium, by the behaviour of sellers if below. At any price other than the equilibrium price, one side or the other of the market is dissatisfied. At prices above equilibrium, for example, sellers are not selling as much as they want to. The impulse of a dissatisfied seller is to reduce the price. In the seafood business, after all, the rule of thumb is "sell it or smell it." At a price of $8 each, 2000 lobsters are being sold, but another 2000 go unclaimed. Each seller reasons, correctly, that if he were to cut his price slightly, while other sellers remained at $8, he could move all his unsold lobsters. Buyers will abandon sellers who charge $8 in favour of those who charge only $7.95. But then the deserted sellers themselves have a motive for cutting price. And if all sellers cut price to $7.95, each will again have a large quantity of unsold lobsters. Downward pressure on price will persist so long as there remain any dissatisfied sellers—that is, until price falls to its equilibrium value.

When price is below $6, buyers are dissatisfied. Under these conditions, sellers will realize that they can increase their prices and still sell as much as they wish to. This upward pressure on price will persist until price reaches its equilibrium value. Put another way, consumers will start bidding against each other in the hope of seeing their demands satisfied.

An extraordinary feature of this equilibrating process is that no one consciously plans or directs it. The actual steps that consumers and producers must take to move toward equilibrium are often indescribably complex. Suppliers looking to expand their operations, for example, must choose from a bewilderingly large menu of equipment options. Buyers, for their part, face literally millions of choices about how to spend their money. And yet the adjustment toward equilibrium results more or less automatically from the natural reactions of self-interested individuals facing either surpluses or shortages.

2.4 SOME WELFARE PROPERTIES OF EQUILIBRIUM

Given the attributes—tastes, abilities, knowledge, incomes, and so on—of buyers and sellers, the equilibrium outcome has some attractive properties. Specifically, we can say that no reallocation can improve some people's position without harming the position of at least some others. *If price and quantity take anything other than their equilibrium values, however, it will always be possible to reallocate so as to make at least some people better off without harming others.*

Sticking with the lobster example, suppose that the price is $4 and that suppliers therefore offer only 2000 lobsters. As indicated in Figure 2-5, when only 2000 lobsters are available, buyers are willing to pay $8 apiece for them. Here, the value to the buyer of the last lobster caught ($8) is higher than the cost of harvesting it ($4), which means that there is room to cut a deal.

Suppose, for example, a dissatisfied buyer were to offer a supplier $5 for a lobster. The supplier would gladly sell an additional lobster at this price (since, at 2000 lobsters, additional lobsters cost only $4 each). This transaction would improve the buyer's position by $3 (the difference between the $8 value he attaches to the lobster and the $5 he paid for it). It would also improve the seller's position by $1 (the difference between the $5 she got and the $4 cost of the extra lobster). No one suffers any harm from this transaction (except the extra lobster!), and the two participants reap a total of $4 additional benefit from it ($3 for the buyer, $1 for the seller). A similar argument can be made

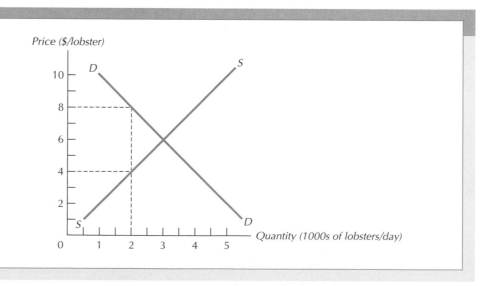

FIGURE 2-5

An Opportunity for Improvement in the Lobster Market
When the quantity traded in the market is below the equilibrium quantity, it is always possible to reallocate resources in such a way that some people are made better off without harming others. Here, a dissatisfied buyer can pay a seller $5 for an additional lobster, thus making both parties better off.

concerning any price that is below the equilibrium value. For any such price, it will always be possible to make some people better off without hurting others.

What if the price had been higher than the equilibrium price to begin with? Suppose that price is $8 and that trading is therefore limited by buyers' demands for 2000 lobsters. (Again, see Figure 2-5.) Now a dissatisfied seller can propose a transaction that will make both the seller and some buyers better off. Suppose, for example, a seller offers an additional lobster for sale for $7. Since buyers value additional lobsters at $8, whoever buys it will be better off by $1. And since lobsters cost only $4 to harvest, the seller will be better off by $3. Again, no one is injured by this transaction, and again the two parties gain a total of $4.

Thus, no matter whether price starts out above or below its equilibrium value, it will always be possible to put together a transaction that benefits all participants. We'll examine the welfare properties of the market system in much greater detail in Chapter 16. But for now, we may observe that the equilibrium price and quantity constitute the best outcome attainable, given the initial attributes and endowments of buyers and sellers.

2.5 COMPETITIVE MARKETS AND EQUITY

The fact that market equilibrium outcomes are efficient in the sense described above does not mean that they are necessarily desirable in any absolute sense. All markets may be in perfect equilibrium, for example, and yet many people may lack sufficient incomes to purchase even the bare necessities of life. The claim that market equilibrium is efficient does not challenge the notion that it is difficult, often even painful, to be poor. Efficiency says merely that, *given the low incomes of the poor,* free exchange enables them to do the best they can. One can hold this view and yet still believe that it is desirable to provide public assistance to people who are unable to earn adequate incomes in the marketplace.

Concern for the well-being of those with low incomes motivates most societies to try to alter market outcomes. The difficulty is that some direct interventions in markets can produce unintended and often harmful consequences. A more thorough understanding of the workings of the market mechanism would prevent many of the most costly consequences of such intervention.

EXAMPLE 2-1 | **Compensation for being "bumped." What are the efficiency and distributional implications of handling excess demand for airline travel through a first-come, first-served policy as opposed to an auction mechanism?**

It has always been a common practice for commercial airlines to issue more reservations than there are seats on a flight. Because many reservation holders fail to show up for their flights, this practice seldom causes difficulty. This overbooking provides airlines with a means of increasing their "load factors" (the proportion of occupied seats to total available seats on any flight), even if there are "no-shows." Since it costs little more to transport 150 passengers than 140 passengers on a plane with a 150-seat capacity, increasing the load factor is extremely important for airline profitability.

Occasionally, however, 160 passengers will show up for a flight on which there are only, say, 150 seats. Before the late 1970s, airlines dealt with overbooked flights by boarding passengers on a first-come, first-served basis. Under this system, a person with a valid reservation who *had* to be at his destination by a certain time would have to arrive at the airport *long* before the flight was called (simply on the off-chance that the flight might be overbooked), in order to protect his place in the queue that *might* occur. His reservation was effectively meaningless as a guarantee of a seat. There was also a question as to whether the airlines were acting in bad faith toward the passengers who

Why is an auction a better way to allocate seats on an overbooked flight than first-come, first-served?

did show up, and basically downloading all of the costs, uncertainty, and inconvenience of overbooking onto these passengers, while reaping all of the benefits themselves.

As a result of government regulatory intervention, initially in the United States and then elsewhere, this inefficient and inequitable system has been replaced by an alternative system. Passengers on an overbooked flight have an option of volunteering to take a later flight to their destination, in exchange for some combination of cash and free travel to compensate them for the delay and inconvenience. Under this system, those who can least afford the delay simply do not volunteer to accept the compensation. Others who have more flexible schedules or who value the compensation package more highly than the cost of the delay receive a net benefit for consenting to being bumped from the flight. The airlines also benefit. By providing the compensation package to a few passengers on those flights where overbooking becomes a problem, airlines can increase their load factors on *all* their flights. Not only that, but from a customer relations standpoint, having customers who are either happy to be flying or happy to have been quite literally "bought off" is preferable to dealing with an irate mob.

One remaining question, however, is whether the compensation system has removed one source of inefficiency and inequity only to replace it by another. Other things being equal, it is the rich who are least likely to volunteer, because they can afford to forgo the compensation package, while lower-income passengers are the ones who are most likely to accept it. The rich therefore end up flying on time, while lower-income passengers stay behind, curled up in uncomfortable chairs in the terminal, waiting for the next flight. Described in these terms, the system may sound inequitable. But that impression is quite misleading. The distribution of income and wealth in society is unequal, and it may even be felt that the degree of inequality is excessive. But it is not the job of the airline compensation system to eliminate these inequalities. *Given* the present distribution of income, what it does do is enable those who would be hurt *least* by waiting to *benefit* by volunteering to wait for a later flight. If a lower-income passenger felt she *had* to arrive at her destination via the original flight, she would simply not volunteer for the compensation option.

For those who believe that government intervention in the private sector invariably leads to inefficiency, there is a certain irony in the fact that in this case it took government regulation to show private corporations the proper use of the market mechanism to increase both efficiency and fairness. This is not an isolated example. We shall see later in the chapter that certain types of government intervention in the market can result in inefficient outcomes. Yet, in later chapters, we shall also see that in a range of cases the unregulated market itself does not produce socially efficient outcomes. In such cases of "market failure," even apart from concerns about equity and fairness, government action may be necessary to restore efficiency.

Some critics of the market system argue that it is unfair to ration goods and services by asking how much people are willing to pay for them. This criterion, they point out, gives short shrift to the interests of the poor. But as Example 2-1 illustrates, serious contradictions are inherent in alternative schemes of allocation. Consider again our hypothetical lobster market. Suppose we are concerned that the equilibrium price of $6 will exclude many deserving poor persons from ever being able to know the pleasure of a lobster dinner. And suppose that, with this in mind, we adopt a system that periodically gives free lobsters to the poor. Wouldn't such a system represent a clear improvement in the eyes of any person who feels compassion for the poor?

The answer, as in Example 2-1, is that for the same cost we can do even better. When a poor person, or indeed a rich person, does not buy lobster because the price is too high, she is saying, in effect, that she would prefer to spend her money on other things. If we gave such a person a lobster, what would she want to do with it? In an ideal world, she would immediately sell it to someone willing to pay the $6 equilibrium price for it. We know there will be such persons because some of the lobsters that would have been bought for $6 were instead given to the poor. The poor person's sale of the lobster to one of these people will bring about a clear improvement for both parties—for the buyer, or else he would not have bought it, and for the seller because the lobster is worth less than $6 to her.

The practical difficulty, as we will see in detail in later chapters, is that it would take time and effort for our hypothetical poor person to find a buyer for the lobster. In the end, she would probably eat it herself. True enough, she might enjoy her lobster dinner. But by her own reckoning, she would have enjoyed the $6 even more.

Rent Controls

Price ceiling
Government-fixed *maximum* price that can be charged for a good.

Rent control is one form of government intervention in the market that can have unintended adverse consequences. Rent control is intended to ensure that a stock of *affordable* rental housing is available, particularly to lower-income families, by placing a **price ceiling** on the rents that can be charged for any given apartment.

Basic supply and demand analysis is again all we need to see clearly the nature of the difficulties. Figure 2-6 depicts the supply and demand schedules for a hypothetical urban apartment market. The equilibrium rent in this market would be $600 per month, and at this level there would be 60,000 apartments traded. The government, however, has passed a law that holds rents at $R_c = $400 per month, or $200 below the market-clearing value. At $400 per month, buyers would like to rent 80,000 apartments, but suppliers are willing to offer only 40,000. There is an excess demand of 40,000 units. And if the rent control level remains fixed at $400 per month, excess demand will tend to grow over time as population grows and rent control makes building new apartments an unattractive investment.

In an unregulated market, the immediate response to such a high level of excess demand would be for rents to rise sharply. But here the law prevents them from rising above R_c. Yet there are other ways the pressures of excess demand can make themselves felt. One is for owners to spend less on maintaining the quality of their rental units. After all, if there are two tenants knocking at the door of each vacant apartment, a landlord has considerable room to manoeuvre. Clogged drains, peeling paint, broken thermostats, and the like are not apt to receive prompt attention when rents are set well below market-clearing levels.

Nor are these the most serious difficulties. With an offering of only 40,000 apartments per month, we see in Figure 2-6 that tenants would be willing to pay as much as $800 per month for an apartment. This pressure almost always finds ways, legal or illegal, of expressing itself. "Finder's fees" or "key deposits" become a common way of artificially raising the rent. Owners who cannot charge a market-clearing rent for an apartment also have the option of converting it to a condominium or co-op, which enables them to sell their asset for a price much closer to its true economic value, and further reduces the rental housing stock.

Even when rent-controlled apartment owners do not hike their prices in these various ways, serious misallocations can result. A widow steadfastly remains in her seven-room apartment even after her children have left home because it is much cheaper than alternative dwellings not covered by rent control. It would be much better for all concerned if she relinquished that space to a larger family. But under rent controls, she has every economic incentive not to do so.

EXAMPLE 2-2

Suppose the rent control is lowered (strengthened) to $200 per month. What is the excess demand, and how does it compare to the excess demand when rents were limited (more loosely) to $400 per month?

At $200 per month, buyers would like to rent 100,000 apartments, but suppliers are willing to offer only 20,000. Thus there is an excess demand of 80,000 units. The excess demand is greater than the excess demand of 40,000 units at the $400 per month rent control.

EXERCISE 2-2

In the market for apartments described in Figure 2-6, what would happen if the rent control level were set at $625 per month?

There are much more effective ways to help low-income individuals than to give them rent-controlled apartments or free lobsters. One way would be to give them additional income and let them decide for themselves how to spend it. Later chapters examine some of the practical difficulties involved in transferring additional purchasing power into the hands of the poor. In brief, the most difficult problem is that it is hard to target cash to the genuinely needy without unnecessarily subsidizing others who could fend for themselves. But as we will see, economic reasoning also suggests practical ways to overcome this difficulty. There are no simple or easy solutions. But given the substantial losses that can be caused by policies that prevent prices from reaching their equilibrium levels, these issues deserve our most serious attention.

FIGURE 2-6

Rent Controls
With the rent control level set at $400 a month, there is an excess demand of 40,000 apartments a month. At a rent control level of $400/month, only 40,000 apartments are supplied. At this quantity, the *marginal* buyer would be willing to pay $800/month for an apartment!

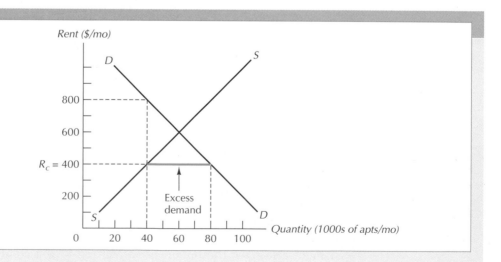

2.6 PRICE SUPPORTS

The rent control example considered a case in which the government imposed a price ceiling to prevent the price from rising to its equilibrium level. For some agricultural products, such as eggs and butter, historically the government established **price support** (or *price floor*) programs. Here, in contrast to the case of rent control, the price is set above the market equilibrium level; the problem is not one of excess demand but of excess supply. In order to maintain the price at the support level, the government must enter the market as a buyer, to absorb the excess supply. Otherwise, farmers would have an incentive to cut their prices.

Figure 2-7 depicts a price support level of P_s in a hypothetical market for butter. Because P_s is above the equilibrium price, the government must purchase the excess supply of 10,000 tonnes of butter per year. It must also arrange to store or otherwise dispose of the butter it has purchased.

A primary purpose of farm price supports is to increase the income of family farms. But such price support programs turned out to be a costly and inefficient method of farm income maintenance. They raised the prices of these products to consumers. Moreover, this burden was borne disproportionately by low-income families, who spend a higher than average percentage of their incomes on food. As well, the government food stockpiles were difficult to dispose of, costly to store, and subject to spoilage. For these and other reasons, such forms of price support have been largely eliminated in Canada, although (as we will see in Chapter 11) other methods of farm income maintenance still generate serious inefficiencies in the agricultural sectors of North America and especially Europe.

2.7 THE RATIONING AND ALLOCATIVE FUNCTIONS OF PRICES

Prices serve two important and distinct functions. First, they ration existing supplies of goods. Scarcity is the universal feature of economic life. People want more of virtually everything than could be supplied at a price of zero. Equilibrium prices serve to curtail

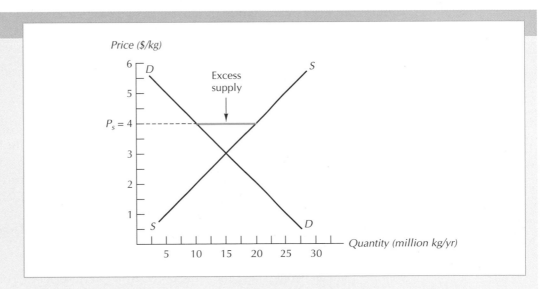

FIGURE 2-7

A Price Support in the Butter Market
For a price support to have any impact, it must be set above the market-clearing price. Its effect is to create excess supply, which the government then purchases.

these excessive claims by rationing scarce supplies to the users who place the highest value on them. This is the *rationing function of price*. It operates principally in the short run, to distribute existing output.

The second function of price is that of a signal to direct productive resources among the different sectors of the economy. In industries in which there is excess demand, firms are able to charge more than they need to cover their costs of production. The resulting profits act as a carrot that lures additional resources into these industries. The other side of this coin is that losses act as the stick that drives resources out of those industries in which there is excess supply. This is the so-called *allocative function of price*, the driving force behind Adam Smith's invisible hand. It operates principally in the longer run, to induce resources to flow from industries with excess supply to those with excess demand.

Rent controls subvert both critical functions of the price mechanism. The rationing function is undercut by the alternative mechanisms that distribute housing with little regard to the value people place on it. The underlying needs of tenants (as measured by their ability and willingness to pay) are relegated to secondary status. Both luck and the people you happen to know are often decisive. Artificially low rents also undercut the allocative function of price by sending a false signal to investors about the need for additional housing. With rent controls in effect, apartment builders earn less than they could by investing their money in other industries. It is hardly surprising, therefore, that many of them do precisely that. The cruel irony is that the pressing need in many communities with rent controls is for more low-income housing units, not fewer— which is precisely what a competitive market would produce on its own if instead money were redistributed to low-income households.

2.8 DETERMINANTS OF SUPPLY AND DEMAND

Supply and demand analysis is useful not only for the normative insight it offers into questions of public policy but also for a rich variety of descriptive purposes. Most importantly, it helps us predict how equilibrium prices and quantities will respond to changes in market forces. Because supply and demand curves intersect to determine equilibrium prices and quantities, anything that shifts these curves will tend to alter equilibrium values in a predictable way. In the next several chapters, we investigate in detail the forces that determine the shape and position of market demand curves. For the moment, let's discuss a few whose roles are intuitively clear.

Determinants of Demand

Incomes. It is obvious that income will influence the amount of most goods and services people will purchase at any given price. For most goods, the quantity demanded at any price will rise with income. Goods that have this property are called *normal goods*. So-called *inferior goods* (such as ground beef with high fat content, at certain income levels) are the exception to this general pattern. For such goods, the quantity demanded at any price will fall as income rises. The reason is that consumers abandon these goods in favour of higher-quality substitutes (such as leaner grades of meat in the ground beef case) as soon as they can afford to.

Tastes. Not all people share the same tastes. In Western societies, culture instills a taste for sitting on padded furniture, whereas in many Eastern societies, people customarily favour sitting cross-legged on the floor. The demand for armchairs hence tends to be

Rationing function of price The process whereby price directs existing supplies of a product to the users who value it most highly.

Allocative function of price The process whereby price acts as a signal that guides resources away from the production of goods whose prices lie below cost toward the production of goods whose prices exceed cost.

larger in the West than in the East. Nor do tastes always remain fixed over time. In response to fashion trends, the demand for skirts with hemlines above the knee can vary sharply from one decade to another.

Prices of Substitutes and Complements. Bacon and eggs play a complementary role in the diets of some people. For such people, a sharp increase in the price of bacon would lead to a reduction not only in the quantity of bacon demanded but also in the demand for eggs. Such goods are considered complements: an increase in the price of one good decreases demand for the other good. In contrast, in the case of close substitutes, such as coffee and tea, an increase in the price of one will tend to increase the demand for the other.

Expectations. People's expectations about future income and price levels also affect their current purchase decisions. For example, someone who expects sharply higher income in the future is likely to spend more today than an otherwise identical person who expects a much smaller income in the future. (After all, with a higher expected income, the need to save for the future diminishes.) Similarly, people will often accelerate their current purchases of goods whose prices are expected to rise sharply in the months to come.

Population. In general, the larger a market, the greater the amount of a good or service that will be purchased at any given price. Thus, in cities with growing populations, the demand for housing increases from year to year, whereas it tends to fall in cities with declining populations.

Figure 2-8 graphically displays some factors that shift demand curves.

FIGURE 2-8

Factors that Shift Demand Curves
Prices of substitutes and complements, incomes, population, expectation of future price and income changes, and tastes all influence the position of the current demand curve for a product.

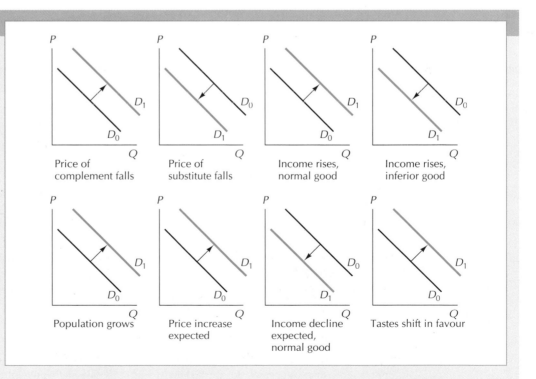

Determinants of Supply

Technology.   The amount suppliers are willing to offer at any price depends first and foremost on their costs of production. These costs, in turn, are closely linked to technology. For instance, the discovery of a more efficient lobster trap will reduce the cost of harvesting lobsters, which results in a rightward shift in the supply schedule.

Factor Prices.   Another important determinant of a supplier's costs is the payment it must make to its factors of production: labour, capital, and so on. If the price of lobster boats rises, or if the wage rate goes up, the supply schedule for lobsters will shift to the left.

The Number of Suppliers.   The more firms that can supply any product, the greater will be the quantity supplied of that product at any given price. The supply schedule of personal computers will shift to the right if more and more companies begin producing them.

Expectations.   Suppliers too will take expected changes in prices into account in their current production decisions. For example, if livestock producers expect beef prices to rise sharply in the future because of a shortage of young cattle, they are likely to withhold current supplies of mature livestock to take advantage of the higher future prices.[1]

Weather.   For some products, particularly agricultural ones, nature has a great deal to say about the placement of the supply schedule. In years of drought, for example, the supply schedule for many foodstuffs will be shifted sharply to the left.

Figure 2-9 shows the effects of some factors that shift supply schedules.

FIGURE 2-9

Factors That Shift Supply Schedules
Technology, input prices, the number of firms, expectations about future prices, and the weather all affect the position of the supply schedule for a given product.

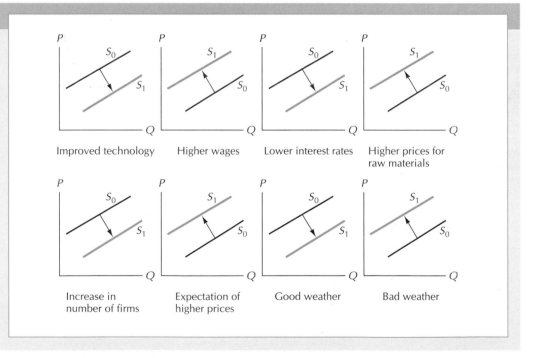

Improved technology   Higher wages   Lower interest rates   Higher prices for raw materials

Increase in number of firms   Expectation of higher prices   Good weather   Bad weather

---

[1]Note that supply is the quantity offered for sale at various prices, not necessarily production (when inventories can be stored). Hence, livestock producers will reduce sales of cattle in the current period, since they can sell them in a later period when prices are higher, provided that the higher expected prices more than compensate for the additional cost of feeding and tending the cattle in the interim.

Neither of the above lists of supply and demand shifters is meant to be exhaustive. We shall revisit them in more detail in Chapters 4 and 10.

Changes in Demand vs. Changes in the Quantity Demanded

When economists use the expression *change in demand*, they mean a shift in the entire demand curve. Thus, when the average income level of buyers changes, the demand curve shifts—there is a change in demand. When we say *change in the quantity demanded*, we mean a movement along the demand curve. When the price of a good falls, for example, the result is an increase in the quantity demanded, not an increase in demand.

Analogous interpretations attach to the expressions *change in supply and change in the quantity supplied*. These terminological distinctions are important for clear communication both in classroom discussion and on exams. And if the experience of previous generations of students is any guide, it requires effort to keep them straight.

2.9 PREDICTING AND EXPLAINING CHANGES IN PRICE AND QUANTITY

To predict or explain changes in equilibrium prices and quantities, we must be able to predict or account for the shifts in the relevant supply and/or demand schedules. When supply and demand curves have the conventional slopes, the following propositions about equilibrium prices and quantities will hold:

- An increase in demand alone will lead to an increase in both the equilibrium price and the equilibrium quantity exchanged.
- A decrease in demand alone will lead to a decrease in both the equilibrium price and the equilibrium quantity exchanged.
- An increase in supply alone will lead to a decrease in the equilibrium price and an increase in the equilibrium quantity exchanged.
- A decrease in supply alone will lead to an increase in the equilibrium price and a decrease in the equilibrium quantity exchanged.

These simple propositions permit us to answer a variety of questions.

Economic Naturalist 2-1

WHY DO THE PRICES OF SOME GOODS, LIKE APPLES, GO DOWN DURING THE MONTHS OF HEAVIEST CONSUMPTION WHILE THOSE OF OTHERS, LIKE BEACHFRONT COTTAGES, GO UP?

The answer is that the seasonal consumption increase is the result of a supply increase in the case of apples, a demand increase in the case of cottages. As shown in Figure 2-10, these shifts produce the observed seasonal relationships between equilibrium prices and quantities. (The subscripts *h* and *l* in Figure 2-10 are used to denote high and low consumption, respectively.) When demand increases (as for cottages), the increase in the equilibrium quantity occurs concurrently with an increase in the equilibrium price. When supply increases (as for apples), the increase in the equilibrium quantity occurs concurrently with a decrease in the equilibrium price.

FIGURE 2-10

Two Sources of Seasonal Variation
Apple consumption is highest in the fall, while cottage rentals are highest in summer. (The subscripts *h* and *l* stand for high and low consumption, respectively.) (a) Apple prices are lowest in fall, because the quantity increase results from increased supply. (b) Cottage prices are highest in summer, because the quantity increase results from increased demand.

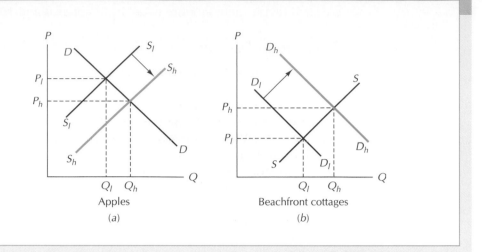

Apples
(a)

Beachfront cottages
(b)

EXERCISE 2-3

What will happen to the equilibrium price and quantity in the fresh fish market if both of the following events *simultaneously* occur: (1) a scientific report is issued saying that fish contains mercury, which is toxic to humans, and (2) the price of diesel fuel (used to operate fishing boats) falls significantly?

EXAMPLE 2-3

If grain is one of the components of cattle feed, how does a price support program in the grain market affect the equilibrium price and quantity of beef?

The price support program raises the price of cattle feed, which causes a leftward shift in the supply schedule for beef. (See Figure 2-11.) This, in turn, results in an increase in the equilibrium price and a reduction in the equilibrium quantity of beef.

FIGURE 2-11

The Effect of Grain Price Supports on the Equilibrium Price and Quantity of Beef
By raising the price of grain, an input used in beef production, the price supports produce a leftward shift in the supply curve of beef. The result is an increase in the equilibrium price and a reduction in the equilibrium quantity.

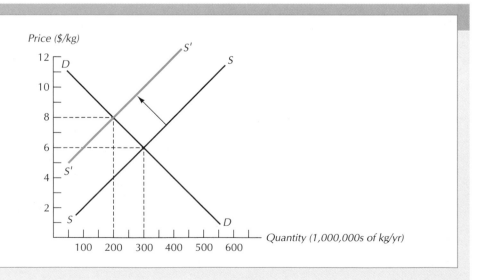

Interpreting Observed Market Changes

Our four basic propositions about changes in supply and demand can be of considerable practical importance in interpreting the changes we observe in actual markets. Often, we don't know the precise form of the supply and demand functions in a particular market. All we actually see are the price and the quantity exchanged in an initial equilibrium and in a subsequent equilibrium. Suppose we know only that supply curves are positively sloped and demand curves are negatively sloped in this market.

Figure 2-12 shows precisely what we can and cannot say about what has caused a shift from an initial equilibrium E_0 (with price P_0 and quantity exchanged Q_0) to a new equilibrium. Figure 2-12(a) shows the three situations possible when both price and quantity *increase* in the new equilibrium. Demand *must* have increased (say, from D_0 to D_1), but supply could have remained constant at S_0 (yielding E_1), decreased to S_1 (yielding E_2), or increased to S_2 (yielding E_3). In short, if the new equilibrium is northeast of E_0, we know that demand has increased, but we cannot know what has happened to supply without further information.

Figure 2-12(b) shows the four zones I to IV, defined relative to an initial equilibrium E_0, and indicates what we can definitely say about any new equilibrium. For the odd-numbered equilibria (E_1, E_3, E_5, and E_7), we know what has happened to *only one* of supply and demand. For the even-numbered equilibria (E_2, E_4, E_6, and E_8), we can definitely say what has happened to *both* supply and demand. At E_6, for example, on the border between zones III and IV, the price is unchanged, but the quantity exchanged is lower than at E_0, which can occur only if both supply and demand *decrease* by the same proportion at P_0. You should use Figure 2-12(b) as a basis for practice in sketching the combinations of supply and demand shifts associated with various price-quantity changes. This exercise should sharpen your economic intuition and hone your skills as an economic naturalist in observing actual market behaviour.

Analyzing Supply-Demand Changes Using Market Data Figure 2-12 *a* shows that if equilibrium *P* and *Q* increase, demand must have increased but supply may have remained constant, decreased, or increased. Figure 2-12 *b* shows what must have happened in each of zones I to IV relative to an initial equilibrium E_0. For the odd-numbered equilibria, we know only how one function (supply *or* demand) must have changed. For even-numbered equilibria on the border between two zones, we know how *both* supply and demand must have changed.

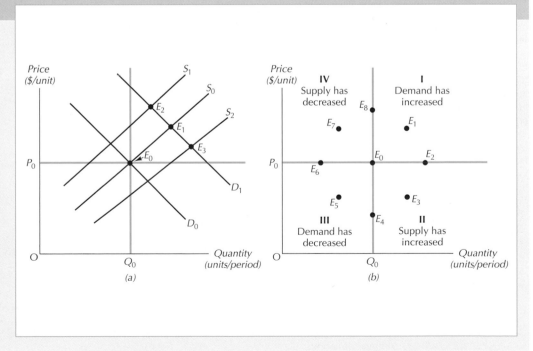

2.10 THE ALGEBRA OF SUPPLY AND DEMAND

The examples thus far have focused on a geometric approach to market equilibrium. This approach is fine for illustrating the basic principles of the theory. But for actually computing numerical values, it usually is more convenient to find equilibrium prices and quantities algebraically. Suppose, for example, the supply schedule for a product is given by

$$Q^s = -\frac{2}{3} + \frac{1}{3}P, \quad \text{or} \quad P = 2 + 3Q^s, \qquad (2.1)$$

and that its demand schedule is given by

$$Q^d = 10 - P, \quad \text{or} \quad P = 10 - Q^d, \qquad (2.2)$$

where P is the product price (measured in \$/unit) and Q^s and Q^d (measured in units per period) stand for the quantity supplied and the quantity demanded, respectively.[2] In equilibrium, we know that $Q^s = Q^d$. Denoting this common value as Q^*, we may then equate the right-hand sides of Equations 2.1 and 2.2 and solve:

$$2 + 3Q^* = 10 - Q^*, \qquad (2.3)$$

which gives $Q^* = 2$ units per period. Substituting $Q^* = 2$ back into either the supply or demand equation gives the equilibrium price, $P^* = \$8$/unit.

Needless to say, we could have graphed Equations 2.1 and 2.2 to arrive at precisely the same solution (see Figure 2-13). The advantage of the algebraic approach is that it is much less painstaking and more accurate than producing drawings of the supply and demand schedules.

FIGURE 2-13

Graphs of Equations 2.1 and 2.2
The algebraic and geometric approaches lead to exactly the same equilibrium prices and quantities. The advantage of the algebraic approach is that exact numerical solutions can be achieved more easily. The geometric approach is useful because it gives a more intuitively clear description of the supply and demand curves.

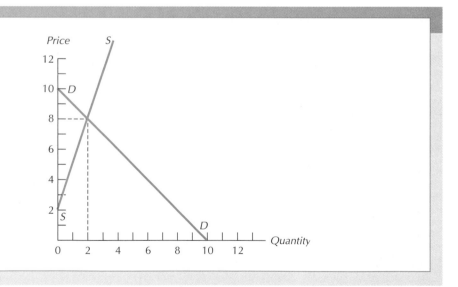

---

[2]The first form of Equations 2.1 and 2.2, with Q^s and Q^d (viewed as the *dependent* variables) on the left-hand side of the equation and P (viewed as the *independent* variable) on the right-hand side of the equation, are often treated by economists as *the* supply and demand functions. The second form of the equations (with P on the left and Q^s and Q^d on the right) are conventionally referred to as the *inverse supply and demand functions*, respectively. See Module 1 of the *Basic Math Review* (especially Sections 1.4 and 1.5) at www.mcgrawhill.ca/college/frank for a discussion of some odd features of the way economists conventionally treat supply and demand graphs and functions, and Modules 2 and 3 for a review of linear equations.

Find the equilibrium price and quantity in a market whose supply and demand curves are given by $P = 4Q^s$ and $P = 12 - 2Q^d$, respectively.

2.11 TAXES

Supply and demand analysis is also a useful tool for analyzing the effects of various taxes. In this section we consider a constant tax per unit of output. How will the equilibrium price and quantity of a product be affected if a tax of $T = \$10/\text{unit}$ is levied on each unit sold by the producer? There are two *equivalent* ways to approach this question. The first is to suppose that the tax is levied on the seller. In Figure 2-14, the line SS denotes the original supply schedule. At a price of $P_0 = \$25/\text{unit}$, sellers were willing to supply Q_0 units of output. When a tax $T = 10$ is levied on sellers, the market price would have to be $P_0 + 10 = \$35/\text{unit}$ for them to get the same net payment that they used to receive when the price was $P_0 = \$25/\text{unit}$. At a price of $\$35/\text{unit}$, then, suppliers will offer the same amount of output they used to offer at a price of $\$25/\text{unit}$. The resulting after-tax supply schedule is the original supply schedule shifted upward by $T = 10$.

In Figure 2-15, DD represents the demand curve facing the sellers who have been taxed $T = \$10$ per unit of output. The effect of the tax is to cause the equilibrium quantity to fall from Q^* to Q_1^*. The price paid by the buyer rises from P^* to P_1^*; and the price, net of the tax, received by the seller falls to $P_1^* - 10$.

Note in Figure 2-15 that even though the seller pays a tax of T on each product purchased, the total amount the seller receives per unit lies less than T below the old equilibrium price. Note also that even though the tax is collected from the seller, its effect is to increase the price paid by buyers. The burden of the tax is thus divided between the buyer and the seller.

Algebraically, the seller's share of the tax, denoted t_s, is the reduction in the price the seller receives, divided by the tax:

$$t_s = \frac{P^* - (P_1^* - T)}{T}. \tag{2.4}$$

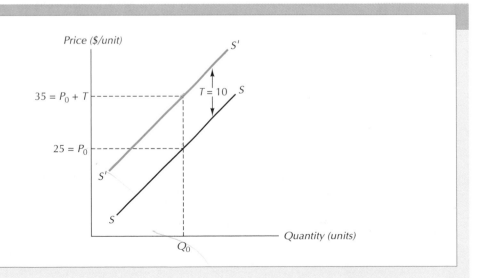

FIGURE 2-14

A Tax of $T = \$10/\text{Unit}$ Levied on the Seller Shifts the Supply Schedule upward by T Units

The original supply schedule tells us what price suppliers must charge in order to cover their costs at any given level of output. From the seller's perspective, a tax of $T = \$10/\text{unit}$ is the same as a unit-cost increase of $10. The new supply curve thus lies $10/\text{unit}$ above the old one.

FIGURE 2-15

Equilibrium Prices and Quantities When a Tax of T = \$10/Unit Is Levied on the Seller
The tax causes a reduction in equilibrium quantity from Q^* to Q_1^*. The new price paid by the buyer rises from P^* to P_1^*. The new price received by the seller falls from P^* to $P_1^* - 10$.

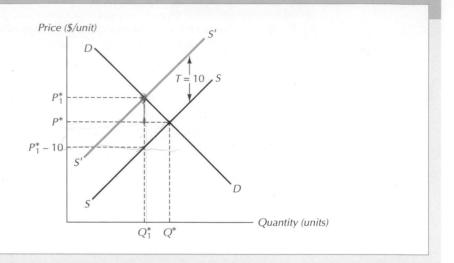

Similarily, the buyer's share of the tax, t_b, is the increase in price (including tax) divided by the tax:

$$t_b = \frac{P_1^* - P^*}{T}. \tag{2.5}$$

EXERCISE 2-5

Verify that $t_s + t_b = 1$.

In general, t_b and t_s depend on the shapes of the supply and demand schedules. If, for example, supply is highly unresponsive to changes in price, t_b will be close to zero, t_s close to 1. Conversely, if demand is highly unresponsive to price, t_b will be close to 1, t_s close to zero. These claims amount to a statement that a tax tends to fall most heavily on the side of the market that can least escape it. If buyers have no substitute products to which they are prepared to turn, the lion's share of the tax will be passed on to them by suppliers. But if suppliers have no alternative other than to go on supplying a product, most of the burden of a tax will fall on them. As long as the supply curve is positively sloped and the demand curve is negatively sloped, however, both t_s and t_b will be positive.

The second way of analyzing the effect of a tax of T = \$10 per unit of output is to imagine that the tax is collected directly from the buyer and to analyze how that would affect the demand curve for the product. In Figure 2-16, the demand curve before the imposition of the tax is denoted by the line DD. At a price of P_1, buyers would demand a quantity of Q_1. After the imposition of the tax, the total amount that buyers have to pay if the product price is P_1 will be $P_1 + 10$. Accordingly, the quantity they demand falls from Q_1 to Q_2. In like fashion, we can reckon the quantity demanded at any other price after imposition of the tax. The resulting after-tax demand curve will be the line $D'D'$ in Figure 2-16. It is simply the original demand curve translated downward by \$10/unit.

If line SS in Figure 2-17 denotes the supply schedule for this market, we can easily trace out the effects of the tax on the equilibrium price and quantity. The equilibrium quantity falls from Q^* to Q_2^*, and the equilibrium price falls from P^* to P_2^*. The total price paid by the buyer after imposition of the tax rises to $P_2^* + 10$.

Is the effect of a tax on the seller any different from the effect of a tax levied on the buyer? Not at all. To illustrate, suppose the supply and demand curves for a market are given by $P = Q^s$ and $P = 10 - Q^d$, respectively, and consider first the effect of a tax of $2 per unit of output imposed on the seller. Figure 2-18a shows the original supply and demand curves and the new after-tax supply curve, $S'S'$. The original equilibrium price and quantity are both equal to 5. The new equilibrium price to the buyer (inclusive of tax) and quantity are $6 per unit and 4 units, respectively. The price received by sellers, net of the tax, is $4 per unit.

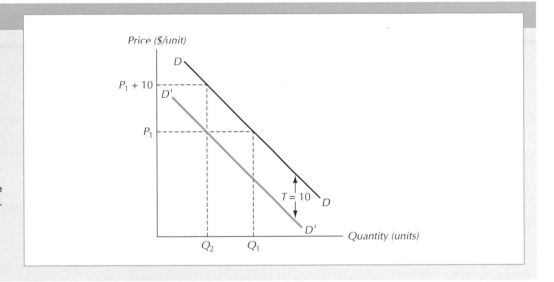

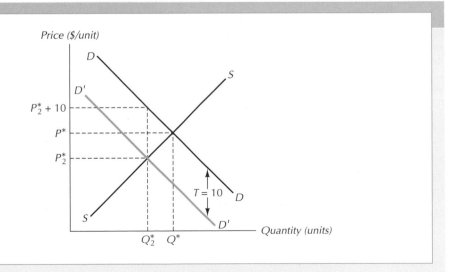

Now, consider a tax of $2 per unit of output imposed on the buyers. Figure 2-18*b* shows the original supply and demand curves and the new after-tax demand curve, $D'D'$. Note that the effects on price and quantity are exactly the same as in the case of the tax levied on sellers shown in panel *a*.

EXERCISE 2-6

Consider a market whose supply and demand curves are given by $P = 4Q^s$ and $P = 12 - 2Q^d$, respectively. How will the equilibrium price and quantity in this market be affected if a tax of $6 per unit of output is imposed on sellers? If the same tax is imposed on buyers?

When tax revenues have to be raised, political leaders may find it expedient to propose a sales tax on corporations because "they can best afford to pay it." But careful analysis of the effects of a sales tax shows that its burden will be the same whether it is imposed on buyers or sellers. The *legal incidence of the tax* (whether it is imposed on buyers or on sellers) has no effect on the *economic incidence* of the tax (the respective shares of the tax burden borne by buyers and sellers). Economically speaking, the entity from which the tax is actually collected is thus a matter of complete indifference.

A word of caution: When we say that the economic burden of the tax does not depend on the party from whom the tax is directly collected, this does not mean that buyers and sellers always share the burden of taxes equally. Their respective shares may, as noted, be highly unequal. The independence of legal incidence and economic incidence simply means that the burden will be shared in the same way no matter where the tax is placed.

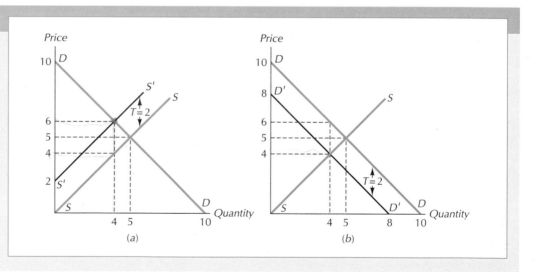

FIGURE 2-18

A Tax on the Buyer Leads to the Same Outcome as a Tax on the Seller
The price received by sellers (net of the tax), the price paid by buyers (including tax), and the equilibrium quantity will all be the same when the tax is collected from sellers (panel *a*) as when it is collected from buyers (panel *b*).

- The supply curve is generally an upward-sloping line that tells what quantity sellers will offer at any given price. The demand curve is generally a downward-sloping line that tells what quantity buyers will demand at any given price. In an unregulated market, the equilibrium price and quantity are determined by the intersection of these two curves.

- If price is above its equilibrium level, there will be dissatisfied sellers, or excess supply. This condition motivates sellers to cut their prices. In contrast, when prices are below equilibrium, there will be dissatisfied buyers, or excess demand. This condition motivates sellers to charge higher prices. The only stable outcome is the one in which excess demand and excess supply are exactly zero.

- Given the attributes of buyers and sellers, the equilibrium price and quantity represent the best attainable outcome, in the sense that any other price-quantity pair would be worse for at least some buyers or sellers.

- The fact that market outcomes are efficient in this sense does not mean they necessarily command society's approval. On the contrary, we often lament the fact that many buyers enter the market with so little income. Concern for the well-being of the poor has motivated governments to intervene in a variety of ways to alter the outcomes of market forces.

- Sometimes these interventions take the form of laws that peg prices above or below their equilibrium levels. Such laws can generate harmful, if unintended, consequences. Programs such as rent control, for example, interfere with both the rationing and allocative functions of the price mechanism. They can lead to black marketeering and deterioration of the stock of rental housing. By the same token, price supports in agriculture tend to enrich larger farms while doing little to ease the plight of marginal family farms. It is often possible to design alternative policies that are more effective and less costly.

- If the difficulty is that the poor have too little money, the solution is to discover ways of boosting their incomes directly. Legislators cannot repeal the laws of supply and demand. But legislatures do have the capacity to alter the underlying forces that govern the shape and position of supply and demand schedules.

- Supply and demand analysis is the economist's basic tool for predicting how equilibrium prices and quantities will change in response to changes in market forces. Four simple propositions guide this task: (1) an increase in demand will lead to an increase in both the equilibrium price and the equilibrium quantity; (2) a decrease in demand will lead to a decrease in both the equilibrium price and the equilibrium quantity; (3) an increase in supply will lead to a decrease in the equilibrium price and an increase in the equilibrium quantity; and (4) a decrease in supply will lead to an increase in the equilibrium price and a decrease in the equilibrium quantity.

- Incomes, tastes, the prices of substitutes and complements, expectations, and population are among the factors that shift demand schedules. Supply schedules, in turn, are governed by such factors as technology, input prices, the number of suppliers, expectations, and, especially for agricultural products, the weather.

- Supply and demand analysis is a useful device for understanding how taxes affect equilibrium prices and quantities. In particular, it helps dispel the myth that a tax is paid primarily by the party on whom it is directly levied. In practice, the burden of a tax falls on whichever side of the market is least able to avoid it.

QUESTIONS FOR REVIEW

1. What is the difference between "scarcity" and "shortage"?
2. What would the supply curve look like for a good that is not scarce? Assuming the good is useful, what would its demand curve look like? Explain why a positive price for a commodity implies that it is scarce.
3. Give two examples of actions taken by the administration of your college or university whose effect is to prevent specific markets from reaching equilibrium. What evidence of excess supply or excess demand can you cite in these examples?
4. What is the difference between "a reduction in supply" and "a reduction in the quantity supplied"?
5. Identify each of the following as (1) a change in demand or (2) a change in the quantity demanded.
   a. Grape consumption falls because of a consumer boycott.
   b. Grape consumption falls because of a tax on grape producers.
   c. Grape consumption rises because of a good harvest.
   d. Grape consumption rises because of a change in tastes.

6. When there is excess supply, why is any single seller who supplies less than the entire market able to sell all she wants to by offering only a small reduction below the current market price?

7. Give an example of a market in which the *allocative* function of price is not very important.

8. The steeper the demand curve for some good relative to the supply curve for that good, the greater the proportion of a tax on that good that will fall on buyers. True or false? Explain, using a diagram.

9. Suppose you are an elected government member and need to collect revenue by taxing a product. For political reasons, you want the burden of the tax to fall mostly on consumers, not firms (who have been substantial contributors to your campaign fund). What should you look for when picking a product to tax?

10. Which would a poor person be more likely to accept and why?
    a. A $50,000 Mercedes (immediate resale value = $30,000)
    b. $35,000 cash

11. Given the following four situations in the Regina market for saskatoon berries, use supply and demand diagrams to explain what *could* have happened (or equivalently, what could *not* have happened) to both supply and demand in the new equilibrium, relative to the initial equilibrium:
    a. Price is higher; quantity exchanged is lower.
    b. Price is unchanged; quantity exchanged is higher.
    c. Price is lower; quantity exchanged is unchanged.
    d. Price is lower; quantity exchanged is lower.

PROBLEMS

1. The government, as a revenue-generating measure, imposes a tax of $2/kg on the retail price of Smarties. It collects the tax from Smarties sellers. The original supply and demand schedules for Smarties are as shown in the diagram. Show, in the same diagram, how the short-run equilibrium price and quantity of Smarties will be affected by the tax. Label all important points clearly. How much tax revenue does the government receive?

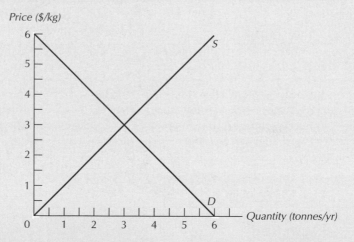

2. In the market for Smarties described in Problem 1 (with no tax), suppose that a price floor of $4/kg results in sales of only 2 tonnes/yr. If the price floor were removed, describe a transaction that would make some buyers and sellers better off without harming others.

3. Suppose the Smarties market in Problem 1, with a tax of $2/kg, experiences growth in the demand for Smarties because of new-found medical uses. The new demand curve is $P = 8 - Q$, where P is in $/kg and Q is in tonnes. Find the change in government tax revenue due to the heightened demand for Smarties.

4. Suppose instead the Smarties market in Problem 2, with no tax but a price floor at $4/kg, suffers a reduction in supply. The new supply curve is $P = 2 + Q$. How does excess supply change due to the reduction in supply? Is the price floor still binding (does it cause price to be above its equilibrium level)?

5. Assume that tea and lemons are complements and that coffee and tea are substitutes.

   a. How, if at all, will the imposition of an effective ceiling price on tea affect the price of lemons? Explain.
   b. How, if at all, will the imposition of an effective ceiling price on tea affect the price of coffee? Explain.

6. The market for DVDs has supply and demand curves given by $P = 2Q^s$ and $P = 42 - Q^d$, respectively, where P is in $/DVD and Q^s and Q^d are in DVDs. Construct and label a diagram.

   a. How many units will be traded at a price of $35? At a price of $14? Which participants will be dissatisfied at these prices?
   b. What quantity of DVDs at what price will be sold in equilibrium?
   c. What is the total revenue from DVD sales? Where is it shown on your diagram?

7. Suppose that in the market described in Problem 6, the government levies a tax of $9 on each DVD sold, collected from sellers.

   a. What quantity of DVDs will be sold in equilibrium?
   b. What price do buyers pay, and how much do they spend in total?
   c. What after-tax price do sellers now receive, and what is their total after-tax revenue?
   d. How much money goes to the government?
   e. Show the above results graphically.

8. For the tax described in Problem 7, what fraction of the tax do the sellers bear and what fraction of the tax do the buyers bear?

*9. The Frug, a subcompact car, is produced only in the small country of Leutonia. The Canadian government, concerned by high levels of Frug imports, negotiates a "voluntary" import quota on Frugs with Leutonian Frug exporters. Some Canadian economic advisers recommend using an import tax (or tariff) instead. If the tariff (at $T per Frug) were set to produce the *same* reduction in imports as the quota, how will the prices paid for Frugs by Canadian consumers compare under the two policies? How much revenue will Frug exporters receive and how much import tariff revenue will the Canadian government receive under each policy? Show your results in a diagram.

10. Hardware and software for computers are complements. Discuss the effects on the equilibrium price and quantity:

    a. In the software market, when the price of computer hardware falls.
    b. In the hardware market, when the price of computer software rises.

11. Suppose a newly released study shows that battery-powered toys harm a child's development and recommends that parents adjust their purchasing behaviour accordingly. Use diagrams to show the effect on price and quantity in each of the following markets:

    a. The market for battery-powered toys
    b. The market for D batteries
    c. The market for yo-yos (which do not require batteries)

12. Using diagrams, show what changes in equilibrium price and quantity exchanged would be expected in the following markets in the situations described:

    a. *Crude oil:* As petroleum reserves decrease, it becomes more difficult to find and recover crude oil.
    b. *Air travel:* Worries about air safety cause travellers to shy away from air travel.
    c. *Rail travel:* Worries about air safety cause travellers to shy away from air travel.
    d. *Hotel rooms in Cuba:* Worries about air safety cause travellers to shy away from air travel.
    e. *Milk:* A drop in hay prices enables milk producers to cut production costs.

13. For each situation in Problem 12, state whether the effect involves a change in demand or just a change in quantity demanded.

*14. Because of concerns that barbecuing meat using charcoal may cause cancer, the government decides to impose a 100 percent tax at the retail level on charcoal briquets. Suppose the daily demand for charcoal was $P = 120 - 2Q$ and the supply was $P = 30 + Q$, where P is in dollars and Q is the number of 10-kg bags of charcoal sold daily.

    a. Give the before-tax charcoal price and quantity exchanged.
    b. Give the after-tax charcoal price to buyers, the quantity exchanged, and total tax revenues.
    c. How is the tax divided among sellers and buyers?

15. In the kumquat market, supply is given by the equation $P = 4Q$, while demand is given by $P = 20$, where P is price in dollars per unit and Q is quantity in units per week.

    a. Find the equilibrium price and quantity (using both algebra and a graph).
    b. If sellers must pay a tax of $T = \$4$ per unit, what happens to the quantity exchanged, the price buyers pay, and the price sellers receive (net of the tax)?
    c. How is the burden of the tax distributed across buyers and sellers and why?

16. Repeat Problem 15, but instead suppose the buyer pays the tax, demand is $P = 28 - Q$, and supply is $P = 20$.

17. Suppose demand for seats at Winless University football games is given by $P = 1900 - (\frac{1}{5})Q$ and supply is fixed at $Q = 9000$ seats.

    a. Find the equilibrium price and quantity of seats for a football game (using algebra and a graph).
    b. Suppose the government prohibits ticket scalping (selling tickets above their face value), and the face value of tickets is $50 (this policy places a price ceiling at $50). How many consumers will be dissatisfied (how large is excess demand)?
    c. Suppose the next game is a major rivalry, and so demand jumps to $P = 2100 - (\frac{1}{5})Q$. How many consumers will be dissatisfied for the big game?
    d. How do the distortions of this price ceiling differ from the more typical case of upward-sloping supply?

18. Suppose the supply of a good is given by the equation $P = Q$ and demand is fixed at $Q = 12$ units per week, with P in dollars per unit.

    a. Find the equilibrium price and quantity.
    b. Suppose the government levies a tax equal to $4 per unit on sellers of the good. Find the equilibrium quantity, price paid by buyers, and price received by the sellers (net of taxes).
    c. How is the tax burden distributed and why?

19. The demand for apartments is given by the equation $P = 1200 - Q$ while the supply is given by the equation $P = Q$ units. The government imposes rent control at $P = \$300$ per month. Suppose demand grows in the market to $P = 1400 - Q$.

    a. How is excess demand affected by the growth in demand for apartments?
    b. At what price would the government have to set the rent control to keep excess demand at the same level as prior to the growth in demand?

20. Suppose demand is given by $P = 300 - .5Q$ and supply is given by $P = .5Q$ in the canola market, where Q is tonnes of canola per year. The government sets a price support at $P = \$250/$ tonne and purchases any excess supply at this price. In response, as a long-run adjustment, farmers switch their crops from wheat to canola, expanding supply to $P = .25Q$.

    a. How does excess supply with the larger supply compare to excess supply prior to the farmers' switching crops?
    b. How much more does the government have to spend to buy up the excess supply?

*21. You are a highly paid market analyst. Using Figure 2-12*b* for reference, explain to your clients what *must* have happened and what *could* have happened to both demand and supply curves in each of the following competitive markets to bring about the *new* equilibrium described, relative to an *initial* equilibrium. Draw supply and demand diagrams to explain your analyses.

    a. In the durum wheat market, both the quantity exchanged and the price have decreased.

    b. In the market for skis, the price has increased but the quantity exchanged has remained the same.

    c. In the market for kumquats, both the quantity exchanged and the price have increased in the new equilibrium.

    d. In the portable music player market, the quantity exchanged has increased, but the price has remained constant.

    e. In the skateboard market, the price has increased but the quantity has decreased.

ANSWERS TO IN-CHAPTER EXERCISES

2-1. At a price of $2 per lobster, the quantity demanded is 5000 lobsters per day and the quantity supplied is 1000 lobsters per day, making excess demand equal to 4000 lobsters per day. At a price of $10 per lobster, excess supply is 4000 lobsters per day.

2-2. A rent control level set above the equilibrium price has no effect. The rent will settle at its equilibrium value of $600 per month.

2-3. The fall in the price of diesel fuel shifts the supply curve to the right. The report on mercury shifts the demand curve to the left. As shown in the following diagrams, the equilibrium price will go down (both panels) but the equilibrium quantity may go either up (panel *b*) or down (panel *a*).

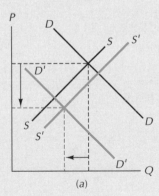

(a)

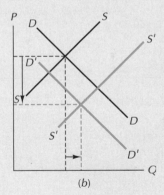

(b)

2-4. $4Q^* = 12 - 2Q^*$, which yields $Q^* = 2$ units and $P^* = 4Q^* = \$8$/unit.

2-5. $t_s + t_b = [(P^* - P_1^* + T) + (P_1^* - P^*)]/T = T/T = 1$.

2-6. The original price and quantity are given by $P^* = \$8$/unit and $Q^* = 2$ units, respectively. The supply curve with the tax is given by $P = 6 + 4Q^s$. Letting P' and Q' denote the new equilibrium values of price and quantity, we now have $6 + 4Q' = 12 - 2Q'$, which yields $Q' = 1$ unit. $P' = \$10$/unit, where P' is the price paid by buyers. $P' - 6 = \$4$/unit is the price received by sellers. Alternatively, the demand curve with a tax of $6/unit levied on buyers is given by $P = 6 - 2Q^d$, and we have $4Q' = 6 - 2Q'$, which again yields $Q' = 1$ unit. $P'' = \$4$/unit, where P'' is the price received by sellers. $P'' + T = P'' + 6 = \$10$/unit is the price paid by buyers, including the tax.

Part 2

THE THEORY OF CONSUMER BEHAVIOUR

These chapters develop the theory of consumer behaviour. Chapter 3 is of special importance, for it lays out the economic theory of how people with limited resources choose among competing alternatives. The methods and tools developed in this chapter recur throughout the remainder of the book, and indeed throughout all of economics. Chapter 4 shows how the theory of rational individual choice can be used to derive individual and market demand curves. Chapter 5 explores numerous applications of rational choice and demand theories, including the theory of choices that involve future consequences.

Chapter 6 shows how the rational choice model can be extended to cover choices that involve uncertainty or incomplete information. Chapter 7 examines the role of unselfish motives in economic and social behaviour and shows why honest people often have an economic advantage over people who cheat. Finally, Chapter 8 looks at a variety of circumstances in which ordinary people have a tendency to make irrational choices. Experience shows that being aware of these tendencies helps people make better decisions.

Chapter 3

RATIONAL CONSUMER CHOICE

Y ou have just cashed your monthly paycheque and are on your way to the local music store to buy the new *Celine Dion Sings Rap Classics* CD you've been wanting. The price of the disc is $20. In situation 1 you lose $20 on your way to the store. In situation 2 you buy the disc and then trip and fall on your way out of the store; the disc shatters as it hits the sidewalk. Try to imagine your frame of mind in each situation.

a. Would you proceed to buy the disc in situation 1?

b. Would you return to buy the disc in situation 2?

Similar questions[1] were put to a large class of undergraduates who had never taken an economics course. In response to the first question, 54 percent answered yes, saying they would buy the disc after losing the $20 bill. But only 32 percent answered yes to the second question—68 percent said they would not buy the disc after having broken the first one. There is, of course, no "correct" answer to either question. The events described will have more of an impact, for example, on a poor consumer than on a rich one. Yet a moment's reflection reveals that your behaviour in one situation logically should be exactly the same as in the other. After all, in both situations, the only economically relevant change is that you now have $20 less to spend than before. This might well mean that you will want to give up having the disc; or it could mean saving less or giving up some other good or service that you would have bought instead. But your choice should not be affected by the particular way you happened to become $20 poorer. In both situations, the cost of the disc is $20, and the benefits you will receive from listening to it are also the same. You should either buy the disc in both situations or not buy it in both situations. And yet, as noted, many people said they would behave differently in the two situations.

---

[1]These questions are patterned after questions posed by decision theorists Daniel Kahneman and Amos Tversky (see Chapter 8).

CHAPTER PREVIEW

Our task in this chapter is to set forth the economist's basic model for answering questions such as the ones asked above. This model is known as the theory of *rational consumer choice*. It underlies all individual purchase decisions, which in turn add up to the demand curves we worked with in the preceding chapter.

Rational choice theory begins with the assumption that consumers enter the marketplace with well-defined preferences. Taking prices as given, their task is to allocate their incomes to best serve these preferences. Two steps are required to carry out this task. Step one is to describe the various combinations of goods the consumer is *able* to buy. We will see that these combinations depend on both her income level and the prices of the goods. Step two then is to select from among the feasible combinations the particular one that she *prefers* to all others. Analysis of step two requires some means of describing her preferences, in particular, a summary of the rank ordering she assigns to all feasible combinations. Formal development of these two elements of the theory occupies our attention throughout this chapter. Because the first element—describing the set of possibilities—is much less abstract than the second, let us begin with it.

3.1 THE BUDGET CONSTRAINT AND THE AFFORDABLE SET

Bundle A particular combination of two or more goods.

For simplicity, let us begin by considering a world with only two goods,[2] food and shelter. A ***bundle*** of goods is the term used to describe a particular combination of food, measured in kilograms per week, and shelter, measured in square metres per week. Thus, in Figure 3-1, one bundle (bundle A) might consist of 5 sq m/wk of shelter and 7 kg/wk of food, while another (bundle B) consists of 3 sq m/wk of shelter and 8 kg/wk of food. For brevity's sake, we may use the notation (5, 7) to denote bundle A and the notation (3, 8) to denote bundle B. More generally, (S_0, F_0) will denote the bundle with S_0 sq m/wk of shelter and F_0 kg/wk of food. By convention, the first number of the pair in any bundle represents the good measured along the horizontal axis.

Note that the units on both axes are *flows*, which means physical quantities per unit of time—kilograms per week, square metres per week. Consumption is always measured as a flow. It is important to keep track of the time dimension because without

---

FIGURE 3-1

Two Bundles of Goods
A bundle is a specific combination of goods. Bundle *A* has 5 units of shelter and 7 units of food. Bundle *B* has 3 units of shelter and 8 units of food.

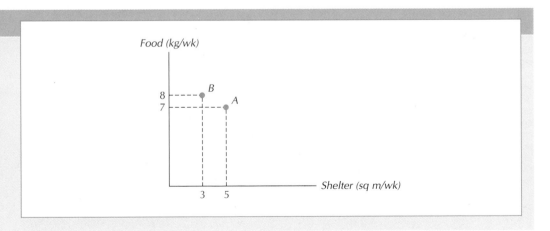

---

[2]As economists use the term, a "good" may refer to either a product or a service.

it there would be no way to evaluate whether a given quantity of consumption was large or small. (Suppose all you know is that your food consumption is 2 kg. If that's how much you eat each day, it's a lot. But if that's all you eat in a month, you're not likely to survive for long.)[3]

Suppose the consumer's income is M = $100 per week, all of which she spends on some combination of food and shelter. (Note that income is also a flow.) Suppose further that the prices of shelter and food are P_S = $5/sq m and P_F = $10/kg, respectively. If the consumer spent all her income on shelter, she could buy M/P_S = ($100/wk) ÷ ($5/sq m) = 20 sq m/wk. That is, she could buy the bundle consisting of 20 sq m/wk of shelter and 0 kg/wk of food, denoted (20, 0). Alternatively, suppose the consumer spent all her income on food. She would then get the bundle consisting of M/P_F = ($100/wk) ÷ ($10/kg), which is 10 kg/wk of food and 0 sq m/wk of shelter, denoted (0, 10).

In Figure 3-2 these polar cases are labelled K and L, respectively. The consumer is also able to purchase any other bundle that lies along the straight line that joins points K and L. (Verify, for example, that the bundle (12, 4) lies on this same line.) This line is called the **budget constraint** and is labelled B in the diagram.

Recall the maxim from high school algebra that the slope of a straight line is its "rise" over its "run" (the change in its vertical position divided by the corresponding change in its horizontal position). Here, note that the slope of the budget constraint is its

Budget constraint
The set of all bundles that can be purchased with given income and prices, if all income is spent.

FIGURE 3-2

The Budget Constraint and the Affordable Set
With M = $100/week, P_F = $10/kg, and P_S = $5/sq m, the shaded area (including the horizontal and vertical axes and the budget constraint, line B) defines the *affordable set* for the consumer. With this money income and these prices, she can afford any point (or *bundle*) in this triangular set. Line B describes the set of all bundles the consumer can purchase if all of income is spent at the given prices. Its slope is the negative of the price of shelter divided by the price of food. This slope is the opportunity cost of an additional unit of shelter along the budget constraint—the number of units of food that must be sacrificed in order to purchase one additional unit of shelter at market prices.

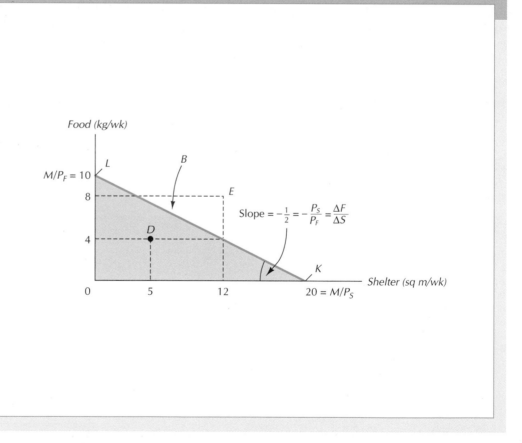

[3]The flow aspect of consumption helps us alleviate some concerns about goods not being divisible. If you consume 1.5 kg/mo, then you consume 18 kg/yr, which is a whole number.

vertical intercept (the rise) divided by its horizontal intercept (the corresponding run): $-(10 \text{ kg/wk})/(20 \text{ sq m/wk}) = -\frac{1}{2} \text{ kg/sq m}$. The minus sign signifies that the budget line falls as it moves to the right—that it has a negative slope. More generally, if M denotes the consumer's weekly income, and P_S and P_F denote the prices of shelter and food, respectively, the horizontal and vertical intercepts will be given by (M/P_S) and (M/P_F), respectively. Thus the general formula for the slope of the budget constraint is given by $-(M/P_F)/(M/P_S) = -P_S/P_F$, which is simply the negative of the price ratio of the two goods. Given their respective prices, it is the rate at which food can be exchanged for shelter. Thus, in Figure 3-2, along the budget constraint 1 kg of food can be exchanged for 2 sq m of shelter. In the language of opportunity cost from Chapter 1, we would say that the opportunity cost of an additional square metre of shelter is $P_S/P_F = \frac{1}{2}$ kg of food.[4]

In addition to being able to buy any of the bundles along her budget constraint, the consumer is also able to purchase any bundle that lies within the budget triangle bounded by it and the two axes. The bundles on or within the budget triangle are referred to as the *feasible set*, or **affordable set**. D is one such bundle in Figure 3-2. Bundle D costs \$65/wk, which is well below the consumer's income of \$100/wk. Since at D the consumer has \$35 unspent, at this point she can purchase more of *either* good *without* sacrificing any of the other good. Hence, as is true at any interior point of the affordable set, the opportunity cost of either good in terms of the other is *zero*! Only along the budget constraint (where all income has been spent) is it the case that some food must be given up to get an additional unit of shelter, or some shelter must be given up to get an additional unit of food. The slope of the budget constraint is $\Delta F/\Delta S$. It is *negative*, since if ΔS is positive—that is, if the quantity of shelter purchased is increased—then ΔF must be negative, since the increased expenditure on shelter means that less food can be purchased with the same income. By similar reasoning, if ΔF is positive then ΔS must be negative. Thus the slope, the ratio $\Delta F/\Delta S$, is necessarily negative, since the numerator and denominator must be of opposite sign. Bundles like E that lie outside the budget triangle are said to be *infeasible*, or *unaffordable*. At a cost of \$140/wk, E is simply beyond the consumer's reach.

If S and F denote the quantities of shelter and food, respectively, the budget constraint must satisfy the following equation:

$$P_S S + P_F F = M, \tag{3.1}$$

which says simply that if she spends all her income, the consumer's weekly expenditure on shelter ($P_S S$) plus her weekly expenditure on food ($P_F F$) must add up to her weekly income (M).[5] We can express the budget constraint in the conventional straight-line formula, $y = a + bx$, where a is the vertical intercept and b is the slope. To do so, we solve Equation 3.1 for F in terms of S, which yields

$$F = \frac{M}{P_F} - \frac{P_S}{P_F}S. \tag{3.2}$$

---

[4]Notice that along the budget constraint, the opportunity cost of an additional kilogram of *food* (in terms of the number of square metres of *shelter* that must be given up to get it) is 2 sq m/kg, or P_F/P_S, which is the *reciprocal* of the opportunity cost of shelter in terms of food.

[5]For bundles in the *interior* of the affordable set such as D, not all of money income is spent, and therefore all such points are described by the inequality $P_S S + P_F F < M$. In contrast, infeasible or unaffordable bundles such as E are described by the inequality $P_S S + P_F F > M$: the expenditure necessary to purchase such bundles would exceed the consumer's money income.

Affordable set
Bundles on or below the budget constraint; bundles for which the required expenditure at given prices is less than or equal to the income available.

Equation 3.2 is another way of seeing that the vertical intercept of the budget constraint is given by M/P_F and its slope by $-(P_S/P_F)$. The equation for the budget constraint in Figure 3-2 is $F = 10 - \frac{1}{2}S$.

Budget Shifts Due to Price or Income Changes

Price Changes.   The slope and position of the budget constraint are fully determined by the consumer's income and the prices of the respective goods. Change any one of these factors and we have a new budget constraint. Figure 3-3 shows the effect of an increase in the price of shelter from $P_{S_1} = \$5/\text{sq m}$ to $P_{S_2} = \$10/\text{sq m}$. Since both weekly income and the price of food are unchanged, the vertical intercept of the consumer's budget constraint stays the same. The rise in the price of shelter rotates the budget constraint inward about this intercept, as shown in the diagram.

Note in Figure 3-3 that even though the price of food has not changed, the new budget constraint, B_2, curtails not only the amount of shelter the consumer can buy but also the amount of food.[6]

EXERCISE 3-1

Show the effect on the budget constraint B_1 in Figure 3-3 of a fall in the price of shelter from \$5/sq m to \$4/sq m.

In Exercise 3-1, you saw that a fall in the price of shelter again leaves the vertical intercept of the budget constraint unchanged. This time the budget constraint rotates outward. Note also in Exercise 3-1 that although the price of food remains unchanged, the new budget constraint enables the consumer to buy bundles that contain not only more shelter but also more food than she could afford on the original budget constraint.

EXERCISE 3-2

Show the effect on the budget constraint B_1 in Figure 3-3 of a rise in the price of food from \$10/kg to \$20/kg.

FIGURE 3-3

The Effect of a Rise in the Price of Shelter
When shelter goes up in price, the vertical intercept of the budget constraint remains the same. The original budget constraint rotates inward about this intercept.

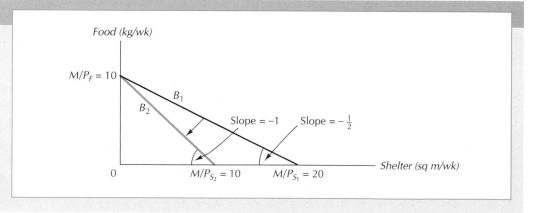

---

[6]The single exception to this statement involves the vertical intercept (0, 10), which lies on both the original and the new budget constraints.

CHAPTER 3: RATIONAL CONSUMER CHOICE

Exercise 3-2 demonstrates that when the price of food changes, the budget constraint rotates about its horizontal intercept. Note also that even though income and the price of shelter remain the same, the new budget constraint curtails not only the amount of food the consumer can buy but also the amount of shelter.

When we change the price of only one good, we necessarily change the slope of the budget constraint, $-P_S/P_F$. The same is true if we change both prices by different proportions. But as Exercise 3-3 will illustrate, changing both prices by exactly the same proportion gives rise to a new budget constraint with the same slope as before.

EXERCISE 3-3

Show the effect on the budget constraint B_1 in Figure 3-3 of a rise in the price of food from \$10/kg to \$20/kg and a rise in the price of shelter from \$5/sq m to \$10/sq m.

Note from Exercise 3-3 that the effect of doubling the prices of both food and shelter is to shift the budget constraint inward and parallel to the original budget constraint. The important lesson of this exercise is that the slope of a budget constraint tells us only about *relative prices*, nothing about how high prices are in absolute terms. When the prices of food and shelter change in the same proportion, the opportunity cost of shelter in terms of food remains the same as before.

Income Changes.   The effect of a change in income is much like the effect of an equal proportional change in all prices. Suppose, for example, that our hypothetical consumer's income is cut by half, from \$100/wk to \$50/wk. The horizontal intercept of the consumer's budget constraint then falls from 20 sq m/wk to 10 sq m/wk, and the vertical intercept falls from 10 kg/wk to 5 kg/wk, as shown in Figure 3-4. Thus the new budget, B_2, is parallel to the old, B_1, each with a slope of $-\frac{1}{2}$. In terms of its effect on what the consumer can buy, cutting income by one-half with prices unchanged is thus no different from doubling each price with money income unchanged. Precisely the same budget constraint results from both changes.

EXERCISE 3-4

Show the effect on the budget constraint B_1 in Figure 3-4 of an increase in income from \$100/wk to \$120/wk.

FIGURE 3-4

The Effect of Cutting Income by Half
Both horizontal and vertical intercepts fall by half. The new budget constraint has the same slope as the old but is closer to the origin.

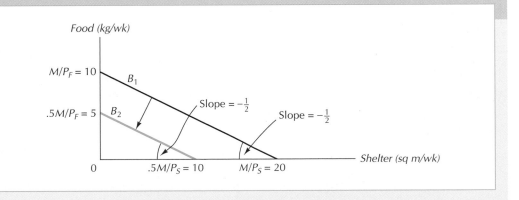

Exercise 3-4 illustrates that an increase in income shifts the budget constraint parallel outward. As in the case of an income reduction, the slope of the budget constraint remains the same.

Budgets Involving More than Two Goods

The examples discussed so far have all been ones in which the consumer is faced with the opportunity to buy only two different goods. Needless to say, not many consumers have such narrow options. In its most general form, the consumer budgeting problem can be posed as a choice between not two but N different goods, where N can be an indefinitely large number. With only two goods ($N = 2$), the budget constraint is a straight line, as we just saw. With three goods ($N = 3$), it is a plane. When we have more than three goods, the budget constraint becomes what mathematicians call a *hyperplane*, or *multidimensional plane*. The only real difficulty is in representing this multidimensional case geometrically. We are just not very good at visualizing surfaces that have more than three dimensions.

Cambridge economist Alfred Marshall (1842–1924) proposed a disarmingly simple solution to this problem. It is to view the consumer's choice as being one between a particular good—call it X—and an amalgam of other goods, denoted Y. This amalgam is generally called the **composite good**. We may think of the composite good as the amount of income the consumer has left over after buying the good X. Equivalently, it is the amount of money the consumer spends on goods other than X.

To illustrate how this concept is used, suppose the consumer has an income level of M/wk, and the price of X is given by P_X. The consumer's budget constraint may then be represented as a straight line in the X, Y plane, as shown in Figure 3-5. For simplicity, the price of a unit of the composite good is taken to be $1, so that if the consumer devotes none of his income to X, he will be able to buy M units of the composite good. All this means is that he will have M available to spend on other goods if he buys no X. Alternatively, if he spends all his income on X, he will be able to purchase the bundle (M/P_X, 0). Since the price of Y is assumed to be $1/unit, the slope of the budget constraint is simply $-P_X$.

As before, the budget constraint summarizes the various combinations of bundles that are affordable. Thus, the consumer can have X_1 units of X and Y_1 units of the composite good in Figure 3-5, or X_2 and Y_2, or any other combination that lies on the budget constraint.

Composite good A hypothetical construct representing all *other* goods on which income could be spent, with their prices relative to each other held constant.

FIGURE 3-5

The Budget Constraint with the Composite Good The vertical axis measures the amount of money spent each month on all goods other than X. The composite good has a price of $1/unit.

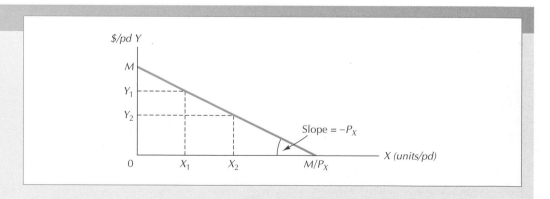

The Budget Constraint and Expenditure Shares

Because the budget constraint gives the set of affordable bundles when *all* income is spent, at every point it also provides us directly with information on the *share* of total expenditure spent on each good. Consider point C in Figure 3-6, where Felicia, a consumer, purchases X_1 of good X and Y_1 of good Y. If she spent 100 percent of her income M on X, she could purchase OE (= M/P_X) kg/week, but she purchases only OG (=X_1) kg/week. Hence s_X ($\equiv P_X X/M$), the share of her total expenditure that is spent on X, equals OG/OE. Since her expenditure share on Y, s_Y ($\equiv P_Y Y/M$), equals $1 - s_X$, we know that $s_Y = OE/OE - OG/OE = GE/OE$. By similar reasoning, measuring on the vertical axis, $s_Y = OF/OA$ and $s_X = FA/OA$. Note that we can obtain this information on expenditure shares even when we do not have precise information on Felicia's money income or the prices of X and Y. This fact is often of use in econometric analysis.

EXAMPLE 3-1

In Figure 3-6, suppose that Felicia's weekly income is \$120, and that she purchases 18 tonnes of Y per week, when she could have bought a maximum of 24 tonnes per week. At this point, she also buys 3 kg/week of X. What is the price of X?

In this Example, there are two basic ways of calculating P_X. First, note that Felicia is spending OF/OA = 18/24 = 75% of her income on Y, and so she is spending 25% (or \$30) on X. Spending \$30/week, she can purchase 3 kg/week of X, and so P_X = 30/3 = \$10/kg.

Alternatively, we can calculate that P_Y = 120/24 = \$5/tonne, and note that the slope of the budget constraint (= $-P_X/P_Y$) = $-6/3$ = -2, so that $P_X = 2P_Y = 2(5)$ = \$10/kg.

In this Example, either method will work. As Exercise 3-5 shows, however, this is not always the case.

EXERCISE 3-5

With his present weekly income, Luke could purchase a maximum of 30 tonnes of Y per week, but instead he purchases only 24 tonnes per week and spends \$120/week on X. What is the price of Y?

FIGURE 3-6

The Budget Constraint and Expenditure Shares At point C, the proportion of total expenditure spent on X, $s_X \equiv P_X X/M$, is $OG/OE = FA/OA$, and the share of expenditure on Y, $s_Y \equiv P_Y Y/M$, is $OF/OA = GE/OE$.

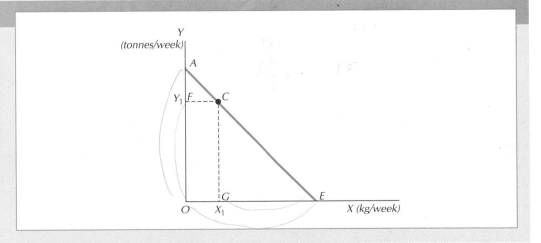

Kinked Budget Constraints

The budget constraints we have seen so far have all been straight lines. When relative prices are constant, the opportunity cost of one good in terms of any other is the same, no matter what bundle of goods we already have. But sometimes the budget constraints we encounter in practice are kinked lines. By way of illustration, consider the following example of quantity discounts.

EXAMPLE 3-2

The Gigawatt Power Company charges \$.10 per kilowatt-hour (kWh) for the first 1000 kWh of power purchased by a residential customer each month, but only \$.05/kWh for all additional kWh. For a residential customer with a monthly income of \$400, graph the budget constraint for electric power and the composite good.

If the consumer buys no electric power at all, he will have \$400 per month available for the purchase of other goods. Thus the vertical intercept of his budget constraint is the point (0, 400). As shown in Figure 3-7, for each of the first 1000 kWh he buys, he must give up \$.10, which means that the slope of his budget constraint starts out at $-\frac{1}{10}$. Then at 1000 kWh/mo, the price falls to \$.05/kWh, which means that the slope of his budget constraint from that point rightward is only $-\frac{1}{20}$.

Note that along the budget constraint shown in Figure 3-7, the opportunity cost of electricity depends on how much electricity the consumer has already purchased. Consider a consumer who now uses 1020 kWh each month and is trying to decide whether to leave his front porch light on all night, which would result in an additional consumption of 20 kWh per month. Leaving his light on will cost him an extra \$1 per month. Had his usual consumption level been only 980 kWh per month, however, the cost of leaving the front porch light on would have been \$2 per month. On the basis of this difference in the opportunity cost of additional electricity, we can predict that people who already use a lot of electricity (more than 1000 kWh per month) should be more likely than others to leave their porch lights burning at night.

FIGURE 3-7

A Quantity Discount Gives Rise to a Nonlinear Budget Constraint
Once electric power consumption reaches 1000 kWh/mo, the opportunity cost of additional power falls from \$.10/kWh to \$.05/kWh.

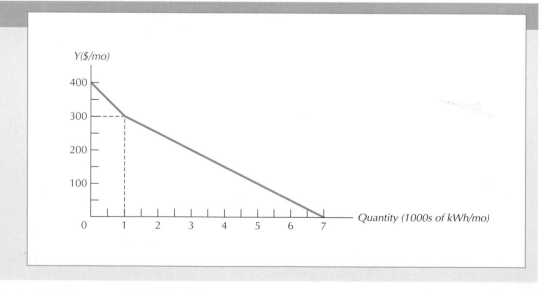

Suppose instead Amperage Electric Power charged $.05/kWh for the first 1000 kWh of power purchased by a residential consumer each month, but $.10/kWh each for all additional kilowatt-hours. For a residential consumer with a monthly income of $400, graph the budget constraint for electric power and the composite good. What if the rate jumps to $.10/kWh for *all* kilowatt-hours if power consumption in a month exceeds 1000 kWh (where the higher rate applies to all, not just the additional, kilowatt-hours)?

If the Budget Constraint Is the Same, the Decision Should Be the Same

Even without knowing anything about the consumer's preferences, we can use budgetary information to make certain inferences about how a rational consumer will behave. Suppose, for example, that the consumer's tastes do not change over time and that he is confronted with exactly the same budget constraint in each of two different situations. If he is rational, he should make exactly the same choice in both cases. As the following example makes clear, however, it may not always be immediately apparent that the budget constraints are in fact the same.

EXAMPLE 3-3

On one occasion, Red Green, a rational consumer, fills his car's tank with gasoline on the evening before his departure on a fishing trip. He awakens to discover that a thief has siphoned out 20L from his gas tank. On another occasion, he plans to stop for gas on his way out the next morning before he goes fishing. He awakens to discover that he has lost $20 from his wallet. If gasoline sells for $1.00/L and the round-trip will consume 20L, how, if at all, should Red's decision about whether to take the fishing trip differ in the two cases? (Assume that, monetary costs aside, the inconvenience of having to refill his tank is negligible.)

Suppose Red's income is $M/mo. Before his loss, his budget constraint is line B_1 in Figure 3-8. In both instances described, his budget constraint at the moment he discovers his loss will shift inward to B_2. If he does not take the trip, he will have $M - $20 available to spend on other goods in both cases. And if he does take the trip, he will have to purchase the required gasoline at $1.00/L in both cases. No matter what the source of the loss, the remaining opportunities are exactly the same. If Red's budget is tight, he may decide to cancel his trip. Otherwise, he may go despite the loss. But because his budget constraint and tastes are the same in the lost-cash case as in the stolen-gas case, it would not be rational for him to take the trip in one instance but not in the other.

Note that the situation described in Example 3-3 has the same structure as the one described in the broken-CD example with which we began this chapter. It too is one in which the decision should be the same in both instances because the budget constraint and preferences are the same in each.

Although the rational choice model makes clear that the decisions *should* be the same if the budget constraints and preferences are the same, people sometimes choose differently. The difficulty is often that the way the different situations are described sometimes causes people to overlook the essential similarities between them. For instance, in Example 3-3, many people erroneously conclude that the cost of taking the trip is higher in the stolen-gas case than in the lost-money case, and so they are less

FIGURE 3-8

Budget Constraints Following Theft of Gasoline, Loss of Cash
A theft of $20 worth of gasoline has exactly the same effect on the budget constraint as the loss of $20 in cash. The bundle chosen should therefore be the same, irrespective of the source of the loss.

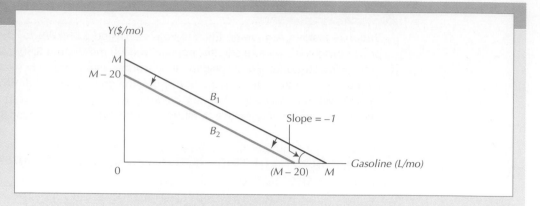

likely to take the trip in the former instance. Similarly, many people were less inclined to buy the disc after having broken the first one than after having lost $20 because they thought, incorrectly, that the disc would cost more in the broken-disc situation. As we have seen, however, the amount that will be saved by not buying the disc, or by not taking the trip, is exactly the same in each case.

To recapitulate briefly, the affordable set, bounded by the budget contraint, summarizes the combinations of bundles that the consumer is able to buy. Its position is determined jointly by income and prices. From the set of feasible bundles, the consumer's task is to pick the particular one she likes best. To identify this bundle, we need some means of summarizing the consumer's preferences over all possible bundles she might consume; we now turn to this task.

3.2 CONSUMER PREFERENCES

Preference ordering
A scheme whereby the consumer ranks all possible consumption bundles in order of preference.

For simplicity, let us again begin by considering a world with only two goods: shelter and food. A *preference ordering* is a scheme that enables the consumer to rank different bundles of goods in terms of their desirability, or order of preference. Consider two bundles, *A* and *B*. For concreteness, suppose that *A* contains 4 sq m/wk of shelter and 2 kg/wk of food, while *B* has 3 sq m/wk of shelter and 3 kg/wk of food. Knowing nothing about a consumer's preferences, we can say nothing about which of these bundles he will prefer. *A* has more shelter, but less food, than *B*. Someone who spends a lot of time at home would probably choose *A*, while someone with a rapid metabolism would be more likely to choose *B*.

In general, we can say that for any two such bundles, the consumer is able to make one of three possible statements: (1) *A* is preferred to *B*, (2) *B* is preferred to *A*, or (3) *A* and *B* are equally preferred. The preference ordering enables the consumer to rank different bundles but not to make more precise quantitative statements about their relative desirability. Thus, the consumer might be able to say that he prefers *A* to *B* but not that *A* provides twice as much satisfaction as *B*.

Preference orderings often differ widely among consumers. One person will prefer Rachmaninoff, another Neil Young. Despite these differences, however, most preference orderings share several important features. More specifically, economists generally assume four simple properties of preference orderings. These properties allow us to construct the concise analytical representation of preferences we need for the budget allocation problem.

1. Completeness. A preference ordering is *complete* if it enables the consumer to rank all possible combinations of goods and services. Taken literally, the completeness assumption is virtually always false, for there are many goods we know too little about to be able to evaluate decisively. It is nonetheless a useful simplifying assumption for the analysis of choices among bundles of goods with which consumers are familiar. Its real intent is to rule out instances like the one portrayed in the fable of Buridan's ass. The hungry animal was unable to choose between two bales of hay in front of him and starved to death as a result.

2. More-Is-Better. The more-is-better or *nonsatiation* property of preference orderings means simply that, other things equal, more of a good is preferred to less. Of course, more of something can make us worse off (as with overeating). But such examples usually contemplate some sort of practical difficulty, such as having a self-control problem or being unable to store a good for future use. As long as people can freely dispose of goods they don't want, having more of something can't make them worse off.

As an example of the application of the more-is-better assumption, consider the two bundles A, which has 12 sq m/wk of shelter and 10 kg/wk of food, and B, which has 12 sq m/wk of shelter and 11 kg/wk of food. The assumption tells us that B is preferred to A, because it has more food and no less shelter.

3. Transitivity. If you like steak better than hamburger, and you like hamburger better than hot dogs, then you probably like steak better than hot dogs. If a consumer's preference ordering is transitive, then for any three bundles A, B, and C, if he prefers A to B and prefers B to C, then he always prefers A to C. For example, suppose A is (4, 2), B is (3, 3), and C is (2, 4). If you prefer (4, 2) over (3, 3) and you prefer (3, 3) over (2, 4), then you must prefer (4, 2) over (2, 4). The preference relationship is thus assumed to be like the relationship used to compare heights of people. If O'Neal is taller than Carter and Carter is taller than Nash, we know that O'Neal must be taller than Nash.

Not all comparative relationships are transitive. The relationship "parent of," for example, is not. If Cathy is the parent of Cecile, who is the parent of Charlie, it does not follow that Cathy is Charlie's parent: she is his *grand*parent! Similarly, the relation "preferred by a majority" is not necessarily transitive. If policy option A is preferred by a majority to option B, and B is preferred by a majority to option C, it is quite possible (if different individuals rank the options differently) that option C is preferred by a majority to option A.

Transitivity is a simple consistency property and applies as well to the relation "equally preferred to" and to any combination of it and the "preferred to" relation. For example, if A is equally preferred to B and B is equally preferred to C, it follows that A is equally preferred to C. Similarly, if A is preferred to B and B is equally preferred to C, it follows that A is preferred to C.

The transitivity assumption can be justified as eliminating the potential for a "money pump" problem. To illustrate, suppose you prefer A to B and B to C, but now suppose you actually prefer C over A, so that your preferences are intransitive. If you start with C, you would trade C for B, trade B for A, and then trade A for C. This cycle could continue forever. If you were charged a tiny fee for each trade, you would spend all your money on trading. Clearly, preferences that permit you to be drained of all your money are not rational.

As reasonable as the transitivity property sounds, we will see examples in later chapters of behaviour that seems inconsistent with it. But it is an accurate description of preferences in most instances, and unless otherwise stated, we will adopt it throughout as a working assumption.

4. Convexity. This assumption implies that mixtures of goods are preferable to extremes. If you are indifferent between two bundles A and B, your preferences are convex if you prefer a bundle that contains half of A and half of B (or any other mixture) to either of the original bundles. For example, suppose you are indifferent between $A = (4, 0)$ and $B = (0, 4)$. If your preferences are convex, you will prefer the bundle $(2, 2)$ to each of the more extreme bundles. This property conveys the sense that we dislike having *too* little of most goods.

Indifference Curves

Let us consider some implications of these assumptions about preference orderings. Most importantly, they enable us to generate a graphical description of the consumer's preferences. To see how, consider first the bundle A in Figure 3-9, which has 12 sq m/wk of shelter and 10 kg/wk of food. The more-is-better assumption tells us that all bundles to the northeast of A are preferred to A, and that A, in turn, is preferred to all those to the southwest of A. Thus, the more-is-better assumption tells us that Z, which has 28 sq m/wk of shelter and 12 kg/wk of food, is preferred to A and that A, in turn, is preferred to W, which has only 6 sq m/wk of shelter and 4 kg/wk of food.

Now consider the set of bundles that lie along the line joining W and Z. Because Z is preferred to A and A is preferred to W, it follows that as we move from Z to W we must encounter a bundle that is equally preferred to A. (The intuition behind this claim is the same as the intuition that tells us that if we climb on any continuous path on a mountainside from one point at 500 metres above sea level to another at 1000 metres, we must pass through every intermediate altitude along the way.) Let B denote the bundle that is equally preferred to A, and suppose it contains 17 sq m/wk of shelter and 8 kg/wk of food. (The exact amounts of each good in B will of course depend on the specific consumer whose preferences we are talking about.) The more-is-better assumption also tells us that there will be only one such bundle on the straight line between W and Z. Points on that line to the northeast of B are all better than B; those to the southwest of B are all worse.

In precisely the same fashion, we can find another point—call it C—that is equally preferred to B. C is shown as the bundle $(20, 7)$, where the specific quantities in C again depend on the preferences of the consumer under consideration. By the transitivity assumption, we know that C is also equally preferred to A (since C is equally preferred to B, which is equally preferred to A).

FIGURE 3-9

Generating Equally Preferred Bundles
Z is preferred to A because it has more of each good than A has. For the same reason, A is preferred to W. It follows that on the line joining W and Z there must be a bundle B that is equally preferred to A. In similar fashion, we can find a bundle C that is equally preferred to B.

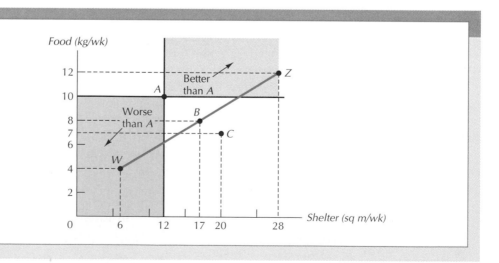

Indifference curve
A set of bundles among which the consumer is indifferent.

We can repeat this process as often as we like, and the end result will be an ***indifference curve***, a set of bundles all of which are equally preferred to the original bundle *A*, and hence also equally preferred to one another. This set is shown as the curve labelled I_0 in Figure 3-9. It is called an indifference curve because the consumer is indifferent among all the bundles that lie along it.

An indifference curve also permits us to compare the satisfaction implicit in bundles that lie along it with those that lie either above or below it. It permits us, for example, to compare bundle *C* (20, 7) to bundle *K* (23, 4), which has less food and more shelter than *C* has. We know that *C* is equally preferred to *D* (25, 6) because both bundles lie along the same indifference curve. *D*, in turn, is preferred to *K* because of the more-is-better assumption: it has 2 sq m/wk more shelter and 2 kg/wk more food than *K* has. Transitivity, finally, tells us that since *C* is equally preferred to *D* and *D* is preferred to *K*, *C* must be preferred to *K*.

By analogous reasoning (run through the argument yourself), we can say that bundle *L* is preferred to *A*. *In general, bundles of goods that lie above an indifference curve are all preferred to the bundles that lie on it. Similarity, bundles that lie on an indifference curve are all preferred to those that lie below it.*

The completeness property of preferences implies that there is an indifference curve that passes through every possible bundle. That being so, we can represent a consumer's preferences with an ***indifference map***, an example of which is shown in Figure 3-11. This indifference map shows just four of the infinitely many indifference curves that, taken together, yield a complete description of the consumer's preferences.

Indifference map
A representative sample of the set of a consumer's indifference curves, used as a graphical summary of her preference ordering.

The numbers $I_1, \ldots, I_4$ in Figure 3-11 are index values used to denote the order of preference that corresponds to the respective indifference curves. Any index numbers would do equally well provided they produced the same ranking as $I_1 < I_2 < I_3 < I_4$. In representing the consumer's preferences, what really counts is the *ranking* of the indifference curves, not the particular numerical values we assign to them.[7]

FIGURE 3-10

An Indifference Curve
An indifference curve is a set of bundles that the consumer prefers equally. For two goods, any bundle, such as *L*, that lies above an indifference curve is preferred to any bundle on the indifference curve. Any bundle on the indifference curve, in turn, is preferred to any bundle, such as *K*, that lies below the indifference curve.

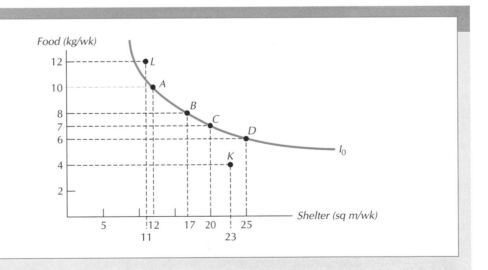

---

[7]Relabelling the indifference curves I_0, $I_{1.7}$, I_{16} and I_{83} respectively, for example, would produce the same ranking, since $0 < 1.7 < 16 < 83$, just as $1 < 2 < 3 < 4$. The crucial point is that the higher the number of an indifference curve, the greater is the level of satisfaction given by the bundles along it. For a more complete discussion of this issue, see Appendix 3A.

FIGURE 3-11

Part of an Indifference Map
The entire set of a consumer's indifference curves is called the consumer's indifference map. Bundles of goods on any indifference curve are less preferred than bundles on a higher indifference curve, and more preferred than bundles on a lower indifference curve.

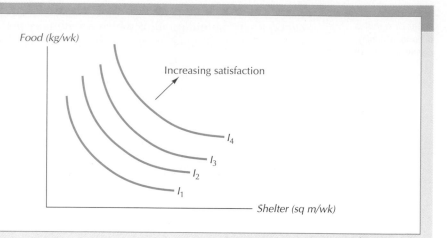

The four properties of preference orderings that we assume in the standard case imply four important properties of indifference curves and indifference maps:

1. Indifference curves for goods are ubiquitous. Any bundle has an indifference curve passing through it. This property is assured by the completeness property of preferences.
2. Indifference curves for goods are downward sloping. An upward-sloping indifference curve would violate the more-is-better property by saying a bundle with more of both goods is equivalent to a bundle with less of both.
3. Indifference curves (from the same indifference map) cannot cross. To see why, suppose that two indifference curves did, in fact, cross as in Figure 3-12. The following statements must then be true:

   E is equally preferred to *D* (because they each lie on the same indifference curve).
   D is equally preferred to *F* (because they each lie on the same indifference curve).
   E is equally preferred to *F* (by the transitivity assumption).

FIGURE 3-12

Why Two Indifference Curves Do Not Cross
If indifference curves were to cross, they would have to violate at least one of the assumed properties of preference orderings.

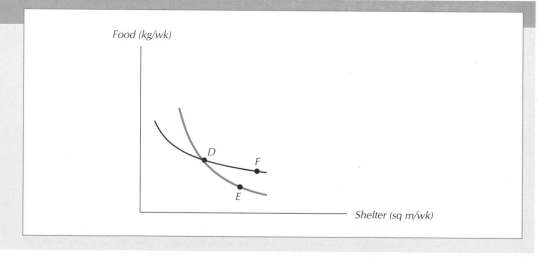

But we also know that

F is preferred to E (because more is better).

Because it is not possible for the statements E is equally preferred to F and F is preferred to E to be true simultaneously, the assumption that two indifference curves cross thus implies a contradiction. The conclusion is that the original proposition must be true, namely, two indifference curves cannot cross.

4. Indifference curves for goods become less steep as we move downward and to the right along them. As discussed below, this property is implied by the convexity property of preferences.

Tradeoffs between Goods

Marginal rate of substitution (MRS)
At any point on an indifference curve, the rate at which the consumer is willing to exchange the good measured along the vertical axis for the good measured along the horizontal axis; equal to the negative of the value of the slope of the indifference curve.

An important property of a consumer's preferences is the rate at which he is willing to exchange, or "trade off," one good for another. This rate is represented at any point on an indifference curve by the *marginal rate of substitution (MRS)*, which is defined as the negative of the value of the slope of the indifference curve at that point. In the left panel of Figure 3-13, for example, the marginal rate of substitution at point A is given by the absolute value of the slope of the tangent to the indifference curve at A, which is the ratio $\Delta F_A / \Delta S_A$. (The notation ΔF_A means "small change in food from the amount at point A.") If we take ΔF_A units of food away from the consumer at point A, we have to give him ΔS_A additional units of shelter to make him just as well off as before. The right panel of the figure shows an enlargement of the region surrounding bundle A. If the marginal rate of substitution at A is 2, this means that the consumer must be given 2 kg/wk of food to make up for the loss of 1 sq m/wk of shelter.[8]

Whereas the slope of the budget constraint tells us the rate at which we can substitute food for shelter without changing total expenditure, the MRS tells us the rate at which we can substitute food for shelter without changing total satisfaction. Put another way, the slope of the budget constraint gives the marginal *cost* of shelter in terms of food, and the MRS gives the marginal *benefit* of shelter in terms of food.

FIGURE 3-13

The Marginal Rate of Substitution
MRS at any point along an indifference curve is defined as the negative of the value of the slope of the indifference curve at that point. It is the amount of food the consumer must be given to compensate for the loss of 1 unit of shelter.

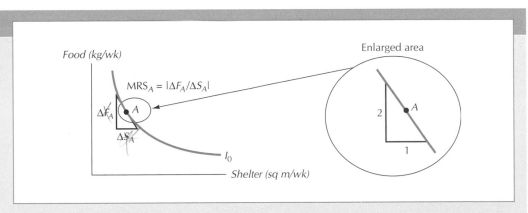

$$MRS = \frac{\Delta F}{\Delta S} \qquad MRS = \frac{\Delta Y}{\Delta X} = \frac{P_X}{P_F}$$

---

[8]More formally, the indifference curve may be expressed as a function $Y = Y(X)$ and the MRS at point A is defined as the negative of the value of the derivative of the indifference curve at that point: $MRS = -dY(X)/dX$. Technically speaking, the 2 kg/sq m ratio refers to *infinitesimal* amounts in the *neighbourhood* of A. Appendix 3A contains a more precise and detailed account.

The convexity property of preferences tells us that along any indifference curve, the more a consumer has of one good, the more she must be given of that good before she will be willing to give up a unit of the other good. Stated differently, the MRS declines as we move downward to the right along an indifference curve. Indifference curves with diminishing rates of marginal substitution are thus convex or bowed inward toward the origin. The indifference curves shown in Figures 3-10, 3-11, and 3-13 all have this property, as does the curve shown in Figure 3-14.

In Figure 3-14, note that at bundle A food is relatively plentiful and the consumer would be willing to sacrifice 3 kg/wk of it in order to obtain an additional square metre of shelter. Her MRS at A is 3. At C, the quantities of food and shelter are more balanced, and there she would be willing to give up only 1 kg/wk to obtain an additional square metre of shelter. Her MRS at C is 1. Finally, note that food is relatively scarce at D, and there she would be willing to give up only $\frac{1}{4}$ kg/wk of food to obtain an additional unit of shelter. Her MRS at D is $\frac{1}{4}$.

Intuitively, diminishing MRS means that consumers like variety. We are usually willing to give up goods we already have a lot of to obtain more of those goods we now have only a little of.

Using Indifference Curves to Describe Preferences

To get a feel for how indifference maps describe a consumer's preferences, let us see how indifference maps can be used to portray differences in preferences between two consumers. Suppose, for example, that both Pete and Rick like potatoes but that Rick likes rice much more than Pete does. This difference in their tastes is captured by the differing slopes of their indifference curves in Figure 3-15. Note in Figure 3-15a, which shows Pete's indifference map, that Pete would be willing to exchange 1 kg of potatoes for 1 kg of rice at bundle A. But at the corresponding bundle in Figure 3-15b, which shows Rick's indifference map, we see that Rick would trade 2 kg of potatoes for an additional 1 kg of rice. Their difference in preferences shows up clearly in this difference in their marginal rates of substitution of potatoes for rice.

FIGURE 3-14

Diminishing Marginal Rate of Substitution
The more food the consumer has, the more she is willing to give up to obtain an additional unit of shelter. The marginal rates of substitution at bundles A, C, and D are 3, 1, and 1/4, respectively.

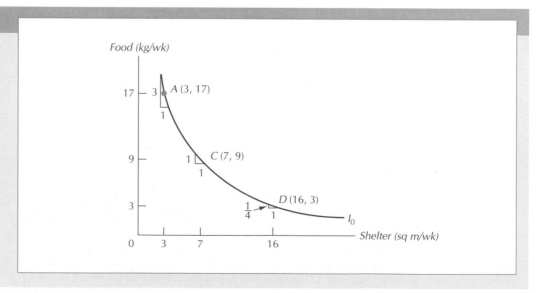

FIGURE 3-15

People with Different Tastes
Relatively speaking, Pete is a potato lover; Rick, a rice lover. This difference shows up in the fact that at any given bundle Pete's marginal rate of substitution of potatoes for rice is smaller than Rick's.

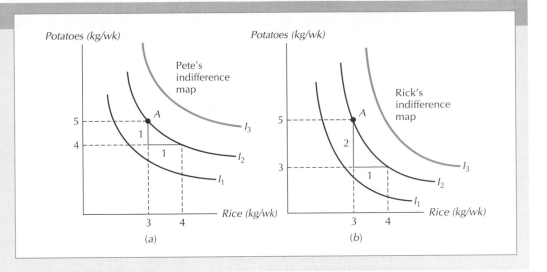

(a)

(b)

3.3 THE BEST FEASIBLE OR AFFORDABLE BUNDLE

We now have all the tools we need to determine how the consumer should allocate his income between two goods. The indifference map tells us how the various bundles are ranked in order of preference. The budget constraint, in turn, tells us which bundles are affordable. The consumer's task is to put the two together and to choose the most preferred or **best affordable bundle.** (Recall from Chapter 1 that we need not suppose that consumers think explicitly about budget constraints and indifference maps when deciding what to buy. It is sufficient to assume that people make decisions as if they were thinking in these terms, just as expert pool players choose between shots *as if* they knew all the relevant laws of Newtonian physics.)

Best affordable bundle
The most preferred bundle of those that are affordable.

For the sake of concreteness, let us again consider the choice between food and shelter that confronts a consumer with an income of $M = \$100/\text{wk}$ facing prices of $P_F = \$10/\text{kg}$ and $P_S = \$5/\text{sq m}$. For simplicity, we assume (unless otherwise specified) throughout this chapter and the next that the consumer can neither borrow nor save. Current income cannot be augmented by borrowing, and income that is not spent this period vanishes in a puff of smoke. Figure 3-16 shows this consumer's budget constraint and part of his indifference map. Of the five labelled bundles—A, D, E, F, and G—in the diagram, G is the most preferred because it lies on the highest indifference curve. G, however, is not affordable, nor is any other bundle that lies beyond the budget constraint. The more-is-better assumption implies that the best affordable bundle must lie *on* the budget constraint, not inside it. (Any bundle inside the budget constraint would be less preferred than one just slightly to the northeast, which would also be affordable.)

Where exactly is the best affordable bundle located along the budget constraint? We know that it cannot be on an indifference curve that lies partly inside the budget constraint. On the indifference curve I_1, for example, the only points that are even candidates for the best affordable bundle are the two that lie on the budget constraint, namely, A and E. But A cannot be the best affordable bundle because it is equally preferred to D, which in turn is less desirable than F by the more-is-better assumption. So by transitivity, A is less desirable than F. For the same reason, E cannot be the best affordable bundle.

Since the best affordable bundle cannot lie on an indifference curve that lies partly inside the budget constraint, and since it must lie on the budget constraint itself, we know it has to lie on an indifference curve that intersects the budget constraint only once. In Figure 3-16, that indifference curve is the one labelled I_2, and the best affordable bundle is F, which lies at the point of tangency between I_2 and the budget constraint. With an income of \$100/wk and facing prices of \$5/sq m for shelter and \$10/kg for food, the best this consumer can do is to buy 6 kg/wk of food and 8 sq m/wk of shelter.

The choice of bundle F makes perfect sense on intuitive grounds. The consumer's goal, after all, is to reach the highest indifference curve he can, given his budget constraint. His strategy is to keep moving to higher and higher indifference curves until he reaches the highest one that is still affordable. For indifference maps for which a tangency point exists, as in Figure 3-16, the best bundle will always lie at the point of tangency.

In Figure 3-16, note that the marginal rate of substitution at F is exactly the same as the absolute value of the slope of the budget constraint. This will always be so when the best affordable bundle occurs at a point of tangency. The condition that must be satisfied in such cases is therefore

$$\text{MRS} = \frac{P_S}{P_F}. \tag{3.3}$$

The right-hand side of Equation 3.3 represents the opportunity cost of shelter in terms of food. Thus, with $P_S = \$5/\text{sq m}$ and $P_F = \$10/\text{kg}$, the opportunity cost of an additional square metre of shelter is $\frac{1}{2}$ kg of food. The left-hand side of Equation 3.3 is $|\Delta F/\Delta S|$, the absolute value of the slope of the indifference curve at the point of tangency. It is the amount of additional food the consumer must be given in order to compensate him fully for the loss of 1 sq m of shelter. In the language of cost-benefit analysis discussed in Chapter 1, the slope of the budget constraint represents the opportunity cost of shelter in terms of food, while the slope of the indifference curve represents the marginal benefit of consuming shelter as compared with that of consuming food. Since the slope of the budget constraint is $-\frac{1}{2}$ in this example, the tangency condition tells us that $\frac{1}{2}$ kg of food would be required to compensate for the benefits given up with the loss of 1 sq m of shelter.

If the consumer were at some bundle on the budget line for which the two slopes are not the same, then it would always be possible for him to purchase a better bundle. To see why, suppose he were at a point where the slope of the indifference curve (in absolute

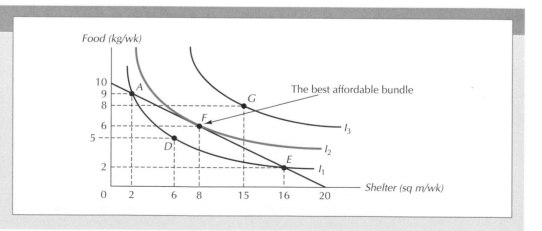

FIGURE 3-16

The Best Affordable Bundle
The best the consumer can do is to choose the bundle on the budget constraint that lies on the highest attainable indifference curve. Here, that is bundle F, which lies at a tangency between the indifference curve and the budget constraint.

value) is less than the slope of the budget constraint, as at point E in Figure 3-16. Suppose, for instance, that the MRS at E is only $\frac{1}{4}$. This tells us that the consumer can be compensated for the loss of 1 sq m of shelter by being given an additional $\frac{1}{4}$ kg of food. But the slope of the budget constraint tells us that by giving up 1 sq m of shelter, he can purchase an additional $\frac{1}{2}$ kg of food. Since this is $\frac{1}{4}$ kg more than he needs to remain equally satisfied, he will clearly be better off if he purchases more food and less shelter than at point E. The opportunity cost of an additional $\frac{1}{2}$ kilogram of food is less than the benefit it confers.

EXERCISE 3-7

Suppose that the marginal rate of substitution at point A in Figure 3-16 is 1.0. Show that this means the consumer will be better off if he purchases less food and more shelter than at A.

Corner Solutions

Corner solution
In a choice between two goods, a case in which the consumer does not consume one of the goods.

The best affordable bundle need not always occur at a point of tangency. In some cases, there may simply *be* no point of tangency—the MRS may be everywhere greater, or less, than the slope of the budget constraint. In this case we get a ***corner solution***, like the one shown in Figure 3-17, where M, P_F, and P_S are again given by \$100/wk, \$10/kg, and \$5/sq m, respectively. The best affordable bundle is the one labelled A, and it lies at the upper end of the budget constraint. At A the MRS is less than the absolute value of the slope of the budget constraint. For the sake of illustration, suppose the MRS at $A = .25$, which means that this consumer would be willing to give up .25 kg of food to get an additional square metre of shelter. But at market prices the opportunity cost of an additional square metre of shelter is .5 kg of food. He increases his satisfaction by continuing to give up shelter for more food until it is no longer possible to do so. Even though this consumer regards shelter as a desirable commodity, the best he can do is to spend all his income on food. Market prices are such that he would have to give up too much food to make the purchase of even a single unit of shelter worthwhile.

The indifference map in Figure 3-17 satisfies the property of diminishing marginal rate of substitution—moving to the right along any indifference curve, the slope becomes smaller in absolute terms. But because the slopes of the indifference curves start out smaller than the slope of the budget constraint here, the two never reach equality.

FIGURE 3-17

A Corner Solution
When the MRS of food for shelter is always less than the slope of the budget constraint, the best the consumer can do is to spend all his income on food.

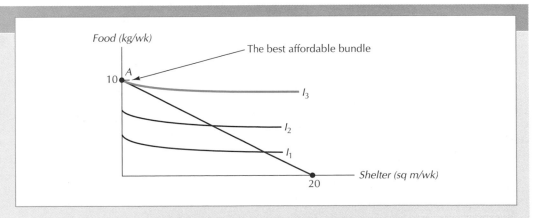

Indifference curves that are not strongly convex are characteristic of goods that are easily substituted for one another. Corner solutions are more likely to occur for such goods, and indeed are almost certain to occur when goods are perfect substitutes. For perfect substitutes, along any given indifference curve, the MRS does not diminish at all; rather, it is everywhere the same. With perfect substitutes, indifference curves are straight lines. If they happen to be steeper than the budget constraint, we get a corner solution on the horizontal axis; if less steep, we get a corner solution on the vertical axis.

EXAMPLE 3-4

Consider the case of Jitters, a caffeinated cola drinker. He spends all his soft drink budget on Coca-Cola and Jolt cola and cares only about the total caffeine content of what he drinks. If Jolt has twice the caffeine of Coke, and if Jolt costs $1/L and Coke costs $.75/L, how will Jitters spend his soft drink budget of $15/wk?

For Jitters, Jolt and Coke are *perfect substitutes*, which means that his indifference curves will not have the usual convex shape but will instead be linear. The top line in Figure 3-18 is the set of all possible Coke-Jolt combinations that provide the same satisfaction as the bundle consisting of 0 L of Jolt per week and 30 L of Coke per week. Since each litre of Jolt has twice the caffeine of a litre of Coke, all bundles along this line contain precisely the same amount of caffeine. The next green line down is the indifference curve for bundles equivalent to bundle (0, 20); and the third green line down is the indifference curve corresponding to (0, 10). Along each of these indifference curves, the marginal rate of substitution of Coke for Jolt is always $\frac{2}{1}$, that is, 2 L of Coke for every litre of Jolt.

In the same diagram, Jitters's budget constraint is shown as line *B*. The slope of his indifference curves is -2; of his budget constraint, $-\frac{4}{3}$. The best affordable bundle is the one labelled *A*, a corner solution in which he spends all his budget on Jolt. This makes intuitive sense in the light of Jitters's peculiar preferences: he cares only about total caffeine content, and at the given prices, Jolt provides more caffeine per dollar than Coke does. If the Jolt-Coke price ratio, P_J/P_C had been $\frac{3}{1}$ (or any other amount greater than $\frac{2}{1}$), Jitters would have spent all his income on Coke. That is, we would again have had a corner solution, only this time on the vertical axis. Only if the price ratio had been exactly $\frac{2}{1}$ might we have seen Jitters spend part of his income on each good. In that case, any combination of Coke and Jolt on his budget constraint would have served him equally well.

Most of the time we will deal with problems that have not corner but *interior solutions*— that is, with problems where the best affordable bundle will lie at a point of tangency. An interior solution, again, is one where the MRS is exactly the same as the slope of the budget constraint.

EXERCISE 3-8

Suppose Albert uses exactly two pats of butter on each piece of toast. If toast costs $.10/slice and butter costs $.20/pat, find Albert's best affordable bundle if he has $12 per month to spend on toast and butter. Suppose Albert starts to watch his cholesterol and therefore alters his preference to using exactly one pat of butter on each piece of toast. How much toast and butter would Albert then consume each month?

FIGURE 3-18

Equilibrium with Perfect Substitutes Here, the MRS of Coke for Jolt is 2 at every point. Whenever the price ratio P_J/P_C is less than 2, a corner solution results in which the consumer buys only Jolt. On the budget constraint B, the consumer does best to buy bundle A.

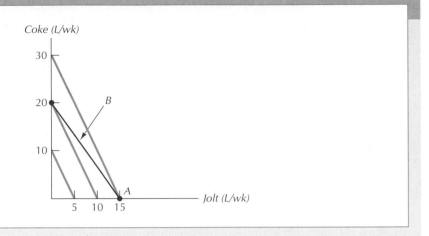

Indifference Curves When There Are More than Two Goods

In the examples discussed so far, the consumer cares about only two goods. Where there are more than two, we can construct indifference curves by using the same device we used earlier to represent multigood budget constraints. We simply view the consumer's choice as being one between a particular good X and an amalgam of other goods Y, which is again called the composite good. As before, the composite good is the amount of income the consumer has left over after buying the good X.

In the multigood case, we may thus continue to represent the consumer's preferences with an indifference map in the XY plane. Here, the indifference curve tells not the rate at which the consumer will exchange some particular good Y for a good X, but the rate at which he will exchange the composite good for X. Just as in the two-good case, equilibrium occurs when the consumer reaches the highest indifference curve attainable on his budget constraint.

3.4 AN APPLICATION OF THE RATIONAL CHOICE MODEL

As the following example makes clear, the composite good construct enables us to deal with more general questions than we could in the simple two-good case.

EXAMPLE 3-5 | **Is it better to provide subsidized housing or cash to low-income families?**

Canada, like most other OECD countries, has employed a wide range of publicly subsidized "assisted housing" programs. One of the main objectives of all of these programs is to provide access to a primary human requirement for those most in need. The current annual cost of housing subsidies in Canada is estimated at over $5 billion. Increasingly, in the allocation of the limited stock of subsidized housing units, the focus is on those high-need, low-income families who have to spend over 30 percent of their family income to rent adequate accommodation.

Rent subsidies are earmarked for accommodation alone. They are typically paid directly (in one form or another) to the landlord, and the "recipients" usually never see the money. Suppose that the housing subsidy to a family costs the government $400 per month. Would the family have been better off if instead it had been given $400 directly in cash? We can use a simple indifference curve model to investigate this question.

Let Y denote the composite good (measured in dollars/month) and X represent shelter (measured in square metres/month), with P_Y as \$1/unit and P_X in \$/sq m. If the family has a monthly income of \$1000, its budget line in Figure 3-19 would be AB. Without the subsidy, it would choose the bundle at M, paying AL dollars for ON sq m of shelter. Assisted housing is allocated in accordance with an *externally* determined standard, based on family size and other criteria. Suppose that for this family, the "standard" amount of housing is OG sq m, for which the family pays AC dollars, leaving OC dollars for other expenditures. Its consumption point is now E, which is on a higher indifference curve than M; the family is better off.

The amount of the subsidy can be expressed in two ways: as the additional amount of shelter the family receives (DE) or as the dollar value of the subsidy (FE). The family's budget constraint for shelter in a single location is now $ADEFB$, with the jut outward at the point given by the standard amount of shelter, although the family could (in a second location) increase the available space, along the line EK.

Would a \$400 cash payment to the family make them better off than the subsidy? Under our assumptions so far, almost certainly. The cash subsidy would shift their budget constraint out to JK, parallel to AB. The indifference curves I_E^1, I_E^2, and I_E^3 passing through point E are for three different families, all of whom are eligible for OG in subsidized shelter. I_E^1 is tangent to JK at E, and so Family 1 will do equally well with the subsidy or the cash: in either case, it will select bundle E. I_E^2, however, is flatter than JK at E, and hence Family 2 would be better off with the cash, since it could then pick a preferred bundle such as E_2 (with less shelter and more of the composite commodity). With the cash grant, space-hungry Family 3 will choose E_3. It could have rented more than OG (along EK) with the subsidy, but not in a single location, and so it too is presumably better off with the cash transfer.

In short, except in the case of Family 1, whose indifference curve is tangent to JK exactly at E, cash transfers appear to provide higher levels of welfare than subsidies in our simple model.

If the conclusions we can draw from such a simple model are so strong, then why are billions of dollars being spent each year to provide subsidized housing, instead of just making cash grants? One *political* reason is that earmarking the subsidy for shelter guarantees that the resources used will put roofs over people's heads, rather than being spent in frivolous or illicit ways. Even if only a small minority of the cash recipients misspent the cash and ended up homeless, the erosion of political support, for the governments involved and for the programs *and* the other families involved in them, would be costly. In this context, the inefficiencies the model highlights can be viewed as "insurance" costs, in relation to maintaining political support for the programs.

A second political factor is that the existing stock of assisted housing units places an upper limit on the cost of the programs for the government. In many centres, there are long waiting lists of *eligible* families. If *all* eligible families were given cash grants, the overall cost of the programs would rise or the cash grant per family could have to be cut. At the same time, administration and control costs would increase. The present system contains inequities, but its "*automatic* cost control" feature makes it politically attractive to governments.

There is also a strictly economic reason that helps explain the use of subsidized housing rather than cash payments. We have assumed so far that \$400 in cash would buy the same amount of shelter as \$400 in subsidized housing. This may, however, not be the case. First, mortgage rates may be lower on government-backed projects because

FIGURE 3-19

For 3 families receiving subsidized housing at E, only Family 1 (with indifference curve I_E^1) is equally well off with the subsidy or an equivalent cash grant. With a cash grant that raised the budget constraint to JK, Family 2 would choose bundle E_2 and Family 3 would choose bundle E_3. Both would be better off than at E. The indifference curves of all 3 families cross at E, reflecting the different MRS for each family at E. Of course, the indifference curves for each individual family do *not* cross.

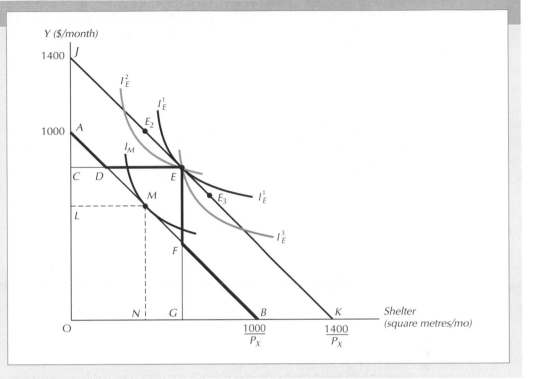

they are less risky than private investments in rental housing. Second, the landlord's risk of nonpayment is different in the two cases. If a family is paying $600 per month in rent out of $1400 in monthly income ($1000 plus the $400 cash grant), the landlord faces a greater risk of default, and a greater loss if there is a default, than if the family is paying only $200 out of $1000 while the government pays a guaranteed $400 per month. The necessary premium to compensate the landlord for the greater risk in the former case raises rents in the private rental market. These two factors and some related ones mean that a cash grant of about $475 is required to provide equivalent shelter to that provided by a $400 subsidy. When the effects of risk are added in, a cash grant program may cost more per square metre than subsidized housing. This additional cost must be set off against the inefficiencies identified in our basic model.

We examine risk and insurance further in Chapter 6. What we can say here is that our simple model has highlighted a genuine limitation of assisted housing programs. The reality is more complex than our model suggests, but the model focuses our attention on the types of questions that need to be asked in assessing the value of *any* social program.

Example 3-5 calls our attention to an issue raised not only with rent subsidies but also with other forms of in-kind transfers. Although the two forms of transfer are sometimes equivalent, cash transfers often seem superior on those occasions when they differ.

Economic Naturalist 3-1

WHY DO PEOPLE OFTEN GIVE GIFTS IN KIND INSTEAD OF CASH?

Occasionally someone receives a gift that is exactly what he would have purchased for himself had he been given an equivalent amount of money. But gifts can miss the mark. Who has never been given an article of clothing that he was embarrassed to wear? The rational economic choice model implies that we could avoid the problem of useless gifts if we followed

"Sweetheart, perhaps we shouldn't exchange gifts this year."

the simple expedient of giving cash. And yet virtually every society continues to engage in ritualized gift giving.

The fact that this custom has persisted should not be taken as evidence that people are irrational. Rather, it suggests that there may be something about gift giving that the rational choice model fails to capture. One purpose of giving a gift is to express affection for the recipient. A thoughtfully made or chosen gift accomplishes this in a way that a gift of cash cannot. Or it may be that some people have difficulty indulging themselves with even small luxuries and would feel compelled to spend cash gifts on purely practical items. For these people, a gift provides a way of enjoying a small luxury without having to feel guilty about it.[9] This interpretation is supported by the observation that we rarely give purely practical gifts like plain cotton underwear or laundry detergent.

Whatever the real reasons people may have for giving in kind rather than in cash, it seems safe to assume that we do not do it because it never occurred to us to give cash. On the contrary, occasionally we do give cash gifts, especially to young relatives with low incomes. But even though there are advantages to gifts in cash, people seem clearly reluctant to abandon the practice of giving in kind.

3.5 CHANGES IN TASTES, PREFERENCES, AND GOODS

The model of consumers' constrained optimizing behaviour we have been developing focuses on how we select the best feasible or affordable bundle from a *given* range of goods, with *given* money income, *given* prices, and *given* tastes or preferences as represented by an indifference map. Yet over time, people's tastes or preferences can change, goods that were once available can disappear from the market, and new goods can appear in the market. Indeed, the fact that new goods appear and existing goods disappear means that in our model, tastes and preferences *have* to change over time. After all, it makes no sense to have a preference ordering over goods that no longer exist, while our completeness assumption means that we have to have preference rankings for new goods as they become available. Even if there is *no* change in the range and quality of goods available, however, tastes can and do change.

We can formally incorporate the effects of changes over time in the range of available goods and in tastes into our model fairly easily. Since each axis of our diagram measures the consumption flow per period of a single specific good, we can represent a change in the number of goods available simply by changing the number of axes and relabelling. Suppose that at time t only goods X_1, X_2, and X_3 are available. Then our indifference contours and budget constraint are defined in the three-dimensional space, with the quantity of one of the goods along each of the three axes. If in period $t + 1$, good X_2 has disappeared but goods X_4 and X_5 are now available, then we define preferences and the budget constraint over the four-dimensional space, with the quantities of X_1, X_3, X_4, and X_5 along the four axes.[10]

---

[9]For a discussion of this interpretation, see R. Thaler, "Mental Accounting and Consumer Choice," *Marketing Science, 4,* Summer 1985.

[10]In practice, for three or more goods, we typically use vector notation and analysis instead, partly because of the difficulties of drawing higher-dimensional diagrams on a two-dimensional page.

Similarly, to represent the effects of changes in tastes over time, we can simply redraw the indifference map. Figure 3-20 illustrates a change in tastes for a consumer, Hedonistica, who consumes only two goods, X and Y. In both periods t and $t + 1$, she faces prices $P_X = \$1/\text{unit}$ and $P_Y = \$2/\text{unit}$. The figure shows her best affordable bundles when her income is $100 ($A$ in period t, A' in period $t + 1$) or $200 ($B$ in period t, B' in period $t + 1$). Note several features of Figure 3-20. First, X is an "inferior" good (see Chapter 4) in period t: with an income of $100, Hedonistica would consume 40 units of X, but with an income of $200, she would consume only 20 units. In period $t + 1$, X has become a normal good. Not only will she consume more X at each income level than she did in period t, but she consumes more X at the higher income level. Second, although the proportion of her income that she spends on X and Y is the same at A and at B', this does not mean that her tastes are the same in both periods; rather, it is a coincidental result of the *change* in tastes. Third, her indifference curves for period $t + 1$ intersect those for period t. This fact does not violate our non-intersection rule, because that rule holds only for *given* tastes. The fourth feature is not as obvious, but is nonetheless very important. When her tastes change, even if her income and prices remain unchanged, we can no longer say whether Hedonistica is "better off" in period t or in period $t + 1$, because from a theoretical standpoint, she is now a "different" person. What we *can* say is how this "different" person, with her changed preferences, will respond to various price and income combinations.

Economists, however, are interested not only in the *effects* of changes in tastes, but also in the *causes*. People's tastes and preferences can change for many reasons. Some needs and preferences are at least partly age-specific. Our favourite TV programs when we were children, not surprisingly, often strike us now as "childish." One of the side benefits of certain kinds of music is that they drive parents crazy. The human life cycle has been described as a progress from diapers to underwear to diapers. A younger population will tend to have greater demands for education; an aging population will have greater

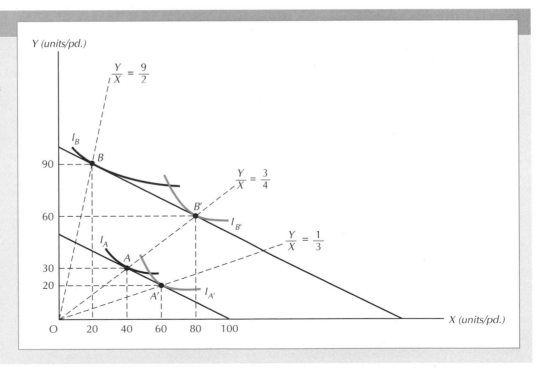

FIGURE 3-20

A Change in Tastes
The blue indifference curves I_A and I_B describe the consumer's preferences in period t; the green indifference curves $I_{A'}$ and $I_{B'}$ describe her preferences in period $t + 1$. Her indifference curves reflect a shift toward a stronger preference for X in period $t + 1$.

demands for health care, medicine, and retirement facilities. Individuals' needs and preferences similarly tend to reflect their ages and to change with age.

A second important source of changes in tastes is learning and experimentation. Our basic model of consumer behaviour assumes *complete* knowledge of the need-satisfying qualities of *all* commodities, and a *complete* preference ordering. In practice, however, there are many goods that most of us have never consumed: small $350 jars of caviar, $1.5 million yachts, and $80 million mansions come to mind. Most of us have not tried even a fraction of the goods that we *could* afford, and with thousands of new products coming onto the market each year, we are destined to be always less than "fully informed consumers." Some of our acts of consumption are, hence, simultaneously experiments—means of learning how (or whether) goods that we don't yet know can satisfy our needs. For those right at the margin of bare subsistence, such experimentation may be an unaffordable luxury. Yet a sharp increase in our income level, or a sharp drop in the price of an unfamiliar good, will increase the chances of experimentation. If the new good has very attractive characteristics, it may well become part of our "normal" consumption pattern. Manufacturers often launch a new product with free samples or deeply discounted prices for this very reason, to increase the number of experimenters.

Preferences can change not only as a result of direct consumption experience but also as a result of indirect or mediated information. Such information could be something as simple as a trusted friend's "Try it, you'll like it!" It could take the form of a government announcement about the health or safety hazards of consuming a particular item, or a consumer advocacy group's call to boycott a polluting company's products. It could also be a skilfully designed TV commercial, which provides new information on the characteristics or uses of a good, or simply generates favourable and memorable emotional associations. In most cases, however, unless the good itself lives up to its advance billing when it is actually consumed, such indirect information is unlikely by itself to result in a change in tastes.

There is, however, one significant potential exception to this rule of thumb, that of fashions, fads, and crazes. Normally we assume that the satisfaction from consuming a good stems from its "innate" want-satisfying characteristics. Yet apart from these inherent characteristics, goods can at times acquire the capacity to confer social status, acceptance, or distinction. We are familiar with lists of "What's hot and what's not!" A self-respecting trend-following consumer would not be caught dead in an outfit that was "out of it" or "uncool." Such "bandwagon" effects not only increase the volatility of tastes, but also complicate our basic model of consumer choice, insofar as we assume that each consumer's choices are independent of those of other consumers. In several later chapters, we analyze some effects of such interdependent preferences, but in this chapter and the next we shall assume that there is no interdependence.[11]

---

[11]For further reading, see David Foot and Daniel Stoffman, *Boom, Bust and Echo,* Toronto: Stoddart, 2000; Harvey Leibenstein, "Bandwagon, Snob, and Veblen Effects in the Theory of Consumers' Demand," *Quarterly Journal of Economics,* May, 1950, pp. 183–207; Paul Ormerod, *Butterfly Economics,* London: Faber and Faber, 1998; and Ian Parker, "Commodities as Sign-systems," in Robert Babe, editor, *Information and Communication in Economics,* Boston: Kluwer, 1994, pp. 69–91.

- Our task in this chapter was to set forth the basic model of rational consumer choice. In all its variants, this model retains certain common features; in particular, it takes consumers' preferences as given and assumes they will try to satisfy them in the most efficient way.

- The first step in solving the budgeting problem is to identify the set of bundles of goods that the consumer is able to buy. In the standard case, the consumer is assumed to have an income level given in advance and to face fixed prices. Prices and income together define the consumer's budget constraint, which, in the simple two-good case, is a downward-sloping line whose slope, in absolute value, is the ratio of the two prices. It is the set of all possible bundles that the consumer might purchase if he spends his entire income.

- The second step in solving the consumer budgeting problem is to summarize the consumer's preferences. Here, we begin with a preference ordering by which the consumer is able to rank all possible bundles of goods. This ranking scheme is assumed to be complete and transitive and to exhibit the more-is-better or nonsatiation property. Preference orderings that satisfy these restrictions give rise to indifference maps, or collections of indifference curves, each of which represents combinations of bundles among which the consumer is indifferent. Preference orderings are also assumed to exhibit a diminishing marginal rate of substitution, which means that, along any indifference curve, the more of a good a consumer has, the more he must be given to induce him to part with a unit of some other good. The diminishing MRS property is what accounts for the characteristic convex shape of indifference curves.

- The budget constraint tells us what combinations of goods the consumer can afford to buy. To summarize the consumer's preferences over various bundles, we may use either an indifference map or a utility function (see Appendix 3A). In the indifference-curve framework, the best affordable bundle occurs at a point of tangency between an indifference curve and the budget constraint. At that point, the marginal rate of substitution is exactly equal to the rate at which the goods can be exchanged for one another at market prices.

- Appendix 3A (which follows immediately) develops the utility function approach to the consumer budgeting problem. Topics covered include cardinal versus ordinal utility, algebraic construction of indifference curves, the use of calculus to maximize utility, goods and "bads," and the characteristics of certain special utility functions.

QUESTIONS FOR REVIEW

1. If the prices of all products are rising at 20 percent per year and your employer gives you a 20 percent salary increase, are you better off, worse off, or equally well off in comparison with your situation a year ago?

2. *True or false:* If you know the slope of the budget constraint (for two goods), you know the prices of the two goods. Explain.

3. *True or false:* The downward slope of indifference curves in the standard case is a consequence of the diminishing marginal rate of substitution.

4. Construct an example of a preference ordering over Coke, Diet Coke, and Diet Pepsi that violates the transitivity assumption.

5. Explain in your own words how the slope of an indifference curve provides information about how much a consumer likes one good relative to another.

6. Explain why a consumer will often buy one bundle of goods even though he prefers another.

7. Why are corner solutions especially likely in the case of perfect substitutes?

8. *True or false:* If the indifference curve map is concave to the origin, then the optimal commodity basket must be at a corner equilibrium, except possibly when there are quantity discounts.

9. If Ralph were given $10, he would spend none of it on tuna fish. But when asked, he claims to be indifferent between receiving $10 worth of tuna fish and a $10 bill. How could this be?

1. The Acme Seed Company charges $2 per kg for the first 10 kg you buy of marigold seeds each week and $1 per kg for every kilogram you buy thereafter. If your income is $100 per week, draw your budget constraint for the composite good and marigold seeds.

2. Same as Problem 1, except now the price for every kilogram over 10 kg per week is $4 per kg.

3. Etta Pistachio likes cashews better than almonds and likes almonds better than walnuts. She likes pecans equally as well as macadamia nuts and prefers macadamia nuts to almonds. Assuming her preferences are transitive, which does she prefer:
   a. Pecans or walnuts?
   b. Macadamia nuts or cashews?

4. Originally P_X is $120/unit and P_Y is $80/unit. *True or false:* If P_X increases by $18/unit and P_Y increases by $12/unit with money income unchanged, the new budget line will be shifted inward and parallel to the old budget line. Explain.

5. Martha has $150 of disposable income to spend each week and cannot borrow money. She buys Malted Milk Balls and the composite good. Suppose that Malted Milk Balls cost $2.50 per bag and the composite good costs $1 per unit.
   a. Sketch Martha's budget constraint.
   b. What is the opportunity cost, in terms of bags of Malted Milk Balls, of an additional unit of the composite good?

6. In Problem 5, suppose that in an inflationary period the cost of the composite good increases to $1.50 per unit, but the cost of Malted Milk Balls remains the same.
   a. Sketch the new budget constraint.
   b. What is the opportunity cost of an additional unit of the composite good?

7. In Problem 6, suppose that Martha demands a pay raise to fight the inflation. Her boss submits and raises her salary so that her disposable income is now $225 per week.
   a. Sketch the new budget constraint. Is Martha better off than in Problem 5?
   b. What is the opportunity cost of an additional unit of the composite good?

8. Kathy, an aggressive skier, spends her entire income on skis and bindings. She wears out one pair of skis for every pair of bindings she wears out.
   a. Graph Kathy's indifference curves for skis and bindings.
   b. Now draw her indifference curves on the assumption that she is such an aggressive skier that she wears out two pairs of skis for every pair of bindings she wears out.

9. Suppose Kathy in Problem 8 has $3600 in income to spend on skis and bindings each year. Find Kathy's best affordable bundle of skis and bindings under both of the preferences described in the previous problem. Skis are $480 per pair and bindings are $240 per pair.

10. For Alexi, coffee and tea are perfect substitutes: one cup of coffee is equivalent to one cup of tea. Suppose Alexi has $90 per month to spend on these beverages, and coffee costs $.90/cup while tea costs $1.20 per cup. Find Alexi's best affordable bundle of tea and coffee. How much could the price of a cup of coffee rise without harming her standard of living? Similarly, how much could the price of a cup of tea rise?

11. Eve likes apples but doesn't care for pears. If apples and pears are the only two goods available, draw her indifference curves.

12. Nicolette and Tarzan both like food but dislike cigarette smoke. The more food Nicolette has, the more she would be willing to give up to achieve a given reduction in cigarette smoke. If the air is smoke free, Tarzan requires a lot of food to compensate him for the introduction of any cigarette smoke, but thereafter he requires increasingly less food to compensate him for a given increase in smoke. Draw their indifference curves for food and smoke.

13. Francis is an ascetic, for whom "more food and shelter is better" until his basic needs are met. After that point, since there is no free disposal, more food or shelter interferes with his spiritual meditation and makes him worse off. Draw his indifference curves.

14. Paula, a former actress, spends all her income attending plays and movies and likes plays exactly three times as much as she likes movies.
    a. Draw her indifference map.
    b. Paula earns $120 per week. If play tickets cost $12 each and movie tickets cost $4 each, show her budget line and highest attainable indifference curve. How many plays will she see?
    c. If play tickets are $12 and movie tickets are $5, how many plays will she attend?

15. For each of the following, sketch:
    a. A typical person's indifference curves between garbage and the composite good.
    b. Indifference curves for the same two commodities for Oscar the Grouch on *Sesame Street*, who loves garbage and has no use for the composite good.

16. Carlo budgets $9 per week for his morning coffee with milk. He likes it only if it is prepared with 4 parts coffee, 1 part milk. Coffee costs $1 per unit, milk $.50/unit. How much coffee and how much milk will Carlo buy per week? How will your answers change if the price of coffee rises to $3.25 per unit? Show your answers graphically.

17. The federal government grants your university $2 million, stipulating that the money must be used for geriatric research only. The graph below shows the university's pre-grant research budget constraint and best attainable indifference curve. How would the university's welfare differ if the grant came without the restriction?

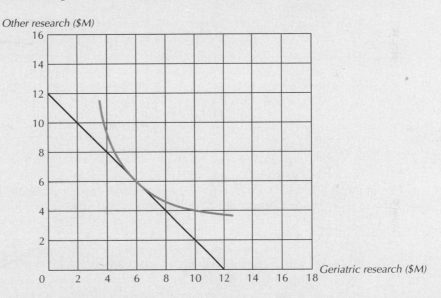

18. The Wishbone Cellular Phone Company offers an optional package for calls whereby each month the subscriber gets the first 50 minutes of calls free, the next 100 minutes at $.05/min, and any additional time at the rate of $.10/minute. Draw the budget constraint for cellular phone calls and the composite good for a subscriber with an income of $80 per month.

19. For the Wishbone subscriber in Problem 18, what is the opportunity cost of making an additional 20 minutes of calls if he currently makes:
    a. 40 minutes of calls each month?
    b. 140 minutes of calls each month?

20. You have the option of renting a car on a daily basis for $40 per day or on a weekly basis for $200 per wk. Draw your budget constraint for a budget of $360 per trip.
    a. Find your best affordable bundle if your travel preferences are such that you require exactly $140 worth of other goods for each day of rental car consumption.
    b. Alternatively, suppose you view a day of rental car consumption as a perfect substitute for $35 worth of other goods.

21. Howard said that he was exactly indifferent between consuming four slices of pizza and one beer versus consuming three slices of pizza and two beers. He also said that he prefers a bundle consisting of one slice of pizza and three beers to either of the first two bundles. Do Howard's preferences exhibit diminishing marginal rates of substitution?

22. Your telephone company has offered you a choice between the following billing plans:

    Plan A: Pay $.05 per call.

    Plan B: Pay an initial $2 per week, which allows you up to 30 calls per week at no charge. Any calls over 30 per week cost $.05 per call.

    If your income is $12 per week and the composite good costs $1 per unit, graph your budget constraints for the composite good and calls under the two plans.

*23. At your school's fund-raising picnic, you pay for soft drinks not with cash but with tickets purchased in advance—one ticket per bottle of soft drink. Tickets are available in sets of three types:

    Set 1: $3 for 3 tickets

    Set 2: $4 for 5 tickets

    Set 3: $5 for 8 tickets

    If the total amount you have to spend is $12 and fractional sets of tickets cannot be bought or sold, graph your budget constraint for soft drinks and the composite good.

24. Consider two Italian restaurants located in identical towns 200 kilometres apart. The restaurants are identical in every respect but their tipping policies. At one, there is a flat $15 service charge, but no other tips are accepted. At the other, a 15 percent tip is added to the bill. The average food bill at the first restaurant, exclusive of the service charge, is $100. How, if at all, do you expect the amount of food eaten in the two restaurants to differ?

*25. Dean Dean Dean, a retired college administrator, consumes only grapes and the composite good Y ($P_Y = \$1$). His income consists of $10,000 per year from his pension plan, plus the proceeds from whatever he sells of the 2000 bushels of grapes he harvests annually from his vineyard. Last year, grapes sold for $2 per bushel, and Dean consumed all 2000 bushels of his grapes in addition to 10,000 units of Y. This year the price of grapes is $3 per bushel, while P_Y remains $1. If his indifference curves have the conventional shape, will this year's consumption of grapes be greater than, smaller than, or the same as last year's? Will this year's consumption of Y be greater than, smaller than, or the same as last year's? Explain.

26. Maizie Forsbey-Witchoo, a *Star Wars* fanatic, currently spends all of her monthly memorabilia budget on *Star Wars* action figures and packs of *Star Wars* collectible cards.

    a. Last month, she bought 16 action figures, although she could have purchased a maximum of 24, and spent the remaining $120 on packs of cards. What is the price of an action figure?

    b. This month, with her budget and prices unchanged, she purchased 80 packs of cards and spent the remaining $60 on action figures. What is the price of a pack of cards, and what is the maximum number of packs she could have purchased? With packs of cards on the horizontal axis, what is the slope of her budget constraint?

ANSWERS TO IN-CHAPTER EXERCISES

3-1.

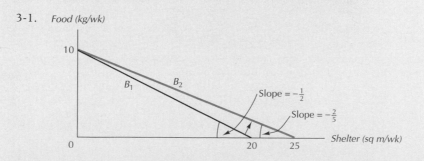

3-2. Food (kg/wk)

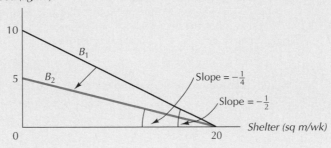

3-3. Food (kg/wk)

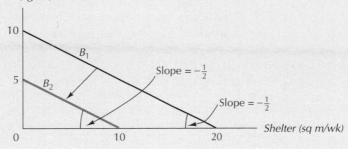

3-4. Food (kg/wk)

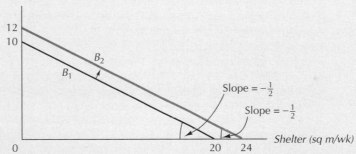

3-5. Luke is spending 24/30 = 80% of his income on Y, and, therefore, the $120 he spends on X is 20% of his weekly income M. Hence $M = 120/.2 = $600/week$, which could purchase a maximum of 30 tonnes of Y per week. Therefore, the price of Y ($=P_Y$) $= 600/30 = $20/tonne$. Note that it is *not* possible to calculate either the price *or* the quantity of X purchased from the information given.

3-6. The budget constraint for a residential consumer with Amperage Electric Power would be kinked outward, as the initial rate for the first 1000 kWh per month is lower. For power consumption X up to 1000 kWh per month, the budget constraint has a slope given by the lower rate $.05/kWh.

$$Y = 400 - .05X \qquad 0 \le X \le 1000 \text{ kWh per month}$$

For power consumption X above 1000 kWh/mo, the budget constraint has a slope given by the higher rate $.10/kWh.

$$Y = 450 - .10X \qquad X > 1000 \text{ kWh per month}$$

The kink occurs where the level of consumption of other goods (when $X = 1000$ kWh/mo) is $Y = 400 - .05X = 400 - 50 = \$350$, or equivalently, $Y = 450 + .10X = 450 - 100 = \$350$. If instead the rate were \$.10/kWh for all kWh that exceeded 1000 kWh/mo, then the budget constraint for $X > 1000$ kWh per month would be

$$Y = 400 - .10X \qquad X > 1000 \text{ kWh/mo}$$

and would have a discrete drop from $Y = \$350$ to $Y = \$300$ at $X = 1000$ kWh per month.

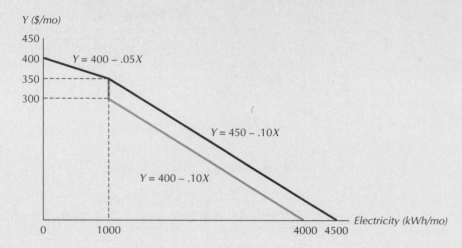

3-7. At bundle A, the consumer is willing to give up 1 kg of food to get an additional square metre of shelter. But at the market prices, if he gives up 1 kg of food, he can actually buy an additional 2 sq m of shelter. It follows that the consumer will be better off than at bundle A if he buys 1 kg less of food and 2 sq m more of shelter.

3-8. Albert's budget constraint is $T = 120 - 2B$. Albert's initial preferences are for two pats of butter for every slice of toast: $B = 2T$. Substituting this equation into his budget constraint yields $T = 120 - 4T$, or $5T = 120$, which solves for $T = 24$ slices of toast, and thus $B = 48$ pats of butter each month. Albert's new preferences are for one pat of butter for every slice of toast: $B = T$. Substituting this equation into his budget constraint yields $T = 120 - 2T$, or $3T = 120$, which solves for $T = 40$ slices of toast, and thus $B = 40$ pats of butter each month. Not only has Albert cut the fat, but he is consuming more fibre too!

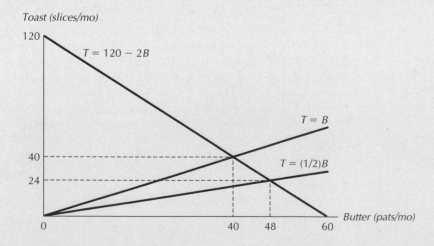

Appendix 3A

THE UTILITY FUNCTION APPROACH TO THE CONSUMER BUDGETING PROBLEM

3A.1 THE UTILITY FUNCTION APPROACH TO CONSUMER CHOICE

Finding the highest attainable indifference curve on a budget constraint is just one way that economists have analyzed the consumer choice problem. For many applications, a second approach has also proved useful. In this approach we represent the consumer's preferences not with an indifference map but with a utility function (a formula that yields a number representing the satisfaction provided by a bundle of goods.)

A utility function is simply a formula that, for each possible bundle of goods, yields a number that represents the amount of satisfaction provided by that bundle. Suppose, for example, that Tom consumes only food and shelter and that his utility function is given by $U = U(F, S) = FS$, where F denotes the number of kilograms of food and S the number of square metres of shelter he consumes per week, and U his satisfaction, measured in "utils" per week.[1] If $F = 4$ kg/wk and $S = 3$ sq m/wk, Tom will receive 12 utils/wk of utility, just as he would if he consumed 3 kg/wk of food and 4 sq m/wk of shelter. In contrast, if he consumed 8 kg/wk of food and 6 sq m/wk of shelter, he would receive 48 utils/wk.

The utility function is analogous to an indifference map in that both provide a complete description of the consumer's preference ordering. In the indifference curve framework, we can rank any two bundles by seeing which one lies on a preferred indifference curve. In the utility-function framework, we can compare any two bundles by seeing which one yields a greater number of utils. Indeed, as the following example illustrates, it is usually straightforward to use a utility function to construct the corresponding indifference map.

---

[1]The term "utils" represents an arbitrary unit. As we shall see, what is important for consumer choice is not the actual number of utils various bundles provide, but the rankings of the bundles based on their associated utilities.

If Tom's utility function is given by U(F, S) = FS, graph the indifference curves that correspond to 1, 2, 3, and 4 utils, respectively.

In the language of utility functions, an indifference curve is all combinations of F and S that yield the same level of utility—the same number of utils. Suppose we look at the indifference curve that corresponds to 1 unit of utility—that is, the combinations of bundles for which $FS = 1$. Solving this equation for S, we have

$$S = \frac{1}{F}, \qquad\qquad (3A.1)$$

which is the indifference curve labelled $U = 1$ in Figure 3A-1. The indifference curve that corresponds to 2 units of utility is generated by solving $FS = 2$ to get $S = 2/F$, and it is shown by the curve labelled $U = 2$ in Figure 3A-1. In similar fashion, we generate the indifference curves for $U = 3$ and $U = 4$, which are correspondingly labelled in the diagram. More generally, we get the indifference curve corresponding to a constant utility level U_0 by solving $FS = U_0$ to get $S = U_0/F$.

In the indifference curve framework, the best attainable bundle of goods is the bundle on the budget constraint that lies on the highest indifference curve. Analogously, the best attainable bundle in the utility-function framework is the bundle on the budget constraint that provides the highest level of utility. In the indifference curve framework, in the standard case (that is, with convex indifference curves and no kinks or corner solutions) the best attainable bundle occurs at a point of tangency between an indifference curve and the budget constraint. At the optimal bundle, the slope of the indifference curve equals the slope of the budget constraint. Suppose that food and shelter are again our two goods, and P_F and P_S are their respective prices. If $\Delta S/\Delta F$ denotes the slope of the highest attainable indifference curve at the optimal bundle, the tangency condition is that $MRS = -\Delta S/\Delta F = P_F/P_S$. What is the analogous condition in the utility-function framework?

To answer this question, we must introduce the concept of marginal utility, which is the rate at which total utility changes as the quantity of either food or shelter changes with the quantity of the other goods unchanged. More specifically, let MU_F ($= \Delta U/\Delta F$) denote the number of additional utils we get for each additional unit of food and MU_S

FIGURE 3A-1

Indifference Curves for the Utility Function $U = FS$

To get the indifference curve that corresponds to all bundles that yield a utility level of U_0, set $FS = U_0$ and solve for S to get $S = U_0/F$.

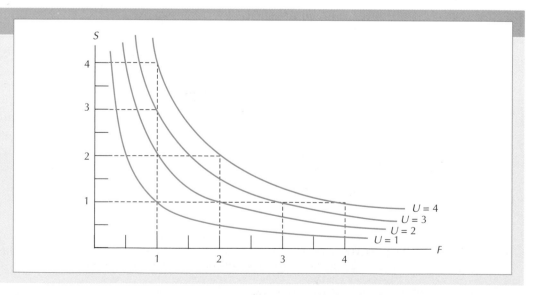

Utility Is Constant Along an Indifference Curve
In moving from K to L, the loss in utility from having less shelter, $MU_S\Delta S$, is exactly offset by the gain in utility from having more food, $MU_F\Delta F$.

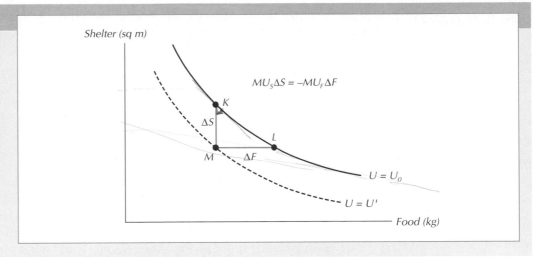

(= $\Delta U/\Delta S$) denote the number of additional utils we get for each additional unit of shelter. In Figure 3A-2, note that bundle K has ΔF fewer units of food and ΔS more units of shelter than bundle L. Note also, in the move from K to L, that ΔS (the move from K to M in Figure 3A-2) has a negative sign (because there is a reduction in the quantity of shelter). However, ΔF (the move from M to L) has a positive sign (since the quantity of food increases). If there is a move from L to K, the signs of ΔS and ΔF will both be reversed, and so they will still have opposite signs. Both MU_F and MU_S are positive in sign, because F and S are both goods ("More is better"), and so an increase in either F or S causes an increase in utility. Thus, if we move from bundle K to bundle L, we gain $MU_F\Delta F$ utils from having more food, but we lose $MU_S\Delta S$ utils from having less shelter.

Because K and L both lie on the same indifference curve, we know that both bundles provide the same level of utility. Thus the utility we lose from having less shelter must be exactly offset by the utility we gain from having more food. This tells us that

$$\Delta U = MU_F\Delta F + MU_S\Delta S = 0, \text{ or equivalently, } MU_F\Delta F = -MU_S\text{v}S. \qquad (3A.2)$$

Cross-multiplying terms in Equation 3A.2 gives

$$\frac{MU_F}{MU_S} = -\frac{\Delta S}{\Delta F} \qquad (3A.3)$$

Suppose that the optimal bundle lies between K and L, which are very close together, so that ΔF and ΔS are both very small. As K and L move closer to the optimal bundle, the ratio $\Delta S/\Delta F$ becomes equal to the slope of the indifference curve at that bundle, the value of which (Equation 3A.3 tells us) equals the negative of the ratio of the marginal utilities of the two goods. And since the slope of the indifference curve at the optimal bundle is the same as that of the budget constraint, the following condition must also hold for the optimal bundle:[2]

---

[2]In the standard case, for this condition to yield a unique optimum, it is also necessary that the curve representing any given level of utility be strictly convex with respect to the origin, or (equivalently, for smooth curves, in calculus terms) that $d^2Y/dX^2 > 0$. This is the mathematical equivalent of a continuously diminishing marginal rate of substitution.

$$\frac{MU_F}{MU_S} = \frac{P_S}{P_F} \qquad (3A.4)$$

Equation 3A.4 is the condition in the utility-function framework that is analogous to the MRS = PF/PS condition in the indifference curve framework. In fact, an alternative way of defining MRS is as the ratio <u>MUF/MUS</u>.

If we cross-multiply terms in Equation 3A.4, we get an equivalent condition that has a very straightforward interpretation:

$$\frac{MU_F}{P_F} = \frac{MU_S}{P_S} \qquad (3A.5)$$

In words, the left-hand side of Equation 3A.5 may be interpreted as the extra utility gained from the last dollar spent on F. Similarly, the right-hand side of the equation is the extra utility gained from the last dollar spent on S. In the standard case, it is easy intuitively to see why at the optimal values of F and S, the extra utility gained from the last dollar spent on each must be the same. Suppose, to the contrary, that the extra utility gained from the last dollar spent on S exceeded the extra utility from the last dollar spent on F. The consumer could then spend a dollar less on F and a dollar more on S and end up with more utility than he had under the original allocation. The conclusion is that the original allocation could not have been optimal. Only when the extra utility gained from the last dollar spent on each good is the same will it not be possible to carry out a similar utility-augmenting reallocation.

EXAMPLE 3A-2

Suppose that the marginal utility of the last dollar John spends on food is greater than the marginal utility of the last dollar he spends on shelter. For example, suppose the prices of food and shelter are \$1/kg and \$2/sq m, respectively, and that the corresponding marginal utilities are 6 utils/kg and 4 utils/sq m. Show that John cannot possibly be maximizing his utility.

For John, MU_F/P_F = (6 utils/kg)/(\$1/kg) = *6 utils per dollar*, while MU_S/P_S = (4 utils/sq m)/(\$2/sq m), or only *2 utils per dollar*. That is, MU_F/P_F = 6 utils/\$ > 2 utils/\$ = MU_S/P_S. John is getting more utils per dollar (more "bang per buck") from the last dollar he spends on food than from the last dollar he spends on shelter. He should therefore shift his expenditures *away from* the good that gives him *less* "bang per buck" and *toward* the good that gives him *more* "bang per buck" for the last dollar spent. Concretely, if John bought 1 sq m/wk less shelter, he would save \$2/wk and would lose 4 utils/wk. But this would enable him to buy 2 kg/wk more food, which would add 12 utils/wk, for a net gain of 8 utils/wk.

In summary, abstracting from special cases such as kinks and corner solutions, a necessary condition for optimal budget allocation is that the last dollar spent on each commodity yield the same increment in utility.

EXAMPLE 3A-3

Utility-maximizing Carmen loves to eat apples (*A*) and bananas (*B*). Her utility function has the following special additive form: $U = U_A + U_B$. U_A is her utility from apples, U_B is her utility from bananas, and all terms are measured in "utils." The additive form involves a strong assumption: it means that the utility she derives from consuming apples or bananas is independent of the quantity she is consuming of the other good. For Carmen, $U_A = 30A - .5A^2$ and $U_B = 20B - .25B^2$. Her corresponding marginal utility functions are as follows: $MU_A = 30 - A$, and

$MU_B = 20 - .5B$. A is the number of baskets of apples she consumes and B is the number of bunches of bananas she consumes per period. MU_A is measured in utils per basket, and MU_B in utils per bunch. Both (linear) marginal utility functions are characterized by continuously diminishing marginal utility and (as is necessarily the case with such linear functions) by *satiation*. $MU_A = 0$ utils/basket when $A = 30$ baskets, and $MU_B = 0$ utils/bunch when $B = 40$ bunches. Beyond these consumption levels, MU_A and MU_B become *negative*, which means that total utilities U_A and U_B are *lowered* by consumption beyond these levels. That is, linear marginal utility functions violate the *nonsatiation* ("More is better") assumption: more is better only up to the point at which marginal utility becomes zero. After that, "More is worse." You *can* have too much of a good thing! This period, Carmen has \$112 to spend, the price of apples (P_A) is \$2/basket, and the price of bananas (P_B) is \$4/bunch. She can neither save, lend, or borrow. How will she allocate her expenditures in order to maximize her utility?

First, if Carmen spends all of her income, she must satisfy her budget constraint: $M = \$112 = 2A + 4B$, or (rearranging and simplifying) $B = 28 - .5A$. Second, she wants $MU_A/P_A = (30 - A)/2 = (20 - .5B)/4 = MU_B/P_B$. Substituting $(28 - .5A)$ into this last equation in place of B and solving for A, she gets $A = 24$ baskets. (Check her calculations.) Substituting this value into the budget constraint, she gets $B = 16$ bunches.

Carmen's total expenditure on apples is $P_A A = 2 \times 24 = \$48$, and on bananas is $P_B B = 4 \times 16 = \$64$, making a total of \$112; she has exactly spent her budget. $MU_A/P_A = (30 - 24)/2 = 3$ utils per dollar, and $MU_B/P_B = [20 - .5(16)]/4 = 3$ utils per dollar as well. That is, she has equalized the "bang per buck" from the last dollar spent on each of the goods.

Her *total* utility from apples is $U_A = 30(24) - .5(24^2) = 432$ utils, and from bananas $= 20(16) - .25(16^2) = 256$ utils, and so her total utility $U = 688$ utils. You can verify that if Carmen shifts her expenditures from this optimum allocation, her total utility will decline. For example, with $A = 22$ baskets and $B = 17$ bunches, or with $A = 26$ baskets and $B = 15$ bunches, her total utility is only 685.75 utils.

Note also that if all of Carmen's utility values were doubled or halved, she would still do best to buy 24 baskets and 16 bunches per period. Consumer choice depends not on the *absolute* number of utils associated with different bundles but instead on the *ordinal ranking* of the utility levels associated with different bundles. Any transformation of the utility function that preserves the ordinal ranking of different bundles (taking its logarithm, or squaring it, or adding 137 to it) will result in Carmen's making the *same* utility-maximizing decision in any situation.

3A.2 CARDINAL VS. ORDINAL UTILITY

In our discussion about how to represent consumer preferences, we assumed that people are able to rank each possible bundle in order of preference. This is called the *ordinal utility* approach to the consumer budgeting problem. It does not require that people be able to make quantitative statements about how much they will like various bundles. Thus it assumes that a consumer will always be able to say whether he prefers A to B, but that he may not be able to make such statements as "A is 6.43 times as good as B."

In the 19th century, economists commonly assumed that people could make the latter type of statement. Today we call theirs the *cardinal utility* approach to the consumer choice problem. In the two-good case, it assumes that the satisfaction provided by any bundle can be assigned a numerical, or cardinal, value by a utility function of the form

$$U = U(X, Y). \tag{3A.6}$$

In three dimensions, the graph of such a utility function will look something like the one shown in Figure 3A-3. It resembles a mountain, but if we make the "more-is-better" assumption, it is a mountain without a summit. The value on the U axis measures the height of the mountain, which continues to increase the more we have of X or Y.

Suppose in Figure 3A-3 we were to fix utility at some constant amount, say, U_0. That is, suppose we cut the utility mountain with a plane parallel to the XY plane, U_0 units above it. The line labelled JK in Figure 3A-3 represents the intersection of that plane and the surface of the utility mountain. All the bundles of goods that lie on JK provide a utility level of U_0. If we then project the line JK downward onto the XY plane, we have what amounts to the U_0 indifference curve, shown in Figure 3A-4.

Suppose we then intersect the utility mountain with another plane, this time U_1 units above the XY plane. In Figure 3A-3, this second plane intersects the utility mountain along the line labelled LN. It represents the set of all bundles that confer the utility level U_1. Projecting LN down onto the XY plane, we thus get the indifference curve labelled U_1 in Figure 3A-4. In like fashion, we can generate an entire indifference map corresponding to the cardinal utility function $U(X, Y)$.

Thus we see that it is possible to start with any cardinal utility function and end up with a unique indifference map. *But it is not possible to go in the other direction!* That is, it is not possible to start with an indifference map and work backward to a unique cardinal utility function. The reason is that there will always be infinitely many such utility functions that give rise to precisely the same indifference map.

FIGURE 3A-3

A Three-Dimensional Utility Surface

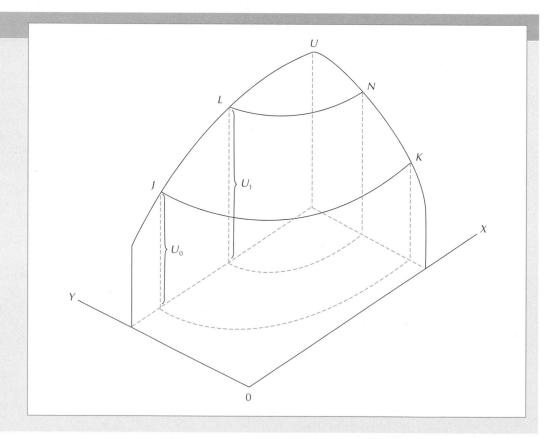

APPENDIX 3A: THE UTILITY FUNCTION APPROACH TO THE CONSUMER BUDGETING PROBLEM

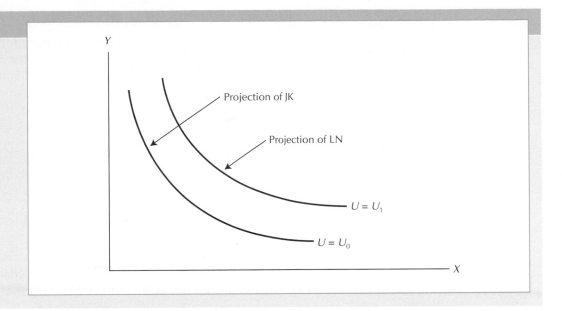

To see why, just imagine that we took the utility function in Equation 3A.4 and doubled it, so that utility is now given by $V = 2U(X, Y)$. When we graph V as a function of X and Y, the shape of the resulting utility mountain will be much the same as before. The difference will be that the altitude at any X, Y point will be twice what it was before. If we pass a plane $2U_0$ units above the XY plane, it would intersect the new utility mountain in precisely the same manner as the plane U_0 units high did originally. If we then project the resulting intersection down onto the XY plane, it will coincide perfectly with the original U_0 indifference curve.

All we do when we multiply (divide, add to, or subtract from) a cardinal utility function is to relabel the indifference curves to which it gives rise. Indeed, we can make an even more general statement: if $U(X, Y)$ is any cardinal utility function and if V is any increasing function, then $U = U(X, Y)$ and $V = V[U(X, Y)]$ will give rise to precisely the same indifference maps. The special property of an increasing function is that it preserves the rank ordering of the values of the original function. That is, if $U(X_1, Y_1) > U(X_2, Y_2)$, the fact that V is an increasing function assures that $V[U(X_1, Y_1)]$ will be greater than $V[U(X_2, Y_2)]$. And as long as that requirement is met, the two functions will give rise to exactly the same indifference curves.

The concept of the indifference map was first discussed by Francis Edgeworth, who derived it from a cardinal utility function in the manner described above. It took the combined insights of Vilfredo Pareto, Irving Fisher, and John Hicks to establish that Edgeworth's apparatus was not uniquely dependent on a supporting cardinal utility function. As we have seen, the only aspect of a consumer's preferences that matters in the standard budget allocation problem is the shape and location of his indifference curves. Consumer choice turns out to be completely independent of the labels we assign to these indifference curves, provided only that higher-numbered curves correspond to higher levels of utility.

Modern economists prefer the ordinal approach because it rests on much weaker assumptions than the cardinal approach. That is, it is much easier to imagine that people can rank different bundles than to suppose that they can make precise quantitative statements about how much satisfaction each provides.

3A.3 GENERATING INDIFFERENCE CURVES ALGEBRAICALLY

Even if we assume that consumers have only ordinal preference rankings, it will often be convenient to represent those preferences with a cardinal utility index. The advantage is that this procedure provides a compact algebraic way of summarizing all the information that is implicit in the graphical representation of preferences.

This is basically what we did when we constructed the indifference map in Figure 3A-1. If we defined a utility function $V = 2U = 2XY$, then the indifference curves in Figure 3A-1 would be *unchanged in shape*, but instead of being numbered U = 1, 2, 3, and 4 they would be numbered V = 2, 4, 6, and 8, respectively. If we defined $W = U^2 = X^2 Y^2$, again the shape of the indifference curves would be unchanged, but they would be renumbered W = 1, 4, 9, and 16 respectively.

Perfect Complements

We can construct an odd-looking utility function to represent the case of perfect complements. If Rotunda always consumes burgers (B) and French fries (F) in the fixed ratio of 2 burgers to 1 large fries, we can write her utility function as follows:

$$U = \min[B/2, F]. \qquad (3A.7)$$

The "min" means, "whichever is the lower of $B/2$ and F."

Figure 3A-5 shows Rotunda's indifference map, derived from this utility function. At L, where $B = 2$ burgers and $F = 1$ fries, $U = \min[2/2, 1] = 1$ util. At P, where $B = 4$ burgers and $F = 1$ fries, $U = \min[4/2, 1] = \min[2, 1] = 1$ util. There is no increase in Rotunda's utility if she has 2 more burgers, because of the absence of the complementary order of fries. Essentially, two of the four burgers are in excess of Rotunda's requirements. Efficiency in consumption therefore requires that $B/2 = F$, or that the fries-burger ratio $F/B = 1/2$.

Along LP the marginal utility of burgers (MU_B) is zero, and along LM, the marginal utility of fries $(MU_F) = 0$. At point M, however, $MU_B = 1/2$ util/burger, and at point P, $MU_F = 1$ util/large fries. Note also that at point L, if we reduce the quantity of either burgers or fries consumed (holding the other constant), Rotunda's utility is proportionally lowered. Hence the coefficients of B and F in the utility function (1/2 and 1, respectively) correspond as indicated to the marginal utilities of burgers and fries.

FIGURE 3A-5

Indifference Curves for the Utility Function $U = \min[B/2, F]$

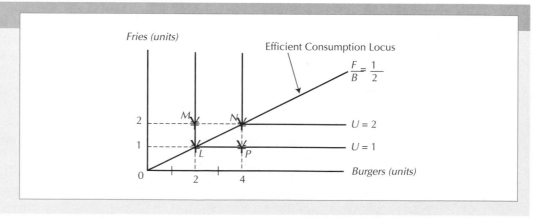

Fries (units)

Efficient Consumption Locus

$\dfrac{F}{B} = \dfrac{1}{2}$

M   N

2 — — — — — — — — — $U = 2$

1 — — — — — — — — — $U = 1$

L   P

0   2   4   Burgers (units)

Indifference Curves for the Utility Function
$U(X,Y) = (2/3)X + 2Y$
The indifference curve that corresponds to all bundles yielding a utility level of U0 is given by $Y = (U_0/2) - (\frac{1}{3})X$.

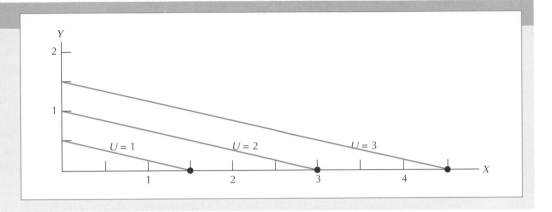

Finally, note that a new function, $V = 100U = 100 \min[B/2, F] = \min[50B, 100 F]$, will generate the *same* indifference map. So will $W = U^2 = \min[(B/2)^2, F^2] = \min[B^2/4, F^2]$. The only thing that changes is the numbering of the indifference curves. (As an exercise, you may want to calculate these numbers for V and W at the four labelled points in Figure 3A-5.)

Perfect Substitutes

Consider another case, where X and Y are perfect substitutes, with $U(X, Y) := (2/3)X + 2Y$. The bundles of X and Y that yield a utility level of U_0 are again found by solving $U(X, Y) = U_0$ for Y. This time we get $Y = U_0/2 - (1/3)X$. The indifference curves corresponding to $U = 1$, $U = 2$, and $U = 3$ are shown in Figure 3A-6. Note that they are all linear, which is what tells us that this particular utility function describes a preference ordering in which X and Y are perfect substitutes. The marginal utilities can be read straight from the utility function. $MU_X = \Delta U/\Delta X = 2/3$ utils/unit of X, because a 1-unit increase in X increases U by 2/3 utils. Similarly, $MU_Y = 2$ utils/unit of Y. The slope of the indifference curves $= -MRS = -MU_X/MU_Y = \Delta Y/\Delta X = -1/3$. Since an additional unit of Y yields 3 times the utils of an additional unit of X ($MU_Y = 2 = 3 \times 2/3 = 3MU_X$), if we give up 1 unit of Y we require 3 units of X to leave us at the same level of utility.

3A.4 USING CALCULUS TO MAXIMIZE UTILITY

Students who have had calculus are able to solve the consumer's budget allocation problem without direct recourse to the geometry of the indifference maps. Let $U(X, Y)$ be the consumer's utility function; and suppose M, P_X, and P_Y denote money income, the price of X, and the price of Y respectively. Formally, the consumer's allocation problem can be stated as follows:

$$\text{Maximize } U(X, Y) \text{ subject to } P_X X + P_Y Y = M.$$
$$X, Y$$

(3A.8)

The appearance of the terms X and Y below the "maximize" expression indicates that these are the variables whose values the consumer must choose.

The Method of Lagrangean Multipliers

As noted earlier, the function $U(X, Y)$ itself has no maximum; it simply keeps on increasing with increases in X or Y. The maximization problem defined in Equation 3A.8 is called a constrained *maximization problem*, which means we want to find the values of X and Y that produce the highest value of U subject to the constraint that the consumer spend only as much as his income. We will examine two different approaches to this problem.

One way of making sure that the budget constraint is satisfied is to use the method of Lagrangean multipliers. In this method we begin by transforming the constrained maximization problem in Equation 3A.8 into the following unconstrained maximization problem:

$$\text{Maximize } \mathcal{L} = U(X, Y) - \lambda(P_X X + P_Y Y - M).$$
$$X, Y, \lambda \tag{3A.9}$$

The term λ is called a Lagrangean multiplier, and its role is to assure that the budget constraint is satisfied. (How it does this will become clear in a moment.) The first-order conditions for a maximum of $\mathcal{L}$ are obtained by taking the first partial derivatives of $\mathcal{L}$ with respect to X, Y, and λ and setting them equal to zero:

$$\frac{\partial \mathcal{L}}{\partial X} = \partial U/\partial X - \lambda P_X = 0, \tag{3A.10}$$

$$\frac{\partial \mathcal{L}}{\partial Y} = \partial U/\partial Y - \lambda P_Y = 0, \tag{3A.11}$$

and

$$\frac{\partial \mathcal{L}}{\partial \lambda} = M - P_X X - P_Y Y = 0. \tag{3A.12}$$

The next step is to solve Equations 3A.10–3A.12 for X, Y, and λ. The solutions for X and Y are the ones that we mainly care about here. The role of the equilibrium value of λ is to guarantee that the budget constraint is satisfied. Note in Equation 3A.12 that setting the first partial derivative of $\mathcal{L}$ with respect to λ equal to zero guarantees this result. λ is often referred to as "the marginal utility of money," because it indicates the increase in utility resulting from a \$1 increase in M.

Specific solutions for the utility-maximizing values of X and Y require a specific functional form for the utility function. We will work through an illustrative example in a moment. But first note that an interesting characteristic of the optimal X and Y values can be obtained by using Equation 3A.10 and Equation 3A.11 to get

$$\frac{MU_X}{MU_Y} \equiv \frac{\partial U/\partial X}{\partial U/\partial Y} = \frac{\lambda P_X}{\lambda P_Y} = \frac{P_X}{P_Y} \tag{3A.13}$$

Thus, using calculus, we have arrived at essentially the same formula we derived in Equation 3A.4.[3]

---

[3]$\partial U/\partial X$ and $\partial U/\partial Y$ are the *partial* derivatives of U with respect to X and Y respectively. They can be interpreted as representing the increase in utility that would result from an infinitesimal increase in *one* of the variables, X or Y, with the *other* variable held constant.

An Example. To illustrate the Lagrangean method, suppose that $U(X, Y) = XY$ and that $M = \$40$, $P_X = \$4/L$, and $P_Y = \$2/kg$. Our constrained maximization problem would then be written as

$$\text{Maximize } \mathcal{L} = XY - \lambda(4X + 2Y - 40).$$
$$X, Y, \lambda \qquad (3A.14)$$

The first-order conditions for a maximum of $\mathcal{L}$ are given by

$$\frac{\partial \mathcal{L}}{\partial X} = \frac{\partial(XY)}{\partial X} - 4\lambda = Y - 4\lambda = 0, \qquad (3A.15)$$

$$\frac{\partial \mathcal{L}}{\partial Y} = \frac{\partial(XY)}{\partial Y} - 2\lambda = X - 2\lambda = 0, \qquad (3A.16)$$

and

$$\frac{\partial \mathcal{L}}{\partial \lambda} = 40 - 4X - 2Y = 0. \qquad (3A.17)$$

Using Equation 3A.15 and Equation 3A.16 and eliminating λ, we get $Y = 2X$; substituting this result into Equation 3A.17 and solving for X, we get $X = 5$ L, which in turn yields $Y = 2X = 10$ kg. Thus (5, 10) is the utility-maximizing bundle.

An Alternative Method

There is an alternative way of making sure that the budget constraint is satisfied, one that involves less cumbersome notation than the Lagrangean approach. In this alternative method, we simply solve the budget constraint for Y in terms of X and substitute the result wherever Y appears in the utility function. Utility then becomes a function of X alone, and we can maximize it by taking its first derivative with respect to X and equating that to zero.[4] The value of X that solves that equation is the optimal value of X, which can then be substituted back into the budget constraint to find the optimal value of Y.

To illustrate, again suppose that $U(X, Y) = XY$, with $M = 40$, $P_X = 4$, and $PY = 2$. The budget constraint is then $4X + 2Y = 40$, which solves for $Y = 20 - 2X$. Substituting this expression back into the utility function, we have $U(X, Y) = X(20 - 2X) - 20X - 2X^2$. Taking the first derivative of U with respect to X and equating the result to zero, we have

$$\frac{dU}{dX} = 20 - 4X = 0, \qquad (3A.18)$$

which solves for $X = 5$. Plugging this value of X back into the budget constraint, we discover that the optimal value of Y is 10. So the optimal bundle is again (5, 10), just as we found using the Lagrangean approach. For these optimal values of X and Y, the consumer will obtain $(5)(10) = 50$ units of utility.

Both algebraic approaches to the budget allocation problem yield precisely the same result as the graphical approach described in Chapter 3. Note in Figure 3A-7 that the $U = 50$ indifference curve is tangent to the budget constraint at the bundle (5, 10).

---

[4]Here, the second-order condition for a local maximum is that $d^2U/dX^2 < 0$.

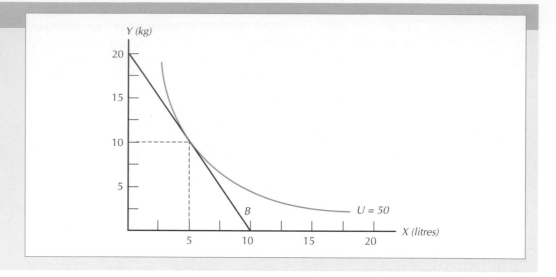

A Simplifying Technique

Suppose our constrained maximization problem is of the general form

$$\text{Maximize } U(X, Y) \text{ subject to } P_X X + P_Y Y = M.$$
$$X, Y$$

$$(3A.19)$$

If (X^*, Y^*) is the optimum bundle for this maximization problem, then we know it will also be the optimum bundle for the utility function $V[U(X, Y)]$, where V is any increasing function.[5] This property often enables us to transform a computationally difficult maximization problem into a simple one. By way of illustration, consider the following example:

$$\text{Maximize } U = X^{1/3}Y^{2/3} \text{ subject to } 4X + 2Y = 24.$$
$$X, Y$$

$$(3A.20)$$

First note what happens when we proceed with the untransformed utility function given in Equation 3A.20. Solving the budget constraint for $Y = 12 - 2X$ and substituting back into the utility function, we have $U = X^{1/3}(12 - 2X)^{2/3}$. Calculating dU/dX is a bit tedious in this case, but if we carry out each step carefully we get the following first-order condition:

$$\frac{dU}{dX} = (\frac{1}{3})X^{-2/3}(12 - 2X)^{2/3} + X^{1/3}(2/3)(12 - 2X)^{-1/3}(-2) = 0, \quad (3A.21)$$

which, after a little more tedious rearrangement, solves for $X = 2$. And from the budget constraint we then get $Y = 8$.

Now suppose we transform the utility function by taking its logarithm:

$$V = \ln[U(X, Y)] = \ln(X^{1/3}Y^{2/3}) = (\frac{1}{3})\ln X + (\frac{2}{3})\ln Y. \qquad (3A.22)$$

---

[5]Again, an increasing function is one for which $V(X_1) > V(X_2)$ whenever $X_1 > X_2$.

Since the logarithm is an increasing function, when we maximize V subject to the budget constraint, we will get the same answer we got using U. The advantage of the logarithmic transformation here is that the derivative of V is much easier to calculate than the derivative of U. Again, solving the budget constraint for $Y = 12 - 2X$ and substituting the result into V, we have $V = (1/3)\ln X + (2/3)\ln(12 - 2X)$. This time the first-order condition follows almost without effort:

$$\frac{dV}{dX} = \frac{1/3}{X} - \frac{2(2/3)}{12-2X} = 0, \qquad (3A.23)$$

which solves easily for $X = 2$. Plugging $X = 2$ back into the budget constraint, we again get $Y = 8$.

The best transformation to make will naturally depend on the particular utility function you start with. The logarithmic transformation greatly simplified matters in the example above, but will not necessarily be helpful for other forms of U.

3A.5 GOODS AND "BADS," BLISS, AND "OPTIMAL" POLLUTION

In the *standard case*, with two goods, X and Y, the negative slope of indifference curves follows from the "more is better" or "nonsatiability" assumption. If we *give up* some of good Y ($\Delta Y < 0$), then our utility is lowered (since $MU_Y \equiv \Delta U/\Delta Y > 0$), and hence we require *more* of good X ($\Delta X > 0$) to restore us to the original level of utility. Figure 3A-8 depicts a more complete set of possibilities. Here the utility mountain *does* reach a summit, a point of maximum satisfaction or *satiation*, at point B (for "Bliss"). ABC is the locus of all points where the slope of indifference curves is zero (since $MU_X = 0$). To the left of ABC, X is a good. To the right of ABC, X is a "bad": at any given level of Y consumption, more X *lowers* utility. In related fashion, DBE is the locus of points where

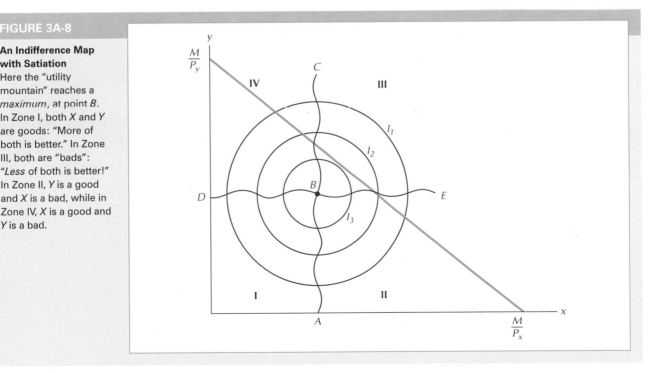

FIGURE 3A-8

An Indifference Map with Satiation
Here the "utility mountain" reaches a *maximum*, at point B. In Zone I, both X and Y are goods: "More of both is better." In Zone III, both are "bads": "*Less* of both is better!" In Zone II, Y is a good and X is a bad, while in Zone IV, X is a good and Y is a bad.

a tangent to the indifference curves is vertical (since $MU_Y = 0$). Below *DBE*, *Y* is a good, but above *DBE*, *Y* is a "bad": at any given level of *X* consumption, more *Y* lowers utility.

ABC and *DBE* thus define four zones, labelled I, II, III, and IV. In Zone I, *X* and *Y* are both goods: "more (of either) is better." In Zone II, *X* is a bad and *Y* is a good. In Zone III, *X* and *Y* are both bads: "less (of either) is better." And in Zone IV, *X* is a good, and *Y* is a bad. In all four zones, the relation MRS $= MU_X/MU_Y = -\Delta Y /\Delta X$ still holds. Yet in Zones II and IV, the slope of the indifference curves $\Delta Y /\Delta X$ is *positive*, and hence the MRS is *negative*. The reason is that in Zone II, *X* is a bad, with $MU_X < 0$, while for the good, Y, $MU_Y > 0$. Since MU_X and MU_Y are of *opposite* sign, their ratio, MRS $= MU_X/MU_Y$, is *negative*, and therefore along each indifference curve $\Delta Y /\Delta X$ (= $-$MRS) is *positive*.

The economic meaning of the positive slope of the indifference curve in Zone II is straightforward. If we have *more* of the bad, *X*, we require a *greater* amount of the good, *Y*, to leave us at the *same* level of utility: therefore the slope of the indifference curves, $\Delta Y/\Delta X$, is *positive*. In Zone IV, the same logic applies, except that here *X* is the good and *Y* is the bad. In Zone III, the indifference curves have a negative slope, as in the *standard* case of Zone I. In Zone III, however, the reason is that both *X* and *Y* are bads ($MU_X < 0$ and $MU_Y < 0$). Hence their *ratio*, the MRS, is *positive* at any point, and the slope of the indifference curve through that point is *negative*. The economic interpretation is simple: if we have more of *one* bad, then we require *less* of the other bad to leave us at the same level of utility.

Figure 3A-8 is not an abstract academic exercise. It highlights some important real-life considerations for consumer choice theory. We first encountered one of them in Example 3A-3 on pages 96–97: it *is* possible to have "too much of a good thing." In a week, it is impossible for one person to consume seven tonnes of ice cream. Even before the maximum physically possible amount is consumed, the marginal utility of an additional bowl will likely have become negative. Economists often assume that *instantaneous and costless disposal of unwanted items* is possible, once satiation or "bliss" is achieved. As a practical matter, of course, disposal is *not* free. If it were, then at a minimum a lot of sanitation and recycling workers would be out of a job! Instead, in the world of Figure 3A-8, we can assume that if the budget constraint (shown in green) is such that point *B* is an *interior* point, then only the fraction of income necessary to purchase the bundle at *B* will be spent.

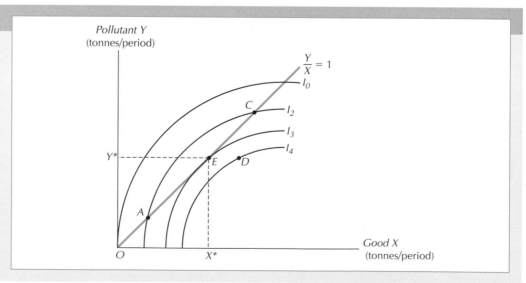

FIGURE 3A-9

Choosing the Optimal Amount of Pollution
The green line *OAEC* gives the possible combinations of good *X* and pollutant *Y*. The level of satisfaction increases as we move *rightward* (to *more* of good *X*) and *downward* (to *less* of pollutant *Y*). Utility is maximized at point *E*. *E* is better than points *A* and *C* (which are feasible but yield lower utility), while point *D* is unattainable.

Zones II and IV in Figure 3A-8 are also of practical importance, as the following example shows.

What is the optimal amount of pollution?

In Figure 3A-9, X is a good and Y is a pollutant that results from production of the good, on a tonne-per-tonne basis, so that $Y/X = 1$. The index numbers of the indifference curves increase as we move *downward* (to lower levels of the pollutant Y) and *to the right* (to higher levels of the good X). As Figure 3A-9 shows, the highest attainable utility level is reached at point E on indifference curve I_3, which is just tangent to the green Y/X curve, with the MRS $= -1$. Attainable points on OE such as A and C lie on the lower indifference curve I_2, while a point such as D on I_4 is unattainable.

Note that if a "zero-tolerance" policy were adopted toward pollution, then with the existing technology, production of X would have to cease entirely, and we would be at the origin, on indifference curve I_0, which yields less utility than point E. Sometimes our economic choices involve choosing how much of a bad we are prepared to tolerate to get more of a good, rather than how much of a good we are prepared to give up in exchange for more of another good.

Of course, if the amount of pollution per tonne of X were lowered by technical change, then the Y/X ray would rotate downward, which would increase the attainable utility level.

A change of preferences so that pollution became less acceptable would be reflected in the indifference curves' becoming flatter. You can verify for yourself that with technology unchanged, this shift of preferences would result in lower levels of consumption of both X and Y.

An Important Qualification: You may have felt a bit uneasy as you were reading the above example. After all, "We all know that pollution is bad!" The basic point the example makes is valid. Sometimes, accepting *some* pollution is an unavoidable cost of getting the good that is produced along with it, although reasonable people can differ about how much pollution is "acceptable." Yet if you did feel uneasy, you also had good reason. Example 3A-4 implicitly assumes that we have *exact* knowledge of the costs resulting from each and every level of pollution. Yet our present degree of scientific ignorance and uncertainty about the short-term—and even more so the long-term—consequences of pollutants, singly and especially in combination, means that a cautious posture may well be warranted.

3A.6 PROPERTIES OF THE COBB-DOUGLAS FUNCTION

Utility functions with the form $U = AX^aY^b$ are known as Cobb-Douglas functions. Cobb-Douglas functions are widely used in both consumption theory and production theory. Although they may look a bit intimidating on first acquaintance, their widespread use is partly due to their mathematical *simplicity*. We have already worked with two special cases of Cobb-Douglas functions in this appendix. The first is that in Example 3A-1, with $U = FS$. Here, $A = 1$, $X = F$, $Y = S$, and $a = b = 1$. The second is that in Equation 3A.20, with $U = X^{1/3}Y^{2/3}$. Here, $A = 1$, $a = 1/3$, and $b = 2/3$. We will look at Cobb-Douglas functions again in Appendix 9A, in the context of production theory, but some of their more interesting properties deserve attention here. These properties are outlined in Table 3A-1, followed by a brief discussion of their significance.

	Symbolic Form	Example 1	Example 2	Example 3
1. Utility Function	$U = AX^aY^b$	$U_1 = 16XY^3$	$U_2 = 2X^{.25}Y^{.75}$	$U_3 = X^2Y$
2. $MU_X \equiv \partial U/\partial X$	$aAX^{a-1}Y^b$	$16Y^3$	$.5X^{-.75}Y^{.75}$	$2XY$
3. $MU_Y \equiv \partial U/\partial Y$	bAX^aY^{b-1}	$48XY^2$	$1.5X^{.25}Y^{-.25}$	X^2
4. $MRS (\equiv MU_X/MU_Y)$	$\dfrac{aY}{bX}$	$\dfrac{Y}{3X}$	$\dfrac{Y}{3X}$	$\dfrac{2Y}{X}$
5. Consumption Efficiency ($MRS = P_X/P_Y$)	$\dfrac{aY}{bX} = \dfrac{P_X}{P_Y}$	$\dfrac{Y}{3X} = \dfrac{P_X}{P_Y}$	$\dfrac{Y}{3X} = \dfrac{P_X}{P_Y}$	$\dfrac{2Y}{X} = \dfrac{P_X}{P_Y}$
6. P_XX/M	$\dfrac{a}{a+b}$	1/4	1/4	2/3
7. P_YY/M	$\dfrac{b}{a+b}$	3/4	3/4	1/3
8. Elasticity of Substitution	1	1	1	1
9. Income-Elasticity of Demand for X, Y	1	1	1	1

Table 3A-1 will repay study, and will be useful for problem solving and review. Calculus is required to derive rows 2 and 3, but rows 4 to 9 can be derived using algebraic manipulation and theory. Let us note briefly a few of the features revealed by the table. First, despite their apparently different form, Examples 1 and 2 give the same results for rows 4 to 7. The reason is that $U_1 = U_2{}^4$, or equivalently that $U_2 = U_1{}^{1/4}$. Each is an order-preserving increasing function of the other.

Second, and perhaps most remarkable, as rows 6 and 7 show, a *constant* proportion of money income (M) will be spent on each of X and Y, *regardless of what P_X and P_Y are*. In Example 3, for instance, if your income is \$900, you will spend $2/3 \times 900 = \$600$ on X and $1/3 \times 900 = \$300$ on Y, no matter what their relative prices are! As a corollary, we can never have a "corner solution" with a Cobb-Douglas function: some of *both* goods will always be consumed at *any* set of positive prices.

A third important property of Cobb-Douglas functions (as shown by row 4) is that their indifference curves are *homothetic* with respect to the origin. This term means that along any straight line (or ray) from the origin, the slopes of *all* the indifference curves will be the same, since $MRS = aY/bX$, and a and b are constants, while on any ray from the origin, Y/X (the slope of the ray) is constant. In Example 2, if $Y = 60$ units and $X = 10$ units, then $MRS = Y/3X = 60/[3(10)] = 2$, and the slope of the indifference curve is -2. The MRS will also be 2 if $Y = 90$ units and $X = 15$ units, and at any point along this ray from the origin with $Y/X = 6$.

This homotheticity property also accounts for the unitary income-elasticity of demand for X and Y recorded in row 9 (which will be taken up in Chapter 4). If prices are constant and the proportion of income spent on each commodity is constant, then a 10 percent increase in money income will result in a 10 percent increase in the quantities of both X and Y purchased.

To sketch another concept, the *elasticity of substitution* along an indifference curve is the percentage change in Y/X associated with a 1 percent increase in P_X/P_Y. It is *zero* in the case of perfect complements. If the elasticity of substitution is *less than 1*, then $P_X X / P_Y Y$, the ratio of expenditures on X to expenditures on Y, will *increase* as X becomes relatively more expensive. If it is *greater than 1*, then $P_X X / P_Y Y$ will *fall* as P_X / P_Y increases. With a Cobb-Douglas function, as can be seen by rearranging row 5, $P_X X / P_Y Y$ = a/b, a constant ratio. A 1 percent increase in P_X / P_Y causes a 1 percent increase in Y/X, so that the ratio of expenditures on the two goods is unchanged, as we saw above.

The results in Table 3A-1 can be used to solve problems in consumption theory involving Cobb-Douglas functions faster and more simply than by using calculus methods, because the calculus is "built into" the formulas. Yet the results should also have highlighted the unrealism of some of the assumptions implicit in Cobb-Douglas models. Part of being a good economist is knowing not just the strengths but also the limits of one's models.

PROBLEMS

**1. Tom spends all his $100 weekly income on two goods, X and Y. His utility function is given by $U(X, Y) = XY$. If P_X = $4/unit and P_Y = $10/unit, how much of each good should he buy?

**2. Same as Problem 1, except now Tom's utility function is given by $U(X, Y) = X^{1/2} Y^{1/2}$. Note the relationship between your answers in Problem 1 and this problem. What accounts for this relationship?

**3. Same as Problem 1, except that P_X increases to $5/unit. How much of each good should he buy now? What is his total expenditure on X? On Y? Compare your results with those in Problems 1 and 2. What explains your results? Draw a graph, with budget lines and indifference curves labelled, that illustrates your findings from all three problems.

4. Sue consumes only two goods, food and clothing. The marginal utility of the last dollar she spends on food is 12, and the marginal utility of the last dollar she spends on clothing is 9. The price of food is $1.20/unit, and the price of clothing is $.90/unit. Is Sue maximizing her utility?

5. In Figure 3A-2, suppose that U' = 320 utils and U_0 = 380 utils. The coordinates of K are (30, 60) and of L are (40, 40). What are the coordinates of point M?

   a. Going from K to L, calculate ΔS, ΔF, $MU_S = \Delta U / \Delta S$, $MU_F = \Delta U / \Delta F$, MRS, and $\Delta S / \Delta F$. Verify that $MU_S \Delta S = -MU_F \Delta F$.

   b. Now suppose that U' = 14 utils and U_0 = 16 utils, with the coordinates of K, L, and M unchanged. Recalculate the variables in (a).

   c. What conclusions do you draw from your findings in (a) and (b)?

6. In Example 3A-3, suppose that everything is unchanged except that Carmen now has $256 to spend. Show that she *can* equalize MU_A / P_A and MU_B / P_B, when she spends all of her income. Show also that she would rather destroy or give away $36 if she can't lend or save money between periods, by comparing her total utility U when she spends $256 efficiently and $220 efficiently.

7. *True or false:* Using the model in Figure 3A-9, an *improvement* in the efficiency of pollution-cleanup technology can result in a *higher* "optimal" level of pollution. Explain your answer, with the use of a diagram.

Chapter 4

INDIVIDUAL AND MARKET DEMAND

A package of salt costs about fifty cents at the grocery store. We would likely use the same amount of salt at that price as we would if it instead sold for five cents or even $5 per package. We would also consume about the same amount of salt if our incomes were ten times higher than they are now.

Salt is an unusual case. The amounts we buy of many other goods are much more sensitive to prices and incomes. Someone moving from Winnipeg to Vancouver or Toronto, where housing prices are over double what they are in Winnipeg, would likely move into accommodation that was substantially smaller than her Winnipeg home. Someone moving from Vancouver to Winnipeg, in contrast, might move into a veritable palace by Vancouver standards.

CHAPTER PREVIEW

Viewed within the framework of the rational choice model, our behaviour with respect to salt and housing purchases is perfectly intelligible. Our focus in this chapter is to use the tools from Chapter 3 to shed additional light on why, exactly, the responses of various purchase decisions to changes in income and price differ so widely. In Chapter 3, we saw how changes in prices and incomes affect the budget constraint. Here we shall see how changes in the budget constraint affect actual purchase decisions. More specifically, we shall use the rational choice model to generate an individual consumer's demand curve for a product and employ our model to construct a relationship that summarizes how individual demands vary with income.

We shall see how the total effect of a price change can be decomposed into two separate effects: (1) the substitution effect, which denotes the change in the quantity demanded that results because the price change makes substitute goods seem either more or less attractive; and (2) the income effect, which denotes the change in quantity demanded that results from the change in purchasing power caused by the price change.

Next, we shall show how individual demand curves can be added to yield the demand curve for the market as a whole. A central analytical concept we will develop in this chapter is the *price elasticity of demand*, a measure of the responsiveness of purchase decisions to small changes in price. We shall also consider the *income elasticity of demand*, a measure of the responsiveness of purchase decisions to small changes in income. And we shall see that, for some goods, the distribution of income, not just its average value, is an important determinant of market demand.

A final elasticity concept in this chapter is the *cross-price elasticity of demand*, which is a measure of the responsiveness of the quantity demanded of one good to small changes in the prices of another good. Cross-price elasticity is the criterion by which pairs of goods are classified as being either substitutes or complements.

These analytical constructs provide a deeper understanding of a variety of market behaviours as well as a stronger foundation for intelligent decision and policy analysis.

4.1 THE EFFECTS OF CHANGES IN PRICE

The Price-Consumption Curve

Recall from Chapter 2 that a market demand curve is a relationship that tells how much of a good the market as a whole wants to purchase at various prices. Suppose we want to generate a demand schedule for a good—say, shelter—not for the market as a whole but for only a single consumer. Holding income, preferences, and the prices of all other goods constant, how will a change in the price of shelter affect the amount of shelter the consumer buys? To answer this question, we begin with this consumer's indifference map, with shelter on the horizontal axis and the composite good Y on the vertical axis. Suppose the consumer's income is $120 per week, and the price of the composite good is again $1 per unit. The vertical intercept of her budget constraint will then be 120. The horizontal intercept will be $120/P_S$, where P_S denotes the price of shelter. Figure 4-1 shows four budget constraints that correspond to four different prices of shelter, namely, $24/sq m, $12/sq m, $6/sq m, and $4/sq m. The corresponding best affordable bundles contain 2.5, 7, 15, and 20 sq m/wk of shelter, respectively. If we repeat this procedure for indefinitely many prices, the resulting points of tangency trace out the line labelled PCC in Figure 4-1. This line is called the **price-consumption curve**, or **PCC**.

For the particular consumer whose indifference map is shown in Figure 4-1, note that each time the price of shelter falls, the budget constraint rotates outward, enabling the consumer to purchase not only more shelter but more of the composite good as well. And each time the price of shelter falls, this consumer chooses a bundle that contains more shelter than in the bundle chosen previously. Note, however, that the amount of money spent on the composite good may either rise or fall when the price of shelter falls. Thus, the amount spent on other goods falls when the price of shelter falls from $24/sq m to $12/sq m but rises when the price of shelter falls from $6/sq m to $4/sq m. Below, we will see why this is a relatively common purchase pattern.

The Individual Consumer's Demand Curve

An individual consumer's demand curve is like the market demand curve in that it tells the quantities the consumer will buy at various prices. All the information we need to construct the individual demand curve is contained in the price-consumption curve. The first step in going from the PCC to the individual demand curve is to record the relevant price-quantity combinations from the PCC in Figure 4-1, as in Table 4-1. We can ascertain the price of shelter (P_S) along any budget constraint in either of two ways. We can use the fact that P_S is given by money income (M) divided by the horizontal intercept of the budget constraint. Alternatively, we can note that the slope of the budget constraint in Figure 4-1

Price-consumption curve (PCC) Holding money income and the prices of all other goods constant, the PCC for a good X is the set of optimal bundles traced on an indifference map as the price of X varies.

FIGURE 4-1

The Price-Consumption Curve
Holding income and the price of Y fixed, we vary the price of shelter. The set of optimal bundles traced out by the various budget lines is called the price-consumption curve, or PCC.

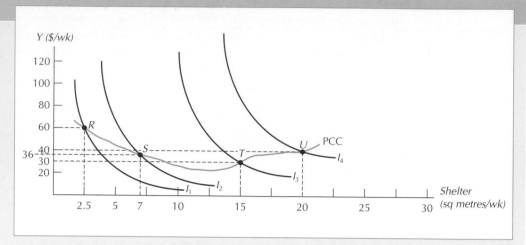

FIGURE 4-2

An Individual Consumer's Demand Curve
Like the market demand curve, the individual demand curve is a relationship that tells how much the consumer wants to purchase at different prices.

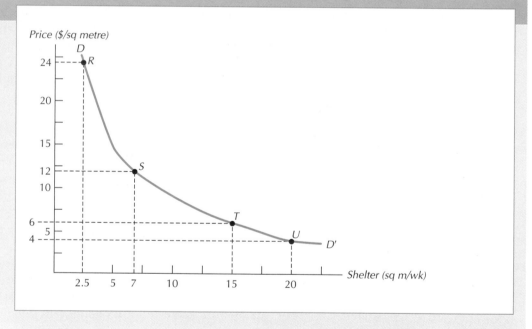

TABLE 4-1

A Demand Schedule
To derive the individual's demand curve for shelter from the PCC in Figure 4-1, begin by recording the quantities of shelter that correspond to the shelter prices on each budget constraint

Point	Price of shelter ($/sq metre)	Quantity of shelter demanded (sq metres/wk)	Total Expenditure on shelter ($/wk)	on Y ($/wk)
R	24	2.5	60	60
S	12	7	84	36
T	6	15	90	30
U	4	20	80	40

is $-P_S/P_Y$. Since P_Y, the price of the composite commodity, has been set at a fixed \$1 per unit, however, the slope of each budget constraint is just $-P_S$, measured in \$/sq m. Thus in Table 4-1, we simply match the absolute value of the *slope* of the budget constraint (P_S) with the optimal quantity of shelter demanded on that budget constraint at that price.

In Figure 4-2, we plot the price of shelter, P_S, on the vertical axis, and the quantity of shelter demanded at each price, given by the optimal points on the PCC, on the horizontal axis, *directly below* the corresponding quantities in Figure 4-1. Then we "connect the dots," to generate the demand curve for shelter, DD', in Figure 4-2. Now that we have derived this demand curve from the individual's underlying preferences and income, we should note several important features. First, in moving from the PCC to the individual's demand curve, we are moving from a graph in which both axes measure *quantities* to one in which the *price* of shelter is plotted against the *quantity* of shelter. Second, the demand curve is constructed holding money income, M, and the price of the composite good, P_Y, constant. If *either* changes, then generally the individual's *PCC*, and correspondingly the demand curve, will shift. Determining *how* they will shift is one of our principal tasks in the rest of this chapter.

A third feature has probably occurred to you. In Figure 4-1, if we know P_Y, the price of the composite commodity, then we can calculate from the diagram what the consumer's money income must be, since the vertical intercept equals M/P_Y. Here, with $P_Y = \$1$ per unit, the vertical intercept $M/P_Y = M/1 = \$M/wk$. Moreover, to every point on DD' corresponds not only the optimal quantity of shelter, but also a definite, optimal quantity of Y. We can observe this quantity directly by consulting the PCC, but we cannot directly observe it using the demand curve. The question thus arises: "Why use the demand curve at all; why not just use the PCC? In strict logic, the demand curve of Figure 4-2 gives us less information than Figure 4-1." The answer is straightforward: the demand curve is simple, memorable, powerful, and easy to manipulate. But behind every demand curve lurks a PCC. We need always to keep in mind that each demand curve is constructed holding money income and other prices constant, and that to every price on the demand curve corresponds not just the optimal quantity of *shelter* at that price—which we observe in Figure 4-2—but also the *un*observed optimal quantity of the *composite commodity*.

4.2 THE EFFECTS OF CHANGES IN INCOME

The Income-Consumption Curve

The PCC and the individual demand schedule are two different ways of summarizing how a consumer's purchase decisions respond to variations in prices. Analogous devices exist to summarize responses to variations in income. The income analogue to the PCC is the ***income-consumption curve***, or **ICC**. To generate the PCC for shelter, we held preferences, income, and the price of the composite good constant while tracing out the effects of a change in the price of shelter. In the case of the ICC, we hold preferences and relative prices constant and trace out the effects of changes in income.

In Figure 4-3, for example, we hold the price of the composite good constant at 1 and the price of shelter constant at \$10/sq m and examine what happens when income takes the values \$40/wk, \$60/wk, \$100/wk, and \$120/wk. Recall from Chapter 3 that a change in income alone shifts the budget constraint parallel to itself. As before, to each budget there corresponds a best affordable bundle. The set of best affordable bundles is denoted as ICC in Figure 4-3. For the consumer whose indifference map is shown, the ICC happens to be a straight line, but this need not always be the case.

Income-consumption curve (ICC) Holding the prices of all goods constant, the ICC is the set of optimal bundles traced on an indifference map as money income varies.

FIGURE 4-3

An Income-Consumption Curve
As income increases, the budget constraint moves outward. Holding preferences and relative prices constant, the ICC traces out how these changes in income affect consumption. It is the set of all tangencies as the budget line moves outward.

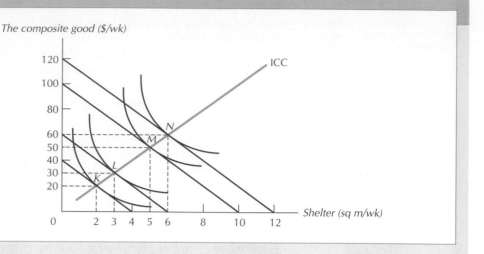

FIGURE 4-4

An Individual Consumer's Engel Curve
Holding preferences and relative prices constant, the Engel curve tells how much shelter the consumer will purchase at various levels of income.

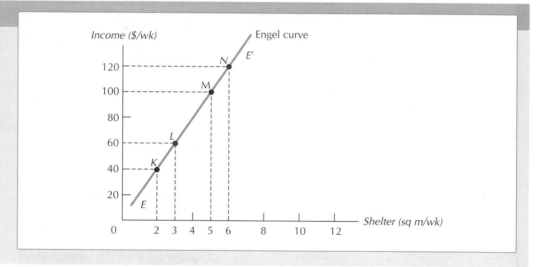

The Engel Curve

Engel curve A curve that plots the relationship between the quantity of a good consumed and income.

The analogue to the individual demand curve in the income domain is the individual *Engel curve.* It takes the quantities of shelter demanded from the ICC and plots them against the corresponding values of income. If we do this for indefinitely many income-consumption pairs for the consumer shown in Figure 4-3 (as illustrated in Table 4-2), we can trace out the line *EE'* shown in Figure 4-4. The Engel curve shown in Figure 4-4 happens to be a straight line through the origin, with a constant 50 percent of income spent on shelter, but Engel curves in general will not be.

Note carefully the distinction between what we measure on the vertical axis of the ICC and what we measure on the vertical axis of the Engel curve. On the vertical axis of the ICC, we measure the amount the consumer spends each week on all goods other than shelter. On the vertical axis of the Engel curve, in contrast, we measure the consumer's total weekly income.

Income ($/wk)	Quantity of shelter demanded (sq m/wk)	Expenditure on shelter ($/wk)	(% of total)
40	2	20	50%
60	3	30	50%
100	5	50	50%
120	6	60	50%

Note also that, as was true with the PCC and individual demand curves, the ICC and Engel curves contain essentially the same information. The advantage of the Engel curve is that it allows us to see at a glance how the quantity demanded varies with income, holding prices constant.

Normal and Inferior Goods

Note that the Engel curve in Figure 4-5a is upward sloping, implying that the more income a consumer has, the more tenderloin steak he will buy each week. Most things we buy have this property, which is the defining characteristic of a *normal good*. Goods that do not have this property are called *inferior goods*. For such goods, an increase in income leads to a reduction in the quantity demanded. Figure 4-5b is an example of an Engel curve for an inferior good. The more income a person has, the less regular ground beef he will buy each week.

Why would someone buy less of a good following an increase in his income? The prototypical inferior good is one for which there are several strongly preferred, but more expensive, substitutes. Supermarkets, for example, generally carry several different grades of ground beef, ranging from regular, which has the highest fat content, to ground sirloin, which has the lowest. A consumer will often tend to switch to a leaner grade of meat as soon as he is able to afford it. For such a consumer, regular ground beef will be an inferior good. At low income levels, regular hamburger may be a normal good, as people substitute it for packaged macaroni and cheese when their income rises.

Indeed, no good (call it X) that is consumed in positive amounts at *some* income level can be an inferior good at *all* income levels, since when income is zero, consumption

FIGURE 4-5

The Engel Curves
for Normal and
Inferior Goods

(a) This Engel curve is
for a normal good. The
quantity demanded
increases with income.
(b) This Engel curve for
regular ground beef
has the negative slope
characteristic of inferior
goods. As the con-
sumer's income grows,
he switches from regular
ground beef to more
desirable cuts of meat.

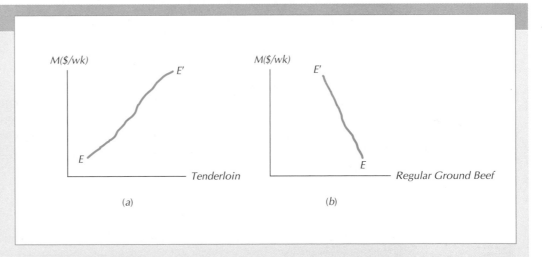

of the good is necessarily zero. Hence if it is demanded at some positive income level, then at least over the range from zero income to this income level, the good *must* be normal: $\Delta X^d/\Delta M > 0$. A good is inferior at given relative prices over some income range not because it is *inherently* "inferior" in some sense, but because at these prices, over this range of money income, an increase in income causes a decrease in demand for the good. At other income levels, or with different relative prices, it could be a normal good.

For any consumer who spends all her income, it is a matter of simple arithmetic that not all goods can be inferior. After all, when income rises, it is mathematically impossible to spend less on all goods at once. From this observation, it follows that the more broadly a good is defined, the less likely it is to be inferior. Thus, while hamburger is an inferior good for many consumers, there are probably very few people for whom the good "meat" is inferior, and fewer still for whom "food" is inferior.[1]

4.3 THE INCOME AND SUBSTITUTION EFFECTS OF A PRICE CHANGE

In Chapter 2 we saw that a change in the price of a good affects purchase decisions for two reasons. For concreteness, we will consider the effects of a price increase. (The effects of a price reduction will be in the opposite direction from those of a price increase.) One effect of a price increase is to make close substitutes of the good more attractive than before. For example, when the price of rice increases, wheat becomes more attractive. This is the so-called **substitution effect** of a price increase.

Substitution effect
That component of the total effect of a change in the price of a good that results from the associated change in the relative attractiveness of other goods.

The second effect of a price increase is to reduce the consumer's purchasing power. For a normal good, this effect too will tend to reduce the amount purchased. But for an inferior good, the effect is just the opposite. The loss in purchasing power, taken by itself, tends to increase the quantity purchased of an inferior good. The change in the quantity purchased attributable to the change in purchasing power is called the **income effect** of the price change.

Income effect That component of the total effect of a price change that results from the associated change in real purchasing power.

The *total effect* of the price increase is the sum of the substitution and income effects. The substitution effect virtually always causes the quantity purchased to move in the opposite direction from the change in price—when price goes up, the quantity demanded goes down; and conversely, when price goes down, the quantity demanded goes up. The direction of the income effect depends on whether the good is normal or inferior. For normal goods, the income effect works in the same direction as the substitution effect—when price goes up (down), the fall (rise) in purchasing power causes the quantity demanded to fall (rise). For inferior goods, in contrast, the income and substitution effects work against one another.

The substitution and income effects of a price increase can be seen most clearly when they are displayed graphically. Let us begin by depicting the total effect of a price increase. In Figure 4-6, the consumer has an initial income of $120 per week and the initial price of shelter is $6/sq m. This gives rise to the budget constraint labelled B_0, and the optimal bundle on that budget is denoted by A, which contains 10 sq m/wk of shelter. Now let the price of shelter increase from $6/sq m to $24/sq m, resulting in the budget labelled B_1. The new optimal bundle is D, which contains 2 sq m/wk of shelter. The movement from A to D is called the total effect of the price increase. Naturally, the

---

[1]Another useful way to partition the set of consumer goods is between so-called *necessities* and *luxuries*. A good is defined as a luxury for a person if (with given relative prices) he spends a larger proportion of his income on it when his income rises. A necessity, in contrast, is one for which he spends a smaller proportion of his income when his income rises. (More on this distinction follows.)

FIGURE 4-6

The Total Effect of a Price Increase

With an income of $120 per week and a price of shelter of $6/sq m, the consumer chooses bundle *A* on the budget constraint B_0. When the price of shelter rises to $24/sq m, with income held constant at $120 per week, the best affordable bundle becomes *D*. The movement from 10 to 2 sq m/wk of shelter is called the total effect of the price increase.

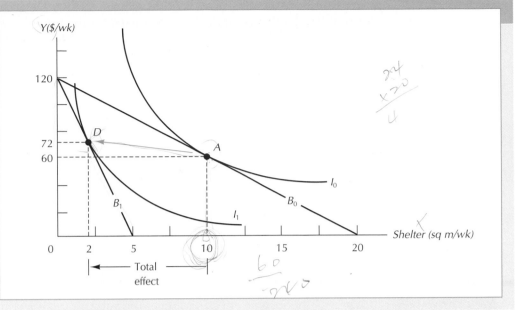

price increase causes the consumer to end up on a lower indifference curve (I_1) than the one he was able to attain on his original budget (I_0).

To decompose the total effect into the income and substitution effects, we begin by asking the following question: How much income would the consumer need to reach his original indifference curve (I_0) after the increase in the price of shelter? Note in Figure 4-7 that the answer is $240 per week. If the consumer were given a total income of that amount, it would undo the injury caused by the loss in purchasing

FIGURE 4-7

The Substitution and Income Effects of a Price Change

To get the substitution effect, slide the new budget B_1 outward parallel to itself until it becomes tangent to the original indifference curve, I_0. The movement from *A* to *C* gives rise to the substitution effect, the reduction in shelter due solely to the fact that shelter is now more expensive relative to other goods. The movement from *C* to *D* gives rise to the income effect. It is the reduction in shelter that results from the loss in purchasing power implicit in the price increase.

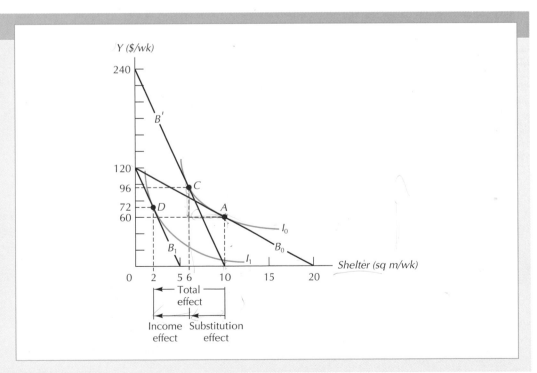

power resulting from the increase in the price of shelter. The budget constraint labelled B' is purely hypothetical, a device constructed for the purpose at hand. It has the same slope as the new budget constraint (B_1)—namely, -24—and it is just far enough out from the origin to be tangent to the original indifference curve, I_0. With the budget constraint B', the optimal bundle is C, which contains 6 sq m/wk of shelter. The movement from A to C gives rise to the substitution effect of the price change—which here involves a reduction of 4 sq m/wk of shelter and an increase of $36 per week of the composite good.

The hypothetical budget constraint B' tells us that even if the consumer had enough income to reach the same indifference curve as before, the increase in the price of shelter would cause him to reduce his consumption of it in favour of other goods and services. *For consumers whose indifference curves have the conventional convex shape, the substitution effect of a price increase will always be to reduce consumption of the good whose price increased.*

The income effect of the price increase stems from the movement from C to D. The particular good shown in Figure 4-7 happens to be a normal good. The hypothetical movement of the consumer's income from $240 per week to $120 per week serves to accentuate the reduction of his consumption of shelter, causing it to fall from 6 sq m/wk at A to 2 sq m/wk at D.

Whereas the income effect reinforces the substitution effect in the case of a normal good, the two effects tend to offset one another in the case of an inferior good. In Figure 4-8, the line B_0 depicts the budget constraint for a consumer with an income of $24 per week who faces a price of hamburger of $1/kg. On B_0 the best affordable bundle is A, which contains 12 kg/wk of hamburger. When the price of hamburger rises to $2/kg, the resulting budget constraint is B_1 and the best affordable bundle is now D, which contains 9 kg/wk of hamburger. The total effect of the price increase is thus to reduce the quantity of hamburger consumed by 3 kg/wk. Budget constraint B' once again is the hypothetical budget constraint that enables the consumer to reach the

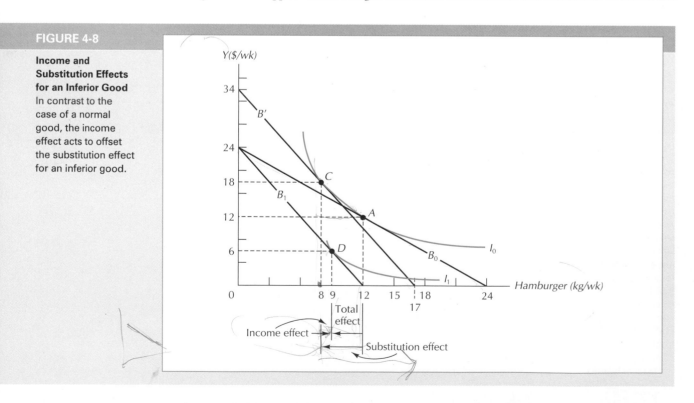

FIGURE 4-8

Income and Substitution Effects for an Inferior Good
In contrast to the case of a normal good, the income effect acts to offset the substitution effect for an inferior good.

original indifference curve at the new price ratio. Note in this case that the substitution effect of the price change (the change in hamburger consumption associated with movement from *A* to *C* in Figure 4-8) is to reduce the quantity of hamburger consumed by 4 kg/wk—that is, to reduce it by more than the value of the total effect. The income effect by itself (the change in hamburger consumption associated with the movement from *C* to *D*) actually serves to increase hamburger consumption by 1 kg/wk. The income effect thus works in the opposite direction from the substitution effect for an inferior good like hamburger.

| EXAMPLE 4-1 | **Income and substitution effects for perfect complements. Suppose skis and bind-ings are perfect, one-for-one complements and Nancy spends all her equipment budget of $1200 per year on these two goods. Skis and bindings each cost $200 per pair. What will be the income and substitution effects of an increase in the price of bindings to $400 per pair?** |

Since our goal here is to examine the effect on two specific goods (skis and bindings), we proceed by devoting one axis to each good and dispense with the composite good. On the original budget constraint, B_0, the optimal bundle is denoted A in Figure 4-9. Nancy buys three pairs of skis per year and three pairs of bindings. When the price of bindings rises from $200 per pair to $400 per pair, we get the new budget constraint, B_1, and the resulting optimal bundle D, which contains two pairs of skis per year and two pairs of bindings. An equipment budget of $1800 per year is what the consumer would need at the new price to attain the same indifference curve she did originally (I_0). (To get this figure, slide B_1 out until it hits I_0, then calculate the cost of buying the bundle at the vertical intercept—here, nine pairs of skis per year at $200 per pair.) Note that because perfect complements have right-angled indifference curves, the budget B' results in an optimal bundle C that is exactly the same as the original bundle A. *For perfect complements, the substitution effect is zero. So for this case, the total effect of the price increase is exactly the same as the income effect of the price increase.*

FIGURE 4-9

Income and Substitution Effects for Perfect Complements
For perfect comple-ments, the substitution effect of an increase in the price of bindings (the movement from *A* to *C*) is equal to zero. The income effect (the movement from *A* to *D*) and the total effect are one and the same.

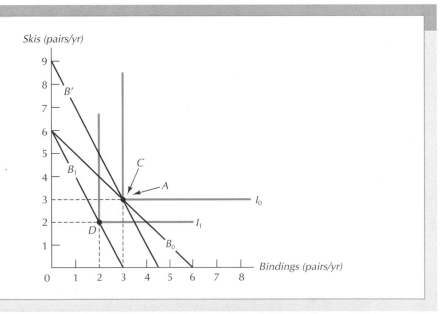

Example 4-1 tells us that if the price of ski bindings goes up relative to the price of skis, people will not alter the proportion of skis and bindings they purchase. But because the price increase lowers their real purchasing power (that is, because it limits the quantities of both goods that they can buy), they will respond by buying fewer units of ski equipment. The income effect will thus cause them to lower their consumption of both skis and bindings by the same proportion.

EXERCISE 4-1

Repeat Example 4-1 with the assumption that pairs of skis and pairs of bindings are perfect two-for-one complements. (That is, assume that Nancy wears out two pairs of skis for every pair of bindings she wears out.)

EXAMPLE 4-2

Income and substitution effects for perfect substitutes. Suppose Pam considers tea and coffee to be perfect one-for-one substitutes and spends her budget of $12 per week on these two beverages. Coffee costs $1 per cup, while tea costs $1.20 per cup. What will be the income and substitution effects of an increase in the price of coffee to $1.50 per cup?

Initially, Pam will demand 12 cups of coffee per week and no cups of tea (point A in Figure 4-10) as they contribute equally to her utility but tea is more expensive. When the price of coffee rises, Pam switches to consuming only tea, buying 10 cups of tea per week and no coffee (point D). Pam would need a budget of $14.40 per week to afford 12 cups of tea (point C), which she likes as well as the 12 cups of coffee she originally consumed. The substitution effect is from (12,0) to (0,12) and the income effect from (0,12) to (0,10), with the total effect from (12,0) to (0,10). *With perfect substitutes, the substitution effect can be very large. For small price changes (near MRS), consumers may switch from consuming all one good to consuming only the other good.*

EXERCISE 4-2

Starting from the original prices, what will be the income and substitution effects of an increase in the price of tea to $1.50 per cup?

FIGURE 4-10

For perfect substitutes, the substitution effect of an increase in the price of coffee (the movement from A to C) can be very large.

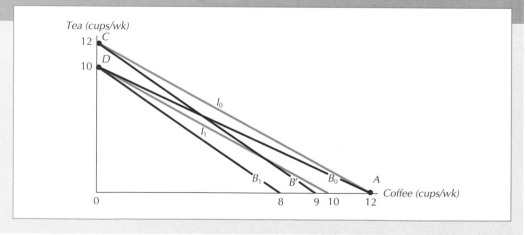

4.4 CONSUMER RESPONSIVENESS TO CHANGES IN PRICE

We began this chapter with the observation that for certain goods, such as salt, consumption is highly insensitive to changes in price while for others, such as housing, it is much more sensitive. The principal reason for studying income and substitution effects is that these devices help us understand such differences.

Let us consider first the case of salt. When analyzing substitution and income effects, there are two salient features to note about salt. First, for most consumers, it has no close substitutes. If someone were forbidden to shake salt onto his steak, he might respond by shaking a little extra pepper, or even by squeezing some lemon juice onto it. But for most people, these alternatives would fall considerably short of the real thing. The second prominent feature of salt is that it occupies an almost imperceptibly small share of total expenditures. An extremely heavy user of salt might consume a package every month. If this person's income were $1200 per month, a doubling of the price of salt—say, from $.30/package to $.60/package—would increase the share of his budget accounted for by salt from .00025 to .0005. For all practical purposes, therefore, the income effect of a price increase of salt is negligible.

It is instructive to represent these two properties of salt diagrammatically. In Figure 4-11, the fact that salt has no close substitutes is represented by indifference curves with a nearly right-angled shape. Salt's negligible budget share is captured by the fact that the cusps of these indifference curves occur at extremely small quantities of salt.

Suppose, as in Figure 4-11, the price of salt is originally $.30/package, resulting in an equilibrium bundle labelled A in the enlarged region, which contains 1.0002 packages per month of salt. A price increase to $.60/package results in a new equilibrium bundle D with 1 package per month of salt. The income and substitution effects are measured in terms of the intermediate bundle C. Geometrically, the income effect is small because the original tangency occurred so near the vertical intercept of the budget constraint.

FIGURE 4-11

Income and Substitution Effects of a Price Increase for Salt
The total effect of a price change will be very small when (1) the original equilibrium bundle lies near the vertical intercept of the budget constraint and (2) the indifference curves have a nearly right-angled shape. The first factor causes the income effect (the reduction in salt consumption associated with the movement from C to D) to be small; the second factor causes the substitution effect (the reduction in salt consumption associated with the movement from A to C) to be small.

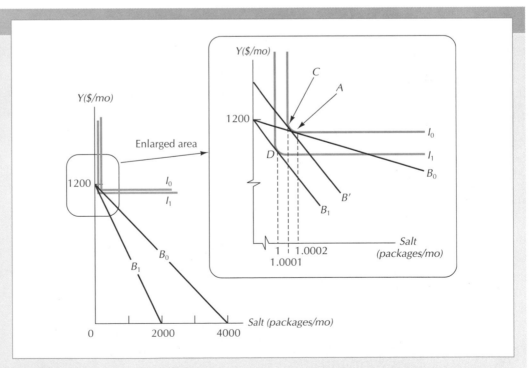

When we are near the pivot point of the budget constraint, even a very large rotation produces only a small movement. The substitution effect, in turn, is small because of the nearly right-angled shape of the indifference curves.

Let us now contrast the salt case with the housing example. With housing, the two salient facts are that (1) it accounts for a substantial share of total expenditures (roughly 30 percent for many people), and (2) most people have considerable latitude to substitute between housing and other goods. The second assertion may not appear obvious at first glance, but on reflection, its plausibility becomes clear. Indeed, there are many ways to substitute away from housing expenditures. The most obvious is to switch from a larger to a smaller dwelling. Many Vancouverites, for example, could afford to live in homes larger than the ones they now occupy, yet they prefer to spend what they save in housing costs on restaurant meals, theatre performances, and the like. Another substitution possibility is to consume less conveniently located housing. Someone who works in Vancouver can live near her job at a high housing cost; alternatively, she can live in Surrey or Coquitlam and pay considerably less. Or she can choose a home in a less fashionable neighbourhood, or one not quite as close to convenient transportation. The point is that there are many different options for housing, and the choice among them will depend strongly on income and relative prices.

In Figure 4-12, the consumer's income is $120 per week and the initial price of shelter is $.60/sq m. The resulting budget constraint is labelled B_0, and the best affordable bundle on it is A, which contains 100 sq m/wk of shelter. An increase in the price of shelter to $2.40/sq m causes the quantity demanded to fall to 20 sq m/wk. The smooth convex shape of the indifference curves represents the high degree of substitution

FIGURE 4-12

Income and Substitution Effects for a Price-Sensitive Good
Because shelter occupies a large share of the budget, its income effect tends to be large. And because it is practical to substitute away from shelter, the substitution effect also tends to be large. The quantities demanded of goods with both large substitution and large income effects are highly responsive to changes in price.

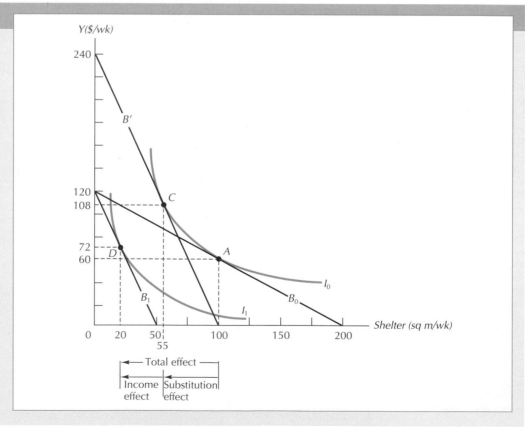

possibilities between housing and other goods and accounts for the relatively large sub-stitution effect (the fall in shelter consumption associated with the movement from *A* to *C*). Note also that the original equilibrium bundle, *A*, was a tangency far from the ver-tical pivot point of the budget constraint. In contrast to the case of salt, here the rotation in the budget constraint caused by the price increase produces a large movement in the location of the relevant segment of the new budget constraint. Accordingly, the income effect for shelter (the fall in shelter consumption associated with the movement from *C* to *D*) is much larger than in the case of salt. With both a large substitution and a large income effect working together, the total effect of an increase in the price of shelter (the fall in shelter consumption associated with the movement from *A* to *D*) is very large.

EXAMPLE 4-3

Deriving individual demand curve for perfect complements. James views car washes and gasoline as perfect complements in a 1-to-10 ratio, requiring one car wash for every 10 litres of gas. Gas costs $1 per litre, and James has $48 per month to spend on gas and car washes. (See Figure 4-13.) Construct James's demand curve for car washes by considering his quantity demanded of car washes at various prices (such as $2, $6, and $14 per wash; see Figure 4-14).

FIGURE 4-13

A Price Increase for Car Washes
With $48 per month, James buys 4 washes per month when the price is $2 per wash (budget constraint *B*), 3 washes per month when the price is $6 per wash (budget constraint *B'*), and 2 washes per month when the price is $14 per wash (budget constraint *B"*).

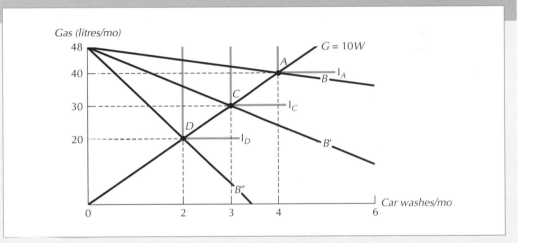

FIGURE 4-14

James's Demand for Car Washes
The quantity of car washes James demands at various prices forms his demand curve for car washes.

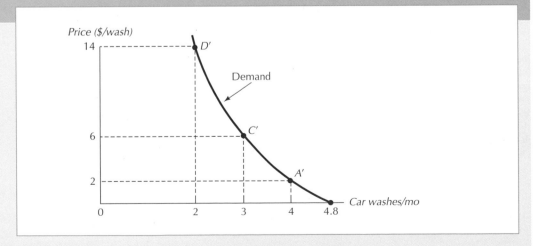

James's preferences dictate that his optimal bundle must satisfy $G = 10W$, as his indifference curves are L-shaped. James's budget constraint is $P_G G + P_W W = 48$, or $G = 48 - P_W W$. Substituting $G = 10W$, his budget constraint is $10W + P_W W = 48$, which implies $(10 + P_W)W = 48$, or $W = 48/(10+P_W)$. This is James's demand function for car washes. At $P_W = 2$, $W = 4$; at $P_W = 6$, $W = 3$; at $P_W = 14$, $W = 2$, as summarized in Table 4-3.

TABLE 4-3

A Demand Schedule for Car Washes

Price of car wash ($/wash)	Quantity of car washes demanded (washes/month)	Expenditure on car washes ($/mo)	(% of income)
2	4	8	16.67%
6	3	18	37.5%
14	2	28	58.33%
38	1	38	79.17%

4.5 MARKET DEMAND: AGGREGATING INDIVIDUAL DEMAND CURVES

Having seen where individual demand curves come from, we are now in a position to see how individual demand curves may be aggregated to form the market demand curve. For simplicity, let us consider a market for a good—for the sake of concreteness, again shelter—that consists of only two potential consumers. Given the demand curves for each of these consumers, how do we generate the market demand curve for shelter? In Figure 4-15, D_1 and D_2 represent the individual demand curves for consumers 1 and 2, respectively. To get the market demand curve, we begin by calling out a price—say, $4/sq m—and adding the quantities demanded by each consumer at that price. This sum, 6 sq m/wk + 2 sq m/wk = 8 sq m/wk, is the total quantity of shelter demanded in the market at the price $4/sq m. We then plot the point (8, 4) as one of the quantity-price pairs on the market demand curve D in the right panel of Figure 4-15. To generate additional points on the market demand curve, we simply repeat this process for other prices. Thus, the price $8/sq m corresponds to a quantity of $4 + 0 = 4$ sq m/wk on the market demand curve for shelter. Proceeding in like fashion for additional

FIGURE 4-15

Generating Market Demand from Individual Demands
The market demand curve (D in the right panel) is the horizontal sum of the individual demand curves, D_1 (left panel) and D_2 (centre panel).

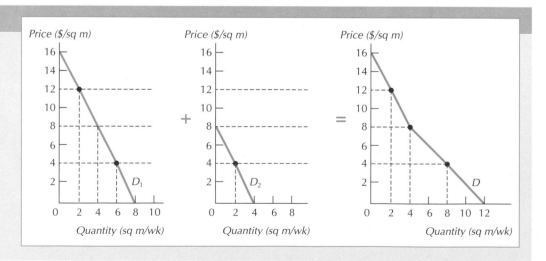

CHAPTER 4: INDIVIDUAL AND MARKET DEMAND

prices, we trace out the entire market demand curve for shelter. Note that for prices above $8/sq m, consumer 2 demands no shelter at all, and so the market demand curve for prices above $8 is identical to the demand curve for consumer 1.

The procedure of announcing a price and adding the individual quantities demanded at that price is called *horizontal summation*. It is carried out the same way whether there are only two consumers in the market or many millions. In both large and small markets, the market demand curve is the horizontal summation of the individual demand curves.

In Chapter 2 we saw that it is often easier to generate numerical solutions when demand and supply curves are expressed algebraically rather than geometrically. Similarly, it will often be convenient to aggregate individual demand curves algebraically rather than graphically. When using the algebraic approach, a common error is to add individual demand curves vertically instead of horizontally. A simple example makes this danger clear.

EXAMPLE 4-4

Smith and Jones are the only consumers in the market for beech saplings in a small town in New Brunswick. Their demand curves are given by $P = 30 - 2Q_J$ and $P = 30 - 3Q_S$, where Q_J and Q_S are the quantities demanded by Jones and Smith, respectively. What is the market demand curve for beech saplings in their town?

When we add demand curves horizontally, we are adding quantities, not prices. Thus it is necessary first to solve the individual demand equations for the respective quantities in terms of price. This yields $Q_J = 15 - (P/2)$ for Jones, and $Q_S = 10 - (P/3)$ for Smith. If the quantity demanded in the market is denoted by Q, we have $Q = Q_J + Q_S = 15 - (P/2) + 10 - (P/3) = 25 - (5P/6)$. Solving back for P, we get the equation for the market demand curve: $P = 30 - (6Q/5)$. We can easily verify that this is the correct market demand curve by adding the individual demand curves graphically, as in Figure 4-16.

The common pitfall is to add the demand functions as originally stated and then solve for P in terms of Q. Here, this would yield $P = 30 - (5Q/2)$, which is obviously not the market demand curve we are looking for.

EXERCISE 4-3

Write the individual demand curves for shelter in Figure 4-15 in algebraic form, then add them algebraically to generate the market demand curve for shelter. (*Hint*: Note that the formula for quantity along D_2 is valid only for prices between 0 and 8. What is the market demand curve for prices between 8 and 16?)

FIGURE 4-16

The Market Demand Curve for Beech Saplings
When adding individual demand curves algebraically, be sure to solve for quantity first before adding.

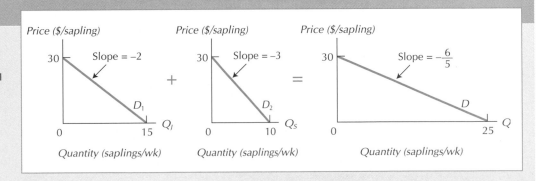

FIGURE 4-17

Market Demand with Identical Consumers
When 10 consumers each have a demand curve $P = 10 - 5Q_i$, the market demand curve is the horizontal summation $P = 10 - (\frac{1}{2})Q$, with the same price intercept and $\frac{1}{10}$ the slope.

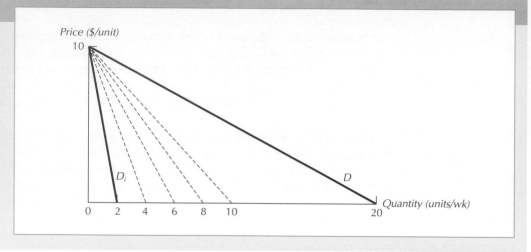

The horizontal summation of individual consumers' demands into market demand has a simple form when the consumers in the market are all identical. Suppose n consumers each have the demand curve $P = a - bQ_i$. To add up the quantities for the n consumers into market demand, we rearrange the consumer demand curve $P = a - bQ_i$ to express quantity alone on one side $Q_i = a/b - (1/b)P$. Then market demand is the sum of the quantities demanded Q_i by each of the n consumers.

$$Q = nQ_i = n\left(\frac{a}{b} - \frac{1}{b}P\right) = \frac{na}{a} - \frac{n}{b}P.$$

We can then rearrange market demand $Q = na/b - (n/b)P$ to return to the form with price alone on one side $P = a - (b/n)Q$. The intuition is that each one unit demanded by the market is $1/n$ unit for each consumer to demand. These calculations suggest a general rule for constructing the market demand curve when consumers are identical. If we have n individual consumer demand curves in the form $P = a - bQ_i$, then the market demand curve may be written $P = a - (b/n)Q$.

EXAMPLE 4-5

Suppose a market has 10 consumers, each with demand curve $P = 10 - 5Q_i$, where P is the price in dollars per unit and Q_i is the number of units demanded per week by the ith consumer (Figure 4-17). Find the market demand curve.

First, we need to rearrange the representative consumer demand curve $P = 10 - 5Q_i$ to have quantity alone on one side:

$$Q_i = 2 - \frac{1}{5}P.$$

Then we multiply by the number of consumers, $n = 10$:

$$Q = nQ_i = 10Q_i = 10\left(2 - \frac{1}{5}P\right) = 20 - 2P.$$

Finally, we rearrange the market demand curve $Q = 20 - 2P$ to have price alone on one side, $P = 10 - (\frac{1}{2})Q$, to return to the slope-intercept form.

Suppose a market has 30 consumers, each with demand curve $P = 120 - 60Q_i$, where P is price in dollars per unit and Q_i is the number of units demanded per week by the ith consumer. Find the market demand curve.

4.6 PRICE ELASTICITY OF DEMAND

Price elasticity of demand The percentage change in the quantity of a good demanded that results from a 1 percent change in its price.

An analytical tool of central importance is the ***price elasticity of demand***. It is a quantitative measure of the responsiveness of purchase decisions to variations in price, and as we will see in both this and later chapters, it is useful for a variety of practical problems. *Price elasticity of demand is defined as the percentage change in the quantity of a good demanded that results from a 1 percent change in its price.* For example, if a 1 percent rise in the price of shelter caused a 2 percent reduction in the quantity of shelter demanded, then the price elasticity of demand for shelter would be −2. The price elasticity of demand will generally be negative (or, in the limit, zero), insofar as price changes move in the opposite direction from changes in quantity demanded.

The demand for a good is said to be elastic with respect to price if its price elasticity is less than −1. The good shelter mentioned in the preceding paragraph would thus be one for which demand is elastic with respect to price. The demand for a good is *inelastic* with respect to price if its price elasticity is between −1 and zero and *unit elastic* with respect to price if its price elasticity is equal to −1. These definitions are portrayed graphically in Figure 4-18.

When interpreting actual demand data, it is often useful to have a more general definition of price elasticity that can accommodate cases where the observed change in price does not happen to be 1 percent. Let P be the current price of a good and let Q be the quantity demanded at that price. And let ΔQ be the change in the quantity demanded that occurs in response to a very small change in price, ΔP. The price elasticity of demand at the current price and quantity will then be given by

$$\eta = \frac{\Delta Q/Q}{\Delta P/P}.\qquad(4.1)$$

The numerator on the right side of Equation 4.1 is the proportional change in quantity. The denominator is the proportional change in price. Equation 4.1 is exactly the same as our earlier definition when ΔP happens to be a 1 percent change in current price. The advantage is that the more general definition also works when ΔP is any other small percentage change in current price.

FIGURE 4-18

Three Categories of Price Elasticity
With respect to price, the demand for a good is elastic if its price elasticity is less than −1, inelastic if its price elasticity exceeds −1, and unit elastic if its price elasticity is equal to −1.

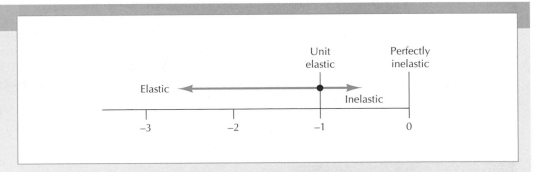

Geometric Interpretations of Price Elasticity

Another way to interpret Equation 4.1 is to rewrite it as

$$\eta = \frac{\Delta Q}{\Delta P} \frac{P}{Q}. \tag{4.2}$$

Equation 4.2 suggests a simple interpretation in terms of the geometry of the market demand curve. When ΔP is small, the ratio $\Delta P/\Delta Q$ is the slope of the demand curve, which means that the ratio $\Delta Q/\Delta P$ is the reciprocal of that slope. Thus the price elasticity of demand may be interpreted as the product of the ratio of price to quantity and the reciprocal of the slope of the demand curve:[2]

$$\eta = \frac{P}{Q} \frac{1}{\text{slope}} \tag{4.3}$$

Equation 4.3 is called the *point-slope* method of calculating price elasticity of demand. By way of illustration, consider the demand curve for shelter shown in Figure 4-19. Because this demand curve is linear, its slope is the same at every point, namely, -2. The reciprocal of this slope is $-\frac{1}{2}$. The price elasticity of demand at point A is therefore given by the ratio of price to quantity at A ($\frac{12}{2}$) multiplied by the reciprocal of the slope at A ($-\frac{1}{2}$), and so we have $\eta_A = (\frac{12}{2})(-\frac{1}{2}) = -3$.

When the market demand curve is linear, as in Figure 4-19, several properties of price elasticity quickly become apparent from this interpretation. The first is that the price elasticity is different at every point along the demand curve. More specifically, we know that the slope of a linear demand curve is constant throughout, which means that the reciprocal of its slope is also constant. The ratio of price to quantity, in contrast, takes a different value at every point along the demand curve. As we approach the vertical intercept, it approaches infinity. It declines steadily as we move downward along the demand curve, finally reaching a value of zero at the horizontal intercept.

A second property of demand elasticity in the standard case is that it is never positive. As noted earlier, with the slope of the demand curve negative, its reciprocal must also be negative; and because the ratio P/Q is always positive, it follows that the price elasticity of demand—which is the product of these two—must always be a negative number (except at the horizontal intercept of the demand curve, where P/Q, and hence elasticity, is zero). For the sake of convenience, however, economists often ignore the negative sign of price elasticity and refer simply to its absolute value. When a good is said to have a "high" price elasticity of demand, this will always mean that its price elasticity is large in absolute value, indicating that the quantity demanded is highly responsive to changes in price. Similarly, a good whose price elasticity is said to be "low" is one for which the absolute value of elasticity is small, indicating that the quantity demanded is relatively unresponsive to changes in price.

A third property of price elasticity at any point along a straight-line demand curve is that it will be inversely related to the slope of the demand curve. The steeper the demand curve, the less elastic is demand at any point along it. This follows from the fact that the reciprocal of the slope of the demand curve is one of the factors used to compute price elasticity.

---

[2]In calculus terms, price elasticity is defined as $\eta = (P/Q)[dQ(P)/dP]$.

$$\eta = \frac{P}{Q} \times \frac{1}{slope}$$

FIGURE 4-19

The Point-Slope Method

The price elasticity of demand at any point is the product of the price-quantity ratio at that point and the reciprocal of the slope of the demand curve at that point. The price elasticity at A is thus $(\frac{12}{2})(-\frac{1}{2}) = -3$.

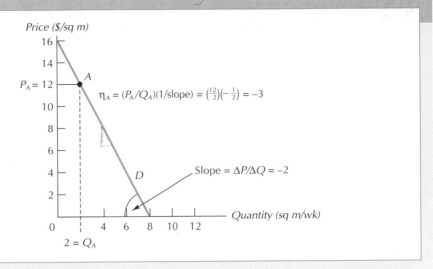

Use the point-slope method (Equation 4.3) to determine the elasticity of the demand curve $P = 32 - Q$ at the point where $P = 24$.

$Q = 32 - 24 = 8$

$.8 \times$ $(\cancel{2}\cancel{A})$ $(a\ P)\ (0, 32)$ $\eta = \frac{24}{8} \times -1 = -3$

$(32, 0)$

Two polar cases of demand elasticity are shown in Figure 4-20. In Figure 4-20a, the horizontal demand curve, with its slope of zero, has an infinitely high price elasticity at every point. Such demand curves are often called *perfectly elastic* and, as we will see, are especially important in the study of competitive firm behaviour. In Figure 4-20b, the vertical demand curve has a price elasticity everywhere equal to zero. Such curves are called *perfectly inelastic*.

As a practical matter, it would be impossible for any demand curve to be perfectly inelastic at all prices. Beyond some sufficiently high price, income effects must curtail consumption of the good. This will be true even for a seemingly essential good with no substitutes, such as surgery for certain malignant tumours. Even so, the demand curve for many such goods and services can be perfectly inelastic over an extremely broad range of prices (recall the salt example discussed earlier in this chapter).

The Unit-free Property of Elasticity

Another way of measuring responsiveness to changes in price is to use the slope of the demand curve. Other things equal, for example, we know that the quantity demanded of a good with a steep demand curve will be less responsive to changes in price than will one with a less steep demand curve.

Since the slope of a demand curve is much simpler to calculate than its elasticity, it may seem natural to ask, "Why bother with elasticity at all?" One important reason is that the slope of the demand curve is very sensitive to the units we use to measure price and quantity, while elasticity is not. By way of illustration, notice that the three demand curves in Figure 4-21 (which all describe the identical demand situation) have slopes ranging from $-.0002$ to -2. This difference occurs solely because of the choice of different units to describe the demand relation. Yet at point C in all three diagrams,

FIGURE 4-20

Two Important Polar Cases
(*a*) The price elasticity of the demand curve is equal to −∞ at every point. Such demand curves are said to be perfectly elastic.
(*b*) The price elasticity of the demand curve is equal to 0 at every point. Such demand curves are said to be perfectly inelastic.

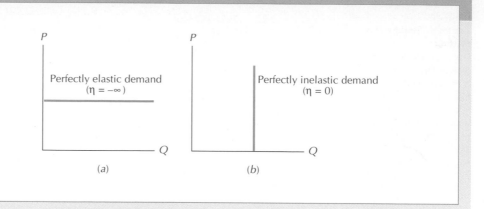

the price elasticity of demand is −3. This will be true no matter how we measure price and quantity. And most people find it much more informative to know that a 1 percent cut in price will lead to a 3 percent increase in the quantity demanded than to know that the slope of the demand curve is −.0002.

Some Representative Elasticity Estimates

As the entries in Table 4-4 show, the price elasticities of demand for different products often differ substantially. The low elasticity for theatre and opera performances probably reflects the fact that buyers in this market have much larger than average incomes, so that income effects of price variations are likely to be small. Income effects for green peas are also likely to be small even for low-income consumers, yet the price elasticity of demand for green peas is more than 14 times larger than for theatre and opera performances. The difference is that there are many more close substitutes for green peas than there are for theatre and opera performances. Later in this chapter we investigate in greater detail the factors that affect the price elasticity of demand for a product.

FIGURE 4-21

Elasticity Is Unit Free
The slope of the demand curve at any point depends on the units in which we measure price and quantity. The slope at point *C* is greater in absolute value in (*b*), with price in cents per litre, and less in (*c*), with quantity in centilitres per day, than in (*a*). The price elasticity at any point, in contrast, is completely independent of units of measurement.

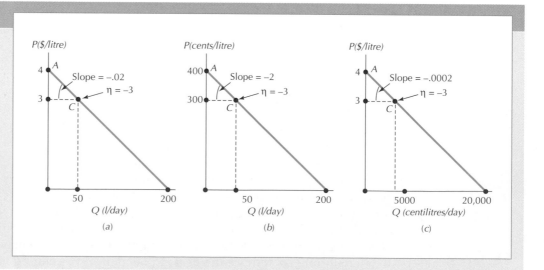

TABLE 4-4

Price Elasticity
Estimates for Selected
Products*

Good or service	Price elasticity
Green peas	−2.8
Electricity	−1.2
Beer	−1.19
Movies	−.87
Air travel (foreign)	−.77
Shoes	−.70
Theatre, opera	−.18

*These short-run elasticity estimates are taken from the following sources: H. S. Houthakker and Lester Taylor, *Consumer Demand in the United States: Analyses and Projections*, 2d ed., Cambridge, MA: Harvard University Press, 1970; L. Taylor, "The Demand for Electricity: A Survey," *Bell Journal of Economics*, Spring 1975; K. Elzinga, "The Beer Industry," in Walter Adams (ed.), *The Structure of American Industry*, New York: Macmillan, 1977.

Elasticity and Total Expenditure

Suppose you are the administrator in charge of setting fares for the Metroville Transit Commission. At the current fare of $1 per trip, 100,000 trips per day are taken. If the price elasticity of demand for trips is −2.0, what will happen to the number of trips taken per day if you raise the fare by 10 percent? With an elasticity of −2.0, a 10 percent increase in price will produce a 20 percent reduction in quantity. Thus the number of trips will fall to 80,000/day. Total expenditure at the higher fare will be (80,000 trips/day)($1.10/trip) = $88,000/day. Note that this is smaller than the total expenditure of $100,000/day that occurred under the $1 fare.

Now suppose that the price elasticity had been not −2.0 but −0.5. How would the number of trips and total expenditure then be affected by a 10 percent increase in the fare? This time the number of trips will fall by 5 percent, to 95,000/day, which means that total expenditure will rise to (95,000 trips/day) ($1.10/trip) = $104,500/day. If your goal as an administrator is to increase the total revenue collected from fares, you will need to know something about the price elasticity of demand for trips before deciding whether to raise the fare or to lower it.

This example illustrates one of the most important relationships in all of economics, namely, the one between price elasticity and total expenditure. The questions we want to be able to answer are often of the form, "If the price of a product changes, how will the total amount spent on the product be affected?" and "Will more be spent on the product if we sell more units at a lower price or fewer units at a higher price?" In Figure 4-22, for example, we might want to know how total expenditures for shelter are affected when the price falls from $12/sq m to $10/sq m.

The total expenditure, R, at any quantity-price pair (Q, P) is given by the product

$$R = PQ. \tag{4.4}$$

In Figure 4-22, the total expenditure at the original quantity-price pair is thus ($12/sq m) (4 sq m/wk) = $48 per week. Geometrically, it is the sum of the two shaded areas E and F. Following the price reduction, the new total expenditure is ($10/sq m)(6 sq m/wk) = $60 per week, which is the sum of the shaded areas F and G. These two total expenditures have in common the shaded area F. The change in total expenditure is thus the dif-

FIGURE 4-22

The Effect on Total Expenditure of a Reduction in Price
When price falls, people spend less on existing units (*E*). But they also buy more units (*G*). Here, *G* is larger than *E*, which means that total expenditure rises.

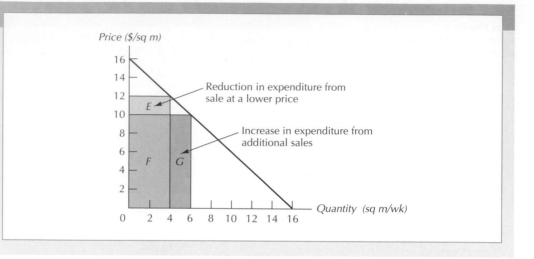

ference in the two shaded areas *E* and *G*. The area *E*, which is ($2/sq m)(4 sq m/wk) = $8 per week, may be interpreted as the reduction in expenditure caused by selling the original 4 sq m/wk at the new, lower price. *G*, in turn, is the increase in expenditure caused by the additional 2 sq m/wk of sales. This area is given by ($10/sq m)(2 sq m/wk) = $20 per week. Whether total expenditure rises or falls thus boils down to whether the gain from additional sales exceeds the loss from lower prices. Here, the gain exceeds the loss by $12, so total expenditure rises by that amount following the price reduction.

If the change in price is small, we can say how total expenditure will move if we know the initial price elasticity of demand. Recall that one way of expressing price elasticity is the percentage change in quantity divided by the corresponding percentage change in price. If the absolute value of that quotient exceeds 1, we know that the percentage change in quantity is larger than the percentage change in price. And when that happens, the increase in expenditure from additional sales will always exceed the reduction from sales of existing units at the lower price. In Figure 4-22, note that the elasticity at the original price of $12 is −3.0, which confirms our earlier observation that the price reduction led to an increase in total expenditure. Suppose, on the contrary, that demand is inelastic. Then the percentage increase in quantity will be smaller than the corresponding percentage decrease in price, and the additional sales will not compensate for the reduction in expenditure from sales at a lower price. Here, a price reduction will lead to a reduction in total expenditure.

EXERCISE 4-6

For the demand curve in Figure 4-22, what is the price elasticity of demand when *P* = $4/sq m? What will happen to total expenditure on shelter when price falls from $4/sq m to $3/sq m?

The general rule for small price reductions, then, is this: *A price reduction will increase total revenue if and only if the absolute value of the price elasticity of demand is greater than 1.* Parallel reasoning leads to an analogous rule for small price increases: *An increase in price will increase total revenue if and only if the absolute value of the price elasticity is less than 1.* These rules are summarized in the top panel of Figure 4-23, where the point *M* is the midpoint of the demand curve.

FIGURE 4-23

Demand and Total Expenditure

When demand is elastic, total expenditure changes in the opposite direction from a change in price. When demand is inelastic, total expenditure and price both move in the same direction. At the midpoint of the demand curve (*M*), total expenditure is at a maximum.

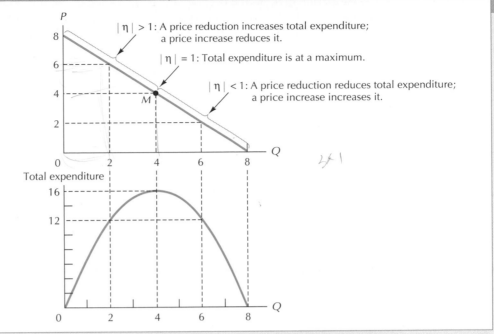

The relationship between elasticity and total expenditure is spelled out in greater detail in the relationship between the top and bottom panels of Figure 4-23. The top panel shows a straight-line demand curve. For each quantity, the bottom panel shows the corresponding total expenditure. As indicated in the bottom panel, total expenditure starts at zero when Q is zero and increases to its maximum value at the quantity corresponding to the midpoint of the demand curve (point M in the top panel). At that same quantity, price elasticity is unitary. Beyond that quantity, total expenditure declines with output, reaching zero at the quantity corresponding to the horizontal intercept of the demand curve.

EXAMPLE 4-6

The market demand curve for bus rides in a small community is given by $P = 100 - (Q/10)$, where P is the fare in cents per ride and Q is the number of rides purchased each day. If the price is \$.50 per ride, how much revenue will the transit system collect each day? What is the price elasticity of demand for bus rides? If the system needs more revenue, should it raise or lower its price? How would your answers have differed if the initial price had been not \$.50 per ride but \$.75?

Total revenue for the bus system is equal to total expenditure by riders, which is the product PQ. First we solve for Q from the demand curve and get $Q = 1000 - 10P$. When P is \$.50 per ride, Q will be 500 rides/day and the resulting total revenue will be \$250/day. To compute the price elasticity of demand, we can use the formula $\eta = (P/Q)(1/\text{slope})$. Here the slope is $-\frac{1}{10}$, so $1/\text{slope} = -10$ (see footnote 3). P/Q takes the value $50/500 = \frac{1}{10}$. Price elasticity is thus the product $(\frac{1}{10})(-10) = -1$. With a unitary price elasticity, total revenue attains its maximum value. If the bus company either raises or lowers its price, it will earn less than it does at the current price.

---

[3]The slope here is from the formula $P = 100 - (Q/10)$.

At a price of $.50, the company was operating at the midpoint of its demand curve. If the current price had instead been $.75, it would be operating above the midpoint. More precisely, it would be halfway between the midpoint and the vertical intercept (point K in Figure 4-24). Quantity would be only 250 rides/day, and price elasticity would have been −3 (computed, for example, by using the ratio of the line segments, *EK/AK*, as shown in Appendix 4A). Operating at an elastic point on its demand curve, the company could increase total revenue by cutting its price.

4.7 DETERMINANTS OF PRICE ELASTICITY OF DEMAND

What factors govern the size of the price elasticity of demand for a product? To answer this question, it is useful to draw first on our earlier discussion of substitution and income effects, which suggests primary roles for the following factors:

- **Substitution possibilities.** The substitution effect of a price change tends to be small for goods for which there are no close substitutes. Consider, for example, the vaccine against rabies. People who have been bitten by rabid animals have nothing to substitute for this vaccine, and the demand for the vaccine will tend to be highly inelastic. We saw that the same was true for a good such as salt. But consider now the demand for a particular brand of salt. Despite the advertising claims of salt manufacturers, one brand of salt is a more-or-less perfect substitute for any other. Because the substitution effect between specific brands of salt will be large, a rise in the price of one brand should sharply curtail the quantity of it demanded. In general, the absolute value of price elasticity will rise with the availability of attractive substitutes.

- **Budget share.** The larger the share of total expenditures accounted for by the product, the more important will be the income effect of a price change. Goods such as salt, rubber bands, cellophane wrap, and a host of others account for such small shares of total expenditures that, for most people, the income effects of a price change are likely to be negligible for these goods. For goods like housing and higher education, in contrast, the income effect of a price increase is likely to be large indeed. In general, other factors the same, the larger the share of total expenditure accounted for by a good, the more price elastic the demand for a normal good will be and the less price elastic the demand for an inferior good will be.

FIGURE 4-24

The Demand for Bus Rides
At a price of $.50 per ride, the bus company is maximizing its total revenues. At a price of $.75 per ride, demand is elastic with respect to price, and so the company can increase its total revenues by cutting its price.

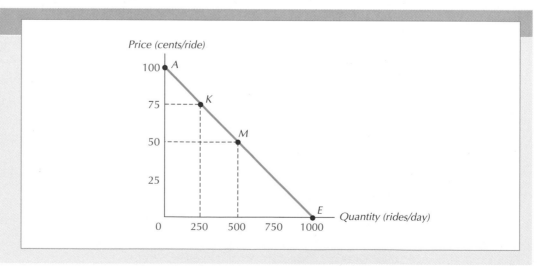

FIGURE 4-25

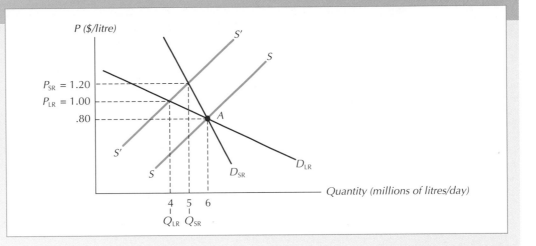

- **Direction of income effect.** A factor closely related to the budget share is the direction—positive or negative—of its income effect. While the budget share tells us whether the income effect of a price change is likely to be large or small, the direction of the income effect tells us whether it will offset or reinforce the substitution effect. Thus, a normal good will tend to have a higher price elasticity than an inferior good, other things equal, because the income effect reinforces the substitution effect for a normal good but offsets it for an inferior good.

- **Time.** Our analysis of individual demand did not focus explicitly on the role of time. But it too has an important effect on people's responses to changes in prices. Consider a sharp, unexpected increase in gas prices. One response of a consumer confronted with a higher price of gasoline is simply to drive less. But many auto trips are part of a larger pattern and cannot be abandoned, or even altered, very quickly. A person cannot simply stop going to work, for example. He can cut down on his daily commute by joining a car pool or by purchasing a house closer to where he works. He can also curtail his gasoline consumption by trading in his current car for one that gets better mileage. But all these steps take time, and as a result, the demand for gasoline will tend to be more elastic in the long run than in the short run.

The short- and long-run effects of a supply shift in the market for gasoline are contrasted in Figure 4-25. The initial equilibrium at A is disturbed by a supply reduction from S to S'. In the short run, the effect is for price to rise to $P_{SR} = \$1.20$/litre and for quantity to fall to $Q_{SR} = 5$ million litres/day. The long-run demand curve is more elastic than the short-run demand curve. As consumers have more time to adjust, therefore, price effects tend to moderate while quantity effects tend to become more pronounced. Thus the new long-run equilibrium in Figure 4-25 occurs at a price of $P_{LR} = \$1.00$/litre and a quantity of $Q_{LR} = 4$ million litres per day.

We see an extreme illustration of the difference between short- and long-run price elasticity values in the case of natural gas used in households. The price elasticity for this product is only $-.1$ in the short run but a whopping -10.7 in the long run![4] This difference reflects the fact that once a consumer has chosen appliances to heat and

---

[4]H. S. Houthakker and Lester Taylor, *Consumer Demand in the United States*: Analyses and Projections, 2d ed., Cambridge, MA: Harvard University Press, 1970.

FIGURE 4-26

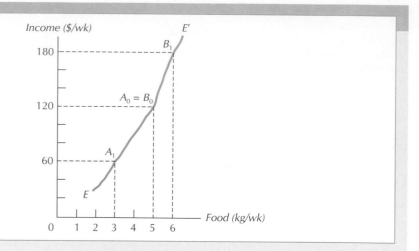

cook with, he or she is virtually locked in for the short run. People aren't going to cook their rice for only 10 minutes just because the price of natural gas has gone up. In the long run, however, consumers can and do switch between fuels when there are significant changes in relative prices.

4.8 THE DEPENDENCE OF MARKET DEMAND ON INCOME

As we have seen, the quantity of a good demanded by any person depends not only on its price but also on the person's income. Since the market demand curve is the horizontal sum of individual demand curves, it too will naturally be influenced by consumer incomes. In some cases, the effect of income on market demand can be accounted for completely if we know only the average income level in the market. This would be the case, for example, if all consumers in the market were alike in terms of preference and all had the same incomes.

In practice, however, a given level of average income in a market will sometimes give rise to different market demands depending on how income is distributed among individuals. A simple example helps make this point clear.

EXAMPLE 4-7

Two consumers, **A** and **B**, are in a market for food. Their tastes are identical, and each has the same initial income level, $120 per week. If their individual Engel curves for food are as given by the locus EE′ in Figure 4-26, how will the market demand curve for food be affected if **A**'s income goes down by 50 percent while **B**'s goes up by 50 percent?

The nonlinear shape of the Engel curve pictured in Figure 4-26 is plausible considering that a consumer can eat only so much food. Beyond some point, increases in income should have no appreciable effect on the amount of food consumed. The implication of this relationship is that B's new income ($180 per week) will produce an increase in his consumption (1 kg per week) that is smaller than the reduction in A's consumption (2 kg per week) caused by A's new income ($60 per week).

What does all this say about the corresponding individual and market demand curves for food? Identical incomes and tastes give rise to identical individual demand curves, denoted D_A and D_B in Figure 4-27. Adding D_A and D_B horizontally, we get the initial market demand curve, denoted D. The nature of the individual Engel curves tells us that B's increase in demand will be smaller than A's reduction in demand following the shift in income distribution. Thus, when we add the new individual demand curves (D'_A and D'_B), we get a new market demand for food (D') that lies to the left of the original demand curve.

The dependence of market demands on the distribution of income is important to bear in mind when the government considers policies to redistribute income. A policy that redistributes income from rich to poor, for example, is likely to increase demand for goods like food and reduce demand for luxury items, such as jewellery and foreign travel.

Demand in many other markets is relatively insensitive to variations in the distribution of income. In particular, the distribution of income is not likely to matter much in markets in which individual demands tend to move roughly in proportion to changes in income.

Engel curves at the market level are schedules that relate the quantity demanded to the average income level in the market. The existence of a stable relationship between average income and quantity demanded is by no means assured for any given product because of the distributional complication just discussed. In particular, note that we cannot construct Engel curves at the market level by simply adding individual Engel curves horizontally. Horizontal summation works as a way of generating market demand curves from individual demand curves because all consumers in the market face the same market price for the product. But when incomes differ widely from one consumer to another, it makes no sense to hold income constant and add quantities across consumers.

As a practical matter, however, reasonably stable relationships between various aggregate income measures and quantities demanded in the market may nonetheless exist. Suppose such a relationship exists for the good X and is as pictured by the locus EE' in Figure 4-28, where Y denotes the average income level of consumers in the market for X, and Q denotes the quantity of X. This locus is the market analog of the individual Engel curves discussed earlier.

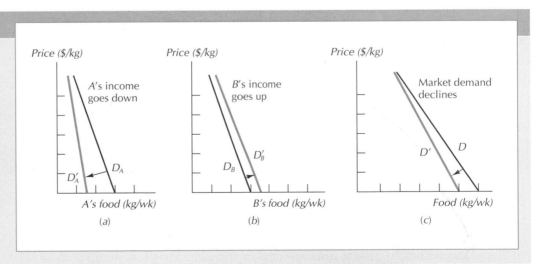

FIGURE 4-27

Market Demand Sometimes Depends on the Distribution of Income
A given increase in income produces a small demand increase for B (b); an income reduction of the same size produces a larger demand reduction for A (a). The redistribution from A to B leaves average income unchanged but reduces market demand (c).

Price ($/kg) · A's income goes down · D'_A · D_A · A's food (kg/wk) · (a)

Price ($/kg) · B's income goes up · D'_B · D_B · B's food (kg/wk) · (b)

Price ($/kg) · Market demand declines · D' · D · Food (kg/wk) · (c)

FIGURE 4-28

An Engel Curve at the Market Level
The market Engel curve tells what quantities will be demanded at various average levels of income.

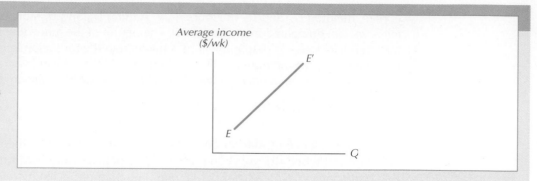

FIGURE 4-29

Engel Curves for Different Types of Goods
(a) This good has income elasticity = 1, and a linear Engel curve passing through the origin. Doubling income from M_0 to $2M_0$ hence doubles quantity demanded from Q_0 to $2Q_0$. (b) These Engel curves show that consumption increases more than proportionally to income for luxuries and less than proportionally for necessities. It *falls* as income increases for an interior good.

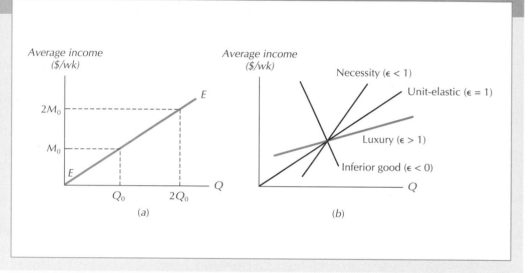

If a good exhibits a stable Engel curve, we may then define its *income elasticity of demand*, a formal measure of the responsiveness of purchase decisions to variations in the average market income. Denoted ϵ, it is given by a formula analogous to the one for price elasticity:[5]

$$\epsilon = \frac{\Delta Q/Q}{\Delta Y/Y} \qquad (4.5)$$

where Y denotes average market income and ΔY is a small change therein.

Goods for which a change in income produces a less than proportional change in the quantity demanded, with prices constant, thus have an income elasticity less than 1. Such goods are called *necessities*, and their income elasticities must take on a value $\epsilon < 1$. Food is a commonly cited example. *Luxuries* are those goods for which $\epsilon < 1$. Common examples are expensive jewellery and foreign travel. Inferior goods are those for which $\epsilon < 0$. Goods for which $\epsilon = 1$ will have Engel curves that are straight lines through the origin, as pictured by the locus *EE* in Figure 4-29a. The market Engel curves for luxuries, necessities, and inferior goods, where these exist and are stable, are pictured in Figure 4-29b.

---

[5]In calculus terms, the corresponding formula is $\epsilon = (Y/Q)\ [dQ(Y)/dY]$.

The income elasticity formula in Equation 4.5 is easier to interpret geometrically if we rewrite it as

$$\epsilon = \frac{Y}{Q} \frac{\Delta Q}{\Delta Y}. \tag{4.6}$$

The first factor on the right side of Equation 4.6 is simply the ratio of income to quantity at a point along the Engel curve. It is the slope of the line from the origin (a ray) to that point. The second factor is the reciprocal of the slope of the Engel curve at that point. If the slope of the ray exceeds the slope of the Engel curve, the product of these two factors must be greater than 1 (the luxury case). If the ray is less steep, ϵ will be less than 1 but still positive, provided the slope of the Engel curve is positive (the necessity case). Thus, in distinguishing between the Engel curves for necessities and luxuries, what counts is not the slopes of the Engel curves themselves but how they compare to the slopes of the corresponding rays from the origin. Finally, if the slope of the Engel curve is negative, ϵ must be less than zero (the inferior good case).[6]

Application: Forecasting Economic Trends

If the income elasticity of demand for every good and service were 1, the composition of GNP would be completely stable over time (assuming that technology and relative prices remained unchanged). The same proportion would be devoted to food, travel, clothing, and indeed to every other consumption category.

As the entries in Table 4-5 show, however, the income elasticities of different consumption categories differ markedly. And therein lies one of the most important applications of the income elasticity concept, namely, forecasting the composition of future purchase patterns. Ever since the industrial revolution in the West, real purchasing power per capita has grown at roughly 2 percent per year. Our knowledge of income elasticity differences enables us to predict how consumption patterns in the future will differ from the ones we see today.

TABLE 4-5

Income Elasticities of Demand for Selected Products*

Good or service	Income elasticity
Automobiles	2.46
Furniture	1.48
Restaurant meals	1.40
Water	1.02
Tobacco	.64
Gasoline and oil	.48
Electricity	.20
Margarine	−.20
Pork products	−.20
Public transportation	−.36

*These estimates come from H. S. Houthakker and Lester Taylor, *Consumer Demand in the United States*: Analyses and Projections, 2d ed., Cambridge, MA: Harvard University Press, 1970; L. Taylor and R. Halvorsen, "Energy Substitution in U.S. Manufacturing," *Review of Economics and Statistics*, November 1977; H. Wold and L. Jureen, *Demand Analysis*, New York: Wiley, 1953.

[6]Note that an inferior good also satisfies the definition of a necessity.

If income elasticities and relative prices remained constant, then a growing share of consumers' budgets would be devoted to goods like restaurant meals and automobiles, whereas ever smaller shares would go to tobacco, fuel, and electricity. Similarly, the absolute amounts spent per person on margarine, pork products, and public transportation would be smaller in the future than they are today. Even if preferences and prices change, such projections provide a useful benchmark.

4.9 CROSS-PRICE ELASTICITIES OF DEMAND

Cross-price elasticity of demand The percentage change in the quantity of one good demanded that results from a 1 percent change in the price of another good.

The quantity of a good purchased in the market depends not only on its price and consumer incomes but also on the prices of related goods. *Cross-price elasticity of demand* is the percentage change in the quantity demanded of one good caused by a 1 percent change in the price of another. More generally, for any two goods, X and Z, the cross-price elasticity of demand may be defined as follows:[7]

$$\eta_{Q_X \bullet P_Z} \equiv \eta_{XZ} = \frac{\Delta Q_X / Q_X}{\Delta P_Z / P_Z},\qquad(4.7)$$

where ΔQ_X is a small change in Q_X, the quantity of X, and ΔP_Z is a small change in P_Z, the price of Z. η_{XZ} measures how the quantity demanded of X responds to a small change in the price of Z.

Unlike the elasticity of demand with respect to a good's own price (the *own-price elasticity*), which in the standard case is never greater than zero, the cross-price elasticity may be either positive or negative. X and Z are defined as *complements* if $\eta_{XZ} < 0$. If $\eta_{XZ} > 0$, they are *substitutes*. Thus, a rise in the price of ham will reduce not only the quantity of ham demanded, but also, because ham and eggs are complements, the demand for eggs. A rise in the price of coffee, in contrast, will tend to increase the demand for tea. Estimates of the cross-price elasticity of demand for selected pairs of products are shown in Table 4-6.

EXERCISE 4-7

Would the cross-price elasticity of demand likely be positive or negative for the following pairs of goods: (a) apples and oranges, (b) airline tickets and automobile tires, (c) computer hardware and software, (d) pens and paper, (e) pens and pencils?

TABLE 4-6

Cross-Price Elasticities for Selected Pairs of Products*

Good or service	Good or service with price change	Cross-price elasticity
Butter	Margarine	+.81
Margarine	Butter	+.67
Natural gas	Fuel oil	+.44
Beef	Pork	+.28
Electricity	Natural gas	+.20
Entertainment	Food	−.72
Cereals	Fresh fish	−.87

*From H. Wold and L. Jureen, *Demand Analysis*, New York: Wiley, 1953; L. Taylor and R. Halvorsen, "Energy Substitution in U.S. Manufacturing," *Review of Economics and Statistics*, November 1977; E. T. Fujii et al., "An Almost Ideal Demand System for Visitor Expenditures," *Journal of Transport Economics and Policy*, 19, May 1985, 161–171; and A. Deaton, "Estimation of Own- and Cross-Price Elasticities from Household Survey Data," *Journal of Econometrics*, 36, 1987: 7–30.

[7]In calculus terms, the corresponding expression is given by $\eta_{XZ} = (P_Z / Q_X)(dQ_X / dP_Z)$. In Appendix 4A, we examine substitutes and complements in more detail.

WHY WOULD A SHARP DECREASE IN RENTAL HOUSING RATES CAUSE A DECREASE IN DEMAND FOR HAMBURGER HELPER?

We normally don't think particularly hard about shelter and Hamburger Helper as *substitutes*, with a positive cross-price elasticity of demand. And it is certainly possible that they could be complements on this measure, for *some* families. Understanding income and substitution effects helps us organize our thinking about the impact of price changes on consumption behaviour. Here, we can reasonably assume that rent represents a significant proportion of a household's expenditure each period. For simplicity, let us also assume that ground beef and Hamburger Helper are perfect complements: a fixed proportion of ground beef meals will be made with Hamburger Helper. Hamburger Helper is unlikely to be a *direct* (or *net*) complement of shelter.[8]

The most likely explanation stems from the fact that the decline in rental rates increases real income by an appreciable amount. Then if ground beef is an inferior good, less ground beef—and therefore less Hamburger Helper—will be consumed. Another possibility, of course, is that hamburger is a normal good, but the demand for shelter is highly price-elastic. In this event, a *higher* proportion of income would be spent on shelter after the drop in rental rates, leaving less to purchase ground beef, Hamburger Helper, and other goods. To test your understanding of the logic underlying these stories, give two situations in which a drop in rents could cause an *increase* in demand for Hamburger Helper, so that shelter and Hamburger Helper would be *complements*.

One of the best ways of becoming better economic naturalists is to practise tracing the interconnections between seemingly *un*connected goods, in terms of income and substitution effects. We may not be able to discover the single correct explanation without further empirical research, but we can at least narrow down the possibilities.

SUMMARY

- Our focus in this chapter was on how individual and market demands respond to variations in prices and incomes. To generate a demand curve for an individual consumer for a specific good *X*, we first trace out the price-consumption curve in the standard indifference curve diagram. The PCC is the line of optimal bundles observed when the price of *X* varies, with both income and preferences held constant. We then take the relevant price-quantity pairs from the PCC and plot them in a separate diagram to get the individual demand curve.

- The income analogue to the PCC is the income-consumption curve, or ICC. It too is constructed using the standard indifference curve diagram. The ICC is the line connecting optimal bundles traced out when we vary the consumer's income, holding preferences, and relative prices constant. The Engel curve is the income analogue to the individual demand curve. We generate

it by retrieving the relevant income-quantity pairs from the ICC and plotting them in a separate diagram.

- Normal goods are those the consumer buys more of when income increases, and inferior goods are those she buys less of as income rises.

- The total effect of a price change can be decomposed into two separate effects: (1) the substitution effect, which denotes the change in the quantity demanded that results because the price change makes substitute goods seem either more or less attractive, and (2) the income effect, which denotes the change in quantity demanded that results from the change in real purchasing power caused by the price change. The substitution effect always moves in the opposite direction from the movement in price: price increases (reductions) always reduce (increase) the quantity

---

[8]Net and gross complements and substitutes are defined and discussed in Section 4A.7 of Appendix 4A, immediately following this chapter.

demanded. For normal goods, the income effect also moves in the opposite direction from the price change, and thus tends to reinforce the substitution effect. For inferior goods, the income effect moves in the same direction as the price change, and thus tends to undercut the substitution effect.

- The fact that the income and substitution effects move in opposite directions for inferior goods suggests the theoretical possibility of a Giffen good, one for which the total effect of a price increase is to increase the quantity demanded. There have been no fully documented examples of the existence of Giffen goods, and in this text we adopt the convention that in the standard case, all goods are demanded in smaller quantities at higher prices. Giffen goods are analyzed in Appendix 4A.

- Goods for which purchase decisions respond most strongly to price tend to be ones that have large income and substitution effects that work in the same direction. For example, a normal good that occupies a large share of total expenditures and for which there are many direct or indirect substitutes will tend to respond sharply to changes in price. For many consumers, housing is a prime example of such a good. The goods least responsive to price changes will be those that account for very small budget shares and for which substitution possibilities are very limited. For most people, salt has both of these properties.

- There are two equivalent techniques for generating market demand curves from individual demand curves. The first is to display the individual curves graphically and then add them horizontally. The second method is algebraic and proceeds by first solving the individual demand curves for the respective Q values, then adding those values, and finally solving the resulting sum for P.

- A central analytical concept in demand theory is the price elasticity of demand, a measure of the responsiveness of purchase decisions to small changes in price. Formally, it is defined as the percentage change in quantity demanded that is caused by a 1 percent change in price. Goods for which the absolute value of elasticity exceeds 1 are said to be elastic; those for which it is less than 1, inelastic; and those for which it is equal to 1, unit elastic.

- Another important relationship is the one between price elasticity and the effect of a price change on total expenditure. When demand is elastic, a price reduction will increase total expenditure; when inelastic, total expenditure falls when the price goes down. When demand is unit elastic, total expenditure remains constant, as a (small) reduction in price is exactly offset by the increase in quantity demanded.

- The value of the price elasticity of demand for a good depends largely on four factors: substitutability, budget share, direction of income effect, and time. (1) Substitutability. The more easily consumers may switch to other goods, the more elastic demand will be. (2) Budget share. Other factors being the same, goods accounting for a large share of total expenditures will have greater income effects. (3) Direction of income effect. Other factors being the same, inferior goods will tend to be less elastic with respect to price than are normal goods. (4) Time. Habits and existing commitments limit the extent to which consumers can respond to price changes in the short run. Price elasticity of demand will tend to be larger, the more time consumers have to adapt.

- Changes in the average income level in a market will generally shift the market demand curve. The income elasticity of demand for a good X is defined analogously to its price elasticity. It is the percentage change in quantity demanded that results from a 1 percent change in income. Goods whose income elasticity of demand exceeds zero are called normal goods; those for which it is less than zero are called inferior; those for which it exceeds 1 are called luxuries; and those for which it is less than 1 are called necessities. For normal goods, an increase in income will shift market demand to the right; and for inferior goods, an increase in income will shift demand to the left. For some goods, the distribution of income, not just its average value, is an important determinant of market demand.

- The cross-price elasticity of demand is a measure of the responsiveness of the quantity demanded of one good to a small change in the price of another. Formally, it is defined as the percentage change in the quantity demanded of one good that results from a 1 percent change in the price of the other. If the cross-price elasticity of demand for X with respect to the price of Z is positive, X and Z are substitutes; and if negative, they are complements. In remembering the formulas for the various elasticities—own price, cross-price, and income—many people find it helpful to note that each is the percentage change in an effect divided by the percentage change in the associated causal factor.

- Appendix 4A (immediately following the chapter) examines a number of additional topics in demand theory, including the constant-elasticity demand curve, the segment-ratio method of calculating elasticity, arc-elasticity, the income-compensated demand curve, Giffen goods, the price-consumption curve and demand elasticity, the Hicks-Allen-Slutsky equation, net and gross substitutes and complements, and using income-elasticities of demand.

1. Why does the quantity of salt demanded tend to be unresponsive to changes in its price?

2. Why is the quantity of automobiles demanded much more responsive than salt is to changes in price?

3. Draw Engel curves for both a normal good and an inferior good.

4. Give two examples of what are, for most students, inferior goods.

5. Can the price-consumption curve for a normal good ever be downward sloping?

6. To get the market demand curve for a standard marketed good, why do we add individual demand curves horizontally rather than vertically?

7. Summarize the relationship between price elasticity, changes in price, and changes in total expenditure.

8. Why don't we measure the responsiveness of demand to price changes by the slope of the demand curve instead of using the more complicated expression for elasticity?

9. For a straight-line demand curve, what is the price elasticity at the revenue-maximizing point? Where is the revenue-maximizing point?

10. Do you think an education at a specific university has a high or low price (tuition) elasticity of demand?

11. How can changes in the distribution of income across consumers affect the market demand for a product?

12. If you expected a long period of declining GNP, what kinds of companies would you choose to invest in?

13. *True or false*: For a budget spent entirely on two goods, an increase in the price of one will necessarily decrease the consumption of both, unless at least one of the goods is inferior. Explain.

14. Mike spends all his income on tennis balls and basketball tickets. His demand curve for tennis balls is elastic. *True or false*: If the price of tennis balls rises, he consumes more tickets. Explain.

15. *True or false*: If each individual in a market has a straight-line demand curve for a good, then the market demand curve for that good must also be a straight line. Explain.

16. Suppose your budget is spent entirely on two goods: bread and butter. If bread is an inferior good, can butter be inferior as well?

*17. *True or false*: If Zelda's demand curve for cubic zirconium nose rings is perfectly inelastic over a certain price range, then over this price range the nose rings are necessarily an *inferior* good for her. Explain your answer, using a diagram.

*18. *True or false*: For a rational consumer facing given relative prices, it is possible for a good X to be a necessity over a lower income range and a luxury over a higher income range. Explain your answer, using a diagram.

*19. *True or false*: For a rational consumer beginning on a given indifference curve, it is possible for a good X to be a necessity at one set of relative prices and a luxury at different relative prices as income increases. Explain your answer, using a diagram.

*20. *True or false*: For a rational consumer beginning on a given indifference curve, it is possible for X to be a normal good at one set of relative prices and an inferior good at different relative prices as income increases. Explain your answer, using a diagram.

*21. *True or false*: For a rational consumer facing given relative prices, it is possible for the income consumption curve to move *vertically* upward or *horizontally* leftward as income increases. Explain your answer, using a diagram.

*22. *True or false*: With relative prices given, it is impossible for a good to be inferior at all income levels. Explain your answer, using a diagram.

*23. *True or false*: If X is a normal good in a two-good (X and Y) world, then from an initial equilibrium, holding money income and P_X constant, it is possible for the demand for X to decrease if the price of Y (P_Y) increases *or* if P_Y decreases. Explain your answer, using a diagram.

*24. *True or false*: If X is a normal good in a two-good (X and Y) world, then from an initial equilibrium, holding money income and P_X constant, it is possible for the demand for X to increase if the price of Y (P_Y) increases *or* if P_Y decreases. Explain your answer, using a diagram.

*25. *True or false*: In a two-good (X and Y) world, relative to an initial equilibrium position, it is possible (holding other determinants unchanged) for a decrease in P_Y to cause an increase in demand for X while a decrease in P_X causes a decrease in demand for Y, so that at this point Y is a complement of X while X is a substitute for Y. Explain your answer, using a diagram.

1. Sam spends $6 per week on orange juice and apple juice. Orange juice costs $2 per cup while apple juice costs $1 per cup. Sam views 1 cup of orange juice as a perfect substitute for 3 cups of apple juice. Find Sam's optimal consumption bundle of orange juice and apple juice each week. Suppose the price of apple juice rises to $2 per cup, while the price of orange juice remains constant. How much additional income would Sam need to afford his original consumption bundle?

2. Bruce has the same income and faces the same prices as Sam, but he views 1 cup of orange juice as a perfect substitute for 1 cup of apple juice. Find Bruce's optimal consumption bundle. How much additional income would Bruce need to afford his original consumption bundle when the price of apple juice doubles?

3. Maureen has the same income and faces the same prices as Sam and Bruce, but Maureen views 1 cup of orange juice and 1 cup of apple juice as perfect complements. Find Maureen's optimal consumption bundle. How much additional income would Maureen need to afford her original consumption bundle when the price of apple juice doubles?

4. The market for lemonade has 10 potential consumers, each having an individual demand curve $P = 101 - 10Q_i$, where P is price in dollars per cup and Q_i is the number of cups demanded per week by the ith consumer. Find the market demand curve using algebra. Draw an individual demand curve and the market demand curve. What is the quantity demanded by each consumer and in the market as a whole when lemonade is priced at $P = \$1$ per cup?

5. a. For a demand curve $P = 60 - .5Q$, find the elasticity at $P = 10$.

   b. If the demand curve shifts parallel to the right, what happens to the elasticity at $P = 10$?

6. Consider the demand curve $Q = 100 - 50P$.

   a. Draw the demand curve and indicate which portion of the curve is elastic, which portion is inelastic, and which portion is unit elastic.

   b. Without doing any additional calculation, state at which point of the curve expenditures on the goods are maximized, and then explain the logic behind your answer.

7. Suppose the demand for crossing the Chargem Bridge is given by $Q = 10,000 - 1000P$, where P is in $/car and Q is the number of cars per day.

   a. If the toll (P) is $2/car, how much revenue is collected daily?

   b. What is the price elasticity of demand at this point?

   c. Could the bridge authorities increase their revenues by changing their price?

   d. The Crazy Canuck Lines, a ferry service that competes with the Chargem Bridge, begins operating hovercrafts that make commuting by ferry much more convenient. How will this affect the elasticity of demand for trips across the Chargem Bridge?

8. Consumer expenditures on safety are thought to have a positive income elasticity. For example, as incomes rise, people tend to buy safer cars (large cars with side air bags), they are more likely to fly on trips rather than drive, they are more likely to get regular health tests, and they are more likely to get medical care for any health problems the tests reveal. Is safety a luxury or a necessity?

9. Professors Adams and Brown make up the entire demand side of the market for summer research assistants in the economics department. If Adams's demand curve is $P = 50 - 2Q_A$ and Brown's is $P = 50 - Q_B$, where Q_A and Q_B are the hours demanded by Adams and Brown, respectively, and P is in dollars per hour, what is the market demand for research hours in the economics department?

10. Suppose that at a price of $400 per ticket, 300 tickets are demanded to fly from Montreal to Vancouver. Now the price rises to $600 per ticket, and 280 tickets are still demanded. Assuming the demand for tickets is linear, find the price elasticities at the quantity-price pairs (300, 400) and (280, 600).

11. The monthly market demand curve for calculators among engineering students is given by $P = 100 - Q$, where P is the price per calculator in dollars and Q is the number of calculators purchased per month. If the price is \$30, how much revenue will calculator makers get each month? Find the price elasticity of demand for calculators at this point. What should calculator makers do to increase revenue?

**12. What price maximizes total expenditure along the demand curve $P = 27 - Q^2$? What are the values for Q and the price elasticity of demand at this price? How would your answers change if instead the demand curve was $P = 27 - 2\sqrt{Q}$?

13. A hot dog vendor faces a daily demand curve of $Q = 1800 - 15P$, where P is the price of a hot dog in cents and Q is the number of hot dogs purchased each day.

    a. If the vendor has been selling 300 hot dogs each day, how much revenue has he been collecting?

    b. What is the price elasticity of demand for hot dogs at this level of sales?

    c. The vendor decides that he wants to generate more revenue. Should he raise or lower the price of his hot dogs?

    d. At what price would he achieve maximum total revenue?

14. Rank the absolute values of the price elasticities of demand at the points *A, B, C, D,* and *E* on the following three demand curves.

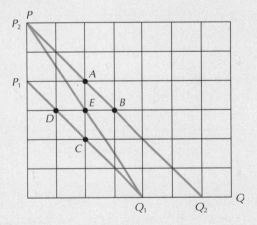

15. Draw the probable Engel curves for the following goods: food, European vacations, and Cheapo brand sneakers at \$9.99 per pair.

16. Is the cross-price elasticity of demand likely positive or negative for the following pairs of items?

    a. Tennis rackets and tennis balls

    b. Peanut butter and jelly

    c. Hot dogs and hamburgers

*17. In 2008, *X* costs \$3/unit and 400 units are sold. That same year, a related good Y costs \$10/unit and 200 units are sold. In 2009, *X* still costs \$3/unit but only 300 units are sold, while 150 units of Y are sold at \$12/unit. Other things unchanged, if the demand for *X* is a linear function of the price of Y, what is the cross-price elasticity of demand for *X* with respect to Y when P_Y is \$10/unit?

*18. Smith cannot tell the difference between rice and wheat and spends all her food budget of \$24 per week on these foodstuffs. If rice costs \$3/kg, draw Smith's price-consumption curve for wheat and the corresponding demand curve.

*19. Repeat the preceding problem on the assumption that rice and wheat are perfect, one-for-one complements.

*20. Suppose your local espresso bar makes the following offer: People who supply their own half-litre carton of milk get to buy a cup of cappuccino for only $1.50 instead of $2.50. Half-litre cartons of milk can be purchased in the adjacent convenience store for $.50. In the wake of this offer, the quantity of cappuccino sold goes up by 60 percent and the convenience store's total revenue from sales of milk exactly doubles.

   a. *True or false*: If there is a small, but significant, amount of hassle involved in supplying one's own milk, it follows that the value of the price elasticity of demand for cappuccino is exactly −3. Explain.

   b. *True or false*: It necessarily follows that demand for the convenience store's milk is elastic with respect to price. Explain.

**21. Based on the situation described in Example 4-3 on page 123, with the price of gas $P_G = \$1/L$ and monthly expenditure of $48 on gas and car washes, do the following:

   a. Give the equations for: (i) the demand function for car washes, $W = f(P_W)$; (ii) the derivative of the demand function, dW/dP_W; (iii) the own-price elasticity of demand for car washes, $\eta = (P_W/W)(dW/dP_W)$; (iv) the inverse demand function, $P_W = f^{-1}(W)$; (v) the slope of the demand function, dP_W/dW; and (vi) the demand for gas (in L/mo) as a function of the price of car washes, $G = g(P_W)$.

   b. Calculate: (i) the values for W, dW/dP_W, η, and G when $P_W = \$2/$car wash and when $P_W = \$4/$car wash; (ii) the values for P_W and dP_W/dW when $W = 2$ and $W = 4$ car washes per month.

   c. Is the demand for car washes elastic or inelastic? At what price of car washes would the elasticity of demand be −1, or unitary?

*22. *True or false*: In Figure 4-1 on page 112, a doubling of both money income *and* the price of the composite commodity would leave the price-consumption curve and the demand curve unchanged. Explain your answer using a diagram.

**23. Mongo, a musician who consumes beans (*B*) and the composite commodity (*Y*), has the following utility function:

$$U = BY^2.$$

His money income each period is $180, and the composite commodity has a price of $1 per unit.

   a. With beans on the horizontal axis, construct Mongo's price-consumption curve (PCC). In a second diagram directly below the first one, construct his demand curve for beans.

   c. If the price of the composite commodity doubles with his money income unchanged, show how this change affects his PCC and his demand curve for beans.

*24. In Figures 4-7 and 4-8 on pages 117 and 118, respectively, show on the *vertical* axes the income, substitution, and total effects of the specified price change. In Figures 4-9, 4-10, and 4-12, on pages 119, 120, and 122, respectively, show the income, substitution, and total effects on *both* axes.

ANSWERS TO IN-CHAPTER EXERCISES

4-1. On Nancy's original budget, B_0, she consumes at bundle *A*. On the new budget, B_1, she consumes at bundle *D*. (To say that *D* has 1.5 pairs of bindings per year means that she consumes three pairs of bindings every two years.) The substitution effect of the price increase (the movement from *A* to *C*) is zero. To purchase the original bundle, Nancy would now need $P_S S + P_B B = 200(4) + 400(2) = \$1600$.

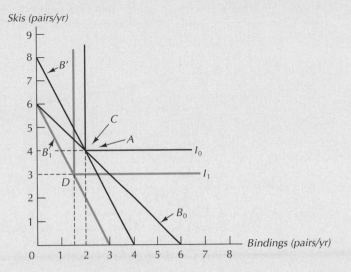

4-2. The income effect, substitution effect, and total effects are all zero because the price change does not alter Pam's optimal consumption bundle. She will still consume at point A. She is neither better off nor worse off if the price of a commodity she did not consume initially (that is, tea) increases.

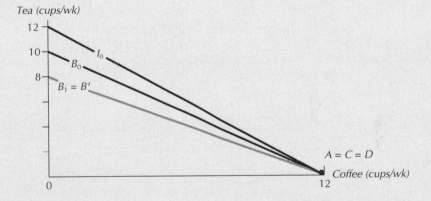

4-3. The formulas for D_1 and D_2 are $P = 16 - 2Q_1$ and $P = 8 - 2Q_2$, respectively. For the region in which $0 \leq P \leq 8$, we have $Q_1 = 8 - (P/2)$ and $Q_2 = 4 - (P/2)$. Adding, we get $Q_1 + Q_2 = Q = 12 - P$, for $0 \leq P \leq 8$. For $8 \leq P \leq 16$, the market demand curve is the same as D_1, namely, $P = 16 - 2Q$.

4-4. First, we need to rearrange the representative consumer demand curve $P = 120 - 60Q_i$ to have quantity alone on one side:

$$Q_i = 2 - \frac{1}{60}P.$$

Then we multiply by the number of consumers, $n = 30$,

$$Q = nQ_i = 30Q_i = 30(2 - \frac{1}{60}P) = 60 - \frac{1}{2}P.$$

Finally, we rearrange the market demand curve $Q = 60 - \frac{1}{2}P$ to have price alone on one side, $P = 120 - 2Q$, to return to the slope-intercept form.

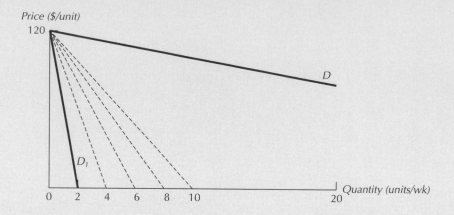

4-5. Since the slope of the demand curve is -1, we have $\eta = -P/Q$. At $P = 24$, $Q = 8$, and so $\eta = -P/Q = \frac{-24}{8} = -3$.

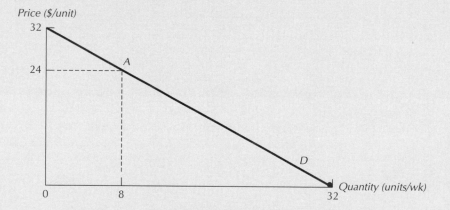

4-6. Elasticity when $P = \$4$/sq m is $-\frac{1}{3}$, so that at that price, demand is inelastic and a price reduction will reduce total expenditure. At $P = \$4$/sq m, total expenditure is $\$48$ per week, which is more than the $\$39$ per week of total expenditure at $P = \$3$/sq m.

4-7. Substitutes, such as a, b, and e, have positive cross-price elasticity (an increase in the price of one good raises quantity demanded of the other good). Complements, such as c and d, have negative cross-price elasticity (an increase in the price of one good lowers quantity demanded of the other good).

Appendix 4A

ADDITIONAL TOPICS IN DEMAND THEORY

4A.1 THE CONSTANT-ELASTICITY DEMAND CURVE

The demand curves discussed so far have been linear demand curves, which have the property that they become more inelastic as we move down the demand curve. Not all demand curves have this property, however; on the contrary, there are demand curves for which price-elasticity can remain constant or even rise with movements down the demand curve. The constant-elasticity demand curve is the name given to a demand curve for which elasticity does not vary with price and quantity. The linear demand curve has the general form $Q = A - BP$, or equivalently $P = a - bQ$, where $a = A/B$ and $b = 1/B$. The constant-elasticity demand curve is instead written

$$Q = KP^{\eta}, \text{ or equivalently } P = kQ^{1/\eta}, \tag{4A.1}$$

where $k = (1/K)^{1/\eta}$ is a positive number, and η is the constant price-elasticity of demand. The specific values of k and η determine the exact shape and position of the demand curve.[1] If $\eta = 0$, then $P^{\eta} = 1$, and hence $Q = K$, a constant. This is the case of the vertical (or perfectly inelastic) demand curve. In the *standard case*, η is negative: a 1 percent *increase* in price *(P)* causes an η percent *decrease* in quantity demanded *(Q)*.

An example with $k = 2$ and $\eta = -1$ is pictured in Figure 4A-1. Let us examine some points on the curve pictured in Figure 4A-1 and verify that they do indeed have the same price-elasticity. Consider first the point $P = 2$, $Q = 1$, and calculate price-elasticity as the product of the ratio P/Q and the reciprocal of the slope of the demand curve. To calculate the slope of the demand curve, we need to calculate the ΔQ that occurs in response to a very small ΔP near the point (1, 2). Suppose, for example, we use a price

---

[1]Using the formal definition of elasticity, it is easy to show that the elasticity at any price-quantity pair along this demand curve is η:

$$\text{Price-elasticity of demand} = \frac{P}{Q} \cdot \frac{dQ(P)}{dP} = \frac{P}{KP^{\eta}} \cdot \eta KP^{\eta-1} = \eta.$$

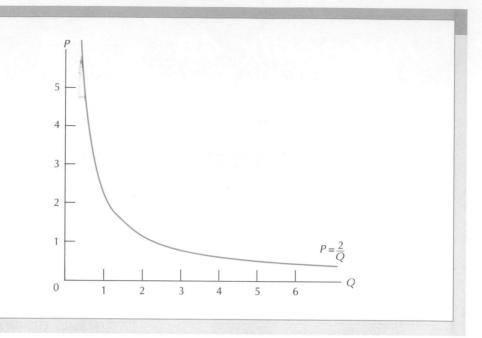

change of $+.001$. If $P = 2.001$, we can solve from the demand curve (that is, from the equation $P = 2/Q$) to get the corresponding $Q = 2/2.001 = .9995$. Thus $\Delta Q = .9995 - 1 = 2.0005$, and the slope of the demand curve at $(1, 2)$ may be calculated as $\Delta P/\Delta Q$, or $.001/(-.0005) = -2$. The reciprocal of the slope is $-1/2$, and so the price-elasticity of demand is $(P/Q)(1/\text{slope}) = 2(-1/2) = -1$.

Consider now the point $(2, 1)$. Again using a ΔP of $.001$, we get a new Q of $2/1.001 = 1.998$, or a ΔQ of $-.002$. Thus the slope of the demand curve at $(2, 1)$ is $.001/(-.002) = -1/2$, and its reciprocal is -2. The price-elasticity of demand at $(2, 1)$ is therefore $(1/2)(-2)$, or again -1.

EXERCISE 4A-1

Try several other points along the demand curve in Figure A4-1 and verify that the price elasticity in every instance is equal to -1. (The answer at the end of the appendix uses the points $(.5, 4)$ and $(4, .5)$, and again takes $\Delta P = .001$.)

The demand curve given by $P = k/Q$ is a special case of the constant-elasticity demand curve called the *constant-expenditure demand curve*. At every point along such a demand curve, total expenditure is given by the product $PQ = k$, where k is again a positive constant. Thus, unlike the case of the straight-line demand curve, here people spend exactly the same amount when price is high as they do when price is low. Someone who spends her entire allowance on compact discs each month, for example, would have a constant-expenditure demand curve for compact discs. The constant k would be equal to the amount of her allowance.

As we saw in Appendix 3A, a consumer with a Cobb-Douglas function of the form $U = X^a Y^b$ and money income M will have constant-expenditure demand functions for *both* X and Y. The demand functions will have the form $X = aM/(a + b)P_X$ or $P_X = aM/(a + b)X$ and $Y = bM/(a + b)P_Y$ or $P_Y = bM/(a + b)Y$.

As we move downward along any constant-elasticity demand curve ($P = kQ^{1/\eta}$), the fall in the ratio P/Q is exactly counterbalanced by the rise in the reciprocal of the slope. An *elastic* constant-elasticity demand curve with $|\eta| > 1$ has the property that a price cut will always increase total expenditures. For an inelastic one with $|\eta| < 1$, in contrast, a price cut will always reduce total expenditures.

4A.2 THE SEGMENT-RATIO METHOD

The price-elasticity at a given point along a straight-line demand curve may be given one other useful geometric interpretation. Suppose we divide the demand curve ACE into two segments AC and EC, as shown in Figure 4A-2. The price elasticity of demand at point C, denoted η_C, will then be equal to the ratio of the two segments:[2]

$$\eta_C = \frac{AC}{EC} = \frac{OF}{AF} = \frac{OG}{EG} \qquad (4A.2)$$

Equation A.4.2 is called the *segment-ratio method* for calculating price elasticity of demand.

Knowing that the price-elasticity of demand at any point along a demand curve is the ratio of two line segments greatly simplifies the task of making quantitative statements about it. Consider the linear demand curve shown in the top panel of Figure 4A-3. At the midpoint of that demand curve (point M), for example, we can see at a glance that the value of price-elasticity is -1. One-quarter of the way down the demand curve (point K in Figure 4A-3), the elasticity is -3; three-quarters of the way down (point L), $-\frac{1}{3}$; and so on. The bottom panel of Figure 4A-3 summarizes the relation between position on a straight-line demand curve and the price-elasticity of demand.

There are four important points to notice about Equation 4A-2. First, the *three* line-segment ratios are *all* equal, because of the fact that triangles AFC and CGE are similar.

---

[2]To see why this is so, we can make use of some simple high school geometry. First, note that the reciprocal of the slope of the demand curve in Figure 4A-2 is the ratio EG/GC and that the ratio of price to quantity at point C is GC/FC. Multiplying these two, we get $\eta_C = (EG/GC)(GC/FC) = EG/FC$. Now note that the triangles AFC and CGE are similar, which means that the ratios of their corresponding sides must be equal. In particular, it means that the ratio EG/FC, which we just saw is equal to the price elasticity of demand at point C, must also be equal to the ratio EC/AC. And this, of course, is just the result we set out to establish. Also, by similar triangles, $EC/AC = OF/AF = EG/OG$.

FIGURE 4A-2

The Segment-Ratio Method
The value of price-elasticity at any point is the ratio of the two demand curve segments from that point. At point C, the value of the price elasticity of demand is equal to $EC/AC = OF/AF = EG/OG$.

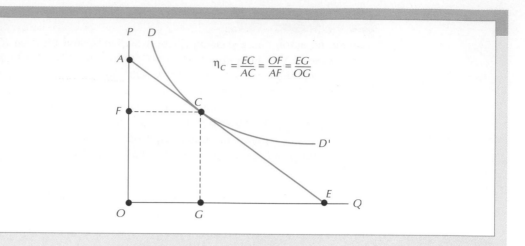

$$\eta_C = \frac{EC}{AC} = \frac{OF}{AF} = \frac{EG}{OG}$$

FIGURE 4A-3

Elasticity at Different Positions Along a Straight-Line Demand Curve
Using the segment-ratio method, the price elasticities at points K, M, and L (top panel) can be calculated in an instant.

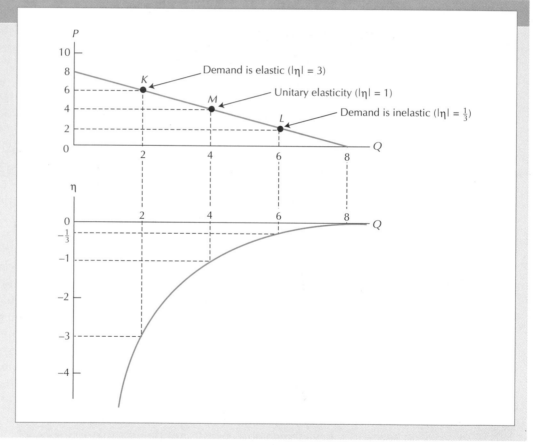

Demand is elastic ($|\eta| = 3$)

Unitary elasticity ($|\eta| = 1$)

Demand is inelastic ($|\eta| = \frac{1}{3}$)

Each of these ratios can be useful, depending on the information we have concerning the demand curve. Second, the fact that the elasticity of demand is *negative* for a downward-sloping demand curve is built into the ratios, since they are all *directed* line segments. Take the middle ratio, OF/AF, for example: OF is *positive* (since it moves *upward* from O to F), while AF is *negative* (since it moves *downward* from A to F). Their *ratio* is therefore *negative*, as is η, the price-elasticity of demand.

APPENDIX 4A: ADDITIONAL TOPICS IN DEMAND THEORY

The third point to observe is that two straight-line demand curves with the same *vertical intercept* but different slopes will have the *same* elasticity at any given *price OF*, since at that price, OF/AF $(= \eta)$ will be the same for both of them. Similarly, linear demand curves with the same *horizontal intercept* but different slopes will have the same elasticity at any given *quantity OG*, since EG/OG will be the same for both. By the same logic, two *parallel* linear demand curves will have the same elasticity at points where they are cut by any given ray from the origin, since at these points the ratios EC/AC will be identical.

The fourth point is perhaps the most significant. We began with the linear demand curve *ACE*. Yet the segment-ratio method can be used to calculate the elasticity at *any* point on *any* demand curve, linear *or* nonlinear! Consider the demand curve *DCD'* in Figure 4A-2, which is tangent to *ACE* at point *C*. What is *its* price-elasticity at *C*? The *same* as that of *ACE*. Its price (*OF*), quantity demanded (*OG*), and slope (*CG/GE*) are the same, and therefore its elasticity (η) is the same! Hence, to find the elasticity at any point *C* on any *nonlinear* demand curve, we simply draw the *tangent ACE* to the demand curve at *C*, and use any of our three ratios to measure the price-elasticity of demand at *C*.

4A.3 THE CONCEPT OF ARC-ELASTICITY

Suppose we start on a hypothetical straight-line demand curve at a point with $P_0 = 10$ and $Q_0 = 100$. Now, let price rise by 10 so that $P_1 = 20$, and suppose the resulting quantity demanded is $Q_1 = 50$. What is the price-elasticity of demand for this good? Suppose we try to answer this question using the formula $\eta = (\Delta Q/Q)/(\Delta P/P)$. It is clear that $\Delta P = 10$ and $\Delta Q = 250$. But what values do we use for P and Q? If we use the initial values, P_0 and Q_0, we get an elasticity of $(-50/100)/(10/10) = (-\frac{1}{2})$. But if we use the new values, P_1 and Q_1, we get an elasticity of $(-50/50)/(10/20) = (-2)$.

Thus, if we reckon price and quantity changes as proportions of their initial values, we get one answer, but if we compute them as proportions of their new values we get another answer. Neither of these answers is incorrect. The fact that they differ is merely a reflection of the fact that the elasticity of demand differs at every point along a straight-line demand curve.

Strictly speaking, the original question ("What is the price-elasticity of demand for this good?") was not well posed. To have elicited a uniquely correct answer, it should have been, "What is the price-elasticity of demand at the point (100, 10)?" or, "What is the price-elasticity of demand at the point (50, 20)?" Economists have nonetheless developed a convention for answering ambiguous questions like the one originally posed. It is to use the formula for the *arc-elasticity of demand*, which is defined by the following equation:

$$\eta = \frac{\Delta Q/[(Q_0 + Q_1)/2]}{\Delta P/[(P_0 + P_1)/2]}. \qquad (4A.3)$$

The arc-elasticity approach thus sidesteps the question of which price-quantity pair to use by using averages of the new and old values. The formula reduces to

$$\eta = \frac{\Delta Q/(Q_0 + Q_1)}{\Delta P/(P_0 + P_1)}. \qquad (4A.4)$$

The arc-elasticity of demand is clearly an imprecise compromise measure. Yet used carefully, it has some strengths relative to the (theoretically) more precise point-elasticity measure. Point-elasticity, again strictly speaking, is defined only for infinitesimal changes around the initial point, or price-quantity pair. The real world, however, has an unfortunate habit of permitting discrete and substantial changes in prices and quantities.

When such *discrete* changes occur, the preconditions for using point-elasticity measures aren't met, and the arc-elasticity measure can provide a reasonable approximate measure, as Exercise 4A-4 indicates.

4A.4 THE INCOME-COMPENSATED DEMAND CURVE

The individual demand curves we constructed in Chapter 4 take into account both the substitution and income effects of price changes. For many applications, such demand curves will be the relevant tool for predicting people's response to a change in price. Suppose, for example, that gasoline prices rise because of a new OPEC agreement. Such a price increase will have both income and substitution effects, and the individual demand curve described earlier will be the appropriate device for predicting a person's response.

There are, however, two reasons, one theoretical and one practical, why this demand curve is not always the appropriate tool for economic analysis. The theoretical reason is that we define *consumer surplus*, and *changes* in consumer surplus as a result of price changes, with real income (in utility terms) held *constant*. Yet as we move downward along an ordinary demand curve, our real income is *increasing*, since at the lower price we could purchase more of *all* goods than we could before. Similarly, as we move upward along the demand curve, our real income falls.

The practical reason arises particularly in the area of tax policy. If the government imposes a sales tax on a particular commodity such as gasoline or cigarettes, the resulting higher price has a direct negative income effect on consumers of that commodity. Yet the tax also generates government *revenues*. Whether these revenues are returned directly to consumers, for example in the form of lower *income* taxes, or are used by government to fund road improvements or lung cancer treatment centres, *positive* income effects will generally result from the disposition or *expenditure* of these tax revenues. The match between those who pay the taxes and those who receive the benefits may not be exact, on a dollar-per-dollar basis. Yet to the extent that the income that is taken away in taxes is returned in some form to those who pay the tax, analysis using the conventional demand curve overstates the loss of income resulting from the tax.

One issue raised by this tax policy example is whether there is a difference to me in the nature of the income effect if the government reduces my other taxes correspondingly (so that my disposable income is unchanged) or if it spends the money in increasing government-financed health service, research and development, educational, or transport system investments. There is one obvious difference, in that I have less *direct* control over *government* expenditures than over how I spend my *personal* budget. At the same time, it is also true that the income effect of government expenditures is real: if the government provides me with additional health services at little or no direct cost, then I do not have to spend my own income on these services, and my real income has risen to that extent. Moreover, if the tax revenues are spent in the provision of *public goods* that could not or would not be provided by the private sector, or if government-financed provision of certain services can be done more efficiently and cost-effectively than by private service-providers, my real income can be *raised* by taxes, once the *full* effects of public fiscal activity are taken into account!

Ordinary vs. Income-Compensated Demand Curves for a Normal Good
The ordinary demand curve plots the substitution and income effects of a price change. The income-compensated demand curve plots only the substitution effect. For a normal good, the income-compensated demand curve will always be steeper than the ordinary demand curve.

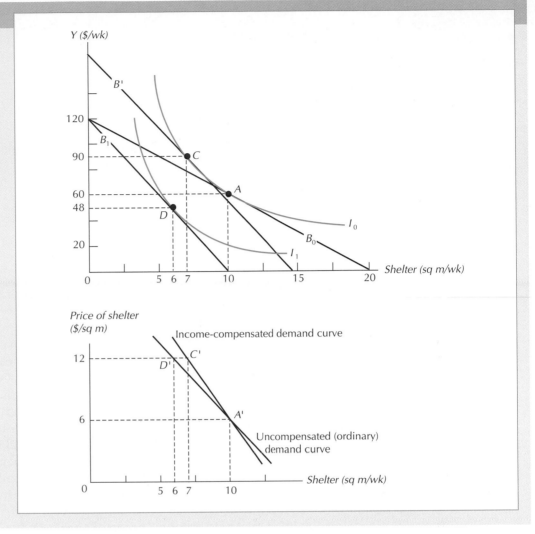

We shall examine this issue more thoroughly in Chapter 18. For now, however, we can say that there are both theoretical and practical reasons to use the income-compensated demand curve, which tells the amounts consumers would buy if they were fully compensated for the income effects of changes in price. To generate this curve for an individual, we simply eliminate the income effect from the total effect of price changes. The top panel of Figure 4A-4 shows the income and substitution effects of an increase in the price of shelter from $6/sq m to $12/sq m for a consumer whose weekly income is $120. The ordinary demand curve for shelter for the individual pictured here would associate a price of $6/sq m with 10 sq m/wk and a price of $12/sq m with 6 sq m/wk. The income-compensated demand curve is always constructed relative to a fixed reference point, the current price. Thus, like the ordinary demand curve, it too associates 10 sq m/wk with the price $6. But with the price $12 it associates not 6 sq m/wk but 7 sq m/wk, which is the amount of shelter the consumer would have bought at $12/sq m if he had been given enough income to remain on the original indifference curve, I_0.

The individual whose responses are described in Figure 4A-4 happens to regard shelter as a normal good, one for which the quantity demanded increases as income rises. For normal goods, the income-compensated demand curve will necessarily be

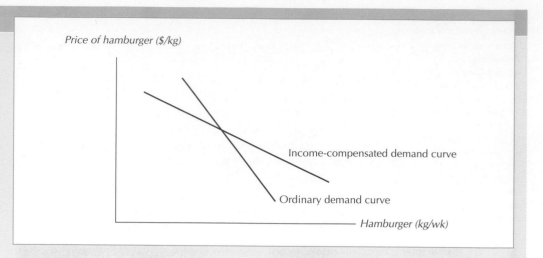

FIGURE 4A-5

Ordinary vs. Income-Compensated Demand Curves for an Inferior Good
The income effect offsets the substitution effect for an inferior good. The income-compensated demand curve, which omits the income effect, is therefore less steep than the ordinary demand curve in the case of an inferior good.

Price of hamburger ($/kg)

Income-compensated demand curve

Ordinary demand curve

Hamburger (kg/wk)

steeper than the ordinary demand curve. In the case of an inferior good, however, the ordinary demand curve will always be the steeper of the two. The relationship between the two demand curves for an inferior good is as pictured in Figure 4A-5.

As a practical matter, the distinction between the two types of demand curves is relevant only for goods for which income effects are large in relation to the corresponding substitution effects. In order for the income effect of a price change for a particular good to be large, it is necessary (but not sufficient) that the good account for a significant share of total expenditures. Many of the individual goods and services we buy, however, account for only a tiny fraction of our total expenditures. Accordingly, for such goods the distinction between the two types of demand curve will be unimportant.

Even for a good that accounts for a large budget share, the income effect of a price change will sometimes be small. If the good is exactly on the boundary between being a normal and being an inferior good, for example, its income-elasticity of demand will be *zero*, and hence so will the income effect, *regardless of the good's share in total expenditure*. If a good on the horizontal axis has zero income-elasticity of demand at all levels of consumption, then the vertical distance between any two given indifference curves will be constant, and the ordinary and income-compensated demand curves for the good will exactly coincide.[3] (You should draw the indifference map for this case, with an initial budget line and the new budget line resulting from a price change, showing the subsitution effect and the income of the price change, to confirm this conclusion).

4A.5 GIFFEN GOODS

A *Giffen good* (a good whose demand curve is upward sloping) is one for which the total effect of a price increase is to increase, not reduce, the quantity purchased. Since the substitution effect of a price increase is always to reduce the quantity purchased, the

---

[3]As an example, the additive utility function $U = a\ln X + bY$ (where a and b are constants) has a zero income-elasticity of demand for X. Note that $MU_X \equiv \partial U/\partial X = a/X$, while $MU_Y \equiv \partial U/\partial Y = b$, so that $MRS \equiv MU_X/MU_Y = a/(bX)$; Y does not appear in the expression for the MRS. Efficiency in consumption requires that $MRS = a/(bX) = P_X/P_Y$, or $X = (aP_Y)/(bP_X)$. Hence, with P_X/P_Y constant, the demand for X is constant *regardless of the level of money income*, and the income-elasticity of demand for X is therefore zero. (See Problem 2 in this Appendix.)

Giffen good must be one whose income effect not only works against but also overpowers the corresponding substitution effect. That is, the Giffen good is a particular kind of inferior good—one so strongly inferior that the income effect is actually larger than the substitution effect.

Alfred Marshall first noted the possibility of a Giffen good in 1895, in the third edition of his classic *Principles of Economics*. He credited Sir Robert Giffen with the observation that for poorer English working-class families, an increase in the price of a major staple food like bread could so lower their real income that "they are forced to curtail their consumption of meat and the more expensive farinaceous foods: and bread being the cheapest food which they can get and will take, they consume more and not less of it." (See Figure 4A-6).

To date, empirical studies concerning the existence of Giffen goods have been rather inconclusive, but Marshall's account does indicate the characteristics a Giffen good would logically have to possess. First, it would not only have to be inferior, but would also have to occupy a large share of the consumer's budget. Otherwise an increase in its price would not create a significant reduction in real purchasing power. (Doubling

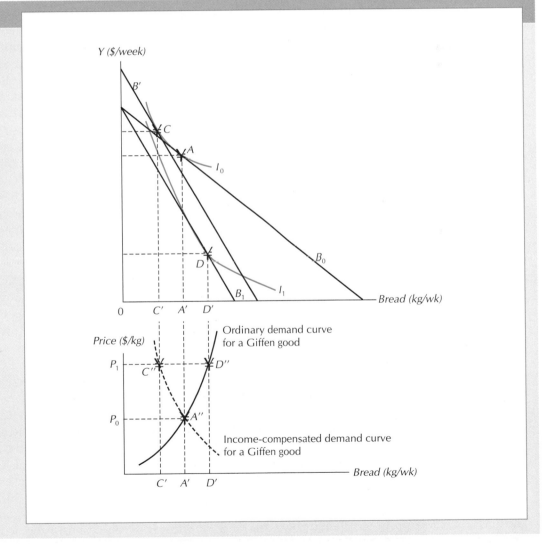

FIGURE 4A-6

Indifference Map and Demand Curve for a Giffen Good
The shift from *A* to *C* (the substitution effect) is swamped by the income effect (*C* to *D*) for a strongly inferior good. Note that the compensated demand curve has the standard downward slope.

the price of keyrings, for example, does not make anyone appreciably poorer.) The second characteristic required of a Giffen good is that it have a relatively small substitution effect, one small enough to be overwhelmed by the income effect.

In practice, it would be unusual for a good to satisfy both properties required of a Giffen good. Most goods, after all, account for only a tiny share of the consumer's total expenditures. Moreover, as noted, the more broadly a good is defined, the less likely it is to be inferior. Finally, inferior goods are often ones for which there are close substitutes. The consumer's tendency to substitute ground sirloin for hamburger, for example, is precisely what makes hamburger tend to be an inferior good.

The Giffen good is an intriguing anomaly, and independently of its empirical importance it is useful for testing our understanding of the subtleties of income and substitution effects. In the remainder of this text, however, we will treat demand curves with the conventional downward slope as "the standard case."

4A.6 THE PRICE-CONSUMPTION CURVE AND THE DEMAND CURVE: SOME EXTENSIONS

In Section 4.1 of Chapter 4, we introduced the price consumption curve (PCC) and showed how the demand curve can be derived from the PCC. This section analyzes that relationship in more detail. We begin with the PCC in Figure 4A-7. Here the consumer has money income (M) of $240 per period, and the price of Y (the composite commodity) is set at $1 per unit. As we move outward along the PCC from A to C to D, we move continuously toward a *lower* price of X (P_X) and toward *higher* indifference curves or levels of satisfaction. The total expenditure along the PCC is a constant $240 per period, but as P_X decreases, our utility necessarily continuously *increases*. This is *also* true of the demand curve for X that we can derive from the PCC: the lower P_X, the higher our utility.

A second feature of the PCC follows from the way in which we construct it. As long as P_X is greater than or equal to zero, no point on the PCC can be higher than point A, since the slope of the budget line from A that intersects the PCC at any point on it equals $-P_X$. Hence if the budget line from A had a *positive* slope, this would imply that P_X was *negative*. Intuitively, the reason that no point on the PCC can be higher than A is that even if the price of X was equal to zero, so that the budget constraint was a horizontal line, point A represents the maximum consumption of Y that is possible with an income of $240 per period.

Third, there are some additional constraints on the form the PCC can take. With a strictly convex indifference map, a single straight line from point A cannot cut the PCC at two separate points, since that would require indifference curves to cross, which—as we saw in Chapter 3—involves a contradiction. (Try drawing this case for yourself, with appropriate indifference curves, to satisfy yourself that this is the case.) It follows that as long as *some X* is being consumed, it is impossible for the PCC to move either vertically *downward* or horizontally to the *left* as the price of X decreases and we move to higher levels of satisfaction.

The fourth important feature of the PCC in Figure 4A-7 is that we can use it directly to determine the price elasticity of demand for X. The reason is simple. Recall from Figure 3-6 of Chapter 3 that at point C, the share of expenditure on Y is given by OC'/OA, and the share of expenditure on X by $C'A/OA$. At D, with a lower price of X, the expenditure share of Y has increased to OD'/OA, while the share of X has decreased to $D'A/OA$. Since total expenditure on X and Y combined ($240) is the same at both C and D, we therefore know that expenditure on X has decreased between C and D, in response to the decrease in the price of X. Over the range of prices between C and D, the demand for X is thus

The PCC and the Elasticity of Demand
Along the price-consumption curve *ACD*, between *A* and *C* the demand curve for *X* is *elastic* ($\eta < -1$): a decrease in the price of *X* causes total expenditure on *X* to *increase*. Between *C* and *D*, the demand for *X* is *inelastic* ($-1 < \eta < 0$): a decrease in the price of *X* causes total expenditure on X to *decrease*.

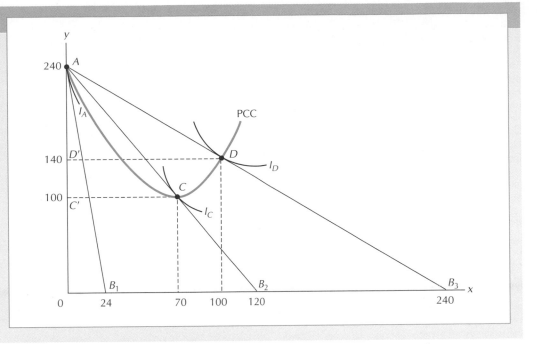

inelastic. In contrast, as P_X decreases between *A* and *C*, expenditure on *X* increases, from zero at *A* to *C'A* dollars per period at *C*. Therefore along *AC*, the demand for *X* is price-*elastic*: a one percent drop in P_X results in a greater than 1 percent increase in quantity demanded.

The price consumption curve and corresponding demand curve *ABCDEFG* of Figure 4A-8 illustrate all of the possibilities that can occur with regard to the price elasticity of demand. These possibilities are detailed in Table 4A-1. Three segments of the PCC and demand curve warrant particular attention. Along *BC*, the horizontal segment of the PCC, a *constant* amount is being spent on *X*, which implies that the price elasticity of demand is *unitary* ($\eta = -1$): on *BC*, a 1 percent decrease in P_X is exactly matched by a 1 percent increase in the quantity of *X* demanded. Along *DE*, the vertical segment of the PCC, the price elasticity of demand for *X* is *zero* ($\eta = 0$). The reduction in P_X as we move from *D* to *E* results in *no change* in the quantity of *X* demanded. Over this range *X* is inferior, and the income and substitution effects are equal in magnitude and opposite in sign. Finally, along *EF*, *X* is a *Giffen good*, and the elasticity of demand is *positive* ($\eta > 0$)! The decrease in P_X from *E* to *F* results in a *decrease* in the quantity of *X* demanded, and

TABLE 4A-1

The Price Consumption Curve and Demand Elasticity in Figure 4A-8

Interval or Point	Price elasticity of demand		As P_X decreases: Quantity of *X*	As P_X decreases: Expenditure P_X *X*
AB	Elastic	$\eta < -1$	increases	increases
BC	Unit-elastic	$\eta = -1$	increases	remains constant
CD	Inelastic	$-1 < \eta < 0$	increases	decreases
DE	Perfectly inelastic	$\eta = 0$	remains constant	decreases
EF	Positively elastic	$0 < \eta$	decreases	decreases
F	Perfectly inelastic	$\eta = 0$	remains constant	decreases
FG	Inelastic	$-1 < \eta < 0$	increases	decreases

A Weird but Possible PCC

The price consumption curve *ABCDEFG* (described in Table 4A-1) has segments where demand for *X* is elastic (*AB*, with $\eta < -1$), unit-elastic (*BC*, with $\eta = -1$), inelastic (*CD* and *FG*, with $-1 < \eta < 0$), perfectly inelastic (*DE*, with $\eta = 0$), and *positively* elastic (the Giffen good segment *EF*, where $\eta > 0$). The sum of expenditures on *X* and the composite commodity *Y* is the same at every point on the PCC and on the demand curve, but the level of satisfaction continually increases as we move out from *A* to *G* along the PCC and (equivalently) to lower prices of *X* on the demand curve.

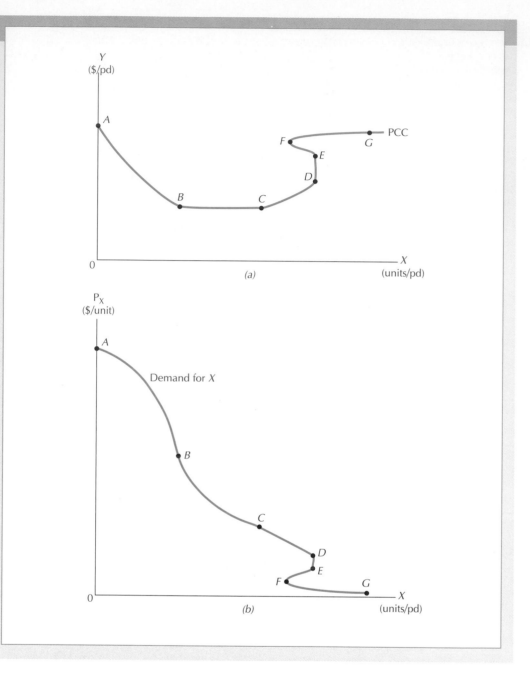

an even greater proportional drop in total expenditure on *X*. Note, however, that the consumer is still better off at *F* than at *E*. The decreased consumption of *X* is more than compensated for by the increased consumption of the composite commodity, and *F* is on a higher indifference curve than is *E*.

4A.7 THE HICKS-ALLEN-SLUTSKY EQUATION

The breaking-down or "decomposition" of the effects of a change in the price of a good into substitution and income effects was first developed by Eugen Slutsky in 1915, and independently rediscovered by J. R. Hicks and R. G. D. Allen in 1934.[4] There are some slight differences between the Slutsky and the Hicks-Allen approaches, but the two are equivalent for infinitesimal price changes.[5] We focus here on the Hicks-Allen version, the one we have used in Chapter 4.

The basic Hicks-Allen-Slutsky equation, describing the effect of a change in the price of a good X on the quantity of X demanded with money income and other prices unchanged, may be written as follows:

$$\frac{\partial X}{\partial P_X} = \left.\frac{\partial X}{\partial P_X}\right|_{U=U_A} - X\frac{\partial X}{\partial M},$$

(4A.5)

where the ∂ symbol represents partial derivatives. (See Figure 4A-9, which depicts a *discrete*—not an infinitesimal—decrease in the price of X, P_X, to facilitate the discussion.)

The left-hand side of the equation refers to the *total* change in the quantity of X demanded as a result of a change in P_X. The first right-hand term refers to the *substitution* effect of the change in P_X. The notation $U = U_A$ indicates that the substitution effect represents the solution to the problem of minimizing the cost of attaining the level of utility at point A, now that P_X has decreased. The budget line B', which is parallel to the new budget line B_1 and tangent to I_A at C, represents this cost-minimizing solution.

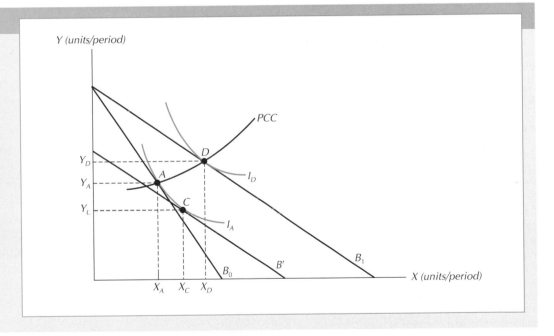

FIGURE 4A-9

The Hicks-Allen-Slutsky Equation: A Decrease in P_X
A decrease in P_X, with X and Y both normal goods and Y a net substitute for X, results here in an *increase* in the quantity purchased of both X and Y. For X, the income and substitution effects are both negative, and work in the same direction to increase the quantity of X purchased. For Y, the substitution effect is positive, while the income effect is negative and stronger.

[4]Eugen Slutsky (1915), "On the Theory of the Budget of the Consumer," in G. J. Stigler and K. E. Boulding (editors), *Readings in Price Theory*, Chicago: Irwin, 1952, 27–56; and J. R. Hicks and R. G. D. Allen, "A Reconsideration of the Theory of Value," *Economica*, February 1934: 52–76, May 1934: 196–219.

[5]The principal difference is that the Hicks-Allen substitution effect holds *utility constant* when a good's price changes, while the Slutsky substitution effect is based on a budget line passing through the *initial consumption point* at the new prices. The Slutsky version of the substitution effect thus generates a higher utility for a price increase *or* a price decrease than the Hicks-Allen substitution effect. Since the *total* effect of a price change is the same in both versions, the Slutsky "income effect" is smaller for a price decrease and larger for a price increase than the Hicks-Allen income effect. As we have noted, however, for infinitesimal price changes, the two approaches converge.

The second right-hand term, $-X \, \partial X/\partial M$, refers to the *income effect* of the decrease in P_X. It represents the solution to the problem of maximizing the increase in utility when the budget line (with the new, lower, P_X) increases from B' to B_1. We can interpret it in intuitive terms as follows. With a budget constraint $M = P_X X + P_Y Y$, a reduction in P_X by \$1/unit *lowers* the cost of purchasing a given (X, Y) bundle by \$$X$: $\partial M/\partial P_X = X$. In *purchasing power* terms, a decrease in P_X is thus equivalent to an increase in money income, while an increase in P_X is equivalent to a decrease in money income. This inverse relationship is shown by the negative sign before the X in the expression for the income effect. The expression $\partial X/\partial M$ is simply the change in expenditure on X associated with a given increase in money income.

With strictly convex indifference curves, the substitution effect is necessarily negative: a decrease in P_X causes an increase in X along I_A, while an increase in P_X results in a decrease in X. The income effect, however, may be positive or negative. It will be negative if X is a normal good with $\partial X/\partial M > 0$, in which case the income effect will reinforce the substitution effect. If X is an inferior good, however, $\partial X/\partial M < 0$, and the income effect will be positive: the income effect of a decrease in P_X is to lower the demand for X, while that of an increase in P_X is to increase the demand for X. With a Giffen good, as we have seen, the income effect outweighs the substitution effect.

As Figure 4A-9 illustrates, a change in P_X also has an effect on the quantity of Y demanded, which is represented in the following equation:

$$\frac{\partial Y}{\partial P_X} = \frac{\partial Y}{\partial P_X}\bigg|_{U=U_A} - X\frac{\partial Y}{\partial M}.$$

(4A.6)

Note that $-X$ also appears in the expression for the income effect in this equation, since the change in purchasing power results from the change in P_X, and hence depends in both equations on the magnitude of X.

As in Equation 4A.5, the income effect $-X \, \partial Y/\partial M$ is negative if Y is a normal good and positive if Y is inferior. With regard to the substitution effect, however, there are two possibilities. If we hold utility constant at the initial level, then as P_X decreases with all other prices constant, the quantity of Y demanded may decrease *or* increase. If we are in a two-good (X and Y) world, or if Y is the composite commodity, then (with strictly convex indifference curves) a decrease in P_X necessarily causes a decrease in the quantity of Y demanded. In this case, we say that X and Y are **net substitutes**. In a world of many goods, a reduction in P_X will still cause an increase in the consumption of X along the initial indifference surface. This increased consumption of X, however, can cause an *increase* in the demand for goods that are commonly consumed together with X. A sharp drop in the price of peanut butter, for example, could cause an increase in the quantity not only of peanut butter but also of jam purchased, holding utility constant, for a consumer who consumed peanut butter and jam in fixed proportions. In this case, we say that peanut butter and jam are **net complements**.

In Chapter 4, we defined substitutes and complements in terms of the *total effect* of a price change: if $\partial Y/\partial P_X > 0$, after accounting for both substitution and income effects, then X is a *substitute* for Y. We will retain that usage. Yet in order to distinguish substitutes on this definition from *net* substitutes, economists often apply the term **gross substitutes** when considering the *total effect* of a price change. Similarly, economists will speak of X and Y as being **gross complements**, rather than simply *complements*, when $\partial Y/\partial P_X < 0$, if there is any danger of ambiguity. Table 4A-2 contains a summary of possible outcomes

Net substitute A good Y is a net substitute for good X if the *substitution* effect of an increase (decrease) in the price of X is an increase (decrease) in the quantity of Y demanded.

Net complement A good Y is a net complement of good X if the *substitution* effect of an increase (decrease) in the price of X is a decrease (increase) in the quantity of Y demanded.

Gross substitute A good Y is a gross substitute for good X if the *total* effect of an increase (decrease) in the price of X is an increase (decrease) in the quantity of Y demanded.

Gross complement A good Y is a gross complement of good X if the *total* effect of an increase (decrease) in the price of X is a decrease (increase) in the quantity of Y demanded.

of a change in P_X. Reading Table 4A-2 takes a bit of practice, but it is straightforward. A plus (+) sign in a cell means that the price of X and the quantity (of X or Y, whichever is being analyzed) move in the *same* direction as a result of the particular effect. A minus (−) sign means that they move in *opposite* directions. As an example, consider the effect of an increase in P_X on the quantity of Y demanded, for the case in Row 2.2.2 of the table with Y inferior and X a net complement of Y. Here the substitution effect has a *minus* sign. The *substitution* effect of an increase in P_X is a *decrease* in the quantity demanded of Y, for which X is a net complement. The *income* effect, however, has a *plus* sign: the increase in P_X, which reduces real income, thereby *increases* the demand for Y, because Y is an inferior good.

Note that the *total* effect of the increase in P_X is *indeterminate*—a question mark (?)—since the substitution and income effects operate in opposite directions. If the substitution effect outweighs the income effect, the total effect will result in X's being a *gross complement* of Y; if the income effect is greater, then X will be a *gross substitute* for Y. Rows 1.2 and 2.1.1 also represent cases where the total effect of a change in P_X is indeterminate. In row 1.2, if the income effect outweighs the substitution effect, X is a *Giffen good*. You should analyze row 2.1.1 with the aid of a few diagrams, to see what determines whether the *total* effect of a change in P_X is positive (so that X is a gross *substitute* of Y) or negative (so that X is a gross *complement* of Y).

TABLE 4A-2

Effects of a Change in P_X on the Quantity Demanded of X and Y

	Good	Substitution effect	Income effect	Total effect
1.	X	$\left.\dfrac{\partial X}{\partial P_X}\right\|_{U=U_0}$	$-X\dfrac{\partial X}{\partial M}$	$\dfrac{\partial X}{\partial P_X}$
1.1	X normal	−	−	−
1.2	X inferior	−	+	?
2.	Y	$\left.\dfrac{\partial Y}{\partial P_X}\right\|_{U=U_0}$	$-X\dfrac{\partial Y}{\partial M}$	$\dfrac{\partial Y}{\partial P_X}$
2.1.1	Y normal, net substitute	+	−	?
2.1.2	Y normal, net complement	−	−	−
2.2.1	Y inferior, net substitute	+	+	+
2.2.2	Y inferior, net complement	−	+	?

4A.8 USING INCOME-ELASTICITIES OF DEMAND

A relationship that we can derive directly from the budget equation is often useful in empirical economic work. We begin with the budget equation for a consumer spending all of her income on only two goods, X and Y, with constant prices P_X and P_Y respectively:

$$P_X X + P_Y Y = M. \qquad (4A.7)$$

When income increases by an amount ΔM, the increase will be spent on X and Y, and so we have

$$P_X \Delta X + P_Y \Delta Y = \Delta M. \qquad (4A.8)$$

We now divide through by ΔM, multiply through by M/M, and multiply the first term on the left-hand side by X/X and the second term by Y/Y, to get

$$\left(\frac{P_X X}{M}\right)\left(\frac{\Delta X}{\Delta M} \cdot \frac{M}{X}\right) + \left(\frac{P_Y Y}{M}\right)\left(\frac{\Delta Y}{\Delta M} \cdot \frac{M}{Y}\right) = 1, \qquad (4A.9)$$

which can be written more simply as

$$s_X \epsilon_X \cdot M + s_Y \epsilon_Y \cdot M = 1, \qquad (4A.10)$$

where s_X and s_Y are the shares of X and Y in total expenditure and $\epsilon_X \cdot M$ and $\epsilon_Y \cdot M$ are their income-elasticities of demand, respectively. Note also that $s_X + s_Y = 1$. This fact enables us to calculate any of the variables if we know any two of the others, including at least one income-elasticity.

EXERCISE 4A-5

Daisy spends all of her flower budget on roses and geraniums. At a point where she is spending 40 percent of her budget on geraniums, her income-elasticity of demand for roses is 2. What is her income-elasticity of demand for geraniums at this point?

QUESTION FOR REVIEW

1. *True or false:* All Giffen goods are inferior. Explain.

PROBLEMS

1. You are given three demand curves: (**I**) $P = 30 - Q$; (**II**) $P = 60 - Q$; and (**III**) $P = 60 - 2Q$.
   a. Graph and label the three demand functions on the *same* diagram.
   b. Using the line-segment method for calculating elasticity, fill in a table with four columns (P, Q, slope, and point-elasticity) for *each* demand curve in the following four cases: (**A**) $P = \$30$/unit; (**B**) $P = \$20$/unit; (**C**) $Q = 15$ units; (**D**) $P = Q$. (You will have 12 rows in total.)
   c. Identify the points where the values for the price elasticity of demand are identical. Comment on your results.

**2. Mike consumes two goods, X and Y, according to the following utility function:

$$U = 10 \ln X + Y.$$

The price of Y, P_Y, is a constant $2 per unit, and initially Mike's money income M is $30 per day and the price of X, P_X, is $1 per unit. (*Hint:* See footnote 3 of this Appendix.)
   a. In the initial situation, how much X and how much Y does Mike consume?

b. If his daily income becomes $40, with prices unchanged, how much X and how much Y does Mike consume?

c. If Mike's daily income is $30, but the price of X becomes $2 per unit, how much X and how much Y does Mike consume?

d. If Mike's daily income is $40, and the price of X becomes $2 per unit, how much X and how much Y does Mike consume?

e. With his daily income at $30, what is the equation for Mike's demand for X, and what is the price elasticity of his demand for X?

f. What is Mike's income-elasticity of demand for X?

**3. Spike consumes X and Y, according to the utility function

$$U = XY^3.$$

His daily income is $16; P_Y, the price of Y is $2 per unit; and initially P_X, the price of X, is $1 per unit.

a. In the initial situation, how many units of X and of Y will Spike consume, and how many utils of satisfaction will he receive, each day?

c. With his income and the price of Y as given, what is the equation for Spike's demand curve for X, and what is its elasticity?

d. By setting Spike's MRS equal to $P_X/P_Y = P_X/2$, solve for the optimal quantity of Y as a function of X, and substitute for Y in Spike's utility function, with utility at the constant level, call it U^0, that you calculated in Part 3a above. Then solve for X as a function of U_0, P_X, and P_Y, to get the formula for the income-compensated demand curve passing through the initial equilibrium point. Compare its elasticity to that of Spike's regular demand curve, as calculated in Part 3b. Interpret your results.

4. *True or false:* If X is a *net substitute* for Y and Y is normal, it is possible for the equilibrium quantity of Y demanded to *increase* if the price of X decreases. Explain your answer with the use of a diagram.

ANSWERS TO IN-APPENDIX EXERCISES

4A-1. First consider the point (.5, 4). If we again let ΔP be .001 so that the new P is 4.001, the resulting Q is 2/4.001 = .499875, which means that ΔQ is −.000125. Price elasticity is therefore equal to $(4/.5)(-.000125/.001) = -1$. Now consider the point (4, .5). If we again let ΔP be .001, so that the new P is .501, the resulting Q is 2/.501 = 3.992, which means that ΔQ is 2.008. Price elasticity is therefore equal to $(.5/4)(-.008/.001) = -1$.

4A-2. (a) The demand curves are $P_C = aM/(a + b)C = .4 (300)/C = 120/C$ and $P_I = bM/(a + b)I = .6(300)/I = 180/I$. With $P_C = $8/meal, he eats 120/8 = 15 Chinese meals per month. With $P_I = $12/meal, he eats 180/12 = 15 Indian meals per month.

(b) With P_C unchanged, Kiefer still consumes 15 Chinese meals per month, spending $120 as before. With $P_I = $3/meal, he eats 180/3 = 60 Indian meals per month, again spending $180.

(c) With $M = $900/month, and $P_I = $3/meal, Kiefer's demand curves become $P_C = aM/(a + b)C = .4(900)/C = 360/C$ and $P_I = bM/(a + b)I = .6(900)/I = 180/I$. With $P_C = $8/meal, he will eat 45 Chinese meals per month. With $P_I = $3/meal, he will eat 180 Indian meals per month. This works out to about 6 Indian meals and 1.5 Chinese meals per day. Kiefer will soon be ready for the "big time"!

4A-3. For $P = $4/unit, we have $4 = 4/\sqrt{Q}$, which yields $Q = 1$ unit, so total expenditure is 4(1) = $4. For $P = $3/unit, we have $3 = 4/\sqrt{Q}$, which yields $Q = 16/9$ units, so total expenditure is $(3)(\frac{16}{9}) = $5.33. So with $\eta = -2$, total expenditure rises with a decrease in price.

4A-4. Using $(P, Q) = (4,1)$, the measured price-elasticity of demand $= (4/1)(-7/9) = -3.111$. With $(P, Q) = (3, 16/9)$, elasticity $= -1.3125$. Using the arc-elasticity formula, elasticity $= [(-7/9)/(25/9)]/(1/7) = -49/25 = -1.96$, instead of -2, or about a 2 percent error. Thus the arc-elasticity measure gives a much closer approximation to the true point-elasticity of demand than do either of the simple elasticity measures, when *discrete* changes in prices and quantities are involved.

4A-5. Substituting into the formula $s_G \epsilon_{G \cdot M} + s_R \epsilon_{R \cdot M} = 1$, with $\epsilon_{R \cdot M} = 2$, $s_G = .4$, and $s_R = 1 - s_G = .6$, we have that Daisy's income elasticity of demand for geraniums $\epsilon_{G \cdot M} = [1 - (.6)(2)]/.4 = -.2/.4 = -.5$: a 1 percent increase in income will lead to a .5 percent decrease in her expenditure on geraniums.

Chapter 5

APPLICATIONS OF RATIONAL CHOICE AND DEMAND THEORIES

Inevitably, some claims for publicly provided social assistance or "welfare" payments involve misrepresentation or fraud. The proportion across Canada has been estimated to be as high as 2 percent of total social assistance payments. Consider a provincial government elected on a platform of "downsizing government" and "ending welfare fraud." As part of their mandate to downsize government, they downsize the welfare fraud investigation unit. Not only does this step reduce government expenditures, but as a result of the increased zeal and productivity of the remaining investigators, the next year witnesses a decline in welfare fraud.

Or does it? Certainly the number of cases of fraud uncovered and investigated has declined. But an alternative explanation is that the total number of cases of potential fraud that can be investigated is roughly proportional to the number of investigators assigned to the detection and documentation of fraud. If a stable proportion of these potential-fraud investigations turn up evidence of *actual* fraud, then the reality is quite different from what the data suggest. With fewer investigators to do the legwork, a larger proportion of cases of actual welfare fraud goes undetected.

Several related misconceptions are at work here. The first is, "If we don't know about it, it's not happening." The second is that "Information is a free good." However, the gathering and production of information consumes resources, particularly when people have a vested interest in concealment. The third related misconception involves treating welfare fraud investigators exclusively in terms of their *cost*, while neglecting the *benefits* that flow from their work. If an additional fraud investigator, costing $80,000 per year, including overhead expenses, can produce annual welfare cost savings of $300,000, then the marginal net "benefit" of laying off that investigator is *minus* $220,000. And this loss is not the end of the story. If laying off fraud investigators increases the likelihood that attempts at welfare fraud will succeed, then we would expect the number of fraudulent claims to increase. Shortsighted downsizing in this case is thus false economy with a vengeance.

CHAPTER PREVIEW

The case of welfare fraud investigation shows the importance of rational choice theory. In this chapter we take up a variety of applications and examples involving the rational choice and demand theories developed in Chapters 3 and 4. We begin with two examples—a gasoline tax and school vouchers—that illustrate how the rational choice model can shed light on important economic policy questions. Next we consider the concept of consumer surplus, a measure of how much the consumer benefits from being able to buy a given product at a given price. And we shall see how the rational choice model can be used to examine how price and income changes affect welfare.

Next on our agenda are some case studies that illustrate the role of price elasticity in policy analysis. Here we examine the effect of a transit fare increase and the effect of liquor taxes on alcohol consumption by heavy drinkers.

Finally, we consider how the rational choice model can be adapted to consider choices that have future consequences.

5.1 USING THE RATIONAL CHOICE MODEL TO ANSWER POLICY QUESTIONS

Many government policies affect not only the incomes that people receive but also the prices they pay for specific goods and services. Sometimes these effects are the deliberate aim of government policy, and on other occasions they are the unintended consequence of policies directed toward other ends. In either case, both common sense and our analysis of the rational choice model tell us that changes in incomes and prices can normally be expected to alter the ways in which consumers spend their money. And as we will see, the rational choice model can yield crucial insights not always available to policy analysts armed with only common sense.

Application: A Gasoline Tax and Rebate Policy

Suppose the Government of Canada determines that a reduction in overall gasoline consumption is desirable, for both environmental and energy-conservation reasons. One method of curtailing gas consumption would be to institute a "conservation surtax" on gasoline. To address concerns that the surtax imposes a hardship on lower-income households, the government decides to use the entire proceeds of the surtax to reduce other taxes. Each individual will therefore receive a lump-sum tax rebate. (Here the term "lump sum" means that the rebate does not vary with the amount of gasoline the individual consumes.) There can still be some distributional effects. A heavy gasoline user will receive a smaller rebate than he has paid in surtax, while pedestrians and cyclists will receive a larger rebate than they have paid in surtax. This bias actually reinforces the objectives of the surtax/rebate policy, by rewarding low gasoline consumption. For simplicity, we shall assume, reasonably, that the costs of administering the policy are negligible.

A critic might ask, "Why bother? If you give *all* the surtax revenues back to people, then they will just go out and spend their rebates on gasoline. Except for the slight redistributive effect you've mentioned, giving the tax proceeds back defeats the purpose of the policy." This argument is incorrect, as illustrated in the example that follows.

Suppose that the current price of gasoline is $1.00/L. A surtax of $.50/L is imposed that results in a $.50 increase in the price of gasoline to consumers.[1] Consider a consumer

---

[1]Recall from Chapter 2 that the rise in equilibrium price will be exactly the same as the tax when the supply curve for gasoline is perfectly horizontal.

whose income is $150 per week, and whose lump-sum tax rebate happens to be *exactly equal* to the amount of gasoline surtax he pays.

This consumer's budget constraint before the imposition of the tax is shown as B_1 in Figure 5-1.[2] On this budget constraint, he chooses bundle C, which contains 58 L/wk of gasoline. His budget constraint with a $1.50/L price of gasoline would be B_2 if he received no rebate. On this budget constraint, he would consume bundle A, which contains only 30 L/wk of gasoline. But how do we find the budget constraint that corresponds to a rebate equal to the amount collected from him in gasoline taxes?

The first step is to note that for any given quantity of gasoline consumed, the vertical distance between budget constraints B_1 and B_2 corresponds to the total amount of tax paid on that amount of gasoline. Thus, at 1 L/wk of gasoline, the vertical distance between B_1 and B_2 would be $.50; at 2 L/wk, it would be $1.00; and so on.

Our next step is to trace out how the consumer's consumption will vary as a function of the size of the rebate. To do this, note that a rebate is like income from any other source, so what we really want to do is to trace out how the consumer responds to changes in income. As we saw in Chapter 4, the appropriate tool for this task is the income-consumption curve, or ICC. Accordingly, we construct the ICC through bundle A, as shown in Figure 5-1.

Now look at bundle D, the point where the ICC through A intersects the original budget constraint B_1. D is the equilibrium bundle on the budget constraint labelled B_3, where the price of gasoline is $1.50/L and the consumer has $(150 + R)/wk = $84/wk of income. This means that if we give the consumer a rebate of $R = $18/wk, he will consume bundle D and pay exactly $18/wk in gasoline taxes. Note, however, that D lies well to the left of the original bundle C, which means that, despite the rebate, the

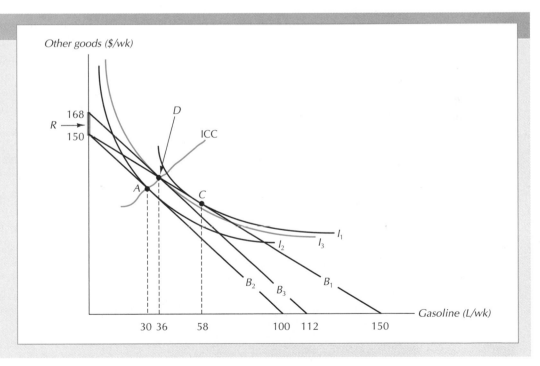

FIGURE 5-1

A Gasoline Tax and Rebate
The tax rotates the original budget constraint from B_1 to B_2. The rebate shifts B_2 out to B_3. The rebate does not alter the fact that the tax makes gasoline 50 percent more expensive relative to all other goods. The consumer shown in the diagram responds by consuming 22 L/wk less gasoline.

[2]The equation for B_1 is $Y = 150 - G$, for B_2 is $Y = 150 - 1.5G$, and for B_3 is $Y = 168 - 1.5G$, where G is gasoline (L/wk) and Y is all other goods ($/wk).

consumer substantially curtails his gasoline consumption. If gasoline is a normal good, the effect of the rebate is to offset partially the income effect of the price increase. It does nothing to alter the substitution effect.

Note also that as a result of the tax-and-rebate policy, the individual is on a *lower* indifference curve than he was initially (I_3 is lower than I_1). The reason is that his indifference curves as drawn give no weight to the benefits of gasoline conservation and reduced environmental damage. If the consumer attaches utility to these effects, then (in a *three*-dimensional diagram) he could view himself as better off. From a *social* perspective, however, by assumption overall welfare has increased even if some individuals disagree with the policy.

Application: School Vouchers

A perennial policy concern in any country is how to ensure the best quality of primary and secondary education for students. One proposal for improving the quality of schooling assumes that a major problem with the present public school system is that it behaves too much like a complacent monopoly. Under this proposal, the present system would be replaced by a *voucher system*, under which each school-age child would be given a voucher that could be applied toward the costs of tuition at *any* school of the family's choosing. Proponents of vouchers argue that tuition-charging private schools cannot currently compete on an equal footing with public schools offering free tuition. According to them, the voucher system would introduce more competition into the market for educational services, and improve educational quality.

We will develop a simple model of the present system and the voucher alternative, and then consider some additional factors that need to be taken into account in appraising their relative merits. Under the present system, with some variations from province to province, public school costs are paid for out of provincial and municipal tax revenues, which are collected from all households, those with and without school-age children. Children are entitled to free public education. If a family chooses to send its children to a private school, it does not receive a refund of an equivalent portion of its taxes, any more than those without children do. It can, however, deduct certain of these private schooling costs—up to a specified maximum amount—in calculating its taxable income.

The present system is depicted in Figure 5-2. We will assume that educational "quality" can be measured, and that it is a linear function of the number of dollars spent on educating a child. Consider a family with after-tax income equal to OB, which it can spend on educational quality for its children or on all other goods. If we set the value of a unit of educational quality at \$1, and the family pays *all* of its children's educational expenses, then the family's budget constraint BCD has a slope of -1, and $OB = OD$. Childless families and individuals will consume at point B, because they have no such educational expenses. Suppose that families are legally required to provide a minimum quality of education (equal to OA) for each child. Then a family with one child will consume along CD, spending at least OA on educational quality and at most AC on other goods. A family with three children will be required to spend at least 3 OA on education, with the balance for other goods. The burden on the family of meeting this socially imposed requirement out of its own resources could represent a genuine hardship. For this reason, and because an educated population is viewed as a social good, the public school system provides OA per child in tuition-free education. For a one-child family, the budget constraint with free public schooling now becomes BE_1F. Along E_1F, the family could augment the quality of education for their child by expenditures on

FIGURE 5-2

With OA in "free" education and marginal tax rate CC'/CE_1, a single-child family's after-tax budget constraint is $BE_1C'D'$. Three families have the same after-tax income OB, *before* their schooling decision. Family 1 chooses E_1, in public school, Family 3 chooses E_3 in private school, and Family 2 is indifferent between E_1 (public school) and E_2 (private school).

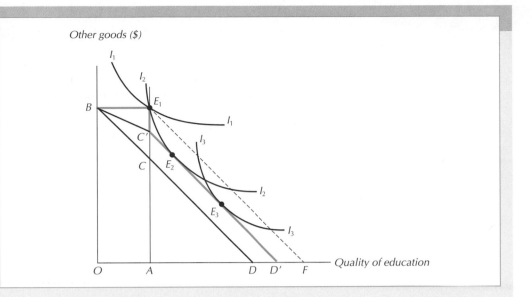

computers, learning software, individual tutoring, extracurricular programs, and the like. We have drawn E_1F as a dotted line, however, to highlight the difference between public schooling and tuition-charging private schooling in a way that is most favourable to voucher system proponents.

We will assume that educational quality is obtainable only during the school day, and that if the family wants more "quality" for its child, it must withdraw her from the public school system and enrol her in a private school. If the maximum tax-deductible education expenditure equals OA, and the family's marginal tax rate over this range is given by CC'/CE_1, then the net *after-tax* cost of OA $(= CE_1)$ of private schooling is only $CE_1 - CC' = C'E_1$. If the family wants to spend more than OA on schooling, it can purchase additional educational quality along $C'D'$. It receives no tax deduction for school expenditures above the maximum deductible amount OA, however, and so the slope of $C'D'$ is -1. The budget constraint is thus $BE_1 C'D'$. Families with *higher* marginal tax rates, typically, higher-income families, pay less in after-tax dollars for private schooling than those with *lower* marginal tax rates, under the present system.

Consider three families, with identical marginal tax rates and after-tax income before making their schooling decision, and indifference curves I_1, I_2 and I_3, respectively. Family 1 reaches its highest indifference curve at E_1, in the public school system. Family 2 is indifferent between consuming at E_1 or E_2, while Family 3 will opt for private school at E_3.

What effect will a voucher system have? Suppose that each family receives one voucher per child equal in value to OA, and there is no tax deduction for additional educational expenditures. As Figure 5-3 shows, the new budget constraint facing all three families will be BE_1F, and E_1F will have a slope of -1. Family 1 will remain at E_1. If educational quality is a normal good, however, then both Family 2 and Family 3 will spend *more* than before on educational quality, at E_2' and E_3' in the private school system. The total additional cost of the voucher system to taxpayers is the *sum* of the amounts $C'E_1$ for *all* children who were in private schools under the *present* system. Establishment of the voucher system involves no additional cost to taxpayers if a child switches from a public to a private school, since that child was already consuming OA in resources under the present system.

FIGURE 5-3

Educational Choice under a Voucher System
Under the voucher system, the budget constraint becomes BE_1F. Family 1's expenditure is unchanged at E_1, but Family 2 and Family 3 both spend *more* on education, at E'_2 and E'_3 respectively.

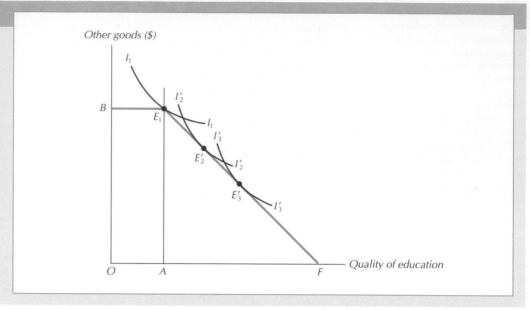

The voucher system therefore increases the taxes paid by childless individuals and families with children in public schools under the present system, and lowers the taxes of those (typically higher-income) families who choose to send their children to private schools under the present system. The voucher system also increases the incentive for families to shift their children from public to private schools. Family 2, which was initially indifferent between public and private schooling, opts for private schooling under the voucher system, as will any single-child family whose MRS at E_1 is greater than 1. Total expenditures on schooling should therefore increase under a voucher system.

Voucher Systems: Further Considerations

The benefit of the voucher system, according to its proponents, is that increased competition will increase educational productivity. This is theoretically possible, and if it were to occur then it could result in cost savings and greater educational quality for the same expenditure of resources. However, we have no universally agreed-upon, one-dimensional measure of what constitutes educational *quality*. What we do have is a wide range of diverse educational *objectives*, and a range of interrelated programs intended to achieve them. The objectives include the development of gross and fine motor skills; a balance of intellectual, physical, and emotional growth; mastery of the three Rs and a number of specific subject areas; general cultural knowledge; familiarity with computers; the ability to work independently, and to cooperate with others; the capacity to benefit from cultural diversity; leadership; and the capacity for critical and creative thought. If we have no real measure of educational quality, then it is even less clear that a doubling of expenditures per student will double the quality of education. We can imagine one school with a stable of polo ponies, and another with ten used soccer balls. The former costs much more per student than the latter, but each program will contribute, in different ways, to the achievement of various educational objectives. If polo costs 500 times more per student than soccer, is its marginal contribution to educational quality 500 times greater than that of soccer? Merely posing the question in this way should suggest the difficulty with our initial assumptions that quality can be measured in a unidimensional way, and that a doubling of educational expenditure doubles quality. Yet the conclusions of our basic model require this assumption.

We can still explore whether the voucher system is likely to be more cost effective, efficient, or productive. Let us note briefly some of the ways in which the shift to a voucher system could *reduce* the efficiency of the system. If private schools are "for-profit" institutions, then from each dollar spent on education a proportion will have to go to the school's owners as profits. Interest costs will also be higher for the private schools, because the risk premium on a loan to a private borrower is greater than on one to government. The public school system may also be able to achieve more economies in the purchase of textbooks, course materials, and school supplies through the use of its mass buying power. Costs of curriculum research and development can likewise be spread over a larger student population. Such costs are hence lower per student within the present system. If the costs of providing *equivalent* education are higher under the voucher system, for the above reasons, then vouchers also increase the risk of school bankruptcies, and the costs of disruption of service they entail.

These added costs of the voucher system relative to the present system are fairly clear. Other potential costs are less obvious. The rise of a whole host of diverse private schools increases what economists call problems of uncertainty and *asymmetric information* (which we will examine further in Chapter 6 and Appendix 6A). The new schools know what sort of education they are providing. Parents, however, do not, and it is generally costly for them to discover the quality of education being provided by a particular school, except after the fact. Impressive brochures and websites are relatively cheap to produce; quality education, however measured, is generally not. One theoretical possibility would be to shift children from school to school until a good match was achieved, but this search process would involve major transactions costs for parents, children, and the educational system as a whole.

If there is greater diversity among schools under the voucher system, then the costs of teacher accreditation, core curriculum approval, and overall educational quality control are also likely to increase. Consider Family 1 in Figure 5-3. They would prefer to spend *less* than OA on their child's education. Fortunately, under the voucher program, the Creative Home Educational Adventure Program school (CHEAP, for short) offers a curriculum where the school's students work entirely at home, surfing the net, "to develop their independent study skills." CHEAP receives OA per child, and then provides a cash rebate to the parents, so that they can purchase "necessary educational supplies," and a diploma at the end of the year. The CHEAP campus is a post office box. Needless to say, CHEAP is not likely to be in business for long, but it will cost resources to put them out of business.

The voucher system, at least in the form outlined here, would also have consequences for children with special needs and their families. In the present system, OA is not the amount that is actually devoted to each public school student, but rather the average amount per student. Students with special needs or disabilities tend to require more than the average amount OA, while other students require less than OA. Under the voucher system, each student receives precisely OA, and the averaging-out that is an integral part of the present system is no longer possible. Students without disabilities benefit from the change, since they received less than OA before, but students with disabilities and their families are disadvantaged under the voucher system, since they receive fewer resources than they do under the present system.

This brief sketch of a few of the potential problems with school voucher systems is not intended to suggest that the voucher idea is not worth exploring further. We will be examining the question of the appropriate balance between public and private provision of goods and services in several subsequent chapters, including Chapter 12 and Chapter 18. Yet it should suggest that policy ideas that look good on paper may have unintended consequences when they are translated into the real world, unless they are implemented with forethought and care.

5.2 CONSUMER SURPLUS

When exchange takes place voluntarily, economists generally assume that it makes all participants better off. Otherwise they would not have engaged in the exchange. It is often useful to have a dollar measure of the extent to which people benefit from a transaction. Such a measure, called *consumer surplus,* is particularly important for the purpose of evaluating potential government programs. It is relatively straightforward to measure the costs of, say, building a new road. But an intelligent decision about whether to build the road cannot be made without a reliable estimate of the extent to which consumers will benefit from it.

Using Demand Curves to Measure Consumer Surplus

The easiest way to measure consumer surplus involves the consumer's demand curve for the product. In both panels in Figure 5-4, the line labelled *D* represents an individual's demand curve for shelter, which sells for a market price of $3/sq m. In panel (*a*), note that the most the consumer would have been willing to pay for the first square metre of shelter is $14. Since shelter costs only $3/sq m, this means that he obtains a surplus of $11 from his purchase of the first square metre of shelter each week. The most he would be willing to pay for the second square metre of shelter is $13, so his surplus from the purchase of that unit will be smaller, only $10. His surplus from the third unit is smaller still, at $9. For shelter or any other perfectly divisible good, the height of the individual's demand curve at any quantity represents the most

FIGURE 5-4

The Demand Curve Measure of Consumer Surplus
(*a*) The height of the demand curve at any quantity measures the most the consumer would be willing to pay for an extra unit of shelter. That amount minus the market price is the surplus he gets from consuming the last unit. (*b*) The total consumer surplus is the shaded area between the demand curve and the market price.

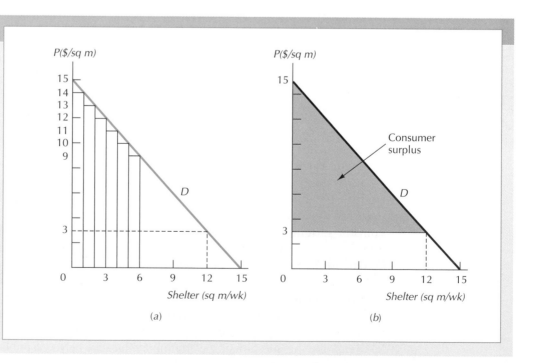

the consumer would pay for an additional unit of it.[3] In this example, if we subtract the purchase price of $3/sq m from that value and sum the resulting differences for every quantity out to 12 sq m/wk, we get roughly the shaded area shown in panel (b). (If we use infinitesimal increments along the horizontal axis, we get exactly the shaded area.) This shaded area represents the individual's consumer surplus from the purchase of 12 sq m/wk of shelter.

EXAMPLE 5-1

An individual's demand curve for gasoline is given by $P = 2.50 - \frac{1}{16}Q$, where P is the price of gasoline ($/L), and Q is the quantity she consumes (L/wk). If the individual's weekly income is $1000 and the current price of gasoline is $.50/L, by how much will her consumer surplus decline if an oil import restriction raises the price to $.75/L?

At a price of $.50/L, she consumes only 32 L of gasoline per week, which amounts to less than 2 percent of her income. The income effect of the price increase is therefore likely to be insignificant, so we can use the demand curve approximation to measure her consumer surplus before and after the price increase. (See footnote 3.) Figure 5-5 displays her demand curve. Her consumer surplus at the price of $.50/L is given by the area of the triangle AEF in Figure 5-5, $CS = \frac{1}{2}(2.5 - .5)(32) = \$32/wk$. Following the price increase, her consumption falls from 32 to 28 L/wk, and her surplus shrinks to the area of the triangle ACD, $CS' = \frac{1}{2}(2.5 - .75)(28) = \$24.50/wk$. Her loss in consumer surplus is the difference between these two areas, which is the area of the trapezoid $DCEF$, the shaded region in Figure 5-5. This area is equal to $CS - CS' = 32 - 24.50 = \$7.50/wk$.

FIGURE 5-5

The Loss in Consumer Surplus from an Oil Price Increase
At a price of $.50/L, consumer surplus is given by the area of triangle AEF. At a price of $.75/L, consumer surplus shrinks to the area of triangle ACD. The loss in consumer surplus is the difference in these two areas, which is the area of the shaded region.

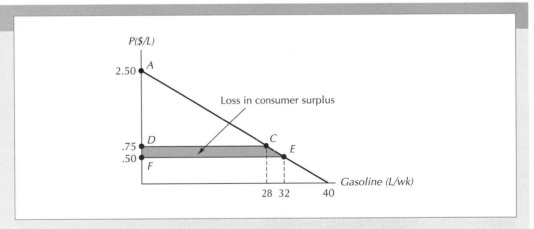

---

[3]These statements about willingness to pay are literally true only if the demand curve we are talking about is an income-compensated demand curve like the one discussed in Appendix 4A. If the demand curve shown were an ordinary demand curve of the sort we have been using, it would tell us that the consumer would be willing to buy 1 unit at a price of $14, 2 units at a price of $13, and so on. From this it would not be strictly correct to conclude that, having already paid $14 for the first unit, the consumer would then be willing to spend an *additional* $13 for the second unit. If the income effect of the demand for the good is positive, the fact that the consumer is now $14 poorer than before means that he would be willing to pay somewhat less than $13 for the second unit. But since income effects for most goods are small, it will generally be an acceptable approximation to measure consumer surplus using the ordinary demand curve. In a widely cited article, Robert Willig has argued that the demand curve method will almost always yield an acceptable approximation of the true value of consumer benefits. See R. Willig, "Consumer Surplus without Apology," *American Economic Review, 66,* 1976: 589–597. Additional measures of consumer surplus are analyzed in Appendix 5A.

By how much would consumer surplus shrink in Example 5-1 if the price of gasoline rose from $.75/L to $1/L?

Application: Two-Part Pricing

Economic reasoning suggests that a voluntary exchange will take place between a buyer and a seller if and only if that exchange makes both parties better off. On the buyer's side, we may say that willingness to exchange depends on the buyer's expectation of receiving consumer surplus from the transaction.

Economic theory does not tell us very much about how the gains from exchange will be divided between the buyer and the seller. Sometimes the buyer will be in an advantageous bargaining position, enabling her to capture most of the benefits. Other times the buyer's options will be more limited, and in these cases, her consumer surplus is likely to be smaller. Indeed, as Economic Naturalist 5-1 illustrates, the seller can sometimes design a pricing strategy that captures *all* the consumer surplus.

Economic Naturalist 5-1

WHY DO SOME TENNIS CLUBS HAVE AN ANNUAL MEMBERSHIP CHARGE IN ADDITION TO THEIR HOURLY COURT FEES?

Why do many tennis clubs have both annual membership fees and court rental fees?

A suburban tennis club rents its courts for $25 per person per hour. John's demand curve for court time, $P = 50 - \frac{1}{4}Q$, measured in hours per year, is given in Figure 5-6. Assuming there were no other tennis clubs in town, what is the maximum annual membership fee John would be willing to pay for the right to buy court time for $25 per hour?

The answer to this question is the consumer surplus John receives from being able to buy as much court time as he wants at the $25 per hour price. This is equal to the area of triangle *ABC* in Figure 5-6, which is $CS = \frac{1}{2}(50 - 25)100 = \$1250/\text{yr}$. If the club charged a fee higher than that, Mano would be better off not renting any court time at all.

FIGURE 5-6

An Individual Demand Curve for Tennis Court Time
At a price of $25 per hour, John receives $1250 per year (the shaded area) of consumer surplus from renting court time. The maximum annual membership fee the club can charge is $1250.

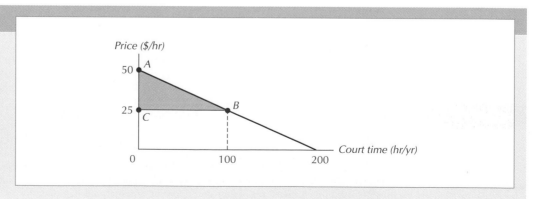

In Economic Naturalist 5-1, how much would the maximum annual membership fee be if the club charged only $20 per hour for court time?

Two-part pricing
Pricing system with a fixed access fee and a charge per unit of a good purchased.

Economic Naturalist 5-1 sheds light on many of the pricing practices we observe throughout the economy. Many amusement parks, for example, charge a fixed admission fee in addition to a charge for each ride. Many telephone companies charge a fixed monthly fee in addition to charges based on actual calls made. And some shopping clubs charge a fixed membership fee for the right to buy items carried in their stores or catalogues. Pricing schemes such as these are often called *two-part pricing*. Their effect is to transfer a portion of the consumer surplus from the buyer of the product to the seller.

Economic Naturalist 5-2

WHY DO SOME AMUSEMENT PARKS CHARGE ONLY A FIXED ADMISSION FEE, WITH NO ADDITIONAL CHARGE EVEN FOR RIDES WITH LONG LINES?

Many amusement parks offer a one-day pass, at a fixed price. This pass includes unlimited access to all rides and attractions in the theme park, the only catch being that on certain rides, waiting lines can be more than an hour long. Given persistent excess demands for some rides at a price of zero, why don't these parks charge an additional fee for each use of their most popular rides?

Economic theory predicts that the price of any good or service will rise in the face of excess demand. Long waiting lines like the ones described above thus pose a challenge for economists. In this case, a possible explanation may be that the people who have to pay for the rides (parents) are different from the ones who demand them (their children). Since their parents are paying, children want to ride the most thrilling rides whether the price is $0 or $5 per ride. At a price high enough to eliminate waiting lines, it would be possible to go on the most popular rides dozens of times a day, and many children would want to do exactly that. Parents could always ration access by saying no, of course. But not many parents look forward to a vacation in which they must spend the entire day saying no to their children. For these parents, this pricing policy is perhaps an ideal solution. It enables them to say to their children, "Go on whichever rides you want, as many times as you want," and then allow waiting lines to perform the essential rationing function.

5.3 OVERALL WELFARE COMPARISONS

The concept of consumer surplus helps us identify the benefits (or costs) of changes that occur in particular markets. Often we will want to assess whether consumers are better or worse off as a result of changes not just in one market but in many. Here too our model of rational choice lets us draw a variety of useful inferences. Consider the following example.

EXAMPLE 5-2

Jones spends all his income on two goods: X and Y. The prices he paid and the quantities he consumed last year are as follows: $P_X = \$10/unit$, $X = 50$ units, $P_Y = \$20/unit$, and $Y = 25$ units. This year P_X and P_Y are both $10/unit, and Jones's income is $750. Assuming his tastes do not change, in which year was Jones better off, last year or this year?

To answer this question, it is helpful to begin by comparing Jones's budget constraints for the two years. To do this, we note first that his income last year was equal to what he spent, namely, $P_X X + P_Y Y = \$1000$. For the prices given, we thus have the budget constraints shown in Figure 5-7a.

In Figure 5-7a, we see that Jones's budget constraint for this year contains the very same bundle he bought last year. Since his tastes have not changed, this tells us he cannot be worse off this year than last. After all, he can still afford to buy the same bundle as before. But our standard assumptions about preference orderings enable us to draw an even stronger inference. In particular, if his indifference curves have the standard smoothly convex shape, we know that an indifference curve—call it I_0—was tangent to last year's budget constraint at the point A in Figure 5-7b. We also know that this year's budget constraint is steeper than last year's, which tells us that part of I_0 must lie inside this year's budget triangle. On I_0, bundle A is equally preferred to bundle C. And because more is better, we know that D is preferred to C. It thus follows that D is preferred to A, and so we know that Jones was able to purchase a bundle of goods this year that he likes better than the one he bought last year. It follows that Jones was better off this year than last.

EXERCISE 5-3

Jacob spends all his income on two goods: X and Y. The prices he paid and the quantities he consumed last year are as follows: $P_X = \$15$/unit, $X = 20$ units, $P_Y = \$25$/unit, and $Y = 30$ units. This year the prices have changed ($P_X = \$15$/unit and $P_Y = \$20$/unit), and Jacob's income is now $900. Assuming his tastes have not changed, in which year was Jacob better off, last year or this year?

Application: The Welfare Effects of Changes in Housing Prices

Consider the following two situations:

1. You have just paid $200,000 in cash for a house. The very next day, the prices of all houses, including the one you just bought, unexpectedly double.

FIGURE 5-7

Budget Constraints for Two Years

(a) If the consumer's budget constraint for this year contains the same bundle he bought last year (bundle A), he will be at least as well off this year as last. (b) If, in addition, relative prices are different in the two years, he will necessarily be able to buy a better bundle this year (bundle D).

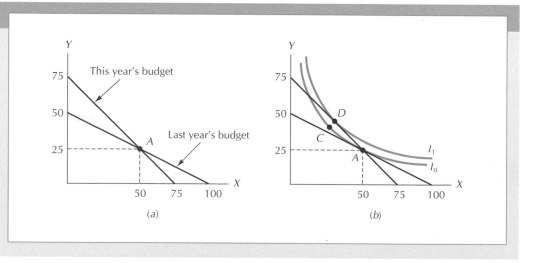

CHAPTER 5: APPLICATIONS OF RATIONAL CHOICE AND DEMAND THEORIES

2. You have just paid $200,000 in cash for a house. The very next day, the prices of all houses, including the one you just bought, unexpectedly fall by half.

In each case, ignoring transactions costs and taxation effects, how does the price change affect your welfare? (Are you better off before the price change or after?)

A class of first-year graduate students in economics was asked these questions. The overwhelming majority responded that you are better off as a result of the price increase in situation 1, but worse off as a result of the price drop in situation 2. Although most students seemed very confident about these two responses, only one turns out to be correct.

To see why, let us first consider the case in which all housing prices double. Suppose your total wealth just before purchasing your house was $400,000. Let the size of your current house correspond to one unit of housing and let the price of other goods (the composite good) be $1 per unit. Your original budget constraint under situation 1 will then correspond to the line labelled B_1 in Figure 5-8. Its vertical intercept, $400,000, is the maximum amount you could have spent on other goods. Its horizontal intercept, 2 units of housing, corresponds to the maximum quantity of housing you could have bought (that is, a house twice as large as your current house). On B_1, the equilibrium at A represents your original purchase. At A, you have 1 unit of housing and $200,000 left for other goods.

After the price of your house doubles, your budget constraint becomes the line labelled B_2 in Figure 5-8. To calculate the vertical intercept of B_2, note that your current house can now be sold for $400,000, which, when added to the $200,000 you had left over after buying your house, yields a maximum of $600,000 available for other goods. The horizontal intercept of B_2 tells us that when the price of housing doubles to $400,000/unit, your $600,000 will buy a maximum of only 1.5 units of housing. Note finally that on B_2 your optimal bundle is C, which contains $H_2 < 1$ units of housing and $O_2 > $200,000 worth of other goods. And since bundle C lies on a higher indifference curve than bundle A, you are better off than before the price increase.

Not surprisingly, when the price of housing goes up, your best response is to buy fewer units of housing and more units of other goods. Note that you are insulated from the harm of the income effect of the price increase because the price increase makes the house you own more valuable.

FIGURE 5-8

Rising Housing Prices and the Welfare of Homeowners
When the price of housing doubles, your budget constraint becomes B_2, which also contains your original bundle A. Because C, the optimal bundle on B_2, lies on a higher indifference curve than A, the effect of the housing price increase is to make you better off.

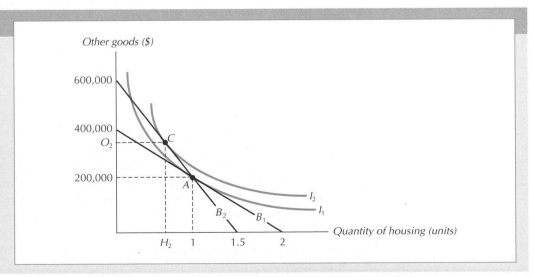

FIGURE 5-9

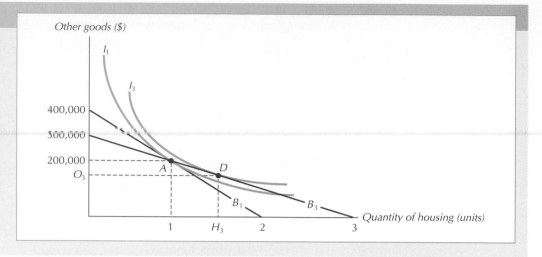

So far, so good. Now let us consider what for many students was the more troubling case—namely, situation 2, in which housing prices fall by half. Again adopting the units of measurement used in situation 1, your budget constraint following the fall in housing prices is the line labelled B_3 in Figure 5-9. To get its vertical intercept, note that sale of your current house will now yield only $100,000, which, when added to the $200,000 you already have, makes a maximum of $300,000 available for the purchase of other goods. To calculate the horizontal intercept of B_3, note that when the price of housing falls to $100,000, your $300,000 will now buy a maximum of 3 units of housing. Given the budget constraint B_3, the best affordable bundle is the one labelled D, which contains $H_3 > 1$ units of housing and $O_3 < 200,000$ units of other goods. As in situation 1, the effect of the relative price change is again to move you to a higher indifference curve. This time, however, your direction of substitution is the opposite of the one in situation 1: because housing is now cheaper than before, you respond by purchasing more units of housing and fewer units of other goods.

In each situation, note that your new budget constraint contains your original bundle, which means that you have to be at least as well off after the price change as before. Note also that in each case the change in relative prices means that your new budget constraint contains bundles that lie beyond your original indifference curve, making it possible to achieve a better outcome in each situation.

Application: A Bias in the Consumer Price Index

The consumer price index (CPI) measures changes in the "cost of living," the amount a consumer must spend to maintain a given standard of living. Published each month by Statistics Canada, the CPI is calculated by first computing the cost of a representative bundle of goods and services during a reference period and then dividing that cost into the current cost of the same bundle. Thus, if it cost $100 to buy the representative bundle in the reference period and $150 to buy the same bundle today, the CPI would be 1.5. Announcing this figure, government spokespersons would explain that it meant the cost of living had increased by 50 percent compared to the reference period.

What the CPI fails to take into account, however, is that when the prices of different goods rise by different proportions, consumers do not generally buy the same bundle of goods they used to buy. Instead, the typical pattern is to substitute away from those goods whose prices have risen the most. By reallocating their budgets in this fashion, consumers are able to escape at least part of the harmful effects of price increases. Because the CPI fails to take substitution into account, it tends to overstate increases in the cost of living.

A simple example using the rational choice model makes this point unmistakably clear. Suppose the only goods in the economy were rice and wheat and that the representative consumer consumed 20 kg/mo of each in the reference period. If rice and wheat each cost $1/kg in the reference period, what will be the CPI in the current period if rice now costs $2/kg and wheat costs $3/kg? The cost of the reference period bundle at reference period prices was $40, while at current prices the same bundle now costs $100. The CPI thus takes the value of $100/$40 = 2.5. But is it really correct to say that the cost of living is now 2.5 times what it was?

To consider an extreme case, suppose our representative consumer regarded rice and wheat as perfect one-for-one substitutes, meaning that her indifference curves are negatively sloped 45° lines. In Figure 5-10, her original bundle is denoted as A and her original indifference curve (which coincides exactly with her original budget constraint) is labelled I_0. Now suppose we ask, how much income would she need in the current period to achieve the same level of satisfaction she achieved in the reference period? At the new prices, the slope of her budget constraint is no longer -1, but $-3/2$. With a budget constraint with this new slope, she could reach her original indifference curve most cheaply by buying the bundle labelled C in Figure 5-10. And since the cost of C at current prices is only $80, we can say that the cost of maintaining the original level of satisfaction is only 2.0, not 2.5 times as great.

FIGURE 5-10

The Bias Inherent in the Consumer Price Index
For this consumer, rice and wheat are perfect substitutes. When the price of each was $1/kg, she bought 20 kg/mo of each in the reference period, for a total expenditure of $40/mo. If the current prices of rice and wheat are $2/kg and $3/kg, respectively, the expenditure required to buy the original bundle is $100/mo. The CPI is the ratio of these two expenditures, $100/$40 = 2.5. But the consumer can attain her original indifference curve, I_0, by buying bundle C, which costs only $80 at current prices. The cost of maintaining the original level of satisfaction is thus only 2.0 times the original level.

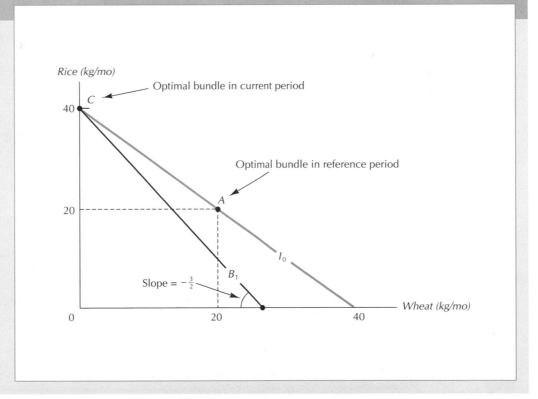

In general, we can say that the extent to which the CPI overstates the cost of living will go up as substitution possibilities increase. The bias will also be larger when there are greater differences in the rates of increase of different prices.

Quality Change: Another Bias in the CPI?

Gathering data on the prices of goods and services might seem like a straightforward task. In practice, however, it is complicated by the existence of discounts, rebates, and other promotional offers in which the actual transaction price may be substantially different from the official list price.

Yet important as they are, accurate price data are not sufficient for estimating changes in the cost of living. We must also account for changes in the quality of what we buy. And this, unfortunately, turns out to be a far more complicated task than measuring changes in prices.

Twenty-five years ago, a hand-held scientific calculator cost $99.95. Now, you can buy a respectable one for $9.95. The price has fallen to a tenth of its former level. But the earlier calculator could perform only 18 functions, while the current one can perform 136 functions. And for less than $99.95, you can now have a programmable hand-held calculator that performs a range of operations that would test the knowledge of a good undergraduate math major.

In the case of automobiles, average automobile prices since the early 1980s have increased at a somewhat higher rate than the Consumer Price Index. Yet at the same time, a number of features that were non-existent, optional, or luxury items then are common or standard now. Airbags, antilock brakes, significantly reduced hydrocarbon and nitrogen oxide emission levels, rear window defrosters, power windows, increased interior room, improved engine performance, increased average fuel economy, greater reliability, crashworthiness, and rust resistance: this is only a partial list of the quality improvements that we now take for granted. If we factor in reasonable estimates of the value of all of these quality changes, then automobile prices have actually risen *less* rapidly than consumer prices generally.

With other goods, there has likely been some *lowering* of quality over time. The replacement of wood flooring by particleboard in housing construction has lowered the rate of increase of housing prices, but has also reduced the strength and durability of the housing stock. A digital wristwatch that keeps accurate time can be obtained for a few dollars, but such wristwatches have become almost disposable items.

One method of dealing with such quality changes is to impute a value to the various product characteristics, and make an adjustment, downward (if there has been an improvement in quality) or upward (in the case of quality deterioration), from the market price actually observed to correct for the quality change. This adjustment will never be exact, because goods come as a *bundle* of characteristics that cannot be sold separately. And there is an arbitrary element in the weights we attach to specific characteristics, separately or in combination. Carefully done, however, such adjustments can provide an approximation of the change in value due to quality change, and thus improve the accuracy of our price indices.[4]

The problem of quality change becomes even more acute, however, with the appearance of completely new products and the disappearance of old ones. The CPI tracks the

---

[4]A good introduction to some of these issues is Statistics Canada, *Your Guide to the Consumer Price Index*, available free online at <http://www.statscan.ca>.

weighted average prices of a representative bundle of consumer goods, where the weights are given by the quantities purchased by consumers in the base year. If the base year is 1950, then the quantity weight assigned to colour televisions, home microwave ovens, Walkmans, personal computers, e-mail services, CD burners, and precooked bacon is *zero*: these products did not exist in 1950. In contrast, if this year is the base year, the quantity weight attached to eight-track tapes is zero, and the weight attached to buggy whips would be almost zero, except for the specialty trade in the back of some adult stores, next to the leather goods section.

Obviously, if a good that appears in the base year bundle is not produced at all in the comparison year, it will have *no* price in the comparison year. Conversely, if it is produced in the comparison year but not in the base year, it *will* have a price, but the quantity weight attached to that price is *zero*. Over time, with the appearance of qualitatively new products and the disappearance of old ones, the CPI starts to develop holes or gaps. In response to this problem, Statistics Canada has adopted the expedient of periodically revising its standard consumption bundle and changing its base year. The price index for the new base year is calculated in two ways: using the quantity weights from the *old* base year *and* using quantity weights derived from the standard commodity bundle of the new base year. This overlap permits the construction of spliced-together **chain indexes**. Economists, business, labour, and government shamelessly use such chain indexes for economic analysis and policy purposes, even when they are fully aware of their defects, simply because there is no generally accepted alternative.

The CPI, warts and all, is of considerable practical importance, since (among its other uses) it is often the basis for cost-of-living adjustment (COLA) provisions in wage settlements and pension plans. We may believe that the CPI is biased, but we will continue to use it as long as it is "the best game in town." We explore price indexes in greater detail in the online Web Supplement at www.mcgrawhill.ca/olc/frank.

Chain index
Single price index series created by splicing together two or more overlapping series based on different reference years with different quantity weights.

5.4 USING PRICE ELASTICITY OF DEMAND

In the sphere of applied economic analysis, few tools are more important than the concept of price elasticity of demand. In this section we examine applications of this concept in two different settings.

Application: TTC Fare Increases

The Toronto Transit Commission (TTC) prides itself on being "the most productive, least subsidized transit authority in North America."[5] From a social standpoint, for reasons we will examine further in Chapter 12, it may even be *under*-subsidized! Traffic congestion on the major road routes in the Greater Toronto Area (GTA) is estimated to cost several billion dollars annually in lost time and wasted fuel, in addition to its environmental costs. If more motorists could be enticed to use public transit through lower TTC fares and increased service, reduced road congestion would result in major time and cost savings. Here we are concerned with a narrower but related and important issue, namely the price elasticity of demand for rides on the TTC.

Between 1995 and 2000 there were three fare increases on the TTC, one of 14.6 percent in 1995, one of 9.3 percent in 1996, and one of 5.2 percent in 1999. We will use the data on fare increases and ridership levels to calculate approximate price elasticity of

---

[5]Toronto Transit Commission, "TTC Year 2000 Operating Budget," December 14, 1999, p. 1.

FIGURE 5-11

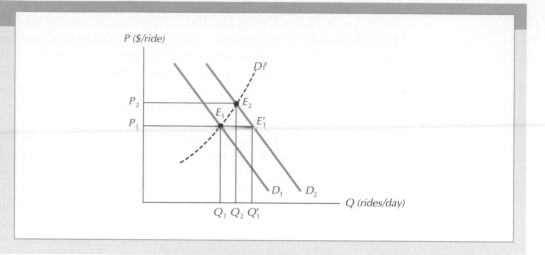

After the fare increases from P_1 to P_2, ridership increases from Q_1 to Q_2 because of two separate shifts: the shift of the demand curve from D_1 to D_2, and the shift along D_2 from E'_1 to E_2. Neglecting the shift from D_1 to D_2 gives the imaginary upward-sloping demand curve, D?

demand estimates. In the process, we will discover some pitfalls to avoid in making such calculations. In the months after the 1995 fare increase, ridership fell from an annualized figure of 392 million to 380 million riders, a 3.06 percent drop. The price elasticity of demand η is simply $(\Delta Q/Q)/(\Delta P/P)$, the ratio of the percentage change in ridership to the percentage change in fares, or $-.0306/.146 = -.21$. This rough-hewn price-elasticity estimate is *negative* and *inelastic* (significantly less than 1 in absolute value): quantity demanded dropped by about .21 percent for each 1 percent increase in fares. The 1995 fare increase resulted in an *increase* in revenues. The 9.6 percent fare increase in 1996 similarly resulted in a decline in annualized ridership from 380 million to 372 million rides, a decline of $8/380 = 2.1$ percent, which yields a rough price-elasticity estimate of $-.021/.096 = -.22$. If we apply the same method to the 5.2 percent fare increase of 1999, however, we encounter a problem: ridership actually *increased* from 387 million to 396 million rides, an *increase* of $9/387 = 2.33$ percent, and so the estimated price elasticity of demand is $.0233/.052 = +.45$! This suggests that the demand curve in 1999 was *upward* sloping, like that of a Giffen good.

What went wrong? After all, we don't really believe that public transit has an upward-sloping demand curve. Figure 5-11 shows what likely occurred. Recall that price elasticity of demand estimates require that *other* determinants of quantity demanded besides price remain *unchanged*. In at least two respects, however, this was not a reasonable assumption. First, the TTC had been shut down for two days by a strike shortly before the fare increase, so that annualized ridership was artificially lower than it would have been under normal circumstances. Second, and equally important, since early 1997 there had been a steady increase in ridership with fares constant in nominal terms (and hence declining slightly in real terms), as a result of increased service and of demographic and other factors. As Figure 5-11 suggests, the shift from E_1 to E_2 was likely the result of a combination of *two* shifts. The shift of *demand* from D_1 to D_2 would have resulted, at the original price P_1, in an increase in ridership from Q_1 to Q'_1. Along D_2, the increase in price from P_1 to P_2 would have resulted in a decrease in quantity demanded from Q'_1 to Q_2. The *price* elasticity of demand relates only to this *second* shift *along* D_2. Ignoring the first shift gives us the illusion that we are measuring the elasticity of the upward-sloping dotted demand curve D?, which does not in fact exist.

Although the price elasticities we calculated using the 1995 and 1996 fare increase data conformed to our expectations, we have no more reason to trust their accuracy than we do the 1999 estimate, unless we are certain that *all factors affecting demand except price did remain constant*. The same warning applies to all empirical elasticity measures, including those included in the tables of Chapter 4. As circumstances change, elasticities typically change as well, and before we rely on such estimates we need to satisfy ourselves that proper estimating procedures were used initially and that circumstances have not altered excessively.

Given the uncertainties about our rough elasticity estimates, which we could refine using more sophisticated econometric methods, can we say anything about the policy issue with which we began this section? Strictly speaking, the answer is "No." But a reasonable hypothesis might be that if demand was shifting outward over the entire 1995–2000 period, then demand is *more* price-elastic than our estimates indicate. Lowering the price would be more effective in attracting new riders than we might have thought. Yet if demand is still fairly price-inelastic, then increasing service, which shifts the demand curve to the right, might be an equally effective way to entice motorists to leave their cars at home, utilize public transit, and relieve traffic congestion.

Application: The Price Elasticity of Demand for Alcohol

How does the consumption of alcoholic beverages respond to changes in their price? For many decades, the conventional wisdom on this subject responded, "not very much." Unfortunately, however, estimates of the price elasticity of demand for alcohol tend to be highly unreliable. The problem is that liquor prices usually don't vary sufficiently to permit an accurate estimate of their effects.

In a careful study,[6] Philip Cook made use of some previously unexploited United States data on significant changes in alcohol prices. He suggested that the price elasticity of demand for alcohol may be much higher than had been thought.

Cook's method was to examine changes in alcohol consumption that occurred in response to changes in U.S. state liquor taxes. Of the 48 contiguous states, 30 license and tax the private sale of liquor. Periodically, most of these states increase their nominal liquor taxes to compensate for the effects of inflation. The pattern is for the real value of a state's liquor tax to be highest right after one of these tax increases, then to erode steadily as the cost of living rises over the next several years. The fact that taxes are not adjusted continuously to keep their real value constant provides the real price variability we need to estimate the responsiveness of alcohol purchases to price changes.

There were 39 liquor tax increases in Cook's 30-state sample during the period 1960–1975. In 30 of these 39 cases, he found that liquor consumption declined relative to the national trend in the year following the tax increase. His estimate of the price elasticity of demand was −1.8, a substantially higher value than had been found in previous studies.

Cook's interpretation of his findings provides an interesting case study in the factors that govern price elasticity. One salient fact about the alcohol market, he noted, is that heavy drinkers, though a small fraction of the total population, account for a large fraction of the total alcohol consumed. This fact has led many people to expect that alcohol consumption would be unresponsive to variations in price. The common view of heavy

---

[6]Philip J. Cook, "The Effect of Liquor Taxes on Drinking, Cirrhosis, and Auto Accidents," in *Alcohol and Public Policy*, Mark Moore and Dean Gerstein (eds.), Washington, DC: National Academy Press, 1982.

drinkers, after all, is that they drink primarily out of habit, not because of rational deliberations about price. Stated another way, analysts always expected the substitution effect to be small for these people. But even if the substitution effect were zero for heavy drinkers, there would remain the income effect to consider. The budget share devoted to alcohol tends to be large among heavy drinkers for two reasons. The obvious one is that heavy drinkers buy a lot of liquor. Less obvious, perhaps, is that their incomes tend to be significantly smaller than average. Many heavy drinkers have difficulty holding steady jobs and often cannot work productively in the jobs they do hold. The result is that the income effect of a substantial increase in the price of liquor forces many heavy drinkers to consume less. In support of this interpretation, Cook observed that mortality from cirrhosis of the liver declines sharply in the years following significant liquor tax increases. This is a disease that for the most part afflicts only people with protracted histories of alcohol abuse, and clinical experience reveals that curtailed drinking can delay or prevent its onset in long-term heavy drinkers.

5.5 THE INTERTEMPORAL CHOICE MODEL

The choices we have considered thus far have involved tradeoffs between alternatives in the present—the choice between food now and clothing now, between travel now and a home entertainment system now, and so on. There was no hint in any of these choices that the alternative chosen today might affect the menu of alternatives available in the future.

Yet such effects are a prominent feature of many of our most important decisions. Our task in this section is to enlarge the basic consumer choice model in Chapter 3 to accommodate them.

Intertemporal Consumption Bundles

When deciding what to do with their incomes, people may either consume them all now or save part for the future. The question we want to be able to answer is, "How would rational consumers distribute their consumption over time?" To keep the analysis manageable, it is helpful to begin by supposing that there are only two time periods, namely, *current* and *future*. In the standard, or *atemporal*, choice model in Chapter 3, the alternatives were different goods that could be consumed in the current period—apples now vs. oranges now, etc. In our simple *intertemporal choice model*, the

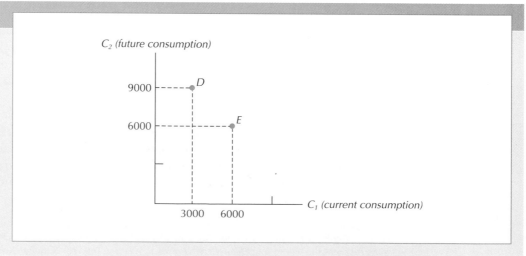

FIGURE 5-12

Intertemporal Consumption Bundles
Alternative combinations of current and future consumption are represented as points in the C_1, C_2 plane. By convention, the horizontal axis measures current consumption; the vertical axis, future consumption.

alternatives instead will be *current consumption* (denoted C_1) vs. *future consumption* (denoted C_2). Each of these is an amalgam—the functional equivalent of the composite good (see Chapter 3). For the sake of simplicity, we set aside the question of how to apportion current and future consumption among the various specific consumption goods and assume that the goods' prices remain constant.

In the atemporal choice model, any bundle of goods can be represented as a point in a simple two-dimensional diagram. We use an analogous procedure in the intertemporal choice model. In Figure 5-12, for example, current consumption of $6000 combined with future consumption of $6000 is represented by the bundle E. Bundle D represents current consumption of $3000 and future consumption of $9000.

The Intertemporal Budget Constraint

Suppose you receive $50,000 income in the current period and $60,000 income in the future period. Suppose also that if you deposit some of your income from the current period in a bank, you can receive your principal plus 20 percent in the future period. Similarly, if you wish to borrow against your future income, you may receive $1 in the current period for every $1.20 you must repay in the future period. (See Figure 5-13.) To construct your intertemporal budget constraint, first note that you can always merely consume your income in each period, so C_1 = $50,000 and C_2 = $60,000 must be a point on your intertemporal budget constraint. Another option is to deposit all $50,000 (maximum lending) and thus receive 1.2(50,000) = $60,000 in addition to your $60,000 future income for C_2 = $120,000 future consumption with no current consumption (C_1 = 0). Yet another option is to borrow 60,000/1.2 = $50,000 (maximum borrowing) in addition to your $50,000 current income for C_1 = $100,000 current consumption with no future consumption (C_2 = 0). The equation for your intertemporal budget constraint is C_2 = 120,000 − 1.2C_1, or, equivalently, 1.2C_1 + C_2 = $120,000.

In general, suppose you receive M_1 of your income in the first period and M_2 in the second, and can either borrow or lend at the interest rate r. Under these circumstances, what is the most you can consume in the future period? Maximum future consumption occurs when you set all your current income aside for future use. Setting aside M_1 in the current period at the interest rate r means your deposit will grow to $M_1(1 + r)$ by the future period. So the most you can possibly consume in the future is that amount plus your future income, or $M_1(1 + r) + M_2$.

FIGURE 5-13

The Intertemporal Budget Constraint For every dollar by which current consumption is reduced, it is possible to increase future consumption by $1.20.

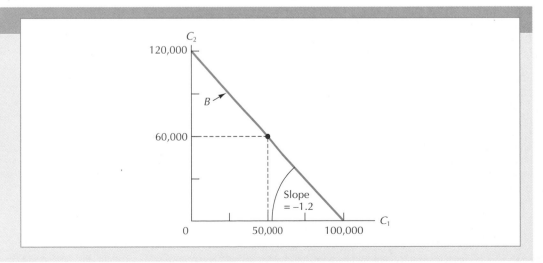

What is the most you could consume in the current period? The answer is your current income plus the maximum amount you can borrow against your future income. The most you can borrow against a future income of M_2 is called the **present value** of M_2, denoted $PV(M_2)$. It is the amount that, if deposited today at the interest rate r, would be worth exactly M_2 in the future period. Accordingly, we can find the present value of M_2 by solving $PV(M_2)(1 + r) = M_2$ for $PV(M_2)$:

$$PV(M_2) = \frac{M_2}{1+r}. \tag{5.1}$$

Present value

The present value of a payment of X dollars T years from now is $X/(1 + r)^T$, where r is the annual rate of interest.

For example, if M_2 were \$110,000 and the interest rate were 10 percent per period (that is, $r = .10$), the present value of M_2 would be \$110,000/1.1 = \$100,000. Present value is a simple equivalence relationship between sums of money that are payable at different points in time. If $r = 10$ percent ($= .10$) per period, then \$100,000 today will be worth \$110,000 in the future, and \$110,000 in the future is worth \$100,000 today.

It is not necessary, of course, to borrow or save the maximum amounts possible. The consumer who wishes to shift some of her future income into the current period can borrow any amount up to the maximum at the rate of $1/(1 + r)$ dollars today for every dollar given up in the future. Or, she can save any amount of her current income and get back $(1 + r)$ dollars in the future for every dollar not consumed today. The intertemporal budget constraint, shown as the locus B in Figure 5-14, is thus the straight line that joins the maximum current consumption and maximum future consumption points. Its slope will be $-(1 + r)$. As in the atemporal model, here too the slope of the budget constraint may be interpreted as a relative price ratio. This time it is the ratio of the prices of current and future consumption. With $r > 0$, current consumption has a higher price than future consumption because of the opportunity cost of the interest forgone when money is spent rather than saved. It is conventional to refer to the horizontal intercept of the intertemporal budget constraint as the *present value of lifetime income*.

Since all income is spent on consumption either in period 1 (C_1) or in period 2 (C_2), we can express the equality of income and consumption as follows:

$$M_1(1 + r) + M_2 = C_1(1 + r) + C_2. \tag{5.2}$$

FIGURE 5-14

Intertemporal Budget Constraint with Income in Both Periods, and Borrowing or Lending at the Rate r

The opportunity cost of \$1 of present consumption is $(1 + r)$ dollars of future consumption. The horizontal intercept of the intertemporal budget constraint is the present value of lifetime income, $M_1 + M_2/(1 + r)$.

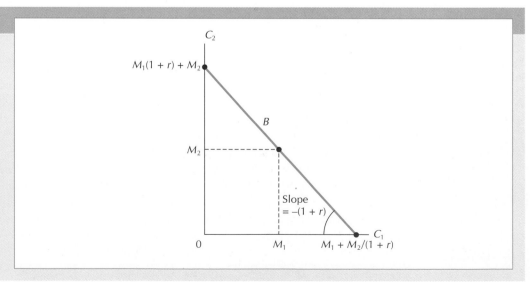

Note that Equation 5.2 expresses the equality in terms of *future* dollars, since both M_1 and C_1 are multiplied by $(1 + r)$, to reflect the fact that a dollar today may be exchanged for $(1 + r)$ dollars in the next period. Dividing all terms in Equation 5.2 by $(1 + r)$ would give us the equality of income and consumption in terms of *present* dollars:

$$M_1 + \frac{M_2}{1 + r} = C_1 + \frac{C_2}{1 + r}. \tag{5.3}$$

We can rearrange Equation 5.2 to give us the intertemporal budget constraint in slope-intercept form:

$$C_2 = [M_1(1 + r) + M_2] - (1 + r)C_1. \tag{5.4}$$

Another illuminating way of rewriting Equation 5.2 is:

$$(M_1 - C_1)(1 + r) = (C_2 - M_2). \tag{5.5}$$

In this form, we can see clearly that if a consumer saves (and loans out) some of her income in period 1 ($M_1 > C_1$), then she will be able to consume more than her income in period 2 ($C_2 > M_2$). For example, if $r = 20$ percent/period and she saves \$1000 in period 1 ($M_1 - C_1 = \$1000$), then in period 2 she will be able to consume $1000(1.2)$ =\$1200 more than her period 2 income ($C_2 - M_2 = \$1200$). In contrast, if she borrows \$1000 in period 1, then $M_1 - C_1 = -\$1000$, and her consumption in period 2 will be \$1200 less than her income ($C_2 - M_2 = -\$1200$).

EXERCISE 5-4

You have \$50,000 of current income and \$42,000 of future income. If the interest rate between the current and future period is 5 percent, what is the present value of your lifetime income? What is the maximum amount you could consume in the future? What is the equation describing your intertemporal budget constraint?

As in the atemporal case considered in Chapter 3, the intertemporal budget constraint is a convenient way of summarizing the consumption bundles that someone is *able* to buy. And as before, it tells us nothing about which particular combination a person will *choose* to buy.

Intertemporal Indifference Curves

To discover which bundle the consumer will select from those that are feasible, we need some convenient way of representing the consumer's preferences over current and future consumption. Here again the analytical device is completely analogous to one we used in the atemporal case. Just as a consumer's preferences over two current consumption goods may be captured by an indifference map, so too may his preferences over current and future goods be represented in this fashion. In Figure 5-15, the consumer is indifferent between the bundles that lie on the locus I_1, each of which is less desirable than the bundles on I_2, and so on.

The absolute value of the slope of the intertemporal indifference curve at any point is the marginal rate of substitution between future and current consumption. At point A in Figure 5-15, it is given by $|\Delta C_2 / \Delta C_1|$, and this ratio is also referred to as the

Marginal rate of time
preference (MRTP)
The number of units
of consumption in
the future a consumer
would exchange for
1 unit of consumption
in the present.

marginal rate of time preference (MRTP) at A (see footnote 7). If $|\Delta C_2/\Delta C_1| > 1$ at A, the consumer is said to exhibit *positive time preference* at that point. This means that he requires more than 1 unit of future consumption to compensate him for the loss of a unit of current consumption. If $|\Delta C_2/\Delta C_1| < 1$ at a point, he is said to exhibit *negative time preference* at that point. Such a person is willing to forgo 1 unit of current consumption in return for less than 1 unit of future consumption. Finally, if $|\Delta C_2/\Delta C_1| = 1$ at a point, the consumer is said to have *neutral time preference* at that point. With neutral time preference, present and future consumption trade off against one another at the rate of 1 to 1.

As in the atemporal case, it appears justified to assume that the marginal rate of time preference declines as one moves downward along an indifference curve. The more current consumption a person already has, the more she will be willing to give up in order to obtain an additional unit of future consumption. For most of us then, the question of whether time preference is positive, negative, or neutral will be a matter of where we happen to be on our indifference maps. The scion of a wealthy family who is unable to borrow against the $5 billion he is due to inherit in 2 years very likely has strongly positive time preference. In contrast, the subsistence farmer whose food stocks are perishable is likely to have negative time preference in the wake of having harvested a bumper crop.

The optimal allocation between current and future consumption is determined exactly as in the atemporal model. The consumer selects the point along his budget constraint that corresponds to the highest attainable indifference curve. If the intertemporal indifference curves have the conventional convex shape, we ordinarily get a tangency solution like the one shown in Figure 5-16. If the MRTP is everywhere larger than (or everywhere smaller than) the absolute value of the slope of the budget constraint, corner solutions result, just as in the atemporal case.

In Figure 5-16, suppose that the consumer has the same income in each time period ($M_1 = M_2$) but consumes more in period 2 than in period 1. Does this pattern imply that she has negative time preference at the optimum point A? Not necessarily. If the rate of interest is positive ($r > 0$), then $1 + r > 1$, and at A she will have positive time preference. What *is* true is that (with an interior solution) her time preference at the optimum point will be positive, neutral, or negative as $r > 0$, $r = 0$, or $r < 0$, respectively.

FIGURE 5-15

An Intertemporal Indifference Map
As in the atemporal model, movements to the northeast represent increasing satisfaction. The absolute value of the slope of an indifference curve at a point is called the marginal rate of time preference (MRTP) at that point. The MRTP at A is $|\Delta C_2/\Delta C_1|$.

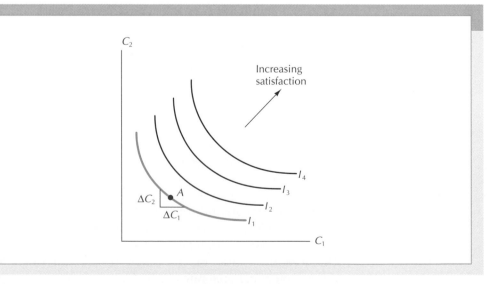

---

[7]In calculus terms, the marginal rate of time preference is given by $|dC_2/dC_1|$.

The optimal allocation will of course be different for different consumers. The optimum shown in Figure 5-17a, for example, is for a consumer whose preferences are much more heavily tilted in favour of future consumption. The one shown in Figure 5-17b, in contrast, is for a consumer who cares much more about present consumption. But in each case, note that the slope of the indifference curve at the optimal point is the same. As long as consumers can borrow and lend at the interest rate r, the marginal rate of time preference at the optimal bundle will be $(1 + r)$ (except, of course, in the case of kinks and corner solutions). Hence with $r > 0$, for interior solutions, positive time preference is the rule, regardless of the consumer's preferences.

If (as we usually assume) both current and future consumption are normal goods, then an increase in the present value of lifetime income, all other factors constant, will cause both current and future consumption to rise.

FIGURE 5-16

The Optimal Intertemporal Allocation

As in the atemporal model, the optimal intertemporal consumption bundle (bundle A) lies on the highest attainable indifference curve. Here, that occurs at a point of tangency, with the consumer saving and loaning $(M_1 - C_1^*)$ in period 1 and consuming $(C_2^* 2 M_2) = (M_1 - C_1^*)(1 + r)$ more than her income in period 2.

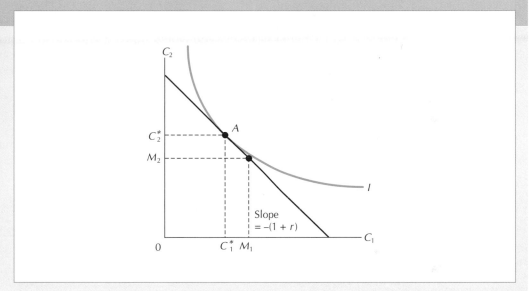

FIGURE 5-17

Patience and Impatience

(a) The patient consumer postpones the bulk of consumption until the future period. (b) The impatient consumer consumes much more heavily in the current period. But in equilibrium, the marginal rate of time preference $|\Delta C_2/\Delta C_1|$ equals $(1 + r)$ for both consumers, and is hence the same for both.

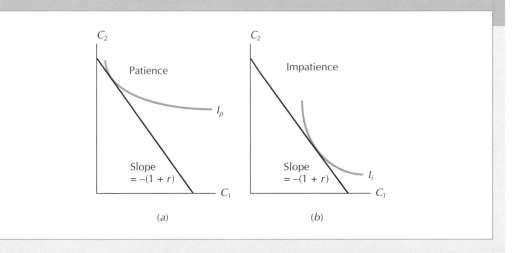

(a)   (b)

EXAMPLE 5-3

In a two-period world, you have current income of $100,000 and future income of $154,000, and can borrow and lend at the rate $r = 10$ percent/period. Under these conditions, you consume exactly your income in each period. Your indifference curves are smooth and convex. *True or false:* **An increase in r to $r = 40$ percent/period will cause you to save some of your current income.**

Line B in Figure 5-18 is the original budget constraint. Its horizontal intercept is the present value of lifetime income when $r = .1$: $100,000 + $154,000/1.1 = $240,000$. Its vertical intercept is future income plus $(1 + r)$ times current income: $154,000 + (1.1)($100,000) = $264,000$. The optimal bundle occurs at A, by assumption, which implies that the MRTP at A is 1.1. When the interest rate rises to .4, the intertemporal budget constraint becomes B'. Its horizontal intercept is $100,000 + $154,000/1.4 = $210,000$. Its vertical intercept is $154,000 + (1.4)($100,000) = $294,000$. Because the MRTP at A is less than the absolute value of the slope of the budget constraint B', it follows that you will be better off by consuming less in the present and more in the future than you did at A. The new bundle is shown at D in Figure 5-18.

Note also that if the interest rate were *lower* than 10 percent per period, you would *also* be better off! Now you would borrow, and consume more in the present and less in the future than at A. This is the exact intertemporal analogue of the housing price example we analyzed earlier, where you were better off if housing prices rose or if housing prices fell.

Suppose, however, that you were either a borrower or a lender at the initial interest rate. How would your consumption and saving or borrowing behaviour be affected by an increase in the interest rate?

FIGURE 5-18

The Effect of a Rise in the Interest Rate
When the interest rate goes up, the intertemporal budget constraint rotates about the current endowment point. If the current endowment point (A) was optimal at the lower interest rate, the new optimal bundle (D) will have less current consumption and more future consumption.

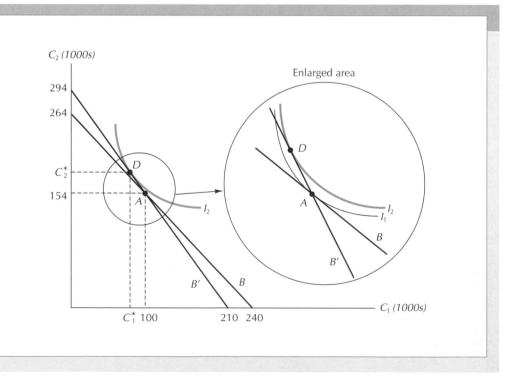

In a two-period world, with current and future consumption both as normal goods, Lenore and Boris have identical preferences, smooth convex indifference curves, and identical intertemporal budget constraints at the initial rate of interest, r_0. The only difference between them is that Lenore's income is $\$M_L$ in period 1 and zero in period 2, while Boris has no income in period 1 and $\$M_B$ in period 2. What can we definitely say about the effect of a higher rate of interest on their consumption and saving or borrowing behaviour?

We can use Figure 5-19 and apply our knowledge of income and substitution effects to answer this question. At the initial rate of interest, r_0, both Lenore in panel (a) and Boris in panel (b) have identical budget constraints, B_0. Hence, with identical tastes, both will choose the same consumption point (call it A). At A, Lenore is a lender, since her income M_L exceeds her consumption C_{1_A} in period 1. Boris, however, is a borrower, since he has no income in period 1 and must borrow $\$C_{1_A}$ to pay for his period 1 consumption. If the interest rate increases to r_1, then both intertemporal budget constraints rotate around the income endowment points (M_L and M_B) to B_1, which has a slope of $-(1 + r_1)$. Lenore the lender is now better off, because her feasible consumption set has expanded, but Boris the borrower is worse off, since his consumption set has contracted. For both Lenore and Boris, the *substitution* effect of the increase in r will operate to increase C_2 and decrease C_1, since the increase in $(1 + r)$ increases the opportunity cost of a unit of consumption in period 1. The income effect, however, works in opposite directions for lender and borrower. Lenore's income has increased, and therefore (since C_1 and C_2 are normal goods), the income effect works to increase C_1 and C_2. Hence for Lenore, the total effect of the increase in r will be to increase C_2. Her C_1, however, may increase (if the income effect dominates) to a point on B_1 such as A', or decrease (if the substitution effect dominates) to a point on B_1 such as A''. At A', Lenore would be saving and lending *less* than she would have at A, while at A'', she would be saving and lending *more* than at A. Thus the effect of the higher interest rate on her level of savings is ambiguous, although she will definitely consume more in period 2.

How an Interest Rate Increase Affects Lenders and Borrowers At interest rate r_0, both the lender in (a) and the borrower in (b) have identical optima at A on B_0. An increase in r causes both intertemporal budget constraints to rotate around the income endowment point to B_1, with slope = $-(1 + r_1)$. The lender is better off and the borrower is worse off. The new optimum for both will be at a point such as A' or A'', along DE in (a) and along M_BD in (b).

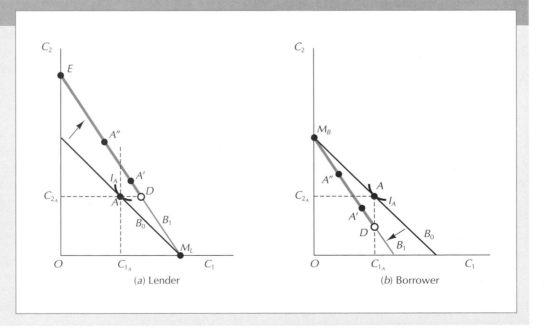

(a) Lender

(b) Borrower

Boris's income, however, has decreased, and therefore the income effect works to *decrease* both C_1 and C_2. Hence for Boris, the total effect of the interest rate increase will be to decrease C_1 (and thus his borrowing), but C_2, his period 2 consumption, may decrease (if the income effect dominates) to a point on B_1 such as A', or increase (if the substitution effect dominates) to a point on B_1 such as A''.

It should be clear that a *lower* interest rate than r_0 would make Lenore worse off and Boris better off. You will likely want to draw the diagrams and trace the income and substitution effects for this case, to show that at a lower interest rate, Boris will definitely borrow more and consume more in period 1, while Lenore will definitely consume less in period 2 but may save and lend more *or* less in period 1 than at A.

This example should indicate not only why debtors tend to push for lower interest rates and "easy money" while creditors push for higher interest rates and "tight money," but also why macroeconomists tend, on the whole, to be agnostic about the effects of higher interest rates on savings behaviour. Two of the most important words in the arsenal of the astute economic naturalist are "It depends."

Application: The Permanent Income and Life-Cycle Hypotheses

Economists once assumed that a person's current consumption depends primarily on her current income. Thus if a consumer received a windfall roughly equal to her current income, the prediction was that her consumption would roughly double.

In the 1950s, however, Milton Friedman, Franco Modigliani, Richard Brumberg, and others argued that the intertemporal choice model suggests otherwise.[8] To illustrate, consider a consumer with current and future incomes both equal to 120, who can borrow and lend at the rate $r = 20$ percent/period. The locus labelled B in Figure 5-20 is the consumer's intertemporal budget constraint, and the optimal bundle along it is denoted by A. Note that the horizontal intercept of B is the present value of lifetime income, namely, $120 + (120/1.2) = 220$.

Notice what happens when this consumer's current income rises from 120 to 240. His budget constraint is now the locus labelled B', and the optimal bundle is D. The effect of increasing current income is thus to increase not only current consumption (from 80 to 150) but also future consumption (from 168 to 228). If intertemporal indifference curves exhibit diminishing marginal rates of time preference,[9] the consumer generally does best not to concentrate too much of his consumption in any one period. By spreading his windfall over both periods, he is able to achieve a better outcome.

Friedman's *permanent income hypothesis* says that the primary determinant of current consumption is not current income but what he called **permanent income.** In terms of our simple intertemporal choice model, permanent income is simply the present value of lifetime income. (Following the increase in current income in Figure 5-20, permanent income is $240 + 120/1.2 = 340$.) When we consider that in reality the future consists of not just one but many additional periods, it becomes clear that current income

Permanent income
The present value of lifetime income.

---

[8]See Franco Modigliani and R. Brumberg, "Utility Analysis and the Consumption Function: An Interpretation of Cross-Section Data," in K. Kurihara (ed.), *Post-Keynesian Economics,* London: Allen & Unwin, 1955; and Milton Friedman, *A Theory of the Consumption Function,* Princeton, NJ: Princeton University Press, 1957.

[9]Recall that diminishing marginal rate of time preference is the intertemporal analogue of diminishing marginal rate of substitution in the atemporal model.

FIGURE 5-20

Permanent Income, Not Current Income, Is the Primary Determinant of Current Consumption
The effect of a rise in current income (from 120 to 240) will be felt as an increase not only in current consumption (from 80 to 150), but also in future consumption (from 168 to 228).

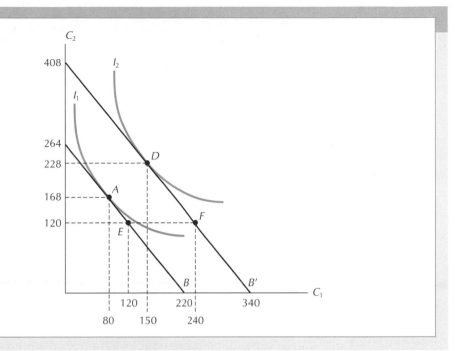

constitutes only a small fraction of permanent income. (If there were 10 such future periods we were concerned about, for example, then a 10 percent increase in current income would cause permanent income to increase by just over 2 percent.)[10] Accordingly, Friedman argued, a given proportional change in current income should give rise to a much smaller proportional change in current consumption, just as we saw in Figure 5-20. (The *life-cycle hypothesis* of Modigliani and Brumberg tells essentially the same story.)

Factors Accounting for Differences in Time Preference

Uncertainty regarding the future is one reason to prefer current to future consumption. In countries at war, for example, people often live as though there were no tomorrow, as indeed for some of them there will not be. In contrast, a peaceful international climate, secure employment, stable social networks, good health, and a variety of similar factors tend to reduce uncertainty about the future, in the process justifying greater weight on future as opposed to current consumption.

Intertemporal indifference maps, like the atemporal variety, will also vary according to the disposition of the individual. As Figure 5-17 (page 191) suggests, for some individuals, like the grasshopper in Aesop's fable, the only problem with immediate gratification is that it takes too long. Others, like Aesop's ant, are reluctant to consume any significant amount until adequate provision is made for the future. Grasshoppers will have very steep intertemporal indifference curves, while those of ants will be flatter. Such differences in individual time preference result from a number of factors, which vary in importance among individuals. There are differences in the intensity of desire for immediate want

---

[10]Again, we assume an interest rate of $r = 20$ percent/period.

satisfaction, in the capacity to gain pleasure from anticipating future consumption, in the degree of risk aversion (given uncertainty about the future), and in the capacity for prevision and planning.

Time preference depends also on the specific circumstances of the choice at hand. Experimental studies have isolated certain situations in which most people have strongly positive time preference, others in which they show strongly negative time preference. Carnegie-Mellon University economist George Loewenstein, for example, told experimental subjects to imagine they had won a kiss from their favourite movie star and then asked them when they would most like to receive it. Even though getting it right away was one of the options, most subjects elected to wait an average of several days. These choices imply negative time preference, and Loewenstein theorized that most subjects simply wanted a little while to savour the anticipation of the kiss.[11] Loewenstein also told a group of subjects to imagine that they were going to receive a painful electric shock and then asked them when they would like to receive it. This time most subjects chose to get it right away. They apparently wanted to spend as little time as possible dreading the shock. But since an electric shock is a "bad" rather than a "good," these choices too imply negative time preference.

These situations where people display negative time preference can be set against instances where people show a preference for present over future consumption. Put a large bowl of hot popcorn down in front of those same subjects shortly before dinner time. Even among those who would prefer the dinner to the popcorn, there are likely some who will "spoil their dinner," because they lack the self-control to wait. Eugen von Böhm-Bawerk (1851–1914) suggested that one reason for such behaviour is that current consumption opportunities confront our senses directly, whereas future ones can be only imagined. Böhm-Bawerk believed that our "faulty telescopic faculty" was no good reason to assign greater weight to current than to future pleasures. Uncertainty aside, he felt that people would reap greater satisfaction from their lives if they weighed the present and the future equally.

Other Factors That Affect Intertemporal Choice

Preference for a Rising Consumption Standard. Some evidence suggests that people prefer a consumption pattern that gives even more weight to future than to current consumption, when satisfaction depends not only on the level of consumption but also on its rate of change. An improving standard of living can often bring greater satisfaction than a static one that is initially at a higher level.

At the most fundamental level, support for this idea comes from our knowledge of how the human nervous system perceives and processes information. As psychologists and biologists explain it, we are much less sensitive to the absolute level of any sensory stimulus than to deviations from norms or reference standards we adopt from experience. The pedestrian in Montreal, for example, often fails to notice the horns that blare at him, whereas small-town residents are often startled by much fainter sounds. Like the din of the metropolis, consumption at any constant level becomes a norm. As such, it is at least partly taken for granted, serving as the standard against which future consumption levels are measured.

---

[11]See George Loewenstein, "Anticipation and the Valuation of Delayed Consumption," *Economic Journal, 97,* September 1987: 666–684.

Level vs. Growing Consumption Profiles Many people declare a strong preference for a growing consumption profile (panel *b*) over a static profile (panel *a*).

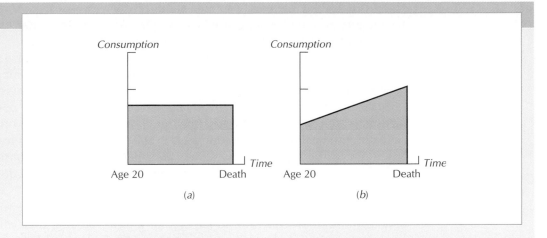

To test your own intuition about the importance of a rising consumption profile, imagine yourself living on a deserted island faced with a once-and-for-all choice between the two consumption profiles shown in Figure 5-21. Which one would you pick?

In a sample of 112 undergraduates who were asked to make a choice similar to the one portrayed in Figure 5-21, 87 (78 percent) chose the rising profile (panel *b*).[12] This pattern seems strongly at odds with Böhm-Bawerk's notion that people generally put too much weight on current consumption. One reason for the apparent discrepancy is that the savings incentives we face individually differ from the ones we face as whole societies. Indeed, as we see in the next section, individuals face strong incentives to concentrate their consumption in the present, even though they might wish that everyone would save more for the future.

Positional Concerns and Intertemporal Choice. Skating excellence is inescapably relative. In 1962, Canadian skater Donald Jackson won the World Championship, largely because he was the first to land a triple lutz jump in competition. Now, triple lutzes and triple axels are part of the standard repertoire of every world-class skater. Kurt Browning was the first to land a quadruple toe loop in competition, at the 1988 Worlds. Now, winning the World Championship typically requires not just a single quad, but rather multiple quads or quads in combination.

Positional good A good whose value depends strongly on how it compares with similar goods consumed by others; also called a *status good*.

The late British economist Fred Hirsch coined the term ***positional goods*** to refer to goods and services whose value is strongly influenced by their *relative quality*.[13] Luxury goods like diamonds are a quintessential example. As with top skaters, a "good" diamond is one that compares favourably with other available diamonds. A good job, similarly, is one that is better than most other jobs. The standards that define a good job in the 21st century are very different from those that applied in the 17th century. Education is likewise a good with a strong positional component. Whether society considers you well educated, and thus qualified for a good job, depends to a large extent on how your education compares with the education received by your peers.

---

[12]See R. Frank and R. Hutchens, "Wages, Seniority, and the Demand for Rising Consumption Profiles," *Journal of Economic Behavior and Organization, 21,* 1993: 251–276.

[13]See Fred Hirsch, *Social Limits to Growth,* Cambridge, MA: Harvard University Press, 1976.

The central feature of a positional good is its *inherent* scarcity. Although it is possible to imagine an environment in which people had more food than they could possibly consume, the same cannot be said of a positional good.

This feature of positional goods shapes a variety of important decisions, including the one of how much to save. A family can save more of its income for retirement, or spend more now for, say, a house in a better school district. For most parents, the lure of providing relative educational advantages for their children is powerful. Yet simple arithmetic tells us that no matter how much each family spends on housing, only 10 percent of the children can occupy seats in the top decile of the educational quality distribution. In the aggregate, saving less and spending more for houses in better school districts in itself serves only to bid up the prices of those houses. It does nothing to alter the relative distribution of educational opportunities.[14]

Spending on positional goods is thus very much like a military arms race. Each side spends more in an effort not to fall behind, but in the end, their efforts merely offset one another. Positional concerns cause the individual payoff from spending to appear spuriously large, the payoff from saving spuriously small. These concerns are thus in direct competition with the desire to have a rising consumption profile. To provide the best possible education for your children, you must spend heavily during the early years of the life cycle. In contrast, to achieve a rising consumption profile, you must save a lot during the early years. If positional concerns are strong, then even people who strongly value a rising consumption profile might nonetheless save very little. Indeed, many families would have grossly inadequate incomes for retirement were it not for the Canada Pension Plan and private forced-savings programs. These programs may be interpreted as collective actions to shelter part of our incomes from spending on positional goods, in the process helping achieve a more preferred lifetime consumption profile.[15]

The importance of positional concerns suggests an important qualification to the life-cycle and permanent income models of savings. If positional concerns are important, people in the lower part of the income distribution will naturally have more difficulty than others in keeping up with community consumption standards. The clear prediction is that the savings rate will rise with position in the income distribution. In every country for which the relevant data are available, savings rates rise sharply with income.

The Self-Control Pitfall.   Another reason for low savings rates coexisting with a preference for a rising consumption profile is that people often seem to have difficulty carrying out plans they believe to be in their own interests. Thomas Schelling notes, for example, that most cigarette smokers say they want to quit.[16] Many of them, with great effort, have done so. Many more, however, have tried to quit and failed.

One way of solving the self-control problem is captured by the example of Homer's Ulysses, who was faced with having to sail past dangerous reefs where the sirens lay. Ulysses realized that once he was within earshot of the sirens' cries, he would be drawn irresistibly toward them and sail to his doom on the reefs. Able to foresee this temporary change in his preferences, he came up with an effective ***commitment device:*** he instructed his crewmen to strap him tightly to the mast and not to release him, even though he might beg them to, until they had sailed safely past.

Commitment device
A device that commits a person to behave in a certain way in the future, even though he may wish to behave otherwise when the time comes.

---

[14]Nor, in itself, does it alter the absolute value of educational services consumed by each student.

[15]For a detailed argument in support of this interpretation, see R. Frank, *Choosing the Right Pond: Human Behavior and the Quest for Status*, New York: Oxford University Press, 1985. Formally, the problem is like the "prisoners' dilemmas" we discuss further in Chapters 7 and 13.

[16]See Thomas Schelling, *Choice and Consequence*, Cambridge, MA: Harvard University Press, 1984.

Similar sorts of commitment devices are familiar in modern life. Fearing they will be tempted to spend their savings, people join "Christmas clubs," special accounts that prohibit withdrawals until late autumn; they buy whole-life insurance policies, which impose substantial penalties on withdrawals before retirement. Fearing they will spoil their dinners, they put the salted nuts out of easy reach. Fearing they will gamble too much, they limit the amount of cash they take to Casino Niagara. Fearing they will stay up too late watching TV, they move the television out of the bedroom.

The moral of the burgeoning self-control literature is that *devising* a rational intertemporal consumption plan is only part of the problem. There is also the task of *implementing* it. But here too, rational deliberation can help us avoid some of the most important pitfalls. The consumer who has just given up smoking, for example, can predict that he will desperately want a cigarette if he goes out drinking with his friends on Friday nights. And he can also insulate himself from that temptation by committing himself to alternative weekend activities for the next month or so. By the same token, the person who wants to shield herself from the temptation to spend too much may have part of her pay diverted automatically into a savings program, and this is precisely what millions of people do.

These issues once again highlight the distinction between the positive and normative roles of the rational choice model discussed in Chapter 1. Because the rational choice model takes no account of self-control problems and the like, it will sometimes fail to predict how people actually behave. But this does not mean that the model, even in its narrowest form, is wrong or useless. For here, as in other instances, it can play the important normative role of guiding people toward better decisions, ones that accord more fully with their real objectives.

SUMMARY

www.mcgrawhill.ca/olc/frank

- In this chapter our primary focus was on applications of the rational choice and demand theories developed in Chapters 3 and 4. We also considered the concept of consumer surplus, which measures the amount by which a consumer benefits by being able to buy a given product at a given price. We saw that consumer surplus is well approximated by the area bounded above by the individual demand curve and below by the market price. Two-part pricing structures are a device by which a portion of consumer surplus is transferred from the buyer to the seller.

- The rational choice model is also useful for evaluating the welfare effects of price and income changes. It suggests why the consumer price index, the government's measure of changes in the cost of living, may often overstate the true cost of achieving a given level of satisfaction.

- The intertemporal choice model is, in every essential respect, analogous to the atemporal choice model in Chapter 3. In the two-dimensional case, it begins with

a commodity graph that depicts current and future consumption levels of a composite good. The consumer's initial endowment is the point, (M_1, M_2), that corresponds to current and future income. If the consumer can borrow and lend at the rate r, his intertemporal budget constraint is then the line passing through the endowment point with a slope of $-(1 + r)$. The opportunity cost of a unit of current consumption is $1 + r$ units of future consumption. The horizontal intercept of the intertemporal budget constraint is the present value of all current and future income, which is also called the present value of lifetime wealth.

- The consumer's intertemporal preferences may be represented by an indifference map with essentially the same properties as in the atemporal case. A consumer is said to exhibit positive, neutral, or negative time preference at a point if his marginal rate of time preference (the absolute value of the slope of his indifference curve) at that point is greater than 1, equal to 1, or less than 1, respectively. In the case of interior solutions, equilibrium occurs at a tangency between the intertemporal budget constraint and an indifference curve. Hence with an interior solution, when $r > 0$, consumers will exhibit positive time preference in equilibrium, irrespective of the shape of their indifference curves.

- An important application of the intertemporal choice model is to the study of decisions about how much to save. The permanent income and life-cycle hypotheses employ the model to demonstrate that it is the present value of lifetime wealth, not current income alone, that governs current consumption (and hence current savings).

- Appendix 5A discusses additional applications of rational choice and demand theories, including the use of indifference curves to measure consumer surplus and compensating and equivalent variation measures of consumer surplus.

QUESTIONS FOR REVIEW

1. Explain in your own words why a gasoline tax whose proceeds are refunded to the consumer in a lump-sum amount will nonetheless reduce the consumption of gasoline.
2. Explain in your own words what a two-part pricing scheme is and why sellers might use one.
3. Do you think a university education has a high or a low price-(tuition-) elasticity of demand?
4. Explain in your own words why even long-term heavy drinkers might be highly responsive to increases in the price of alcohol.
5. Explain why 1 plus the interest rate in the intertemporal choice model is analogous to the relative price ratio in the consumer choice model discussed in Chapter 3.

6. Public transit services are generally more energy efficient than individuals using cars to commute to work. However, the trend over the past 30 years has been a decline in the proportion of commuters using public transit, despite an increase in real energy prices. Why?
7. Jennifer, who earns an annual salary of $20,000, wins $25,000 in the lottery. Explain why she most likely will not spend all her winnings during the next year.
8. For Lenore and Boris in Example 5-4, if the initial situation is unchanged but the new interest rate is lower than r_0, explain in terms of income and substitution effects and with diagrams how their consumption, saving, and borrowing choices will necessarily change.

PROBLEMS

1. Using a diagram like Figure 5-2 (page 171), explain why, under our current method of educational finance, a rich family is much more likely than a poor family to send its children to a private school.

2. When the price of gasoline is $1.00/L, you consume 2000 L/yr. Then two things happen: (1) The price of gasoline rises to $2/L and (2) a distant uncle dies, with the instruction to his executor to send you a cheque for $2000/yr. If no other changes in prices or income occur, do these two changes leave you better off than before?

3. Larry demands strawberries according to the schedule $P = 4 - (Q/2)$, where P is the price of strawberries ($/pack) and Q is the quantity (packs/wk). Assuming that the income effect is negligible, how much will he be hurt if the price of strawberries goes from $1/pack to $2/pack?

4. The only video rental club available to you charges $4 per movie per day. If your demand curve for movie rentals is given by $P = 20 - 2Q$, where P is the rental price ($/day) and Q is the quantity demanded (movies per year), what is the maximum annual membership fee you would be willing to pay to join this club? What is the average amount you would pay per video movie, counting membership and rental costs?

5. Jane spends all her income on hot dogs and caviar. Her demand curve for caviar is inelastic over the relevant price range. Unfortunately, overfishing has caused the supply of caviar to fall and the price to rise. If Jane's preferences and income and the price of hot dogs are unchanged, what has happened to Jane's consumption of hot dogs? Explain.

6. Jones spends all his income on two goods, X and Y. The prices he paid and the quantities he consumed last year are as follows: $P_X = \$15/\text{unit}$, $X = 20$ units, $P_Y = \$25/\text{unit}$, and $Y = 30$ units. If the prices next year are $P_X = \$6/\text{unit}$ and $P_Y = \$30/\text{unit}$, and Jones's income is $1020, will he be better or worse off than he was in the previous year? (Assume that his tastes do not change.)

7. Smith lives in a world with two time periods, this period and the next period. His income in each period, which he receives at the beginning of each period, is $210. If the interest rate is 5 percent/period, what is the present value of his lifetime income? Draw his intertemporal budget constraint. On the same axes, draw Smith's intertemporal budget constraint when $r = 20$ percent/period.

8. Suppose Smith from Problem 7 views current and future consumption as perfect, one-for-one substitutes for one another. Find his optimal consumption bundle, in both cases.

9. Suppose Smith from Problem 7 views current and future consumption as one-to-one complements. Find his optimal consumption bundle, in both cases.

10. Karen earns $75,000 in the current period and will earn $75,000 in the future.
    a. Assuming that these are the only two periods, and that banks in her country borrow and lend at an interest rate $r = 0$, draw her intertemporal budget constraint.
    b. Now suppose banks offer 10 percent interest on funds deposited during the current period, and offer loans at this same rate. Draw her new intertemporal budget constraint.

11. Find the present value of $50,000 to be received after 1 year if the rate of interest for 1 year is
    a. 8 percent.
    b. 10 percent.
    c. 12 percent.

12. Crusoe will live this period and the next period as the lone inhabitant of his island. His only income is a crop of 100 coconuts that he harvests at the beginning of each period. Coconuts not consumed in the current period spoil at the rate of 10 percent per period.
    a. Draw Crusoe's intertemporal budget constraint. What will be his consumption in each period if he regards future consumption as a perfect, one-for-one substitute for current consumption?
    b. What will he consume each period if he regards .8 unit of future consumption as being worth 1 unit of current consumption?

13. This fall, Crusoe puts 50 coconuts from his harvest into a cave just before a family of shipwrecked circus bears goes in to hibernate. As a result, he is unable to get the coconuts out before the bears emerge the following period. Coconuts spoil at the same rate no matter where he stores them. Why might he do this?

14. Kathy earns $55,000 in the current period and will earn $60,000 in the future period. What is the maximum interest rate that would allow her to spend $105,000 in the current period? What is the minimum interest rate that would allow her to spend $120,500 in the future period?

15. Smith receives $100 of income this period and $100 next period. At an interest rate of 10 percent per period, he consumes all his current income in each period. He has a diminishing marginal rate of time preference between consumption next period and consumption this period. *True or false*: If the interest rate rises to 20 percent, Smith will save some of his income this period. Explain.

16. At current prices, housing costs $50 per unit and the composite good has a price of $1 per unit. A wealthy benefactor has given Joe, a penniless person, 1 unit of housing and 50 units of the composite good. Now the price of housing falls by half. *True or false*: Joe is necessarily better off as a result of the price change. Explain.

*17. Tom and Karen are economists. In an attempt to limit their son Harry's use of the family car, they charge him a user fee of $.20/km. At that price he still uses the car more than they would like, but they do not want simply to raise the price further. So Tom and Karen ask him the following question: "What is the minimum increase in your weekly allowance you would accept in return for having the fee raised to $.40/km?" Harry, who is a known truth-teller and has conventional preferences, answers, "$10/wk."

    a. If Tom and Karen increase Harry's allowance by $10/wk and charge him 40 cents/km, will he drive less than before? Explain.

    b. Will the additional revenue from the higher charges per kilometre be more than, less than, or equal to $10/wk? Explain.

*18. All book buyers have the same preferences, and under current arrangements, those who buy used books at $22 receive the same utility as those who buy new books at $50. The annual interest rate is 10 percent, and there are no transaction costs involved in the buying and selling of used books. Each new textbook costs m to produce and lasts for two years.

    a. What is the buyer's reservation price for the use of a new book for one year?

    b. How low would m have to be before a publisher would find it worthwhile to print books with disappearing ink—ink that vanishes one year from the point of sale of a new book, thus eliminating the used-book market? (Assume that eliminating the used-book market will exactly double the publisher's annual sales.)

**19. Herb wants to work exactly 12 hr/wk to supplement his graduate fellowship. He can either work as a clerk in the library at $6/hr or individually tutor first-year graduate students in economics. Pay differences aside, he is indifferent between these two jobs. Each of three first-year students has a demand curve for tutoring given by $P = 10 - Q$, where P is the price in dollars per hour, and Q is the number of hours per week. If Herb has the option of setting a two-part tariff for his tutoring services, how many hours per week should he tutor and how many hours should he work in the library? If he does any tutoring, what should his rate structure be?

**20. How would your answer to the preceding question change if Herb could earn $7 per hour in the library?

**21. Grace Hopper and her Aunt Prudence live in a two-period universe. Both have an income of $60,000 in period 1, and no income in period 2. The interest rate is zero. Grace's utility function has the form $U = (C_1)^2 C_2$, while Aunt Prudence chooses to consume exactly the same amount in each period. How much will each spend in each period? (*Hint*: If you do not have calculus, see Appendix 3A.)

**22. How will your answers to the preceding question change if the interest rate increases to 100 percent per period?

**23. In a two-period universe, Max Borlen has an income of $60 in period 1 and $120 in period 2. His utility function has the form $U = (C_1)^2 C_2$, where U is in utils and C_1 and C_2 are in dollars.

    a. If the interest rate is zero, how much will Max consume in each period, how much (if any) will he borrow or lend, and what is his utility (in utils)?

    b. If instead the interest rate is 100 percent per period, how much will Max consume in each period, how much (if any) will he borrow or lend, and what is his utility (in utils)?

    c. Is Max better off in (a) or in (b)? Briefly explain your answer.

    d. How would your answers to (a), (b), and (c) change if Max's utility function were instead $U = C_1(C_2)^2$? (*Hint*: If you do not have calculus, see Appendix 3A.)

**24. Iona Bentley has the following intertemporal utility function:

$$U = (C_1)^{.6}(C_2)^{.4}.$$

Her income is $4000 in period 1 and $4000 in period 2.

    a. If the interest rate is zero, how much will she consume in each period, and how much (if any) will she borrow or lend?

    b. If the interest rate is 100 percent per period, how much will she consume in each period, and how much (if any) will she borrow or lend?

    c. Is she better off in the situation of 24.a or that of 24.b?

d. How would your answers to Parts 24a, b, and c change if instead her utility function was $U = (C_1)^{.4}(C_2)^{.6}$?

*25. Harry runs a small movie theatre, whose customers all have identical tastes. Each customer's reservation price just to see a movie is $5, and lower prices will not induce them to attend more frequently. Each customer's demand curve for popcorn at Harry's concession stand is given by $P_c = 4 - Q_c$, where P_c is the price of popcorn in dollars per container and Q_c is the number of containers purchased. Customers treat seeing a movie and eating popcorn at it as a unified "theatre-going experience." If the marginal cost of allowing another patron to watch the movie is zero, and the marginal cost of popcorn is $1, at what price should Harry sell tickets and popcorn if his goal is to maximize his profits? (Assume that Harry is able to advertise his cost structure costlessly to potential patrons.)

ANSWERS TO IN-CHAPTER EXERCISES

5-1. Initial consumer surplus at $P = \$.75/L$ (and $Q = 28$ L/wk) is $CS = \frac{1}{2}(2.5 - .75)(28) = \$24.50/wk$. Consumer surplus at the higher price $P' = \$1/L$ (and $Q' = 24$ L/wk) is $CS' = \frac{1}{2}(2.5 - 1)(24) = \$18/wk$. The loss in consumer surplus is given by the area of $DCEF$, which equals $24.50 - 18 = \$6.50/wk$.

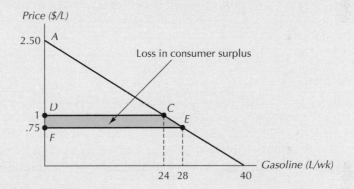

5-2. The maximum membership fee is now given by the area of triangle $AB'C'$, which is $CS = \frac{1}{2}(50 - 20)120 = \$1800/yr$.

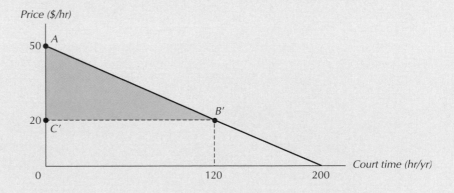

5-3. The two budget lines and last year's optimal bundle are shown in the diagram. A closer look at the tangency point (enlarged area) shows that this year Jacob can now afford to purchase a bundle he prefers to the one he bought last year.

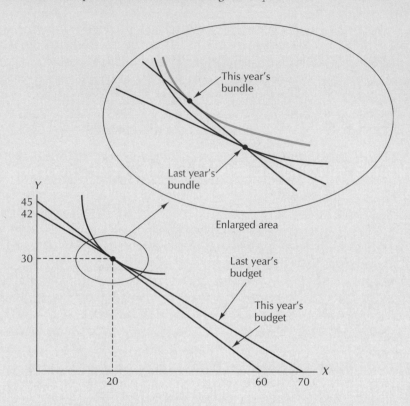

5-4. PV = $50,000 + $42,000/1.05 = $90,000. Maximum future consumption = $50,000(1.05) + $42,000 = $94,500. The equation for your intertemporal budget constraint is $C_2 = 94,500 - 1.05C_1$.

Appendix 5A

ADDITIONAL APPLICATIONS OF RATIONAL CHOICE AND DEMAND THEORIES

5A.1 USING INDIFFERENCE CURVES TO MEASURE CONSUMER SURPLUS

An alternative method of measuring consumer surplus to that using income-compensated demand curves involves the direct use of indifference curves. To illustrate, consider a consumer who eats many of his meals at a Thai restaurant that recently opened in his neighbourhood. The price per meal at this restaurant is $20, and with his current income of $1200/mo, he eats 20 Thai meals per month. In Figure 5A-1, this places him at bundle A on the budget constraint B_0. One way of approximating the benefit he derives from having access to this restaurant is to pose the following question: What is the difference between the most he would be willing to pay for the 20 meals and the amount he currently pays for them? In Figure 5A-1, if our consumer lacked access to the Thai restaurant, he would be located at the bundle D, (0, 1200). On I_1, the indifference curve through bundle D, the bundle labelled C is the one that contains 20 meals per month.

We know that he is indifferent between bundle D and bundle C because they both lie along I_1. This tells us that the most he would be willing to pay for 20 Thai meals per month is $1200 - $500 = $700. But if he is able to purchase 20 Thai meals per month at the market price of $20/meal, he will spend only $400. The difference between the most he would be willing to spend for 20 meals and the amount he actually must spend for the same 20 meals if allowed to purchase them at the market price is $700 - $400 = $300. This difference is a measure of the net benefit to him of being able to eat at the Thai restaurant, and is thus a measure of the consumer surplus provided by that option.[1]

---

[1] The indifference curve method described above yields only an approximation of the true net benefit a consumer receives from the existence of any given market. We examine more precise measures in Section 5A.2. There is a special case in which more precise measures of consumer surplus would be exactly the same as the measure described in Figure 5A-1. This would occur if the hypothetical budget line with the same slope as the original one happened to be tangent to I_1 at bundle C. This, in turn, would mean that the demand for the good on the horizontal axis is unaffected by changes in income. (See Appendix 4A, footnote 3.) Accordingly, we may say that for goods whose income effects are small, the indifference curve measure of consumer surplus will yield approximately the same results as and be essentially indistinguishable from the demand curve measure discussed earlier.

Using Indifference Curves to Measure Consumer Surplus
Given the option of eating at the Thai restaurant, the consumer chooses bundle A, which contains 20 meals/mo. Without that option, he would consume bundle D, which lies on indifference curve I_1. Bundle C is the bundle on I_1 that contains 20 meals/mo, which tells us that the consumer would be willing to sacrifice up to $700/mo of the composite good in exchange for 20 meals/mo. If he has the option of buying those meals at $20 each, he will spend only $400 on them. The difference, $700 − $400 = $300, is the consumer's monthly surplus from being able to eat at the Thai restaurant.

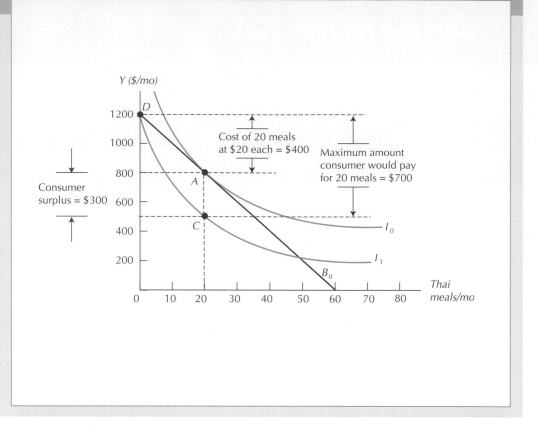

Your budget is $600 per term for evening meals, and your favourite restaurant near campus is Pizza Palace. When the price of a dinner there is $5, you eat 20 Pizza Palace dinners a term. If the price were $15 per dinner, you would be indifferent between eating there 20 times a term and not eating there at all. What is your consumer surplus each term from being able to eat dinners for $5 each at Pizza Palace?

Whether to use the demand curve measure of consumer surplus or the indifference curve measure will in general depend on the nature of the problem at hand. The information provided in Exercise 5A-1, for example, does not permit us to use the demand curve measure. As a practical matter, however, economists are more likely to have information about demand curves than about indifference curves. And for this reason, the demand curve measure is much more widely used in policy studies.

5A.2 COMPENSATING VARIATION AND EQUIVALENT VARIATION

In most cases, the method we developed in Section 5A-1 provides a convenient method of approximating the dollar value of consumer surplus. In this section, we examine two related money measures of the change in a consumer's welfare that results from a change in the price of a good. These measures are known as the *compensating variation* in income and the *equivalent variation* in income.

Consider a consumer with the preferences depicted in Figure 5A-2a and corresponding demand curves, shown in Figure 5A-2b. She derives utility from two commodities, X and the composite commodity Y (which has a fixed price of \$1 per unit). Initially, with money income $M = M_0$ and P_X (the price of X) $= P_{XA}$, she maximizes her utility by consuming the bundle at point A.

Suppose that the price of X decreases to P_{XD}, so that her optimal consumption bundle is now at point D. Her real income has increased as a result of the decrease in P_X. Can we derive a monetary measure of the extent to which she is better off as a result of the price decrease? In fact, we can derive *two* such measures. First, given the new, lower price of X, P_{XD}, we can ask, "By how much could her money income be lowered while still leaving her utility at the same level as at point A?" The answer will be familiar: it is directly related to the substitution effect. At the *new* prices, point C on indifference curve I_A is the cost-minimizing consumption bundle. The money income necessary to purchase the bundle at C is M_1, the vertical intercept of the budget line B'. The ***compensating variation*** in money income is thus the *reduction* in money income $(OM_1 - OM_0 = -M_1M_0 = M_0M_1)$ at the new prices that would leave the consumer at her initial level of utility. The reduction of money income (which lowers her utility) precisely compensates for (or offsets) the effect of the lower P_X in raising her utility.

Alternatively, we could focus on the consumer's new optimal consumption bundle at D. Here her utility level has increased to the level of I_D, because of the decrease in P_X from P_{XA} to P_{XD}. We could now ask, "By how much would money income have to *increase* to attain this new, higher, utility level, if prices had remained at their *original* level?" At the *original* prices, point E on I_D, where MRS $= P_{XA}/P_Y$, is the efficient or cost-minimizing consumption bundle. To purchase the bundle at E at the original prices, however, money income would have had to increase from M_0 to M_2, the vertical intercept of the budget line B''. The ***equivalent variation*** in money income is thus the *increase* in money income $(OM_2 - OM_0 = M_0M_2)$ that would yield an equivalent increase in utility to that resulting from the price decrease, if prices had remained at their initial level.

We can also use Figure 5A-2a to show the compensating and equivalent variations in income corresponding to an *increase* in the price of X from P_{XD} to P_{XA}. In this case, the initial optimal consumption bundle is at D, and the *new* optimal bundle with $P_X = P_{XA}$ is at A. The *compensating* variation for the price increase from P_{XD} to P_{XA} is hence, not surprisingly, an *increase* in income of M_0M_2. As we have already seen, M_0M_2 is the *equivalent* variation for a price *decrease* from P_{XA} to P_{XD}. Similarly, the *equivalent* variation in money income for a price *increase* (which is M_0M_1) equals the *compensating* variation for a price *decrease*.

Compensating variation for a price change
The change in money income that would enable a consumer to attain the *original* level of utility at the *new* set of prices.

Equivalent variation for a price change
The change in money income that would enable a consumer to attain the *new* level of utility at the *original* set of prices.

Standard and Constant-Utility Demand Curves

Figure 5A-2b depicts the demand curves for X that correspond to the consumption choice situation in Figure 5A-2b. The standard, uncompensated demand curve for X is shown as AD. It corresponds to the price-consumption curve (PCC) of Figure 5A-2a.[2] AC is the constant-utility demand curve for X corresponding to I_A. Every point on the demand curve AC corresponds, for each value of P_X, to the cost-minimizing point on I_A. As P_X decreases, the cost of attaining the same level of utility as at A also continuously decreases. DE is the constant-utility demand curve for X corresponding to I_D. Every point on the demand curve DE corresponds to the cost-minimizing point on I_D for each value of P_X. As P_X increases from P_{XD} to P_{XA}, the cost of attaining the same level of utility as at D likewise continuously increases.

---

[2]We derive the demand curve AD from the price-consumption curve in the same way that we derived Figures 4-2 and 4-14 from Figures 4-1 and 4-13, respectively, in Chapter 4.

(a) A decrease in P_X shifts the budget line from B_0 to B_1 and the optimal consumption point from A to D. The compensating variation in income for a price *decrease* is the decrease in income M_0M_1, and the equivalent variation in income is the increase in income M_0M_2. The compensating variation in income for a price *increase* is the increase in income M_0M_2, and the equivalent variation in income is the decrease in income M_0M_1.
(b) The uncompensated demand curve AD is bracketed by two constant-utility demand curves, AC and DE. The (constant) utility level along AC equals the utility level of I_A, while utility along DE equals that of I_D. The area $ACGF$ is equal in absolute value to M_0M_1, and the area $DGFE$ is equal in absolute value to M_0M_2.

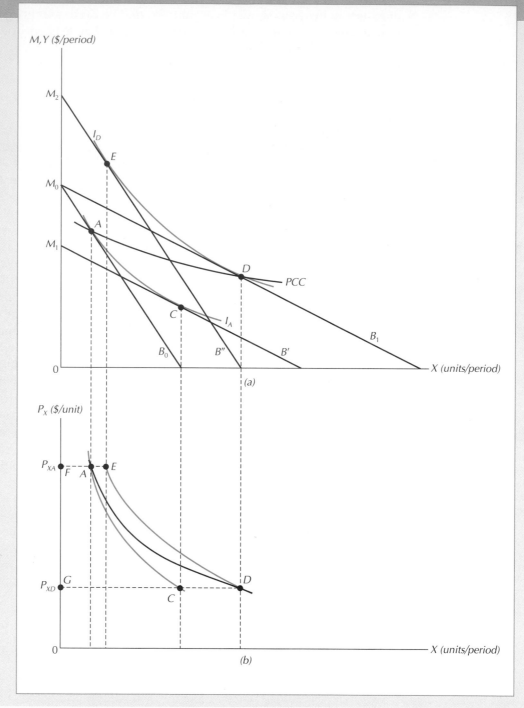

We are now in a position to appreciate a quite remarkable fact. The area $ACGF$ in Figure 5A-2 is equal to M_0M_1 in absolute value. It corresponds to the compensating variation in income when P_X decreases from P_{XA} to P_{XD}, or to the equivalent variation in income when P_X increases from P_{XD} to P_{XA}. Similarly, the area $DGFE$ in Figure 5A-2*b* is equal to M_0M_2 in absolute value. It corresponds to the equivalent variation in income when P_X decreases from P_{XA} to P_{XD}, or to the compensating variation in income when P_X increases from P_{XD} to P_{XA}.[3]

The explanation for these relationships is quite simple. The decrease in P_X has two effects that lower the cost of attaining a given level of utility. First, the cost of purchasing any given quantity of X decreases, by the same proportion that P_X decreases. Second, since P_Y remains constant, the decrease in P_X/P_Y means that X is becoming relatively cheaper. Hence, fewer units of Y are purchased as the consumer substitutes purchases of X for the now relatively more expensive Y.

The area $ACGF$ represents how much money income the consumer would give up to have the opportunity of purchasing X at the lower price P_{XD} rather than at the higher price P_{XA}. The consumer would be willing to give up this amount of money because her utility level at C (with $ACGF$ less expenditure required at the lower P_X) is exactly the same as at A. But this is just the definition of the compensating variation of income for a decrease in P_X from P_{XA} to P_{XD}, which (as we saw in Figure 5A-2) is M_0M_1. It is the fact that the consumer would be *willing* to pay this amount but does not have to that constitutes her net benefit from the decrease in P_X. You should verify the other three relationships for yourself, but the logic is the same in all four cases.

Normal and Inferior Goods

In the case depicted in Figures 5A-2a and 5A-2b, the compensating variation in income is less than the equivalent variation for a decrease in P_X, and greater for an increase in P_X. This fact is readily seen in Figure 5A-2b, since E is to the right of A at P_{XA} and D is to the right of C at P_{XD}, and hence $ACGF < DGFE$. This relationship, however, does not invariably hold. If we consult Figure 5A-2a, we see that the reason it holds here is that X is a *normal* good, with a *positive* income-elasticity of demand ($\varepsilon_{X \cdot M} > 0$). Hence an increase in the budget constraint from B_0 to B'' causes an increase in the optimal quantity of X purchased at E relative to A. Similarly, an increase in the budget constraint from B' to B_1 causes an increase in the optimal quantity of X purchased at D relative to C.

Suppose, however, that X is an *inferior* good, with a negative income-elasticity of demand ($\varepsilon_{X \cdot M} < 0$) over the relevant range of income and prices. Then E will be to the left of A and D will be to the left of C, as we saw in Section 4A.4 of Appendix 4. In this case, the compensating variation for a decrease in P_X ($ACGF$) will be *greater* than the equivalent variation ($DGFE$). And if $\varepsilon_{X \cdot M} = 0$, then in a diagram like Figure 5A-2a, E will be directly above A and D will be directly above C. In this case, the three demand curves in Figure 5A-2b will exactly coincide, and the compensating variation and equivalent variation measures will be equal! Although the three curves coincide, however, they are not identical. AC will still everywhere have the utility level of I_A, while DE will everywhere have the (higher) utility level of I_D, since consumption of Y will be higher along I_D than along I_A at any given quantity of X. These results are summarized in Table 5A-1.

---

[3]Denoting the constant-utility demand curve AC by $D^*(P_X, P_Y, U_A)$, the area $ACGF$ is given by

$$\int_{P_{XD}}^{P_{XA}} D^*(P_X, P_Y, U_A)dP_X.$$

Denoting the constant-utility demand curve DE by $D^*(P_X, P_Y, U_D)$, the area $DGFE$ is given by

$$\int_{P_{XD}}^{P_{XA}} D^*(P_X, P_Y, U_D)dP_X.$$

TABLE 5A-1

Compensating
Variation (C.V.) and
Equivalent Variation
(E.V.) Measures of
Consumer Net Benefit:
Possible Cases

Income-Elasticity of Demand for X ($\epsilon_{X \cdot M}$)	Relative Positions of Points A and E, C and D, in a Figure like 5A-2	Decrease in P_X ($A \to D$) C.V. $= ACGF = M_0M_1$ E.V. $= DGFE = M_0M_2$	Increase in P_X ($D \to A$) C.V. $= DGFE = M_0M_2$ E.V. $= ACGF = M_0M_1$
$\epsilon_{X \cdot M} > 0$ (X normal)	A left of E, C left of D	C.V. $<$ E.V.	C.V. $>$ E.V.
$\epsilon_{X \cdot M} = 0$	A directly below E, C directly below D	C.V. $=$ E.V.	C.V. $=$ E.V.
$\epsilon_{X \cdot M} < 0$ (X inferior)	A right of E, C right of D	C.V. $>$ E.V.	C.V. $<$ E.V.

EXAMPLE 5A-1

Felicia, a rational consumer, has $1200 to spend on good X and on Y, the composite commodity. Her utility function is given by the equation

$$U = X^{1/2} + Y^{1/2}.$$

The price of the composite commodity Y is fixed at $1 per unit. P_X, the price of X, is initially $3 per unit and then decreases to $1 per unit. Derive Felicia's regular, uncompensated demand curves for X and for Y. Then determine how much she will purchase when $P_X = $3 per unit and when $P_X = $1 per unit, and calculate her utility from each bundle. Using her constant-utility demand curves for X and Y, calculate the compensating variation and the equivalent variation in income corresponding to this decrease in P_X.

In solving this example, we shall refer to Figure 5A-2a, which was constructed using the numbers in the example. Felicia's MRS is simply $(\partial U/\partial X)/(\partial U/\partial Y) = (X^{-1/2})/(Y^{-1/2}) = (Y/X)^{1/2}$. For efficiency in consumption she must have MRS $\equiv (Y/X)^{1/2} = P_X/P_Y$. With $P_Y = 1$, this means that at efficient consumption points, it must be the case that $Y = (P_X)^2X$. Substituting this relation into the budget constraint, $M = P_XX + P_YY = P_XX + Y$ gives $M = X[P_X + (P_X)^2]$. Rearranging gives us Felicia's regular, uncompensated demand curve:

$$X = \frac{M}{P_X + (P_X)^2} = \frac{1200}{P_X + (P_X)^2}.$$

Since at efficient consumption points $X = Y/(P_X)^2$, we can similarly substitute into the budget equation $M = P_XX + P_YY = P_XX + Y$ to get the uncompensated demand for Y as a function of P_X:

$$Y = \frac{P_XM}{(1 + P_X)} = \frac{1200P_X}{(1 + P_X)}.$$

Hence, when $P_X = $3/unit, we have $X = 1200/[P_X + (P_X)^2] = 1200/12 = 100$ units, while $Y = 1200P_X/(1 + P_X) = 3600/4 = 900$ units. Felicia's utility at this point (call it A) is $U_A = X^{1/2} + Y^{1/2} = 100^{1/2} + 900^{1/2} = 10 + 30 = 40$ utils. When $P_X = $1/unit, $X = 1200/[P_X + (P_X)^2] = 1200/2 = 600$ units, while $Y = 1200P_X/(1 + P_X) = 1200/2 = 600$ units. Felicia's utility at this point (call it D) is $U_D = X^{1/2} + Y^{1/2} = 600^{1/2} + 600^{1/2} = 10\sqrt{6} + 10\sqrt{6} = 20\sqrt{6}$ (≈ 48.99) utils.

Felicia's constant-utility demand curve for X, for any level of utility U_0, may be derived from her utility function $U = X^{1/2} + Y^{1/2}$ and the efficient consumption condition $Y = (P_X)^2X$. Given that $U_0 = X^{1/2} + Y^{1/2} = X^{1/2} + P_XX^{1/2} = (1 + P_X)X^{1/2}$, the constant-utility demand curve for X is simply

$$X = \left(\frac{U_0}{1 + P_X}\right)^2.$$

By a similar procedure, we can derive the constant-utility demand curve for Y as a function of P_X:

$$Y = \left(\frac{P_X U_0}{1 + P_X}\right)^2.$$

At A, $U_0 = 40$ utils, and so the constant-utility demand curve for X passing through A has the form $X = [40/(1 + P_X)]^2 = 1600/(1 + P_X)^2$. At A, where $PX = \$3$/unit, $X = 1600/(1 + 3)^2 = 100$ units, as we have already seen. The constant-utility and regular demand curves intersect at this point. At point C, where $P_X = \$1$/unit, $X = 1600/(1 + 1)^2 = 400$ units, and $Y = [40P_X/(1 + P_X)]^2 = [40/(1 + 1)]^2 = 400$ units. Here $U = X^{1/2} + Y^{1/2} = 400^{1/2} + 400^{1/2} = 40$ utils, as required. The total expenditure at $C = P_X X + P_Y Y = (1)(400) + (1)(400) = \$800$. The *compensating variation* in income for a decrease in P_X from \$3/unit to \$1/unit is therefore $800 - 1200 = -\$400$. With P_X at \$1/unit, Felicia could attain the *same* level of utility as at A (40 utils) by spending \$400 less than at A.

To find the *equivalent variation* in income, we need to ask, "How much would it cost Felicia to achieve a utility of $20\sqrt{6}$ (≈ 48.99) utils (the same as at point D) if P_X were still at its initial level of \$3/unit?" At point E, $X = [U_0/(1 + P_X)]^2 = [20\sqrt{6}/(1 + 3)]^2 = 150$ units, and $Y = [P_X U_0/(1 + P_X)]^2 = [60\sqrt{6}/(1 + 3)]^2 = 1350$ units. The cost of this consumption bundle is $P_X X + P_Y Y = (3)(150) + (1)(1350) = \$1800$. The equivalent variation in money income that would yield the same utility as at D with $P_X = \$3$ per unit is hence $1800 - 1200 = \$600$. Felicia would need \$600 more to attain the utility level at D, if P_X had remained at its initial level of \$3 per unit.

Which is the better measure of the change in consumer welfare resulting from a price change, the compensating variation or the equivalent variation measure? There is no definitive answer to this question, since the two are measuring different hypothetical situations. Let us note by way of conclusion, however, that the measure of consumer surplus derived from the regular, uncompensated demand curve (area $ADGF$ in Figure 5A-2b) will always be intermediate between the other two measures. For this reason, particularly when income effects are small, we may be able, in Robert Willig's words, to use "consumer surplus without apology."[4]

---

[4]See Chapter 5, footnote 3.

www.mcgrawhill.ca/olc/frank

1. Alfredo Fettucine budgets \$500 per year for eating out. One of his favourite restaurants is "Ace's." When the price of a dinner at Ace's is \$25, he maximizes his utility by eating there six times a year. Al feels that if the price were to double, he would be indifferent between eating there six times a year and not eating there at all. What is the yearly consumer's surplus Al receives from his meals at Ace's when the price per meal is \$25?

2. The campus vending machines sell cans of pop for \$.55. Suppose you bought eight cans per week and you had a weekly discretionary income of \$10. The university announces a new price of \$.75 per can. At this price you are indifferent between buying eight cans a week and buying none. How much consumer surplus did you lose from this price increase? Use a diagram to illustrate your answer.

3. Max Lagrange has an income of $120 per period and consumes only good X and the composite commodity Y, according to the following utility function:

$$U = XY^2.$$

Initially, the price of X (P_X) is $2 per kilogram and the price of Y (P_Y) is $1 per unit. Then the price of X decreases to $1 per unit, with his money income and the price of Y unchanged.

    a. Calculate Max's optimal purchases of X and Y and his utility (in utils) in the initial situation and after the decrease in P_X.

    b. What is the compensating variation in income corresponding to the price change? What is the equivalent variation?

    c. If instead the initial price of X had been $1 per kilogram, and P_X had risen to $2 per kilogram, give the compensating variation and the equivalent variation in income corresponding to this change in P_X.

ANSWER TO IN-APPENDIX EXERCISE

5A-1. The key to answering this question lies in recognizing how to make use of the information that you would be indifferent between eating 20 Pizza Palace dinners per term at $15 each and eating none. Graphically, to eat no Pizza Palace dinners means to consume the bundle labelled D in the following diagram. To eat 20 dinners per term at a price of $15 each means to consume bundle C in the same diagram. The fact that you are indifferent between these two alternatives means that both bundles lie on the same indifference curve, labelled I_1 in the diagram. It follows that the most you would be willing to pay for the 20 dinners is $300 per term (the vertical distance between C and D). When you are free to eat at Pizza Palace as often as you wish at a price of $5 per dinner, you consume bundle A, which puts you on the indifference curve labelled I_0. On your original budget constraint (B0) you have to pay only $100 for the same 20 meals. Your consumer surplus is the difference between the most you would be willing to pay for the 20 meals and the amount you actually pay for them: $300 − $100 = $200/term.

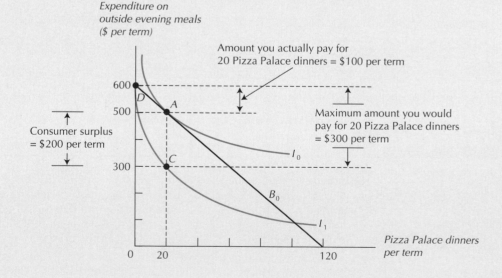

Chapter 6

THE ECONOMICS OF INFORMATION AND CHOICE UNDER UNCERTAINTY

When a toad and his rival vie for the same mate, each faces an important strategic decision. Should he fight for her or set off in search of another? To fight is to risk injury, but to continue searching has costs as well. At the very least, it will consume time. And there is no guarantee that the next potential mate will not herself be the object of some other toad's affections.

In deciding between these alternatives, each toad's assessment of the other's fighting capabilities plays an important role. If one's rival is considerably larger, the likelihood of prevailing will be low and the likelihood of injury high, so it will be prudent to continue searching. Otherwise, it may pay to fight.

Many of these decisions must be made at night, when it is hard to see. Toads have therefore found it expedient to rely on various nonvisual clues; the most reliable is the pitch of the rival's croak. In general, the larger a toad is, the longer and thicker are its vocal cords, and hence the deeper its croak. Hearing a deep croak in the night, a toad may reasonably infer that a big toad made it. Indeed, experiments have shown that the common toad is much more likely to be intimidated by a deep croak than by a high-pitched one.[1]

CHAPTER PREVIEW

Information is an important input for decision making, not only for toads, but also for consumers and firms. Our models in previous chapters assumed perfect information. In practice, however, we are often woefully ill informed. Our concern in the first part of this chapter is with the question of how we gather and evaluate relevant information.

All information has biases and limits, and information varies in its credibility and reliability, or value. We require information in order to make decisions, but one of our

---

[1] See John Krebs and Richard Dawkins, "Animal Signals: Mind Reading and Manipulation," in J. Krebs and N. Davies (eds.), *Behavioral Ecology: An Evolutionary Approach*, 2d ed., Sunderland, MA: Sinauer Associates, 1984.

basic decisions is how much trust to place in the information *itself*. We need to make two judgments in evaluating information from any outside source. First, does the source actually have the information we require? Second, is it in the source's interest to provide us with full and accurate information, or might he benefit in some way from providing us with partial, misleading, or inaccurate information?

Assuming that the source has the information, we might imagine that a source who is our ally will always provide us with all of the information we need, whereas our enemies will always attempt to deceive us. Yet an *exact* coincidence of interests may not exist, even among close friends. Moreover, since communication activities involve real costs in time and resources, even among allies an economic decision is still involved as to how much or how little information to communicate. Perhaps more surprising, a real or potential *adversary* will often have an incentive to communicate *accurate* information to us. This is true even if the information is only a threat ("If you don't do X for me, then I will do Y to you") or a promise ("If you do X for me, then I will do Y for you"). The problem for the information source in a potentially adversarial relationship is how to make her information, threats, or promises *credible* to the recipient.

Between the ally or teammate and the enemy or potential adversary is the source whose *business* is the provision of information. Economic and management consultants are typically paid directly by their clients for providing information. The reference librarian at a public library earns both her pay and her job satisfaction from linking up information searchers with the information they are looking for. The sign at one library information desk we know says simply, "Please disturb." Internet search engines, even in their present crude form, are a powerful means of gaining access to information, although the relevance and reliability of the information sources they locate is often open to question.

Because many of the issues that will concern us arise in simple form in the context of the toad's problem, it provides a convenient starting point for our discussion. We shall see that the principles that govern communication between toads help us understand such diverse issues as product warranties, hiring practices, and even how people choose partners in personal relationships. We shall also examine statistical discrimination, the process by which people use group characteristics to help estimate the characteristics of specific individuals.

Although the quality of decisions can often be improved by the intelligent gathering of information, it is almost impossible to acquire all potentially relevant information. Our task in the second part of this chapter is to expand the consumer choice model in Chapter 3 to accommodate decisions made under uncertainty.

6.A THE ECONOMICS OF INFORMATION

6.1 COMMUNICATION BETWEEN POTENTIAL ADVERSARIES

The problems of communication between parties whose goals are potentially in conflict are fundamentally different from those involving parties with common goals. Toads searching for mates obviously fall into the former category, as in general will any two parties to an economic exchange. The seller, for example, sometimes has an incentive to overstate the quality of his product. The buyer, likewise, often has an incentive to understate the amount she is willing to pay for it. The potential employee may be tempted to misrepresent his qualifications for the job, while the employer may misrepresent the job's attractiveness.

Bridge partners, in contrast, clearly share common goals. When a bridge player uses the standard bidding conventions to tell his partner something, there is no reason for his partner not to take the message at face value. Neither player has anything to gain by deceiving the other. Communication here is a pure problem of information transfer. A message need only be decipherable. Error aside, its credibility is not in question.

A very different logic applies, however, when the interests of would-be communicators are in conflict, or even potentially so. Suppose, for example, the bridge player whispers to the opponent on her left, "I always bid conservatively." What is the opponent to make of such a remark? It is perfectly intelligible. Yet if all parties are believed to be rational, the relationship between them is such that the statement can convey no real information. If being known as a conservative bidder would be an advantage, that would be reason enough for a player to call himself one, true or not. In itself, the statement is neither credible nor incredible; it simply contains no information.

The streetwise shopper knows to be wary of inflated claims about product quality. But how exactly does she distinguish a good product from a bad one? How, similarly, does a producer persuade a potential rival that he will cut his price sharply if the rival enters his market? Statements like "I will cut my price" are problematic in the sense illustrated by the opposing bridge players. Since the producer has an incentive to utter such statements whether true or not, they should convey no information.

We do know, however, that adversaries can communicate information that has strategic value. Toads, after all, are able to broadcast information of this sort. But they do not do it merely by saying "I am a big toad." The big toad's implicit claim is credible only because of the physical barriers that prevent the small toad from uttering a deep croak. The toad's croak is an example of a signal: a means of conveying information.

The toad example illustrates two important properties of **signalling** between potential adversaries: (1) signals must be costly to fake; and (2) if some individuals use signals that convey favourable information about themselves, others will be forced to reveal information even when it is considerably less favourable. Each principle is important for understanding how economic agents gather and interpret information. Let's begin by stating each principle in terms of its application in the toad example and then examining its application in a variety of economic contexts.

Signalling
Communication that conveys information.

6.2 THE COSTLY-TO-FAKE PRINCIPLE

For a signal between adversaries to be credible, it must be costly (or, more generally, difficult) to fake. If small toads could costlessly imitate the deep croak that is characteristic of big toads, a deep croak would no longer *be* characteristic of big toads. But they cannot. Big toads have a natural advantage, and it is that fact alone that enables deepness of croak to emerge as a reliable signal.

Costly-to-fake principle
For a signal to an adversary to be credible, it must be costly to fake.

This *costly-to-fake principle* has clear application to signals between people. On April 12, 1980, Terry Fox, a 21-year-old cancer patient whose right leg had been amputated above the knee, set out from St. John's, Newfoundland, on his Marathon of Hope, a cross-Canada run to raise money for cancer research. The run had to be ended on September 1, 1980, just outside Thunder Bay, after 143 days and 5373 kilometres, because the cancer had spread. Terry died in hospital in New Westminster, B.C. on June 28, 1981. Since then, however, the total of money raised in his name for cancer research has reached over $360 million. Between 1985 and 1987, Rick Hansen's 40,000-kilometre around-the-world "Man in Motion" wheelchair tour raised public awareness of spinal cord injury paralysis and millions of dollars for research and rehabilitation.

Both men are rightly regarded as Canadian heroes: as individuals who triumphed in the face of adversity. Their names still have the power to encourage practical support of their goals, in large measure because their own actions provide compelling evidence of their courage, commitment, and dedication to those goals. It is simply not credible that someone without such a strong commitment would have incurred the costs they bore and made the sacrifices they were prepared to make.

We turn now to some economic applications of the costly-to-fake principle.

Product Quality Assurance

Many products are so complex that consumers cannot inspect their quality directly. In such cases, firms that offer high quality need some means of communicating this fact to potential buyers. Otherwise, they will not be able to charge high enough prices to cover their added costs.

One way to solve this problem is for the firm to develop a reputation for delivering high quality.[2] But conditions will not always allow a firm to do this. Consider the case of sidewalk vendors who sell wristwatches on the streets. If such a "firm" decides to go out of business, it can do so with virtually no losses. It has no headquarters, no costly capital equipment, no loyal customers to worry about—indeed, no sunk costs of any kind. Even if a vendor had supplied quality products on the same street corner for years, that would provide no assurance that he would still be in business tomorrow. And if he *were* planning to go out of business, his incentive would be to sell the lowest-quality merchandise he could pass off. In short, a firm with no obvious stake in the future has an inherently difficult time persuading potential customers it will make good on its promises.

The incentives are different for a firm with extensive sunk costs. If such a firm goes out of business, it loses the value of substantial investments that cannot be liquidated. Accordingly, the material interests of these firms favour doing everything they can to remain in business. And if buyers know that, they can place much greater trust in the promise of a high-quality product. If such a firm charged a price commensurate with high quality and then delivered shoddy merchandise, it would get too little repeat business to survive, and would thus have incurred its sunk costs in vain.

These observations suggest a reason for believing that heavily advertised products may in fact turn out to have higher quality, just as their slogans proclaim. An extensive national advertising campaign is a sunk cost, its value lost forever if the firm goes out of business. Having made such an investment, the firm then has every incentive to deliver. That firms believe many consumers have spotted this pattern is evidenced by the fact that they often say "… as seen on national TV …" in their magazine ads.

Choosing a Person for a Position of Trust

In many situations employees have an opportunity to cheat their employers. Many productive activities would have to be abandoned if firms could not identify and hire employees who behaved honestly in these situations. The firm needs a signal that identifies a prospective employee as trustworthy. One basis for such a signal might be the relationship between a person's character and the costs or benefits of membership in specific groups. For example, perhaps trustworthy people generally enjoy working in volunteer charitable organizations, which untrustworthy people instead tend to consider highly burdensome. In such cases, the groups people decide to join will convey statistically reliable information about their character.

---

[2]This illustration is based on Benjamin Klein and Keith Leffler, "The Role of Market Forces in Assuring Contractual Performance," *Journal of Political Economy*, August 1981.

The costly-to-fake principle is also at work in relation to the members of religious orders who take vows of poverty, chastity, and obedience. If material wealth, a fulfilling sexual relationship, and freedom in determining how one spends one's time are viewed as goods, then membership in such an order entails real personal costs or sacrifices. For this reason, it seems reasonable to trust the good faith and commitment to spiritual values of an individual who has taken these vows. Even when these specific forms of abstinence are not required, some process of training, initiation, and ordination or swearing of vows is common. Like the deepness of a toad's croak as a signal of its size, membership in such an order is taken as a good signal of trustworthiness, because it would be so costly for an opportunistic person to emulate.

The public outrage at instances of child abuse in Canadian religiously run orphanages and residential schools stems directly from the general abhorrence of any such abuse of a position of trust. Yet the outrage is also related to the fact that some of the perpetrators of those acts broke their vows, and in the process devalued those vows as a signal of trustworthiness.

Choosing a Hard-Working, Smart Employee

As a final illustration of the costly-to-fake principle, consider a degree with honours from an elite university. Employers are looking for people who are smart and willing to work hard. There are obviously a great many people in the world who have both these traits yet do not have an elite degree. Even so, employers are reasonably safe in assuming that a person who has such a degree is both smart and hard working, for it is not obvious how anyone without that combination of traits could go about getting an elite degree with honours.

No one really questions the fact that the graduates of elite institutions generally turn out to be productive employees. But there is a lively debate indeed about the extent to which attendance at these institutions actually *causes* high productivity. People who think it does point to the fact that the graduates of elite institutions earn significantly higher salaries. Skeptics caution, however, that the entire differential cannot be attributed to the quality of their education. The problem is that the students at the best institutions were undoubtedly more productive to begin with. These institutions, after all, screen their applicants carefully and accept only those with the strongest records of achievement.

6.3 THE FULL-DISCLOSURE PRINCIPLE

Full-disclosure principle Individuals must disclose even unfavourable qualities about themselves, lest their silence be taken to mean that they have something even worse to hide.

A second important principle illustrated by the toad example can be called the *full-disclosure principle*, which says that if some individuals stand to benefit by revealing a favourable value of some trait, others will be forced to disclose their less favourable values. This principle helps answer the initially puzzling question of why the smaller toads bother to croak at all.[3] By croaking, they tell other toads how small they are. Why not just remain silent and let them wonder?

Suppose all toads with croaks pitched higher than some threshold did, in fact, remain silent. Imagine an index from 0 to 10 that measures the pitch of a toad's croak, with 10 being the highest and 0 the lowest; and suppose, arbitrarily, that toads with an index value above 6 kept quiet (see Figure 6-1).It is easy to see why any such pattern would be inherently unstable. Consider a toad with an index of 6.1, just above the cutoff. If he remains silent, what will other toads think? From experience, they will know that *because* he is silent, his croak must be pitched higher than 6. But how much higher?

---

[3]See Krebs and Dawkins, 1984.

FIGURE 6-1

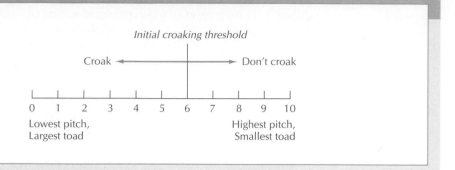

Lacking information about this particular toad, they cannot say exactly. It generally will be possible, however, to make a statistical guess. Suppose toads were uniformly scattered along the pitch scale. This means that if we picked a toad at random from the entire population of toads, the pitch of its croak would be equally likely to take any value along the pitch scale. With the croaking threshold at 6, however, a toad who remained silent would be systematically different from a randomly selected toad. In particular, experience would tell that the average index for toads who remain silent is 8 (halfway between 6 and 10). Any toad with an index less than 8 would, by the fact of his silence, create the impression that he is smaller than he really is. Our toad with an index of 6.1 would therefore do far better to croak than not.

Thus, if the threshold for remaining silent were 6, it would pay all toads with an index less than 8 to croak. If they do, of course, the threshold will not remain at 6. It will shift to 8. But a threshold of 8 will not be stable either. With the cutoff at that level, it will pay all toads with an index less than 9 to croak. *Any* threshold less than 10 is for similar reasons destined to unravel. This process happens not because the small toads want to call attention to their smallness by croaking. Rather, they are forced to do so in order to keep from appearing smaller than they really are.

The full-disclosure principle derives from the fact that potential adversaries do not all have access to the same information. In the toad case, the asymmetry is that the silent toad knows exactly how big he is, while his rival can make only an informed guess. As the following illustrations demonstrate, similar asymmetries give rise to important signals between economic agents.

Product Warranties

Information asymmetries help explain, for example, why the producer of a low-quality product might disclose that fact by offering only very limited warranty coverage. The asymmetry here is that producers know much more than consumers about how good their products are. The firm that knows it has the best product has a strong incentive to disclose that information to consumers. A credible means of doing so is to provide a liberal guarantee against product defects. (This device is credible because of the costly-to-fake principle—a low-quality product would break down frequently, making it too costly to offer a liberal guarantee.)

Once this product appears with its liberal guarantee, consumers immediately know more than before, not only about *its* quality, but about the quality of all remaining products as well. In particular, they know that the ones without guarantees cannot be of the highest quality. Lacking any other information about an unguaranteed product, a prudent consumer would estimate its quality as the average level for such products. But this means consumers will underestimate the quality of those products that are just slightly inferior to the best product.

Consider the situation confronting the producer of the second-best product. If it continues to offer no guarantee, consumers will think its product is worse than it really is. Accordingly, this producer will do better to offer a guarantee of its own. But because of its product's slightly lower quality, the terms of its guarantee cannot be quite so liberal as those for the best product.

With the second-best product now guaranteed, the class of remaining unguaranteed products is of still lower average quality than before. The unravelling process is set in motion, and in the end, all producers must either offer guarantees or live with the knowledge that consumers rank their products lowest in quality. The terms of the guarantees will in general be less liberal the lower a product's quality. Producers clearly do not want to announce their low quality levels by offering stingy warranty coverage. Their problem is that failure to do so would make consumers peg their quality levels even lower than they really are.

When a car manufacturer declares, "We back them better because we build them better," we cannot be 100 percent sure it is telling the literal truth. But if the claim were grossly misleading—that is, if its cars were significantly more likely to break down than others—it would be a costly lie indeed. And therein lies a rational motive for consumers to credit its statement.

Regulating the Employment Interviewer

Another illuminating application of the full-disclosure principle is the difficulty that the principle predicts for government policies that try to restrict the amount of information corporations can demand of job applicants. With some minor exceptions and variations from province to province, Canadian provincial human rights codes generally prohibit employers from asking about marital status and family status, including plans for having children. Before the enactment of this legislation, employers routinely solicited such information, particularly from female job candidates. The information is correlated with the likelihood of withdrawal from the labour force, and the employer's motive in asking for it was to avoid investing in the hiring and training of workers who would not stay long. Since the demographic information is costly to fake (few people would refrain from marrying in order to appear less likely to drop out of the labour force), it can be a signal between parties whose interests might be in conflict. The purpose of the legislation was to prevent employers from favouring job candidates on the basis of demographic status.

To achieve this, however, it is not sufficient merely to prohibit employers from asking about demographic categories. For if a woman realizes that her own particular characteristics place her in the most favoured hiring category, she has every incentive to *volunteer* information about them. This sets up the familiar unravelling process whereby all but the least favourable information will eventually be volunteered freely by job candidates. The candidate who fails to volunteer information, however unfavourable, is simply assumed to be in the least favourable category. If the legislation were to achieve its desired intent, it would somehow have to prohibit job candidates from volunteering the information at issue.

People and things belong to categories. Categories, in turn, often exist in hierarchies. Some categories are, by consensus, better than others. To be trustworthy is better than to be untrustworthy, hard working better than lazy, and so on. The general message of the full-disclosure principle is that lack of evidence that something resides in a favoured category will often suggest that it belongs to a less-favoured one. Stated in this form, the principle seems transparently simple. And yet its implications are sometimes far from obvious.

The Lemons Principle

For example, as the following Economic Naturalist illustrates, the full-disclosure principle helps resolve the long-standing paradox of why new cars usually lose a large fraction of their market value the moment they are driven from the showroom.

Economic Naturalist 6.1

WHY DO "ALMOST NEW" USED CARS SELL FOR SO MUCH LESS THAN BRAND-NEW CARS?

A new car purchased for $30,000 on Monday might sell for only $22,000 on Friday. The explanation for this large price drop clearly cannot be that the car has suffered physical depreciation of more than 25 percent in less than a week. Economists struggled for years to make sense out of this curious pattern of events. In an uncomfortable departure from their characteristic professional posture, some even speculated that consumers held irrational prejudices against used cars. George Akerlof, however, suggested that mysterious superstitions might not be necessary. In his "The Market for 'Lemons,'" he offered an ingenious alternative explanation that is considered the first clear statement of the full-disclosure principle.[4]

Akerlof began with the assumption that new cars are, roughly speaking, of two basic types: good ones and "lemons." The two types look alike. But the owner of any given car knows from experience which type she owns. Since prospective buyers cannot tell which type is which, good cars and lemons must sell for the same price. We are tempted to think the common price will be a weighted average of the respective values of the two types, with the weights being the proportions accounted for by each type. In the new-car market, in fact, this intuition proves roughly correct.

Why do used cars sell for such deep discounts?

In the used-car market, however, things work out differently. Since good cars are worth more to their owners than lemons are to theirs, a much larger fraction of the lemons finds its way quickly into the used-car market. As used-car buyers notice the pattern, the price of used cars begins to fall. This fall in price then reinforces the original tendency of owners of good cars not to sell. In extreme cases, the *only* used cars for sale will be lemons.

Akerlof's insight was to realize that the mere fact that a car was for sale constituted important information about its quality. This is not to say that having a lemon is the only reason that prompts people to sell their cars. Even if it were just a minor reason, however, it would still keep the owner of a good car from getting full value for it in the secondhand market. And that may be all that is needed to initiate the by now familiar unravelling process. Indeed, trouble-free cars rarely find their way into the used-car market except as a result of heavy pressure from external circumstances. ("Going overseas, must sell my Volvo station wagon" or "Injured hand, must sell stick shift.")

Akerlof's explanation thus vindicates our intuition that physical depreciation is an insufficient reason for the sharp price differential between new and used cars. The gap is much more plausibly understood as a reflection of the fact that cars offered for sale, taken as a group, are simply of lower average quality than cars not offered for sale.

---

[4]George Akerlof, "The Market for 'Lemons,'" *Quarterly Journal of Economics*, 1970.

The Stigma of the Newcomer

The full-disclosure principle also suggests why it might once have been more difficult than it is now to escape the effects of a bad reputation by moving. In the current environment, where mobility is high, a dishonest person would be attracted to the strategy of moving to a new location each time he got caught cheating. But in less mobile times, this strategy would have been much less effective, for when societies were more stable, trustworthy people had much more to gain by staying put and reaping the harvest of the good reputation they worked to develop. In the same sense that it is not in the interests of the owner of a good car to sell, it was not in the interests of an honest person to move. In generally stable environments, movers, like used cars, were suspect. Nowadays, however, there are so many *external* pressures to move that the mere fact of being a newcomer carries almost no such presumption.

Choosing a Relationship

Most people want mates who are kind, caring, healthy, intelligent, physically attractive, and so on. Information about physical attractiveness may be gathered at a glance. But many of the other traits people seek in a mate are difficult to observe, and people often rely on behavioural signals that reveal them. To be effective, such signals must be costly to fake. Someone who is looking for, say, a highly disciplined partner might thus do well to take special interest in people who run marathons in less than two and a half hours. Even the degree of interest a person shows in a prospective partner will sometimes reveal a lot.

Economic Naturalist 6.2

WHY IS COYNESS OFTEN AN ATTRACTIVE ATTRIBUTE?

Groucho Marx once said he wouldn't join any club that would have him as a member. To follow a similar strategy in the search for a relationship would obviously result in frustration. And yet Groucho was clearly onto something. There may be good reasons for avoiding a seemingly attractive searcher who is too eager. If this person is as attractive as he or she seems, why such eagerness? Such a posture will often suggest unfavourable values for traits that are difficult to observe. The properties of effective signals thus make it clear why coyness, within limits, is so adaptive. It is very difficult, apparently, for eager persons to disguise their eagerness.

The same properties also have implications for the institutional arrangements under which people search for partners. An often decried difficulty of modern urban life is that heavy work schedules make it hard for people to meet one another. In response, commercial dating services emerged offering to match people with ostensibly similar interests and tastes. Participants in these services were thus spared the time and expense of getting to know people with whom they have few interests in common. They also avoided uncertainty about whether their prospective partner was interested in meeting someone. And yet while marriages have sometimes resulted from commercial dating services, the consensus appears to be that they are a bad investment. The apparent reason is that, without meaning to, they act as a screening device that identifies people who have trouble initiating their own relationships. To be sure, sometimes a participant's trouble is merely that he or she is too busy. But often it is the result of personality problems or other, more worrisome difficulties. People who participate in dating services are indeed easier to meet, just as the advertisements say. But basic signalling theory says that, on the average, they are less worth meeting.

MATE MART

The picture has changed somewhat in recent years, complicating this basic story. Time pressures have not disappeared, and increased mobility has increased the demand for ways of meeting new people quickly. Computerized dating services have refined their methods, adding elements such as psychologically more sophisticated questionnaires and videotaped messages to increase selectivity in matchups. A number of services have gone online, thereby lowering the time-cost of checking out the potential pool relative to alternative ways of meeting new prospects. These changes have increased the number of people using these services *and* the average quality of the participants. The result has been a decrease in the stigma attached to trying a dating service: indeed, in some circles it is a sign of being adventuresome.

At the same time, however, technological change in the "meet market" has meant that dating services now face increased competition not only from traditional sources such as newspaper "personal" ads—which have grown rapidly, in both family-rated and R-rated versions—but also from online chat rooms. Despite their potential risks, including the informational asymmetries and false self-advertising they permit, chat rooms and such person-to-person (P2P) online media reduce the need for the relationship broker. Signalling theory is still relevant, but the landscape in which we apply it is rapidly changing.

6.4 CONSPICUOUS CONSUMPTION AS ABILITY SIGNALLING

Suppose that you have been unjustly accused of a serious crime and are looking for a lawyer to represent you. And suppose your choice is between two lawyers who, so far as you know, are identical in all respects, except for their standard of consumption. One wears a threadbare polyester suit off the rack and arrives at the courthouse in a 15-year-old, rust-eaten Chevy Citation. The other wears an impeccably tailored sharkskin suit and drives a new BMW 750i. Which one would you hire?

Our simple signalling principles suggest that the latter lawyer is probably a better bet. The reason is that a lawyer's ability level in a competitive market is likely to be mirrored closely by his income, which in turn will be positively correlated with his consumption. There is obviously no guarantee that the lawyer who spends more on consumption will have higher ability. But here, as in other situations involving risk, people must be guided by the laws of probability. And these laws say unequivocally to choose the better-dressed lawyer.

Where important decisions involving people we do not know well are involved, even weak signals of ability are often decisive. Close employment decisions are an obvious example. First impressions count for a lot during job interviews, and as apparel manufacturers are fond of reminding us, we never get a second chance to make a first impression. Placement counsellors have always stressed the importance of quality attire and a good address in the job search process. Even when the employer *knows* how good an applicant is, she may still care a great deal about how that person will come across to others. This will be especially true in jobs that involve extensive contact with outsiders who do *not* know how good the employee is.

Judging from their spending behaviour, many single people seem to believe that their marriage prospects hinge critically on what clothes they wear and what cars they drive. At first glance, this seems curious because by the time most people marry, they presumably know one another well enough for such things not to count for much. Even so, many potential mates have been rejected at the outset for seeming "unsuitable." The trappings of success do not guarantee that a person will marry well, but they do strengthen the chances of drawing a second glance.

The importance of consumption goods as signals of ability will be different for different occupations. Earnings and the abilities that count most among research professors are not strongly correlated, and most professors think nothing of continuing to drive a 15-year-old automobile if it still serves them reliably. But it would be a big mistake for an aspiring investment banker to drive such a car in the presence of his potential clients.

Note that conspicuous consumption as an ability signal confronts us with a dilemma. The concept of a tasteful wardrobe, like the notion of a fast car, is inescapably relative. To make a good first impression, it is not sufficient to wear clothes that are clean and mended. We must wear something that looks better than what most others wear. This creates an incentive for everyone to save less and spend more on clothing. But when *everyone* spends more on clothing, relative appearance remains unchanged. Conspicuous consumption is thus essentially a positional good (see Chapter 5). In the familiar stadium metaphor, all spectators leap to their feet to get a better view of an exciting play, only to find the view no better than if all had remained seated. Here, too, the aggregate outcome of individually rational behaviour is markedly different from what people had hoped.

As a group, it might pay to spend much less on conspicuous consumption and to save much more for retirement. But if conspicuous consumption strongly influences estimates of ability, it will not pay any individual, acting alone, to take this step.

6.B CHOICE UNDER UNCERTAINTY

No matter how much time and energy we spend gathering information, most choices must be made without complete knowledge about the relevant alternatives. The choice between, say, taking a ski trip or buying a new CD player can be made more intelligently if we consult sources like the Weather Channel and *Consumer Reports.* And yet, in the end, we simply cannot rule out possibilities like bad weather or defective computer chips. Such risks are a prominent feature of many of our most important decisions. Our task in the remainder of this chapter is to enlarge the basic consumer choice model in Chapter 3 to accommodate them.

6.5 PROBABILITY AND EXPECTED VALUE

Choosing a university to attend, a person to marry, an occupation to pursue, even a movie to see—in each case there are likely to be important characteristics of the alternatives that you are uncertain about at the moment of choice. Sometimes your choice is between two alternatives that are equally risky (the choice, for example, between two blind dates); other times it will be between a little-known alternative and a relatively familiar one (for instance, the decision whether to transfer to another university or to stay where you are).

Economic decisions made under uncertainty are essentially gambles. We have a variety of intuitions about what makes for an attractive gamble, and many of these intuitions carry over into the realm of economic choices. To illustrate, consider the following series of gambles involving the toss of a fair coin.

Gamble 1.   If the coin comes up heads, you win $100; if tails, you lose $.50.

This is a gamble you are unlikely ever to be offered in a profit-making casino. The winning outcome is 200 times larger than the losing outcome and the two outcomes are equally likely. Only people whose religious faith proscribes gambling would consider turning this gamble down, and even for them, the choice might be difficult. (They might, for example, think it best to take the gamble and donate their winnings to charity.)

Gamble 2.   If heads, you win $200; if tails, you lose $100.

With a winning outcome only twice as large as the losing outcome, this bet is obviously less attractive than the first, but it too would be accepted by many people.

Finally, consider a third gamble. It is the same as the second except the payoffs are multiplied by 100.

Gamble 3.   If heads, you win $20,000; if tails, you lose $10,000; losers are allowed to pay off their loss in small monthly payments spread out over 30 years.

If put to the test, most people would refuse this bet, even though its payoffs are in exactly the same proportion as those in gamble 2. It is the task of a theory of choice under uncertainty to explain this pattern of behaviour.

Expected value
The weighted sum of all possible outcomes, with each outcome weighted by its probability of occurrence.

One important property of a gamble is its *expected value*, a weighted average of all its possible outcomes, where the weights are the respective probabilities. The probability that a fair coin comes up heads when tossed is 50 percent. One way of interpreting this statement is to say that it means that if a fair coin were tossed a very large number of times, it would come up heads almost exactly half the time, tails the remaining times. Thus, the three bets described above have expected values of

$$EV_1 = (1/2)(\$100) + (1/2)(-\$.50) = \$49.75; \qquad (6.1)$$

$$EV_2 = (1/2)(\$200) + (1/2)(-\$100) = \$50; \qquad (6.2)$$

and

$$EV_3 = (1/2)(\$20,000) + (1/2)(-\$10,000) = \$5000, \qquad (6.3)$$

where the notation EV_i denotes the expected value of gamble i, where $i = 1, 2, 3$.

A gamble is clearly more attractive if it has a positive expected value rather than a negative one. But from the way most people respond to these three hypothetical gambles, it is clear that having a positive expected value is by no means sufficient to make a gamble attractive. On the contrary, gamble 3 has the highest expected value of the three, yet is the one least likely to be accepted. In contrast, gamble 1, which has the lowest expected value, is the one most likely to be chosen.

Now, the lesson is obviously not that having a higher expected value is a bad thing in itself. Rather, it is that in addition to the expected value of a gamble, most people also consider how they feel about each of its possible outcomes. The feature that makes gamble 3 so unattractive to most people is that there is a 50–50 chance of the extremely unpleasant outcome of losing \$10,000. Gamble 2 also contains an unpleasant possibility, namely, a 50–50 chance of losing \$100. But this is an outcome many people feel they could live with. Gamble 1 is by far the easiest choice for most people because its positive outcome is large enough to make a difference, while its negative outcome is too small to really matter.

6.6 THE VON NEUMANN–MORGENSTERN EXPECTED UTILITY MODEL

Expected utility
The expected utility of a gamble is the expected value of utility over all possible outcomes.

The formal economic theory of choice between uncertain alternatives was advanced by John von Neumann and Oskar Morgenstern. Its central premise is that people choose the alternative that has not the highest expected value but the highest *expected utility*. Their theory of expected utility maximization assumes a utility function U that assigns a numerical measure to the satisfaction associated with different outcomes. *The expected utility of a gamble is the expected value of utility over all possible outcomes.*

For the sake of simplicity, we will consider the outcome of a gamble to be defined uniquely by the amount of total wealth to which it corresponds. For example, if a consumer with an initial wealth level of 1000 accepted gamble 1 above and won, the outcome would be a total wealth of $1000 + 100 = 1100$, and the consumer's utility would be $U(1100)$. If he lost, his wealth would be $1000 - .50 = 999.50$, his utility $U(999.50)$. More generally, if M_0 is the consumer's initial wealth level, the expected utility of accepting the first gamble would be

$$EU_1 = (1/2) U(M_0 + 100) + (1/2) U(M_0 - .50). \qquad (6.4)$$

If your choice is between accepting gamble 1 or refusing it, and you refuse it, your expected utility will simply be the utility of the wealth level M_0, namely, $U(M_0)$. Faced with this choice, the von Neumann–Morgenstern expected utility criterion tells you to accept the gamble if and only if EU_1 is larger than $U(M_0)$.

EXAMPLE 6-1

Suppose Lee's utility function is given by $U(M) = \sqrt{M}$. If Lee has an initial wealth of \$10,000, which of the above gambles has the highest expected utility?

The three expected utilities are given by

$$EU_1 = (1/2)\sqrt{10,100} + (1/2)\sqrt{9999.50} = 100.248,$$
$$EU_2 = (1/2)\sqrt{10,200} + (1/2)\sqrt{9900} = 100.247,$$

and

$$EU_3 = (1/2)\sqrt{30,000} + (1/2)\sqrt{0} = 86.603,$$

so gamble 1 is the most attractive of the three for Lee.

The key insight of the theory is that the expected values of the outcomes of a set of alternatives need not have the same ranking as the expected utilities of the alternatives. Differences in these orderings arise because utility is often a nonlinear function of final wealth. In the empirically most common case, utility is assumed to be a *concave* function of total wealth, which means that the utility function has the characteristic profile shown in Figure 6-2. More formally, a function $U(M)$ is said to be concave if for any pair of values M_1 and M_2, the function lies above the chord joining the points $[M_1, U(M_1)]$ and $[M_2, U(M_2)]$. The utility function $U = \sqrt{M}$ is a concave function of M. A utility function that is concave in M is also said to exhibit **diminishing marginal utility** of wealth. Marginal utility is simply the slope of the utility function,[5] and a utility function with diminishing marginal utility is one whose slope declines as M increases. Intuitively, the meaning of diminishing marginal utility of wealth is that the more wealth a consumer has, the smaller will be the increase in his utility caused by a 1-unit increase in wealth.

Individuals whose utility functions are concave in total wealth are said to be **risk averse**, which means that they would always refuse a gamble whose expected value is zero. Gambles with an expected value of zero are called **fair gambles**.

Consider, for example, a gamble G in which you win $30 if the coin comes up heads, but lose $30 if tails. The expected value of this gamble is $(1/2)30 + (1/2)(-30) = 0$, so it is a fair gamble. For a person with an initial wealth level of $40, and utility function given by $U = U(M)$, where U is measured in "utils," the expected utility of this gamble is

$$EU_G = .5U(40 - 30) + .5U(40 + 30) = .5U(10) + .5U(70). \qquad (6.5)$$

For any fair gamble, the expected value of your wealth if you accept the gamble is the same as the certain value of your wealth if you refuse the gamble. Here, the expected value of wealth when you take the gamble is equal to $40. If you refuse the gamble, you will have a certain wealth level of $40, which yields utility equal to $U(40)$. Expected utility theory says that if $EU_G > U(40)$, you should accept the gamble; if $EU_G < U(40)$, you should refuse it; and if $EU_G = U(40)$, you should be indifferent between accepting or refusing it.

The expected utility of a gamble has a straightforward geometric interpretation. We first construct the chord that joins the points on the utility function that correspond to

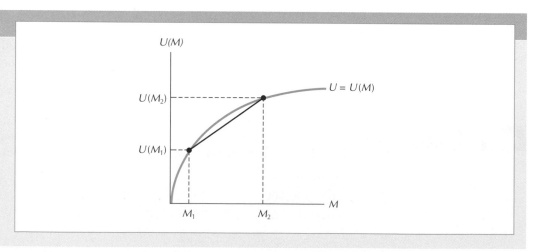

FIGURE 6-2

A Concave Utility Function
Any arc of a concave utility function lies above the corresponding chord.

---

[5]See Appendix 3A for a more extended discussion of marginal utility and Module 7 of the online *Basic Math Review* for weights.

losing and winning the gamble, respectively (that is, the points *A* and *C* in Figure 6-3). For the utility function shown in Figure 6-3, the expected utility of the gamble is equal to .5(18) + .5(38) = 28 utils. Note that this value corresponds to the point on the chord between *A* and *C* that lies directly above the expected value of wealth under the gamble ($40). Note that the expected utility of refusing the gamble is simply *U*(40) = 32 utils, which is clearly larger than the expected utility of the gamble itself.

Indeed, it is clear from Figure 6-3 that a risk-averse person will refuse not only fair gambles but even some that have positive expected value. For the particular utility function shown, all gambles that result in an expected value of final wealth less than $54 yield a lower expected utility than that of standing pat with the initial wealth level of $40.

The gambles we have considered so far have been ones decided by the toss of a coin. With probability 50 percent, a good outcome occurred; with probability 50 percent, a bad outcome. In general, however, the probability of winning a gamble can be any number between 0 and 1. But as the following example and exercise illustrate, the expected utility of a gamble may still be interpreted as a point on the chord joining the winning and losing endpoints, even when the probability of winning is something other than $\frac{1}{2}$.

<table>
<tr><td>EXAMPLE 6-2</td><td>**Your utility function is $U(M) = \sqrt{M}$ and your initial wealth is $36. Will you accept a gamble in which you win $13 with probability 2/3 and lose $11 with probability 1/3?**</td></tr>
</table>

The expected utility of the gamble is given by

$$EU_G = (2/3)\sqrt{36 + 13} + (1/3)\sqrt{36 - 11} = 14/3 + 5/3 = 19/3.$$

If you refuse the gamble, your utility will be $\sqrt{36}$ = 6 utils, which is smaller than 19/3 utils, so you should accept the gamble.

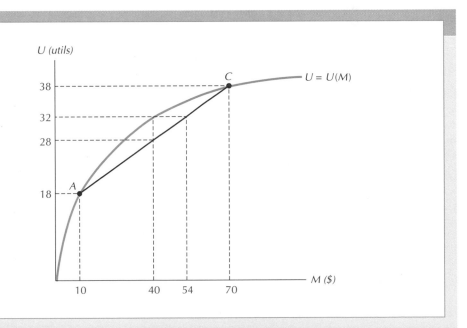

FIGURE 6-3

A Risk-Averse Person Will Always Refuse a Fair Gamble
The expected utility of a gamble lies on the chord joining points *A* and *C*. If the probability of winning is 1/2, the expected utility lies halfway between *A* and *C*. Since a point on the arc of a concave function always lies above the corresponding point on the chord, the expected utility of a fair gamble will always be less than the utility of refusing the gamble.

Graph the utility function in Example 6-2 for $0 < M < 50$. Locate the points on the utility function that correspond to the winning and losing outcomes of the gamble in Example 6-2. Draw the chord between these two points, labelling the winning endpoint C, the losing endpoint A. What fraction of AC must you move from C before reaching the expected utility of the gamble?

The general rule illustrated by Exercise 6-1 is that if the probability of winning is p and the probability of losing is $1 - p$, then the expected utility lies on the chord AC, $(1 - p)AC$ to the left of C, the winning endpoint of the chord. If $p = 1$, so that you are certain of winning, then $1 - p = 0$, and your expected utility coincides with the utility at point C. If $p = 0$, so that you are certain of losing, then $1 - p = 1$, and your expected utility coincides with that at point A.

One intuitive rationale for the assumption that most people are risk averse is that increments to total wealth yield diminishing marginal utility—which, again, means that the more wealth a consumer has, the smaller will be the increase in his utility caused by a one-unit increase in wealth. Most of us are comfortable with the idea that an extra $100 means more to a person if his total wealth is $4000 than it would if his total wealth were $1 million. Note that this intuition is equivalent to saying that the utility function is concave in total wealth—which in turn implies that a given gain in wealth produces a gain in utility that is *smaller* than the utility loss that would be caused by an identical loss in wealth.

Whether people are risk averse is of course an empirical question. We do know that at least some people are not risk averse some of the time (such as those who climb sheer rock cliffs, or go hang-gliding in gusty winds). And we also know that most of us are not risk averse at least some of the time (as, for example, when we buy a lottery ticket, or play roulette in Casino Niagara, or any other game of chance with negative expected value).

Risk seeking Preferences described by a utility function with increasing marginal utility of wealth.

Consider a person with an initial wealth of M_0 who is confronted with a gamble that pays B with probability $1/2$ and $-B$ with probability of $1/2$. If this person is a ***risk seeker***, her utility function will look like the one pictured in Figure 6-4. It is *convex* in total wealth, which implies that the expected utility of accepting a fair gamble, EU_G, will be larger than the utility of refusing it, $U(M_0)$. Geometrically, a convex utility function is one whose slope increases with total wealth.

FIGURE 6-4

The Utility Function of a Risk-Seeking Person Is Convex in Total Wealth
Any arc of a convex function lies below the corresponding chord. For a risk seeker, the expected utility of a fair gamble, EU_G, will always exceed the utility of refusing the gamble, $U(M_0)$.

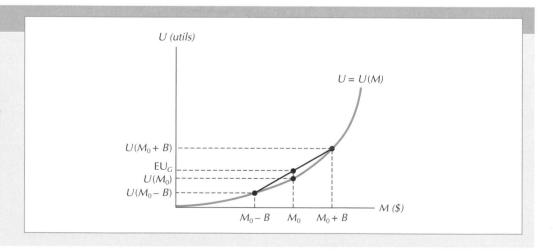

Consider a person with an initial wealth level of $100 who faces a chance to win $20 with probability 1/2 and to lose $20 with probability 1/2. If this person's utility function is given by $U(M) = M^2$, where U is measured in utils, will she accept this gamble?

Risk neutral Preferences described by a utility function with constant marginal utility of wealth.

A person is said to be **risk neutral**, finally, if he is generally indifferent between accepting or refusing a fair gamble. The utility function of a risk-neutral person will be linear, like the one shown in Figure 6-5.

Consider a person with an initial wealth level of $100 who faces a chance to win $20 with probability 1/2 and to lose $20 with probability 1/2. If this person's utility function is given by $U(M) = M$, where U is measured in utils, will she accept this gamble?

EXAMPLE 6-3

Suppose it is known that some fraction z of all personal computers are defective. The defective ones, however, cannot be identified except by those who own them. Consumers are risk neutral and value nondefective computers at $2000 each. Computers do not depreciate physically with use. There is no technical change in computers, and the lemons principle applies. New computers sell for $1000, used ones for $500. What is z?

Because of the lemons principle, we know that all used computers that are for sale must be defective. (The owners of nondefective computers could not sell them for what they are worth in the used market, so they hold on to them.) Accordingly, the price of a used computer is the same as the value of a new defective one. (Recall that being used, by itself, doesn't cause the machines to depreciate.) Because consumers are risk neutral, the price of a new computer—$1000—is simply a weighted average of the values of nondefective and defective computers, where the weights are the respective probabilities. Thus we have

$$\$1000 = \$500z + \$2000(1 - z), \qquad (6.6)$$

which solves for $z = 2/3$.

FIGURE 6-5

Risk Neutrality
A risk-neutral consumer is indifferent between accepting or refusing a fair gamble, because the expected utility of accepting, EU_G, is the same as the certain utility of refusing, $U(M_0)$.

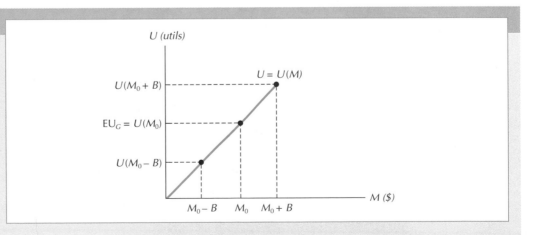

Suppose one in every four new personal computers is defective. The defective ones, however, cannot be identified except by those who own them. Consumers are risk neutral and value nondefective computers at $2000 each. Computers do not depreciate physically with use, and there is no technical change. If used computers sell for $600, how much do new ones sell for?

The gambles we have considered thus far have had only two outcomes. In general, however, a gamble can have any number of possible outcomes. The expected value of a gamble with more than two outcomes is, as before, a weighted sum of the possible outcomes, where the weights are again the respective probabilities. For example, a gamble with three possible outcomes, B_1, B_2, and B_3, which occur with probabilities p_1, p_2, and p_3, respectively, has an expected value of $p_1 B_1 + p_2 B_2 + p_3 B_3$. Because the probabilities must add up to 1, we know that $p_3 = (1 - p_1 - p_2)$. The expected utility of this gamble is therefore $p_1 U(B_1) + p_2 U(B_2) + (1 - p_1 - p_2)U(B_3)$.

To gain added facility with the concepts of the expected utility model, it is helpful to work through some simple numerical examples. In the next example we use a payoff tree to illustrate the outcomes and probabilities for a decision under uncertainty.

EXAMPLE 6-4

Sarah has a von Neumann–Morgenstern utility function given by $U = 1 - 1/M$, where M is the present value of her lifetime income. If Sarah becomes a teacher, she will make $M = 5$ with probability 1. If she becomes an actress, she will make $M = 400$ if she becomes a star, but only $M = 2$ if she fails to become a star. The probability of her becoming a star is .01. Smith is an infallible judge of acting talent. After a brief interview, he can state with certainty whether Sarah will become a star. What is the most she would be willing to pay for this information?

To answer this question, we must first calculate Sarah's expected utility if she lacks access to Smith's information. If she were to become a teacher, she will have a lifetime income of 5 with probability 1, so her expected utility would be simply

$$U_T = 1 - 1/5 = .8.$$

If instead she pursued an acting career, her expected utility would be

$$EU_A = .01(1 - 1/400) + .99(1 - 1/2) = .505.$$

Because her expected utility is higher by becoming a teacher rather than an actress, she will become a teacher and have an expected utility of .8.

Now suppose that she has access to an interview with Smith that will reveal with certainty whether she would become a star if she pursued an acting career. And suppose that the charge for this interview is P, where P is measured in the same units as M (see Figure 6-6).

The clear advantage of having the information Smith provided is that if he says she would succeed as an actress, she can then avail herself of that lucrative, but otherwise too risky, career path. If Smith says she would not succeed, however, she can choose teaching with no regrets. Her expected utility if she pays P for the interview is given by

$$EU_I = .01[1 - 1/(400 - P)] + .99[1 - 1/(5 - P)]. \qquad (6.7)$$

FIGURE 6-6

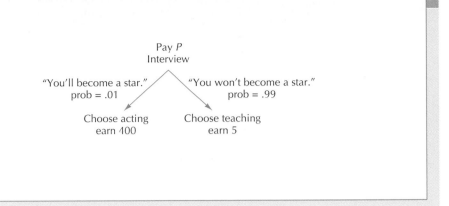

To find the maximum amount that Smith can charge for an interview, we set EU_I equal to Sarah's expected utility if she lacks information and solve for P (recall that if she lacks information, she becomes a teacher and gets $U_T = .8$):

$$EU_I = .01[1 - 1/(400 - P)] + .99[1 - 1/(5 - P)] = U_T = .8. \qquad (6.8)$$

As an exercise, you can verify that a value of P of approximately .0482 solves this equation. For any price less than that, Sarah should pay Smith for his evaluation. But if Smith charges more than .0482, Sarah should skip the interview and become a teacher.

As the preceding example clearly illustrates, information that helps reduce uncertainty has economic value. And this is reflected in the fact that we employ vocational testing services, guidance counsellors, and a variety of other professionals to generate just this type of information.

EXAMPLE 6-5

Suppose you have been accepted by two universities, A and B. A is a much more demanding and also a more prestigious institution than B. In all respects other than the possible influence each school will have on your career prospects, you are indifferent between the two. B is a safe option in the sense that you know you will do reasonably well academically there, and that after graduation you will land an "adequate" job. If you manage to survive academically at A, you will land a "great" job; but it is also possible that you will do poorly there, in which case you will end up in a "bad" job. Figure 6-7 shows the lifetime wealth levels for each type of job and the corresponding probabilities of getting each type for the two schools.

If your utility function of lifetime wealth is $U(M) = M$, which university should you attend?

Your expected utilities of attending the two universities are given by

$$EU_A = .6\sqrt{1,000,000} + .4\sqrt{250,000} = 800 \text{ utils} \qquad (6.9)$$

and

$$EU_B = \sqrt{690,000} = 830.7 \text{ utils}, \qquad (6.10)$$

and since EU_B is greater than EU_A, you should attend B. Notice, however, that your expected lifetime wealth after attending A [namely, .6(1,000,000) + .4(250,000) = $700,000] would be higher than after attending B ($690,000). That B is nonetheless more attractive to you is a consequence of the fact that your utility function, $U = \sqrt{M}$, is concave. The slightly higher expected wealth from attending A is not sufficient to compensate for the risk associated with that choice (see Figure 6-8).

EXERCISE 6-5

In Example 6-5, how low would the lifetime wealth of the adequate job have had to be before university A would have been more attractive?

FIGURE 6-7

Career Prospects After Attending Universities A and B
If you go to university B, you get an adequate job with certainty. If you go to the more prestigious university A, you get a great job with probability .6. But with probability .4 you will flunk out of A, in which case you will get a bad job.

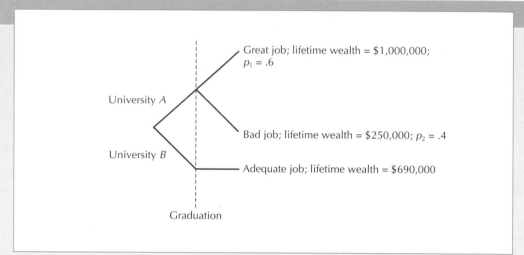

FIGURE 6-8

The Expected Utilities of Alternative University Choices
The expected value of lifetime wealth is higher when you go to A ($700,000) than when you go to B ($690,000). But a risk-averse person will nonetheless choose B, because it has higher expected utility (830.6) than A (800).

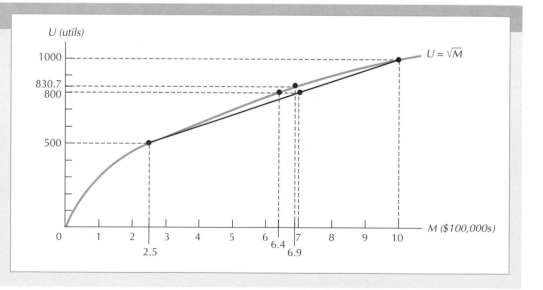

CHAPTER 6: THE ECONOMICS OF INFORMATION AND CHOICE UNDER UNCERTAINTY

Certainty equivalent value The certainty equivalent value of a gamble is the sum of money for which an individual would be indifferent between receiving that sum and taking the gamble.

The answer to the question asked in Exercise 6-5 is called the ***certainty equivalent value*** of the gamble associated with attending university A. The certainty equivalent value of a gamble is the sum of money for which an individual would be indifferent between receiving that sum and taking the gamble.

Exposure to risk is an undesirable thing for risk-averse consumers, enough so that they are often willing to sacrifice substantial resources in order to reduce it. Thus, the certainty equivalent value of a gamble is less than the expected value of a gamble for risk-averse consumers. As you showed in Exercise 6-5, the consumer in Example 6-5 would have been willing to accept an outcome with $60,000 less in expected lifetime wealth in order to avoid the possibility of landing in a bad job.

6.7 INSURING AGAINST BAD OUTCOMES

When the risks that different consumers confront are independent of one another (that is, when the likelihood of a bad outcome happening to one consumer is *independent* of the likelihood of one happening to another), it will often be possible for consumers to act collectively to achieve a result they all prefer.

Risk Pooling

Suppose, for example, that 1000 people like the one in Example 6-5 made an agreement to attend university A and then pool their incomes afterward. If the individual probabilities of finding good jobs are independent, the proportion of people in a large group finding good jobs will be almost exactly 60 percent. (More on this point below.) And with 60 percent of the people getting good jobs and the remaining 40 percent getting bad ones, each person's share in the total wealth in the pool would be $700,000.

By agreeing to pool their incomes, then, people could eliminate virtually all the uncertainty associated with attending university *A*. If the alternative were to attend university *B* and earn $690,000, people would be willing to pay up to $10,000 each for the privilege of joining an income pool. As long as the costs of organizing the pool are less than $10,000/person, everyone can benefit by such a *risk-sharing* arrangement.

Law of large numbers A statistical law that says that if an event happens independently with probability *p* in each of *N* instances, the proportion of cases in which the event occurs approaches *p* as *N* grows larger.

Risk sharing, or *risk pooling,* works because of a statistical property called the ***law of large numbers***. This law says that if an event happens independently with probability p for each of a large number of individuals, then the *proportion* to whom it happens in a given year will almost never deviate significantly from p. Suppose the event is that of a fire destroying a private home, and that it happens with probability .001 for each home in a given year. For a small collection of individual homes, the proportion destroyed by fire can vary sharply from year to year. But in a sample of, say, 1,000,000 homes, we can be reasonably sure that the number destroyed by fire in a given year will be very close to 1000 (so that the proportion destroyed—1000/1,000,000—would be .001).

The law of large numbers also shows up clearly in the proportion of heads observed in N flips of a fair coin. The probability of getting heads on a single toss of a fair coin is $\frac{1}{2}$, and it is not at all unlikely to get heads $\frac{2}{3}$ of the time or more when you toss a coin only, say, six times. (You can expect at least four heads in six tosses 34.4 percent of the time, and *exactly* three heads only 31.25 percent of the time!) But toss a fair coin 10,000 times and the percentage of heads will lie between 49 and 51 percent more than 95 percent of the time.

For individuals, or even small groups of individuals, accidental losses pose a problem of inherent uncertainty. But for a large group of individuals, the proportion of people who will have accidents is extremely stable and predictable. And this property of the law of large numbers makes it possible for people to reduce their risk exposure through pooling arrangements.

Another method of risk sharing is the practice of joint ownership of business enterprises. When a new business starts, two things can happen. The business can succeed, in which case its owners earn a lot of money. Alternatively—and much more likely—it can fail, in which case they lose all or part of their initial investments. Starting a business is thus a gamble, much like any other. Consider a business venture that requires an initial investment of $10,000. Suppose that with probability $\frac{1}{2}$ you lose this initial investment, and with probability $\frac{1}{2}$ you not only get it back but also earn a dividend of $20,000. This venture is thus essentially the same as gamble 3 considered earlier. It is clear that while the expected value of this enterprise is positive (namely, $5000), many people would find it unacceptably risky. But if 100 people pooled their resources and shared the investment, the venture would suddenly look exactly like gamble 2—each person would stand to lose $100 with probability $\frac{1}{2}$ or gain $200 with probability $\frac{1}{2}$. Without changing the business venture itself at all, it has suddenly become attractive to a great many more people.

Partnerships, joint stock companies, racehorse syndicates, and a host of other similar institutional arrangements enable people to translate unacceptably large risks into much more palatable small ones. Someone with a lot of wealth to invest can keep her risk to a minimum by investing it in numerous independent projects. There is a good chance that *some* of these projects will fail, but very little chance that a substantial portion of them will.

Another example of collective action to reduce uncertainty is the operation of insurance markets. Consider the case of automobile liability insurance. An accident that causes death or serious injury could involve costs of millions of dollars. A judgment that a driver was at fault in the accident and liable for these damages could financially ruin an uninsured individual. The likelihood of such an outcome is remote, but the consequences are so severe that few families could bear them. Most individuals would therefore prefer to pay a few hundred dollars a year into a pool, to insure themselves against this possibility. The law of large numbers makes it possible to predict accurately the revenue pool needed to cover all benefit claims. Across Canada, basic liability insurance is compulsory, whether provided by the private sector or (as in British Columbia, Saskatchewan, and Manitoba) by government-owned insurers. Yet many Canadians carry as much as 20 times the compulsory amount of liability coverage: a small extra premium apparently buys a lot of peace of mind.

For the average consumer, insurance for sale in a private marketplace will always be an unfair gamble, in the specific sense defined earlier. To see why, note first that if an insurance company paid out exactly the same amount in benefits as it collected in premiums, then buying insurance would be a fair gamble—the amount a policyholder got back in benefits would be equal, on the average, to the amount she paid in premiums. But a private insurance company must collect more in premiums than it pays out in benefits, because it must also cover its administrative costs and profit. That most people prefer a small unfair gamble (buying insurance) to a much larger fair one (taking their chances without insurance) is often cited as evidence that most people are risk averse.

The Reservation Price for Insurance

What is the most a consumer would pay for insurance against a loss? Suppose a risk-averse consumer with an initial wealth of $700 has the utility function $U(M)$, as shown in Figure 6-9. If he faces the prospect of a loss of $600 with probability 1/3, his expected utility is $(1/3)U(100) + (2/3)U(700) = (1/3)(18) + (2/3)(36) = 30$ utils. (See Figure 6-9, and note that his expected utility lies on the chord joining A and C at the point directly above $M = \$500$, his expected wealth without insurance.) Now suppose this consumer could buy an insurance policy that completely covered the loss. What is the most he would be willing to pay for such a policy? From Figure 6-9, we see that if he paid \$330 for it, his utility would be $U(700 - 330) = U(370) = 30$ utils, whether or not a loss occurred. Since this is exactly the same as his expected utility if he did not buy the policy, he would be indifferent between buying and not buying it. The amount \$330 is thus his *reservation price* for the policy, the most he would be willing to pay for it. Note that $700 - 330 = \$370$ is the *certainty equivalent value* of the gamble of getting $\$700 - \$600$ with probability 1/3 and \$700 with probability 2/3. If I is the actual price of the insurance, and is less than \$330, then the consumer will buy the policy and get consumer surplus from it of $\$330 - I$.

More generally, suppose a risk-averse consumer with an initial wealth of M_0 has the utility function $U(M)$ shown in Figure 6-10. If she faces the prospect of a loss L with

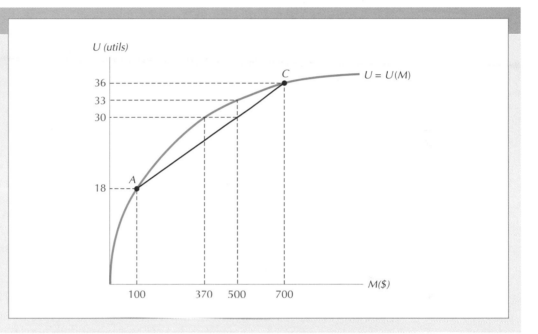

FIGURE 6-9

The Reservation Price for Insurance
The consumer's initial wealth is \$700, and he faces a loss of \$600 with probability 1/3. His expected utility is 30 utils. Because he gets the same expected utility from a certain wealth level of \$370, he would be willing to pay as much as \$700 2 \$370 5 \$330 for insurance against the loss.

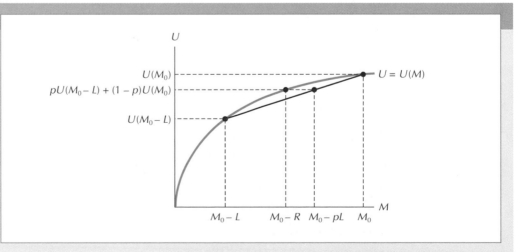

FIGURE 6-10

The Reservation Price for Insurance Against a Loss L Occurring with Probability p
If this consumer paid R for an insurance policy against a loss of L that occurred with probability p, her utility, $U(M_0 - R)$, would be the same as her expected utility without the insurance, $pU(M_0 - L) + (1 - p)U(M_0)$.

probability p, her expected utility is $pU(M_0 - L) + (1 - p)U(M_0)$. From Figure 6-10, we see that if she paid R for an insurance policy against this loss, her utility would be $U(M_0 - R)$, whether or not a loss occurred. Since this is exactly the same as her expected utility if she did not buy the policy, she would be indifferent between buying and not buying it. In this more general case, R is her reservation price. $M_0 - R$ is the certainty equivalent value of the gamble of getting $M_0 - L$ with probability p and M_0 with probability $1 - p$. Finally, if I is the actual price of the insurance, and is less than R, then the consumer will buy the policy and get consumer surplus of $R - I$.

6.8 ADVERSE SELECTION

When a trading opportunity is presented to a heterogeneous group of potential traders, those who accept it will be different—and in some specific sense, worse—on the average, than those who do not. For example, the used cars that are for sale are on average of lower quality than the used cars that are not for sale; and the participants in dating services can be less worth meeting than others. Both illustrate the lemons principle, and are also sometimes referred to as examples of ***adverse selection***. Adverse selection is the process by which "undesirable" members of a population of buyers or sellers are more likely to participate in a voluntary exchange.

Adverse selection
Process by which the less desirable potential trading partners volunteer to exchange.

Adverse selection is especially important in insurance markets, where it often eliminates exchange possibilities that would be beneficial to both consumers and insurance companies alike. To remain in business, an insurance company must have revenues from premiums that cover the claims it pays out plus its administrative expenses and profits. Its premiums therefore must closely reflect the likelihood of claims being filed. Not all potential consumers, however, are equally likely to file claims. In the automobile collision insurance case, for example, some drivers are several times more likely to have accidents than others.

If insurance companies could identify the most risky drivers, they could adjust their premiums accordingly. To some extent, of course, they attempt to do precisely that, charging higher rates for drivers with a history of accidents or serious traffic violations or even for those having no prior insurance history. (More below on how they also set different rates for people with identical records who belong to different groups.) But these adjustments are at best imperfect. Some people who have had neither an accident nor a traffic ticket are nonetheless much more at risk than many drivers with blemished records. Within any broad category of policy, there will inevitably be wide variation in the riskiness of potential policyholders.

Competitive pressure in the insurance market will in general force premiums to reflect the average level of risk for policies in a given category. This means that drivers who know they are much riskier than average face an attractive price on insurance. The other side of this coin, however, is that the same premium is unattractive to drivers who know they are much less risky than average. The result is that many of the least risky drivers will be induced to self-insure. And when that happens, the average riskiness of the drivers who do buy insurance goes up, which necessitates a rise in premiums. This increase, in turn, makes the insurance even less attractive to less risky drivers, inducing still more of them to self-insure. In the end, all but the worst drivers may be excluded from participation in the insurance market. This is an unfortunate outcome for many careful drivers, who would gladly pay an insurance premium that was anywhere close to the expected value of their losses.

6.9 MORAL HAZARD

Moral hazard The incentive for people to change their behaviour in a situation where the behaviour cannot be costlessly observed and they do not bear all of the costs of the changed behaviour.

Another phenomenon with important implications for insurance markets and many other spheres is *moral hazard*. Moral hazard arises when an individual's behaviour in the absence of a contract differs from his behaviour once the contract exists, and where his behaviour cannot be costlessly observed, but has real economic consequences. We find many examples in the insurance market. In the absence of collision damage insurance, Marvin Meek is a careful, defensive driver, since he will bear all the repair costs of an accident. With collision coverage, he is transformed into "Road-Rage Man," a daredevil of the highways and an accident waiting to happen. Without burglary insurance, Homer Housepoor checks all of his windows, doors, locks, and alarm systems every morning and every night, to ensure that they are secured. Once insured, Homer becomes more lax in his security precautions, and the probability of a successful break-in increases.

In these cases, the existence of insurance coverage increases the likelihood of traffic accidents and burglaries, respectively, because it alters the incentive structure. Once insured, both Marvin and Homer are less inclined to exercise care, because they are shielded from at least some of the costs and adverse consequences of their changed behaviour. Even if the insurance company puts clauses into the insurance policies requiring "a reasonable standard of care," those clauses will be ineffective unless the insurance company can monitor the relevant behaviour at negligible cost. Marvin and Homer may or may not be fully conscious of the extent to which their being insured alters their behaviour: it may be that neither has any conscious intent to deceive. As far as the insurance company is concerned, however, what matters is not their intent but their behaviour. If the insurance company's actuaries have calculated accident or burglary policy rates based on the *whole* population, insured *and* uninsured, and if the fact of being insured increases the likelihood of an accident or burglary, then moral hazard will cause such policies to be unprofitable at the originally estimated premium.

Moral hazard also relates to cases of outright fraud. Ace Lumber Supplies is a money-losing business, with creditors knocking at the door. Ace takes out a fire insurance policy, and two weeks later, a mysterious fire burns down its lumber warehouse, totally destroying the building and its entire lumber inventory. The insurance payments save Ace from having to declare bankruptcy; it certainly was lucky that Ace decided to insure against this disaster! Of course, this "lucky" coincidence will bring out the arson unit of the insurance company's fraud investigation department in full force. Moral hazard of this sort results in a number of types of inefficiency, in social terms. First, there will be more fires than in the absence of insurance. Second, when fraud artists successfully perpetrate insurance scams, the premiums of legitimate policyholders increase, relative to what they would have been in the absence of moral hazard. This premium hike has the added effect of causing some people who would have purchased insurance before to self-insure, which for them is a second-best option. Even if there were no additional claims, however, the mere possibility that moral hazard *could* exist forces insurance companies to incur the cost of fraud investigation departments, which itself tends to increase premium rates. Moreover, policyholders with a *legitimate* claim can find—apart from the typical slowness of some insurance companies in reimbursing policyholders, and the haggling over payment amounts that people have experienced—that they are subject to interrogations, delay, repeated demands for further documentation, and suggestions that they may have behaved fraudulently. The inefficiency and costs associated with such situations result from the mere *possibility* of moral hazard.

Insurance companies can take a number of steps to reduce the adverse effects of moral hazard. They can raise premium rates to cover the additional claims resulting from the operation of moral hazard, although in so doing they are imposing the cost of those whose behaviour changes once insured on those whose behaviour does not, and also driving away some good risks. Where monitoring costs are low, they can insert "standard of care" provisions into their insurance policies. They can offer lower premium rates to people who own security devices (for example, home burglar alarm systems, automobile anti-theft devices, and smoke and carbon monoxide detectors) that reduce the probability or the expected amount of a claim. As already noted, they can devote resources to fraud detection. They can provide insurance with "deductible" provisions. If there is an auto accident claim, for example, the insured pays the first $500, or $1000, of repair costs and the insurance company pays only the balance. "Deductible" provisions have the effect of increasing the cost to the insured of changing behaviour, and thereby provide an incentive to exercise appropriate care. It is also not uncommon for insurance companies to increase policy renewal premium rates dramatically for a driver who has made an accident claim, on the grounds that she belongs in a higher risk class simply by virtue of having been involved in an accident, regardless of who was at fault. The result is that the driver can end up paying the entire cost of the accident claim *or more*, in the form of elevated premiums over the next three or four years.

Principal–agent situation
A situation in which one economic actor (the principal) contracts with another (the agent) to act on the principal's behalf, and where the economic interests of the two parties may not coincide.

Moral hazard also exists in many other realms besides insurance. In ***principal–agent*** situations, where one party, the principal, hires or designates an agent to act on her behalf in some economic activity, the interests of principal and agent often do not fully coincide. In such situations, it is often difficult for the principal to monitor — sometimes even to understand fully—the actions of the agent.[6] Two examples of this form of moral hazard that frequently make headlines occur when chief executive officers (CEOs) or other senior corporate managers are charged with falsifying a corporation's accounts, to give a misleading impression of the company's profitability, or with ***insider trading*** for personal gain. Another moral hazard problem in a principal–agent relationship occurs when the administrator of a trust fund manages the assets of the fund in ways that benefit the trustee himself rather than the intended beneficiaries of the trust.

Insider trading
Using privileged information that will affect the price of a company's stock before the information has been made public, to conduct personally advantageous transactions.

Such abuses of trust in situations characterized by asymmetric information and moral hazard have led many Canadian professions, such as law, medicine, accountancy, and engineering, to have self-governing regulatory and disciplinary bodies. These bodies are intended not only to ensure the competence of their members but also ensure that members conform to the ethical standards of their profession. Indeed, much of the direct regulatory activity of federal and provincial governments can be interpreted as a strategy for minimizing abuses and inefficiencies arising in situations involving potential moral hazard.

Moral hazard also arises within firms. Managers typically have an interest in getting as much work as possible from workers while paying as little as possible, while workers have an interest in receiving the highest possible labour income for the least possible amount of work. There is therefore an incentive for *both* parties to the labour contract to engage in opportunistic post-contractual behaviour. Bosses have an incentive to extract more production from each worker through the introduction of "speed-ups" and "stretch-outs," while workers have an incentive to exaggerate the difficulty of their tasks and to minimize their effort, particularly when they are not under direct supervision. The development of labour unions on the one side, and attempts on the part of management to develop more effective, incentive-compatible payment schemes and supervision methods on the other, can both be regarded as responses to problems of moral hazard.

---

[6] The implications of monitoring costs in situations of moral hazard are examined in more detail in Section 7.4 of Chapter 7: "Illustration: The Cheating Problem."

6.10 STATISTICAL DISCRIMINATION

As noted earlier, automobile insurance companies often try to tailor their rates to the driving records of individual policyholders. In addition, most companies charge different rates to people with identical driving records if they happen to belong to groups with significantly different average risk. Perhaps the most conspicuous example is the extremely high rate for single male drivers under 25 years of age. The average accident rate for drivers in this group is much higher than for any other demographic category. Even so, plenty of males under 25 are exceptionally good drivers. The difficulty is that insurance companies cannot identify these drivers at reasonable cost.

Similarly, many Canadian auto insurance companies charge different rates depending on which postal code zone you live in. Their rationale is that traffic congestion, theft, vandalism, uninsured drivers, and other factors that influence claims differ greatly from area to area. The awkward result, however, is that people who live just 50 metres from one another in adjacent postal code zones sometimes end up paying substantially different insurance rates.

Many have complained that such rate differentials are inherently unfair. But before judging the insurance companies, it is important to understand what would happen to one that abandoned these differentials. Suppose, for example, that a company decided to sell insurance at the same price to all drivers with clean records. If it retained its current list of policyholders, this would mean lowering its current rates for people in unsafe neighbourhoods, teenage males, and other high-risk groups, and raising them for everyone else. But why should older drivers from safe neighbourhoods then remain with the company? They could save by switching to a company that had stuck with the old rate structure, and many of them would surely do so. By the same token, members of high-risk groups who now hold policies with other companies would have a strong incentive to switch to the one with the new rate structure. In the end, the company would be left with only policyholders from high-risk groups. The company could stick with its new program of charging the same rate for everyone, but that rate would have to be high enough to cover the claims generated by the highest-risk group of all.

In a landmark 1992 judgment, *Zurich Insurance Co. vs. Ontario (Human Rights Commission)*, by a 5–2 split decision the Supreme Court of Canada upheld the right of the insurance industry to set an individual's insurance rates based on the individual's membership in a particular risk class, essentially accepting the above argument. Yet in dissent, Madam Justice L'Heureux-Dubé stated that "the mere statistical correlation between a group and a higher risk cannot suffice to justify discrimination on prohibited grounds." Even Justice Sopinka, writing the majority decision, emphasized that "the insurance industry must strive to avoid setting premiums based on enumerated [discriminatory] grounds."[7] Thus there remains an irreducible contradiction between individual human rights and the private insurer's need to create risk classes composed of many similar individuals, to enable profitable pooling of risks.

Application: Always Self-Insure against Small Losses

As noted earlier, insurance provided in private markets will have negative expected value because of the resources used by the company to administer its policies. The phenomenon of *adverse selection* provides another reason to self-insure when the size of the potential loss is manageable. It says that insurance premiums must be large

---

[7]*Zurich Insurance Co. v. Ontario (Human Rights Commission)*, [1992] 2 S.C.R.

enough to cover the cost of serving the typical policyholder, who will have a greater risk of losses than the average person. Still another reason that insurance premiums exceed the expected value of the average person's losses is the problem of *moral hazard*.

Despite the fact that insurance premiums must cover administrative expenses, profits, and increased costs due to adverse selection and moral hazard, most of us still find it prudent to insure against major losses, like damage to our homes by fire. But many people also insure against a host of much smaller losses.

Buying insurance against minor losses violates the strategy of always picking the alternative with the highest expected outcome when only small outcomes are at stake. Automobile collision insurance policies typically offer a choice of the amount of each claim to leave uncovered—the "deductible provision," as it is called. If you choose the $200 deductible provision, for example, your insurance policy will cover all but the first $200 of any damage claim. Policies with this provision are cheaper than those without, because the company not only does not have to pay the first $200 in damages, but it also avoids the trouble and expense of processing numerous small damage claims. Because of this additional cost reduction, the amount you expect to save in premiums is larger than the extra amount you expect to spend on repairs. And the higher deductible provision you choose, the greater the expected savings will be. Rather than insure fully against collision damage, it thus makes much more sense to choose a large deductible provision and deposit the savings in an interest-bearing account.

How large a deductible provision? The larger the better, subject to the proviso that you have enough resources on hand to take care of the uncovered portion of any damage claim. Indeed, for many middle- and upper-income consumers, and for those with older cars that are not worth very much, the most sensible strategy is not to buy automobile collision insurance at all.

But what if you follow this strategy and then someone smashes your new $20,000 automobile beyond repair? Naturally, you will feel bad. But be careful not to fall victim to the bad-outcome-implies-bad-decision fallacy. After all, the odds of such an accident were very low to begin with, and even having had one, your premium savings over the course of a lifetime will be more than enough to cover the damages. Relative to the alternative of buying collision insurance, going without collision insurance is a better-than-fair gamble, and if you are wealthy enough to withstand the worst outcome, you should take it.

Caution: Always Insure against Major Losses.   Lest there be any misunderstanding, the advice of the last section does not apply to major losses. If a major loss is defined as one that will deprive you of a significant fraction of your lifetime wealth, you should always insure against such losses. You should carry major medical insurance, with deep coverage against both catastrophic illness and loss of income from disability; you should carry an umbrella liability insurance policy against the possibility of a ruinous court judgment; if you live on a flood plain, you should carry flood insurance; and so on.

Ironically, however, many people leave these life-shattering risks uncovered, while at the same time insuring themselves fully against the possible theft of their television sets. The savvy expected utility maximizer will know to avoid this ill-advised pattern of behaviour.

- Potential parties to an economic exchange often share many common goals, but in an important respect they must be viewed as adversaries. In both product and labour markets, both buyers and sellers face powerful incentives to misrepresent their offerings.

- For messages between potential adversaries to be credible, they must be costly to fake. A firm with extensive sunk costs, for example, can communicate credibly that it offers a reliable product because if it fails to satisfy its customers, the firm stands to lose a lot of money. In contrast, a street vendor, for whom the costs of going out of business are very low, has a much more difficult time persuading buyers he offers high quality.

- Messages between potential adversaries must also satisfy the full-disclosure principle, which means that if one party is able to disclose favourable information about itself, others will feel pressure to disclose parallel information, even if considerably less favourable. The producer of a low-quality product does not want to signal his product's inferior status by offering only limited warranty coverage. But unless he does so, many buyers will make an even less favourable assessment.

- When a trading opportunity confronts a mixed group of potential traders, the ones who accept it will be different—and in some way, worse—on the average, than those who reject it. Cars that are offered for sale in the secondhand market are of lower quality than those that are not for sale; participants in dating services may be less worth meeting than others; and so on. These are illustrations of the lemons principle, and are also sometimes referred to as examples of adverse selection.

- Because of the problem of adverse selection, firms are under heavy competitive pressure to find out all the information they possibly can about potential buyers and employees. These pressures often translate into the phenomenon of statistical discrimination. In insurance markets, people from groups with different accident rates will often pay different premiums, even though their individual driving records are identical. This pricing pattern creates an understandable sense of injustice on the part of individuals adversely affected by it. In competitive markets, however, any firm that abandoned this policy could not expect to survive for long.

- An important analytical tool for dealing with choice under uncertainty is the von Neumann–Morgenstern expected utility model. This model begins with a utility function that assigns a numerical measure of satisfaction to each outcome, where outcomes are defined in terms of the final wealth to which they correspond. The model says that a rational consumer will choose between uncertain alternatives so as to maximize his expected utility, a weighted sum of the utilities of the outcomes, where the weights are their respective probabilities of occurrence.

- The central insight of the expected utility model is that the ordering of the expected values of a collection of gambles will often be different from the ordering of the expected utilities of those gambles. The differences in these rankings arise because of non-linearities in the utility function, which in turn summarize the consumer's attitude toward risk. The concave utility function, any arc of which always lies above the corresponding chord, leads to risk-averse behaviour. Someone with such a utility function will always refuse a fair gamble, which is defined as one with an expected value of zero. A person with a convex utility function, any arc of which lies below the corresponding chord, is said to be a risk seeker. Such a person will always accept a fair gamble. A person with a linear utility function is said to be risk neutral, and is always indifferent between accepting and refusing a fair gamble.

- Insurance purchased in private markets is generally an unfair gamble, not only because of the administrative costs included in insurance premiums, but also because of adverse selection and moral hazard. The fact that most people nonetheless buy substantial amounts of insurance is taken as evidence that risk aversion is the most empirically relevant case. This observation is further supported by the pervasiveness of risk-sharing arrangements like joint stock ownership.

- Appendix 6A discusses search theory, the winner's curse, and the Allais paradox.

1. Why must a signal between potential adversaries be costly to fake?
2. Explain why, despite the potential adversary relationship between sellers and buyers, commercial advertising nonetheless transmits information about product quality.
3. What practical difficulty confronts laws that try to regulate what questions can be asked of job applicants during employment interviews?
4. How does statistical discrimination affect the distribution of insurance premiums within a group?
5. How does statistical discrimination affect the average insurance premium paid by members of different groups?
6. Why is it intuitively plausible to assume that most people are risk averse?
7. Give some examples of behaviour that seem inconsistent with the assumption of risk aversion.
8. Explain, in your own words, why it makes sense to self-insure against minor losses.
9. Give some examples in which people do not self-insure against minor losses.

PROBLEMS

1. Suppose the messiness of apartments is measured on an objective scale from 0 to 100, with 0 the cleanest and 100 the messiest. Suppose also that the distribution of apartments by messiness is as shown in the diagram. That is, suppose 10 percent of the apartments lie between 0 and 20, 20 percent between 20 and 40, and so on.

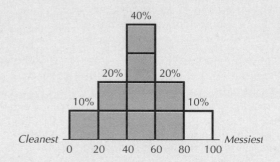

Suppose, finally, that all parents tried to teach their children never to let anyone in to see their apartments if they were over 80 on the messiness scale. If such a rule of thumb were widely observed, what would be your best estimate of the messiness index of someone who said, "You can't come in now, my place is a pit"? In a world in which everyone makes use of all available information, would you expect this rule of thumb to be stable? What do you conclude from the fact that people really do sometimes refuse admission on the grounds that their apartments are too messy?

2. Explain in detail what will happen to a competitive insurance company that charges teenage males the same rates for automobile insurance as it charges its other customers.

3. It is known that some fraction d of all new cars is defective. Defective cars cannot be identified as such except by the people who own them. Each consumer is risk neutral and values a nondefective car at $30,000. New cars sell for $20,000 each, used ones for $5,000. If cars do not depreciate physically with use, what is d?

4. A new motorcycle sells for $9000, while a used motorcycle sells for $1000. If there is no depreciation, the "lemons" principal has operated, and risk-neutral consumers know that 20 percent of all new motorcycles are defective, what value do consumers assign to a nondefective motorcycle?

5. The exhaust system on your 1996 Escort needs to be replaced, and you suspect that the price of a new exhaust system is the same as what you would get if you tried to sell the car. If you know that the car is otherwise okay, what relevance does Akerlof's model of lemons have to your decision about whether to purchase a new exhaust system?

6. What grounds are there for assuming that a randomly chosen social worker is less likely to cheat you in cards than a randomly chosen person?

7. Consider the three gambles in Example 6-1 (page 225). (*Hint:* calculate your results to 4 decimal places.)
    a. Suppose that Lee has the same utility function, $U(M) = \sqrt{M} = M^{.5}$, but his initial wealth is now $1,000,000. Rank the three gambles from highest to lowest utility.
    b. Suppose now that Lee has initial wealth of $10,000, as originally, but that his utility function has the form $U(M) = M^{.75}$. Again, rank the three gambles.
    c. Interpret your results.

8. What is the expected value of a random toss of a fair six-sided die? How frequently will you expect to observe the expected value?

9. A fair coin is flipped twice and the following payoffs are assigned to each of the four possible outcomes:

   H-H: win $20; H-T: win $9; T-H: lose $7; T-T: lose $16.

   What is the expected value of this gamble?

10. Suppose your utility function is given by $U = \sqrt{M}$, where M is your total wealth. If M has an initial value of $16, will you accept the gamble in the preceding problem? If M has an initial value of $100, will you accept the same gamble?

11. Suppose you have $10,000 to invest. A broker phones you with some information you requested on certain junk bonds. If the company issuing the bonds posts a profit this year, it will pay you a 40 percent interest rate on the bond. If the company files for bankruptcy, you will lose all you invested. If the company breaks even, you will earn a 10 percent interest rate. Your broker tells you there is a 50 percent chance that the company will break even and a 20 percent chance that it will file for bankruptcy. Your other option is to invest in a risk-free government bond that will guarantee 8 percent interest for one year.
    a. What is the expected interest rate for the junk bond investment?
    b. Which investment will you choose if your utility function is given by $U = M^2$?
    c. Which investment will you choose if your utility function is given by $U = \sqrt{M}$?

12. Suppose your current wealth, M, is $100 and your utility function is $U = M^2$. In addition, you have a lottery ticket that pays $10 with a probability of .25 and $0 with a probability of .75. What is the minimum amount for which you would be willing to sell this ticket?

13. Your utility function is $= \sqrt{M}$. Your current wealth is $400,000. There is a .00001 probability that your legal liability in an automobile accident will reduce your wealth to $0. What is the most you would pay for insurance to cover this risk?

14. A farmer's hens lay 1000 eggs/day, which he sells for $.10 each, his sole source of income. His utility function is $U = \sqrt{M}$, where M is his daily income. Each time a farmer carries eggs in from the henhouse, there is a 50 percent chance he will fall and break all the eggs. Assuming he assigns no value to his time, is he better off by carrying all the eggs in one trip or by carrying 500 in each of two trips? (*Hint:* There are three possibilities when he takes two trips: 1000 broken eggs, 500 broken eggs, and no broken eggs. What is the probability of each of these outcomes?)

15. Your current wealth level is $M = $49 and you are forced to make the following wager: if a fair coin comes up heads, you get $15; you lose $13 if it comes up tails. Your utility function is $U = \sqrt{M}$.
    a. What is the expected value of this gamble?
    b. What is its expected utility?

c. What is the most you would pay to get out of this gamble?

d. How would your answers change if the payoff for tails fell to a loss of $15?

16. Smith has an investment opportunity that pays $33 with probability .5 and loses $30 with probability .5.

a. If his current wealth is $M = \$111$ and his utility function is $U = \sqrt{M}$, will he make this investment?

b. Will he make it if he has two equal partners? (Be sure to calculate the relevant expected utilities to at least two decimal places.)

17. John has a von Neumann–Morgenstern utility function given by $U = \sqrt{M}$, where M is his annual income. If he becomes an economics professor, he will make $M = \$81$/yr with probability 1. If he becomes a lawyer, he will make $M = \$900$/yr if he becomes a partner in a Bay Street firm, but only $M = \$25$/yr if he fails to make partner. The probability of his becoming a partner is .2. Smith is an infallible judge of legal talent. After a brief interview, he can state with certainty whether John will become a partner. Assuming no discounting, what is the most John would be willing to pay as an annual deduction from his earnings for this information? (Set up the relevant equation. You don't need to solve it.)

*18. In the preceding question, assuming that the interview is costless for Smith to conduct, is he getting the highest possible expected income for himself by charging John the same fee regardless of the outcome of the interview?

*19. There are two groups of equal size, each with a utility function given by $U(M) = \sqrt{M}$, where $M = \$100$ is the initial wealth level for every individual. Each member of group 1 faces a loss of $36 with probability .5. Each member of group 2 faces the same loss with probability .1.

a. What is the most a member of each group would be willing to pay to insure against this loss?

b. In 19.a, if it is impossible for outsiders to discover which individuals belong to which group, will it be practical for members of group 2 to insure against this loss with an insurance company? (For simplicity, you may assume that the insurance company charges only enough in premiums to cover its expected benefit payments, and that people will always buy insurance when its price is equal to or below their reservation price.) Explain.

c. Now suppose that the insurance company in 19.b has an imperfect test for identifying which individuals belong to which group. If the test says that a person belongs to a particular group, the probability that he really does belong to that group is $x < 1.0$. How large must x be in order to alter your answer to 19.b?

*20. There are two groups, each with a utility function given by $U(M) = \sqrt{M}$, where $M = \$144$ is the initial wealth level for every individual. Each member of group 1 faces a loss of $44 with probability .5. Each member of group 2 faces the same loss with probability .1.

a. What is the most a member of each group would be willing to pay to insure against this loss?

b. If it is impossible for outsiders to discover which individuals belong to which group, how large a share of the potential client pool can the members of group 1 be before it becomes impossible for a private company with a zero-profit constraint to provide insurance for the members of group 2? (For simplicity, you may assume that insurance companies charge only enough in premiums to cover their expected benefit payments and that people will always buy insurance when its price is equal to or below their reservation price.) Explain.

*21. Given a choice between A (a sure win of $100) and B (an 80 percent chance to win $150 and a 20 percent chance to win $0), Smith picks A. But when he is given a choice between C (a 50 percent chance to win $100 and a 50 percent chance to win $0) and D (a 40 percent chance to win $150 and a 60 percent chance to win $0), he picks D. Show that Smith's choices are inconsistent with expected utility maximization.

**22. Newt and Aversa have identical farms, and both face the same crop decision: whether to plant wheat or THC-free hemp. Their profits (M, measured in dollars) for each crop depend on the amount of rainfall as shown in the following matrix:

Crop	Low rainfall	High rainfall
Wheat	$8100	$2500
Hemp	$3600	$6400

Newt's utility function has the form $U = M$, while Aversa's has the form $U = \sqrt{M}$. The probability of a low-rainfall growing season is p, and of a high-rainfall growing season is $(1 - p)$.

   a. If each can grow only one of the two crops, at what value of p will Newt be indifferent between growing wheat or hemp? At what value of p will Aversa be indifferent?

   b. Suppose that the probability of a low-rainfall season is 27/56. Which crop will Newt grow? Which one will Aversa grow? Which one made the right decision? Explain your answer.

   c. Now suppose instead that $p = 1/2$, and that Newt and Aversa can each grow a combination of the two crops, with w as the proportion in wheat and $(1 - w)$ as the proportion in hemp. What will the utility-maximizing proportion w be for Newt and what will it be for Aversa?

ANSWERS TO IN-CHAPTER EXERCISES

6-1. The expected utility of the gamble corresponds to point D, which lies one-third of the way from C to A.

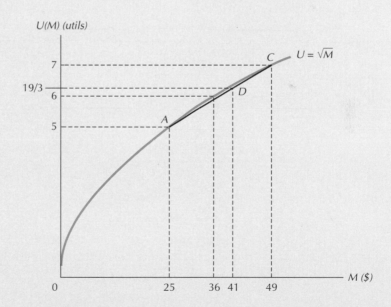

6-2. If she accepts the gamble, her expected utility is given by $EU_G = (1/2)(120^2) + (1/2)(80^2) = 10,400$ utils. Her utility if she refuses the gamble is only $100^2 = 10,000$ utils, and so she should accept the gamble.

6-3. If she accepts the gamble, her expected utility is given by $EU_G = (1/2)(120) + (1/2)(80) = 100$ utils. Her utility if she refuses the gamble is also 100 utils, and so she is indifferent between accepting and refusing the gamble.

6-4. As in Example 6-3, the key step here is to see that the only used computers for sale will be defective. Because of the lemons principle, the owner of a good computer could not sell it for what it is worth to him in the secondhand market. So if the value of a defective computer is \$600, then the value of a new computer to a risk-neutral buyer must be $(1/4)(\$600) + (3/4)(\$2000) = \$1650$.

6-5. Equate the expected utility of attending A to the utility of a job with a lifetime wealth of M', and solve for M':

$$EU_A = 800 = M',$$

which yields $M' = \$640,000$. If the adequate job yields a lifetime wealth of \$640,000, you would be indifferent between university B and university A. Hence, if it is less than \$640,000 (say, \$639,999), you would choose university A.

Appendix 6A

SEARCH THEORY AND THE WINNER'S CURSE

6A.1 THE SEARCH FOR HIGH WAGES AND LOW PRICES

If all jobs paid the same and were in all other respects equally desirable, there would be no reason to continue searching once you received your first job offer. But jobs are, of course, not all the same. In particular, some make much fuller use of your particular mix of talents, training, and skills than others. The better the requirements of a given job match your inventory of personal characteristics, the more productive you will be, and the more your employer will be able to pay you. If you are a slick-fielding shortstop who can hit 30 home runs and steal 30 bases each year, for example, you are worth a lot more to the Toronto Blue Jays than to a local Tim Hortons.

Whatever your mix of skills, your problem is to find the right job for you. The first thing to note is that your search cannot—indeed, should not—be exhaustive. After all, there are more job openings in Canada at any moment than a single person could possibly hope to investigate. Even if it were somehow possible to investigate them all, such a strategy would be so costly—in terms of both money and time—that it would surely not be sensible.

For simplicity, suppose we abstract from all other dimensions of job variation other than wage earnings. That is, let us assume that there is a distribution of possible job vacancies to examine, each of which carries with it a different wage. Also for simplicity, suppose that you are risk neutral, that you plan to work for one period of time, and that the per-period wage payments for the population of job vacancies are uniformly distributed between $100 and $200, as shown in Figure 6A.1. This means that if you examine a job vacancy at random, its wage payment is equally likely to take any of the values between $100 and $200. Suppose, finally, that it costs $5 to examine a job vacancy.

You have begun your search and the first job you examine pays $150. Should you accept it, or pay $5 and look at another? (If you do examine another job and it turns out to be worse than your current offer, you can still accept the current offer.) To decide intelligently here, you must compare the cost of examining another offer with

A Hypothetical Uniform Wage Distribution
The wage paid by a randomly selected new job offer is equally likely to take any of the values between $100 and $200 per time period. On the average, a new job offer will pay $150.

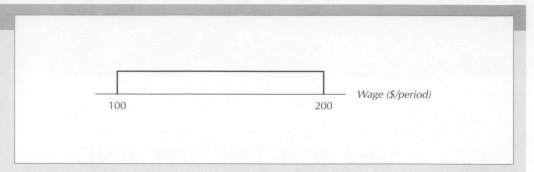

The Expected Value of an Offer That Is Greater than $150
The probability that the next job offer will exceed $150 is .5. An offer that is known to exceed $150 is equally likely to lie anywhere between $150 and $200. Its expected value will be $175.

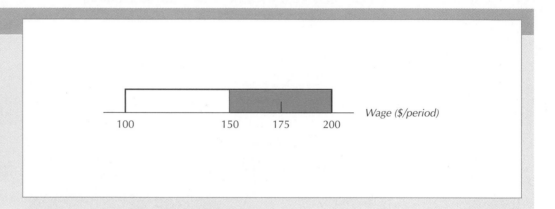

the expected benefits. If there are to be any benefits at all, the new offer must be greater than $150. The probability of that happening is .5 (in Figure A6-2, the ratio of the area of the shaded rectangle to the area of the total rectangle).

Suppose the new offer does, in fact, exceed $150. What is its expected value? In Figure 6A-2, note that since an offer greater than $150 is equally likely to fall anywhere in the interval from $150 to $200, its average value will be $175, which is a gain of $25 over your current offer. Hence the expected gain from sampling another offer when you have a $150 offer in hand—call it EG(150)—is the product of these two factors: (1) the probability that the new offer exceeds the old one, and (2) the expected gain if it does. Thus we have

$$EG(150) = (1/2)(\$25) = \$12.50. \qquad (6A.1)$$

Since the expected gain of sampling another offer exceeds the $5 cost, you should continue searching.

How large should an offer be before you should accept it? The answer to this question is called the *acceptance wage*, denoted w^*. If you are risk neutral, it is the wage for which the expected monetary benefits of sampling another offer are exactly equal to the costs. More generally, it would be the wage for which the expected utility gain from sampling another offer is exactly offset by the loss in utility from the cost of search. The risk-neutral case is much simpler to analyze, and still illuminates the most important issues.

If the current offer *is* w^*, note in Figure 6A-3 that the probability of getting a better one is $(200 - w^*)/100$ (which is again the ratio of the area of the shaded rectangle to the area of the total rectangle). Assuming the new offer does land between w^* and 200,

The Acceptance Wage
The acceptance wage, w^*, is the wage level for which the cost of an additional search exactly equals its expected benefit. The expected benefit is the product of the probability that a new offer will pay more than w^*, $[(200 - w^*)/100]$, and the average gain when it does so, $[(200 - w^*)/2]$. To find w^*, set this product equal to the cost of search (here $5) and solve for w^*.

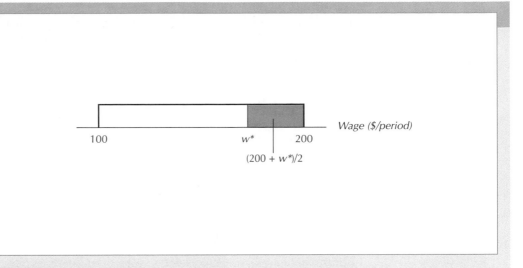

its expected value will be halfway between the two, or $(200 + w^*)/2$. This expected value is $(200 - w^*)/2$ units bigger than w^*.

The expected gain of sampling another offer is again the probability that the new offer exceeds w^* times the expected wage increase if it does. Thus we have

$$\text{EG}(w^*) = \left(\frac{200 - w^*}{100}\right)\left(\frac{200 - w^*}{2}\right) = \frac{(200 - w^*)^2}{200}. \qquad (6A.2)$$

By the definition of the acceptance wage for a risk-neutral searcher, this expected gain is equal to the cost of sampling another offer:

$$\frac{(200 - w^*)^2}{200} = 5, \qquad (6A.3)$$

which reduces to

$$w^* = 200 - \sqrt{1000} = \$168.38. \qquad (6A.4)$$

In this example, then, the optimal decision rule will be to continue searching until you find an offer at least as high as $168.38. When wages are uniformly distributed, as here, you should end up, on the average, with a wage that is midway between $200 and w^*. Note, however, that following this rule does not necessarily mean you will always do better than if you accept a current offer that is less than w^*. If you are extremely unlucky, for example, you might start off with an offer of $160 and then search 20 times before finding an offer greater than w^*. Your total earnings net of search costs could then be at most $100, which is obviously worse than $160.

EXERCISE A.6-1

If you are risk neutral, the cost of search is $1, and wage offers are uniformly distributed between 10 and 60, what is the smallest wage you should accept?

Analogous reasoning leads to a similar optimal decision rule for someone who is searching for a low-priced product. As we see in Chapter 13, most firms employ a variety of discount pricing methods, with the result that there will generally exist a relatively broad distribution of prices in the markets for most products. Again for simplicity, assume a price distribution that is uniform on the interval (0, P), as shown in Figure 6A-4.

The acceptance price, $P*$, is determined in much the same way as the acceptance wage from the job search case. If the price of the product you have just sampled is $P*$, the probability of getting a lower price on your next try is $P*/P$ (as before, the ratio of the area of the shaded rectangle to the area of the total rectangle). If you do find a lower price, your savings, on the average, will be $P*/2$. Your expected gain from another search at $P*$ is therefore

$$EG(P*) = \left(\frac{P*}{2}\right)\left(\frac{P*}{P}\right) = \frac{(P*)^2}{2P}.$$ (6A.5)

If the cost of another search is C, the expression for the acceptance price will be

$$P* = \sqrt{2PC}.$$ (6A.6)

In both the wage- and price-search cases, the acceptance levels depend on the cost of search: when the cost of examining an additional option rises, your acceptance wage falls, and your acceptance price rises. In the price-search case, the relationship between $P*$ and C (as given in Equation 6A.6) is shown in Figure 6A-5.

EXAMPLE 6A-1	**Suppose you are searching for a low price on a price distribution that is uniform on the interval ($1, $2). How will your acceptance price change if the cost of search rises from $.05 to $.10 per search?**

The expression for the acceptance price given in Equation 6A.6 is for a price distribution that is uniform on the interval (0, P). Note that the minimum value of the price distribution here is not 0 but $1/unit. The acceptance price for this price distribution will be exactly $1 higher than the acceptance price for a uniform price distribution on the interval (0, 1). With a cost of $.05/search we see from Equation 6A.6 that the latter acceptance price will be $\sqrt{.10} = .316$, which means that the acceptance price for the uniform price distribution on (1, 2) will be about $1.32. With a cost of $.10/search, the acceptance price for the uniform distribution on (0, 1) rises to $\sqrt{.20} = .447$, so the new acceptance price for the uniform distribution on (1, 2) will be about $1.45.

FIGURE 6A-4

A Hypothetical Price Distribution
The price of a product selected randomly from this distribution is equally likely to be any number between 0 and P. The probability of finding a price below $P*$ is $P*/P$, which is simply the fraction of all prices that lie below $P*$. A price that is known to be below $P*$ has an average value of $P*/2$.

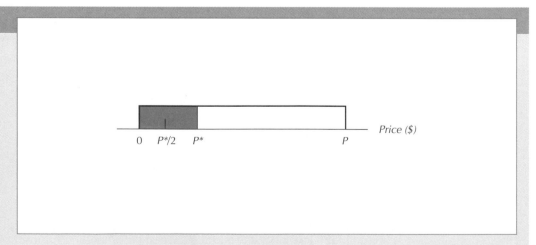

| 0 | $P*/2$ | $P*$ | | | P | Price ($) |

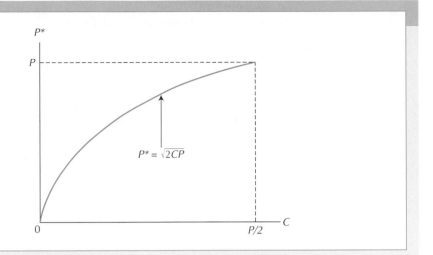

Note the essential similarity between the wage- and price-search problems and the toad's decision considered at the beginning of Chapter 6. Like the rational wage- or price-searcher, a rational toad would weigh the costs of additional search against the expected benefits. He would arrive at an "acceptance pitch," such that if his rival's croak were pitched any higher he would stay and fight.

6A.2 THE WINNER'S CURSE

Some years back, Max Bazerman and William Samuelson performed the following experiment in their microeconomics classes.[1] First they placed $8 worth of coins in a clear glass jar. After giving their students a chance to examine the jar carefully, they then auctioned it off—coins and all—to the highest bidder. They also asked each student to submit a written estimate of the value of the coins in the jar.

On the average, students behaved conservatively, both with respect to their bids and to the estimates they submitted. Indeed, the average estimate was only $5.13, about one-third less than the actual value of the coins. Similarly, most students dropped out of the bidding well before the auction price reached $8.

Yet the size of the winning bid in any auction depends not on the behaviour of the *average* bidder, but on the behaviour of the *highest* bidder. In 48 repetitions of this experiment, the top bid averaged $10.01, more than 20 percent more than the coins were worth. Bazerman and Samuelson thus made almost $100 profit at the collective expense of their winning bidders.

At that price, the winners may consider it an important lesson learned very cheaply. Governments in Canada and elsewhere have used auctions in the allocation of rights to utilize public natural resources, such as oil leases and logging rights, and interest in such auctions has grown in the last few decades. Auctions have been used or considered for the allocation not only of traditional natural resource–based rights, but also of municipal taxi licences, the right to erect billboards, and (in Europe) even pollution-emission rights. Some of the most dramatic auctions were the multi-*billion* dollar auctions held

---

[1]For a more detailed account of this experiment, see David Warsh, "The Winner's Curse," *The Boston Globe*, April 17, 1988.

in Europe in 2000 of cellphone bandwidth frequencies. Rights to use chunks of the electromagnetic spectrum itself (as a scarce public natural resource) were auctioned off, using principles from game theory in designing the sequential-auction method that was used!

Auctions have been used to allocate such rights because under conditions of competition and perfect information, they provide an efficient mechanism for appropriating the economic rents or quasi-rents for the public resource owners or rights-holders. Under conditions of uncertainty and imperfect information, however, it is possible (just as in the penny auction example) that the winning bidders may pay *more* than the rights are worth.

The general principle that the winning bid for an item often exceeds its true value is known as the *winner's curse*. The startling thing about the winner's curse is that it does not require anyone to use a biased estimate of the value of the prize. The problem is that all estimates involve at least some element of randomness. An estimate is said to be *unbiased* if, on the average, it is equal to the true value. Temperature forecasts, for instance, are unbiased; they are too high some days, too low others, but their long-run average values track actual temperatures almost perfectly. By the same token, even if each bidder's estimate is unbiased, it will on some occasions be too high, on others too low. And the winner of the auction will of course be the bidder whose estimate happens to be too high by the greatest margin.

A fully rational bidder will take into account the fact that the winning bid tends to be too high. Referring again to the coin auction, suppose that someone's best estimate of the value of the coins in the jar is $9. Knowing that the winning bid will tend to be too high, he can then protect himself by adjusting the amount he bids downward. If other bidders are fully rational, they too will perform downward revisions of their bids, and the identity of the winning bidder should be the same as before.

How big should the downward adjustment be? A moment's reflection makes it clear that the more bidders there are, the larger the adjustment should be. Suppose the true value of the good being auctioned is $1000. To illustrate what is meant by an unbiased estimate, imagine that each potential bidder draws a ball from an urn containing 201 balls consecutively numbered from 900 to 1100. (Once its number is inspected, each ball is returned to the urn.) The expected value of the number on any given ball is 1000, no matter how many bidders there are. But the expected value of the *highest* number drawn will increase with the number of bidders. (If a million people drew balls from such urns, it is almost certain that someone would get 1100, the maximum possible value; but if only five people drew, the highest number would be much smaller, on the average.) Accordingly, the more bidders there are, the more you should adjust your estimate downward.

To illustrate the mechanics of the adjustment process, consider an auction in which the true value of the item for sale is .5, and in which each bidder uses an estimate that is uniformly distributed between 0 and 1. This estimate is equally likely to take any value between 0 and 1, so it has an expected value of .5, which means it is unbiased (see Figure 6A-6).

If there were only one bidder at this auction, the expected value of the highest estimate would be .5, and so there would be no need for him to make an adjustment. If there were N bidders, however, what would be the expected value of the highest estimate? Suppose we put the N estimates in ascending order and call them $X_1, X_2, ..., X_N$ so that X_N denotes the highest of the N estimates. Since the estimates all come from a uniform distribution, the expected values of $X_1, X_2, ..., X_N$ will be evenly spaced along the interval. As noted, when $N = 1$ we have only X_1, and its expected value, .5, lies right in the middle of the interval.

FIGURE 6A-6

An Unbiased Estimate with a Uniform Distribution
Each potential bidder has an estimate of the value of the resource that is equally likely to take any value between 0 and 1. The true value of the resource is the average value of these estimates, which is .5.

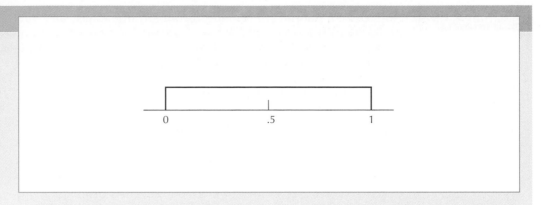

What about when $N = 2$? Now our two estimates are X_1 and X_2, and their expected values are as shown in the second panel of Figure 6A-7. This time the highest estimate has an expected value of 2/3. In the third panel note that the highest of three estimates has an expected value of 3/4. In the bottom panel, finally, the highest of four estimates has an expected value of 4/5. In general, the highest of N estimates will have an expected value of $N/(N + 1)$ (see footnote 2).

If the estimates were all drawn from a uniform distribution on $(0, C)$, not on $(0, 1)$, the expected value of the highest estimate would be $CN/(N + 1)$.

FIGURE 6A-7

The Expected Value of the Highest Estimate, $N = 1, 2, 3,$ and 4
When more people make estimates of the value of a resource, the expected value of the highest estimate increases. When the estimates are uniformly distributed on the interval $(0, 1)$, the largest of N estimates (X_N) has an average value of $N/(N + 1)$.

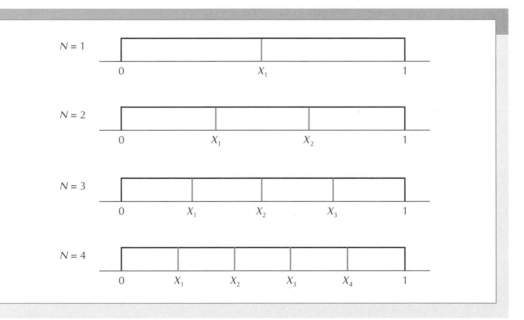

---

[2]The random variables $X_1, ..., X_N$ are known as the "order statistics" of a sample of size N. To find the expected value of X_N, note first that X_N is less than any value z if and only if *each* of the N sampled values is less than z. For the uniform distribution on $(0, 1)$, the probability of that event is simply z^N. This is the cumulative distribution function of X_N. The probability density function of X_N is therefore $d(z^N)/dz$, or Nz^{N-1}. The expected value of X_N is thus given by

$$\int_0^1 zNz^{N-1}dz = \frac{N}{N + 1}.$$

Suppose 50 people are bidding for an antique clock, and each has an unbiased estimate of the true value of the clock that is drawn from a uniform distribution on the interval $(0, C)$, where C is unknown. Your own estimate of the value of the clock is $400. How much should you bid?

Your problem is to adjust your estimate so that if it happens to be the highest of the 50, you will not bid more, on the average, than the true value of the clock, which is $C/2$. The expected value of the highest of 50 estimates is $(50/51)C$, so if your estimate of 400 happens to be the highest, we have, on the average,

$$(50/51)C = 400, \qquad\qquad (6A.7)$$

which solves for $C = 408$. This is your adjusted estimate of the value of C on the assumption that yours was the highest of the 50 unadjusted estimates. Since the true value of the clock is $C/2$, you should therefore bid only $204.

EXERCISE A.6-2

If there had been only four bidders in Example 6A-2, how much should you have bid?

As a practical matter, do bidders really adjust their behaviour to eliminate the winner's curse? An evolutionary argument can be made to the effect that there will be an automatic tendency for this to happen. The idea is that bidders who fail to adjust their estimates downward will end up losing money each time they win an auction, and will eventually go bankrupt. Those who survive may not understand the winner's curse at all. They may simply be people who happen for other reasons to bid cautiously.

When extremely large sums of money are at stake and bankruptcy is a real possibility, the evolutionary argument has some force. Yet in its simplest form, the argument is *too* simple. If the losses incurred by "winning" a single auction are not devastatingly high relative to the wealth of the winner, then it will require a *series* of cursed wins to drive the winner into bankruptcy. For this to occur, however, it is not sufficient that our winner be overly optimistic in every auction: he must be consistently and systematically the *most* over-optimistic of *all* bidders. Otherwise, he won't win the other auctions, and instead, other "successful" bidders will incur the winner's curse. If the "wins" are spread around, then the *relative* positions of the competitors will not be altered significantly, which is the critical factor in an evolutionary context.

Given that he has won the auction and paid more than the true value (or equivalently, that he has submitted an excessively *low* bid on a tender to provide, say, municipal garbage collection services), let's take the analysis a step further. He may not actually *lose* money, provided that he works longer and harder than he had planned, to compensate for his excessive optimism. His utility will be lower, but his economic survival will not be at stake. Moreover, in the process he should increase his stock of knowledge, in two ways. He will now have more accurate information on actual costs of garbage collection than his competitors. In addition, "learning by doing" and the need to innovate in response to cost pressures can result in his developing more cost-efficient methods of garbage collection, which enable him to underbid his competitors *and* make a profit when the collection contract is next let out to tender.

In this extended evolutionary model, it is not just that if he fails to adjust his estimates of the costs of garbage removal upward he will "become extinct" (go bankrupt). Rather, the process of fulfilling the contract *itself* gives him the knowledge to make a more realistic estimate next time, as well as the opportunity to develop cost-efficient systems that will make his bid more competitive. (The fact that in this auction he was a bad *estimator* doesn't imply that he's a poor manager in *other* respects.) In this version, which allows for the possibility of learning, "Nothing succeeds like failure." In the long run (if our winner survives into the long run), the winner's curse *can* be a blessing in disguise.

There are two further problems with the simple evolutionary argument. First, it doesn't address the question of how those who lost the auction (because they bid more realistically) survive. If they have other sources of income, then our winner is surely entitled to have other sources of income as well, and the profits from his profitable activities can offset the losses resulting from the winner's curse. This, incidentally, is one further argument for diversification and spreading your risks.

Second, aided by the pennies example, we slipped in several assumptions that you may have already noticed: first, that there is such a thing as *the* "true value" of an item at auction. For something like pennies (assuming that there are no rare ones in the jar), the "true" value is unambiguous: money is money. But consider Harry, whose taste is all in his mouth, and who buys an absolutely hideous statue at an auction. He was willing to pay $50 for it. He got it for only $7.50. His wife Madge says, "But Harry, it's ugly!" "Maybe, but what a bargain!" For Harry, part of the utility he derives from auctions comes from the pleasure of getting a "bargain." If Madge has her way, the statue may turn up at next year's yard sale, but in the meantime Harry is content: he "got his money's worth." Now consider Louise, who wants a picture with lots of sky blue in it for her study, and finds one at a country auction (a bit dusty, and in an old frame, but with just the shade of blue she's after), which she gets for $40. The "true" value *for her* was what she paid for it, because it complements *her* room. Actually, that's not the "true" value, either, because in dusting it off, she notices the signature "A.Y. Jackson" in the corner. She now has a lost original "Group of Seven" painting, the *market* value of which turns out to be $80,000 when she resells it at an auction a few months later, because she has decided to repaint her study.

These examples suggest four final points about auctions and the winner's curse. First, for a *unique* item there is no issue of whether it could be purchased more cheaply elsewhere: it can't. Therefore the only test my bid has to pass is whether the item is worth that much to me. Second, asymmetries in information among the bidders can alter the outcome of the auction. Had a knowledgeable art dealer happened to be at Louise's auction, Louise would never have won the auction. The art dealer would have got the painting, for whatever bid it took to induce Louise to drop out of the bidding. Third, in an open auction with possible informational asymmetries, the bidding process *itself* can generate information about the value of the item for less well-informed bidders. An auction thus has a game-theoretic dimension, with some bidders using early bids to set up a low value for the final successful bid, known art collectors and dealers using agents to bid on their behalf, and unscrupulous auctioneers using confederates or "stooges" to bid up the price to artificially high levels. Fourth, while the specific formulas we have developed depend on the assumptions made (such as the uniform distribution and risk-neutrality assumptions), the *principle* of the winner's curse is applicable to *any* situation in which there is a distribution of estimates around a true value.

EXAMPLE 6A-3	**Suppose you are the economic adviser for a firm that is trying to decide whether to acquire the Bumbler Oil Company, whose only asset is an oil field that has a net value X under its current management. The owners of Bumbler know the**

exact value of X, but your company knows only that X is a random number that is uniformly distributed between 0 and 100. Because of your company's superior management, Bumbler's oil field would be worth $1.5X$ in its hands. What is the highest value of P that you can bid and still expect not to take a loss if your company acquires Bumbler Oil?

If your company bids P and X is greater than P, then Bumbler will refuse the offer and the deal is off. Your company earns zero profit in that case. If Bumbler accepts your company's offer, then we know that $X \leq P$. Since X is uniformly distributed between 0 and 100, then for any value of P you pick, the *expected* value of X for $X \leq P$ is $P/2$. This means that the expected value of Bumbler's oil field to your company is 1.5 times that, or $.75P$. If your company bids P and Bumbler accepts, then the expected profit of your company will be $.75P - P = -.25P$. So for *any* positive P, your company expects to lose $.25P$ if Bumbler accepts its offer. Your company's best strategy is therefore not to bid at all.

6A.3 SOME PITFALLS FOR THE EXPECTED UTILITY MAXIMIZER

The expected utility model offers guidance about how to choose rationally in the face of uncertainty. Yet some experiments on decision making in the face of risk have generated apparently paradoxical results, when judged by the expected utility-maximization criterion. One well-known example, based on the work of the French economist M. Allais, suggests that most people behave inconsistently with respect to certain kinds of choices. To illustrate, first consider the following pair of alternatives:

A: A sure win of $30
vs.
A': An 80 percent chance to win $45.

Confronted with these alternatives, most people choose A, the sure win.[3] If a person is risk averse, there is nothing surprising about this choice, even though the expected value of alternative A' is $36.

Now consider the following pair of alternatives:

B: A 25 percent chance to win $30
vs.
B': A 20 percent chance to win $45.

This time most people choose the less certain alternative, namely, B'. Taken in isolation, this choice is also unsurprising, for the expected value of B ($7.50) is significantly lower than that of B' ($9), and both alternatives involve some risk. The problem is that the most popular pair of choices (A and B'), taken together, contradict the assumption of expected utility maximization. To see why, suppose the chooser is a utility maximizer with a utility function $U(M)$ and an initial wealth level of M_0. His choice of A over A' then implies that

$$U(M_0 + 30) > .8U(M_0 + 45) + .2U(M_0). \qquad (6A.8)$$

---

[3]See Amos Tversky and Daniel Kahneman, "The Framing of Decisions and the Psychology of Choice," *Science*, 211, 1981: 453–458.

In turn, his choice of B' over B implies that

$$.2U(M_0 + 45) + .8U(M_0) > .25U(M_0 + 30) + .75U(M_0). \qquad (6A.9)$$

Rearranging the terms of inequality 6A.9, we have

$$.25U(M_0 + 30) < .2U(M_0 + 45) + .05U(M_0). \qquad (6A.10)$$

Dividing both sides of inequality 6A.10 by .25, finally, we have

$$U(M_0 + 30) < .8U(M_0 + 45) + .2U(M_0), \qquad (6A.11)$$

which is precisely the reverse order of inequality 6A.8., the one implied by the choice of A over A'. And hence the contradiction.

Psychologists Daniel Kahneman and Amos Tversky have labelled this kind of inconsistency the "certainty effect." As a purely descriptive matter, they argue that "a reduction in the probability of an outcome by a constant factor has a larger impact when the outcome was initially certain than when it was merely probable."[4] Thus, in the first pair of alternatives, the movement from A to A' represented a 20 percent reduction in the chances of winning (from 100 to 80 percent), the same as the reduction when moving from B to B' (25 to 20 percent). But because the first reduction was from an initially certain outcome, it was much less attractive.

Note that Kahneman and Tversky are not saying that there is anything irrational about liking a sure thing. Their point is simply that our choices in situations where both alternatives are risky seem to imply a lesser degree of risk aversion than does our behaviour in situations where one of the alternatives is risk free.

Part of the attraction of the sure alternative is the regret many people expect to feel when they take a gamble and lose. The expected utility maximizer will want to be careful, however, to avoid the "bad-outcome-implies-bad-decision" fallacy. To illustrate this fallacy, suppose someone offers you the following gamble: You are to draw a single ball from an urn containing 999 white balls and one red ball. If you draw a white ball, as you most probably will, you win $1000. If you draw the lone red ball, however, you lose $1. Suppose you accept the gamble and then draw the red ball. You lose $1. Do you now say you made a bad decision? If you do, you commit the fallacy. The decision, when you made it, was obviously a good one. Almost every rational person would have decided in the same way. The fact that you lost is too bad, but it tells you nothing about the quality of your decision. By the same token, if you choose an 80 percent chance to win $45 rather than a sure win of $30, there is no reason to regret the quality of your decision if you happen to lose.

As a general rule, humans typically prefer certainty to risk. At the same time, however, risk is an inescapable part of the environment. People generally want the largest possible gain *and* the smallest possible risk, but most of the time we are forced to trade risk and gain off against one another. When choosing between two risky alternatives, we are forced to recognize this tradeoff explicitly. In such cases, we cannot escape the cognitive effort required to reach a sensible decision. But when one of the alternatives is riskless, it is often easier simply to choose it and not waste too much effort on the decision. What this pattern of behaviour fails to recognize, however, is that choosing a sure win of $30 over an 80 percent chance to win $45 does precious little to reduce any of the uncertainty that really matters in life.

---

[4]Ibid., p. 456.

On the contrary, *when only small sums of money are at stake, a compelling case can be made that the only sensible strategy is to choose the alternative with the highest expected value.* The argument for this strategy, like the argument for buying insurance, rests on the law of large numbers. Here, the law tells us that if we take a large number of independent gambles and pool them, we can be very confident of getting almost exactly the sum of their expected values. As a decision maker, the trick is to remind yourself that each small risky choice is simply part of a much larger collection. After all, it takes the sting out of an occasional small loss to know that following any other strategy would have led to a virtually certain large loss.

To illustrate, consider again the choice between the sure gain of $30 and the 80 percent chance to win $45, and suppose you were confronted with the equivalent of one sure choice each week. Recall that the gamble has an expected value of $36, $6 more than the sure thing. By always choosing the "risky" alternative, your expected gain—over and beyond the gain from the sure alternative—will be $312 each year. Students who have had an introductory course in probability can easily show that the probability you would have come out better by choosing the sure alternative in any year is less than 1 percent. *The long-run opportunity cost of following a risk-averse strategy for repeated decisions involving identical small outcomes is an almost sure loss of considerable magnitude.* By thinking of your problem as that of choosing a policy for dealing with a large number of choices of the same type, a seemingly risky strategy is transformed into an obviously very safe one.

PROBLEMS

1. You are searching for a high wage from a wage distribution that is uniform on the interval ($5, $8). The cost of each search is $.06. What is the smallest wage you should accept?

2. A class of 100 students is participating in an auction to see who gets a large jar of quarters. Each student has an unbiased estimate of the total value of the coins. If these estimates are drawn from the interval $(0, C)$, where C is not known, and your own estimate is $50, how much should you bid?

**3. Suppose you are the economic adviser for a firm that is trying to decide whether to acquire the Bumbler Oil Company, whose only asset is an oil field that has a net value X under its current management. The owners of Bumbler know the exact value of X but your company knows only that X is a random number that is uniformly distributed between 0 and 100. Because of your company's superior management, Bumbler's oil field would be worth $X + 40$ in its hands.
    a. What is the most your company can bid and not expect to take a loss?
    b. Assuming your company is the only bidder, what bid maximizes your company's expected profits?

4. If the wages you are offered are uniformly distributed between $75 and $150, and if the cost of looking for another job is $2, what is the minimum wage you should consider?

5. The Earthly Bliss dating service charges $100 per date that it arranges. All of its dates will accept an offer of marriage. In your estimation the quality of the potential spouses offered by the dating service can be measured by an index that runs from 0 to 100. The potential spouses are uniformly distributed over this range. Suppose you value a spouse at $50 per index point. If your dates were drawn at random from the Earthly Bliss pool, at what value of the index would you stop searching?

6. You are a buyer for a used-car dealer. You attend car auctions and bid on cars that will be sold at the dealer. The cars are sold "as is" and there is seldom an opportunity to make a thorough inspection. Under these conditions, the lower bound for the value of a car can be zero. A 1995 Dodge Aries has been offered at the auction. You are one of 20 bidders. Your estimate of the value of the car is $200. If all the bidders have unbiased estimates drawn from a uniform distribution with an unknown upper bound, what should you bid for the car?

ANSWERS TO IN-APPENDIX EXERCISES

A6-1. Let w^* again denote the acceptance wage. The probability of finding a higher wage is $(60 - w^*)/50$. The average gain, given that you do find a higher wage, is $(60 - w^*)/2$. So the expected gain is the product of these, $(60 - w^*)^2/100$. Equating this to the cost per search, 1, and solving for w^*, we have $w^* = \$50$.

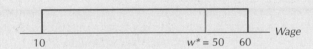

A6-2. With four bidders, the expected value of the largest estimate is $(4/5)C$. Equating this to 400, and solving, we get $C = 500$, and so you should bid $250.

Chapter 7

EXPLAINING TASTES: THE IMPORTANCE OF ALTRUISM AND OTHER NONEGOISTIC BEHAVIOUR

The central assumption of microeconomic analysis is that people are rational. There is far from universal agreement, however, on just what this means. In Chapter 1 we explored two definitions of rationality, the *present-aim* and the egoistic or *self-interest* standards of rationality.[1] We discovered that both have limitations as characterizations of actual economic behaviour. The pure self-interest standard involves unrealistic assumptions as to an individual's capacity for knowledge, including self-knowledge. It fails to account satisfactorily for such observable human motives as altruism, fidelity to principle, a desire for justice, and envy. Moreover, unbridled self-interest rationality is socially and individually highly wasteful, and on this criterion is "irrational."

For these reasons, in textbook accounts of rational choice, the present-aim standard is often initially adopted. Tastes are assumed to be given exogenously, and are not subject to criticism on logical or other grounds. Jeremy Bentham (1748–1832) put the assumption in strong form: "Prejudice apart, the game of push-pin is of equal value with the arts and sciences of music and poetry. If the game of push-pin furnish more pleasure, it is more valuable than either." Yet in *applying* the rationality concept, most economists typically assume some version of the self-interest standard of rationality. This is in fact the approach we took in the preceding chapters and, as we have seen, it generates many powerful insights into human behaviour. It helps explain, for example, why car pools form in the wake of increases in gasoline prices; why the members of "service" organizations, such as the Rotary and Kiwanis clubs, are more likely to be real estate salespersons, dentists, insurance agents, and others with something to sell than to be postal employees or airline pilots; and so on. Without question, self-interest is an important human motive.

Yet narrow self-interest is surely not the only human motive. Travellers on highways leave tips for waitresses they will never see again. Participants in bloody family feuds

---

[1]See Derek Parfit, *Reasons and Persons,* Oxford: Clarendon, 1984.

Bob Haverluck,
Artist and theologian,
Winnipeg, Manitoba.

seek revenge even at ruinous cost to themselves. People walk away from profitable transactions whose terms they believe to be "unfair." Individuals make large *anonymous* donations to causes in which they believe. Nations engaged in arms races, with the objective of Mutual Assured Destruction (MAD), stockpile enough nuclear weapons to destroy the world many times over, whereas even with sloppy aim and allowing for employment effects in the destruction industry, double the required amount would likely be sufficient. In these and countless other ways, people do not seem to be maximizing utility functions of the egoistic sort.

CHAPTER PREVIEW

The self-interest model ignores the fact that most of us pursue a variety of goals that seem to conflict with narrow self-interest. We begin this chapter with an example of how unselfish motivations can be incorporated into the rational choice model—in this case, a straightforward application of the present-aim standard. But our real challenge is to explore how such motivations might have come to be held in the first place. We are all comfortable with the notion that someone who deliberately strives to be more spontaneous is doomed to fail. So, too, we shall see that individuals whose only goal is to promote their own interests face a difficulty of a similar sort. There are important problems that selfish people simply are not able to solve very well.

In the descriptive realm, we will see that it is possible to do a much better job of predicting people's behaviour when we take certain nonegoistic sources of motivation into account.

7.1 AN APPLICATION OF THE PRESENT-AIM STANDARD: ALTRUISTIC PREFERENCES

Because we know from experience that not everyone has the narrowly selfish preferences assumed by the self-interest model, it is tempting to broaden the analysis by simply adding additional tastes—by assuming, for example, that people derive satisfaction from a behaviour that conflicts with narrowly defined self-interest, such as donating to charity, voting, disposing of litter properly, and so on. Let us explore how the notion that some people have altruistic preferences can be incorporated formally into our model of rational choice.

Consider, for example, the case of Anne, who cares not only about her own income level but also about Gilbert's. Such preferences can be represented in the form of an indifference map defined over their respective income levels, and might look something like the one shown in Figure 7-1. Note that Anne's indifference curves are negatively sloped, which means that she is willing to tolerate a reduction in her own income in return for a sufficiently large increase in Gilbert's. Note also that her indifference curves exhibit diminishing MRS, which means that the more income Anne has, the more she is willing to give up in order to see Gilbert have more.

The question that Anne confronts is whether she would be better off if she gave some of her income to Gilbert. In order to answer this question, we first need to display the relevant budget constraint confronting Anne. Suppose her initial income level is $50,000 per year and that Gilbert's is $10,000, as denoted by the point labelled

FIGURE 7-1

**The Indifference
Map for Anne, an
Altruistic Person**
Anne would be willing
to have less income
in order for Gilbert
to have more.

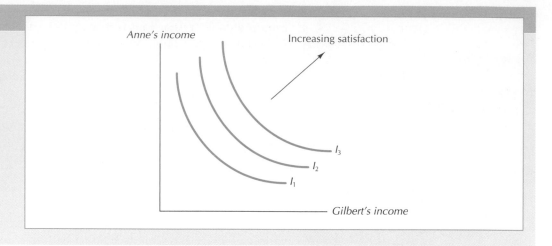

A in Figure 7-2. Anne can retain all her income, in which case she stays at A. Or she can give some of it to Gilbert, in which case she will have $1 less than $50,000 for every $1 she gives him. Her budget constraint here is thus the locus labelled B in Figure 7-2, which has a slope of 21.

If Anne keeps all her income, she ends up on the indifference curve labelled I_1 in Figure 7-2. But because her MRS exceeds the absolute value of the slope of her budget constraint at A, it is clear that she can do better. The fact that MRS > 1 at A tells us that she is willing to give up more than a dollar of her own income to see Gilbert have an extra dollar. But the slope of her budget constraint tells us that it costs her only a dollar to give Gilbert an extra dollar. She is therefore better off if she gives some of her income to Gilbert. The optimal transfer is represented by the tangency point labelled C in Figure 7-2. The best she can do is to give $19,000 of her income to Gilbert.

Note, however, that the conclusion would have been much different if Anne had started not at A but at D in Figure 7-2. Then her budget constraint would have been

FIGURE 7-2

**The Optimal Income
Transfer from an
Altruistic Person**
At point C, Anne's
MRS between her
income and Gilbert's
is exactly equal to the
absolute value of the
slope of her budget
constraint. Given her
preferences, the best
she can do is give
$19,000 of her original
$50,000 income to
Gilbert, keeping
$31,000 for herself.

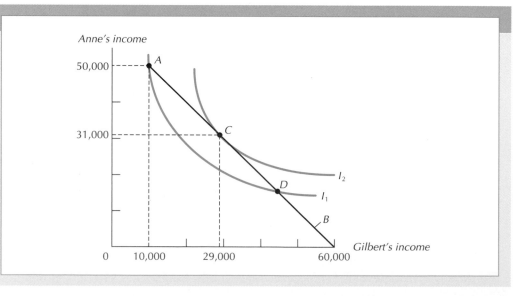

CHAPTER 7: EXPLAINING TASTES: THE IMPORTANCE OF ALTRUISM AND OTHER NONEGOISTIC BEHAVIOUR

only that portion of the locus B that lies below *D*. (She does not have the option of making negative gifts to Gilbert!) And since her MRS at *D* is less than 1, she will do best to give no money to Gilbert at all. (Recall from Chapter 3 that such outcomes are called corner solutions.)

EXAMPLE 7-1

Smith's utility function is given by $U_S = M_S M_J$, where M_S is Smith's wealth level and M_J is Jones's. Initially, Smith has 90 units of wealth and Jones has 10. If Smith is a utility maximizer, should he transfer some of his wealth to Jones, and if so, how much? Draw Smith's initial indifference curve and the indifference curve when each has 50 units of wealth. Also draw Smith's budget constraint in the $M_S M_J$ plane.

Together, Smith and Jones have a total of 100 units of wealth. This means that if Smith's wealth is M_S, then Jones's is $100 - M_S$. Smith's utility function may thus be written as $U_S = M_S(100 - M_S)$, which is plotted in the top panel of Figure 7-3. Note that Smith's utility attains a maximum of 2500 when $M_S = 50$. At the initial allocation of wealth, Smith's utility is only 900. So if Smith is a utility maximizer, he should transfer 40 units of his wealth to Jones. The heavy line in the bottom panel is Smith's budget constraint in the $M_S M_J$ plane. Note that the $U_S = 2500$ indifference curve is tangent to this budget constraint when $M_S = M_J = 50$.

FIGURE 7-3

A Utility-Maximizing Altruist
The top panel shows that Smith's utility is maximized by keeping only 50 units of wealth for himself. The heavy line in the bottom panel is Smith's budget constraint in the $M_S M_J$ plane. Note that the $U_S = 2500$ indifference curve is tangent to that budget constraint at $M_S = 50$.

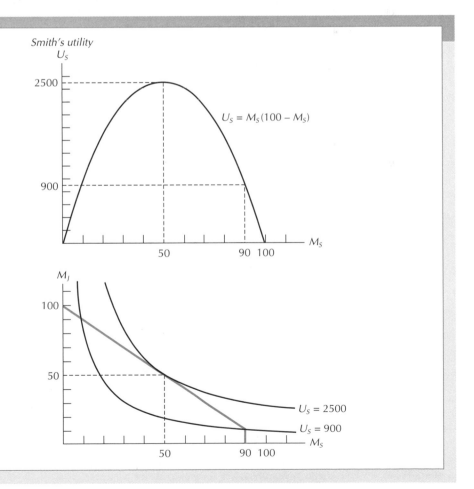

7.2 THE STRATEGIC ROLE OF PREFERENCES

The attractive feature of the present-aim standard of rationality is that it lets us broaden our analysis to embrace nonegoistic motives whose existence is empirically well documented. Yet as we noted in Chapter 1, the lingering methodological difficulty is that unless we impose some constraints on ourselves, the present-aim standard allows us to explain virtually any bizarre behaviour by simply positing a taste for it. Our dilemma is how to expand our view of human motives without at the same time falling into the "anything goes" trap.

Biologists have discovered a way out of this dilemma, one that rests on an analysis that is quintessentially microeconomic in character. In biology, an organism's tastes are not arbitrarily given, as they are in economic models. Rather, biologists assume that tastes are forged by the pressures of natural selection to help organisms solve important problems in their environments. Consider the example of the common human taste for sweets. How would biologists explain such a taste? Their argument is straightforward. It begins with the observation that certain kinds of sugars—in particular, those commonly found in ripened fruit—were more easily digested than other sugars by our primate ancestors. The next step is to assume an initial degree of variability of tastes across individuals—that is, to assume that some individuals were more predisposed than others to "like" the kinds of sugars found in ripened fruit. Motivated by this taste, these primates were more likely than others to eat ripened fruit. Because the sugars in ripened fruit are more easily digested, individuals who liked these sugars were more likely than others to survive and leave offspring. And because of this advantage, the genes for liking the kinds of sugars found in ripened fruit eventually spread throughout the population. Thus, in the biologist's account, our taste for sweets is a characteristic we inherited from our ancestors, in whom it evolved for functional reasons.

There is evidence that this particular taste is less functional in our current environment. In earlier times, the sugars found in ripened fruits were sufficiently scarce that there was no practical danger of overconsuming them. Now, with sweets so plentiful, our taste for them sometimes leads us to overindulge, from a health standpoint. If the consequences for survival and reproduction were sufficiently acute, and those with the strongest taste for sweets were incapable of moderation, then evolutionary pressures would eventually diminish the average human taste for sweets. For the next hundred generations or so, however, it is almost certainly a taste we are stuck with at the biological level.

The taste for sweets is a simple preference, in the sense that it would have been useful to an individual irrespective of whether others in the population shared that taste. Other tastes, however, are more complex, in the sense that the usefulness of having them depends on the fraction of other individuals in the population who share them. This second type we will call a *strategic preference*, one that helps the individual solve important problems of social interaction. An early example of a strategic preference in the biological literature focused on the taste for aggressive behaviour. A simple version of the biologist's model of the evolution of this taste helps fix ideas for our subsequent analysis of a variety of other important strategic preferences.

A Parable of Hawks and Doves

To begin, consider a population that consists of individuals who are the same except with respect to their taste for aggressive behaviour. One type of individual, called a "hawk," has a strong preference for such behaviour.[2] The other type, called a "dove,"

---

[2]The names "hawk" and "dove" are used metaphorically here to describe members of the same species who have different tastes for aggressive behaviour.

strictly prefers to avoid aggressive behaviour. Which of these two types an individual happens to be matters only when it comes into conflict with another individual over an important resource—food, a mate, whatever. The hawk's strategy is always to fight for the resource. The dove's strategy is never to fight.

If these two types compete for the scarce resources required for survival, which type will win out? At first glance, it might seem as if the hawks would, since they would always prevail in their conflicts with doves. But this view overlooks what happens when two hawks confront one another. Since both individuals are now predisposed to be aggressive, a bitter fight may ensue. Depending on the consequences of such a fight, it may thus be a risky proposition indeed to be a hawk.

The potential disadvantage of being a hawk becomes even clearer when we examine what happens when two doves confront one another over an important resource. In these encounters, the costs of a bloody battle are avoided, and the doves share the resource.

In our hypothetical population, pairs of individuals interact with one another at random and there are three possible pairings: (1) two doves, (2) two hawks, and (3) a hawk and a dove. To see how this population will evolve, we need to know the payoffs for each of these three types of interaction. To make our analysis manageable, let us assume that a biologist has gathered data that enable us to express these payoffs in units of some common measure—say, calories. Suppose the conflict involves food that contains 12 calories. When two doves interact, they share the food so that each receives a payoff of 6 calories. When a hawk and a dove interact, the dove defers to the hawk, so the hawk gets 12 calories, the dove none. Finally, when two hawks interact, the winner of the ensuing fight gets the 12 calories, the loser none. The fight itself, however, consumes 10 calories for each hawk, which means that the net payoff is $12 - 10 = 2$ calories for the winning hawk, and -10 calories for the losing hawk. Over the course of many encounters between hawks, any given hawk can expect to win half the time and lose half the time. Thinking of hawks as a whole, then, the average payoff from hawk–hawk encounters is $(2 - 10)/2 = -4$ calories per individual.

If we let X and Y represent two individuals from the population, the average payoffs for the different combinations of interactions are summarized in Table 7-1.

As biologists view the matter, the question of whether it is better to be a hawk or to be a dove is answered by computing which type gets more calories on the average. To do this, we must first know the likelihood of each type of interaction. To illustrate, suppose

TABLE 7-1

The Hawk–Dove Payoff Matrix

Two individuals are in conflict over food worth 12 calories. When two hawks meet, a fight ensues that consumes 10 calories each, leaving an average net payoff of −4 calories per hawk. When doves and hawks meet, doves defer, so hawks get 12 calories, doves 0. When two doves meet, they share the food, so each gets 6 calories.

		Individual Y	
		Hawk	**Dove**
Individual X	**Hawk**	−4 calories for each	12 calories for X 0 calories for Y
	Dove	0 calories for X 12 calories for Y	6 calories for each

that half the population initially consists of hawks, the other half of doves. Then, half of each individual's interactions would be with hawks, the other half with doves. For a hawk, then, the average payoff, denoted P_H, would be a weighted average of the two payoff values:

$$P_H = (\tfrac{1}{2})(-4) + (\tfrac{1}{2})(12) = 4. \tag{7.1}$$

The corresponding average payoff for a dove, denoted P_D, would be

$$P_D = (\tfrac{1}{2})(0) + (\tfrac{1}{2})6 = 3. \tag{7.2}$$

The implicit assumption in the biologist's view of the competition between hawks and doves is that whichever type garners a larger number of calories will tend to raise larger families and will thus make up an increasing share of the total population. We have just seen that in a population initially split 50–50 between the two types, the hawks will get more calories than the doves, and this means that the hawks' share of the total population will grow.

Suppose we use h to denote the fraction of the population that consists of hawks (so that, in the example just considered, we had $h = \tfrac{1}{2}$). Then, since the population shares of the two types must sum to 1, we know that $1 - h$ will be the fraction of the population that consists of doves. For such a population, the average payoff for hawks is again a weighted average of the two types of hawk payoffs, where now the weights are the respective population shares, h and $(1 - h)$:

$$P_H = (h)(-4) + (1 - h)(12) = 12 - 16h. \tag{7.3}$$

The corresponding general expression for the average payoff for doves is

$$P_D = (h)(0) + (1 - h)6 = 6 - 6h. \tag{7.4}$$

For example, if the share consisting of hawks were four-fifths, hawks would encounter other hawks in their interactions four-fifths of the time, doves the remaining one-fifth of the time, making the average payoff for hawks $P_H = (\tfrac{4}{5})(-4) + (\tfrac{1}{5})(12) = -.8$. The corresponding average for doves would be $P_D = (\tfrac{4}{5})(0) + (\tfrac{4}{5})(6) = 1.2$. So when hawks make up four-fifths of the population, their average payoff will be smaller than the average payoff for doves, and this means that the hawks' share of the population will begin to fall.

To see whether the population shares will settle at some equilibrium, we plot the average payoff curves for the two types and look for a point at which they cross. As shown in Figure 7-4, this occurs when $h = .6$. This means that when 60 percent of the population consists of hawks, the remaining 40 percent of doves, each type will receive an average payoff of 2.4 calories per interaction. With equal average payoffs, the two types will tend to have equally many offspring, which implies that their respective shares of the population will remain unchanged.

Note that the equilibrium point identified in Figure 7-4 is stable: if the population share of hawks were ever to deviate from .6, there would immediately be forces pulling it back to .6. For example, if the share of hawks for some reason dipped to .5, the average payoff curves in Figure 7-4 show that the average payoff for hawks would exceed the average payoff for doves, and this would cause the hawks' population share to rise. Conversely, if the share of hawks somehow rose to .7, then the hawks' average payoff would be smaller than the doves', and this would cause the hawks' population share to fall.

FIGURE 7-4

Average Payoffs for Hawks and Doves
The average payoffs for both hawks and doves are declining functions of the share of the population consisting of hawks. The mixture of the two types is in equilibrium when the average payoffs are the same for the two types.

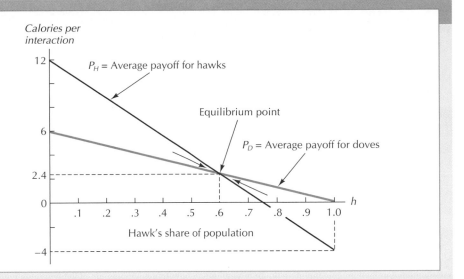

In the example discussed above, suppose now that the payoffs are altered as follows: When two doves interact, each earns 3 units; when two hawks interact, each earns 1 unit; and when a dove and a hawk interact, the former gets a payoff of 2 units, the latter a payoff of 6 units. What will be the equilibrium population share of each type?

The hawks and doves example illustrates how the usefulness of a preference for a certain mode of behaviour depends on the frequency with which others in the population also prefer that behaviour. Being a hawk (preferring aggression) can be advantageous, but only up to a point. For once hawks become sufficiently numerous, it then becomes advantageous to be a dove. The population is in equilibrium only when the average payoffs for the two tastes are the same.

Note also in Figure 7-4 that the population as a whole would be better off if there were no hawks at all ($h = 0$). For in a population consisting only of doves, all individuals would receive 6 calories per interaction, a dramatic improvement over the equilibrium value of 2.4. But a population consisting only of doves would not be evolutionarily stable. Hawks could invade such a population and make rapid headway because of their success when interacting with doves.

The rational choice model introduced in Chapter 3 regards the consumer's tastes as given, a set of goals the consumer strives to fulfill. Ecological models like the hawks and doves example take a step back and ask where those tastes come from. These models view preferences not as ends in themselves but as a means by which individuals achieve important material objectives (in the hawks and doves case, the acquisition of calories needed to survive and reproduce).

With the workings of the hawks and doves model firmly in mind, we are now in a position to analyze how a variety of other tastes might have emerged. In particular, we focus on how certain unselfish motives often help people solve an important class of problems that arise in economic and social interaction.

7.3 THE COMMITMENT PROBLEM

One of the most frequently discussed examples in which the pursuit of self-interest is self-defeating is the so-called *prisoner's dilemma*. The mathematician A. W. Tucker is credited with having discovered this simple game, whose name derives from the anecdote originally used to illustrate it. Two prisoners are held in separate cells for a serious crime that they did, in fact, commit. The prosecutor, however, has only enough hard evidence to convict them of a minor offence, for which the penalty is, say, a year in jail. Each prisoner is told that if one confesses while the other remains silent, the confessor will go scot-free while the other will spend 20 years in prison. If both confess, they will get an intermediate sentence, say, 5 years. Table 7-2 summarizes these payoffs. The two prisoners are not allowed to communicate with one another.

The dominant strategy in the prisoner's dilemma is to confess. No matter what Y does, X gets a lighter sentence by speaking out—if Y too confesses, X gets 5 years instead of 20; and if Y remains silent, X goes free instead of spending a year in jail. The payoffs are perfectly symmetric, so Y also does better to confess, no matter what X does. The difficulty is that when each behaves in a self-interested way, both do worse than if each had shown restraint. Thus, when both confess, they get five years, instead of the one year they could have gotten by remaining silent.

Although the prisoners are not allowed to communicate with one another, it would be a mistake to assume that this is the real source of difficulty. Their problem is rather a lack of *trust*. A simple promise not to confess does not change the material payoffs of the game. (If each could promise not to confess, each would *still* do better if he broke his promise.)

The prisoner's dilemma is an example of a broader class of problems called *commitment problems*. The common feature of these problems is that people can do better if they can commit themselves to behave in a way that will later be inconsistent with their own material interests. In the prisoner's dilemma, for example, if the prisoners could commit themselves to remain silent, they would do better than if left free to pursue their narrow material interests.

Thomas Schelling[3] provided another vivid illustration of a commitment problem. Schelling described a kidnapper who suddenly gets cold feet. He wants to set his victim free but is afraid he will go to the police. In return for his freedom, the victim gladly promises not to do so. The problem, however, is that both realize it will no longer be

TABLE 7-2

The Prisoner's Dilemma
No matter what the other player does, each player always gets a shorter sentence by confessing. And if each player confesses, each gets 5 years. Yet if both players had remained silent, each would have gotten only 1 year in jail. Here the individual pursuit of self-interest produces a worse outcome for each player.

		Prisoner Y	
		Confess	**Remain silent**
Prisoner X	**Confess**	5 years for each	0 years for X 20 years for Y
	Remain silent	20 years for X 0 years for Y	1 year for each

---

[3]Thomas Schelling, *The Strategy of Conflict,* Cambridge, MA: Harvard University Press, 1960.

in the victim's interest to keep this promise once he is free. And so the kidnapper reluctantly concludes that he must kill him. The kidnapper's belief that the victim will act in a rational, self-interested way spells apparent doom for the victim.

Schelling suggested the following way out of the dilemma: "If the victim has committed an act whose disclosure could lead to blackmail, he may confess it; if not, he might commit one in the presence of his captor, to create a bond that will ensure his silence."[4] The blackmailable act serves here as a *commitment device*, something that provides the victim with an incentive to keep his promise.[5] Keeping it will still be unpleasant for him once he is freed, but clearly less so than not being able to make a credible promise in the first place.

In everyday economic and social interaction, we repeatedly encounter commitment problems like the prisoner's dilemma, or like the one confronting Schelling's kidnapper and victim. The solution Schelling suggested tries to eliminate the problem by altering the relevant material incentives. Unfortunately, however, this approach will not always be practical. An alternative approach relies on the *psychological* rewards governing behaviour. For example, if the kidnapper knew that the kidnap victim would rather die than break a promise, and hence would not go to the police even if it were in his material interest to do so, then the kidnapper *could* safely set him free.

7.4 ILLUSTRATION: THE CHEATING PROBLEM

The functional role of unselfish motives can be seen more clearly with the help of an example of a simple ecology in which egoists are pitted against nonegoists in a struggle to survive. The commitment problem they face arises in joint business ventures, each of which consists of a pair of individuals. In these ventures each person can behave in either of two ways: he can "cooperate," which means to deal honestly with his partner, or he can "defect," which means to cheat his partner. The payoffs to each of two representative partners, Smith and Jones, depend on the combination of behaviours chosen in the manner shown in Table 7-3. These payoffs confront the partners with a monetary version of the prisoner's dilemma. Note that Jones gets a higher payoff by defecting, no matter what Smith does, and that the same is true for Smith. If Jones believes Smith will behave in a self-interested way, he will predict that Smith will defect. And if only to protect himself, he may feel compelled to defect as well. When both defect, each gets only a two-unit payoff. The frustration, as in all dilemmas of this sort, is that both could have done better. Had they cooperated, each would have gotten a four-unit payoff.

Now suppose we have not just Smith and Jones but also a large population. Pairs of people again form joint ventures and the relationship between behaviour and payoffs for the members of each pair is again as given in Table 7-3. Suppose further that everyone in the population is of one of two types—cooperator or defector. A cooperator is someone who, possibly through intensive cultural conditioning, has developed a heritable capacity to experience a moral sentiment that predisposes him to cooperate. A defector is someone who either lacks this capacity or has failed to develop it.

In this scheme, cooperators are altruists in the sense that they refrain from cheating even when there is no possibility of being detected. Viewed in the narrow context of

---

[4]Ibid., pp. 43–44.
[5]Note the analogy to the commitment devices we discussed in Chapter 5, whereby people forced themselves to save.

TABLE 7-3

		Smith	
		Defect	**Cooperate**
Jones	**Defect**	2 for each	0 for Smith 6 for Jones
	Cooperate	6 for Smith 0 for Jones	4 for each

the choice at hand, this behaviour is clearly contrary to their material interests. Defectors, by contrast, are pure opportunists. They always make whatever choice will maximize their personal payoffs. As in the hawks and doves example considered earlier, our task here is to determine what will happen when people from the two groups are thrown into a survival struggle against one another. As we will see, the answer depends critically on how easily the two types may be distinguished from one another. We consider several possibilities in turn.

Population Movements When Cooperators and Defectors Look Alike

Suppose, for argument's sake, that cooperators and defectors look exactly alike, thus making it impossible to distinguish the two types. In this hypothetical ecology, this means that, as in the hawks and doves example, individuals will pair at random. Naturally, cooperators (and defectors, for that matter) would like nothing better than to pair with cooperators, but they have no choice in the matter. Because everyone looks the same, they must take their chances. The expected payoffs to both defectors and cooperators therefore depend on the likelihood of pairing with a cooperator, which in turn depends on the proportion of cooperators in the population.

Let c denote the fraction of the population that consists of cooperators. If a cooperator interacts with a randomly chosen person from the population, the probability of that person's also being a cooperator will be c. The probability of that person's being a defector is $1 - c$. Since a cooperator gets a payoff of four units when he interacts with another cooperator and a payoff of zero when he interacts with a defector, the expected, or average, payoff for each cooperator in this case can be written as

$$P_C = c(4) + (1 - c)(0) = 4c. \tag{7.5}$$

The corresponding expression for the average payoff for defectors is given by

$$P_D = 6c + 2(1 - c) = 2 + 4c. \tag{7.6}$$

When half of the population consists of cooperators ($c = \frac{1}{2}$), a cooperator has a 50–50 chance of interacting with another cooperator, in which case he will get 4 units, and a 50–50 chance of interacting with a defector, in which case he will get 0 units. His expected payoff here is a weighted average of these two outcomes, namely, 2 units. The expected payoff to a defector is 4 units.

EXERCISE 7-2

What are the average payoffs for cooperators and defectors when $c = .9$?

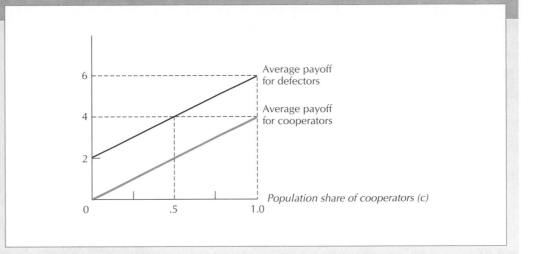

FIGURE 7-5

Average Payoffs When Cooperators and Defectors Look Alike
The expected payoffs for both cooperators and defectors increase with the percentage of cooperators in the population. But no matter what the initial population share of cooperators is, cooperators earn a lower average payoff than defectors. This means that cooperators are destined for extinction.

The average payoff relationships for the monetary values assumed in this illustration are shown in Figure 7-5.

When cooperators and defectors look exactly the same, how will the population evolve over time? As in the hawks and doves example, the rule here is that each individual reproduces in proportion to its average payoff: those with larger material payoffs have the resources necessary to raise larger numbers of offspring.[6] Recall that in the hawks and doves example the average payoff curves for the two types intersected, resulting in a stable population share for each type. In the current case, however, the average payoff curves do not intersect. Since defectors always receive a higher average payoff here, their share of the population will grow over time. Cooperators, even if they make up almost the entire population to begin with, are thus destined for extinction. When cooperators and defectors look alike, genuine cooperation cannot emerge. In a crude way, this case provides the underlying rationale for the self-interest model's assumption of egoistic behaviour.

Note in Figure 7-5 that in a population consisting only of cooperators ($c = 1.0$), everyone's payoff would be four units, or twice as much as everyone gets in the equilibrium consisting only of defectors. As in the hawks and doves example, however, such a population would not survive if it were invaded by defectors, who are more successful than cooperators, given *this* payoff matrix.

Population Movements When Cooperators Are Easily Identified

Now suppose everything is just as before except that cooperators and defectors are perfectly distinguishable from each other. For concreteness, suppose that sympathy is the emotion that motivates cooperation, and that there is an observable symptom present in people who

---

[6]In practice, we do not require intergenerational transfer of "cooperator" and "defector" genes as the sole mechanism explaining the relative expansion or decline over time of one group or the other. In human societies, an individual can in all sincerity "convert" from one group (or mode of behaviour) to the other, in response to information (gained from experience) about the "success" or the ethical implications of pursuing one strategy or the other. The possibility of "conversion" implies that equilibrium can be reached more rapidly than an intergenerational genetic-transfer model would suggest.

FIGURE 7-6

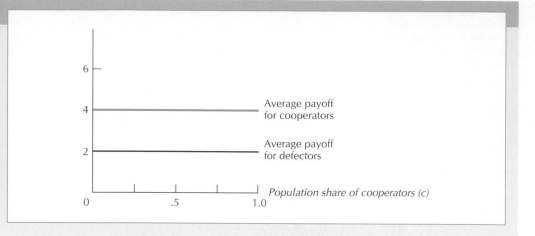

experience this emotion (perhaps a "sympathetic manner"). Defectors lack this observable symptom; or, more generally, they may try to mimic it, but fail to get it exactly right.

If this symptom is observable at a glance, the tables are completely turned. Cooperators can now interact selectively with one another and be assured of a payoff of four units. No cooperator need ever interact with a defector. Defectors are left to interact with one another, for which they get a payoff of only two units.

Since all element of chance has been removed from the interaction process, payoffs no longer depend on the proportion of cooperators in the population (see Figure 7-6). Cooperators always get four, defectors always get two.

This time the cooperators' larger payoffs enable *them* to raise larger families, which means they will make up an ever-growing share of the population. When cooperators can be easily identified, it is the defectors who face extinction.

Mimicry Without Cost or Delay

The defectors need not go quietly into the night, however. Suppose there arises a mutant strain of defectors, one that behaves exactly like other defectors but in which each individual has precisely the same symptoms of trustworthiness as cooperators. Since this particular strain of defectors looks exactly the same as cooperators, it is impossible for cooperators to discriminate against them. Each impostor is therefore just as likely to interact with a cooperator as a genuine cooperator is. This, in turn, means that the mutant defectors will have a higher expected payoff than the cooperators.

The nonmutant defectors—those who continue to look different from cooperators—will have a lower payoff than both of these groups and, as before, are destined for extinction. But unless the cooperators adapt in some way, they too face the same fate. When defectors can perfectly mimic the distinguishing feature of cooperators with neither cost nor delay, the feature loses all power to distinguish. Cooperators and the surviving defectors again look exactly alike, which again spells doom for the cooperators.

Imperfect Mimicry and the Cost of Vigilance

Defectors, of course, have no monopoly on the power to adapt. If random mutations alter the cooperators' distinguishing characteristic, the defectors will be faced with a moving target. Imagine that symptoms by which cooperators originally managed to distinguish themselves can be imperfectly mimicked by defectors. If the two types could be distinguished at a glance, defectors would again be doomed. But suppose it requires effort to differentiate between a cooperator and a defector. For concreteness, suppose inspection costs one unit. Paying this cost is like buying a pair of invisible glasses that enable cooperators and defectors to be distinguished at a glance. For those who do not pay, the two types remain perfectly indistinguishable.

To see what happens this time, suppose the payoffs are again as given in Table 7-3, and consider the decision facing a cooperator who is trying to decide whether to pay the cost of vigilance. If he pays it, he can be assured of interacting with another cooperator and will thus get a payoff of $4 - 1 = 3$ units. If he does not, his payoff is uncertain. Cooperators and defectors will look exactly alike to him and he must take his chances. If he happens to interact with another cooperator, he will get four units. But if he interacts with a defector, he will get zero. Whether it makes sense to pay the one-unit cost of vigilance thus depends on the likelihood of those two outcomes.

Suppose the population share of cooperators is 90 percent. By not paying the cost of vigilance, a cooperator will interact with another cooperator 90 percent of the time, with a defector only 10 percent. His payoff will thus have an average value of $(.9)(4) + (.1)(0) = 3.6$ units. Since this is higher than the three-unit net payoff he would get if he paid the cost of vigilance, it is clearly better not to pay it.

Now suppose the population share of cooperators is not 90 percent but 50 percent. If our cooperator does not pay the cost of vigilance, he will now have only a 50–50 chance of interacting with a cooperator. His average payoff will thus be only two units, or one unit less than if he had paid the cost. On these odds, it would clearly be better to pay it.

The numbers in this example imply a "breakeven point" obtained by solving the following equation for c:

$$4c = 3, \tag{7.7}$$

which yields $c = .75$. Thus, when the population share of cooperators is 75 percent, a cooperator's expected payoff if he does not pay the cost of vigilance ($4c$) is exactly equal to his certain payoff if he does (3). A cooperator who does not pay the cost has a 75 percent chance at a payoff of 4 units, and a 25 percent chance of getting zero, which means an average payoff of 3 units, the same as if he had paid the cost. When the population share of cooperators is below 75 percent, it will always be better for him to pay the cost of vigilance. When the population share of cooperators is above 75 percent, it will never be better for him to pay the cost of vigilance.

EXERCISE 7-3

In a population with 60 percent cooperators and a cost of vigilance equal to 1.5, should a cooperator pay the cost of vigilance?

With the breakeven rule in mind, we can now say something about how the population will evolve over time. When the population share of cooperators is below 75 percent, cooperators will all pay the cost of vigilance and get a payoff of three units by cooperating with one another. It will not be in the interests of defectors to bear this cost, because the vigilant cooperators would not interact with them anyway. The defectors are left to interact with one another and get a payoff of only two units. Thus, if we start with a population share of cooperators less than 75 percent, the cooperators will get a higher average payoff, which means that their share of the population will grow.

In populations that consist of more than 75 percent cooperators, the tables are turned. Now it no longer makes sense to pay the cost of vigilance. Cooperators and defectors will thus interact at random, which means that defectors will have a higher average payoff. This difference in payoffs, in turn, will cause the population share of cooperators to shrink.

For the values assumed in this example, the average payoff schedules for the two groups are plotted in Figure 7-7. As noted, the cooperators' schedule lies above the defectors' for shares smaller than 75 percent, but below it for larger shares. The sharp discontinuity in the defectors' schedule reflects the fact that, to the left of 75 percent, all cooperators pay for vigilance, while to the right of 75 percent, none of them does. Once the population share of cooperators passes 75 percent, defectors suddenly gain access to their victims. The evolutionary rule, once again, is that higher relative payoffs result in a growing population share. This rule makes it clear that the population in this example will stabilize at 75 percent cooperators.

Now, there is obviously nothing magic about this 75 percent figure. Had the cost of vigilance been lower than one unit, for example, the population share of cooperators would have been larger.

EXERCISE 7-4

What will be the equilibrium population share of cooperators if the cost of vigilance is .5 unit?

An increase in the payoff when cooperators pair with one another would also increase the equilibrium population share of cooperators. The point of the example is that when there are costs of vigilance, there will be pressures that pull the population toward some stable mix of cooperators and defectors. As in the hawks and doves example considered earlier, once the population settles at this mix, members of both groups have the same average payoff and are therefore equally likely to survive. There is an ecological niche, in other words, for both groups. This result stands in stark contrast to the view that only opportunism can survive in a bitterly competitive material world.

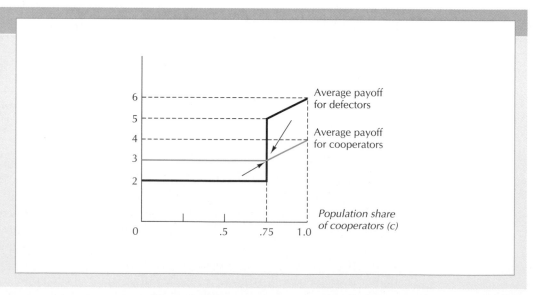

FIGURE 7-7

Average Payoffs with Costs of Vigilance
From any starting point, the population eventually stabilizes at 75 percent cooperators. Below 75 percent, cooperators pay vigilance costs, avoid interaction with defectors, and grow more rapidly than defectors. Above 75 percent, cooperators do not pay vigilance costs. Hence *defectors* receive higher average payoffs and grow more rapidly.

FIGURE 7-8

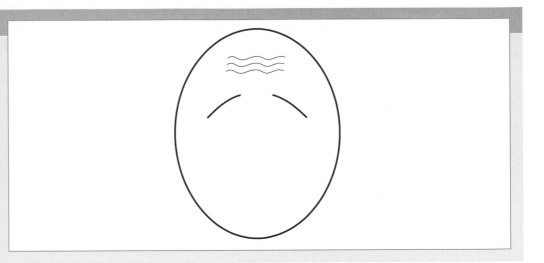

The central assumption behind the claim that certain nonegoistic motives or preferences can help solve commitment problems is that the presence of these motives can somehow be discovered by others. Consider, for instance, the schematic expression in Figure 7-8. The distinct configuration of the eyebrows—elevated in the centre of the brow, sloping downward toward the sides—is produced by a specific combination of the pyramidal muscles (located near the bridge of the nose) and the corrugator muscles (located near the centre of the brow). Only 15 percent of experimental subjects are able to produce this expression on demand. In contrast, virtually all subjects exhibit it spontaneously when they experience grief, sadness, or concern.

Psychologists have also found that posture and other elements of body language, the pitch and timbre of the voice, the rate of respiration, and even the cadence of speech are systematically linked to underlying motivational states. Because the relevant linkages are beyond conscious control in most people, it is difficult to conceal from others the experience of certain emotions, and equally difficult to feign the characteristic expressions of these emotions on occasions when they are not actually experienced. For this reason, we are able to use such clues to form estimates of the emotional makeup of others, which in turn help us to form judgments about their preferences.[7] In addition to facial expressions and other physical symptoms of emotion, we rely on reputation and a variety of other clues to predict the behaviour of potential partners.[8]

7.5 A SIMPLE THOUGHT EXPERIMENT

Perhaps the following simple thought experiment will help you decide whether you think you are able to make reliable character judgments about other people.

Imagine you have just gotten home from a crowded concert and discover you have lost $1000 in cash. The cash had been in your coat pocket in a plain envelope with your name written on it. Do you know anyone, not related to you by blood or marriage, who you feel certain would return it to you if he or she found it?

---

[7]The term "preferences" may not fully capture the essence of what we are trying to assess in potential partners. "Character" or "moral sentiments" may come closer.

[8]On the role of reputation and other factors, see Robert H. Frank, *Passions Within Reason*, New York: Norton, 1988, Chapter 4; and Paul Milgrom and John Roberts, *Economics, Organization and Management*, Upper Saddle River, NJ: Prentice-Hall, 1992, Chapter 8.

For the sake of discussion, we will assume that you are not in the unenviable position of having to answer no. Think for a moment about the person you are sure would return your cash; call her "Faith." Try to explain *why* you feel so confident about her. Note that, if she had kept the cash, you could not have known it. On the basis of your other experiences with her, the most you could possibly know is that she did not cheat you in *every* such instance in the past. Even if, for example, she returned some lost money of yours in the past, that would not prove she didn't cheat you on some other occasion. (After all, if she *had* cheated you in a similar situation, you wouldn't know it.) In any event, you almost certainly have no logical basis in experience for inferring that Faith would not cheat you now. If you are like most participants in this thought experiment, you simply believe you can fathom her inner motives. You are sure she would return your cash because you are sure she would feel terrible if she did not.

For preferences to serve as commitment devices, it is not necessary to be able to predict other people's preferences with certainty. Just as a weather forecast of 20 percent chance of rain can be invaluable to someone who must plan outdoor activities, so can probabilistic assessments of character traits be of use to people who must choose someone to trust. It would obviously be nice to be accurate in every instance. But it will often suffice to be right only a fraction of the time. And most people firmly believe they can make reasonably accurate character judgments about people they know well. If you share this belief, you are in a position to see clearly why the unbridled pursuit of self-interest will often be self-defeating.

Here are two more examples of commitment problems and how nonegoistic preferences can help solve them:

- **The deterrence problem.** Suppose Jones has a $200 leather briefcase that Smith covets. If Smith steals it, Jones must decide whether to press charges. If he does, he will have to go to court. He will get his briefcase back and Smith will spend 60 days in jail, but the day in court will cost him $300 in lost earnings. Since this is more than the briefcase is worth, it would clearly not be in his material interest to press charges. (To eliminate an obvious complication, suppose Jones is about to move to a distant city, so there is no point in his adopting a tough stance in order to deter future theft.) Thus, if Smith knows Jones is a purely rational, self-interested person, he is free to steal the briefcase with impunity. Jones may threaten to press charges, but his threat would be empty.

    But suppose that Jones is *not* a pure egoist—that if Smith steals his briefcase, he will become outraged and think nothing of losing a day's earnings, or even a week's, in order to see justice done. If Smith knows this, he will let the briefcase be. If people expect us to respond "irrationally" (by the self-interest standard) to the theft of our property, we will seldom need to because it will not be in their interests to steal it. Being predisposed to respond irrationally serves much better here than being guided only by material self-interest.

- **The bargaining problem.** In this example, Smith and Jones again face the opportunity of a profitable joint venture. There is some task that they alone can do, which will net them $1000 total. Suppose Jones has no pressing need for extra money, but Smith has important bills to pay. It is a fundamental principle of bargaining theory that the party who needs the transaction least is in the strongest position. The difference in their circumstances thus gives Jones the advantage. Needing the gain less, he can threaten, credibly, to walk away from the transaction unless he gets the lion's share of the take, say, $900. Rather than see the transaction fall through, it will then be in Smith's interest to capitulate.

But suppose Jones knows that Smith cares not only about how much money he receives in absolute terms but also about how the total is divided between them. More specifically, suppose Jones knows that Smith is committed to a norm of fairness that calls for the total to be divided evenly. If Smith's commitment to this norm is sufficiently strong, he will refuse Jones's one-sided offer, even though he would do better, in purely material terms, by accepting it. The irony is that if Jones knows this, he will not confront Smith with a one-sided offer in the first place.

7.6 ALTRUISM, SURVIVAL, AND THE PRODUCTION OF PREFERENCES

We are in a position now to take stock of the models developed so far in the chapter, and to place them in context. In order to develop the core principles clearly, we have made some strong assumptions. It is possible, however, to relax these assumptions significantly and to reach basically the same conclusions. To begin with, in practice we rarely find pure "hawks" or pure "doves." When we do, we often call the former "sociopaths" or "war heroes" and the latter "wimps" or "saints," depending on the situation and our own biases. Most of us have in our repertoire some aggressive and some cooperative tastes or modes of behaviour, although the proportion differs significantly from person to person. The reason is simple: at the level of both individuals and society, *both* modes of behaviour can have survival value. Suppose, for example, that cooperation (literally, operating or working together) is the primary source of higher productivity, as Adam Smith argued in the brilliant first three chapters of the *Wealth of Nations* on the division of labour. Then egalitarian cooperative behaviour can produce equal shares of a *bigger* pie, whereas predatory or parasitic defection may gain a more-than-equal share of a *smaller* pie. Which strategy offers a bigger payoff, and hence a greater chance of evolutionary success, depends critically on the structure of the payoff matrix.

We have so far treated the payoff matrices we have studied as given and unchanging. We have noted, however, that even slight changes in the payoff matrix can dramatically change the equilibrium proportion of hawks and doves, or of hawkish and dovish behaviour. Over periods much shorter than those on a natural-evolutionary time scale, changes in the environment can sharply alter the absolute and relative payoffs to cooperation and defection. A major natural disaster, like the 1997 Winnipeg flood, the 1998 Quebec-Ontario ice storm, or the 2004 Asian *tsunami*, can call forth literally millions of volunteer labour-days, and place a premium on cooperative behaviour. Here what is at stake is the survival or reconstruction of the social *system* itself, without which the *individual* interactions would be virtually impossible in their original form, at the original payoff levels. Mobilization in wartime, in a union organizing drive, or in a mass social movement again places a premium on cooperation within the group in relation to the common adversary: "United we stand, divided we fall." In such situations, moreover, there will be a role for "cooperative hawks," if they can channel their taste for aggression toward the *external* threat.

If success of the group increases the individual group member's selective advantage or probability of success, then a taste for cooperation is an aspect of "fitness" in the evolutionary sense. This is true of a wolf pack or a herd of caribou, and it is equally true of a Girl Guide troop, a street gang, or the participants in a microeconomics course organizing pre-exam study groups. Similarly, since human infants are basically helpless at birth and for an extended period thereafter, cooperation in the form of parental love and nurture appears to be selectively advantageous for human doves *and* hawks. That all human societies have religious, educational, and legal institutions does not in itself answer the question as to whether humans have a *taste* for cooperation. It could be argued that humans are *not* by nature cooperative, and so cooperation has to be obtained by the investment of scarce resources in brainwashing or coercion. It is also possible, however, that a mere taste for cooperation does not guarantee that people will know *how* best to cooperate. In this view, resources need to be devoted to ensure that everyone understands "the rules of the game," the ever-changing list of prescribed, permitted, and proscribed forms of behaviour, and the consequences of following and of deviating from the rules.

Our initial examples in the chapter were drawn from biological models where the primary mechanism of relative population increase and decrease involves transmission of genetic characteristics, predispositions, or tastes. We have seen, however, that with human populations we can allow for the effects of both "nature" *and* "nurture," biological *and* cultural transmission of traits or tastes. The message sent by both types of model is that microeconomics does not have to rest on the assumption of exogenously given tastes. We can use microeconomic analysis itself to understand the production, reproduction, and distribution of tastes in an economic system. This field of research is still one of the frontier areas of economics. Even our current level of knowledge, however, calls into question the adequacy of the self-interest standard of rationality, and provides us with means of introducing nonegoistic motives and tastes into our analysis of economic behaviour.

Economic Naturalist 7-1

WHY DO PEOPLE VOTE IN FEDERAL ELECTIONS, AND WHAT DETERMINES VOTER TURNOUT?

In Example 1.11 of Chapter 1, we saw that egoistically rational people would not vote in elections. For a person who has come to believe that it is a citizen's duty to vote, however, voting now becomes an end in itself, something that provides satisfaction.[9] A simple model enables us to see how this change affects the decision on whether to vote. Consider a consumer whose utility is given by the following function:

$$U = 2M + 150V, \tag{7.8}$$

where M is the dollar value of her annual consumption of the composite good, and V takes the value 1 if she votes and 0 if she does not. Suppose further that this consumer can earn $50 per hour for as many hours as she chooses to work.

Let t denote the time (in hours) she spends travelling to and from the polls and waiting in line to vote. Suppose that she regards this time as neither more nor less unpleasant than working an equivalent amount of time at her job. Then the opportunity cost of voting, in terms of forgone income, is $M = \$50t$, which would have given her $2M = 100t$ units of utility. The benefit of voting is 150 units of utility. Costs and benefits will be equal when $t = 150/100 = 1.5$ hours. If total expected voting time exceeds 1.5 hours, she won't vote; if it is less than 1.5 hours, she will; and if it is exactly 1.5 hours, she will be indifferent between voting and not voting. She will be more likely to vote the greater the utility of V relative to that of M, the closer she lives to the polling station, and the shorter the lineups for voting. The model also shows how a storm that increases travel time to the polls will tend to reduce voter turnout.

Since elections are never decided by a single vote, why do people incur the cost of going to the polls?

---

[9]Here too, it might seem more descriptive to say that a person votes not because it gives her pleasure but because she thinks it is the right thing to do. Analytically, however, both descriptions may be represented by saying that the act of voting augments utility.

Application: Concerns About Fairness

As an additional illustration of how predictions change when we take nonegoistic motives into account, consider the following simple game developed by German economist Werner Guth, to test for the presence of concerns about fairness.

The game is called the *ultimatum bargaining game* and involves two players, an *allocator* and a *receiver*. It begins by giving the allocator a fixed sum of money, say, $20. The allocator must then make a proposal about how the money should be divided between him and the receiver—for example, he might propose $10 for himself and $10 for the receiver. The receiver's task is then either to accept or to reject the proposal. If he accepts it, then they each receive the amounts proposed. If he rejects it, however, each player receives nothing. The $20 simply reverts to the experimenters. The players in the game are strangers to one another and will play the game only once.

The Pure Self-Interest Model

What does the self-interest model predict will happen here? To answer this question, we begin by assuming that each player cares only about his final wealth level, not about how much the other player gets. Now suppose the allocator proposes to keep $P_A = \$15$ for himself and to give the remaining $\$20 - P_A = \$5$ to the receiver, and that the receiver accepts this proposal. If M_A and M_R were their respective wealth levels before the experiment, their final wealth levels will then be $M_A + \$15$ and $M_R + \$5$.

If, on the other hand, the receiver rejects the allocator's proposal, then their final wealth levels will be M_A and M_R. Knowing this, the allocator can conclude that the receiver will get a higher wealth level by accepting the proposal than by rejecting it, provided only that P_A is less than $20. If the money cannot be divided into intervals any smaller than one cent, the self-interest model thus predicts unequivocally that the allocator will propose to keep $19.99 for himself and to give the remaining one cent to the receiver. The receiver may not be pleased about this one-sided offer, but the self-interest model says he will accept it nonetheless, because $M_R + \$.01 > M_R$. By the logic of the self-interest model, the receiver reasons that whereas a gain of one cent is not much, it is better than nothing, which is what he would get if he refused the offer. Because the game is played only once, there is no point in refusing in the hope of encouraging a more favourable offer next time.

When Fairness Matters

What prediction would we reach if we acknowledge that the receiver cares not just about his final wealth level but also about fairness? It is natural to say that the fairest split of the surplus in an ultimatum bargaining game is 50–50. Let S (= $20) denote the total sum of money to be divided, and let $P_R/S = (20 - P_A)/20$ be the share of this surplus the receiver would get if he accepted the proposal. A convenient way to express the receiver's concern about fairness is by saying that his satisfaction declines as the ratio P_R/S deviates—in either direction—from the value .5. Thus, the receiver's indifference map defined over M_R and P_R/S might look roughly as shown in Figure 7-9. The indifference curves shown embody the additional assumption that a one-sided division is more objectionable if it favours the other person—which is another way of saying that the M_RS rises more sharply when we move to the left from $P_R/S = .5$ than when we move to the right.[10]

---

[10]The point made in this example would be essentially the same if the receiver's indifference curves in Figure 7-9 were downward sloping throughout.

The Tradeoff between Absolute Wealth and Relative Gain
In many situations, the fairest division of surplus is when each party receives an equal share. When people value fairness for its own sake, the indifference curves between final wealth and own share of the surplus are U-shaped, which means that people need to be compensated for accepting divisions that deviate from equality.

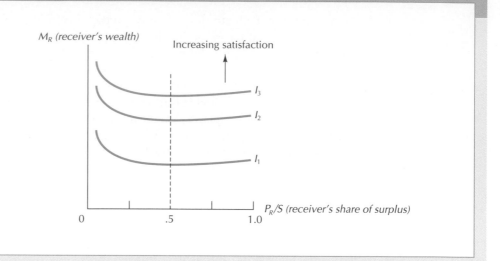

Let us now evaluate the one-sided proposal predicted by the standard self-interest model, where $P_A = \$19.99$ and $P_R = \$.01$. If the receiver accepts this proposal, he will end up at the point ($\$.01/20$, $M_R + \$.01$), labelled C in Figure 7-10. If, on the other hand, he rejects the proposal, he will have virtually the same wealth level, M_R. If rejecting may be considered to result in a P_R/S value of .5 (since neither party gains ground at the other's expense), the receiver will thus end up at point D in Figure 7-10. And because D lies on a higher indifference curve than C, he does best to reject the proposal. (If he accepted it, the trivial increase in his wealth would be insufficient to compensate for the disutility of the one-sided transaction.) More important, if the allocator knows that the receiver has such preferences, he will never make a one-sided offer in the first place.

In the forgoing example, it cost the receiver only a penny to punish the allocator for making a one-sided offer. Guth and his colleagues found that, even with amounts as large as $50, it is common to see the receiver reject if the allocator offers less than 20 percent of the total.

The Gain from Rejecting a One-Sided Offer
Accepting a one-sided offer places the receiver at point C. By refusing the offer, he ends up at D, where, even though his final wealth is slightly lower, he is on a higher indifference curve.

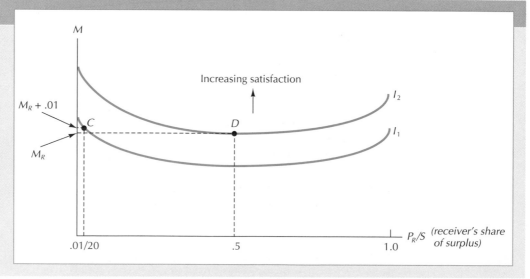

CHAPTER 7: EXPLAINING TASTES: THE IMPORTANCE OF ALTRUISM AND OTHER NONEGOISTIC BEHAVIOUR

At some point, of course, concerns about fairness are likely to give way to concerns about the absolute gain itself. It would be surprising indeed if the receiver rejected a proposal that he get 10 percent of, say, $1 million. Here, most people would surely find the pair $(.1, M_R + \$100,000)$ more attractive than $(.5, M_R)$.

EXAMPLE 7-2

Capulet's utility function is given by $U_C = M_C / \sqrt{M_M}$, where M_C is Capulet's wealth level and M_M is Montagu's. Montagu's utility function takes a similar form: $U_M = M_M / \sqrt{M_C}$. Suppose $M_C = M_M = 4$ units initially, and suppose there is a task, neither pleasant nor unpleasant, that Capulet and Montagu can perform together and that will generate an additional two units of wealth for the two men to divide. Neither man can perform the task alone or with anyone else. What is the smallest payment Capulet would accept in return for this task? (Montagu is paid the difference between 2 and the amount paid to Capulet.) Is this task feasible?

The utility functions in this example are ones in which each person feels better when his own wealth increases but feels worse when the other person's wealth increases. The effect of the task is to increase the wealth of both people. The question is thus whether the positive effect of having more income from performing the task outweighs the negative effect of the other person's also having more income. Capulet's initial utility level is $4 / \sqrt{4} = 2$. Suppose he does the task with Montagu and receives a payment of P, leaving $2 - P$ for Montagu. Capulet's utility level would then be $U_C = (4 + P) / \sqrt{(4 + 2 - P)} = (4 + P) / \sqrt{(6 - P)}$. The lowest acceptable utility payment for Capulet is the one that keeps his utility at the same level as if he did not participate: $(4 + P) / \sqrt{(6 - P)} = 2$. Rearranging terms, we have $P^2 + 12P - 8 = 0$, which solves for $P = .63$ (see footnote 11). Since the problem is symmetric, this is also the minimum payment that would be acceptable to Montagu. And since the total gain from doing the project (2) is more than enough for each person to get .63, they will do it. For example, if each takes a payment of 1, each will have a utility level of $(4 + 1) / \sqrt{(4 + 1)} = \sqrt{5}$, which is greater than the initial utility level of 2.

7.7 THE IMPORTANCE OF TASTES

The self-interest model assumes certain tastes and constraints, and then calculates what actions will best serve those tastes. This model is widely used by economists, other social scientists, game theorists, military strategists, philosophers, and others. Its results influence decisions that affect us all. In its standard form, it assumes purely egoistic tastes—namely, for present and future consumption goods of various sorts, leisure, and so on. Envy, guilt, rage, honour, sympathy, love, and the like typically play no role.

The examples in this chapter, in contrast, emphasize the role of these emotions in behaviour. The rationalists speak of tastes, not emotions, but for analytical purposes, the two play exactly parallel roles. Thus, a person who is motivated to avoid the emotion of guilt or shame may be equivalently described as someone with a "taste" for honest behaviour.

Tastes have important consequences for action. The inclusion of tastes that help solve commitment problems substantially alters the predictions of self-interest models.

---

[11]Recall that the solution to an equation of the form $ax^2 + bx + c = 0$ is given by $x = \dfrac{-b \pm \sqrt{b^2 - 4ac}}{2a}$.

We saw that it may pay people to feel concerned about fairness for its own sake, because feeling that way makes them better bargainers. Without taking into account concerns about fairness, we cannot hope to predict what prices stores will charge, what wages workers will demand, how long business executives will resist a strike, what taxes governments will levy, how fast military budgets will grow, or whether a union leader will be re-elected.

The presence of conscience also alters the predictions of self-interest models. These models predict clearly that when interactions between people are not repeated, people will cheat if they know they can get away with it. Yet evidence consistently shows that in most cases, people do not cheat under these circumstances. Self-interest models also suggest that the owner of a small business will not contribute to the lobbying efforts of trade associations. Like one man's vote, her own contribution will seem too small a part of the total to make any difference. Yet many small businesses do pay dues to trade associations, and many people do vote. Charitable institutions also exist on a far grander scale than would ever be predicted by self-interest models.

There is nothing mystical about the emotions that drive these behaviours. On the contrary, they are an obvious part of most people's psychological makeup. What we have seen is why it might be advantageous, even in purely material terms, to have concerns that motivate unselfish behaviour.

Is Material Gain an "Appropriate" Motive for Morality?

Some may object that the prospect of material gain is somehow an improper motive for adopting moral values. But this objection misconstrues the fundamental message of this chapter, which is that nonegoistic motives confer material advantage only if the satisfaction people take from doing the right thing is *intrinsic* to the behaviour itself. Otherwise, the person will lack the necessary motivation to make self-sacrificing choices when no one is looking, and once other people sense that aspect of his character, material advantages will not, in fact, follow. By the very nature of the commitment problem, moral sentiments rarely lead to material advantage unless they are heartfelt.

- Prisoner's dilemmas and other forms of commitment problems abound in economic transactions. Being known not to have strictly self-interested preferences can be extremely useful for solving these problems.

- In order for such preferences to be advantageous, others must be able to discern that one has them. If preferences could be observed without cost or uncertainty, there would be only cooperative people in the world. But because costs and uncertainty are an inherent part of the process, there will virtually always be an ecological niche for at least some of the opportunistic people assumed in conventional self-interest models. The chapter has also illustrated that the predominance of one group or mode of behaviour can be highly sensitive to the structure of rewards in the payoff matrix.

- The two main points of this chapter are (1) the self-interest model, which assumes that everyone behaves opportunistically, is destined to make important errors in predicting actual behaviour; and (2) people who are concerned about the interests of others need not suffer on that account, even in purely material terms. Because others can recognize the kind of people they are, opportunities will be open to them that would not be open to the opportunist.

QUESTIONS FOR REVIEW

1. Summarize in your own words the major difficulties of the present-aim and self-interest standards of rationality.
2. Explain the role of rational analysis in the psychologist's model of human motivation.
3. Try to think of at least two commitment problems you personally encountered during the last year.
4. In the commitment model, what role is played by the observability of preferences?
5. Explain how a military arms race has some of the same formal characteristics as a prisoner's dilemma.

PROBLEMS

1. A population consists of two types, "friendlies" and "aggressives." Each individual interacts with a randomly chosen member of the population. When two friendlies interact, each earns 3 units. When two aggressives interact, each earns zero units. When a friendly and an aggressive interact, the former gets a payoff of 1 unit, the latter a payoff of 5 units. The growth rate of each type is proportional to its average payoff. What will be the equilibrium population shares of each type?

2. Consider a population with two types of people, Cs and Ds. Interactions among various combinations of the two types produce the following payoffs:

   C-C: 6 each
   C-D: 8 for D, 0 for C
   D-D: 4 each

   Goggles are available, at a cost of 1 unit per pair, which enable the wearer to identify each person's type with certainty. Without the goggles the two types are indistinguishable.
   a. What will be the equilibrium population shares of the two types?
   b. How would your answer differ if the payoff for D-D interactions was 5.5 each?

**3. Alphonse's utility function is given by

$$U_A = (M_A)^2 M_G,$$

where M_A and M_G are the wealth levels of Alphonse and Gaston, respectively. If Alphonse's initial wealth level is 100 while Gaston's is only 20, how much of his wealth will Alphonse give to Gaston? (Hint: Use calculus or Appendix 3A.)

**4. Anne and Gilbert have the following utility functions:

$$\text{Anne:} \quad U_A = M_A \, M_G \quad \text{and} \quad \text{Gilbert:} \quad U_G = (M_A)^2 M_G,$$

where M_A is Anne's wealth and M_G is Gilbert's wealth.

   a. If their total wealth, $M_A + M_G$, = \$180, then what final distribution would maximize Anne's utility? What final distribution would maximize Gilbert's utility?
   b. If Gilbert initially has \$150 and Anne has \$30, what will the final distribution be? If Anne initially has \$150 and Gilbert has \$30, what will the final distribution be? Briefly interpret your results.

**5. Abner's utility function is given by

$$U_A = \frac{(M_A)^2}{M_B},$$

where M_A is Abner's wealth level and M_B is Benjamin's wealth level. Benjamin's utility function is given by

$$U_B = \frac{(M_B)^2}{M_A}.$$

Suppose $M_A = M_B = 10$ initially, and suppose there is a joint project that Abner and Benjamin can undertake that will generate an additional 10 units of wealth to divide between them. The project is neither pleasant nor unpleasant. What is the minimum payment Abner must be given to secure his agreement to perform the project? What is the minimum payment Benjamin must be given? Will they perform the project?

**6. Repeat Problem 5, except that now $U_A = M_A/(M_B)^2$ and $U_B = M_B/(M_A)^2$.

   7. Ed and Fred, two mutually envious individuals, have the following utility functions:

$$\text{Ed:} \quad U_E = M_E - 1.2M_F \quad \text{and} \quad \text{Fred:} \quad U_F = M_F - .5M_E.$$

Each has an initial wealth level of 100 units ($M_E = M_F = 100$ units), and they can participate in a joint project that will pay them an additional 20 units, to be divided between them in some way. Is there room for a deal? If a deal can be struck, what is the possible range of payments to Ed and to Fred?

*8. Suppose that the situation is exactly as in Problem 7, except that $U_F = M_F - aM_E$, where a is a positive constant measuring Fred's degree of envy or positional concerns. What is the highest value a can assume before there is no possibility of a deal?

   9. A turf war seems imminent between two rival street gangs, Satan's Spawn and the Devil's Brood. Satan's Spawn members are deciding between two candidates for gang leader, Crazy Louie (who has promised a fight to the finish if the Brood encroach on Spawn territory), and Eddie the Con (who proposes a "summit" with the Brood to work out boundaries and neutral zones). As a Spawn member, whom do you vote for, and why? Under what circumstances would you change your vote?

   10. Harold's utility is given by $U = 3M + 60V$, where M is the dollar value of his annual consumption of the composite good and V takes the value 1 if he votes and 0 if he does not. Harold finances his consumption by working at a job that pays \$30 per hour for as many hours as he chooses to work. In order to vote he must spend a total of 20 minutes travelling to and from the polling place, where he must stand in line before casting his ballot. If he regards his transit time and waiting time as neither more nor less unpleasant than working an equivalent amount of time at his job, how long (in minutes of waiting time) must the line at the polls be before Harold will decide not to vote?

7-1. Let h denote the share of hawks in the population, so that $1 - h$ denotes the share of doves. Since the two types interact at random with other members of the population, the expected payoff for doves is given by

$$P_D = 3(1 - h) + 2(h) = 3 - h.$$

The corresponding expected payoff for hawks is

$$P_H = 6(1 - h) + 1(h) = 6 - 5h.$$

The population mix is in equilibrium when the expected payoffs of the two types are the same. If h^* denotes the equilibrium share of hawks, we have

$$3 - h^* = 6 - 5h^*,$$

which solves for $h^* = \frac{3}{4}$. The equilibrium share of doves is $1 - h^* = \frac{1}{4}$.

7-2. $P_C = .9(4) + .1(0) = 3.6$. $P_D = .1(2) + .9(6) = 5.6$.

7-3. If all cooperators pay the cost of vigilance, each will get a payoff of $4 - 1.5 = 2.5$. If none pays the cost of vigilance, the expected payoff will be

$$P_C = .6(4) + .4(0) = 2.4,$$

which is less than 2.5. So they should pay the cost of vigilance.

7-4. The payoff net of the cost of vigilance is now $4 - .5 = 3.5$. If Cs do not pay the cost of vigilance, their expected payoff is again given by $P_C = 4c$. To find the breakeven level of c, we solve $4c' = 3.5$, which yields $c' = \frac{7}{8}$.

For $c < \frac{7}{8}$, the Cs have a higher expected payoff if they pay the cost. For $c > \frac{7}{8}$, they have a higher expected payoff if they simply take their chances. For $c < \frac{7}{8}$, the Ds will be forced to interact with one another, which gives the Ds a payoff of 2. Once $c > \frac{7}{8}$, however, the Cs stop paying the cost and the expected payoff for the Ds becomes

$$P_D = c(6) + (1 - c)(2) = 2 + 4c.$$

The expected payoff functions for the Cs and Ds are now as shown in the diagram:

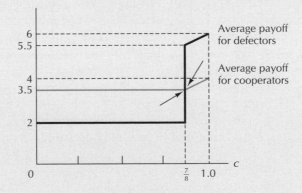

Note that the average payoff for Cs is greater than for Ds whenever $c < \frac{7}{8}$, while the expected payoff for Ds exceeds that of Cs whenever $c > \frac{7}{8}$. The result is that if we start with $c > \frac{7}{8}$, the population share of Cs will shrink to $\frac{7}{8}$, because the growth rate of Ds will be faster than that of Cs. If we start with $c < \frac{7}{8}$, the population share of Cs will grow to $\frac{7}{8}$.

Chapter 8

COGNITIVE LIMITATIONS AND CONSUMER BEHAVIOUR

You are a tennis fanatic, and belong to a club that has beautiful outdoor courts, as well as indoor courts where you can play through the winter. You pay a fixed annual fee that gives you access to both indoor and outdoor courts. There is no additional charge to play on the outdoor courts. To play on the indoor courts, however, you must book a court and pay a nonrefundable, $15 per time-slot court fee in advance. This late autumn day, the forecast was for rain, cold, and strong winds. You and your playing partner had therefore booked and paid for an indoor court, for the only time you both were free that day. When you both arrive at the courts, however, it is sunny and warm, with a light breeze—ideal outdoor tennis weather—and some of the outdoor courts are unoccupied.

As an economist, you note that playing on the outdoor courts is the only sensible thing to do. "But we've already paid for the indoor court," your partner exclaims. You ask, "If both courts cost the same, which would you choose?" She replies, "Outdoors, of course." Then you explain that both courts *do* cost the same, because the cost of the time is going to be $15 no matter where you play, or even if you don't play. The $15 is a sunk cost, and should have no effect on your decision. After some thought, your partner agrees, and you have a wonderful outdoor match, spoiled only by the fact that she beats you in straight sets. The $15 was "wasted," in the sense that you did not actually utilize the indoor court time for which you had already paid. Playing indoors simply to prevent this "waste," however, would have resulted in an even greater waste. You would have wasted the opportunity of playing outdoors at no extra cost, an opportunity which both of you valued more highly than playing indoors.

In this case, the net loss from not understanding the principle of sunk costs is the difference in enjoyment from playing outdoors rather than indoors. In other situations, the costs can be significantly higher. A pharmaceutical company commits an additional $5 million to a drug research project that has already cost $10 million with no discernible results. Managers reason that if they don't spend another $5 million, the $10 million will have been wasted. This is the sunk costs fallacy with a vengeance, and a prescription for creating a bottomless "money pit." The $10 million are already unrecoverable sunk costs. If the results to date are so unpromising that the additional $5 million are unlikely to produce results, *now* is the time to turn off the money tap. Yet vanity, vested interests, and company politics can lead to a neglect of the sunk costs principle and to the perpetuation of such projects long past their proper expiry date.

CHAPTER PREVIEW

In Chapter 7 we saw why motives other than self-interest might be important. These motives often lead people to behave in ways that are considered irrational under the self-interest model. But irrational or not, actions like tipping on the road or returning lost wallets to their owners are undertaken without regret. If a "self-interest" rationalist were to point out that there is no way a waiter in a distant city could retaliate for not having been left a tip, most of us would respond, "So what?" We would not suddenly regret having left tips all our lives.

Our focus in this chapter is on irrational behaviour of an altogether different sort, behaviour that is the result of failure to see clearly how best to achieve a desired result. Failure to ignore the sunk costs of the indoor tennis court is one example. Unlike the behaviours considered in the last chapter, people often *do* want to alter these behaviours once their consequences become clear to them.

In addition to failing to ignore sunk costs, we shall see that people violate the prescriptions of rational choice models in a variety of other ways. The important point, for our purposes, is that these violations are often systematic. We shall examine several behavioural models of choice that often do a much better job of predicting actual decisions than the rational choice model. It is important to remember, however, that these behavioural models claim no normative significance. They tell us, for instance, that we often *do* tend to be influenced in our decisions by sunk costs, not that we *should* be influenced by them.

The rational choice model says we can make better decisions by ignoring sunk costs, and most people, on reflection, strongly agree. The value of behavioural models is that they call our attention to situations in which we are likely to make mistakes. They are an important tool for helping us avoid common pitfalls in decision making.

8.1 BOUNDED RATIONALITY

Nobel laureate Herbert Simon was among the first to impress upon economists that human beings are incapable of behaving like the rational beings portrayed in standard rational choice models. Simon, a pioneer in the field of artificial intelligence, stumbled upon this realization in the process of trying to instruct a computer to "reason" about a problem. He discovered that when we ourselves confront a puzzle, we rarely reach a solution in a neat, linear fashion. Rather, we search in a haphazard way for potentially relevant facts and information, and usually quit once our understanding reaches a certain threshold. Our conclusions are often inconsistent, even flatly incorrect. But much of the time, we come up with serviceable, if imperfect, solutions. In Simon's terms, we are "satisficers," not maximizers.

Subsequent economists have taken Simon's lead and developed a sophisticated literature on decision making under incomplete information. We now realize that when information is costly to gather, and cognitive processing ability is limited, it is not even rational to make fully informed choices of the sort portrayed in simple models. Paradoxically, it is irrational to be completely well informed! The literature on decision making under incomplete information, far from being a challenge to the rational choice model, has in some respects bolstered our confidence in it.

But there is another offshoot of Simon's work, one that is less friendly to the rational choice model. This research, strongly influenced by the work of cognitive psychologists like Daniel Kahneman and Amos Tversky, demonstrates that even with transparently simple problems, people often violate the most fundamental axioms of rational choice. Choosing whether to play tennis indoors or out is a case in point. The relevant facts in this problem could hardly be any simpler, and yet, as noted, people often choose irrationally.

Such examples are by no means isolated. One of the most cherished tenets of the rational choice model is that wealth is fungible. Fungibility implies, among other things, that our total wealth, not the amount we have in any particular account, determines what we buy. Kahneman and Tversky, however, provided a vivid experimental demonstration to the contrary.[1] They tell one group of people to imagine that, having earlier purchased tickets for $10, they arrive at the theatre to discover they have lost them. Members of a second group are told to picture themselves arriving just before the performance to buy their tickets when they find each of them has lost $10 on the way to the theatre. People in both groups are then asked whether they will continue with their plans to attend the performance. In the rational choice model, the forces governing this decision are the same for both groups. Losing a $10 ticket should have precisely the same effect as losing a $10 bill. (Recall from Chapter 3 the rule that if tastes and budget constraints are the same, decisions should also be the same.) And yet, in repeated trials, most people in the lost-ticket group say they would not attend the performance, while an overwhelming majority—88 percent—in the lost-bill group say they would.

Kahneman and Tversky hypothesized that people apparently organize their spending into separate "mental accounts" for food, housing, entertainment, general expenses, and so on. People who lose their tickets act as if they debit $10 from their mental entertainment accounts, while those who lose $10 debit their general expense account. For people in the former group, the loss makes the apparent cost of seeing the show rise from $10 to $20, whereas for those in the second it remains $10.

The rational choice model makes clear that the second group's assessment is the correct one. And on reflection, most people do, in fact, agree that losing a ticket is no better reason not to see the performance than losing a $10 bill.

8.2 THE ASYMMETRIC VALUE FUNCTION

The rational choice model says that people should evaluate events, or collections of events, in terms of their overall effect on total wealth. Suppose A is the event that you get an unexpected gift of $100 and B is the event that you return from vacation to find an $80 invoice from the city for the repair of a broken water line on your property. According to the rational choice model, you should regard the occurrence of these two events as a good thing, because their net effect is a $20 increase in your total wealth.

Kahneman and Tversky found, however, that people seem to weigh each event separately, and attach considerably less importance to the gain than to the loss—so much less that many people actually refuse to accept pairs of events that would increase their overall wealth!

In the rational choice model, this of course can never happen. Confronted with the two events A and B described above, a person with an initial wealth of M_0 knows exactly how to react. The combined effect of A (a $100 gain) and B (an $80 loss) is to

---

[1]See Amos Tversky and Daniel Kahneman, "The Framing of Decisions and the Psychology of Choice," *Science, 211,* 1981: 453–458.

FIGURE 8-1

Utility of a Pair of Events That Increases Total Wealth
Under the rational choice model, any combination of events that increases total wealth will also increase total utility.

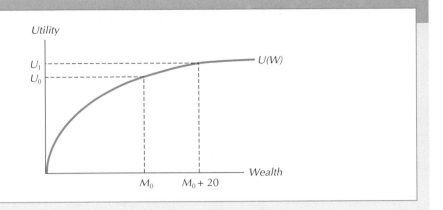

increase his wealth to $M_0 + 20$. And since utility is an increasing function of total wealth, the two events taken together cause utility to increase from U_0 to U_1, as shown in Figure 8-1.

Kahneman and Tversky proposed that people evaluate alternatives not with the conventional utility function, but instead with a *value function* that is defined over *changes* in wealth. One important property of this value function is that it is much steeper in losses than in gains. In Figure 8-2, for example, note how it assigns a much larger value, in absolute terms, to a loss of $80 than to a gain of $100. Note also that the value function is concave in gains and convex in losses. This property is the analogue of diminishing marginal utility in the traditional model. It says that the impact of incremental gains or losses diminishes as the gains or losses become larger.

Kahneman and Tversky emphasized that their value function is a purely descriptive device. They are trying to summarize regularities in the ways people actually seem to make choices. They make no claim that people *should* choose in the ways predicted by their value function.

FIGURE 8-2

The Kahneman-Tversky Value Function
Unlike the traditional utility function, the value function is defined over *changes* in total wealth. It is steeper in losses than in gains, concave in gains, and convex in losses.

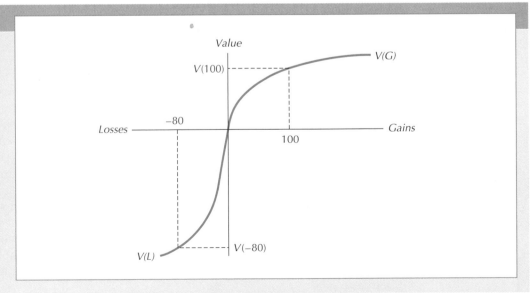

According to Kahneman and Tversky, it is very common for people to evaluate each item of a collection of events separately and then make decisions on the basis of the sum of the separate values. In this example, $V(100)$ is much smaller, in absolute terms, than $V(-80)$. Because the algebraic sum of the two is less than zero, anyone who employs this decision mechanism will refuse the pair of opportunities A and B, even though their net effect is to increase total wealth by $20.

There are really two important features of the Kahneman and Tversky value function. One is that people treat gains and losses asymmetrically, giving the latter much heavier weight in their decisions than the former. The second is that people evaluate events first and then add the separate values together. The first of these features does not necessarily imply irrational behaviour. There is nothing inconsistent, after all, about feeling that a loss causes more pain than the happiness caused by a gain of the same magnitude. What *does* often appear irrational is the second step—treating each event separately, rather than considering their combined effect.

This is essentially a question about how to frame events. If someone pointed out to a person that the net effect of two events A and B was to increase her wealth by $20, she would probably quickly agree to allow the events to happen. Framed as an entity, they are obviously an improvement over the status quo. The problem is that, in actual decisions, it may seem more natural to frame the events separately.

Another example helps illustrate this point. A corporation makes available to its employees a new medical insurance plan. The old plan paid 100 percent of all covered medical expenses, and the premium was approximately $500 per year per family. The new plan has a $200 deductible feature—people must pay the first $200 in medical expenses each year, but once that threshold is reached, the insurance again pays 100 percent. The premium for the new plan is $250 per year, half that of the old plan. Employees have the option of staying with the old plan or switching to the new.

Seen through the lens of the rational choice model, the new plan dominates the old. The $250 savings in premiums is more than enough to compensate for the $200 deductible feature. Families that incur less than $200 per year in medical expenses do even better under the new plan. Nonetheless, many employees are adamant in their wish to remain on the old plan. If some people code the $250 premium savings and the $200 extra in medical bills as separate events, the asymmetric value function predicts just such behaviour. As indicated in Figure 8-3, the $200 loss weighs in more heavily than the $250 gain.

8.3 SUNK COSTS

Another basic tenet of the rational choice model is that sunk costs should be ignored in decisions. In the tennis example at the beginning of this chapter, we saw that it is this *principle*, rather than sunk costs, that is sometimes ignored. Economist Richard Thaler argued that such examples are not isolated, that people in fact show a general tendency not to ignore sunk costs. Thaler is the author of the all-you-can-eat pizza experiment we discussed in Chapter 1. Recall that in the experiment the diners whose admission charges were refunded ate substantially fewer slices of pizza than the others. Thaler offered several other vivid illustrations of the pattern.

One is a thought experiment in which you are asked first to imagine that you have bought a pair of fashionable shoes for $200, only to discover that they are painfully tight. They improve slightly after being broken in, but still cause considerable discomfort. What do you do with these shoes, continue wearing them or give them away? Would your response be any different if you had not bought the shoes but instead had received them as a gift?

FIGURE 8-3

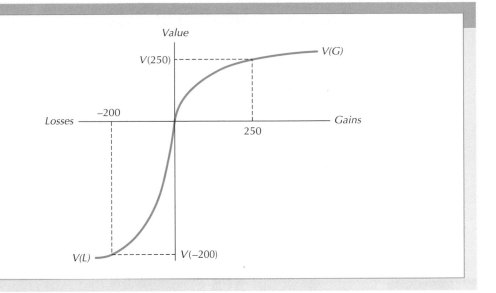

Rejection of a Dominant Insurance Plan
Because the savings in premiums ($250) is larger than the largest possible increase in uncovered expenses ($200), the new plan is necessarily better than the old. But if people code gains and losses separately, they may nonetheless refuse to switch to the new policy

Under the rational choice model, it should not matter whether you bought the shoes or were given them. Either way, you own them now, and the only question is whether the discomfort they cause is serious enough to discontinue wearing them. People in both categories should be equally likely to discontinue wearing the shoes. Contrary to this prediction, however, people are much more likely to say they would abandon the shoes if they received them as a gift. Having shelled out $200 apparently makes many people determined to endure them.

One final sunk cost example: suppose you have just paid $40 for tickets to a basketball game to be played tonight in an arena 100 km from your home. Suddenly it starts snowing heavily and the roads, while passable, are difficult. Do you still go to the game? Would your answer have been different if, instead of having bought the tickets, you had received them for free? Thaler finds that most people who bought the tickets would go, whereas most of those who were given them say they would stay home. According to the rational choice model, of course, the decision should be the same in either case. If your expected pleasure of seeing the game exceeds the expected hassle of the drive, you should go; otherwise stay home. Neither element in this cost-benefit calculation should depend on how you obtained the tickets.

8.4 OUT-OF-POCKET COSTS VS. OPPORTUNITY COSTS

Thaler suggested that our tendency not to ignore sunk costs may be given a simple interpretation in terms of the Kahneman and Tversky value function. In the tennis example, failure to play on the outdoor courts on a nice day is coded mentally as a forgone gain, whereas not playing on the $15 indoor court you have already paid for is coded as a loss. Even though the gain is larger than the loss here, the greater steepness of the value function in the loss domain creates a bias in favour of the indoor court.

Much the same interpretation is supported by a number of other plausible examples.[2] Consider a person who in 1955 bought a case of wine for $5 per bottle. Today the same wine sells at the retail level for $100 per bottle. A wine connoisseur offers him $60 per

[2]See R. Thaler, "Toward a Positive Theory of Consumer Choice," *Journal of Economic Behavior and Organization*, 1980.

bottle for it and he refuses, even though the most he would pay for the same wine today is $35 per bottle. If he is neither bargaining nor speculating on being able to sell the wine to someone else for more than $60 per bottle, then the rational choice model rules out such behaviour. But if out-of-pocket expenses (for example, for the purchase of additional wine) are coded as losses, while opportunity costs (for example, of not selling the wine to the connoisseur) are coded as forgone gains, then the asymmetric value function allows for just such a response.

An even more common example is the case of tickets to premium entertainment events. Stanley Cup final tickets that sold for $100 each through official channels can fetch up to $1000 in the open market, but many fans use their $100 tickets to attend the games, thus passing up the opportunity to sell them for $1000. Few of these fans, however, would have paid $1000 for a ticket, and it is improbable that transaction costs of selling the tickets fully explain their behaviour.

Thaler offered the parallel example of the man who would refuse to mow his neighbour's lawn for $20 yet mows his own identical lawn, even though his neighbour's son would be willing to mow it for him for only $8. This behaviour, as well as the behaviour of the Stanley Cup fans, is also consistent with the notion that out-of-pocket expenses are coded as losses, opportunity costs as forgone gains.

8.5 HEDONIC FRAMING

Kahneman and Tversky's value function suggested specific ways that sellers, gift givers, and others might frame their offerings to enhance their appeal.[3] Thaler mentioned these four specific strategies:

- **Segregate gains.** Because the value function is concave in gains, a higher total value results when we decompose a large gain into two (or more) smaller ones. Thus, Figure 8-4 shows that a gain of 100 creates more total value if decomposed into two separate gains of 60 and 40. The moral here, as Thaler said, is "Don't wrap all the presents in a single box."

  Thaler tested the empirical validity of this recommendation by asking people which of the following two individuals they thought would be happier: A, who is given two lottery tickets, one of which wins $50, the other $25; or B, who is given one lottery ticket, which wins $75. Of the people he asked, 64 percent responded that A would be happier, 18 percent said B, and 17 percent thought the two would be equally happy. The rational choice model, of course, says that both would be equally happy.

- **Combine losses.** The convexity of the value function in the loss domain implies that two separate losses will appear less painful if they are combined into a single, larger loss. As shown in Figure 8-5, for example, separate losses of 20 and 30 have a combined value that is larger, in absolute terms, than the value of a loss of 50.

  To test this prediction about the efficacy of combining losses, a sample of subjects was asked who would feel worse: A, who gets one letter from the government saying he owes $150 in taxes; or B, who gets letters from two separate branches of government, one saying he owes $100, another saying he owes $50. (The subjects were also told that there would be no repercussions other than the additional tax payments themselves.) Here are their responses: 76 percent said that B would feel worse, 16 percent said A, and 8 percent said there would be no difference. The rational choice model, again, says that the two should feel the same.

---

[3]The material in this section draws extensively on the arguments and evidence presented in R. Thaler, "Mental Accounting and Consumer Choice," *Marketing Science*, 4, 1985.

Marketers seem to have discovered the principle that losses are less painful when combined than when taken separately. A $2000 Jacuzzi, for example, seems much cheaper when its price is added together with that of a $150,000 house than it does when it is evaluated in isolation. The $150,000 expense of the house already has the buyer so far out on the flattened part of the value function that an extra $2000 seems to cause very little additional injury.

FIGURE 8-4

The Benefit of Segregating Gains
Because the value function is concave in gains, the total value of two small gains taken separately [$V(60) + V(40)$] is larger than the value of their sum [$V(100)$].

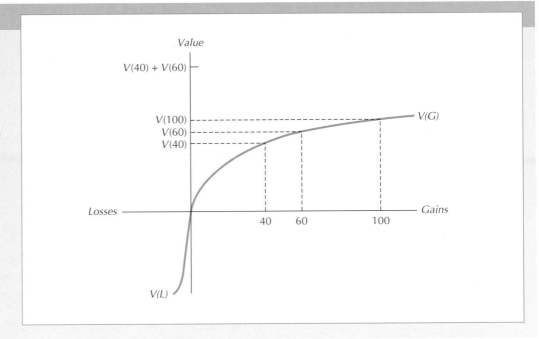

FIGURE 8-5

The Benefit of Combining Losses
Because the value function is convex in losses, the effect of two losses taken separately [$V(-20) + V(-30)$] is more painful than the effect of their sum [$V(-50)$].

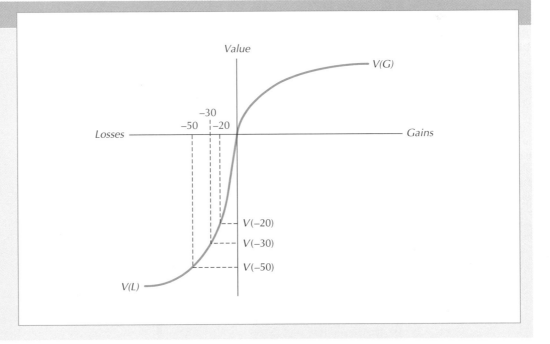

- **Offset a small loss with a larger gain.** The greater steepness of the value function in the loss domain can be avoided whenever a loss can be combined with a larger gain. Thus, the effect of a gain of 250 and a loss of 200, evaluated separately, is to produce a net value that is negative. As shown in Figure 8-6, however, the effect of lumping the two together is clearly positive.

    To test your intuition about the advantage of offsetting a loss with a larger gain, ask yourself which person you think would be happier: A, who wins $100 in the lottery but the same day drops a bottle of ink and does $80 worth of damage (including the trouble and inconvenience of cleanup) to his living room rug; or B, who wins $20 in the lottery? Of a large sample of subjects who were asked this question, 70 percent responded B, 25 percent said A, and 5 percent thought the two would be equally happy.[4] The rational choice model, which predicts the third outcome, is again in conflict with the majority view.

    Recall our earlier discussion of the company whose employees were reluctant to adopt the new medical insurance plan. This company might have won much stronger acceptance for the plan had it framed the decision in terms of the net effect, rather than as a separate loss and gain.

- **Segregate small gains from large losses.** A sample of subjects were asked which of these individuals is more upset: A, whose car sustains $200 damage in the parking lot the same day he wins $25 in the office football pool; or B, whose car sustains $175 damage in the parking lot? Of those responding, 72 percent said B would be more upset, 22 percent picked A, and 6 percent said they would be equally upset. The rational choice model predicts they would be equally upset, because they suffer exactly the same reduction in their wealth. The Kahneman and Tversky value function, in contrast, predicts that B would be more upset, which accords with most people's responses.

    Thaler called the segregation of a small gain from a big loss the "silver-lining effect" and argued that it may help explain why so many merchants offer cash rebates on

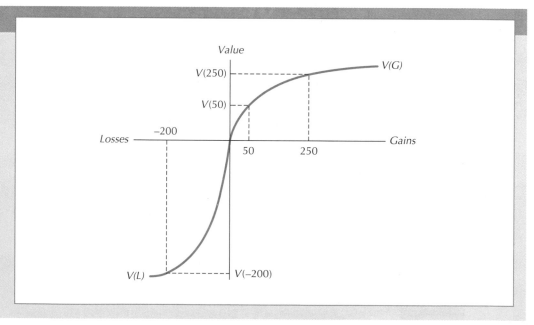

FIGURE 8-6

The Benefit of Offsetting a Loss with a Larger Gain
Because the value function is steeper in losses than in gains, the pain of a loss [V(−200)] will often exceed the pleasure of a slightly larger gain [V(250)]. The pain of such a loss can be avoided when it is possible to combine it with the larger gain to produce a positive net effect [V(50)].

[4]R. Thaler, op. cit., 1985.

FIGURE 8-7

The Silver-Lining Effect and Cash Rebates
If a cash rebate is coded as a separate gain [*V*(1200)], and the price of the product as a loss [*V*(−11,200)], then the total effect [*V*(1200)] + [*VV*(−11,200)] is less painful than when the product is offered at a lower price *V*(−10,000)].

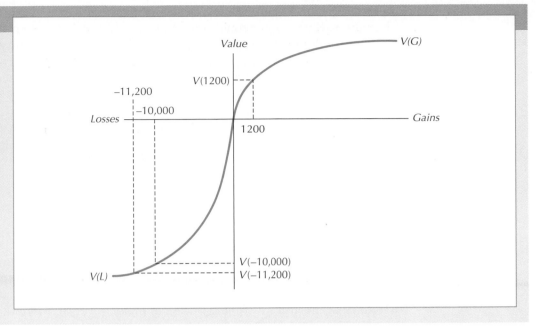

their products. ("Buy a new Ford before October 1st and get $1200 cash back!") Viewed in the context of the rational choice model, this practice seems to be dominated by the simple alternative of reducing the price of the product. The reason is that the buyer must pay sales tax on the whole price of the item, including any amount he gets back as a rebate. Considering Goods and Services Tax (GST) alone, a $1200 price reduction is worth $72 more to the consumer than a $1200 rebate. And yet the practice persists. If it leads people to code the price of the product as a loss and the rebate as a gain (see Figure 8-7), the value function approach makes clear why it might be so effective.

8.6 CHOICE UNDER UNCERTAINTY

The standard model of rational choice under uncertainty is the von Neumann–Morgenstern expected utility model discussed in Chapter 6. This model provides valuable *guidance* about how best to choose between uncertain alternatives. But Kahneman and Tversky showed that it does not always provide a good *description* of the way people actually decide.[5] To illustrate, they presented a series of choices to a group of volunteer subjects. They began with the following problem, which elicited responses that were perfectly consistent with the expected utility model:

Problem 1. Choose between

  A: A sure gain of $240   (84 percent)

and

  B: A 25 percent chance of getting $1000 and a 75 percent chance of getting $0. (16 percent)

---

[5]See Amos Tversky and Daniel Kahneman, "Judgment Under Uncertainty: Heuristics and Biases," *Science, 185,* 1974: 1124–1131.

The numbers in parentheses indicate the percentage of subjects who picked each alternative. Here, most people chose the sure gain of $240, even though the expected value of the lottery, at $250, was $10 higher. To verify that this pattern is consistent with the expected utility model, let U denote a subject's utility function, defined on total wealth, and let M denote her initial wealth in dollars. Then the expected utility of choice A is $U(M + 240)$, whereas the expected utility of choice B is $.25U(M + 1000) + .75U(M)$. If utility is a concave function of total wealth (that is, if people are risk averse), we see in Figure 8-8 why A might easily have been more attractive than B.

Subjects were then asked to consider an apparently very similar problem:

Problem 2.   Choose between

   C: A sure loss of $750   (13 percent)

   and

   D: A 75 percent chance of losing $1000 and a 25 percent chance of losing $0. (87 percent)

This time the lottery has the same expected value as the sure option. Under the expected utility model, risk-averse subjects therefore ought to choose the sure alternative once again. But this time we see a dramatic reversal. More than 6 times as many people chose the lottery as chose the sure loss of $750.

Finally, the subjects were asked to consider the following problem:

Problem 3.   Choose between

   E: A 25 percent chance of getting $240 and a 75 percent chance of losing $760 (0 percent)

   and

   F: A 25 percent chance of getting $250 and a 75 percent chance of losing $750. (100 percent)

Viewed in isolation, the responses to Problem 3 are completely unsurprising. The lottery in E is simply worse in every way than the one in F, and only someone who

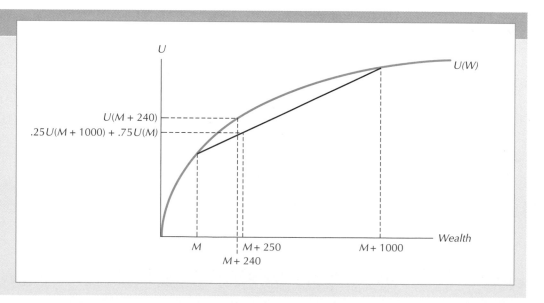

FIGURE 8-8

A Risk-Averse Person Will Usually Prefer a Sure Gain to a Lottery with Slightly Higher Expected Value
If the utility function is sufficiently concave, $U(M + 240)$ will exceed the expected utility of a gamble with positive expected value, $.25U(M + 1000) + .75U(M)$.

wasn't paying attention would have chosen E. But note that lottery E is what we get when we combine choices A and D from Problems 1 and 2; and that, similarly, lottery F is the result of combining choices B and C from the two earlier problems. In the first two problems, the combination of B and C was chosen by fewer subjects (3 percent) than any other, whereas the combination A and D was by far the most popular (chosen by 73 percent of all subjects)—even though the combination of A and D is strictly dominated by the combination of B and C. Such findings, needless to say, pose a sharp challenge to the expected utility model.

Kahneman and Tversky argued that the observed pattern is exactly what would have been predicted using their asymmetric value function. In Problem 1, for example, note that the choice is between a certain gain and a lottery whose possible outcomes are non-negative. Since the value function is concave in gains, and since the expected value of the lottery is only slightly larger than the sure alternative, it predicts the choice of the latter.

In Problem 2, in contrast, the choice is between a certain loss, on the one hand, and a lottery, each of whose outcomes is a loss, on the other. Since the value function is convex in losses, it predicts risk-seeking behaviour with respect to such a choice, and this, of course, is just what we saw. Because Problem 3 forced people to amalgamate the relevant gains and losses, subjects were easily able to see that one pair of alternatives dominated the other, and chose accordingly.

It is tempting to suppose that violations of the expected utility model occur only when the problem is sufficiently complicated that people have difficulty computing what the model prescribes. But Kahneman and Tversky showed that the outcomes of even the simplest of decisions can be manipulated by framing the alternatives slightly differently.

For example, they asked a group of subjects to choose between various policy responses to a rare disease that would claim 600 lives if we did nothing. One group was asked to choose either program A, which would save exactly 200 lives with certainty, or program B, which would save 600 lives with probability 1/3 and zero lives with probability 2/3. Here, 72 percent of all subjects chose program A. A second group was asked to choose either program C, under which exactly 400 people would die, or program D, under which there is a 1/3 chance no one will die and 2/3 chance that all 600 will die. This time, 78 percent of all subjects chose program D.

A moment's reflection reveals that programs A and C are exactly the same, as are programs B and D. And yet subjects from the two groups chose dramatically differently. Kahneman and Tversky explained that the first group coded "lives saved" as gains, and were therefore risk averse in choosing between A and B. Similarly, the second group coded deaths as losses, which led them to be risk seeking in the choice between C and D.

It is also tempting to suppose that behaviour inconsistent with the prescriptions of the expected utility model is largely confined to situations involving novice decision makers, or situations where little of importance is at stake. Kahneman and Tversky found, however, that even experienced physicians make similarly inconsistent recommendations about treatment regimens when the problems are framed in slightly different ways. The moral is that we are all well advised to be cautious when making decisions under uncertainty. Try framing the relevant alternatives in different ways and see if it makes any difference. And if it does, try to reflect on which of the formulations best captures your underlying concerns.

8.7 JUDGMENTAL HEURISTICS AND BIASES

Many of the examples considered so far make it clear that even when people have precisely the relevant facts at their fingertips, they often fail to make rational decisions.

There is yet another difficulty confronting the rational choice model, namely, that we often draw erroneous inferences about what the relevant facts are. More important, many of the errors we make are systematic, not random. Kahneman and Tversky identified three particularly simple heuristics, or rules of thumb, that people use to make judgments and inferences about the environment.[6] These heuristics are efficient in the sense that they help us economize on cognitive effort and give roughly correct answers much of the time. But they also give rise to large, predictable errors in many cases. Let us consider each of the three heuristics in turn.

Availability

We often estimate the frequency of an event, or class of events, by the ease with which we can summon examples from memory. Much of the time, there is a close positive correlation between the ease with which we can do so and the true frequency of occurrence. It is easier, after all, to recall examples of things that happen often.

But frequency of occurrence is not the only factor that determines ease of recall. If people were asked, for example, whether there are more murders than suicides in Toronto each year, many would confidently answer yes. And yet there are always more suicides! Kahneman and Tversky explained that we think there are more murders because murders are more "available" in memory. Memory research demonstrates that it is much easier to recall an event the more vivid or sensational it is. Even if we had heard about equally many suicides as murders, it is on this account likely that we will be able to remember a much larger proportion of the murders.

Other elements in the mechanics of memory can also affect the availability of different events. Ask yourself, for example, whether more words in the English language start with the letter *r* than words that have *r* as their third letter. Most people answer confidently that many more words start with *r*, but in fact many more words have *r* as their third letter. We store words in memory much as they are stored in a dictionary—alphabetically, beginning with the first letter. We know plenty of words with *r* as their third letter, but it is no easier to remember them than it is to find them in a dictionary.

Events also tend to be more available in memory if they have happened more recently. A large body of research indicates that people tend to assign too much weight to recent information when making assessments about relative performance. In baseball, for example, a player's lifetime batting average against a certain pitcher is usually the best available predictor of how he will do against that pitcher in his next time at bat. It is apparently not uncommon, however, for a manager to bench a hitter against a pitcher he has performed poorly against the last couple of times out, even though he has hit against that same pitcher very well over a span of many years. The problem occurs when the manager estimates the player's performance by examples of it that spring easily to mind. And the most recent examples are the easiest ones to think of.

Interestingly, increased use of computer programs to analyze baseball performance statistics may have reduced the frequency of such occurrences: computers tend to have better memories than managers.

Economically, the availability bias is important because we often have to estimate the relative performance of alternative economic options. Managers of companies, for example, must weigh the merits of different employees for promotion. The most effective managers will be those who guard against the natural tendency to put too much weight on recent performance.

---

[6]See Tversky and Kahneman, ibid.

Representativeness

Kahneman and Tversky also discovered an interesting bias in the way we attempt to answer questions of the type, "What is the likelihood that object *A* belongs to class B?" For example, suppose Steve is a shy person and we want to estimate the likelihood that he is a librarian rather than a salesperson. Most people respond that Steve is much more likely to be a librarian, because shyness is thought to be a representative trait for librarians, but rather an unusual one for salespersons. Such responses are often biased, however, because the likelihood of belonging to the category in question is influenced by many other important factors besides representativeness. Here, it is heavily influenced by the relative frequencies of salespersons and librarians in the overall population.

A simple example conveys the essence of the problem. Suppose that 80 percent of all librarians are shy, but only 20 percent of all salespeople are. Suppose further that there are nine salespeople in the population for every librarian. Under these reasonable assumptions, if we know that Steve is shy and that he is either a librarian or a salesperson, what is the probability that he is a librarian? The relevant numbers for answering this question are displayed in Figure 8-9. There, we see that even though a much larger proportion of librarians are shy, there are more than twice as many shy salespersons as there are shy librarians. The reason, of course, is that there are so many more salespeople than librarians. Out of every 100 people here, 26 of them are shy—18 salespersons and 8 librarians. This means that the odds of a shy person being a librarian are only 8/26, or just under one-third. Yet most people who confront this example are reluctant to say that Steve is a salesperson, because shyness is so unrepresentative of salespersons.

EXERCISE 8-1

Suppose 90 percent of all librarians are shy but only 20 percent of all salespersons are, and that there are four times as many salespersons as librarians. What is the likelihood that a randomly chosen shy person is a librarian, given that he is either a salesperson or a librarian?

FIGURE 8-9

Distribution by Type of Librarians and Salespersons
Even though shyness is more representative of librarians than of salespersons, a shy person is much more likely to be a salesperson than a librarian. The reason is that there are many more salespersons than librarians.

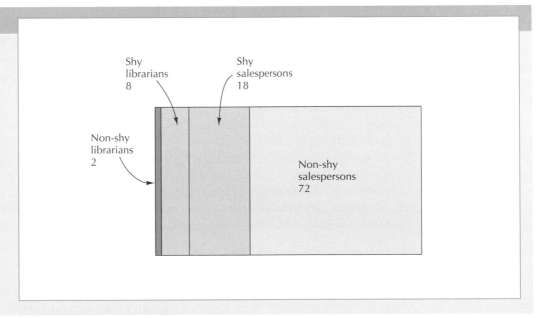

Shy librarians 8

Shy salespersons 18

Non-shy librarians 2

Non-shy salespersons 72

Another example of the representativeness bias is the statistical phenomenon known as the *regression effect, or regression to the mean*. Suppose a standard IQ test is administered to 100 people and that the 20 who score highest have an average score of 122, or 22 points above the average for the population. If these same 20 people are then tested a second time, their average score will almost always be substantially smaller than 122. The reason is that there is a certain amount of randomness in performance on IQ tests, and the people who did best on the first test are likely to include disproportionately many whose performances happened to be better than usual on that particular test.

We have substantial firsthand experience with regression effects in our daily lives (for example, the sons of unusually tall fathers tend to be shorter than their fathers). Kahneman and Tversky noted, however, that we often fail to make adequate allowance for it in our judgments because, they conjectured, we feel intuitively that an output (for example, an offspring) should be representative of the input (for example, the parent) that produced it.

It has long been observed that the rookie of the year in professional sports leagues often has a mediocre second season. This has been attributed to the "sophomore jinx." A related phenomenon often occurs in the music industry. Alanis Morissette's breakthrough 1995 album, *Jagged Little Pill*, sold over 30 million copies worldwide, the most ever by a female recording artist. *Jagged Little Pill* was technically not her first (or "rookie") album, but this fact does not affect the argument. Her 1998 follow-up album, *Supposed Former Infatuation Junkie*, received strong reviews and garnered numerous awards. Almost inevitably, however, it did not match the sales record of *Jagged Little Pill*. Both these phenomena are easily explained as the result of regression to the mean. Someone gets to be rookie of the year only after having had an extraordinarily good season. Similarly, an unusually successful "new" artist is news because of the degree of success itself, because the artist *is* new and therefore becomes the subject of more "Who is … ?" articles, and because new artists do *not* usually have that degree of success. The subsequent sales performance, even if it is very respectable, will seem like confirmation of the "jinx," because expectations are so high while sales will likely be below the level that first attracted all the attention.

An especially pernicious consequence of our failure to take into account regression to the mean is the effect it has on our estimates of the relative efficacy of praise and blame. Psychologists have long demonstrated that praise and other forms of positive reinforcement are much more effective than punishment or blame for teaching desired skills. But people would be unlikely to draw this inference from experience if they were unmindful of the importance of regression to the mean.

The reason is that, quite independently of whether a person is praised or blamed, a good performance is likely to be followed by a lesser one and a bad performance by a better one. Someone who praises good performances is therefore likely to conclude, erroneously, that praise perversely *causes* worse performance. Conversely, someone who denigrates poor performance is likely, spuriously, to attribute to his action the improvement that in fact results from regression effects. The co-movements of praise, blame, and performance would convince all but the most sophisticated analyst that blame works and praise doesn't. Managers who are trying to elicit the most effective performances from their employees can ill afford to make this mistake.

Anchoring and Adjustment

In one common strategy of estimation, known as "anchoring and adjustment," people first choose a preliminary estimate—an anchor—and then adjust it in accordance with

CHAPTER 8: COGNITIVE LIMITATIONS AND CONSUMER BEHAVIOUR

whatever additional information they have that appears relevant. Kahneman and Tversky have discovered that this procedure often leads to biased estimates, for two reasons. First, the initial anchor may be completely unrelated to the value to be estimated. And second, even when it is related, people tend to adjust too little from it.

To demonstrate the anchoring and adjustment bias, Kahneman and Tversky asked a sample of students to estimate the percentage of African countries that are members of the United Nations. Each person was first asked to spin a wheel that generated a number between 1 and 100. The student was then asked whether his estimate was higher or lower than that number. And finally, the student was asked for his numerical estimate of the percentage. The results were nothing short of astonishing. Students who got a 10 or below on the spin of the wheel had a median estimate of 25 percent, whereas the corresponding figure for those who got a 65 or above was 45 percent.

Each student surely *knew* that the initial random number had no possible relevance for estimating the percentage of African nations that belong to the U.N. Nonetheless, the numbers had a dramatic effect on the estimates they reported. In similar problems, any number close at hand seems to provide a convenient starting point. Kahneman and Tversky reported that giving the students monetary payoffs for accuracy did not alter the size of the bias.

In another illustration, two groups of high school students were asked to estimate the product of eight numbers within five seconds. The first group was given this expression:

$$8 \times 7 \times 6 \times 5 \times 4 \times 3 \times 2 \times 1,$$

while the second group was given exactly the same numbers in reverse order:

$$1 \times 2 \times 3 \times 4 \times 5 \times 6 \times 7 \times 8.$$

The time limit prevented most students from performing the entire calculation, which would lead to the correct answer of 40,320. What many of them apparently did was to perform the first few multiplications (their anchor), and then to project an estimate of the final result. For both groups of students, these anchors turned out not to be very appropriate and the projections turned out to be grossly insufficient. The resulting bias displays exactly the predicted pattern: the median estimate for the first group was 2250; for the second group, only 512.

An important economic application of the anchoring and adjustment bias is in estimating the failure rates of complex projects. Consider, for example, starting a new business. To succeed, it is necessary that each of a large number of events happens. Satisfactory financing must be obtained, a workable location found, a low-cost production process designed, sufficiently skilled labour hired, an effective marketing campaign implemented, and so on. The enterprise will fail if any one of these steps fails. When many steps are involved, the failure rate is invariably high, even when each step has a high probability of success. For example, a program involving 10 steps, each with a success rate of 90 percent, will fail 65 percent of the time. When estimating failure rates for such processes, people tend to anchor on the low failure rate for the typical step, from which they make grossly insufficient adjustments. The anchoring and adjustment bias may thus help explain why the overwhelming majority of new businesses fail.

Weber-Fechner law
The property of perception whereby the just noticeable difference in a stimulus tends to be proportioned to the value of the stimulus.

8.8 THE PSYCHOPHYSICS OF PERCEPTION

There is yet another pattern to the way we perceive and process information that has importance in economic applications. It is related to the so-called ***Weber-Fechner law*** of psychophysics. Weber and Fechner set out to discover how large the change in a stimulus had to be before we could perceive the difference in intensity. Most people, for example, are unable to distinguish a 100-watt light bulb from a 100.5-watt light bulb. But how large does the difference in brightness have to be before people can reliably identify it? Weber and Fechner found that the minimally perceptible difference is roughly proportional to the original intensity of the stimulus. Thus the more intense the stimulus is, the larger the difference has to be, in absolute terms, before we can tell the difference.

Thaler suggested that an analogue of the Weber-Fechner law seems to be at work when people decide whether price differences are worth worrying about. Suppose, for example, you are about to buy a clock radio in a store for $25 when a friend informs you that the same radio is selling for only $20 in another store only 10 minutes away. Do you go to the other store? Would your answer have been different if you had been about to buy a television for $500 and your friend told you the same set was available at the other store for only $495? Thaler found that most people answer yes to the first question and no to the second.

In the rational choice model, it is inconsistent to answer differently for the two cases. A rational person will travel to the other store if and only if the benefits of doing so exceed the costs. The benefit is $5 in both cases. The cost is also the same for each trip, whether it is to buy a radio or a television. If it makes sense to go in one case, it also makes sense in the other.

8.9 THE DIFFICULTY OF ACTUALLY DECIDING

In the rational choice model, there should be no difficult decisions. If the choice between two alternatives is a close call—that is, if the two alternatives are predicted to yield approximately the same utility—then it should not make much difference which is chosen. Alternatively, if one of the options clearly has a higher expected utility, the choice should again be easy. Either way, the chooser has no obvious reasons to experience anxiety and indecision.

In reality, of course, we all know that difficult decisions are more the rule than the exception. There are many pairs of alternatives over which our utility functions just don't seem to assign clear, unambiguous preference rankings. The difficulty is most pronounced when the alternatives differ along dimensions that are hard to compare. If the three things we care about in a car are, say, comfort, fuel economy, and safety, it will be easy to decide between two cars if one is safer and more comfortable and has lower fuel consumption than the other. But what if one is much more comfortable and has much higher fuel consumption? In theory, we are supposed to have indifference curves that tell us the rate at which we would be willing to trade one characteristic for the other. In practice, however, we may not. We tend to know our tradeoffs best where we already have some consumption experience: acts of consumption are also learning experiences. In the absence of a complete preference pre-ordering, we can be uncertain about our precise tradeoff among characteristics in a given situation. Our uncertainty is compounded by the fact that the situation may change, and in the new situation our relative valuation of the characteristics could be different. ("If I pick the more comfortable car, what will happen if I then get transferred to a job that requires a long daily commute?") At times, it may seem as though there is a special Murphy's Law of Decision-making: "Whatever choice you make, you'll regret it."

With imperfect information and bounded rationality, "stewing about a decision" can be a vital part of the decision process, if it helps to focus attention on salient aspects of the alternatives that are *not* initially fully appreciated. Yet it can play havoc with a fundamental axiom of rational choice theory, namely, that choices should be independent of irrelevant alternatives. This axiom is often illustrated by a story like the following. A man comes into a delicatessen and asks what kind of sandwiches there are. The attendant answers that they have roast beef and chicken. The patron deliberates for a few moments and finally asks for a roast beef sandwich. The counterman says, "Oh, I forgot to mention, we also have tuna." To this the patron responds, "Well, in that case I guess I'll have chicken." According to the rational choice model, the availability of tuna should matter only if it is the alternative the patron most prefers. There is no intelligible basis for its availability to cause a switch from roast beef to chicken.

Tversky performed some intriguing experiments that suggest choice may not, in fact, always be independent of irrelevant alternatives. One of his examples is the choice between apartments that differ along two dimensions, monthly rent and distance from campus. From a student's point of view, an apartment is more attractive the closer it is to campus and the lower its monthly rent. A group of students was asked to choose between two apartments like the pair shown in Figure 8-10. Notice in the figure that neither apartment dominates the other. *A* is more expensive, but *B* is farther from campus. We expect that students who are relatively more concerned about rent will choose apartment *B*, while those who care primarily about commuting time will pick *A*. By manipulating the distance and rent, it is easy to get a group of students to divide roughly 50–50 between the two apartments.

So far, no surprises. But now Tversky adds a third apartment, *C*, to the list of choices, giving us the set depicted in Figure 8-11. Notice that *C* is dominated by *B*—that is, it is both farther from campus *and* more expensive than *B*. In terms of the rational choice

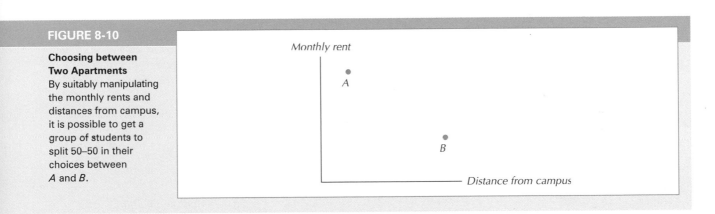

FIGURE 8-10

Choosing between Two Apartments
By suitably manipulating the monthly rents and distances from campus, it is possible to get a group of students to split 50–50 in their choices between *A* and *B*.

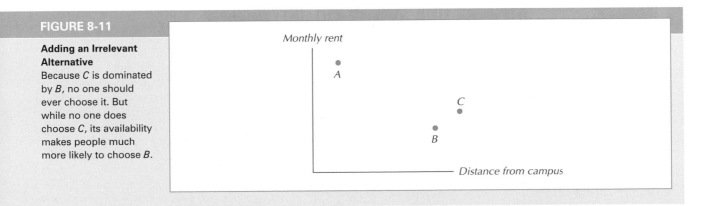

FIGURE 8-11

Adding an Irrelevant Alternative
Because *C* is dominated by *B*, no one should ever choose it. But while no one does choose *C*, its availability makes people much more likely to choose *B*.

model, it is a classic example of an irrelevant alternative. Faced with the choice *A*, *B*, and *C*, no rational consumer would ever choose *C*. And indeed, in actual experiments, hardly anyone ever does.

The surprise is that options like *C* turn out to affect people's choices between the remaining options. Tversky and his colleagues discovered that when an apartment like *C* is added to the pair *A* and *B*, the effect is to shift people's choices substantially in favour of *B*. Before *C* was available, students divided 50–50 between *A* and *B*. Once *C* was added, however, more than 70 percent of the students chose *B*, the option that dominates *C*.

Many people apparently find the original choice between *A* and *B* a difficult one to make. The appearance of *C* gives them a comparison they can make comfortably, namely, the one between *B* and *C*. Tversky hypothesized that this creates a "halo effect" for *B*, which makes it much more likely to be chosen over *A*. Perhaps a similar effect might cause the availability of tuna to cause someone to switch his decision from roast beef to chicken. Whatever the reason for such behaviour, it is clear that it violates the axiom that choice is independent of irrelevant alternatives.

Economic Naturalist 8-1	**WHY DO REAL ESTATE AGENTS OFTEN SHOW CLIENTS TWO HOUSES THAT ARE NEARLY IDENTICAL, EVEN THOUGH ONE IS BOTH CHEAPER AND IN BETTER CONDITION THAN THE OTHER?** As in the examples just discussed, the fact that one house dominates another may endow the first house with a halo that makes it more attractive relative to houses that are better than it on at least some dimensions. For example, an agent might have a client who is having difficulty making up her mind between a Greek revival house and a Queen Anne Victorian. By showing the client a similar Queen Anne Victorian that is priced higher and is less well maintained than the first, she might clinch the sale in favour of the dominant Queen Anne Victorian. Again, people seem to dislike choosing between alternatives that are difficult to compare. Experienced real estate agents often avoid this problem by giving their clients an opportunity to focus on an easy choice.

SUMMARY

www.mcgrawhill.ca/olc/frank

- Numerous examples of behaviour contradict the predictions of the standard rational choice model. People apparently often fail to ignore sunk costs. They play tennis indoors when, by their own account, they would prefer to play outside. They behave differently when they lose a ticket than when they lose an equivalent amount of cash. Psychologists argue that such behaviour is the result of limitations in human cognitive capacity. People use mental accounting systems that reduce the complexity of their decisions, sometimes at the expense of consistency with the axioms of rational choice.

- An important class of departures from rational choice appears to result from the asymmetric value function described by Kahneman and Tversky. In contrast to the rational choice model, which uses a utility function defined on total wealth, Kahneman and Tversky's descriptive theory uses a value function defined over changes in wealth. Unlike the traditional model, it gives losses much heavier decision weight than gains. This feature makes decisions extremely sensitive to how the alternatives are framed. A pair of gains, for example, is more attractive if presented separately than if lumped together. Losses, in contrast, have less impact if amalgamated than if taken separately. Also, a loss combined with a slightly larger gain produces a positive effect, whereas taken separately their net effect is negative; and finally, a small gain segregated from a large loss produces less of a negative effect than the two lumped together. The rational choice model, in contrast, says that none of these framing effects should matter.

- Decisions under uncertainty also often violate the prescriptions of the expected utility model. And again, the asymmetric value function provides a consistent description of several important patterns. People tend to be risk averse in the domain of gains but risk seeking in the domain of losses. The result is that subtle differences in the framing of the problem can shift the mental reference point used for reckoning gains and losses, which, in turn, can produce radically different patterns of choice.

- Another important departure from rational choice occurs in the heuristics, or rules of thumb, people use to make estimates of important decision factors. The *availability* heuristic says that one way people estimate the frequency of a given class of events is by the ease with which they can recall relevant examples. This leads to predictable biases because actual frequency is not the only factor that governs how easy it is to recall examples. People tend to overestimate the frequency of vivid or salient events, and of other events that are especially easy to retrieve from memory.

- Another important heuristic is *representativeness*. People estimate the likelihood that an item belongs to a given class by how representative it is of that class. We saw that this often leads to substantial bias because representativeness is only one of many factors that govern this likelihood. Shyness may indeed be a trait representative of librarians, but if there are many more salespeople than librarians, it is more likely that a randomly chosen shy person is a salesperson rather than a librarian.

- *Anchoring and adjustment* is a third heuristic that often leads to biased estimates of important decision factors. This heuristic says that people often make numerical estimates by first picking a convenient, but sometimes irrelevant, anchor and then adjusting from it (usually insufficiently) on the basis of other potentially relevant information. This procedure often causes people to underestimate the failure rate of projects with many steps. If such a project fails when any one of its essential elements fails, then even if the failure rate of each

element is extremely low, a project with many elements is nonetheless very likely to fail. Because people tend to anchor on the failure rate for the typical step, and adjust insufficiently from it, they often grossly overestimate the likelihood of success. This may help explain the naive optimism of people who start new businesses.

- Another departure from rational choice is analogous to a phenomenon in the psychophysics of perception. Psychologists have discovered that the just perceptible change in any stimulus tends to be proportional to its initial level. A related pattern seems to apply when the stimulus in question is the price of a good or service. People think nothing of driving across town to save $5 on a $25 radio, but would never dream of doing so to save $5 on a $500 TV set.

- Finally, departures from rational choice may occur because people simply have difficulty choosing between alternatives that are hard to compare. The rational choice model assumes that we have complete preference orderings, but, in practice, it often seems to require a great deal of effort for us to decide how we feel about even very simple alternatives.

- Behavioural models of choice often do a much better job of predicting actual decisions than the rational choice model. It is important to remember, however, that the behavioural models claim no normative significance. That is, the mere fact that people are often influenced in their decisions by sunk costs should not be taken to mean that people should be influenced by them. The rational choice model says we can make better decisions by ignoring sunk costs, and most people, on reflection, strongly agree. In this respect, behavioural models of choice are an important tool for helping us avoid common pitfalls in decision making.

1. Suppose you were the owner of a small business and were asked the maximum you would be willing to pay in order to attend a course in the traditional theory of rational choice. In which case would your answer be larger: (1) if it were known that people almost always behave in strict accordance with the predictions of rational choice theory; or (2) if it were known that people's behaviour often departs systematically from the predictions of rational choice theory?

2. Why is it rational to make decisions with less than complete information?

3. Distinguish between (1) the best decision and (2) the decision that leads to the best possible outcome.

4. Is there anything irrational about weighing gains less heavily than losses?

5. The policy of one school was to punish students for being late, while the corresponding policy in an otherwise identical school was to reward students for being on time. If effectiveness is measured by behaviour on the day following punishment or reward, which policy would seem to be more effective? Is this standard of effectiveness a good one?

PROBLEMS

1. Suppose your happiness is given by a Kahneman-Tversky value function like the one shown in the diagram.

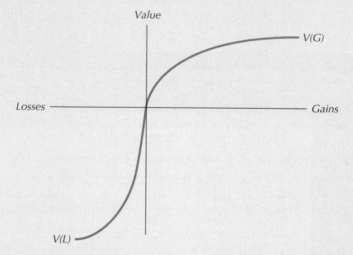

You have decided to apply the principles of hedonic framing to put the most favourable spin on the various combinations of events that occur in your life. How should you then frame the following combinations of events?

   a. A gain of $500 and a loss of $50.
   b. A gain of $50 and a loss of $500.
   c. A gain of $500 and a gain of $600.
   d. A loss of $500 and a loss of $600.

2. The Bay has hired you as a consultant to give it marketing advice about how to sell its deluxe home entertainment system. On the basis of the material covered in this chapter, suggest two specific marketing strategies for The Bay to consider.

3. Give two examples of how the framing of alternatives tends to produce systematic effects on people's choices.

4. Studies have shown that in the Toronto subway, crime rates fall in the months following increased police patrols. Does this pattern prove that the increased patrols are the cause of the crime reductions?

5. Eppie Curus is a gourmet. He makes it a point never to visit a restaurant a second time unless he has been served a superb meal on his first visit. He is puzzled at how seldom the quality of his second meal is as high as the first. Should he be?

6. Dalgleish the detective will correctly identify a lying suspect as a liar 80 percent of the time, and a truthful subject as truthful 80 percent of the time. Dalgleish says that Jones is lying and Smith is telling the truth. The polygraph expert, who is right 100 percent of the time, says that 40 percent of the subjects interviewed by Dalgleish have been telling the truth. What is the probability that Jones is lying? that Smith is telling the truth?

7. A witness testifies that the taxicab that struck and injured Smith in a dark alley was green. On investigation, the lawyer for Green Taxi Company discovers that the witness identifies the correct colour of a taxi in a dark alley 80 percent of the time. There are two taxi companies in town, Green and Blue. Green operates 15 percent of all local taxis. The law says that the Green Taxi Company is liable for Smith's injuries if and only if the probability that it caused them is greater than .5. Is Green liable? Explain.

*8. In Problem 7, with all other elements unchanged:
   a. What is the *lowest* percent identification accuracy that the witness would have to have for the Green Taxi Company to be liable?
   b. If the required probability of a correct identification for Green to be held liable were .6 instead of .5, then what identification accuracy would the witness have to have?

9. Last week your travel agent called to tell you that she had found a great fare, $667, for your trip to the United Kingdom later this month. This fare was almost $400 below the advance purchase excursion fare. You told her to book it immediately and went around the department telling everyone about your great bargain. An hour later she called you back and told you that the reservation agent at Icarus Airways had made a mistake and that the quoted fare did not exist. Your agent said she would hunt around and do the best she could for you. A few days later she found a ticket consolidator that could book you on the same Icarus Airways flight for $708, a figure still well below what you originally had expected to pay. This time you didn't go around the department bragging about your bargain. How might the material in this chapter be used to shed light on your behaviour?

10. In planning your next vacation, you have narrowed your choices down to two packages offered by your travel agent, a week in Cuba for $1200 or a week in Cancun for $1000. You are indifferent between these choices. You see an ad in the travel section of the newspaper for a week in Cuba, with accommodations identical to those offered by your agent, for $1500. According to the theory of rational choice, should the information in the newspaper ad influence your vacation plans? Explain.

11. Mary will drive across town to take advantage of a 40 percent–off sale on a $40 blouse but will not do so to take advantage of a 5 percent–off sale on a $1000 television. Assuming that her alternative is to pay list price for both products at the department store next to her home, is her behaviour rational?

12. Hal is having difficulty choosing between two tennis rackets, A and B. As shown in the diagram, B has more power than A, but less control. According to the rational choice model, how will the availability of a third alternative—racket C—influence Hal's final decision? If Hal behaves like most ordinary decision makers in this situation, how will the addition of C to his choice set matter?

*13. An investment project has 20 interdependent stages. If any one of these stages is not properly completed, the entire project will fail, but fortunately each stage has a success rate of 95 percent. What is the probability that the project will fail?

*14. For the project described in Problem 13, if all 20 stages have the same success rate, how high must this rate be in order for the overall project to have a 75 percent likelihood of success?

ANSWER TO IN-CHAPTER EXERCISE

8-1. If there are four times as many salespersons as librarians, then there will be 80 salespersons for every 20 librarians. Of the 80 salespersons, 20 percent, or 16, will be shy. Of the 20 librarians, 90 percent, or 18, will be shy. Thus, the likelihood that a shy person is a librarian is $18/(18 + 16) = .53$.

Part 3

THE THEORY OF THE FIRM AND MARKET STRUCTURE

The standard economic theory of the firm assumes that the firm's primary goal is to maximize profits. Profit maximization requires the firm to expand or to contract its output whenever the benefits of doing so exceed the costs. Our agenda in the first two chapters of Part 3 is to develop the cost side of this calculation. Chapter 9 begins with the theory of production, which shows how labour, capital, and other inputs are combined to produce output. Making use of this theory, Chapter 10 then describes how the firm's costs vary with the amount of output it produces.

The next three chapters consider the benefit side of the firm's calculation under four different forms of market structure. Chapter 11 looks at the perfectly competitive firm, for which the benefit of selling an extra unit of output is exactly equal to its price. Chapter 12 examines the monopoly firm, or sole supplier of a good for which there are no close substitutes. For such a firm, the benefit of selling an extra unit of output is generally less than its price because it must cut its price on existing sales in order to expand its output. Chapter 13 looks at two intermediate forms of market structure, monopolistic competition and oligopoly. In making decisions about output levels, monopolistically competitive firms behave like monopolists. In contrast, the oligopolist must take account of strategic responses of its rivals when it calculates the benefits of expanding or contracting output.

Chapter 9

PRODUCTION

Many people think of production as a highly structured, often mechanical process whereby raw materials are transformed into finished goods. And without doubt, a great deal of production—like a mason's laying bricks for the walls of a house—is of roughly this sort. Economists emphasize, however, that production is also a much more general concept, encompassing many activities not ordinarily thought of as such. We define it as *any activity that creates present or future utility*.

Thus, the simple act of telling a joke constitutes production. In *Annie Hall*, Woody Allen (Figure 9-1) tells the story of the man who complains to his analyst that his brother thinks he's a chicken. "Why don't you tell him he's *not* a chicken?" asks the analyst, to which the man responds, "I can't, I need the eggs." Once a joke is told, it may leave no more tangible trace than a pleasant memory. But under the economic definition of production, Woody Allen is as much a production worker as the artisan whose chisel and lathe mould an ashwood log into a Louisville Slugger baseball bat. The person who delivers a singing telegram is also engaged in production; so is the doctor who gives a child a tetanus shot; the lawyer who draws up your will; the people who collect your garbage; the postal worker who delivers your tax return to Canada Revenue Agency; and even the economists who write about production.

CHAPTER PREVIEW

In our discussions of consumer choice during the preceding chapters, an existing menu of goods and services was taken for granted. But where do these goods and services come from? In this chapter we shall see that their production involves a decision process very similar to the one we examined in earlier chapters. Whereas our focus in earlier chapters was on the economic decisions that underlie the demand side of the market relationship, our focus in the next six chapters is on the economic decisions that underlie the supply side.

FIGURE 9-1

A Production Worker

Photograph by Phillippe Halsman © Yvonne Halsman

In this chapter we describe the production possibilities available to us for a given state of technology and resource endowments. We want to know how output varies with the application of productive inputs in both the short run and the long run. Answers to these questions will set the stage for our efforts in the next chapter to describe how firms choose among technically feasible alternative methods of producing a given level of output.

9.1 THE INPUT–OUTPUT RELATIONSHIP, OR PRODUCTION FUNCTION

There are several ways to define production. One definition, mentioned above, is that it is any activity that creates present or future utility. Production may be equivalently described as a process that transforms inputs (factors of production) into outputs. (The two descriptions are equivalent insofar as output is something that creates present or future utility.) Among the inputs into production, economists have traditionally included land, labour, capital, and the more elusive category called entrepreneurship. To this list, it has become increasingly common to add such factors as knowledge or technology, organization, and energy.[1]

Production function
A means of describing the technically efficient quantities of output corresponding to all possible combinations of inputs.

A *production function* is the relationship by which inputs are combined to produce output. Schematically, it may be represented as the box in Figure 9-2. Inputs are fed into it, and output is discharged from it. The box implicitly embodies the existing state of technology, which has been improving steadily over time. Thus, a given combination of productive inputs will yield a larger number of cars, or cars having more features, with today's technology than with the technology of 1990.

---

[1]Some of these inputs are more readily measured than others. "Entrepreneurship," for example, typically involves some combination of risk-taking and deal-making ability, creative vision, and managerial responsibility. We have no good measures of any of these aspects of entrepreneurship, much less of entrepreneurship as a whole.

FIGURE 9-2

**The Production
Function**
The production function
transforms inputs like
land, labour, capital,
and management into
output. The box in the
diagram embodies the
existing state of tech-
nological knowledge.
Because knowledge
has been accumulating
over time, we get more
output from a given
combination of inputs
today than we would
have in the past.

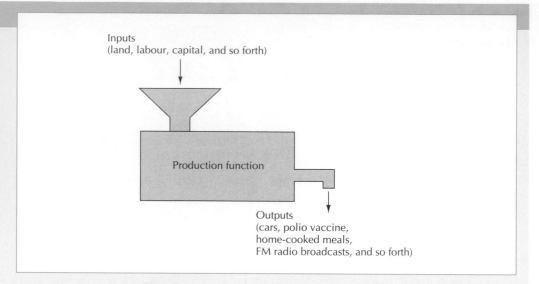

A production function may also be thought of as a cooking recipe. It lists the ingredients and tells you, say, how many pancakes of what type you will get if you manipulate the ingredients in a certain way.[2]

Yet another way of describing the production function is to cast it in the form of a
mathematical equation. Consider a production process that employs two inputs, capital
(K) and labour (L), to produce meals (Q). The relationship between K, L, and Q may
be expressed as

$$Q = F(K, L), \tag{9.1}$$

where F is a mathematical function that summarizes the process depicted in Figure 9-2. It
is no more than a simple rule that tells how much Q we get when we employ specific
quantities of K and L in a *technically efficient* way. By way of illustration, suppose the production function for meals is given by $F(K, L) = 2KL$, where K is measured in equipment-
hours per week,[3] L is measured in person-hours per week, and output is measured in
meals per week. For example, 2 equipment-hours per week combined with 3 person-
hours per week would yield $2(2)(3) = 12$ meals per week with this particular production function. The relationship between K, L, and weekly output of meals for the
production function $Q = 2KL$ is summarized in Table 9-1.

Technical efficiency
Attaining the maximum
possible output from
a given combination
of inputs.

Technical Efficiency: A Cautionary Note

At a basic level, ***technical efficiency*** is an intuitively obvious concept: it means getting
the most output possible from any given combination of inputs, in the present state of
knowledge. It should be carefully distinguished from ***economic efficiency*** in production,

Economic efficiency
Producing a given
level of output at
minimum cost.

---

[2]In some recipes, the ingredients must be mixed in fixed proportions. Other recipes allow substitution
between ingredients, as in a pancake recipe that allows milk and oil to be substituted for eggs. Production
functions can be of either of these two types.

[3]Here, 1 frying pan–hour per week is 1 frying pan used for 1 hour during the course of a week. Thus, a
frying pan that is in use for 8 hours per day for each day of a 5-day work week would constitute 40
frying pan–hours per week of capital input.

CHAPTER 9: PRODUCTION

TABLE 9-1

The Production Function $Q = 2KL$
The entries in the table represent output, measured in meals per week, and are calculated using the formula $Q = 2KL$.

		\multicolumn{5}{c}{Labour (person-hours/wk)}				
		1	2	3	4	5
Capital (equipment-hours/wk)	1	2	4	6	8	10
	2	4	8	12	16	20
	3	6	12	18	24	30
	4	8	16	24	32	40
	5	10	20	30	40	50

which is our focus in Chapter 10. Attaining economic efficiency means minimizing the cost of producing a given level of output, or (equivalently) maximizing the output that we produce for a given level of expenditure on inputs. A production process may be operated in a technically efficient way, in that output is at the maximum level attainable with a given combination of inputs. Yet it is not economically efficient if the same level of output could be achieved at a lower cost, using a different and cheaper combination of inputs.

Our definition of technical efficiency, however, should alert us to some potential complicating factors. We shall note them here and then boldly proceed to assume them away. First, technical efficiency is defined relative to a *given* body of scientific, technological, and organizational knowledge. With the advance of knowledge, processes that were formerly considered technically efficient can become technically *in*efficient. This means that in a world where the advance of knowledge is more or less continuous, *most* of the processes that have been in existence for some time are technically *inefficient*, to some degree. They remain in existence because *some* of the costs associated with their use are *sunk* costs, and hence can be ignored, whereas *all* of the costs of introducing the newest, "best practice," technically efficient processes are *real* costs. Anyone just starting out to produce a particular good, however, will adopt the technically efficient method of producing it, unless that method is unavailable because of patent or other restrictions.

The second definitional difficulty is a more technical one, but is nonetheless significant. The problem does not arise if a given production process produces only one output. For this reason, we shall assume in this chapter and the next one that only one output is produced. Suppose, however, that two outputs are being produced, and that with the same inputs Process A produces more of good 1 but less of good 2 than Process B. We cannot simply add the two goods together, because they are qualitatively different, and we cannot weight the outputs by their prices, since those prices are determined by other factors such as the demand for the two goods, and not purely by technical factors. Hence in this case, all we can say with strict accuracy is that Process A is more technically efficient in producing the combination of outputs it produces, while Process B is more technically efficient in producing its output combination! If both processes can be operated at any level of outputs, however, then a *weighted combination of both processes* could represent the technically efficient way of producing any intermediate proportions of good 1 and good 2, for all joint output levels of the two goods.

A third qualification of the technical efficiency concept is important when there are two or more distinct production processes for producing a good. Suppose that one process is more technically efficient in producing a given level of output at high capital–labour ratios, while another is more efficient at low capital–labour ratios. If we can choose only one of the processes and cannot costlessly shift from one to the other, then in a world of uncertainty about future relative input prices, we will choose the process that will be technically *and* economically efficient at the input prices we expect to materialize. If we guess wrong, however, we may be locked into a process that is both technically *and* economically *in*efficient. In this chapter and the next, we shall therefore assume that all inputs are perfectly divisible and that all existing processes can be costlessly combined in any proportions. Under the above assumptions, our intuitive notion of technical efficiency is applicable.

Intermediate Products and Value Added

Capital (as embodied, for example, in the form of stoves and frying pans) and labour (as embodied in the services of a chef) are clearly by themselves insufficient to produce meals. Raw foodstuffs are also necessary. The production process described by Equation 9.1 is one that transforms raw foodstuffs into the finished product we call meals. In this process, foodstuffs are **intermediate products**, ones that are transformed into something more valuable by the activity of production. Strictly speaking, the output of this process is not the meals themselves, but the *value added* to the raw foodstuffs. For example, if a chef and her equipment transformed $50 worth of raw foodstuffs into meals with a total value of $150, the resulting output would be measured as the $100 of value added.

> **Intermediate products** Products that are transformed by a production process into products of greater value.

For the sake of simplicity, we will ignore the complication of intermediate goods in the examples we discuss in this chapter. But this feature could be built into all these examples without changing any of our essential conclusions.

Fixed and Variable Inputs

The production function tells us how output will vary if some or all of the inputs are varied. In practice, there are many production processes in which the quantities of at least some inputs cannot be altered quickly. The FM radio broadcast transmission of classical music is one such process. To carry it out, complex electronic equipment is needed, and also a music library and a large transmission tower. Records and compact discs can be purchased in a matter of hours. But it may take weeks to acquire the needed equipment to launch a new station, and months or even years to obtain regulatory approval, purchase a suitable location, and construct a new transmission tower.

> **Long run** The shortest period of time required to alter the amounts of all inputs used in a production process.

The **long run** for a particular production process is defined as the shortest period of time required to alter the amounts of *every* input. An input whose quantity may be freely altered is called a *variable input*. One whose quantity cannot be altered—except perhaps at prohibitive cost—within a given time period is called a *fixed input* with respect to that time period. In the long run, all inputs are variable inputs, by definition. The **short run**, in contrast, is defined as that period during which one or more inputs cannot be varied. In the classical music broadcast example, records and compact discs are variable inputs in the short run, but the broadcast tower is a fixed input. If sufficient time elapses, however, even it becomes a variable input. In some production activities, like those of a street-corner hot dog cart, even the long run does not involve an extended period of time.

> **Short run** The longest period of time during which at least one of the inputs used in a production process cannot be varied.

9.2 PRODUCTION IN THE SHORT RUN

Consider again the production process described by $Q = F(K, L) = 2KL$, the simple two-input production function described in Table 9-1. And suppose we are concerned with production in the short run—here, a period of time in which the labour input is freely variable but the capital input is fixed, say, at the value $K = K_0 = 1$. With capital held constant, output becomes, in effect, a function of only the variable input, labour: $F(K, L) = 2K_0 L = 2L$. This means we can plot the production function in a two-dimensional diagram, as in Figure 9-3a. For this particular $F(K, L)$, the short-run production function is a straight line through the origin whose slope is 2 times the fixed value of K: Thus, $\Delta Q / \Delta L = 2K_0$. In Figure 9-3$b$, note that the short-run production function rotates upward to $F(K_1, L) = 6L$ when K rises to $K_1 = 3$.

EXERCISE 9-1

Graph the short-run production function for $F(K, L) = \sqrt{K} \sqrt{L}$ when K is fixed at $K_0 = 4$.

As you saw in Exercise 9-1, the graphs of short-run production functions will not always be straight lines. The short-run production function shown in Figure 9-4 has several properties that are commonly found in production functions observed in practice. First, it passes through the origin, which is to say that we get no output if we use no variable input. Second, initially the addition of variable inputs augments output at an increasing rate: moving from 1 to 2 units of labour yields 10 extra units of output, while moving from 2 to 3 units of labour gives 13 additional units. Finally, the function shown in Figure 9-4 has the property that beyond some point ($L = 4$ in the diagram), additional units of the variable input give rise to smaller and smaller increments in output. Thus, the move from 5 to 6 units of labour yields 14 extra units of output, while the move from 6 to 7 units of labour yields only 9. For some production functions, the level of output may eventually decline with additional units of the variable input beyond some point, as happens here for $L > 8$. With a limited amount of capital to work with, additional workers may eventually begin to get in one another's way.

The property that output initially grows at an increasing rate may stem from the benefits of division of tasks and specialization of labour. With one employee, all tasks must be done by the same person, while with two or more employees, tasks may be divided and employees may better perform their dedicated tasks. (Similar logic applies to specializing in one task within any period of time.)

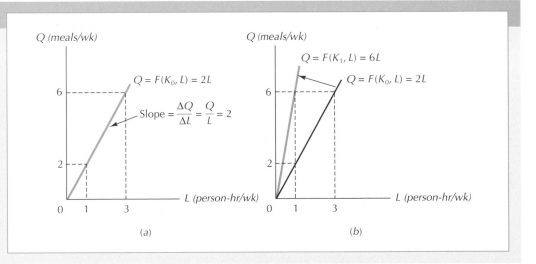

FIGURE 9-3

A Specific Short-Run Production Function
Panel a shows the production function, $Q = 2KL$, with K fixed at $K_0 = 1$. Panel b shows how the short-run production function shifts when K is increased to $K_1 = 3$.

FIGURE 9-4

Another Short-Run Production Function
The curvilinear shape shown here is common to many short-run production functions. Output initially grows at an increasing rate as labour increases. Beyond $L = 4$, output grows at a diminishing rate with increases in labour.

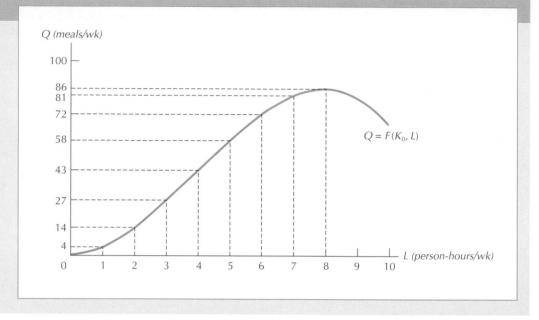

Law of diminishing returns If other inputs are fixed, the increase in output from an increase in the variable input must eventually decline.

The final property noted about the short-run production function in Figure 9-4—that beyond some point, output grows at a diminishing rate with increases in the variable input—is known as the ***law of diminishing returns***. And although it too is not a universal property of short-run production functions, it is extremely common. The law of diminishing returns is a short-run phenomenon. Formally, it may be stated as follows:

If equal amounts of a variable input are added and all other inputs are held fixed, the resulting increments to output will eventually diminish.[4]

Economic Naturalist 9-1

WHY CAN'T ALL THE WORLD'S PEOPLE BE FED FROM THE AMOUNT OF GRAIN GROWN IN A SINGLE FLOWERPOT?

The law of diminishing returns suggests that no matter how much labour, fertilizer, water, seed, capital equipment, and other inputs were used, only a limited amount of grain could be grown in a single flowerpot. With the land input fixed at such a low level, increases in other inputs would quickly cease to have any effect on total output.

---

[4]The "law" in this form is more accurately referred to as the *"law" of eventually diminishing marginal productivity of a variable input,* as the next section makes clear. Despite its ambiguities, however, "diminishing returns" has a long pedigree and wide currency in economics. We are therefore stuck with the term, and need to ensure that we understand precisely what it does and doesn't mean.

Employing the logic of Economic Naturalist 9-1, the British economist Thomas Malthus argued in 1798 that, with unchecked population growth, the law of diminishing returns implied eventual misery for the human race. The difficulty is that agricultural land is fixed and, beyond some point, the application of additional labour will yield ever smaller increases in food production. The inevitable result, as Malthus saw it, is that population growth will drive average food consumption down to the starvation level.

Whether Malthus's conclusion will be borne out in the future remains to be seen. But he would never have imagined that food production per capita would grow more than twenty-fold during the ensuing two centuries. Note carefully, however, that the experience of the last 200 years does not contradict the law of diminishing returns. What Malthus did not foresee was the explosive growth in agricultural technology that has far outstripped the effect of a fixed supply of land. Still, the ruthless logic of Malthus's observation remains. No matter how advanced our technology, if population continues to grow, it is just a matter of time before limits on arable land spell persistent food shortages.

The world's population has grown rapidly during the years since Malthus wrote, more than doubling during the last 50 years alone. Are we in fact doomed to eventual starvation? Perhaps not. As the late economist Herbert Stein once famously remarked, "If something can't go on forever, it won't." And indeed, population specialists now predict that the earth's population will peak by the year 2070 and then begin to decline.[5] There is thus a good chance that we will escape the dire fate of the basic Malthusian model.

Technological improvements in production are represented graphically by an upward shift in the production function. In Figure 9.5, for example, the curves labelled F_1 and F_2 are used to denote the agricultural production functions at time t_1 and t_2, respectively. The law of diminishing returns applies to each of these curves, and yet the growth in food production has kept pace with the increase in labour input during the period shown, and productivity per worker (given by the slope of the rays OA and OB, not drawn) actually rises.

FIGURE 9-5

The Effect of Technological Progress in Food Production
F_1 is the production function for food in the year t_1. F_2 is the corresponding function for t_2. Technological progress in food production causes F_2 to lie above F_1. Even though "diminishing returns" applies to both F_1 and F_2, food production grows more rapidly than labour inputs between t_1 and t_2.

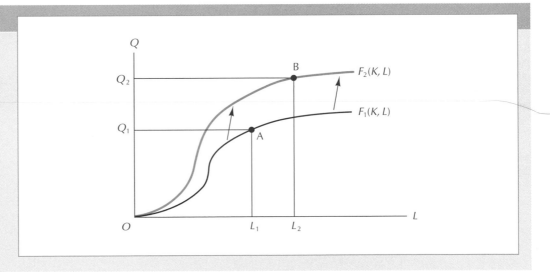

[5] See "The End of World Population Growth," Wolfgang Lutz, Warren Sanderson, and Sergei Sherbov, *Nature*, 412, August 2, 2001: 543–545.

Total, Marginal, and Average Products

Total product curve
A curve showing the amount of output as a function of the amount of a variable input.

Short-run production functions like the one shown in Figures 9-4 and 9-5 are often referred to as **total product curves**. They relate the total amount of output to the quantity of the variable input. Also of interest in many applications is the **marginal product** of a variable input. It is defined as *the change in the total product that occurs in response to a unit change in the variable input (all other inputs held fixed).* A business manager trying to decide whether to hire or fire another worker has an obvious interest in knowing what the *marginal* product of labour is.

Marginal product
Change in total product due to a one-unit change in the variable input.

More formally, if ΔL denotes a small change in the variable input, and ΔQ denotes the resulting change in output, then the marginal product of L, denoted MP_L, is defined as

$$MP_L = \frac{\Delta Q}{\Delta L}. \qquad (9.2)$$

Geometrically, the marginal product at any point is simply the slope of the total product curve at that point, as shown in the top panel of Figure 9-6.[6] For example, the marginal product of labour when $L = 2$ is $MP_{L=2} = 12$ meals/person-hour. Likewise, $MP_{L=4} = 16$ and $MP_{L=7} = 6$ for the total product curve shown in Figure 9-6. Note, finally, that MP_L is negative for values of L greater than 8.

FIGURE 9-6

The Marginal Product of a Variable Input
At any point, the marginal product of labour, MP_L, is the slope of the total product curve at that point (top panel). For the production function shown in the top panel, the marginal product curve (bottom panel) initially increases as labour increases. Beyond $L = 4$, however, the marginal product of labour decreases as labour increases. For $L > 8$ the total product curve declines with L, which means that the marginal product of labour is negative in that region.

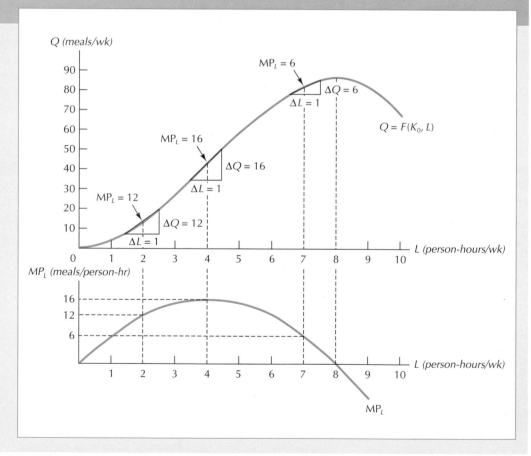

[6]The formal definition of the marginal product of the variable input L is given by $MP_L \equiv \partial F(K, L)/\partial L$, where the "$\partial$" denotes a partial derivative. See Appendix 9A.

The marginal product curve itself is plotted in the bottom panel in Figure 9-6. Note that it rises at first, reaches a maximum at $L = 4$, and then declines, finally becoming negative for values of L greater than 8. Note in the diagram that the maximum point on the marginal product curve corresponds to the inflection point on the total product curve, the point where its curvature switches from convex (increasing at an increasing rate) to concave (increasing at a decreasing rate). Note also that the marginal product curve reaches zero at the value of L at which the total product curve reaches a maximum.

As we shall see in later chapters, the importance of the marginal product concept lies in the fact that decisions about running an enterprise often arise in the form of decisions about *changes*. Should we hire another engineer or accountant? Should we reduce the size of the maintenance staff? Should we install another Xerox machine? Should we lease another delivery truck?

To answer such questions intelligently, we must compare the benefit of the change in question with its cost. And as we will see, the marginal product concept plays a pivotal role in the calculation of the benefits when we alter the level of a productive input. Looking at Figure 9-6, we may identify a range of values of the variable input that a rational manager would never employ. In particular, as long as labour commands a positive wage, such a manager would never want to employ the variable input in the region where its marginal product is negative ($L > 8$ in Figure 9-6). Equivalently, he would never employ a variable input past the point where the total product curve reaches its maximum value (where $MP_L = 0$).

EXERCISE 9-2

What is the marginal product of labour when $L = 3$ person-hours per week in the short-run production function shown in Figure 9-3a? When $L = 1$? Does this short-run production function exhibit "diminishing returns" to (diminishing marginal productivity of) labour?

Average product
Total output divided by the quantity of the variable input.

The ***average product*** of a variable input is defined as the total product divided by the quantity of that input. Denoted AP_L, it is thus given by

$$AP_L = \frac{Q}{L}. \qquad (9.3)$$

Geometrically, the average product is the slope of the line joining the origin to the corresponding point on the total product curve. Three such lines, R_1, R_2, and R_3, are drawn to the total product curve shown in the top panel in Figure 9-7. The average product at $L = 2$ is the slope of R_1, which is $\frac{14}{2} = 7$. Note that R_2 intersects the total product curve in two places—first, directly above $L = 4$, and then directly above $L = 8$. Accordingly, the average products for these two values of L will be the same—namely, the slope of R_2, which is $\frac{43}{4} = \frac{86}{8} = 10.75$. R_3 intersects the total product curve at only one point, directly above $L = 6$. The average product for $L = 6$ is thus the slope of R_3, $\frac{72}{6} = 12$ meals per person-hour. Note also that at $L = 6$, where AP_L reaches its maximum value, $AP_L = MP_L$ (see footnote 8 on page 421).

EXERCISE 9-3

For the short-run production function shown in Figure 9-3a, what is the average product of labour at $L = 3$? At $L = 1$? How does average product compare to marginal product at these points?

FIGURE 9-7

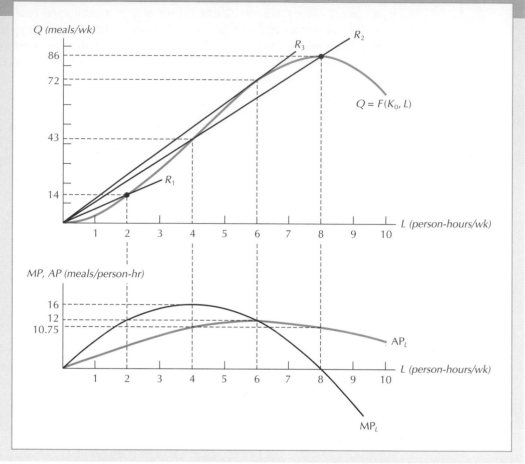

9.3 THE RELATIONSHIPS AMONG TOTAL, MARGINAL, AND AVERAGE PRODUCT CURVES

Because of the way the total, marginal, and average products are defined, systematic relationships exist among them. The top panel in Figure 9-7 shows a total product curve and three of the rays whose slopes define the average product of the variable input. The steepest of the three rays, R_3, is tangent to the total product curve at $L = 6$. Its slope, $Q/L = \frac{72}{6} = 12$, is the average product of labour at $L = 6$. The marginal product of labour at $L = 6$ is defined as the slope of the total product curve at $L = 6$, which happens to be exactly the slope of R_3, since R_3 is tangent to the total product curve. Thus $AP_{L=6} = MP_{L=6}$, as shown in the bottom panel by the fact that the AP_L curve intersects the MP_L curve for $L = 6$.

For values of L less than 6, note in the top panel in Figure 9-7 that the slope of the total product curve is larger than the slope of the ray to the corresponding point. Thus, for $L < 6$, $MP_L > AP_L$, as reflected in the bottom panel. Note also in the top panel that for values of L greater than 6, the slope of the total product curve is smaller than the slope of the ray to the corresponding point. This means that for $L > 6$, we have $AP_L > MP_L$, as shown in the bottom panel in Figure 9-7.

Note finally in Figure 9-7 that for extremely small values of L, the slope of the ray to the total product curve becomes indistinguishable from the slope of the total product curve itself. This tells us that as L approaches zero, average and marginal products converge, which is reflected in the bottom panel in Figure 9-7 by the fact that both curves emanate from the same point.[7]

The relationship between the marginal and average product curves may be summarized as follows: *When the marginal product curve lies above the average product curve, the average product curve must be rising; and when the marginal product curve lies below the average product curve, the average product curve must be falling. The two curves intersect at the maximum value of the average product curve.* A moment's reflection on the definitions of the two curves makes the intuitive basis for this relationship clear. If the contribution to output of an additional unit of the variable input exceeds the average contribution of the variable inputs used thus far, the average contribution must rise. This effect is analogous to what happens when a student with a 3.8 grade point average joins a club whose other members have an average GPA of 2.2: the new member's presence causes the group's GPA to rise. Conversely, adding a variable input whose marginal product is less than the average product of existing units is like adding a new club member with a GPA of 1.7. Here, the effect is for the existing average to fall.[8]

EXERCISE 9-4

Consider a short-run production process for which $AP_{L=10} = 7$ and $MP_{L=10} = 12$. Will $AP_{L=10.1}$ be larger or smaller than $AP_{L=10}$ for this process?

9.4 THE PRACTICAL SIGNIFICANCE OF THE AVERAGE–MARGINAL DISTINCTION

The distinction between average and marginal products is of central importance to anyone who must allocate a scarce resource between two or more productive activities. The specific question is, how should the resource be allocated in order to maximize total output? The following examples make clear the issues posed by this problem and the general rule required to solve it.

Read through the following case carefully and try to answer the question posed at the end:

> Suppose you own a fishing fleet consisting of a given number of boats, and can send your boats in whatever numbers you wish to either of two ends of an extremely wide lake, east or west. Under your current allocation of boats, the ones fishing at the east end return daily with 100 kg of fish each, while those in the west return daily with 120 kg each. The fish populations at each end of the lake are completely independent, and your current yields can be sustained indefinitely. Should you alter your current allocation of boats?

Most people, especially those who have not had a good course in microeconomics, answer confidently that the current allocation should be altered. Specifically, they say that the fishing fleet owner should send more boats to the west side of the lake. Yet, as

---

[7]For the production function shown, that point happens to be the origin, but in general it need not be. Technically, Q/L is not defined when L is *exactly* zero.

[8]Mathematically, the result that MP_L intersects AP_L at the maximum value of AP_L can be shown by noting that the necessary condition for a maximum of AP_L is that its first partial derivative with respect to L be zero:

$$\partial(Q/L)/\partial L = [L(\partial Q/\partial L) - Q]/L^2 = 0,$$

from which it follows that $\partial Q/\partial L = Q/L$. See Figure 9-7, at $L = 6$ person-hours/week.

the following example illustrates, even a rudimentary understanding of the distinction between the average and marginal products of a productive resource makes clear that this response is not justified.

EXAMPLE 9-1 In the fishing fleet case just described, suppose the relationship between the number of boats sent to each end and the number of kilograms caught per boat is as summarized in Table 9-2. Suppose further that you have four boats in your fleet, and that two currently fish the east end while the other two fish the west end. (Note that all of these suppositions are completely consistent with the facts outlined in the scenario.) Should you move one of your boats from the east end to the west end?

From the entries in Table 9-2, it follows that your total output under the current allocation is 440 kg of fish per day (100 kg from each of the two boats at the east end, 120 from each of the two at the west end). Now suppose you transfer one boat from the east end to the west end, which means you now have three boats in the west and only one in the east. From the figures in Table 9-2, we see that your total output will now be only 430 kg per day, or 10 kg per day less than under the current allocation. So, no, you should not move an extra boat to the west end. Neither, for that matter, should you send one of the west-end boats to the east end. Loss of a boat from the west end would reduce the total daily catch at that end by 110 kg (the difference between the 240 kg caught by two boats and the 130 that would be caught by one), which is more than the extra 100 kg you would get by having an extra boat at the east end. The current allocation of two boats to each end is optimal.

TABLE 9-2

Average Product, Total Product, and Marginal Product (Kg/Day) for Two Fishing Areas
The average catch per boat is constant at 100 kg per boat for boats sent to the east end of the lake. The average catch per boat is a declining function of the number of boats sent to the west end.

Number of boats	East end			West end		
	AP	TP	MP	AP	TP	MP
0	—	0		—	0	
			100			130
1	100	100		130	130	
			100			110
2	100	200		120	240	
			100			90
3	100	300		110	330	
			100			70
4	100	400		100	400	

The general rule for allocating a resource efficiently across different production activities is to allocate each unit of the resource to the production activity where its marginal product is highest. This form of the rule applies to resources, such as boats, that are not perfectly divisible, and also to cases where the marginal product of a resource is always higher in one activity than in another.[9] For a resource that is perfectly divisible, and for activities for which the marginal product of the resource is not always higher in one than in the other activities, the rule is to *allocate the resource so that its marginal product is the same in every activity.*

---

[9]See Example 9-2.

Many people, however, "solve" these kinds of problems by allocating resources to the activity with the highest *average* product, or by trying to equalize *average* products across activities. The reason that this particular wrong answer often has appeal is that people often focus on only part of the relevant production process. By sending only two boats to the west end, the average catch at that end is 20 kg per day greater than the average catch per boat at the east end. But note that if you send a third boat to the west end, that boat's contribution to the total amount of fish caught at the west end will be only 90 kg per day (the difference between the 330 kg caught by three boats and 240 kg caught by two). What people often tend to overlook is that the third boat at the west end catches some of the fish that would otherwise have been caught by the first two.

As the figures in Table 9-2 illustrate, the opportunity cost of sending a third boat to the west end is the 100 kg of fish that will no longer be caught at the east end. But since that third boat will add only 90 kg to the daily catch at the west end, the best that can be done is to keep sending two boats to each end of the lake. The fact that either of the two boats currently fishing at the east end could catch 10 kg per day more by moving to the west end is no cause for concern to a fishing fleet owner who understands the distinction between average and marginal products.

EXERCISE 9-5

Explain why we cannot necessarily conclude that the baseball pitcher should throw more fastballs in the following situation. You are a baseball pitcher who throws two different kinds of pitches: fastball and curve. Your team statistician tells you that at the current rate at which you employ these pitches, batters hit .275 against your curve, only .200 against your fastball. Should you alter your current mix of pitches?

Example 9-1 produced what economists call an *interior solution*—one in which each of the production activities is actually employed. But not all problems of this sort have interior solutions. As the next example will make clear, there are cases where one activity simply dominates the other.

EXAMPLE 9-2

Same as Example 9-1, except now the average product in the west end is a constant 120 kg per boat per day.

The difference between this example and Example 9-1 is that this time there is no drop-off in the rate at which fish are caught as more boats are sent to the west end of the lake. So this time the average product of boats sent to the west end is identical to their marginal product. And since the marginal product is always higher for boats sent to the west end, the optimal allocation is to send all four boats to that end.

Cases like the one illustrated in Example 9-2 are by no means unusual. But by far the more common, and more interesting, production decisions are the ones that involve interior solutions like the one we saw in Example 9-1, where some positive quantity of the productive input must be allocated to each activity.

EXAMPLE 9-3

Suppose that from the last minute you devoted to Problem 1 on your first economics exam you earned 4 extra points, while from the last minute devoted to Problem 2 you earned 6 extra points. The total number of points you earned

on these two questions were 20 and 12, respectively, and the total time you spent on each was the same. If time scarcity was the sole factor, and total obtainable marks were the same for both questions, how—if at all—should you have reallocated your time between them?

The rule for efficient allocation of time spent on exams is the same as the rule for efficient allocation of any resource: the marginal product of the resource should be the same in each activity. From the information given, the marginal product of your last minute spent on question 2 was 6 points, or 2 points more than the marginal product of the last minute spent on question 1. Even though the average product of your time spent on question 1 was higher than on question 2, you would have scored more points if you had spent less time on question 1 and more time on question 2.

9.5 PRODUCTION IN THE LONG RUN

The examples discussed thus far have involved production in the short run, where at least one productive input cannot be varied. In the long run, in contrast, all factors of production are by definition variable. In the short run, with K held fixed in the production function $Q = F(K, L)$, we were able to describe the production function in a simple two-dimensional diagram. With both K and L variable, however, we now require three dimensions instead of two. And when there are more than two variable inputs, we require even more dimensions.

This creates a problem similar to the one we encountered in Chapter 3 when the consumer was faced with a choice between two or more products: We are not very adept at graphical representations involving three or more dimensions. For production with two variable inputs, the solution to this problem is similar to the one we adopted in Chapter 3.

To illustrate, consider again the production function we discussed earlier in this chapter:

$$Q = F(K, L) = 2KL, \qquad (9.4)$$

and suppose we want to describe all possible combinations of K and L that give rise to a particular level of output—say, $Q = 16$. To do this, we solve $Q = 2KL = 16$ for K in terms of L, which yields

$$K = \frac{8}{L}. \qquad (9.5)$$

Isoquant The set of all technically efficient input combinations that yield a given level of output.

The (L, K) pairs that satisfy Equation 9.5 are shown by the curve labelled $Q = 16$ in Figure 9-8. The (L, K) pairs that yield 32 and 64 units of output are shown in Figure 9-8 as the curves labelled $Q = 32$ and $Q = 64$, respectively. Such curves are called ***isoquants***, and are defined formally *as all technically efficient combinations of inputs that yield a given level of output.*

Note the clear analogy between the isoquant and the indifference curve of consumer theory. Just as an indifference map provides a concise representation of a consumer's preferences, an *isoquant map* provides a concise representation of a production process.

On an indifference map, movements to the northeast correspond to increasing levels of satisfaction. Similar movements on an isoquant map correspond to increasing levels of output. A point on an indifference curve is preferred to any point that lies below that indifference curve, and less preferred than any point that lies above it. Likewise, any input bundle on an isoquant yields more output than any input bundle that lies below

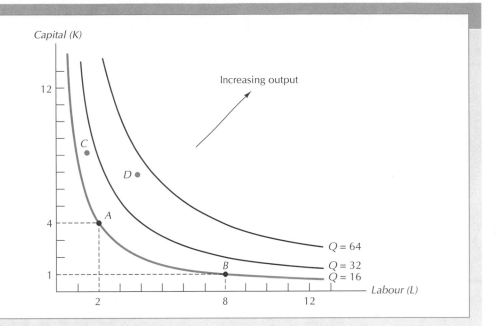

that isoquant, and less output than any input bundle that lies above it. Thus, bundle *C* in Figure 9-8 yields more output than bundle *A*, but less output than bundle *D*.

The only substantive respect in which the analogy between isoquant maps and indifference maps is incomplete has to do with the significance of the labels attached to the two types of curves. From Chapter 3 recall that the actual numbers assigned to each indifference curve were used to indicate only the relative rankings of the bundles on different indifference curves. The number we assign to an isoquant, in contrast, corresponds to the actual level of output we get from an input bundle along that isoquant. With indifference maps, we are free to relabel the indifference curves in any way that preserves the original ranking of bundles. But with isoquant maps, the labels are determined uniquely by the production function.

The Marginal Rate of Technical Substitution

Recall from our discussion of consumer theory in Chapter 3 that the marginal rate of substitution is the rate at which the consumer is willing to exchange one good for another along an indifference curve. The analogous concept in production theory is called the ***marginal rate of technical substitution***, or ***MRTS***. It is the rate at which one input can be exchanged for another without altering output. In Figure 9-9, for example, the MRTS at *A* is defined as the absolute value of the slope of the isoquant at *A*, $|\Delta K/\Delta L|$.

Marginal rate of technical substitution (MRTS) The rate at which one input can be exchanged for another without altering the total level of output.

In consumer theory, we assumed that the marginal rate of substitution diminishes with downward movements along an indifference curve. For most production functions, the MRTS displays a similar property. Holding output constant, the less we have of one input, the more we must add of the other input to compensate for a one-unit reduction in the first input.

A simple but very important relationship exists between the MRTS at any point and the marginal products of the respective inputs at that point. In a small neighbourhood of point *A* in Figure 9-9, suppose we reduce *K* by ΔK and augment *L* by an amount ΔL

FIGURE 9-9

The Marginal Rate of Technical Substitution The MRTS is the rate at which one input can be exchanged for another without altering total output. The MRTS at any point is the absolute value of the slope of the isoquant that passes through that point. If ΔK units of capital are removed at point A, and ΔL units of L are added, output will remain the same at Q_0 units.

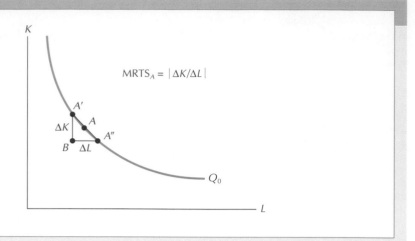

just sufficient to maintain the original level of output. If MP_{KA} denotes the marginal product of capital at A, then the reduction in output caused by the loss of ΔK is equal to $MP_{KA}\Delta K$. Using MP_{LA} to denote the marginal product of L at A, it follows similarly that the gain in output resulting from the extra ΔL is equal to $MP_{LA}\Delta L$. Finally, since the reduction in output from having less K is exactly offset by the gain in output from having more L, it follows that $\Delta Q = MP_{KA}\ \Delta K + MP_{LA}\ \Delta L = 0$, or

$$MP_{KA}\Delta K = -MP_{LA}\Delta L. \tag{9.6}$$

Cross-multiplying, we get

$$\frac{MP_{LA}}{MP_{KA}} = -\frac{\Delta K}{\Delta L} = \left|\frac{\Delta K}{\Delta L}\right| = MRTS_A, \tag{9.7}$$

which says that the MRTS at A is simply the ratio of the marginal product of L to the marginal product of K. (Note that MP_{KA} and MP_{LA} are positive, ΔK is negative, and ΔL is positive.)[10] This relationship will have an important application in the next chapter, where we will take up the question of how to produce a given level of output at the lowest possible cost.

EXERCISE 9-6

Given a firm's current level of capital and labour inputs, the marginal product of labour for its production process is equal to 3 units of output per unit of labour input. If the marginal rate of technical substitution between K and L is 9, what is the marginal product of capital?

---

[10]Strictly speaking, the Δ notation applies to *finite* changes. Hence in Figure 9-9, $MP_{KA} \equiv \Delta Q/\Delta K$ is shorthand for the reduction in output Q when we move from A' to B, and $MP_{LA} \equiv \Delta Q/\Delta L$ refers to the increase in Q when we move from B to A''. Formally, in the limit, as A', A'', and thus B approach A, $\Delta K/\Delta L$ becomes dK/dL, $MP_{KA} \equiv \Delta Q/\Delta K$ becomes $(\partial Q/\partial K)_A$, and $MP_{LA} \equiv \Delta Q/\Delta L$ becomes $(\partial Q/\partial L)_A$, where the ∂ notation refers to partial derivatives. See the discussion in Section 3A.1 of Appendix 3A, which applies to production functions and isoquants as well as to utility functions and indifference curves.

FIGURE 9-10

Isoquant Maps for Perfect Substitutes and Perfect Complements
In panel *a*, we get the same number of trips from a given total quantity of gasoline, no matter how we mix the two brands. Esso and Shell are perfect substitutes in the production of automobile trips. In panel *b*, word processors and typists are perfect complements in the process of typing letters.

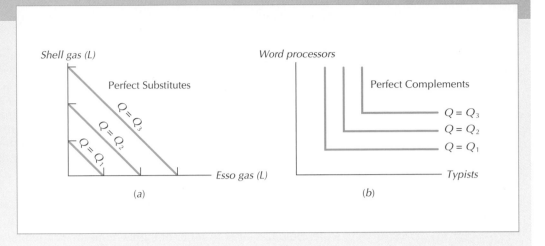

In consumer theory, the shape of the indifference curve tells us how the consumer is willing to substitute one good for another. In production theory, an essentially similar story is told by the shape of the isoquant. Figure 9-10 illustrates the extreme cases of inputs that are perfect substitutes (*a*) and perfect complements (*b*). Figure 9-10*a* describes a production process in which cars and gasoline are combined to produce trips. The input of gasoline comes in two brands, Shell and Esso, which are perfect substitutes for one another. We can substitute 1L of Shell for 1L of Esso and still produce the same number of trips as before. The MRTS between Shell and Esso remains constant at 1 as we move downward along any isoquant.

Figure 9-10*b* describes a production process for typing letters using the two inputs of word processors and typists. In this process, the two inputs are perfect complements. Here, inputs are most effectively combined in fixed proportions. Having more than one word processor per typist doesn't augment production, nor does having more than one typist per word processor.

9.6 RETURNS TO SCALE

A question of central importance for the organization of industry is whether production takes place most efficiently at large scale rather than small scale (where "large" and "small" are defined relative to the scale of the relevant market). This question is important because the answer dictates whether an industry will end up being served by many small firms or only a few large ones.

The technical property of the production function used to describe the relationship between scale and efficiency is called *returns to scale*. The term tells us what happens to output when *all* inputs are increased by exactly the same proportion. Because returns to scale refer to a situation in which all inputs are variable, *the concept of returns to scale is an inherently long-run concept.*

Increasing returns to scale The property of a production process whereby a proportional increase in every input yields a more than proportional increase in output.

A production function for which proportional changes in all inputs lead to a more than proportional change in output is said to exhibit **increasing returns to scale**. For example, if we double all inputs in a production function with increasing returns to scale, we get more than twice as much output as before. As we will see in Chapters 12 and 13, such production functions generally give rise to conditions in which a small number of firms supply most of the relevant market.

Increasing returns to scale often result from the greater possibilities for specialization and cooperation in large organizations. Adam Smith illustrated this point by describing the division of labour in a pin factory:

> One man draws out the wire, another straights it, a third cuts it, a fourth points it, a fifth grinds it at the top for receiving the head; to make the head requires two or three distinct operations .... I have seen a small manufactory of this kind where ten men only were employed ... [who] could, when they exerted themselves, make among them about twelve pounds of pins in a day. There are in a pound upwards of four thousand pins of a middling size. Those ten persons, therefore, could make among them upwards of forty-eight thousand pins in a day. Each person, therefore, making a tenth part of forty-eight thousand pins, might be considered as making four thousand eight hundred pins in a day. But if they had all wrought separately and independently ... they certainly could not each of them have made twenty, perhaps not one pin in a day ....[11]

The airline industry is often cited as a modern example of an industry with increasing returns to scale. Having a large number of flights helps an airline fill each flight by feeding passengers from its incoming flights to its outgoing flights. Local airport activities also exhibit increasing returns to scale. Ticket-counter space, ticket agents, reservations equipment, baggage-handling equipment, ground crews, and passenger-boarding facilities are all resources that are utilized more efficiently at high activity levels than at low activity levels. (The ticket counters, gates, and agents of a carrier with only a few flights a day will stand idle much of the time.) As a consequence of the law of large numbers,[12] moreover, it follows that maintenance operations, flight crew scheduling, and other inventory-related activities are all accomplished more efficiently on a large scale than on a small scale. Increasing returns to scale in commercial air transport help to explain increases in industry concentration, of which the Air Canada takeover of Canadian Airlines (see Appendix 13A) is just one instance.

Canadian auto parts manufacturer Magna International, with its headquarters in Aurora, Ontario, is one of the world's largest parts suppliers, with over 80,000 employees and over $20 billion in annual sales. In Magna's case, increasing returns to scale have resulted in part from the long production runs on many of its principal products, which maximize the utilization of its plant and workforce.

Constant returns to scale The property of a production process whereby a proportional increase in every input yields an equal proportional increase in output.

A production function for which a proportional change in all inputs causes output to change by the same proportion is said to exhibit **constant returns to scale**. In such cases, doubling all inputs results in a doubling of output. In industries in which production takes place under constant returns to scale, large size is neither an advantage nor a disadvantage.

Decreasing returns to scale The property of a production process whereby a proportional increase in every input yields a less than proportional increase in output.

Finally, a production function for which a proportional change in all inputs causes a less than proportional change in output is said to exhibit **decreasing returns to scale**. Here large size is a handicap, and we do not expect to see large firms in an industry in which production takes place with decreasing returns to scale. As we will see in Chapter 11, the constant and decreasing returns cases often enable many sellers to coexist within the same narrowly defined markets.

A production function need not exhibit the same degree of returns to scale over the entire range of output. On the contrary, a commonly observed pattern is for there to be increasing returns to scale at low levels of output, followed by constant returns to

---

[11]Adam Smith, *An Inquiry into the Nature and Causes of The Wealth of Nations*, ed. Edwin Cannan, Book 1, Chapter 2, Chicago: University of Chicago Press, 1976, 8–9.

[12]See Chapter 6.

scale at intermediate levels of output, followed finally by decreasing returns to scale at high levels of output. The isoquant map for such a production function is discussed after the following Economic Naturalist example.

WHY DO BUILDERS USE PREFABRICATED FRAMES FOR ROOFS BUT NOT FOR WALLS?

When construction crews build a wood-frame house, they usually construct framing for the walls at the construction site. In contrast, they often buy prefabricated framing for the roof. Why this difference?

There are two key differences between wall framing and roof framing: (1) cutting the lumber for roof framing involves many complicated angle cuts, whereas the right-angle cuts required for wall framing are much simpler (see Figure 9-11); and (2) sections of roof framing of a given size are all alike, whereas wall sections differ according to the placement of window and door openings. Both properties of roof framing lead to substantial economies of scale in production. First, the angle cuts they require can be made much more rapidly if a frame or "jig" can be built that guides the lumber past the saw-blade at just the proper angle. It is economical to set up such jigs in a factory where thousands of cuts are made each day, but it usually does not pay to use this method for the limited number of cuts required at any one construction site. Likewise, automated methods are easy to employ for roof framing by virtue of its uniformity. The idiosyncratic nature of wall framing, by contrast, militates against the use of automated methods.

So the fact that there are much greater economies of scale in the construction of roof framing than wall framing helps account for why wall framing is usually built at the construction site while roof framing is more often prefabricated.

Showing Returns to Scale on the Isoquant Map

A simple relationship exists between a production function's returns to scale and the spacing of its isoquants. Consider the isoquant map in Figure 9-12. As we move outward into the isoquant map along the ray labelled R, each input grows by exactly the same proportion. The particular production function whose isoquant map is shown in the diagram exhibits increasing returns to scale in the region from A to C. Note, for

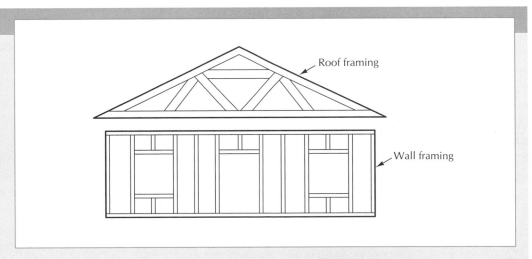

FIGURE 9-11

Prefabricated vs. On-Site Construction
The angular cuts and standard shapes characteristic of roof framing are more conducive to economies of scale than are the rectangular cuts and idiosyncratic layouts of wall framing. This difference helps explain why wall framing is generally built at the construction site while roof framing is more often prefabricated.

Roof framing

Wall framing

FIGURE 9-12

Return to Scale Shown on the Isoquant Map
In the region from *A* to *C*, this production function has increasing returns to scale. Proportional increases in input yield more than proportional increases in output. In the region from *C* to *F*, there are constant returns to scale. Inputs and output grow by the same proportion in this region. In the region northeast of *F*, there are decreasing returns to scale. Proportional increases in both inputs yield less than proportional increases in output.

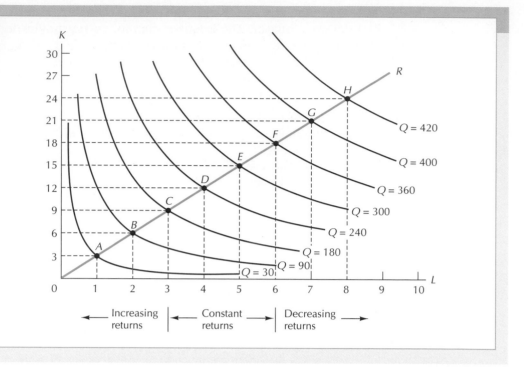

example, that when we move from *A* to *B*, both inputs double while output goes up by a factor of 3; likewise, when we move from *B* to *C*, both inputs grow by 50 percent while output grows by 100 percent. In the region from *C* to *F*, this same production function exhibits constant returns to scale. Note, for example, that when we move from *D* to *E*, both inputs grow by 25 percent and output also grows by 25 percent. Finally, the production function whose isoquant map is shown in Figure 9-12 exhibits decreasing returns to scale in the region to the northeast of *F*. Thus, when we move from *F* to *G*, both inputs increase by 16.7 percent while output grows by only 11.1 percent.[13]

The Distinction between Diminishing Returns and Decreasing Returns to Scale

It is important to bear in mind that decreasing returns to scale have nothing whatsoever to do with the law of diminishing returns. Decreasing returns to scale refer to what happens when *all* inputs are varied by some proportion. The law of diminishing returns, in contrast, refers to the case in which one input varies while all others are held fixed. As an empirical generalization, it applies with equal force to production functions having increasing, constant, or decreasing returns to scale.

The Logical Puzzle of Decreasing Returns to Scale

If the production function $Q = F(K, L)$ is a complete description of the corresponding production process, it is difficult to see how any production function could ever exhibit decreasing returns to scale in practice. The difficulty is that we ought to be able to

[13]The discussion in this section applies to *homothetic* production functions, an important class of production functions defined by the property that the slopes of all isoquants are constant at points along any ray or straight line from the origin. See Appendixes 3A and 9A.

duplicate the process used to produce any given level of output, and thereby achieve constant returns to scale. To illustrate, suppose first that $Q_0 = F(K_0, L_0)$. If we now want to produce $2Q_0$ units of output, we can always do so by again doing what we did the first time—namely, by again combining K_0 and L_0 to get Q_0 and adding that to the Q_0 we already have. Similarly, we can get $3Q_0$ by carrying out $F(K_0, L_0)$ three times in succession. Simply by carrying out the process again and again, we can get output to grow in the same proportion as inputs, which means constant returns to scale. And for reasons similar to the ones discussed above for the airline industry, it will often be possible to do even better than that.

In cases where it is not possible to at least double our output by doubling both K and L, we seem forced to conclude that there must be some important input besides K and L that we are failing to increase at the same time. This input has been referred to as "organization" or "communication," the idea being that when a firm gets past a certain size, it somehow starts to get out of control. Others claim that it is the shortage of managerial or entrepreneurial resources that creates bottlenecks in production. If there is indeed some unmeasured input that is being held fixed as we expand K and L, then we are still in the short run by definition. And there is no reason to expect to be able to double our output by doubling only some of our inputs. We use the concept in practice, because we are not sure exactly what the mysterious "other input" is. But the logical puzzle remains.

SUMMARY

www.mcgrawhill.ca/olc/frank

- Production is any activity that creates current or future utility. A production function summarizes the relationship between inputs and outputs. The short run is defined as that period during which at least some inputs are fixed. In the two-input case, it is the period during which one input is fixed, the other freely variable.

- The marginal product of a variable input is defined as the change in output brought forth by an additional unit of the variable input, all other inputs held fixed. The law of diminishing returns says that beyond some point the marginal product declines with additional units of the variable input.

- The average product of a variable input is the ratio of total output to the quantity of the variable input. Whenever marginal product lies above average product, the average product will increase with increases in the variable input. Conversely, when marginal product lies below average product, average product will decline with increases in the variable input.

- An important practical problem is that of how to allocate an input across two productive activities in such a way as to generate the maximum possible output. In general, two types of solutions are possible. A corner solution occurs when the marginal product of the input

is always higher in one activity than in the other. In that case, the best thing to do is to concentrate all the input in the activity where it is most productive.

- An interior solution occurs whenever the marginal product of the variable input, when all of it is placed in one activity, is lower than the marginal product of the first unit of the input in the other activity. In this case, the output-maximizing rule is to distribute the input across the two activities, if it is perfectly divisible, in such a way that its marginal product is the same in both. Even experienced decision makers often violate this simple rule. The pitfall to be on guard against is the tendency to equate not marginal but average products in the two activities.

- The long run is defined as the period required for all inputs to be variable. The actual length of time that corresponds to the short and long runs will differ markedly in different cases. In the two-input case, all of the relevant information about production in the long run can be summarized graphically by the isoquant map. The marginal rate of technical substitution is defined as the rate at which one input can be substituted for another without altering the level of output. The MRTS at any point is simply the absolute value of the slope of the isoquant at that point. For most production functions, the MRTS will diminish as we move downward to the right along an isoquant.

- A production function is said to exhibit constant returns to scale if a given proportional increase in all inputs produces the same proportional increase in output. A production function is said to exhibit decreasing returns to scale if a given proportional increase in all inputs results in a smaller proportional increase in output. And, finally, a production function is said to exhibit increasing returns to scale if a given proportional increase

in all inputs causes a greater proportional increase in output. Production functions with increasing returns to scale are also said to exhibit economies of scale. Returns to scale constitute a critically important factor in determining the structure of industrial organization.

- Appendix 9A considers several mathematical extensions of production theory. Topics covered include applications of the average-marginal distinction, specific mathematical forms of the production function, and a mathematical treatment of returns to scale in production.

QUESTIONS FOR REVIEW

1. List three examples of production that a noneconomist might not ordinarily think of as production.
2. Give an example of production in which the short run lasts at least one year.
3. Why should a person in charge of hiring productive inputs care more about marginal products than about average products?
4. Robert Solow is said to have remarked that when Paul Samuelson switched from physics to economics, the average IQ in both disciplines went up. A bystander responded that Solow's claim must be wrong, because it implies that the average IQ for academia as a whole (which is a weighted average of the average IQ levels for each discipline) must also have gone up as a result of the switch, which is clearly impossible. Was the bystander right? Explain.

5. How is an isoquant map like an indifference map? In what important respect do the two constructs differ?
6. Distinguish between diminishing returns to a variable input and decreasing returns to scale.
7. *True or false:* If the marginal product is decreasing, then the average product must also be decreasing. Explain.
8. A factory adds a worker and subsequently discovers that the average product of its workers has risen. *True or false*: The marginal product of the new worker is less than the average product of the plant's workers before the new employee's arrival.
9. Currently, 2 units of labour and 1 unit of capital produce 1 unit of output. If you double both the inputs (4 units of labour and 2 units of capital), what can you conclude about the output produced under constant returns to scale? Decreasing returns to scale? Increasing returns to scale?

PROBLEMS

1. Graph the short-run total product curves for each of the following production functions if K is fixed at $K_0 = 4$.

   a. $Q = F(K, L) = 2K + 3L$.

   b. $Q = F(K, L) = K^2 L^2$.

   c. $Q = F(K, L) = KL^{\frac{1}{2}}$.

   d. $Q = F(K, L) = K^{\frac{1}{2}} L^{\frac{1}{2}}$.

2. Are the four production functions in Problem 1 characterized by constant returns to scale, increasing returns to scale, or decreasing returns to scale? Are they characterized by constant, increasing, or diminishing marginal productivity of labour? Are they characterized by constant, increasing, or diminishing marginal productivity of capital?

3. Suppose the marginal product of labour is currently equal to its average product. If you were one of ten new workers the firm was about to hire, would you prefer to be paid the value of your average product or the value of your marginal product? Would it be in the interests of an employer to pay you the value of your average product?

4. The following table provides partial information on total product, average product, and marginal product for a production function. Using the relationships between these properties, fill in the missing cells.

Labour	Total product	Average product	Marginal product
0	0		
1		180	
			140
2			
3	420		
4		120	

5. The Melonville Police Department must decide how to allocate police officers between West Melonville and Centre City. The average product, total product, and marginal product in each of these two areas are given in the table below. Currently the police department allocates 200 police officers to Centre City and 300 to West Melonville. If police can be redeployed only in groups of 100, how, if at all, should the police department reallocate its officers to achieve the maximum number of arrests?

Number of police	West Melonville			Centre City		
	AP	TP (arrests/hr)	MP	AP (arrests/hr)	TP	MP
0	—	0		—	0	
			40			45
100	40	40		45	45	
			40			35
200	40	80		40	80	
			40			25
300	40	120		35	105	
			40			15
400	40	160		30	120	
			40			5
500	40	200		25	125	

6. Suppose a crime wave hits West Melonville, so that the marginal product and average product of police officers are now 60 arrests per hour for any number of groups of 100 police officers. What is the optimal allocation of 500 police officers between the two areas now?

7. A firm's short-run production function is given by

$$Q = \frac{5}{4}L^2 \quad \text{for } 0 \le L \le 2$$

and

$$Q = 3L - \frac{1}{4}L^2 \quad \text{for } 2 < L \le 7.$$

   a. Sketch the production function.

   b. Find the maximum attainable production. How much labour is used at that level?

   c. Identify the ranges of L utilization over which the marginal product of labour is increasing and decreasing.

   d. Identify the range over which the marginal product of labour is negative.

8. Is it possible to construct two isoquants, for $Q = 100$ units and $Q = 200$ units, such that at a high K/L ratio there are *decreasing* returns to scale, at a low K/L ratio there are *increasing* returns to scale, and at an intermediate K/L ratio there are *constant* returns to scale? If it is possible, do it. If it is impossible, explain why.

9. Suppose capital is fixed at 4 units in the production function $Q = KL$. Draw the total, marginal, and average product curves for the labour input.

**10. Why can a production function with the form $Q = L^a K^b$, with $a < 1$ and $b < 1$, never generate graphs like those in Figure 9-7? Calculate the formulas for AP_L and MP_L and then graph the total, average, and marginal product of labour curves for $Q = L^{.5} K^{.75}$, with K fixed at 16 units. Explain the differences between your graphs and those in Figure 9-7.

*11. In Figure 9-8, re-label the three isoquants ($Q = ?$) if, instead of $Q = 2KL$:

   a. $Q = KL$.

   b. $Q = 8K^{.5}L^{.5}$.

   c. $Q = .25K^2L^2$.

   (*Hint:* Find a point ($K = ?$, $L = ?$) on each isoquant and then calculate Q.)

**12. For the *four* production function in Problem 11, give the formulas for the marginal and average products of labour and capital. When $K = 4$ units and $L = 2$ units, calculate the numerical values for MP_L, AP_L, MP_K, and AP_K.

13. Identify the regions of increasing, constant, and decreasing returns to scale on the isoquant map below.

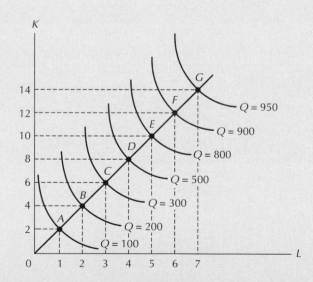

*14. Is it possible at all points to have diminishing MP_L and MP_K and at the same time increasing returns to scale? Is it possible at all points to have increasing MP_L and MP_K and at the same time decreasing returns to scale? Explain.

9-1. For $K = 4$, $Q = \sqrt{4}\sqrt{L} = 2\sqrt{L}$ (Also, $AP_L = Q/L = 2/\sqrt{L}$, and $MP_L = 1/\sqrt{L}$.)

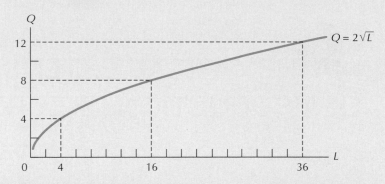

9-2. The slope of the total product curve in Figure 9-3a is 2 for all values of L. So $MP_{L=3} = 2$, and the short-run production function doesn't exhibit "diminishing returns."

9-3. The slope of the ray to any point on the total product curve is 2, and so $AP_{L=3} = 2$. When the total product curve is a ray or straight line from the origin, as here, $AP_L = MP_L$ is constant for all values of L.

9-4. Because $AP_{L=10} < MP_{L=10}$, AP_L will rise when L increases, and so $AP_{L=10.1} > AP_{L=10}$.

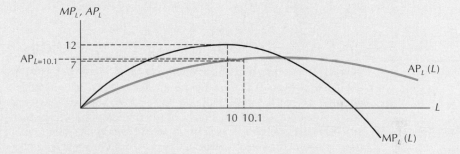

9-5. We cannot say that the pitcher should throw more fastballs without first knowing how a change in the proportion of pitches thrown would alter the effectiveness of both types of pitches. In particular, throwing more fastballs is likely to decrease the effectiveness not only of the additional fastballs thrown, but of all other fastballs as well. And if this loss exceeds the gain from switching from curves to fastballs, more fastballs should not be thrown.

9-6. From the relationship $MP_L/MP_K = MRTS$, we have $3/MP_K = 9$, which yields $MP_K = \frac{1}{3}$ unit of output per additional unit of capital.

Appendix 9A

MATHEMATICAL EXTENSIONS OF PRODUCTION THEORY

This appendix discusses several mathematical extensions and applications of the concepts developed in Chapter 9.

9A.1 APPLICATION: THE AVERAGE-MARGINAL DISTINCTION

Suppose that when your tennis opponent comes to the net, your best response is either to lob (hit the ball over his head) or to pass (hit the ball out of reach on either side). Each type of shot is more effective if it catches your opponent by surprise. Suppose that someone who lobs all the time will win a given point only 10 percent of the time with a lob, but that someone who virtually never lobs wins the point on 90 percent of the rare occasions when he does lob. Similarly, suppose that someone who tries passing shots all the time wins any given point only 30 percent of the time with a passing shot, but that someone who virtually never tries to pass wins 40 percent of the time when he does try. Suppose, finally, that the rate at which each type of shot becomes less effective with use declines linearly with the proportion of times a player uses it. What is the best proportion of lobs and passing shots to use when your opponent comes to the net?[1]

The payoffs from the two types of shots are summarized graphically in Figure 9A-1. Here, the "production" problem is to produce the greatest possible percentage of winning shots when your opponent comes to the net. $F(L)$ tells you the percentage of points you will win with a lob as a function of the proportion of times you lob (L). $F(L)$ is thus, in effect, the average product of L. $G(L)$ tells you the percentage of points you will win with a passing shot, again as a function of the proportion of times you lob. The negative slope of $F(L)$ reflects the fact that lobs become less effective the more you use them. Similarly, the positive slope of $G(L)$ says that passing shots become more effective the more you lob. Your problem is to choose L^*, the best proportion of times to lob.

To find the optimal value of L, we must first discover how the percentage of total points won, denoted W, varies with L. For any value of L, W is simply a weighted average of the percentages won with each type of shot. The weight used for each type of shot is simply the proportion of times it is used. Noting that $(1 - L)$ is the proportion of passing shots when L is the proportion of lobs, we have

---

[1]This example was suggested by Harvard psychologists Richard Herrnstein and James Mazur, in "Making Up Our Minds: A New Model of Economic Behavior," *The Sciences*, November/December 1987: 40–47.

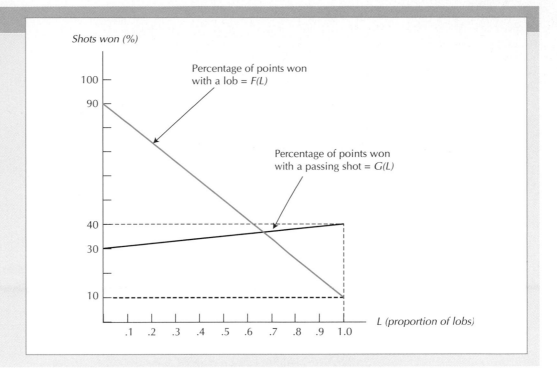

$$W = LF(L) + (1 - L)G(L). \tag{9A.1}$$

The expression $LF(L)$ is the percentage of total points won on lobs. $(1 - L)G(L)$, similarly, is the percentage of total points won on passing shots. From Figure 9A-1, we see that the algebraic formulas for $F(L)$ and $G(L)$ are given by $F(L) = 90 - 80L$ and $G(L) = 30 + 10L$. Substituting these relationships into Equation 9A.1 gives

$$W = 30 + 70L - 90L^2, \tag{9A.2}$$

which is plotted in Figure 9A-2. The value of L that maximizes W turns out to be $L^* = .389$, and the corresponding value of W is 43.61 percent.[2]

Note in Figure 9A-3 that at the optimal value of L, the likelihood of winning with a lob, is almost twice as high (58.9 percent) as that of winning with a passing shot (33.9 percent). Many people seem to find this state of affairs extremely uncomfortable—so much so that they refuse to have anything to do with it. In extensive experimental studies, Harvard psychologists Richard Herrnstein and James Mazur have found that people tend to divide their shots not to maximize their overall chances of winning, but to equate the *average product* of each type. Note in Figure 9A-3 that this occurs when $L = 2/3$, or 66.7 percent, at which point the percentage of points won with either shot is 36.7 percent. At this value of L, however, the *marginal product* of a passing shot will be much higher than for a lob, because it will strongly increase the effectiveness of all your *other* lobs. (Of course, an extra passing shot will also reduce the effectiveness of your other passing shots, but by a much smaller margin.)

---

[2]The calculus-trained student can find L^* without having to plot W as a function of L simply by solving

$$dW/dL = 70 - 180L = 0,$$

which yields $L^* = \frac{7}{18} = .389$, which, upon substitution into Equation 9A.2, yields $W = 43.61$ percent. Alternatively, note in Figure 9A-3 that the dotted *marginal* curves ($90 - 160L$ for lobs and $40 - 20P = 40 - 20(1 - L) = 20 + 20L$ for passing shots) corresponding to these average curves, which have the same vertical intercepts and twice the slope of the corresponding (linear) average curves, *do* intersect at $L^* = 7/18 = .389$ or (reading from right to left) at $P^* = 11/18 = .611$. The proportion of passing shots, P, is read from *right to left*, and the winning percentage on passing shots *falls* as the proportion of passing shots *increases*.

The Optimal Proportion of Lobs

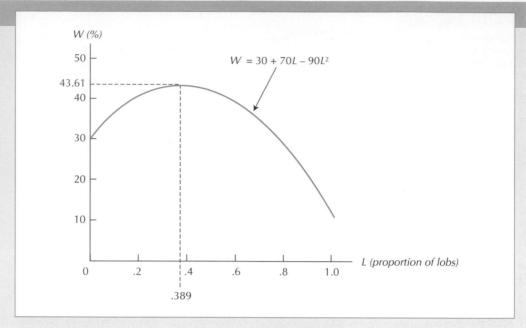

$W = 30 + 70L - 90L^2$

At the Optimizing Point, the Likelihood of Winning with a Lob Is Much Greater than of Winning with a Passing Shot

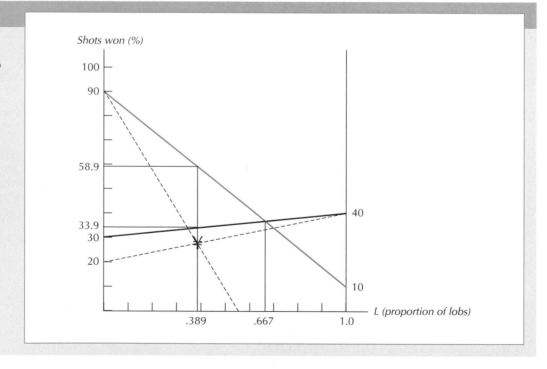

The situation here is analogous to the allocation problem involving the boats, mentioned in Chapter 9. There is no more reason to want the average return to each tennis shot to be the same than there is to want the average product on each end of the lake to be the same. And yet the tendency to equate average rather than marginal products is a very common pitfall, one that even experienced maximizers have to be on guard against. Let us consider one final example.

True or false? The best football coach is the one who always chooses the play that will gain the most yardage.

If you answered "true," you have not been paying attention. The best coach is the one who selects the best mix of plays, just as the best tennis player is the one who selects the best mix of shots. In the Canadian Football League (CFL) in 1999, completed passes gained an average of 13.57 yards, or 160 percent more than the 5.22-yard average gain per run. Correcting with the average pass completion percentage of 58.6 percent, passing plays gained 7.95 yards on average, or 52.3 percent higher than running plays. Only the Edmonton Eskimos gained more yards on average per running play than per passing play (6.60 yards to 6.56 yards), and the Montreal Alouettes gained 95 percent more per passing play than per running play. Why don't coaches call more passes? Because the passing game loses effectiveness if it is used too frequently. From the big difference in average gains for the two types of plays, it is apparent that most coaches are aware that the run is necessary to set up the pass. But many ostensibly expert commentators seem completely oblivious to this point. Trailing by four points with 20 seconds to go, with third and goal at the 4-yard line, a team is more likely to score a touchdown if it throws the ball. However, a team will win more games over the long run if it nonetheless uses a running play in this situation every once in a while. But let a coach call a running play and fail in this situation, and both the fans in the stands and the announcers in the booth will insist that he is an idiot.

9A.2 ISOQUANT MAPS AND THE PRODUCTION MOUNTAIN

Previously, we derived isoquants algebraically by holding output constant in the production function and then solving for K in terms of L. But there is also a geometric technique for deriving the isoquant map, one that is similar to the derivation of the indifference map discussed in Appendix 3A. This approach begins with a three-dimensional graph of the production function, perhaps something like the one shown in Figure 9A-4. It resembles the sloping surface of a mountain. The value on the Q axis measures the height of the mountain, or total output, which continues to increase as we employ more of K or L.

Suppose in Figure 9A-4 we were to fix output at some constant amount, say, Q_0. That is, suppose we cut the production mountain with a plane parallel to the KL plane, Q_0 units above it. The line labelled AB in Figure 9A-4 represents the intersection of that plane and the surface of the production mountain. All the input bundles that lie on AB yield an output level of Q_0. If we then project line AB downward onto the KL plane, we get the Q_0 isoquant shown in Figure 9A-5. As defined in Chapter 9, an isoquant is a locus of K, L pairs that produce the same level of output.

Suppose we then intersect the production mountain with another plane, this time Q_1 units above the KL plane. In Figure 9A-4, the second plane intersects the production mountain along the line labelled CD. It represents the locus of all input bundles that yield output level Q_1. Projecting CD down onto the KL plane, we thus get the isoquant labelled Q_1 in Figure 9A-5. In like fashion, we can generate an entire isoquant map corresponding to the production function $Q = F(K, L)$.

If we cut the production mountain with a *vertical* plane, passing through a point K_0 on the K axis and parallel to the L axis, and project the set of points of intersection onto the LQ plane, we can trace the level of output Q as a function of the variable input L, with K fixed at K_0. The slope of this function at any point will be the marginal product of labour for $K = K_0$, as depicted in Figure 9-6 of Chapter 9 on page 318.

9A.3 THE COBB-DOUGLAS AND LEONTIEF PRODUCTION FUNCTIONS

In this section we will examine two of the many different production functions that are commonly used in economic analysis, the Cobb-Douglas and Leontief production functions. You should consult Appendix 3A at this point. The reason is that the *formal* properties of the two utility functions discussed there can all be translated into production terms, although there are a few important differences in *interpretation*. In order to facilitate the comparison, in *this* subsection we have used parallel notation: the first term on the right-hand side of both utility and production functions is the variable on the *horizontal* axis of the indifference and isoquant map diagrams, while the second term refers to the variable on the *vertical* axis. This order, however,

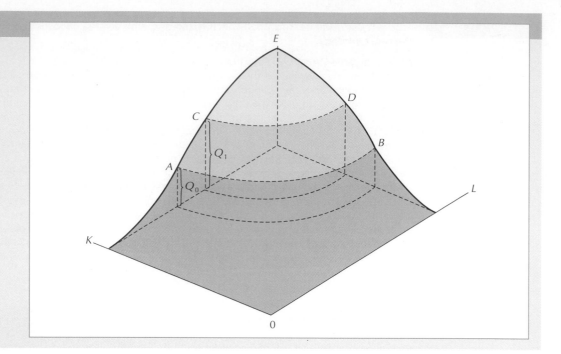

FIGURE 9A-5

The Isoquant Map
Derived from the
Production Mountain

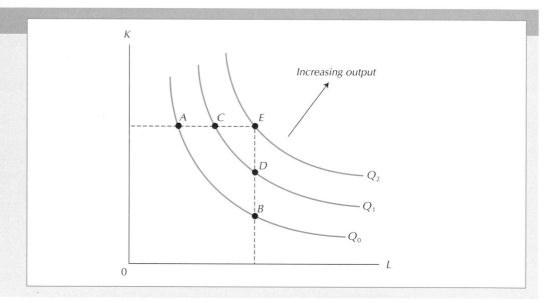

has no theoretical significance: if the order of the terms is reversed, the production functions are unchanged. Once we have shown the parallels between these special production and utility functions, you will therefore see both $Q = F(L, K)$ and $Q = F(K, L)$. At that point you will want to understand the relationships, and not merely to have memorized the formulas.

The Cobb-Douglas Production Function

Perhaps the most widely used production function of all is the Cobb-Douglas, which in the two-input case takes the form

$$Q = AL^a K^b.$$

(9A.3)

Here A can be any positive number, and for there to be diminishing marginal productivity of labour and capital, a and b respectively must be between 0 and 1.

To generate an equation for the Q_0 isoquant, we fix Q at Q_0 and then solve for K in terms of L. In the Cobb-Douglas case, this yields

$$K = \left(\frac{Q_0}{A}\right)^{\frac{1}{b}} (L)^{\frac{-a}{b}} \qquad (9A.4)$$

For the particular Cobb-Douglas function $Q = L^{1/2}K^{1/2}$, the Q_0 isoquant will be

$$K = (Q_0)^2/L. \qquad (9A.5)$$

A portion of the isoquant map for this particular Cobb-Douglas production function is shown in Figure 9A-6.

The number assigned to each particular isoquant in Figure 9A-6 is exactly the level of output to which it corresponds. For example, when we have 2 units of K and 2 units of L, we get $Q = \sqrt{2} \cdot \sqrt{2} = 2$ units of output. Recall from Chapter 3 that the numbers we used to label the indifference curves on an indifference map conveyed information only about *relative* levels of satisfaction. All that was required of our indexing scheme in that context was that the *order* of the numbers we assigned to the indifference curves reflect the proper ranking of the corresponding satisfaction levels. With isoquants, the situation is altogether different. We have, in effect, no choice about what labels to assign to them.

Calculus-trained students can easily verify the following expressions for the marginal products of labour and capital in the Cobb-Douglas case:

$$MP_L \equiv \frac{\partial Q}{\partial L} = aAL^{a-1}K^b \qquad (9A.6)$$

and

$$MP_K \equiv \frac{\partial Q}{\partial K} = bAL^aK^{b-1}. \qquad (9A.7)$$

What interpretation do we give to the coefficients a and b? With $Q = AL^aK^b$, note that a 1 percent increase in L alone, with K constant, will yield an a percent increase in Q, and so a is the point-elasticity of output with respect to labour. Similarly, b is the point-elasticity of output with respect

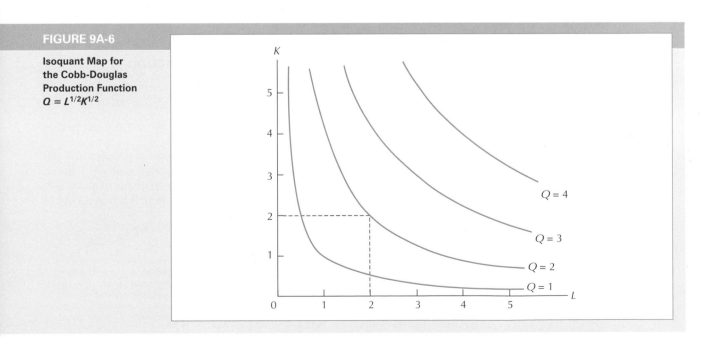

FIGURE 9A-6

Isoquant Map for the Cobb-Douglas Production Function $Q = L^{1/2}K^{1/2}$

to capital.[3] The output-elasticities with respect to both labour and capital are *constant*, and for a, $b<1$ we have continuously *diminishing marginal productivity*, or "diminishing returns." Note, however, from the fact that a and b are *positive* constants *or* directly from Equations 9A.6 and 9A.7 that the marginal productivities will always remain positive. (As an exercise, you may want to graph the MP_L curve for a specific Cobb-Douglas production function for several convenient values of K.)

Given that $MRTS = MP_L/MP_K$, we can take the ratio of 9A.6 and 9A.7 and simplify to get

$$MRTS = aK/bL, \qquad (9A.8)$$

which will remind you of the expression for *MRS* in row 4 of Table 3A.1 on page 108. Note that Equation 9A.8 implies that Cobb-Douglas production functions are *homothetic* with respect to the origin: a and b are both constants, and on any ray from the origin, the K/L ratio is constant, and therefore on *any* isoquant with K/L at a specified value, $MRTS$ $(= aK/bL)$ is constant.

In Chapter 10, we show that the long-run cost-minimization condition for a price-taking firm is $MRTS = w/r$, the wage-rental ratio. In the Cobb-Douglas case, this condition together with Equation 9A.8 implies that at any cost-minimizing point,

$$wL/rK = a/b \qquad (9A.9)$$

That is, at *any* wage-rental ratio, the cost-minimizing ratio of the wage bill (wL) to total capital rental costs (rK) is a *constant*, equal to a/b. Hence, similarly to rows 6 and 7 in Table 3A-1 on page 108, the efficient proportion of total costs represented by wages, $wL/(wL + rK)$, is equal to $a/(a + b)$, and the proportion of total costs represented by capital rental costs, $rK/(wL + rK)$, equals $b/(a + b)$. In other words, regardless of how high or how low w is relative to r, a *constant* proportion of total input costs, $a/(a + b)$, will be spent on labour inputs, and a constant proportion, $b/(a + b)$, will be spent on capital inputs.

EXERCISE 9A-1

The production function for Crunchy-Wunchies Cereal—"Absolutely *no* food value, but *fantastic prizes!*"—has the following form:

$$Q = 2L^{3/4}K^{1/2},$$

where Q is in tonnes per period. When $L = 16$ labour-days per period and $K = 64$ machine-days per period, what are the values (with correct units) for Q, MP_L, MP_K, AP_L $(= Q/L)$, AP_K $(= Q/K)$, and $MRTS$?

The Leontief, or Fixed-Proportions, Production Function

The simplest among all production functions that are widely used is the Leontief, named for the Nobel laureate Wassily Leontief, who devised it. For the two-input case, it is given by

$$Q = \min(aL, bK). \qquad (9A.10)$$

As with the perfect complements utility function in Appendix 3A, its interpretation is simply that Q is equal to either aL or bK, whichever of the two is *smaller*. Suppose, for example, that $a = 3$, $b = 2$, $L = 3$, and $K = 4$. Then, $Q = \min(3 \times 3, 2 \times 4) = \min(9, 8) = 8$. The isoquant map for $Q = \min(3L, 2K)$ is shown in Figure 9A-7. At point A, with $L = 3$ and $K = 4$, there is an excess of 1/3 unit of labour relative to what is required.

---

[3]Students with calculus can verify that since the point-elasticity of output with respect to labour is defined as $\epsilon_{QL} = (\partial Q/\partial L)/(Q/L) = MP_L/AP_L$, therefore $\epsilon_{QL} = (aAL^{a-1}K^b) \times (L/AL^aK^b) = a$, and similarly $\epsilon_{QK} = b$. Others should try some numerical examples to convince themselves. For instance, let $Q = L^{.75} K^{.25}$, and set $(L, K) = (1, 1)$, $(1.01, 1)$, and $(1, 1.01)$. Solve for Q in all three cases, and verify that a 1 percent increase in L alone causes about a .75 percent increase in Q, while a 1 percent increase in K alone causes about a .25 percent increase in Q. (The slight imprecision results, of course, from the fact that even a 1 percent change is a *discrete* change, not an infinitesimal one.)

Isoquant Map for the Leontief Production Function $Q = \min(3L, 2K)$

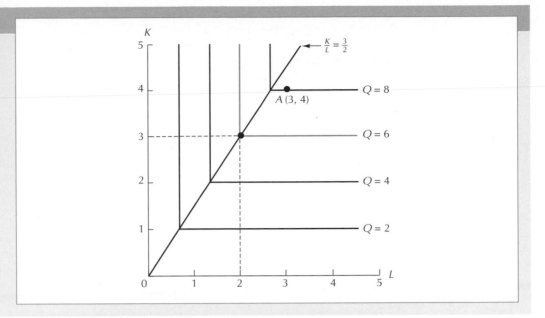

To see why the Leontief is also called the fixed-proportions production function, note first in Figure 9A-7 that if we start with 3 units of K and 2 units of L, we get 6 units of output. If we then add more L—so that we have, say, 3 units of L instead of 2—we still get only $Q = \min(3 \times 3, 2 \times 3) = \min(9, 6) = 6$ units of output. By the same token, adding more K when we are at $K = 3$ and $L = 2$ will not lead to any additional output. In the Leontief case, K and L are used most effectively when $aL = bK$—in the example at hand, when $3L = 2K$. In Figure 9A-7, the locus of points for which $3L = 2K$ is shown as the ray $K = \left(\frac{a}{b}\right)L = \left(\frac{3}{2}\right)L$. It is along this ray that the cusps of all the right-angled isoquants of this Leontief production function will lie.

Recall from Chapter 3 and Appendix 3A that in the case of perfect complements, the indifference curves had the same right-angled shape as the isoquants for the Leontief production function. This meant that the MRS was infinite on the vertical arm of the indifference curve, zero on the horizontal arm, and undefined at the cusp. For exactly parallel reasons, the MRTS in the Leontief case will be infinite on the vertical arm of the isoquant, zero on the horizontal, and undefined at the cusp.

9A.4 A MATHEMATICAL DEFINITION OF RETURNS TO SCALE

Mathematically, to increase all inputs in the same proportion means simply to multiply all inputs by the same number $c > 1$. By way of illustration, consider the production function we discussed in Chapter 9, $Q = F(K, L) = 2KL$. For this particular function, when we multiply each input by c we get

$$F(cK, cL) = 2(cK)(cL) = c^2 2KL = c^2 F(K, L). \qquad (9A.11)$$

The result of multiplying each input by c in this production function is thus to multiply the original output level by c^2. Output thus grows more than in proportion to input growth in this case—with proportional growth, we would have had output equal to $cF(K, L)$—so this production function has increasing returns to scale. Thus, for example, if $c = 2$ (a doubling of each input), we get $F(2K, 2L) = 2(2K)(2L) = 4(2KL)$, a quadrupling of output.

Drawing on these observations, the definitions of our three cases may be summarized as follows:

Increasing returns:	$F(cK, cL) > cF(K, L);$	*(9A.12)*
Constant returns:	$F(cK, cL) = cF(K, L);$	*(9A.13)*

and

Decreasing returns:	$F(cK, cL) < cF(K, L).$	*(9A.14)*

The following two exercises will help cement your ability to apply these definitions to specific examples.

EXERCISE 9A-2

Does the production function $Q = \sqrt{K}\ \sqrt{L}$ have increasing, constant, or decreasing returns to scale?

EXERCISE 9A-3

Does the production function $Q = L^{1/3}K^{1/3}$ have increasing, constant, or decreasing returns to scale?

In the case of the Cobb-Douglas production function, $Q = AL^aK^b$, Equations 9A.12 through 9A.14 imply a simple relationship between the parameters a and b and the degree of returns to scale. Specifically, if $a + b > 1$, there are increasing returns to scale; $a + b = 1$ means constant returns to scale; and $a + b < 1$ means decreasing returns to scale. To illustrate for the constant returns case, suppose $Q = F(L, K) = AL^aK^b$, with $a + b = 1$.

Then we have

$$F(cL, cK) = A(cL)^a(cK)^b, \tag{9A.15}$$

which reduces to

$$c^{(a + b)}AL^aK^b = cAL^aK^b = cF(L, K), \tag{9A.16}$$

which, by Equation 9A.13, is the defining characteristic of constant returns to scale. Similarly, if $a + b > 1$, $c^{(a + b)}$ is greater than c, implying *increasing* returns to scale, while if $a + b < 1$, $c^{(a + b)}$ is less than c, and we have *decreasing* returns to scale.

PROBLEMS

www.mcgrawhill.ca/olc/frank

1. Do the following production functions have increasing, decreasing, or constant returns to scale? Which ones fail to satisfy the "law of diminishing returns" (eventually diminishing marginal productivity of the variable input)?
   a. $Q = 4K^{1/2}L^{1/2}$
   b. $Q = aK^2 + bL^2$
   c. $Q = \min(aK, bL)$
   d. $Q = 4K + 2L$
   e. $Q = K^{.5}L^{.6}$
   f. $Q = K_1^{.3}K_2^{.3}L^{.3}$

**2. What is the formula for the marginal product of labour in the production function $Q = 2K^{1/3}L^{1/3}$ if K is fixed at 27? (For this question, you should use calculus if you have it, but if not, you can substitute into Equation 9A.6.)

3. Can the Cobb-Douglas production function be used to portray a production process in which returns to scale are increasing at low output levels and are constant or decreasing at high output levels?

4. Suppose that a firm with the production function

$$Q = \min(2K, 3L)$$

is currently using 6 units of capital and 5 units of labour. What are the marginal products of K and L in this case?

5. The average number of yards gained by a university football team on a passing play is $8 + 12r$, where r is the fraction of their total plays that are running plays. Their average gain per running play is $10 - 8r$. What is their optimal fraction of running plays? At this value of r, what is the average gain per pass? The average gain per run? (This problem and the next one are similar to the tennis example considered earlier. [You can use calculus, or you can refer to the marginal curves in Figure 9A-3 for guidance.])

6. Suppose you are a baseball pitcher with two pitches, fastball and curve. Your opponents' batting averages against these two pitches are as shown in the diagram below. If your goal is to minimize your opponents' overall batting average, what is the optimal proportion of fastballs? At this proportion, what are opponents' batting averages against your two pitches?

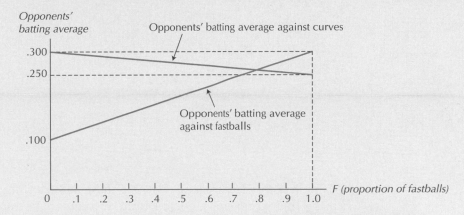

**7. The production function for Hogwarts Remover, an anti-magic potion, has the form

$$Q = K^{.5}L^{.5},$$

where Q is in bottles per period and K and L are in machine-days and labour-days per period, respectively.
   a. Graph the unit isoquant ($Q = 1$) and the isoquant for $Q = 2$.
   b. Calculate the formulas for MP_L, MP_K, and MRTS.
   c. When $Q = 4$ and $L = 9$, give the long-run efficient value for K and the MRTS at this point.
   d. If instead the production function had the form $Q = KL$, repeat problems 7a to 7c.

**8. With a firm's production function given by $Q = 6L^{2/3}K^{1/3}$, calculate the efficient long-run value of K and the MRS when Q is 648 units per period and L is 216 labour-hours per period. Do the same calculations when Q is 1296 units per period and L is 432 labour-hours per period.

ANSWERS TO IN-APPENDIX EXERCISES

A9-1. Substituting into the appropriate formulas, $Q = 128$ tonnes/period, $MP_L = 1.5\ K^{1/2}/L^{1/4} = 6$ tonnes/labour-day; $MP_K = L^{3/4}/K^{1/2} = 1$ tonne/machine-day; $AP_L\ (= Q/L) = 128/16 = 8$ tonnes/labour-day; $AP_K\ (= Q/K) = 128/64 = 2$ tonnes/machine-day; and MRTS $= MP_L/MP_K = 6$ machine-days/labour-day. Note also that $MP_L/AP_L = 6/8 = 3/4$, the elasticity of output with respect to labour-days, and that $MP_K/AP_K = 1/2$, the elasticity of output with respect to machine-days.

A9-2. $F(K, L) = \sqrt{KL}$, so $F(cK, cL) = \sqrt{(cK)(cL)} = \sqrt{c^2KL} = cF(K, L)$, and so it has constant returns to scale.

A9-3. $F(K, L) = K^{1/3}L^{1/3}$, so $F(cK, cL) = (cK)^{1/3}(cL)^{1/3} = c^{2/3}K^{1/3}L^{1/3} = c^{2/3}F(K, L) < cF(K, L)$, and so it has decreasing returns to scale.

Chapter 10

COSTS

O
n a small two-hectare *shamba*, or field, an East African peasant family is harvesting their grain crop. Ten people are working in the *shamba*, some of the adults bent over with sickles, cutting sheaves. Others (including the children) gather the sheaves into larger bundles to be taken back home, winnowed using sticks and large flat wicker baskets, and stored for family consumption and as seed for the next planting. On a mid-sized, two-section (500-hectare) Saskatchewan wheat farm, two workers on combine harvesters cut wide swaths through the golden fields. Virtually all of the crop is destined for market. The seed for next year's crop will be purchased, along with most of the other inputs except for the machinery and the farmer's managerial and planning expertise and physical labour. The total value of the capital equipment on the East African farm is about $100, while on a Saskatchewan farm, machinery and equipment alone can be valued at over $1 million.

One might think that if it were not for the poverty of the East African farmers, which prevents them from purchasing the equipment available to the Canadian farmer, they would not be forced to use such "inefficient" methods of production. But this view misunderstands the nature of cost-efficiency in production. Because labour is so much cheaper relative to capital equipment in East Africa than in Canada, *both* farms could in fact be using the most cost-efficient production methods in their respective situations.

CHAPTER PREVIEW

In this chapter we translate the theory of production developed in Chapter 9 into a coherent theory of costs. Our task in Chapter 9 was to establish the relationship between the quantities of inputs employed and the corresponding level of output, but here we forge the link between the quantity of output produced and the cost of producing it.

Our first step is to tackle the question of how costs vary with output in the short run. This question turns out to be more involved than it sounds, for there are seven different types of costs to keep track of, namely, total cost, variable cost, fixed cost, marginal cost, average total cost, average variable cost, and average fixed cost. This array sounds bewildering at first, but the links between the different cost concepts are actually very clear and simple. And each turns out to be important for the study of firm behaviour, which is our principal concern in the chapters to follow.

Of even greater importance for the structure and conduct of industry is the question of how costs vary with output in the long run. We begin with the question of how to produce a given level of output—say, a tonne of grain, either here or in some other country—at the lowest possible cost. A given quantity can be produced in many ways. We need to find the cheapest way, the most appropriate method for existing factor prices. The answer to this question enables us to explore how costs are related to returns to scale in production.

10.1 COSTS IN THE SHORT RUN

To see how costs vary with output in the short run, it is convenient to begin with a simple production example of the sort we discussed in Chapter 9. Suppose Kelly's Cleaners washes bags of laundry using labour (L) and capital (K). Labour is purchased in the open market at a wage rate $w = \$10$ per person-hour.[1] Capital is fixed in the short run. The relationship between the variable input and the total number of bags washed per hour is summarized in Table 10-1. Note that output initially grows at an increasing rate with additional units of the variable input (as L grows from 0 to 4 units), then grows at a diminishing rate (as L grows from 4 to 8 units).

The total cost of producing the various levels of output is simply the cost of all the factors of production employed. If Kelly owns his own capital, its rental value is an implicit cost, the money Kelly could have earned if he had sold his capital and invested the proceeds in, say, a government bond (see Chapter 1). Suppose Kelly's capital is fixed at 120 machine-hours per hour, the rental value of each of which is $r = \$.25$ per machine-hour,[2] for a total capital rental of $30 per hour. This cost is **fixed cost (FC)**, which means that it does not vary in the short run as the level of output varies. More generally, if K_0 denotes the amount of capital and r is its rental price per unit, we have

Fixed cost (FC) Cost that does not vary with the level of output in the short run.

$$FC = rK_0. \qquad (10.1)$$

TABLE 10-1

The Short-Run Production Function for Kelly's Cleaners
The entries in each row of the right column tell the quantity of output produced by the quantity of variable input in the corresponding row of the left column. This production function initially exhibits increasing, then diminishing, returns to the variable input.

Quantity of labour (person-hr/hr)	Quantity of output (bags/hr)
0	0
1	4
2	14
3	27
4	43
5	58
6	72
7	81
8	86

[1] A person-hour is one person working for one hour. In Chapter 14 we will consider how input prices are determined. For the present, we simply take them as given.

[2] A machine-hour is one machine working for one hour.

Other examples of fixed cost might include property taxes, insurance payments, interest on loans, and other payments to which the firm is committed in the short run and that do not vary as the level of output varies. Business managers often refer to fixed costs as *overhead costs.*

Variable cost (VC)
Cost that varies with the level of output in the short run.

Variable cost (VC) is defined as the total cost of the variable factor of production at each level of output.[3] To calculate VC for any given level of output in this example, we simply multiply the amount of labour needed to produce that level of output by the hourly wage rate. Thus, the variable cost of 27 bags per hour is ($10 per person-hour) (3 person-hours/hour) = $30/hr. More generally, if L_1 is the quantity of labour required to produce an output level of Q_1 and w is the hourly wage rate, we have

$$VC_{Q_1} = wL_1. \tag{10.2}$$

Note the explicit dependence of VC on output in the notation on the left-hand side of Equation 10.2, which is lacking in Equation 10.1. This is to emphasize that variable cost depends on the output level produced, whereas fixed cost does not.

Total cost (TC) All costs of production: the sum of variable cost and fixed cost.

Total cost (TC) is the sum of FC and VC. If Kelly wishes to wash 43 bags/hr, the total cost of doing so will be $30 per hour + ($10 per person-hour)(4 person-hours per hour) = $70/hour. More generally, the expression for total cost of producing an output level of Q_1 is written

$$TC_{Q_1} = FC + VC_{Q_1} = rK_0 + wL_1. \tag{10.3}$$

Table 10-2 shows fixed, variable, and total cost for corresponding output levels for the production function given in Table 10-1. The relationships among the various cost categories are most clearly seen by displaying the information graphically, not in tabular form. The short-run production function from Table 10-1 is plotted in Figure 10-1. Recall from Chapter 9 that the initial region of upward curvature ($0 \leq L \leq 4$) of the production function corresponds to increasing marginal productivity of the variable input. Beyond the point $L = 4$, the production function exhibits diminishing marginal productivity of the variable input.

Graphing the Total, Variable, and Fixed Cost Curves

Not surprisingly, the shape of the variable cost curve is systematically related to the shape of the short-run production function. The connection arises because the production function tells us how much labour we need to produce a given level of output, and this quantity of labour, when multiplied by the wage rate, gives us variable cost. Suppose, for example, we want to plot the variable cost of producing 58 units of output. We first note from the production function shown in Figure 10-1 that 58 units of output require 5 units of labour, which, at a wage rate of $10 per person-hour, gives rise to a variable cost of (5)(10) = $50 per hour. So in Figure 10-2 (on page 350), the output level of 58 is plotted against a variable cost of $50 per hour, Similarly, note from the production function that 43 units of output require 4 units of labour, which, at the $10 wage rate, gives rise in Figure 10-2 to a variable cost of $40 per hour. In like fashion, we can generate as many additional points on the variable cost curve as we choose.

Of particular interest is the relationship between the curvature of the production function and that of the variable cost curve. Note in Figure 10-1 that $L = 4$ is the point

---

[3] In production processes with more than one scarce variable input, variable cost refers to the cost of all such inputs.

FIGURE 10-1

Output as a Function of One Variable Input
This production process shows increasing marginal productivity of the variable input up to $L = 4$, and diminishing marginal productivity thereafter.

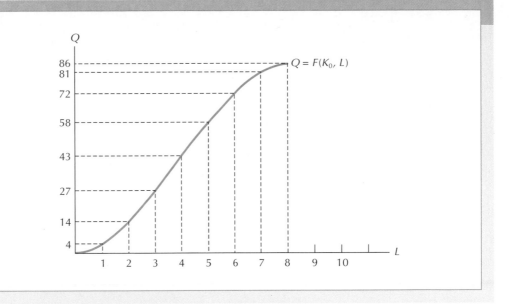

TABLE 10-2

Outputs and Costs
The fixed cost of capital is $30/hr, and the cost per unit of the variable factor (L) is $10/hr. Total cost is calculated as the sum of fixed cost and variable cost. See Figure 10-2.

Q	FC	VC	TC
0	30	0	30
4	30	10	40
14	30	20	50
27	30	30	60
43	30	40	70
58	30	50	80
72	30	60	90
81	30	70	100
86	30	80	110

at which decreasing marginal productivity of the variable factor of production sets in. For values of L less than 4, the marginal productivity of labour is increasing, which means that increments in L produce successively larger increments in Q in that region. Put another way, in this region a given increase in output, Q, requires successively smaller increments in the variable input, L. As a result, variable cost grows at a diminishing rate for output levels less than 43. This is reflected in Figure 10-2 by the decreasing slope of the variable cost curve as output increases from 0 to 43.

Once L exceeds 4 in Figure 10-1, we enter the region of "diminishing returns," or decreasing MP_L. Here, successively larger increments in L are required to produce a given increment in Q. In consequence, variable cost grows at an increasing rate in this region. This is reflected in the increasingly steep slope of the variable cost curve in Figure 10-2 for output levels in excess of 43.

Because fixed costs do not vary with the level of output, their graph is simply a horizontal line. Figure 10-2 shows the fixed, variable, and total cost curves (FC, VC, and TC) for a representative production function. Note in the figure that the variable cost curve passes through the origin, which means simply that variable cost is zero when

FIGURE 10-2

The Total, Variable, and Fixed Cost Curves
These curves are for the production function for Kelly's Cleaners, shown in Figure 10-1. The variable cost curve passes through the origin, which means that the variable cost of producing zero units of output is equal to zero. The TC curve, which is the sum of the FC and VC curves, is parallel to the VC curve and lies FC = $30/hour above it. See Table 10-2.

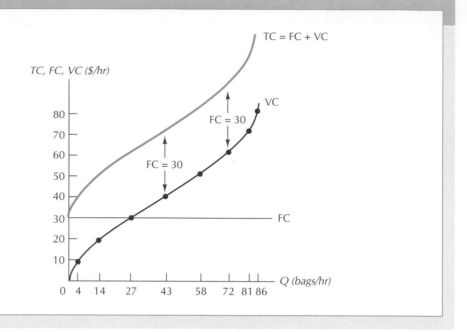

we produce no output. The total cost of producing zero output is equal to fixed costs, FC. Note also in the figure that the vertical distance between the VC and TC curves is everywhere equal to FC. This means that the total cost curve is parallel to the variable cost curve and lies FC units above it.

EXAMPLE 10-1

Suppose the production function is given by $Q = 3KL$, where K denotes capital and L denotes labour. The price of capital is $2/machine-hr, the price of labour is $24/person-hr, and capital is fixed at 4 machine-hr/hr in the short run. Graph the TC, VC, and FC curves for this production process.

Unlike the production process shown in Figure 10-1, the process in this example is one with constant marginal productivity of the variable factor of production. As shown in Figure 10-3, output here is strictly proportional to the variable input.

To derive the total cost function from this production function, we must first discover how much capital and labour are required to produce a given level of output in the short run. Since K is fixed at 4 machine-hr/hr, the required amount of labour input is found by solving $Q = 3KL = 3(4)L$ for $L = Q/12$. The total cost of producing Q units of output per hour is therefore given by

$$TC(Q) = (\$2/\text{machine-hr})(4 \text{ machine-hr/hr})$$
$$+ (\$24/\text{person-hr})\left(\frac{Q}{12} \text{ person-hr/hr}\right) = \$8/\text{hr} + \$2Q/\text{hr}. \qquad (10.4)$$

The $8/hr expenditure on capital constitutes fixed cost. Variable cost is total cost less fixed cost, or

$$VC_Q = 2Q. \qquad (10.5)$$

The total, variable, and fixed cost curves are plotted in Figure 10-4.

FIGURE 10-3

The Production Function Q = 3KL, with K = 4
This short-run production function exhibits constant marginal productivity of L over the entire range of L. There is neither a region of increasing nor a region of diminishing marginal productivity of L.

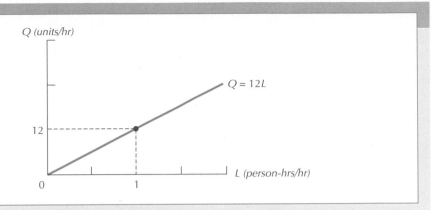

FIGURE 10-4

The Total, Variable, and Fixed Cost Curves for the Production Function Q = 3KL
With K fixed at 4 machine-hr/hr in the short run and a price of K of r = $2/machine-hr, fixed costs are $8/hr. To produce Q units of output per hour requires Q/12 person-hr/hr of labour. With a price of labour of $24/person-hr, variable cost is $2Q/hr. Total cost is $8/hr + $2Q/hr.

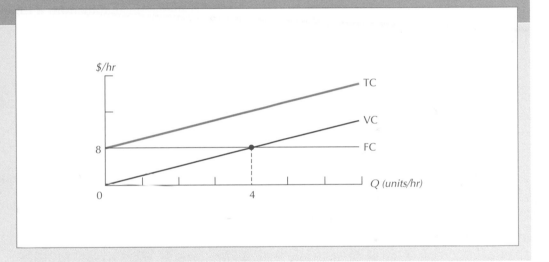

EXERCISE 10-1

Same as Example 10-1 except the price of capital r = $4/machine-hr.

Other Short-Run Costs

Average fixed cost (AFC) Fixed cost divided by the quantity of output.

Average fixed cost (AFC) is fixed cost divided by the quantity of output. For example, the average fixed cost of washing 58 bags/hr is ($30/hr) ÷ (58 bags/hr) = $.517/bag. More generally, the average fixed cost of producing an output level of Q_1 is written

$$AFC_{Q_1} = \frac{FC}{Q_1} = \frac{rK_0}{Q_1}. \qquad (10.6)$$

Note in Equation 10.6 that, unlike FC, AFC depends on the level of output produced.

Average variable cost (AVC) Variable cost divided by the quantity of output.

Average variable cost (AVC) is variable cost divided by the quantity of output. If Kelly washes 72 bags/hr, his AVC will be ($10/person-hr)(6 person-hr/hr) ÷ 72 bags/hr = $.833/bag. The average variable cost of producing an output level Q_1 may be written as

$$AVC_{Q_1} = \frac{VC_{Q_1}}{Q_1} = \frac{wL_1}{Q_1}. \qquad (10.7)$$

Average total cost
(ATC) Total cost
divided by the quantity
of output.

Average total cost (ATC) is total cost divided by the quantity of output. And since total cost is the sum of total fixed cost and total variable cost, it follows that ATC is the sum of AFC and AVC. For example, the ATC of washing 58 bags/hr is ($30/hr) ÷ (58 bags/hr) + ($10/person-hr)(5 person-hr/hr) ÷ (58 bags/hr) = $.517/bag + $.862/bag = $1.379/bag. The average total cost of producing Q_1 units of output is given by

$$ATC_{Q_1} = AFC_{Q_1} + AVC_{Q_1} = \frac{rK_0 + wL_1}{Q_1}. \qquad (10.8)$$

Marginal cost (MC), finally, is the change in total cost that results from producing an additional unit of output.[4] In going from 58 to 72 bags/hr, for example, total costs go up by $10/hr, which is the cost of hiring the extra worker needed to achieve that increase in output. Since the extra worker washes an extra 14 bags/hr, the marginal cost of the additional output in per-bag terms is ($10/hr) ÷ (14 bags/hr) = $.714/bag. More generally, if ΔQ denotes the change in output from an initial level of Q_1, and ΔTC_{Q_1} denotes the corresponding change in total cost, marginal cost at Q_1 is given by

$$MC_{Q_1} = \frac{\Delta TC_{Q_1}}{\Delta Q}. \qquad (10.9)$$

Because fixed cost does not vary with the level of output, the change in total cost when we produce ΔQ additional units of output is the same as the change in variable cost. Thus an equivalent expression for marginal cost is

$$MC_{Q_1} = \frac{\Delta VC_{Q_1}}{\Delta Q}, \qquad (10.10)$$

where ΔVC_{Q_1} represents the change in variable cost when we produce ΔQ units of additional output.

Graphing the Short-Run Average and Marginal Cost Curves

Since FC does not vary with output, average fixed cost declines steadily as output increases. This fact alone provides an important explanation for the precarious position of Canadian cultural industries as compared with those of the United States. Consider two books, one aimed mainly at the Canadian market and one at the U.S. market. Both books have fixed costs of $200,000. With sales of 2000 copies, AFC would be $100 per book. Sales of 40,000 copies are very respectable in the Canadian market, and would bring AFC down to $5 per book. But if sales of the U.S. book reflected relative market size, then 400,000 copies would be sold, and U.S. AFC would become $.50 per book. Being able to spread fixed costs over a market that is 10 times as large gives U.S. cultural industry producers a significant edge over their Canadian counterparts.

For the fixed cost curve FC shown in the top panel in Figure 10-5, the corresponding average fixed cost curve is shown in the bottom panel as the curve labelled AFC. Like all other AFC curves, it takes the form of a rectangular hyperbola. As output shrinks toward zero, AFC grows without bounds, and it falls ever closer to zero as output increases. Note that the units on the vertical axis of the AFC curve are dollars per unit ($/unit) of output, and that the vertical axis of the FC curve, in contrast, is measured in dollars per hour ($/hr).

---

[4]In calculus terms, the definition of marginal cost is simply $MC_Q = dTC_Q/dQ$, that is, the derivative or slope of the TC (total cost) curve.

FIGURE 10-5

The Marginal, Average Total, Average Variable, and Average Fixed Cost Curves
The MC curve intersects the ATC and AVC curves at their respective minimum points. With TC curves having this form, it is always the case that minimum MC occurs to the left of minimum AVC, which is left of minimum ATC.

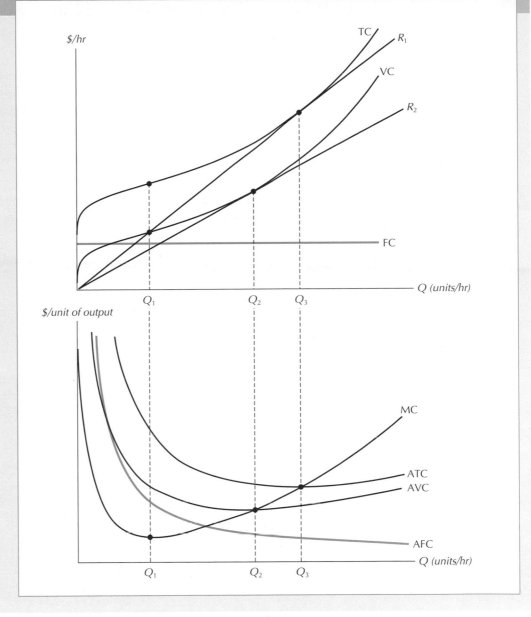

Geometrically, average variable cost at any level of output Q, which is equal to VC/Q, may be interpreted as the slope of a ray to the variable cost curve at Q. Notice in the top panel in Figure 10-5 that the slope of a ray to the VC curve declines with output up to the output level Q_2; thereafter it begins to increase. The corresponding average variable cost curve, shown in the bottom panel in Figure 10-5, therefore reaches its minimum value at Q_2, the output level at which the ray R_2 is tangent to the variable cost curve. Beyond that point, the AVC curve increases with output.

The graph of the ATC curve is generated in an analogous fashion. For any level of output, ATC is the slope of the ray to the total cost curve at that output level. For the total cost curve in the top panel in Figure 10-5, the corresponding ATC curve is plotted in the bottom panel of the diagram. Note that the minimum point on ATC in the bottom panel occurs at Q_3, the output level for which the ray R_1 is tangent to the TC curve in the top panel.

Recall that because TC = FC + VC, it follows that ATC = AFC + AVC (simply divide both sides of the former equation by output). This means that the vertical distance between the ATC and AVC curves at any level of output will always be the corresponding level of AFC. Thus the vertical distance between ATC and AVC approaches infinity as output declines toward zero, and shrinks toward zero as output grows toward infinity. Note also in Figure 10-5 that the minimum point on the AVC curve occurs at a lower level of output than does the minimum point on the ATC curve. Because AFC declines continuously, ATC continues falling even after AVC has begun to turn upward.

EXAMPLE 10-2

Construct a table showing the average fixed costs, average variable cost, average total cost, and marginal cost using the information in Table 10-1 for Kelly's Cleaners. Then graph these average costs.

We calculate the average fixed cost as fixed costs divided by quantity (AFC = FC/Q), average variable cost as variable cost divided by quantity (AVC = VC/Q), and average total cost as total cost divided by quantity (ATC = TC/Q). We calculate marginal cost by finding the difference in total cost divided by the difference in quantity (MC = ΔTC/ΔQ) to fill in the table below. Circled numbers are minimum points. The average cost curves are illustrated in Figure 10-6.

Outputs (in bags) and Costs (in $/bag)				
Q	AFC	AVC	ATC	MC*
0	∞	–	∞	
				2.50
4	7.50	2.50	10.00	
				1.00
14	2.14	1.43	3.57	
				.77
27	1.11	1.11	2.22	
				(.63)
43	.70	.93	1.63	
				.67
58	.52	.86	1.38	
				.71
72	.42	(.83)	1.25	
				1.11
81	.37	.86	(1.23)	
				2.00
86	.35	.93	1.28	

*The marginal cost entries are placed between the lines of the table to indicate that each entry represents the cost of moving from the preceding output level to the next.

EXERCISE 10-2

If FC takes the value $20/hour, what is the vertical distance between the ATC and AVC curves in Figure 10-5 when $Q = 10$ units/hour?

FIGURE 10-6

Quantity vs. Average Costs
ATC is the sum of AVC and AFC. AFC is declining for all values of Q. Values of the curves are based on the table in Example 10-2.

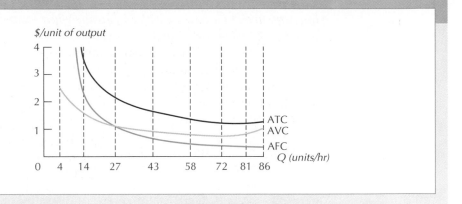

In terms of its role in the firm's decision of how much output to produce, by far the most important of the seven cost curves is the *marginal cost curve*. The reason, as we will see in the coming chapters, is that the firm's typical operating decision involves the question of whether to expand or contract its current level of output. To make this decision intelligently, the firm must compare the relevant costs and benefits. The cost of expanding output (or the savings from contracting) is by definition equal to marginal cost.

Geometrically, marginal cost at any level of output may be interpreted as the slope of the total cost curve at that level of output. And since the total cost and variable cost curves are parallel, marginal cost is also equal to the slope of the variable cost curve. (Recall that the variable cost component is all that varies when total cost varies, which means that the change in total cost per unit of output must be the same as the change in variable cost per unit of output.)

Notice in the top panel in Figure 10-5 that the slope of the total cost curve decreases with output up to Q_1, and rises with output thereafter.[5] This tells us that the marginal cost curve, labelled MC in the bottom panel, will be downward sloping up to Q_1 and upward sloping thereafter. Q_1 is the point at which "diminishing returns" set in for this production function, and diminishing returns are what accounts for the upward slope of the short-run marginal cost curve.

At the output level Q_3, the slope of the total cost curve is exactly the same as the slope of the ray to the total cost curve (the ray labelled R_1 in the top panel in Figure 10-5). This tells us that marginal cost and average total cost will take precisely the same value at Q_3. To the left of Q_3, the slope of the total cost curve is less than the slope of the corresponding ray, which means that marginal cost will be less than average total cost in that region. For output levels in excess of Q_3, the slope of the total cost curve is greater than the slope of the corresponding ray, so marginal cost will be greater than average total cost for output levels larger than Q_3. These relationships are reflected in the average total cost and marginal cost curves shown in the bottom panel in Figure 10-5. Notice that the relationship between the MC and AVC curves is qualitatively similar to the relationship between the MC and ATC curves. One common feature is that MC intersects each curve at its minimum point. Both average cost curves have the

---

[5]A point at which the curvature changes is called an *inflection point*. In calculus terms, $MC_Q = dTC_Q/dQ > 0$ as long as TC_Q is an increasing function of Q. The *second* derivative of TC_Q with respect to Q, d^2TC_Q/dQ^2, however, is less than zero to the left of the inflection point Q_1 (where MC_Q is falling), greater than zero to the right of Q_1 (where MC_Q is rising), and equal to zero at the point of inflection Q_1, where MC_Q is at its minimum value.

additional property that *when MC is less than average cost (either ATC or AVC), the average cost curve must be decreasing with output; and when MC is greater than average cost, average cost must be increasing with output.*

Note also that both of these relationships are very much like the ones among marginal and average product curves discussed in Chapter 9. They follow directly from the definition of marginal cost. Producing an additional unit whose cost exceeds the average (either total or variable) cost incurred thus far has the effect of pulling the average cost up. Conversely, an extra unit whose cost is less than the average will necessarily pull down the average.

Finally, note in the bottom panel in Figure 10-5 that the units on the vertical axis of the marginal cost curve diagram are again dollars per unit ($/unit) of output, the same as for the three short-run average cost curves. All four of these curves can thus be displayed in a single diagram. But you must never, *ever*, attempt to place any of these four curves on the same axes with the total cost, variable cost, or fixed cost curves, where the vertical axis is in dollars/hour. The units measured along the vertical axes are simply not compatible.[6]

EXAMPLE 10-3

Suppose output is given by the production function $Q = 3KL$, where K denotes capital and L denotes labour. The price of capital is \$2/machine-hr, the price of labour is \$24/person-hr, and capital is fixed at 4 units in the short run (these are the same production function and input prices as in Example 10-1). Graph the ATC, AVC, AFC, and MC curves.

Recall from Example 10-1 that the total cost curve for this process is given by

$$TC_Q = 8 + 2Q. \qquad (10.11)$$

Marginal cost is the slope of the total cost curve, which here is equal to \$2/unit of output:

$$MC_Q = \frac{\Delta TC_Q}{\Delta Q} = 2. \qquad (10.12)$$

Average variable cost is given by VC_Q/Q, which is also \$2/unit of output:

$$AVC_Q = \frac{2Q}{Q} = 2. \qquad (10.13)$$

When marginal cost is constant, as in this production process, it will always be equal to AVC.

Average fixed cost is given by

$$AFC_Q = \frac{8}{Q} \qquad (10.14)$$

and average total cost is given by

$$ATC_Q = 2 + \frac{8}{Q} \qquad (10.15)$$

in this example. The marginal and average cost curves are as shown in the bottom panel in Figure 10-7, where the top panel reproduces the corresponding total, variable, and fixed cost curves.

---

[6]A colleague tells of an occasion when he issued this warning forcefully to his class of intermediate microeconomics students. He was team-teaching the course that semester with a professor whose competence was very much in doubt. All doubt was resolved when, in the very next class meeting, his coteacher began his lecture by drawing the TC, ATC, and MC curves on a single set of axes.

FIGURE 10-7

Cost Curves for a Specific Production Process
For production processes with constant marginal cost, average variable cost and marginal cost are identical. Marginal cost always lies below ATC for such processes.

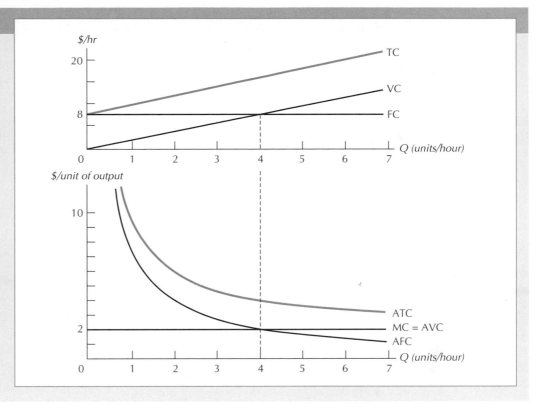

10.2 ALLOCATING PRODUCTION BETWEEN TWO PROCESSES

In Chapter 9, we saw that the problem of allocating a fixed resource between two production activities is solved by the allocation that equates the marginal product of the resource in each. There is a very closely related problem that can be solved with the cost concepts developed in this chapter. Here, the problem is to divide a given production quota between two production processes in such a way as to produce the quota at the lowest possible cost.

Let Q^T be the total amount to be produced, and let Q^A and Q^B be the amounts produced in processes A and B, respectively. And suppose the marginal cost in either process at very low levels of output is lower than the marginal cost at Q^T units of output in the other (which ensures that both processes will be used),[7] and that inputs are perfectly divisible. *The values of Q^A and Q^B that solve this problem will then be the ones that result in equal marginal costs for the two processes.*

To see why, suppose the contrary—that is, suppose that the cost-minimizing allocation resulted in higher marginal costs in one process than in the other. We could then shift one unit of output from the process with the higher marginal cost to the one with the lower. Because the result would be the *same* total output as before at *lower* cost, the initial division could not have been the cost-minimizing one.

---

[7]Suppose the marginal cost at $Q = Q^T$ using production function A was less than the marginal cost at $Q = 0$ for production process B: $MC^A_{Q^T} < MC^B_0$. Then the cheapest way of producing Q^T would be to use only process A.

In Chapter 9 we saw that two production processes could have equal marginal products even though their average products differed substantially. Here, too, it is possible for two production processes to have equal marginal costs even though their average costs differ markedly. The cost-minimizing condition does not require average cost levels in the two processes to be the same, and indeed, in practice, they will often take substantially different values.

Suppose production processes A and B give rise to the following marginal and average total cost curves, where MC and ATC are in \$/unit of output:

$$MC^A = 12Q^A, \quad ATC^A = 16/Q^A + 6Q^A,$$
$$MC^B = 4Q^B, \quad ATC^B = 240/Q^B + 2Q^B,$$

where the superscripts denote processes A and B, respectively. What is the least costly way to produce a total of 32 units of output?

The minimum-cost condition is that $MC^A_{Q^A} = MC^B_{Q^B}$, with $Q^A + Q^B = 32$. Equating marginal costs, we have

$$12Q^A = 4Q^B. \qquad (10.16)$$

Substituting $Q^B = 32 - Q^A$ into Equation 10.16, we have

$$12Q^A = 4(32 - Q^A) = 128 - 4Q^A \qquad (10.17)$$

which solves for $Q^A = 8$. $Q^B = 32 - 8 = 24$ takes care of the remaining output, and at these output levels, marginal cost in both plants will be \$96/unit of output (see Figure 10-8). The line $MC^T = 3Q^T$ is the horizontal sum of MC^A and MC^B.[8] We can also see the output that equates marginal cost by summarizing the marginal cost information in a table as below.

Q	MC^A	MC^B	MC^T
0	0	0	0
8	96	32	24
16	192	64	48
24	288	96	72
32	384	128	96

The average total cost values that correspond to this allocation are $ATC^A = \$50$/unit of output and $ATC^B = \$58$/unit of output. From the average total cost curves we can deduce total cost curves in this example (just multiply ATC by Q).[9] They are given by $TC^A = 16 + 6(Q^A)^2$ and $TC^B = 240 + 2(Q^B)^2$. The cost-minimizing allocation results in $TC^A = \$400$ and $TC^B = \$1392$, illustrating that the cost-minimizing allocation does not require equality of total costs either.

Same as Example 10-3 except the total output is 12 units.

---

[8]MC^T is found by solving $Q^T = Q^A + Q^B = MC/12 + MC/4 = MC/3$ for $MC^T = 3Q^T$.

[9]Note that $MC^A = dTC^A/dQ^A = d[16 + 6(Q^A)^2]/dQ^A = 12Q^A$ and $MC^B = dTC^B/dQ^B = d[240 + 2(Q^B)^2]/dQ^B = 4Q^B$.

FIGURE 10-8

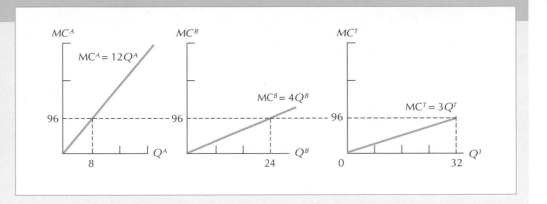

10.3 THE RELATIONSHIP AMONG MP, AP, MC, AND AVC

In Chapter 9, we saw that the marginal product of labour curve cuts the average product of labour curve at the maximum value of the AP_L curve. And in this chapter, we saw that the marginal cost curve cuts the average variable cost curve at the minimum value of the AVC curve. There is a direct link between these relationships. To see the connection, note first that from the definition of marginal cost we have $MC = \Delta VC/\Delta Q$. When labour is the only variable factor, $\Delta VC = \Delta wL$ so that $\Delta VC/\Delta Q$ is equal to $\Delta wL/\Delta Q$. If w is constant, this is the same as $w\Delta L/\Delta Q$. And since $\Delta L/\Delta Q$ is equal to $1/MP_L$, it follows that

$$MC = \frac{w}{MP_L}. \qquad (10.18)$$

In similar fashion, note from the definition of average variable cost that $AVC = VC/Q = wL/Q$, and since L/Q is equal to $1/AP_L$, it follows that

$$AVC = \frac{w}{AP_L}. \qquad (10.19)$$

From Equation 10.18, we see that the minimum value of marginal cost corresponds to the maximum value of MP_L. Likewise, it follows from Equation 10.19 that the minimum value of AVC corresponds to the maximum value of AP_L. The top panel in Figure 10-9 plots the AP_L and MP_L curves as functions of L. The bottom panel uses Equations 10.18 and 10.19 to plot the corresponding MC and AVC curves as functions of L. (Normally, the MC and AVC curves are plotted as functions of Q. The value of Q that corresponds to a given value of L in the bottom panel may be calculated by multiplying L times the corresponding value of AP_L.) Note that the MP_L curve in the top panel takes its maximum value at $L = L_1$, and that the minimum value of the MC curve in the bottom panel occurs at the output level (Q_1) that corresponds to $L = L_1$. Note also that the AP_L curve in the top panel takes its maximum value at $L = L_2$, and that the minimum value of the AVC curve in the bottom panel occurs at the output level (Q_2) that corresponds to $L = L_2$.

There are several related pitfalls to avoid in interpreting Figure 10-9. Here is how to avoid them. First, note that at L_M, $MPL = 0$, which means that at L_M, Q is at its maximum value, Q_M. Any increase in L past L_M actually *lowers* Q, as shown by the fact that $MP_L < 0$ to the right of L_M. Second, as Figure 10-9 shows, since $MP_L = 0$ at L_M, $MC(= w/MP_L)$

FIGURE 10-9

The Relationship between MP_L, AP_L, MC, and AVC
Normally, the MC and AVC curves are plotted with Q on the horizontal axis. In the bottom panel, they are shown as functions of L. The value of Q that corresponds to a given value of L is found by multiplying L times the corresponding value of AP_L. The maximum value of the MP_L curve, at $L = L_1$, top panel, corresponds to the minimum value of the MC curve, at $Q = Q_1$, bottom panel. Similarly, the maximum value of the AP_L curve, at $L = L_2$, top panel, corresponds to the minimum value of the AVC curve, at $Q = Q_2$, bottom panel.

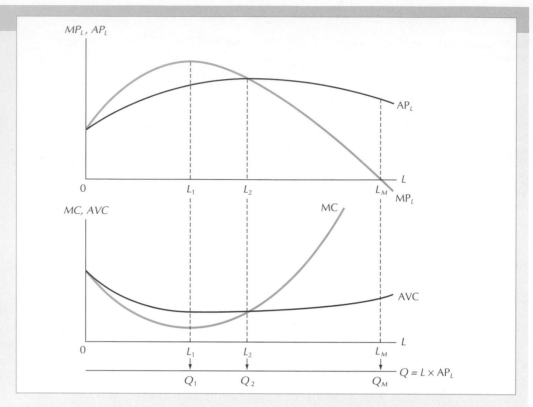

tends to infinity as L approaches L_M and MP_L approaches zero. This just says that the cost of producing one unit more than the *maximum* level of output is infinite: we simply *can't* produce more than the maximum! The third major pitfall is to assume that Q bears a constant proportional relationship to L. Since AP_L varies as L increases, however, first rising and then falling, the scale along the Q ($= AP_L \times L$) axis *cannot* remain constant. In fact, as we noted above, moving to the right of L_M and Q_M actually *lowers* the value of Q below the value at Q_M, since in this region AP_L falls by a greater proportion than L rises.[10] The important point that emerges is the same one we noted in discussing Figure 9-6. As long as the wage rate is positive, a rational manager will never hire more than L_M person-hours, since if she did, total cost would be higher and Q lower than at L_M.

EXERCISE 10-4

For a production function at a given level of output in the short run, the marginal product of labour is greater than the average product of labour. If the wage rate is constant, how will marginal cost at that output level compare with average variable cost?

---

[10]The relationship between Q and L is not constant, but it does vary systematically. Let us define ϵ_{QL}, the elasticity of output with respect to labour, as the percentage increase in Q resulting from a 1 percent increase in L, with other inputs held constant. Then $\epsilon_{QL} = (\Delta Q/Q)/(\Delta L/L) = (\Delta Q/\Delta L)/(Q/L) = MP_L/AP_L$, the ratio of the marginal product of labour to the average product of labour. Between 0 and L_2, $\epsilon_{QL} > 1$ (since $MP_L > AP_L$), and therefore a 1 percent increase in L causes a greater than 1 percent increase in Q. At L_2, $\epsilon_{QL} = 1$. Between L_2 and L_M, $0 < \epsilon_{QL} < 1$ (since $0 < MP_L < AP_L$), and at L_M, $\epsilon_{QL} = 0$ (since $MP_L = 0$). To the right of L_M, ϵ_{QL} is negative, and hence a 1 percent increase in L causes an ϵ_{QL} percent *decrease* in Q.

10.4 COSTS IN THE LONG RUN

In the long run all inputs are, by definition, freely variable. If the manager of the firm wishes to produce a given level of output at the lowest possible cost and is free to choose any input combination she pleases, which one should she choose? As we will see in the next section, the answer to this question depends on the relative prices of capital and labour.

Choosing the Optimal Input Combination

No matter what the structure of industry may be—monopolistic or atomistically competitive, capitalist or socialist, industrialized or less developed—the objective of most producers is to produce a given level and quality of output at the lowest possible cost. Equivalently, the producer wants to produce as much output as possible from any given expenditure on inputs.

Let us begin with the case of a firm that wants to maximize output from a given level of expenditure. Suppose it uses only two inputs, capital (K) and labour (L), whose prices, measured in dollars per unit of input per day, are $r = 2$ and $w = 4$, respectively. What different combinations of inputs can this firm purchase for a total expenditure of $C = \$200/\text{day}$? Notice that this question has the very same structure as the one we encountered in the theory of consumer behaviour in Chapter 3: with an income of M, and facing prices of P_X and P_Y, what combinations of X and Y can the consumer buy? In the consumer's case, recall, the answer was easily summarized by the budget constraint. The parallel information in the case of the firm is summarized by the *isocost line*, shown in Figure 10-10 for the example given. Any of the input combinations on the locus labelled B can be purchased for a total expenditure of \$200/day. Analogously to the budget constraint case, the slope of the isocost line is the negative of the ratio of the input prices, $-w/r$.

EXERCISE 10-5

If $w = \$3/\text{labour-day}$ and $r = \$6/\text{machine-day}$, draw the isocost lines that correspond to total expenditure of \$90 and \$180 per day.

FIGURE 10-10

The Isocost Line
For given input prices ($r = 2$ and $w = 4$ in the diagram), the isocost line is the locus of all possible input bundles that can be purchased for a given level of total expenditure C (\$200 in the diagram). The slope of the isocost line is the negative of the input price ratio, $-w/r$.

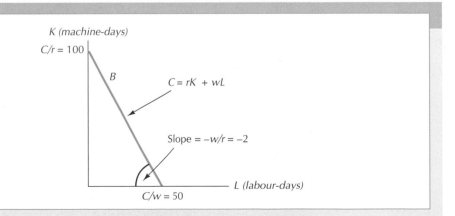

The analytic approach for finding the maximum output that can be produced for a given cost turns out to be very similar to the one for finding the optimal consumption bundle. Just as a given level of satisfaction can be achieved by any of a multitude of possible consumption bundles (all of which lie on the same indifference curve), so too can a given amount of output be produced by any of a host of different input combinations (all of which lie on the same isoquant). In the consumer case, we found the optimum bundle by superimposing the budget constraint onto the indifference map and locating the relevant point of tangency.[11] Here, we superimpose the isocost line onto the isoquant map. In Figure 10-11, the tangency point (L^*, K^*) is the input combination that yields the highest possible output (Q_1) for an expenditure of C.

FIGURE 10-11

The Maximum Output for a Given Expenditure
A firm that is trying to produce the largest possible output for an expenditure of C will select the input combination at which the isocost line for C is tangent to an isoquant.

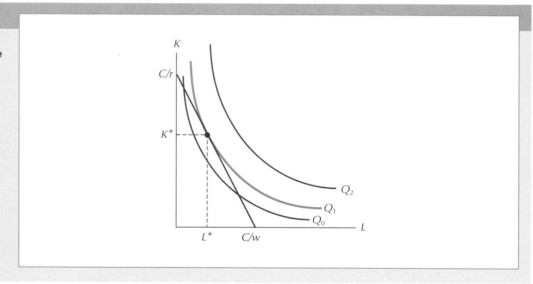

FIGURE 10-12

The Minimum Cost for a Given Level of Output
A firm that is trying to produce a given level of output, Q_1, at the lowest possible cost will select the input combination at which an isocost line is tangent to the Q_1 isoquant.

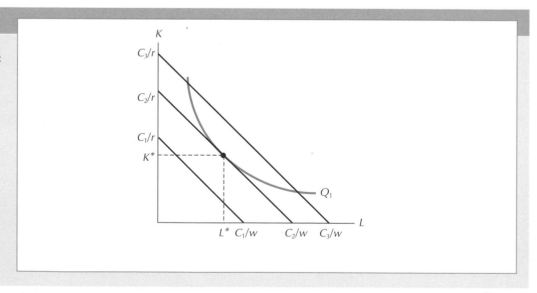

---

[11]Except, of course, in the case of corner solutions, kinks, or indivisibilities.

CHAPTER 10: COSTS

As noted, the problem of producing the largest output for a given expenditure is solved in essentially the same way as the problem of producing a given level of output for the lowest possible cost. The only difference is that in the latter case we begin with a specific isoquant (the one that corresponds to the level of output we are trying to produce), then superimpose a map of isocost lines, each corresponding to a different cost level. In our first exercise, cost was fixed and output varied; this time, output is fixed and costs vary. As shown in Figure 10-12, the least-cost input bundle (L^*, K^*) corresponds to the point of tangency between an isocost line and the specified isoquant (Q_1).

Recall from Chapter 9 that the slope of the isoquant at any point is equal to $-MP_L/MP_K$, the negative of the ratio of the marginal product of L to the marginal product of K at that point. (Recall also from Chapter 9 that the ratio MP_L/MP_K is called the marginal rate of technical substitution.) Combining this with the result that minimum cost occurs at a point of tangency with the isocost line (whose slope is $-w/r$), it follows that at the cost-minimizing point, with an interior solution,

$$\text{MRTS} = \frac{MP_{L^*}}{MP_{K^*}} = \frac{w}{r}, \tag{10.20}$$

where K^* and L^* again denote the minimum-cost values of K and L. Cross-multiplying, we have

$$\frac{MP_{L^*}}{w} = \frac{MP_{K^*}}{r}. \tag{10.21}$$

Equation 10.21 has a straightforward economic interpretation. Note first that MP_{L^*} is simply the extra output obtained from an extra unit of L at the cost-minimizing point. w is the cost, in dollars, of an extra unit of L. The ratio MP_{L^*}/w is thus the extra output we get from the last dollar spent on L. Similarly, MP_{K^*}/r is the extra output we get from the last dollar spent on K. In words, Equation 10.21 tells us that when costs are at a minimum, the extra output we get from the last dollar spent on an input must be the same for all inputs.

It is easy to show why, if that were not the case, costs would not be at a minimum. Suppose, for example, that the last units of both labour and capital increased output by 4 units. That is, suppose $MP_L = MP_K = 4$. And again, suppose that $r = P_K = \$2$/unit of capital and $w = P_L = \$4$/unit of labour. We would then have gotten only 1 unit of output for the last dollar spent on L, but 2 units for the last dollar spent on K. We could reduce spending on L by a dollar, increase spending on K by only \$.50, and get the same output level as before, saving \$.50 in the process. Whenever the ratios of marginal products to input prices differ across inputs, it will always be possible to make a similar cost-saving substitution in favour of the input with the higher MP/P ratio.[12]

More generally, we may consider a production process that employs not two but N inputs, $X_1, X_2, \dots, X_N$. In this case, the condition for production at minimum cost is a straightforward generalization of Equation 10.21:

$$\frac{MP_{X_1}}{P_{X_1}} = \frac{MP_{X_2}}{P_{X_2}} = \dots = \frac{MP_{X_N}}{P_{X_N}}. \tag{10.22}$$

---

[12]Again, this statement is true except in the case of corner solutions, kinks, or indivisibilities.

WHY IS GRAIN FARMING SO LABOUR INTENSIVE FOR EAST AFRICAN PEASANTS AND SO CAPITAL INTENSIVE IN SASKATCHEWAN?

This question, to which the answer seems so obvious, is actually quite complex. Here we shall focus on just one basic but crucial part of the puzzle. For simplicity, suppose that only two scarce inputs, capital (K) and labour (L) are involved in grain production, because land is abundant in both places. Any of the input combinations on the isoquant labelled $Q = 1$ tonne in Figure 10-13 will yield 1 tonne of grain. The combination (L_S^*, K_S^*) corresponds to the highly capital-intensive technique used in Saskatchewan, (L_{EA}^*, K_{EA}^*) to the highly labour-intensive technique used in East Africa.

Farm machinery prices are somewhat higher in East Africa, and hence so is r, the rental rate per machine-day. By far the most important factor, however, is that the daily wage rate in parts of East Africa is about 2 percent of the equivalent Canadian wage rate. Hence the isocost line is much flatter in East Africa. As shown in Figure 10-13, this fact alone is sufficient to account for the dramatic difference in production techniques. East African grain farming does not have high productivity per person, but in *both* places the choice of production techniques is cost efficient, given relative input prices.

EXERCISE 10-6

Suppose capital and labour are perfect complements in a one-to-one ratio. That is, suppose that $Q = \min(L, K)$. Currently, the wage rate is $w = 5$ and the rental rate is $r = 10$. What are the minimum cost and method of producing $Q = 20$ units of output? Suppose the wage rises to $w' = 20$. If we keep total cost the same, what level of output can now be produced and what method of production (input mix) is used?

EXERCISE 10-7

Repeat the previous exercise but now suppose capital and labour are perfect substitutes in a one-to-one ratio: $Q = K + L$.

FIGURE 10-13

Different Ways of Producing 1 Tonne of Grain
Countries where labour is cheap relative to capital will select labour-intensive techniques of production. Those where labour is more expensive will employ relatively more capital-intensive techniques.

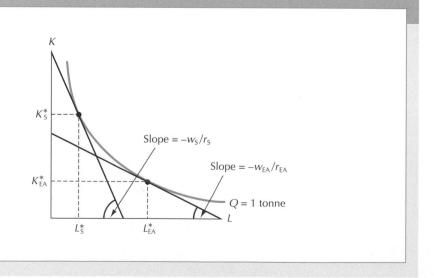

WHY DO UNIONS SUPPORT MINIMUM WAGE LAWS?

Canadian labour unions have actively supported minimum wage legislation and increases in the level of the minimum wage, federally and in each province. They have also supported a broad range of social programs, the benefits of which do not directly accrue exclusively or even primarily to union members. In this respect, the Canadian union movement has historically been less narrowly "economistic" in its goals than organized labour in the United States. We will examine both unions and the minimum wage issue in more detail in Chapter 14. Here, we simply want to show how minimum wage legislation could benefit union members, even if all union members earned substantially more than the minimum wage and had no humanitarian concern for the welfare of nonunion workers.

An understanding of the condition for production at minimum cost helps show why. On average, union workers tend to be more skilled than nonunion workers. Unskilled labour and skilled labour are substitutes for one another in many production processes, giving rise to isoquants shaped something like the one shown in Figure 10-14. What mix of the two skill categories the firm chooses to use will depend strongly on relative prices. Figure 10-14 shows the least costly mix for producing $Q = Q_0$ both before and after the enactment of the minimum wage statute. The wage rate for skilled labour is denoted by w. The prelegislation price of unskilled labour is w_1, which rises to w_2 after enactment of the law. The immediate effect is to increase the absolute value of the slope of the isocost line from w_1/w to w_2/w, causing the firm to increase its employment of skilled labour from S_1 to S_2, simultaneously reducing its employment of unskilled (nonunion) labour from U_1 to U_2. Hence, although most union workers are not affected directly by the minimum wage laws, these laws have the indirect consequence of increasing the demand for skilled (and thus union) labour.[13]

FIGURE 10-14

The Effect of a Minimum Wage Law on Employment of Skilled Labour
Unskilled labour and skilled labour are substitutes for one another in many production processes. When the price of un-skilled labour rises, the slope of the isocost line rises, causing many firms to increase their employment of skilled (unionized) labour.

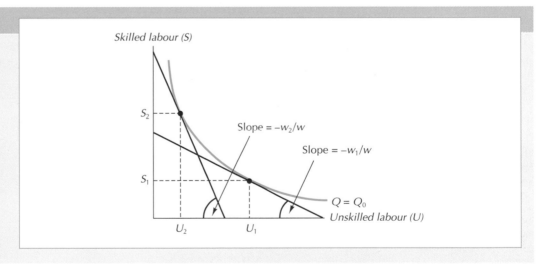

---

[13]This example assumes that the firm will produce the same level of output after the minimum wage hike as before. As Chapter 11 shows, however, a perfectly competitive firm will generally produce less output than before. If the output reduction is large enough, it could offset the firm's switch to skilled labour. Chapter 14 shows how a minimum wage can actually *increase* output and employment!

WHY WOULD A MANUFACTURER BAKE THE IMAGE OF A HOUSEFLY INTO THE CENTRE OF ITS CERAMIC URINALS?

Changes in the capital–labour ratio are sometimes motivated not by a change in factor prices, but by the introduction of new ideas. Consider, for example, the "official toilet project" initiated some years ago by Jos van Bedaf, head manager of cleaning for the Schiphol airport in Amsterdam.[14] His problem was that the airport men's rooms, which were used by more than 100,000 patrons a year, had a tendency to become messy and smelly despite frequent cleanings. Mr. van Bedaf's solution was not to intensify the efforts of maintenance crews but to make a minor change in the restroom equipment. Specifically, he requested that his sanitation equipment manufacturer supply the airport with urinals with the image of a housefly baked onto the centre of each fixture's glazed ceramic surface. His theory was that the presence of this target would cause patrons to be much more accurate in their use of the facilities. The result? Dramatically cleaner facilities and a 20 percent reduction in cleaning costs. A national newspaper in the Netherlands rated the Schiphol facilities first on a list of clean restrooms.

The Relationship between Optimal Input Choice and Long-Run Costs

Given sufficient time to adjust, the firm can always buy the cost-minimizing input bundle that corresponds to any particular output level and relative input prices. To see how the firm's costs vary with output in the long run, we need only compare the costs of the respective optimal input bundles.

The curve labelled *EE* in Figure 10-15 shows the firm's ***output expansion path***. It is the set of cost-minimizing input bundles when the input price ratio is fixed at w/r. Thus, when the price of K is r and the price of L is w, the cheapest way to produce Q_1 units of output is to use the input bundle S, which contains K_1^* units of K, L_1^* units of L, and costs TC_1. The bundle S is therefore one point on the output expansion path. In like fashion, the output level Q_2 is associated with bundle T, which has a

Output expansion path
The locus of tangencies (minimum-cost input combinations) traced out by an isocost line of given slope as it shifts outward into the isoquant map for a production process.

FIGURE 10-15

The Long-Run Output Expansion Path
With fixed input prices r and w, bundles S, T, U, and others along the locus *EE* represent the least costly ways of producing the corresponding levels of output.

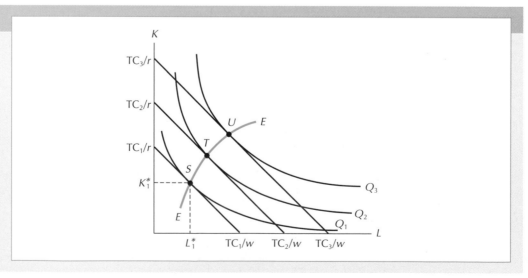

---

[14]This example is based on Stefan Verhagen, "Fly in the Pot," *Cornell Business*, April 21, 1992.

total cost of TC_2; Q_3 is associated with U, which costs TC_3; and so on. In the theory of firm behaviour, the long-run expansion path is the analogue to the income-consumption curve in the theory of the consumer.

To go from the long-run expansion path to the long-run total cost curve, we simply plot the relevant quantity-cost pairs from Figure 10-15. Thus, the output level Q_1 corresponds to a long-run total cost of TC_1, Q_2 to TC_2, and so on. The result is the curve labelled LTC in the top panel in Figure 10-16. In the long run there is no need to distinguish among total, fixed, and variable costs, since all costs are variable.

The LTC curve will always pass through the origin because in the long run the firm can liquidate all of its inputs. If the firm elects to produce no output, it need not retain, or pay for, the services of any of its inputs. The shape of the LTC curve shown in the top panel looks very much like that of the short-run total cost curve shown in Figure 10-2. But this need not always be the case, as we will presently see. For the moment, though, let us take the shape of the LTC curve in the top panel in Figure 10-16 as given and ask what it implies for the long-run average and marginal cost curves.

Analogously to the short-run case, long-run marginal cost (LMC) is the slope of the long-run total cost curve:

$$LMC_Q = \frac{\Delta LTC_Q}{\Delta Q}. \qquad (10.23)$$

In words, LMC is the cost to the firm, in the long run, of expanding its output by one unit.

Long-run average cost (LAC) is the ratio of long-run total cost to output:

$$LAC_Q = \frac{LTC_Q}{Q} \qquad (10.24)$$

Again, there is no need to discuss the distinctions among average total, fixed, and variable costs, since all long-run costs are variable.

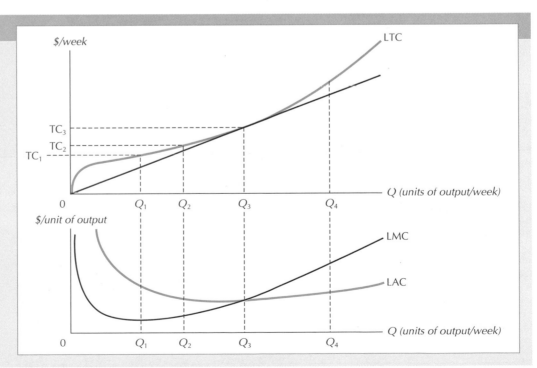

FIGURE 10-16

The Long-Run Total, Average, and Marginal Cost Curves
In the long run, the firm always has the option of ceasing operations and ridding itself of all its inputs. This means that the long-run total cost curve (top panel) will always pass through the origin. The long-run average and long-run marginal cost curves (bottom panel) are derived from the long-run total cost curves in a manner completely analogous to the short-run case.

The bottom panel in Figure 10-16 shows the LAC and LMC curves that correspond to the LTC curve shown in the top panel. The slope of the LTC curve is diminishing up to the output level Q_1 and increasing thereafter, which means that the LMC curve takes its minimum value at Q_1. The slope of LTC and the slope of the ray to LTC are the same at Q_3, which means that LAC and LMC intersect at that level of output. And again as before, the traditional average-marginal relationship holds: LAC is declining whenever LMC lies below it, and rising whenever LMC lies above it.

For a constant returns to scale production function with constant input prices, doubling output exactly doubles costs. Tripling all inputs triples output and triples costs, and so on. For the case of constant returns to scale, long-run total costs are thus exactly proportional to output. As shown in Figure 10-17a, the LTC curve for a production function with constant returns to scale is a straight line through the origin. Because the slope of LTC is constant, the associated LMC curve is a horizontal line, and coincides with the LAC curve (Figure 10-17b).

When the production function has decreasing returns to scale, a given proportional increase in output requires a greater proportional increase in all inputs and hence, with constant input prices, a greater proportional increase in costs. The LTC, LMC, and LAC curves for a production function with decreasing returns to scale are shown in Figure 10-18. For the particular LTC curve shown in Figure 10-18a, the

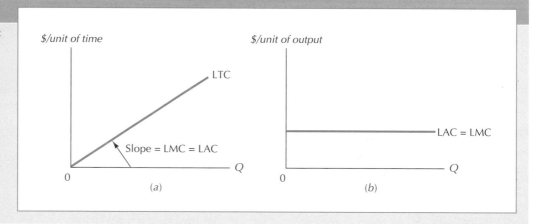

FIGURE 10-17

The LTC, LMC, and LAC Curves with Constant Returns to Scale
(a) With constant returns, long-run total cost is strictly proportional to output. (b) Long-run marginal cost is constant and equal to long-run average cost.

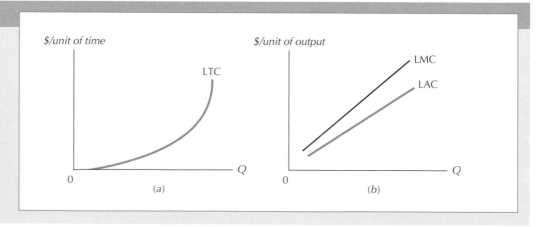

FIGURE 10-18

The LTC, LAC, and LMC Curves for a Production Process with Decreasing Returns to Scale
Under decreasing returns, output grows less than in proportion to the growth in inputs, which means that total cost grows more than in proportion to growth in output.

FIGURE 10-19

The LTC, LAC, and LMC Curves for a Production Process with Increasing Returns to Scale
With increasing returns, the large-scale firm has lower average and marginal costs than the smaller-scale firm.

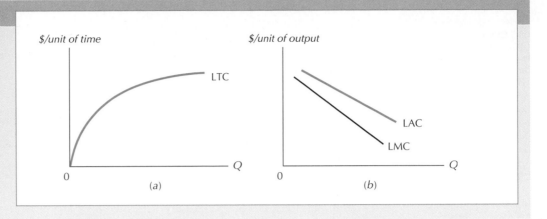

associated LAC and LMC curves happen to be linear (Figure 10-18*b*), but this need not always happen. The general property of the decreasing returns case is that it gives rise to an upward-curving LTC curve, and upward-sloping LAC and LMC curves. Note yet another application of the average-marginal relationship: the fact that LMC exceeds LAC ensures that LAC must rise with output.

Consider, finally, the case of increasing returns to scale. Here, output grows more than in proportion to the increase in inputs. In consequence, again assuming constant input prices, long-run total cost rises less than in proportion to increases in output, as shown in Figure 10-17*a*. The accompanying LAC and LMC curves are shown in Figure 10-17*b*. The distinguishing feature of the LAC and LMC curves under increasing returns to scale is not the linear form shown in this particular example, but the fact that they are downward sloping.

The production processes whose long-run cost curves are pictured in Figure 10-17 to Figure 10-19 are "pure cases," exhibiting constant, decreasing, and increasing returns to scale, respectively, over their entire ranges of output. As discussed in Chapter 9, however, the degree of returns to scale of a production function need not be the same over the whole range of output.

10.5 LONG-RUN COSTS AND THE STRUCTURE OF INDUSTRY

As noted in the preview to this chapter, long-run costs are important because of their effect on the structure of industry. A detailed elaboration of this role will be the subject of the coming chapters. Here, a brief overview of the key issues will help set the stage for that discussion.

When, as in Figure 10-20*a*, there are declining long-run average costs throughout, the tendency will be for a single firm to serve the market. If two firms attempted to serve such a market, with each producing only part of the total output sold, each would have higher average costs than if one of them alone served the market. The tendency in such a market will be for the firm that happens to grow larger to have a cost advantage that enables it to eliminate its rival. Markets characterized by declining long-run average cost curves are for this reason often referred to as **natural monopolies**.

Natural monopoly
An industry whose market output is produced at the lowest cost when production is concentrated in the hands of a single firm.

Consider now the LAC curve shown in Figure 10-20*b*. The minimum point on this curve occurs at the output level Q_0. At that output level, the firm achieves its lowest possible unit cost of production. The output level Q_0 may be called the *minimum efficient scale:* the level of production required for LAC to reach its minimum level. If Q_0 constitutes

FIGURE 10-20

LAC Curves Characteristic of Highly Concentrated Industrial Structures
(a) LAC curves that slope continuously downward generate natural monopolies. Unit costs are lowest when one firm serves the market. *(b)* U-shaped LAC curves with minima at a substantial share of total market output generate markets served by a few firms.

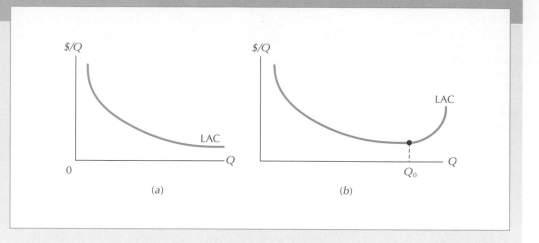

a substantial share of industry output—more than, say, 20 percent—the industry will tend to be dominated by a small handful of firms. As in the natural monopoly case, a large number of small firms would be unlikely to survive in such a market, since each would have much higher average costs than larger firms. In contrast to the natural monopoly case, however, the upturn in the LAC beyond Q_0 will make it difficult for a single firm to serve the entire market. Markets served by firms with LACs like the one in Figure 10-20*b* are likely to be "highly concentrated," which means that a small number of firms will tend to account for the lion's share of all output sold.

The long-run average cost curve associated with a market served by many firms is likely to take one of the three forms shown in Figure 10-21. If Q_0, the minimum point on the U-shaped average cost curve in panel *a*, constitutes only a small fraction of total industry output, we expect to see an industry populated by numerous firms, each of which produces only a small percentage of total industry output. Small size is also not a disadvantage when the production process is one that gives rise to a horizontal LAC curve like the one shown in panel *b*. For such processes, all firms—large or small— have the same unit costs of production. For the upward-sloping LAC curve shown in panel *c* in Figure 10-21, small size is not only compatible with survival in the market-place but positively required, since large firms will always have higher average costs than smaller ones. As a practical matter, however, it is very unlikely that there could

FIGURE 10-21

LAC Curves Characteristic of Unconcentrated Industry Structures
For survival in any market, a firm must have the lowest possible unit costs. If the minimum point of a U-shaped LAC (Q_0 in *a*) occurs at a small fraction of market output, or if LAC is everywhere flat or rising (*b* and *c*, respectively), then small size and survival are compatible.

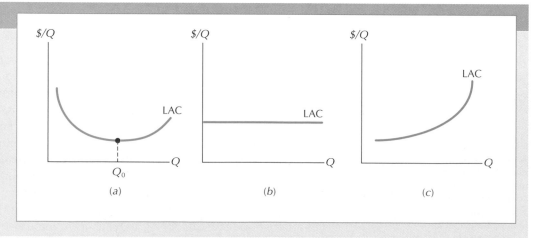

ever be an LAC curve that is upward sloping even at extremely small levels of output. (Imagine, for example, the unit costs of a firm that tried to produce one gram of sugar.)

The relationship between market structure and the shape of the long-run average cost curve derives from the fact that, in the face of competition, market survival requires firms to have the lowest unit costs possible under existing production technology. Whether that happens at low or high levels of output depends entirely on the shape of the LAC curve.

10.6 THE RELATIONSHIP BETWEEN LONG-RUN AND SHORT-RUN COST CURVES

One way of thinking of the LAC curve is as an "envelope" of all the short-run average cost (SAC) curves. Suppose the SAC curves that correspond to 10,000 different levels of K were drawn in a diagram like Figure 10-22. If we then took a string and moulded it to the outer contour of these SAC curves, it would trace out the shape of the LAC curve. In Figure 10-22, note that for the output level at which a given SAC is tangent to the LAC, the long-run marginal cost (LMC) of producing that level of output is the same as the short-run marginal cost (SMC). Thus, $LMC(Q_1) = SMC(Q_1)$, $LMC(Q_2) = SMC(Q_2)$, and $LMC(Q_3) = SMC(Q_3)$ (see footnote 15). Note also that each point along a given SAC curve, except for the tangency point, lies above the corresponding point on the LAC curve. Note, finally, that at the minimum point on the LAC curve in Figure 10-22 ($Q = Q_2$), the long-run and short-run marginal and average costs all take exactly the same value.

Some intuition about the SAC-LAC relationship for a given SAC curve is afforded by noting that to the left of the SAC-LAC tangency, the firm has "too much" capital, with the result that its fixed costs are higher than necessary; and that to the right of the tangency, the firm has "too little" capital, so that diminishing marginal productivity of labour drives its costs up. Only at the tangency point does the firm have the optimal quantities of both labour and capital for producing the corresponding level of output.

FIGURE 10-22

The Family of Cost Curves Associated with a U-Shaped LAC
The LAC curve is the "outer envelope" of the SAC curves. LMC = SMC at the Q value for which the SAC is tangent to the LAC. At the minimum point on the LAC, LMC = SMC = SAC = LAC. All marginal cost curves, short run and long run, intersect their corresponding average cost curves at their minimum points.

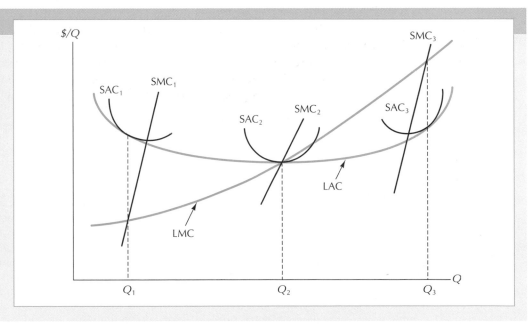

---

[15]These relationships are developed in greater detail in Appendix 10A.

- Of all the topics covered in an intermediate microeconomics text, students usually find the material on cost curves by far the most difficult to digest. And for good reason, since the sheer volume of specific concepts can easily seem overwhelming at first encounter. It is important to bear in mind, therefore, that all the various cost curves can be derived from the underlying production relationships in a very simple and straightforward manner.

- Short-run cost curves, for example, all follow directly from the short-run production function. All short-run production functions we have discussed involved one fixed factor and one variable factor, but the theory would be exactly the same in the case of more than one fixed or variable input. Short-run total costs are decomposed into fixed and variable costs, which correspond, respectively, to payments to the fixed and variable factors of production. Because of the law of diminishing returns, beyond some point we require ever larger increments of the variable input to produce an extra unit of output. The result is that short-run marginal cost, which is the slope of the short-run total cost curve, is increasing with output in the region of diminishing returns. Diminishing returns are also responsible for the fact that short-run average total and average variable cost curves—which are, respectively, the slopes of the rays to the short-run total and variable cost curves—eventually rise with output. Average fixed costs always take the form of a rectangular hyperbola, approaching infinity as output shrinks toward zero, and falling toward zero as output grows increasingly large.

- The problem of allocating a given production quota to two different production facilities is similar to the problem of allocating an available input across two different facilities. In the latter case, the goal is to maximize the amount of output that can be produced with a given amount of input. In the former, it is to produce a given level of output at the lowest total cost. The solution is to allocate the production quota so that the marginal cost is the same in each production process. This solution does not require that average costs be the same in each process and, in practice, they often differ substantially.

- The optimal input bundle for producing a given output level in the long run will depend on the relative prices of the factors of production. These relative prices determine the slope of the isocost line, which is the locus of input bundles that can be purchased for a given total cost. The optimal input bundle will be the one that lies at the point of tangency between an isocost line and the desired isoquant. At the cost-minimizing point, with perfectly divisible inputs and no corner solutions, the ratio of the marginal product of an input to its price will be the same for every input. Put another way, the extra output obtained from the last dollar spent on one input must be the same as the extra output obtained from the last dollar spent on any other input. Still another way of stating the minimum-cost condition is that the marginal rate of technical substitution at the optimizing bundle must be the same as the absolute value of the slope of the isocost line.

- These properties of production at minimum cost help us understand why methods of production often differ sharply when relative factor prices differ sharply. We saw, for example, that it helps explain why developing countries often use labour-intensive techniques while their industrial counterparts choose much more capital-intensive ones, and why labour unions might lobby on behalf of increased minimum wages, even though virtually all of their members earn more than the minimum wage to begin with.

- For a given level of output, long-run total costs can never be larger than short-run total costs for the simple reason that we have the opportunity to adjust all of our inputs in the long run, only some of them in the short run. The slope of the long-run average cost curve is a direct reflection of the degree of returns to scale in production. With constant input prices, when there are increasing returns, LAC declines with output. With decreasing returns, in contrast, LAC rises with output. And finally, constant returns in production give rise to a horizontal LAC function. A U-shaped LAC curve is one that corresponds to a production process that exhibits first increasing, then constant, and finally decreasing returns to scale. No matter what its shape, the LAC curve will always be an envelope of the corresponding family of SAC curves, each of which will be tangent to the LAC at one and only one point. At the output levels that correspond to these points of tangency, LMC and the corresponding SMC will be the same.

- The relationship between market structure and long-run costs derives from the fact that survival in the marketplace requires firms to have the lowest costs possible with available production technologies. If the LAC curve is downward sloping, lowest costs occur when only one firm serves the market. If the LAC curve is U-shaped and its minimum point occurs at a quantity that corresponds to a substantial share of total market output, the lowest costs will occur when only a few firms serve the market. In contrast, if the minimum point on a U-shaped LAC curve corresponds to only a small fraction of total industry output, the market is likely to be served by many competing firms. The same will be true when the LAC curve is either horizontal or upward sloping.

- Appendix 10A, "Mathematical Extensions of the Theory of Costs," considers the relationship between long-run and short-run costs in greater detail. It also develops the calculus approach to cost minimization, and shows how to use production functions to derive cost functions.

QUESTIONS FOR REVIEW

1. What is the relationship between the "law of diminishing returns" (or eventually diminishing marginal productivity of the variable input) and the curvature of the variable cost curve?
2. What is the relationship between the law of diminishing returns and the slope of the short-run marginal cost curve?
3. In which production process is fixed cost likely to be a larger percentage of short-run total costs, book publishing or landscape gardening?

4. Why does the short-run MC curve cut both the ATC and AVC curves at their minimum points?
5. If the LAC curve is rising beyond some point and input prices are constant, what can we say about the degree of returns to scale in production?
6. Assuming no indivisibilities or corner solutions, why should the production of a fixed output be allocated between two production activities so that the marginal cost is the same in each?

PROBLEMS

1. The Preservation Embalming Company's cost data have been partially entered in the table below. Following the sudden and unexpected death of the company's accountant, you are called on to fill in the missing entries. Columns 2–4 are in \$/day, and columns 5–8 are in \$/body.

Bodies embalmed	Total cost	Fixed cost	Variable cost	ATC	AVC	AFC	MC
0	24			—	—	—	
							16
1							
2			50				
3	108						
							52
4							
5					39.2		
6				47			

2. Sketch the short-run TC, VC, FC, ATC, AVC, AFC, and MC curves for the production function

$$Q = 3KL,$$

where K is fixed at 2 units in the short run, with $r = $3/capital-unit$ and $w = $2/labour-unit$.

3. With constant input prices, when the average product of labour is the same as the marginal product of labour, how will marginal cost compare with average variable cost?

4. A firm has access to two production processes with the following marginal cost curves: $MC_1 = .4Q_1$ and $MC_2 = 2 + .2Q_2$, where both MCs are in \$/unit of output.
   a. If it wants to produce 8 units of output, how much should it produce with each process?
   b. If it wants to produce 4 units of output?

5. A firm uses two inputs, K and L, in its production process and finds that no matter how much output it produces or how input prices vary, it always minimizes its costs by buying only one or the other of the two inputs. Draw this firm's isoquant map.

6. A firm finds that no matter how much output it produces and no matter how input prices vary, it always minimizes its costs by buying half as many units of capital as of labour. Draw this firm's isoquant map.

7. A firm purchases capital and labour in competitive markets at prices of $r = \$6$/machine-hour and $w = \$4$/labour-hour, respectively. With the firm's current input mix, the marginal product of capital is 12kg/machine-hour and the marginal product of labour is 18kg/labour-hour. Is this firm minimizing its costs? If so, explain how you know. If not, explain what the firm ought to do.

8. A firm has a production function $Q = F(K, L)$ with constant returns to scale. Input prices are $r = \$2$/$K$-unit and $w = \$1$/$L$-unit. The output-expansion path for this production function at these input prices is a straight line through the origin. When it produces 5 units of output, it uses 2 units of K and 3 units of L. How much K and L will it use when its long-run total cost is equal to $70, how much will Q be, and what is its LAC?

9. A firm with the production function $Q = F(K, L)$ is producing an output level Q^* at minimum cost in the long run. At Q^*, how will its short-run marginal cost when K is fixed compare with its short-run marginal cost when L is fixed?

10. A firm employs a production function $Q = F(K, L)$ for which only two values of K are possible, K_1 and K_2. Its SAC curve when $K = K_1$ is given by $SAC_1 = Q^2 - 4Q + 6$. The corresponding curve for $K = K_2$ is $SAC_2 = Q^2 - 8Q + 18$. What is this firm's LAC curve? At what value of Q will $SAC_1 = SAC_2$?

11. If a firm's LMC curve lies above its SMC curve at a given level of output, what will be the relationship between its SAC and LAC curves at that output level? If LMC lies *below* SMC, what is the relationship between SAC and LAC?

**12. A firm has a long-run total cost function:

$$LTC(Q) = Q^3 - 20Q^2 + 220Q.$$

Derive expressions for long-run average cost and marginal cost, and sketch these curves.

**13. For the total cost function

$$TC(Q) = Q^2 + 10,$$

sketch ATC, AVC, AFC, and MC.

**14. Consolidated Rip-off Artist Productions has followed up its success with Ridiculous Putty, Mr. Tomatohead, and the Tickle-Me-Elmer talking plush toy by producing Megapokéyugibots (MPYBs): "They're not just a toy, they're a way of life!" The firm can produce MPYBs using two processes, defined by the following two total cost functions, where TC^A and TC^B are in dollars per period and Q^A and Q^B are in MPYBs per period:

Process A: $TC^A = 20 + 2Q^A + .5(Q^A)^2$
Process B: $TC^B = 40 + 7Q^B + .25(Q^B)^2$

a. Give the formulas for MC^A and MC^B. Also calculate the formula for MC^T as a function of $Q^T = Q^A + Q^B$, for $Q^T \geq 5$.

b. When the firm efficiently produces $Q^T = 11$ MPYBs per period, give the values for MC^T, Q^A, Q^B, ATC^A, ATC^B, and ATC^T.

c. Repeat 14b when $Q^T = 32$ units. Which process is used more intensively when $Q^T = 11$ and which is used more intensively when $Q^T = 32$ units? Explain why.

**15. Soundscape Enterprises manufactures Sonoblast, a device that produces a high-pitched reminder to telemarketers that they have once again disturbed you just when you were sitting down to dinner. The production function for Sonoblasts is given by the formula $Q = 2KL^{1/2}$, where Q is in units of output per period, K is in machine-weeks per period, and L is in labour-weeks per period. The machine rental rate r is \$512 per machine-week and the wage rate w is \$128 per labour-week. In the short run, K is fixed at 4 machine-weeks per period.

a. Give the formulas for the short-run production function and the marginal product of labour (MP_L) function.

b. Express variable cost (VC), total cost (TC), and marginal cost (MC) as functions of L *and* as functions of Q; and average variable cost (AVC), average fixed cost (AFC) and average total cost (ATC) as functions of Q.

c. At what level of Q is ATC minimized? What are the values of ATC and of MC at this level of output?

d. If K is increased to a fixed 16 units, at what level of Q is ATC minimized, and what are the values of ATC and of MC at this level of output?

e. In the long run, with all inputs variable, what is the optimal K/L ratio with input prices unchanged? How many units of L and of K would be required to produce the levels of output in 15c and in 15d and what is the average cost of producing Sonoblasts in each case? Explain the relation between your results here and those for 15c and 15d.

ANSWERS TO IN-CHAPTER EXERCISES

10-1. The variable cost curve is the same as before; the FC and TC curves are shifted upward by 8 units. (See the following graph.)

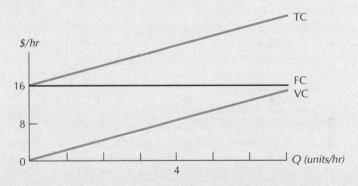

10-2. The vertical distance between the ATC and AVC curves is AFC. So we have $\text{ATC}_{10} - \text{AVC}_{10}$ $= \text{AFC}_{10} = \text{FC}/10 = 20/10 = \$2/\text{unit}$.

10-3. Equating marginal costs, we have $12Q^A = 4Q^B$. Substituting $Q^B = 12 - Q^A$ yields $12Q^A = 48 - 4Q^A$, which solves for $Q^A = 3$. $Q^B = 12 - 3 = 9$ takes care of remaining output, and at these output levels, marginal cost in both plants will be \$36/unit of output.

10-4. When marginal product lies above average product, marginal cost lies below average variable cost. (See Figure 10-9.)

10-5.

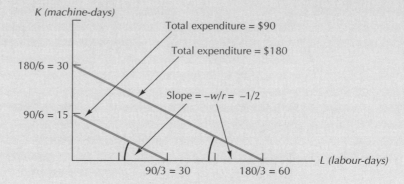

10-6. To produce 20 units of output efficiently, we will need $L = K = 20$. As $r = \$10/K$-unit and $w = \$5/L$-unit, costs are

$$C = 10K + 5L = 200 + 100 = \$300,$$

which may be rewritten as $K = 30 - \frac{1}{2}L$ in slope-intercept form. When the wage rises to $w = \$20/L$-unit, keeping costs at $C = \$300$ requires that we find the point at which $K = L$ on the new isocost curve

$$C' = 10K + 20L = 300,$$

which may be rewritten as $K = 30 - 2L$ in slope-intercept form. Setting $K = L$, we have

$10K + 20L = 300 \Rightarrow 10L + 20L = 300 \Rightarrow 30L = 300 \Rightarrow L = 10$ labour-units.

Thus, $L = K = 10$ and we produce $Q = 10$ units of output.

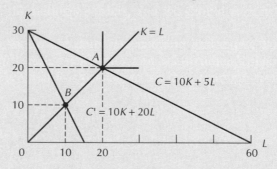

10-7. To produce 20 units of output, we need $L = 20$ or $K = 20$. Since $r = 10$ and $w = 5$, costs are

$$C = \min\{10K, 5L\} = \min\{200, 100\} = \$100.$$

When the wage rises to $w = \$20/L$-unit, keeping costs at $C = \$100$ implies that

$$Q = \max\left\{\frac{100}{r}, \frac{100}{w}\right\} = \max\{10,5\} = 10 \text{ units.}$$

Thus, we use no labour ($L = 0$), all capital ($K = 10$), and produce $Q = 10$ units.

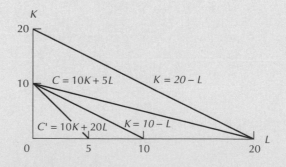

Appendix 10A

MATHEMATICAL EXTENSIONS OF THE THEORY OF COSTS

This appendix discusses some extensions of the concepts developed in Chapter 10.

10A.1 THE RELATIONSHIP BETWEEN LONG-RUN AND SHORT-RUN COST CURVES

Let us consider first in greater detail the relationship between long- and short-run total costs, for a perfectly competitive firm acting as a buyer in input markets and facing a constant wage rate (w) and rental rate on capital (r).

Recall that the LTC curve is generated by plotting the Q value for a given isoquant against the corresponding total cost level for the isocost line tangent to that isoquant. As we saw in Figures 10-11, 10-12, and 10-15, with given values for w and r, the tangency condition MRTS $= w/r$ determines the *cost-minimizing* combination of K and L to produce the quantity of output Q associated with any particular isoquant. Thus, for example, in Figure 10A-1, $Q = 1$ is associated with a long-run total cost of LTC_1, $Q = 2$ with LTC_2, and so on.

When K is variable, as it and all other factors are in the long run, the expansion path is given by the line OV. Now suppose, however, that K is fixed at K_2^*, the level that is optimal for the production $Q = 2$. The short-run expansion path will then be the horizontal line through the point $(0, K_2^*)$, which includes the input bundles X, T, and Z. The short-run total cost of producing a given level of output—say, $Q = 1$—is simply the total cost associated with the isocost line that passes through the intersection of the short-run expansion path and the $Q = 1$ isoquant (point X in Figure 10A-1), namely, STC_1.

Note in Figure 10A-1 that short- and long-run total costs take the same value for $Q = 2$, the output level for which the short- and long-run expansion paths cross. For all other output levels, the isocost line that passes through the intersection of the corresponding isoquant and the short-run expansion path will lie above the isocost line that is tangent to the isoquant. Thus, for all output levels other than $Q = 2$, short-run total cost will be higher than long-run total cost.

The short- and long-run total cost curves that correspond to the isoquant map of Figure 10A-1 are shown in Figure 10A-2. Note in Figure 10A-1 that the closer output is to $Q = 2$, the smaller the difference will be between long-run and short-run total cost. This property is reflected in

The Short-Run and Long-Run Expansion Paths
The long-run expansion path is the line OV. With K fixed at K_2^*, the short-run expansion path is a horizontal line through the point $(0, K_2^*)$. Because K_2^* is the optimal amount of K for producing 2 units of output, the long-run and short-run expansion paths intersect at T. The short-run total cost of producing a given level of output is the cost associated with the isocost line that passes through the intersection of the relevant isoquant and the short-run expansion path. Thus, for example, STC_3 is the short-run total cost of producing 3 units of output, at Z.

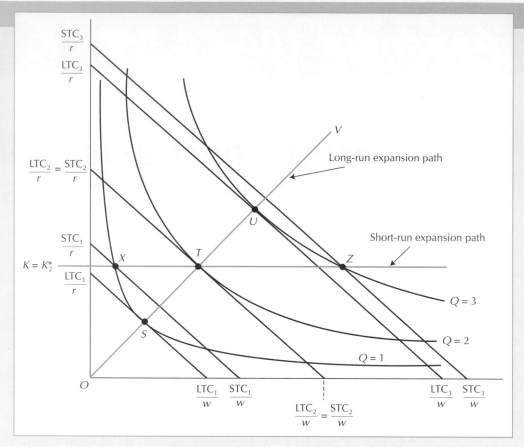

Figure 10A-2 by the fact that the STC curve is tangent to the LTC curve at $Q = 2$: the closer Q is to 2, the closer STC_Q is to $STC_2 = LTC_2$. Note also in Figure 10A-2 that the STC curve intersects the vertical axis at rK_2^*, the fixed cost associated with K_2^* units of K.

The production process whose isoquant map is shown in Figure 10A-1 happens to be one with constant returns to scale. Accordingly, since w and r are constant, its long-run average and marginal cost curves will be the same horizontal line. The height of this line is determined by the slope of the LTC curve in Figure 10A-2. The associated SAC curve will be U-shaped and tangent to the LAC curve at $Q = 2$, as shown in Figure 10A-3.

There are short-run cost curves not just for $K = K_2^*$, but for every other level of the fixed input as well. For example, the short-run average cost curve when K is fixed at K_3^* (the optimal amount of K for producing $Q = 3$) is shown in Figure 10A-3 as the curve labelled $SAC_{K=K_3^*}$. Like the SAC curve associated with K_2^*, it too is U-shaped, and is tangent to the LAC curve at $Q = 3$. The SAC curves will in general be U-shaped and tangent to the LAC curve at the output level for which the level of the fixed input happens to be optimal. In the present example, the SMC and SAVC curves for $K = K_3^*$ lie everywhere below the corresponding curves for $K = K_2^*$, because the MP_L function *increases* as K increases. Hence SMC ($= w/MP_L$) decreases as K increases. Since (with constant returns to scale and w and r constant) $K_3^* = 1.5\ K_2^*$, average fixed costs at the cost-minimizing points will be equal: $AB\ (= rK_2^*/2) = CD\ (= rK_3^*/3)$. To the left of point E, $SAC_{K=K_2^*}$ (the short-run average cost curve for $K = K_2^*$) is lower than $SAC_{K=K_3^*}$ (the short-run average cost curve for $K = K_3^*$). To the right of E, $SAC_{K=K_3^*} < SAC_{K=K_2^*}$. At E, the lower average fixed costs with $K = K_2^*$ are exactly offset by the lower average variable costs with $K = K_3^*$.

A similar relationship between SAC and LAC exists in the case of production processes that give rise to U-shaped LAC curves. For such a process, the LAC curve and three of its associated SAC curves are shown in Figure 10A-4. When the LAC curve is U-shaped, note that the tangencies between it and the associated SAC curves do not in general occur at the minimum points on the

The LTC and STC Curves Associated with the Isoquant Map in Figure 10A-1
As Q approaches 2, the level of output for which the fixed factor is at its optimal level, STC_Q approaches LTC_Q. The two curves are tangent at $Q = 2$.

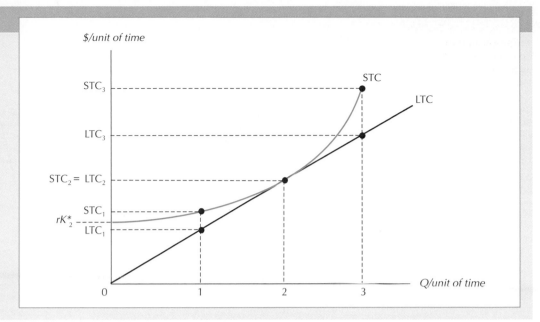

SAC, SAVC, and SMC Curves Associated with Figure 10A-1

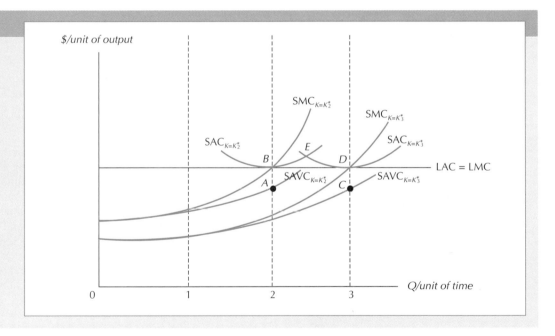

SAC curves. The lone exception is the SAC curve that is tangent to the minimum point of the U-shaped LAC (SAC_2 in Figure 10A-4). On the downward-sloping portion of the LAC curve, the tangencies will lie to the left of the minimum points of the corresponding SAC curves; and on the upward-sloping portion of the LAC curve, the tangencies will lie to the right of the minimum points.

In the text, we noted that one way of thinking of the LAC curve is as an "envelope" of all the SAC curves, like the one shown in Figure 10A-4. At the output level at which a given SAC is tangent to the LAC, the long-run marginal cost (LMC) of producing that level of output is the same as the short-run marginal cost (SMC). To see why this is so, recall that the tangency point represents the quantity level that is optimal for the fixed factor level that corresponds to the particular SAC curve. If we change output by a very small amount in the short run—by either increasing or reducing the amount of the variable input—we will end up with an input mix that

**The Family of Cost
Curves Associated
with a U-Shaped LAC**
The LAC curve is the
"outer envelope" of the
SAC curves. LMC =
SMC at the Q value for
which the SAC is tan-
gent to the LAC. At the
minimum point on the
LAC, LMC = SMC =
SAC = LAC.

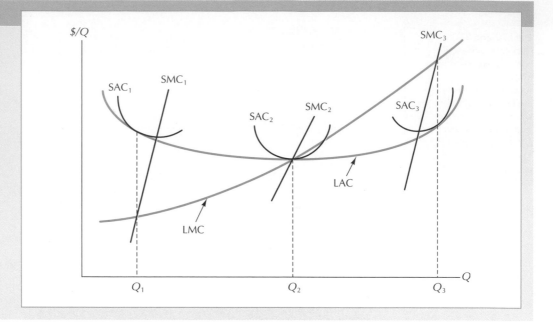

is only marginally different from the optimal one, and whose cost is therefore approximately the same as that of the optimal mix. Accordingly, for output levels very near the relevant tangency point, SMC and LMC are approximately the same.

Note also, as Figure 10A-4 indicates, that the SMC curves will always cut the LMC curve from below. The reason is implicit in our discussion of why LMC and SMC are nearly the same in a neighbourhood of the tangency points. Starting at a tangency point—say, at Q_1 in Figure 10A-4—suppose we want to produce an extra unit of output in the short run. To do so, we will have to move from an input mix that is optimal to one that contains slightly more L and slightly less K than would be optimal for producing $Q_1 + 1$ in the long run. So the cost of that extra unit will be higher in the short run than in the long run, which is another way of saying $\text{SMC}_{Q_1+1} > \text{LMC}_{Q_1+1}$.

Now suppose that we start at Q_1 and want to produce one unit of output less than before. To do so, we will have to move to an input bundle that contains less L and more K than would be optimal for producing $Q_1 - 1$. In consequence, our cost savings will be smaller in the short run than they would be in the long run, when we are free to adjust both L and K. This tells us that $\text{LMC}_{Q_1-1} > \text{SMC}_{Q_1-1}$. To say that LMC exceeds SMC whenever output is less than Q_1, but is less than SMC when output is greater than Q_1, is the same thing as saying that at Q_1, the slope of the LMC curve is less than that of the SMC curve.[1] It is still true, however, that both to the right and to the left of Q_1, SAC_1 is greater than LAC, because AFC_1 must be added to AVC_1 to equal SAC_1, whereas by definition, for LAC fixed costs are zero.

EXERCISE 10A-1

Consider a production function $Q = F(K, L)$ for which only two values of K are possible. These two values of K give rise to the SAC curves shown in the diagram. What is the LAC curve for this firm?

---

[1]The SMC curve must cut the LMC curve from below. Equivalently, the slope of the SMC curve must be *greater* than that of the LMC curve at their intersection point. Hence, in Figure 10A-4, the SMC curve is *steeper* than the LMC curve. The *same* condition means that if the LMC and SMC curves are both *downward* sloping over some range of Q, then at their intersection the SMC curve will be *flatter* than the LMC curve. With *negatively* sloped curves, the slope of the *flatter* curve has the higher value. In calculus terms, the condition is that $d^2\text{LTC}/dQ^2 < d^2\text{STC}/dQ^2$.

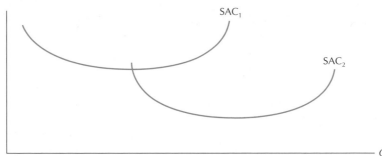

10A.2 THE CALCULUS APPROACH TO COST MINIMIZATION

Using the Lagrangean technique discussed in Appendix 3A, we can show that the equality of MP/P ratios (Equation 10.22 in Chapter 10) emerges as a necessary condition for the following cost-minimization problem:

$$\min_{K,\,L} P_K K + P_L L \text{ subject to } F(K, L) = Q_0. \tag{10A.1}$$

To find the values of K and L that minimize the cost of producing Q_0, we first form the Lagrangean expression:

$$\mathcal{L} = P_K K + P_L L + \lambda[F(K, L) - Q_0]. \tag{10A.2}$$

The first-order conditions for a minimum are given by

$$\frac{\partial \mathcal{L}}{\partial K} = P_K + \frac{\lambda \partial F}{\partial K} = 0, \tag{10A.3}$$

$$\frac{\partial \mathcal{L}}{\partial L} = P_L + \frac{\lambda \partial F}{\partial L} = 0, \tag{10A.4}$$

and

$$\frac{\partial \mathcal{L}}{\partial \lambda} = F(K, L) - Q_0 = 0. \tag{10A.5}$$

Using Equation 10A.3 and Equation 10A.4, eliminating λ and rearranging terms, we have

$$\frac{\partial F/\partial K}{P_K} \equiv \frac{MP_K}{P_K} = \frac{MP_L}{P_L} \equiv \frac{\partial F/\partial L}{P_L}, \tag{10A.6}$$

which is the result of Equation 10.21 in Chapter 10. (As an exercise, derive the same result by finding the first-order conditions for a maximum level of output subject to a cost limit of C.)

An alternative to the Lagrangean technique is to solve the production function constraint in Equation 10A.1 for K in terms of L, then substitute the result back into the expression for total cost. To illustrate this alternative approach, consider the following example.

EXAMPLE 10A-1

For the production function $Q = F(K, L) = \sqrt{K}\,\sqrt{L}$ with $P_K = 4$ and $P_L = 2$, find the values of K and L that minimize the cost of producing 2 units of output.

Our problem here is to minimize $4K + 2L$ subject to $F(K, L) = \sqrt{K}\,\sqrt{L} = 2$. Here the production function constraint is $Q = 2 = \sqrt{K}\,\sqrt{L}$, which yields $K = 4/L$. So our problem is to minimize $4(4/L) + 2L$ with respect to L. The first-order condition for a minimum is given by

$$\frac{d[(16/L) + 2L]}{dL} = 2 - \frac{16}{L^2} = 0, \tag{10A.7}$$

which yields $L = 2\sqrt{2}$. Substituting back into the production function constraint, we have $K = 4/(2\sqrt{2}) = \sqrt{2}$.

10A.3 FROM PRODUCTION FUNCTIONS TO COST FUNCTIONS

We normally want to express total cost, TC, as well as VC, ATC, AFC, AVC, and MC, as functions of Q, the level of *output*. Yet the simplest formula for total costs is as a function of *input* prices and quantities:

$$TC = rK + wL. \qquad (10A.8)$$

In this section, we outline a method for getting from Equation 10A.8 to short run and long-run cost functions in their standard form, using the relationships we have developed in Chapters 9 and 10.

For simplicity, in all of the examples that follow, we measure output Q in kilograms/ period, labour inputs L in labour-days/period, and capital inputs K in machine-days/ period, and w and r in dollars per labour-day and dollars per machine-day, respectively. We continue to assume that in the short run, K is the fixed input and L is the variable input.[2]

Although the details vary slightly, the same method applies in the short run and the long run:

Step 1: Express output Q as a function of L alone, and then compute L as a function of Q (the inverse function).

Step 2: Calculate total cost TC as a function of L alone, and then substitute Q for L in the TC function.

From the TC function, it is straightforward to calculate the corresponding average and marginal cost functions in terms of output, Q.

EXAMPLE 10A-2

With $K = K_0$, and w and r given, a firm's short-run production function has the form

$$Q = bL - aL^2, \text{ with } a > 0, b > 0.$$

Compute its TC, AFC, AVC, and MC equations as functions of Q.

We can rewrite the production function in the form

$$aL^2 - bL + Q = 0$$

and solve for L to get $L = [b - (b^2 - 4aQ)^{1/2}]/2a$. (Notice that we do not use the solution $L = [b + (b^2 - 4aQ)^{1/2}]/2a$. The reason is that Q reaches a maximum when $L = b/2a$, with $MP_L = 0$, and when L exceeds $b/2a$, MP_L is negative, so that no profit-maximizing firm will ever hire labour inputs in this region.)

Total cost is therefore $TC = rK_0 + wL = rK_0 + w[b - (b^2 - 4aQ)^{1/2}]/2a$. Fixed cost FC is simply rK_0, and hence $AFC = rK_0/Q$.

From the production function, we have $AP_L = Q/L = b - aL$ and $MP_L = dQ/dL = b - 2aL$.

Since $AVC = w/AP_L = w/(b - aL)$, substituting for L in this expression and simplifying, we have

$$AVC = 2w[b + (b^2 - 4aQ)^{1/2}]^{-1}.$$

Similarly, since $MC = w/MP_L = w/(b - 2aL)$, we have, substituting for L and simplifying,

$$MC = w(b^2 - 4aQ)^{-1/2}.$$

We now have TC, AFC, AVC, and MC as functions of output Q, rather than of L.

---

[2]The method in the text can readily be generalized to the case of two or more variable and fixed inputs. For example, suppose that $Q = F(L_1, L_2, K_1, K_2)$. L_1 and L_2 are two types of labour input, both variable in the short run, with wage rates w_1 and w_2, respectively. K_1 and K_2 are two types of capital input, both fixed at levels K_{10} and K_{20} in the short run, with rental rates r_1 and r_2, respectively. Then fixed costs $FC = r_1K_{10} + r_2K_{20}$, and we can write the short-run production function as $Q = F_0(L_1, L_2)$, where F_0 is the function F with $K_1 = K_{10}$ and $K_2 = K_{20}$. Since L_1 and L_2 are *both* variable, cost minimization in the short run for any level of output requires $MPL_1/w_1 = MPL_2/w_2$, as shown in Section 10A.2. Using this relation and the value calculated for FC, we can calculate short-run total cost (STC) as a function of Q, using the method of this section.

EXERCISE 10A-2

With $K = K_0 = 10$ machine-days per period, $w = \$40$/labour-day, and $r = \$5$/machine-day, a firm's short-run production function has the form

$$Q = 20L - L^2.$$

Compute its TC, AFC, AVC, and MC equations as functions of Q.

Cost Functions for Cobb-Douglas Production Functions

The general formula for Cobb-Douglas production functions is

$$Q = AL^aK^b. \tag{10A.9}$$

The properties of Cobb-Douglas functions have been described previously in Appendices 3A and 9A, and we have seen examples of them in Chapter 10 and in this Appendix. Table 10A-1 provides general formulas and examples for cost functions derived from Cobb-Douglas production functions, using the steps outlined at the beginning of this section.

Several points are worth noting in analyzing Table 10A-1. The first is probably the most important. The symbolic forms of the functions look fairly intimidating, but as the table shows, once all of the cancellation and simplification is completed, the specific examples take a much simpler form.

Consider, for example, the equations for long-run total cost (LTC) in row 5 of the table, which all simplify to the form LTC $= BQ^{1/(a + b)}$, where B is a constant. We have seen equations with this form before, i.e., the equations for constant-elasticity demand curves in Appendix 3A. The exponent, $1/(a + b)$, is the elasticity of long-run total cost with respect to output. With increasing returns to scale, as in Example 1, $(a + b)$ is greater than 1, and thus $1/(a + b)$ is less than 1. Hence a 1 percent increase in output will result in a less than 1 percent increase in LTC, resulting in a decreasing, or negatively sloped, LAC curve, as in Figure 10-19. In contrast, Example 3 has $(a + b) < 1$, or decreasing returns to scale, and hence $1/(a + b)$ is greater than 1, generating increasing LAC, as in Figure 10-18. Example 2, with $(a + b) = 1$, or constant returns to scale, has $1/(a + b) = 1$, generating constant LAC, as in Figure 10-17.

We can actually say even more than this about the elasticity exponent, $1/(a + b)$. The elasticity of long-run total cost with respect to output is $(\Delta LTC/LTC)/(\Delta Q/Q) = (\Delta LTC/\Delta Q)/(LTC/Q)$ $=$ LMC/LAC. That is, LMC $=$ LAC/$(a + b)$ at any value of Q. Comparing lines 7 and 6 in Table 10A-1, we find that LMC $= 2/3$ of LAC in Example 1, LMC $= 4/3$ of LAC in Example 3, and LMC $=$ LAC in Example 2. Thus, if we know the value of $(a + b)$ from the production function and the value of LMC at a particular value of Q, we can calculate the value of LAC, and vice versa.

Another feature of the examples that is worth recalling is that in all three cases, the value of the exponent a, the elasticity of output with respect to labour inputs, is twice that of b, the elasticity of output with respect to capital inputs. Hence, even though the three production functions are characterized by differing types of returns to scale, in all three cases, in the long run with both inputs variable, twice as much will be spent on labour inputs as on capital inputs, regardless of the wage rate and the rental rate on capital.

Another feature of importance is the coefficient A, which measures the productivity of the inputs and which hence also affects long-run average cost. For instance, in Example 1, we have $Q = .25LK^{1/2}$. Suppose that A increases from .25 to 2, that is, by a factor of 8. By how much will the cost per unit, the LAC, decrease? The answer may be a bit surprising. For any given quantity of L and K, output would increase to 8 times its initial level as a result of the increase in A. Because Example 1 is characterized by *increasing* returns to scale, the same increase in output would result from a *quadrupling* of inputs of both L and K, since $(a + b) = 3/2$, and $4^{3/2} = 8$. Hence LAC would fall to one-quarter of its initial level as a result of the eightfold increase in A. In Example 2, however, with *constant* returns to scale, LAC would fall to *one-eighth* of its initial level if A increased by a factor of 8 from .5 to 4. You should satisfy yourself that in Example 3, with an eightfold increase in A (from 8 to 64), LAC would decrease to *one-sixteenth* ($= 8^{-4/3}$) of its initial level.

The final consideration concerns the effect on costs of changes in input prices. In Example 1, if input prices dropped to $\$.75$/labour-day and $\$1.50$/machine-day, that is, to one-quarter their initial level, the change would have the same effect on LAC as the increase in A from .25 to 2, as you can readily verify.

	Symbolic form	Example 1	Example 2	Example 3
Long run (L, K both variable)				
1. Production function	$Q = AL^aK^b$	$Q = .25LK^{1/2}$ $w = 3, r = 6$	$Q = .5L^{2/3}K^{1/3}$ $w = 4, r = 16$	$Q = 8L^{1/2}K^{1/4}$ $w = 8, r = 4$
2.a. Efficiency condition	$MRTS = \dfrac{aK}{bL} = \dfrac{w}{r}$	$MRTS = \dfrac{2K}{L}$ $= \dfrac{3}{6} = \dfrac{1}{2}$	$MRTS = \dfrac{2K}{L}$ $= \dfrac{4}{16} = \dfrac{1}{4}$	$MRTS = \dfrac{2K}{L}$ $= \dfrac{8}{4} = 2$
2.b. Efficient K/L ratio	$K = \dfrac{b}{a}\dfrac{w}{r}L$	$K = L/4$	$K = L/8$	$K = L$
3. Q as a function of L*	$Q = k\,L^{a+b}$	$Q = (1/8)L^{3/2}$	$Q = L/4$	$Q = 8L^{3/4}$
4. L as a function of Q*	$L = k^{-\frac{1}{a+b}}\,Q^{\frac{1}{a+b}}$	$L = 4Q^{2/3}$	$L = 4Q$	$L = \dfrac{Q^{4/3}}{16}$
5. Long-run Total Cost*	$LTC = \dfrac{(a+b)w}{a}\,k^{-\frac{1}{a+b}}\,Q^{\frac{1}{a+b}}$	$LTC = 18Q^{2/3}$	$LTC = 24Q$	$LTC = \dfrac{3Q^{4/3}}{4}$
6. Long-run Average Cost*	$LAC = \dfrac{(a+b)w}{a}\,k^{-\frac{1}{a+b}}\,Q^{\frac{1-a-b}{a+b}}$	$LAC = 18Q^{-1/3}$	$LAC = 24$	$LAC = \dfrac{3Q^{1/3}}{4}$
7. Long-run Marginal Cost*	$LMC = \dfrac{w}{a}\,k^{-\frac{1}{a+b}}\,Q^{\frac{1-a-b}{a+b}}$	$LMC = 12Q^{-1/3}$	$LMC = 24$	$LMC = Q^{1/3}$
Short run ($K = K_0$)				
8. Production function	$Q = AK_0^bL^a$	$Q = .25L\,K_0^{1/2}$ $K_0 = 64$	$Q = .5L^{2/3}K_0^{1/3}$ $K_0 = 8$	$Q = 8L^{1/2}\,K_0^{1/4}$ $K_0 = 16$
9. L as a function of Q	$L = (AK_0^b)^{-\frac{1}{a}}\,Q^{\frac{1}{a}}$	$L = .5Q$	$L = Q^{3/2}$	$L = Q^2/256$
10. STC	$STC = rK_0 + w(AK_0^b)^{-\frac{1}{a}}\,Q^{\frac{1}{a}}$	$STC = 384 + 1.5Q$	$STC = 128 + 4Q^{3/2}$	$STC = 64 + Q^2/32$
11. SATC	$SATC = \dfrac{rK_0}{Q} + w(AK_0^b)^{-\frac{1}{a}}\,Q^{\frac{1}{a}}$	$SATC = 384/Q + 1.5$	$SATC = 128/Q + 4Q^{\frac{1}{2}}$	$SATC = \dfrac{64}{Q} + \dfrac{Q}{32}$
12. SAFC	$SAFC = rK_0/Q$	$SAFC = 384/Q$	$SAFC = 128/Q$	$SAFC = 64/Q$
13. SAVC	$SAVC = w(AK_0^b)^{-\frac{1}{a}}\,Q^{\frac{1-a}{a}}$	$SAVC = 1.5$	$SAVC = 4Q^{1/2}$	$SAVC = Q/32$
14. SMC	$SMC = \dfrac{w}{a}(AK_0^b)^{-\frac{1}{a}}\,Q^{\frac{1-a}{a}}$	$SMC = 1.5$	$SMC = 6Q^{1/2}$	$SMC = Q/16$

*$k = [A\left(\dfrac{b}{a}\dfrac{w}{r}\right)^b]$

EXERCISE 10A-3

In Examples 2 and 3 of Table 10A-1, what changes in w and r would cause the same change in long-run average cost as an eightfold increase in the productivity coefficient, A?

**1. A firm produces output with the production function
$$Q = \sqrt{K} \sqrt{L} = K^{1/2}L^{1/2},$$
where K and L denote its capital and labour inputs, respectively. If the price of labour is $1/unit and the price of capital is $4/unit, what quantities of capital and labour should it employ if its goal is to produce 2 units of output? (You will need either calculus or the results on Cobb-Douglas functions in Appendix 3A and Appendix 9A.)

2. Sketch LTC, LAC, and LMC curves for the production function given in Problem 1. Does this production function have constant, increasing, or decreasing returns to scale?

**3. Suppose that a firm has the following production function:
$$Q(K, L) = 2L\sqrt{K} = 2LK^{1/2}.$$
   a. If the price of labour is $2/unit and the price of capital is $4/unit, what is the optimal ratio of capital to labour?
   b. For an output level of $Q = 1000$ units, how much of each input will be used and what will be the average cost of a unit of output? What would your answers be for $Q = 8000$ units?

**4. A firm with the production function
$$Q(K, L) = 2\sqrt{KL} = 2K^{1/2}L^{1/2}$$
is currently utilizing 8 units of labour and 2 units of capital. If this is the optimal input mix, and if total costs are equal to $16, what are the prices of capital and labour?

**5. Primo Salt, Inc., manufactures salt, according to the following production function:
$$Q(K, L) = 2L^{1/2}K^{1/3},$$
where output Q is measured in tonnes, L in labour-days, and K in machine-days. With both L and K variable, it is maximizing its output for an expenditure of $800, hiring 64 labour-days with the rental rate on machines $r = $40 per machine day.
   a. Give the wage rate w (in $/labour-day), the number of machine-days rented (K), Q, and average cost per tonne (ATC).
   b. Suppose that w and r are unchanged, but that Primo can rent only one machine-day. If it still spends $800, give its output level and cost per tonne.
   c. If Primo decides instead to produce the same output as in 5a, with $K = 1$ machine-day, give the values for L, total cost, and cost per tonne.
   d. If Primo doubles the quantity of inputs it utilizes relative to 5a, give the values for the total costs, Q, and cost per tonne.

**6. Crunchy-Wunchy Flakes ("Absolutely no food value, but we have great prizes!") are produced using fixed inputs of 20 machine-days/period, with wage rate w at $20/labour-day and rental rate r at $10/machine-day. Its short-run production function is given by the equation
$$Q = 30L - .5L^2,$$
where Q is in tonnes/period. Calculate its average product of labour and marginal product of labour functions, and then give its total cost, average fixed cost, average variable cost, and average total cost equations as functions of Q.

**7. Two firms, Ace Novelties, Inc., and Deuce Very Good Copies, Ltd., both produce knick-knacks, although for different markets. Both face wage rates of $8/labour-day and rental rates of $1/machine-day. Knickknack output is measured in kilograms/period. Their production functions are as follows:
      Ace: $Q = L^{2/3}K^{2/3}$.
      Deuce: $Q = L^{1/3}K^{1/3}$.
   a. Give the efficient K/L ratio, and the share of long-run total costs (LTC) devoted to labour costs (wL/LTC) and to capital costs (rK/LTC), for each firm.
   b. Give the formulas for long-run total cost (LTC), average cost (LAC), and marginal cost (LMC) for each firm as a function of its output, Q.
   c. Give the unit cost (LAC) for each firm when $Q = 1$ kilogram/period and when $Q = 16$ kilograms/period.

A10-1. The LAC curve (bottom panel) is the outer envelope of the two SAC curves (top panel). Given that only two values for K are possible, the LAC represents the minimum cost of producing any level of output Q when all *possible* adjustments to input combinations have been made.

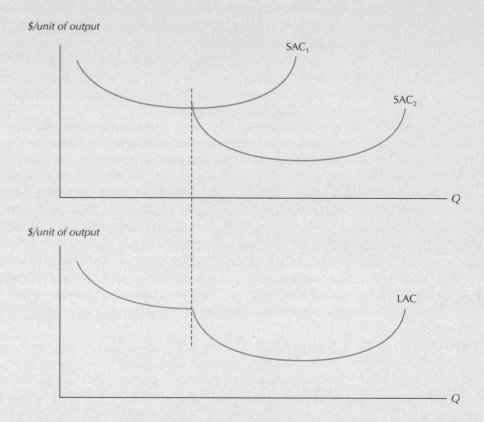

A10-2. The firm's average product of labour (AP_L) function is given by $AP_L = Q/L = 20 - L$, and its marginal product of labour (MP_L) function is given by $MP_L = dQ/dL = 20 - 2L$. Given $Q = 20L - L^2$, we can solve for L to get $L = 10 - (100 - Q)^{1/2}$. $TC = rK_0 + wL = 50 + 40L = 50 + 400 - 40(100 - Q)^{1/2} = 450 - 40(100 - Q)^{1/2}$. Average fixed cost $AFC = FC/Q = 50/Q$. Average variable cost $AVC = wL/Q = w/AP_L = 40/(20 - L) = 40/[10 + (100 - Q)^{1/2}]$. Marginal cost $MC = w/MP_L = 40/(20 - 2L) = 40/[2(100 - Q)^{1/2}] = 20/(100 - Q)^{1/2}$.

A10-3. To cause the same change in LAC as an eightfold increase in the productivity coefficient A, in Example 2 of Table 10A-1 (which is characterized by *constant* returns to scale), w and r would both have to decrease to one-eighth of their initial levels, or to \$.50/labour-day and \$2/machine-day. In Example 3 (which is characterized by *decreasing* returns to scale), the input prices would have to fall to 1/16 of their initial level, or to \$.50/labour-day and to \$.25/machine-day.

Chapter 11

PERFECT COMPETITION

Imagine that you are a legislator in the country of Bucolica. You have been asked to vote for a bill whose purpose is to alleviate poverty among farmers in the southern region of the country. Farmers in that region rent their farmland from landowners and are allowed to keep the proceeds from the sale of the crops they grow. Because of limited rainfall, their crops are usually meagre, resulting in very low incomes for the average farmer. The bill under consideration would authorize public funds to construct an irrigation system that would double the crop yields on the land in the region.

You strongly favour the objective of the bill and are about to vote in favour of it when you meet with your legislative assistant, who majored in economics at university. She urges you in the strongest possible terms not to vote for the bill. She concedes that the project would double crop yields, and she too is sympathetic to the goal of providing improved conditions for farmers. Even so, she insists that the bill would have little or no long-run effect on the earnings of farmers. Your aide has given you sound advice on similar matters in the past, and you decide to hear her out.

CHAPTER PREVIEW

In this chapter we will develop the analytical tools necessary for our hypothetical legislator to assess the assistant's advice, including a model of price and output determination in perfectly competitive markets. Our first step is to characterize the competitive firm's objective as that of earning the highest possible profits. This is clearly not the only goal a firm might pursue, but we shall see several reasons firms might often behave as if profits were all they cared about.

We then consider the four conditions that define a perfectly competitive market: (1) the existence of a standardized product, (2) price-taking behaviour on the part of firms, (3) perfect long-run mobility of factors of production, and (4) perfect information on the part of consumers and firms. It turns out that none of these conditions is likely to be completely satisfied in practice for any industry. Nonetheless, we shall see that the economic model of perfect competition often generates useful insights even when its structural preconditions are only approximately satisfied.

Next, using the cost curves discussed in Chapter 10, we derive the necessary condition for profit maximization in the short run. The rule calls for the firm to produce an output level at which its short-run marginal cost is equal to the price of the product. We shall see that implementation of this rule fortunately does not require that firms have a detailed understanding of the economist's concept of marginal cost.

From the individual firm's supply decision, we move to the issue of industrywide supply. The technique for generating the industry supply schedule turns out to be closely analogous to the one for aggregating individual demand curves into a market demand curve: we simply add the individual firms' supply curves horizontally.

The industry short-run supply and demand curves interact to determine the short-run market price, which forms the basis for output decisions by individual firms. We shall see that a firm's short-run profitability acts as a signal governing the movement of resources into and out of the industry—more specifically, that profits prompt resources to enter while losses prompt them to leave.

We shall see that in the long run, if tastes and technology are unchanging, a competitive industry whose firms have U-shaped LAC curves will settle at an equilibrium price equal to the minimum value of the LAC curve. Under certain conditions in a perfectly competitive equilibrium, it is impossible to conduct any further transaction at any price that will equally benefit both parties. The competitive equilibrium is thus self-sustaining and efficient under some economic welfare criteria.

11.1 THE GOAL OF PROFIT MAXIMIZATION

In studying not only perfect competition but also a variety of other market structures, economists traditionally assume that the firm's central objective is to maximize profit. Making this assumption imposes two tasks. The first is to clarify just what is meant by the term "profit," and the second is to explain why it often makes sense to assume that firms try to maximize it.

What Do We Mean by "Profit"?

Economic profit
Total revenue minus total explicit *and* *implicit* costs incurred.

Accounting profit
Total revenue minus total explicit costs incurred.

Profit—or, more precisely, **economic profit**—is defined as the difference between total revenue and total cost, where total cost includes all costs—both explicit and implicit—associated with resources used by the firm. This definition is significantly different from the one used by accountants and many other noneconomists, which does not subtract opportunity or implicit costs from total revenue. **Accounting profit** is simply total revenue less all explicit costs incurred.

To illustrate the distinction, suppose a firm produces 100 units of output per week by using 11 units of capital and 10 units of labour. Suppose the weekly price of each factor is $10 per unit, and the firm owns its 11 units of capital. If output sells for $2.50 per unit, the firm's total revenue will be $250 per week. To calculate the week's economic profit, we subtract from $250 the $100 spent on labour (an explicit cost) and the $110 opportunity cost of capital (an implicit cost), which leaves $40. (Under the assumption that the firm could have rented its capital to some other firm at the weekly rate of $10 per unit, the $110 opportunity cost is simply the earnings forgone by using the capital in its own operation.) The week's accounting profit for this firm, in contrast, is $150, the difference between the $250 total revenue and the $100 out-of-pocket expenditure for labour.

Accounting profit may be thought of as the sum of two components: (1) *normal profit*, which is the opportunity cost of the resources owned by the firm (in this example, $110), and (2) economic profit, as defined above (here, $40). *Economic profit* is profit over and above the normal profit level.

The importance of the distinction between accounting and economic profits is driven home forcefully—if a bit fancifully—by the following example.

EXAMPLE 11-1

Mike runs a miniature golf course in Canmore, Alberta. He rents the course and equipment from a large recreational supply company and supplies his own labour. His monthly earnings, net of rental payments, are $800, and he considers working at the golf course just as attractive as his only other alternative, working as a grocery clerk for $800 per month.

Now Mike learns that his Uncle Bobby has died and left him some land in Toronto (the parcel bounded by the streets shown in Figure 11-1). The land has been cleared, and Mike discovers that a construction company is willing to install and maintain a miniature golf course on it for a payment of $4000 per month. Mike also commissions a market survey, which reveals that he would collect $16,000 per month in revenue by operating a miniature golf course there. (After all, there are many more potential golfers in Toronto than in Canmore.) After deducting the $4000 per month payment to the construction company, this would leave him with $12,000 per month free and clear. Given these figures, and assuming that the cost of living is the same in Toronto as in Canmore, should Mike, a profit maximizer, switch his operation to Toronto?

Since he is a profit maximizer, he should switch to Toronto only if his economic profit there will be higher than in Canmore. Suppose, however, that Mike is unfamiliar with the concept of economic profit and instead compares his accounting profits in the two locations. In Canmore, his accounting profit is $800 per month, the amount he has left over after paying all his bills. In Toronto, the corresponding figure will be $12,000 per month. On this comparison, he would quickly forsake Canmore for Toronto.

If he compares economic profits, however, he will reach precisely the opposite conclusion. In Canmore, his economic profit is zero once we account for the opportunity cost of his labour. (He could have earned $800 per month as a grocery clerk, exactly the amount of his accounting profit.) To calculate what his economic profits would be in Toronto, we must deduct from his $12,000 per month accounting profits not only the $800 monthly opportunity cost of his labour, but also the opportunity cost of his land. The Toronto site is in a prime location. Suppose we conservatively estimate that Mike's land would sell for $20,000,000 in today's real estate market, and suppose that the interest rate is .5 percent per month. The opportunity cost of devoting the land to a miniature golf course will then be (.005) × $20,000,000 = $100,000 per month, which makes his monthly economic profit in Toronto equal to $12,000 − $800 − $100,000 = −$88,800. Thus, if we assign any reasonable value to the opportunity cost of his land, it will obviously be better for Mike to sell or rent it and remain in Canmore. The reason Toronto real estate is so expensive is that people can build skyscrapers on it and charge high rents to a multitude of tenants. To build a miniature golf course in downtown Toronto would be like wearing diamonds on the soles of your shoes.

EXERCISE 11-1

In Example 11-1, how low would the monthly interest rate have to be before Mike should relocate to Toronto?

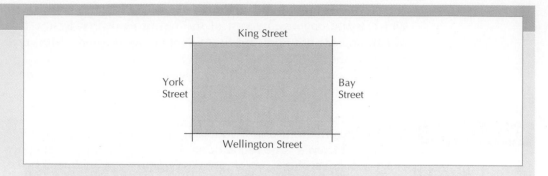

FIGURE 11-1

Potential Site for a Downtown Toronto Miniature Golf Course

Why Profit Maximize?

Let's turn now to the assumption of profit maximization. In order to predict what any entity—a firm, person, committee, or government—will do under specific conditions, some sort of assumption must be made about its goals. After all, if we know where people want to go, it's much easier to predict what they'll do to get there. Economists assume that the goal of firms is to maximize economic profits; then they try to discover what specific behaviours contribute to that objective.

Numerous challenges have been raised to the profit-maximization assumption. Some critics say the firm's goal is to maximize its chances of survival; others believe that it wants to maximize total sales or total revenues; and some even claim that firms don't try to maximize anything at all.

One reason for such skepticism is that examples abound in which the managers of firms appear incompetent and too poorly informed to take the kinds of actions required for maximizing profits. It is important to understand, however, that the assumption of profit maximization is not refuted by the existence of incompetent managers. On the contrary, a case can be made that, even in a world in which the actions of firms are initially random, there will be a long-run tendency for profit-maximizing behaviour eventually to dominate.[1]

The argument is directly analogous to Charles Darwin's theory of evolution by natural selection, and it goes roughly as follows. First, in a world of random action, some firms will, purely by chance, come much closer than others to profit-maximizing behaviour. The result will be that the former firms will have greater surplus revenues at their disposal, which will enable them to grow faster than their rivals. The other side of this coin is that firms whose behaviour deviates most sharply from profit maximization are the ones most likely to go bankrupt. In the animal kingdom, food is an essential resource for survival, and profits play a parallel role in the competitive marketplace. Those firms with the highest profits are often considerably more likely to survive. The evolutionary argument concludes that, over long periods of time, behaviour will tend toward profit maximization purely as a result of selection pressures in the competitive environment.

But the forces in support of profit maximization are not limited to the unintentional pressures of natural selection. They also include the actions of people who are very consciously pursuing their own interests. Bankers and other moneylenders, for example, are eager to keep their risks to a minimum and, for this reason, they prefer to do busi-

---

[1]See, for example, Armen Alchian, "Uncertainty, Evolution, and Economic Theory," *Journal of Political Economy*, 1950.

ness with highly profitable firms. In addition to having more internal resources, such firms thus have easier access to external sources of capital to finance their growth. Another important force supporting profit-maximizing behaviour is the threat of an outside takeover. The price of shares of stock in a firm is based on the firm's profitability (more on this point in Chapter 15), with the result that shares of stock of a non-profit-maximizing firm will often sell for much less than their potential value. This creates an opportunity for an outsider to buy the stock at a bargain price and then drive its price upward by altering the firm's behaviour.

Another pressure in favour of profit maximization is that the owners of many firms compensate their managers in part by giving them a share of the firm's profits or options to purchase the company's stock. Some firms extend such incentives to their workers. This provides a clear financial incentive for employees to enhance profitability whenever and wherever opportunities arise for them to do so. As cases such as those of Enron, Arthur Andersen, and other corporations illustrate, it can also provide an incentive to create the *illusion* of profitability by fraudulent means, which at least has the economic benefit of increasing employment in the paper-shredder industry. This issue is addressed in Chapter 15.

Let us note, finally, that the assumption of profit maximization does not imply that firms conduct their operations in the most efficient conceivable manner at all times. In the world we live in there are not only many intelligent, competent managers, but also a multitude who possess neither of these attributes. Needless to say, not every task can be assigned to the most competent person in the universe. In a sensible world, the most important tasks will be carried out by the best managers, the less important tasks by less competent ones. So the mere fact that we often observe firms doing silly things does not establish that they are not maximizing profits. To maximize profits means simply to do the best one can under the circumstances, and that will sometimes mean having to muddle along with uninspired managers.

Taken as a whole, the forgoing observations lend support to the assumption of profit maximization. But they obviously do not establish conclusively that firms always pursue profits at the expense of all other goals. This remains an empirical question, and in the chapters to come we will see some evidence that firms sometimes fall short. Even so, the assumption of profit maximization is a good place to begin our analysis of firm behaviour, and there is no question but that it provides useful insights into how firms respond to changes in input or product prices, taxes, and other important features of their operating environments.

We need to recognize, however, that there can be a difference between short-run and long-run profit maximization, particularly when industries are imperfectly competitive and the strategic behaviour of firms is important. In Chapter 13, we shall see that in some situations, certain strategies—such as maximizing market share even at the expense of current profitability, or engaging in a costly price war to establish the credibility of a future threat to meet and beat all competitors' prices—can serve to maximize a firm's profits over the long term, even if they cut into present profits. The implications of the profit-maximization hypothesis for behaviour are generally dependent on the time horizon specified.

11.2 THE FOUR CONDITIONS FOR PERFECT COMPETITION

To predict how much output a competitive firm will produce, economists have developed the *theory of perfect competition*. Four conditions define the existence of a perfectly competitive market. Let us consider each of them in turn.

1. Firms Sell a Standardized Product. In a perfectly competitive market, the product sold by one firm is assumed to be a perfect substitute for the product sold by any other. Interpreted literally, this is a condition that is rarely if ever satisfied. Connoisseurs of fine wines, for example, insist that they can tell the difference between wines made from the same variety of grape grown on estates only a few kilometres apart. It is also difficult to speak of a market for even such a simple commodity as shirts, because shirts come in so many different styles and quality levels. If we define the market sufficiently narrowly, however, it is sometimes possible to achieve a reasonable degree of similarity among the products produced by competing firms. For instance, "Canadian No. 1 Durum wheat" may not be exactly the same on different farms, but it is close enough that most buyers don't care very much which farm the wheat comes from.

2. Firms Are Price Takers. This means that the individual firm treats the market price of the product as given. More specifically, it must believe that the market price will not be affected by how much output it produces. This condition is likely to be satisfied when the market is served by a large number of firms, each one of which produces an all but imperceptible fraction of total industry output. But a large number of firms is not always necessary for price-taking behaviour. Even if there are only two firms in a market, for example, each may behave as a price taker if it believes that other firms stand ready to enter the market at a moment's notice.

3. Factors of Production Are Perfectly Mobile in the Long Run. One implication of this condition is that if a firm perceives a profitable business opportunity at a given time and location, it will be able to hire the factors of production it needs in order to take advantage of it. Similarly, if its current venture no longer appears attractive in relation to alternative business ventures, it is free to discharge its factors of production, which will then move to industries where opportunities are stronger. Of course, no one believes that resources are perfectly mobile. Labour, in particular, is not likely to satisfy this condition. People buy homes, make friends, enroll their children in schools, and establish a host of other commitments that make it difficult to move from one place to another. Nonetheless, the perfect mobility assumption is often reasonably well satisfied in practice, especially if we take into account that it is not always necessary for labour to move geographically in order for it to be mobile in an economic sense. In larger urban labour markets, for instance, workers with portable skills who are laid off by one firm can often find work with another firm in a related industry in the same area, without incurring relocation costs. Sometimes firms may move to the worker. A case in point is the relocation of many Hollywood film and television productions to Canadian cities like Toronto and Vancouver, in response to the increase in the Canadian value of the U.S. dollar and the availability of a film production infrastructure.

4. Firms and Consumers Have Perfect Information. Short of bankruptcy, a firm has no reason to leave its current industry if it has no way of knowing about the existence of more profitable opportunities elsewhere. Similarly, a consumer has no motive to switch from a high-priced product to a lower-priced one of identical quality unless she has information about the existence of the latter. Here too the required condition is never satisfied in a literal sense. The world is sufficiently complex that there will inevitably be relevant features of it hidden from view. As a practical matter, the assumption of perfect information is usually interpreted to mean that people can acquire most of the information that is most relevant to their choices without great difficulty. Even this more limited condition will fail in many cases. As we saw in Chapter 8, people often have the relevant information right at their fingertips and yet fail to make sensible use of it. These observations notwithstanding, the state of knowledge can often be sufficient to provide a reasonable approximation to the perfect information condition.

To help assess whether the assumptions underlying the model of perfect competition are hopelessly restrictive, it is useful to compare them to the assumptions that underlie the physicist's model of objects in motion. If you have taken a high school or college physics course, then you know (or once knew) that a force applied to an object on a frictionless surface causes that object to accelerate at a rate inversely proportional to its mass. Thus, a given force applied to a 10-kg object will cause that object to accelerate at twice the rate we observe when the same force is applied to a 20-kg object.

To illustrate this theory, physics teachers show us films of what happens when various forces are applied to a hockey puck atop a large surface of dry ice. These physicists understand perfectly well that there is an easily measured amount of friction between the puck and the dry ice. But they are also aware that the friction levels there are so low that the model still provides reasonably accurate predictions.

In the kinds of situations we are most likely to encounter in practice, friction is seldom as low as between a puck and a dry ice surface. This will be painfully apparent to you, for example, if you have just taken a spill on your Harley Sportster. But even here the physicist's laws of motion apply, and we can make adjustments for friction in order to estimate just how far a fallen rider will slide. And even where the model cannot be calibrated precisely, it tells us that the rider will slide farther the faster he was going when he fell, and that he will slide farther if the pavement is wet or covered with sand or gravel than if it is clean and dry.

With the economic model of perfect competition, the issues are very similar. In some markets, most notably for agricultural products, the four conditions come close to being satisfied. The predictions of the competitive model in these cases can be almost as precise as those of the physicist's model applied to the puck on dry ice. In other markets, such as those for garbage trucks or earth-moving equipment, at least some of the conditions are not even approximately satisfied. Yet even in these cases, the competitive model can tell us something useful if we interpret it with sufficient care.

11.3 THE SHORT-RUN CONDITION FOR PROFIT MAXIMIZATION

The first question we want our model of competitive firm behaviour to be able to answer is, "How does a firm choose its output level in the short run?" Under the assumption that the firm's goal is to maximize economic profit, it will choose that level of output for which the difference between total revenue and total cost is largest.

Consider a firm with the short-run total cost curve labelled TC in the top panel in Figure 11-2. Like many of the firms we discussed in Chapter 10, this firm experiences first increasing, then decreasing, marginal productivity of its variable input, which produces the familiar pattern of curvature in its total cost curve. Suppose this firm can sell its output at a price of $P_0 = \$18$ per unit. Its total revenue per week will then be $18 per unit of output times the number of units of output sold each week. For example, if the firm sells no output, it earns zero total revenue; if it sells 10 units of output per week, it earns $180 per week; if it sells 20 units per week, it earns $360 per week; and so on. So for the perfectly competitive firm, which can sell as much or as little output as it chooses at a constant market price, total revenue is exactly proportional to output. For the firm in this example, the total revenue curve is the line labelled TR in the top panel in Figure 11-2. It is a ray whose slope is equal to the product price, $P_0 = \$18$ per unit.

FIGURE 11-2

Revenue, Cost, and Economic Profit
The total revenue curve is the ray labelled TR in the top panel. The difference between it and total cost (TC in the top panel) is economic profit (Π_Q in the bottom panel). At $Q = 0$, $\Pi_Q = -FC = -\$30$/wk. Economic profit reaches a maximum ($\$12.60$/wk) for $Q = 7.4$ units/wk.

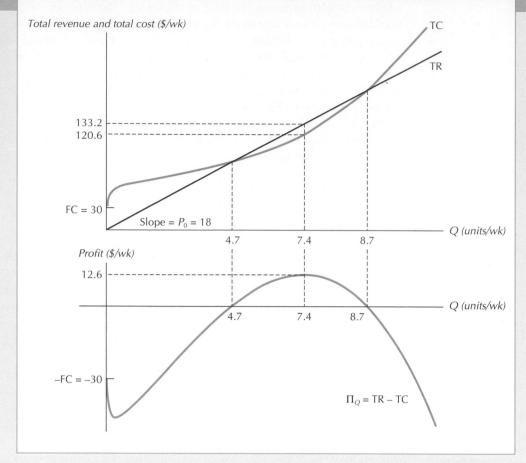

The bottom panel in Figure 11-2 plots the difference between TR and TC, which is the curve labelled Π_Q, the notation traditionally used in economics to represent economic profit. Here, Π_Q is positive for output levels between $Q = 4.7$ and $Q = 8.7$, and reaches a maximum at $Q = 7.4$ units/week. For output levels less than 4.7 or greater than 8.7, the firm is earning economic losses, which is simply another way of saying that its economic profits are negative for those values of Q.

In the bottom panel in Figure 11-2, note also that the vertical intercept of the profit curve is equal to $-\$30$ per week, the negative of the firm's fixed cost. When the firm produces no output, it earns no revenue and incurs no variable cost but must still pay its fixed costs, so its profit when $Q = 0$ is simply $-FC$. If there were no positive output level for which the firm could earn higher profit than $-FC$, its best option would be to produce zero output in the short run.

The maximum profit point can also be characterized in terms of the relationship between marginal revenue and short-run marginal cost. ***Marginal revenue (MR)*** is equal to the slope of the total revenue curve at any given point:

Marginal revenue (MR)
The change in total revenue that occurs as a result of a one-unit change in quantity sold.

$$MR_Q = \frac{\Delta TR_Q}{\Delta Q}. \qquad (11.1)$$

Marginal revenue is formally defined as *the change in revenue that occurs when the sale of output changes by one unit*. In the cost-benefit language of Chapter 1, MR is the benefit to the firm of selling an additional unit of output. If the firm wants to maximize its profits, it must weigh this benefit against the cost of selling an extra unit of output, which is its marginal cost. As Figure 11-2 shows, in the special case of a perfectly competitive firm (which faces a *constant* price P for its output), the total revenue curve is a straight line or ray from the origin, with a constant slope equal to its product price. Hence for a perfect competitor, at all levels of output and sales, marginal revenue is equal to the price of the product:[2]

$$MR_Q = \frac{\Delta TR_Q}{\Delta Q} = P. \qquad (11.2)$$

The short-run marginal and average variable cost curves that correspond to the TC curve in Figure 11-2 are shown in Figure 11-3, where we again suppose that the firm can sell its output at a price of $P_0 = \$18$ per unit. To maximize its economic profits, the firm should follow this rule: Provided P_0 is larger than the minimum value of AVC (more on the reason for this condition below), *the firm should produce a level of output for which marginal revenue, MR = P_0 = 18, is equal to marginal cost on the rising portion of the MC curve*. For the particular cost curves shown in Figure 11-3, $P_0 = 18$ is indeed larger than the minimum value of AVC, and is equal to marginal cost at the quantity level $Q^* = 7.4$ units/week. The requirement that marginal revenue intersect marginal cost on the rising portion of marginal cost implies that marginal revenue intersects marginal cost from above. Thus marginal revenue lies below marginal cost past this point of intersection, and the firm has no incentive to expand output beyond this point: additional units would *reduce* profits.

FIGURE 11-3

The Profit-Maximizing Output Level in the Short Run

A necessary condition for profit maximization is that price equal marginal cost on the rising portion of the marginal cost curve. Here, this happens at the output level $Q^* = 7.4$ units/wk.

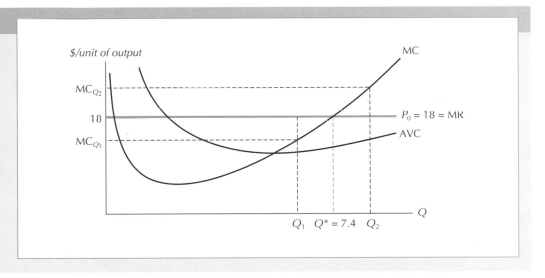

[2]For profits to be at a maximum, the slope or derivative of the profit function Π_Q (= $TR_Q - TC_Q$) with respect to Q must equal zero: $d\Pi_Q/dQ = 0$. Note that this is the case in the lower panel of Figure 11-2 at Q = 7.4 units/week. That is, in the general case, we require $d\Pi_Q/dQ = dTR_Q/dQ - dTC_Q/dQ = 0$, or MR_Q ($\equiv dTR_Q/dQ$) = MC_Q ($\equiv dTC_Q/dQ$). For a perfectly competitive firm, $MR_Q = P$, and hence we can write the (first-order) condition for profit-maximization for a perfect competitor as $MR_Q = P = MC_Q$: price must be equal to marginal cost. Footnote 3 on the following page provides the second-order condition for profit maximization. As we shall see in footnote 3 and in Chapter 12, output price and marginal revenue are not the same for a monopolist.

As the following exercise demonstrates, the definitions of MR and MC tell us something about the relative values of the slopes of the TR and TC curves at the maximum-profit point in Figure 11-2.

How do the slopes of the TC and TR curves compare at $Q = 7.4$ in Figure 11-2?

Why is "price = marginal cost" a necessary condition for profit maximization? Suppose we picked some other level of output, say, Q_1, that is less than $Q^* = 7.4$. The benefit to the firm of selling an additional unit of output will be $P_0 = \$18$ (its marginal revenue). The addition to total cost of producing an extra unit of output at Q_1 will be its marginal cost at the level of output, MC_{Q1}, which in Figure 11-3 is clearly less than 18. It follows that for any level of output on the rising portion of the MC curve to the left of $Q^* = 7.4$, the benefit of expanding (as measured by marginal revenue) will be greater than the cost of expanding (as measured by marginal cost). This amounts to saying that profit will increase when we expand output from Q_1.

Now consider any level of output to the right of $Q^* = 7.4$, such as Q_2. At Q_2, the benefit of contracting output by one unit will be the resulting cost savings, which is marginal cost at that level of output, namely, MC_{Q2}. (Note here that we are using the term *benefit* to refer to the avoidance of a cost.) The cost to the firm of contracting output by 1 unit will be its marginal revenue, $P_0 = 18$, the loss in total revenue when it sells 1 unit less. (Here, not getting a benefit is a cost.) Since $MC_{Q2} > \$18$, the firm will save more than it loses when it contracts output by 1 unit. It follows that for any output level greater than $Q^* = 7.4$, the firm's profit will grow when it contracts output. The only output level at which the firm cannot earn higher profit by either expanding or contracting is $Q^* = 7.4$, the level for which the cost of any move is exactly equal to its benefit.[3]

---

[3]The firm's problem is to maximize $\Pi = PQ - TC_Q$, where TC_Q is the short-run total cost of producing Q units of output. In the general case, $MR_Q = dTR_Q/dQ = dPQ/dQ = P(dQ/dQ) + Q(dP/dQ) = P + Q(dP/dQ)$. For a perfect competitor, however, P is constant. Hence $dP/dQ = 0$, and so $MR_Q = dPQ/dQ = P$. The first-order condition for profit maximization for a perfect competitor is therefore:

$$\frac{d\Pi}{dQ} = P - \frac{dTC_Q}{dQ} = P - MC_Q = 0.$$

which gives the condition $P = MC_Q$. The general second-order condition for a maximum is given by

$$\frac{d^2\Pi}{dQ^2} = \frac{dMR_Q}{dQ} - \frac{dMC_Q}{dQ} < 0, \text{ or } \frac{dMR_Q}{dQ} < \frac{dMC_Q}{dQ}.$$

This may be expressed by saying that the MC curve must cut the MR curve from below, meaning that the MC curve is below the MR curve to the left of their intersection, and above the MR curve to the right of the intersection. When $MR_Q = P$ (a constant), however,

$$\frac{dMR_Q}{dQ} = \frac{dP}{dQ} = 0.$$

Hence under perfect competition, the second-order condition reduces to

$$\frac{d^2\Pi}{dQ^2} = \frac{-dMC_Q}{dQ} < 0 \qquad \text{or} \qquad \frac{dMC_Q}{dQ} > 0.$$

This tells us why for a perfect competitor we must be at a point on the *rising* portion of the marginal cost curve. In Figure 11-3, the left-hand intersection of P and MC_Q (where MC_Q is *downward* sloping) is what is called a point of local profit-*minimization*. As the corresponding points in Figure 11-2 show, profits *increase* to the left *and* right of this intersection.

The Shutdown Condition

Shutdown condition
If price falls below the minimum of average variable cost, the firm should shut down in the short run.

Recall that the rule for short-run profit maximization is to set price equal to marginal cost, provided price exceeds the minimum value of average variable cost. Why must price be greater than the minimum point of the AVC curve? The answer is that unless this condition is met, the firm will do better to shut down—that is, to produce no output—in the short run. To see why, note that the firm's *average revenue* (*AR*) per unit of output sold is simply the price at which it sells its product. (When price is constant for all levels of output, average revenue and marginal revenue are the same, and AR = TR/Q = PQ/Q = P.) If average revenue is less than average variable cost, the firm is taking a loss on each unit of output it sells, *in addition to the loss—equal to the negative of its fixed costs—it would sustain if it shut down in the short run*. The firm's total revenue (average revenue times quantity) will be less than its total variable cost (AVC times quantity), and this means that it would do better by not producing any output at all.

As we saw in Figure 11-2, a firm that produces zero output will earn economic profit equal to the negative of its fixed costs. If the price of its product is less than the minimum value of its average variable costs, it would have even greater economic losses if it produced a positive level of output.

The two rules—(1) that price must equal marginal cost on a rising portion of the marginal cost curve and (2) that price must exceed the minimum value of the average variable cost curve—together define the short-run supply curve of the perfectly competitive firm. The firm's supply curve tells how much output the firm wants to produce at various prices. As shown by the heavy locus in Figure 11-4, it is the rising portion of the short-run marginal cost curve that lies above the minimum value of the average variable cost curve (which is $12 per unit of output in this example). Below P = 12, the supply curve coincides with the vertical axis, indicating that the firm supplies zero output when price is less than min AVC. For prices above 12, the firm will supply the output level for which P = MC. Thus, prices of 14 and 20 will cause this firm to supply 6.4 and 7.8 units of output, respectively. The competitive firm acts here as both a price taker and a profit maximizer: taking the market price as given, it chooses the level of output that maximizes economic profit at that price.

Note in Figure 11-4 that the firm supplies positive output whenever price exceeds min AVC, and recall that average variable cost is less than average total cost, the difference

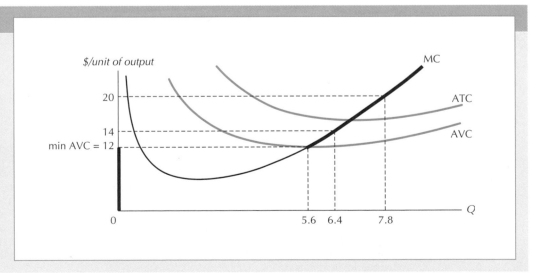

FIGURE 11-4

The Short-Run Supply Curve of a Perfectly Competitive Firm
When price lies below the minimum value of average variable cost (here $12/unit of output), the firm will make losses at every level of output, and will keep its losses to a minimum by producing zero. For prices above min AVC, the firm will supply that level of output for which P = MC on the rising portion of its MC curve.

being average fixed cost. It follows that no matter how small AFC is, there will be a range of prices that lie between the AVC and ATC curves. For any price in this range, the firm supplies the level of output for which P = MC, which means that it will lose money because P is less than ATC. For example, the firm whose cost curves are shown in Figure 11-4 cannot cover all its costs at a price of $14 per unit. Even so, its best option is to supply 6.4 units of output per week, because it would lose even more money if it were to shut down. Being able to cover variable costs does not assure the firm of a positive level of economic profit. But it is sufficient to induce the firm to supply output in the short run.

Note also in Figure 11-4 that the firm's short-run supply curve is upward sloping. This is because the relevant portion of the firm's short-run marginal cost curve is upward sloping, which, in turn, is a direct consequence of the law of diminishing returns, or of eventually diminishing marginal productivity of the variable input.[4]

11.4 SHORT-RUN COMPETITIVE INDUSTRY SUPPLY

The short-run supply curve for a competitive industry is generated in a manner analogous to the one we used to generate the market demand curve in Chapter 5. In this case we simply announce a price and then add together the amounts each firm wishes to supply at that price. The resulting sum is industry supply at that price. Additional points on the industry supply curve are generated by pairing other prices with the sums of individual firm supplies at those prices.

FIGURE 11-5

The Short-Run Competitive Industry Supply Curve
To get the industry supply curve (right panel), we simply add the individual firm supply curves (left and centre panels) horizontally.

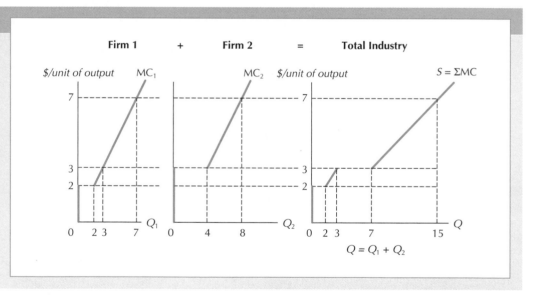

---

[4]The condition that ensures that a perfectly competitive firm will *not* shut down in the short run can be written P = MC > AVC. The *equivalent* condition in the *input* market can be simply derived. Recall from Chapter 10, for a perfect competitor hiring a single variable input, L, that MC = w/MP_L, and that AVC = w/AP_L. The condition MC > AVC is hence equivalent to the condition in the *input* market that $w/MP_L > w/AP_L$, or (simplifying) that $MP_L < AP_L$. This condition can be seen in Figure 10-9 on page 360. The competitive firm will shut down if P = MC to the *left* of Q_2 in Figure 10-9. This is equivalent to saying that it will shut down if employment is less than L_2 units of labour at the point where P = MC = w/MP_L and MP_L = w/P, since it is only in the range from L_2 to L_M that $AP_L > MP_L > 0$. The relation between input and output markets is discussed further in Chapter 14 and in Module 4, Example 8 of the online *Basic Math Review*.

Figure 11-5 illustrates the procedure for one of the simplest cases, an industry consisting of only two firms. At a price of $2 per unit of output, only firm 1 (left panel) wishes to supply any output, and so its offering, $Q_1 = 2$ units of output per week, constitutes the entire industry supply at $P = 2$ (right panel). At $P = 3$, firm 2 enters the market (centre panel) with an offering of $Q_2 = 4$. Added to firm 1's offering at $P = 3$—namely, $Q_1 = 3$—the resulting industry supply at $P = 3$ is $Q = 7$ (right panel). In like fashion, we see that industry supply at $P = 7$ is $Q = 7 + 8 = 15$. In Chapter 4, we saw that the market demand curve is the horizontal summation of the individual consumer demand curves. Here, we see that the market supply curve is the horizontal summation of the individual firm supply curves.

The horizontal summation of an individual firm's supplies into industry supply has a simple form when the firms in the industry are all identical. Suppose n firms each have supply curve $P = c + dQ_i$. To add up the quantities for the n firms into industry supply, we rearrange the firm supply curve $P = c + dQ_i$ to express quantity alone on one side $Q_i = -(c/d) + (1/d)P$. Then industry supply is the sum of the quantities supplied Q_i by each of the n firms,

$$Q = nQ_i = n\left(-\frac{c}{d} + \frac{1}{d}P\right) = -\frac{nc}{d} + \frac{n}{d}P$$

We can then rearrange industry supply $Q = -(nc/d) + (n/d)P$ to get it back in the form of price alone on one side: $P = c + (d/n)Q$. The intuition is that each one unit supplied by the industry is $1/n$ unit for each firm to supply. These calculations suggest a general rule for constructing the industry supply curve when firms are identical. If we have n individual firm supply curves $P = c + dQ_i$, then the industry supply curve is $P = c + (d/n)Q$.

| **EXAMPLE 11-2** | **Suppose an industry has 200 firms, each with supply curve $P = 100 + 1000Q_i$. What is the industry supply curve?** |

First, we need to rearrange the representative firm supply curve $P = 100 + 1000Q_i$ to have quantity alone on one side:

$$Q_i = -\frac{1}{10} + \frac{1}{1000}P$$

Then we multiply by the number of firms $n = 200$:

$$Q = nQ_i = 200Q_i = 200\left(-\frac{1}{10} + \frac{1}{1000}P\right) = -20 + \frac{1}{5}P$$

Finally, we rearrange the industry supply curve $Q = -20 + \left(\frac{1}{5}\right)P$ to have price alone on one side $(P = 100 + 5Q)$, to return to slope-intercept form.

EXERCISE 11-3

Suppose an industry has 30 firms, each with supply curve $P = 20 + 90Q_i$. What is the industry supply curve?

11.5 SHORT-RUN COMPETITIVE EQUILIBRIUM

The individual competitive firm must choose the most profitable level of output to pro-duce in response to a given price. But where does that price come from? As we saw in Chapter 2, it comes from the intersection of the supply and demand curves for the product. Recall that at the equilibrium price sellers are selling the quantity they wish to sell and buyers are buying the quantity they wish to buy.

In the left panel in Figure 11-6, the curve labelled D is the market demand curve for a product sold in a perfectly competitive industry. The curve labelled S is the corre-sponding short-run industry supply curve, the horizontal summation of the relevant portions of the individual short-run marginal cost curves.[5] These two curves intersect to establish the short-run competitive equilibrium price, here denoted $P^* = \$20$ per unit of output. $P^* = 20$, in turn, is the price on which individual firms base their output decisions.

The conditions confronting a typical firm are shown in the right panel in Figure 11-6. The demand curve facing this firm is a horizontal line at $P^* = 20$. This means that it can sell as much or as little as it chooses at the market price of $20 per unit. Put another way, any single firm can sell as much as it wants to without significantly affecting the market price. If a firm charged more than the $20, it would sell no output at all because buyers would switch to a competing firm that sells for $20. A firm could charge less than $20, of course, but would have no motive to do so if its objective were to maxi-mize economic profit, since it can already sell as much as it wants to at $20. The result is that even though the market demand curve is downward sloping, the demand curve facing the individual firm is perfectly elastic. (Recall from the definition of price elas-ticity in Chapter 4 that a horizontal demand curve has infinite price elasticity, which is the defining characteristic of the term "perfectly elastic.")

FIGURE 11-6

Short-Run Price and Output Determination under Perfect Competition

The short-run supply and demand curves intersect to determine the short-run equilibrium price, $P^* = 20$ (left panel). The firm's demand curve is a horizontal line at $P^* = 20$ (right panel). Taking $P^* = 20$ as given, the firm maximizes economic profit by producing $Q_i^* = 80$ units/wk, for which it earns an economic profit of $\Pi_i = \$640$/wk (the shaded rectangle in the right panel).

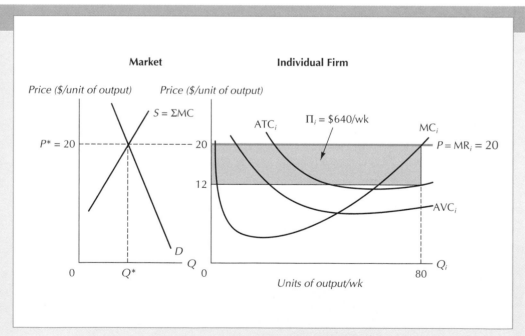

---

[5]Here, the "relevant portions" are those that lie above the respective values of min AVC.

TABLE 11-1

Economic Profits vs. Economic Losses
At a price of 20, the firm earns economic profits, but at a price of 10, it suffers economic losses. The circled numbers represent the *maximum* profits (*minimum* losses) corresponding to the given price in each case.

Q	ATC	MC	$\Pi(P = 20)$ (Figure 11-6)	$\Pi(P = 10)$ (Figure 11-7)
40	14	6	240	−160
60	12	10	480	(−120)
80	12	20	(640)	−160
100	15	31	500	−500

In the right panel in Figure 11-6, the representative firm maximizes its profit by equating $P^* = \$20$ per unit to marginal cost at an output level of $Q^*i = 80$ units per week. At that output level its total revenue is $P^*Q_i^* = \$1600$ per week and its total costs are $ATC_{Qi}^*Q_i^* = (\$12$ per unit$)(80$ units per week$) = \$960$ per week. Its economic profit is the difference between total revenue and total cost, $\$1600$ per week $- \$960$ per week $= \$640$ per week, and is represented by the shaded rectangle denoted Π_i. Equivalently, profits can be calculated as the difference between price ($\$20$ per unit) and average total cost ($\$12$ per unit) times the quantity sold (80 units/week).

Recall that the opportunity cost of resources owned by the firm constitutes part of the cost included in its average total cost curve. This is why we say that total revenues over and above total costs constitute economic profit. If the firm's revenue were exactly equal to its total cost, it would earn only a normal profit—which is to say, zero economic profit.

Facing a price equal to average total cost implies that total cost equals total revenue, and the firm earns zero economic profits. Thus price equal to the minimum of average total cost can be called the breakeven point—the lowest price at which the firm will not suffer negative economic profits in the short run.

The situation portrayed in Figure 11-6 and Table 11-1 is one in which the short-run equilibrium price enables the firm to make a positive economic profit. Another possibility

FIGURE 11-7

A Short-Run Equilibrium Price That Results in Economic Losses
The short-run supply and demand curves sometimes intersect to produce an equilibrium price $P^* = \$10$/unit of output (left panel) that lies below the minimum value of the ATC curve for the typical firm (right panel), but above the minimum point of its AVC curve. At the profit-maximizing level of output, $Q_i^* = 60$ units/wk, the firm earns an economic loss of $\Pi_i = -\$120$/wk.

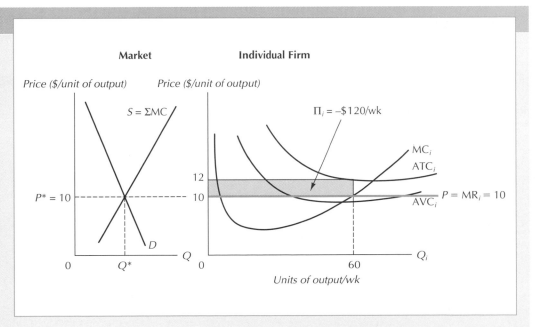

is that the short-run supply and demand curves will intersect at an equilibrium price that is sufficiently high to induce firms to supply output, but not high enough to enable them to cover all their costs. This situation is shown in Figure 11-7 and Table 11-1. In the left panel, supply and demand intersect at a price $P^* = \$10$ per unit of output, which lies above the minimum value of the AVC curve of the firm shown in the right panel, but below that firm's ATC curve at the profit-maximizing level of output, $Q_i^* = 60$ units of output per week. The result is that the firm makes an economic loss of $P^*Q_i^* - \text{ATC}_{Q_i^*}Q_i^* = -\$120$ per week. This loss is shown in the right panel in Figure 11-7 by the shaded rectangle labelled Π_i. Note that this loss is less than $-\text{TFC}$, the value of economic profit when output is zero. We know this because TFC is the rectangle given by $(\text{ATC}_{Q_i^*} - \text{AVC}_{Q_i^*})Q_i^*$, and with P^* greater than $\text{AVC}_{Q_i^*}$, the area of TFC exceeds that of the shaded rectangle. Thus it makes sense to produce even when economic profit falls below zero in the short run.

11.6 THE EFFICIENCY OF SHORT-RUN COMPETITIVE EQUILIBRIUM

Allocative efficiency
A condition in which all possible gains from exchange are realized.

One of the most attractive features of perfectly competitive markets is the fact that they result in ***allocative efficiency***, which means that they fully exploit the possibilities for mutual gains through exchange. To illustrate, let us consider the short-run equilibrium pictured in the left panel of Figure 11-8, and suppose that the cost curves pictured in the right panel are the same for each of 1000 firms in the industry.

In a competitive market in the short run, consumers give firms money, which firms use to buy variable inputs to produce the output that goes to consumers. To say that the competitive equilibrium leaves no room for further mutually beneficial exchange is the same thing as saying that there is no way for any producer and consumer to agree to a private transaction at any price other than $10. Of course, consumers would gladly pay less than $10 for an additional unit of output. But since $10 is equal to the

FIGURE 11-8

Short-Run Competitive Equilibrium Is Efficient
At the equilibrium price and quantity, the value of the additional resources required to make the last unit of output produced by each firm (MC in the right panel) is exactly equal to the value of the last unit of output to buyers (the demand price in the left panel). This means that further mutually beneficial trades do not exist.

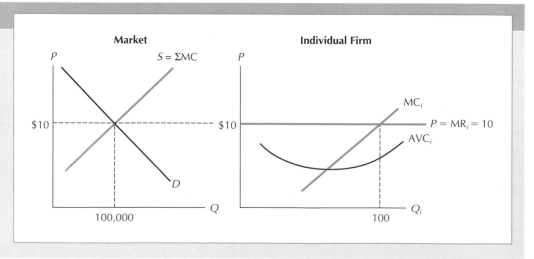

value of the resources required to produce another unit (MC_i in the right panel of Figure 11-8), no firm would be willing to respond. Firms, for their part, would gladly produce an extra unit of output if the price were higher than $10. But with 100,000 units of output already in the market, there are no consumers left who are willing to pay more than $10 (left panel of Figure 11-8). At the short-run competitive equilibrium price and quantity, the value of the resources used to produce the last unit of output (as measured by short-run marginal cost) is exactly equal to the value of that unit of output to consumers (as measured by the price they are willing to pay for it). Firms may wish that prices were higher, and consumers may complain that prices are too high already. But no two parties have any incentive to trade at any price other than the equilibrium price.

11.7 PRODUCER SURPLUS

To say that a competitive market is efficient is to say that it maximizes the net benefits to its participants. In policy analysis, it is often useful to estimate the actual amount by which people and firms gain from their participation in specific markets. Suppose, for example, that the government of a less developed country (LDC) knows it can open up new markets for seafood by building a road from its coast to an interior region. If its goal is to use the country's resources as efficiently as possible, its decision about whether to build the road will depend on whether the benefits people and firms reap from these new markets exceed the cost of building the road.

Producer surplus
The difference between total revenue and variable cost at a given level of output; equivalently, the sum of fixed cost and economic profit.

In Chapter 5 we discussed the concept of consumer surplus as a measure of the benefit to the consumer of engaging in a market exchange. An analogous measure exists for producers. We call it **producer surplus**, and it measures how much better off the firm is as a result of having supplied its profit-maximizing level of output. It may seem tempting to say that the firm's producer surplus is simply its economic profit, but that will not generally be the case. To see why, first recall that in the short run if the firm produces nothing, it will sustain a loss equal to its fixed cost. If the price exceeds the minimum value of AVC, however, it can do better by supplying a positive level of output. How much better? The firm's gain compared with the alternative of producing nothing is the difference between total revenue and total variable cost at the output level where $P = MC$. Now recall that economic profit is the difference between total revenue and total cost, and that total cost differs from variable cost by fixed cost; it follows that producer surplus is the sum of economic profit and fixed cost.[6] Diagrammatically, it is the area of the shaded rectangle shown in the left panel in Figure 11-9. In the short run, producer surplus is thus larger than economic profit, because the firm would lose more than its economic profit if it were prevented from participating in the market.

The right panel in Figure 11-9 shows an equivalent way of representing producer surplus. The alternative measure makes use of the fact that variable cost at any level of output is equal to the area under the marginal cost curve (below the shaded area in the right panel). To see why this is so, note that the variable cost of producing 1 unit of output is equal to marginal cost at 1 unit, MC_1; VC for 2 units is the sum of MC_1 and MC_2, and so on, so that $VC_Q = MC_1 + MC_2 + \ldots + MC_Q$, which is just the area under the MC curve. Hence the difference between the total revenue and total variable cost may also be expressed as the upper shaded area in the right panel in Figure 11-9.

---

[6]If $\Pi = TR - TC$ and $TC = VC + FC$, then producer surplus = $TR - VC = TR - TC + FC = \Pi + FC$.

FIGURE 11-9

Two Equivalent Measures of Producer Surplus
The difference between total revenue and total variable cost is a measure of producer surplus, the gain to the producer from producing Q_i^* units of output rather than zero. It can be measured as the difference between $P^*Q_i^*$ and $AVC_{Q_i}^*Q_i^*$ (shaded rectangle, left panel), or as the difference between $P^*Q_i^*$ and the area under the marginal cost curve (upper shaded area, right panel).

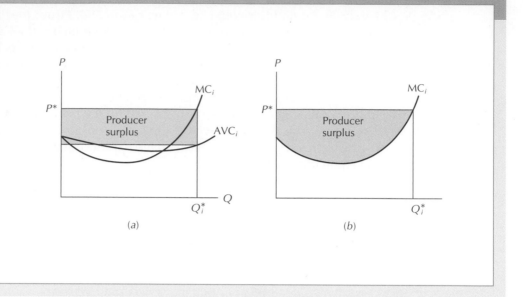

Which of the two ways of measuring producer surplus is most useful will depend on the specific context at hand. If we are interested in the change in an existing producer surplus, the method shown in the right panel in Figure 11-9 will usually be easiest to work with. But when we want to measure total producer surplus, it will often be easier to calculate the surplus by using the method shown in the left panel.

To measure aggregate producer surplus for a market, we simply add the producer surplus for each firm that participates. In cases where each firm's marginal cost curve is upward sloping for the bulk of its range, aggregate producer surplus will be well approximated by the area between the supply curve and the equilibrium price line, P^*, as shown in Figure 11-10.

FIGURE 11-10

Aggregate Producer Surplus When Individual Marginal Cost Curves Are Upward Sloping Throughout
For any quantity, the supply curve measures the minimum price at which firms would be willing to supply it. The difference between the market price and the supply price is the marginal contribution to aggregate producer surplus at that output level. Adding these marginal contributions up to the equilibrium quantity Q^*, we get the shaded area, which is aggregate producer surplus.

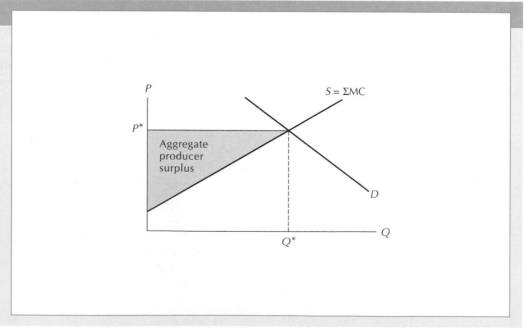

FIGURE 11-11

The Total Benefit from Exchange in a Market
The sum of aggregate producer surplus (shaded lower triangle) and consumer surplus (shaded upper triangle) measures the total benefit from exchange.

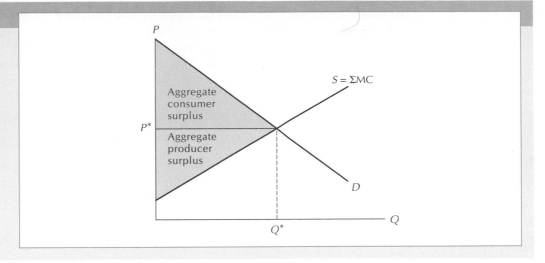

Recall from Chapter 5 that a rough approximation of consumer surplus for the market as a whole is given by the area between the demand curve and the equilibrium price line, as indicated by the shaded upper triangle in Figure 11-11.[7] The total benefits from exchange in the marketplace may be measured by the sum of consumer and producer surpluses.

EXAMPLE 11-3

Suppose there are two types of users of fireworks: careless and careful. Careful users never get hurt, but careless ones sometimes injure not only themselves, but also innocent bystanders. The short-run marginal cost curves of each of the 1000 firms in the fireworks industry are given by MC = 10 + Q, where Q is measured in kilograms of cherry bombs per year and MC is measured in dollars per kilogram of cherry bombs. The demand curve for fireworks by careful users is given by P = 50 − .001Q (same units as for MC). The government would like to continue to permit careful users to enjoy fireworks. But since it is impractical to distinguish between the two types of users, the government has decided to outlaw fireworks altogether. How much better off would consumers and producers be if the government had the means to effect a partial ban?

If the entire fireworks market is banned completely, the total of consumer and producer surplus will be zero. So to measure the benefits of a partial ban, we need to find the sum of consumer and producer surplus for a fireworks market restricted to careful users. To generate the supply curve for this market, we simply add the marginal cost curves of the individual firms horizontally, which results in the curve labelled S in Figure 11-12. The demand curve for careful users would intersect S at an equilibrium price of $30/kg and an equilibrium quantity of 20,000 kg/yr.

By outlawing the sale of fireworks altogether, legislators eliminate producer and consumer surplus values given by the areas of the two shaded triangles in Figure 11-12, which sum to $400,000/yr. In the language of cost-benefit analysis, this is the cost imposed on producers and careful users. The benefit of the ban is whatever value the public assigns to the injuries prevented (net of the cost of denying careless users the right to continue). It is obviously no simple matter to put a dollar value on the pain and

---

[7]Recall also that this measure of consumer surplus is most accurate when income effects are small, or if the demand curve is an income-compensated one.

suffering associated with fingers blown off by cherry bombs. In Chapter 14, we will discuss how at least rough estimates have been attempted in similar situations. But even in the absence of a formal quantitative measure of the value of injuries prevented, the public can ask itself whether the forgone surplus is a reasonable price to pay. The restrictions in most provinces on the private sale and use of fireworks, and the emphasis on community fireworks displays run by trained pyrotechnicians, suggest that the answer to this question is yes.

EXERCISE 11-5

What would the sum of consumer and producer surplus be in Example 11-3 if the demand curve for careful users were instead given by $P = 30 - .001Q$?

11.8 ADJUSTMENTS IN THE LONG RUN

The firm's objective, in both the long run and the short run, is to earn the highest economic profit it can. In the preceding section we saw that a firm will sometimes find it in its interest to continue supplying output in the short run even though it is making economic losses. In the long run, however, a firm would prefer to go out of business if it could not earn at least a normal profit (that is, zero economic profit) in its current industry.

Analyzing long-run adjustment processes is a challenging task. Every market is subject to change as a result of three main forces: technical change within the industry supplying the market, changes in input prices, and changes in market demand. For the moment, we shall hold technology and input prices constant and restrict our attention to changes in demand. Yet even this simplification by no means eliminates the complexity, because by definition time enters in an essential way into long-run adjustment processes. In analyzing short-run equilibrium, we assume that the number of firms is fixed and that each firm has certain fixed inputs, the quantity of which cannot readily be varied except at prohibitive cost. In the long run, however, the number of firms in the industry can change, as a result of the entry of new firms attracted by extranormal (economic) profits or the exit of existing firms that have been sustaining economic losses. Moreover, firms that remain in the industry may change their scale of efficient operation by increasing or decreasing their level of employment of inputs that were fixed in the short run.

FIGURE 11-12

Producer and Consumer Surplus in a Market Consisting of Careful Fireworks Users
The upper shaded triangle is consumer surplus ($200,000/yr). The lower shaded triangle is producer surplus ($200,000/yr). The total benefit of keeping this market open is the sum of the two, or $400,000/yr.

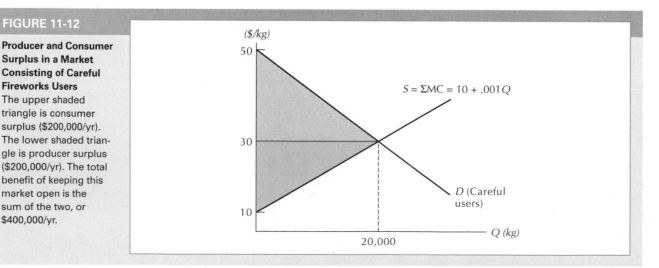

The precise nature of the long-run adjustment process in a particular industry hinges on the answers to a number of questions. Are the firms in the industry absolutely identical, or do they differ in size, technology, cost structure, and efficiency? Is there any difference in the relative speed of different adjustment processes? For example, is the speed of exit more rapid than the speed of entry? Can an existing firm adjust its capital stock in less time than it takes a new entrant to build a new plant from the ground up? Do all firms, existing firms and potential entrants alike, have the same expectations regarding relative speeds of the various adjustment processes and the nature of the industry in the long run? Do they have perfect foresight, or do they behave more or less myopically? If all firms in the industry are identical and are currently sustaining economic losses, which ones among the firms exit the industry? As the curtain rises, are all firms in the industry in short-run *and* long-run equilibrium, or are they in various stages of adjustment to past historical events?

Depending on the assumptions we make, we can produce a wide range of models of long-run firm and industry adjustment. Let us instead focus on the following simple hypothetical situation, and ask whether it is sustainable in the long run. Suppose that in the initial short-run equilibrium, firms in the industry have somehow adjusted their capital stocks so that they are producing at the level where the short-run market equilibrium price $P = \text{SMC} = \text{LMC}$. Industry supply and demand intersect at the price level $P = 10$, as shown in the left panel in Figure 11-13. The cost curves for a representative firm are shown in the right panel in Figure 11-13. At $Q = 200$ units/period the price of \$10 per unit of output exceeds SAC_2, with the result that the firm earns economic profit of \$600 each time period. This profit is indicated by the shaded rectangle.

The situation depicted in Figure 11-13 is inherently unstable. The reason is that the existence of positive economic profits creates a powerful incentive for outsiders to enter the industry. Recall that the average cost curves already include the opportunity cost of the capital that a firm requires to do business. This means that an outsider can buy everything needed to duplicate the operations of one of the existing firms in the industry, and in the process earn an economic profit of \$600 each time period.

As additional firms enter the industry, their short-run marginal cost curves are added to those of existing firms, which shifts the industry supply curve to the right.

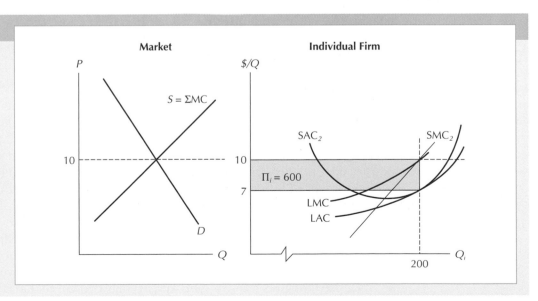

FIGURE 11-13

A Price Level That Generates Economic Profit
At the price level $P =$ \$10/unit, the firm has adjusted its plant size so that $\text{SMC}_2 = \text{LMC} = 10$. At the profit-maximizing level of output, $Q = 200$, the firm earns an economic profit equal to \$600 each time period, indicated by the area of the shaded rectangle.

FIGURE 11-14

A Step along the Path toward Long-Run Equilibrium
Entry of new firms causes supply to shift rightward, lowering price from 10 to 8. The lower price causes existing firms to adjust their capital stocks downward, giving rise to the new short-run cost curves SAC₃ and SMC₃. As long as price remains above short-run average cost (here, $SAC_3 = 5$), economic profits will be positive ($\Pi = \$540$ per time period), and incentives for new firms to enter will remain.

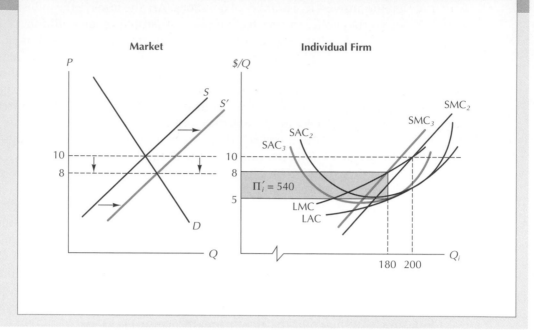

If only one firm entered the industry, there would be no significant effect on price. And with price virtually the same as before, each firm in the industry would continue to earn economic profits of nearly $600 per time period. These profits will continue to act as a carrot to lure additional firms into the industry, and the accumulating rightward supply shift will gradually cause price to fall.

The left panel in Figure 11-14 portrays the rightward shift in industry supply that results from a significant amount of entry. The new supply schedule, S', intersects the demand schedule at $P = \$8$ per unit. If the existing firms expected this price level to continue, they would have an incentive to reduce their capital stocks. In the right panel in Figure 11-14, note that the amount of capital that gives rise to the short-run cost curves SAC_3 and SMC_3 is optimal for the price level $P = \$8$ per unit. The profit-maximizing level of output for $P = \$8$ per unit is $Q = 180$ units/period. This results in an economic profit of $540 per time period, as indicated by the shaded rectangle.

Note that the adjustment by existing firms to the lower price level shifts each of their short-run marginal cost curves to the left. In terms of its effect on the industry supply curve, this adjustment thus works in the opposite direction from the adjustment caused by the entry of new firms. But the *net* effect of the two adjustments must be to shift industry supply to the right. If it were not, price wouldn't have fallen in the first place, and there would have been no reason for existing firms to reduce their capital stocks.

Even after the adjustments described above take place, new and existing firms in the industry continue to earn positive economic profits. The new profit level is lower than before, but will still act as an incentive for additional entry into the industry. Further entry sets off yet another round of adjustment, as the continuing fall in price renders existing capital stocks too large. For industries whose firms have U-shaped long-run average cost curves, entry, falling prices, and capital stock adjustment will continue until these two conditions are met: (1) price reaches the minimum point on the LAC curve (P^* in the right panel in Figure 11-15), and (2) all firms have moved to the capital stock size that gives rise to a short-run average cost curve that is tangent to the LAC

FIGURE 11-15

The Long-Run Equilibrium under Perfect Competition
If price starts above P^*, entry keeps occurring and capital stocks of existing firms keep adjusting until the rightward movement of the industry supply curve causes price to fall to P^*. At P^*, the profit-maximizing level of output for each firm is Q_i^*, the output level for which $P^* = SMC^* = LMC = SAC^* = LAC$. Economic profits of all firms are equal to zero.

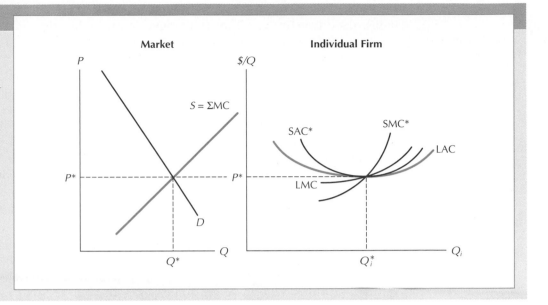

curve at its minimum point (SAC* in the right panel in Figure 11-15). Note in the right panel in Figure 11-15 that once all firms have reached this position, economic profit for each will be zero. The short-run marginal cost curve in the right panel is like the short-run marginal cost curve of all other firms in the industry, and when these curves are added horizontally, we get the industry supply curve shown in the left panel, which intersects the market demand curve at the long-run equilibrium price of P^*. This is the long-run competitive equilibrium position for the industry. Once it is reached, there will be no further incentive for new firms to enter the industry, because existing firms will all be earning an economic profit of zero.

In discussing the movement toward long-run competitive equilibrium, we began with an initial situation in which price was above the minimum value of long-run average cost and existing firms were all earning an economic profit. Suppose we had instead started with a hypothetical situation in which price had fallen below the minimum value of LAC. In that case, existing firms would be earning negative economic profits (that is, economic losses), which would be an incentive for some of them to leave the industry. The exodus would shift the supply curve leftward, causing an increase in price. This process would continue until all firms settled into the long-run equilibrium position portrayed in the right panel in Figure 11-15.

11.9 THE INVISIBLE HAND: SOME WRINKLES

Over two centuries ago, Adam Smith presented the first statement of a remarkable and important thesis. Smith argued that in a market society, although individuals in their actions intend only their individual security and private gain, they will be "led by an invisible hand to promote an end which was no part of [their] intention," the maximization of "the annual revenue of the society."[8] Smith's "invisible hand" is, in fact, the powerful network of communication, coordination, and control of a vast range of interconnected economic activities: the perfectly competitive market, or price system.

---

[8]Adam Smith, *An Inquiry into the Nature and Causes of the Wealth of Nations*, ed. Edwin Cannan, Book 4, Chapter 2, Chicago: University of Chicago Press, 1976, 477.

In an ideal (costless and perfectly functioning) competitive market, individuals and industries, driven by the self-interest motive, informed by price signals, and guided by the carrot of economic profit and the stick of economic losses, arrive at their respective long-run equilibrium positions. Remarkably, almost paradoxically, even if no firm consciously intends to promote the general social welfare, the long-run competitive equilibrium has, socially, some very desirable properties. Price is equal to marginal cost, both long run and short run, which means that the equilibrium is efficient in the sense previously discussed: it exhausts all possibilities for mutually beneficial trades. The last unit of output consumed is worth exactly the same to the buyer as the resources required to produce it. Moreover, price is equal to the minimum point on the long-run average cost curve, which means that there is no less costly way of producing the product. Finally, all producers earn only a normal rate of profit, which is the opportunity cost of the resources they have invested in their firms. The public pays not a penny more than what it cost the firms to serve them.

As remarkable as these efficiency properties is the sheer scale and volume of activity that is coordinated by the market mechanism. The next time you are in a supermarket, count the number of countries represented by the food and household products for sale in that one store. When you get home, take out your Yellow Pages and skim all the goods and services, from A to Z, that are available with a single phone call. These goods are available not as a result of a single centralized plan, but rather because of the profit-seeking behaviour of a multitude of economic agents, whose actions are coordinated by price signals sent by a multitude of interlinked markets.

In a pure centralized command economy, resources are allocated not by markets but by decisions reached by central planning committees. However, with limitations on the amount of information such committees can process, plans may not exactly reflect the final demand for goods, and planned targets may be incorrect. The famous Russian cartoon reprinted on this page, for example, shows the strategy of a nail factory manager who realizes that the easiest way to fulfil August's planned quota of 5000 kg of nails is to produce a single 5000-kg nail!

The competitive market is a powerful medium of communication. One of its principal strengths is that it economizes on the information required by each economic agent. The price signals generated by markets enable significant decentralization of decision making. A competitive firm does not need to know the internal production details of all of its potential input suppliers, merely the prices they charge for their outputs. Similarly, a firm needs to know only how much buyers are prepared to pay for its products.

Yet the market itself is not costless. It has a number of resource-consuming prerequisites, which those who have grown up in a market economy tend simply to assume. It has been said that "There is no such thing as a free lunch," because of the opportunity cost of the resources devoted to providing "free" school lunches or Meals on Wheels. A corollary is that "There is no such thing as a free market." Ironically, one of the clearest demonstrations of the substantial costs of creating and maintaining a market system has come from the formerly planned economies of the Soviet bloc, where market institutions were previously less well developed than in the advanced capitalist countries. There the virtual abandonment of central planning in the period after 1985 resulted in severe economic disruption, in some cases verging on chaos. The reason? Fully developed market institutions did not simply spring spontaneously and costlessly into existence to take over all of the coordinating functions formerly performed by centralized planning.

The modern market has evolved over a great number of years, alongside other social and economic institutions and customs that have sustained and been sustained by the

"Who needs a nail as big as that?"

"Who cares? The important thing is we fulfilled the plan for nails in one fell swoop."

market. The competitive market system depends on low-cost systems for disseminating accurate information on the prices and characteristics of goods, in order to minimize search and other transactions costs. It requires that people have basic numerical skills, so that they can use its price information in their decision making. The competitive market functions best in a peaceful, secure, and stable environment, where exchanges can be conducted without the threat of violence. It requires a widely understood and enforceable system of property rights. It requires legal institutions and law enforcement, in order to establish the rules of the game, to resolve contractual and other commercial disputes, and to impose penalties on those who cheat, defraud, or extort resources from the other players.

One of the principal institutions for providing these prerequisites of an efficient market system is government. Government and the market are viewed by some as polar opposites, even antagonists. However, without many of the activities of government, the market system would be unsustainable in its present form. The costs of these government activities may therefore be regarded as social overhead costs of maintaining the market system. Recognizing that "there is no such thing as a free market" should in no way diminish our recognition of the power of the market mechanism as a means of organizing and coordinating economic activity. It merely means that, as with all social institutions, we need to weigh the benefits of the market against its costs.

In later chapters, we will see that in certain situations, market systems can fall short of the mark. Moreover, competitive market allocations are "efficient" relative to an initial distribution of resources among the members of society. If you do not believe that the underlying distribution of resources is fair, there is no compelling reason for you to approve of the pattern of goods and services served up by the market mechanism. Understanding clearly the limitations of the market increases our ability to appreciate its remarkable capacities, without falling into the trap of assuming that it will always function automatically, costlessly, and without problems.

11.10 THE COST OF EXTRAORDINARY INPUTS

The Irrigation Project

We are in a position now to return to the question with which we began this chapter, namely, whether a state-supported irrigation system that doubles crop yields will raise the incomes of poor farmers. Recall that the farmers in question live in an isolated region of Bucolica and rent their farms from landowners.

First, let's consider the current situation in which no irrigation system exists. Farmers here may be viewed as the operators of small competitive firms. They rent land and supply their own labour, and keep the proceeds from selling their grain in a market so large that their own offerings have no appreciable effect on the price of grain, which is, say, $10 per bushel. For the sake of simplicity, let us ignore the cost of seed, tools, and other minor inputs.

Suppose that an individual farmer can farm 20 hectares and that without irrigation the land will yield 60 bushels of grain per hectare per year. His total revenue from the sale of his grain will then be $12,000/yr, from which he must deduct the rent for his land. How will that rent be determined?

Suppose the alternative to working as a farmer is to work in a factory for $6000/yr, and that factory work is generally regarded as neither more nor less pleasant than farming. If the land rent were only, say, $5000/yr for a 20-ha farm, then all the region's workers would prefer farming to working in the factories, because their net earnings would be $7000 instead of $6000. Assuming that there are many more factory workers than could farm the region's limited supply of farmland, there would be excess demand for farms at a rental price of $5000/yr. Factory workers would bid against one another, and the bidding would continue until the rental price for a 20-hectare parcel reached $6000/yr. At that price, a worker would have $6000 left over from the sale of his crops, which would leave him indifferent between the options of farming and factory work. By similar reasoning, the land rent could never exceed $6000 for very long under these conditions, for if it did, net farm incomes would fall below $6000/yr and everyone would want factory work instead of farming.

Now let's see what happens with the introduction of the irrigation project. With grain yields now 120 bushels/hectare instead of 60, a 20-ha farm will produce $24,000 in annual total revenue instead of $12,000. If the land rent remained at its original $6000/yr level, a farmer would earn $18,000/yr instead of $6000. Indeed, it was the prospect of such a dramatic rise in farmers' incomes that attracted so much support for the irrigation bill in the first place.

What the supporters of the bill have failed to recognize, however, is that land rents will not remain at $6000/yr after the introduction of the irrigation system. Needless to say, factory workers would bid vigorously for an opportunity to rent a farm parcel that would raise their income from $6000 to $18,000/yr. In the face of this bidding pressure, the rental price of farmland will continue to rise until it reaches a level of $18,000/yr. (If it were only $17,000, for example, a factory worker could switch to farming and raise his annual income from $6000 to $7000.) Once the annual rent for a 20-ha farm reaches $18,000, the balance between farm and factory opportunities will be restored.

Our hypothetical aide recommended against the irrigation project on the grounds that it would not raise the incomes of farmers in the long run. She perceived correctly that the beneficiaries of the state-supported irrigation project would be not the impoverished farmers but the owners of the land. If these owners already have high incomes, then the objective of the project will not be met by spending tax dollars solely to increase landowners' incomes.[9] This example illustrates the important idea that strong forces tend to equalize the average total costs of different firms in a competitive industry. Here, land prices adjusted to bring the average costs of the irrigated farms into balance with the average costs of growing crops elsewhere.

Would the aide's recommendation have differed if the farmers had individually owned their plots of land? Yes, since in this case, the increase in land prices as a result of the project would in fact have directly benefited the farmers. Yet in many less developed countries, land ownership is highly concentrated in a few hands, and there the aide's objections would apply. Is the situation any different in Canadian agriculture, where farmers typically have title to most of the land they farm, but the property is often heavily mortgaged? In this case, since the value of the mortgage is fixed in nominal terms, any increase in land prices *would* in fact directly benefit the farmers. This fact helps to answer the following Economic Naturalist question.

---

[9]Of course, the irrigation project would still be attractive if its cost were less than the value of the extra grain that resulted.

Over the past few decades, in several provinces, particularly Ontario, urban sprawl has gobbled up many square kilometres of prime farmland in the vicinity of larger and smaller urban centres. In response, governments have proposed or enacted legislation restricting the sale in certain areas of some grades of agricultural land for non-agricultural purposes. It might seem that most farmers would be pleased at these attempts to preserve farmland against urban encroachment. Yet farmers have been among the most vocal opponents of these measures.

The reason is not hard to find. As discussed further in Section 11.13 of the chapter, many of the smaller agricultural enterprises are barely viable in economic terms. Running a family farm is a demanding business, and the immediate material rewards are not always proportional to the effort. Moreover, even among those who know and love farming as a way of life, the system of passing on the farm to the younger generation has been challenged, as the younger generation is drawn away by more attractive non-agricultural opportunities. Hence, a significant number of farmers have come to view themselves as the last generation of farmers in the family. Their land thus becomes their "retirement fund." They plan to work the land until they retire, and then sell the land and retire on the proceeds. The market value of the land, however, is much lower in agricultural uses than if it is parcelled out for non-agricultural uses such as housing subdivisions or industrial parks. Legislation that restricts the non-agricultural use of prime farmland operates in the opposite direction from our hypothetical irrigation project, by lowering the expected value of the land and thus sharply reducing the value of farmers' retirement funds. Viewed from this perspective, it is not surprising that many farmers are less than pleased with legislation aimed at preserving farmland.

An Efficient Manager

Suppose one firm is like all others except that it employs an extraordinarily efficient manager. This manager is so efficient that the firm earns $500,000 of economic profit annually in an industry where the economic profit of the other firms hovers very close to zero. If she received the same salary as all other managers, the firm that employed her would have much lower costs than all other firms in the industry. But then there would be a strong incentive for some other firm to bid this manager away by offering her a higher salary.

Suppose a new firm offered her $300,000 more than her current annual salary and she accepted. That new firm would then earn an economic profit of $200,000/yr. That's less than an economic profit of $500,000/yr, but it is $200,000/yr better than the normal profit her original employer will earn without her.

Still other firms would have an incentive to offer even more for this manager. The bidding should continue until the cost savings for which she is responsible are entirely incorporated into her salary—that is, until her salary is $500,000/yr higher than the salary of an ordinary manager. And once her salary is bid up to that level, the firm that hires her will no longer enjoy a cost advantage over the other firms in the industry. The existence of such competitive bidding for inputs makes it plausible to assume that all the firms in a competitive industry have roughly the same average total costs in equilibrium.

Suppose all firms in an industry have "competent" managers and earn zero economic profit. The manager of one of the firms suddenly leaves and the firm finds that only incompetent applicants respond when the position is advertised at the original salary of $50,000/yr (which is the going rate for competent managers in this industry). Under an incompetent manager paid this salary, the firm will experience an economic loss of $20,000/yr. At what salary would it make sense for this firm to hire an incompetent manager?

11.11 THE LONG-RUN COMPETITIVE INDUSTRY SUPPLY CURVE

We saw that the short-run supply curve for a perfectly competitive industry is the horizontal summation of the short-run marginal cost curves of its individual firms. But the corresponding long-run supply curve for a competitive industry is not the horizontal summation of the long-run marginal cost curves of individual firms. Our task in the next sections is to derive the long-run supply curve for competitive industries operating under a variety of different cost conditions.

Long-Run Supply Curve with U-Shaped LAC Curves

What does the long-run supply curve look like in an industry in which all firms have identical U-shaped long-run average cost (LAC) curves? Suppose, in particular, that these LAC curves are like the one labelled LAC_i in the right panel in Figure 11-16. Suppose the demand curve facing the industry is initially the one labelled D_1 in the left panel. Given this demand curve, the industry will be in long-run equilibrium when each firm installs the capital stock that gives rise to the short-run marginal cost curve labelled SMC_i in the right panel. The number of firms in the industry will adjust so that the short-run supply curve, denoted S_{SR} in the left panel, intersects D_1 at a price equal to the minimum value of LAC_i. (If there were more firms than that or fewer, each would be making either an economic loss or a profit.)

Now suppose demand shifts rightward from D_1 to D_2, intersecting the short-run industry supply curve at the price P_2. The short-run effect will be for each firm to increase its output from Q^*_{i1} to Q^*_{i2}, which will lead to an economic profit measured by the shaded rectangle in the right panel in Figure 11-16. With the passage of time, these

FIGURE 11-16

The Long-Run Competitive Industry Supply Curve
When firms are free to enter or leave the market, price cannot depart from the minimum value of the LAC curve in the long run. If input prices are unaffected by changes in industry output, the long-run supply curve is S_{LR}, a horizontal line at the minimum value of LAC.

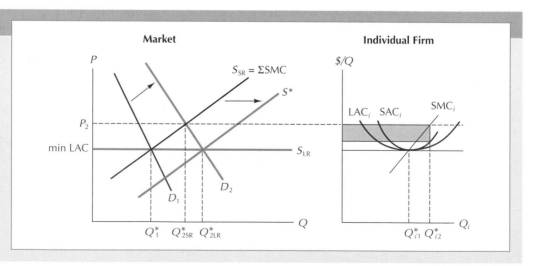

profits will lure additional firms into the industry until the rightward supply shift (to $S*$ in the left panel) again results in a price of min LAC. The long-run response to an increase in demand, then, is to increase industry output by increasing the number of firms in the industry. As long as the expansion of industry output does not cause the prices of capital, labour, and other inputs to rise, there will be no long-run increase in the price of the product.[10]

If demand had shifted to the left from D_1, a parallel story would have unfolded: Price would have fallen in the short run, firms would have reduced their offerings, and the resulting economic losses would have induced some firms to leave the industry. The exodus would shift industry supply to the left until price had again risen to min LAC. Here again the long-run response to a shift in demand is accommodated by a change in the number of firms. With U-shaped LAC curves, there is no tendency for a fall in demand to produce a long-run decline in price.

In summary, the long-run supply curve for a competitive industry with U-shaped LAC curves and constant input prices is a horizontal line at the minimum value of the LAC curve. In the long run, all the adjustment to variations in demand occurs not through changing prices but through variations in the number of firms serving the market. Following possibly substantial deviations in the short run, price shows a persistent tendency to gravitate to the minimum value of long-run average cost.

Industry Supply When Each LAC Curve Is Horizontal

As in the case of U-shaped LAC curves, the long-run industry supply curve when each firm's LAC curve is horizontal will again be a horizontal line (again assuming that input prices do not change with changes in industry output). But there is one salient difference between the two cases: When firms have identical U-shaped LAC curves, we can predict that each firm will produce the quantity that corresponds to the minimum point on its LAC. We thus get an industry composed of firms that all produce the same level of output.

In the case of horizontal LAC curves, in contrast, there is simply no unique minimum-cost point. LAC is the same at any level of output, which leads to an indeterminacy not present in the earlier case. We just cannot predict what the size distribution of firms will look like in the case of horizontal LAC curves. There may be a handful of large firms, many small ones, or a mixture of different sizes. All we can say with confidence is that price in the long run will gravitate toward the value of LAC.

The Effect on Supply of Changing Input Prices

In our analysis of cost curves in Chapter 10, which forms the basis of our analysis of supply under perfect competition, an important assumption was that input prices do not vary with the amount of output produced. For a single firm whose input purchases constitute only a small fraction of the total input market, this assumption is plausible. In many cases, moreover, even the entire industry's demands for inputs constitute only a small share of the overall input market. For example, even if the insurance industry issues 20 percent more policies this year than last, it employs such a small percentage of the total available supplies of secretaries, computers, executives, and other inputs that the prices of these inputs should not be significantly affected. So here too we may reasonably assume that input prices do not depend on output.

---

[10]In the section below we show on the next page what happens when changes in industry output cause changes in input prices.

But there are at least some industries in which the volume of inputs purchased constitutes an appreciable share of the entire input market. The market for commercial airliners, for example, consumes a significant share of the total amount of titanium sold each year. In such cases, a large increase in industry output will often be accompanied by significant increases in input prices.

When that happens, we have what is known as a ***pecuniary diseconomy***, a bidding up of input prices when industry output increases.[11] Even though the industry can expand output indefinitely without using more inputs per unit of output, the minimum point on each firm's LAC curve is nonetheless a rising function of industry output. For example, note in the left panel in Figure 11-17 that the firm's LAC curve for an industry output of Q_2 lies above its LAC curve for an industry output of $Q_1 < Q_2$, and that the LAC curve for an industry output of $Q_3 > Q_2$ lies higher still. To each industry output level there corresponds a different LAC curve, because input prices are different at every level of industry output. The long-run supply curve for such an industry will trace out the minimum points of these LAC curves. Thus, on the long-run industry supply curve (SLR, right panel), Q_1 corresponds to the minimum point on the firm's LAC curve when industry output is Q_1 (left panel); Q_2 corresponds to the minimum point for the LAC curve for Q_2; and so on. With pecuniary diseconomies, the long-run supply curve will be upward sloping even though each individual firm's LAC curve is U-shaped. Pecuniary diseconomies also produce an upward-sloping industry supply curve when each firm's LAC curve is horizontal. Competitive industries in which rising input prices lead to upward-sloping supply curves are called *increasing cost industries*.

There are also cases in which the prices of inputs may fall significantly with expanding industry output. This will happen, for example, if inputs are manufactured using technologies in which there are substantial economies of scale. A dramatic increase

---

FIGURE 11-17

Long-Run Supply Curve for an Increasing Cost Industry
When input prices rise with industry output, each firm's LAC curve will also rise with industry output (left panel). Thus the firm's LAC curve when industry output is Q_2 lies above its LAC curve when industry output is Q_1 (left panel). Firms will still gravitate to the minimum points on their LAC curves (Q_i^*, left panel), but because this minimum point depends on industry output, the long-run industry supply curve (SLR, right panel) will now be upward sloping.

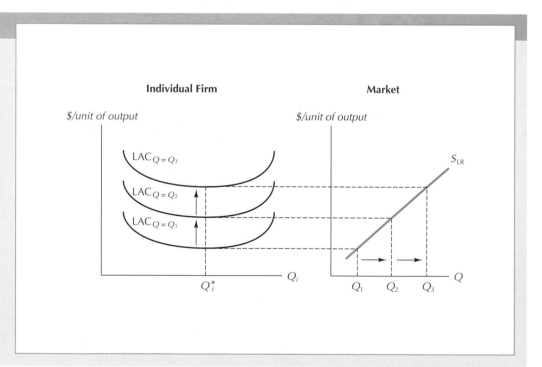

---

[11]A *pecuniary diseconomy* thus implies that input prices will fall when industry output contracts.

Pecuniary economy
A decrease in production cost that occurs when an expansion of industry output causes a fall in the prices of inputs.

in road building, for example, might facilitate greater exploitation of economies of scale in the production of earthmoving equipment, resulting in a lower price for that input. Such cases are called ***pecuniary economies***, and give rise to a downward-sloping long-run industry supply curve, even where each firm's LAC curve is either horizontal or U-shaped. Competitive industries in which falling input prices lead to downward-sloping supply curves are called *decreasing cost industries*.[12]

Economic Naturalist 11-2

WHY DO FILM-BASED COLOUR PHOTOGRAPHS COST LESS THAN BLACK-AND-WHITE PHOTOGRAPHS?

In the 1950s, colour photographs were a luxury, costing several times as much as black and white. Today, it costs about $17.99 to develop and print a 36-exposure roll of black-and-white film, but only $6.99 for the same size roll of colour film. This fall in the relative price of colour photos has occurred despite the fact that the colour process remains more complex than the one for black and white.

If colour processing is more complex than black and white, why does it cost less? The answer is in part because of economies of scale in the production of the machinery used to make both types of prints. When colour photography was in its infancy, film was expensive and the colours tended to fade rapidly, so most people used black and white. The high volume of black-and-white photo processing, in turn, made it possible to produce processing machines cheaply because of economies of scale. As the price of colour film declined over time and its quality rose, more people began to use it and the demand for colour-processing equipment gradually grew. And again because of economies of scale in the production of processing equipment, this led to a fall in the cost of an important input for colour print-making—a pecuniary economy. At the same time, with pecuniary economies, the *decline* in production of black-and-white processing equipment led to an *increase* in its price.

The resulting changes in the equilibrium prices and quantities of the two types of prints are roughly as shown in Figure 11-18. Note that the relative positions of the two supply curves are the same for both years. This means that the printmaking industry would be willing to supply any given total quantity of black-and-white prints for a lower price than for the same quantity of colour prints in both years. It is the change in demand patterns, together with downward-sloping supply curves in both markets, that explains the observed reversal in relative prices.

Of course, over the past decade, technological change has been altering the picture dramatically. The rapid rise of digital cameras, the sharp drop in the prices of basic and high mega-pixel digital cameras, and the increased sophistication of computerized home and online photo design and printing systems have revolutionized photography. In the process, the sharp line between black-and-white and colour photos has been almost completely erased in the digital realm. At the same time, sales of traditional silver-halide film have taken a sharp hit, as memory cards have increasingly displaced film. Significantly, the model of pecuniary economies enables us to predict the effects of these changes on the future cost of both black-and-white *and* colour *film*-based pictures.

---

[12]Note that as the left panel of Figure 11-17 is drawn, the firm's minimum LAC point, Q_i^*, does not change as industry output increases. This will be the case if *all* input prices rise proportionally as industry output increases. If the input prices increase by different proportions, however, firms' output expansion paths—and thus the shape of their LAC curves—can change, and hence so can Q_i^* at different industry output levels. The same principle also applies for decreasing cost industries.

FIGURE 11-18

Because of economies of scale in the production of equipment used to process film, the long-run supply curves of both colour and black-and-white prints are downward sloping. In 1955, when the quality of colour film was poor, most people demanded black and white, resulting in lower prices. Now, in contrast, demand for colour is much greater than for black and white. The result is that colour prints are now less expensive than black and white, even though colour-processing equipment remains more complicated.

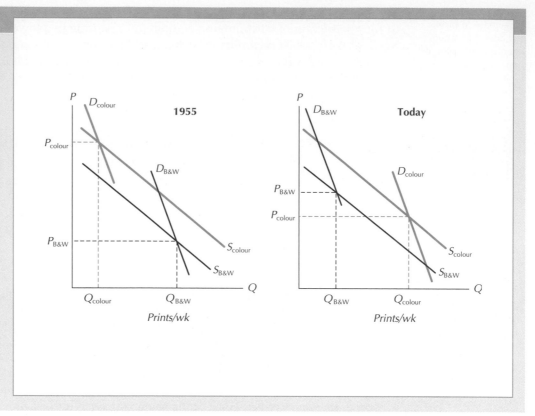

11.12 THE ELASTICITY OF SUPPLY

In Chapter 4 we defined the price elasticity of demand as a measure of the responsiveness of the quantity demanded to variations in price. An analogous concept exists for measuring the responsiveness of the quantity supplied to variations in price. Naturally, it is called the price elasticity of supply. Suppose we are at a point (Q, P) on the industry supply curve shown in Figure 11-19, where a change in price of ΔP gives rise to a change of ΔQ in the quantity supplied. The price elasticity of supply, denoted ϵ^S, is then given by

$$\epsilon^S = \frac{\Delta Q}{\Delta P} \frac{P}{Q} \quad \text{(see footnote 13)}. \tag{11.3}$$

As in the case of elasticity of demand, supply elasticity has a simple interpretation in terms of the geometry of the industry supply curve. When ΔP is small, the ratio $\Delta P/\Delta Q$ is the slope of the supply curve, which means that the ratio $\Delta Q/\Delta P$ is the reciprocal of that slope. Thus the price elasticity of supply may be interpreted as the product of the ratio of price to quantity and the reciprocal of the slope of the supply curve:

$$\epsilon^S = \frac{P}{Q} \frac{1}{\text{slope}} \tag{11.4}$$

---

[13]In calculus terms, supply elasticity is defined by $\epsilon^S = (dQ/Q)/(dP/P) = (P/Q)(dQ/dP)$.

FIGURE 11-19

The Elasticity of Supply
In the neighbourhood of point A, the elasticity of supply is given by $\epsilon^S = (\Delta Q/\Delta P)(P/Q)$. If the short-run supply curve is upward sloping, the short-run elasticity of supply will always be positive. In the long run, elasticity of supply can be positive, zero, or negative.

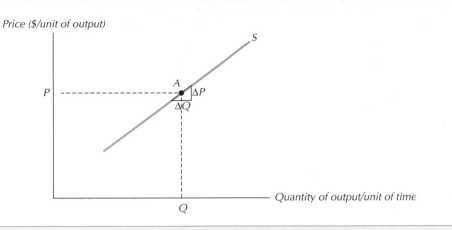

Price ($/unit of output)

Quantity of output/unit of time

EXAMPLE 11-4

Suppose the industry supply curve is $P = -30 + 2Q$, for $Q \geq 15$. What is the price elasticity of supply when $Q = 20$? When $Q = 25$?

At $Q = 20$, price is $P = -30 + 2Q = -30 + 2(20) = 10$ (see Figure 11-20). The slope of the linear supply curve is constant at

$$m = \frac{\text{rise}}{\text{run}} = \frac{\Delta P}{\Delta Q} = 2.$$

Thus the elasticity of supply at ($P = 10$, $Q = 20$) is

$$\epsilon^s = \frac{1}{\text{slope}}\left(\frac{P}{Q}\right) = \frac{1}{2}\left(\frac{10}{20}\right) = \frac{1}{4}.$$

When $Q = 25$, price $P = 20$, and the elasticity of supply therefore increases to $\left(\frac{1}{2}\right)\left(\frac{20}{25}\right) = \frac{2}{5}$.

FIGURE 11-20

A Case of Inelastic Supply
The elasticity of supply at $Q = 20$ and $P = 10$, $\epsilon^s = \frac{1}{\text{slope}}(P/Q) = \frac{1}{2}(10/20) = \frac{1}{4} < 1$, and hence supply is inelastic. At $Q = 25$ and $P = 20$, $\epsilon^s = (1/2)(20/25) = 2/5$. With this inelastic linear supply curve, as Q increases, so does the supply elasticity, until for very large Q, ϵ^s becomes almost unitary.

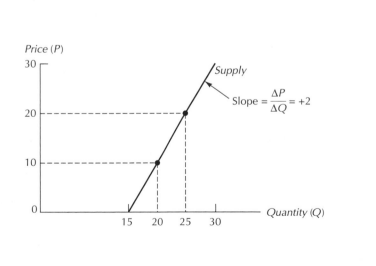

Price (P)

Quantity (Q)

What is the elasticity of supply at point *A* in Figure 11-19 if the price and quantity at *A* are given by 24 and 40, respectively, and the slope of the supply curve is .5?

With diminishing marginal productivity of variable inputs, the short-run competitive industry supply curve will be upward sloping, which means that the short-run elasticity of supply will be positive. For industries with a horizontal long-run supply curve, the long-run elasticity of supply is infinite. Output can be expanded indefinitely without a change in price. With pecuniary economies and diseconomies, long-run competitive industry supply curves may also be either downward or upward sloping in specific cases. The corresponding long-run elasticities of supply in these cases will be either negative or positive, respectively.

We have already noted that most industries employ only a relatively small share of the total volume of inputs traded in the marketplace, which means that modest variations in industry output should have no significant effect on input prices in most industries. In practical applications of the competitive model, therefore, economists often adopt the working hypothesis that long-run supply curves are horizontal. Of course, this hypothesis can always be modified when there is evidence that pecuniary economies or diseconomies are important.[14]

11.13 APPLYING THE COMPETITIVE MODEL

As noted earlier in the chapter, economists recognize that no industry strictly satisfies the four requirements for perfect competition—a standardized product, firms as price takers, perfect factor mobility, and perfect information. For practical purposes, the important question is how far an industry can fall short of these conditions before general tendencies of the competitive model fail to apply. Unfortunately, there are no hard-and-fast rules for making this judgment. In industries where entry and exit are relatively easy, a firm may behave as a price taker even in a market where it is the only competitor. In industries where entry and exit are more difficult, even the existence of a relatively large number of established firms does not guarantee price-taking behaviour. In the short run, especially, firms may be able to work out tacit agreements to restrain price competition even when there are extranormal profits.

Despite this difficulty, experience has shown that some of the most important long-run properties of the competitive model apply in many industries, with the notable exception of those where the government erects legal barriers to entry (for example, by requiring a government licence in order to participate in a market, as is the case with the CRTC and radio and television broadcast licences).

By way of illustration, let's consider three brief applications that highlight some of the insights afforded by the perfectly competitive model.

Price Supports as a Device for Saving "Marginal" Farms

In 1900, more than 40 percent of the Canadian labour force earned its living by farming. Today, the corresponding figure is less than 3 percent. This change is obviously not the result of a dramatic decline in food consumption. Rather, it is one of the many consequences of farming methods' having become vastly more productive during the last century.

---

[14] For further results on the elasticity of supply, see Module 6 of the Online *Basic Math Review*.

There is no single history of Canadian agriculture. The great regional diversity in types of farm and the differing market and policy environments for different agricultural products mean that generalizations about the agricultural sector can be difficult. The challenges faced by a prairie grain farmer are different from those faced by a prairie livestock producer. These challenges differ in turn from those of an Okanagan or Annapolis Valley or Niagara Peninsula orchard operation, or a Prince Edward Island potato farm. Canada has four main types of farms: livestock farms (including feedlots, dairy operations, and poultry and egg producers), grain farms, special-crop farms (including tobacco and market gardening operations) and mixed farms. The marijuana industry, located primarily in British Columbia, which produces an estimated 800 tonnes of pot a year with a street value of about $9 billion, faces its own distinct challenges, not the least of which is that it is illegal.

However, some important patterns are fairly clear. The 2001 Census of Agriculture found approximately 247,000 farms in Canada. The number of farms has declined continuously from census to census since the historical peak of 730,000 farms was reached in 1941. Over the same period, average farm size, in terms of area, gross sales, and capitalization, has been increasing. In recent years, so has the use of computers and the Internet in managing farm operations. The average age of farm operators, however, has also been rising. This is an indication that young men and women from farm families are not following in their parents' footsteps in great numbers. On many Canadian farms, particularly the smaller ones, the net income from farm operations, even before deducting the opportunity cost of the time spent working the farm, represents less than 50 percent of the total income of the farm families, with earnings from outside jobs representing more than 50 percent of total family income.

Interpreting correctly the numbers for the farms with the lowest net farm incomes poses a challenge. The reason is that two distinct groups of farms are included in this category. The first group is made up of farms that are simply too small to be viable. With poor soil or too little land and capital to achieve an efficient scale of production, they are marginal. Even in good times, a farm family cannot sustain itself by farming alone, and working away from the farm is necessary to supplement net farm income. The second group is owned by people who are basically recreational, land-speculating, or tax-break farmers. For members of this group, owning a farm is basically a consumption or a speculative choice, not a production choice. They enjoy the benefits of country living, their income—often quite a good income—is derived from sources away from the farm, and any revenue they earn from their farm operations is a bonus. Effective policies for low-income farms have to take into account the existence of these two different groups.

One of the most significant features of Canadian agriculture is that 95 percent of farms are *family* farms. This is in sharp contrast to the situation in the United States, where corporate agribusiness has come to play a much larger role in overall agricultural production. A second important feature is one that Canadian agriculture shares with that of the United States and the European Community. Agricultural production is fairly heavily subsidized. Under the umbrella of the federal Agricultural Stabilization Act, a range of price support, subsidy, supply management, and disaster relief programs are in place. The specific programs available vary from commodity to commodity, and even from province to province. Most of these programs have multiple objectives: to ensure a secure domestic supply of agricultural products; to stabilize farm incomes from year to year; and to provide relief for the poorest farmers.

Simplified models of two types of agricultural stabilization programs can provide us with a basis for assessing the effectiveness of these programs in achieving their objectives.

FIGURE 11-21

**Marketing Board
Supply Management**
Restriction of supply
by a marketing board
increases producer
surplus by the area
(1 minus 3), but increases
the price to consumers
from P_C to P_M, reduces
consumer surplus by
(1 + 2), and results in a
deadweight efficiency
loss of (2 + 3).

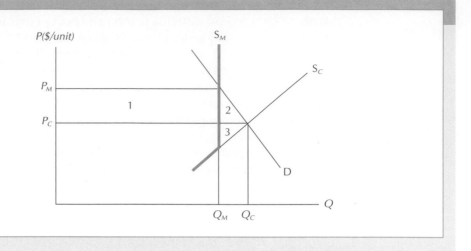

One type of program, illustrated in Figure 11-21, involves the use of agricultural product marketing boards, which engage in supply management to maintain product prices at profitable levels. Suppose that an egg marketing board is established for egg producers, as the sole agency that can sell eggs to consumers. In our simple model, only member producers are permitted to sell eggs, and they sell them through the marketing board. The board restricts the egg supply by allocating quotas to its members, causing the supply curve to become vertical at Q_M. Under competition, consumers would have paid P_C, but they now pay P_M. If demand is inelastic, as it is reasonable to assume, the restriction of supply increases the total revenue of egg producers. Consumer surplus will be reduced by the area (1 + 2), while producer surplus increases by an amount equal to area 1 minus area 3. The deadweight efficiency loss will be the area (2 + 3), while area 1 will be redistributed from consumers to egg producers. In the long run, if quotas can be transferred from one producer to another, the value of the quotas will be capitalized, just as taxi licences are when the number of taxis is controlled. Whether individual egg producers can realize the capitalized value of their quotas by selling them to another producer depends on the mechanism by which quotas are allocated. There is still an incentive for egg producers to innovate and cut costs. But the most effective innovators will not be able to increase their share of market supply if quotas cannot be transferred. Industry productivity will therefore be lower than in the absence of the quota system.

A second type of program involves the establishment by government of a support price or price floor for an agricultural product. If the price falls below this level, the government will purchase any excess supply at the support price. Such programs have a number of effects, including the accumulation by the government of enormous stockpiles of the commodity. Let us focus, however, on the question of whether they provide assistance to smaller farmers effectively and at low social cost. Figure 11-22 shows the short-run cost curves for two types of farms, small (S) farms and large (L) farms. Under competition, with the market price equal to P^*, both large and small farms would produce where their SMC curves intersect the horizontal line through P^*. Large farms would produce at the minimum point on the LAC curve, earning zero economic profits, while small farms would sustain substantial losses. Figure 11-22 depicts the situation *after* the support price P_G is in place. Both types of farm expand output, small farms to Q_S and large farms to Q_L. The losses of the small farms have been reduced

FIGURE 11-22

The Short-Run Effect of Agricultural Price Supports
Price supports initially reduce the losses of small farms, while creating economic profits for large farms. In the long run, however, they serve only to bid up land prices.

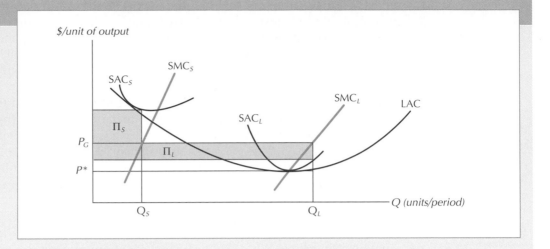

to an amount equal to the area of the green rectangle Π_S, while large farms earn an economic profit indicated by the shaded rectangle Π_L. These positive economic profits lead to bidding for farmland by outsiders eager to get in on the extranormal profits. The end result will be an increase in land prices and thus cost curves. In the long run there is little benefit to small farmers except when they sell their land, if by that time it is not mortgaged up to the hilt to cover past losses and they still own it free and clear. Although it is not directly shown in Figure 11-22, we should not forget that instituting the support price at a level above the competitive market price also has the effect of reducing consumer surplus.

These two simple models are both important in understanding the prospects for Canadian agriculture. There are many supply management marketing boards in Canada, although not all marketing boards are of this type. As Figure 11-21 suggests, they tend to result in higher food prices for consumers and in deadweight efficiency losses. A number of commentators have suggested that in many cases the costs of such marketing boards outweigh any benefits. The second model is important for a different reason. While some forms of price support have been and are used in Canada, price supports and subsidies are quantitatively much more important in the United States and Europe—on the order of $450 billion per year! For grain products in particular, even if Canadian farmers can produce at lower cost than farmers elsewhere, once subsidies are incorporated it is more difficult for Canadian farmers to compete in export markets. The costs to Canada of becoming involved in a competitive international subsidy war would be immense, even if it were able to under World Trade Organization (WTO) rules. Yet the WTO has found that removing entrenched agricultural subsidy programs is the toughest nut it has had to crack, and Canadian grain exports are one of the casualties of the present system.

Why Taxing Business Can Be a Taxing Business

As noted in Chapter 2, political leaders often find it easier to propose new taxes on business than to collect additional taxes from individuals. Proposals to tax business usually include statements to the effect that "wealthy corporations can better afford to pay extra taxes than struggling workers can." Suppose that the government decides to levy a tax on business: specifically, on the firms of a particular perfectly competitive industry. What sort of tax should it impose? Let's say that it opts initially for a tax on the output of the industry. The industry is one in which individual firms have identical U-shaped LAC curves like the one labelled LAC_i in the right panel in Figure 11-23. With constant input prices, the long-run industry supply curve will be a horizontal line at the minimum point of LAC_i (the curve labelled SLR in the left panel). If D is the market demand curve, then the equilibrium price will be Q_1^*.

If a tax of T dollars is collected on each unit of output sold in the market, the tax shifts the LAC and SMC curves of each firm upward by T dollars (right panel in Figure 11-23). The new long-run industry supply curve is again a horizontal line at the minimum value of the LAC curve—this time the curve $S_{LR} + T$ in the left panel in Figure 11-23. The effect of the tax is to increase the price of the product by exactly T dollars. Industry output contracts from Q_1^* to Q_2^* (left panel), and this contraction is achieved by firms leaving the industry.

The net result of the output tax is that in the long run the burden of this tax on business falls entirely on consumers! This was the wrong sort of tax to achieve the government's objectives. What about a surtax on extranormal or economic profits instead? This tax will not be passed on to consumers. Unfortunately, it also has the drawback that it will not raise any revenues, since in long-run competitive equilibrium each firm earns zero economic profits. Alternatively, suppose that the government decides to put a surtax on the normal (accounting) profits of the industry. If it does so, then the industry will disappear completely, because after the surtax is deducted from normal profits (which represent zero economic profits), each firm will be making economic losses and will exit from the industry. Perhaps then it should increase the corporate tax rate on all businesses, so that there is "no place to hide." Unfortunately, in a world where capital is increasingly mobile internationally, there are "places to hide." The problem is that they are outside the nation's borders, and we should expect "capital flight" to occur in this case.

Governments obviously do use corporate taxation and excise taxes on particular commodities as means of revenue generation and as instruments of government policy. In Chapter 12, we shall see that it is possible to tax the economic profits of a *monopolist*

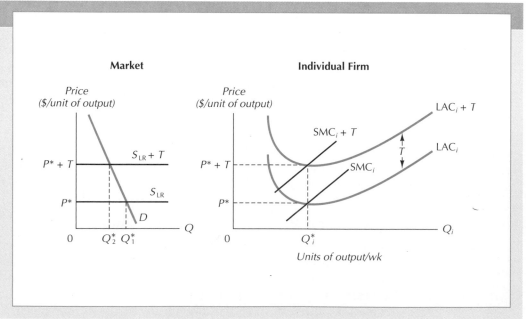

FIGURE 11-23

The Effect of a Tax on the Output of a Perfectly Competitive Industry
A tax of T dollars per unit of output raises the LAC and SMC curves by T dollars (right panel). The new long-run industry supply curve is again a horizontal line at the minimum value of LAC (left panel). Equilibrium price rises by T dollars (left panel), which means that 100 percent of the tax is passed on to consumers.

without thereby causing changes in its behaviour. In Chapter 16, we shall see why, in a general-equilibrium context, a tax on the output of *competitive* industries can offset monopoly-induced distortions and increase economic efficiency. What this section has shown is that taxing business out of political expediency, without adequate economic analysis, can have negative consequences. In the case of a perfectly competitive industry, the long-run results can be exactly the opposite of what was intended.

The Adoption of Cost-Saving Innovations

The economist's emphasis on the competitive firm as a price taker sometimes creates the impression that competitive firms do little more than passively respond to impersonal price signals served up by the environment. This impression is deeply misleading. While it is true, for example, that an individual trucker can do little to affect trucking rates set in the open market, there is a great deal he can and must do to ensure his continued survival.

The short-run response to the dramatic fuel price increases of the 1970s automatically led to just the sorts of adjustments predicted by the competitive model: short-term losses, exit from the industry, gradually rising prices, and a gradual restoration of profitability for surviving firms. But the change in the environment also created opportunities that some firms actively exploited to their own advantage. A case in point is the subject of Economic Naturalist 11-2.

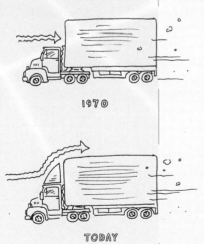

1970

TODAY

Why did airfoils suddenly appear on large trucks in the mid-1970s?

Economic Naturalist 11-3

WHY DID 18-WHEELERS SUDDENLY BEGIN USING AIRFOILS IN THE MID-1970S?

Before 1970, the profile of the typical 18-wheel semi tractor-trailer truck was like the one shown at the top of the figure in the margin. The broad, flat expanse of the front of the trailer was directly exposed to the force of the oncoming wind, which at highway speeds was substantial. But with the low cost of diesel fuel in 1970, the penalty from having to run the engine a little harder was not large.

With the tripling of diesel prices by the early 1980s, however, that penalty became much more important—so much so that entrepreneurs devised ways of reducing it. One of the most successful innovations was the simple airfoil that now adorns the cab of virtually every large truck on the road. Shown at the bottom of the figure in the margin, its purpose is to deflect the wind to the top of the trailer. The profile of today's semi is still no aerodynamic masterpiece, but truckers estimate that the reduced wind resistance decreases their fuel consumption by 10 to 15 percent at highway speeds.

The first truckers to install the airfoils did so when the industry price level was determined by the higher costs of running trucks that lacked them. As a result, these early adopters earned economic profits from their efforts. As time passed, however, more and more trucks began to sport the devices, and the industry price level gradually declined in response to the lower costs they made possible. Now it is rare to see an 18-wheeler that lacks an airfoil. It is safe to assume that the resultant cost savings have been fully reflected in lower trucking rates. The result is that the owner of a truck must now install an airfoil merely to be able to earn a normal rate of profit. Those who fail to install them pay the penalty of earning economic losses.

The lesson of this example is that the entrepreneur who earns economic profits is the one who adopts cost-saving innovations ahead of the competition. It is the search for such innovations that keeps even the price-taking firm from being merely a passive reactor to economic forces beyond its control.

- The assumed objective of the firm is to maximize its economic profits. Competitive pressures in the marketplace may render this a plausible assumption, even though it seems to impute an unrealistically high degree of purposefulness to the actions of many managers. Economic profit is the difference between total revenue and cost—both explicit and implicit—of all resources used in production. Economic profit is not to be confused with accounting profit, which is the difference between total revenue and the explicit cost of resources used.

- The economic model of perfect competition assumes a standardized product, price-taking behaviour on the part of the firms, perfect mobility of resources, and perfect information on the part of buyers and firms. In this sense, it is similar to the physicist's model of motion on frictionless surfaces. Both models describe idealized conditions that are rarely if ever met in practice, and yet each generates useful predictions and explanations of events we observe in the world.

- The rule for profit maximization in the short run is to produce the level of output for which price is equal to short-run marginal cost on the rising portion of that curve. If price falls below the minimum value of average variable cost, the firm does best to produce no output in the short run. The individual firm's short-run supply curve is thus the rising portion of its short-run marginal cost curve that lies above the minimum point of its average variable cost curve.

- The short-run industry supply curve is the horizontal summation of the individual firm's supply curves. It intersects the industry demand curve to determine the short-run equilibrium price. The individual competitive firm's demand curve is a horizontal line at the equilibrium price. If that price happens to lie above the minimum value of a firm's long-run average cost curve, the firm will earn positive economic profits. If price is less than that value, the firm will suffer economic losses.

- Long-run adjustments consist not only of alterations in the size of existing firms' capital stocks, but also of entry and exit of firms. Where firms have identical U-shaped LAC curves, the long-run equilibrium price will be the minimum value of that LAC curve, and each firm will produce the corresponding quantity.

- Both long-run and short-run equilibrium positions are efficient in the sense that the value of the resources used in making the last unit of output is exactly equal to the value of that output to the buyer. This means that the equilibrium position exhausts all possibilities for mutually beneficial exchange. The long-run equilibrium has two additional attractive features: (1) output is produced at the lowest possible unit cost, and (2) the seller is paid only the cost of producing the product. No economic profit is extracted from the buyer.

- Under perfect competition with constant input prices, the long-run industry supply curve is a horizontal line, not only when LAC curves are horizontal, but also when they are U-shaped. When input prices are an increasing function of industry output, the industry supply curves in both cases will be upward sloping. When input prices decline with industry output, the competitive industry supply curve will be downward sloping.

- The effect of competition for the purchase of unusually high quality inputs is to raise the price of those inputs until they no longer enable the firm that employs them to earn an economic profit. This is an extremely important part of the long-run adjustment process, and failure to account for it lies behind the failure of many well-intended economic policies.

- Even price-taking firms must actively seek out means of reducing their costs of doing business. To the early adopters of cost-saving innovations goes a temporary stream of economic profit, while late adopters must suffer through periods of economic losses.

1. What is the difference between economic profit and accounting profit, and how does this difference matter for actual business decisions?

2. Under what conditions will we expect firms to behave as price takers even though there are only a small number of other firms in the industry?

3. Would the market for dry cleaning be perfectly competitive in large cities such as Edmonton or Montreal? Why or why not? How about in a smaller centre such as Dauphin, Manitoba, or Antigonish, Nova Scotia?

4. A firm's total revenue curve is given by $TR = 3Q - .02Q^2$. Is this a perfectly competitive firm? Explain why or why not.

5. Does the fact that a business manager may not know the definition of marginal cost contradict the theory of perfect competition?

6. *True or false:* If marginal cost lies below average fixed cost, the firm should necessarily shut down in the short run. Explain.

7. What do economists mean when they say that the short-run competitive equilibrium is efficient?

8. *True or false:* In a constant cost industry where individual firms have U-shaped long-run average cost curves, a tax of a constant, fixed amount on each unit of output sold will not affect the amount of output sold by a perfectly competitive firm that remains in the industry in the long run. Explain.

9. Suppose all firms in a competitive industry are operating at output levels for which price is equal to long-run marginal cost. True or false: This industry is necessarily in long-run equilibrium.

10. *True or false:* Consumer surplus is the area between the demand curve and the price line. For a perfectly competitive firm the demand curve equals the price line. Thus, a perfectly competitive industry produces no consumer surplus.

11. Why are pecuniary economies and diseconomies said to be the exception rather than the rule?

12. In a perfectly competitive industry, would you expect a firm that adopts cost-saving innovations faster than 80 percent of all firms in the industry to earn economic profits? If so, will there be any tendency for these profits to be bid away?

13. True or false: Initially, an industry is in short-run and long-run equilibrium. Then a government program provides an annual lump-sum subsidy (one that does not vary with the level of production) to each firm in the industry. In the long run, the output of each of the original firms in the industry will rise.

PROBLEMS

1. A competitive firm has the cost structure described in the following table. Graph the marginal cost, average variable cost, and average total cost curves. How many units of output will it produce at a market price of $32 per unit? Calculate its profits and show them in your graph.

Q	ATC	AVC	MC
1	44	4	8
2	28	8	16
4	26	16	32
6	30.67	24	48
8	37	32	64

2. If the short-run marginal and average variable cost curves for a competitive firm are given by $SMC = 2 + 4Q$ and $AVC = 2 + 2Q$, where SMC and AVC are in $ per unit and Q is in units, how many units of output will it produce at a market price of $10 per unit? At what level of fixed cost will this firm earn zero economic profit?

3. Each of 1000 identical firms in the competitive peanut butter industry has a short-run marginal cost curve given by

$$SMC_Q = 4 + Q.$$

If the demand curve for this industry is

$$P = 10 - .002Q,$$

what will be the short-run loss in producer and consumer surplus if an outbreak of aflatoxin suddenly makes it impossible to produce any peanut butter?

4. Assuming the aflatoxin outbreak in Problem 3 persists, will the long-run loss in producer and consumer surplus be larger than, smaller than, or the same as the short-run loss? (An exact numerical answer is not required.)

5. A perfectly competitive firm faces a price of $10 per unit and is currently producing at a level of output where marginal cost is equal to $10 per unit on a rising portion of its short-run marginal cost curve. At this output level, its long-run marginal cost is equal to $12 per unit and short-run average variable cost is equal to $8 per unit. The minimum point on its long-run average cost curve is equal to $10 per unit. Is this firm earning an economic profit in the short run? Should it alter its output in the short run? In the long run, what should this firm do?

**6. All firms in a competitive, constant-cost industry have long-run total cost curves given by

$$LTC_Q = Q^3 - 10Q^2 + 36Q,$$

where Q is the firm's level of output. What will be the industry's long-run equilibrium price? (*Hint:* Use either calculus or a graph to find the minimum value of the associated long-run average cost curve.) What will be the long-run equilibrium output level of the representative firm?

**7. Same as Problem 6, except now

$$LTC_Q = Q^2 + 4Q.$$

Could any firm actually have this particular LTC curve? Why or why not?

8. The marginal and average cost curves of taxis in Metropolis are constant at $.20/km. The demand curve for taxi trips in Metropolis is given by $P = 1 - .00001Q$, where P is the fare, in dollars per kilometre, and Q is measured in kilometres per year. If the industry is perfectly competitive and each cab can provide exactly 10,000 km/yr of service, how many cabs will there be in equilibrium and what will be the equilibrium fare?

9. Now suppose that the city council of Metropolis decides to curb congestion in the downtown area by limiting the number of taxis to six. Applicants participate in a lottery, and the six winners get a medallion, which is a permanent licence to operate a taxi in Metropolis. What will the equilibrium fare be now? How much economic profit will each medallion holder earn? If medallions can be traded in the marketplace and the rate of interest is 10 percent/yr, how much will the medallions sell for? (*Hint:* How much money would you have to deposit in a bank to earn annual interest equal to the profit made by a taxi medallion?) Will the person who buys a medallion at this price earn a positive economic profit?

**10. Merlin is like all other managers in a perfectly competitive industry except in one respect: because of his great sense of humour, people are willing to work for him for half the going wage rate. All firms in the industry have short-run total cost curves given by

$$STC_Q = M + 10Q + wQ^2 \quad \text{(see footnote 15)},$$

where Q is units of output per day, M is the salary paid to the manager and w is the wage rate paid by the firm. If all firms in the industry face an output price of $28 per unit, and if the going wage rate is $2/labour-day, how much more will Merlin be paid than the other managers in the industry?

---

[15]As a general rule (as can be verified with calculus), if $TC_Q = a + bQ + cQ^2$, then the associated MC_Q curve is $dTC_Q/dQ = MC_Q = b + 2cQ$; $AVC_Q = b + cQ$; $AFC_Q = a/Q$; and $ATC_Q = AFC_Q + AVC_Q = a/Q + b + cQ$. The *minimum* value of ATC occurs where $dATC_Q/dQ = c - a/Q^2 = 0$, or where $Q = (a/c)^{1/2}$. Hence, for example, in Problem 10, $MC_Q = 10 + 2wQ$. (As an exercise, you should calculate MC_Q, AVC_Q, AFC_Q, and ATC_Q for Problems 10, 11, 13, and 16.)

**11. You are the owner/manager of a small competitive firm that manufactures house paints. You and all your 1000 competitors in this constant-cost industry have short-run total cost curves given by

$$STC = 8 + 2Q + 2Q^2,$$

and the industry is in long-run equilibrium. (Use calculus or see footnote 15.)

Now you are approached by an inventor who holds a patent on a process that will reduce your costs by half at each level of output.
    a. What is the most you would be willing to pay for the exclusive right to use this invention?
    b. Would the inventor be willing to sell at that price?

12. In the short run, a perfectly competitive firm produces output using capital services (a fixed input) and labour services (a variable input). At its profit-maximizing level of output, the marginal product of labour is equal to the average product of labour.
    a. What is the relationship at the profit-maximizing point between this firm's average variable cost and its marginal cost? Explain.
    b. If the firm has 10 units of capital and the rental price of each unit is $4/day, what will be the firm's profit? Should it remain open in the short run?

**13. A firm in a competitive industry has a total cost function of $TC = .2Q^2 - 5Q + 30$. What is its corresponding marginal cost curve? If the firm faces a price of $6 per unit, what quantity should it sell? What profit does the firm make at this price? Should the firm shut down? (Use calculus or see footnote 15.)

14. The demand for gasoline is $P = 5 - .002Q$ and the supply is $P = .2 + .004Q$, where P is in dollars per litre and Q is in litres. If a tax of $1.20/L is placed on gasoline, what is the incidence of the tax? What is the lost consumer surplus? What is the lost producer surplus? What are the tax revenue and the deadweight loss?

15. Suppose that bicycles are produced by a perfectly competitive, constant cost industry. Which of the following will have a larger effect on the long-run price of bicycles: (1) a government program to advertise the health benefits of bicycling, or (2) a government program that increases the demand for steel, an input in the manufacture of bicycles that is produced in an increasing cost industry?

**16. Suppose a representative firm in a perfectly competitive, constant cost industry has a cost function $TC = 4Q^2 + 100Q + 100$. (Use calculus or see footnote 15.)
    a. What is the long-run equilibrium price for this industry?
    b. If market demand is given by the function $Q = 1000 - P$, where P denotes price, how many firms will operate in this long-run equilibrium?
    c. Suppose the government grants a lump-sum subsidy to each firm that manufactures the product. If this lump-sum subsidy equals $36/firm, what would be the new long-run equilibrium price for the industry?

17. The domestic supply and demand curves for left-handed backscratchers (LHBs) are given by $P = 10 + Q$ and $P = 100 - 2Q$, respectively, where P is the price in dollars per LHB, and Q is the quantity in LHBs per year. Canada produces and consumes only a trivial fraction of world LHB output, and the current world price of $30/LHB is unaffected by events in the Canadian market. Transportation costs are also negligible.
    a. How much will Canadian consumers pay for LHBs and how many LHBs per year will they consume?
    b. How will your answers to 17a change if the government imposes a tariff of $20/backscratcher?
    c. What total effect on domestic producer and consumer surplus will the tariff have? How much revenue will the tariff raise?

18. An Australian researcher has discovered a drug that weakens a sheep's wool fibres just above the sheep's skin. The drug sharply reduces the cost of shearing (cutting the wool off) sheep because the entire coat pulls off easily in one piece. The quality of the wool thus obtained is not affected. The world wool market is reasonably close to the model of perfect competition in both the product and factor sides. Trace out all of the effects of the introduction of this new drug.

19. Using Figure 11-17 (page 416) as a basis, draw the industry long-run supply curve and the LAC curves of a representative firm for a decreasing-cost industry:
    a. If all input prices decrease by the same proportion as industry output expands.
    b. If input prices decrease by different proportions as industry output expands.

**20. In the perfectly competitive gold ring market, B. and F. Baggins Enterprises is one of a number of identical firms supplying the market. The firm's long-run total cost function has the form

$$LTC_i = 504Q_i - 36(Q_i)^2 + (Q_i)^3,$$

where LTC_i is in dollars per period, Q_i is in rings per period, and the i subscript refers to the individual firm. Market demand is given by the equation

$$P = 270 - .01Q,$$

where Q is the number of rings demanded by the entire market and P is in dollars per ring.

    a. Derive expressions for Baggins Enterprises' long-run average cost (LAC_i) and long-run marginal cost (LMC_i) as functions of Q_i.
    b. Determine the levels of Q_i at which LAC_i and LMC_i reach their minimum values.
    c. In long-run equilibrium, what are the price and quantity of gold rings exchanged and the total number of firms in the industry?
    d. Repeat Problem 20c if (beginning at the equilibrium in c) market demand becomes $P = 243 - .01Q$, and briefly describe the adjustment process toward the new long-run equilibrium.

21. In Figure 11-20, where $P = -30 + 2Q$, calculate the elasticity of supply when $Q = 15$ and when $Q = 30$. Then, by substituting $(-30 + 2Q)$ for P in the formula for elasticity of supply and simplifying, derive the formula for the supply elasticity as a function of Q, and use this formula to explain what happens to elasticity as Q increases.

**22. For each of the following supply curves, calculate the level of output Q at which the elasticity of supply = 1, and indicate whether supply is elastic or inelastic at levels of Q less than this point and at levels of Q greater than this point.
    a. $P = 16 + .01Q^2$.
    b. $P = -4 + Q^{1/2}$, for $Q \geqslant 16$.
    c. $P = 6Q$.

ANSWERS TO IN-CHAPTER EXERCISES

11-1. Let r^* be the monthly interest rate for which Mike's economic profit would be zero. Then r^* must satisfy \$16,000 − \$4,000 − \$800 − r^* (\$20,000,000) = 0, which yields $r^* = .00056$, or .056 percent per month. Mike should relocate only if the interest rate is lower than r^*.

11-2. Marginal cost is the slope of the total cost curve, and marginal revenue is the slope of the total revenue curve. At the maximum profit point, $Q = 7.4$, the slopes of these two curves are exactly the same.

11-3. First, we need to rearrange the representative firm supply curve $P = 20 + 90Q_i$ to have quantity alone on one side.

$$Q_i = -\frac{2}{9} + \frac{1}{90} P.$$

Then we multiply by the number of firms $n = 30$.

$$Q = nQ_i = 30Q_i = 30\left(-\frac{2}{9} + \frac{1}{90}P\right) = -\frac{20}{3} + \frac{1}{3}P.$$

Finally, we rearrange the industry supply curve $Q = -\frac{20}{3} + \frac{1}{3}P$ to have price alone on one side, $P = 20 + 3Q$, to return to slope-intercept form.

11-4. Short-run profit maximization for a perfectly competitive firm occurs at the quantity where price equals marginal cost, $P = MC$, provided $P \geqslant$ min AVC (otherwise, the firm shuts down). Since marginal cost is $MC = 2Q$, the market price $P = 12$ equals marginal cost ($12 = 2Q$) at quantity $Q = 6$. Note that min AVC = 0 in this case, so that with *any* $P > 0$, the firm will not shut down. We can express profits (with fixed costs separated out) as $\pi = (P - AVC)Q - FC$. Since average variable cost is $AVC = Q = 6$, the firm would earn profits of

$$\pi = (12 - 6)6 - FC = 36 - FC.$$

Thus, with fixed cost FC = $36, the firm would earn zero profits.

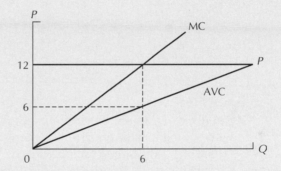

11-5. Total surplus is equal to the sum of the two shaded triangles shown below, which is $100,000 per year.

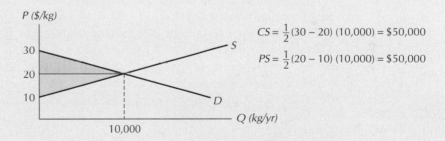

$CS = \frac{1}{2}(30 - 20)(10,000) = \$50,000$

$PS = \frac{1}{2}(20 - 10)(10,000) = \$50,000$

11-6. If the firm pays an incompetent manager only $30,000, it will continue to earn zero economic profit. It cannot pay any more than that without suffering an economic loss.

11-7. Using the formula $\epsilon^s = (P/Q)(1/\text{slope})$, we have $\epsilon^s = (\frac{24}{40})(\frac{1}{.5}) = 1.2$. This means that a 1 percent increase in price results in a 1.2 percent increase in quantity supplied. The supply curve is *elastic* at this point.

Chapter 12

MONOPOLY

Virtually every movie theatre charges different admission prices to moviegoers who belong to different groups. Often there will be different prices for children, "students," adults, and "senior citizens." Some theatres sell ten-packs of movie tickets at a much lower unit price than the tickets they sell at the door. And people who attend weekday matinee showings sometimes pay much less than those who attend evening showings. None of these practices would be expected in our model of perfect competition, where all buyers pay a single price for a completely standardized product (the so-called *law of one price*).

The same theatre operators who charge different ticket prices to different groups follow a very different practice when it comes to the sale of concession items. Here, the law of one price almost always prevails. Students, adults, senior citizens, major league baseball players, the clergy, service station attendants, and all other patrons pay exactly the same price for their popcorn. The same observation applies to the prices of soft drinks and candy. These prices, however, are usually much higher than we see for the same items sold in grocery stores and other retail establishments, certainly far greater than any reasonable measure of the marginal cost of providing them.

Both behaviours—charging differential admission prices on the one hand and uniformly high concession prices on the other—are, as we shall see, perfectly consistent with what the economic model predicts about the single seller of a good or service.

CHAPTER PREVIEW

In this chapter, we examine the market structure that least resembles perfect competition—namely, *monopoly*, the case of a market served by a single seller of a product with no close substitutes. We shall discuss five factors that lead to this market structure: (1) control over key inputs, (2) economies of scale, (3) patents, (4) network economies, and (5) government licences. We shall see that the monopolist's rule for maximizing profits in the short run is the same as that used by perfectly competitive firms. The monopolist will expand output if the gain in revenue exceeds the increase in costs, and will contract output if the loss in revenue is smaller than the reduction in costs.

Next, we shall examine the monopolist's behaviour when confronted with the options of selling in several separate markets. Here again, the logic of cost-benefit analysis will provide a convenient framework for analyzing the firm's decision about whether to alter its current behaviour.

Our next step is to examine the efficiency properties of the standard monopoly equilibrium. We shall see that, unlike the perfectly competitive case, the monopoly equilibrium does not exhaust the potential gains from exchange. In general, the value to society of an additional unit of output will exceed the cost to the monopolist of the resources required to produce it. We shall see that this finding has often been interpreted to mean that monopoly is less efficient than perfect competition. We shall also see, however, that this interpretation can be of limited practical significance, insofar as the conditions that give rise to monopoly differ from those required for perfect competition.

Our policy focus in the chapter is on the question of how the government should treat natural monopolies—markets characterized by downward-sloping long-run average cost curves. We shall consider five policy alternatives: (1) state ownership, (2) private ownership with government price regulation, (3) competitive bidding by private firms for the right to be the sole provider of service, (4) vigorous enforcement of antitrust laws designed to prevent monopoly, and finally, (5) a complete *laissez-faire*, or hands-off, policy. Problems are inherent in each alternative, and we shall see that the best policy generally will be different in different circumstances.

12.1 DEFINING MONOPOLY

Monopoly
A market served by a single seller of a product with no close substitutes.

A *monopoly* is a market structure in which a single seller of a product with no close substitutes serves the entire market. This definition could hardly appear any simpler, and yet it turns out to be exceedingly difficult to apply in practice. Consider the example of movie theatres with which the chapter began. Is a local movie house a monopoly under our definition? In smaller centres, at least, it is likely to be the only one showing a given film at a given time. Whether it is a monopoly obviously depends on what we mean by a close substitute. If, for example, the theatre is currently showing *Halloween Part 37: The Final Final Chapter*, there is likely to be a rich variety of close substitutes for its product. A host of such films are released each year, and the potential patrons of these films generally do not have to look far if they are dissatisfied with the terms available at any particular theatre.

But what about a theatre that is in the midst of an exclusive engagement of a new IMAX feature? Practically speaking, there is no close substitute, and anyone who wants to see it has only one seller to deal with.

The key feature that differentiates the monopoly from the competitive firm is the price elasticity of demand facing the firm. In the case of the perfectly competitive firm, recall, price elasticity is infinite. If a perfectly competitive firm raises its price only slightly, it will lose all its sales. A monopoly, in contrast, has significant control over the price it charges.

Empirically, one practical measure for deciding whether a firm enjoys significant monopoly power is to examine the cross-price elasticity of demand for its closest substitutes. In one famous U.S. antitrust case, the DuPont Corporation was charged with having an effective monopoly on the sale of cellophane. Even though the company sold more than 80 percent of all cellophane traded, it was able to defend itself against this charge by arguing that the cross-price elasticities between cellophane and its close substitutes—at the time, mainly waxed paper and aluminum foil—were sufficiently high to justify lumping all of these flexible-wrap products into a single market. DuPont sold less than 20 percent of total industry output under this broader market definition. In a controversial decision, the court deemed that small enough to sustain effective competition.

This is not to say, however, that cross-price elasticity provides a clear, unambiguous measure that distinguishes a product with close substitutes from one without. While there may not be any other movie system quite like IMAX, there have always been lots of alternative ways to entertain oneself for two hours. For the person whose heart is set on seeing the IMAX feature, the theatre operator is a monopolist, but for the person merely out in search of a good movie, the same theatre operator faces stiff competition. The difference between perfect competition and monopoly often boils down to the question of which of these two types of buyers is more numerous. As in so many other cases in economics, the task of distinguishing between competition and monopoly remains as much an art as a science.

Note carefully that the distinction between monopoly and competition does not lie in any difference between the respective price elasticities of the *market* demand curves for the two cases. On the contrary, the market price elasticity of demand for products supplied by competitive firms is often much smaller than the price elasticity of demand facing a monopolist. The price elasticity of demand is smaller for wheat than for Polaroid cameras, even though wheat is produced under nearly perfectly competitive conditions while Polaroid's patents make it the only legal seller in most of its markets. The important distinction between monopoly and competition is that the demand curve facing the individual competitive firm is horizontal (irrespective of the price elasticity of the corresponding market demand curve), while the monopolist's demand curve is simply the downward-sloping demand curve for the entire market.

12.2 FIVE SOURCES OF MONOPOLY

How does a firm come to be the only one that serves its market? Economists discuss five factors, any one or combination of which can enable a firm to become a monopoly. Let's consider these factors in turn.

1. Exclusive Control over Important Inputs. The Perrier Corporation of France sells bottled mineral water. It spends millions of dollars each year advertising the unique properties of this water, which are the result, it says, of a once-in-eternity confluence of geological factors that created its mineral spring. Other companies provide similar products, some of which are basically just tap water saturated with carbon dioxide gas. Some people find it hard to tell the difference between this enhanced tap water and the mineral water. But others feel differently, and for many of them there is simply no satisfactory substitute for Perrier. Perrier's monopoly position with respect to these buyers is the result of its exclusive control over an input that cannot easily be duplicated.

A similar monopoly position has resulted from DeBeers' high degree of control over most of the world's supply of raw diamonds. Synthetic diamonds have now risen in quality to the point where they can occasionally fool even an experienced jeweller. But for many buyers, the preference for a stone that was mined from the earth is not a simple matter of greater hardness and refractive brilliance. They want *real* diamonds, and DeBeers is the dominant company that has them.

Exclusive control of key inputs is not a guarantee of permanent monopoly power. The preference for having a real diamond, for example, is based largely on the fact that mined diamonds have historically been genuinely superior to synthetic ones. But assuming that synthetic diamonds eventually do become completely indistinguishable from real ones, there will no longer be any basis for this preference. And as a result, DeBeers' control over the supply of mined diamonds will cease to confer monopoly power. This is one of the reasons that DeBeers has also become a world leader in synthetic diamond research and sales. New ways are constantly being devised of producing existing products, and the exclusive input that generates today's monopoly can become obsolete tomorrow.

2. Economies of Scale. When the long-run average cost curve (given fixed input prices) is downward sloping, the least costly way to serve the market is to concentrate production in the hands of a single firm. In Figure 12-1, for example, note that a single firm can produce an industry output of Q^* at an average cost of LAC_{Q^*}, while with two firms sharing the same market, average cost rises to $LAC_{Q^*/2}$. A market that is most cheaply served by a single firm is called a *natural monopoly*. A frequently cited example is local water supply.

Recall from Chapter 11 that it is possible for the LAC curve to be downward sloping even in the absence of economies of scale. This can happen, for example, if the price of an important input falls significantly when industry output expands (a *pecuniary economy*, in the language of Chapter 11). Note carefully, however, that this case is *not* one that gives rise to natural monopoly. Input prices here depend on the level of industry output, not on the output of any one firm. Pecuniary economies will apply with equal force whether one or many firms serve the market.

Strictly speaking, then, it is the degree of returns to scale, not the slope of the LAC curve, that determines whether we have a natural monopoly. With fixed input prices, of course, there is always a one-to-one relationship between returns to scale and the slope of the LAC curve (see Chapter 10).

3. Patents. Most countries of the world protect inventions through some sort of patent system. A patent typically confers the right to exclusive benefit from all exchanges involving the invention to which it applies. There are costs as well as benefits to patents. On the cost side, the monopoly it creates usually leads, as we will see, to higher prices for consumers. On the benefit side, the patent makes possible a great many inventions that would not otherwise occur. Although some inventions are serendipitous, most are the result of long effort and expense in sophisticated research

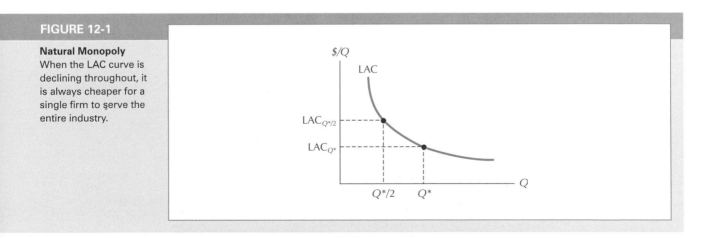

FIGURE 12-1

Natural Monopoly
When the LAC curve is declining throughout, it is always cheaper for a single firm to serve the entire industry.

laboratories. If a firm were unable to sell its product for a sufficiently high price to recoup these outlays, it would have no economic reason to undertake research and development. Without a patent, competition would force price down to marginal cost, and the pace of innovation would be slowed dramatically. The protection from competition afforded by a patent is what makes it possible for the firm to recover its costs of innovation. In Canada, the life of a patent is 20 years, a compromise figure that is likely too long for many inventions, too short for others.[1]

4. Network Economies   On the demand side of many markets, a product becomes more valuable as greater numbers of consumers use it.[2] A vivid illustration is the VHS technology's defeat of the competing Beta format in home video recorders. The attraction of VHS over the initial versions of Beta was that it permitted longer recording times. Beta later corrected this deficiency, and on most important technical dimensions became widely regarded by experts as superior to VHS. Yet the initial sales advantage of VHS proved insuperable. Once the fraction of consumers owning VHS passed a critical threshold, the reasons for choosing it became compelling—variety and availability of tape rentals, access to repair facilities, the capability to exchange tapes with friends, and so on.

In extreme cases, such *network economies* function like economies of scale as a source of natural monopoly. Microsoft's Windows operating system, for example, achieved its dominant market position on the strength of powerful network economies. Because Microsoft's initial sales advantage gave software developers a strong incentive to write for the Windows format, the inventory of available software in the Windows format is by now vastly larger than for any competing operating system. And although general-purpose software such as word processors and spreadsheets continues to be available for multiple operating systems, specialized professional software and games usually appear first in the Windows format and often only in that format. This software gap has given people a good reason for choosing Windows, even if, as in the case of many Apple Macintosh users, they believe a competing system is otherwise superior. The end result is that more than 90 percent of the world's personal computers now run Microsoft's Windows operating system. If that's not a pure monopoly, it comes awfully close.

5. Government and Other Licences or Franchises.   In many markets, the law prevents anyone but a government-licensed firm from doing business. Service station and fast-food restaurant sites in the rest areas on many limited-access highways, for example, are allocated by the government based on competitive bids. To the extent that more than one establishment per rest area is not economically efficient, the government licence as a source of monopoly is really a scale economy acting in another form. Yet government licences are also required in other markets, such as the one for taxis, where scale economies do not seem to be as important. To raise revenues, some college campuses have granted exclusive rights for vending machines sales. Some government licences, such as the broadcast licences issued by the CRTC, are accompanied by strict requirements (such as Canadian content quotas), which applicants must agree to meet

---

[1]The brand-name pharmaceutical lobby in particular has argued that the extended testing period before a new drug is approved for the market results in too short a period of patent protection.

[2]See, for example, Joseph Farrell and Garth Saloner, "Standardization, Compatibility, and Innovation," *Rand Journal of Economics*, 16, 1985: 70–83.; M. L. Katz and Carl Shapiro, "Systems Competition and Network Effects," *Journal of Economic Perspectives*, Spring 1994: 93–115; Oz Shy, *The Economics of Network Industries*, Cambridge, Cambridge University Press, 2001.

as a condition of being awarded a licence. In some cases, prices that a licensee can charge are controlled, while in other cases (as in many airports) licences are auctioned off to the highest bidder, who is then permitted to charge "what the traffic will bear." Despite the range of forms such licensing arrangements can take, they all have the effect of establishing a monopoly position for successful licensees.

By far the most important of the five factors for explaining monopolies that endure in the long run is economies of scale. Production processes are likely to change over time, which makes exclusive control over important inputs only a transitory source of monopoly. Patents too are inherently transitory. Network economies, once firmly entrenched, can be as persistent a source of natural monopoly as economies of scale. Strictly speaking, network economies work through the demand side of the market by affecting what buyers are willing to pay for a product. But they may be equivalently conceptualized on the supply side as yet another feature of product quality. The more people who own the product, the higher its effective quality level. It may thus be said of a product that benefits from network economies that any given quality level can be produced at lower cost as sales volume increases. Viewed in this way, network economies are just another form of economies of scale in production, and that's how we shall view them in the discussion that follows. Government licences can persist for extended periods, but many of these licences are themselves merely an implicit recognition of scale economies that would lead to monopoly in any event.

Information as a Growing Source of Economies of Scale

In 1984, at the dawn of the personal computing age, approximately 80 percent of the cost of a personal computer was accounted for by its hardware, only 20 percent by its software. Only six years later, those percentages were exactly reversed. Now all but a tiny fraction of the total costs of bringing a personal computer to market are associated in one way or another with the production of information. Although this transformation has been especially dramatic in the case of personal computers, an essentially similar transformation has been occurring for most other products as well.

The distinctive feature about information is that virtually all costs associated with the production of information are fixed—in contrast to hardware, for which a large share of production costs is roughly proportional to the volume of production. The upshot is that the production of information-rich products is often characterized by enormous economies of scale.

As a practical matter, however, large one-time costs, including product research and other costs associated with generating information, are often incurred before a product is launched. Typically these costs never recur, even during a product life cycle spanning several decades. Strictly speaking, these costs are not fixed, since the inputs used for generating the information could be varied in principle. Yet when the product is launched, there is simply no economic reason for varying them. So for practical purposes these costs are essentially fixed. In any case, the important point is that the firm's long-run average cost curve is likely to be downward sloping whenever a substantial share of its total cost is associated with initial investments in information.

A case in point is the microprocessor that powers personal computers and a growing array of other products. The fixed investment required to produce the latest Intel Pentium chip is roughly $3 billion. Once the chip has been designed and the manufacturing facility built, however, the marginal cost of producing each chip is only a few cents. It is hardly a surprise, therefore, that Intel currently supplies more than 80 percent of all microprocessors sold today.

Economies of scale have always been an important feature of the modern industrial landscape. But as more and more of the value embedded in products consists of information, the importance of economies of scale can only grow further.

With this brief overview of the causes of monopoly in mind, let us turn now to the question of what the consequences of monopoly are. In order to do this, we will proceed in much the same fashion as we did in our study of the competitive firm. That is, we will examine the firm's output decision and ask whether it leads to a situation in which all possible gains from exchange are exhausted. It will turn out that the answer to the latter question is generally no. But in formulating a government policy to improve on the results of unregulated monopoly, we will see that it is critical to understand the original source of monopoly.

12.3 THE PROFIT-MAXIMIZING MONOPOLIST

As in the competitive case, we assume that the monopolist's goal is to maximize economic profit. And again as before, in the short run this means to choose the level of output for which the difference between total revenue and short-run total cost is greatest. The case for this motive is less compelling than in the case of perfect competition. After all, the monopolist's survival is less under siege than the competitor's, and so the evolutionary argument for profit maximization applies with less force in the monopoly case. Nonetheless, we will explore just what behaviours follow from the monopolist's goal of profit maximization.

The Monopolist's Total Revenue Curve

The key difference between the monopolist and the perfect competitor is the way in which total, and hence marginal, revenue varies with output. Recall from Chapter 11 that the demand curve facing the perfect competitor is simply a horizontal line at the short-run equilibrium market price—call it P^*. The competitive firm is a price taker, often because its own output is too small to have any discernible influence on the market price. Under these circumstances, the perfectly competitive firm's total revenue curve is a ray from the origin with slope P^*, as shown in Figure 12-2.

Now consider a monopolist with the downward-sloping demand curve $P = 80 - (\frac{1}{5})Q$ pictured in the top panel in Figure 12-3. For this firm too, total revenue is the product of price and quantity. At point A on its demand curve, for example, it sells 100 units of output per week at a price of $60 per unit, giving a total revenue of $6000 per week.

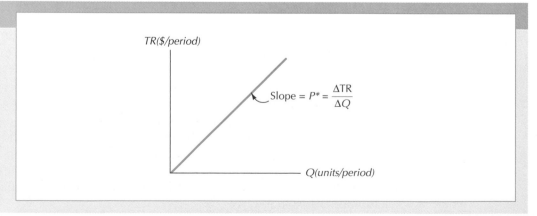

FIGURE 12-2

The Total Revenue Curve for a *Perfectly Competitive Firm*
Price for the perfect competitor remains at the short-run equilibrium level P^* irrespective of the firm's output. Its total revenue is thus the product of P^* and the quantity it sells: $TR = P^*Q$.

TR($/period)

Slope $= P^* = \dfrac{\Delta TR}{\Delta Q}$

Q(units/period)

At *B*, it sells 200 units at a price of $40, so its total revenue at *B* will be $8000 per week, and so on. The difference between the monopolist and the competitor is that for the monopolist to sell a larger amount of output, he must cut his price—not only for the marginal unit but for all preceding units as well. As we saw in Chapter 5, the effect of a downward-sloping demand curve is that total revenue is no longer proportional to output sold. As in the competitive case, the monopolist's total revenue curve (middle panel in Figure 12-3) passes through the origin, because in each case selling no output generates no revenue. But as price falls, total revenue for the monopolist does not rise linearly with output. Instead, it reaches a maximum value at the quantity corresponding to the midpoint of the linear demand curve (*B* in the top panel), after which it again begins to fall. The corresponding values of the price elasticity of demand are shown in the bottom panel in Figure 12-3. Note that total revenue reaches its maximum value when the price elasticity of demand η is -1.

FIGURE 12-3

Demand, Total Revenue, and Elasticity
For the monopolist to increase sales, it is necessary to cut price (top panel). Total revenue rises with quantity, reaches a maximum value, and then declines (middle panel). The quantity level for which the price elasticity of demand is unitary (= −1) corresponds to the midpoint of the demand curve, and at that value total revenue is maximized.

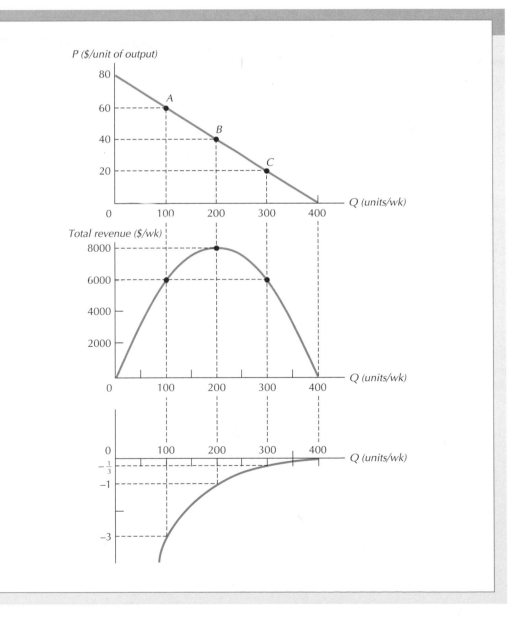

Sketch the total revenue curve for a monopolist whose demand curve is given by $P = 100 - 2Q$.

The top panel in Figure 12-4 portrays the short-run total cost curve and total revenue curve for a monopolist facing the demand curve shown in Figure 12-3. Economic profit, plotted in the bottom panel, is positive in the interval from $Q = 45$ to $Q = 305$, and is negative elsewhere. The maximum profit point occurs at $Q^* = 175$ units per week, which lies to the left of the output level for which total revenue is a maximum ($Q = 200$).

Notice in Figure 12-4 that the vertical distance between the short-run total cost and total revenue curves is greatest when the two curves are parallel (when $Q = 175$ units/week). Suppose this were not the case. For example, suppose that at the maximum-profit point the total cost curve were steeper than the total revenue curve. It would then be possible to earn higher profits by producing less output, because costs would go down by more than the corresponding reduction in total revenue. Conversely, if the total cost curve were less steep than the total revenue curve, the monopolist could earn higher profits by expanding output, because total revenue would go up by more than total cost.

Marginal Revenue

The slope of the total cost curve at any level of output is by definition equal to marginal cost at that output level. By the same token, the slope of the total revenue curve is the

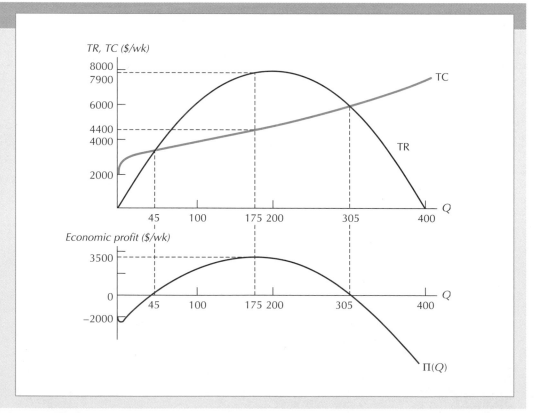

FIGURE 12-4

Total Cost, Revenue, and Profit Curves for a Monopolist
Economic profit [$\Pi(Q)$ in the bottom panel] is the vertical distance between total revenue and total cost (TR and TC in the top panel). Note that the maximum-profit point, $Q^* = 175$, lies to the *left* of the output level at which TR is a maximum ($Q = 200$).

definition of *marginal revenue*.[3] As in the case of the perfectly competitive firm, we can think of marginal revenue as the change in total revenue when the sale of output changes by one unit. More precisely, suppose ΔTR_Q is the change in total revenue that occurs in response to a small change in output, ΔQ. Marginal revenue, denoted MR_Q, is then given by

$$MR_Q = \frac{\Delta TR_Q}{\Delta Q}. \tag{12.1}$$

Using this definition, a profit-maximizing monopolist in the short run will choose that level of output Q^* for which

$$MC_{Q^*} = MR_{Q^*} \text{ (see footnote 4)}, \tag{12.2}$$

provided marginal revenue intersects marginal cost from above. The monopolist wants to sell all units for which marginal revenue exceeds marginal cost, so marginal revenue should lie above marginal cost prior to the intersection. (For some cost structures, marginal cost may decline initially and then increase, leading to two intersections of marginal cost and marginal revenue.)

Recall that the analogous condition for the perfectly competitive firm is to choose the output level for which price and marginal cost are equal. Recalling that marginal revenue and price (P) are exactly the same for the competitive firm (when such a firm expands output by one unit, its total revenue goes up by P), we see that the profit-maximizing condition for the perfectly competitive firm is simply a special case of Equation 12.2.

In the case of the monopoly firm, marginal revenue will always be less than price.[5] To see why, consider the demand curve pictured in Figure 12-5, and suppose that the monopolist wishes to increase output from $Q_0 = 100$ to $Q_0 + \Delta Q = 150$ units/wk. His total revenue from selling 100 units/wk is ($60/unit) (100 units/wk) = $6000/wk. To sell an additional $\Delta Q = 50$ units/wk, he must cut his price to $50 per unit: $\Delta P = 50 - 60 = -\$10$ per unit. His new total revenue will be ($50/unit)(150 units/wk), which is equal to $7500/wk. To calculate marginal revenue, we simply subtract the original total revenue, $6000/wk, from the new total revenue, and divide by the change in output, $\Delta Q = 50$ units/wk. This yields $MR_{Q_0=100} = (\$7500/\text{wk} - \$6000/\text{wk})/(50 \text{ units/wk}) = \$30$ per unit, which is clearly less than the original price of $60 per unit.

Another useful way of thinking about marginal revenue is to view it as the sum of the gain in revenue from new sales and the loss in revenue from selling the previous output level at the new, lower price. In Figure 12-5, the area of rectangle B ($2500/wk) represents the gain in revenue from the additional sales at the lower price. The area of rectangle A ($1000/wk) represents the loss in revenue from selling the original 100 units/wk at $50 per unit instead of $60. Marginal revenue is the difference between the gain in revenue from additional sales and the loss in revenue from sales at a lower price, divided by the change in quantity. This yields ($2500/wk − $1000/wk)/(50 units/wk), which is again equal to $30 per unit.

---

[3] In calculus terms, marginal revenue is defined as the derivative $d\text{TR}/dQ$. The relationship between total, average, and marginal revenue is discussed further in Module 5 of the online *Basic Math Review*.

[4] This condition can also be justified by noting that the first-order condition for maximum profit is given by

$$\frac{d\Pi}{dQ} = \frac{d(\text{TR} - \text{TC})}{dQ} = MR - MC = 0.$$

[5] There is actually one exception to this claim, namely, the case of the perfectly discriminating monopolist, discussed below.

FIGURE 12-5

Changes in Total Revenue Resulting from a Price Cut
The area of rectangle A ($1000/wk) is the loss in revenue from selling the previous output level at a lower price. The area of rectangle B ($2500/wk) is the gain in revenue from selling the additional output at the new, lower price. Marginal revenue is the difference of these two areas ($2500 − $1000 = $1500/wk) divided by the change in output (50 units/wk). Here MR equals $30/unit, which is less than the old price of $60/unit.

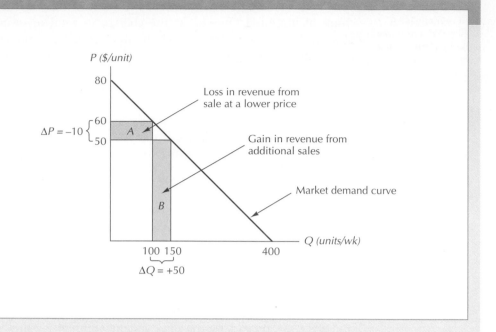

To explore how marginal revenue varies as we move along a straight-line demand curve, consider the demand curve pictured in Figure 12-6, and suppose that the monopolist wishes to increase output from Q_0 to $Q_0 + \Delta Q$ units. His total revenue from selling Q_0 units is $P_0 Q_0$. To sell an additional ΔQ units, he must *cut* his price: ΔP is therefore *negative*, so that $(P_0 + \Delta P)$ is less than P_0. His new total revenue will be $(P_0 + \Delta P)(Q_0 + \Delta Q)$, which is equal to $P_0 Q_0 + P_0 \Delta Q + \Delta P Q_0 + \Delta P \Delta Q$. To calculate marginal revenue, simply subtract the original total revenue, $P_0 Q_0$, from the new total revenue, and divide by the change in output, ΔQ. This leaves $MR_{Q_0} = P_0 + (\Delta P/\Delta Q)Q_0 + \Delta P$, which is clearly less than P_0. As ΔP approaches zero, the expression for marginal revenue thus approaches[6]

$$MR_{Q_0} = P_0 + \frac{\Delta P}{\Delta Q}Q_0. \tag{12.3}$$

Equation 12.3 makes intuitive sense if we think of ΔQ as being a one-unit change in output; P_0 would then be the gain in revenue from the sale of that extra unit, and $(\Delta P/\Delta Q)Q_0 = \Delta P Q_0$ would be the loss in revenue from the sale of the existing units at the lower price. Since $(\Delta P/\Delta Q)$ is negative, the second term on the right-hand side of Equation 12.3 is also negative. Thus Equation 12.3 shows that marginal revenue is less than price for all positive levels of output.

The fact that area B is larger than area A in Figure 12-6 means that marginal revenue is positive at Q_0. Once output moves past the midpoint (M in Figure 12-6) on a straight-line demand curve, however, the marginal revenue of a further expansion will be negative. The area of rectangle C is larger than the area of rectangle D in Figure 12-6, which means that marginal revenue at the output level Q_1 is less than zero.

---

[6]Note that when ΔP shrinks toward zero, the corresponding ΔQ does so as well. Because ΔP and ΔQ are of opposite signs, the ratio $\Delta P/\Delta Q$, which is simply the slope of the demand curve, is negative.

FIGURE 12-6

Marginal Revenue and Position on the Demand Curve
When Q is to the left of the midpoint (M) of a straight-line demand curve (for example, $Q = Q_0$), the gain from added sales (area B) outweighs the loss from a lower price for existing sales (area A). When Q is to the right of the mid-point (for example, $Q = Q_1$), the gain from added sales (area D) is smaller than the loss from a lower price for existing sales (area C). At the mid-point of the demand curve, the gain and the loss are equal, which means marginal revenue is zero.

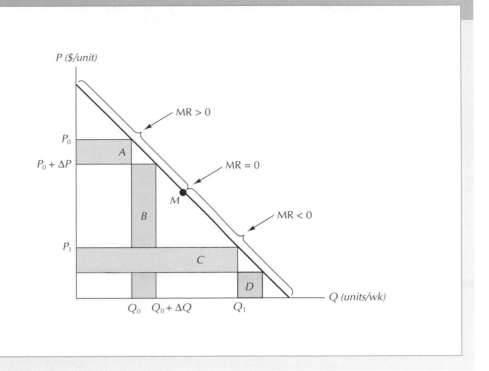

Marginal Revenue and Elasticity

Yet another useful relationship links marginal revenue to the price elasticity of demand at the corresponding point on the demand curve. Recall from Chapter 4 that the price elasticity of demand at a point (Q, P) is given by

$$\eta = \frac{\Delta Q}{\Delta P} \frac{P}{Q}. \tag{12.4}$$

In Equation 12.4, the terms ΔQ and ΔP have opposite signs when the demand curve is downward sloping, so that η is negative: a 1 percent *increase* in P causes an η percent *decrease* in Q. We take the *absolute* value of elasticity as follows:

$$|\eta| = -\eta = -\frac{\Delta Q}{\Delta P} \frac{P}{Q}. \tag{12.5}$$

Recall that the higher the absolute value of η, the more elastic the demand curve. We can relate marginal revenue and elasticity by noting that the expression $(\Delta P/\Delta Q)Q$ in Equation 12.3 is equal to P/η. Hence by substitution we get

$$\mathrm{MR}_Q = P\left(1 + \frac{1}{\eta}\right) = P\left(1 - \frac{1}{|\eta|}\right). \tag{12.6}$$

Equation 12.6 tells us that the less elastic demand is with respect to price, the greater the proportion by which price will exceed marginal revenue.[7] It also tells us that when

---

[7]Equation 12.6 can be derived using calculus as follows:

$$\mathrm{MR} = \frac{d\mathrm{TR}}{dQ} = \frac{d(PQ)}{dQ} = P + \frac{QdP}{dQ} = P\left(1 + \frac{Q}{P}\frac{dP}{dQ}\right) = P\left(1 + \frac{1}{\eta}\right) = P\left(1 - \frac{1}{|\eta|}\right).$$

elasticity is unitary ($\eta = -1$), then $MR_Q = 0$. And in the limiting case of infinite price elasticity, marginal revenue and price are exactly the same. (Recall from Chapter 11 that price and marginal revenue are the same for the competitive firm, which faces a horizontal, or infinitely elastic, demand curve.)

Graphing Marginal Revenue

Equation 12.6 also provides a convenient way to plot the marginal revenue values that correspond to different points along a demand curve. To illustrate, consider the straight-line demand curve in Figure 12-7, which intersects the vertical axis at a price value of $P = 80$. The elasticity of demand is infinite at that point, which means that $MR_0 = 80(1 - 1/|\eta|) = \$80$ per unit. Although marginal revenue will generally be less than price for a monopolist, the two are exactly the same when quantity is zero. The reason is that at zero output there are no existing sales for a price cut to affect.

Now suppose we move, say, one-quarter of the way down the demand curve to point A, (100, 60). At that point, $|\eta| = 3$ (recall from Appendix 4A that the elasticity of demand at any point on a straight-line demand curve is simply the ratio of the bottom segment to the top segment of the demand curve at that point). Thus we have $MR_{100} = (60)(1 - \frac{1}{3}) = \$40$ per unit.

Halfway down the demand curve, at point B, (200, 40), $|\eta| = 1$, which gives us $MR_{200} = (40)(1 - \frac{1}{1}) = 0$. This confirms our earlier finding (Chapter 4) that total revenue is at a maximum at the midpoint of a straight-line demand curve, where elasticity is unitary.

Finally, consider point C, (300, 20), which is three-quarters of the way down the demand curve. Here $|\eta| = \frac{1}{3}$, so we have $MR_{300} = (20)[1 - (1/\frac{1}{3})] = (20)(-2) = -\$40$ per unit. Thus, at $Q = 300$, the effect of selling an extra unit of output is to *reduce* total revenue by \$40/wk.

Filling in additional points in the same fashion, we quickly see that the marginal revenue curve associated with a straight-line demand curve is itself a straight line, one whose slope is twice that of the demand curve. The marginal revenue curve cuts

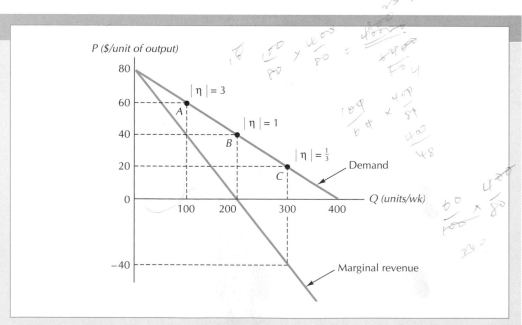

FIGURE 12-7

The Demand Curve and Corresponding Marginal Revenue Curve

For the case of a straight-line demand curve, the corresponding marginal revenue curve is also a straight line. It has the same vertical intercept as and twice the slope of the demand curve. Its horizontal intercept is therefore half that of the demand curve. When $MR \equiv \Delta TR/\Delta Q = 0$, total revenue is at a maximum. See Figure 12-3.

the horizontal axis directly below the *midpoint* of the linear demand curve, and for all quantities larger than that, marginal revenue is negative. Note that all points to the right of the midpoint of the demand curve have price elasticity values less than 1 in absolute value. The fact that marginal revenue is negative in this region thus fits our observation from Chapter 4 that a cut in price will reduce total revenue whenever demand is inelastic with respect to price.

| EXAMPLE 12-1 | **Find the marginal revenue curve that corresponds to the demand curve $P = 12 - 3Q$.** |

The marginal revenue curve will have the same intercept as and twice the slope of the demand curve, which gives us MR $= 12 - 6Q$, as plotted in Figure 12-8.

The general formula for a linear demand curve is $P = a - bQ$, where a and b are positive numbers. The corresponding marginal revenue curve will be MR $= a - 2bQ$ (see footnote 8).

EXERCISE 12-2

Sketch demand and marginal revenue curves for a monopolist whose market demand curve is given by $P = 100 - 2Q$.

Graphical Interpretation of the Short-Run Profit Maximization Condition

Recall from Chapter 11 the graphical representation of the maximum-profit point for the competitive firm in the short run. An analogous graphical representation exists for the monopolist. Consider a monopolist with the demand, marginal revenue, and short-

FIGURE 12-8

A Specific Linear Demand Curve and the Corresponding Marginal Revenue Curve
The marginal revenue curve has the same vertical intercept as and twice the slope of the corresponding linear demand curve.

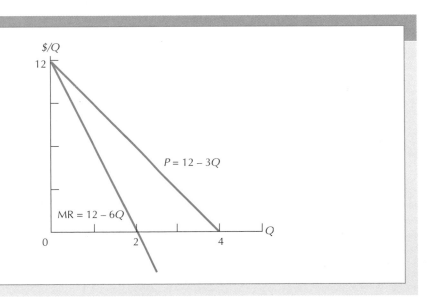

---

[8]Note that total revenue for the demand curve $P = a - bQ$ is given by TR $= PQ = aQ - bQ^2$. The corresponding marginal revenue curve is

$$MR = \frac{d\,TR}{dQ} = a - 2bQ.$$

run cost curves pictured in Figure 12-9. The profit-maximizing level of output for this firm is Q^*, the one for which the marginal revenue and marginal cost curves intersect. At that quantity level, the monopolist can charge a price of P^*, and by so doing will earn an economic profit equal to the shaded rectangle labelled Π.

EXAMPLE 12-2

A monopolist faces a demand curve of $P = 100 - 2Q$ and a short-run total cost curve of TC $= 640 + 20Q$. The associated marginal cost curve is MC $= \$20$ per unit. What is the profit-maximizing price? How much will the monopolist sell, and how much economic profit will it earn at that price?

The marginal revenue curve for this demand curve is MR $= 100 - 4Q$. Marginal cost is the slope of the total cost curve, which is constant at \$20 per unit in this example. Setting MR $=$ MC, we have $100 - 4Q = 20$, which yields the profit-maximizing quantity, $Q^* = 20$ units. Plugging $Q^* = 20$ back into the demand curve, we get the profit-maximizing price, $P^* = \$60$ per unit. This solution is shown graphically in Figure 12-10, which also displays the average total cost curve for the monopolist. Note that at Q^* the ATC is \$52 per unit, which means the monopolist earns an economic profit of $60 - 52 = \$8$ on each unit sold. With $Q^* = 20$, that makes for a total economic profit of \$160.

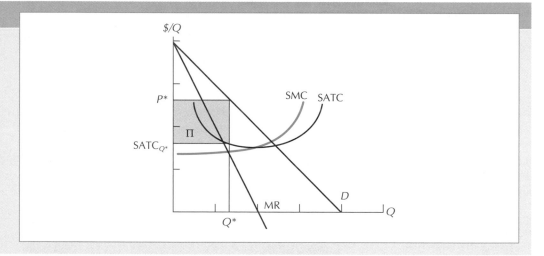

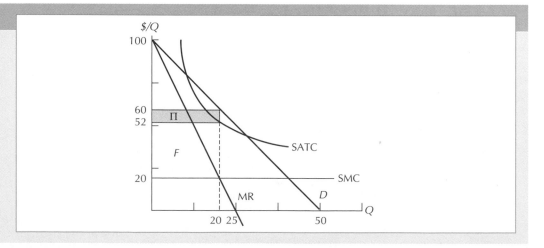

Note in Figure 12-10 that the monopolist's fixed cost was irrelevant to the determination of the profit-maximizing output level and price. This makes sense intuitively, because fixed cost has no bearing on the gains and losses that occur when output changes.

A Profit-Maximizing Monopolist Will Never Produce on the Inelastic Portion of the Demand Curve

If a monopolist's goal is to maximize profits, it follows directly that with marginal costs positive, she will never produce an output level on the inelastic portion of her demand curve. If she were to increase her price at such an output level, the effect would be to increase total revenue. The price increase would also reduce the quantity demanded, which, in turn, would reduce the monopolist's total cost. Since economic profit is the difference between total revenue and total cost, profit would necessarily increase in response to a price increase from an initial position on the inelastic portion of the demand curve. The profit-maximizing level of output must therefore lie on the elastic portion of the demand curve, where further price increases would cause both costs *and* revenue to go down.

The Profit-Maximizing Markup

The profit-maximization condition MR = MC can be combined with Equation 12.6, which says MR = $P[1 - (1/|\eta|)]$, to derive the profit-maximizing markup for the monopolist:

$$\frac{P - \text{MC}}{\text{MC}} = -\frac{1}{\eta + 1} = \frac{1}{|\eta| - 1}, \qquad (12.7)$$

which is the difference between the profit-maximizing price and marginal cost, expressed as a fraction of marginal cost. For example, if the price elasticity of demand facing a monopolist were equal to −2, the profit-maximizing markup would be $1/(2 - 1) = 1$ or 100 percent, which implies that the profit-maximizing price is twice marginal cost. Equation 12.7 tells us that the profit-maximizing markup grows smaller as demand grows more elastic. In the limiting case of infinitely elastic demand, the profit-maximizing markup is zero (which implies $P = \text{MC}$), the same as in the perfectly competitive case.

The Monopolist's Shutdown Condition

In the case of the perfectly competitive firm, we saw that it paid to shut down in the short run whenever the price fell below the minimum value of average variable cost (AVC). The analogous condition for the monopolist is that there exists no quantity for which the demand curve lies above the average variable cost curve. The monopolist whose demand, marginal revenue, SMC, and AVC curves are shown in Figure 12-11,

FIGURE 12-11

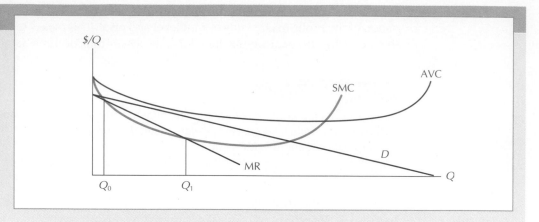

for example, has no positive level of output for which price exceeds AVC, and so the monopolist does best by ceasing production in the short run. He will then sustain a short-run economic loss equal to his fixed costs, but he would do even worse at any positive level of output.

Another way of stating the shutdown condition for a monopolist is to say that he should cease production whenever average revenue is less than average variable cost at every level of output. Average revenue is simply another name for price—the value of P along the monopolist's demand curve.[9]

Figure 12-11 also illustrates the important point that MR = MC is a necessary, but not sufficient, condition for maximum profit. Note in the figure that marginal revenue is equal to marginal cost at the output level Q_0. Why isn't this the maximum-profit point? Recall that in the case of the perfectly competitive firm, the maximum-profit condition called for price to equal marginal cost on a rising portion of the marginal cost curve, above the minimum point on the AVC curve. A somewhat different condition applies in the case of the monopolist. In Figure 12-11, note that at Q_0 the MR curve intersects the MC curve from below.[10] This means not only that Q_0 is not the maximum-profit point, but also that it actually corresponds to a *lower* profit level than any of the other output levels nearby. For example, consider an output level just less than Q_0. At any such output level the gains from contracting output (MC) will exceed the losses (MR), so the firm does better to contract from Q_0. Now consider an output level just slightly larger than Q_0. For such an output level, the gains from expanding (MR) exceed the costs (MC), so the firm does better to expand. Thus, when the firm is at Q_0, it can earn higher profits by either contracting *or* expanding. Q_0 is called a *local minimum* profit point.[11]

Note also in Figure 12-11 that the MR curve intersects the MC curve a second time at the output level Q_1. This time the intersection occurs from above, and you can easily

---

[9]More formally, note that average revenue = TR/Q = PQ/Q = P.

[10]"MR intersects MC from below at Q_0" means that as Q approaches Q_0 from the left, MR lies below MC and then crosses MC when $Q = Q_0$. See footnote 11.

[11]The second-order condition for maximum profit is given by

$$\frac{d(MR - MC)}{dQ} = \frac{dMR}{dQ} - \frac{dMC}{dQ} < 0, \text{ or } \frac{d^2TR}{dQ^2} - \frac{d^2TC}{dQ^2} < 0,$$

which says that the slope of the marginal revenue curve must be *less* than that of the marginal cost curve. At Q_0, this condition is not met, since MR is *flatter* (and hence has a *greater* slope) than MC.

show as an exercise that Q_1 yields higher profits than any of the other output levels close by. (The argument runs exactly parallel to the one in the preceding paragraph.) We refer to points like Q_1 as *local maximum* profit points. But although Q_1 yields more profit than any nearby output level, the firm fails to cover its average variable cost at the level of output, and so does better simply to produce nothing at all. The point Q^* we saw earlier in Figure 12-9 is both a local maximum profit point and a *global maximum* profit point, the latter designation indicating that no other output level, including zero, yields higher profit. For a monopolist, a global maximum profit point might occur either on the rising or on the falling portion of the MC curve. But it must be at a point where the MR curve intersects the MC curve from above.

<hr>

EXERCISE 12-4

Find the optimal price and quantity for the monopolist described by the information in the following table.

Q	P	MR	SMC	AVC
0	100	100	150	150
15	85	70	70	107
25	75	50	41	84
34	66	32	32	72
50	50	0	63	63

To recapitulate briefly, we have seen that the monopolist behaves like a perfectly competitive firm in the sense that each chooses an output level by weighing the benefits of expanding (or contracting) output against the corresponding costs. For both the perfect competitor and the monopolist, marginal cost is the relevant measure of the cost of expanding output. Fixed costs are irrelevant for short-run output decisions in both cases. For both the monopolist and the perfect competitor, the benefits of expanding output are measured by their respective values of marginal revenue. For the competitor, marginal revenue and price are one and the same. For the monopolist, in contrast, marginal revenue is less than price. The competitor maximizes profit by expanding output until marginal cost equals price. The monopolist maximizes profit by expanding output until marginal cost equals marginal revenue, and thus chooses a lower output level than if he had used the competitor's criterion. Both the monopolist and the perfect competitor do best to shut down in the short run if price is less than average variable cost for all possible levels of output.

12.4 A MONOPOLIST HAS NO SUPPLY CURVE

As we saw in Chapter 11, the competitive firm has a well-defined supply curve. It takes market price as given and responds by choosing the output level for which marginal cost and price are equal. At the industry level, a shifting demand curve will trace out a well-defined industry supply curve, which is the horizontal summation of the individual firm supply curves.

There is no similar supply curve for the monopolist. The reason is that the monopolist is not a price taker, which means that there is no unique correspondence between price and marginal revenue when the market demand curve shifts. Thus, a given marginal revenue value for one demand curve can correspond to one price, while the same value of marginal revenue for a second demand curve corresponds to a different price. As a result, it is possible to observe the monopolist producing Q^*_1 and selling at P^* in one period, and then selling Q^*_2 at P^* in another period.

To illustrate, consider a monopolist with a demand curve of $P = 100 - Q$ and with the same cost curves as in Example 12-2, in particular with MC = $20 per unit. The marginal revenue curve for this monopolist is given by MR = $100 - 2Q$, and equating MR to MC yields a profit-maximizing output level of $Q^* = 40$ units. The corresponding profit-maximizing price is $P^* = \$60$ per unit. Note that this is the same as the profit-maximizing price we saw for the monopolist in Example 12-2, even though the demand curve here lies to the right of the earlier one.

When the monopolist's demand curve shifts, the price elasticity of demand at a given price generally will also shift. But these shifts need not occur in the same direction. When demand shifts rightward, for example, elasticity at a given price may either increase or decrease, and the same is true when demand shifts leftward. The result is that there can be no unique correspondence between the price a monopolist charges and the amount she chooses to produce. And hence we say that the monopolist has no supply curve. Rather, she has a *supply rule*, which is to equate marginal revenue and marginal cost.

12.5 ADJUSTMENTS IN THE LONG RUN

In the long run, the monopolist is of course free to adjust all inputs, just as the competitive firm is. What is the optimal quantity in the long run for a monopolist with a given technology? The best the monopolist can do is to produce the quantity for which long-run marginal cost is equal to marginal revenue. In Figure 12-12, that will mean choosing a capital stock that gives rise to the short-run average and marginal cost curves labelled SAC* and SMC*. For that level of capital stock, the short-run marginal cost curve passes through the intersection of the long-run marginal cost and marginal revenue curves. Q^* will be the profit-maximizing quantity in the long run, and it will sell at a price of P^*. For the conditions pictured in Figure 12-12, the long-run economic profit level, Π, will be positive, and is indicated by the area of the shaded rectangle.

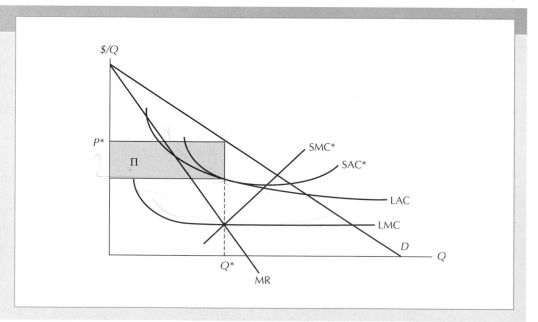

FIGURE 12-12

Long-Run Equilibrium for a Profit-maximizing Monopolist
The profit-maximizing quantity in the long run is Q^*, the output level for which LMC = MR. The profit-maximizing price in the long run is P^*. The optimal capital stock in the long run gives rise to the short-run marginal cost curve SMC*, which passes through the intersection of LMC and MR.

As we saw in Chapter 11, economic profits tend to vanish in the long run in perfectly competitive industries. This tendency will sometimes be present for monopoly. To the extent that the factors that gave rise to the firm's monopoly position come under attack in the long run, there will be downward pressure on its profits. For example, competing firms may develop substitutes for important inputs that were previously under the control of the monopolist. Or in the case of patented products, competitors may develop close substitutes that do not infringe on existing patents, which are in any event only temporary.

But in other cases, monopoly profits may persist even in the long run. The firm shown in Figure 12-12, for example, has a declining long-run average cost curve, which means that it may enjoy a persistent cost advantage over potential rivals. In such natural monopolies, economic profits may be highly stable over time. And the same, of course, may be true for a firm whose monopoly comes from having a government licence. Persistent economic profits are indeed one of the major policy concerns about monopoly, as we discuss further later in the chapter.

12.6 PRICE DISCRIMINATION

Our discussion thus far has assumed that the monopolist sells all its output at a single price. In reality, however, monopolists often charge different prices to different buyers, a practice that is known as *price discrimination*. The movie theatre discount tickets discussed at the beginning of this chapter constitute one example. In the following sections, we analyze how the profit-maximizing monopolist behaves when it is possible to charge different prices to different buyers. When price discrimination is possible, a monopolist can transfer some of the gains from consumers into its own profits. However, we shall see that not all the higher profits under price discrimination come at the expense of consumers. Efficiency is enhanced as the monopolist expands output toward the level at which demand intersects marginal cost.

Sale in Different Markets

Suppose the monopolist has two completely distinct markets in which she can sell her output. Perhaps she is the only supplier in the domestic market for her product, and the only one in a foreign market as well. If she is a profit maximizer, what prices should she charge and what quantities should she sell in each market?

Suppose the demand and marginal revenue curves for the two markets are as given in the left and middle panels in Figure 12-13. First note that if the monopolist is maximizing profit, her marginal revenue should be the same in each market. (If it weren't, she could sell one fewer unit in the market with lower MR and one unit more in the market with higher MR, and in the process increase her profit.) Given that MR in the two markets must be the same, the profit-maximizing total quantity will be the one for which this common value is the same as marginal cost. Graphically, the solution is to add the marginal revenue curves horizontally across the two markets, and produce the level of output for which the resulting curve intersects the marginal cost curve. In the right panel in Figure 12-13, the optimal total output is indicated by $Q^* = 10$ units. Q_1^* = 4 of it is sold in market 1 at a price of P_1^*, and the remaining $Q_2^* = 6$ in market 2 at a price of P_2^*.

FIGURE 12-13

The Profit-maximizing Monopolist Who Sells in Two Markets
The marginal revenue curve for a monopolist who sells in two markets is the horizontal sum of the respective marginal revenue curves. The profit-maximizing output level is where the SMR curve intersects the MC curve, here, $Q^* = 10$. Marginal revenue in each market will be the same when $Q_1^* = 4$ and $Q_2^* = 6$ are sold in markets 1 and 2, respectively.

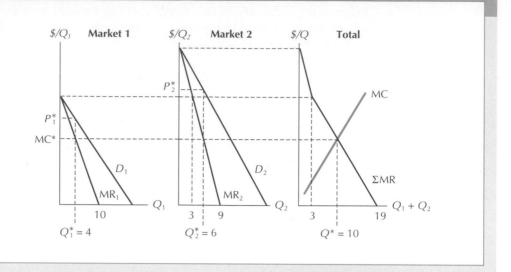

EXAMPLE 12-3

A monopolist has marginal costs $MC = Q$ and home market demand $P = 30 - Q$. The monopolist can also sell to a foreign market at a constant price $P_F = 12$. Find and graph the quantity produced, quantity sold in the home market, quantity sold in the foreign market, and price charged in the home market. Explain why the monopolist's profits would fall if it were to produce the same quantity but sell more in the home market.

The linear demand curve $P = 30 - Q$ has associated marginal revenue $MR = 30 - 2Q$. The profit-maximizing level of output for a monopolist selling to segmented markets occurs where $\Sigma MR = MC$. The horizontal sum of the marginal revenues across markets is the home marginal revenue function MR_H up to home output where $MR_F = MR_H$, and then the foreign marginal revenue function $MR_F = \$12$ per unit for any further units (see Figure 12-14). Total marginal revenue equals marginal cost at $MR_F = MC$, which solves for $Q = 12$ units. Marginal cost for this level of output equals home marginal revenue at $30 - 2Q_H = \$12$ per unit, so $Q_H = 9$ units, with the remaining units sold abroad:

$$Q_F = Q - Q_H = 12 - 9 = 3.$$

In the home market, the monopolist charges

$$P_H = 30 - Q_H = 30 - 9 = \$21 \text{ per unit.}$$

Any further units sold at home would yield marginal revenue less than $12 per unit. Since sales to the foreign market yield a constant marginal revenue of $12 per unit, shifting sales to the home market would decrease profits, because of the lost marginal revenue for each unit shifted.

FIGURE 12-14

A Monopolist with a Perfectly Elastic Foreign Market
The marginal revenue curve ΣMR follows MR$_H$ as long as MR$_H \geq$ MR$_F$, and then follows MR$_F$. The profit-maximizing output level is where the ΣMR curve intersects the MC curve, here $Q^* = 12$.

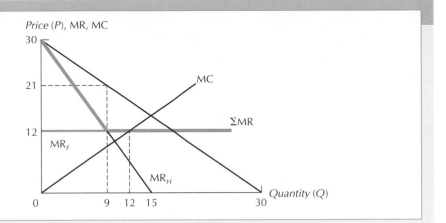

Suppose a monopolist sells in two separate markets, with demand curves given by $P_1 = 10 - Q_1$ and $P_2 = 20 - Q_2$, respectively. If her total cost curve is given by TC $= 5 + 2Q$ (for which the associated marginal cost curve is given by MC $= 2$), what quantities should she sell and what prices should she charge in the two markets?

Note in Exercise 12-5 that the monopolist who sells in two markets charges a higher price in the market where demand is less elastic with respect to price.[12] Charging different prices to buyers in completely separate markets is often referred to as *third-degree price discrimination*. There is no special significance to the term "third-degree" beyond the fact that this type of price discrimination was the third one in A.C. Pigou's classic taxonomy.

Examples of third-degree price discrimination abound. This textbook, for instance, is offered in an international student edition that sells for roughly half the price of the Canadian edition. Because the incomes of students are generally much lower in foreign markets than in Canada, the price elasticity of demand tends to be much higher in foreign than in Canadian markets. The price that maximizes profits in the Canadian market would discourage many students in developing countries from buying.

Charging different patrons different admission prices for the same movie is another example. The higher price elasticities of senior citizens and students make it a good strategy for theatre operators to set lower prices for these groups. Businesses that offer discount prices to students, senior citizens, and others sometimes portray their behaviour as having been motivated by concern for the economic hardships confronting these groups. This concern is no doubt often heartfelt. But notice that the same pattern of behaviour would be seen on the part of monopolists interested only in the bottom line.

Notice also that price discrimination is feasible only when it is impossible, or at least impractical, for buyers to trade among themselves. If students in other lands could trade with those in Canada, for example, it would not be possible to sell essentially the same book for $50 in Calcutta and $100 in Canada. Entrepreneurial students would

---

[12]This result follows from Equation 12.6, which says that MR $= P(1 - 1/|\eta|)$. Setting MR$_1 =$ MR$_2$ yields $P_1/P_2 = (1 - 1/|\eta_2|)/(1 - 1/|\eta_1|)$. Hence the higher price will be charged to customers with the lower price elasticity of demand.

buy $50 books abroad and sell them to Canadian students for, say, $95; others, hoping to get in on the action, would cut the price even further, and eventually the price differential would vanish. Buying at a low price from one source and reselling at a higher price is often called ***arbitrage***. Where arbitrage is practical, large price differentials for a single product cannot persist. Arbitrage ensures, for example, that the price of gold in London can never differ significantly from the price of gold in Toronto, New York, or Tokyo.

Arbitrage The purchase of something for costless risk-free resale at a higher price.

The Perfectly Discriminating Monopolist

First-degree price discrimination is the term used to describe the largest possible extent of market segmentation. To illustrate, suppose a monopolist has N potential customers, each one of whom has a downward-sloping demand curve like the one labelled D_i in Figure 12-15. What is the most revenue the monopolist could extract from the sale of Q' units of output to such a customer? If the monopolist had to sell all units at the same price, the best he could do would be to charge P', which would yield a total revenue of $P'Q'$. But if he can charge different prices for different units of output, he can do much better. For example, he can sell the first Q_1 units at a price of P_1, the next $Q_2 - Q_1$ units at a price of P_2, and so on. If the intervals into which the monopolist can partition the product are arbitrarily small, this form of pricing will augment total revenue by the area of the shaded triangle in Figure 12-15.

Had the monopolist been forced to charge the single price P' for all units, that shaded triangle would have been consumer surplus. When he is able to charge different prices for each unit, however, the monopolist captures all the consumer surplus. The consumer pays the maximum he would have been willing to pay for each unit, and as a result receives no surplus.

How much output will a profit-maximizing, perfectly discriminating monopolist produce? As always, the rule is to equate marginal revenue to marginal cost. Figure 12-16 portrays the demand, short-run marginal, and average total cost curves for a perfectly discriminating monopolist. But what is the marginal revenue curve for this monopolist?

FIGURE 12-15

Perfect Price Discrimination
If the monopolist can sell each unit of output at a different price, he will charge the maximum the buyer is willing to pay for each unit. In this situation, the monopolist captures all the consumer surplus.

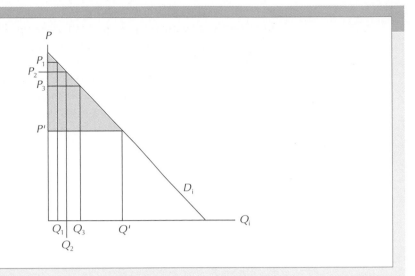

FIGURE 12-16

The Perfectly Discriminating Monopolist
The marginal revenue curve for the monopolist who can discriminate perfectly is exactly the same as his demand curve. The profit-maximizing output is Q^*, the one for which the SMC and demand curves intersect. Economic profit (Π) is given by the shaded area.

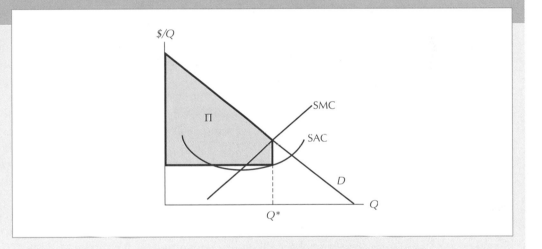

It is exactly the same as his demand curve. Because he can discriminate perfectly, he can lower his price to sell additional output without having to cut price on the output originally sold. Price and marginal revenue are one and the same, just as in the case of perfect competition. The best this firm can do is to produce Q^* units of output, each of which it sells at the highest price each of its buyers is willing to pay.

There are two salient points of comparison between the perfectly discriminating monopolist and the monopolist who cannot discriminate at all. The first is that the perfect discriminator produces a higher level of output because he need not be concerned with the effect of a price cut on the revenue from output produced thus far. He can cut price to the people who would not otherwise buy, and maintain higher prices to those who are willing to pay them.

A second important difference is that there generally is positive consumer surplus under the nondiscriminating monopolist, but none under the perfect discriminator. Because the nondiscriminator must charge the same price to all buyers, there is pressure on him not to set his price too high. If he sets it at the level the least elastic demanders are willing to pay, he will lose the patronage of all others. As a result, the monopolist will not do this, and the least elastic demanders end up paying a price well below their respective reservation prices—hence the consumer surplus.

Perfect price discrimination is a never-attained theoretical limit. If a customer's demand curve were tattooed on his forehead, it might be possible for a seller to tailor each price to extract the maximum possible amount from every buyer. But in general, the details of individual demand are only imperfectly known to the seller. Merchants often estimate individual elasticity on the basis of information known about groups to which the individual belongs. An e-merchant, for example, could sell virtually the identical organizer-planner at two different prices, charging a healthy premium for the "deluxe professional edition." Of course it would be harder to use this ploy in a walk-in retail outlet where both versions were displayed side by side.

Perhaps the closest thing we see to an in-depth assessment of individual elasticities is in the behaviour of merchants in bazaars in the Middle East. The seasoned camel trader has had many years of experience in trying to assess how much a buyer with a given demographic and psychological profile is willing to pay. His stock in trade is to interpret the incongruous gesture, the inadvertent eye movement. But even here, the clever buyer may know how to conceal his eagerness to own the camel.

Second-Degree Price Discrimination

Yet another form of price discrimination is the practice by which many sellers post not a single price, but a schedule along which price declines with the quantity you buy. Thus, many electric utilities employ what are called *declining tail-block rate structures* by which the first, say, 300 kilowatt-hours per month are billed at 10 cents each, the next 700 at 8 cents, and all quantities over 1000 kilowatt-hours per month at 5 cents each. Such rate structures are a form of *second-degree price discrimination*.

Figure 12-17 illustrates the effect of such a rate structure for a consumer with the demand curve labelled D_i. In comparison with the alternative of charging a price of P_3 for every unit, the quantity discount scheme increases the consumer's total payment by an amount equal to the shaded area.

Second-degree price discrimination is like first-degree in that it tries to extract consumer surplus from each buyer. The two principal differences are these: (1) The same rate structure is available to every consumer under second-degree schemes, which means that there is no attempt to tailor charges to elasticity differences among buyers; and (2) the limited number of rate categories tends to limit the amount of consumer surplus that can be captured under second-degree schemes. First-degree schemes get the whole triangle, whereas Figure 12-17 shows that second-degree schemes capture only part of it.

The Hurdle Model of Price Discrimination

Hurdle model of price discrimination Price discrimination using an obstacle that must be surmounted to become eligible for a discount price.

Every seller would like to practise perfect price discrimination. The difficulty, as noted earlier, is that sellers lack the information on individual demand curves necessary to do so. Yet another important form of price discrimination consists of a technique whereby the firm induces the most elastic buyers to identify themselves. This is the **hurdle model of price discrimination**. The basic idea is that the seller sets up a hurdle of some sort and makes a discount price available to those buyers who elect to jump over it. The logic is that those buyers who are most sensitive to price will be much more likely than others to jump the hurdle.

FIGURE 12-17

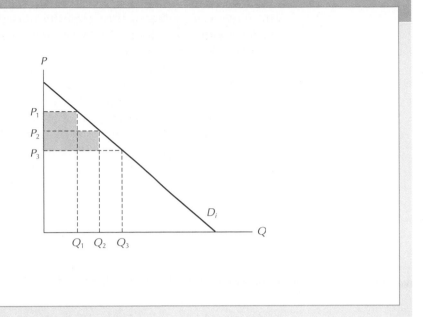

The seller offers the first block of consumption (0 to Q_1) at a high price (P_1), the second block (Q_1 to Q_2) at a lower price (P_2), the third block (Q_2 to Q_3) at a still lower price (P_3), and so on. Even though second-degree price discrimination makes no attempt to tailor rates to the characteristics of individuals or specific groups, it often enables the monopolist to capture a substantial share of consumer surplus (the shaded area).

One example of a hurdle is a rebate form included in the product package. To jump over the hurdle here means to go to the trouble of filling in the form, finding a stamp and an envelope, and then getting to the post office to mail it in. The firm's hope is that people who don't care much about price will be less likely than others to bother going through this process. If so, then people whose demands are less elastic at any given price end up paying the "regular" price, while those with more elastic demands pay the lower discount price.

It is a rare product whose seller does not use the hurdle model of differential pricing. Book publishers often offer only high-priced hardback editions in the first year of publication. Buyers who don't care strongly about price buy these editions when they first come out. Others wait a year or two and then buy the much less expensive softcover edition. Here, the hurdle is having to endure the wait. Appliance sellers offer regular "scratch-'n-dent" sales at which machines with trivial cosmetic imperfections are sold for less than half their regular price. Here, there are two hurdles: having to find out when and where the sale takes place and having to put up with a scratch or dent (which often will be out of sight). Airlines offer "super-saver" discounts of up to half off the regular coach fare. Here also there are two hurdles: having to make reservations a week or more in advance and having to stay over a Saturday night. Many retailers include discount coupons in their newspaper ads. Here, the hurdles are having to read the ads, clip the coupons, and get to the store before they expire. Some sellers post signs behind the counter saying "Ask about our special low price." Here, the hurdle is merely having to do the asking. But even this trivial hurdle can be remarkably effective, because many well-heeled buyers would find asking about a special price too unseemly even to contemplate.

None of these schemes perfectly segregates high-elasticity from low-elasticity buyers. For instance, there are some people who wait for the January white sales to buy their towels even though they would buy just as many if the sales weren't offered. But on the whole, the hurdles seem to function much as intended. A perfect hurdle would be one that imposes only a negligible cost on the buyers who jump it, yet perfectly separates buyers according to their elasticity of demand. Analytically, the effect of such a hurdle is portrayed in Figure 12-18, where P_H represents the "regular," higher price and P_L represents the lower, discount price. Basically, the hurdle functions much like a tax, in that it imposes a per-unit transaction cost T on those who choose to jump it. A buyer will not jump the hurdle if on her valuation $T > (P_H - P_L)$, and will jump it if $T < (P_H - P_L)$. The perceived cost of jumping the hurdle, however, can vary considerably from buyer to buyer, because people place different valuations on the costs of time, delay, inconvenience, uncertainty, and lowered status (for those who view "bargain hunting" as beneath their dignity). With a perfect hurdle, none of the people who pay the discount price has a reservation price greater than or equal to the regular price, which means that all of them would have been excluded from the market had only the regular price been available.

In theory, the hurdle model could backfire on the monopolist. Suppose that on average, high-elasticity buyers have a higher valuation of the cost of jumping the hurdle than do low-elasticity buyers. This situation could arise if high-elasticity buyers were wealthier than low-elasticity buyers, but perceived other goods as closer substitutes for the monopolist's product than did the low-elasticity buyers. In this case, the *low*-elasticity buyers would jump the hurdle and pay the lower price, while the *high*-elasticity buyers would not purchase the monopolist's product at all. Consequently, profits would fall. (You will have a chance to analyze this case in Problem 20 at the end of the chapter.) Yet the widespread use of hurdles as a method of price discrimination suggests that for many producers, it can be an effective means of increasing profits.

The hurdle model need not be limited to the two-price version depicted in Figure 12-18. On the contrary, many sellers have developed it into a highly complex art form involving literally dozens of price-hurdle combinations. On its Toronto–Vancouver route for example, Air Canada offers a wide range of fares, each with its own set of restrictions. But no matter how simple or complex the scheme may be, its goal is the same—to give discounts to customers who would not otherwise buy the product.

The hurdle model is like first-degree price discrimination in that it tries to tailor prices to the elasticities of individual buyers. The principal difference is that even in its most sophisticated form, the hurdle model cannot hope to capture all the consumer surplus.

12.7 THE EFFICIENCY LOSS FROM MONOPOLY

Recall from Chapter 11 the claim that perfect competition led to an efficient allocation of resources. This claim was based on the observation that in long-run competitive

FIGURE 12-18

A Perfect Hurdle
When a hurdle is perfect, the only buyers who become eligible for the discount price (PL) by jumping it are those who would not have been willing to pay the regular price (PH). A perfect hurdle also imposes no significant costs on those who jump it.

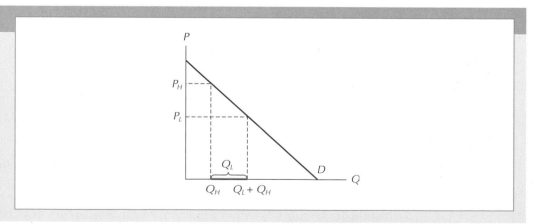

equilibrium, there are no possibilities for additional gains from exchange. The value to buyers of the last unit of output is exactly the same as the market value of the resources required to produce it.

How does the long-run equilibrium under monopoly measure up on the same criterion? Not very well, it turns out. To illustrate, consider a monopolist with constant long-run average and marginal costs and the demand structure shown in Figure 12-19. The profit-maximizing quantity for this monopolist is Q^*, which he will sell at a price of P^*. Note that at Q^*, the value of an additional unit of output to buyers is P^*, which is greater than the cost of producing an additional unit, LMC. This means that the single-price monopolist does not exhaust all possible gains from exchange. As we saw earlier, if it were possible for the monopolist to charge different prices to every buyer, output would expand to Q_C, which is the same amount we would see in a perfectly competitive industry under the same demand and cost conditions. If output expanded from Q^* to Q_C under perfect price discrimination, the gain in producer surplus would be equal to the combined areas of the triangles labelled S_1 and S_2. Under perfect competition, the triangle S_1 (along with the areas S_2 and Π) would instead be part of consumer surplus. The cost to society of having such a market served by a single-price monopolist, rather than by a perfectly discriminating monopolist *or* by perfectly competitive sellers, is the loss of consumer surplus, S_1.

In pure efficiency terms, the perfectly discriminating monopolist and the perfectly competitive industry lead to the same result. The difference is that in the former case all the benefit comes in the form of *producer* surplus, in the latter case all in the form of *consumer* surplus. The *efficiency* loss from monopoly can thus be viewed as the result of failure to price discriminate perfectly! This loss (the area of triangle S_1 in Figure 12-19) is called the *deadweight loss from monopoly*.

In the preceding analysis, it made sense to speak of the welfare loss from having monopoly rather than competition because the cost structure was one that is compatible

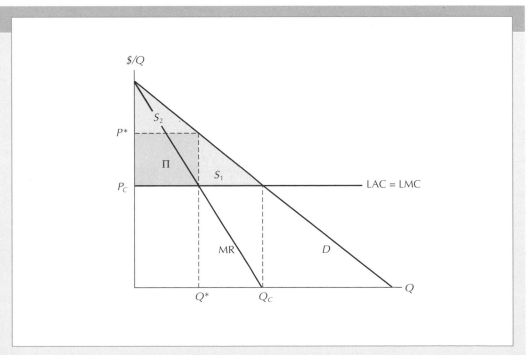

FIGURE 12-19

The Welfare Loss from a Single-Price Monopoly

A monopolist who charges a single price to all buyers will produce Q^* and sell at P^*. A competitive industry operating under the same cost conditions would produce Q_c and sell at P_c. In comparison with the perfectly competitive outcome, single-price monopoly results in a loss of consumer surplus equal to the area of $\Pi + S_1$. Since the monopolist earns Π, the cost to society is S_1— called the deadweight loss from monopoly.

with the existence of perfect competition. But with that kind of cost structure, only legal barriers could prevent the emergence of competition. The existence of economic profits (Π in Figure 12-19) would lure competitors into the industry until price and quantity were driven to P_C and Q_C, respectively.

Suppose the reason for having a monopoly with a flat LAC curve is that the firm enjoys patent protection for its product. Can we now say that the welfare loss from having a single-price monopoly is equal to the lost consumer surplus measured in Figure 12-19? Before answering, we must first ask, "What is the alternative to the current situation?" If it is a society without patent protection, we may well have never gotten the product in the first place, so it hardly makes sense to complain that, compared with pure competition, monopoly produces a welfare loss. True enough, the patent-protected single-price monopoly does not exhaust all possible gains from trade. But with the patent-protected monopoly, we do get a consumer surplus of S_2 plus producer surplus of Π, whereas we might have gotten nothing at all without the patent protection.

12.8 PUBLIC POLICY TOWARD NATURAL MONOPOLY

These observations make clear that the relevant question is not whether monopoly is efficient in comparison with some unattainable theoretical ideal, but how it compares with the alternatives we actually confront. This question is nowhere more important than in the case of natural monopoly.

To keep the analysis simple, consider a technology in which total cost is given by

$$TC = F + MQ, \qquad (12.8)$$

where Q is the level of output and M is the constant marginal cost (in dollars per unit). Suppose the demand and marginal revenue curves for a single-price monopolist producing with this technology are as shown in Figure 12-20. The theoretical ideal allocation for this market would be to produce a quantity of Q^{**} and sell it at marginal cost, which here is equal to M. In contrast, the single-price monopoly produces only Q^* and sells it for P^*.

There are basically two objections to the equilibrium price-quantity pair of the single-price natural monopoly: (1) the *fairness objection*, which is that the producer earns an economic profit (Π); and (2) the *efficiency objection*, which is that price is above marginal cost, resulting in a deadweight loss of consumer surplus (S).

If the natural monopoly sold Q^{**} at a price equal to MC = M, it would receive no producer surplus and would sustain economic losses equal to total fixed costs, F, while the entire area between the demand curve and MC would be consumer surplus. With the price at P^*, the loss of consumer surplus equals the area ($\Pi + F + S$). Of this amount, the monopolist receives producer surplus of ($\Pi + F$), leaving S as a deadweight loss of consumer surplus.

Policymakers may respond in a variety of ways to the fairness and efficiency objections. The five options considered below account for the most important alternatives.

1. State Ownership and Management

Efficiency requires that price be equal to marginal cost. The difficulty this creates is that, for a natural monopoly, marginal cost is below average total cost. Because private firms are not able to charge prices less than average cost and remain in business in the long run, the single-price firm has no alternative but to charge more than marginal cost. An option for getting around this particular difficulty is to have the state take over the industry. One attractive feature of this option is that the government is not bound, the way a private firm is, to earn at least a normal profit. It would thus be able to set a price equal to marginal cost, and absorb the resulting economic losses out of general tax revenues.

Government-owned enterprises have historically been more important in Canada than in the United States, and less important than in some European countries. Some of these enterprises have the characteristics of natural monopolies. So-called "public utilities" such as electrical power, water supply, and sewage services are classic examples of industries with elements of increasing returns to scale. Many of these utilities *have* in fact been publicly owned in Canada. The public utilities that have not been publicly owned, however, have typically been government regulated, in the manner discussed in the next section.

Government enterprises are currently operated by all three levels of government: federal, provincial, and local. These enterprises have historically been run in a variety of ways: directly, as departments of government; as government-owned Crown corporations; and as public–private collaborative enterprises. The Crown corporation Canada Post has a legislated monopoly position with first-class mail delivery that may be justified in part by natural monopoly considerations, but it also competes directly with private courier companies in providing express delivery services. A number of other ventures owned or run by Canadian governments, however, do not appear to have a "natural monopoly" basis. The sale of alcohol in a number of provinces through provincial liquor control board outlets rather than by private retailers, for example, cannot be adequately explained in natural monopoly terms. In Quebec and Alberta, liquor is sold by the private sector, and in Ontario some wineries have retail outlets for their products. Where governments have entered liquor retailing it has usually been to achieve other social policy objectives, as is also the case with the entry of government into the lottery and gaming industries.

Since the 1970s, in most of the OECD countries including Canada, there has been an active debate as to the desirability of privatizing government enterprises. Supporters

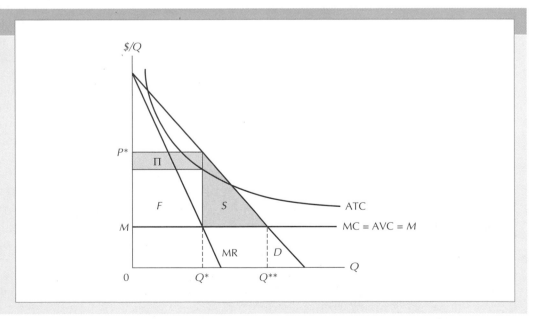

FIGURE 12-20

A Natural Monopoly
The two main objections to single-price natural monopoly are that it earns economic profit (Π) and that it results in the deadweight loss of consumer surplus (S).

of privatization argue that government ownership can weaken incentives for cost-conscious, efficient management. Harvey Leibenstein has argued that an organization's costs depend not just on its technology, but also on the vigour with which it pursues efficiency. An organization that does not act energetically to curb costs is said, in Leibenstein's terms, to exhibit **X-inefficiency**.[13] Leibenstein argued that the extent to which X-inefficiency is a problem will depend on economic incentives. Proponents of privatization argue that it is likely to be more widespread in government. When a private firm cuts a dollar from its costs, its profit goes up by a dollar. In contrast, when the person in charge of a government agency cuts a dollar from her agency's budget, the effect is merely to shrink her fiefdom.

Moreover, they argue, when a private firm fails to cut costs, it is disciplined by the market. If a government-run firm fails to cut costs it can still perpetuate itself, because it is not required to make a profit and because it can rely on a subsidy out of government revenues. This line of argument has some merit, and we shall consider some cases below where private contractors have been able to offer services equivalent to those provided by municipal government employees, at lower cost.

Those who are skeptical that privatization is a panacea for "all that ails us," however, are not without ammunition in this debate. First, they argue, the notion that government bureaucrats are motivated exclusively by empire-building ambitions is significantly oversimplified.[14] Second, particularly after decades of government downsizing and the introduction of new management information and control systems and performance criteria, if a government bureaucrat wanted to empire build, the way for her to increase her budget, in competition with all the empire builders in other departments, would be to show *results*. She would have to demonstrate that an additional dollar spent by her department would generate more "bang per buck" than if it were spent elsewhere. Third, government-owned arm's-length institutions, such as Crown corporations, can offer essentially the same performance bonuses and incentives as the private sector.

Skeptics also point out that inefficiency and bureaucracy are by no means a government monopoly. Large *private* corporations also have large bureaucracies: the misadventures of the cartoon anti-hero, Dilbert, emerge from the frustrations of working in the *private* sector's "cubicle culture." For every horror story you have about waiting in line at a government office to renew a driver's licence, you likely have one about waiting in line behind ten shopping carts at the supermarket while many of the cash registers are idle, or searching a department store to find a clerk (*any* clerk) who can tell you where they have hidden the sale items. These examples suggest that one method of cost cutting for a private company is to download costs (increased waiting time and frustration) onto consumers. These costs do not show up directly in conventional profit-and-loss accounts. The success of such cost-cutting measures will be greatest for a natural monopoly because, by definition, it is "the only game in town." Moreover, if an unregulated private natural monopolist is X-inefficient, its extranormal profits will buffer it from the discipline of the market.

A further limitation on the private sector drive for cost efficiency in the name of profit-maximization exists. Several private Canadian companies responsible for the disposal of hazardous industrial waste, an activity that is costly when it is properly done, have

---

[13]Harvey Leibenstein, "Allocative Efficiency vs. X-Efficiency," *American Economic Review*, June 1966: 392–415.

[14]The traditional view, as advanced in William Niskanen, *Bureaucracy and Representative Government*, Chicago: Aldine-Atherton, 1971, and Gordon Tullock, *The Politics of Bureaucracy*, Washington, DC: Public Affairs Press, 1965, has been criticized in Albert Breton and Ronald Wintrobe, *The Logic of Bureaucratic Conduct*, Cambridge University Press, 1982.

cut costs by using substandard containers or by simply dumping the hazardous waste, without containers, into regular landfill sites. Such activities are illegal, but as long as the company is not caught, these cost-cutting measures sharply increase profitability. In a senior citizens' extended care facility, "effective" cost minimization can involve reductions in food quantity and quality, facility maintenance, recreational programs and outings, and the staff-to-client ratio. The profit-maximizing ideal, from the facility's standpoint, would be a form of senior citizen "warehousing." Again, such profit-maximizing neglect *has* occurred in privately run Canadian care facilities. Critics of wholesale privatization argue, in the light of such examples, that private profitability data are not strictly comparable with those of government facilities, because the social costs of private profit maximization are not fully accounted for, and because the costs of government inspection to ensure compliance with the applicable laws need to be included as one of the costs of privatization.

A final argument relates to popular perceptions. If a government-run natural monopoly loses money because it is supplying a service at marginal cost and therefore requires government subsidization out of tax revenues, this is proof to a large segment of the public that government enterprises are inefficient. They fail to appreciate that in *this* situation, economic *profits* would be a sign of inefficiency, since profits would mean that consumer surplus was not being maximized.

Any generalization about government vs. private ownership is likely to be an over-generalization. Good decisions regarding the proper balance between public and private enterprise require detailed empirical economic analysis of explicit *and* hidden social costs and benefits of specific alternatives. In some cases, government-run natural monopoly may be the best solution, and in others, one of the following alternatives may be preferable.

2. State Regulation of Private Monopolies

One alternative is to leave ownership in private hands, while providing guidelines or regulations that limit pricing and other discretion. The stereotypical example of this approach is public regulation of private companies that provide electricity, water, and telephone service.

A common form of government price regulation employed in Canada is known as *rate-of-return regulation*, in which prices are set to allow the firm to earn a predetermined rate of return on its invested capital. Ideally, this rate of return would allow the firm to recover exactly the opportunity cost of its capital, so that it would ideally be the same as the competitive rate of return on investment.

In practice, however, regulatory agencies can never be certain what the competitive rate of return will be in any period. If the rate they set lies below the competitive return, the firm will have an incentive to reduce the quality of its service, and eventually to go out of business. In contrast, if regulators set too high a rate of return, prices will be higher than necessary and the firm will earn extranormal profits. Neither of these outcomes is attractive, but regulatory agencies have tended to view the problems caused by an insufficient rate of return as more serious than those caused by an excessive one.

Harvey Averch and Leland Johnson were the first to explore in detail the consequences of a regulatory rate of return set higher than the cost of capital.[15] Their conclusion, in

---

[15]Harvey Averch and Leland Johnson, "Behavior of the Firm under Regulatory Constraint," *American Economic Review*, December 1962: 1052–1069. See also R. M. Spann, "Rate of Return Regulation and Efficiency in Production: An Empirical Test of the Averch-Johnson Thesis," *Bell Journal of Economics*, Spring 1974: 38–52.

a nutshell, is that this practice gives the firm an incentive to substitute capital for other inputs in a way that inflates the cost of doing business. If the regulated utility's goal is to maximize profit, the behavioural path it will follow will be to make its "rate base"—the invested capital on which it earns the allowed rate of return—as large as possible. If the regulated monopolist can borrow capital at 8 percent per year and is allowed to earn 10 percent per year on each dollar invested, it can clear $20,000 of extra profit for every extra $1,000,000 of borrowed funds it invests.

At least two important distortions follow from the discrepancy between the allowed rate of return and the actual cost of capital. The first we may call the *gold-plated water cooler effect*. Note that the regulated monopolist has an incentive to purchase more capital equipment than is actually necessary to produce any given level of output. Faced with a choice between buying a regular water cooler, for example, and a more expensive gold-plated one, the regulated monopolist has an incentive to opt for the latter. Regulatory agencies try to prevent the purchase of unnecessary equipment, but the complexities of day-to-day operations are too great to allow every decision to be monitored carefully.

A second distortion induced by rate-of-return regulation is peculiar to the monopolist who serves more than one separate market, and we may call it the *cross-subsidy effect*. Because the allowed rate of return exceeds the cost of capital, such a monopolist has an incentive to sell below cost in the more elastic market, and cross-subsidize the resulting losses by selling above cost in the less elastic market. The idea is that the below-cost price in the elastic market boosts sales by more than the above-cost price in the less elastic market curtails them. The resulting increase in output increases the requirements for capital to produce it, and hence increases the profits allowed by regulation.

To illustrate, consider the regulated monopolist whose demand and cost curves for two markets are shown in Figure 12-21. The ATC curves are constructed to include the allowed rate of profit, which exceeds the cost of capital. Thus, when the monopolist is earning a zero profit in terms of the cost curves shown in Figure 12-21, he is really earning

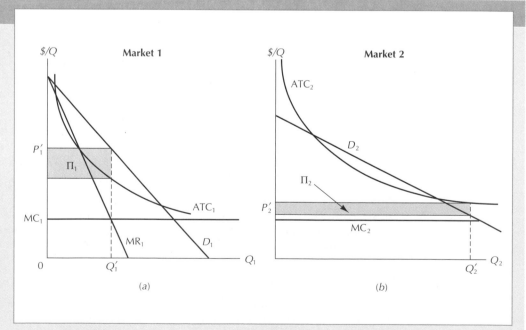

FIGURE 12-21

Cross-Subsidization to Boost Total Output
A regulated monopolist is generally allowed to earn a rate of return that exceeds the actual cost of capital, which provides an incentive to acquire as much capital as possible. To increase output (thereby to increase the required capital stock), the monopolist can sell above cost in his less elastic market (market 1 in panel a) and use the resultant profits ($\Pi_1 > 0$) to subsidize the losses ($\Pi_2 < 0$) sustained by selling below cost in his more elastic market.

$$\Pi = (r^a - r^c)K, \qquad\qquad (12.9)$$

where r^a is the allowed rate of return, r^c the actual cost of capital, and K the size of the total capital stock. To maximize profit, the monopolist thus wants to make K as big as possible, which in turn means making the sum of the outputs sold in the two markets as large as possible. To do that, he will set MR = MC in the market with the less elastic demand (market 1 in panel a) and use the profits earned in that market (Π_1) to subsidize a price below average cost in the market with more elastic demand (market 2 in panel b). The aim, again, is to boost sales in the latter market by more than they are curtailed in the former. By selling the largest possible output, the monopolist is able to employ the largest possible capital stock, and thereby is able to earn the largest possible profit.

Despite these difficulties, governments in virtually every part of the world continue to regulate the price and output decisions of important natural monopolies like electric utilities and telephone service. The net benefits of such regulation are difficult to quantify precisely. But at a minimum they serve an important psychological function for a public that feels understandably uncomfortable about not having a buffer between itself and the sole supplier of a critical good or service.

3. Exclusive Contracting for Natural Monopoly

In the title of a widely quoted article, Harold Demsetz asked the disarmingly simple question, "Why Regulate Monopoly?"[16] His point was that even though cost conditions may dictate that a market be served by a single supplier, there can still be vigorous competition to see who gets to be that supplier. In Demsetz's proposal, the government would specify in detail the service it wanted provided—fire protection, garbage collection, postal delivery, whatever—and then call for private companies to submit bids to supply the service. And to the low bidder would then go the contract. In a number of cases, shifting from direct municipal government provision of services to private contractors has resulted in substantial cost savings, with no apparent reduction in the quality of service.[17] Such schemes are more widespread in the United States than in Canada. Yet every level of government in Canada uses tender systems extensively in purchasing goods and services from the private sector. In this context, Demsetz's proposal is basically an extension of a long-standing government practice. It is also related to the "make or buy" decision of a private sector firm: "Do we produce this service ourselves or purchase it from outside the firm?" The decision should hinge on which strategy provides the best service at the lowest cost.

The exclusive contracting proposal has the advantage of administrative simplicity when compared to the other alternatives. Despite this apparent advantage, private contracting is not necessarily a superior solution in every instance. Because the contract must specify the details of the service to be provided, it must go into extraordinary detail in the case of a complex service, such as telecommunications. Moreover, it must make provisions for how new contractors are to be selected. For electric utilities, changing contractors necessarily involves the transfer of a vast, complex array of generation and distribution equipment. At what price should this equipment be sold? By the time all the i's are dotted and the t's crossed, exclusive contracts for providing monopoly service may be so detailed as to be indistinguishable from direct economic regulation.

---

[16]Harold Demsetz, "Why Regulate Monopoly?" *Journal of Law and Economics*, April 1968: 55–65.

[17]For an extended survey of studies comparing private costs and public costs, see E. S. Savas, *Privatizing the Public Sector*, Chatham, NJ: Chatham House Publishers, 1982.

4. Vigorous Enforcement of Competition Policy

Government competition policy is a further means of dealing with monopoly power. Combines legislation in Canada dates back to the fairly toothless Act of 1889, but since 1986 the main instrument of federal competition policy has been the Competition Act. The Competition Act actually deals with a broader range of issues than just those posed by anti-competitive activities or unfair business practices of existing monopolies. It contains provisions regarding misleading advertising and predatory pricing—the sale of products at prices below cost in an attempt to drive a potential rival out of business. But these policies apply to highly concentrated market structures generally, and not simply to monopolies. The Competition Act also restricts collusion between firms in price setting, bidding on tenders, or partitioning the market. Finally, the Competition Act requires government approval of any mergers that would significantly increase the degree of concentration in an industry.

In certain industries, the Canadian market is relatively small, in comparison with the minimum efficient scale of firm output. Partly for this reason, Canadian competition policy has tended to permit a greater degree of industrial concentration than does U.S. policy. In Canada, more weight has been given to the potential efficiency gains from mergers than to the increased monopoly power that results. Canada has no parallel to the 1911 breakup of Standard Oil and the American Tobacco Company or the breakup of Microsoft (subsequently put on indefinite hold) ordered by a lower court in 2000 under United States antitrust law. Three Canadian cases provide some evidence regarding the future direction of Canadian competition policy. In December 1998, the federal government rejected two merger proposals involving four of Canada's major banks, although bank mergers continue to be an active policy issue. In December 1999, however, it approved Air Canada's takeover of Canadian Airlines. (See Appendix 13A on these two apparently contradictory decisions.)

The third, least publicized but in some ways most significant, case was the split decision of the Canadian Competition Tribunal on August 30, 2000, allowing the merger of Superior Propane and ICG Propane. On the basis of econometric evidence regarding cross-elasticities of demand, the majority of the Tribunal determined that the relevant market was not the "fuel" market, where the companies' market share was only about 2 percent, as the companies had argued. Rather, the relevant markets were the propane delivery and national account coordination services markets. They also found that a national monopoly would be created in the latter market and that monopoly or reduced competition would occur in 65 local propane delivery markets served by the merged firm. In addition, they found that consumer surplus would be reduced by the merger, and that efficiency gains would be captured exclusively by the companies. Still, they allowed the merger, because on the majority's calculation, the potential efficiency gains outweighed the deadweight loss from greater monopoly. The decision signalled the Tribunal's willingness to permit an increase in monopoly power if there were potential efficiency gains, regardless of how those gains were distributed and whether consumers were harmed or layoffs occurred in the process.

5. A *Laissez-Faire* Policy toward Natural Monopoly

As a fifth and final alternative for dealing with natural monopoly, let us consider the possibility of *laissez faire*, or doing nothing—just letting the monopolist produce whatever quantity she chooses and sell it at whatever price the market will bear. The obvious objections to this policy are the two we began with, namely, the fairness and efficiency problems. In this section, however, we shall see that in some circumstances, the seriousness of these problems may be reduced.

Consider, in particular, a natural monopolist who uses the hurdle model of differential pricing. To keep the discussion simple, let's suppose she charges a regular price and also a discount price, the latter available to customers who clear some hurdle, such as mailing in a rebate form. How does the presence of this differential pricing device affect the fairness and efficiency objections to natural monopoly?

Consider first the efficiency objection. Recall that the problem is that the single-price monopolist charges a price above marginal cost, which excludes many potential buyers from the market, ones who value the product more highly than the value of the resources required to produce it.

For illustrative purposes, let's examine a natural monopolist with a total cost curve given by $F + MQ$ and a linear demand curve given by $P = A - BQ$. Figure 12-22a shows the demand and marginal cost curves for such a monopolist. If she is a single-price profit maximizer, she will produce Q^* and sell for P^*. But if she is able to charge one price to the buyers along the upper part of the demand curve and a lower price to all other buyers (Figure 12-22b), her profit-maximizing strategy will be to sell Q_H at the price P_H and $Q_L = Q - Q_H$ at the price P_L.[18]

Note that the deadweight efficiency loss associated with the two-price monopolist (the area of triangle Z in panel b) is much smaller than the corresponding loss for the single-price monopolist (the area of triangle W in panel a). As panel b shows, the two-price monopolist receives producer surplus equal to the area $(2 + 4 + 5)$. Those who pay P_H receive consumer surplus equal to area 1, while those who pay the lower price P_L receive consumer surplus equal to area 3. The total *consumer* surplus (areas $1 + 3$ in panel b) is less than in the single-price case (area $1 + 2$ in panel a). The two-price *producer* surplus, however, *exceeds* the single-price monopoly's producer surplus (area $3 + 4$ in panel a) by an even *greater* amount. Hence with the two-price monopoly, the *sum* of producer and consumer surpluses is greater, and the deadweight efficiency loss is lower, than under a single-price monopoly regime.

In general, the more finely the monopolist can partition her market under the hurdle model, the smaller the efficiency loss will be. As noted earlier, it is not uncommon to see a whole menu of different discount prices, each with a different set of restrictions

---

[18]For the single-price monopolist the profit function is given by

$$\Pi_1 = (A - BQ)Q - F - MQ.$$

The first-order condition for a maximum is given by

$$\frac{d\Pi_1}{dQ} = A - 2BQ - M = 0,$$

which yields a profit-maximizing quantity of $Q^* = (A - M)/2B$, and a corresponding price of $P^* = (A + M)/2$.

The profit function for the two-price monopolist, in contrast, is given by

$$\Pi_2 = TR - TC = (P_H Q_H + P_L Q_L) - TC,$$

where $Q = Q_H + Q_L$ and $TC = F + MQ$. Substituting into the profit function the values for P_H $(= A + BQ_H)$, P_L $(= A - BQ)$, and TC $(= F + MQ)$, and setting $Q = Q_H + Q_L$ gives

$$\Pi_2 = (A - BQ_H)Q_H + (A - BQ_H - BQ_L)Q_L - [F + M(Q_H + Q_L)].$$

The first-order conditions for a maximum are given by

$$\frac{\partial\Pi_2}{\partial Q_H} = A - 2BQ_H - BQ_L - M = 0 \quad \text{and} \quad \frac{\partial\Pi_2}{\partial Q_L} = A - BQ_H - 2BQ_L - M = 0,$$

which can be solved for

$$Q_H = \frac{A - M}{3B} = Q_L \quad \text{and} \quad P_L = \frac{A + 2M}{3} \quad \text{and} \quad P_H = \frac{2A + M}{3}.$$

FIGURE 12-22

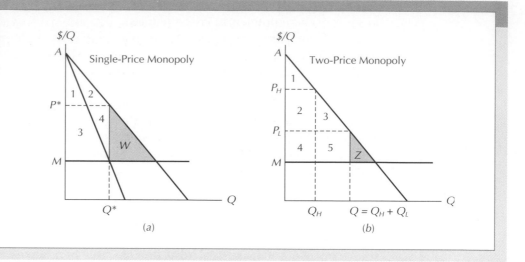

(the deeper the discount, the more stringent the restriction). When natural monopolies use hurdle pricing extensively to expand their markets, the magnitude of the efficiency problem will be reduced.

What about the fairness problem? First, what is this problem? The popular perception of it is that the monopolist transfers resources from people who desperately need them (namely, poor consumers) to others who have more than they need to begin with (namely, wealthy shareholders). Under unconstrained natural monopoly, this redistribution of resources from consumers to shareholders undeniably occurs. Yet we will see that under certain circumstances, the actual extent of the redistribution can be less than we might initially think.

The more general question of what constitutes a fair distribution of society's resources is a deep philosophical one, beyond the scope of our discussion here. We might say that no economic agent should be entitled to acquire, through force or coercion, the power to extract excessive resources from other economic agents. Yet unless we have fairly clear definitions of what constitutes coercion and how much is excessive, this principle doesn't get us very far. For instance, in a democracy, the coercive power vested by citizens in the *government* is viewed as a necessary condition of a stable and secure society and economy. Moreover, Albert Breton has argued that from an economic standpoint, much of what passes for normal business practice by firms contains an element of coercion.[19] While the meaning of coercion hence raises difficulties, the even more difficult question of how much extraction of resources is "excessive" lands us right back in the philosophical minefield. Let us suppose, however, that we are considering a natural monopoly that has become the lone seller in its market by wholly benevolent means. This is not impossible. By definition, its costs are lower than if other firms also served the market, and it might have entrenched its position through courteous and efficient customer service. Is it "unjust" for the firm to charge prices in excess of marginal cost?

Certainly consumers would be happier to pay only the marginal cost of production. But marginal cost is less than average cost in a natural monopoly, and so it is not possible for *everyone* to pay marginal cost and have the supplier remain in business. At best, *some*

---

[19]See Albert Breton, "Presidential Address: The Growth of Competitive Governments," *Canadian Journal of Economics*, November 1989: 717–750, on "post-contractual opportunistic behaviour" by firms.

consumers can pay prices close to marginal cost, but then others will have to pay more. More to the point, if the monopolist is earning extranormal or economic profits, we know that buyers are paying more, on the average, than the cost of the resources required to serve them. Can this be defended in the name of fairness?

The simple answer is no, even if every person who purchases the monopolist's output has the alternative of simply not purchasing it. If the monopolist employs a hurdle model of discriminatory pricing, however, not only does the market move toward a more *efficient* outcome but also the hurdle pricing system can mitigate the degree of *unfairness* arising from the unconstrained use of monopoly power.

For a monopolist using the hurdle model of pricing, consider first the source of a given dollar of monopoly profit. From which buyers does this dollar come? It is straightforward to show that it cannot have come from the discount price buyer. Typical discount prices range from 15 to 50 percent off the so-called regular price, and seldom do more than half of all buyers pay the discount price. Taking an illustrative case in which the discount is 30 percent and half of all buyers receive it, we see that the monopolist's revenue would fall by 15 percent if everyone paid the discount price. Very few firms would remain profitable in the face of a 15 percent decline in total revenue.

It follows that if the monopolist is earning economic profit, the primary source of that profit is the buyer who pays the regular price. The fact that this buyer could have paid a discount price if he had been willing to jump the requisite hurdle tells us that the burden imposed on him is no greater than the trouble of jumping the hurdle. This is obviously not the same as saying that the regular-price buyer makes a voluntary charitable contribution to the monopolist. But it does mean that in this situation, most of the burden of monopoly profits is borne by those who are prepared to bear it.

So much for the source of monopoly profit. What about its disposition? Who gets it? If we assume a 50 percent corporate income tax rate, then about half of each dollar of before-tax profits will go into government treasuries. The remainder is paid out to shareholders, either directly through dividends or indirectly by reinvesting it into the company. The average income of shareholders is greater than that of citizens as a whole. But there are many lower-income shareholders in Canada. Many employee pension funds, for example, are invested in the stock market, as are the private insurance holdings of many lower-income individuals. So a considerable fraction of any dollar of monopoly profit will wind up in the hands of lower-income shareholders.

When shareholders actually receive their dividends, those dividends will be subject to personal income tax. Insofar as the personal income tax is a progressive tax, larger-income shareholders will remit a larger proportion of their dividend income to the government than lower-income shareholders. The potentially adverse distributional effects of unconstrained monopoly profits can thus be significantly offset in practice by factors such as monopoly hurdle-pricing systems and a progressive tax structure.

This conclusion requires some qualifications. Not all natural monopolies utilize hurdle pricing. Indeed, some monopoly pricing policies, such as quantity discounts or preferential prices for major customers, tend to operate in the opposite direction. Moreover, hurdles are seldom *perfect*: they screen out some buyers who will not buy at the regular price, and sometimes real resources must be expended to jump over these hurdles. Finally, the services of creative tax accountants tend to have an income elasticity of demand that is greater than unity: the rich are more able to afford their services, and are likely to receive more benefit from their services in avoiding taxes, than lower- and middle-income taxpayers. Even allowing for these considerations, in some cases the element of unfairness associated with monopoly profits may be reduced, if not completely eliminated.

So what are we to conclude from this brief analysis of the five policy options for dealing with natural monopoly? The short answer is that each has problems. None completely eliminates the difficulties that arise when a single seller serves the market. Sometimes the least costly solution will be competitive contracting, other times direct state ownership. Regulation will continue to play a role in specific industries, particularly the traditional public utilities. And despite their shortcomings, competition laws serve the public well by discouraging price fixing and other anticompetitive practices. But in some cases, particularly those in which the monopolist has devised means of richly segmenting the market, the best option may be simply not to intervene at all.

Does Monopoly Suppress Innovation?

Economic conspiracy buffs and others have suggested that monopolists deprive consumers of a spectrum of valuable technological innovations. This suggestion has some empirical and theoretical support. In the early 1960s, Gillette dominated the North American razor blade market. It had the know-how to produce a stainless steel blade but did not do so, because of management's concern that introducing a longer-lasting blade would cut profits. Wilkinson Sword, a newcomer to the industry, introduced the coated stainless steel blade in 1961–62. Over the next three years, Gillette lost about 30 percent of its market, before fighting back with its own stainless steel blade and re-establishing its predominance.

We can construct models under which a monopoly will not innovate or will delay the introduction of an innovation, in comparison with what we would expect under competition. As the following example shows, however, it is not correct to assume that a monopoly will always suppress innovation.

EXAMPLE 12-4	**Suppose that all lightbulbs are produced by a monopolist. The current lightbulb design lasts 1000 hours. Now the lightbulb monopolist discovers how to make a bulb that lasts 10,000 hours for the same per-bulb cost of production. Will the monopolist introduce the new bulb?**

Suppose we measure the quantity produced by the monopolist not as lightbulbs per se, but as the number of bulb-hours of lighting services. Thus, if the cost of producing the current design is, say, $1.00/kilohour, then the cost of the new design is only $.10/kilohour. In Figure 12-23, D represents the market demand curve for lighting and MR the associated marginal revenue curve.

Note that the profit-maximizing price and quantity for the current design, whose marginal cost is $1/kilohour, are P_1 and Q_1, respectively. For the new design, whose marginal cost is $.10/kilohour, the profit-maximizing price and quantity are P_2 and Q_2. The monopolist's profit under the current design is the area of the rectangle $ABCE$. For the new design, the corresponding profit value is the area of the rectangle $FGHK$. And because the monopolist's profit is higher under the new design, it has every incentive to make that design available.

Note that in this model, we have assumed that demand and marginal revenue are linear, and that average cost curves are horizontal. Horizontal cost curves mean that the monopolist must have patent protection for both the old and the new lightbulbs. Note also that with constant costs, competition would result in production of the new bulbs at Q_C, at a price of $.10 per kilohour. Under monopoly, not all of the potential benefits of the innovation are being realized.

FIGURE 12-23

Does Monopoly Supress Innovation?
The cost of producing the new, efficient lightbulb, at $.10/kilohour, is only one-tenth the cost of producing the current design, $1/kilohour. Because the monopolist's profits with the efficient design (area of *FGHK*) exceed its profits with the current design (area of *ABCE*), it will offer the new design.

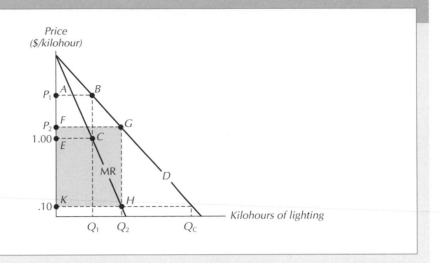

In a world of uncertainty and rapid technological change, however, monopoly may even foster innovation. If the monopolist views its present market as potentially vulnerable to entry, it may focus on innovation as a defensive strategy to increase barriers to entry. At the same time, monopoly profits provide a cushion or security zone within which innovation may flourish. Retained earnings can provide funding directly for research and development, while the firm's secure monopoly position may give it access to borrowed funds at preferential rates, reflecting its low risk premium. Innovation almost inevitably involves making mistakes. Monopoly profits mean that a monopolist can *afford* to make mistakes.

A large monopolist is also well positioned to engage in "cherry picking." In addition to its own R and D investment, it can monitor the innovations of smaller potential competitors. Most of these innovations will be failures, but the monopolist can simply buy up the successful small firms and their patents, at premium prices. At this point, it can either exploit the innovations or just shelve them, having eliminated a potential source of competition. In short, there is no a *priori* reason to assume that monopoly in and of itself will invariably either retard or accelerate innovation. If we assume that unconstrained monopolies are profit maximizers, we should expect to find examples of both inhibition and encouragement of innovation.

SUMMARY

www.mcgrawhill.ca/olc/frank

- Monopoly is the name given to the market structure in which a single firm serves the entire market. Five main factors, acting alone or in combination, give rise to monopoly: (1) control over key inputs, (2) economies of scale, (3) patents, (4) network economies, and (5) government licences. In the long run, generally the most important of these is economies of scale, in part because it is often an element in network economies and government licences.

- Because the monopolist is the only seller in the market, his demand curve is the downward-sloping market demand curve. Unlike the perfect competitor, who can sell as much as he chooses at the market price, the monopolist must cut price in order to expand his output. The monopolist's rule for maximizing profits is the same as the one used by perfectly competitive firms. It is to expand output if the gain in revenue (marginal revenue) exceeds the increase in costs (marginal cost), and to contract if the loss in revenue is smaller than the reduction in costs. The pivotal difference is that marginal revenue is less than price for the monopolist, but equal to price for the perfect competitor.

- When the monopolist can sell in several separate markets, he distributes output among them so that marginal revenue is the same in each. Here again, the familiar logic of cost-benefit analysis provides a convenient framework for analyzing the firm's decision about whether to alter its current behaviour.

- Unlike the perfectly competitive case, the monopoly equilibrium generally does not exhaust the potential gains from exchange. In general, the value to society of an additional unit of output will exceed the cost to the monopolist of the resources required to produce it. This finding has often been interpreted to mean that monopoly is less efficient than perfect competition. But this interpretation is of only limited practical significance, because the conditions that give rise to monopoly—in particular, economies of scale in production—are rarely compatible with those required for perfect competition.

- Our policy focus in the chapter was on the question of how the government should treat natural monopolies— markets characterized by downward-sloping long-run average cost curves. We considered five policy alternatives: (1) state ownership, (2) private ownership with government price regulation, (3) competitive bidding by private firms for the right to be the sole provider of service, (4) vigorous enforcement of competition laws designed to prevent monopoly, and finally (5) a complete *laissez-faire*, or hands-off, policy. Problems arise with each of these alternatives, and the best policy will in general be different in different circumstances. In markets where the monopolist employs the hurdle model of differential pricing, the *laissez-faire* approach is less inefficient and inequitable than it otherwise would be. Allowing buyers to decide for themselves whether to become eligible for a discount price reduces both the inefficiency and inequity costs of natural monopoly.

QUESTIONS FOR REVIEW

1. What five factors give rise to monopoly? In the long run, why are economies of scale generally the most important factor?

2. If Canada has hundreds of cement producers but a small town has only one, can this cement producer really be a monopolist? Explain.

3. When is marginal revenue less than price for a monopolist? Explain.

4. Why does a profit-maximizing monopolist never produce on an inelastic portion of the demand curve? Would a revenue-maximizing monopolist ever produce on the inelastic portion of the demand curve?

5. Why is an output level at which MR intersects MC from *below* never the profit-maximizing level of output?

6. What effect will the imposition of a 50 percent tax on economic profit have on a monopolist's price and output decisions? (*Hint:* Recall that the assumed objective is to choose the level of output that maximizes economic profit.)

7. Suppose that at a monopolist's profit-maximizing point, the elasticity of demand is $\eta = -3$. By what percentage does price exceed marginal cost? How does this markup of price over marginal cost compare with perfect competition?

8. *True or false:* A lump-sum tax on a monopolist will always increase the price charged by the monopolist and lower the quantity of output sold.

9. *True or false:* If a monopolist faces a perfectly horizontal demand curve, then the deadweight loss to the economy is zero.

10. What forces work against X-inefficiency in privately owned monopolies?

11. How does the hurdle method of price discrimination mitigate both the efficiency and fairness problems associated with monopoly?

1. You are a self-employed profit-maximization consultant. Five monopolies facing downward-sloping demand curves are currently seeking your advice, and although the information they have supplied to you is incomplete, your expert knowledge allows you to make a definite recommendation in each case. Select one of the following recommendations for each firm in the short run:
   a. Remain at the current output level.
   b. Increase output.
   c. Reduce output.
   d. Shut down.
   e. Go back and recalculate your figures because the ones supplied can't possibly be right.

Firm	P	MR	TR	Q	TC	MC	ATC	AVC	Your recommendation
A	3.90	3.00		2000	7400	2.90		3.24	
B	5.90			10,000		5.90	4.74	4.24	
C		9.00	44,000	4000		9.00	11.90	10.74	
D	35.90	37.90		5000		37.90	35.90		
E	35.00		3990	1000	3300		at min value	23.94	

2. A monopolist has a demand curve given by $P = 100 - Q$ and a total cost curve given by TC $= 16 + Q^2$. The associated marginal cost curve is MC $= 2Q$. Find the monopolist's profit-maximizing quantity and price. How much economic profit will the monopolist earn?

3. Now suppose the monopolist in Problem 2 has a total cost curve given by TC $= 32 + Q^2$. The corresponding marginal cost curve is still MC $= 2Q$, but fixed costs have doubled. Find the monopolist's profit-maximizing quantity and price. How much economic profit does the monopolist earn?

4. Now suppose the monopolist in Problem 2 has a total cost curve given by TC $= 16 + 4Q^2$. The corresponding marginal cost curve is now MC $= 8Q$, and fixed costs are back to the original level. Find the monopolist's profit-maximizing quantity and price. How much economic profit does the monopolist earn?

5. Now suppose the monopolist in Problem 2 also has access to a foreign market in which he can sell whatever quantity he chooses at a constant price of $60 per unit. How much will he sell in the foreign market? What will his new quantity and price be in the original market? How much will his total profits be?

6. Now suppose the monopolist in Problem 2 has a long-run marginal cost curve of MC $= 20$. Find the monopolist's profit-maximizing quantity and price. Find the efficiency loss from this monopoly.

7. Suppose that each period a perfectly discriminating monopolist faces market demand $P = 100 - 10Q$ and has constant marginal cost MC $= 20$ (with no fixed costs). How much does the monopolist sell? How much profit does the monopolist earn? What is the maximum per-period licence fee the government could charge the firm and have it still stay in business?

8. The demand by senior citizens for showings at a local movie house has a constant price elasticity equal to -4. The demand curve for all other patrons has a constant price elasticity equal to -2. If the marginal cost per patron is $1.20 per showing, how much should the theatre charge members of each group?

9. During the Iran–Iraq war, the same arms merchant often sold weapons to both sides of the conflict. In this situation, a different price could be offered to each side because there was little danger that the country offered the lower price would sell arms to its rival to profit from the difference in prices. Suppose a French arms merchant has a monopoly of Exocet air-to-sea missiles and is willing to sell them to both sides. Iraq's demand for Exocets is $P = 400 - .5Q$ and Iran's is $P = 300 - Q$, where P is in millions of dollars. The marginal cost of Exocets is $MC = Q$. What price will be charged to each country? What is each country's elasticity of demand for missiles at this point?

10. If you have ever gone grocery shopping on a weekday afternoon, you may have noticed some elderly shoppers going slowly down the aisles checking their coupon book for a coupon that matches each of their purchases. How is this behaviour explained by the hurdle model of price discrimination?

11. A profit-maximizing monopolist's price is $10 per unit. At this price the absolute value of the elasticity of demand is –2. What is the monopolist's marginal cost? What would the marginal cost be if instead the elasticity of demand were –4?

*12. Suppose the government imposed a price ceiling on a monopolist (an upper bound on the price the monopolist can charge). Let $\bar{P}$ denote the price ceiling, and suppose the monopolist incurs no costs in producing output. *True or false:* If the demand curve faced by the monopolist is inelastic at the price $\bar{P}$, then the monopolist would be no better off if the government removed the price ceiling. In a diagram, show where the monopolist will produce with the price ceiling.

13. *The Globe and Post*, a profit-maximizing newspaper, faces a downward-sloping demand schedule for advertisements. When advertising for itself in its own pages (for example, an ad saying "Our news has fewer calories"), is the opportunity cost of a given-size ad simply the price it charges its outside advertisers? Explain.

**14. Crazy Harry, a monopolist, has a total cost curve given by $TC = 5Q + 15$. He sets two prices for his product, a regular price, P_H, and a discount price, P_L. Everyone is eligible to purchase the product at P_H. To be eligible to buy at P_L, it is necessary to present a copy of the latest Crazy Harry newspaper ad to the salesclerk. Suppose the only buyers who present the ad are those who would not have been willing to buy the product at P_H. (*Hint:* Use the method described in footnote 18.)

   a. If Crazy Harry's demand curve is given by $P = 20 - 5Q$, what are the profit-maximizing values of P_H and P_L?
   b. How much economic profit does Harry make?
   c. How much profit would he have made if he had been forced to charge the same price to all buyers?
   d. Are buyers better or worse off as a result of Harry's being able to charge two prices?

15. An author has signed a contract in which the publisher promises to pay her $10,000 plus 20 percent of gross receipts from the sale of her book. *True or false*: If both the publisher and the author care only about their own financial return from the project, then the author will prefer a higher book price than the publisher.

16. A film director has signed a contract in which the production studio promises to pay her $1,000,000 plus 5 percent of the studio's rental revenues from the film, all of whose costs of production and distribution are *fixed*. *True or false*: If both the director and the studio care only about their own financial return from the project, then the director will prefer a lower film rental price than the studio.

**17. In the situation described in Exercise 12-5, suppose that demand is unchanged but that the monopolist's Total Cost function is given by $TC = .25Q^2$. Calculate its MC equation, the level of Q_T where $MR_T = MC$, and the values at this point for Q_1, Q_2, P_1, P_2, and total profit in the two markets.

**18. The demand function for Sweet Chunks Cereal ("If we could make it more than 100 percent sugar, we would!") is given by the equation

$$Q = 64P^{-2}.$$

a. Give the formulas for price (P), total revenue (TR), and marginal revenue (MR) as functions of Q.

b. Calculate the profit-maximizing Q, P, percent markup ($P - MC$)/MC, profit, and elasticity if:
   i. TC $= 6 + .5Q$.
   ii. TC $= 6 + Q$.
   iii. TC $= 6 + 2Q$.

**19. Ecotripper Enterprises is the sole producer of Sunblast solar-powered skateboards, "the green alternative." Market demand for Sunblasts is given by the formula

$$P = 120 - .5Q,$$

where P is in dollars per skateboard and Q is in skateboards per week. Total costs, in dollars per week, are given by the formula

$$TC = 100 + 20Q.$$

a. Derive the expression for the marginal cost (MC) and marginal revenue (MR) functions, and calculate the profit-maximizing price, quantity sold, and profit.

b. If the government imposes a price ceiling of $85 per skateboard, what is the effect on the equilibrium described in 19a?

c. Repeat 19b if the price ceiling is set at $65 per skateboard.

d. If the government wanted Ecotripper to produce the socially efficient quantity of skateboards, what price ceiling could it set in the short run? What would the result be in the long run?

e. If the government decided to set the price ceiling so that consumer surplus was maximized subject to Ecotripper's earning zero profits, what would be the level of the price ceiling (to the nearest cent per unit), the quantity sold (to the nearest unit), and the consumer surplus?

**20. Hardy Hurdley owns a clear spring, which produces mineral water that is viewed as having unique restorative properties. Hardy has no fixed costs, and the water is available at zero marginal cost. It is demanded by two groups, Group A and Group B, whose demand functions for the water take the following forms:

Group A $P = 20 - 2Q_A$
Group B $P = 10 - Q_B,$

where Q_i is in litres and P is in dollars per litre.

a. If Hardy sets a single price for the water, give the price he will charge, the quantity purchased by Group A and by Group B, Hardy's profits, and the consumer surplus of Group A and of Group B. (*Hint:* What is Hardy's marginal revenue (MR) curve?)

b. Hardy decides to charge two prices for the water, a "regular" price (P_H), which involves no waiting, and a lower price (P_L), which is available only after waiting one hour per litre purchased. Group A members assess the cost of the wait at $8/hour, while Group B members treat the waiting cost as zero. What prices would Hardy set if he knew the demand curves and the valuations of the cost of the wait? Calculate Hardy's profits and the consumer surplus of Group A and of Group B under this hurdle pricing system.

c. Suppose that P_H and P_L are as in 20b, but that now Group B members evaluate the waiting-time hurdle at a cost of $8/hour, while Group A members treat the waiting cost as zero. Calculate Hardy's profits and the consumer surplus of Group A and of Group B in this situation.

d. Compare the three situations. In which situation is the sum of consumer surplus and producer surplus greatest? In which situation is it smallest? How do these sums compare with the competitive outcome?

12-1.

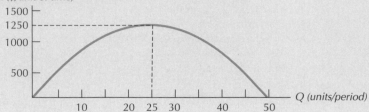

12-2.

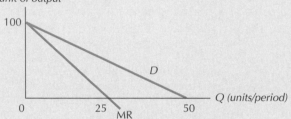

12-3. MC = 40 = 100 − 4Q, which solves for $Q^* = 15$ units, $P^* = 100 - 2Q^* = \$70$ per unit, and losses = \$190.

12-4. The profit-maximizing level of output for a single-price monopolist occurs where MR = MC. Marginal revenue equals marginal cost at both $Q = 15$ and $Q = 34$, but $Q = 34$ has marginal revenue intersect from above and thus is the maximal one. However, even at $Q = 34$, price does not cover average variable cost ($66 = P < \text{AVC} = 72$). The average variable cost curve lies everywhere above the demand curve (see figure), so the firm can do no better than earn profits equal to the negative of the fixed costs. Thus, the optimal quantity is $Q = 0$: the firm should shut down!

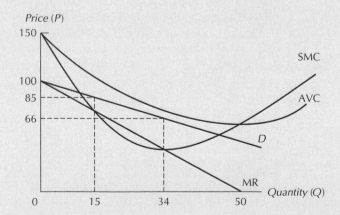

12-5. $MR_1 = 10 - 2Q_1$ (left panel), and $MR_2 = 20 - 2Q_2$ (centre panel), so the horizontal summation of the MR curves is given by ΣMR (right panel). Rewriting the MR equations, we have $Q_1 = 5 - .5MR_1$ and $Q_2 = 10 - .5MR_2$. Since we want MR = MC in *both* markets, we have $MR_1 = MR_2 = MR_T$. We can therefore write the formula relating Q_T and MR_T as follows: $Q_T = Q_1 + Q_2 = (5 + 10) - (.5 + .5) MR_T = 15 - MR_T$, or equivalently, $MR_T = 15 - Q_T$, for $Q_T \geq 5$ ($MR_T \leq 10$). For $Q_T \leq 5$ ($MR_T \geq 10$), the MR_T curve coincides with the MR_2 curve. The profit-maximizing quantity is 13, of which 4 should be sold in market 1, the remaining 9 in market 2. The profit-maximizing prices are $P_1^* = \$6$ per unit and $P_2^* = \$11$ per unit.

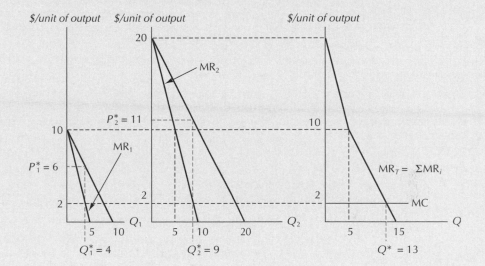

Chapter 13

OLIGOPOLY AND MONOPOLISTIC COMPETITION

Two children are playing Tic Tac Toe. At first the older one wins or draws every time, whether she starts or plays second. When the younger one threatens to quit playing because "I never win," the older one lets him win a few times. Gradually, the younger one learns the ropes. After a while, they both get bored with Tic Tac Toe, because every game ends in a draw, and they go outside to play soccer.

Two grandmasters are hunched over a chessboard. They have played against each other often, each knows the other's style of play, and they are roughly even in matches won. But Vish's last move was unexpected, a sharp departure from his usual line of attack. Despite the time pressures, Kaspar knows he will have to analyze the move carefully before making his response.

Two months from now, Megapop Enterprises will be conducting an expensive and top secret marketing test in Edmonton for a new line of soft drinks. The information this test generates will be crucial in planning the Canada-wide launch of the new line early next year. In a conference room at the head office of Gigafizz Corporation, Megapop's major competitor, some senior executives are discussing a photocopy of Megapop's top secret test plan. Exactly how they obtained the plan document is not important, although it does involve a new Hummer in the driveway of the executive secretary to a Megapop senior vice-president. Gigafizz is now planning a saturation advertising and price-cutting blitz focused on Edmonton, which coincidentally is scheduled to begin in seven weeks and to last for several months. Retaining its share of the Edmonton soft drink market is only a secondary objective of the blitz. Management's major objective is to create so much "noise" that the information Megapop generates from its Edmonton market testing will be of no use for the national product launch. Meanwhile, in a Megapop conference room, some senior Megapop executives (and one executive secretary) are enjoying a champagne toast. Then they will get down to putting the finishing touches on plans for their expensive, ultra-secret market test of the new soft drink line, which will occur in two months time … in Hamilton.

The hostility between two neighbouring countries, Armoria and Bellicosa, goes back for centuries, and has involved many periods of active warfare and uneasy peace. Neither trusts the intentions of the other, and each maintains an extensive military establishment. Armorian military intelligence sources have heard rumours of an arms buildup in Bellicosa. The Armorian generals successfully argue for an increase in military expenditures as insurance against an unprovoked surprise attack by the Bellicosan aggressors. This Armorian arms buildup becomes known to the Bellicosan high command. They in turn argue (successfully) that peace-loving Bellicosa needs to spend more on defence, as insurance in light of this proof of Armoria's perfidious attempt to create an "armaments gap." Bellicosa's actions do not go unnoticed in Armoria, however, and the competitive cycle of escalating expenditures continues. In the ensuing arms race, or "Richardson process" (named after Lewis Richardson, who was the first to subject what he called "deadly quarrels" to mathematical and statistical treatment[1]), both countries are left worse off. Non-military consumption and investment is reduced to free up the resources required for the arms buildups, and productivity growth lags. Equally significant, the "insurance" analogy breaks down. Both countries are less secure now, because each is now capable of inflicting much more damage on the other than before the arms race began, and the arms race itself has increased levels of hostility and mistrust in both countries.

CHAPTER PREVIEW

The four situations with which we began this chapter have something in common. In very different ways, they all involve *strategic interaction* among the players in a contest. The "best" course of action for each player depends not only on the nature of the contest (the "rules of the game") but also on the specific actions taken by the other player or players. This type of strategic interaction between firms was ruled out in the market structures we studied in the last two chapters. In the perfect competition model, firms were assumed to ignore the actions of their adversaries. And in monopoly, the firm simply had no rivals to worry about. Both perfect competition and monopoly represent idealized forms. They are extraordinarily useful for generating insights about general tendencies but are rarely, if ever, encountered in practice. Our task in this chapter is to describe and explore the hybrid forms of industrial organization we deal with on a daily basis—namely, oligopoly and monopolistic competition.

Oligopoly An industry in which there are only a few important sellers.

Oligopoly refers to an industry in which there are only a few important sellers. These firms produce all, or most, of their industry's output. The logic of strategic interaction among oligopolistic rivals often has much the same flavour as the above examples. Among oligopolists, strategic interaction is not only present but occupies centre stage.

We begin by comparing several simple models of interdependence in which firms make alternative assumptions about the behaviour of their rivals. We shall then see how collusive behaviour and other forms of strategic interaction are illuminated by the mathematical theory of games; and we shall explore some simple models of the games oligopolists play.

Monopolistic competition An industry in which each of a number of firms produces a product that is an imperfect substitute for the products of the other firms and where there is free entry and exit of firms.

Monopolistic competition is defined by two seemingly simple conditions: (1) the existence of numerous firms each producing a product that is a close, but imperfect, substitute for the products of other firms; and (2) free entry and exit of firms. We begin with a traditional model of monopolistic competition, and then develop a simple spatial

---

[1]See Lewis Richardson, *Arms and Insecurity*, Chicago: Quadrangle, 1960; and *The Statistics of Deadly Quarrels*, Chicago: Quadrangle, 1960.

model of monopolistic competition. In this model, customers have particular locations or product characteristics that they most prefer. The result, we will see, is that firms tend to compete most intensively for the buyers of products that are most similar to their own.

13.A OLIGOPOLY

13.1 THE COURNOT MODEL

If a firm is considering a change in its output level or selling price, there are many possible assumptions it could make about the reactions of its rivals. It could assume, for example, that its rivals will continue producing at their current levels of output. Alternatively, it could assume that they would continue to charge their current prices. Or it could assume that rivals would react in various specific ways to its own price and output changes. In the sections that follow, we explore the implications of various such assumptions.

We begin with the simplest case, the so-called **Cournot model**, in which each firm assumes that its rivals will continue producing at their current levels of output. Named for the French economist Auguste Cournot, who introduced it in 1838, this model describes the behaviour of two firms that sell bottled water from identical mineral springs. A two-firm oligopoly is called a *duopoly*, and the Cournot model is sometimes referred to as the *Cournot duopoly model*, although its conclusions can easily be generalized to more than two firms.

The central assumption of the Cournot model is that each duopolist treats the other's quantity of output as a fixed number, one that will not respond to its own production decisions. This form of interdependence leads to an outcome in which the behaviour of each firm substantially affects its rival.

Suppose the total market demand curve for mineral water is given by

$$P = a - b(Q_1 + Q_2), \qquad (13.1)$$

where a and b are positive numbers and Q_1 and Q_2 are the outputs of firms 1 and 2, respectively. Cournot assumed that the water could be produced at zero marginal cost, but this assumption is merely for convenience. Essentially similar conclusions would emerge if each firm had a constant positive marginal cost.

Let us look first at the profit-maximization problem facing firm 1. Given its assumption that firm 2's output is fixed at Q_2, the demand curve for firm 1's water is given by

$$P_1 = (a - bQ_2) - bQ_1, \qquad (13.2)$$

which is rewritten to emphasize the fact that firm 1 treats Q_2 as given.

As Equation 13.2 shows, for any level of Q_2 we get the demand curve for firm 1 by subtracting bQ_2 from the vertical intercept of the market demand curve. The idea is that firm 2 has skimmed off the first Q_2 units of the market demand curve, leaving firm 1 the remainder to work with.

If Q_2 were equal to zero, firm 1 would have the entire market demand curve to itself, as is indicated by D in Figure 13-1. If Q_2 is positive, we get firm 1's demand curve by shifting the vertical axis of the demand diagram rightward by Q_2 units. Firm 1's demand curve is that portion of the original demand curve that lies to the right of this new vertical axis, and for this reason it is sometimes called a *residual demand curve*. The associated marginal revenue curve is labelled MR_1. Firm 1's rule for profit maximization is the same as for any other firm that faces a downward-sloping demand curve, namely, to equate marginal revenue and marginal cost. Marginal cost in this example is assumed to be zero, so the profit-maximizing level of output for firm 1 is that level for which its marginal revenue curve takes the value of zero, for any given value of Q_2.

The equilibrium outputs for a Cournot duopoly can be deduced from the residual demand diagram. Given that firm 2 is producing Q_2, firm 1 maximizes its profits by producing where marginal revenue equals marginal cost. Marginal revenue for firm 1 is given by $MR_1 = (a - bQ_2) - 2bQ_1$. Marginal revenue has twice the slope as demand, so marginal revenue intersects zero marginal cost at half the distance from the $Q_1 = 0$ axis to the horizontal intercept of the demand curve. By symmetry (the two firms are identical so they must behave the same), $Q_2 = Q_1$, which means that Figure 13-1 actually depicts the equilibrium position, when each of the three segments shown on the horizontal axis has the same length. And this implies that each firm produces output equal to one-third of the distance from the origin to the horizontal intercept of the demand curve. The demand curve $P = a - bQ$ has a horizontal intercept of $Q = a/b$; hence, $Q_1 = Q_2 = a/(3b)$. A more general approach is to set marginal revenue equal to marginal cost and solve for the output of firm 1 in terms of the output of firm 2.[2] When marginal cost is zero for firm 1,

$$Q_1^* = \frac{a - bQ_2}{2b}. \qquad (13.3)$$

Reaction function
A curve that tells the profit-maximizing level of output for one oligopolist for each amount supplied by another.

Economists often call Equation 13.3 firm 1's **reaction function**, and denote it by $Q_1^* = R_1(Q_2)$. This notation is suggestive because the reaction function tells how firm 1's quantity will react to the quantity level offered by firm 2.

Because the Cournot duopoly problem is completely symmetric, firm 2's reaction function has precisely the same structure:

FIGURE 13-1

The Profit-Maximizing Cournot Duopolist
The Cournot duopolist's demand curve is obtained by shifting the vertical axis rightward by the amount produced by the other duopolist (Q_2 in the diagram). The portion of the original market demand curve that lies to the right of this new vertical axis is the demand curve facing firm 1. Firm 1 then maximizes profit by equating marginal revenue and marginal cost, the latter of which is zero.

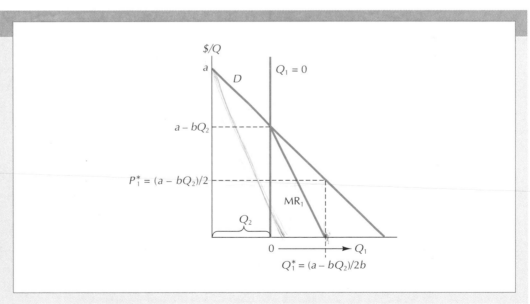

[2]This more general approach is needed if firms are asymmetric (not identical)—for instance, if they have different marginal cost functions, and thus would not necessarily both produce the same level of output.

FIGURE 13-2

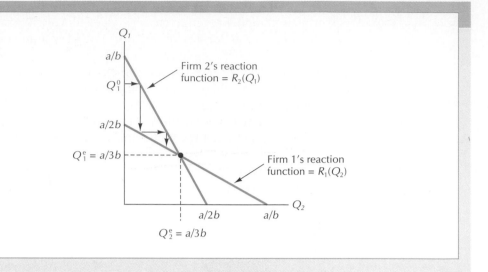

$$Q_2^* = R_2(Q_1) = \frac{a - bQ_1}{2b} \qquad (13.4)$$

The two reaction functions are plotted in Figure 13-2. To illustrate the workings of the reaction function concept, suppose firm 1 initially produced a quantity of Q_1^0. Firm 2 would then produce the level of output that corresponds to Q_1^0 on its reaction function. Firm 1 would respond to that output level by picking the corresponding point on its own reaction function. Firm 2 would then respond by picking the corresponding point on its reaction function, and so on. Note that the firm on the horizontal axis adjusts horizontally to its reaction function, while the firm on the vertical axis adjusts vertically to its reaction function. The end result of this process is a stable equilibrium at the intersection of the two reaction functions. When both firms are producing a/3b units of output, neither has any incentive to change.[3] Each is maximizing its profits, given the output decision of the other.

How profitable are the Cournot duopolists? Since their combined output is $2a/3b$, the market price will be $P = a - b(2a/3b) = a/3$. At this price, each will have total revenue equal to $(a/3)(a/3b) = a^2/9b$. And since neither firm has any production costs, total revenues and economic profits here are one and the same.

---

[3]Equilibrium requires that $Q_1^* = R_1(Q_2^*)$ and that $Q_2^* = R_2(Q_1^*)$. In other words, it requires that the two reaction curves intersect, so that for firm 1, $Q_2^* \to Q_1^*$, while for firm 2, $Q_1^* \to Q_2^*$. Consider the more general case where two Cournot duopolists have zero fixed costs and constant marginal costs equal to c_1 and c_2, respectively. Firm 1's equilibrium profit-maximizing level of output is derived by setting $MR_1 = a - bQ_2 - 2bQ_1 = c_1 = MC_1$. This gives

$$Q_1^* = \frac{a - c_1 - bQ_2^*}{2b}, \text{ and similarly, } Q_2^* = \frac{a - c_2 - bQ_1^*}{2b}.$$

Substituting the value for Q_2^* into the equation for Q_1^* and simplifying gives

$$Q_1^* = \frac{a - 2c_1 + c_2}{3b}, \text{ and similarly, } Q_2^* = \frac{a - 2c_2 + c_1}{3b},$$

subject to both Q_1^* and Q_2^* being nonnegative. When the marginal costs of the two firms are equal ($c_1 = c_2 = c$), we have $Q_1^* = Q_2^* = (a - c)/3b$. When $c_1 = c_2 = 0$, as in our present example, the general formula simplifies to $Q_1^* = Q_2^* = a/3b$. Try substituting different sets of values for a, b, c_1, and c_2 into these equations to see the effect of changes in these values on the equilibrium position.

EXAMPLE 13-1

Cournot duopolists face a market demand curve given by $P = 56 - 2Q$, where Q is total market demand. Each can produce output at a constant marginal cost of $20/unit. Graph their reaction functions and find the equilibrium price and quantity.

Figure 13-3a shows the residual demand curve facing firm 1 when firm 2 produces Q_2 units. Firm 1's marginal revenue curve has the same vertical intercept as its demand curve and is twice as steep. Thus the equation for firm 1's marginal revenue curve is $MR_1 = 56 - 2Q_2 - 4Q_1$. Equating MR_1 to marginal cost ($= 20$), we solve for firm 1's reaction function, $Q_1^* = R_1 = 9 - (Q_2/2)$. By symmetry, firm 2's reaction function is $R_2 = 9 - (Q_1/2)$. The two reaction functions are shown in Figure 13-3b, where they intersect at $Q_1 = Q_2 = 6$ units. Total market output will be $Q_1 + Q_2 = 12$ units. Consulting the market demand curve, we see that the market price will be $P = 56 - 2(12) = \$32/unit$.

EXERCISE 13-1

Repeat Example 13-1 with the two firms facing a market demand curve of $P = 44 - Q$.

You may be wondering why the Cournot duopolists assume that their own production decisions will be ignored by their rivals. If so, you have asked a penetrating question, the same one posed by Cournot's critic, the French economist Joseph Bertrand. Let's now consider his alternative solution to the duopoly problem.

13.2 THE BERTRAND MODEL

Bertrand duopoly model An industry in which two firms produce identical goods and each firm chooses its price taking its rival's price as given.

The insight of the **Bertrand duopoly model** was that, from the buyer's perspective, what really counts is how the prices charged by the two firms compare. Since the duopolists are selling identical mineral water, every buyer will naturally want to buy from the seller with the lower price. Bertrand proposed that each firm chooses its price on the

FIGURE 13-3

Deriving the Reaction Functions for Specific Duopolists
Panel a shows the profit-maximizing output level for firm 1 (Q_1^*) when firm 2 produces Q_2. That and the parallel expression for firm 2 constitute the reaction functions plotted in panel b.

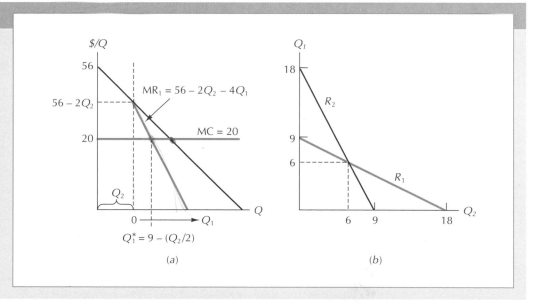

assumption that its rival's price would remain fixed. On its face, this assumption seems no more plausible than Cournot's, and since prices and quantities correspond uniquely along market demand curves, it may seem natural to wonder whether Bertrand's assumption even leads to a different outcome. On investigation, however, the outcomes turn out to be very different indeed.

To illustrate, suppose the market demand and cost conditions are the same as in the Cournot example. And suppose firm 1 charges an initial price of P_0^1. Firm 2 then faces essentially three choices: (1) it can charge more than firm 1, in which case it will sell nothing; (2) it can charge the same as firm 1, in which case we will assume that the two firms split the market demand equally at that price; or (3) it can sell at a marginally lower price than firm 1, in which case it will capture the entire market demand at that price. The third of these options will always be by far the most profitable.[4]

As in the Cournot model, the situations of the duopolists are completely symmetric in the Bertrand model, which means that the option of selling at a marginally lower price than the competition will be the strategy of choice for both firms. Needless to say, there can be no stable equilibrium in which each firm undersells the other. The back-and-forth process of price-cutting will continue until it reaches its economic limit—namely, marginal cost, which in the mineral spring example is zero. (If instead we had considered an example in which both firms have the same positive marginal cost, price would have fallen to that value.) Once each firm has cut its price to marginal cost, it will have no incentive to cut further. With each firm selling at marginal cost, as we have assumed, the duopolists will share the market equally.

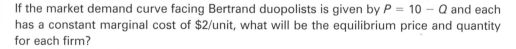

| EXAMPLE 13-2 | **Bertrand duopolists face a market demand curve given by $P = 56 - 2Q$. Each can produce output at a constant marginal cost of \$20/unit. Find the equilibrium price and quantity.** |

The solution is that both firms price at marginal cost: $P = $ MC $ = \$20/$unit. Industry output is determined by market demand: $20 = 56 - 2Q$ implies $Q = 18$ units. If the firms split the market equally, then each firm produces half of industry output: $Q_1 = Q_2 = Q/2 = 9$ units.

EXERCISE 13-2

If the market demand curve facing Bertrand duopolists is given by $P = 10 - Q$ and each has a constant marginal cost of \$2/unit, what will be the equilibrium price and quantity for each firm?

So we see that a seemingly minor change in the initial assumptions about firm behaviour—that each duopolist takes its rival's price, not quantity, as given—leads to a sharply different equilibrium. Now we consider how another small change in the initial assumptions about firm behaviour can lead to yet another equilibrium.

13.3 THE STACKELBERG MODEL

In 1934, the German economist Heinrich von Stackelberg asked the simple but provocative question, "What would a firm do if it knew its only rival were a naïve

---

[4]In the case of a price only infinitesimally smaller than firm 1's price, firm 2's profit will be virtually twice as large under option 3 as under option 2.

Cournot duopolist?" In the **Stackelberg model**, it would want to choose its own output level by taking into account the effect that choice would have on the output level of its rival.

Returning to our original Cournot model, suppose firm 1 knows that firm 2 will treat firm 1's output level as given. How can it make strategic use of that knowledge? To answer this question, recall that firm 2's reaction function is given by $Q_2^* = R_2(Q_1) = (a - bQ_1)/2b$. Knowing that firm 2's output will depend on Q_1 in this fashion, firm 1 can then substitute $R_2(Q_1)$ for Q_2 in the equation for the market demand curve, which yields the following expression for its own demand curve:

$$P = a - b[Q_1 + R_2(Q_1)] = a - b\left(Q_1 + \frac{a - bQ_1}{2b}\right) = \frac{a - bQ_1}{2} \qquad (13.5)$$

This demand curve and the associated marginal revenue curve are shown as D_1 and MR_1 in Figure 13-4. Since marginal cost is assumed to be zero in the mineral spring example, firm 1's profit-maximizing output level will be the one for which MR_1 is zero, namely, $Q_1^* = a/2b$. $Q_2^* = a/4b$ and the price $P^* = a - bQ^* = a - b(Q_1^* + Q_2^*) = a/4$. (See footnote 5.)

EXAMPLE 13-3

A Stackelberg leader (firm 1) and follower (firm 2) face a market demand curve given by $P = 56 - 2Q$. Each can produce output at a constant marginal cost of $20/unit. Find the equilibrium price and quantity.

The solution is found by substituting firm 2's reaction function $Q_2 = 9 - Q_1/2$ into the demand facing firm 1, $P = (56 - 2Q_2) - 2Q_1$, to find $P = 38 - Q_1$ with corresponding marginal revenue $MR_1 = 38 - 2Q_1$. Setting marginal revenue equal to marginal cost yields firm 1's output $Q_1 = 9$ units. Inserting firm 1's output into firm 2's reaction function yields firm 2's output $Q_2 = 4.5$ units. Total industry output is $Q = Q_1 + Q_2 = 13.5$ units, with price $P = 56 - 2Q = 56 - 27 = $29/unit.

EXERCISE 13-3

The market demand curve for a Stackelberg leader and follower is given by $P = 10 - Q$. If each has a marginal cost of $2/unit, what will be the equilibrium price and quantity for each?

---

[5]When marginal costs $MC_1 = MC_2 = 0$, the profit of firm 1 is given by $\Pi_1 = P(Q) \cdot Q_1$. The price $P = a - bQ = a - b(Q_1 + Q_2) = a - b[Q_1 + R_2(Q_1)] = a - b[Q_1 + (a - bQ_1)/2b] = (a - bQ_1)/2$. Hence

$$\Pi_1 = PQ_1 = (aQ_1 - bQ_1^2)/2.$$

That is, to each value of Q_1, from $Q_1 = 0$ (where firm 1 supplies none of the market demand) to $Q_1 = a/b$ (where firm 1 supplies the maximum quantity demanded by the market), corresponds a particular level of profit, *taking into account the quantity that firm 2 will produce given that firm 1's output = Q_1*. To maximize profit, firm 1 sets

$$\frac{d\Pi_1}{dQ_1} = a/2 - bQ_1 = 0,$$

and so $Q_1^* = a/2b$. Given that $Q_1 = a/2b$, firm 2's profit function is given by

$$\Pi_2 = PQ_2 = [a - b(a/2b + Q_2)] \cdot Q_2,$$

which simplifies to $\Pi_2 = [aQ_2/2 - b(Q_2)^2]$. To maximize its profit, firm 2 sets

$$\frac{d\Pi_2}{dQ_2} = a/2 - 2bQ_2 = 0,$$

which gives $Q_2^* = a/4b$.

FIGURE 13-4

**The Stackelberg
Leader's Demand,
Marginal Revenue,
and Profit Functions**
(*a*) When firm 1 knows
firm 2 is a Cournot
duopolist, it can take
account of the effect of
its own behaviour on
firm 2's quantity choice.
The result is that it
knows exactly what its
(residual) demand curve
will be. (*b*) Firm 1's profit
function, with zero costs,
is $\Pi_1 = PQ_1 = (aQ_1 - bQ_1^2)/2$, which reaches
a maximum at $Q_1^* = a/(2b)$, with $\Pi_1^* = a^2/8b$.

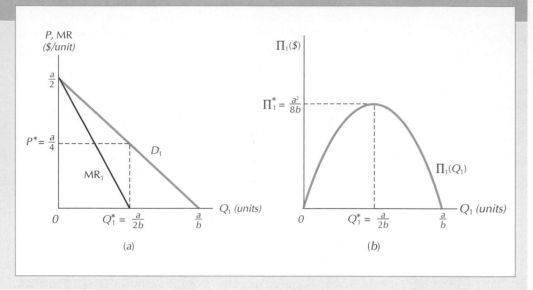

(*a*)   (*b*)

For obvious reasons, firm 1 is referred to as a *Stackelberg leader. Stackelberg follower* is the term used to describe firm 2. To help place the Stackelberg leader's behaviour in clearer perspective, let's again consider the graph of the two firms' Cournot reaction functions, reproduced here as Figure 13-5. As we saw in Figure 13-4, $a/2b$ is the best output for firm 1 to produce once it takes into account that firm 2 will respond to its choice according to the reaction function $R_2(Q_1)$. Once firm 1 produces $a/2b$, firm 2 will consult R_2 and respond by producing $a/4b$. Now here is the crucial step. If firm 1 thought that firm 2 would stay at $a/4b$ no matter what, its best bet would be to consult its own reaction function and produce the corresponding quantity, namely, $3a/8b$. By doing so, it would earn more than by producing $a/2b$. The problem is that firm 1 realizes that if it cuts back to $3a/8b$, this will elicit a further reaction from firm 2, culminating in a downward spiral to the intersection point of the two reaction functions. Firm 1 would do better to move to $3a/8b$ if it could somehow induce firm 2 to remain at $a/4b$. But it cannot. The best option open to firm 1 is therefore to grit its teeth and stay put at $a/2b$. At this point it earns more profit than at the intersection of the reaction curves, but does not give firm 2 any incentive to increase output.

13.4 COMPARISON OF OUTCOMES

Now that we have considered three different types of behaviour for duopolists, let's compare the outcomes of the different models, in the case where the two firms are identical and marginal costs are zero. A monopoly confronting the same demand and cost conditions as Cournot duopolists would have produced $a/2b$ units of output at a price of $a/2$, earning an economic profit of $a^2/4b$ (see Figure 13-6). The interdependence between the (identical) Cournot duopolists thus causes price to be one-third lower and total quantity to be one-third higher than the corresponding values in the monopoly case.[6]

---

[6]As a fraction of the output for a perfectly competitive industry facing linear demand, industry output under a Cournot N-opoly is $N/(N + 1)$ with N identical firms. As the number of firms N becomes large, the Cournot industry output (and therefore price and profit) approaches that of a perfectly competitive industry. In this sense, Cournot duopoly (or N-opoly) is truly between monopoly and perfect competition.

FIGURE 13-5

The Stackelberg Equilibrium
In the Stackelberg model, firm 1 ignores its own reaction function from the Cournot model. It chooses its own quantity to maximize profit, taking into account the effect that its own quantity will have on the quantity offered by firm 2.

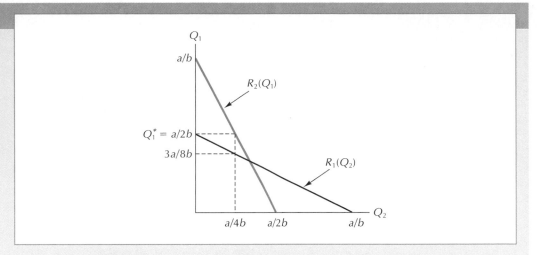

Whereas the equilibrium price and quantity in the Cournot model differed by only a factor of one-third from those in the monopoly case, in the Bertrand model they are precisely the same as in the competitive case.[7]

How well should the Stackelberg duopolists do? Naturally, the leader fares better since it is the one strategically manipulating the behaviour of the follower. Referring to Figure 13-4, we see that firm 1's profit is $a^2/8b$, which is twice that of firm 2. As it happens, this is exactly what firm 1 would have earned had it and firm 2 colluded to charge the monopoly price, $a/2$, and split the market evenly (see Figure 13-6). The combined output of the two firms in the Stackelberg case is $3a/4b$, which is slightly higher than in the Cournot case, with the result that the market price, $a/4$, is slightly lower than in the Cournot case ($a/3$). The results of the four possibilities considered thus far are summarized in Table 13-1.

The Stackelberg model represents a clear improvement over the Cournot and Bertrand models in that it allows at least one of the firms to behave strategically. But why should only one firm behave in this fashion? If firm 1 can make strategic use of its rival's reaction function, why can't firm 2 do likewise? Suppose, in fact, that both firms try to be Stackelberg leaders. Each will then ignore its own reaction function and produce $a/2b$, with the result that total industry output and price will be a/b and 0, respectively, the same as in the Bertrand model. From the standpoint of consumers,

TABLE 13-1

Comparison of Oligopoly Models
All five models assume a market demand curve of $P = a - bQ$ and two identical firms with marginal cost equal to zero. (Of course, if marginal cost is not zero, some entries will differ from the ones shown.)

Model	Industry output Q	Market price P	Industry profit Π
Shared monopoly	$Q_m = a/(2b)$	$P_m = a/2$	$\Pi_m = a^2/(4b)$
Cournot	$(4/3)Q_m$	$(2/3)P_m$	$(8/9)\Pi_m$
Stackelberg	$(3/2)Q_m$	$(1/2)P_m$	$(3/4)\Pi_m$
Bertrand	$2Q_m$	0	0
Perfect competition	$2Q_m$	0	0

---

[7]If firms choose capacity and then price, the outcome matches the Cournot equilibrium. See David Kreps and Jose Scheinkman, "Quantity Precommitment and Bertrand Competition Yield Cournot Outcomes," *Bell Journal of Economics, 14*, 1983: 326–337.

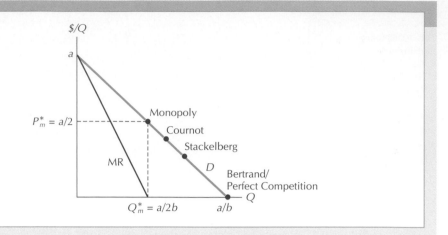

FIGURE 13-6

Comparing Equilibrium Price and Quantity
The monopolist would maximize profit where marginal revenue equals zero, since there are no marginal production costs. The equilibrium price will be higher, and the equilibrium quantity lower, than in the Cournot, Stackelberg, and Bertrand cases.

this is a very desirable outcome, of course. But for the owners of the firms, universal strategic behaviour leads to the worst possible outcome.

13.5 GAME THEORY: A PRIMER

In working through these models of duopoly firm behaviour, you may have found yourself asking some questions. How could a Cournot duopolist be so foolish as to assume that its rival's output will not adjust if the first duopolist changes its own level of output? At *any* point except the Cournot equilibrium, the rival would have an incentive (in the form of increased profits) to do just that. Surely the behaviour of the Bertrand duopolist is even more foolish. Does he really believe that his rival will quietly acquiesce in the loss of all of its sales and profits, when the rival, by adjusting its price slightly downward, can capture 100 percent of the market? Don't both of them realize that the first to default and undercut the other's price is setting them both on the path to zero profitability? Why can the two Stackelberg duopolists not simply agree on a mechanism to split the monopoly level of output and monopoly profits between them? After all, if the Stackelberg leader could produce by itself at the monopoly output level, it would have more than enough profits in hand to bribe or compensate the Stackelberg follower for ceasing production completely. Then both of them could be receiving higher profits than they would at the Stackelberg equilibrium.

There are in fact practical constraints (such as government competition legislation) on the possibilities for cooperation and collusion among oligopolists. But there are also structural features of oligopolistic competition which make it difficult for cooperation to occur. One of the principal tools economists have developed for understanding these features is the theory of games, which traces its origins to the pioneering work of John von Neumann and Oskar Morgenstern[8] in the 1940s and which has since become a growth industry within economics. Game theorists have produced a wide range of models of interactive strategic behaviour, and applied them to an even wider range of economic decision situations. The four elements that characterize all of the games with which we shall be concerned, however, are (1) the players, (2) the list of possible strategies for each player, (3) the payoffs that correspond to each combination of strategies, and (4) the decision-rule for each player in choosing among alternate strategies.

---

[8]See John von Neumann and Oskar Morgenstern, *Theory of Games and Economic Behavior,* 3d ed., Princeton, NJ: Princeton University Press, 1953.

Although they have these four basic elements in common, game-theoretical models come in many forms. Games can be modelled as *cooperative* or *noncooperative*. They can be *two-person* or many-player (*N-person*) games. The payoff function or matrix can be *zero-sum* (so that one person's gain is another's loss) or *non-zero-sum*. The players can all have *perfect information*, or there can be *asymmetric information* (information known to some players but not to all). Games can be played *one time only*, or *repeated* a definite finite number of times, or an indefinite finite number of times, or (what is sometimes almost equivalent) an infinite number of times. The players can make their moves *simultaneously* or by turns (*sequentially*). Games can also differ in the *extent of communication* permitted among the players, the *costs of communication*, the possibility of *side payments* ("bribes") from one player to another, and hence the ease or difficulty of *coalition formation*.

With all the permutations of these categories, game theory provides us with a rich inventory of ways to understand strategic interaction among firms and individuals. We have in fact already used a number of elements of game theory in several other chapters. In Chapters 5 and 7, we used the prisoner's dilemma, one of the simplest, deepest, and most fruitful classic games, to illuminate both the paradoxes of positional goods and the role of "commitment devices" in escaping prisoner's dilemma situations. In Chapter 7, we also explored the ultimatum bargaining game, to show how a reputation for being *non*rational (being willing to sacrifice one's own self-interest out of a concern for fairness or justice, or for that matter simply for revenge) can actually increase a player's bargaining power. In Chapter 6, we showed how one of the fundamental problems of the economics of information in a *strategic* setting is establishing credibility and trust among potential rivals, and demonstrated the importance of the "costly to fake" and "full disclosure" principles in establishing credibility. Again in Chapter 7, we utilized payoff matrixes in a *non*-strategic way to illustrate the evolution over time of populations of hawks and doves, cooperators and defectors. You are therefore already familiar with elements of the game-theoretic approach to economic behaviour that we will be exploring further here.

The term "game" is sometimes extended to include situations of individual decision making under uncertainty. Suppose you are deciding whether or not to take an umbrella with you when you leave your home in the morning. You assess the probability of rain, weigh the inconvenience of toting the umbrella around all day against the inconvenience of being caught umbrellaless in the rain, and make your decision. Such decisions, along with bets you make on the outcome of games of chance, are sometimes referred to as "games against nature." Such "games" are important, especially in the economics of information and uncertainty. They lack one element that characterizes the games with which economic game theorists are most concerned: that of strategic interaction. It may seem, especially to believers in Murphy's Law, that leaving your umbrella at home practically guarantees a downpour. Yet the meteorological consensus is that your umbrella decision has no effect on the likelihood of rain. In contrast, the decision by a Bertrand duopolist to lower its price will almost certainly produce a strategic response from its rival, as we have already seen and will explore further below.

Game Theory Decision Rules

In the above context, what constraints do we place on the structure of our game-theoretical models? We typically require the players in a game to be "rational." If we don't assume that all of the players are rational, then the standard results of game theory do not hold. Rationality is normally taken as equivalent to what we described in Chapters 1 and 7 as "self-interest rationality." We assume that all players know what is in their own best interests. They know the outcome or payoff to all players resulting from all possible strategy combinations.They are also assumed to be capable of determining the strategy that will result in the best outcome for themselves, given the strategies that will be followed by the other self-interested players faced by the same payoff combinations. They do not allow the payoffs to others to influence their own choices. They can, however, use the knowledge of those payoffs and of the fact that the other players are also rational to deduce the courses of action the others are likely to take.

These assumptions are strong ones, which are rarely satisfied in reality. For one reason, as the number of players and the number of strategies per player increase, the information-processing demands on each player increase exponentially. In the simple two-player matrices with two strategies per player we shall be using, there are only four cells and eight individual payoffs to keep track of. In a game with 10 players, each of whom has 10 possible strategies, the payoff matrix will have 10^{10}, or 10 billion cells, and 100 billion individual payoffs! In practice, a player may find it quite costly and difficult to determine the precise payoffs to all other players resulting from all possible sets of strategies. This difficulty is accentuated when—as is often the case—players have an incentive to conceal their true preferences.

The assumption that the monetary payoffs to other players have no influence on a player's strategic choices can pose an additional difficulty. A player may in fact be indifferent to all payoffs except his own. As we saw in Chapter 7, however, an Altruist, if his own income level is given, will attain a *higher* level of satisfaction if the incomes of others increase. We have also seen in Chapter 5 that relative as well as absolute income levels can matter, as in the case of *positional goods*. In this case, a person (let us call him a Misanthropist) at a given level of income will attain a higher level of satisfaction if the incomes of others *decrease*. If a player's utility is dependent not only on his own monetary payoff but also on the payoffs to others, then the decision-making process becomes significantly more complicated.

Now comes the crucial question. What decision criterion should a rational player use in choosing among his or her strategies? In order to answer that question, you will need to play some games. Table 13-2 contains the payoff matrices for four simple games. Each game has two players, Ron (who plays one of his two *row* strategies, r_1 or r_2) and Colleen (who plays one of her *column* strategies, c_1 or c_2). Each pair of strategies results in a payoff to each player: $\prod_R$ is Ron's payoff, and $\prod_C$ is Colleen's. Both payoffs are measured in dollars. If the payoff is negative, money is taken away from the player. The rules are the same for each of the four games. Both players are compelled to play the game. The game is played only once. There is no communication among the players, and neither has any specific knowledge about the other. No side payments are permitted, from Ron to Colleen or *vice versa*. Your task is to play each game, first as Ron and then as Colleen, and determine the optimal strategy for each. Payoff matrix (a) provides Ron with a clear choice: regardless of which strategy Colleen adopts, he receives $2 more by choosing r_1 than if he chooses r_2. He should therefore choose r_1. We call r_1 his **dominant strategy**. Colleen also has a dominant strategy. Regardless of which strategy Ron adopts, she gains $1 more by choosing c_2 than if she chooses c_1. Her dominant strategy is therefore c_2, and when the game is played the pair of strategies selected will be (r_1, c_2). The northeast cell of the payoff matrix corresponding to this pair of strategies gives Ron $3 and Colleen $5.

In matrices (b), (c) and (d), Ron's payoffs are all $1, no matter which strategy he selects *or* Colleen selects. He has no obvious dominant strategy in any of the three games. His strategy choices, however, do affect the payoffs to Colleen. Playing as Ron, what

Dominant strategy A strategy in a game that (if it exists) produces the best outcome for a player regardless of the strategy chosen by the other player.

TABLE 13-2

Why Minimax?
In game (a), each player has a dominant strategy: the equilibrium is in the northeast cell of the matrix. In games (b), (c), and (d), Ron has no dominant strategy. In game (b), Colleen's dominant strategy (c_1) minimizes her losses regardless of Ron's strategy. In games (c) and (d), Colleen has no dominant strategy, but her "minimax" strategy (c_1) minimizes the maximum loss she could sustain.

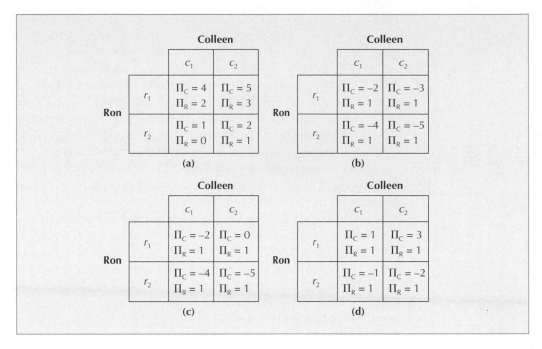

would you do? On consulting the three matrices, you notice that if you choose r_1, in every case Colleen's payoff can be higher than if you choose r_2. You could therefore decide to act as an Altruistic Egoist: as long as you do no worse by choosing r_1 than by choosing r_2, while Colleen does better, you will choose r_1. A second possibility, however, is that you could decide to act as a Misanthropic Egoist, and choose r_2: after all, what has Colleen ever done for you? A third possibility would be to opt for r_1 with matrices (b) and (c), where Colleen can be made better off than otherwise (but will not gain as much as you), but to choose r_2 in game (d), where she could gain more than you. In this case, you would be acting as a Semi-Altruistic Egoist. A final possibility is that you could act as an Indifferent Egoist, and simply flip a coin (heads r_1, tails r_2) to determine your strategy.

Could all of Ron's possible decision rules qualify as "rational"? At a practical level, the answer is "yes." What we have called Altruistic Egoism could be a (costless) means of creating goodwill, as part of a coalition-building exercise or to generate indebtedness chips that could be cashed in future. Similarly, so-called Misanthropic Egoism can simply be a means of increasing your own relative economic power by (costlessly) weakening a competitor. Semi-Altruistic Egoism combines elements of both of the preceding strategies. And if there are in fact costs of decision making but *some* decision must be made, then flipping a coin economizes on decision-making costs.

But now put yourself in Colleen's place. Ron has no dominant strategy, and as we have seen, in all three games he could play either r_1 or r_2. In game (b), Colleen does have a dominant strategy. Regardless of whether Ron plays r_1 or r_2, her best strategy is c_1, since in either case her losses are lower with c_1 than with c_2. In games (c) and (d), however, she has no dominant strategy, and she cannot be certain how Ron (playing rationally) will play.

Let's focus on matrix (d). If Colleen were certain that Ron would play as an Altruistic Egoist and choose r_1, she would choose c_2, ending up with the payoff of \$3 in the northeast cell. If she were certain that Ron was either a Misanthropic Egoist or a Semi-Altruistic Egoist and would therefore choose r_2, she would pick c_1. She would then end up in the southwest cell, losing \$1 (which is better than losing \$2 in the southeast cell).

Finally, if she knew he was an Indifferent Egoist, she would also know that when he flipped the coin there would be a 50 percent chance of his choosing r_1 and a 50 percent chance of his choosing r_2. In this case, if she chose c_1, her expected payoff would be $.5(1) + .5(-1) = 0$. If she chose c_2, her expected payoff would be $.5(3) + .5(-2) = \$.50$. Hence if she wanted to maximize her expected payoff, she would choose c_2. If instead she wanted to minimize her maximum possible loss, she would choose c_1, where the most she could lose would be \$1 (if the coin came up tails, or r_2). In short, in this case she could *rationally* choose *either* c_2 or c_1, depending on which decision rule she used ("maximize expected payoff" *vs.* "minimize maximum loss").

You have examined the possibilities. In Colleen's place, which decision rule would you follow, and which strategy would you adopt, c_1 or c_2? You may be relieved at this point to know that there is in fact no absolutely right answer. Colleen does not know precisely which type of rational Egoist Ron is. If she knew that, she could simply apply her decision criterion *knowing what he would do in matrix (d)*. This information would thus have value for her. The ancient Chinese general Sun Tzu is reputed to have said, "If you know the enemy and know yourself, you need not fear the result of a hundred battles." The fact that such knowledge has value helps to explain why (as in the Megapop and Gigafizz example with which we began the chapter) an oligopolistic firm may invest resources in industrial espionage to discover its rivals' plans. It also explains why the rivals might engage in *counter*-espionage, spending resources on security systems or deliberately leaking *mis*information to that firm in a "sting" operation to mislead it about their intentions.

In the situation we are analyzing, however, Colleen has no way of acquiring this information. Suppose, though, that she did in fact have the additional outside information that Ron had played r_1 in earlier games with others, featuring matrix (c). Would this information help her? Unfortunately not, because it would not tell her whether Ron was acting as an Altruistic Egoist or a Semi-Altruistic Egoist, both of whom would definitely play r_1 given payoff matrix (c). It is also possible that in the earlier games Ron was acting as an Indifferent Egoist who just happened to flip a sequence of heads (and therefore chose r_1) in those games. Colleen could not even completely rule out the possibility that Ron was acting in those games as a higher-order Misanthropic Egoist, attempting to set up a sting. We saw in Chapter 1 that a rational egoist might invest resources in acts of generosity to create a reputation for benevolence or trustworthiness, if the expected discounted future benefits of such a strategy outweighed the present costs. In Chapter 7, we saw how such "mimicry" could have survival value. The same possibility exists here. In short, even if Colleen has the additional information that Ron has played a sequence of r_1 moves in earlier games with matrix (c), this does not give her any certain information about what strategy he will adopt in the game *she* is playing with him, using payoff matrix (d).

Note by way of contrast that if Colleen knew that Ron had earlier played r_2 in a sequence of games with matrix (c), she could say with certainty that he was neither an Altruistic Egoist nor a Semi-Altruistic Egoist. But she would still not have sufficient information to determine whether he was a Misanthropic Egoist or an Indifferent Egoist who just happened to flip a string of tails (and therefore chose r_2). There is no avoiding the fact that even with information on Ron's past pattern of play, Colleen cannot definitely determine what type of player he is, nor which strategy he will adopt in the game with her.

If Colleen could estimate the probability that Ron would play r_1 (call it p_1), she could determine which strategy (c_1 or c_2) would maximize her expected payoff. Her expected payoff from playing c_1 is $E(\Pi_1) = p_1(1) + (1 - p_1)(-1) = 2p_1 - 1$. Her expected payoff from playing c_2 is $E(\Pi_2) = p_1(3) + (1 - p_1)(-2) = 5\,p_1 - 2$. Solving for p_1, we find that if $p_1 > 1/3$, she should play c_2; if $p_1 < 1/3$, she should play c_1; and if $p_1 = 1/3$, she should be indifferent between the two strategies. But the fact of the matter is that she has no rational basis for determining p_1.

Why Minimax?

Minimax strategy
Choosing the option that minimizes the maximum loss (maximizes the minimum gain) one receives.

It is this fact that provides the rationale for using the ***"minimax" (or "maximin") criterion*** as a decision rule. "Minimax" is shorthand for "minimize the maximum loss"; "maximin" means "maximize the minimum gain." Since a loss is a negative gain, for our purposes we can treat the two terms as equivalent. The minimax criterion works very simply. If Colleen knows which strategy Ron will pick (because Ron has a dominant strategy), she should select her strategy so that she maximizes her payoff (or minimizes her loss), *given Ron's strategy*. If she doesn't know for certain which strategy Ron will select, as is the case with matrix (d), then she should pick the strategy that will minimize her maximum possible loss, *regardless of which strategy Ron picks*. Faced by matrix (d), as a minimax decision maker she will pick strategy c_1, because the worst she will do with c_1 is lose \$1 (if Ron picks r_2), whereas she could have lost \$2 had she picked strategy c_2 and Ron picked r_2.

Note that in a very real sense the minimax criterion is a conservative, "prepare for the worst case" decision rule. To see how conservative, replace the 3 in the northeast corner of matrix (d) by 300, and recalculate the value of p_1 for which choosing c_2 would maximize Colleen's expected payoff. If there is even one chance in 300 that Ron will pick r_1, Colleen maximizes her expected payoff by choosing c_2. The minimax criterion still says, "Pick c_1, because no matter what Ron does, you can't lose more than \$1." The minimax criterion thus performs well against Misanthropic Egoists, but considerably less well in situations where cooperation (collaboration, coalition, and collusion) could mutually benefit *both* players.

We have devoted considerable attention to the question of decision rules, because in a very real way they are at the heart of formal game theory. The decision rule that rational players adopt is important in itself. But knowledge of the rule being followed also enables players to deduce how *other* rational players will behave when faced by a particular payoff matrix, even when no communication is permitted between players or when players have an incentive to try to mislead other players about their intentions. Such deductions are valid only if there is a common understanding among players of what constitutes a "rational" decision rule.

In the rest of the section, we shall be applying a number of simple game-theoretical models to some basic issues in the economics of oligopoly, and showing how the principles they illustrate can also be applied to a wider range of social phenomena. In order to illustrate the basic principles of game theory in their clearest form, we have adopted the strong assumptions outlined above. Yet it is important to note that attempts to apply *overly* simple game-theoretical models directly to practical strategic situations can come to grief. In such cases, the problem is not with the models themselves. Rather, it stems from a failure to take into account the consequences for strategic behaviour when the assumptions of the models do not hold.

We shall first see that the situation facing Bertrand duopolists can be modelled as a prisoner's dilemma, and that this perspective clarifies the incentive for each duopolist to defect. We analyze the circumstances in which a firm's decision as to whether to advertise or not can also become a prisoner's dilemma. We use the example of advertising

TABLE 13-3

The Prisoner's Dilemma
Each player believes he
will always get a shorter
sentence by confessing,
no matter what the other
player does. And if each
player confesses, each
gets five years. Yet if both
players had remained
silent, each would have
gotten only one year in
jail. Here, the individual
pursuit of self-interest
produces a worse out-
come for each player.

		Prisoner Y	
		Confess	Remain silent
Prisoner X	Confess	5 years for each	0 years for X 20 years for Y
	Remain silent	20 years for X 0 years for Y	1 year for each

to explore the concept of a "Nash equilibrium," one of the pivotal notions in game theory. We then examine *repeated* games, and in particular the remarkably simple and simply remarkable "tit-for-tat" strategy for playing repeated prisoner's dilemmas. We develop a *sequential* game model to analyze the strategic options open to an incumbent firm that wishes to deter outside firms from entering an industry, and show its relation to the theory of contestable markets. We conclude with some observations on the scope and limits of the game-theoretic approach in understanding contemporary oligopolistic behaviour.

13.6 THE "DUOPOLIST'S DILEMMA"

Our exploration begins with a look at two Bertrand duopolists who have decided to collude, charge the monopoly price, and divide the market equally between themselves. As attractive as the collusive outcome is from the perspective of the firms involved, it turns out to be surprisingly difficult to sustain. Indeed, a recurring theme in the economics of oligopoly is that what it pays each firm to do individually often turns out to be very harmful to the interests of firms taken as a whole, although it can be in the interests of consumers.

The basic problem confronting colluding oligopolists often has the same structure as the prisoner's dilemma game we saw in Chapter 7. Recall that in the original story used to illustrate the prisoner's dilemma, two prisoners are held in separate cells for a serious crime that they did in fact commit. The prosecutor, however, has only enough hard evidence to convict them of a minor offence, for which the penalty is, say, a year in jail. Each prisoner is told that if one confesses while the other remains silent, the confessor will go scot-free while the other spends 20 years in prison. If both confess, they will get an intermediate sentence, say, 5 years. The two prisoners are not allowed to communicate with one another. In Table 13-3, the two players in the game are prisoner X and prisoner Y. Each player has two strategies: confess and remain silent. The payoffs to each combination of strategies are the sentences they receive, which are summarized in the *payoff matrix* shown in Table 13-3.

The prisoner's dilemma does have a *dominant strategy*, a strategy that produces better results no matter what strategy the opposing player follows. The dominant strategy in the prisoner's dilemma is to confess. No matter what Y does, X gets a lighter sentence by speaking out: if Y too confesses, X gets 5 years instead of 20; and if Y remains silent, X goes free instead of spending a year in jail. The payoffs are perfectly symmetric, so Y also does better to confess, no matter what X does. The difficulty is that when each behaves in a self-interested way, both do worse than if each had shown restraint. Thus, when both confess, they get five years, instead of the one year they could have gotten by remaining silent.

To illustrate the relationship between the prisoner's dilemma and the problem confronting the two duopolists who are trying to collude, we will use the same demand

TABLE 13-4

Profits to Cooperation and Defection

The dominant strategy is for each firm to defect, for by so doing it earns higher profit no matter which option its rival chooses. Yet when both defect, each earns less than when each cooperates.

		Firm 1	
		Cooperate (P = 10)	Defect (P = 9)
Firm 2	**Cooperate** (P = 10)	$\Pi_1 = 50$ $\Pi_2 = 50$	$\Pi_1 = 99$ $\Pi_2 = 0$
	Defect (P = 9)	$\Pi_1 = 0$ $\Pi_2 = 99$	$\Pi_1 = 49.50$ $\Pi_2 = 49.50$

and cost conditions as in the mineral spring example. For the sake of concreteness, suppose that the market demand curve takes the specific form $P = 20 - Q$. The two firms have the possibility of a collusive agreement under which each produces half the monopoly output and offers it for sale at the monopoly price. For the specific demand curve assumed, the monopoly price is $10/unit, and the monopoly quantity is 10 units. If the firms enter into, and abide by, this agreement, each will sell 5 units at a price of $10/unit, thus making an economic profit of $50. On a strict profit criterion, there is no possibility for both firms to do better than that.

Yet this does not assure that each firm will abide by the agreement. Note that the payoffs to each firm depend on the combination of behaviours they choose. Each firm has two options—namely, to abide by the agreement or to defect. Again for the sake of concreteness, suppose that to defect means to cut price by $1/unit, from $10 to $9/unit. If one firm abides by the agreement while the other defects, what will happen? Since the two firms are selling identical products, the defecting firm will capture the entire market because of its lower price. Selling 11 units at a price of $9/unit, it will earn a profit of $99; the trusting cooperator sells no output and thus earns zero profit.

If both firms defect, they will end up splitting the 11 units of output sold at a price of $9/unit, and each will make an economic profit of $49.50. Since each firm has two options—(1) cooperate, or abide by the agreement to charge $10; and (2) defect, or charge $9—there are four possible combinations of behaviour. These combinations, and the profits that result from each, are summarized in Table 13-4.

Note in the table that it is a dominant strategy for each firm to defect. That is, each firm gets a higher payoff by defecting, no matter which option the other firm chooses. To illustrate, consider the choice facing firm 2. It says to itself, "Suppose firm 1 cooperates; which choice is best for me?" By cooperating when firm 1 cooperates, the firms end up in the upper left cell of the profit matrix in Table 13-4, which means each earns $50. But if firm 2 defects, the result will be the lower left cell, where it would end up earning $99. Now firm 2 says, "Suppose firm 1 defects. Which choice is best for me this time?" If firm 2 cooperates, we get the upper right cell of the profit matrix, where it earns 0. But if firm 2 defects, it earns $49.50. Thus, no matter which choice firm 1 makes, firm 2 earns higher profit by defecting.

By exactly parallel reasoning, defection is also a dominant strategy for firm 1. Note, however, that when each firm defects, each does worse than if each had cooperated. In this situation, behaviour that is in the interest of each individual firm adds up to a result that is not in the interest of firms generally.

As this example is set up, the firms don't do much worse when each defects than when each cooperates. But firms that find it in their interest to defect once are likely to find it in their interest to do so again. If one now charges $8/unit while the other remains at $9/unit, for example, the former will earn a profit of $96, while the latter earns 0. A firm need not feel a compelling desire to outdo its rival in order for defection to be an attractive option. On the contrary, its motive may be purely self-protective, the very rational fear that its rival will defect. As we saw in the Bertrand model, the resulting process of competitive price cutting will terminate only when price has plummeted all the way down to marginal cost. At that point, recall, neither firm earns any profit at all. So the cost of failing to abide by a cooperative agreement can be very high indeed.

Oligopolists compete not only along the price dimension, but through the use of advertising as well. Here too we see that what is in the interests of an individual firm is often not in the interests of firms taken as a whole, as the following Economic Naturalist indicates.

Economic Naturalist 13-1

WHY COULD A BAN ON ADVERTISING INCREASE TOBACCO COMPANY PROFITS?

When a firm in any given industry advertises its product, its demand increases for two reasons. First, people who never used that type of product before learn about it, and some will buy it. Second, other people who already consume a different brand of the same product may switch brands because of advertising. The first effect boosts sales for the industry as a whole. The second merely redistributes existing sales within the industry.

The cigarette industry is an example of one in which the most important effect of advertising is believed to be brand switching. In such industries, the decision of whether to advertise often confronts individual firms with a prisoner's dilemma. Table 13-5 shows the profits to a hypothetical pair of cigarette producers under the four possible combinations of their advertise/don't advertise decisions. If both firms advertise (lower right cell), each earns a profit of only 250, as compared with a profit of 500 each if neither advertises (upper left cell). So it is clearly better for neither firm to advertise than for both to advertise.

Yet note the incentives confronting the individual firm. Firm 1 sees that if firm 2 doesn't advertise, firm 1 can earn higher profits by advertising (750) than by not advertising (500). Firm 1 also sees that if firm 2 does advertise, firm 1 will again earn more by advertising (250) than by not advertising (0). It is thus a dominant strategy for firm 1 to advertise. And because the payoffs are symmetric, it is also a dominant strategy for firm 2 to advertise. So here too when each firm does what is rational from its own point of view, firms as a group do worse than if they had acted in concert.

The cigarette industry in North America has been increasingly under siege since scientific evidence on the health hazards of smoking began to accumulate in the early 1960s. The industry has had to respond to declining numbers of smokers, restrictions on smoking in public places, restrictions on advertising, mandatory health warnings on cigarette packages, and (most recently) a host of multi–billion dollar lawsuits and settlements, including suits by provincial governments to recover the health care costs attributable to smoking-related illnesses. Under the 1997 Tobacco Act (Bill C-71), cigarette advertising (including event sponsorship) was severely curtailed, although extensions were granted for certain forms of advertising. Ironically, if cigarette advertising is relatively ineffective in increasing demand and thus involves a prisoner's dilemma, one effect of restrictions on cigarette advertising may have been to increase profitability for the tobacco manufacturers, relative to a situation with no restrictions.

TABLE 13-5

The Advertising Decision as a Prisoner's Dilemma
In many industries the primary effect of advertising is to cause consumers to switch brands. In such industries, the dominant strategy is to advertise heavily (lower right cell), even though firms taken as a whole would do better by not advertising (upper left cell).

		Firm 1	
		Don't advertise	Advertise
Firm 2	**Don't advertise**	$\Pi_1 = 500$ $\Pi_2 = 500$	$\Pi_1 = 750$ $\Pi_2 = 0$
	Advertise	$\Pi_1 = 0$ $\Pi_2 = 750$	$\Pi_1 = 250$ $\Pi_2 = 250$

13.7 THE NASH EQUILIBRIUM CONCEPT

When, as in the prisoner's dilemma, both parties have a dominant strategy in a game, the equilibrium for the game occurs when each plays the dominant strategy. But there are many games in which not every player has a dominant strategy. Consider, for example, the variation on the advertising game shown in Table 13-6. No matter what firm 2 does, firm 1 does better to advertise; so advertise is the dominant strategy for firm 1. But now the same cannot be said of firm 2. If firm 1 advertises, firm 2 does best also to advertise. But if firm 1 does not advertise, firm 2 does best not to advertise. In contrast to the prisoner's dilemma, here the best strategy for firm 2 depends on the particular strategy chosen by firm 1.

Even though firm 2 does not have a dominant strategy in this game, we can say something about what is likely to happen. In particular, firm 2 is able to predict that firm 1 will advertise because that is a dominant strategy for firm 1. And since firm 2 knows this, it knows that its own best strategy is also to advertise. In this game, the lower right cell is called a **_Nash equilibrium_**,[9] which is defined as a combination of strategies such that each player's strategy is the best he can choose given the strategy chosen by the other player. Thus, at a Nash equilibrium, neither player has any incentive to deviate from its current strategy. Note that when each player follows his dominant strategy in a prisoner's dilemma, the result is a Nash equilibrium. But as we have seen, a Nash equilibrium does not require both players to have a dominant strategy.

Nash equilibrium
The combination of strategies in a game such that no player has an incentive to change strategies, given the strategy adopted by each of his opponents.

TABLE 13-6

A Game in Which Firm 2 Has No Dominant Strategy
Firm 1 earns higher profits by advertising, no matter what firm 2 does. Its dominant strategy is to advertise. But firm 2 has no dominant strategy. If firm 1 advertises, firm 2 does best also to advertise, but if firm 1 does not advertise, firm 2 does best not to advertise.

		Firm 1	
		Don't advertise	Advertise
Firm 2	**Don't advertise**	$\Pi_1 = 500$ $\Pi_2 = 400$	$\Pi_1 = 750$ $\Pi_2 = 0$
	Advertise	$\Pi_1 = 0$ $\Pi_2 = 300$	$\Pi_1 = 300$ $\Pi_2 = 200$

---

[9]After John F. Nash, the Nobel Prize–winning mathematician who introduced the concept in 1951.

Does either firm have a dominant strategy in the game below? Does the game have a Nash equilibrium?

		Firm 1	
		High research budget	**Low research budget**
	High research budget	$\Pi_1 = 200$ $\Pi_2 = 40$	$\Pi_1 = 60$ $\Pi_2 = 100$
Firm 2	**Low research budget**	$\Pi_1 = \varnothing$ $\Pi_2 = 30$	$\Pi_1 = 40$ $\Pi_2 = 80$

13.8 REPEATED GAMES AND THE TIT-FOR-TAT STRATEGY

To say that the costs of failing to cooperate are high is simply another way of saying that there are powerful financial incentives to find some way to hold collusive agreements together. What the potential participants to a collusive agreement need is some way to penalize those who defect, thereby making it in their material interests not to do so. When a prisoner's dilemma confronts parties who will interact only once, this turns out to be very difficult to achieve. But when the participants expect to interact repeatedly in the future, new possibilities emerge.

Experimental research in the 1960s identified a very simple strategy that proves remarkably effective at keeping potential defectors in check.[10] The strategy is called *tit-for-tat*, and it works as follows: The first time you interact with someone, you cooperate. In each subsequent interaction you simply do what that person did in the previous interaction. Thus, if your partner defected on your first interaction, you would then defect on your next interaction with her. If she then cooperates, your move next time will be to cooperate as well.

Tit-for-tat is described as a "nice" strategy because of the propensity of players to cooperate on the first interaction. If two tit-for-tat players interact together over a long period of time, the result will be cooperation in each and every interaction. Tit-for-tat is also a "tough" strategy, however, because those who follow it always stand ready to punish defectors in the next interaction. Finally, it is a "forgiving" strategy, in the sense that a player is willing to cooperate with a former defector once she shows evidence of willingness to cooperate.

Robert Axelrod conducted an extensive analysis of how well the tit-for-tat strategy performs against other strategies for playing the repeated prisoner's dilemma game.[11] In an early round of Axelrod's computer simulations, tit-for-tat was the most successful strategy, in the sense that people who followed it earned more, on average, than those using any of the other strategies tested. Axelrod then published this finding and invited experts from all over the world to try to design a better strategy. His challenge produced a host of ingenious counterstrategies. Axelrod found, however, that even these strategies, many of which had been put together for the specific purpose of defeating tit-for-tat, did not survive against it.

---

[10]See Anatol Rapoport and A. Chammah, *Prisoner's Dilemma*, Ann Arbor: University of Michigan Press, 1965.

[11]Robert Axelrod, *The Evolution of Cooperation*, New York: Basic Books, 1984.

The success of tit-for-tat requires a reasonably stable set of players, each of whom can remember what other players have done in previous interactions. It also requires that players have a significant stake in what happens in the future, for it is only the fear of retaliation that keeps people from defecting. When these conditions are met, cooperators can identify one another and discriminate against defectors.

The conditions called for by the tit-for-tat strategy are often met in human populations. Many people do interact repeatedly, and most keep track of how others treat them. Axelrod has assembled persuasive evidence that these forces help explain how people actually behave. Perhaps the most impressive of all this evidence comes from accounts of the "live-and-let-live" system that developed in the trench warfare in Europe during World War I. In many areas of the war, the same enemy units lay encamped opposite one another in the trenches over a period of several years. Units were often closely matched, with the result that neither side had much hope of quickly defeating the other. Their choices were to fight intensively, with both sides sustaining heavy casualties, or to exercise restraint.

The conditions of interaction described by historian Tony Ashworth in his account of the trench fighting closely resemble those required for the success of tit-for-tat.[12] The identities of the players were more or less stable. Interactions between them were repeated, often several times daily, for extended periods. Each side could easily tell when the other side defected from the strategy. And each side had a clear stake in keeping its future losses to a minimum.

There is little doubt that tit-for-tat often did emerge as the strategy of choice for both Allied and German fighting units in World War I. Although strongly discouraged as a matter of official policy, restraint was sometimes conspicuously apparent. Referring to night patrol squads operating out of the trenches, Ashworth writes:

> … both British and Germans on quiet sectors assumed that should a chance face-to-face encounter occur, neither patrol would initiate aggression, but each would move to avoid the other. Each patrol gave peace to the other where aggression was not only possible, but prescribed, provided, of course, the gesture was reciprocated, for if one patrol fired so would the other.[13]

In the words of one of the participants in the conflict:

> We suddenly confronted, round some mound or excavation, a German patrol. … We were perhaps twenty yards from one another, fully visible. I waved a weary hand, as if to say, what is the use of killing each other? The German officer seemed to understand, and both parties turned and made their way back to their own trenches.[14]

Often, bombardments would occur only at specified times of day and would be directed away from the most vulnerable positions. Mealtimes and hospital tents, for example, were usually tacitly off limits.

The conditions discussed by Axelrod help to explain not only when people will cooperate, but also when they are most likely to *refrain* from cooperation. For example, he notes that mutual restraint in trench warfare began to break down once the end of the war was clearly in sight.

As in warfare, so, too, in the world of business. Companies pay their bills on time, Axelrod suggests, not because it is the right thing to do but because they require future

---

[12]Tony Ashworth, *Trench Warfare: The Live and Let Live System*, New York: Holmes and Meier, 1980.

[13]Ibid., p. 103.

[14]Herbert Read, quoted in ibid., p. 104.

shipments from the same suppliers. When future interactions appear unlikely, this tendency to cooperate often breaks down:

> [An] example is the case where a business is on the edge of bankruptcy and sells its accounts receivable to an outsider called a 'factor.' This sale is made at a very substantial discount because once a manufacturer begins to go under, even his best customers begin refusing payment for merchandise, claiming defects in quality, failure to meet specifications, tardy delivery, or what-have-you. The great enforcer of morality in commerce is the continuing relationship, the belief that one will have to do business again with this customer, or this supplier, and when a failing company loses this automatic enforcer, not even a strong-arm factor is likely to find a substitute.[15]

One additional requirement for the success of tit-for-tat is that there not be a known, fixed number of future interactions. Indeed, if players know exactly how many times they will interact, then mutual cooperation on every move cannot be a Nash equilibrium. To see why, suppose each firm knew it was going to interact with its rival for, say, exactly 1000 more times. Each would then know that the other would defect on the last interaction, because there would be no possibility of being punished for doing so. But since each firm realizes that, it will also have no reason not to defect on the 999th interaction. After all, a defection will occur on the 1000th interaction no matter what it does on the round before. The same argument can be applied step-by-step back to the first interaction, with the result that the tit-for-tat strategy completely unravels.

The unravelling problem does not arise if there is not a known, fixed number of interactions.[16] If we suppose, for example, that there is always some positive probability that a further interaction will ensue, then no interaction can ever be identified as being the last one, which means the threat of future punishment will always have at least some force. In the situations in which most firms find themselves (an exception being the bankruptcy case cited earlier), it seems plausible to assume that there will always be some probability of interaction in the future.

Is it inevitable, then, that the tit-for-tat strategy will produce widespread collusion among firms? By no means. One difficulty is that tit-for-tat's effectiveness depends on there being only two players in the game. In competitive and monopolistically competitive industries there are generally many firms, and even in oligopolies there are often several. When there are more than two firms, and one defects this period, how do the cooperators selectively punish the defector next period? By cutting price? That will penalize everyone, not just the defector. Even if there are only two firms in an industry, the problem remains that some other firm may enter the industry. So the would-be cooperators have to worry not only about each other, but also about the entire list of firms that might decide to compete with them. Each firm may see this as a hopeless task and decide to defect now, hoping to reap at least some extranormal profit in the short run.

We will consider the threat of potential entry in greater detail in the sections to follow. For the moment, we may note that, as a purely empirical matter, cartel agreements and other forms of collusion have occurred frequently in the past but have tended to be highly unstable. Apparently the practical problems involved in implementing tit-for-tat in the environments confronting firms make it very difficult to hold collusive agreements together for long.

---

[15]Mayer, quoted in Axelrod, op. cit., pp. 59, 60.

[16]Another way the unravelling problem is avoided is if there is some positive probability that others will follow the tit-for-tat strategy even though, strictly speaking, it is not rational for them to do so. See David Kreps, Paul Milgrom, John Roberts, and Robert Wilson, "Rational Cooperation in Finitely Repeated Prisoner's Dilemmas," *Journal of Economic Theory*, 27, 1982: 245–252.

One situation in which tit-for-tat can be effective occurs when there is a dominant producer in the industry, who can take a price-leadership or quantity-leadership role to discourage cheaters or defectors. Some commentators have argued that the relatively high degree of success and longevity of OPEC compared to most modern cartels can be attributed to the fact that Saudi Arabia is in a position to play this "policeman" role within the OPEC cartel. By opening the valves, it can lower the price of oil sharply to punish OPEC members trying to evade their production quotas. Other OPEC members are also hurt by the price drop in the short run. To the extent that their anger is directed primarily at the defector rather than at Saudi Arabia, this is an additional source of internal discipline. The key is whether Saudi Arabia can provide a *credible* threat that it will act against its own *short-term* interests to enforce discipline. If enforcement can increase its *long-run* revenues, then the threat becomes more credible. If it has actually punished defectors in this way in the past, this fact adds to the credibility of the threat. The most effective threat is the one that does *not* have to be acted upon, because the other players believe that it would be, should the occasion arise.

We said earlier that tit-for-tat was a remarkable strategy. One of its most remarkable and powerful features is its simplicity, which gives it considerable communicative power. It can communicate a clear message, in very few moves, *even when no communication between players is permitted*. The message is simple: "If you defect, I will punish you by defecting. If you cooperate, I'll reward you by cooperating." The expected value for each player of an infinite sequence of paired cooperative moves exceeds that from sequences involving defection and retaliation. Hence the sooner the lesson is learned that cooperation pays and defection doesn't, the better for both parties. One of tit-for-tat's main advantages over other strategies is the speed with which it gets this message across.

If we compare tit-for-tat with an *ultimatum* strategy ("If you defect once, I will defect forever after that point"), we can see the benefit of what we have called tit-for-tat's "forgiving" character. The ultimatum strategy allows for no learning or repentance by a defecting player. Its initial threat potential is high, but if a player makes a single experiment in defection (or even a mistake), both players are thereafter locked into the inferior (defect, defect) sequence of payoffs. An ultimatum strategy thus lacks flexibility. Because the consequences for the ultimatum maker (of *permanently* abiding by the "defect" strategy after an opponent has defected only *once*) are so adverse, it may even lack credibility, as both players may discover at high cost. Note also that its informational requirements are greater than those of tit-for-tat: if others do not know from the outset that you are playing an ultimatum strategy, then by the time they find out, it will be too late.

Try another conceptual experiment with tit-for-tat. Suppose that two tit-for-tat players are playing each other. If all goes well, they both cooperate in the first game and hence in all subsequent games. But now suppose that there is (for one game only) a bit of "noise" in the system. Player 1 cooperates, but Player 2 believes that Player 1 has defected. Trace the moves of each in the next five games. Here is the question: do you think that one or both will realize (after some finite number of games) that they are both playing a tit-for-tat strategy, and that at some point in the past some glitch must have occurred? If so, can they escape the trap? Experiments suggest that the answer is a qualified "yes." But note that to escape the trap, one player (the one due to play "defect") must instead play "cooperate," and risk being defected on twice in a row. This decision is not a decision *within* the game, but rather a *meta*-decision that involves "breaking the rules" to get back on track. Here again, the *simplicity* of tit-for-tat increases the likelihood of being able to pinpoint the fact that some noise must have crept into the system. The message sent is, "Don't look at my last move. Look at the sequence of my moves, and correlate them with your own. This is the kind of player I am. Trust me." Making the above meta-decision requires a modicum of trust; tit-for-tat provides a basis for such trust, at least for *one* move, which is all it takes to get the game back on track.

13.9 SEQUENTIAL GAMES

The games we have considered so far have been ones in which both players must pick their strategies simultaneously. Each player had to choose his strategy knowing only the incentives facing his opponent, not the opponent's actual choice of strategy. But in many games, one player moves first, and the other is then able to choose his strategy with full knowledge of the first player's choice. It can be, but is not always, an advantage to move first. In warfare, with two armies readying themselves for battle, one side (even if it is not itself fully prepared) may launch a ***pre-emptive strike*** against the other. It hopes to catch the enemy by surprise and inflict serious damage on them before they can react. But it also hopes to pre-empt many of the basic *strategic* decisions about the battle: when it will begin, obviously, but also the terrain over which it will be fought, and which configuration of forces will define its course. A bridge player with a strong hand may make a high initial pre-emptive bid, in order to limit the length of the auction and thereby minimize the amount of information the opponents can share before the hand is played.

In more directly economic situations as well, there can be advantages to moving first. Consider two mutual funds, both holding large blocks of shares in a high-tech firm. Both are poised to buy or sell, depending on today's quarterly results. Omnifund's "reliable sources" get the information to it 15 minutes before the news hits Globalfund. The news is bad, and Omnifund has already unloaded its block, driving down the share price in the process, before Globalfund has had time to react. Omnifund does some healthy profit taking, while all Globalfund takes is a bath. In security markets, "being first" can often be measured in minutes. For a second instance, suppose that an Alberta town has room enough for only one large all-purpose store. Then the first firm into that market has effectively "captured" it. The firm becomes an incumbent monopoly; it can make positive profits indefinitely. Other firms know that by entering the market, they can cause the incumbent firm to lose money, but as long as it is there, they will sustain losses themselves. It is therefore not in their rational self-interest to enter the market.

In other situations, however, there can be advantages to being second. In the scramble to get competing new software systems out into the market first, it can happen that "haste makes waste." If a company rushes its software into the stores before all the bugs have been ironed out, a more patient and methodical competitor can learn from the mistakes of the first company. When its own product is finally released, it can dominate the market, simply because its software is better. Before the home videogame market became a multi-horse race (with the entry of Sony's Play Station 2 and Microsoft's X-Box into the market) and Sega decided to focus on game software, Sega often beat Nintendo into the market with its next-generation systems. Nintendo, taking a longer development time, was able to parlay consumer loyalty, a larger game inventory, and a few more bells and whistles into a dominant share of the market.

Being second can also be preferable in an industry characterized by price leadership, where the price leader sets the market price and adjusts its own output to maintain that price. The price follower determines its output level by equating its marginal cost to the set price, thereby maximizing its producer surplus. In response, the leader may have to cut back its own output in order to maintain the price it has set. The price follower can actually do better than the price leader. From a strategic standpoint, in short, sometimes "He who hesitates is lost," and sometimes it's better to "Look before you leap."

Pre-emptive action
An initial action, taken by one player in a sequential game, that restricts the strategic options available to other players.

Strategic Entry Deterrence and Costs of Entry

In *one* set of cases, where there is *already* an incumbent monopoly firm in a market, there is no question as to who is going to be first. The incumbent is. But the question arises as to why its economic profits don't attract new entrants to the market. In our Alberta example above, we basically assumed the problem of entry away by treating the town as a "natural monopoly" situation. This is not an unrealistic assumption in many smaller Canadian centres. At a more general level, however, the issue of barriers to entry and strategic behaviour by incumbent firms to discourage entry by new firms is not this simple. We shall therefore now explore some simple sequential-game models that cast some light on ways by which firms in concentrated industries can keep new entrants out, and on situations in which they can't.

Economic Naturalist 13-2

WHY MIGHT A COMPANY MAKE AN INVESTMENT IT KNOWS IT WILL NEVER USE?

The city of Melonville currently has one amusement park, Funland. The Joyworld Corporation is considering establishing a Joyworld theme park in the Greater Melonville Area, featuring the Stratocoaster ride, a major attraction. Both Funland and Joyworld realize that they are participants in a sequential game of the sort pictured in Figure 13-7. The game starts at point *A*, where Joyworld must decide whether to enter the Melonville market. If it does not, then Funland will receive a payoff of 100, Joyworld a payoff of 0. If Joyworld enters, however, the game moves to point *B*, where Funland must decide whether to counter by building the Devil Twist ride or to stand pat. Suppose that if Funland builds the Devil Twist, its payoff will be 30, while Joyworld will earn a payoff of –50; and that if Funland doesn't build, its payoff will be 40, while Joyworld will get a payoff of 60. Funland naturally wants Joyworld not to enter, and announces that if Joyworld is built, it will definitely proceed with building the Devil Twist. The problem is that its threat is not credible. The Joyworld executives know that if Joyworld enters Melonville, Funland's best option is to stand pat. The Nash equilibrium of this sequential game is point *E*, where Joyworld enters and Funland stands pat.

Now suppose that before Funland was originally built, it was possible to purchase and clear additional land and thus lower the construction cost of the Devil Twist. The land costs 10 units, but reduces the construction cost by 20 units. If Funland had bought the land, the sequential game between it and Joyworld would then be as portrayed by the game tree in Figure 13-8. Funland's payoff at point *D* is now 40 (it saves 20 on construction costs less the 10-unit cost of the land). Its payoffs at *C* and *E* are each 10 units less than in Figure 13-7 (reflecting the cost of the land). Despite the small magnitude of these changes in payoffs, the purchase of the land dramatically alters the outcome of the game. This time the Joyworld executives can predict that if they enter with the Stratocoaster, it will be in Funland's interest to counter with the Devil Twist, which means that Joyworld will receive a payoff of –50. As a result, Joyworld will not find it worthwhile to enter Melonville, and so the game will end at point *C*. The payoff to Funland at *C* is 90 (the original 100 minus the 10-unit cost of the land). Its 10-unit investment in the additional land thus increases its net payoff by 50 (the difference between the 90-unit payoff it receives with the land and the 40-unit payoff it would have received without it).

FIGURE 13-7

Theme Park Decision
If Joyworld enters, then
Funland must decide
whether to build the
Devil Twist. Since
Funland earns a higher
profit at *E* than at *D*, it
will not build the Devil
Twist. Hence Joyworld
will enter the market.

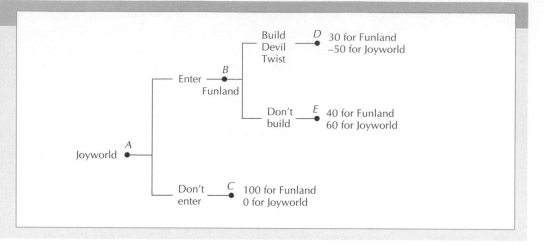

FIGURE 13-8

**Strategic Entry
Deterrence**
Had it originally pur-
chased the additional
land, Funland could
earn more profits by
building the Devil Twist
than by not building it,
if Joyworld entered.
Hence Joyworld
doesn't enter. The Nash
equilibrium of the altered
game is now at point *C*.

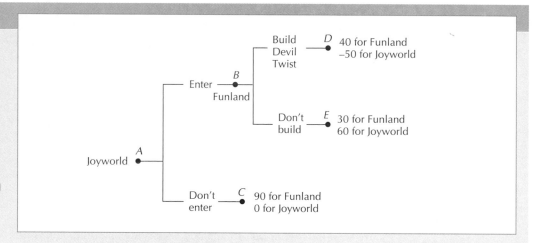

In this case, the strategic investment by Funland, by altering the payoff-structure of the decision-tree, provided an effective entry deterrent. In other situations, deterring entry may be more difficult. All of the factors we discussed in Chapter 12 that operate to sustain a monopoly can represent barriers to entry in an oligopolistic industry. Factors such as customer loyalty or brand familiarity (possibly enhanced by advertising or an established reputation for reliability and good service) can also constitute barriers to entry. If consumers incur either search costs or switching costs (say, penalties for prematurely terminating a service contract) in switching to a new firm, then they may prefer the *status quo*. This (rational) consumer preference constitutes an additional barrier to entry for potential entrants.

WHY WOULD A FIRM BUILD A FACTORY WITH MORE CAPACITY THAN IT WOULD EVER NEED?

Larger production facilities typically have higher fixed costs and lower marginal costs than smaller ones. So the question can be rephrased as follows: Why might it be in a firm's interest to have a factory with very low marginal cost, even if the result were to make its total cost higher than for a smaller facility?

A possible answer is that the larger factory constitutes another example of strategic entry deterrence. If potential entrants knew that an incumbent firm had extremely low marginal cost, they could predict that it would be in the incumbent's interest to remain in business even at a price level too low for entrants to earn a normal profit. In that case, it would not be rational for rivals to enter the market. And their absence, in turn, would enable the incumbent to charge a price sufficiently high to cover the costs of the larger facility.

Why might a firm build a bigger factory than it needed?

Entry with No Fixed Entry Costs

Let us now consider a market where there are *no* entry costs, there is one incumbent firm, and entry is limited to one firm per period. For simplicity, we will assume (as with our two Bertrand duopolists earlier) that the marginal costs of the incumbent and of all potential entrants are zero, and that market demand is given by the function $P = 20 - Q$. Can our incumbent deter entry? In the initial period, before entry, she maximizes profits by equating marginal cost and marginal revenue, which results in output of 10 units, a price of $10/unit and profits of $100. The first potential entrant knows that if she maintains this level of output, his profit-maximizing output level will be 5 units, the Stackelberg follower level. Hence in the second period, if he enters the market, total output will be 15 units, price will be $5/unit, the incumbent will make $50 in profits and the newcomer will make $25.

The incumbent's profits are lower after entry, and so she wants to deter the newcomer from entering the market. Suppose she says that *if* he enters, she will produce 15 units herself, so that $Q = 20$ units, driving the price to zero; therefore, he might as well stay out. As we saw in the Funland case, however, the problem is that her threat is not credible. The incumbent's profit-maximizing output level after entry is 10 units, and the entrant will not believe that she would throw away $50. Can she demonstrate her resolve by producing 15 units *this* period? If she does, then her profits this period drop to $75, and the entrant (taking the 15 units as given) finds that his profit-maximizing output level is now 2.5 units. Total output next period becomes 17.5 units, the price falls to $2.50 per unit, and her profits fall to $2.50 \times 15 = $37.50. By attempting deterrence in this manner, she thus lowers her profits in *both* periods. Short of producing all 20 units in the initial period, and forgoing the $100 in profits she could have earned, there is no way

FIGURE 13-9

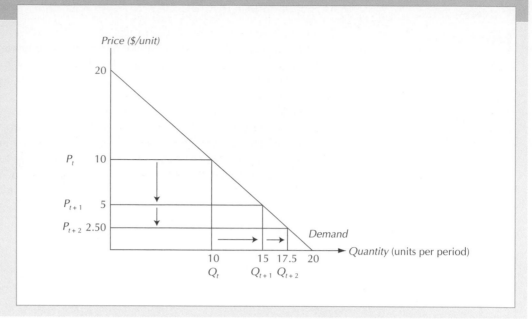

for her to deter entry. The Nash equilibrium in this situation is in fact the Stackelberg quantity leadership equilibrium. In the third period, using identical reasoning, we can show that the two incumbents' best strategy is to allow entry by the second potential entrant, who will produce 2.5 units. You can carry this process on for a few more periods if you wish, but the eventual outcome should be clear. Industry output will expand toward the competitive level of 20 units, and the price will tend in the limit to zero, because there is no way for incumbents to deter the entry of newcomers. The original monopolist and all subsequent entrants will make profits, but the profits for each in every period will be half what they were in the preceding period. The Nash-equilibrium time path of industry output and prices is shown in Figure 13-9.

Potential Entry with Fixed Costs of Entry: The Limit-Price Strategy

Suppose, however, that marginal costs are the same for the incumbent firm and potential entrants but there *are* fixed costs of entry. In this case, it *is* possible for the incumbent to deter potential entrants. To see what her optimal deterrence strategy is, note that if the fixed costs of entry were just over $25 in the above example, then it would not pay potential entrants to enter, since their maximum profits with zero entry costs were only $25. The incumbent could therefore continue to produce at the monopoly level with impunity. If entry costs were only $16 and the incumbent produced 10 units, however, then the new firm could make profits of 25 − 16 = $9, and would be in the market in the second period. Knowing this, the incumbent can consult the potential entrant's residual demand curve, and calculate the level of output she must produce so that the total revenues of the newcomer would be *just equal to the fixed costs of entry*.

In this case, if the incumbent produces 12 units in the first period, her profits are only $96 instead of $100. But the newcomer knows that his residual demand curve is now $P = (20 − 12) − Q_N$, where the subscript stands for "newcomer." Now if he produces his profit-maximizing level of output ($Q_N^* = 4$ units), he will earn *zero* profits, and might

Limit pricing/output strategy A strategy whereby an incumbent sets its output level so that the market price is just low enough to keep out a potential entrant with given fixed costs of entry.

as well stay out.[17] With this ***"limit pricing" (or "limit output") strategy***, the incumbent adjusts her output level just enough to limit entry by any newcomers, for any given level of entry costs. Note that one effect of even the *possibility* of entry, however, is to increase output and decrease price in the market, and that the lower the costs of entry, the closer the market equilibrium is to the competitive outcome. We consider one theory that builds on this fact in the next section.[18]

13.10 CONTESTABLE MARKETS

In a widely discussed book, economists William Baumol, John Panzer, and Robert Willig suggested that oligopolies and even monopolies will sometimes behave much like perfectly competitive firms.[19] The specific condition under which this will happen, according to their theory, is that entry and exit be perfectly free. With costless entry, a new firm will quickly enter if an incumbent firm dares to charge a price above average cost. The name "contestable markets" refers to the fact that when entry is costless, we often see a contest between potential competitors to see which firms will serve the market.

Costless entry does not mean that it costs no money to obtain a production facility to serve a market. It means that there are no *sunk* costs associated with entry and exit. The most important piece of equipment required to provide air service in the Montreal–London market, for example, is a wide-bodied aircraft, which carries a price tag of about $100 million. This is a hefty investment, to be sure, but it is not a sunk cost. If a firm wants to leave the market, it can sell or lease the aircraft to another firm, or make use of it in some other market. Contrast this case with that of a cement producer, which must spend a similar sum to build a manufacturing facility. Once built, the cement plant has essentially no alternative use. The resources that go into it are sunk costs, beyond recovery if the firm suddenly decides it no longer wants to participate in that market.

Why are sunk costs so important? Consider again the contrast between the air service market and the cement market. In each case we have a local monopoly. Because of economies of scale, there is room for only one cement factory in a given area and only one flight at a given time of day. Suppose in each case that incumbent firms are charging prices well in excess of average costs, and that in each case a new firm enters and captures some of the excess profit. And suppose, finally, that the incumbents react by lowering their

---

[17]The mathematics behind this numerical example is straightforward. With zero production costs, the potential entrant's profits (if he enters) are given by $\Pi_N = \Pi Q_N^* - F$, where F is the fixed cost per period (into the indefinite future) of amortizing the initial investment necessary to gain entry into the market. The incumbent is already *in* the market, and so for it, $F = 0$. The incumbent wants to set her output level so that if the newcomer entered the market and produced his profit-maximizing quantity *given the incumbent's level of output*, the resultant market price would leave the newcomer with zero profit, and hence no incentive to enter.

Recall from footnote 3 on page 482 that with demand given by $P = a - bQ = a - b(Q_I + Q_N)$ and marginal costs equal to zero, $Q_N^* = (a - bQ_I)/2b$. Hence the market price after entry would be $\Pi = a - b(Q_I + Q_N^*)$. Substituting the value for Q_N^* into this expression gives $\Pi = (a - bQ_I)/2$. Hence the incumbent can discourage the newcomer from entering by setting her output level so that $PQ_N^* = [(a - bQ_I)/2][(a - bQ_I)/2b] = F$, or equivalently, $(a - bQ_I)^2 = 4bF$. Solving for Q_I^*, we have $Q_I^* = (a - 2\sqrt{bF})/b$. In our numerical example, with $a = 20$ and $b = 1$, this becomes $Q_I^* = 20 - 2\sqrt{F}$.

Note that if the fixed costs of entry $F = 0$, then the only way for the incumbent to deter entry is to produce 20 units, the competitive output level, as we saw earlier. Note also that if $F > \$25$, the incumbent will produce 10 units (the profit-maximizing level of monopoly output) and not less, since in this case there is no threat of entry.

[18]The struggle between Netscape and Microsoft Explorer had many of the characteristics of a strategic entry deterrence game. The U.S. courts have long been engaged in determining whether (here and in other areas) Microsoft has played the game according to the rules.

[19]William Baumol, John Panzer, and Robert Willig, *Contestable Markets and the Theory of Industry Structure*, San Diego, CA: Harcourt Brace Jovanovich, 1982. For an accessible summary, see Baumol, "Contestable Markets: An Uprising in the Theory of Industry Structure," *American Economic Review*, 72, March 1982: 1–15.

prices, with the result that all the firms, entrants and incumbents alike, are losing money. In the cement market case, the entrant will then be stuck with a huge capital facility that will not cover its costs. The airline case, in contrast, carries no similar risk. If the market becomes unprofitable, the entrant can quickly pull out and deploy its asset elsewhere.

The contestable market theory is like other theories of market structure in saying that cost conditions determine how many firms will end up serving a given market. Where there are economies of scale, we expect to see only a single firm. Where there are U-shaped LAC curves whose minimum points occur at a substantial fraction of industry output, we expect only a few firms. With constant costs, there may be many firms. Where the contestable market theory differs from others is in saying that there is no clear relationship between the *actual* number of competitors in a market and the extent to which price and quantity resemble what we would see under perfect competition. Where the threat of entry is credible, incumbent firms are simply not free to charge prices that are significantly above cost.

Critics of the contestable market theory counter that there are important sunk costs involved in participation in *every* market.[20] Granted, in the airline case it is possible to lease an aircraft on a short-term basis; but that alone is not sufficient to start a viable operation. Counter space must be obtained at the airport terminal; potential passengers must be alerted to the existence of the new service, usually with an expensive advertising campaign. Reservations, baggage handling, and check-in facilities must be arranged. Ground service contracts for the aircraft must be signed, and so on. Each step involves irretrievable commitments of resources, and they add up to enough to make a brief stay in the market very costly indeed. The fiercest critics contend that so long as there are any sunk costs involved in entry and exit, the contestable market theory breaks down.

All the returns are not in yet on the contestable market theory. The critics have raised some formidable objections, but there do appear to be at least some settings where the insights hold up. In the intercity bus market, for example, one or two firms usually provide all of the scheduled service in any given city-pair market. Traditional theories of market structure suggest that prices would be likely to rise steeply during holiday weekends, when substantially larger numbers of people travel. What we see in some markets, however, is that small charter bus companies offer special holiday service at fares no higher than normal. These companies often do little more than post a few leaflets on college campuses, stating their prices and schedules and giving a telephone number to call for reservations. The circumstances of the intercity bus industry come very close to the free-entry ideal contemplated by the contestable market theory, and the results are much as it predicts. Much more remains to be said about just when the threat of entry will be a significant disciplining force, a subject we consider in more detail in Appendix 13A.

13.11 GAMES OLIGOPOLISTS PLAY

The boundaries of applied game theory are not static. You should now have some flavour of the style of strategic thinking imbedded in the game-theoretical approach. But the potential scope of applied game theory is as wide as there are situations in which strategic behaviour plays a role.[21] Some of the most rapidly growing areas involve issues that

---

[20]W.G. Shepherd, "Contestability vs. Competition," *American Economic Review, 74,* September 1984: 572–587.

[21]Five lucid works, of varying degrees of difficulty, are recommended for students who want to explore further: Avinash Dixit and Susan Skeath, *Games of Strategy,* New York: Norton, 2004; Herbert Gintis, *Game Theory Evolving,* Princeton University Press, 2000; Jack Hirshleifer and John G. Riley, *The Analytics of Uncertainty and Information,* Cambridge University Press, 1993; Paul Milgrom and John Roberts, *Economics, Organization and Management,* Upper Saddle River, NJ: Prentice Hall, 1992; and Karl Sigmund, *Games of Life,* London: Penguin, 1995.

we have examined in other chapters. The rationality requirement that is central to formal game theory, for example, makes heavy (perhaps unrealistically high) demands on the players. We have already noted that even in a game with only 10 players, each of whom has 10 strategies, the payoff matrix will have 10^{10}, or 10 billion cells. Even with high-powered computers, the information-processing demands are heavy, and the assumption that perfectly rational behaviour is costless may stretch credulity. In such situations, the limitations on rationality that we considered in Chapter 8 may manifest themselves. The question of how best to simplify decision situations *strategically*, so that they become more manageable but no less useful for the players, is one of the open questions in game-theoretical research.

Some of the games we have studied, such as the advertising "arms race" and those we examined in Chapters 5 and 7, are *socially* wasteful, as well as disadvantageous to the players themselves. With other games, in contrast, consumers derive benefit from the fact that the players are busy shooting themselves in the foot. In the case of the non-cooperative Bertrand duopolists, for instance, consumer surplus is eventually maximized as the two firms wend their way toward the competitive market outcome. At the level of the players themselves, there are obviously reasons to develop means of avoiding prisoner's dilemma–type situations. Writing up costly binding contracts lowers the net payoffs in all four cells, but contracts can make defection *much* more costly. For the same reason, the threat of a lawsuit can curb defection. Finally, reputation matters. If a player develops a reputation for defection and other players are not compelled to play with that player, they won't. In contrast, a reputation for honesty and fair dealing can be a customer magnet and can reduce the likelihood that other players will defect for pre-cautionary reasons. The item for "goodwill" that appears on many firms' balance sheets can be an accurate measure of the capitalized value of the firms' reputations.

A perceived threat directed at two players by an external party can increase the benefits they perceive of cooperation and coalition formation between themselves. If the outside threat is diminished, then the two players may cease to behave as cooperatively with each other.

One method of escape from a prisoner's dilemma situation is for the two opposing players to merge. A merger has the effect of converting a competitive situation into a noncompetitive one. If many of the costs of oligopolistic competition were socially wasteful, then society as a whole may have an interest in the merger, if the effect of the merger is not simply to increase the monopoly power of the newly merged firm. This issue is considered further in Appendix 13A.

We have seen that the time factor is important in game-theoretical approaches. The cooperative approach to a repeated prisoner's dilemma can unravel if the game is played for a known finite number of times. A player may act against her short-term self-interest as an investment in increasing her long-term discounted expected payoffs. At a high enough discount rate, however, an infinite stream of potential future net benefits may be outweighed by the present net costs of getting into that stream. Outside observers, comparing the differing behaviour of two players faced by identical situations, may not be able to determine whether one player is behaving rationally and the other irra-tionally, or whether both are behaving rationally and simply have different marginal rates of time preference. Not just time but also *timing* matters. In some sequential games it pays to move first, and in others it pays to let the other player commit himself and then respond: as in chess and boxing, the counter-puncher sometimes wins.

As it developed historically, for a number of reasons game theory began on a founda-tion of the theory of rational self-interest. This starting point may have been necessary, but as a result game theory in its early development tended to focus on the *difficulties* of cooperation and on the primacy of competition and predation. Some of the most exciting recent developments in game theory focus on the preconditions for cooperation, the possibility of "network effects" that make cooperation more necessary and beneficial, and the role of meta-strategies such as mergers as means of capturing these network effects. As we move into the increasingly interconnected global economy of the 21st century, this direction for the future evolution of the game-theoretical understanding of strategic behaviour appears to be not only promising but also essential.

13.B MONOPOLISTIC COMPETITION

13.12 A CHAMBERLINIAN MODEL OF MONOPOLISTIC COMPETITION

One market structure close to perfect competition, what economists call "monopolistic competition," occurs if there is free entry but one firm's products are not perfect substitutes for the products of other firms. The degree of substitutability between products then determines how close monopolistic competition gets to the perfectly competitive outcome.

The traditional economic model of monopolistic competition was developed independently during the 1930s by Edward Chamberlin and by Cambridge economist Joan Robinson. There are significant differences, as well as some formal similarities, between the Robinson and Chamberlin models. Chamberlin viewed his version as a *general* model of the economics of firms, on a continuum ranging from purely competitive firms to monopolies. He was skeptical about the concept of "an industry," since industries are often defined on *technological* criteria. In Chamberlin's view, for a monopolistically competitive firm, it was often less important which industry it belonged to than which other firms provided close substitutes for the firm's products. In some cases, other firms could provide very close substitutes even if they were not in the "same" industry, technologically defined. He therefore did not assume, in general, that all of these firms were "identical" in some sense. Yet the standard "Chamberlinian" model that derived from his work abstracted from these issues. In this section, we outline that Chamberlinian model.

The model begins with the assumption of a clearly defined "industry group," which consists of a large number of producers of products that are close, but imperfect, substitutes for one another. The market for men's dress shirts provides a convenient illustration. Shirts made by Gant serve essentially the same purpose as those made by Van Heusen, Sero, Ralph Lauren, or Arrow. And yet, for many consumers, it is hardly a matter of indifference which brand they buy.

Two important implications follow from these assumptions about industry structure. The first is that because the products are viewed as close but not perfect substitutes, each firm will confront a downward-sloping demand schedule. Someone who has a particular liking for Gant shirts would be willing to pay more for one than for a shirt from some other manufacturer. But let Gant raise its price sufficiently and even these buyers will eventually switch to another brand. The second implication, which follows from the assumption of a large number of independent firms, is that each firm will act as if its own price and quantity decisions have no effect on the behaviour of other firms in the industry. And because the products are close substitutes, this in turn means that each firm perceives its demand schedule as being highly elastic.

A fundamental feature of the Chamberlinian model is the perfect symmetry of the position of all firms in the industry. In metaphorical terms, the Chamberlinian firm may be thought of as one of many fishing boats, each of which has a number of fishing lines in the water. If any one boat were to set its hooks with a more alluring bait while others used the same bait as before, the effect would be for the innovator to increase its share of the total catch by a substantial margin. After all, its lines have become more attractive not only in absolute terms, but also relative to the lines of other boats. Because the situation is perfectly symmetric, however, if it makes sense for one boat to use more attractive bait, so will it for others. Yet when all use better bait, the innovator's lines are no more attractive in relative terms than before. Accordingly, the addition to its total catch will be much smaller than if others had held to their original behaviour.

The analogy between the fishing example above and pricing behaviour by the Chamberlinian monopolistically competitive firm is complete. In contemplating the demand for its own product, the firm assumes that its competitors do not respond in any way to its price and quantity decisions. Like the operators of the fishing boats, the firm is correct in assuming that a change in its own behaviour will not *cause* others to change theirs. Yet the symmetry between firms assures that if it makes sense for one firm to alter its price, it will make sense for all others to do likewise.

The result is that the firm really confronts two different demand curves—one that describes what will happen when it alone changes its price and a second that describes what will happen when all prices change in unison. Thus, for example, the curve *dd* in Figure 13-10 represents the demand curve facing the Chamberlinian firm if it alone varies its price; the curve *DD* is the demand curve when all firms change prices together. At an initial situation in which all firms charge P', each will sell Q'. If only one firm lowers its price to P'', it will sell Q'''. But if others match its price cut, each will sell only Q''.

It is important to stress that individual firms need not fail to realize that the prices of similarly situated firms tend to move together. On the contrary, each firm may be perfectly aware of that. But it also realizes that its own price movements are not what cause other firms to change their behaviour. When it is thinking about the consequences of a price move, therefore, it is forced to think in terms of movements along *dd*, not along the demand curve that describes what happens when all prices change in unison (*DD*).[22]

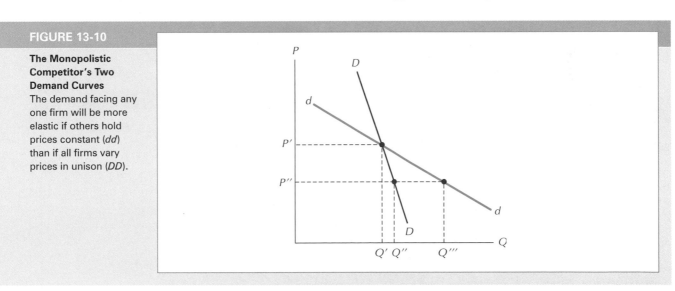

FIGURE 13-10

The Monopolistic Competitor's Two Demand Curves
The demand facing any one firm will be more elastic if others hold prices constant (*dd*) than if all firms vary prices in unison (*DD*).

---

[22]The issue here is much the same as the one confronting participants in the prisoner's dilemma. (See above and Chapters 5 and 7.) Each person may know that it is rational for the other person to defect and may therefore expect him to do so. But each person also knows that his own behaviour will not affect what the other person does.

Chamberlinian Equilibrium in the Short Run

For illustrative purposes, let us consider the monopolistically competitive firm whose demand (the *dd* curve), marginal revenue, average total cost, and short-run marginal cost curves are portrayed in Figure 13-11. Following precisely the same argument we employed in the case of the pure monopoly, we can easily show that the short-run profit-maximizing quantity is Q^*, the one for which the marginal revenue curve intersects the short-run marginal cost curve. The profit-maximizing price is P^*, the value that corresponds to Q^* on the demand curve *dd*.

In Figure 13-11, note also that the demand curve *DD* intersects the demand curve *dd* at the profit-maximizing price, P^*. This is yet another consequence of the fundamental symmetry that exists within Chamberlinian firms. The *DD* curve, recall, is the locus along which each firm's quantity would move with price if the prices of all firms moved in unison. The *dd* curve, by contrast, is the locus along which the firm's quantity will move with price when the prices of all other firms are fixed. Because the situation confronting each firm is the same, if P^* is the profit-maximizing price for one, it must also be for the rest. The price level at which other firms' prices are fixed along *dd* is thus P^*, which implies that at P^* on *dd*, the price of *every* firm will be P^*. And this is why *dd* intersects *DD* at P^*.

Chamberlinian Equilibrium in the Long Run

As in the perfectly competitive case, the fact that there are economic profits in the short run will have the effect of luring additional firms into the monopolistically competitive industry. What is the effect of the entry of these firms? In the competitive case, we saw that it was to shift the industry supply curve rightward, causing a reduction in the short-run equilibrium price. Put another way, the effect of entry in the perfectly competitive model is to cause each firm's horizontal demand curve to shift downward. In the Chamberlinian model, the analogous effect is to shift each firm's demand curve to the left. More precisely, on the assumption that each firm competes on an equal footing for a share of total industry demand, the effect of entry is to cause an equal proportional reduction in the quantity that each firm can sell at any given price. Each firm in the market essentially claims an equal share of industry demand, and with more firms in the industry, that share necessarily declines.

FIGURE 13-11

Short-Run Equilibrium for the Chamberlinian Firm
The Chamberlinian monopolistically competitive firm maximizes economic profit in the short run by equating marginal revenue and short-run marginal cost. Economic profit is Π, the area of the shaded rectangle.

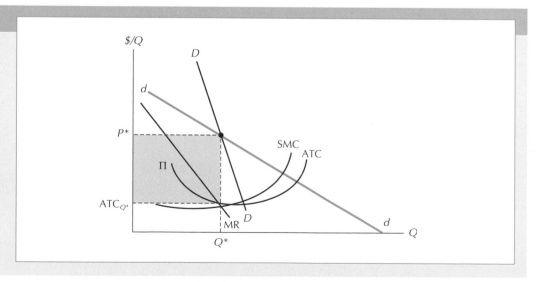

Each of 20 firms in a Chamberlinian monopolistically competitive industry faces a *dd* curve given by $P = 10 - .001Q$. What will each firm's *dd* curve be following the entry of five new firms?

Following the leftward shift in demand caused by entry, each firm has the opportunity to readjust the size of its capital stock and to choose its new profit-maximizing level of output. If extra-normal profit still remains, entry will continue.

The long-run equilibrium position is one in which the demand curve *dd* has shifted left to the point that it is tangent to the long-run average cost curve (and tangent as well to the associated short-run average cost curve). Note in Figure 13-12 that Q^*, the profit-maximizing level of output by the MR = MC criterion, is exactly the same as the output level for which the *dd* curve is tangent to the long- and short-run average cost curves. This is no mere coincidence. We can argue independently of the MR = MC condition that the tangency point must be the maximum-profit point. At that point, the firm earns zero economic profit, while at any other output level, average cost would exceed average revenue, which means that economic profit would be negative.

Note again in Figure 13-12 that the demand curve *DD* intersects *dd* at the equilibrium price P^* for the reasons discussed earlier. If all firms raised price from P^*, each would move upward along *DD*, and each would earn an economic profit. But in the absence of a binding collusive agreement, it would not be in the interest of any firm to maintain its price above P^*, because at any such price its marginal revenue (along the MR curve associated with *dd*) would exceed its marginal cost. At any price above P^*, it could earn higher profits by cutting price and selling more output. The only stable outcome is the tangency point shown in Figure 13-12.

Perfect Competition vs. Chamberlinian Monopolistic Competition

There are several obvious points of comparison between the long-run equilibrium positions of perfect competition and Chamberlinian monopolistic competition. First, competition meets the test of allocative efficiency, while monopolistic competition does

FIGURE 13-12

Long-Run Equilibrium in the Chamberlinian Model
Entry occurs, shifting *dd* leftward until it becomes tangent to the LAC curve. The firm produces Q^*, sells for P^*, and earns zero economic profit.

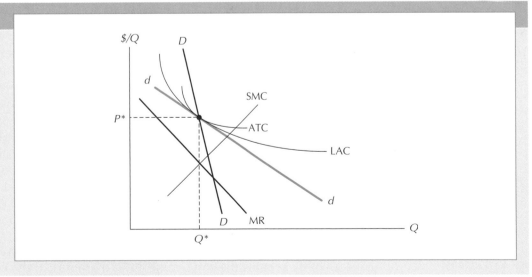

not. Under competition, price is exactly equal to long-run marginal cost, which means that there are no unexploited possibilities for mutual gains through exchange. Under monopolistic competition, in contrast, price will exceed marginal cost, even in the long run. This means that there will be people in society who value an additional unit of output more highly than the value of the resources required to produce it. If monopolistic competitors could come up with a way to cut price to such buyers without cutting price on existing sales, they would gladly do so, making everyone better off in the process. As we saw in the case of the monopolist, such selective price cutting is sometimes possible. But it is inherently imperfect, and on this account monopolistic competition is destined to fall short of perfect competition on the narrow efficiency standard.

Some economists also argue that monopolistic competition is less efficient than perfect competition because in the former case firms do not produce at the minimum points of their long-run average cost (LAC) curves. This is not a very telling comparison, however, because other aspects of the two cases are so different. The relevant question is whether people who currently buy from monopolistic competitors would be happier if all products were exactly the same and cost a little less. This is not an easy question, and, lacking an answer to it, we cannot conclude that monopolistic competition is inefficient merely because firms don't produce at the minimum points of their LAC curves.

There is at least one important sense, related to the discussion in the preceding paragraph, in which the Chamberlinian model is strikingly more realistic than the competitive model. In the perfectly competitive case, recall, price and marginal cost are the same in equilibrium. This implies that the firm should react with sleepy-eyed indifference to an opportunity to fill a new order at the current market price. In the monopolistically competitive case, in contrast, price exceeds marginal cost, which implies that the firm should greet a new order at the current market price with enthusiasm. Periods of temporary shortages apart, we know of very few instances of the former reaction. Almost every businessperson who ever lived is delighted to accept new orders at the current market price.

In terms of long-run profitability, finally, the equilibrium positions of both the perfect competitor and the Chamberlinian monopolistic competitor are precisely the same. Freedom of entry in each case holds long-run economic profit at zero. By the same token, freedom of exit assures that there will be no long-run economic losses in either case.

13.13 A SPATIAL MODEL OF MONOPOLISTIC COMPETITION

As we noted earlier, the extent to which one monopolistically competitive firm's product is an effective substitute for another's determines how closely their market behaviour will resemble that of perfect competition. One concrete way of thinking about incomplete substitutability is in terms of distance. Gas across town is not a perfect substitute for gas at the nearest corner, for instance, especially not when your tank is reading below empty.

Imagine yourself a resident of a small island nation with a large lake in the middle of it. Business activity there is naturally restricted to the doughnut-shaped piece of land that constitutes the island's periphery. There is considerable specialization of labour on your island. People toil all day at their respective tasks and then take their evening meals at restaurants. People on your island lack the customary preference for culinary diversity. Instead, you and your neighbours prefer to eat baked potatoes and grilled chicken every night. Meals in any given restaurant are produced under increasing returns to scale—the more meals produced, the lower the average cost per meal.

How many restaurants should there be in this island nation? We are tempted to say only one, thereby keeping the cost per meal to a minimum. If the circumference of the island were, say, only 300 metres, this would almost surely be the correct answer. But for a much larger island, the direct cost of meals is not likely to be the only item of concern to you and your fellow residents. You will also care about the cost of getting to and from the nearest restaurant. If the island were 300 kilometres around, for example, the cost savings from having only a single restaurant could hardly begin to compensate for the travel costs incurred by those who live on the far side of the island.

The market for evening meals on this island is in one respect the same as the markets we have considered in earlier chapters: a single, standardized meal is served in every restaurant. But the type of food served is not the only important characteristic of a meal. Buyers care also about *where* the meal is served. When products differ along one or more important dimensions—location, size, flavour, quality, and so on—we immediately confront the general question of how much product diversity there should be. Should an economy have 5 different brands of cars, 10, or 50? How many different kinds of tennis racquets should there be?

To help fix ideas, suppose there are initially four restaurants evenly spaced around the periphery of the island, as represented by the heavy black squares in Figure 13-13. Suppose the circumference of the island is 1 km. The distance between adjacent restaurants will then be $\frac{1}{4}$ km, and no one can possibly live more than $\frac{1}{8}$ km away from the nearest restaurant, the one-way trip length required for someone who lives exactly halfway between two restaurants.

To fill out the structure of the environment, suppose there are L consumers scattered uniformly about the circle, and suppose the cost of travel is t dollars per kilometre. Thus, for example, if t were equal to \$24/km, the transportation cost incurred by someone who lives $d = \frac{1}{16}$ km from the nearest restaurant would be the product of the round-trip distance ($2d$) and the travel cost per kilometre (t): $2dt = 2(\frac{1}{16}$ km$)(\$24$/km$) = \$3$.

Suppose further that each consumer will eat exactly 1 meal per day at the restaurant for which the total price (which is the price charged for the meal plus transportation costs) is lowest. And suppose, finally, that each restaurant has a total cost curve given by

$$\text{TC} = F + MQ. \tag{13.6}$$

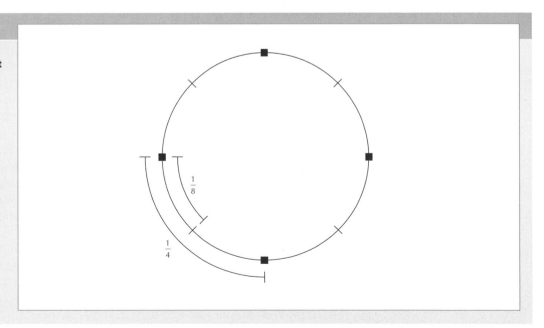

FIGURE 13-13

An Industry in Which Location Is the Important Differentiating Feature
Restaurants (heavy black squares) are the same except for their geographic location. Each person dines at the restaurant closest to home. If the circumference of the loop is 1 km, this means that the distance between restaurants will be $\frac{1}{4}$ km, giving rise to a maximum one-way trip length of $\frac{1}{8}$ km.

Recall from earlier chapters that the total cost curve in Equation 13.6 is one in which there is a fixed cost F and a constant marginal cost M. Here, F may be thought of as the sum of equipment rental fees, opportunity costs of invested capital, and other fixed costs associated with operating a restaurant; and M is the sum of the labour, raw material, and other variable costs incurred in producing an additional meal.

Recall also that average total cost (ATC) is simply total cost divided by output. With a total cost function given by $TC = F + MQ$, average total cost is thus equal to $F/Q + M$. This means that the more customers that are served in a given location, the lower the average total cost will be.

Suppose, for example, that each of our four restaurants has a total cost curve, measured in dollars per day, given by $TC = 50 + 5Q$, where Q is the number of meals it serves each day. If the population, L, is equal to 100 persons, each restaurant will serve $(100/4) = 25$ meals/day, and its total cost will be given by $TC = 50 + 5(25) = \$175$/day. Average total cost in each restaurant will be $TC/25 = (\$175/\text{day})/(25 \text{ meals/day}) = \$7$/meal. In comparison, if there were only two restaurants, each would serve 50 meals/day and have an average total cost of only $6/meal.

What will be the average cost of transportation when there are four restaurants? This cost will depend on unit transportation costs (t) and on how far apart the restaurants are. Recall that the distance between adjacent restaurants will be $\frac{1}{4}$ km when there are four restaurants. Some people will live right next door to a restaurant, and for these people the transportation cost will be zero. With four restaurants, the farthest someone can live from a restaurant is $\frac{1}{8}$ km, the one-way distance for a person who lives halfway between two adjacent restaurants. For this person, the round-trip will cover $\frac{1}{4}$ km; and if t is again equal to $24/km, the travel cost for this patron will be $(\$24/\text{km})(\frac{1}{4} \text{ km}) = \$6$. Since people are uniformly scattered about the loop, the average round-trip will be halfway between these two extremes; it will thus cover a distance of $\frac{1}{8}$ km, and its cost will be $3.

The *overall average cost per meal* is the sum of average total meal cost ($7/meal in the four-restaurant example) and average transportation cost (here, $3/meal), which comes to $10/meal.

The Optimal Number of Locations

If unit transportation cost (t) were zero, it would then clearly be optimal to have only a single restaurant, because that would minimize the overall average cost per meal. But if transportation cost were sufficiently high, a single restaurant would not be optimal because the average patron would have to travel too great a distance. The optimal number of locations is thus the result of a tradeoff between the start-up and other fixed costs (F) of opening new locations, on the one hand, and the savings from lower transportation costs, on the other.

What is the best number of outlets to have? Our strategy for answering this question will be to ask whether the overall average cost per meal served (average total cost plus average transportation cost) would decline if we had one more restaurant than we have now. If so, we should add another restaurant and ask the same question again. Once the overall average cost stops declining, we will have reached the optimal number of restaurants.

To illustrate, suppose we increase the number of restaurants in our earlier example from four to five. How will this affect overall average cost? Again supposing that the restaurants are evenly spaced around the loop, each will now attract only one-fifth of the island's 100 inhabitants, which means that each will serve 20 meals/day. The ATC for each restaurant will thus be $[50 + 5(20)]/20 = \$7.50$/meal, up $.50/meal from the previous value. (Recall that ATC with four restaurants was \$7/meal.) The distance between adjacent restaurants is $\frac{1}{5}$ km when there are five restaurants. This means that the average one-way trip with five restaurants is $\frac{1}{20}$ km, which in turn means that the average round-trip length is $\frac{1}{10}$ km. Average transportation cost is thus ($\frac{1}{10}$ km)(\$24/km) = \$2.40. Note that this is \$.60 less than the previous average transportation cost of \$3, reflecting the decline in average trip length. Adding average total meal cost and average transportation cost, we see that the overall average cost with five restaurants is \$7.50 + \$2.40 = \$9.90/meal.

EXERCISE 13-6

In the preceding example, what is the overall average cost per meal if there are *six* identical restaurants, equally spaced around the loop?

Your calculation in Exercise 13-6 demonstrates that overall average cost per meal goes up when we increase the number of restaurants from five to six. And since the overall average cost declined when we moved from four to five, this means the optimal number of restaurants for our island nation is five.

We can make the preceding analysis more general by supposing that there are N outlets around the loop, as shown by the heavy black squares in Figure 13-14. Now the distance between adjacent outlets will be $1/N$, and the maximum one-way trip length will be half that, or $1/(2N)$. If we again suppose that people are uniformly distributed around the loop, it follows that the average one-way distance to the nearest outlet is $1/(4N)$—which is halfway between 0, the distance of the person closest to a given outlet, and $1/(2N)$, the distance of the person farthest from it. The average round-trip distance is twice the average one-way distance, and is thus equal to $1/(2N)$.

Because the distance between restaurants declines as the number of restaurants grows, the total transportation cost, denoted C_{trans}, will be a decreasing function of the

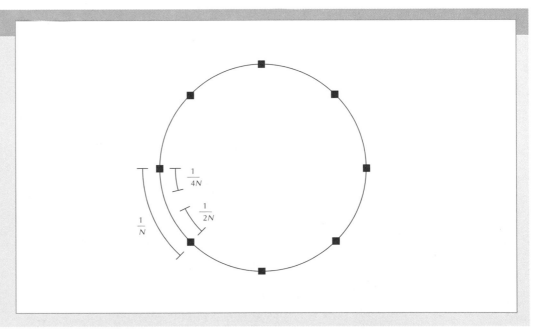

FIGURE 13-14

Distances with
N Outlets

With N outlets, the distance between adjacent outlets will be $1/N$. The farthest a person can live from an outlet is $1/(2N)$. And the average one-way distance people must travel to reach the nearest outlet is $1/(4N)$. The average round-trip distance is $1/(2N)$.

number of outlets. Since transportation cost is t dollars per person per kilometre travelled, total transportation cost will equal the cost per person/km (t) times the number of persons (L) times the average round-trip length ($1/2N$ km):

$$C_{\text{trans}} = tL \frac{1}{2N}. \qquad (13.7)$$

The total cost of meals served, denoted C_{meals}, also depends on both population and the number of outlets. It is given by

$$C_{\text{meals}} = LM + NF, \qquad (13.8)$$

where the first term on the right reflects the fact that each of the L people eats a meal whose marginal cost is M, and the second term is the total fixed cost for N outlets. The object is to choose N to minimize the sum of the two types of costs, $C_{\text{trans}} + C_{\text{meals}}$.

The two cost functions and their sum are shown graphically in Figure 13-15, where N^* denotes the cost-minimizing number of outlets.[23]

The slope of the C_{meals} curve is equal to F, which represents the cost of an additional outlet. The slope of the C_{trans} curve is equal to $-tL/2N^2$ and represents the savings in transportation cost from adding an additional outlet.[24] If the slope of C_{meals} is less than

FIGURE 13-15

The Optimal Number of Outlets
Total transportation cost (C_{trans}) declines with the number of outlets (N), while total cost of meals served (C_{meals}) increases with N. The optimal number of outlets (N^*) is the one that minimizes the sum of these costs.

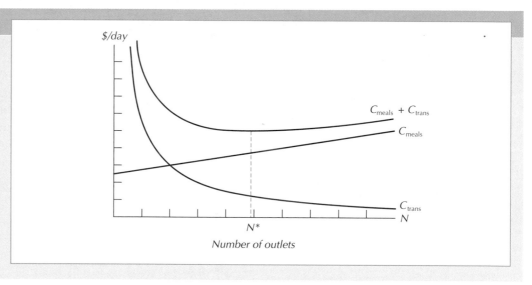

$/day

$C_{\text{meals}} + C_{\text{trans}}$

C_{meals}

C_{trans}

N

N^*

Number of outlets

---

[23]These functions are plotted as if N were a continuous variable, not an integer. For industries involving large numbers of firms, the continuous approximation will introduce only minimal error.

[24]This slope is found by taking the derivative

$$\frac{d(C_{\text{trans}})}{dN} = \frac{-tL}{2N^2}$$

again treating N as if it were continuously variable. Students who haven't had calculus can convince themselves that this expression is correct by letting ΔN be, say, .001 and then calculating the resulting change in C_{trans},

$$\Delta C_{\text{trans}} = \frac{tL}{2(N + .001)} - \frac{tL}{2N} = \frac{-.001tL}{2N(N + .001)}.$$

Dividing the term for ΔC_{trans} by ΔN ($= .001$), we get the ratio $\Delta C_{\text{trans}}/\Delta N$:

$$\frac{\Delta C_{\text{trans}}}{\Delta N} = \frac{-tL}{2N(N + .001)} = \frac{-tL}{2N^2 + .002N} \approx \frac{-tL}{2N^2}.$$

the absolute value of the slope of C_{trans}, the reduction in transportation cost from adding another outlet will more than compensate for the extra fixed cost from adding that outlet. The optimal number of outlets, N^*, is the one for which the slope of the C_{meals} curve is the same as the absolute value of the slope of the C_{trans} curve. N^* must thus satisfy

$$\frac{tL}{2(N^*)^2} = F,\qquad (13.9)$$

which yields

$$N^* = \sqrt{\frac{tL}{2F}}.\qquad (13.10)$$

This expression for the optimal number of outlets has a straightforward economic interpretation. Note first that if transportation cost rises, N^* will also rise. This makes sense because the whole point of adding additional outlets is to economize on transportation costs. Note that N^* also increases with population density, L. The more people there are who live on each segment of the loop, the more people there are who will benefit if the average distance to the nearest outlet becomes shorter. And note, finally, that N^* increases with declines in F, the start-up cost of an additional outlet, which is also just as expected.

Applying Equation 13.10 to our restaurant example in which $L = 100$, $t = 24$, and $F = 50$, we get $N^* = \ = 4.9$. Needless to say, it is impossible to have 4.9 restaurants, so we choose the integer nearest 4.9, namely, 5. And indeed, just as our earlier calculations indicated, having five restaurants results in a lower overall average cost than does having either four or six.

EXERCISE 13-7

How would N^* change in the preceding example if there were 400 people on the island instead of 100?

Will the independent actions of private, profit-seeking firms result in the optimal number of outlets around the loop? This question sounds very simple, but turns out to be exceedingly difficult to answer. We now know that under some conditions there will tend to be more than the optimal number, while under other conditions there will be fewer.[25] But for the moment let us note that the number of outlets that emerges from the independent actions of profit-seeking firms will in general be related to the optimal number of outlets in the following simple way: any environmental change that leads to a change in the optimal number of outlets (here, any change in population density, transportation cost, or fixed cost) will lead to a change in the same direction in the equilibrium number of outlets. For example, a fall in transportation cost will tend to decrease both the optimal number of outlets and the number of outlets we actually observe in practice.

---

[25]A detailed technical discussion of some of the relevant issues can be found in Avinash Dixit and Joseph Stiglitz, "Monopolistic Competition and Optimal Product Diversity," *American Economic Review*, 1977: 297–308; and A. Michael Spence, "Product Selection, Fixed Costs, and Monopolistic Competition," *Review of Economic Studies*, 1976: 217–235.

WHY ARE THERE SO MANY FEWER GROCERY STORES IN MOST CITIES NOW THAN THERE WERE IN 1930? AND WHY DO RESIDENTIAL NEIGHBOURHOODS IN MONTREAL TEND TO HAVE MORE GROCERY STORES THAN RESIDENTIAL NEIGHBOURHOODS IN VANCOUVER?

Grocery retailing, like many other forms of retailing, is characterized by strong economies of scale. It thus confronts the usual tradeoff between direct production cost, on the one hand, and transportation cost, on the other. Over the last century, changing patterns of automobile ownership have affected the pattern of grocery store size and location in Canada. In 1930, most families did not own cars and had to do their shopping on foot. In terms of our expression for the optimal number of outlets (Equation 13.10), this meant a high value of t, unit transportation cost. Today, of course, most families have a car, which has led people to take advantage of the lower prices that are possible in larger stores. In the Greater Vancouver area, partly for geographical reasons, population density is lower and a family car is more of an economic necessity than in Montreal, which has the Métro subway system. The result is a greater concentration of neighbourhood groceries in Montreal. Across Canada, one factor that has offset the trend away from neighbourhood grocery stores toward supermarkets has been the growth of the aptly named "convenience" store. Despite having higher prices, convenience stores survive by offering not only proximity but also extended hours, for which people are willing to pay a premium. Once the supermarkets close, as most of them do, the convenience stores are in a monopoly position until the next morning.

13.14 PRODUCT CHARACTERISTICS AND THE "DISTANCE" BETWEEN PRODUCTS

The power of the spatial interpretation of monopolistic competition is that it can be applied not only to geographic location, but also to a variety of other product characteristics. Consider, for example, the various airline flights between any two cities on a given day. People have different preferences for travelling at various times of day, just as they have different preferences about where to eat or shop. Figure 13-16 depicts an air-travel market (for example, Winnipeg to Calgary) with four flights per day, scheduled at midnight, 6 A.M., noon, and 6 P.M. With the choice of an airline flight, just as with the choice of a place to dine, people will tend to select the alternative that lies closest to their most preferred option. Thus, a person who would most prefer to go at 7 P.M. will probably choose the 6 P.M. flight. In terms of our spatial model, having to wait for a flight is the analogue of having to travel a certain distance in order to get to a store.

Why not have a flight leaving every five minutes, so that no one would be forced to travel at an inconvenient time? The answer again has to do with the tradeoff between cost and convenience. The larger an aircraft is, the lower its average cost per seat is. If people want frequent flights, airlines are forced to use smaller planes and charge higher fares. Conversely, if people didn't care when they travelled, the airline could use the largest possible aircraft and fly at whatever interval was required to accumulate enough passengers to fill the plane. But most passengers have schedules to keep and are willing to pay a little extra for more conveniently timed flights. The result is the same sort of compromise we saw in the restaurant and grocery store examples.

Virtually every consumer product can be interpreted fruitfully within the context of the spatial model. In the automobile market, for example, the available permutations of turbo versus nonturbo, automatic versus standard, coupe versus convertible, sedan versus station wagon, two doors versus four doors, bucket seats versus bench seats, air

FIGURE 13-16

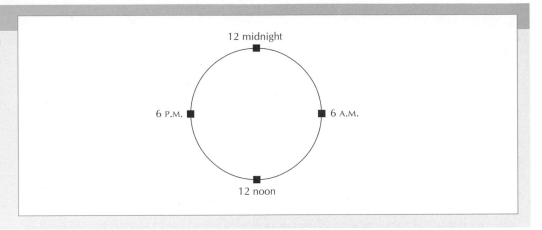

conditioned versus not air conditioned, metallic indigo versus forest green, and so on, lead to an extraordinarily large number of possibilities. It would be considerably cheaper, of course, if we had only a single standard model. But people are willing to pay a little extra for genuine variety, just as they are willing to pay a little extra for a more conveniently located store. In the parlance of the spatial model, car manufacturers are said to "locate" their models in a "product space" or "market niche." Their aim is to see that few buyers are left without a choice that lies "close" to the car that would best suit them. Similar interpretations apply to cameras, stereos, vacations, bicycles, wristwatches, wedding bands, and virtually every other good for which people have a taste for variety. Appendix 13A examines why the costs of variety tend to be borne largely by those customers who most demand it.

13.15 HISTORICAL NOTE: HOTELLING'S HOT DOG VENDORS

In Harold Hotelling's seminal paper on the spatial model of monopolistic competition,[26] he discussed a problem that we can visualize in terms of two hot dog vendors who are free to position themselves wherever they wish along a stretch of beach. Suppose the beach is 1 km long and bounded at each end by some natural obstacle. Suppose also that the vendors charge the same price, customers are evenly distributed along the beach, and each customer buys one hot dog from the nearest vendor. If the vendors' goal is to sell as many hot dogs as possible, where should they position themselves?

Suppose, as in Figure 13-17, that vendor 1 stands at point A and vendor 2 stands at point B, where both A and B are $\frac{1}{4}$ kilometre from the midpoint of the beach located at C. In this configuration, all customers to the left of C are closest to vendor 1 and will buy from him, while those to the right of C will buy from vendor 2. Each vendor thus gets half the market. The greatest one-way distance any customer has to travel is $\frac{1}{4}$ km, and the average one-way distance between customers and their nearest vendor is half that, or $\frac{1}{8}$ km.

Mathematically inclined readers can verify that A and B are in fact the socially optimal locations, those that minimize average travel distance for all consumers. And yet these locations are clearly not optimal from the perspective of either vendor. To see why, suppose vendor 1 were to move 10 steps toward B. The customers to the left of

---

[26]Harold Hotelling, "Stability in Competition," *The Economic Journal, 39,* 1929: 41–57.

FIGURE 13-17

The Hot Dog Vendor Location Problem
Each hot dog vendor does best by positioning himself at the centre of the beach, even though that location does not minimize the average distance that their customers must travel.

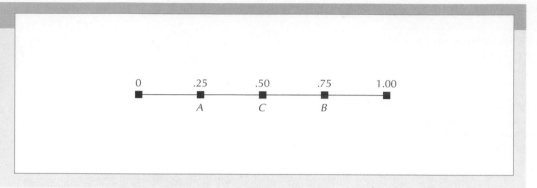

C would continue to find him the closest vendor. But now those customers less than 5 steps to the right of *C*—people who used to be closest to vendor 2—will suddenly find themselves switching to vendor 1. Moving farther to the right will increase vendor 1's sales still further. Vendor 1 will maximize his sales by positioning himself as close as he can get to vendor 2 on the side of vendor 2 that is closer to the centre of the beach.

Vendor 2, of course, can reason in the same fashion, so his strategy will be perfectly symmetric: he will try to get as close to vendor 1 on the side of vendor 1 that is closest to the centre. And when both vendors behave in this fashion, the only stable outcome is for each to locate at *C*, the centre of the beach. At *C*, each gets half of the market, just as he did originally. But the average one-way distance that customers must travel is now $\frac{1}{4}$ km, twice what it was when the vendors were located at *A* and *B*.

Having both vendors at the middle of the beach is thus not optimal from the vantage point of customers, and yet neither vendor would be better off if he were to move unilaterally. The hot dog vendor location problem is thus not one of those cases in which Adam Smith's invisible hand guides resources so as to produce the greatest good for all.

Application: A Spatial Perspective on Political Competition

Hotelling's hot dog vendor location problem illuminates a commonly observed pattern of political competition. Let us suppose for simplicity that an election is being fought on a single policy issue, the level of expenditure on a particular government program. The electorate is uniformly distributed along a continuum between two extreme views: cut program expenditures by $5 million (−5) and increase program expenditures by $5 million (+5). The midpoint (0) represents the view that program expenditures should remain at their present level. Voters will vote for the party with the platform closest to their beliefs. We will assume that only two parties are contesting the election: the Anti-Policy Enterprise party (with an initial platform position at *A* in Figure 13-18) and the Bold Urban-Rural Partnership party, initially at *B*.

In order to win the election, each party must receive a majority of the votes cast. For this reason, like Hotelling's hot dog vendors, both parties have an incentive to "reinterpret" their policies in a way that shifts each closer to the centre of the political spectrum (to *A*′ and *B*′, respectively). They thereby hope to capture a share of the electorate on the other side of the centre point. The end result of this competitive political game is two political platforms that are virtually indistinguishable from each other.

Of course, to apply the model in the real world, we need to add some more realistic elements. In the first place, despite the tendencies to oversimplification that election campaigns often promote, virtually all elections involve many issues, not just one. Second,

FIGURE 13-18

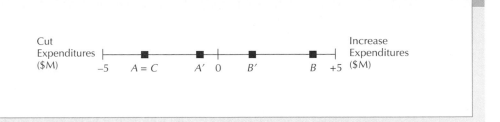

the parties in an election are not perfectly symmetrical, since one party has formed the government and (except in the case of a coalition government) the others haven't. Hence any election tends to involve two opposing sentiments: one is "Throw the rascals out," and the other is, "Better the devil you know than the devil you don't." Incumbent government party members tend to benefit from periods of prosperity, regardless of whether their policies contributed to that prosperity, while opposition parties can benefit from an economic downturn. Also, political scandals can damage the chances of government party members. Third, experience and administrative ability count, independently of policies: both government and opposition incumbents often benefit from this perception. Fourth, on occasion voters will vote for the "best" candidate, rather than along party lines.

A fifth factor is that regionalism often matters. Our initial model assumed that voters were *uniformly* distributed along the continuum in Figure 13-18. If the voters in one region are clustered to the left of the midpoint, however, while those of another region are clustered to the right, it is very difficult for a single party to dominate both regions. Finally, as each party moves closer to the centre, it runs the risk of alienating its hard-core supporters *and* of allowing space in the ideological spectrum for entry into the political market of new competing parties on its side of the continuum but farther from the centre of political indifference. One of the practical effects of this process can be seen using Figure 13-18. Suppose that as the APE party moves from A to A', its place at A is taken by a third (C) party. All voters to the left of A and half of those between *A* and *A'* will vote for the third party. The BURP party will take all the votes to the right of *B'* and half the votes between *B'* and *A'*, and the APE party will be squeezed in the middle. The BURP party will win the election because of this vote-splitting, but with only a plurality, less than 50 percent of the popular vote.

13.16 CONSUMER PREFERENCES AND ADVERTISING

In perfectly competitive markets it would never pay a producer to advertise her product. Being only one of many producers of identical products, the firm that advertised would attract only an insignificant share of any resulting increase in demand. In monopolistically competitive and oligopolistic markets, the incentives are different. Because products are differentiated, producers can often shift their demand curves outward significantly by advertising.

How does advertising affect the efficiency with which markets allocate resources? In the description of the world offered by rational choice theory, producers are essentially agents of consumers. Consumers vote with their purchase dollars, and producers are quick to do their bidding. This description has been called the *traditional sequence*, and Canadian-born Harvard economist John Kenneth Galbraith was one of its most prominent critics. In its place, he proposed a *revised sequence* in which the producer, not the consumer, sits in the driver's seat. In Galbraith's scheme, the corporation decides which products are cheapest and most convenient to produce, and then uses advertising and other promotional devices to create a demand for them.

Galbraith's revised sequence recasts Adam Smith's invisible hand in an unflattering new light. Smith's story, recall, was that producers motivated only by self-interest would provide the products that best meet consumers' desires. Those who behaved otherwise would fail to attract customers and go out of business. If Galbraith is correct, however, this story is turned on its head: it is like saying the all-too-visible hand of advertising guides consumers to serve the interests of large corporations.

Galbraith's revised sequence is not without intuitive appeal. Many people are understandably skeptical, for example, when an economist says that the purpose of advertising is to make consumers better informed. The plain fact, after all, is that this is often anything but its intent. TV ads featuring a pick-up hockey game in the middle of a busy street, or a rant that ends, "I am … Canadian," are not part of the process whereby we become more knowledgeable about the nutritional merits of beer consumption.

But for all the obvious hype in advertising messages, the Galbraith view of the process underweights the fact that it is easier to sell a good product than a bad one. All an advertisement can reasonably hope to accomplish is to induce the consumer to *try* the product. If it is one she tries and likes, she will probably buy it again and again. She will also recommend it to friends. If it is one she doesn't like, however, the process usually ends there. Even if a firm were to succeed in getting *everyone* to try it once, it still wouldn't necessarily be able to maintain a profitable, ongoing venture.

Imagine two alternative products, one that meets real human needs but is costly to produce, and another that meets no real need but is somewhat cheaper. Which of these two types would a profit-hungry producer do best to advertise? Given the importance of repeat business and word-of-mouth endorsements, the first will generally be more attractive. The fact that it costs more to produce will not deter consumers unless its extra benefits do not justify those extra costs.

New products usually go through extensive market testing before they ever land on the shelves. Millions of dollars are spent analyzing test subjects' reactions to them. In the end, most products that enter this testing process never see the light of day. Usually a firm requires concrete evidence that a product is likely to be well received before it commits the millions of dollars required for an intensive national advertising campaign. For this reason, as we saw in Chapter 6, a company's advertising sunk costs can serve as an indicator of quality, or at least of the company's *belief* that a product has sufficient quality to survive in the market.

The Galbraith argument has more weight when the products being advertised are not necessities, so that the "needs" they satisfy have a greater status or positional-goods component. *Want*-creation is a more likely possibility than *need*-creation, as many who have observed the process with young children watching the Saturday morning cartoon TV ads will testify. With fashions and fads, by definition repeat business is less important than with other products. In realms where success is a roll of the dice, often the biggest splash makes the waves. A similar logic underlies the practice of "fourwalling" new movies with saturation TV and Internet advertising, where the best 30 seconds of the movie (on occasion the *only* good 30 seconds of the movie) are set out as bait for those who "need" to see the movie when it first hits the theatres.

Advertising and other efforts to persuade consumers can be viewed as part of a pump-priming process. Given the enormous costs, it usually pays to promote products that consumers are likely to want to purchase repeatedly, or to speak well of to their friends. There is evidence that most firms follow precisely this strategy. Frozen-dinner producers tend to advertise their fancy entrées, not their chicken pot pies. Publishers advertise books that seem likely to become best-sellers, not their titles with more limited appeal.

Because producers have a greater incentive to advertise those products that consumers are most likely to find satisfying, the so-called traditional sequence is more plausible than Galbraith and other critics make it out to be. True enough, where the quality differences between competing goods are small, advertising may have a significant influence on which brand a consumer chooses. But as a first approximation, it still makes sense to assume that consumers have reasonably well-defined notions of what they like, and that producers spend much effort on trying to cater to those notions.

This is not to say, however, that market incentives lead to the amount of advertising that is best from society's point of view. As we saw earlier in this chapter, strategic competition between rivals may sometimes lead firms to spend excessively on advertising. In Appendix 13A, we discuss the strategy of creating "pseudo-variety," where advertising expenditure increases without a corresponding increase in consumer choice.

SUMMARY

- The characteristic feature of oligopolistic markets is interdependence among firms. In the Cournot model, each firm takes the quantities produced by its rivals as given; in the Bertrand model, in contrast, each firm takes its rivals' prices as given. Although the behavioural orientation of firms sounds very much the same in these two cases, the results are strikingly different. The Cournot model yields a slightly lower price and a slightly higher quantity than we would see if the firms colluded to achieve the monopoly outcome. In contrast, the Bertrand model leads to essentially the same outcome we saw under perfect competition.

- A slightly more sophisticated form of interdependence among firms is assumed in the Stackelberg model, in which one firm plays a leadership role and its rivals merely follow. This model is similar in structure to the Cournot model, except that where the Cournot firms took one another's quantities as given, the Stackelberg leader strategically manipulated the quantity decisions of its rivals.

- The interdependences among oligopolistic firms are often successfully analyzed using the mathematical theory of games. The four basic elements of any game are the players, the set of possible strategies, the payoff matrix, and the decision rule. A Nash equilibrium occurs when each player's strategy is optimal given the other player's choice of strategy. A strategy is called dominant if it is optimal no matter what strategy the other player chooses.

- The incentives facing firms who attempt to collude are similar to the ones facing participants in the prisoner's dilemma. The difficulty in holding cartels together is that the dominant strategy for each member is to cheat on the agreement. Repeated interactions between a very small number of firms can support collusive behaviour under circumstances in which strategies like tit-for-tat are effective.

- Incumbent firms may sometimes act strategically to deter potential rivals from entering their markets. Often this involves incurring higher costs or accepting lower prices than would otherwise be necessary.

- The basic idea of the theory of contestable markets is that when the cost of entry and exit is very low, the mere threat of entry can be sufficient to produce an allocation similar to the one we see under perfect competition. Critics of this theory have stressed that there are almost always nontrivial sunk costs associated with entry and exit, and that even small sunk costs leave considerable room for strategic entry deterrence.

- Monopolistic competition is defined by two simple conditions: (1) the existence of numerous firms each producing a product that is a close, but imperfect, substitute for the products of other firms; and (2) free entry and exit of firms. In the spatial model of monopolistic competition, customers have particular locations or product characteristics they most prefer. The result is that firms tend to compete most intensively for the business of products most similar to their own.

- A central feature of the spatial model of monopolistic competition is the tradeoff between the desire for lower cost, on the one hand, and greater variety or locational convenience, on the other. The optimum degree of product diversity depends on several factors. Greater diversity is expected with greater population density and higher transportation costs (where, in the general case, "transportation costs" measure willingness to pay for desired product features). Optimal product diversity is negatively related to the start-up costs of adding new product characteristics or locations. The market metes out a certain rough justice in that the costs of additional variety tend to be borne most heavily by those to whom variety is most important.

- Appendix 13A discusses entry and entry deterrence in more detail, and addresses the question of who pays for variety. The Web Supplement for Chapter 13 provides an expanded model of spatial competition.

QUESTIONS FOR REVIEW

1. What are the fundamental differences among the Cournot, Bertrand, and Stackelberg models of oligopoly?
2. How can the problem of oligopoly collusion be similar in structure to the prisoner's dilemma?
3. What are the difficulties that can arise with the tit-for-tat strategy as a possible solution to the oligopoly collusion problem?
4. Does the equilibrium in the Cournot model satisfy the definition of a Nash equilibrium?
5. What role does the assumption of sunk costs play in the theory of contestable markets?

6. Describe the tradeoff between cost and variety.
7. How is the optimal number of fast food restaurants in a city related to population density? To transportation cost? To the fixed costs per restaurant?
8. What is the difference between the dd and DD curves in the Chamberlinian model? Why is the former more elastic at any price?
9. Criticize the claim that monopolistic competition is inefficient because firms do not produce at the minimum points of their long-run average cost curves.

PROBLEMS

1. The market demand curve for mineral water is given by $P = 15 - Q$. If there are two firms that produce mineral water, each with no fixed cost and constant marginal cost of \$3 per unit, fill in the entries for each of the four duopoly models indicated in the table. (In the Stackelberg model, assume that firm 1 is the leader.)

Model	Q_1	Q_2	$Q_1 + Q_2$	P	Π_1	Π_2	$\Pi_1 + \Pi_2$
Shared monopoly							
Cournot							
Bertrand							
Stackelberg							

2. The market demand curve for a pair of Cournot duopolists is given as $P = 36 - 3Q$, where $Q = Q_1 + Q_2$. For each duopolist, the constant per unit marginal cost is \$18/unit and fixed costs are zero. Find the Cournot equilibrium price, quantity, and profits.

3. Solve the preceding problem for Bertrand duopolists.

4. Given the situation in Problem 2, find the equilibrium price, quantity, and profit for each firm, assuming the firms act as a Stackelberg leader and follower, with firm 1 as the leader.

5. Because of their unique expertise with explosives, the Zambino brothers have long enjoyed a monopoly of the Canadian market for public fireworks displays for crowds of 50,000 or more people. The annual demand for these fireworks displays is $P = 140 - Q$. The marginal cost of putting on a fireworks display is $20, and fixed costs are zero. A family dispute split the firm in two. Alfredo Zambino now runs one firm and Luigi Zambino runs the other. They still have the same marginal costs, but now they are Cournot duopolists. How much profit has the family lost?

*6. Augie and Corinne are mineral spring duopolists facing a market demand given by the equation $P = 24 - Q$. Fixed costs are zero for both, but Augie has a constant marginal cost of $6 per unit, while Corinne's marginal cost is zero.
  a. If they both behave as Cournot duopolists, give the equations for the two reaction curves, equilibrium levels of output, the market price, the profits of each, and the value of consumer surplus.
  b. Suppose instead that they both behave as noncooperative Bertrand duopolists, and calculate the market price, the levels of output and profits of each, and the value of consumer surplus.
  c. If Corinne could effectively bribe Augie to shut down his production completely, regardless of the market price, so that she supplied the entire market, what is the maximum amount she would be willing to pay? What is the minimum amount he would accept?

7. Suppose A and B know that they will interact in a noncommunicating prisoner's dilemma exactly four times. Explain why the tit-for-tat strategy will not be an effective means for assuring cooperation.

8. Firm 1 and firm 2 are automobile producers. Each has the option of producing either a big car or a small car. The payoffs to each of the four possible combinations of choices are as given in the following payoff matrix. Each firm must make its choice without knowing what the other has chosen.

		Firm 1	
		Big car	**Small car**
Firm 2	**Big car**	$\Pi_1 = 400$ $\Pi_2 = 400$	$\Pi_1 = 800$ $\Pi_2 = 1000$
	Small car	$\Pi_1 = 1000$ $\Pi_2 = 800$	$\Pi_1 = 500$ $\Pi_2 = 500$

  a. Does either firm have a dominant strategy?
  b. There are two Nash equilibria for this game. Identify them.

9. Suppose we have the same payoff matrix as in Problem 8 except now firm 1 gets to move first and knows that firm 2 will see the results of this choice before deciding which type of car to build.
  a. Draw the game tree for this sequential game.
  b. What is the Nash equilibrium for this game? Is it better to move first or second?

10. The government has announced its plans to license two firms to serve a market whose demand curve is given by $P = 100 - Q$. The technology is such that each can produce any given level of output at zero cost, but once each firm's output is chosen, it cannot be altered.
  a. What is the most you would be willing to pay for one of these licences if you knew you would be able to choose your level of output first (assuming your choice was observable by the rival firm)?
  b. How much would your rival be willing to pay for the right to choose second?

**11. Firm 1 and firm 2 are competing for a cable television licence. The present value of the net revenues generated by the licence is equal to R. Each firm's probability of winning the licence is given by its proportion of the total spent by the two firms on lobbying the CRTC. That is, if I_1 and I_2 represent the lobbying expenditures of firms 1 and 2, respectively, then firm 1's probability of winning is given by $I_1/(I_1 + I_2)$, while firm 2's probability of winning is $I_2/(I_1 + I_2)$. If each firm assumes that the other firm's spending is independent of its own, what is the equilibrium level of spending for each firm?

For Problems 12 to 15, state whether the proposition is true or false and briefly explain why.

12. A Chamberlinian monopolistically competitive firm in long-run equilibrium will always produce on a downward-sloping portion of its long-run average cost curve.

13. If a new firm enters a Chamberlinian industry with 30 incumbent firms and all, including the entrant, charge the same price, then all firms will sell $\frac{1}{31}$ of the total industry output.

14. The existing firms in a Chamberlinian industry are currently earning economic profits at the short-run equilibrium price. The long-run equilibrium price will necessarily be lower than the current price.

15. If a business owner is delighted to accept additional orders at the current price, he or she cannot have been a profit-maximizing, perfectly competitive producer.

**16. The government is planning to license garages for tow trucks along a 100-km circular highway. Each garage has a fixed cost of $5000. Towing jobs are equally likely along any point of the highway and cost *per kilometre towed* is $50. If there were 2500 towing jobs per day, what number of equally spaced garages would minimize the sum of the fixed costs and towing costs?

17. The 1000 residents of Great Donut Island are all fishermen. Every morning they go to the nearest port to launch their fishing boats and then return in the evening with their catch. The residents are evenly distributed along the 10-km perimeter of the island. Each port has a fixed cost of $1000/day. If the optimal number of ports is exactly 2, what must be the per-kilometre travel cost?

ANSWERS TO IN-CHAPTER EXERCISES

13-1.

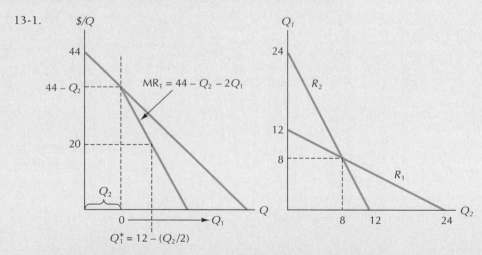

13-2. Price will settle at marginal cost, and so P = $2/unit. The corresponding market demand, $Q = 8$, will be shared equally by the two firms: $Q_1 = Q_2 = 4$ units.

13-3. Let firm 1 be the Stackelberg leader. Firm 2's marginal revenue curve is given by $10 - Q_1 - 2Q_2$. Setting MR = MC = 2, we have firm 2's reaction function, $R_2(Q_1) = Q_2^* = 4 - (Q_1/2)$. Substituting into firm 1's demand function, we get $P_1 = 10 - Q_1 - 4 + (Q_1/2) = 6 - (Q_1/2)$, and the corresponding marginal review curve, $MR_1 = 6 - Q_1$. $MR_1 = MC = 2$ solves for $Q_1^* = 4$ units. This means that Q_2 will be 2 units, for a total market output of 6 units. The market price will be $10 - 6 = $4/unit.

13-4. Regardless of firm 1's strategy, firm 2 does best with a big research budget. The choice of a big research budget is thus a dominant strategy for firm 2. Firm 1 does not have a dominant strategy. If firm 2 chooses a low research budget, then firm 1 does best by choosing a low research budget. But if firm 2 chooses a high research budget, then firm 1 does best by choosing a high research budget. Since firm 1 can predict that firm 2 will choose a high research budget, firm 1's best strategy is to choose a high research budget. The combination of "High research budget—High research budget" is a Nash equilibrium.

13-5. Each firm initially got $\frac{1}{20}$ = 5 percent of total demand, but will now get only $\frac{1}{25}$ = 4 percent. This means that at every price, the quantity demanded will be 20 percent lower than before (see the graph below). The new *dd* curve is $P = 10 - .00125Q$.

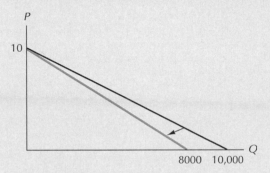

13-6. With six restaurants the average round-trip distance is $\frac{1}{12}$ km, which yields an average transportation cost of $2. On average, each restaurant will attract 100/6 people per day, which yields an ATC of [50 + 5(100/6)]/(100/6) = $8/day. Overall average cost with six restaurants is thus $10/day.

13-7. N^* will now be $\sqrt{[(24)(400)/100]} \approx 9.8$, so there should now be 10 restaurants.

Appendix 13A

ADDITIONAL MODELS OF OLIGOPOLY AND MONOPOLISTIC COMPETITION

13A.1 COMPETITION WHEN THERE ARE INCREASING RETURNS TO SCALE

Consider the case of a duopoly in an industry with increasing returns to scale. How would two firms survive in such an industry, whose cost conditions make it a natural monopoly? It is easy enough to imagine two firms starting out at an early stage of a new product's development, each serving a largely different segment of the market. But now suppose the industry has matured, and a single, nationwide market exists for the product. Should we expect that one firm will drive the other out of business and take over the role of natural monopolist? And if so, what price will it charge?

To make our discussion concrete, suppose that the technology is one with constant marginal cost and declining average total cost, as shown in Figure 13A-1. For simplicity, suppose that the size of the total market is fixed at Q_0. With two identical firms in the industry, each producing half that amount, average cost is AC'. If there were only one firm, its average cost would only be AC_0. By what process do we expect that one firm might eliminate the other?

One obvious strategy for the two firms would be to merge. Rather than having both firms incur the fixed costs represented by the rectangle $(AC' - MC) \times Q_0/2 = (AC_0 - MC) \times Q_0$, a single merged firm could over time eliminate the duplicated facilities and produce at Q_0, at lower total cost. The Competition Act and federal government policy, however, usually restrict such strategies, because of concerns regarding the economic and social effects of increased industrial concentration. The government's December 1998 rejection of the mergers that had been proposed between the Bank of Montreal and the Royal Bank and between the Toronto-Dominion and the Canadian Imperial Bank of Commerce was justified by the government in these terms. It adopted a similar stance toward the subsequent bank merger talks of 2002.

Yet on December 21, 1999, the Competition Bureau of the federal government did approve Air Canada's takeover of Canadian Airlines. The two airlines *were* close to being duopolists in relation to domestic air transport, and the degree of concentration that resulted from their merger was much higher than would have been the case in the financial sector had the bank mergers been permitted. Was the government being inconsistent? Not necessarily. In the situation depicted in Figure 13A-1, there is a social tradeoff between the efficiency gains resulting from a merger and the efficiency losses due to increased monopoly power after the merger.

There were a number of differences between the two sets of mergers: differences in the regulatory environments of the two industries; in the perceived economies of scale expected from the mergers; and in the financial health of the firms involved. The banks were earning substantial

Sharing a Market with Increasing Returns
With two firms in the market, costs are higher than with one. Yet there may be no tendency for one firm to drive the other out of business.

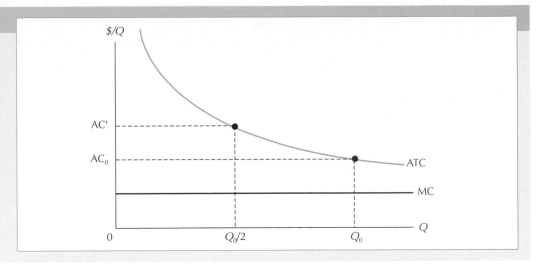

profits when they proposed their mergers, whereas Canadian Airlines in particular was experiencing difficulties related to its high debt load and its smaller market share. There was a legitimate concern that a period of extended cutthroat competition (of the sort described immediately below) could cause substantial bleeding, a weakening of the financial health of the sector as a whole, and disruptions in the provision of essential air transport services. Yet even though the government decided that on balance the airline merger was beneficial, it imposed a number of conditions and performance guarantees on Air Canada before the airline merger was allowed, and also stated that it was prepared to consider greater competition from foreign carriers on domestic routes.

Interestingly, after the merger there was a sharp increase in the number of passenger complaints about airline service. Some increase in complaints would be expected as the normal result of transitional reorganization. Both the government and the airline, however, had strong incentives to minimize the number of complaints, at least in the short run. Paying the same amount for lower-quality service is effectively the same as a price hike, and one of the conditions for permitting the merger was that Air Canada not use its near-monopoly position to penalize consumers. Several factors have made it difficult to achieve a balanced assessment of the effects of the Air Canada merger. The global airline industry was going through a slow stretch in the postmerger period, even before the September 11, 2001, terrorist attacks. The attacks, which drastically reduced the volume of air travel and increased the growth rate of alternatives like teleconferencing, affected not just Air Canada but all passenger airlines. In addition, Air Canada has faced new forms of competition domestically and internationally. It will therefore likely take several years more before a full assessment of the degree of success of the merger can be achieved.

Suppose, however, that the government refused to allow a merger, and that we abstract from regulatory considerations. What alternative possibilities could emerge? One of the firms could announce a pre-emptive price cut, hoping to drive the other out of business. Suppose, for example, that it charges AC_0, what its average cost would be if in fact its strategy proved successful. How will its rival respond? It can either match the price cut and again split the market or refuse and sell nothing. Since its marginal cost is less than AC_0, it will do better by matching. At that price, however, both firms will lose money; and if the price holds, it is just a matter of time before one of them goes out of business. It might take a long time, though, and even the surviving firm could suffer substantial losses in the interim.

More important, from the perspective of the firm considering whether to initiate a price cut, if the firms are identical duopolists, there is no assurance that it would be the one to survive. So if we view the decision from the point of view of the firm, initiating a price war looks like a very risky proposition indeed. Without the threat of entry, it is easy to see why a live-and-let-live strategy might be compellingly attractive.

But let us suppose, for the sake of discussion, that one firm does somehow manage to capture the entire market, and suppose further that potential entrants face substantial sunk costs if they enter this market. Will the surviving firm then be free to charge the monopoly price? In Chapter 13, we examined the monopolist's limit-price/limit-output strategy. Now let us look at the problem from a different perspective.

For the same reasons that a duopolist would be reluctant to initiate a price war, an outsider would be wary about entering the industry to face a possibly ruinous battle with the incumbent firm. It may be possible, though, for an outside firm to write contracts with buyers. If it offered a lower price than the incumbent firm, it could then assure itself of the entire market. But an outside firm realizes that it would be in the interest of the incumbent to match or beat any price it could offer. The potential entrant, after all, must charge enough to cover its prospective sunk costs if entry into the market is to be profitable, whereas the incumbent need only cover its variable costs. Of course, the incumbent would be delighted to cover *all* its costs. But rather than be driven from the market, it would be rational for the incumbent to accept a price that just barely covered its variable costs.

Because of this asymmetry, it will never pay a new firm to take the initiative to enter a natural monopolist's market (unless the new firm happens, for some reason, to have a substantial cost advantage). Any money it spent on market surveys, contract negotiations, and the like would be lost as soon as the incumbent made a better offer, which it would always be in the incumbent's interest to do.

There is one remaining avenue along which the threat of entry might serve to discipline an incumbent natural monopolist. Although it would never pay a potential entrant to incur expenses to try to penetrate this type of market, it might very well pay *buyers* in the market to bear the expense of approaching a potential entrant. If the buyers absorb this expense, they can again expect that the incumbent will agree to offer a competitive price on the product. (If the incumbent does not, they can simply sign an agreement to buy from the outside firm.) So if it is practical for buyers to act collectively at their own expense to negotiate with potential entrants, even an incumbent natural monopolist may be forced to sell at close to a competitive price. By way of illustration, as we noted in Appendix 6A, most local governments act as purchasing agents for their communities by negotiating contracts with potential monopoly suppliers of community services or by calling for tenders where a number of firms are competing to become the monopoly supplier.

In markets for privately sold goods, buyers are often too numerous to organize themselves to act collectively in this fashion. Few people want to go to a town meeting every night to discuss negotiations with potential suppliers of countless different products. Where it is impractical for buyers to organize direct collective action, it may nonetheless be possible for private agents to accomplish much the same objective on their behalf.

Certain department stores and supermarket chains might be interpreted as acting in this role. The Hudson's Bay Company was founded in 1670 as a fur trading venture, and its first retail store, built in Winnipeg in 1881, was still attached to a fur storage warehouse. By the twentieth century, however, like Eaton's and Simpson's (both casualties of the competitive wars), its primary business was the provision of retail consumer goods. Its function was to act as a purchasing agent for the community, negotiating contracts with single-source suppliers. It earned a reputation for driving hard bargains with these suppliers and for passing at least some of the savings along to its customers. The growth in market share of "store" brands (such as the Bay's "Beaumark" brand, Canadian Tire's "Motomaster" and "Mastercraft" products, and the "No Name" and "President's Choice" lines pioneered by Loblaw's) represents another means of strengthening the market leverage of department store, automotive and home improvement, and grocery retailers. Large retail chains can use their market power to strike favourable deals with potential suppliers: "If you want us to stock your brand name products, you will provide us with equivalent, competitive products under the *chain's* brand name. If you can't deliver, we'll find another supplier that can." Why should these retail chains pass the resultant savings along in the form of lower prices? Merchants are in competition with one another not only for the sale of products produced by natural monopolists, but for an enormous list of competitively produced products as well. To have a reputation for delivering quality merchandise at reasonable prices is an essential element in the marketing strategies of many of these merchants, and consumers are potentially the ultimate beneficiaries.

13A.2 PAYING FOR VARIETY

Variety, as we have seen, is costly. Many critics claim that market economies serve up wastefully high degrees of product variety. Wouldn't the world be a better place, these critics ask, if we had a simpler array of products to choose from, each costing less than the highly specific models we see today? The extra costs of product variety may indeed seem an unnecessary burden imposed on consumers who neither desire nor can easily afford it. Here we should distinguish between *genuine* variety and "pseudo-variety." The latter is exemplified by the case of laundry detergents, where detergents with *identical* formulas have been sold by a single manufacturer under different brand names, with different packaging, in the same markets. Both brands require substantial advertising expenditure, and to the extent that there are fixed costs of marketing, we can reinterpret Figure 13A-1 as saying that two brands, each selling $Q_0/2$ boxes of the identical soap, cost more than one brand selling Q_0 boxes.

Why would companies waste resources in this way? Part of the answer was provided by an Imperial Tobacco executive in an interview with one of the authors. A woman had written to Imperial complaining about a Player's cigarette ad, and saying that as a protest she had switched to smoking Matinée. Since Imperial manufactured *both* brands, her protest was likely not as devastating to the company as she had hoped. If brand loyalty declines in importance as a determinant of consumer behaviour, and brand switching and experimentation increase, it may pay a company to engage in *brand proliferation*, even if there are *no* discernible differences among its brands except for packaging and advertising. In this way, the company increases the probability that consumers switching from a competitor's brand *or* from one of its own brands will switch *to* one of its own brands.

The provision of multiple brands characterized by pseudo-variety may be an effective strategy for the corporation, in preserving or increasing its *aggregate* market share. The pseudo-variety strategy, however, entails two types of cost that are socially inefficient. First, there are the excess fixed marketing costs that we noted above. Second, in the absence of perfect information about the characteristics of each brand, brand proliferation based on pseudo-variety tends to increase consumers' search costs *without* actually increasing their real range of choice. These additional search costs represent a socially inefficient use of resources. Even when the variety is *genuine*, and not merely pseudo-variety, the increase in search costs that accompanies an increase in the range of choice is a real cost that needs to be deducted from the benefits of greater choice.

The critics' case is strongest in relation to pseudo-variety, and is not without merit even with genuine variety, if search costs are high. Yet notwithstanding their arguments, increased variety is generally treated as a "good thing," and in more detailed models of spatial competition than those we have developed, the problems mentioned above are potentially less serious.

In our simple model, we assumed that each buyer faced the same unit transportation cost. This assumption is unrealistic even in models where the only dimension of variety is geographic location. Buyers who own automobiles, for example, will have lower transportation costs than those who don't; likewise, buyers whose time is worth little, in opportunity cost terms, have lower transportation costs than those whose time is more valuable. The issue is the same for product variety. Those who care a lot about special product features will have higher "transport costs" than those who do not, which means simply that people in the former group are willing to pay more than others for a product whose special features suit their particular tastes.

It is also true, as a general proposition, that the demand for variety increases sharply with income. In the language of Chapter 4, variety is a luxury, not a necessity. The association between income and the demand for variety plays a pivotal role in the way most producers market their products. To illustrate, consider the array of automobiles offered by General Motors, ranging from the subcompact Chevrolet Cavalier to the full-sized Cadillac Seville. All these cars incorporate a variety of specialized features, which are the result of costly research and development. The research and development costs are largely fixed, which gives rise to a substantial scale economy in the production of cars. If GM (or any other company) could sell more cars in a given year, it could produce each of them at a lower cost.

When marginal cost lies below average cost, it is not possible to charge each buyer a price equal to marginal cost and still earn a normal profit. (Recall from Chapter 10 that a firm's average cost includes a normal rate of profit.) As we saw in Chapter 12, the firm with a scale economy has an incentive to expand its market by setting price close to marginal cost if it can do that without altering its prices on existing sales. But we also saw that if some buyers pay prices below average cost, others must pay prices above it.

The car manufacturer's response to this situation is to set the prices of its better models above average cost, while pricing its lesser models below average cost. Panels (*a*) and (*b*) in Figure 13A-2, for example, show the cost and demand conditions for Chevrolets and Cadillacs, respectively. The marginal cost of producing a Cadillac is only slightly higher than that of producing a Chevrolet.

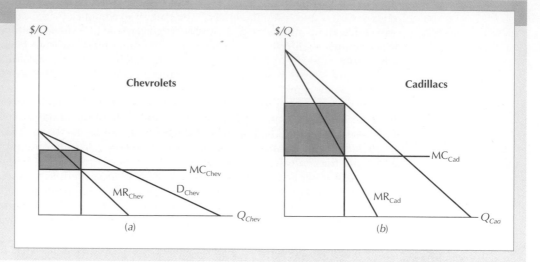

The basic design innovations are available to the company for both cars, and the hardware produced for the Cadillac is only slightly more costly than that used in the Chevrolet. But because the buyers who care most about variety are willing to pay much more for a Cadillac than for a Chevrolet, the company can set sharply different prices for the two models. In an average year, the surplus of total revenue above variable cost for all models (which is the sum of the two shaded rectangles in Figure 13A-2) is enough to cover the company's research and development and other fixed costs.

Variety is costly, just as the critics claim. But the cost of variety is not distributed evenly among all buyers. In the example above, it was paid by the buyers of Cadillacs, not by the buyers of Chevrolets. By the same token, people who buy the Saab 9-3 Sedan enjoy almost all the important advantages of the extensive Saab research program for about $6000 less than the people who buy the 9-3 SE Sedan. Even by the yardstick used by some critics of the market system, this seems a better outcome than the one they urge, which is that all buyers have a standardized "people's car." Under current marketing arrangements, people who don't place high value on variety get to enjoy it at the expense of those who care most about having it. The alternative would be to deny variety to the people who care most about it, without producing real cost savings for the buyers who would be satisfied with a standardized product. Even Volkswagen, which once touted the virtues of a single, standardized model, now offers several dozen versions of its Golf, Jetta, and Passat lines, as well as the revived "Beetle with a price tag."

Similar pricing strategies affect recovery of the costs of variety in virtually every industry. Consider again the restaurant industry. In a city in which most people had cars, and where there was no problem parking, the cheapest way to provide restaurant meals could be to have a single restaurant with only one item on the menu. An army of chefs would labour over gigantic cauldrons of peas and mashed potatoes, while others operated huge ovens filled with roasting chickens. But people don't want the same meal every night, any more than they all want the same kind of car. Even in smaller cities like Guelph, Ontario, there are Indian, Mexican, Lebanese, Chinese, Japanese, Korean, Greek, Italian, French, Vietnamese, and Hungarian restaurants in addition to the usual fare and fast-food chains.

How are the extra costs of all this variety apportioned? Most restaurants price the different items on their menus in differing multiples of marginal cost. Alcoholic beverages, desserts, and coffee, in particular, are almost always priced at several times marginal cost, whereas the markup on most entrées is much smaller. Many restaurants also offer some daily specials, entrées that are priced very close to marginal cost. The result is that the diner who wants to economize on the cost of eating out, either because he has low income or for whatever other reason, will order only the basic meal, taking before-dinner drinks and dessert and coffee at home (or doing without those extras). Such diners end up paying a price not much more than the marginal cost of being served. Other diners who are willing or able to do so will purchase the more costly option of having the entire package at the restaurant. The diners who pursue the latter strategy are much more likely than others to be the ones who feel strongly about variety (again, because the demand for variety is strongly linked to income). Under current marketing arrangements, they are the ones who end up paying most of its cost. Those who care less about variety are still able to enjoy a lamb vindaloo dinner one night and Szechuan chicken the next; and if they don't order drinks and dessert, they pay little more than they would have to in a standardized soup kitchen.

As a final illustration of how the costs of variety are apportioned in monopolistically competitive markets, consider the case of airline ticket pricing. As discussed earlier, the important dimension of variety here is the timing of flights. Not all travellers have equally pressing demands for frequently scheduled flights. Some are willing to pay substantially extra for a slightly earlier departure time, while others would wait a week rather than pay even $5 more. To the extent that airlines use smaller, more costly (per seat) aircraft in order to offer more frequent flights, it is to accommodate the needs of the former group.

Who pays the added costs of the smaller flights? Virtually every airline employs the hurdle model of differential pricing described in Chapter 12. One variant the airlines use offers discounts of up to 50 percent to passengers who satisfy two restrictions: (1) they must buy their tickets in advance, usually at least seven days before flight time; and (2) their journey must include a Saturday night. The effect of these two restrictions together is to eliminate most travellers who demand maximum travel flexibility. In particular, business travellers, whose schedules tend to be much tighter than those of vacation travellers, almost always end up paying the regular coach fare under the current marketing system. In contrast, very few vacation travellers fail to qualify for at least some form of discount.

A second, related, pricing-strategy variant that airlines use to increase their "load factors" (the ratio of total passenger air-miles travelled to capacity passenger air-miles) underlies the growth of "last-minute" clubs. If a particular flight has a substantial number of unsold seats on a particular flight a few days before departure, a proportion of those seats will be made available at a discount via last-minute clubs. Here the hurdle the passengers face is the uncertainty about getting a flight to a particular destination on a particular day. For passengers who just want to go "somewhere, anywhere" for a particular period, or who have some flexibility in their departure date to a particular destination, substantial savings are possible. Internet airfare "comparison-shopping" sites lower the search costs for such passengers (as well as providing additional competition to traditional travel agencies).

If it is largely the scheduling demands of business travellers that dictate the use of smaller, more costly aircraft, this apportioning of the costs appears not only fair but also efficient. Discount tickets enable airlines to attract passengers who would not fly otherwise, and these passengers make possible the use of larger, less costly aircraft. Business travellers end up getting the frequent service they want, and leisure travellers are not forced to pay the added costs of it.[1]

As the above examples suggest, it is often the case that the costs of variety are borne primarily by those who attach a premium to variety, and that those who are less concerned with variety can largely escape these costs. We have also seen that the arguments of critics of "excessive" brand-proliferation do have some merit, particularly when "pseudo-variety" is involved. It is possible to generate formal models in which monopolistic competition results in excessive variety, and others in which it does not.

There is, however, one further consideration that needs to be weighed in the balance. In the real world, new varieties of products are often the result of research and development, the outcome of which is very difficult to predict in advance. If we froze the existing models of automobiles in place forever, it might very well be true that we would be better off with fewer varieties. But the process that leads to these varieties has stimulated extraordinary technological innovation, with application to the production of not only new kinds of cars, but also a host of other products. The costs and fruits of this innovation would have to be accounted for in a more complete comparison of optimal and equilibrium amounts of variety.

---

[1]For a more detailed discussion of this issue, see R. Frank, "When Are Price Differentials Discriminatory?" *Journal of Policy Analysis and Management*, 2, Winter 1983: 238–255.

1. In a world where all consumers had perfect information about the characteristics of all products, would the costs of brand-proliferation based on pseudo-variety still exist? Would firms have any incentive to provide pseudo-variety? Explain.
2. How does the hurdle model of differential pricing affect the distribution of the cost of variety among different buyers?

PROBLEMS

**1. Two mineral water vendors, A and B, occupy fixed locations at opposite ends of a 1-km beach:

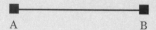

   There are 1000 people distributed uniformly over the beach and each person buys one bottle of mineral water from the vendor whose inclusive price (money price plus round-trip transportation cost) is lowest. Unit transportation cost is equal to $.25 per kilometre. If the marginal cost of mineral water is zero, and A is committed to charge a money price of $1 per bottle, what is the profit-maximizing price for B?

2. A patent monopolist has a total cost curve given by $TC = 40 + 6Q$. If $P = 20 - Q$, what are her profit-maximizing price and quantity?

3. Now the monopolist's patent expires and potential entrants have access to the formerly patented technology. Because of the original firm's experience, however, the cost curves of potential entrants lie above that of the incumbent. If each of these cost curves is given by $TC' = 40 + 7Q$, if there are no sunk costs in production or entry, and if no firm is able to price-discriminate, what will be the new equilibrium level of output and price?

4. How, if at all, will your answer to the preceding problem be different if the fixed cost of 40 in each firm's cost function is now a sunk cost incurred on entry?

For Problems 5 and 6, state whether the proposition is true or false and briefly explain why.

*5. Price discrimination can never survive in the long run in a market in which there are complete freedom of entry and exit and no sunk costs associated with movements into and out of the market.

6. If there are economies of scale in the production of each model of automobile, then the poor would pay much less for their cars if we produced many fewer models than we do now.

Part 4

FACTOR MARKETS

CHAPTER 14:   Labour

CHAPTER 15:   Capital

In these two chapters we examine the workings of markets for productive inputs. In Chapter 14 we see that although the labour market behaves like the market for ordinary goods and services in many respects, in other important ways it is very different. Chapter 15 discusses the markets for real and financial capital. One feature that sets capital apart from other inputs, we shall see, is that while other inputs are usually hired on a period-by-period basis, capital equipment is often owned outright by the firm.

Chapter 14

LABOUR

In 1999, as Prime Minister of Canada, Jean Chrétien earned under $300,000 in salary and benefits, excluding his accommodation at 24 Sussex Drive. In the same year, comedian Jim Carrey is estimated to have earned over $65 million, or about 237 times what the prime minister made. Some would say the difference just means that Jim Carrey was 237 times as funny as the prime minister, although others might disagree. The 1999 earnings estimate for Shania Twain was in the neighbourhood of $72 million, about 250 times what the Prime Minister earned, but of course that year she had more hits than he did.

Productivity differences, however measured, cannot wholly account for pay differences among workers. For example, there is considerable movement of employees back and forth between the public and private sectors. Almost invariably, highly productive persons earn substantially less when they move from the private to the public sector. Then why move? The public sector offers some people the opportunity to shape the broad direction of social and economic policy, others the trappings of power, still others the satisfaction of public service. The package, taken as a whole, must be sufficiently attractive to compensate for the drop in pay.

Entertainers like Shania Twain and Jim Carrey would very likely have continued working even if they had been paid substantially less than they were in 1999. Céline Dion, however, earned an estimated $64.5 million in 1999, but decided not to give any concerts during 2000, so that she could concentrate on producing a son, René Charles, born on January 25, 2001. She made a conscious choice between labour and labour.

CHAPTER PREVIEW

Our goal in this chapter is to examine the economic forces that govern wages and other conditions of employment. Relatively simple models of the labour market shed light on a variety of interesting questions, such as: How much will a worker with a given set of skills earn? Why do working conditions differ from one occupation to another? What do unions do? And so on.

We begin by deriving the demand curve for labour in both the short run and long run. We then approach the supply side of the labour market from the standpoint of an individual worker trying to decide how much to work at a given wage rate.

We then apply the economic theory of labour markets to such topics as unions, discrimination, and minimum wage laws. We conclude by looking at why differences in pay sometimes seem to overstate differences in productivity.

14.1 THE PERFECTLY COMPETITIVE FIRM'S SHORT-RUN DEMAND FOR LABOUR

Consider a firm that produces output by the use of two inputs, capital (K) and labour (L). Suppose that in the short run, its capital stock is fixed. If this firm sells all its output in a perfectly competitive market at the going market price, and if it can hire any quantity of labour it wishes at a wage rate of $12/labour-day, how many units of labour should it hire?

If the manager of the firm is thinking like an economist, she will reason as follows: "The benefit of hiring an extra unit of labour will be the amount for which I can sell the extra output I will get. The cost will be the wage rate. Thus I should hire an extra unit of labour as long as the former exceeds the latter. If the latter exceeds the former, however, I should reduce the amount of labour I hire."

This reasoning is easily translated into a simple graphical hiring rule. Figure 14-1*a* shows the marginal product curve for the labour input when capital is fixed (see Chapter 9). The marginal product curve, recall, tells how much extra output the firm will get when it hires an extra labour-day. For example, when there are 40 labour-days employed, hiring an extra unit will yield 8 units of output. The downward slope of the marginal product curve reflects the law of diminishing returns.

Figure 14-1*b* simply multiplies the marginal product curve by the price of output, here $P = \$2$ per unit. The product of output price and marginal product, $P \times MP_L$, is called the **value of the marginal product of labour**—denoted VMP_L, which is the extra revenue the firm will get by selling the extra output produced by the extra unit of labour. *The hiring rule for the firm is to choose that amount of labour for which the wage rate is equal to the VMP_L.* In Figure 14-1*b*, the rule thus tells the firm it should hire 80 labour-days per day when the wage rate is $12/labour-day.

Value of marginal product (VMP) The value, at current market prices, of the extra output produced by an additional unit of input.

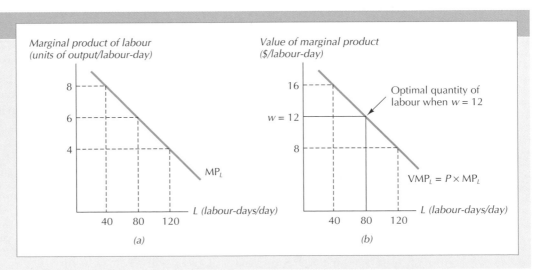

FIGURE 14-1

The Competitive Firm's Short-Run Demand for Labour
When the wage rate is $12/labour-day and the output price is $2/unit (panel *b*), the perfectly competitive firm will hire 80 labour-days per day, the amount for which VMP$_L$ and the wage rate are the same.

To illustrate the logic of the rule, suppose that the firm had instead hired only 40 labour-days. At that level of employment, the value of extra output produced by an extra worker ($16) is greater than the cost of hiring the worker ($12), and so the firm can increase its profit by hiring more workers. Alternatively, suppose that the firm had hired 120 labour-days. VMP_L at $L = 120$ labour-days is only $8/labour-day, which is less than the wage rate of $12/labour-day, and so the firm can increase its profit by discharging workers. Only at $L = 80$ labour-days per day will the firm be unable to take additional steps to increase its profit.[1] Figure 14-1a is drawn for $\text{MP}_L = 10 - (\frac{1}{20})L$. When $P = \$2$ per unit of output, the value of the marginal product of labour, depicted in Figure 14-1b, is

$$\text{VMP}_L = P(\text{MP}_L) = 2(10 - \frac{1}{20}L) = 20 - \frac{1}{10}L.$$

If the wage is $w = \$12$/labour-day, then the quantity of labour demanded by the firm can be calculated as follows:

$$w = \text{VMP}_L \Rightarrow 12 = 20 - \frac{1}{10}L \Rightarrow 8 = \frac{1}{10}L \Rightarrow L^* = 80 \text{ labour-days per day.}$$

EXERCISE 14-1

At a wage rate of $12/labour-day, how many labour-days per day would the firm shown in Figure 14-1 hire if its product sold not for $2 per unit but for $3 per unit?

14.2 THE PERFECTLY COMPETITIVE FIRM'S LONG-RUN DEMAND FOR LABOUR

In the short run, the only way for the firm to respond to a reduction in the wage rate is to hire more labour. In the long run, however, all inputs are completely variable. As we saw in Chapter 9, a reduction in the price of labour will cause the firm to substitute labour for capital, reducing its marginal cost still further. This additional cost reduction will cause an even greater expansion of output than before. It follows that the firm's long-run hiring response to a change in the wage rate will be larger than its short-run response. The relationship between the two labour demand curves is portrayed in Figure 14-2.

The firm's demand for labour will also tend to be more elastic the more elastic the demand is for its product. If a price reduction stimulates a large increase in the quantity of the product demanded, it will also stimulate a large increase in the amount of labour required to produce it. Finally, the firm's demand for labour will tend to be more elastic the more it is able to substitute the services of labour for those of other inputs. Other things equal, the firm with L-shaped isoquants will have the least elastic demand curve for labour.

---

[1] There is one important limitation to the application of the $w = \text{VMP}_L$ rule. Suppose the wage rate were above the value of the average product of labour, which is the product of price and the average product of labour, denoted VAP_L. If the firm pays a wage rate higher than VAP_L, its labour costs alone will exceed the total value of what workers produce, which means that it incurs a loss on each worker it hires. For values of w above VAP_L then, the perfectly competitive firm will demand no labour at all. The condition $\text{VAP}_L \geq w$ is equivalent to the condition with which we are already familiar, that $P \geq \text{AVC}$ or else the firm should shut down in the short run. See Chapter 11 footnote 4 (page 398), Equations 10.18 and 10.19 (page 359), and Figures 10–9 and 11–4 (pages 360 and 397, respectively).

FIGURE 14-2

Short- and Long-Run Demand Curves for Labour
The demand for labour is more elastic in the long run because the firm has the opportunity to substitute labour for capital. In the short run, its only avenue of response is to increase output.

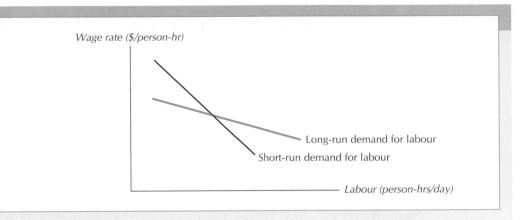

14.3 THE MARKET DEMAND CURVE FOR LABOUR

Recall from Chapter 5 that the technique for deriving a market demand curve for a product is to add the individual consumer demand curves horizontally. The technique for generating the market demand curve for labour is similar except for one important difference. In Figure 14-3, the curve labelled ΣVMP_L, $P = P_1$ is the horizontal summation of the individual VMP_L curves when the output price is equal to P_1. At that value of the price of output, firms taken as a whole demand L_1 units of labour per time period when the wage rate is equal to w_1. Now let the wage rate fall to w_2. Each firm will hire more labour, in the process moving downward along its own individual demand curve for labour. As each firm responds in this way, it offers more of its product for sale in the market. Such action by any one firm in a competitive market would leave the price of output unchanged. But the effect of all firms acting in concert is to produce a downward movement along the industry product demand curve.

This increase in output will necessarily involve a reduction in output price. And in turn this will cause the VMP_L curve for each firm to shift downward. If output price falls from P_1 to P_2, the aggregate demand for labour will be given by the point that corresponds to w_2 on the curve labelled ΣVMP_L, $P = P_2$. By this reasoning, we see that the

FIGURE 14-3

The Market Demand Curve for Labour
When the wage rate falls from w_1 to w_2, each firm hires more labour and produces more output. The increase in output causes output price to fall, which reduces the value of labour's marginal product. The market demand curve for labour is thus more steep than the horizontal summation of the individual demand curves.

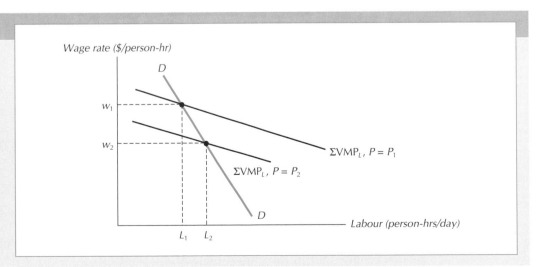

market demand curve for labour (the curve labelled *DD*) will be steeper than the horizontal summation of the VMP_L curves.

The preceding discussion implicitly assumed that there is only one type of labour and that all of it is employed by a single competitive industry. In the real world, of course, matters are more complicated. There are almost countless categories of labour—carpenters, electricians, physicists, lawyers, high school teachers, and so on—and any one type finds employment in many different industries. Thus, electricians are employed in the residential construction, automobile, commercial office building, steel, computer, and fishing industries, to name but a small sample. The market demand curve for electricians is therefore made up of the individual demands of firms in not just one industry but many.

Suppose the payments to electricians by firms in each separate industry constitute only a small fraction—say, .1 percent—of their respective total costs. A small change—say, 10 percent—in the wage paid to electricians would then produce an all but imperceptible change—namely, .01 percent—in each industry's total costs, and hence no appreciable effect on their respective output prices. Under these circumstances, the demand for electricians will be closely approximated by the horizontal summation of the various individual firm demand curves, and the complication discussed in connection with Figure 14-3 may be ignored.

14.4 AN IMPERFECT COMPETITOR'S DEMAND FOR LABOUR

Our discussion of the demand for labour has assumed that the firm faces a perfectly elastic demand for its product. Any additional output produced by additional workers could be sold at the same price as existing output. With an imperfect competitor, of course, this will not be so. Such firms face downward-sloping demand curves, and if they hire additional workers, they must cut their prices in order to sell the additional output.

Marginal revenue product (MRP) The amount by which total revenue changes with the employment of an additional unit of an input.

We saw that with a perfect competitor, the value of the extra output obtained by hiring an extra worker is the product of price and the marginal product of labour. With an imperfect competitor, in contrast, it is the product of marginal revenue and marginal product. This product is called the ***marginal revenue product of labour,*** and is denoted MRP_L. In terms of the definitions of marginal revenue and marginal product, MRP_L is thus given by

$$MRP_L = MR \bullet MP_L = \frac{\Delta TR}{\Delta Q} \bullet \frac{\Delta Q}{\Delta L}, \qquad (14.1)$$

which reduces to

$$MRP_L = \frac{\Delta TR}{\Delta L}. \qquad (14.2)$$

VMP_L and MRP_L are alike in that each represents the addition to total revenue that results from the addition of a unit of labour. The difference between them is that the MRP_L takes into account that the sale of additional output requires a cut in price for the imperfect competitor. VMP_L values the extra output at the existing product price, which is unaffected by variations in the perfect competitor's output. MRP_L values the additional output at its marginal revenue, which is less than its price.

How much labour will a perfect competitor in the labour market hire if it faces a downward-sloping demand curve for its *output*? The answer is that *it will hire that quantity for which the wage rate and MRP_L are equal, where $w = MRP_L$.* The argument for this claim is essentially similar to the one offered for the $w = VMP_L$ condition for the perfect competitor in the output market.

In the case of the perfect competitor in the output market, the short-run demand for labour is downward sloping when the law of diminishing returns operates. The more labour the firm hires, the lower the MP_L will be and hence the lower the VMP_L will be. For the monopolist, too, the law of diminishing returns will cause the short-run demand curve for labour to be downward sloping. But there is an additional reason in the case of the monopolist, which is that its marginal revenue curve is also downward sloping.

For the same reasons discussed in the perfectly competitive case, the monopolist's long-run demand for labour will be more elastic than his short-run demand. But we need not make any additional adjustments to the MRP_L curve when moving from the firm to the industry demand curve, in either the long run or the short run. The monopolist's demand for labour *is* the industry demand for labour. It already takes account of the fact that extra output means a lower product price.

14.5 THE SUPPLY OF LABOUR

For simplicity, let's again imagine that there is only one category of labour and that the choice confronting each worker is how many hours to work each day. The alternative to working is to spend time in "leisure activities," which here will include play, sleep, eating, and any other activity besides paid work in the labour market. If the worker will be paid at a constant rate of $10 for each hour he works, how many hours should he work?

On reflection, this turns out to be a simple consumer choice problem of the very same sort we took up in Chapter 3. The choice in this context is between two goods we may call "income" and "leisure." As in the standard consumer choice problem, the individual is assumed to have preferences over the two goods that can be summarized in the form of an indifference map. In Figure 14-4, the curves labelled I_1, I_2, and I_3 represent three such curves for a hypothetical worker.

The line labelled B in the same diagram represents the individual's budget constraint. If he spent the entire day in leisure activities, he would earn no income, which

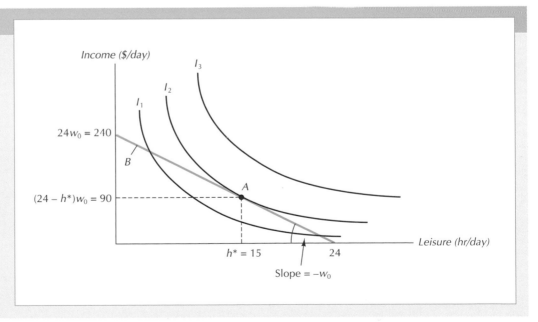

FIGURE 14-4

The Optimal Choice of Leisure and Income
The optimal amount of leisure is $h^* = 15$ hours per day, which corresponds to a point of tangency between the budget constraint (B) and the indifference curve I_2. The corresponding amount of paid labour is $24 - h^* = 9$ hours per day, which yields a daily wage income of $w_0 (24 - h^*)$ = $90 per day.

says that the point (24, 0) must be the horizontal intercept of B. Alternatively, if he worked 24 hours per day at the wage rate of $w_0 = \$10/hr$, his daily income would be $24w_0 = \$240$, which tells us that the point (0, 240) must be the vertical intercept of B. The remainder of B is the straight line that joins these two points. Its equation is $M = w(24 - h) = 10(24 - h) = 240 - 10h$, where M is daily income in dollars and h is the number of leisure-hours per day. The slope of B is simply the negative of the hourly wage rate, $-w_0 = -10$.

Given his preferences and budget constraint, the best this hypothetical consumer can do is to move to point A in Figure 14-4, the tangency between B and the indifference curve I_2. Here, the optimal bundle corresponds to spending $h^* = 15$ hours per day in leisure, the remaining $24 - h^* = 9$ hours in paid work. The consumer's daily income in dollars will be $(24 - h^*)w_0 = \$90$. At A, the marginal rate of substitution between leisure and income is exactly w_0, the hourly wage rate. This means that at the optimal bundle, the marginal value of an extra hour of leisure is exactly equal to the opportunity cost of acquiring it—namely, the \$10 the consumer would have earned had he worked that extra hour.

EXERCISE 14-2

Suppose the wage rate is $w = \$20/hr$. Find the equation for the income/leisure budget constraint and graph it. Suppose that, facing this wage, an individual chooses $h = 14$ hours of leisure per day. Find the worker's income M per day for this amount of leisure.

To generate a worker's supply curve of labour, we simply ask how the optimal amount of paid work varies as the wage rate varies. Figure 14-5 looks at the optimal leisure choices for three different hourly wage rates, $w = \$4$, $w = \$10$, and $w = \$14$. The supply of labour corresponding to $w = \$4$ is $24 - h_1^* = 6$ hours; to $w = \$10$, $24 - h_2^* = 9$ hours; and to $w = \$14$, $24 - h_3^* = 7$ hours.

FIGURE 14-5

Optimal Leisure Choices for Different Wage Rates
When the hourly wage rises from \$4 to \$10, the optimal amount of leisure falls from 18 to 15 hours per day. But when the wage rises still further to \$14, the optimal amount of leisure rises to 17 hours per day.

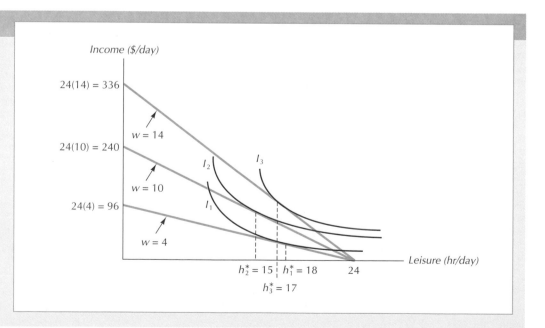

FIGURE 14-6

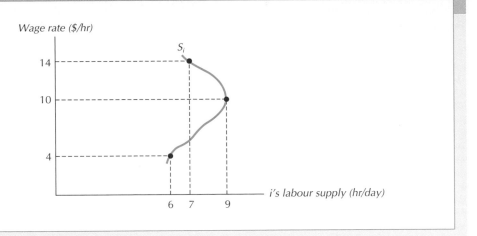

The Labour Supply Curve for the *i*th Worker
For this worker, an increase in the wage rate elicits greater labour supply when the wage rate is less than $10 per hour, but smaller labour supply when the wage rate is above $10 per hour.

Figure 14-6 plots the relationship between the wage rate and the hours of work supplied by the hypothetical worker whose indifference map is shown in Figure 14-5. Calling this person the *i*th worker of many, we see that his supply curve is the line denoted S_i. When compared with other supply curves we have encountered, the salient feature of S_i is that it is not everywhere upward sloping.[2] In particular, it is "backward bending" for values of w larger than $10/hr, which is another way of saying that, in that region, higher wages lead to fewer hours of work supplied.

Colonialists who employed unskilled labour in less developed countries once thought it a sign of "backwardness" that their employees worked fewer hours whenever their wages rose. But as the following example makes clear, such behaviour is consistent with the rational pursuit of a perfectly coherent objective.

EXAMPLE 14-1

Smith wants to earn $200 per day because with that amount he can live comfortably and meet all his financial obligations. Graph Smith's labour supply curve.

If L^S denotes the number of hours per day Smith chooses to work, it must satisfy $wL^S = 200$, where w is Smith's hourly wage rate in dollars. Smith's supply curve will thus be given by $L^S = 200/w$, which is shown in Figure 14-7.

Attempting to earn a target level of income is obviously not the only goal a rational person might pursue. But there is certainly nothing retrograde about it either. A person who holds this goal will always work less whenever the wage rate rises.

EXERCISE 14-3

Draw the labour supply curve for a person with a daily target income of $120.

---

[2]As our analysis in Chapter 5 showed, the supply of savings can behave similarly as the interest rate rises.

FIGURE 14-7

The Labour Supply Curve for a Worker Seeking a Target Level of Income
The higher his hourly wage rate, the fewer hours Smith has to work to earn his daily target of $200.

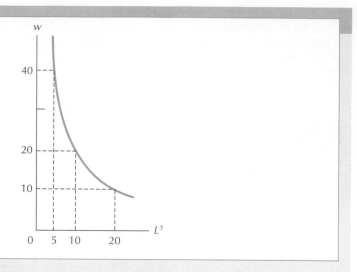

Economic Naturalist 14-1

Why do many taxis disappear when it starts raining?

WHY IS IT SO HARD TO FIND A TAXI ON RAINY DAYS?

In many big cities, one can generally hail a taxicab within a matter of seconds during good weather. But on rainy days, finding one is usually extremely difficult. Why this difference?

Perhaps the most obvious reason is that many people who would be willing to walk short distances during good weather prefer to take a cab instead when it rains. But there is an additional contributing factor—namely, that taxi drivers tend to work shorter days during bad weather. The reason, according to one study, is that many drivers work only as long as necessary to reach a target level of income each day.[3] On low-demand sunny days, they must spend much of their day cruising for passengers, so it takes longer to reach any target income level. The same target is reached much more quickly on high-demand rainy days, when their cabs tend to be full most of the time.

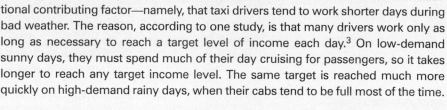

EXERCISE 14-4

Suppose instead that a cab driver's goal were to earn a target level of earnings not for each day, but rather for each week. The driver also prefers to drive no more hours than necessary to reach his target, and in his city it always rains two days each week. How would this driver's hours driven on rainy days compare with his hours driven on sunny days?

Not all individuals exhibit backward-bending labour supply curves. An increase in the wage rate has both an income and a substitution effect on the quantity of leisure demanded. By making leisure more expensive, a wage rate increase leads people to

---

[3]L. Babcock, C. Camerer, G. Loewenstein, and R. Thaler, "Labor Supply of New York City Cab Drivers: One Day at a Time," *Quarterly Journal of Economics*, 111, 1997: 408–441.

consume less of it, and hence to work more—the substitution effect. But an increase in the wage rate also gives people more real purchasing power and, on the plausible assumption that leisure is a normal good, causes them to demand more of it—the income effect. If the income effect dominates the substitution effect over some range of wage rates, we see a backward-bending labour supply curve over that range. Otherwise, the labour supply curve will be everywhere upward sloping.

EXAMPLE 14-2 | **Find the optimal leisure demand for wage rate w = \$20/hr for someone who views income and leisure as perfect complements in a 10-1 ratio (who requires 1 hour of leisure for every \$10 of income).**

The income/leisure budget constraint is

$$M = w(24 - h) = 20(24 - h) = 480 - 20h.$$

Since the individual requires 1 hour of leisure for every \$10 of income, the consumption point must lie on the line M = 10h. The intersection of the budget constraint and this consumption line (see Figure 14-8) yields the leisure demand:

$$480 - 20h = 10h \Rightarrow 480 = 30h \Rightarrow h = 16 \text{ hr/day}.$$

EXERCISE 14-5

Find the optimal leisure demand for wage rate w = \$20 per hour for someone who views income and leisure as perfect substitutes in a 10-1 ratio, and is willing to sacrifice 1 hour of leisure for \$10 of income. Hint: This person's indifference curves are straight lines $M = a - 10h$ for various values of a.

Often we can judge whether a change in income possibilities leaves people better off or worse off without detailed information about their preferences. Knowing their two budget constraints, before and after, and their initial choice of leisure can suffice. If the initial choice of leisure lies on the new budget constraint but the wage rate at that point has changed, the individual must be better off. The individual can be no worse off since she can still afford the same leisure and income. Now, the worker can adjust leisure choice (more leisure if the wage rate fell, less leisure if the wage rate rose) to reach a higher indifference curve.

FIGURE 14-8

When Leisure and Income Are Perfect Complements
If income and leisure are perfect complements in a 10-1 ratio, an individual will consume leisure at a point on the budget constraint that satisfies $M = 10h$.

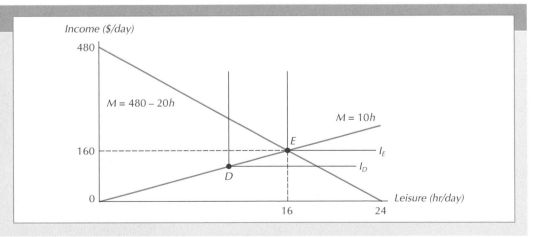

For many people, the wage rate varies with the number of hours they work. Overtime work, for example, often commands a higher wage rate. Maynard has smooth convex indifference curves between leisure and income. He can work as many hours as he chooses. In his current job, Maynard is paid $5 per hour for the first 8 hours he works and $20 for each hour over 8. Faced with this payment schedule, Maynard chooses to work 12 hours a day. If Maynard is offered a new, equally satisfying job that pays $10 for every hour he works, will he take the new job? Explain.

The theory of labour supply plays a crucial role in the logic of welfare reform. The primary goal of most social assistance programs is to provide additional income to the poor. One concern, however, is that welfare assistance may weaken incentives to work. In this respect, the specific form taken by welfare assistance is important. For example, as the following exercise shows, lump sum transfers are more likely to reduce labour supply than wage subsidies, because such transfers result in a greater income effect relative to the substitution effect in labour supply.

Consider the following two antipoverty programs: a payment of $24 per day or a payment of 40 percent of wage income. Assuming that low-income people have the option of working at $5 per hour, show how each program would affect the budget constraint of a representative low-income worker. Which program would be most likely to reduce the number of hours worked?

14.6 IS LEISURE A GIFFEN GOOD?

In the standard consumer choice problem considered in Chapter 4, we saw that the individual demand curve for a product is downward sloping except in the anomalous case of the Giffen good. Here we have seen that the supply curve of labour can be backward bending, which is just another way of saying that the demand curve for leisure can be upward sloping. Does this mean that in such cases leisure is a Giffen good? The answer is "No." Recall that in the Giffen good case, if we hold money income *constant* and increase the price of a strongly *inferior* good, then the quantity demanded of the good increases. In contrast, as the wage rate increases both the opportunity cost of leisure and (for any given number of hours worked) money income *increase*. With a higher opportunity cost of leisure relative to other goods, the substitution effect *reduces* the demand for leisure, while (if leisure is a *normal* good) the added income *increases* the demand for leisure. Only when the second effect of the wage rate increase outweighs the first one will the labour supply curve be backward bending. It follows that if leisure is an inferior good then the labour supply curve can never be backward bending, and if the labour supply curve is backward bending then leisure must be a normal good and hence cannot be a Giffen good.

14.7 THE NONECONOMIST'S REACTION TO THE LABOUR SUPPLY MODEL

Seeing the economic model of labour supply for the first time, many noneconomists consider it a most unrealistic description of the way people actually allocate their time between labour and leisure. Most jobs, after all, offer little choice in the number of hours to work each day. One can of course choose between part-time and full-time work, but the jobs in the part-time category are often so unattractive that many workers view this as a choice not even worth considering.

In part, such criticism of the labour supply model is based on too narrow an understanding of it. The model does not say that people literally choose the number of hours they work each day. Critics are completely correct in pointing out that this is simply not a choice open to most workers. But over the span of several months or years, it may be possible to have considerably more say over the amount of time spent at work. Law school graduates, for example, can go to work for fast-track law firms where associates routinely put in 14-hour days 7 days a week; or they can choose firms where everyone is out by 5 P.M. People can choose jobs that provide longer vacations or greater discretionary time. They can moonlight. And they can change jobs frequently, taking time off in between.

Even allowing for all these possible sources of flexibility, however, it is still fair to say that the options for most people are limited. If firms could offer complete flexibility with no loss in productivity, it would be to their advantage to do so. But most firms hire groups of workers who must interact, and things begin to break down if people are not all on the premises during the same hours of the day. In some occupations, pagers, increasingly smart cellphones, e-mail and other electronic office–home links have reduced the need for direct interaction in a single location. Except where it is possible to use electronic monitoring of task performance, however, many businesses are still reluctant to give up the degree of management supervision and control that the workplace environment enables. One effect of many of these devices has been effectively to *lengthen* the workday, when businesses require that employees be accessible even in their "off-hours."

So for many people it is probably fair to say that the amount of time they work is more a result of the constraints imposed by employers than of any deliberate choices of their own. The need for supervision by management and coworker interaction explains the existence of a common workweek, but not why that workweek is 40 hours long instead of 30 or 50. This is the question that the economic model of labour supply helps to answer. In a perfectly competitive market, the workweek would be 40 hours long because, on the average, that's how long workers wanted it to be. If most people found an extra hour of leisure much more valuable than an extra hour's wage, profit-seeking employers would have an incentive to reduce the length of the workweek. Here again a simple theory helps explain what people do, even when they themselves correctly perceive that the proximate reasons for their actions are forces beyond their control.

14.8 THE MARKET SUPPLY CURVE

The market supply curve for any given category of labour is obtained by horizontally adding the individual supply curves for the potential suppliers of labour in that category. Even though many individuals may have backward-bending supply curves—indeed, even though the nation as a whole may have a backward-bending supply curve—the supply curve for any particular category of labour is nonetheless almost certain to be upward sloping. The reason is that wage increases in one category of labour

labour not only change the number of hours worked by people already in that category, but also lure people into that category from other categories. Just as an increase in the price of barley causes many wheat farmers to shift toward barley, an increase in the wages of hairstylists causes file clerks, department store salespersons, and others to try their hand at cutting hair.

| EXAMPLE 14-3 | Rising enrolments in MBA programs have increased the demand for economics faculty in business schools. If most economists are teaching in liberal arts programs, how will this increase in business school demands affect salaries and employment of economists in the two environments? |

The right panel in Figure 14-9 shows the market supply curve of economists as the line labelled S. It is upward sloping on the assumption that higher wage rates for economists will induce some people to choose economics over other professions. The demand curve for economists by liberal arts programs is shown in the left panel. In the centre panel, the original and new demand curves for economists by business schools are labelled D_{B_1} and D_{B_2}, respectively. Adding the liberal arts and business school demand curves horizontally (on the assumption that the salaries paid to economists are too small a share of total university costs to affect tuition significantly), we get both the original and new total demand curve for economists in the right panel, labelled $D_A + D_{B_1}$ and $D_A + D_{B_2}$, respectively.

Note that the increased demand by business schools causes the wage rate for economists in both environments to rise from w_1 to w_2. To see how employment in the two environments is affected, we simply trace w_2 leftward to the respective demand curves. The increase in business school employment of economists is $Q_{B_2} - Q_{B_1}$, while the reduction in liberal arts employment is $Q_{A_1} - Q_{A_2}$. The gain in business school employment will be equal to the sum of the movements out of liberal arts positions $(Q_{A_1} - Q_{A_2})$ and the overall movement into the economics profession from the outside $(Q_2 - Q_1)$.

This example illustrates two points of particular interest. First is the tendency of salaries for workers in a given occupation to equalize across sectors of the economy that employ that occupation. If the demand for carpenters goes up because of a boom in commercial construction projects, the homeowner who wants to add a recreation

FIGURE 14-9

An Increase in Demand by One Category of Employer
The demand for economists to teach in business schools rises (centre panel), causing the total market demand curve for economists to rise (right panel). Employment at the new higher wage is determined by consulting the respective demand curves of the liberal arts sector (left panel) and business school sector (centre panel).

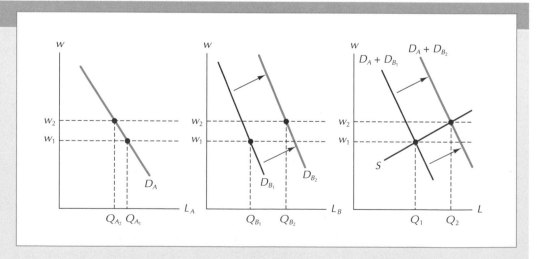

room in her basement soon finds herself paying more as well. The idea here is very simple: unless the wages of carpenters employed in residential construction also rose, many of them would leave that sector for commercial construction. Provided that work in the two environments is in other respects equally desirable, the only stable outcome is for the wage to be the same in each.

The second point suggested by the example is that a small occupational subsector can experience a large proportional rise in demand without appreciably bidding up wages throughout the occupation. Because business schools employed only a small fraction of the total number of academic economists to begin with, these schools could increase their employment substantially without having to pay dramatically higher wages. The general rule is that the effective elasticity of supply to any small occupational subsector will be much higher than to the occupational market taken as a whole.

As a strictly empirical matter, economists who teach in business schools earn higher average salaries than those who teach in liberal arts programs. The difference is large enough to suggest that something must be missing from our theory that calls for equal wages in each sector. The implicit assumption in our model most likely to be invalid is that economists regard the two working environments as being equally attractive.

14.9 MONOPSONY

The classic illustration of a single-employer labour market is the so-called company town. Workers either cannot or will not leave the area, and new firms cannot enter. A firm in this position is called a *monopsonist*—for "sole buyer"—in its labour market. Does it follow that a monopsonist will exploit its workers by paying them too little and offering them too little safety?

Let's consider first the question of wages. A firm that hires labour in a perfectly competitive labour market faces a supply curve of labour that is a horizontal line at the market wage rate. Its own hiring decisions have essentially no effect on the market wage rate. For the monopsonist, in contrast, the labour supply curve is the market supply curve itself. Suppose, for the sake of discussion, that it is upward sloping, like the curve labelled *S* in Figure 14-10. *S* is also called the **average factor cost**, or **AFC**, curve, because it tells the average payment per labour-hour necessary to achieve any given level of employment. The total cost of a given level of employment—called **total factor cost**, or **TFC**—is simply the product of that employment level and the corresponding value of AFC. Thus, the total factor cost of an employment level of 100 labour-hours per hour in Figure 14-10 is equal to 100 × $4/labour-hour = $400 per hour.

Now suppose the firm already has 100 workers and is considering the cost of adding the 101st. To increase its employment by 1 unit, it must raise its wage rate by $.04/labour-hour, not only for the additional unit of labour it hires, but for the current 100 units as well. The total factor cost of 101 labour-hours is $4.04 × 101 = $408.04. The **marginal factor cost**, or **MFC**, of the 101st worker is the amount by which total factor cost changes as a result of hiring that worker:

$$MFC = \frac{\Delta TFC}{\Delta L}. \qquad (14.3)$$

For the example given in Figure 14-10, we thus have MFC = $408.04 − $400 = $8.04 per hour. The MFC of the 101st worker is the sum of the $4.04 per hour he is paid directly and the extra $4 per hour that must be divided among the existing 100 workers. When hiring an extra worker means paying more to existing workers, the MFC curve

Average factor cost (AFC) Another name for the supply curve for an input.

Total factor cost (TFC) The product of the employment level of an input and its average factor cost.

Marginal factor cost (MFC) The amount by which total factor cost changes with the employment of an additional unit of input.

FIGURE 14-10

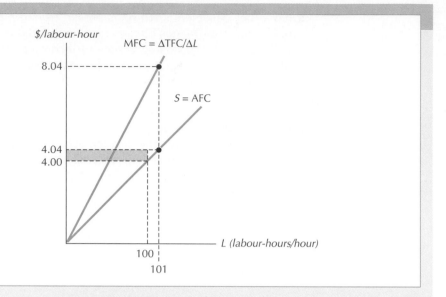

Average and Marginal Factor Cost
When the supply curve (*S*) facing a monopsonist is upward sloping, the cost of hiring an additional unit of labour (MFC) is no longer merely the wage he must be paid. To that wage must be added the additional payment that must be made to existing workers (shaded rectangle).

will always lie above the corresponding AFC curve. If the AFC curve is a straight line with the formula AFC = $a + bL$, then the corresponding MFC curve will be a straight line with the same intercept and twice the slope as the AFC curve: MFC = $a + 2bL$ (see footnote 4).

Figure 14-11 describes the equilibrium wage and employment levels for a monopsonist. The profit-maximizing level of employment is at L^*, where the MRP_L curve intersects the MFC curve. At L^*, the firm pays the wage rate given by the value on the labour supply curve, namely w^*.

The argument that L^* is the profit-maximizing level of employment takes much the same form as the one we saw in the other labour market structures. The MRP_L represents the increase in the firm's total revenue that results from hiring an additional unit of labour, while the MFC curve represents the corresponding addition to its total costs. To the left of L^*, the former exceeds the latter, so the firm's profit will rise if it expands employment. To the right, the latter exceeds the former, so it will do better if it contracts.

This argument has an interesting implication. Just as we said in Chapter 12 that "a monopolist has no supply curve," so we can say that a *monopsonist has no demand curve*. In the present case, this means that there is not a unique relationship between the wage rate w and the quantity of labour inputs the monopsonist demands. To see why, note that the *general* condition for the profit-maximizing level of employment is that MRP_L = MFC. In Figure 14-11, this level of employment is L^*, at which point the wage rate is w^*. In the *special* case of a perfect competitor in both input and output markets, $MRP_L = VMP_L$, since the firm faces a horizontal demand curve for its output at price P, and so MR = P. Similarly, MFC = AFC = w, since the firm faces a horizontal supply curve for its labour inputs. For a perfect competitor in both markets, the condition

---

[4]In calculus terms, MFC is defined as

$$\text{MFC} = \frac{d(\text{TCF})}{dL}.$$

Thus, if AFC = $a + bL$, then TFC = AFC $\times L = aL + bL^2$, which yields MFC = $a + 2bL$. Note that for a perfect competitor who faces a horizontal labour supply curve, $b = 0$, and hence AFC = MFC = a and TFC = aL.

FIGURE 14-11

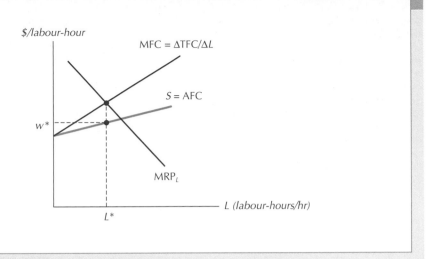

MRP$_L$ = MFC thus becomes MRP$_L$ = VMP$_L$ = w, as we showed earlier. To each wage rate corresponds a definite quantity of labour inputs demanded. For a monopsonist with a given MRP$_L$ curve, however, the point at which MRP$_L$ equals MFC can correspond to an infinite number of wage rates, depending on the shape of the labour supply (AFC) curve. Hence there is no direct, one-to-one relationship between the wage rate and the quantity of labour inputs the monopsonist demands, or in other words, no monopsonist's demand curve.

EXERCISE 14-8

A monopsonist's MRP$_L$ curve is given by MRP$_L$ = 12 − L. If her AFC curve is given by w = 2 + 2L, then (using footnote 4) give the equation for her MFC curve, and calculate the quantity of labour she will hire and the wage rate she will pay. How do your answers change if her AFC curve is given by w = 4 + .5L?

How do the wage and employment levels under monopsony compare with those in competitive labour markets? If the MRP$_L$ curve were the *competitive* industry labour demand curve, then the level of employment would rise to L^{**}, the point at which demand intersects the supply curve in Figure 14-12. The wage rate, too, would rise, from w^* to w^{**}.

In comparison with this competitive norm, the monopsony equilibrium is inefficient in much the same sense that the monopoly equilibrium in the product market is inefficient—it does not exhaust all potential gains from trade. Note in Figure 14-12 that when the employment level is L^*, workers would be willing to supply an additional hour of labour for a payment of only w^*, whereas the extra revenue that would be produced by that extra unit is MRP$_L^*$ = MFC* > w. If the firm could somehow increase total employment by one unit without paying its existing workers more, both it and the extra worker would be better off. To the extent that such exchanges are blocked by the calculus of profit maximization, the monopsony structure is less efficient than the competitive ideal.

FIGURE 14-12

Comparing Monopsony and Competition in the Labour Market
Because the monopsonist takes into account the effect of employment expansions on wages paid to existing workers, it will employ less and pay less than the corresponding values under competition.

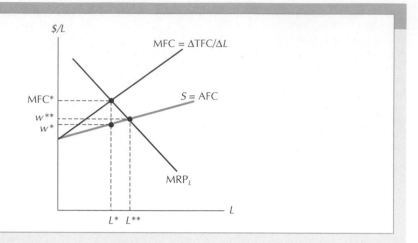

For the monopsony firm, then, wages will indeed be lower than under competition. What about other elements of compensation, such as safety equipment? Here, too, there will be a tendency for the monopsonist to offer less, for exactly parallel reasons. It does not follow, however, that employees of a monopsonist would necessarily be made better off by a regulation requiring additional safety equipment. The monopsonist's incentives cause it to offer a compensation package—consisting of wages, safety equipment, and other fringe benefits—that is worth less than the corresponding package under competition. But the monopsonist generally has an incentive to allocate the total amount spent on compensation within that package in the way that workers would want. Suppose, for example, a safety device was worth $10 per week to each worker and cost only $9 per week per worker to install and operate. This device would meet the standard cost-benefit test, and the monopsonist would earn higher profits by installing it. Workers, after all, would tolerate up to a $10 per week pay cut rather than do without the device. Alternatively, suppose the device cost $11 per week. Then both the firm and the workers would do better by not installing it. We examine the issue of workplace health and safety further in the Web Supplement for Chapter 14.

How important is the problem of monopsony? Recall that the requirement for perfect competition in the labour market is that workers be freely mobile. Recent studies of mobility in Canada suggest that interindustry mobility is substantially greater than interprovincial mobility, and that job availability tends to be more important than comparative wage rates in determining mobility. The studies also suggest that younger workers are more mobile, while older, married workers with children are less mobile. As you might expect, interprovincial migration rates are higher for smaller provinces. They are lower than average for those whose first language is French and for residents of smaller cities, towns, and especially rural areas.[5] The limited mobility of some groups does not necessarily imply that monopsony power is widespread. At the entry level, most workers are relatively free to move. No firm can survive for long without a steady inflow of new workers; and without a competitive compensation package, it would be difficult to attract entry-level workers.

---

[5]See Lars Osberg, Gordon Daniel, and Zhengxi Lin, "Interregional Migration and Interindustry Labour Mobility in Canada: A Simultaneous Approach," *Canadian Journal of Economics*, 1994; Ross Finnie, "Who Moves? A Panel Logit Model Analysis of Inter-Provincial Migration in Canada," Statistics Canada Research Paper Series, 2000.

Wouldn't it be possible, however, for a firm to offer competitive terms to entry-level workers but then cut wages and benefits (or have them grow insufficiently) once these workers have put down roots? The difficulty is that firms develop reputations in the labour market, much as they do in the product market. Other things the same, a firm with a reputation for paying competitive wages to all its workers will be able to lure the best entry-level workers away from firms with reputations for exploiting older workers.

But even if *no* workers were willing or able to move, firms might still not be able to pay less than competitive wages in the long run. If firms in a labour market area paid much less than the value of what their workers produce, new firms could move into the area to compete for the services of those workers. In Chapter 13, we saw that an incumbent monopoly could use *limit pricing* in order to deter entry to the market for its output, as long as potential competitors had to incur fixed costs of entry into that market. The monopolist there set its *output* price at a *lower* level than the price where MR = MC, to discourage competitors. Similarly, a monopsonist can apply a limit pricing strategy in setting the wage rate for its "captive" labour force, so that the *wage rate* it pays is *higher* than at the point where MRP_L = MFC. This strategy works to deter entry, however, only if potential competitors for the available supply of labour incur fixed costs of entry into the labour market. Note, moreover, that even the threat of entry will raise the wage paid by the monopsonist and bring it closer to the competitive wage.

The larger the size of the labour market in a particular centre, the less likely it is that a single firm will be the sole purchaser of labour services, the more mobile—geographically and between industries—the labour force will be, and hence the higher the elasticity of labour supply will tend to be.[6] Consequently, to the extent that monopsony exists, it is likely to be concentrated in relatively small centres or "company towns." Moreover, even here, monopsony efficiency losses can persist in the long run only if entry by other firms can be prevented and the supply of labour does not become more elastic over time.

14.10 MINIMUM WAGE LAWS

As labour policy has been primarily a provincial responsibility since 1867, each province has its own minimum wage legislation. In 1965, the first federal minimum wage, covering those workers under federal jurisdiction, was set at \$1.25/hour. At the time, provincial hourly minimum wage rates ranged from \$.50 for women and \$.70 for men in Newfoundland to \$1.00 in British Columbia. In 1996, the federal rate became the adult rate of the province in which it applied, which in 2000 ranged from \$5.50 in Newfoundland to \$7.60 in British Columbia. In real terms, after correcting for inflation, the minimum wage has increased across Canada since 1965, although not as rapidly as average hourly wages. The intent of such legislation is to raise the wages of unskilled workers sufficiently to provide them with a standard of living above the poverty line. In certain circumstances, however, minimum wage laws can have some undesirable consequences.

The simple model in Figure 14-13 shows the demand and supply curves for unskilled labour, which intersect at an equilibrium real wage of w_0, at which employment is L_0. If the statutory minimum wage is set at w_m, the effect is to reduce employment to D_m, while increasing the quantity of labour supplied to S_m. The difference, $S_m - D_m$, is the unemployment that results from the minimum wage.

---

[6]In Equation 12.6 and footnote 7 of Chapter 12 on page 443, we derived the relationship MR = $P(1 + 1/\eta)$, relating marginal revenue, price, and the price elasticity of demand. With $\eta < 0$, MR < P. The corresponding equation for labour supply is MFC = $w(1 + 1/\epsilon)$, where ϵ is the price elasticity of supply of labour. With $\epsilon > 0$, MFC is greater than w. If the supply of labour becomes more elastic over time, then the divergence between MFC and w will decrease. In the limit, as ϵ approaches infinity and the supply curve facing the firm becomes horizontal, w = MFC and monopsony power disappears.

FIGURE 14-13

A Statutory Minimum Wage
The effect of the minimum wage is to reduce employment of unskilled labour from L_0 to D_m, while increasing supply from L_0 to S_m. The resulting difference, $S_m - D_m$, is the unemployment attributable to the minimum wage.

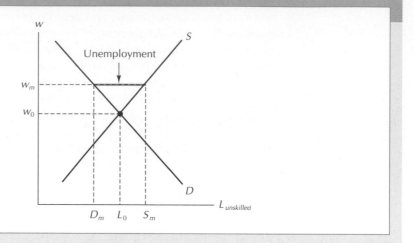

In Figure 14-13, there are both winners and losers from the imposition of the minimum wage. The unskilled workers who retain their jobs earn more as a result. Those who lose their jobs obviously earn less. Whether the net effect is to increase the amount of income earned by unskilled workers depends on the elasticity of demand for that category of labour. If it is elastic, earnings will fall; if it is inelastic, they will rise. The more elastic both supply and demand are, the higher is the unemployment that results. Empirical estimates of demand elasticity vary, but for the most part are below 1 in absolute value, suggesting that the net effect is to increase wage payments to unskilled labour.[7] Some U.S. studies even suggest that minimum wage laws may not raise overall unemployment at all.[8]

There is a strong consensus, however, that minimum wage legislation has significantly reduced the employment of teenagers. The size of any group's employment reduction will depend not only on the elasticity of demand, but also on the extent to which the minimum wage exceeds the market-clearing level. Teenagers as a group are much less productive than adults, if only because they have less education and experience, and so the statutory minimum creates a larger employment gap for them than for other groups.

An interesting exception exists to the general proposition that minimum wages imply a reduction in employment. Figure 14-14 shows the case of a monopsony firm that without a minimum wage would hire L^* workers at a wage of w^*. Confronted with a minimum wage of w_m, its marginal factor cost curve suddenly becomes horizontal over the region from 0 to L_1. No matter how much labour it hires in that region, the marginal cost of an additional worker is constant at w_m. If it wants to expand employment

---

[7]See, for example, Daniel Hamermesh, "Economic Studies of Labor Demand and Their Applications to Public Policy," *Journal of Human Resources*, Fall 1976: 507–525; Edward M. Gramlich, "Impact of Minimum Wages on Other Wages, Employment, and Family Incomes," *Brookings Papers on Economic Activity*, 2, 1976; Jacob Mincer, "Unemployment Effects of Minimum Wages," *Journal of Political Economy*, August 1976; Sar Levitan and Richard Belous, *More Than Subsistence: Minimum Wages for the Working Poor*, Baltimore: Johns Hopkins University Press, 1979; and Finis Welch, *Minimum Wages: Issues and Evidence*, Washington, DC: American Enterprise Institute, 1978. For a review, see Chapter 4 in Ronald Ehrenberg and Robert S. Smith, *Modern Labor Economics*, Glenview, IL: Scott, Foresman, 1982.

[8]See David Card, "Using Regional Variations in Wages to Measure the Effects of the Federal Minimum Wage," *Industrial and Labor Relations Review*, October 1992: 22–37.

FIGURE 14-14

The Minimum Wage Law in the Case of Monopsony
The effect of a minimum wage at w_m is to make the monoposonist's MFC curve horizontal in the region from 0 to L_1, which increases employment from L^* to L_m.

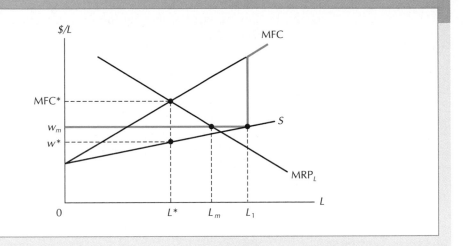

beyond L_1, it must offer a higher wage than w_m, as indicated along the original supply curve. With the minimum wage in effect, the monopsonist's MRP_L curve intersects its new MFC curve at L_m. The effect of the law is thus to increase both the wage *and* the employment level for the monopsonist. Note also that if w_m passes through the intersection of the MRP_L and supply curves, it can actually generate the efficient competitive market equilibrium.

Minimum wages will not always increase employment in monopsony labour markets. If the minimum wage were set above MFC*, for example, the effect would be to reduce employment. And no matter where the minimum wage is set in the region above w^*, the effect will be to reduce the monopsonist's overall rate of return on investment. If the monopsonist's profit were close to normal to begin with, the long-run effect could thus be to induce him to leave the market. Needless to say, this too would result in a reduction of employment for unskilled workers.

EXERCISE 14-9

A monopsonist's MRP_L curve is given by $MRP_L = 12 - L$. If she originally faced an AFC curve given by $w = 2 + 2L$, give her MFC equation. Calculate how her wage and employment offers will be affected by the passage of a law requiring $w \geq \$8$/labour-unit, and then of a law requiring $w \geq \$10$/labour-unit.

Minimum wage legislation affects a large number of Canadian firms and low-income workers. Moreover, its consequences, both positive and negative, are highly dependent on specific market conditions. It merits more empirical study than it has so far received.

14.11 LABOUR UNIONS

About one in three workers in the nonfarm sector of the Canadian economy is a member of a labour union. This proportion is about twice as high as that in the United States, but less than half that of countries like Sweden and Denmark. The primary difference between unionized and nonunionized employment is simple. Unionized workers bargain collectively over the terms and conditions of employment; to nonunionized workers, the firm simply announces its offer, which the workers can either accept or reject, by staying with or leaving the firm. Unions may also facilitate communication between labour and management.

The traditional economic analysis of unions treats them as a form of labour cartel. It focuses on the loss of efficiency if all firms are perfect competitors faced by such a cartel. We can illustrate this analysis with the following simple model. Consider a simple economy with two sectors, one unionized, the other not. Suppose that the total supply of labour to the two sectors is fixed at S_0, and that the union and nonunion labour demand curves are as shown by D_U and D_N in the left and right panels of Figure 14-15, respectively. Without union bargaining, the same wage, w_0, would prevail in each sector, and employment levels in the two sectors would be L_{U_0} and L_{N_0}, respectively, where $L_{U_0} + L_{N_0} = S_0$.

Collective bargaining fixes the wage in the union sector at $w_U > w_0$. The demand for labour is downward sloping, and this causes firms in the union sector to reduce employment from L_{U_0} to L_{U_1}. The displaced workers in the union sector are then forced to seek employment in the nonunion sector, which drives the wage down to w_N in that sector.

At first glance, the process resembles a zero-sum game, one in which the gains of the union workers are exactly offset by the losses of nonunion workers. On closer inspection, however, we see that the process actually reduces the value of total output. Recall from Chapter 9 that the condition for output maximization with two production processes is for the value of the marginal product of the resource to be the same in each process. With the wage set initially at w_0 in both sectors, that condition was satisfied. But with the divergence in wages caused by the collective bargaining process, the value of total output can no longer be at a maximum. Note that if a worker is taken out of the nonunion sector, the reduction in the value of output there will be only w_N, which is less than w_U, the gain in the value of output when that same worker is added to the union sector.

The economic distortion implied by the analysis in Figure 14-15 is exaggerated. If the union firm is required to pay a higher wage, it will attract an excess supply of workers. In practice, the skill levels of workers differ a great deal, and the natural response of the union firm will be to select the most qualified of its job applicants. The other side of the same coin is that nonunion firms will be left to hire workers who are less productive than average. Some studies suggest that the union premium not accounted for

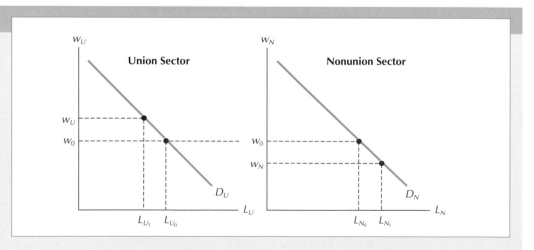

FIGURE 14-15

The Allocative Effects of Collective Bargaining
Without collective bargaining, the same wage, w_0, prevails in each sector. With the union wage pegged at w_U, employment falls in the union sector. The displaced workers seek employment in the nonunion sector, driving wages down there. The result is a reduction in national output.

by differences in worker quality is only about 10 percent. This means that the gain from shifting workers from the nonunion to the union sector will be smaller than it first appeared. Even if the union wage premium is only 10 percent, however, we should be puzzled about the ability of union firms to compete successfully against their nonunion counterparts. If their costs are significantly higher, how do the union firms manage to survive?

Researchers have begun to discover a variety of ways in which unions may actually boost productivity.[9] The revisionist view stresses their role in communicating worker preferences to management. When channels of communication between labour and management do not flow freely, the only option open to a dissatisfied worker is to leave the firm to search for a better situation. The union's role, in the revisionist account, is to offer the worker a voice as an alternative to leaving. The organization of formal grievance procedures, combined with the higher level of monetary compensation, boosts morale among union workers, which in turn leads to higher productivity. Quit rates in union firms, for example, are significantly lower than in nonunion firms, enabling them to economize on hiring and training costs. Recent empirical work suggests that union productivity may be sufficiently high, in fact, to compensate for the premium in union wages. That is to say, even though monetary wages are higher in union firms, labour costs per unit of output may not be. If this conclusion is correct, it resolves the paradox of how union firms survive in competition with their nonunion rivals.

But in so doing, it raises an even more troubling question: if unions lead to higher morale and increased wages, and don't raise unit labour costs, why don't all firms have unions? The proportion of unionized workers in Canada peaked in 1983, at about 40 percent of the nonfarm labour force, and since then it has been gradually declining. A number of factors help explain this trend. First, most nonunionized firms do not want unionization. There may well be net benefits to a firm of unionization, but these benefits tend to be seen as distant and uncertain, whereas the introduction of a union is seen as immediately reducing management's flexibility and freedom to manoeuvre. Second, it has always been costly to launch a union certification drive, and recent economic trends have made it even more costly. By law, certification cannot be done at the company-wide level, but only at the establishment level. With multibranch banks and fast-food franchises, the organizing cost per new union member is high. The rapid growth of "nonstandard"—part-time, short-term or contract, temporary help agency, and "free-lance"—forms of employment have reinforced this factor. Over 4 million workers, about 30 percent of the labour force, now hold such jobs, and about half of new job creation is of this type. Workers in such jobs are much more difficult to organize than those in traditional full-time jobs. Most of the easiest workplaces to organize have already been organized, and so union growth increasingly depends on getting certification in establishments that are costlier to organize. Hence, in the absence of significant changes in labour relations legislation at the federal level and in each of the provinces, a reversal of the decline in the unionized proportion of the labour force is unlikely.

14.12 DISCRIMINATION IN THE LABOUR MARKET

One of the most emotionally volatile issues in all of economics is the phenomenon of discrimination in the labour market. Discussions of it almost always begin by noting the large disparities in earnings that exist between different groups in the labour force.

---

[9]See, in particular, Albert O. Hirschman, *Exit, Voice, and Loyalty*, Cambridge, MA: Harvard University Press, 1973; and Richard B. Freeman and James Medoff, *What Do Unions Do?*, New York: Basic Books, 1985.

For example, the average earnings of women in Canada are roughly 66 percent of those for men.

Everyone recognizes that at least some components of these differentials have nothing to do with discrimination by individual employers. Part of the male–female differential, for example, reflects the historical pattern in which females' labour force participation was more intermittent than males'. Salaries increase most sharply when a worker follows the orderly career progression characteristic of male employment patterns. The female pattern has been to drop out of the labour force several times in connection with childrearing, which has often meant starting over each time at or near the bottom of the employment ladder, or taking on one of the "nonstandard"—and lower-paying— jobs we referred to above.

Each such effect, however, is almost surely the result of *some* sort of discrimination against the affected groups. Few people deny that the asymmetric distribution of child-care responsibilities between the sexes is at least in part the result of discriminatory social attitudes about sex roles. For present purposes, however, it is important to emphasize that from any individual employer's point of view, such effects are examples of *nonmarket* discrimination—effects that lower productivity before job applicants even make contact with the employer. The wage differences for which nonmarket discrimination is responsible cannot logically be attributed to the employer's current hiring behaviour. A completely nondiscriminatory employer would have to pay similar wage differentials on the basis of these effects, or else be forced out of business by competitors who did.

Our concern here is with that portion of the wage differentials that cannot be attributed to nonmarket discrimination. In particular, we are concerned with the case in which a firm pays a lower wage to a female or a minority group member than it would to an equally productive white male (or, in the more extreme case, simply refuses to hire members of those groups). There have been numerous theories offered to explain why firms might behave in this fashion.

One theory is that the firm's customers do not wish to deal with female or minority employees. When employment discrimination is the result of attitudes of the firm's customers, collective action through legislation is one logical way, perhaps even the only practical way, to resolve the problem. The reason is that, without the legislation, discrimination may be the only strategy open to firms that is consistent with profit maximization, and hence with survival.

Such considerations may apply, for example, to a law firm's decision about whether to hire female lawyers. Suppose that some clients, or even judges, are less likely to take counsel from a female lawyer seriously. The law firm might believe firmly that clients and judges would change their minds about female lawyers if given enough experience in dealing with them. But if it hires female lawyers while its competitors do not, its business may suffer in the short run. Hence legislation requiring equal treatment in hiring may be the only effective way to end the impasse.

Customer discrimination is a powerful explanation of employment discrimination in cases such as these. But it cannot account for wage differentials in the cases of workers—such as manufacturing production workers—who never come in contact with customers. Wage differentials in such cases have sometimes been explained as the result of *coworker discrimination*. White workers who feel uneasy about working with members of visible minorities, for example, might prefer employment in firms that hire only white workers. Or the fragile egos of some males might be unable to deal with the idea of taking orders from a female supervisor.

Such preferences imply employment segregation, but not a pattern of wage differentials for equally productive workers. For example, an employer in an all-female establishment who paid lower wages than were received by males of the same productivity would have lower costs, and hence higher profits, than the all-male employers. This would provide an incentive for a new firm to bid for that employer's workers, an incentive that should persist until all wage differentials had been eliminated.

Employer discrimination is the term generally used to describe wage differentials that arise from an arbitrary preference by the employer for one group of worker over another. Since this is the type envisioned by popular accounts of discrimination in the labour market, let us examine it in some detail. To describe the process formally, let us suppose that there are two labour force groups, the *M*s and the *F*s, and that there are no productivity differences between them. More specifically, suppose that the values of their respective marginal products are the same:

$$VMP_F = VMP_M = V_0, \qquad (14.4)$$

and that discriminating employers pay a wage of V_0 to *M*s, but only $V_0 - d$ to *F*s.

Labour costs for a discriminating employer will be a weighted average of V_0 and $V_0 - d$, where the weights are the respective shares of the two groups in the employer's work force. Thus, the more *M*s the employer hires, the higher his costs will be.

Apart from the isolated cases in which customer discrimination might be a relevant factor, a consumer will be unwilling to pay more for a product produced by an *M*. If product price is unaffected by the composition of the work force that produces the product, a firm's profit will be smaller the more *M*s it employs. The most profitable firm will be one that employs only *F*s.

Given our initial assumption that *M*s are paid the value of their marginal product, firms that employ only *M*s will earn a normal profit, while those that hire a mix will earn a positive economic profit. The initial wage differential provides an opportunity for employers who hire mostly *F*s to grow at the expense of their rivals. Indeed, because such firms make an extranormal profit on the sale of each unit of output, their incentive is to expand as rapidly as they possibly can. And to do that, they will naturally want to continue hiring only the *F*s.

But as profit-seeking firms continue to pursue this strategy, the supply of *F*s at the wage rate $V_0 - d$ will not be adequate for further expansion. The short-run solution is to offer the *F*s a slightly higher wage. But this strategy works only if other firms do not pursue it. Once they too start offering a higher wage, the *F*s will again be in short supply. In the end, of course, the only solution is for the wage of the *F*s to be bid up all the way to V_0, thereby eliminating further opportunities for profitable expansion by hiring additional *F*s.

Any employer who wants to voice a preference for hiring *M*s must now do so by paying *M*s a wage in excess of V_0. Employers can discriminate against *F*s if they want to, but only if they are willing to pay premium wages to the *M*s out of their own profits. Few firms could continue to attract capital for long at profit rates that were significantly below normal.

The competitive labour market model suggests that the persistence of significant employer discrimination requires the owners of the firm to supply capital at a rate of return substantially below what they could earn by investing their money elsewhere. The theory of competitive labour markets tells us that unless we can come up with a plausible reason to suppose they might do so, we should concentrate our search for the sources of wage differentials on factors other than employer discrimination. Or else we should look for additional ways in which the theory of competitive labour markets provides an incomplete description of reality.

14.13 STATISTICAL DISCRIMINATION

In Chapter 6 we saw how insurance companies employed data on average claims by various groups to arrive at differential rates for policyholders whose individual claim records were identical. A similar kind of statistical discrimination is pervasive in the labour market. The theory of competitive labour markets tells us that workers will be paid the values of their respective marginal products. But an employee's marginal product is not like a number tattooed on his forehead, there for everyone to observe at a glance. On the contrary, because people often work together in complicated team activities, it is often exceedingly difficult, even after many years on the job, to estimate what any one worker contributes. The problem of estimating the productivity of job applicants, with whom the employer has had no direct experience, is obviously even more difficult.

Still, the task is not hopeless. Just as insurance companies know from long experience that adolescent males are much more likely than other drivers to file accident claims, so too do employers know that applicants from certain groups are likely to be much more productive than others. The average university graduate, for example, will be more productive than the average high school graduate, even though many high school graduates are much more productive than their university counterparts.

In the insurance case in Chapter 6, we saw that even when two people had identical driving records, competitive pressures led to different rates if they happened to belong to groups with differing accident records. We see closely analogous results in the labour market. Even when the employer's information indicates that two individuals have exactly the same productivity, there will be competitive pressure to pay higher wages to the person who belongs to the group with higher average productivity. The problem is, unless the employer's information about individual productivity is perfect, group membership conveys relevant information about likely productivity differences, information a firm can ignore only at its peril.

To illustrate how group membership influences the estimation of individual productivity, consider a labour market group—call it group *A*—the VMPs of whose members are *uniformly distributed* between $10/hr and $30/hr, as shown in Figure 14-16. This means that if we were to choose a person at random from group *A*, the value of his marginal product would be equally likely to be any number from $10/hr to $30/hr.

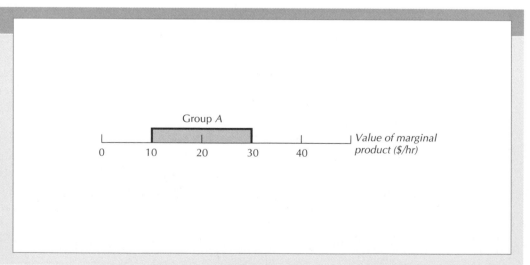

FIGURE 14-16

A Hypothetical Uniform Productivity Distribution The productivity values for members of this group are uniformly distributed between $10/hr and $30/hr. This means that the VMP of a person chosen at random from the group is equally likely to be any number from $10/hr to $30/hr. The average VMP for members of this group is $20/hr.

If we knew nothing about this person other than that he was from group *A*, the expected value of his productivity would simply be the average for members of that group, which is \$20/hr.

If there were no practical way to learn anything about a specific individual's productivity, and if the productivity distribution of his group were known, competitive pressures would require that members of group *A* be paid \$20/hr. Suppose an employer offered less, say \$15/hr. Then a competing firm could offer \$16/hr and lure them away. And since group *A* workers are worth an average of \$20/hr each, this competing firm would augment its expected profits by \$4/hr for each worker it hired. But for the same reason, it too would eventually lose the workers to yet another competing firm. Alternatively, a firm that paid \$25/hr to workers from group *A* would lose an average of \$5/hr for every worker from group *A* it hired, and unless it had some source of extranormal profits, it would sooner or later be forced out of business.

If individual productivity values cannot be measured, the only competitively stable outcome is for members of group *A* to be paid \$20/hr. Some of them will end up being paid much more than they are worth, others much less. But the firms that hire at this rate will cover all their costs, on the average, and can expect to remain in business. Any other policy will result in failure.

Now suppose that employers have a productivity test. This test is not perfect, but it does provide information about individual productivity values. To keep the analysis simple, suppose that the test is 100 percent accurate half of the time, but has no value at all the other half of the time (that is, it yields a random number drawn from the group's productivity distribution); and suppose that employers have no way of knowing when the test is accurate.

Suppose further that this test is administered to a worker from group *A* and yields a value of \$24/hr. What is our best estimate of this worker's true productivity? The test is 100 percent accurate half of the time, and if we knew this was one of those times, the answer would, of course, be \$24. Alternatively, if we knew that this was one of the times the test was worthless, our best estimate would be the expected value of a random number drawn from the uniform distribution between \$10/hr and \$30/hr, namely, \$20/hr, the average productivity value for group *A*. The problem is that we don't know which particular mode this test result falls into. So the best we can do is to take a weighted average of the two results (where the weights are the respective probabilities of occurrence). Our best estimate of the VMP of a worker from group *A* with a test score of \$24 per hour, denoted VMP(24), is thus given by

$$\text{VMP}(24) = (\tfrac{1}{2})(\$24/hr) + (\tfrac{1}{2})(\$20/hr) = \$22/hr \text{ (see footnote 10)}. \qquad (14.5)$$

This means that if we took a large number of individuals from group *A* who happened to score \$24 per hour on the test, their average productivity value would turn out to be \$22/hr.

Suppose instead that we had observed a test result of \$16/hr for a member of group *A*. Our best estimate of his VMP would then be

$$\text{VMP}(16) = (\tfrac{1}{2})(\$16/hr) + (\tfrac{1}{2})(\$20/hr) = \$18/hr. \qquad (14.6)$$

This time note that the effect of the uncertainty in the test causes us to revise upward the estimate of the individual's productivity. *In general, the rule is that when a test is less*

---

[10]Note the similarity of this adjustment procedure to the one discussed in Chapter 8, whereby we estimated the probability that a given shy person was a librarian.

than completely accurate, our best estimate of a worker's productivity will lie between his actual test score and the average productivity of the group to which he belongs. And again, the prediction of competitive labour market theory is that any firm that did not pay its workers according to the best available estimates of their respective VMPs would eventually be driven from the market by the forces of competition.

EXERCISE 14-10

In the example above, what is the best available estimate of the VMP of a person with a test score of 12?

Now suppose an employer confronts job applicants not only from group A, but also from group B. And suppose the VMP distribution for group B is uniform between $20/hr and $40/hr, as shown in Figure 14-17. Suppose, finally, that two applicants, one from group A, and the other from group B, both get a score of 28 on the test (the same test as before). What are the employer's best estimates of their respective productivity values?

In both cases, the imperfection in the test calls for an adjustment toward the relevant group average. Specifically, the best estimate of the VMP for the worker from group A, denoted $\text{VMP}_A(28)$, is

$$\text{VMPA}(28) = (\frac{1}{2})(\$28/\text{hr}) + (\frac{1}{2})(\$20/\text{hr}) = \$24/\text{hr}, \qquad (14.7)$$

while the corresponding estimate for the worker from group B is

$$\text{VMPB}(28) = (\frac{1}{2})(\$28/\text{hr}) + (\frac{1}{2})(\$30/\text{hr}) = \$29/\text{hr}. \qquad (14.8)$$

Thus, even though the two workers earn exactly the same score on the test, the employer adjusts downward in one case, upward in the other. And again, note that if the firm fails to pay its workers according to the best available estimates of their VMPs, it is in

---

FIGURE 14-17

Productivity Distributions for Two Groups
The VMP values of members of group A are uniformly distributed between $10/hr and $30/hr, while those of members of group B are uniformly distributed between $20/hr and $40/hr. If we know only the groups to which people belong, our best estimates of an individual's VMP would be the average VMP for his or her group—$20/hr for group A, $30/hr for group B.

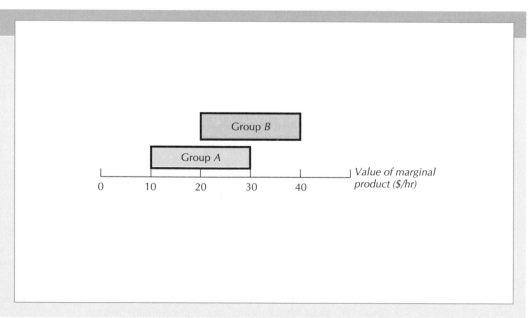

danger of extinction. It is a cruel understatement to say that such competitive imperatives have caused great pain for both employees and employers. The many talented and productive members of group *A* cannot help but feel chagrined when their group identity causes them to be treated differently from the members of other groups. And surely there cannot be many employers who feel comfortable offering different salaries to people whose records look just the same.

Note carefully that statistical discrimination is the result, not the cause, of average productivity differences between groups. Its sole effect is to reduce wage variation within each group. If employers suddenly were able to switch to a policy of setting wages strictly on the basis of individual-specific information, the average wage differential between groups would remain the same as before.

14.14 WINNER-TAKE-ALL MARKETS

In this section we see that differences in rank sometimes cause small differences in ability to translate into large differences in the values of marginal products.[11] The essence of the idea is captured in the following simple example. Imagine that your company, General Dynamics, has been sued by Unidyne for $100 million for patent infringement. On the merits, the case is so close that it is certain to be decided in favour of the side that hires the better lawyer. Suppose Bludgen and Barbe are the top two lawyers in the country, and that while they are almost equally talented in every respect, Barbe is just perceptibly better.

Naturally, both GD and Unidyne will want to hire Barbe, and so both start bidding vigorously for his services. How much will the winner have to pay him? On a moment's reflection, it should be clear that the answer must be $100 million. If Unidyne offered only $99 million, it would be in GD's interest to bid still higher because the alternative is to lose the lawsuit. But then Unidyne will respond by raising its own bid, for its alternative too is to lose the lawsuit. Unless GD and Unidyne can collude successfully, the only stable outcome is for Barbe to be paid $100 million. Bludgen's value, even though he is only a shade less talented, is exactly zero, for by assumption, the side that hires him will lose the lawsuit.

The example is a caricature, but it captures the flavour of what happens in a variety of labour market contexts. Consider, for example, the pay structure in professional tennis. Given the limited amount of time most people are willing to spend watching tennis matches on television, it is practical to see only a handful of players in action during any given year. And given a choice, most fans would be willing to pay a little extra to see the top-ranked players play. The result is that the demand for tennis players ranked in the top 10 is hundreds of times greater than for players ranked around 100. And yet the differences in playing ability between the two categories are often very small. Let the 101st-ranked player meet the 102nd-ranked player and fans will see almost as exciting a match as when the 1st-ranked player meets the 2nd-ranked player. The problem, from the perspective of the lower-ranked pair, is that most fans have time to watch only a single match and would naturally prefer to see the top-ranked pair. The result is that top-ranked players earn millions each year, while those in the second tier earn barely enough to cover their expenses on the tour.

---

[11]The discussion in this section draws on R. Frank, "The Economics of Buying the Best," Cornell University Department of Economics Working Paper, 1978; Sherwin Rosen, "The Economics of Superstars," *American Economic Review,* September 1981; and R. Frank and P. Cook, *The Winner-Take-All Society,* New York: The Free Press, 1995. As is so often the case, one of the earliest discussions of some crucial aspects of winner-take-all markets can be found in Adam Smith (*Wealth of Nations,* Book I, Chapter 10).

The recent rapid growth in demand for *women's* tennis—manifested in increased viewership, higher women's tournament prizes, and greater endorsement income—reveals a further important aspect of such *superstar effects*. Top-flight ability in a sport, narrowly defined, is not the sole determinant of an outstanding individual's earnings in such markets. Anna Kournikova, for example, is a very gifted tennis player, yet in all likelihood her total annual remuneration has not depended exclusively on her on-court performance, but also on her sartorial and other attributes. "Personality" (whether genuine or created by the media) and the "recognition factor" are often worth millions of dollars annually to advertisers aiming to increase their own brand-recognition by association with a celebrity endorser. Moreover, as long as *over*exposure is avoided, the very fact of being presented as a "celebrity" in the ads for one firm confers added value on the celebrity's appearances for other firms. Each set of advertisements legitimizes and thereby increases the cumulative value of the other advertisements, in a self-reinforcing process. At some point, almost independently of having ability, a celebrity can achieve celebrity simply by "being a celebrity."

Similar superstar effects are observed in virtually every professional sport, in the world of entertainment, and even in the ordinary workings of business. Three tenors earn the bulk of the royalties from the compact discs purchased by opera lovers. Regulated companies spend vast sums bidding for the services of a handful of expert witnesses. A small number of actors and actresses have their pick of the best roles.

For the superstar effect to occur, there must be a winner-take-all effect somewhere in the production process. In tennis it is that the top players capture virtually the entire viewing audience. In the lawsuit example, it was that the better lawyer wins the suit. For the superstar effect to be important, the stakes in the contest must be high, as they are in each of these examples.

The marginal productivity theory of pay determination has been criticized on the grounds that workers with nearly identical abilities are often paid vastly different amounts. At first glance, such observations do indeed seem to contradict the theory. But in these circumstances, small differences in ability sometimes translate into very large differences in the values of marginal products.

SUMMARY

- Our goal in this chapter was to examine the economic forces that govern wages and other conditions of employment. The perfectly competitive firm's hiring rule in the short run is to keep hiring until the value of what the last worker produces—the VMP_L—is exactly equal to the wage rate. In the long run, the firm's demand curve for labour is more elastic than in the short run, because the firm faces the additional possibility of substituting labour for capital.

- To aggregate the individual firm demand curves into an industry demand curve for labour involves more than a simple horizontal summation of the individual firm demand curves. An adjustment has to be made for the fact that increasing industry output brings a lower product price.

- The demand curve for labour for a monopolist in the product market is constructed by comparing the wage not with the value of the output the worker produces, but with the amount by which the worker's output will change total revenue—MRP_L. Unlike the perfectly competitive firm, monopolists must take into account that an increase in output requires them to sell existing output at a lower price.

- We began our approach to the supply side of the labour market by considering the individual worker's decision of how much to work at a given wage rate. The more she works, the more she will earn, but the less time she will have available for other activities. The result is a standard consumer choice problem of the kind we examined in Chapter 4. In the consumer case, a price increase of a product is accompanied by a reduction in the quantity demanded (except in the case of the anomalous Giffen good). In contrast, in the labour supply context, it is not uncommon for people to supply fewer hours of labour when wage rates rise. To generate the market supply curve, we add the individual supply curves horizontally. The market supply and demand curves intersect to determine the industry wage level and total volume of industry employment.

- The conventional view of labour unions is that they increase labour's bargaining power vis-à-vis management, thereby increasing labour's share of a fixed economic pie. Recent research, however, suggests that unions may actually improve the productivity of workers, thereby enlarging not only their slice of the economic pie but also management's.

- Proponents of minimum wage laws say they are needed to protect workers from being exploited by employers with excessive market power. Whether the legislation actually serves this goal, however, turns out to be a difficult empirical question.

- Critics claim that many firms pay members of certain groups—notably visible minorities and females—less than they pay white males with the same productivity. Such charges would pose a fundamental challenge to microeconomic theory, for they imply that firms are passing up opportunities to enhance their profits. We saw several reasons, including discrimination by institutions other than firms, that people in the affected groups appear to earn lower salaries.

- An apparent anomaly is the fact that people whose abilities differ only slightly sometimes earn vastly different salaries. The key to resolving the contradiction is to observe that in many contexts, the value of what someone produces depends not only on the absolute level of his or her skills, but on how those skills compare with others'. In arm wrestling, being just a little stronger than your opponent means you win just about every time. In the labour market as well, being just a little better than the competition sometimes means earning vastly more than they do.

- The Web Supplement for Chapter 14 analyzes the internal wage structure of firms and examines a number of factors that affect decisions regarding workplace safety.

QUESTIONS FOR REVIEW

1. What is the difference between the perfect competitor's VMP_L curve and the imperfect competitor's MRP_L curve?

2. If a monopolist bought all the firms in a formerly competitive industry and acquired the legal right to exclude entry, how would the quantity of labour employed be affected?

3. Why might local employers pay workers the value of what they produce even if workers are unable or unwilling to move to another area to accept a better job?

4. Why does economic theory place more emphasis on discrimination by persons and institutions other than employers as a cause of wage differences that exceed productivity differences?

PROBLEMS

1. Given the information in the following table, fill in the value of the marginal product of labour VMP_L for output price $P = \$4$ per unit. Find the perfectly competitive firm's optimal quantity of labour demanded for a wage $w = \$4$ per hour.

L (labour/hours)	MP_L (units per labour-hour)	VMP_L ($ per labour-hour)
0	4	
10	3	
20	2	
30	1	
40	0	

2. Fill in the table below and graph the budget constraint betwen leisure-hours (h) and income per day (M) for $w = \$6$/labour-hour. Then repeat the exercise for h and M', when $w = \$12$/labour-hour. How do the slopes of the two budget constraints compare, and why?

h (leisure-hrs per day)	M ($ per day)	M' ($ per day)
0		
6		
12		
18		
24		

3. Given the information in the accompanying table, find the monopsonist's optimal quantity of labour hired and wage rate paid.

L (labour-hours)	AFC ($ per labour-hour)	TFC ($)	MFC ($ per labour-hour)	MRP_L ($ per labour-hour)
0	0	0	0	16
10	2	20	4	12
20	4	80	8	8
30	6	180	12	4

4. A perfectly competitive firm has $MP_L = 22 - L$. Find and graph its value of the marginal product of labour (VMP_L) function at output price $P = \$5$ per unit of output. Find its optimal quantity demanded of labour at wage rate $w = \$10$/labour-hour.

5. In his current job, Smith can work as many hours per day as he chooses, and he will be paid $1/hr for the first 8 hours he works, $2.50/hr for each hour over 8. Faced with this payment schedule, Smith chooses to work 12 hours per day. If Smith is offered a new job that pays $1.50/hr for as many hours as he chooses to work, will he take it? Explain.

6. Consider the following two antipoverty programs: (1) a payment of $10 per day is to be given this year to each eligible person; *or* (2) each eligible person will be given a benefit equal to 20 percent of the wage income he earns each day this year.

    a. Assuming that eligible persons have the option of working at $4/hr, show how each program would affect the daily budget constraint of a representative eligible worker during the current year.

    b. Which program would be most likely to reduce the number of hours worked?

**7. Douglas Cobb, a utility-maximizing worker, has the following utility function in making his labour-leisure choice:

$$U = hM^2,$$

where h is in leisure-hours per day, he works l hours per day, his labour income M is in dollars per day, and his budget constraint at wage rate w/hr takes the form $M = wl = w(24 - h)$.

    a. Give the formula for Douglas's marginal rate of substitution (MRS) and determine the number of labour-hours he will supply per day by setting MRS $= w$ when $w = \$4$/hr and when $w = \$8$/hour. What is the equation for Douglas's labour supply curve?

    b. Douglas's brother, Cornelius ("Corny") Cobb, has the following utility function:

$$U = h^2M.$$

Answer the questions in 7a for Corny.

8. A monopsonist's marginal revenue product of labour (MRP_L) curve is given by $MRP_L = 12 - 2L$, where w is the hourly wage rate and L is the number of person-hours hired.

    a. If the monopsonist's supply (AFC) curve is given by $w = 2L$, what is the equation for his MFC curve, how many units of labour will he employ and what wage rate will he pay? (*Hint:* use calculus or footnote 4.)

    b. How would your answers to 8a be different if the monopsonist were confronted with a minimum wage bill requiring him to pay at least $7/hr?

    c. How would your answers to 8a be different if the employer in question were required to behave as a perfect competitor in the market for labour? What minimum wage would achieve this result?

9. Acme is the sole supplier of security systems in the product market and the sole employer of locksmiths in the labour market. The demand curve for security systems is given by $P = 100 - Q$, where Q is the number of systems installed per week. The short-run production function for security systems is given by $Q = 4L$, where L is the number of full-time locksmiths employed per week. The supply curve for locksmiths is given by $w = 40 + 2L$, where w is the weekly wage for each locksmith. How many locksmiths will Acme hire, what wage will it pay, how many systems will be installed, and how much will its total revenue be? (*Hint:* use calculus or footnote 4.)

10. The MRP_L curve of a monopsonist is given as $MRP_L = 54 - 2L$; the supply curve (AFC) for this monopsonist is $w = 6 + L$, where w represents the hourly wage rate and L is the number of person-hours hired.

    a. Give the MFC function, and find the optimal quantity of labour and wage rate for this profit-maximizing monopsonist. (*Hint:* use calculus or footnote 4.)

    b. Suppose a minimum wage law imposed a $22/hr minimum wage. How would this affect the quantity of labour demanded by this firm?

11. A monopolist can hire any quantity of labour for $10/labour-hour. If his marginal product of labour is currently 2 units/labour-hour, and his current product price is $5 per unit, should he increase or decrease the amount of labour hired?

12. The Ajax Coal Company is the only employer in its area. Its only variable input is labour, which has a constant marginal product equal to 5 units/person-hour. Because it is the only employer in the area, the firm faces a supply curve for labour given by $w = 10 + L$, where w is the wage rate and L is the number of person-hours employed. Suppose the firm can sell all it wishes at a constant price of $8 per unit of output.

    a. Give the equation for Ajax's MFC curve, and calculate how much labour the firm employs, how much output it produces, and the wage rate it pays.

    b. Suppose now the firm sells a special kind of coal such that it faces a downward-sloping demand curve for its output. In particular, assume that Ajax faces the demand curve given by $P = 102 - 1.96Q$. How much labour does it employ, how much output does it produce, what price does it set for the output, and what is the wage rate?

13. Suppose vacation time comes in one-week intervals, and that the total willingness to pay for total vacation time by younger and older workers in a competitive industry is as given in the table at the top of the next page.

    Suppose $VMP_L = $150 per week for younger workers, $175 per week for older workers, and that existing firms give all their workers, young and old, 5 weeks per year of vacation time. Can these firms be maximizing their profits? If so, explain why. If not, say what changes they should make, and how much extra profit will result.

| Total vacation time, weeks | Total willingness to pay ($) | |
	Younger workers	Older workers
1	300	500
2	475	800
3	600	1050
4	700	1250
5	750	1400

14. Members of two groups, the blues and the greens, have productivity values that range from $5 to $15/hr. The average productivity of the blues is $6/hr and the corresponding average for the greens is $12/hr. A costless productivity test is known to have the property that it gives the correct productivity value with probability 1/3, and a random productivity value drawn from the relevant group distribution with probability 2/3.

    a. Assuming labour markets are competitive, how much will a blue with a test value of 9 be paid?

    b. How much will a green with the same test value be paid?

    c. Is it correct to say that statistical discrimination accounts for why the greens, as a group, are paid more than the blues?

15. A firm has a task to carry out that involves opportunities to shirk with a low probability of detection. If it can hire a nonshirking employee for this task, it will make a lot of money. Its strategy for finding a nonshirker is to pay a very low wage at first, then increase the wage gradually each year so that, by the time the worker has been with the firm for 10 years, he will be earning more than he could elsewhere. The present value of the wage premiums in the later years is larger than the present value of the shortfall in the early years.

    a. Explain how this strategy helps to attract a nonshirking employee. Would the same strategy work if the probability of detecting shirking were zero?

    b. Explain why the ability of the firm to implement this strategy might depend to an extent on its own reputation in the labour market.

16. Consider a two-sector economy that employs a total of 80 units of a single input, labour. N_1 of these units are allocated to sector 1, where the wage is 100 for the top five workers in that sector and zero for all others. (Both the wage for the top workers and the number who receive that wage are invariant to changes in N_1.) The remaining $N_2 = 80 - N_1$ units of labour serve in sector 2, where every worker receives a wage of 10. All workers in sector 1 have an equal probability of being among the top five workers, $5/N_1$, and all workers are risk neutral.

    a. How many workers will work in sector 1?

    b. What will be the value of GNP for the economy?

    c. How would your answers differ if there were a 50 percent tax on the earnings of workers in sector 1?

**17. A competitive firm produces output according to the production function $Q = K^{1/2}L^{1/2}$. If it sells its output in a perfectly competitive market at a price of $10 per unit, and if K is fixed at 4 units, what is this firm's short-run demand curve for labour?

**18. How would your answer to the preceding problem be different if the employer in question sold his product according to the demand schedule $P = 20 - Q$?

14-1. When the product price rises to $3 per unit, the VMPL curve is as shown in panel *b* of the diagram below. The new quantity of labour demanded at $w = \$12$/labour-day is 120 labour-days per day.

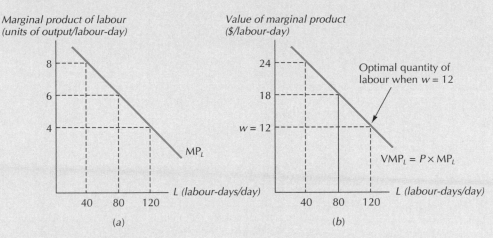

(a)   (b)

The value of the marginal product is

$$\mathrm{VMP}_L = P(\mathrm{MP}_L) = 3(10 - \frac{1}{20}L) = 30 - \frac{3}{20}L.$$

The profit-maximizing level of hiring occurs where

$$w = \mathrm{VMP}_L \Rightarrow 12 = 30 - \frac{3}{20}L \Rightarrow 18 = \frac{3}{20}L \Rightarrow L^* = 120 \text{ labour-days}$$

14-2. With $w = \$20$/hr, the income/leisure budget constraint is

$$M = w(24 - h) = 20(24 - h) = 480 - 20h.$$

With leisure $h = 14$ hours per day, income per day is

$$M = 20(24 - h) = 20(24 - 14) = 20(10) = \$200.$$

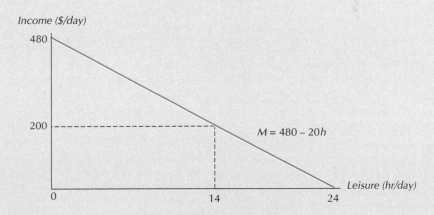

14-3.

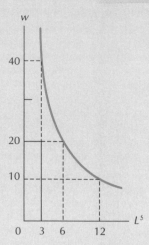

14-4. The driver can reach his weekly income target in fewer total hours per week if he works longer hours during the rainy days and shorter hours during the nonrainy days.

14-5. The budget constraint remains $M = 480 - 20h$. As the individual is willing to sacrifice 1 hour of leisure for $10 of income, indifference curves are straight lines of the general form $M = a - 10h$ provided in the hint. The highest indifference curve that shares a point with the income/leisure constraint is $M = 480 - 10h$, with optimal leisure demand $h = 0$. This form of preferences exhibits extreme substitution effects: the individual will consume no leisure for any $w > 10$ and all leisure for any $w < 10$.

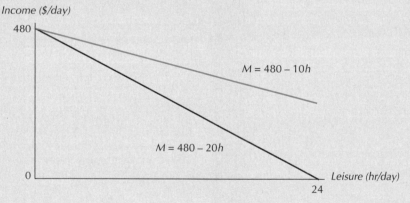

14-6. In his current job, Maynard's maximum income from working all 24 hours is the sum of 8 hours at $5/hr and the remaining 16 hours at $20/hr:

$$8(5) + 16(20) = 40 + 320 = \$360 \text{ per day.}$$

Each hour of leisure requires sacrifice of $20 up to $h = 16$ hr, but only $5 beyond 16 hr. Consuming $h = 16$ hr of leisure and working $24 - h = 24 - 16 = 8$ hr yields $8(5) = \$40$ of income (at the kink in the budget constraint). Maynard's original budget constraint is thus

$$M_1 = \begin{cases} 360 - 20h; \ 0 \leq h \leq 16 \\ 120 - 5h; \ 16 \leq h \leq 24 \end{cases}.$$

The budget constraint has two segments reflecting the two wage rates (regular and overtime). If Maynard works 12 hours, then he enjoys $h_1 = 12$ hours of leisure per day, and thus with the original budget constraint earns income

$$M_1 = 360 - 20h = 360 - 20(12) = 360 - 240 = \$120 \text{ per day.}$$

In his potential new job, Maynard's maximum income from working all 24 hours would be 24(10) = \$240. An hour of leisure requires sacrifice of \$10 of income, up to a maximum of 24 hours per day. Maynard's new budget constraint is

$$M_2 = 240 - 10h.$$

Here the budget constraint is a simple straight line. Maynard's original optimal labour supply choice would still be feasible with the new budget constraint: Maynard could earn the same income with the same amount of leisure of time under the new budget constraint:

$$M_2 = 240 - 10h = 240 - 10(12) = 240 - 120 = \$120 \text{ per day.}$$

Thus, Maynard can be no worse off with the new budget constraint. However, Maynard will have an opportunity cost of leisure time of $w = \$10/hr$ with the new budget constraint rather than $w = \$20/hr$ with the old budget constraint. Therefore, if Maynard has smooth, convex indifference curves, in order to reach his optimum position he must reduce the number of labour-hours he provides, in favour of more leisure. Maynard will be happier at his new optimal labour supply choice. He reaches a higher income-leisure indifference curve (I_2), and so he will accept the new job.

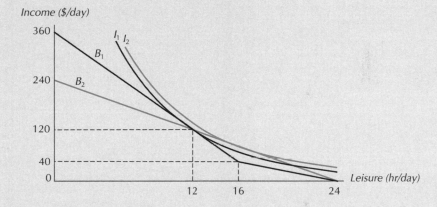

14-7. The original budget constraint is

$$M_0 = w(24 - h) = 5(24 - h) = 120 - 5h.$$

The first program yields a budget constraint

$$M_1 = S + w(24 - h) = 24 + 5(24 - h) = 144 - 5h.$$

The second program yields a budget constraint

$$M_2 = (1 + s)w(24 - h) = (1 + .4)5(24 - h)$$
$$= 7(24 - h) = 168 - 7h.$$

The first program is more likely to reduce hours worked because it increases income but leaves the opportunity cost of leisure unchanged: assuming leisure is a normal good, higher income leads to more leisure consumed. In contrast, the second program increases the opportunity cost of leisure: for low levels of the wage rate, an increase in the wage rate generally increases labour supply as the substitution effect dominates the income effect. Thus, a low-income worker will likely work less under the first program and more under the second program, provided that she works fewer than 12 hours per day in either program.

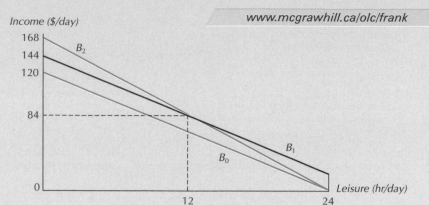

14-8.

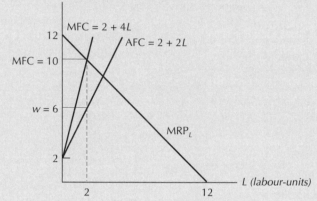

The initial case is shown here. You should draw the case with AFC = w = 4 + .5L, MFC = 4 + L, L^* = 4 labour-units, and w = \$6 per labour-unit. Note that with w = \$6 per labour-unit, the monopsonist will hire *either 2 or 4* labour-units, depending on the shape of the labour supply (AFC) and MFC functions. That is, the monopsonist has no demand curve.

14-9. When the minimum wage is \$8/labour-unit, the monopsonist's MFC curve is the heavy locus with the discontinuity at L = 3. The MRP_L curve passes through this discontinuity, which means that the monopsonist will hire 3 units of labour at a wage of \$8/labour-unit. When the minimum wage is 10, the monopsonist will pay w = \$10/labour-unit and hire 2 units of labour, the same quantity she would have hired in the absence of a minimum wage.

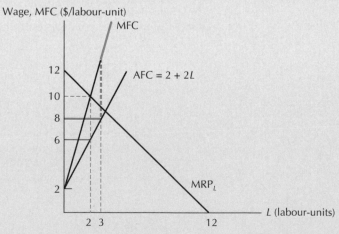

14-10. VMP(12) = ($\frac{1}{20}$)(\$12 per hour) + ($\frac{1}{20}$)(\$20 per hour) = \$16 per hour.

Chapter 15

CAPITAL

S ome newspapers, including the *Toronto Star*, periodically run stock portfolio-picking contests for their readers, young and old alike. At the same time, the *Star* usually invites some expert investment analysts from the major brokerage houses to make their "best-bet" picks. And just for good measure, the *Star* picks a "random" portfolio, basically by throwing darts at the financial page. These imaginary portfolios cannot be changed for the duration of the contest, and the grand winner is the one whose portfolio gains the most in value. The expert analysts rarely if ever win the contest, and their picks have often been outperformed by the average return for the stock market taken as a whole. Some of the "expert" portfolios have gone down in flames. To add insult to injury, there are usually some grade school students among the top ten winners, and the dartboard picks have often fared better than the "experts."

Similar results have been observed with respect to the investment advice published in investment newsletters. Subscriptions to some of these newsletters, whether mailed out or on the Internet, cost several hundred dollars per year. Yet the stocks recommended in most of these newsletters perform no better, on average, than would a random selection of listed stocks.

As anomalous as these patterns may appear at first glance, we shall see that they are consistent with at least one theory of how financial capital markets function. Indeed, with investment newsletters, the real anomaly may be not that the stocks they recommend do no better than others, but that people continue to pay such high prices for this kind of advice.

CHAPTER PREVIEW

In this chapter we examine the market for services of capital inputs. In many respects, the results from our study of labour inputs will carry forward intact. One feature that often sets capital apart from other inputs is that whereas other inputs are usually hired on a period-by-period basis, capital equipment is often owned outright by the firm. In our first exercise we examine the factors that govern the firm's decision to buy a piece of capital equipment.

We then examine the distinction between real and nominal rates of interest. This distinction will help make clear why the interest rates banks and other lenders charge tend to rise hand in hand with the overall rate of inflation.

Next we see how interest rates are determined in the market for loanable funds. A topic of special focus is the market for stocks and bonds; we take up the apparent anomalies mentioned in the chapter introduction. Additional items on our agenda include economic rent and peak-load pricing.

15.1 FINANCIAL CAPITAL AND REAL CAPITAL

When people use the term "capital" they usually mean one of two very different things. They may have in mind *financial capital*, which essentially means money or some other form of paper asset that functions like money. Or they may mean *real capital*, which includes all means of production that generate a flow of productive services over time: lathes, printing presses, barns, factory and office buildings, roads and railway lines, mineshafts, computers, combine harvesters, and orchards. There is an argument for also including computer software and other types of intellectual property as forms of real capital, notwithstanding the fact that the role of capitalized knowledge as a productive input involves genuine conceptual and measurement problems. What should strike us about this catalogue is the diversity or *heterogeneity* of real capital. We shall speak of "the marginal product of capital" in the chapter. Strictly speaking, however, we should speak of "the marginal product of the flow of services from a *particular* machine, used for a *particular* duration, in conjunction with a *particular* combination of labour and other real capital services." This more long-winded expression should be assumed whenever we use the term "marginal product of capital." Alternatively, we could think of the total real capital of a firm as a *composite* commodity, made up of all of its different components in fixed proportions. Here, however, we would have to assume that all of the components are perfectly divisible, which is not in practice a realistic assumption.

When we refer to capital as a factor of production, we are almost always talking about real capital.[1] When people talk about the "capital market" they generally mean the market for financial capital, such as bank loans, corporate stocks, and bonds. Our direct concern in this chapter is with real capital, but because firms require financial capital to purchase real capital, we must consider markets for financial capital as well.

15.2 THE DEMAND FOR REAL CAPITAL

Our theory of the individual firm's demand for labour developed in Chapter 14 applies without modification to the demand for other inputs. In the short run, if the firm can acquire the services of as much capital as it wishes at a constant rental rate of r per year, it should employ capital up to the point at which its marginal revenue product (MRP_K) is exactly equal to the rental rate:

---

[1]Some economists would include "working capital," money the firm keeps on hand to facilitate timely payment of debts when current revenues fall short, as a factor of production, because it enables the firm to function more efficiently. Others argue, however, that working capital does not belong in the production function, because money in and of itself does not produce anything. This debate, which relates to the foundations of monetary theory, is beyond the scope of our discussion here.

$$\text{MRP}_K = \text{MR} \times \text{MP}_K = r, \qquad\qquad (15.1)$$

where MR is the firm's marginal revenue and MP_K is the marginal product of capital.

If the firm happens to be a perfect competitor in its product market, so that its marginal revenue is the same as its product price, then Equation 15.1 reduces to the simpler form:

$$\text{VMP}_K = P \times \text{MP}_K = r, \qquad\qquad (15.2)$$

where VMP_K denotes the value of the marginal product of capital and P is the price of the firm's output.

For firms in a perfectly competitive industry, aggregation of individual firm demand curves into an industry demand curve for capital involves essentially the same complication we saw for labour. We must take into account that an expansion of industry output involves a reduction in the product price, with attendant reductions in the quantities of capital demanded. Again as before, this effect is already accounted for in the monopolist's MRP_K curve.

One salient difference between capital and labour markets is that whereas workers tend to specialize in particular types of activities, new sources of capital (financial capital) are almost completely fungible. Thus, a given sum of money can just as easily fund the construction of a machine to make soft ice cream as it can a printing press, or the production of an animated cartoon. Once financial capital has been used to purchase real capital, however, the firm's flexibility is significantly limited. Whereas labour can, at some expense, be retrained to perform new tasks when conditions change, it is much more difficult to transform a drill press into a sewing machine.

15.3 THE RELATIONSHIP BETWEEN THE RENTAL RATE AND THE INTEREST RATE

How is the rental price of a unit of real capital equipment related to the interest rate at which money can be borrowed? To answer this question, put yourself in the position of a firm whose business is to rent machines. Suppose the purchase price of a particular machine is $1000 and the interest rate at which money can be borrowed or loaned is 5 percent per year. To cover just the opportunity cost of the $1000 you have tied up in the machine, you would have to charge $50 per year for it. But in general there will be additional costs as well. Suppose the machine requires $100 per year worth of maintenance. Your breakeven rental will then have risen to $150 per year. Finally, you must consider changes in the future price of the machine.

For simplicity, suppose that the overall level of prices in the economy is stable. (We analyze below what happens when we relax this assumption.) Even a well-maintained machine will lose some of its value each year. Indeed, if newer, more efficient machines are being designed each year, an existing machine may lose its economic value overnight, even though it continues to function exactly as it did when new. This phenomenon is called **technological obsolescence**. If the net result of these factors—physical wear and tear and technological obsolescence—is for the price of the machine in our example to fall by $100 per year, the total cost of supplying it will then be $250 per year—$50 in forgone interest, $100 in maintenance, and $100 in lost market value. Any additional costs you incur as a rental business—such as wages for your staff—would have to be added to that figure.

Let m stand for annual maintenance expenses, expressed as a fraction of the price of the capital good, and let ∂ stand for physical and technological depreciation, similarly

Technological obsolescence
The process by which a good loses value not because of physical depreciation, but because improvements in technology make substitute products more attractive.

expressed. If i denotes the market rate of interest, expressed in decimal form, then the annual rental price of capital, r, will be the sum of i, m, and ∂:

$$r = i + m + \partial. \qquad (15.3)$$

Sometimes a machine will actually grow, rather than depreciate, in value over time. This can happen, for example, when a key input used in making the machine becomes more expensive. In such cases, the term ∂ in Equation 15.3 would be negative. For example, if the rental firm from our earlier example expected the price of a machine to go *up* by $100 in the year to come, it could break even at a rental fee of only $50, $200 lower than if the price of the machine went down by $100. Expectations of asset price increases appear to explain why, when housing prices are rising rapidly, rents are often lower than the corresponding mortgage payments.

EXERCISE 15-1

Suppose the purchase price of a Coke machine is $5000. If the interest rate is 8 percent per year, the maintenance rate is 2 percent per year, and the rate of physical and technological depreciation is 10 percent per year, how much will the machine's annual rental fee be?

15.4 THE CRITERION FOR BUYING A CAPITAL GOOD

Another factor that sets capital apart from labour is that firms have the option of purchasing capital equipment. Exclusive rights to the athletic services of professional athletes are sometimes bought and sold, but even professional athletes cannot be forced to play for a team indefinitely against their wishes. Labour contracts in general permit workers to move whenever the terms of employment are no longer attractive, the primary reason being that it is impractical to make a disgruntled employee work effectively on the firm's behalf. Moreover, although slavery still exists in some parts of the world, nations have made chattel slavery (the treatment of human beings as property or "capital goods") illegal. The machine, of course, enjoys no such right. It goes to the highest bidder.

What factors govern a firm's decision about whether to buy a given piece of capital equipment? As always, the firm will wish to weigh the benefits of owning the machine against its costs. On the benefit side, the machine will bolster the firm's rate of production not only in the current period, but also in the future. Suppose the extra output made possible by the machine will enhance the firm's total revenue by R for each of the next N years. Suppose further that the machine costs M each year to maintain, and that at the end of N years it has a scrap value of S dollars. R and M are both paid at the *end* of each year. Suppose, finally, that the firm is given this machine and expects to operate it for N years, at which point it will sell it for scrap. How much will the present value of the firm's stream of profits go up?

To answer this question, we must translate net revenues the firm will receive in the future into an equivalent present value. As we saw in Chapter 6, the present value of a dollar to be received 1 year from now is $\$1/(1 + i)$, where i denotes the market rate of interest. The net present value of the stream of returns produced by the machine, including the proceeds from sale for scrap, is therefore given by

$$\text{PV} = \frac{R - M}{1 + i} + \frac{R - M}{(1 + i)^2} + \cdots + \frac{R - M}{(1 + i)^N} + \frac{S}{(1 + i)^N}. \qquad (15.4)$$

The cost of the machine is simply its purchase price, P_K. The firm's decision criterion should be to buy the machine if and only if PV is greater than or equal to P_K. We see from Equation 15.4 that PV is inversely related to the market rate of interest. Thus, as with the firm that rents its equipment, the firm that owns its capital goods will want to employ more of them the lower the market rate of interest is.

EXERCISE 15-2

Suppose a machine generates $121 worth of revenue at the end of each of the next 2 years, at which time it can be sold to a salvage company for $242. If the rate of interest is 10 percent per year, what is the maximum amount a business would pay for this machine?

15.5 INTEREST RATE DETERMINATION

To recapitulate, a firm's demand for capital equipment depends on the rate of interest, the purchase price of capital, and the rates of technological and physical depreciation. Interest rates, in turn, are determined by the intersection of the supply and demand curves for loanable funds. Because financial capital is perfectly fungible, the market for loanable funds is an almost literal embodiment of the ideal of a perfectly homogeneous, standardized product. The result is a national—indeed international—market for loanable funds in which, apart from uncertainty about future foreign exchange rates, the interest rate charged to a given type of borrower is virtually the same everywhere.

How is the demand for loanable funds related to the demand for real capital? A firm's demand for capital tells us how much real capital it would like to employ at any given rental price of capital, r. If it is a firm that has already been in operation for some time, it presumably has already acquired much of the real capital it needs.

For simplicity, let us assume that in the current year the firm wishes to bridge the entire gap between the amount of real capital it has and the amount it would like to have. This gap then constitutes its demand for loanable funds. At the industry level, similarly, the demand for loanable funds is the difference between the amount of capital firms as a whole would like to have and the amount they already do have. The price that is used to ration money in the loanable funds market is the interest rate.

Firms are not the only borrowers in the loanable funds market. Consumers borrow to finance the purchase of houses and other goods. Governments borrow to build roads and schools, and to finance general budget deficits. The demand curve for loanable funds is the horizontal summation of the demands from all these sources.

On the supply side, there are also multiple sources of loanable funds. Consumer savings supplement funds made available by firms out of profits. Firms that currently have excess liquidity—more money in hand than they can foreseeably require for transactions, precautionary or speculative purposes—supply their surplus funds via financial intermediaries to the loanable funds market. In so doing, they increase their return on what would otherwise be "idle," non-interest-bearing, cash balances. Historically in Canada, particularly since the early nineteenth century, foreign sources of loanable funds have also been important, first in the development of canals and railways and later in industry generally. During the twentieth century, however, *direct* foreign investment—capital inflows in equity, or ownership, form—became relatively more important in Canada than *indirect*—debt, or loan—foreign capital inflows.

As we saw in Chapter 5, the theory of consumer behaviour tells us that a rise in interest rates may either raise or lower consumer savings. The total effect is the net result of

FIGURE 15-1

Equilibrium in the Market for Loanable Funds
The quantity of loanable funds demanded at any interest rate (*D*) is the difference between the desired stock of capital at that interest rate and the amount of capital stock already in place. The supply of loanable funds (*S*) comes from consumers, firms, and international lenders. The globalization of international finance assures that the supply curve of loanable funds will not be downward sloping.

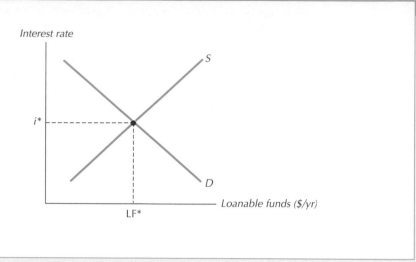

offsetting income and substitution effects, and theory alone does not tell us which will dominate. Empirical studies suggest that in fact the elasticity of consumer savings with respect to interest rates is sometimes positive, sometimes negative, but in any event almost certainly very small.

For savings by private firms, there is no analogue to the income effect in the consumer case, so the quantity of loanable funds supplied by firms will respond positively to interest rates. Most foreign lenders are happy to supply funds to Canadian borrowers whenever the interest rate meets or exceeds what they can earn at home. By the same token, if Canadian interest rates are even slightly lower than those in foreign markets, a large outflow of loanable funds can be the result. Adding all sources of supply horizontally, we obtain the aggregate supply curve of loanable funds. The globalization of the market for loanable funds and the increased volume of international financial capital flows in recent years suggest that this factor is responsible for most of the elasticity we see in the supply curve of loanable funds. The intersection of this curve with the aggregate demand curve for loanable funds, shown in Figure 15-1, determines both the market rate of interest, *i**, and the total volume of funds exchanged, LF*.

15.6 REAL VS. NOMINAL INTEREST RATES

Suppose you borrow $1000 from a bank, which you agree to repay in a year's time at 5 percent interest. And suppose that once the year passes, the overall price level in the economy has risen by 10 percent (as, for example, would happen if each and every price rose by 10 percent). What has been the real cost to you of your loan?

To answer this question, imagine that when you first borrowed the money, you used it to buy $1000 worth of uncut gems. The price of gems, like every other price, is assumed to be rising at 10 percent per year. This means that when your loan comes due, you can sell your gems for $1100, or $50 more than the $1050 you need to repay the bank. The real cost to you of the loan, measured in dollars on its due date, is therefore *minus* $50. Not only did it not cost you any real resources to borrow the money, but you actually came out $50 ahead. On the reciprocal end of this transaction, the bank that loaned you the money came out $50 behind.

Needless to say, a bank could hardly hope to remain in business if it continued to loan money at such unfavourable terms. When banks expect the overall level of prices to rise, they will charge an interest premium to counteract the erosion of the real purchasing power of future loan payments. The actual number that appears on the bank loan contract is called the *nominal rate of interest*—5 percent per year in our example. If n denotes the nominal annual rate of interest, expressed as a fraction, and q denotes the annual rate of inflation, also expressed as a fraction, then the *real rate of interest, i,* is given by

$$i = \frac{n - q}{1 + q} \qquad (15.5)$$

Using the values from our hypothetical example, we have $i = (.05 - .10)/1.10 = -.0455$, or -4.55 percent per year. We can see from Equation 15.5 that when the rate of inflation is small, the real interest rate is approximately equal to the difference between the nominal rate of interest and the rate of inflation, $n - q$. In all our prior examples, the interest rate has been implicitly assumed to be the real interest rate. In its investment decisions, the firm wants to compare the real costs of capital against the real benefits, and proceed only if the latter exceed the former.

15.7 THE MARKET FOR STOCKS AND BONDS

One common method by which firms raise money for new investments is by issuing corporate bonds. A bond is essentially a promissory note issued by the firm. An investor gives the firm some money—say, $10,000—and in return the firm hands the investor a handsomely engraved certificate that promises to pay the investor a fixed rate of interest—say, 10 percent—for a specified time. The *face value* of the bond is the amount for which it was sold to the investor who bought it from the firm. The lifetimes of corporate bonds vary considerably. *Short-term bonds* often promise to return their face value in full within 90 days. Many *long-term bonds* reach maturity only after 30 years, and some have even longer lifetimes.

Once bought, a bond may be traded in the open market. If it is a short-term bond, its price will almost always be close to its face value. For longer-term bonds, however, the price fetched in the open market can differ substantially from face value.

To see why, suppose the market rate of interest is 10 percent when an investor buys a $10,000 bond from a corporation; the bond promises to pay her $1000 per year interest for the next 30 years and then return her $10,000 in full. As long as the interest rate remains 10 percent, the bond will continue to be "worth" $10,000 in the sense that its $1000 annual interest payment fully compensates the investor for the opportunity cost of doing without her money. But suppose the interest rate unexpectedly falls to 5 percent. Now the opportunity cost of doing without $10,000 suddenly falls from $1000 per year to only $500 per year. The investor who holds a bond that promises to give her $1000 per year would not be willing to sell it for only $10,000, because with the interest rate at 5 percent, she would need $20,000 in order to earn the $1000 per year interest she will get by keeping the bond.

The price of the bond in this example will not rise all the way to $20,000, however, because the new buyer knows that the bond will be worth only $10,000 when it reaches maturity. If the due date is imminent, the price will be close to $10,000 no matter what the interest rate is. But the farther away the maturity date of the bond is, the less its face value will affect its current market price. Indeed, there is a particular type of bond, called a *perpetual bond* or *consol,* for which the face value does not matter at all. A perpetual bond is a promise to pay its bearer a fixed sum of money each year forever. As a close approximation, the current market price of a consol is the amount of money that would be needed, if the current market interest rate were expected to continue into the future, to generate the same amount of interest as is paid by the consol. Thus, for example, a consol that promises to pay $1000 per year will be worth $10,000 when the interest rate is 10 percent, and $20,000 when the interest rate is 5 percent. More generally, if I represents the consol's annual payment and i is the market rate of interest, then the price of the consol, P_C, will be given by

$$P_C = \frac{I}{i}. \tag{15.6}$$

EXERCISE 15-3

Consider a perpetual bond that pays $120 per year to its owner. By how much would the price of this bond rise if the interest rate fell from 10 to 5 percent, and was expected to stay there?

Corporations are not the only institutions that issue bonds. Governments at the federal, provincial, and local level do so as well. The examples discussed earlier implicitly assumed that there is a single, uniform market rate of interest at any moment, but in fact there are many different interest rates. The general rule is that the greater the risk is that a borrower will not repay a loan, the greater the interest rate that borrower will pay. Government of Canada bonds carry the lowest risk of default available in the bond market, and the government therefore pays lower rates of interest than do the issuers of other bonds. Suppose, for example, that 10-year, $10,000 Bell Canada bonds pay 8 percent annual interest, while the same type of bond issued by the federal government pays only 6 percent. The 2 percent interest rate differential is called a ***risk premium***, and it compensates the investor for the fact that Bell has a higher likelihood of not repaying its loan than does the federal government.

Risk premium A payment differential necessary to compensate the supplier of a good or service for having to endure risk.

Someone who owns a corporate bond does not have an ownership share in the corporation. The bondholder's financial position is similar to that of a bank that has issued the corporation a loan. The corporation's shareholders are the people who actually own it. A firm that wants to raise money to invest in capital equipment can hire a broker to arrange a new issue of stock certificates. The broker then prepares a description of the firm's investment proposal and, with the cooperation of a network of other brokers, offers the new stock for sale to the public.

If a firm sells 1,000,000 shares of stock, each share constitutes a claim against $\frac{1}{1,000,000}$ of the current and future profits of the firm. Profits may be distributed to shareholders directly in the form of dividends, or they may be reinvested in the company, which will increase the value of the company's future profits.

What price will each share of stock command? Suppose the present value of the current and future profits of our 1,000,000-share hypothetical company is known with certainty to be $500 million. Its stock should then trade at exactly $500/share. At a price any lower than that, investors could increase their wealth immediately by buying it. And at any price above $500, no one would have any economic incentive to own it.

Seldom, if ever, is a company's future profit stream known with certainty. The price people are willing to pay for shares depends on their best estimates of the firm's prospects. For new firms, or for firms that are moving into uncharted territory, the risk

FIGURE 15-2

The Tradeoff between Safety and Expected Return
Because most investors are averse to risk, they will not buy a risky stock unless its expected return is greater than that of less risky stocks. Which type of stock to buy depends on the buyer's preferences. Relatively cautious investors will prefer safer stocks like *C*. Less cautious investors will give up some safety for the greater expected return on investments like *A*.

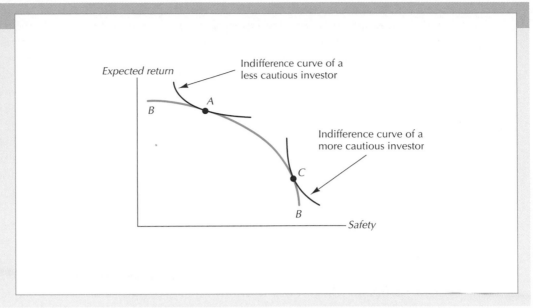

of low earnings can be very substantial indeed. If a genetic engineering company comes up with a way to clone a protein that destroys the AIDS virus, its profits will be virtually unbounded. But many companies are struggling to be first in that race, and the destiny of most of them is to fail.

In other areas of the economy, the economic prospects of a company are easier to predict. Alcan has been in the aluminum business for many decades now, and no major surprises appear to be on the horizon. Alcan stands almost no chance of hitting a big jackpot. But by the same token, its odds of continuing to survive are relatively high.

Consider two firms with the same expected value of current and future profits. The present value of firm 1's profit stream is $100 million with certainty. The present value of firm 2's profit stream, in contrast, has a 50–50 chance of being either $200 million or zero. If the stock prices of the two firms were the same, which one would you prefer to buy? If you are like most investors, you are risk averse (see Chapter 6) and therefore prefer firm 1, the safer investment of the two.

Because most people have this preference, the stocks of firms with risky future earnings generally sell at lower prices, just as riskier bonds generally must pay higher interest rates. As an investor confronting the stock market, you face a budget constraint something like the curve labelled *BB* in Figure 15-2. Along *BB*, the safer the investment, the lower its expected return. Investors with relatively low marginal rates of substitution between return and safety will choose risky investments such as *A*, which offer relatively high expected returns. Those with higher marginal rates of substitution between return and safety will choose safer investments such as *C*. Virtually everyone would like to own stocks with high expected returns *and* high safety. But the terms available in the market force people to choose between these attributes.

The Efficient Markets Hypothesis

Many economists believe that the stock market is generally efficient. By this we mean that the price of a stock embodies all available information that is relevant to its current and future earnings prospects. To illustrate, consider a hypothetical example involving

Dynogene, a highly successful genetic engineering company. Suppose that on the strength of its earnings prospects, the current value of a share of Dynogene is $100. Now suppose that one of Dynogene's researchers suddenly stumbles onto a miracle cure for cancer. The discovery is simple and easy to patent. The company is certain to win government approval for its discovery, at which point its revenues will soar dramatically. But because of bureaucratic red tape, the approval process never takes less than three years. You read in the *Financial Post* about Dynogene's discovery and decide to buy stock in the company. Is this a shrewd move on your part?

The answer is almost certainly no, but not because the company does not have the rosy future that has been forecast for it. The difficulty, according to the efficient markets hypothesis, is that the value of the new discovery will be almost instantaneously bid into the market price of its stock. By the time you hear about it, the rise in price for which it is responsible will have long since occurred.

Note in this context that a divergence between the price-earnings (PE) ratios of two companies' stocks does not refute the efficient markets hypothesis. The PE ratio is a rough-hewn measure that includes only *current* earnings, whereas share prices also reflect the capitalized value of expected *future* profits of the two companies. A company's stock may have a relatively low PE ratio because it is currently undervalued, *or* because the company's future prospects are not that promising. Similarly, a high PE ratio may reflect overvaluation of the stock, *or* an extremely promising expected future earnings stream. The efficient markets hypothesis, moreover, implies that undervaluation and overvaluation are unlikely to persist for long. The market price of a stock at any time should *fully* reflect *all* of the information that bears on the value of that stock.

Economic Naturalist 15-1

WHY IS OWNING STOCK IN A MONOPOLY NO BETTER THAN OWNING STOCK IN A PERFECTLY COMPETITIVE FIRM?

Many people believe that it is better to buy stock in a highly profitable company than in one with only an average profit level. An important implication of the efficient markets hypothesis, however, is that this belief is wrong. To see why, consider two firms identical in all respects except that one is a monopoly and earns twice the profit earned by the other. If the prices of the two stocks were the same, everyone would naturally want to own stock in the monopoly. But for that very reason, the prices of the two stocks cannot be the same. The excess profit of the monopoly will result in its stock selling for twice the price of the other firm's stock. From the perspective of the person buying the stock, therefore, the rate of return will be exactly the same for the two firms. True enough, the monopoly is twice as profitable, but its stock will cost twice as much to acquire.

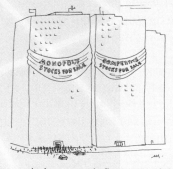

Are stocks in monopoly firms a good deal?

Economic Naturalist 15-1 also helps to explain why, in the example with which we began the chapter, the expert investment analysts' "best picks" were often outperformed by those of schoolchildren, or by the dartboard method. Recall that each portfolio chosen is "locked in" for the duration of the contest. If the experts select the stocks of companies that have excellent management and solid growth prospects, the stock market has usually already factored these strengths into the value of the shares, and so it is unlikely that they will significantly outperform the market as a whole.

Large gains in the value of a stock are principally due to *unanticipated* good news about the company's prospects that emerges during the contest. Unanticipated *bad* news can cause a sharp and rapid *drop* in a stock's value, as the market rapidly moves to incorporate the implications of the new information into the value of the stock. If the news, good or bad, is *genuinely* unanticipated, then by definition, without "inside information" the experts are on roughly an equal footing with all of the other contest participants. In this setting, a "lucky" amateur, one who guesses right, can outperform the pros. For similar reasons, investment newsletters containing "hot tips" on what to buy and sell are unlikely to "beat the market." In the time it takes to produce and distribute them, other investors with access to this information—including the writers of the newsletters themselves—should have already bid the stocks' prices up or down to the level that reflects any new information.

Some Qualifications

At this point, you may be feeling a bit skeptical. Surely *some* people are making money in the stock market in response to emergent new information, by buying a stock just before it rises or selling a stock just before it falls. In this vein, economists tell the story of two believers in the efficient markets hypothesis who are walking down the street one day when they notice a twenty-dollar bill lying on the sidewalk. One of them reaches down for it. The other says, "Don't bother. If it were really there, somebody else would already have picked it up." The efficient markets hypothesis has not been properly understood by these two true believers, although some descriptions of the hypothesis may sound suspiciously close to the version in the story.

You may be skeptical on another count. The volatility of stock markets in recent years may, as the efficient market hypothesis holds, be simply be a response to new information. But some of the market volatility smacks of "bandwagon" effects and herd psychology, like the tulip mania we noted at the start of Chapter 2.

Can we reconcile the efficient markets hypothesis with such phenomena? The difficulty is that for a number of reasons it is virtually impossible to test the hypothesis empirically. In the first place, new information doesn't come in the form, "The price of this stock should immediately move from $100 to $114.50 per share." Rather, it may emerge gradually over a period of weeks or months, in vague or uncertain form: as a company's public announcement of a potential technological breakthrough now in the early testing phases, or even as a rumour of uncertain origin and reliability. A company may attempt to conceal certain information in order to gain a competitive advantage, but some leaks may occur. Alternatively, as the Bre-X Minerals, Enron, and other cases illustrate, a company may make public announcements containing information that at least some people in the company know to be *false*. In short, the information on which judgments regarding the appropriate valuation of a stock are based requires *weighing and interpretation*.

Even if the information is properly interpreted, this does not eliminate the risk and uncertainty involved in purchasing a share. The share is a claim to a stream of *anticipated* future earnings, not guaranteed future earnings. For this reason, the notion that any given price is "*the* right price" for a share is not sustainable. What different investors would regard as a "reasonable" price for a share can diverge. The divergence can result from differences in interpretations of news about the share, estimates of the degree of riskiness attached to the share's expected yield, general attitudes toward risk, current wealth levels, and riskiness of the assets currently in their portfolios. After the fact, one could say that investors were likely overly optimistic or unduly pessimistic about the company's prospects, but "hindsight is 20–20."

Investors do differ in their knowledge, expectations, degree of sophistication and involvement in the market, distance from "insider information," and attitudes toward risk. Given this fact, it becomes important that, in simplest terms, there are two ways to benefit from owning a share. One is to *hold* it, and collect the stream of dividends paid out of a company's profits to its owners. The other is to *sell* it, and reap the capital gains measured by the difference between what you sell it for and what you paid for it. Obviously, this difference can be negative: it is possible to sustain capital *losses* on selling a share. Since there are two ways of benefitting from owning a share, two types of belief affect your decision as to whether to buy a particular share at its current price. The first concerns whether the share price correctly reflects the future earnings prospects and riskiness of the stock. The second concerns whether any other investor would be prepared to pay *more* in the future for the share than its current price.

If another investor exists who would be prepared to pay more than the current price, then that investor would surely view the current price as a bargain. Why is he not already in the market, buying shares *before* the price is bid up? Here your beliefs about the characteristics of other investors come into play. You might speculate that at least *some* other investors are not continuously in the market, or that it will take them longer to process new information than you, or that you have received the new information before them, or that a steady increase in the share's price will induce them to believe that the share's price could rise still higher, because still other investors are even slower getting into the market than they are. At this point, playing the market rationally starts to resemble the children's game of "hot potato." Someone will get stuck with the hot potato, in the form of an overvalued stock, but as long as you have already sold it at a higher price than you paid, you can curl up with your capital gains. The following story has a similar moral. Two hikers are getting into their sleeping bags one night, in a region noted for bears, when one notices that the other is still wearing his running shoes. "Why bother?" he asks. "You'll never be able to outrun a bear." "I don't have to outrun the bear," his friend replies, "I only have to outrun you."

Over the past decade, significant technical and economic change has occurred in stock markets globally. The extension of computerized markets, the dramatic increase in stock transactions via the Internet, the drop in brokerage fees, the shortening of transactions times, and the use of automated buy-and-sell programs have been accompanied by an influx of relatively inexperienced investors, trading on their own account. Some of these developments reinforce the efficient markets hypothesis, since they have reduced the transactions costs of portfolio adjustment in response to new information. Some, however, have increased the potential for stock market speculation based on expectations about others' expectations, rather than on expectations about how particular companies should perform in the future. The efficient markets hypothesis is still important, however, even if a proportion of stock market trading is of this speculative type. What it says is that an investor who tries to profit by playing "hot potato" stands a good chance of getting his fingers burnt.

15.8 TAX POLICY AND THE CAPITAL MARKET

Government tax policies toward capital can significantly affect people's economic decisions. These policies are only part, although an important part, of the complex and interconnected set of policies that make up the fiscal system as a whole. The fiscal system, on taxation and expenditure sides, has a number of objectives, including both fairness or equity and efficiency. The success of the fiscal system in meeting these objectives is almost inevitably only partial, because the objectives are not necessarily all compatible. There is likely no fiscal system in the world that meets with the complete approval of all those subject to its provisions. Tradeoffs are often involved (for example, between greater equity and greater efficiency), and working fiscal systems are typically products of compromise. Tinkering with only part of the system can create problems in other parts of the system. The effects of any fiscal system must be analyzed and evaluated as a whole.

In this context, it is still worth isolating some major effects of the tax treatment of capital. One of the more important of these effects stems from the taxation of interest and dividends in the personal income tax. In our discussion of intertemporal consumer choice in Chapter 5, we implicitly assumed that interest earnings were not taxed. Yet suppose that you purchase a bond for $10,000 that pays 8 percent per year. Your annual interest income is $800. If your marginal tax rate were 10 percent, you would pay $80 in tax on that interest, and the after-tax interest rate would be 7.2 percent per year. If your marginal tax rate were 30 percent, you would pay $240 in tax, and the after-tax interest rate would be only 5.6 percent. Such differences in after-tax interest rates can affect household saving behaviour. Note by way of contrast that if you borrow $10,000 at 8 percent interest for a consumer loan or mortgage, you cannot deduct your $800 interest payment in calculating your taxable income. Hence, in comparison with Figure 5-14 on page 188, even apart from any differences between financial institutions' borrowing rates and lending rates, your after-tax intertemporal budget constraint has a kink at your initial endowment point. It is flatter above the endowment point and steeper below the endowment point.

In the United States, mortgage interest payments have historically been tax-deductible, as part of a strategy to stimulate home ownership and hence the construction industry. The Canadian government has relied instead on a combination of preferential interest rates for housing construction, housing subsidy programs, and fairly modest home ownership savings programs. These programs achieve similar objectives to the U.S. tax policy. From the government's standpoint, however, they have the advantage that if they are scaled back or eliminated, they directly affect a smaller number of economic agents. In the United States, removing the mortgage interest deduction could result in a major taxpayers' revolt. This comparison suggests two thoughts. First, there are usually a number of different ways of achieving a given policy objective. Hence comparing individual tax policies in isolation rather than as part of different fiscal systems will almost invariably be misleading, although this fact doesn't stop lobbyists from trying to do just that. Second, just as it is said that "an old tax is a good tax," because people are used to it, so an old tax deduction comes to be thought of as an entrenched right, especially by those who benefit from it. This is one reason "tax reform" is almost always a politically charged and difficult process.

Tax policy also affects a firm's decision on whether to buy or lease its capital equipment. Firms are granted a depreciation allowance for all capital equipment they own. The details of this allowance are complex, but a simple example will help make the essential point. If a firm owns a machine with, say, a 10-year life span, it is permitted to deduct 10 percent of the purchase price of the machine from its corporate profit each year in reflection of the machine's depreciation in value. By so doing, it avoids having to pay tax on that portion of its profit. This makes good economic sense, because wear and tear on equipment is a legitimate operating expense for the firm. It should no more have to pay tax on such an expense than on its expenses for labour, paper, or any other input.

The depreciation allowance reduces the firm's income tax only if it has to pay income tax in the first place. If a firm experiences not a profit but a loss, or if it is a nonprofit firm, then it owes no tax to the government, and its depreciation allowance essentially goes unclaimed. This fact has opened up an opportunity for entrepreneurs who start companies to lease capital equipment to firms that owe little or no corporate income tax. Because the leasing company can claim the full value of the depreciation allowance, it can essentially supply capital to its clients more cheaply than they can supply it to themselves. From the point of view of society as a whole, however, there is no saving of resources. What the companies save under this arrangement, the government loses in tax revenue, and resources are expended to organize the leasing companies.

As a final example of how tax policy influences investment behaviour, let us consider the government's treatment of income earned from capital gains. A capital gain is income earned by the sale of an asset—such as a stock or a piece of real estate—that has gone up in price during the time it was held. Historically, capital gains have been taxed at a lower rate than other forms of income. Between 1999 and 2005, the federal government lowered the taxable portion of capital gains in stages from 3/4 to 1/2. Under this provision, if you realized $30,000 in capital gains through the sale of an asset, you would pay tax on only $15,000. If you were in the 50 percent marginal tax bracket, you would pay $7500 in taxes. If capital gains were treated like any other income, you would instead have paid $15,000 in taxes.

With preferential tax treatment of capital gains relative to dividend income, shareholders would prefer that companies lower their dividend payments and increase retained earnings out of after-tax profits. The higher retained earnings would be reflected in a higher price per share. When a shareholder came to sell some of her stock, she would pay less tax on the capital gains she received than she would have paid if the profits had been paid out as dividends. In order to reduce the disparity in tax treatment of dividends and capital gains *and* to encourage investment in Canadian companies, federal and provincial governments have therefore introduced tax credits for dividends from Canadian corporations. The effective tax on such dividends is currently even lower than the tax on capital gains! These tax policies are intended to stimulate investment. They also tend, however, to lower government tax revenues and to favour the wealthier segment of society (a larger proportion of whose income is in the form of interest, dividends, and capital gains). Again, however, the capital gains policy should be evaluated not in isolation but rather as a component of the overall fiscal system.

15.9 ECONOMIC RENT

Economic rent The difference between what a factor of production is paid and the minimum amount necessary to induce it to remain in its current use.

In everyday usage, the term "rent" refers to the payment received by a landlord, a rental car company, or some other owner in return for the use of a real economic asset. In economic analysis, however, the term has taken on a slightly different definition. *Economic rent* is the difference between the payment actually received by the owner of a factor of production and his reservation price (the minimum amount necessary to induce him to employ it in its current use). For example, if a landlord would rather see his land lie fallow than let someone else farm it for a payment of less than $100 per month, then only $150 of the $250 monthly payment he currently gets for his land is economic rent.

If an input is supplied perfectly inelastically (that is, if its owner would supply it no matter how low the price), then the entire payment to the owner is economic rent. This situation is shown in Figure 15-3a. Suppose, however, that the owner of an input has an upward-sloping supply curve, which intersects the demand curve for the input at a price of r_1^* as shown in Figure 15-3b. If buyers of the input could collude and make the owner a take-it-or-leave-it offer for K_1^* units of the input, the lowest amount the owner would accept is equal to the area under the supply curve up to K_1^* (the lower shaded area in panel b). But if buyers do not collude, the owner receives a price of r_1^*

FIGURE 15-3

Economic Rent
(a) When an input is supplied perfectly inelastically, the entire payment it receives is an economic rent. (b) The economic rent received by an input with an upward-sloping supply curve is the shaded area above the supply curve.

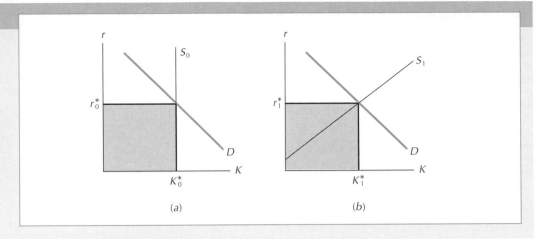

(a)   (b)

on each unit sold, and thus receives more than this minimum amount. His economic rent is the shaded area above the supply curve.

Economic rent is the factor market analogue of producer surplus in the goods market. Producer surplus, recall, is the revenue in excess of the minimum required to call forth a given supply of output in the goods market. As with producer surplus, economic rent will be greater, other things equal, the more inelastic the supply curve of the product.

Though rent is strongly associated in the public mind with payments to the owners of capital inputs, economic rents are often of equal or greater importance in the labour market. Recall, in particular, our discussion of the economics of winner-take-all markets in Chapter 14. People of rare talent or ability often command exceptionally high salaries, even though, in many instances, they would be willing to perform their services for a much lower amount. The multimillion-dollar salaries of top entertainers and professional athletes, for example, are for the most part economic rent, not compensation for the inconvenience of sacrificing leisure.

15.10 PEAK-LOAD PRICING

A firm's demand for capital will depend not only on the rental rate of capital, but also on how it apportions the costs of its capital equipment among the buyers of its product. To illustrate the nature of this relationship, and at the same time to help shed light on an extremely important policy issue, let us consider the case of a regulated electric utility whose demands differ sharply at different hours of the day. One possible rate structure would involve a single, uniform price for electricity, regardless of when it is consumed. This price would just cover all costs, including a normal rate of return on investment. Alternatively, prices could be directly related to the intensity of overall use at the time of consumption, so that a higher price is charged for electricity used during periods of peak demand, say during business hours, than for electricity used during other times of the day. Such rate structures are commonly referred to as *peak-load pricing.*

Peak-load pricing
The practice whereby higher prices are charged for goods or services during the periods in which they are consumed most intensively.

To illustrate the effects of peak-load pricing, consider an electric utility that uses only two inputs, generators and fuel. Suppose that customer demands for electricity in the short run vary by time of day according to the pattern shown in Figure 15-4. The demand curve during business hours is labelled "Peak demand." The demand curve during the rest of the day is labelled "Off-peak demand." Suppose the company initially sells all its power at the same rate, 10 cents/kWh, and that its revenues at that rate

FIGURE 15-4

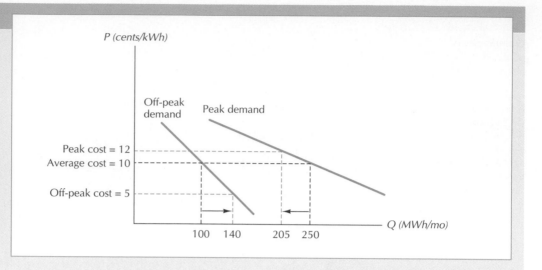

exactly cover all its costs. Note in the diagram that when all power sells for 10 cents/kWh, peak demand is 250 MWh per month.

If the average cost of production is 10 cents/kWh, we know that the marginal cost of serving off-peak users must be less than 10 cents/kWh, while the marginal cost of serving peak users must be more. This follows because we can serve an extra off-peak user without having to add any more generating equipment, whereas we must add new generators to serve additional peak users. The only cost of serving an off-peak user will be the extra fuel required to run some of the generating capacity that would otherwise be idle during that period. Suppose this off-peak marginal cost is 5 cents/kWh. The extra cost during the peak period will include not only the cost of fuel, but also the cost of the required extra capital. For purposes of illustration, suppose that these peak-period costs add to 12 cents/kWh.

And suppose, finally, that the utility charges 12 cents/kWh to peak-period users and only 5 cents/kWh to off-peak users. Note in Figure 15-4 that the effect is to reduce peak-period consumption by 45 MWh per month, most of which shifts to the off-peak period. The shift is achieved in a variety of ways. For example, people may buy timers that operate water heaters, air conditioners, and space heaters only during off-peak hours. Similarly, they may avoid using dishwashers, washing machines, and clothes dryers during the peak period. The net result of such consumption shifts is that a utility can serve its customers with much smaller generating capacity. The resulting cost savings represent a real increase in customer living standards.

As a practical matter, one of the difficulties with peak-load pricing is that it requires significantly more sophisticated use-monitoring systems than are currently in place throughout most of Canada. A single meter-reading every month or even less frequently, which is now the norm for residential users, would have to be supplanted by *continuous-monitoring* systems that could take and process readings on an hour-by-hour basis. The capital costs of new monitoring systems would have to be balanced against the capital savings on generating capacity. Yet even a more widespread use of such monitoring systems among large and medium-sized commercial and industrial electricity users could generate net benefits for the industrial users themselves and for residential customers.

Economic Naturalist 15-2

WHY DO SOME CELLPHONE PLANS OFFER 1000 "FREE" MONTHLY MINUTES AT NIGHT AND ON WEEKENDS, AT THE SAME TIME THAT THEY PROVIDE ONLY 50 FREE MINUTES PER MONTH FOR WEEKDAY CALLS?

The rate structure of these plans may seem odd at first glance. Yet it is a rational response by oligopolistic cellphone companies faced by bandwidth capacity constraints, peak load problems, and the need to attract large numbers of subscribers. The plans typically involve a fixed monthly charge, and a certain number of weekday and of night/weekend minutes per month. High per-minute charges kick in only after these limits are reached. In many plans, there is no rebate if the subscriber does not use all of her allotted free minutes.

But couldn't the cellphone companies increase their profits by charging a lower rate during the day, to encourage greater cellphone use? The problem is that the companies do not *want* to encourage cellphone use during the day! Business cellphone demand is naturally much higher in the daytime, during "normal business hours." If bandwidth capacity constraints are reached because of high call volume, subscribers experience "denial of service," which translates into customer dissatisfaction. The high rate for extra daytime minutes operates as a *rationing* mechanism, to reduce the number of calls during the peak-volume period.

But why is the number of "free" night and weekend minutes as much as twenty times as great as the number of weekday minutes? Two considerations apply. First, as long as system capacity limits have not been reached, the marginal cost to the companies of one more call is effectively zero. Second, there has been intense competition among the companies for subscribers, and for now, abundant night and weekend minutes are a relatively low-cost competitive carrot that can be used to attract new subscribers.

Currently, well over half of Canadian households have at least one cellphone, as the result of remarkable growth over the past decade. The number of cellphone users will increase still further, the range of cellphone functions will continue to expand, and the average monthly minutes per subscriber will likely increase. It is therefore quite possible that in future, the cellphone companies will *have* to reduce the number of free night-time and weekend minutes on their plans, simply as a means of rationing *night*-time demand. Watch for it on your cellphone bill!

Peak-load pricing is by no means limited to the electric utility and telecommunication industries. Airlines employ peak-load pricing, cancelling some or all of their discount seats during heavy travel periods. Many ski areas have higher lift prices on major holiday weekends. Seasonal price differences are a common practice among resort hotels. And as noted in Chapter 12, many movie theatres charge lower prices during weekday matinees. Experience with these pricing practices tells us that when capital costs are assigned to the users responsible for their incurrence, the overall level of capital required can be reduced significantly.

- Our task in this chapter was to examine the market for services of capital inputs. Many of the results from our study of labour inputs apply to capital as well. Thus, for example, the demand for the services of a capital input by a perfect competitor in the input market is the marginal revenue product of that input—which, for a perfect competitor in the output market, is the same as the value of capital's marginal product.

- One feature that often sets capital apart from other inputs is that while other inputs are usually hired on a period-by-period basis, capital equipment is often owned outright by the firm. In considering whether to purchase a machine, the firm must ask how much its output will increase not only in the current period, but also in future periods. The firm's decision rule is to acquire the machine if and only if the present value of the current and future increases in net revenue made possible by the machine exceeds its purchase price. This rule illustrates the factors that determine the rental rate of capital. These include the interest rate, or the opportunity cost of borrowed funds, maintenance costs, the rates of physical and technological depreciation, and expected future movements in the price of the capital good.

- The real rate of interest measures interest in terms of equivalent quantities of real goods or services. If, for example, a bank lends 100 oz of gold and requires a repayment of 105 oz after 1 year, the real interest rate would be 5 percent per year. When the rate of inflation is small, the nominal rate of interest is approximately equal to the real rate of interest plus the rate of inflation. This relationship helps make clear why the interest rates charged by banks and other lenders tend to rise hand in hand with the overall rate of inflation.

- A firm's demand for borrowed money depends on how the amount of capital equipment it would like to have compares with the amount it actually does have. The supply of loanable funds is highly responsive to interest rates because of the international nature of capital markets. The market interest rate and equilibrium level of borrowing are determined by the intersection of the supply and demand curves for loanable funds.

- The market for stocks and bonds is one of the principal sources of funds to finance new capital equipment. A corporate bond is essentially a loan from the purchaser of the bond to the corporation. As a bond nears maturity, its price must converge to its face value. But for bonds that are far from maturity, there will be a significant inverse relationship between current interest rates and the price of the bond. The price of a given stock is the present value, suitably discounted for risk, of the current and future profits to which it provides a claim.

- The "efficient markets hypothesis" says that, holding risk constant, all available information about current and future earnings of a firm is immediately incorporated into the price of its stock. The implication is that an investor should do equally well no matter which stocks he or she purchases. The efficient markets hypothesis thus helps explain why the investment tips of "experts" are of little or no value. The relevance of the hypothesis is undercut to the extent that speculative fever, bandwagon effects, ignorance, and outright deception play a significant role in securities markets.

- Tax policy has numerous effects on capital market decisions. Differing marginal tax rates yield different after-tax rates and can thus affect savings decisions. Tax policy also sometimes induces firms to lease, rather than buy, their capital equipment. And tax policy provides an incentive for firms to reinvest their profits, rather than pay them directly to shareholders as dividends.

- The term "rent" as used by economists has a somewhat different meaning from the one familiar from everyday usage. It is the payment to a factor of production in excess of the minimum value required to keep that factor in its current use. A significant share of the payments received by owners of capital constitutes economic rent under this definition. Rents can constitute a large share of incomes generated in the labour market as well.

- In peak-load pricing schemes, firms and regulatory agencies must decide how much to charge for the use of capital equipment when the intensity of demand varies greatly. As ever, the rule for efficient allocation is to set prices on the basis of marginal cost. Peak-load pricing enables firms to serve their markets while using significantly smaller amounts of capital equipment.

- Appendix 15A discusses the use of natural resources, both renewable and exhaustible, as inputs in production. Interest and growth rates are treated further in Module 9 of the online *Basic Math Review*.

1. What is the difference between real capital and financial capital? Why does concern with one type of capital invariably involve concern with the other?
2. Explain why depreciation is an economic cost just like any other.
3. Why do higher interest rates make future events economically less important?
4. Why do nominal interest rates rise approximately 1-for-1 with increases in inflation?
5. Why are bond prices and interest rates inversely related?
6. Why is published investment advice unlikely to be worth very much?
7. Give three examples of peak-load pricing used in your community.
8. Who will typically aim at achieving a higher expected return on their investments: young investors or older investors with more immediate need for retirement income?

PROBLEMS

1. You are deciding which of two computers to purchase. The interest rate is 9 percent per year and the maintenance rate of both machines is 1 percent per year. The first computer costs $4000 and has a rate of physical and technological depreciation of 10 percent per year. The second computer, on the verge of obsolescence, has a rate of physical and technological depreciation of 30 percent per year. If the annual rental rate for the two computers is the same, how much must the purchase price of the second computer be?

2. A maintenance-free machine that costs $100 will yield returns of $30 at the end of each of the next 3 years, at which time it will be sold as scrap for $30. If the interest rate facing this firm is 10 percent per year, should it purchase this machine?

3. Suppose a perpetual bond pays $3000 per year to its owner. What is the price of the bond if the interest rate is 5 percent per year? 6 percent per year?

4. Tony's barbershop has four chairs and four barbers. Most of the time at least one barber is idle, except on Saturday mornings when all four are continuously booked. Explain, in terms a noneconomist could understand, why the cost of providing a haircut on Saturday morning is higher than at other times of the week.

5. Suppose that 58 percent of investors have decided *not* to own shares in the ten firms identified as the "Top Ten Canadian Polluters" in a recent Greenprobe study. How, if at all, will the returns on the stocks of these ten companies differ from the returns on the stocks of other companies?

6. If the nominal interest rate in a 2-period world (see Chapter 5) is 6 percent per period, and all prices fall at a rate of 4 percent, then what is the real interest rate? If Shirley Eugest has the same income in each period, and at her initial endowment point her marginal rate of time preference (MRTP) is 1.03, then should she become a lender or a borrower?

*7. Risk-neutral Ron T. Hay has $100,000 in Canadian funds. He wants to purchase a 1-year bond and end up with Canadian funds. He can purchase 1-year Canadian bonds paying 10 percent per year or 1-year British bonds paying 20 percent per year. The inflation rate in Canada is 2 percent per year, and in Britain it is 14 percent per year. The Canadian dollar is expected to appreciate against the British pound by 8 percent over the year. There are no transaction costs. What is the *real* interest rate he receives on the bonds that give him his best return, and how much does he end up with in Canadian funds?

**8. The production function for perfectly competitive Ace Skyhooks takes the form $Q = L^{.6}K^{.3}$, where Q is the number of skyhooks, L is in labour-years, and K is in machine-years. The wage rate is $600 per labour-year. Each machine costs $1000, the interest rate is 8 percent per year, depreciation occurs at a rate of 20 percent per year, and maintenance costs $120 per machine per year. The firm has determined that its desired level of employment is 60 labour-years per year, and it will purchase enough machines to minimize unit costs at this level of employment. How much will it invest in machines, how many skyhooks will it produce annually, and what is the price of skyhooks?

*9. Risk-neutral Phil Theeritch has some loanable funds available with which he wishes to purchase either bonds maturing exactly 3 years from today, with a redemption value at maturity of $1000 per bond, or a sequence of 1-year bonds paying a nominal interest rate of 8 percent per year. The rate of inflation over the next 3 years is expected to be 2 percent per year in each of the 3 years.

    a. At what current market price of the three-year bonds would Phil *just* prefer to purchase them rather than a sequence of the one-year bonds?

    b. How, if at all, would your answer to 9a change if the one-year bonds paid 4 percent per year this year, 8 percent per year in the next year, and 12 percent per year in the third year, with the expected inflation rate at 2 percent per year?

    c. How, if at all, would your answer to 9a change if the one-year bonds paid 12 percent per year this year, 8 percent per year in the next year, and 4 percent per year in the third year, with the expected inflation rate at 2 percent per year?

ANSWERS TO IN-CHAPTER EXERCISES

15-1. Since $r = i + m + -$, we have $r = .08 + .02 + .10 = .20$. So the annual rental payment will be $r(\$5000) = \$1000$.

15-2. $PV = (121/1.1) + (121/1.1^2) + (242/1.1^2) = 110 + 100 + 200 = \$410$.

15-3. The price at 10 percent is $\$120/.10 = \$1200$. At 5 percent the price will be $\$120/.05 = \$2400$, so the increase in price is $2400 - 1200 = \$1200$.

Appendix 15A

A MORE DETAILED LOOK AT RENEWABLE AND EXHAUSTIBLE RESOURCE ALLOCATION

15A.1 NATURAL RESOURCES AS INPUTS IN PRODUCTION

In addition to human-made machines and other equipment, natural resources are also important inputs in many production processes, including the production of machines and equipment! For purposes of analysis, it is common to partition natural resources into two distinct categories: (1) renewable resources, such as fish and trees; and (2) exhaustible resources, ones that exist in finite quantities that cannot be replaced once expended. This rough categorization of natural resources is useful, and we will adopt it in this appendix. Yet it is worth examining the categories a bit more closely before we begin. Some natural resources, such as solar energy and the rivers and the waterfalls that generate hydroelectric energy, are not strictly "renewable," but they are *effectively inexhaustible*. At one time in Canada, clean pure water and the ozone layer might have seemed like effectively inexhaustible resources, but human products such as acid rain, industrial chemical effluents, agribusiness sewage containing *E. coli* bacteria and other sources of disease, and chlorofluorocarbon and nitrogen oxide emissions have posed serious threats to both. The moratorium on cod fishing on the Grand Banks and concerns about the long-term viability of the Pacific coast salmon fisheries remind us that even for resources like fish, which would normally be considered *renewable* resources, overfishing or ecological damage to their habitat can threaten their survival and in some cases lead to extinction. It has been estimated that every hour over five living species disappear from the earth: extinction is exhaustion.

In contrast, bauxite and iron ore are "exhaustible" resources that exist in finite quantities. Yet recycling of aluminum cans and scrap iron can significantly reduce the annual rate of extraction of ore necessary to supply any given level of final demand. Such recycling is not exclusive to exhaustible resources. It has also proved important for renewable resources such as pulpwood. Some paper products are now composed of 100 percent recycled fibres, resulting in reduced pressure on forest resources, energy savings, and (as an intended by-product) "green" profits. At present, fossil fuels such as coal, methane (natural gas), and petroleum products such as gasoline, kerosene, and bunker oil are genuinely exhausted in the process of combustion. After combustion, their main contribution is to produce smog and global warming. (The push in many countries of the world to ratify and implement the 1997 Kyoto Protocol on reducing the use of carbon-based fuel was a response to concerns about these effects.) Yet a significant proportion of petroleum-derived engine oil can be recycled. Apart from traditional renewable fuel sources like wood and peat, methane from anaerobic animal waste and plant decomposition could become another commercially important *renewable* energy resource.

We will be examining some simplified models of renewable and exhaustible resources, which reveal some basic principles of resource utilization. The above examples are meant to underline the fact that in applying these principles, we cannot simply decide in the abstract whether a particular resource is inexhaustible or renewable, and then apply the corresponding model. In the natural resource sphere, in order to be good "economic naturalists" we need to be good ecological naturalists as well.

15A.2 RENEWABLE RESOURCES

To illustrate some of the economic issues that arise in connection with renewable resources as inputs, consider the case of a lumber company whose business it is to produce lumber from the trees grown on land to which it has rights into the indefinite future. Its objective is to plant, care for, and harvest trees in such a way as to maximize the present value of its current and future profits.

An agricultural specialist advises the firm about how far apart to plant its trees, what fertilizers to apply, and so on. The economist's expertise lies in answering the question of when the trees should be harvested. (Of course, if different spacings and fertilizer applications produced different growth paths for the total volume of lumber on a given area, or different harvesting costs, she would also advise on those aspects of the profit-maximizing strategy. Here, we abstract from those complications.) Each year the firm must decide whether to cut a tree down or let it grow another year. The benefit of cutting it down now is to get the revenue from selling it right away. If the firm waits a year, it loses the use of that revenue for the time being, but in the meantime the tree continues to grow.

Suppose trees grow over time according to the growth curve labelled B in Figure 15A-1. Suppose also that the price of lumber remains constant through time, that we can neglect logging costs, and that the real market rate of interest remains constant at i/yr. At what age should a tree then be harvested for its lumber?

The revenue from the sale of the tree is proportional to the volume of lumber in it. The slope of the growth curve, $\Delta B/\Delta t$, tells us how much extra lumber the firm will get by waiting an additional Δt units. The rate at which revenue will grow if the tree is left alone is the extra lumber divided by the size of the tree, $(\Delta B/\Delta t)/B$. Thus, if Δt is 1 year and if $\Delta B = .10B$, then the rate at which lumber—and hence total revenue—grows will be .10/yr or 10 percent/yr. Because the slope of the B curve eventually declines over time (see Figure 15A-1), it follows that the value of $(\Delta B/\Delta t)/B$ will also eventually decrease over time, as shown in Figure 15A-2.

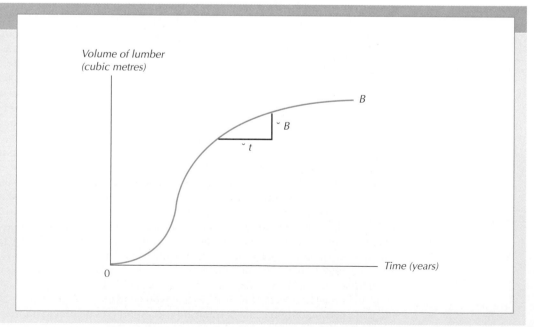

The Growth Curve for a Tree
The curve labelled B tells the volume of lumber in the tree as a function of its age in years. The slope of the curve at a point is given by the ratio $\Delta B/\Delta t$.

Volume of lumber (cubic metres)

B

$\check{} B$

$\check{} t$

0

Time (years)

The Optimal Time of Harvest
The optimal harvest time, t^*, occurs when the growth rate of the tree, $(\Delta B/\Delta t)/B$, is exactly equal to the real rate of interest, i. At that point the extra revenue from leaving the tree in the ground for Δt longer is exactly equal to the interest that could be earned by harvesting the tree and investing the proceeds at i.

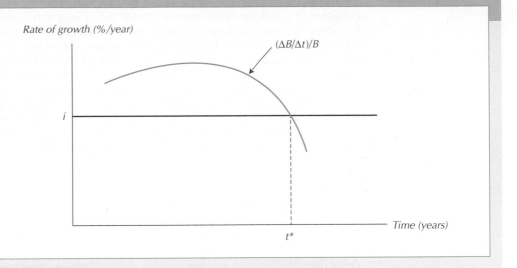

Rate of growth (%/year)

$(\Delta B/\Delta t)/B$

i

Time (years)

t^*

If instead of letting the tree continue to grow, the firm cuts it down now and invests the proceeds at the market rate of interest i, its revenue will grow at the rate of i/yr. It follows that the tree should be harvested as soon as

$$\frac{\Delta B/\Delta t}{B} = i, \qquad (15A.1)$$

which will happen for $t = t^*$ in Figure A.15-2. For values of t to the left of t^*, the growth rate of the tree exceeds the growth rate of money deposited at i/yr, which means that the firm should wait a little longer. For values of t greater than t^*, in contrast, money deposited at i/yr will grow faster than the lumber in the tree, so the firm should harvest the tree a little sooner.[1]

EXERCISE 15A-1

The volume of lumber in a tree is given by $B = 80\sqrt{t}$, the slope of which curve at any point is given by $\Delta B/\Delta t = 40/\sqrt{t}$. If the interest rate is 2 percent/year, prices are constant, and we can neglect harvesting costs, at what age should the tree be harvested?

---

[1]We have assumed that we can neglect logging costs. Technically speaking, this is possible only when logging costs are directly proportional to the value (and with constant prices, the volume) of the lumber. Including the costs of logging, with all prices constant and logging costs (C) expressed in cubic metres of lumber, the optimal harvest time is given by

$$(\Delta B/\Delta t - \Delta C/\Delta t)/(B - C) = i.$$

Let's consider two cases. First, suppose that costs are proportional to the volume of lumber harvested: $C = aB$, with $a < 1$ if harvesting is to occur at all. Hence, $\Delta C/\Delta t = a\Delta B/\Delta t$, and the above expression becomes

$$[(\Delta B/\Delta t)(1 - a)]/[B(1 - a)] = (\Delta B/\Delta t)/B = i,$$

as in Equation 15A.1.

Second, suppose that costs (measured in cubic metres) are constant: $C = C_0$. In this case $\Delta C/\Delta t = 0$, and the expression characterizing t^* becomes

$$(\Delta B/\Delta t)/(B - C_0) = i.$$

Since the denominator is lowered by the amount of the cutting costs, while at any time t the numerator is unchanged, here inclusion of logging costs delays the optimal harvesting time. The higher the logging costs and the more gradual the decline in the growth rate, the greater will be the effect of logging costs in postponing t^*.

Note that the optimal time for harvesting a tree is not when it is as big as it will possibly get. On the contrary, it is still growing at the rate $i > 0$ at the optimal time of harvest. The company's objective is not to get the maximum possible quantity of lumber out of any one tree, but to maximize the net revenues that result from an ongoing process of growing trees. And this will necessarily mean clearing out slower-growing mature trees to make room for faster-growing young ones.

Many observers complain that lumber companies often harvest trees wastefully, even by the standard of Equation 15A.1. Several factors account for this waste when it occurs. If timber were growing on a tract of commonly held land and were free for the taking, on a first-come, first-served basis, it would almost certainly be harvested well before it reached economic maturity. Like the problem of overfishing, it is an example of what has been called "the tragedy of the commons" (discussed in Chapter 17). Each firm operating on the tract might want to allow the trees to grow longer, but none would trust the others to wait. Under these circumstances, each firm cuts down as much timber as it can, as fast as it can.

Provided that an appropriate resource rent can be established, granting logging rights to a *single* firm provides a partial solution. Yet if the rights are not granted for an extended period, the problem still arises. As the end of the lease period approaches, if the firm has no guarantee that the lease will be renewed, it has an incentive to cut wastefully, and long before then its incentive to do proper replanting will have diminished.

Two other factors are important. The first is logging costs. Forestry companies viewed methods such as clear-cutting of whole tracts as economizing on logging costs, with the consequence that smaller trees were cut down prematurely, by the standard of Equation 15A.1. The second factor is in some senses even more critical. If we view forests as *multi-use* resources (with recreational, wildlife sanctuary, climate control, scientific, and other uses in addition to their value as sources of wood), then forestry operations generate significant *externalities*. Clear-cutting methods can affect soil structure and accelerate soil erosion. Forestry is a messy (as well as a dangerous) business. Forestry operations increase soil, waterway, and noise pollution, and thereby reduce the value of the forests in their other uses, but these costs are *external* to the companies' private cost-benefit calculations.

Public protests, government and company research and investigations, new methods of harvesting old-growth forest on a more selective basis, and improved private cost-benefit accounting by the forestry companies themselves have led to a relative decline in the use of clear-cutting methods in Canada. For the long run, key factors in the forest sector will be increased emphasis on *integrated* scientific forest management, improved resource-rent allocation mechanisms, and the development of systems that "internalize the externalities" efficiently (see Chapters 17 and 18), while still permitting profitable forest industry operation.

15A.3 EXHAUSTIBLE RESOURCES

An exhaustible resource is one that cannot be replenished by people. Oil, gold, titanium, and aluminum are examples. Once the earth's initial stock of these substances runs out, even with recycling, we will have to do the best we can without them. How does a competitive market allocate exhaustible resources?

As we saw for a renewable resource, the owner of an exhaustible resource has two options: (1) she can hold the resource for the time being, or (2) she can sell it. Again as before, there is an opportunity cost implicit in the first option. It is the interest that could have been earned had the resource been sold and the proceeds deposited in a bank (or used to purchase a stock or bond). For the tree owner, the compensation for incurring this opportunity cost was the fact that the tree grew larger while it was left in the ground.

But exhaustible resources do not grow over time the way trees do. So the only economic reason the owner of such a resource would have for holding it is the expectation that its price will rise relative to the prices of other goods and services. We will assume that the oil market is characterized by perfect competition, that the initial stock of oil is fixed and perfectly known, that demand is constant over time, that there is a complete set of costless futures markets, and that we can neglect extraction costs. Suppose you are the owner of several million barrels of oil, which sells at a current price of $20 per barrel. If the real interest rate is 5 percent per year, how much will the price of oil have to rise in the next year for you to be willing to hold at least some

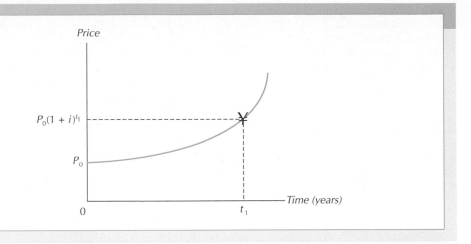

of your oil? Suppose the price rises to $22 per barrel. If you sold all your oil now and deposited the proceeds in an account at 5 percent, your total wealth would grow by 5 percent during the next year. If instead you hold on to your oil, your total wealth will grow by 10 percent. Since the second option is obviously more attractive, the likelihood is that you will not sell any of your oil. In contrast, if the price of oil were expected to rise to only $20.50/barrel in the next year, your best bet would be to unload all your oil now and invest the proceeds at 5 percent. A $.50 rise in the price of a $20 barrel of oil means that the oil you hold will grow by only 2.5 percent in value.

It should be clear from this example that for a competitive market for an exhaustible resource to be in equilibrium, the price of the resource must be rising at precisely the real rate of interest. A growth in price any smaller than that would result in *all* owners trying to sell. And one any higher would result in a complete shutdown of trading. Suppose P_0 denotes the current price of an exhaustible resource—say, oil. If this price grows at the rate of i/yr, then the mathematical expression for the price after t years will be given by[2]

$$P_t = P_0(1 + i)^t, \tag{15A.2}$$

a plot of which is shown in Figure 15A-3.

Two important conclusions follow from the fact that exhaustible resource prices will tend to grow at the real rate of interest. First, because the demand curves for exhaustible resources are downward sloping like any others, with demand unchanged the gradual rise in price will cause a gradual reduction in the quantity of the resource demanded. This, in turn, means that the initial stock of the resource will be used up gradually, not precipitously. As less and less of the original stock remains, higher prices will slow the rate at which it is drawn down further.

A second important effect of rising prices is to stimulate the production of substitutes for the exhaustible resource. Sooner or later, the world is going to run out of oil. The activities we use oil for today will someday have to be done using some other means, or else not be done at all. As oil gets more expensive, entrepreneurs will have strong incentives to discover alternative ways of carrying out the activities that require oil.

All exhaustible sources of energy will eventually run out, at which point we will be forced to rely on renewable sources of energy. Our task in this appendix is to investigate in greater detail the process of transition from exhaustible to renewable energy sources.

Again for simplicity, assume that oil is the only exhaustible energy source and that when it is used up, we will switch to solar energy. Recall from above that equilibrium in the oil market requires that the price of oil rise at the rate of interest. Figure 15.A-4, in which D is the demand curve for oil, summarizes the effect of rising oil prices on the rate at which oil is consumed.

---

[2]If the growth in price is continuous, the exact relationship will be

$$P_t = P_0 e^{it},$$

where e denotes the constant 2.7183. Equation 15A.2 provides a close approximation to this relationship.

The Effect of Rising Prices on the Use of an Exhaustible Resource
The demand curve for an exhaustible resource, like any other, is downward sloping. Gradually rising prices thus lead to gradual reductions in the quantities by which the stock is depleted each year.

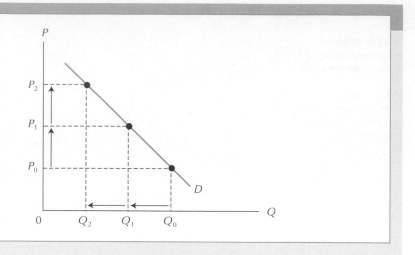

If we know how the price of oil will grow over time, and if we know the demand curve for oil, it is a simple matter to calculate the amount of oil that will be left at any moment in time. Suppose the current stock of oil is S_0 and its current price is P_0. Consulting the demand curve for oil (Figure 15A-4), we see that consumers will use Q_0 units of oil this year, leaving $S_0 - Q_0$ units remaining at the beginning of next year. At next year's price of P_1, they will use Q_1 units, leaving $S_0 - Q_0 - Q_1$ at the beginning of the following year; and so on. Plotting the quantity of oil remaining at each moment in time, we have the *stock exhaustion path*, shown in Figure 15A-5.

Suppose that the price of solar energy is P^* per unit and is expected to remain constant through time. Suppose also that our current stock of oil embodies S_0 units of energy. On our assumptions, the theory of exhaustible resource markets tells us that the price of energy in the form of oil will grow at the real rate of interest. But the theory also predicts that the last drop of oil will be used up at the very moment that its price (measured in dollars per unit of energy) reaches P^*, the level at which it becomes economical to use solar energy.

To see why this second prediction must be expected to hold, suppose that the owners of oil expected it not to. First, suppose they expect that when the price of oil reaches P^*, they will have some additional oil left. The locus labelled SEP_0 in the top panel of Figure 15A-6 depicts the stock exhaustion path corresponding to an initial stock of S_0, with an initial price of P_0. Starting at P_0,

The Stock Exhaustion Path
In the current moment ($t = 0$), the stock of oil is S_0 units. Given its current price of P_0, we consult the demand curve (Figure 15.A-4) to get this year's consumption (Q_0). The stock remaining at the beginning of next year ($t = 1$) will be $S_0 - Q_0$. At next year's price of $P_0(1 + i) = P_1$, consumption will be Q_1, which means that the stock remaining at the beginning of the following year will be $S_0 - Q_0 - Q_1$; and so on.

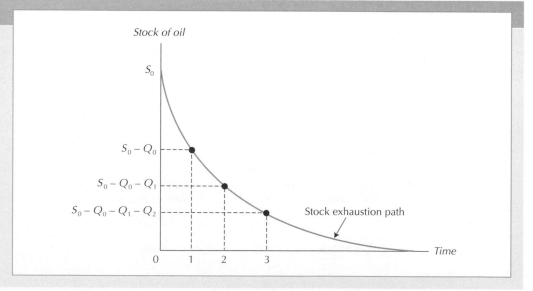

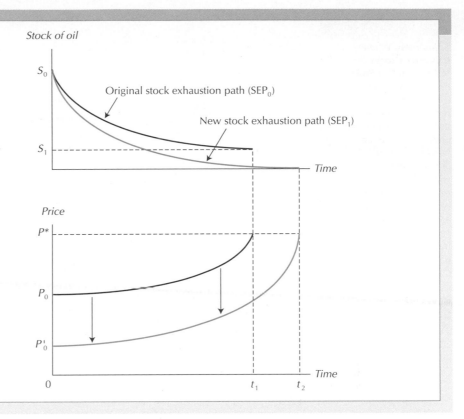

price rises at the real rate of interest over time, intersecting P^* when time $= t_1$ (bottom panel of Figure 15A-6). Note in the top panel that at t_1 there are S_1 units of oil remaining. But the owners of oil know that once its price reaches P^*, it can increase no further. After all, why should anyone be willing to pay more than P^* for oil if solar energy can be had for that price? If the owners have oil left over when the price reaches P^*, they will be able to sell it only at the rate at which people demand energy at that price. This means they will end up having to hold on to an asset—namely, what's left of their oil—whose price doesn't grow, and no investor wants to do that.

Individual owners can avoid that outcome by selling their oil right now. And since all owners face the same incentive to sell, it follows that the current price will fall—from P_0 to P'_0 in the bottom panel of Figure 15A-6. This fall in price will accomplish two things: (1) when price again grows at the real rate of interest, it will take longer than before to reach P^*; and (2) oil use levels will be higher, both now and in the future (because the demand curve for oil is downward sloping). In Figure 15A-6, the first effect is reflected in the fact that $t_2 > t_1$, the second in the fact that the new stock exhaustion locus (SEP$_1$) lies below the original one. Both of these effects will tend to reduce the amount of oil left over when the price reaches P^*. As Figure 15A-6 is drawn, the last drop of oil is used at the exact moment the new price path reaches P*. If owners had still expected some to be left over at t_2, the current price would have fallen still further.

Alternatively, suppose that the owners think they will run out of oil before its price reaches P^*. That is, suppose, as in Figure 15A-7, that we start with an initial stock of S_0 and price of P_0, and that we run out of oil at t_1, before its price reaches P^*. Once oil runs out, people will have to pay P^* per unit of energy since solar energy will be the only source available. So owners can foresee that at t_1 they will be able to charge not Pt_1, but P^* for their oil. This means that by holding on to their oil until t_1, they can earn more than the real rate of interest. So if the owners of oil expect it to run out before its price reaches P*, they will have an immediate incentive to stop selling oil right now. This produces an increase in the current price of oil, from P_0 to P'_0 in the bottom panel of Figure 15A-7, which in turn causes an upward shift in the stock exhaustion path (top panel). The upward movement in price will continue until owners expect that the new price path will reach P^* at the exact moment the corresponding stock exhaustion path reaches zero.

FIGURE 15A-7

Adjustment When Investors Expect Oil to Run Out Too Soon
If oil is expected to run out before price reaches P^*, owners will conclude that they can earn more than the real rate of interest by holding on to their oil. This will cause current price to rise (bottom panel), which in turn will cause an upward shift in the stock exhaustion path (top panel). The upward price adjustment will continue until investors expect price to reach P^* at the moment all stocks are exhausted.

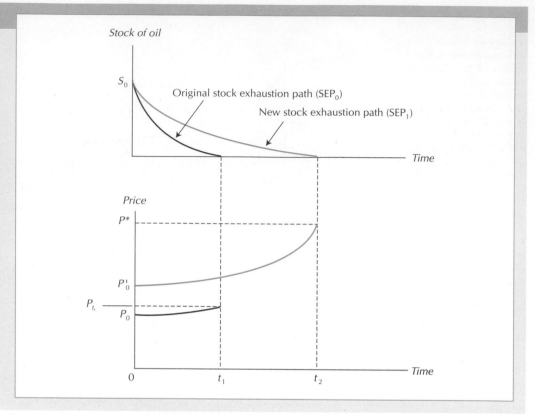

The theory of exhaustible resource markets discussed above implicitly assumes that investors know how much oil remains in the ground at any moment. In practice, however, no one is really sure. Similarly, we don't know exactly how much solar energy will cost once we run out of oil, for that depends on technological developments that are difficult to foretell. In place of known values of oil reserves and known values of the prices of alternative energy sources, the market must rely on estimates. These estimates are often highly imprecise, and always subject to revision as we acquire new information. If someone discovers a massive new oil field, or a substantially cheaper method of harnessing solar energy, current energy prices may change dramatically, as the following example illustrates.

EXAMPLE 15A-1

Suppose that because of a breakthrough in superconductor technology, the price of solar energy falls by half, from P^* to $P^*/2$. Show how this affects the time path of oil prices and the time at which we switch from oil to solar power.

Suppose the original stock adjustment and price paths are as given in Figure 15A-8. With a solar energy price of P^*, the last drop of oil would be used when $t = t_1$, the moment when the price of oil reaches P^*. If the price of oil continued on its original path after the price of solar energy fell, it would reach $P^*/2$ at $t = t'$, when there would be S_t units of oil remaining. For the reasons discussed earlier, this would cause the current price of oil to fall. It would continue falling until it reached a level (P_0 in Figure 15A-8) for which the new price path reaches $P^*/2$ at the same moment the corresponding stock adjustment path reaches zero. As shown in the diagram, the effect of the price reduction in solar energy is to produce downward shifts in both the price and stock adjustment paths for oil. Whereas the age of solar power originally would have begun at $t = t_1$, it will now begin much sooner at $t = t_2$.

Our competitive model of exhaustible resource allocation, despite its strong simplifying assumptions, highlights some of the central features of resource economics. What happens when we

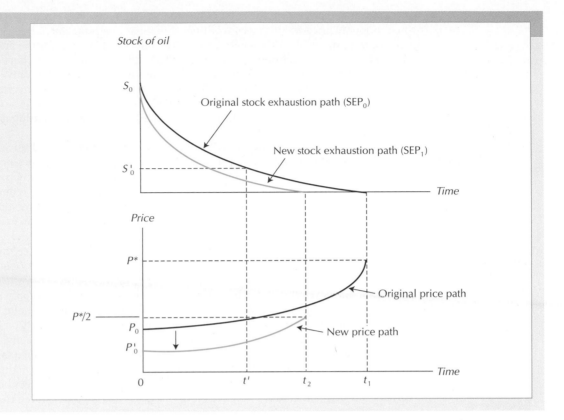

relax some of our assumptions? Most obviously, if global population and income per capita increase, other things being equal, with oil as a normal good we expect the quantity of oil demanded at any price to increase. Hence the annual rate of depletion should increase and the depletion path should shift downward.

One of the remarkable facts about the global petroleum economy is that annual consumption *has* increased steadily over the past three decades, and yet EURRs (Estimated Ultimately Recoverable Reserves) have *also* increased! Three factors account for this apparently paradoxical result. Oil exploration has generated new discoveries; advances in geological knowledge have enabled more refined (and on balance higher) estimates of "how much oil is down there"; and improved oil-extraction techniques have increased the proportion of oil that is recoverable from a reserve of given size. These advances have bought some time, but the total quantity of petroleum globally (known and still undiscovered) is still fixed and diminishing each year. What has happened is that the "known" proportion of total reserves has increased.

One of the more serious limits of our basic model, as we noted above, is that it abstracts from uncertainty and assumes a complete set of costless futures markets. Under uncertainty, however, risk-averse resource holders will have an incentive to deplete their stocks more rapidly, in order to avoid being left holding devalued stocks of the resource in future. The effect of their actions is to lower the rate of increase in prices below the real interest rate (by the amount of their risk premium) and to shift the stock-depletion path downward.

A final limit of the model is its assumption of perfect competition. There are clearly imperfectly competitive elements in the global petroleum market, to mention only OPEC (the Organization of Petroleum Exporting Countries), which owns a significant share of internationally traded oil, and the major oil companies. Yet as we have seen in the text, oligopoly can involve fairly intense competition. As for OPEC, while it has sometimes served as a scapegoat for high oil prices, assessments of its degree of success as a cartel are mixed, and its role in global petroleum pricing is more complex than some stereotypes would suggest.

To see why, let us first note the effect of a shift from competitive to monopoly pricing in the market for an exhaustible resource like oil that has constant demand over time. The price will increase immediately from the competitive to the monopoly level. From that point on, however, the monopoly price will increase over time *at the same rate as the real interest rate*, just as the competitive price did, and for the same reasons. The effect will be to lower the annual depletion rate and shift the stock exhaustion path upward. The shift to monopoly in effect acts as a conservation measure, buying time and increasing the incentive to develop alternative energy sources. In short, monopoly acts in the opposite direction to risk aversion under uncertainty. If risk-averse behaviour is present, monopoly in an exhaustible resource market can produce a rate of depletion that is closer to the social optimum. (Of course, it also has distributional consequences that may be viewed as undesirable.)

This is the theory. In practice, OPEC members have demonstrated an interest (even apart from political considerations) in ensuring that the price of petroleum does not rise too high, too rapidly. If sharp and discontinuous price increases cause either economic slowdowns or inflationary pressures among their trading partners, OPEC pays in terms of reduced demand for its oil exports or higher prices for its imports, or both. Moreover, as we observed above, the higher oil prices are, the greater is the incentive to develop alternative energy sources and less petroleum-intensive production methods.

Is OPEC responsible for high gas prices at the pump? Yes and no. Since the late 1990s, crude oil costs (including resource rents, extraction costs, and transport and storage costs, only some of which reflect OPEC's influence on the world petroleum market) have risen significantly, so that crude oil now represents about half of the pump price of gas. Supply problems resulting from military actions and natural disasters such as Hurricane Katrina have contributed to the increase in world crude oil prices. Refiner and marketer costs add under 20 percent, and federal and provincial taxes represent over 30 percent of the pump price. Yet gas in Canada is still cheap relative to gas in Europe, where gas prices are as much as double the Canadian level, and where government taxes make up almost 2/3 of the pump price. European gas tax policy thus provides a strong incentive to conserve gas, increase fuel efficiency, and reduce greenhouse gas emissions. Perhaps our problem in North America is not that gas prices are too high but that they are too low!

SUMMARY

www.mcgrawhill.ca/olc/frank

- We can usefully distinguish between renewable resources (such as forests and fish) and exhaustible resources (such as petroleum and titanium). If the real interest rate i and the price of a renewable resource are constant, if harvesting costs can be neglected, and if after a point its growth rate g_t declines, the optimal harvest time occurs when $g_t = i$.

- In competitive markets for exhaustible resources, prices tend to rise at the real rate of interest. This not only curtails the rate at which exhaustible resources are used, but also stimulates the rate at which new sub-

stitutes are developed. It also assures a smooth transition between the use of an exhaustible resource and its eventual substitute. With monopoly in the market for an exhaustible resource, the price at any given time will be higher than under competition, but the monopoly price will still increase at a rate equal to the real rate of interest. With uncertainty and risk aversion, the rate of increase of the price of the resource will tend to be lower than the interest rate and the rate of depletion of the resource correspondingly higher.

1. Why does equilibrium require the price of exhaustible resources to rise at the real rate of interest?
2. How do harvesting costs affect the optimal time to harvest a renewable resource?

PROBLEMS

1. Suppose solar energy can be produced at a cost of $2 per unit of energy. Suppose the current price of oil is $1.80 per unit of energy and that there is presently enough oil to last 100 more years at current use levels. If the real rate of interest is 5 percent per year, what do you expect to happen to the current price of oil? (An *exact* numerical answer is not possible, on the basis of the information provided.)

2. There are two remaining exhaustible energy sources, underground oil and offshore oil, with extraction costs of $2 per barrel and $6 per barrel, respectively. There is also solar energy with the price of $12 per energy equivalent of a barrel of oil. Everyone believes that there are currently S_1 barrels of underground oil and S_2 barrels of offshore oil remaining. How would the discovery of A additional barrels of underground oil affect the time and the gross price at which offshore oil will first be extracted? How will the discovery affect the length of the "offshore oil age," that is, the length of the time interval during which we use offshore oil? (An exact numerical answer is not required.)

3. Suppose a certain species of tree grows according to the function $B = 2t$, where B is the volume of lumber in the tree, measured in cubic metres, and t is the tree's age in years. If the interest rate is a constant 5 percent per year and harvesting costs can be neglected, at what age should the trees be cut if the goal is to maximize long-run profit? If instead the interest rate is a constant 2.5 percent per year, when should the trees be cut?

4. Suppose there are two kinds of oil left, underground oil and shale oil. Total reserves of each kind of oil are known with certainty and there is perfect competition. The cost of extracting a unit of underground oil is $2 per barrel, of shale oil $10 per barrel. Once extracted from the earth, the two kinds of oil are identical. Explain, in terms a noneconomist could understand, why it does not make sense to begin using the shale oil until all the underground oil has been exhausted.

ANSWER TO IN-APPENDIX EXERCISE

A.15-1. $(\Delta B/\Delta t)/B = (40/\sqrt{t})/80\sqrt{t} = 1/(2t) = .02$, which solves for $t = 25$ years.

Part 5

GENERAL EQUILIBRIUM AND WELFARE

This part of the text examines in greater detail the conditions under which unregulated markets tend to produce efficient outcomes. Chapter 16 uses the theory of consumer and firm behaviour to help identify these conditions and also offers an assessment of when these conditions are not likely to be satisfied in practice. Chapter 17 examines the role of a well-defined system of property rights in the functioning of markets and the consequences of externalities, both positive and negative. Chapter 18 concludes by examining what microeconomic theory can tell us about the role of government.

Chapter 16

GENERAL EQUILIBRIUM AND MARKET EFFICIENCY

B arbers earn more today than they did 50 years ago, not because they cut hair any faster than they did then but because productivity has grown so rapidly in the other occupations they could have chosen. By the same token, computer paper now sells in much greater quantities, not because we have discovered a cheaper way to produce it but because so many more people now own their own computers. And we know that when a frost kills half the coffee crop in Brazil, the price of tea grown in Darjeeling usually rises substantially.

In the preceding chapters we saw occasional glimpses of the rich linkages between markets in the real world. But for the most part, we ignored these linkages in favour of what economists call *partial equilibrium analysis*—the study of how individual markets function in isolation. One of our tasks in this chapter is to investigate the properties of an interconnected system of markets. This is called **general equilibrium analysis**, and its focus is to make explicit the links that exist between individual markets. It takes into account, for example, the fact that inputs supplied to one market are unavailable for any other and that an increase in demand in one market implies a reduction in demand in others.

General equilibrium analysis The study of how conditions in each market in a set of related markets affect equilibrium outcomes in other markets in that set.

CHAPTER PREVIEW

We begin with one of the simplest possible general equilibrium models, a pure exchange economy with only two consumers and two goods. We shall see that for any given initial allocation of the two goods between the two consumers, a competitive exchange process will always exhaust all possible mutually beneficial gains from trade.

Next we add the possibility of production, again using one of the simplest possible models, one with only two inputs whose total supply is fixed. We shall see that here too competitive trading exploits all mutually beneficial gains from exchange.

We then add the possibility of international trade, assuming that prices are given externally in world markets. We shall see that even though trade leaves domestic production possibilities unchanged, its immediate effect is to increase the value of goods available for domestic consumption.

From trade, we move to the question of how taxes affect the allocation of resources. We conclude with a brief discussion of factors that interfere with the efficient allocation of resources.

16.1 A SIMPLE EXCHANGE ECONOMY

Imagine a simple economy in which there are only two consumers—Ann and Bill—and two goods, food and clothing. Food and clothing are not produced in this economy. Rather, they arrive in fixed quantities in each time period, just like manna from heaven. To help fix ideas, suppose there is a total of 100 units of food each time period and a total of 200 units of clothing. An *allocation* is defined as an assignment of these total amounts between Ann and Bill. An example is the allocation in which Ann receives 70 units of clothing and 75 units of food, with the remaining 130 units of clothing and 25 units of food going to Bill. In general, if Ann receives F_A units of food and C_A units of clothing, then Bill will get $100 - F_A$ units of food and $200 - C_A$ units of clothing. The amounts of the two goods with which Ann and Bill begin each time period are called their *initial endowments*.

In the next section we'll have more to say about where these initial endowments come from, but for now let's take them as externally determined. The question before us here is "What will Ann and Bill do with their initial endowments?" One possibility is that they might simply consume them, but only in rare circumstances will that be the best option available. To see why, it is helpful to begin by portraying the initial endowments diagrammatically. Consider again the case in which Ann receives 70 units of clothing and 75 units of food, with the remaining 130 units of clothing and 25 units of food going to Bill. From earlier chapters, we know how to represent these initial endowments as bundles in two separate food-clothing diagrams. The same allocation can also be represented as a point in a single rectangular diagram—namely, point R in Figure 16-1. The height of the rectangle corresponds to the total amount of food available per time period, 100 units. Its width is equal to the total amount of clothing, 200 units. O^A is the origin for Ann, and the left and bottom sides of the rectangle are the axes that

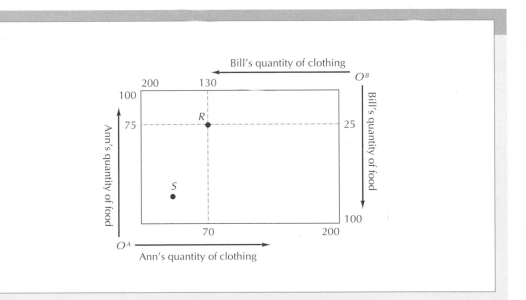

FIGURE 16-1

An Edgeworth Exchange Box
Ann's quantity of food at any point is measured by how far the point lies above O^A. Ann's clothing is measured by how far the point lies to the right of O^A. Bill's clothing is measured leftward from O^B, and his food downward from O^B. At any point within the Edgeworth box, the individual quantities of food and clothing sum to the total amounts available.

measure her quantities of food and clothing, respectively. O^B is the origin for Bill, and movements to the left from O^B correspond to increases in his amount of clothing. Downward movements from O^B correspond to increases in Bill's amount of food.

Because of the special way the rectangle is constructed, every point that lies within it corresponds to an allocation that exactly exhausts the total quantities of food and clothing available. Thus, point R is 70 units to the right of O^A and 130 units to the left of O^B, which means 70 units of clothing for Ann and 130 units for Bill, for a total of 200. R also lies 75 units above O^A and 25 units below O^B, which means 75 units of food for Ann and 25 for Bill, for a total of 100. The rectangular diagram in Figure 16-1 is often referred to as an ***Edgeworth exchange box***, after the British economist Francis Y. Edgeworth, who introduced it.

Edgeworth exchange box A diagram used to analyze the general equilibrium of an exchange economy.

EXERCISE 16-1

Suppose endowment point S in Figure 16-1 lies 25 units above O^A and 25 units to the right of O^A. Verify that Bill's initial endowment at S is 75 units of food and 175 units of clothing.

If Ann and Bill are egoistically rational and have the initial endowments represented by R, what will they do with them? Their possibilities are either to consume what they already have or to engage in exchange with one another. Exchange is purely voluntary, so trades can take place only if they make both parties better off. We shall assume that exchange is costless.

Our criterion for saying an exchange makes someone better off is very simple: it must place him or her on a higher indifference curve. In the Edgeworth box in Figure 16-2, Ann's indifference map has the conventional orientation, while Bill's is rotated 180°. Thus the curves labelled I_{A_1}, I_{A_2}, and I_{A_3} are representative curves from Ann's indifference map, while I_{B_1}, I_{B_2}, and I_{B_3} play the corresponding role for Bill. Ann's satisfaction increases as we move to the northeast in the box; Bill's as we move to the southwest.

FIGURE 16-2

Gains from Exchange
By moving from R to T, each party attains a higher indifference curve.

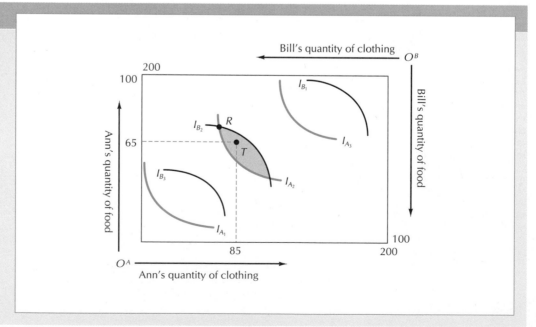

CHAPTER 16: GENERAL EQUILIBRIUM AND MARKET EFFICIENCY

Because we assume that preference orderings are complete, we know that each party will have an indifference curve passing through the initial endowment point R. In Figure 16-2 these curves are labelled I_{A_2} and I_{B_2}. Note that Ann's MRS between food and clothing at R (that is, the absolute value of the slope of her indifference curve) is much larger than Bill's (where the MRS for Bill is measured with respect to his own food and clothing axes). Suppose, for example, that Ann requires 2 units of food in order to be willing to part with a unit of clothing, while Bill requires only $\frac{1}{2}$ unit of food to make the same exchange. Both parties will then be better off if Ann gives Bill a unit of food in exchange for a unit of clothing. Indeed, any point in the lens-shaped shaded region in Figure 16-2 is one for which each party lies on a higher indifference curve than at R. Point T, at which Ann has 65 units of food and 85 units of clothing, is one such point. The two parties can move from R to T by having Ann give Bill 10 units of food in exchange for 15 units of clothing.

But the movement from R to T does not exhaust all possible gains from exchange. Note in Figure 16-3 that there is an additional, albeit smaller, lens-shaped region enclosed by the indifference curves that pass through T by both parties.

Through a process of repeated exchanges *or* through a *single* exchange at the correct exchange ratio, Ann and Bill can finally reach a point at which further mutual gains from trade are no longer possible. The indifference curves for the two parties that pass through any such point will necessarily be tangent to one another, as at point M in Figure 16-4. (If they were not tangent, they would necessarily enclose yet another lens-shaped region in which further gains from exchange would be possible.) Note that at M the marginal rates of substitution of Ann and Bill are exactly the same. It was a difference in these rates that provided the original basis for exchange, and once they are the same, all voluntary trading will cease.

One allocation is said to be *Pareto preferred* or ***Pareto superior*** to another if at least one party prefers it and the other party likes it at least as well. Allocations like the one at M are called ***Pareto optimal***. A Pareto-optimal allocation is one for which there is no other feasible reallocation that is preferred by one party and liked at least equally well by the other party. The concept of Pareto optimality was introduced by the Italian economist Vilfredo Pareto. Pareto-optimal allocations are essentially ones from which further mutually beneficial moves are impossible.

Pareto-superior allocation
An allocation that at least one individual prefers and others like at least as well.

Pareto optimal The term used to describe situations in which it is impossible to make one person better off without making at least one other worse off.

FIGURE 16-3

Further Gains from Exchange
Any point in the shaded region lies on a higher indifference curve for both parties than the ones that pass through T.

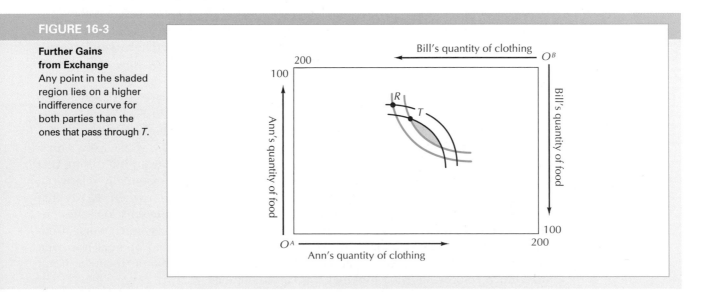

FIGURE 16-4

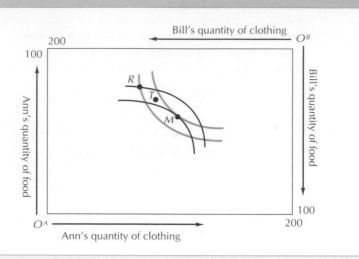

**A Pareto-Optimal
Allocation**
At the allocation *M*, no
further mutually beneficial
exchange is possible.
The marginal rate of
substitution of food
for clothing is the same
for both parties at *M*.

EXERCISE 16-2

Suppose Ann has an initial allocation of 50 units of food and 100 units of clothing in Figure 16-3. She regards food and clothing as perfect, 1-for-1 substitutes. Bill regards them as perfect, 1-for-1 complements, always wanting to consume 1 unit of clothing for every unit of food. Describe the set of allocations that are Pareto preferred to the initial allocation.

Contract curve
A curve along which all final, voluntary contracts must lie.

In any Edgeworth exchange box, there will be not one but an infinite number of mutual tangencies, as illustrated in Figure 16-5. The locus of these tangencies is called the ***contract curve***, a name that was chosen because it describes where all final, voluntary contracts between rational, well-informed persons must lie. Put another way, the contract curve identifies all the efficient ways of dividing the two goods between the two consumers.

Where Ann and Bill end up on the contract curve naturally depends on the initial endowments with which they start. Suppose they start with the one labelled *F* in Figure 16-6. We can then say that they will end up somewhere on the contract curve between points *U* and *V*. Given that they are starting from *F*, the best possible outcome from Ann's point of view is to end up at *V*. Bill, of course, would most prefer *U*. Whether they end up closer to *U* or to *V* depends on the relative bargaining skills of the two traders. Had they instead started at the allocation *G*, they would have ended up between *W* and *Z* on the contract curve.

The uses and limitations of the two Pareto criteria—Pareto preferred and Pareto optimal—can be seen by an examination of some of the points in Figure 16-6. Note, for example, that both *W* and *Z* are Pareto preferred to the original allocation *G*. This follows because *W* is better than *G* from Bill's point of view and no worse from Ann's; and similarly, *Z* is better from Ann's point of view and no worse from Bill's. Note that both points are also Pareto optimal. The two Pareto criteria are essentially relative in nature. Thus, when we say that *U* is Pareto preferred to *F*, or even when we say that *U* is Pareto optimal, we are not saying that *U* is good in any absolute sense. On the contrary, Ann is hardly likely to find *U* very attractive, and it is certainly much worse, from her standpoint, than an allocation like *G*, which is neither Pareto optimal nor even Pareto preferred to *U*. If Ann is starving to death in a tattered coat at *U*, she will not take much comfort in being told that *U* is Pareto optimal.

FIGURE 16-5

The Contract Curve
The locus of mutual tangencies in the Edgeworth exchange box is called the contract curve. Any point that does not lie on the contract curve cannot be the final outcome of a voluntary exchange because both parties will always prefer a move from that point in the direction of the contract curve.

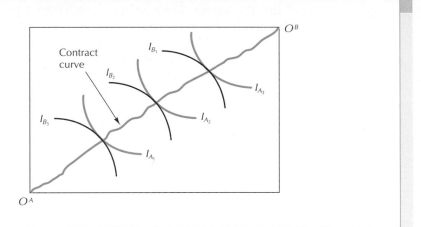

FIGURE 16-6

Initial Endowments Constrain Final Outcomes
Starting from F, traders will move to a point on the contract curve between U and V. They will land closer to V the better Ann's bargaining skills are relative to Bill's. If they start at G, they will end up between W and Z on the contract curve.

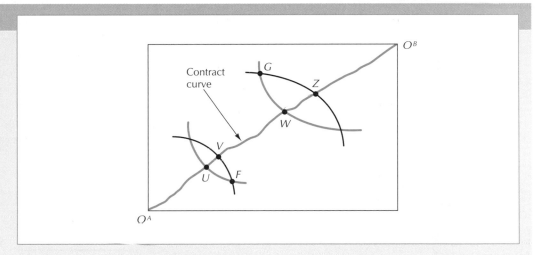

The Pareto criteria thus have force only in relation to the allocation with which the two players begin. Rather than remain at an initial allocation, both will always agree to move to one that is Pareto preferred and, indeed, to keep on moving until they reach one that is Pareto optimal.

In the simple, two-person economy described above, exchange took place through a process of personal bargaining. In market economies, in contrast, most exchanges have a much more impersonal character. People have given endowments and face given prices, and then decide how much of the various goods and services they want to buy and sell. We can introduce market-type exchange into our simple economy by the simple expedient of assuming that there is a third person who plays the role of an auctioneer. His function is to keep adjusting relative prices until the quantities demanded of each good match the quantities supplied.

Suppose Ann and Bill start with the allocation at E in Figure 16-7, in which each has 50 units of food and 100 units of clothing. Suppose also that the ratio of food to clothing prices announced by the auctioneer is $P_{C_0}/P_{F_0} = 1$, meaning that food and clothing both sell for the same price. When the prices of the two goods are the same, the auctioneer stands ready to exchange 1 unit of clothing for 1 unit of food. (More generally, he will exchange clothing for food at the rate of P_{C_0}/P_{F_0} units of food for each unit of clothing.) Note that with the given initial endowments, this rate of exchange uniquely determines the budget constraints for both Ann and Bill. We know that E has to be a point on each person's budget constraint because each has the option of simply consuming all of his or her initial endowment. But suppose that Ann wants to sell some food and use the proceeds to buy more clothing. She can do this by moving downward from E along the line labelled HH'. Alternatively, if she wants to sell clothing to buy more food, she can move upward along HH'. The same HH', seen from Bill's point of view, constitutes the budget constraint for Bill.

Given their budget constraints and preferences, Ann and Bill face a simple choice problem of the sort we discussed in Chapter 3. The optimal bundle for Ann on the budget HH' is the one labelled A_0^* in Figure 16-7, in which she consumes 30 units of food and 120 units of clothing. The corresponding bundle for Bill is labelled B_0^*, and it too contains 30 units of food and 120 units of clothing. Note that by choosing A_0^*, Ann indicates that she wants to sell 20 units of her initial endowment of food in order to buy 20 units of additional clothing. Similarly, by choosing B_0^*, Bill indicates that he too wants to sell 20 units of food and buy 20 more units of clothing.

This creates a problem, however. There are only 200 units of clothing to begin with, and the initial endowments of clothing at E add to precisely that amount. It is thus mathematically impossible for both individuals to have more clothing. By the same token, it is not possible for both persons to sell food. The auctioneer in this exercise is a figment, a hypothetical person who calls out relative prices in the hope of stimulating mutually beneficial exchange. He acts as a costless middleman, arranging for clothing to be exchanged for an equivalent value of food. But if *everyone* wants to sell food and buy clothing, there is no such exchange he can arrange.

FIGURE 16-7

A Disequilibrium Relative Price Ratio
At the price ratio $P_{C_0}/P_{F_0} = 1$, both Ann and Bill want to sell 20 units of food and buy 20 more units of clothing. But in general equilibrium, the amount sold by one party must equal the amount bought by the other. Both the food and clothing markets are out of equilibrium here.

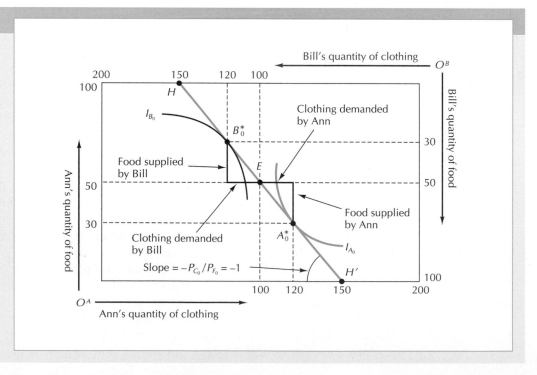

FIGURE 16-8

General Equilibrium
A simple exchange economy is in equilibrium when excess demands for both products are exactly equal to zero. At the price ratio $(P_C/P_F)^* = \frac{6}{5}$, Ann wants to buy 12 units of food, which is exactly the amount Bill wants to sell; also, Ann wants to sell 10 units of clothing, which is exactly the amount Bill wants to buy.

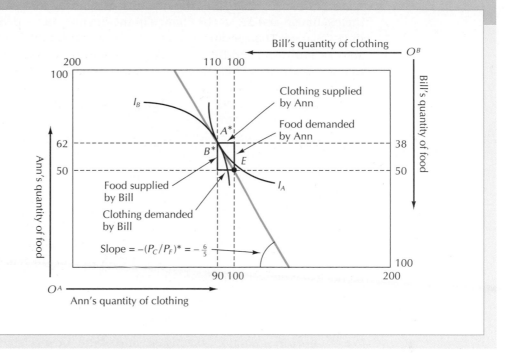

At the price ratio $P_{C_0}/P_{F_0} = 1$, there is excess demand for clothing and excess supply of food. At this price ratio the markets are not in general equilibrium. The solution to this problem is straightforward: the auctioneer simply calls out a new price ratio in which the price of clothing relative to food is higher than before. If there is still excess demand for clothing, he calls out a still higher price ratio, and so on, until the excess demand in each market is exactly zero.[1] Starting with the allocation at E, the price ratio $(P_C/P_F)^*$ that produces general equilibrium is shown in Figure 16-8. On the budget line through E with slope $(P_C/P_F)^*$, the highest attainable indifference curves for Ann and Bill are tangent. In order to move from E to the bundle A^*, Ann must purchase exactly the quantity of food (12 units) that Bill wishes to sell. And for Bill to move from E to the bundle B^*, he must purchase exactly the quantity of clothing (10 units) that Ann wishes to sell. In this illustration, excess demands for both products are exactly equal to zero at the price ratio $(P_C/P_F)^* = \frac{6}{5}$.

We can hence express the condition for consumption efficiency in our exchange economy as follows. At the equilibrium point, it must be the case that

$$\text{MRS}_A = (P_C/P_F)^* = \text{MRS}_B, \qquad (16.1)$$

where MRS_A and MRS_B are Ann's and Bill's marginal rates of substitution at the equilibrium point, respectively. It must also be the case that the price ratio $(P_C/P_F)^*$ satisfies the condition:

$$P_C \Delta C_A + P_F \Delta F_A = 0, \qquad (16.2)$$

---

[1]In advanced courses, we show that a competitive equilibrium will exist in a simple exchange economy if the sum of all individual excess demands is a continuous function of relative prices. This will always happen whenever individual indifference curves have the conventional convex shape.

where ΔC_A is the change in the quantity of clothing that Ann possesses as a result of the exchange and ΔF_A is the change in the quantity of food she possesses as a result of the exchange. This condition on $(P_C/P_F)^*$ ensures that the equilibrium bundle is affordable for both Ann and Bill. Since $\Delta C_A = -\Delta C_B$, the change in the quantity of clothing Bill possesses, and similarly $\Delta F_A = -\Delta F_B$, it is also the case that

$$P_C \Delta C_B + P_F \Delta F_B = 0. \qquad (16.3)$$

Only Relative Prices Are Determined

From the information given in our simple exchange model, note that we are able to determine only the *ratio* of clothing to food prices, not the actual value of individual prices. If, for example, $P_C = 6$ and $P_F = 5$ produce a budget constraint with the slope shown in Figure 16-8, then so will the prices $P_C = 12$ and $P_F = 10$, or indeed any other pair of prices whose ratio is $\frac{6}{5}$. Doubling or halving all prices will double or halve the dollar value of each consumer's initial endowment. In real terms, such price movements leave budget constraints unchanged.

The Invisible Hand Theorem

We are now in a position to consider one of the most celebrated claims in intellectual history, namely, Adam Smith's *theorem of the invisible hand.* In the context of our simple exchange economy, the theorem can be stated as follows:

> An equilibrium produced by perfectly competitive markets will exhaust all possible gains from exchange.

The invisible hand theorem is also known as the *first theorem of welfare economics,* and an alternative way of stating it is that *equilibrium in competitive markets is Pareto optimal.* To see why this must be so, recall that at the general equilibrium allocation, the optimizing indifference curves are tangent to one another. The possible allocations that Ann regards as better than the equilibrium allocation all lie beyond her budget constraint, and the same is true for Bill. And since the two budget constraints coincide in the Edgeworth box, this means that there is no allocation that both prefer to the equilibrium allocation, which is just another way of saying that the equilibrium allocation is Pareto optimal.

The invisible hand theorem tells us that every competitive equilibrium allocation—like D in Figure 16-9—is efficient. But suppose you are a social critic and don't like that particular allocation; you feel that Bill gets too much of each good and Ann too little. The problem, in your view, was that the initial endowment point—J in the diagram—is unjustly favourable to Bill. Suppose there is some other allocation on the contract curve—such as E—that you find much more equitable. Is there a set of initial endowments and relative prices for which E will be a competitive equilibrium? The *second theorem of welfare economics* says that, under relatively unrestrictive conditions:

> *Any* allocation on the contract curve can be sustained as a competitive equilibrium.

The basic condition that assures this result is that consumer indifference curves be convex when viewed from the origin. We know that an allocation like E, or any other efficient allocation, lies at a point of tangency between indifference curves. In Figure 16-9, the locus HH' is the mutual tangent between I_{A_2} and I_{B_2}. If the indifference curves are convex, any initial endowment along HH'—such as M—will lead to a competitive equi-

FIGURE 16-9

If indifference curves are convex, any efficient allocation can be sustained through a suitable choice of initial endowments and relative prices. To sustain *E*, for example, we announce a relative price ratio equal to the slope of *HH'*, the mutual tangent to I_{A_2} and I_{B_2}, and give consumers an initial endowment bundle that lies anywhere on *HH'*, such as *M*.

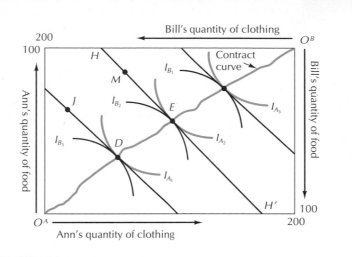

librium at *E*. If we redistribute the initial endowments from *J* to *M*, and announce a price ratio equal to the slope of *HH'*, Ann and Bill will then be led by the invisible hand to *E*. Indeed, any point along the contract curve can be reached in this fashion by a suitable choice of initial endowments and relative prices.

In the context of this simple, two-good, two-person exchange economy, it may not seem like a major accomplishment to be able to sustain all efficient allocations in the manner described by the second welfare theorem. After all, if we are free to redistribute initial endowments, why not simply redistribute them so as to achieve the desired final outcome directly? Why even bother with the intermediate steps of announcing prices and allowing people to make trades? If we are free to move from *J* to *M* in Figure 16-9, then we ought to be able to move directly to *E* and cut out the intervening steps.

The difficulty in practice is that the social institutions responsible for redistributing income have little idea of the shapes and locations of individual consumer indifference curves. People know their own preferences much better than governments do. And for an initial endowment of given value, self-interested rational individuals will generally achieve a much better result if they are free to make their own purchase decisions. *The significance of the second welfare theorem is that under our assumptions the issue of equity in distribution is logically separable from the issue of efficiency in allocation.* As the nineteenth-century British economist John Stuart Mill saw clearly, society can redistribute incomes in accordance with whatever norms of justice it deems fitting, at the same time relying on market forces to assure that those incomes are spent to achieve the most good.

16.2 EFFICIENCY IN PRODUCTION

In our simple exchange model, the total supply of each good was given externally. In practice, however, the product mix in the economy is the result of purposeful decisions about the allocation of productive inputs. Suppose we now add a productive sector to our exchange economy, one with two firms, each of which employs two freely variable inputs—capital (*K*) and labour (*L*)—to produce either of two products, food (*F*) or clothing (*C*). Suppose firm *C* produces clothing and firm *F* produces food. In order to keep the model simple, suppose that the total quantities of the two inputs are *fixed* at *K* = 50 and

FIGURE 16-10

An Edgeworth Production Box
Firm C's quantity of capital at any point is measured by how far the point lies above O^C. Firm C's quantity of labour is measured by how far the point lies to the right of O^C. The corresponding values of firm F's inputs are measured downward and leftward, respectively, from O^F. At any point within the Edgeworth production box, the separate input allocations to the two firms add up to the total amounts available, $K = 50$ for capital, $L = 100$ for labour. The contract curve is the locus of tangencies between isoquants.

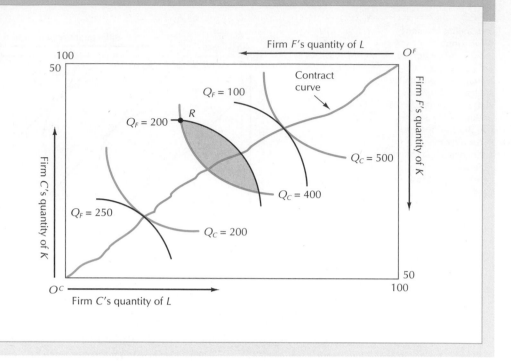

Edgeworth production box A diagram used to analyze feasible and efficient quantities of two outputs using fixed quantities of two inputs.

$L = 100$, respectively. Suppose, finally, that the production processes employed by the two firms give rise to conventional, convex-shaped isoquants.

Just as the Edgeworth exchange box provided a convenient way to summarize the conditions required for efficiency in consumption, a similar analysis serves an analogous purpose in the case of production. Figure 16-10 is called an **Edgeworth production box**. O^C represents the origin of the clothing firm's isoquant map, O^F the origin of the food firm's. Any point within the box represents an allocation of the total inputs to firm C and firm F. Firm C's isoquants correspond to increasing quantities of clothing as we move to the northeast in the box; firm F's correspond to increasing quantities of food as we move to the southwest.

Suppose the initial allocation of inputs is at point R in Figure 16-10. We know that this allocation cannot be efficient because we can move to any point within the shaded lens-shaped region and obtain both more food and more clothing. As in the consumption case, the contract curve is the locus of efficient allocations, which here is the locus of tangencies between isoquants. Recall from Chapter 9 that the absolute value of the slope of an isoquant at any point is called the marginal rate of technical substitution (MRTS) at that point. It is the ratio at which labour can be exchanged for capital without altering the total amount of output. Note that the MRTS between K and L must be the same for both firms at every point along the contract curve.

Suppose the equilibrium food and clothing prices are P_F^* and P_C^*, respectively. Suppose also that the two firms hire labour and capital in perfectly competitive markets at the hourly rates of w and r, respectively. If the firms maximize their profits, is there any reason to suppose that the resulting general equilibrium will satisfy the requirements of efficiency in production? That is, is there any reason to suppose that the MRTS between capital and labour will be the same for each firm? If both firms have conventional, convex-shaped isoquants, the answer is yes.

To see why, first note that a firm that maximizes its profits must also be minimizing its costs. Recall from Chapter 10 that the following conditions must be satisfied if the firms are minimizing costs:

$$\text{MRTS}_C = \frac{\text{MPL}_C}{\text{MPK}_C} = \frac{w}{r} \qquad (16.4)$$

and

$$\text{MRTS}_F = \frac{\text{MPL}_F}{\text{MPK}_F} = \frac{w}{r} \qquad (16.5)$$

where MPL_C and MPK_C are the marginal products of labour and capital in clothing production and MPL_F and MPK_F are the corresponding marginal products in food production. Recall, too, that the ratio of marginal products of the two inputs is equal to the marginal rate of technical substitution. Since both firms pay the same prices for labour and capital, Equations 16.4 and 16.5 tell us that the marginal rates of technical substitution for the two firms will be equal in competitive equilibrium. And this tells us, finally, that competitive general equilibrium is efficient, not only in the allocation of a given endowment of consumption goods, but also in the allocation of the factors used to produce those goods.

EXERCISE 16-3

For an economy like the one described above, suppose the price per unit of labour and the price per unit of capital are both equal to \$4 per hour. Suppose also that in clothing production we have $\text{MPL}_C/\text{MPK}_C = 2$ and that in food production we have $\text{MPL}_F/\text{MPK}_F = \frac{1}{2}$. Is this economy efficient in production? If not, how should it reallocate its inputs?

16.3 EFFICIENCY IN PRODUCT MIX

An economy could be efficient in production and at the same time efficient in consumption and yet do a poor job of satisfying the wants of its members. This could happen if, for example, the economy for some reason devoted almost all its resources to producing clothing, almost none to food. The tiny quantity of food that resulted could be allocated efficiently. And the inputs could be allocated efficiently in the production of this lopsided product mix. But everyone would be happier if there were less clothing and more food. There is thus one additional efficiency criterion of concern, namely, whether the economy has an efficient mix of the two products.

Production possibilities frontier The set of output combinations such that (with a fixed endowment of factor inputs) the production of each good is maximized for any given level of efficient production of all other goods.

To define an efficient product mix, it is helpful first to translate the contract curve from the Edgeworth production box into a ***production possibilities frontier***, the set of all possible efficient output combinations that can be produced with given quantities of capital and labour. Every point along the contract curve gives rise to specific quantities of clothing and food. Suppose $F_C(K, L)$ and $F_F(K, L)$ denote the production functions for clothing (firm C) and food (firm F), respectively. Point O^C in the top panel in Figure 16-11 represents what happens when we allocate all the inputs (50 units of capital, 100 units of labour) to food production and none to clothing. If $F_F(50, 100) = 275$, then the product mix to which this allocation gives rise has zero units of clothing and 275 units of food, and is shown by point O^C in the bottom panel. Point O^F in the top panel in Figure 16-11 represents what happens when we allocate all the inputs to clothing

FIGURE 16-11

Generating the Production Possibilities Frontier
Each point on the contract curve in the Edgeworth production box (top panel) gives rise to specific quantities of food and clothing production. The food–clothing pairs that lie along the contract curve are plotted in the bottom panel, and their locus is called the production possibilities frontier. Movements to the northeast along the contract curve correspond to movements downward along the production possibilities frontier.

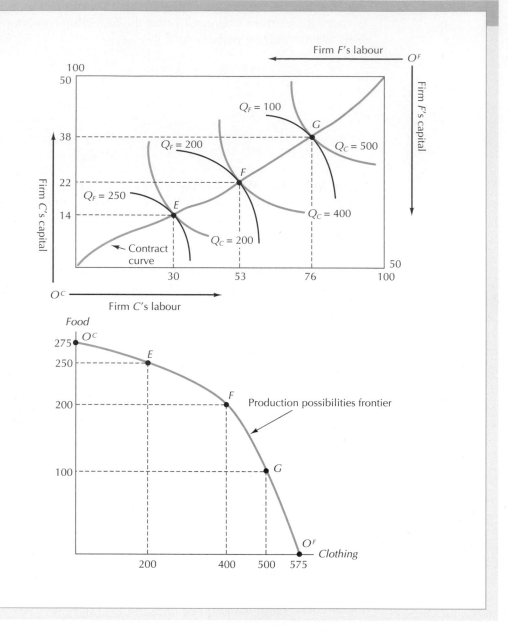

production and none to food. If $F_C(50, 100) = 575$, then the product mix to which this allocation gives rise has 575 units of clothing and zero units of food, and is shown by point O^F in the bottom panel. The product mix corresponding to point E in the top panel has $F_C(14, 30) = 200$ units of clothing and $F_F(36, 70) = 250$ units of food, and is shown by point E in the bottom panel. Similarly, the product mix at F in the top panel has $F_C(22, 53) = 400$ units of clothing and $F_F(28, 47) = 200$ units of food, and corresponds to F in the bottom panel. Likewise, G in the top panel has $F_C(38, 76) = 500$ units of clothing and $F_F(12, 24) = 100$ units of food, and corresponds to G in the bottom panel. By plotting other correspondences in like fashion, we can generate the entire production possibilities frontier shown in the bottom panel.

In the economy shown in Figure 16-11, suppose that a technical change occurs in the clothing industry that makes any given combination of labour and capital yield twice as much clothing as before. Show the effect of this change on the production possibilities frontier.

Marginal rate of transformation (MRT) The rate at which one output can be transformed into another at a point along the production possibilities frontier.

As we move downward along the production possibilities frontier, we give up food for additional clothing. The absolute value of the slope of the production possibilities frontier at any point is called the ***marginal rate of transformation (MRT)*** at that point, and it measures the opportunity cost of clothing in terms of food. For the economy shown, the production possibilities frontier bows out from the origin, which means that the MRT increases as we move to the right. As long as both production functions have constant or decreasing returns to scale, the production possibilities frontier cannot bow in toward the origin.

In order for an economy to be efficient in terms of its product mix, it is necessary that the marginal rate of substitution for every consumer be equal to the marginal rate of transformation. To see why, consider a product mix for which some consumer's MRS is greater or less than the corresponding MRT. The product mix Z in panel (a) in Figure 16-12, for instance, has an MRT of 1, while Ann's consumption bundle at W in panel (b) shows that her MRS is 2. This means that Ann is willing to give up 2 units of food in order to obtain an additional unit of clothing, but that an additional unit of clothing can be produced at a cost of only 1 unit of food. With the capital and labour saved by producing 2 fewer units of food for Ann, we can produce 2 additional units of clothing. We can give 1.5 units of this extra clothing to Ann and the remaining .5 unit to Bill, making both parties better off. It follows that the original product mix cannot have been efficient (where, again, efficient means Pareto optimal).

We are now in a position to ask, finally, whether a market in general competitive equilibrium will be efficient in terms of its product mix. Here, too, the answer turns out to be yes, provided the production possibilities frontier bows out from the origin. Let P_F^* and P_C^* again denote competitive equilibrium prices for clothing and food. As we have already seen in the case of the simple exchange economy, the MRS of every consumer in equilibrium will be equal to the ratio of these prices, P_C^*/P_F^*. What we must show is that the MRT will also be equal to P_C^*/P_F^*

FIGURE 16-12

An Inefficient Product Mix
At the product mix Z (panel a) the MRT is smaller than Ann's MRS at W (panel b). By producing 2 fewer units of food, we can produce 2 additional units of clothing. If we give 1.5 of these extra units to Ann and the remaining .5 unit to Bill, both parties will be better off. Efficiency requires that every consumer's MRS be exactly equal to the economy's MRT.

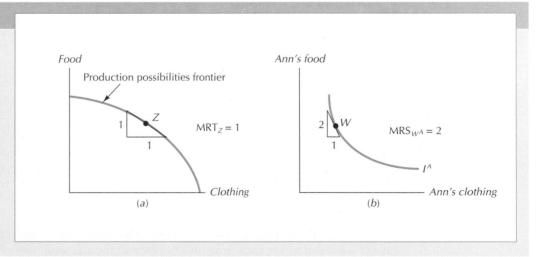

FIGURE 16-13

MRT Equals the Ratio of Marginal Costs
At Z, to produce an extra unit of clothing requires MC_C worth of labour and capital. Each unit less of food we produce at Z frees up MC_F worth of labour and capital. To get an extra unit of C, we must give up MC_C/MC_F units of food, and so the marginal rate of transformation is equal to MC_C/MC_F.

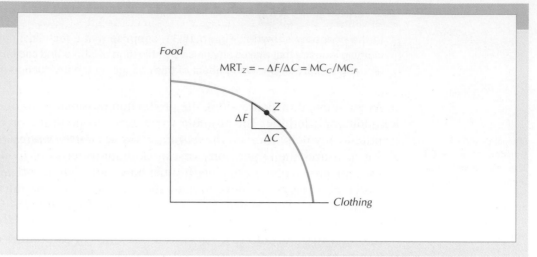

To do this, note first that the MRT at any point along the production possibilities frontier is equal to the ratio of the marginal cost of clothing (MC_C) to the marginal cost of food (MC_F). Suppose, for example, that MC_C at point Z in Figure 16-13 is $100 per unit of clothing and that MC_F is $50 per unit of food. The marginal rate of transformation at Z is $-\Delta F/\Delta C$, the amount of food we have to give up to get an extra unit of clothing. Since MC_C is $100, we need $100 worth of extra labour and capital to produce an extra unit of clothing. And since MC_F is $50, we have to produce 2 fewer units of food in order to free up $100 worth of labour and capital. MRT at Z is therefore equal to 2, which is exactly the ratio of MC_C to MC_F:

$$\text{MRT} = \frac{MC_C}{MC_F}. \qquad (16.6)$$

We also know that the equilibrium condition for competitive food and clothing producers is that product prices be equal to the corresponding values of marginal cost:

$$P_F^* = MC_F \qquad (16.7)$$

and

$$P_C^* = MC_C. \qquad (16.8)$$

Dividing Equation 16.8 by Equation 16.7, we have

$$\frac{P_C^*}{P_F^*} = \frac{MC_C}{MC_F} = \text{MRT}, \qquad (16.9)$$

which establishes that the equilibrium product price ratio is indeed equal to the marginal rate of transformation. Recalling Equation 16.1, we also have

$$\text{MRS}_A = \text{MRS}_B = (P_C/P_F)^* = \text{MRT}, \qquad (16.10)$$

which expresses the condition for efficiency in the choice of product mix that the marginal rate of substitution for each consumer is equal to the marginal rate of transformation.

To summarize, we have now established that an economy in competitive general equilibrium will, under certain conditions, be simultaneously efficient (Pareto optimal) in consumption, in production, and in the choice of product mix. As we have already seen, a society with a Pareto-optimal allocation of resources is not necessarily a good society. The final equilibrium in the marketplace depends very strongly on the distribution of initial endowments, and if this distribution isn't fair, we have no reason to expect the competitive equilibrium to be fair. Even so, it is truly remarkable to be able to claim, as Adam Smith did, that each person, merely by pursuing his own interests, is "led by an invisible hand to promote an end which was no part of his intention"—namely, the exploitation of all gains from exchange possible under given initial endowments.

16.4 GAINS FROM INTERNATIONAL TRADE

In our simple model of exchange and production, we saw why efficiency requires that every consumer's MRS be equal to the economy's MRT. This same requirement must be satisfied even for an economy that is free to engage in foreign trade. To illustrate, consider an economy just like the one we discussed, and suppose that its competitive general equilibrium in the absence of international trade occurs at point V in Figure 16-14. Now suppose that country opens its borders to international trade. If the country is small relative to the rest of the world, output prices will no longer be determined in its own internal markets, but in the much larger international markets. Suppose, in particular, that world prices for food and clothing are P_F^W and P_C^W, respectively. The best option available to this economy will no longer be to produce and consume at V. On the contrary, it should now produce at Z, the point on its production possibilities frontier at which the MRT is exactly equal to the international price ratio, P_C^W/P_F^W. Z is the point that maximizes the value of its output in world markets. Having produced at Z, the country is then free to choose any point along its "international budget constraint," BB'. Since the original competitive equilibrium point, V, lies within BB', we know that it is now possible for every person in the economy to have more of each good than before.

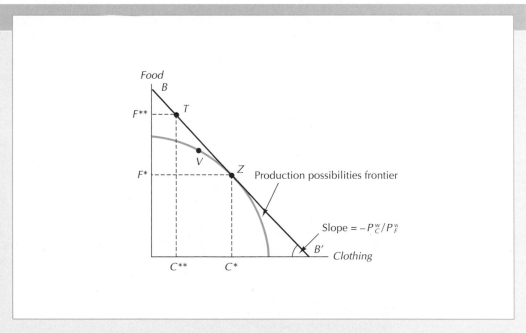

Which of the infinitely many bundles along BB' should be chosen? The best outcome is the one for which P_C^w/P_F^w is equal to every consumer's MRS. We know that without international trade the common value of MRS was equal to the MRT at V, which is smaller than the MRT at Z. Suppose T is the combination of food and clothing that equates everyone's MRS to P_C^w/P_F^w. This economy will then do best by exporting C^* − C^{**} units of clothing and using the proceeds to import F^{**} − F^* units of food.[2]

As noted, the fact that the international budget constraint contains the original competitive equilibrium point means that it is possible to make everyone better off than before. But the impersonal workings of international trading markets provide no guarantee that every single person will in fact be made better off by trade. In the illustration given, international trading possibilities led the economy to produce more clothing and less food than it used to. The effect will be to increase the demand for factors of production used in clothing production and to reduce the demand for those used in food production. If factors of production are used with equal intensity in the two production processes, there will be no change in the intensity of demand for each factor. But suppose that food production is relatively intensive in the use of labour and that clothing production is relatively intensive in the use of capital. Depending on the specific magnitudes involved, the shift in product mix might then drive up the price of capital and drive down the price of labour. In this case, the primary beneficiaries from trade would be the owners of capital. People whose incomes come exclusively from the sale of their own labour would actually do worse than before, even though the value of total output is higher. What our general equilibrium analysis shows is that trade makes it *possible* to give everyone more of everything. It does not prove that everyone necessarily *will* get more.

EXAMPLE 16-1

You are the leader of a small island nation that has never engaged in trade with any other nation. You are considering the possibility of opening the economy to international trade. The chief economist of the island's only labour union, to which every worker belongs, tells you that free trade will reduce the real purchasing power of labour, and you have no reason to doubt him. You are determined to remain in office and need the union's support in order to do so. The union will never support a candidate whose policies adversely affect the welfare of its members. Does this mean you should keep the island closed to trade?

The answer is yes only if there is no way to redistribute the gains that trade will produce. Our general equilibrium analysis establishes that trade will increase the total value of output, which makes it possible for everyone to do better. If the alternative is for the island to remain closed, the owners of capital should readily agree to transfer some of their gains to labour. The only leader who would fail to open the island's economy is one who is unable to negotiate an agreement under which every party ends up with more of everything than before.

---

[2]For the sake of completeness, let us note that it is possible for the post-trade equilibrium to lie to the *southeast* of Z on BB'. The paragraph immediately below in the text suggests how this could occur. Suppose that the opening of trade redistributes income toward the owners of capital, and that at any given P_C/P_F, capital owners spend a much higher proportion of their income on clothing than do wage earners. In this case, the opening of foreign trade could result in the country's exporting food and importing clothing! If we can represent collective preferences by a convex, distribution-invariant community indifference map, however, once foreign trade occurs the economy will move *northwest* of Z along BB' to a point such as T.

Much has been written about the tradeoff between equity and efficiency, the notion that greater distributional fairness may require some sacrifice in efficiency. The lesson in Example 16-1 is that when people are able to negotiate *costlessly* with one another, there is not necessarily any conflict between equity and efficiency. When the total size of the economic pie grows larger, it is always possible for everyone to have a larger slice than before. Efficiency is achieved when we have made the economic pie as large as possible. Attaining the largest possible pie, however, typically requires some cooperation among economic agents. In this case, prior agreement among the agents as to what constitutes a fair division of the pie may be a prerequisite of the cooperation that generates efficiency. There may not alway be a *tradeoff* between equity and efficiency, but factors such as trust and concepts of fairness can thus play a direct role in attaining efficiency.

16.5 TAXES IN GENERAL EQUILIBRIUM

Suppose we are back in our simple production economy without the added complication of international trading opportunities. The economy is in competitive general equilibrium at point V in Figure 16-15, where the marginal rate of transformation is equal to the competitive equilibrium product price ratio, P_C^*/P_F^*. Now suppose the government decides to raise revenue by taxing food at the rate of t/dollar. Every time a producer sells a unit of food for P_F^*, she gets to keep only $(1 - t)P_F^*$. How will such a tax affect resource allocation?

The immediate effect of the tax is to raise the relative price ratio, as seen by *producers*, from P_C^*/P_F^* to $P_C^*/(1 - t)P_F^*$. Producers who were once content to produce at V on the production possibilities frontier will now find that they can increase their profits (or reduce their losses) by producing more clothing and less food than before. Suppose that, in the end, the effect is to cause producers to relocate at point Z along the production possibilities frontier. Recall that the MRT at V was equal to the common value of MRS at V. Since Z has more clothing and less food than V, the MRS of consumers at Z will be smaller than at V. It follows that the MRT at Z will be higher than the MRS at Z, which means that the economy will no longer have an efficient product mix. The original allocation at V was Pareto optimal. The new allocation has too much clothing, too little food.

Note that a tax on food does not alter the fact that consumers will all have a common value of MRS in equilibrium. Nor does it alter the fact that producers will all have a common value of MRTS. Even with such a tax, the economy remains efficient in consumption and production. The real problem created by the tax is that it causes producers to see

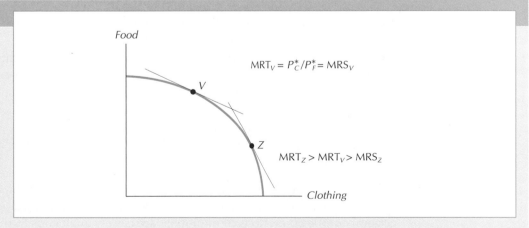

FIGURE 16-15

Taxes Affect Product Mix

A tax on food causes a shift away from food toward clothing consumption. If the original allocation was Pareto optimal, the new one will not be. The marginal rate of transformation will exceed the marginal rate of substitution. There will be too much clothing and too little food.

$$\text{MRT}_V = P_C^*/P_F^* = \text{MRS}_V$$

$$\text{MRT}_Z > \text{MRT}_V > \text{MRS}_Z$$

a different price ratio from the one seen by consumers. Consumption decisions are based on *gross prices*—that is, on prices inclusive of taxes. Production decisions, in contrast, are guided by *net prices*—the amount producers get to keep after the tax has been paid. When producers confront a different price ratio from the one that guides consumers, the MRS can never be equal to the MRT in equilibrium. By driving a wedge between the price ratios seen by producers and consumers, the tax leads to an inefficient product mix.

Subsidies, like taxes, also upset the conditions required for efficiency. The problem with a taxed product is that it appears too cheap to its producer. In contrast, the problem with a subsidized product is that it appears too expensive. In general equilibrium, we get too much of the subsidized product and too little of the unsubsidized one.

The distortionary effects of taxes and subsidies identified by our simple general equilibrium analysis form the cornerstone of the so-called supply-side school of economic policy. Supply-siders are ever ready to argue that taxes almost always lead to some sort of inefficiency in the allocation of resources.

Does it then follow that the world would be better off if we simply *abolished* all taxes? Hardly, for in such a world there could be no goods or services provided by government, and as we will presently see, there are many valuable goods and services that are unlikely to be provided in any other way. The practical message of general equilibrium analysis is that care should be taken to design taxes that keep distortions to a minimum. Note that in our simple model, the problem would have been eliminated had we taxed not just food but also clothing at the same rate *t*. Relative prices would then have stayed the same, and producers and consumers would again be motivated by a consistent set of price signals.

In more realistic general equilibrium models, however, even a general commodity tax could have distortionary effects. With no possibility of saving, a tax on all commodities is essentially the same as a tax on income, including the income earned from the sale of one's own labour. In our simple model, the supply of labour was assumed to be fixed, but in practice it may be sensitive to the real, after-tax wage rate. In a fuller model that included this relationship, a general commodity tax might thus lead to a distortion in decisions about the allocation of time between labour and leisure—for example, people might work too little and consume too much leisure.

From the standpoint of efficiency, a better tax would be a *head tax* (also called a *lump-sum tax*), one that is levied on each person irrespective of his or her labour supply decisions. The problem with this kind of tax is that many object to it on equity grounds. If we levied the same tax on every person, the burden of taxation would fall much more heavily on the poor than it does under our current system, which collects taxes roughly in proportion to individual income.

Of course, in a full general equilibrium model, we must take explicit account not only of the effects of taxation but also of the effects of government expenditure on the economy. Yet on the taxation side, on efficiency grounds, the very best tax of all is one levied on activities of which there would otherwise be too much. And as we will see below and in the next chapter, there are many such activities—perhaps enough to raise most of the tax revenue we need.

16.6 OTHER SOURCES OF INEFFICIENCY

Monopoly

Taxes are but one of many factors that can stand in the way of achieving Pareto optimality in the allocation of resources. One other source of inefficiency is monopoly. The general equilibrium effects of monopoly are closely analogous to those of a commodity tax. Consider again our simple production economy with two goods, and suppose that food is produced by a monopolist, clothing by a price taker. The competitive producer selects an output level for which marginal cost is equal to the price of clothing; the monopolist, as we saw in Chapter 12, selects one for which marginal cost is equal to marginal revenue. Because price always exceeds marginal revenue along a downward-sloping demand curve, this means that price will exceed marginal cost for the monopolist.

From the standpoint of efficiency, this wedge between price and marginal cost functions exactly like a tax on the monopolist's product. The marginal rate of transformation, which is the ratio of the marginal cost of clothing to the marginal cost of food, will no longer be equal to the ratio of product prices. Producers will be responding to one set of relative prices, consumers to another. The result is that too few of the economy's resources will be devoted to the production of food (the monopolized product) and too many to the production of clothing (the competitive product).

The general equilibrium analysis of the effect of monopoly adds an important dimension to our partial equilibrium analysis from Chapter 12. The partial analysis called our attention to the fact that there would be too little output produced by the monopolist. The general equilibrium analysis forcefully reminds us that there is another side of this coin, which is that the resources not used by the monopolist will be employed by the competitive sector of the economy. Thus, if monopoly output is too small, competitive output is too big. The additional competitive output does not undo the damage caused by monopoly, but it partially compensates for it.

Externalities

Another source of inefficiency occurs when production or consumption activities involve benefits or costs that fall on people not directly involved in the activities. Such benefits and costs are usually referred to as **externalities**. A standard example of a *negative externality* is the case of pollution, in which a production activity results in emissions that adversely affect people other than those who consume the product. The planting of additional apple trees, whose blossoms augment the output of honey in nearby beehives, is an example of a *positive externality*. And so is the case of the beekeeper who adds bees to his hive, unmindful of the higher pollination rates they will produce in nearby apple orchards.

Externality Either a benefit or a cost of an action that accrues to someone other than the people directly involved in the action.

Externalities are both widespread and important. We will discuss them in great detail in Chapter 17. For now, let us note that the problem they create for efficiency stems from the fact that, like taxes, they cause producers and consumers to respond to different sets of relative prices. When the orchard owner decides how many trees to plant, he looks only at the price of apples, not at the price of honey. By the same token, when the consumer decides how much honey to buy, he ignores the effects of his purchases on the quantity and price of apples.

In the case of negative externalities in production, the effect on efficiency is much the same as that of a subsidy. In deciding what quantity of the product to produce, the producer equates price and his own private marginal cost. The problem is that the negative externalities impose additional costs on others, and these are ignored by the producer. As with the subsidized product, we end up with too much of the product with negative externalities and too little of all other products. With positive externalities, the reverse occurs. We end up with too little of such products and too much of others.

Taxes as a Solution to Externalities and Monopoly

As noted earlier, the best tax from an efficiency standpoint is one levied on an activity there would otherwise be too much of. This suggests that the welfare losses from monopoly can be mitigated by placing an excise tax on the good produced in the competitive sector. Properly chosen, such a tax could exactly offset the wedge that is created by the disparity between the monopolist's price and marginal cost.

In the case of negative externalities, the difficulty is that individuals regard the product as being cheaper than it really is from the standpoint of society as a whole. By taxing the product with negative externalities at a suitable rate, the efficiency loss can be undone. For products accompanied by positive externalities, the corresponding solution is a subsidy. In view of what was said earlier about the potentially distorting effects of taxes, it is worth underlining this point. Where monopoly or externalities exist, carefully designed taxes and subsidies not only do not create distortions, but also can actually offset or eliminate them and enable the economy to perform efficiently.

Public Goods

One additional factor that stands in the way of achieving efficient allocations through private markets is the existence of *public goods*. A pure public good is one with two specific properties: (1) *nondiminishability*, also called *nonrivalry*, which means that one person's use of the good does not diminish the amount of it available for others; and (2) *nonexcludability*, which means that it is either impossible or prohibitively costly to exclude people who do not pay from using the good. Before the introduction of cable and satellite systems and signal-scrambling technology, broadcast ("over the air") television and radio signals were an example of a pure public good. For those who use rabbit-ears and outdoor antennas, they still are. Your watching an over-the-air TV movie does not make that movie less available to anyone else. Once the signal has gone out over the air, there is no practical way to exclude anyone from using it. National defence is another example of a pure public good. The fact that Smith enjoys the benefits of national defence does not make those benefits any less available to Jones. And it is exceedingly difficult for the government to protect some of its citizens from foreign attack while denying the same protection to others.

There is no reason to presume that private markets will supply optimal quantities of pure public goods. Indeed, if it is impossible to exclude people from using the good, it might seem impossible for a profit-seeking firm to supply any quantity of it at all. But profit-seeking firms often show great ingenuity in devising schemes for providing pure public goods. Commercial broadcast television, for example, covers its costs by charging advertisers for access to the audience it attracts with its programming. But even in these cases, there is no reason to suppose that the amount and kind of television programming we get under this arrangement is economically efficient. (More on this specific issue in Chapter 18.)

The problem is less acute in the case of goods that have the nondiminishability but not the nonexcludability property. When a household receives its television signals exclusively by cable or satellite, it is possible to deny it access to the signals if the household doesn't pay its monthly bill or pay-per-view fee. But even here, there are likely to be inefficiencies. Once a TV program has been produced, it costs society nothing to let an extra person see it. If there is a positive price for watching the program, however, all those who value seeing it at less than that price will not tune in. It is inefficient to exclude these viewers, since their viewing the program would not diminish its usefulness for anyone else.

The inefficiencies highlighted by the example of television are just the tip of the iceberg, as Economic Naturalist 16-1 suggests.

WHY IS ELIMINATING PEER-TO-PEER (P2P) FILE-SHARING OF COPYRIGHT MUSIC, MOVIES, AND SOFTWARE AN ALMOST IMPOSSIBLE TASK?

In theory, it might seem—after a period of relatively uncontrolled P2P file sharing—that the major record companies and other copyright holders have gained the upper hand in controlling unauthorized file sharing. Legal victories in the United States against Napster and MP3, the U.S. Digital Millennium Copyright Act, and the development of online pay-per-download sites all seem to suggest that "the problem is under control." Yet at the same time, global file sharing, and the multi-billion-dollar annual sales of pirated CDs, DVDs, and computer software, have reached historically unprecedented levels. The root of the problem is the public-goods aspect of digitalized informational property. Copying the information leaves the information intact, and the marginal costs of copying are negligible. At the same time, the costs of enforcement of informational property rights have risen sharply, because high-memory digital computers and iPods, CD- and DVD-burning technology, DVD players, and Internet access have become so affordable, widespread, and spatially decentralized. In Canada, enforcement costs are even higher, because of a series of Supreme Court decisions that place a significantly lower burden on Internet Service Providers for copyright enforcement than is the case in the United States. The Supreme Court's decisions gave greater weight to privacy rights and to open access to *non*-copyright file-sharing than in the United States. One of the effects of their judgments, however, was to make enforcement of copyright violations more difficult for copyright holders in Canada.

SUMMARY

www.mcgrawhill.ca/olc/frank

- One of the simplest possible general equilibrium models is a pure exchange economy with only two consumers and two goods. For any given initial allocation of the two goods between the two consumers in this model, a costless competitive exchange process will always exhaust all possible mutually beneficial gains from trade. This result is known as the invisible hand theorem and is also called the first theorem of welfare economics.

- If consumers have convex indifference curves, any efficient allocation can be sustained as a competitive equilibrium. This result is known as the second theorem of welfare economics. Its significance is that it demonstrates that the issues of efficiency and distributional equity are logically distinct. If costless redistribution is possible, then society can redistribute initial endowments according to accepted norms of distributive justice and rely on markets to assure that endowments are used efficiently.

- An economy is efficient in production if the marginal rate of technical substitution is the same for all producers. In the input market, too, competitive trading exploits all mutually beneficial gains from exchange.

- Even though international trade leaves domestic production possibilities unchanged, its immediate effect is to increase the value of goods available for domestic consumption. With a suitable costless redistribution of initial endowments, a free trade economy will always be Pareto superior to a non-free trade economy.

- Taxes can interfere with efficient resource allocation, usually because they cause consumers and producers to respond to different price ratios. The costs of tax-induced distortions must always be balanced against the benefits derived from the government expenditures financed by taxes, including government provision of public goods. The practical significance of this result is to guide us in the search for taxes that minimize distortions. The best tax, from an efficiency standpoint, is one levied on an activity that would otherwise be pursued too intensively.

- Monopoly, externalities, and public goods are three other factors that limit society's capacity to achieve an efficient allocation of resources using the market mechanism alone.

1. Why does efficiency in consumption require the MRS of all consumers to be the same?
2. Distinguish among the terms "Pareto superior," "Pareto preferred," and "Pareto optimal."
3. Why might voters in a country choose a non-Pareto-optimal allocation over another that is Pareto optimal?
4. How do the initial endowments constrain where we end up on the contract curve?
5. In general equilibrium, can there be excess demand for every good?
6. How might an economist or a social critic respond to the claim that governmental involvement in the economy is unjustified because of the invisible hand theorem?
7. Why is the slope of the production possibilities frontier equal to the ratio of marginal production costs?
8. How might a critical economist respond to the claim that taxes always make the allocation of resources less efficient?

PROBLEMS

1. Bert has an initial endowment consisting of 10 units of food and 10 units of clothing. Ernie's initial endowment consists of 10 units of food and 20 units of clothing. Represent these initial endowments in an Edgeworth exchange box.

2. Bert regards food and clothing as perfect 1-for-1 substitutes. Ernie regards them as perfect complements, always wanting to consume 3 units of clothing for every 2 units of food.
   a. Describe the set of allocations that are Pareto preferred to the one given in Problem 1.
   b. Describe the contract curve for the total endowment in Problem 1.
   c. What price ratio will be required to sustain an allocation on the contract curve?

3. How will your answers to Problem 2 differ if 5 units of Ernie's clothing endowment are given to Bert?

4. Consider a simple economy with two goods, food and clothing, and two consumers, A and B, both with convex indifference maps. For a given initial endowment, when the ratio of food to clothing prices in an economy is 3/1, A wants to buy 6 units of clothing while B wants to sell 2 units of food. Is $P_F/P_C = 3$ an equilibrium price ratio? If so, explain why. If not, state in which direction it will tend to change.

5. How will your answer to Problem 4 change if A wants to sell 3 units of clothing and B wants to sell 2 units of food?

6. Suppose Sarah has an endowment of 2 units of X and 4 units of Y and has indifference curves that satisfy our four basic assumptions (see Chapter 3). Suppose Brian has an endowment of 4 units of X and 2 units of Y, and has preferences given by the utility function $U(X, Y) = \min\{X, Y\}$, where

$$\min(X, Y) = \begin{cases} X & \text{if } X \leq Y \\ Y & \text{if } Y \leq X \end{cases}.$$

On an Edgeworth box diagram, indicate the set of Pareto-superior bundles.

7. A simple economy produces two goods, food and clothing, with two inputs, capital and labour. Given the current allocation of capital and labour between the two industries, the marginal rate of technical substitution between capital and labour in food production is 4, while the corresponding MRTS in clothing production is 2. Is this economy efficient in production? If so, explain why. If not, describe a reallocation that will lead to a Pareto improvement.

8. Given the current allocation of productive inputs, the marginal rate of transformation of food for clothing in a simple two-good economy is equal to 2. At the current allocation of consumption goods, each consumer's marginal rate of substitution between food and clothing is 1.5. Is this economy efficient in terms of its product mix? If so, explain why. If not, describe a reallocation that will lead to a Pareto improvement.

9. Crusoe can make 5 units of food per day if he devotes all his time to food production. He can make 10 units of clothing if he spends the whole day at clothing production. If he divides his time between the two activities, his output of each good will be proportional to the time spent on each. The corresponding figures for Friday are 10 units of food and 15 units of clothing. Describe the production possibilities frontier for their economy.

10. If Crusoe and Friday both regard food and clothing as perfect one-for-one substitutes, what should each produce?

11. Now suppose a trading ship visits the island each day and offers to buy or sell food and clothing at the price ratio $P_F/P_C = 4$. How, if at all, will the presence of this ship alter the production and consumption decisions of Crusoe and Friday?

12. How will your answers to Problems 9, 10, and 11 differ if Friday's maximum production figures change to 20 units of food and 50 units of clothing?

13. There are two industries in a simple economy, each of which faces the same marginal cost of production. One of the industries is perfectly competitive, the other a pure monopoly. Describe a reallocation of resources that will lead to a Pareto improvement for this economy.

14. Suppose capital and labour are perfect substitutes in production for clothing: 2 units of capital *or* 2 units of labour produce 1 unit of clothing. Suppose capital and labour are perfect complements in production for food: 1 unit of capital *and* 1 unit of labour produce 1 unit of food. Suppose the economy has an endowment of 100 units of capital and 200 units of labour. Describe the set of efficient allocations of the factors to the two sectors (determine the contract curve in an Edgeworth production box).

15. Construct the production possibilities frontier for the economy described in Problem 14. What is the opportunity cost of clothing in terms of food?

16. Construct the production possibilities frontier for an economy just like the one described in Problem 14, except that its endowment of capital is 200 units.

**17. Allie (*A*) and Bubba (*B*) are price-taking consumers in a two-person, two-good exchange economy with a fixed endowment of 40 units of good X (of which Allie initially has 12 units while Bubba has the remainder) and 80 units of good Y (of which Bubba initially has 50 units, with Allie having the rest). Allie's utility function is given by $U_A = (X_A)^2 Y_A$, and Bubba's is given by $U_B = X_B Y_B$. Exchange is voluntary and costless.

   a. Give the formula for the contract curve in terms of Y_A^* expressed as a function of X_A^*, the total endowment of X (= 40 units), and the total endowment of Y (= 80 units). Also give the formula for the contract curve in terms of Y_B^* expressed as a function of X_B^*, the total endowment of X, and the total endowment of Y. (*Hints:* Use the fact that at every point on the contract curve, $MRS_A = MRS_B$. If you do not have calculus, see Appendix 3A to calculate the formulas for MRS_A and MRS_B.)

   b. Calculate Allie's MRS_A and Bubba's MRS_B at the initial endowment point, explain why this point is not a Pareto-efficient exchange equilibrium, and indicate who will want to sell X and who will want to sell Y.

   c. Combine the relation that holds on the contract curve ($MRS_A = P_X/P_Y = MRS_B$) with the exchange condition that $P_X \Delta X_A + P_Y \Delta Y_A = 0$ to calculate the equilibrium values for X_A, X_B, Y_A, Y_B, and P_X/P_Y.

   d. With *total* initial endowments unchanged, how would your answers to 17b and 17c differ if Allie had an initial endowment of 15 units of Y and Bubba had an initial endowment of 22 units of X?

   e. With *total* initial endowments unchanged, how would your answers to 17b and 17c differ if Allie had an initial endowment of 30 units of X and Bubba had an initial endowment of 50 units of Y?

   f. In which of the three final equilibria is Allie's utility level highest? In which of the three final equilibria is Bubba's utility level highest? Briefly discuss the significance of your results.

16-1. Bill's endowment of food = 100 − Ann's endowment = 75. Bill's endowment of clothing = 200 − Ann's endowment = 175.

16-2. Let M denote the initial allocation. Ann's indifference curve through M is a straight line with slope 5 −1. Bill's indifference curve through M is right-angled, as shown in the following diagram. The set of Pareto-superior allocations is indicated by the shaded triangle.

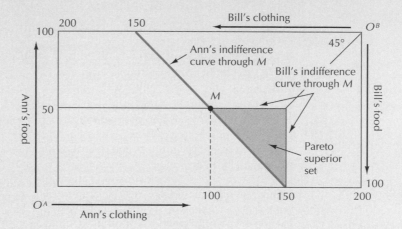

16-3. Here, $P_L/P_K = 1$, which is half as big as MPL_C/MPK_C:

$$\frac{P_L}{P_K} = \frac{1}{2}\frac{MPL_C}{MPK_C},$$

from which it follows that

$$\frac{MPK_C}{P_K} = \frac{1}{2}\frac{MPL_C}{P_L}.$$

In words, this says that the last dollar spent on capital in clothing production produces only half as much extra output as does the last dollar spent on labour in clothing production. It follows that clothing producers can get more output for the same cost by hiring less capital and more labour. Parallel reasoning tells us that food producers can increase food production at no extra cost by hiring less labour and more capital.

Hence initially the economy is not operating efficiently, and *both* food and clothing production can be increased by shifting labour from food to clothing production and capital from clothing to food production. Only when these producers have reached a cost-minimizing input mix characteristic of a competitive equilibrium will efficiency in production be achieved.

16-4. On the new production possibilities frontier, the maximum quantity of food that can be produced (when *all* of the labour and capital is devoted to food production) is unchanged. At every level of food production, the corresponding amount of clothing that can be produced (moving horizontally) is exactly double the amount on the original production possibilities frontier.

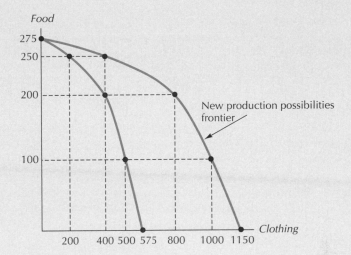

Chapter 17

EXTERNALITIES, PROPERTY RIGHTS, AND THE COASE THEOREM

In the early days of development of the Canadian West, cattle ranchers outnumbered farmers in some areas, and farmers were obliged to fence in their land to prevent stray cattle from trampling or eating their crops. Over time, the number of farmers rose, and eventually exceeded the number of ranchers. It now became the legal responsibility of ranchers to fence in their cattle, and farmers acquired the right not to have their farms harmed by strays.

This change in the structure of property rights is related to an experience you might have had. You are wakened from a deep sleep at 3 a.m. by the loud throbbing of an electric bass and drums, blaring from the outdoor speakers of a party four houses away. You have three midterms to write over the next day and a half, and you are already working on a major case of sleep deprivation. You do the only sensible thing: you call the police. But what gives you the right? A friend lives just off the highway. All night long, eighteen-wheelers whiz by her home, generating about the same decibel level, but she wouldn't dream of calling the police to stop the noise. Another friend's home is on the approach to the airport, and the thunder of planes taking off and landing can sometimes rattle his dishes. He has the right to exclude someone from constructing a building in the airspace above his property, but every day the planes fly low through his airspace without paying him a penny. This pattern of rights is not a matter of historical accident. It has emerged, as we shall see, as a means of making the most efficient use of property when it is difficult to negotiate agreements on a case-by-case basis.

CHAPTER PREVIEW

Our subjects in this chapter are externalities and property rights. We begin with a series of examples illustrating what happens when an action by one party harms another and the parties are able to negotiate costlessly with one another. Next we consider a related set of examples in which negotiation is costly. We then apply the principles that emerge from these examples to a variety of questions regarding the design of property rights. The answers to these questions, we shall see, depend on the kinds of accommodations people would reach among themselves if they were free to negotiate costlessly with one another.

Next we apply the theory of property rights and externalities to the topic of contests for relative position. We conclude this chapter with an examination of taxation as a possible solution to the problem of negative externalities.

17.1 THE RECIPROCAL NATURE OF EXTERNALITIES

In 1992, Ronald H. Coase[1] was awarded the Nobel Prize in economics, largely on the basis of the most influential and widely cited economics paper of the postwar era. Titled "The Problem of Social Cost,"[2] this paper profoundly changed the way economists, legal scholars, political philosophers, and others thought about externalities and the legal and social institutions that have evolved to deal with them.

Coase began with an example involving a doctor whose ability to examine patients was disrupted by the noise of machinery operated by a confectioner (candy maker) in an adjacent building. Historically, the economic and legal view toward such a situation was simple and clear: the confectioner's noise was harming the doctor and it ought to be restrained. Coase's seminal insight was that this view completely overlooks the reciprocal nature of the problem. True enough, the confectioner's noise does harm the doctor. *But if we prevent the noise, we harm the confectioner.* After all, the confectioner makes the noise, not for the purpose of harming the doctor, but in pursuit of his own livelihood. In such situations, there will be harm to *someone,* no matter what happens. Whether the harm caused to the doctor by the noise is greater than the harm that would be caused to the confectioner if he were prohibited from making it is strictly an empirical question. The common interest of each party, Coase recognized, is to avoid the larger of these two unpleasant outcomes.

The earlier, one-sided view of externalities led to a legal tradition in which the confectioner was generally held liable for any damage his noise caused to the doctor. Coase pointed out, however, that if the doctor and the confectioner were able to negotiate costlessly with one another, the most efficient outcome would occur regardless of whether the confectioner was liable. His simple and elegant argument in support of this claim is illustrated in the following series of numerical examples.

EXAMPLE 17-1	**Suppose the benefit to the confectioner of continuing to make noise is 40, while the cost of the noise to the doctor is 60 (see footnote 3). If the confectioner's only alternative to making the noise is to produce nothing, what will happen if he is made liable for the noise damage? (To be liable for the damage means being required to compensate the doctor for any damage caused by the noise.)**

The confectioner will examine his two options—shutting down or compensating the doctor—and choose the one that makes him best off. If he stays open, he will earn 40, but will have to pay 60 to the doctor, for a net loss of 20. If he shuts down, his net gain is 0, and since this is clearly better than losing 20, he will discontinue operation.

Alternatively, suppose the confectioner had not been liable for noise damage. That is, suppose the law grants him the right to continue operating without compensation to the doctor. Coase argued that in this case the doctor will pay the confectioner to

---

[1]Rhymes with "dose."

[2]*Journal of Law and Economics, 3,* 1960: 144–171.

[3]The numerical cost and benefit values used in this and in the following examples represent the present values of all current and future costs and benefits to the parties in question.

shut down. If the confectioner stays open, he will gain only 40 while the doctor will lose 60. But the doctor can compensate the confectioner for the loss of shutting down and still have enough left over to be better off than if the confectioner had stayed open. Suppose, for example, the doctor pays the confectioner 50 to shut down. The confectioner's net gain will now be 10 more than if he had stayed open. And the doctor's net gain of 10 is 10 more than if the noise had continued.

If P denotes the payment the doctor makes to the confectioner to compensate him for shutting down, we know that P must be at least 40 (what the confectioner would get by staying open) and no larger than 60 (what the doctor would get if there were no noise). The net results under the two legal regimes (confectioner liable vs. confectioner not liable) are summarized in Table 17-1.

Note that because the gain to the confectioner of operating his machinery (40) is smaller than the noise damage it imposes on the doctor (60), the most efficient outcome is for the confectioner to shut down. Example 17-1 makes clear that if both the doctor and confectioner are rational and can negotiate costlessly with one another, this will happen regardless of whether the confectioner is liable for noise damage. On efficiency grounds, the legal regime is thus a matter of complete indifference here. On distributional grounds, however, the parties will be anything but neutral about liability. If the confectioner is not liable, his gain is $P \geq 40$, whereas he will be forced to shut down and earn nothing if he is liable. The doctor's net gain will be 60 if the confectioner is liable, but only $60 - P$ if the confectioner is not liable.

TABLE 17-1

Outcome and Payoff Summary for Example 17-1
The gain to the confectioner from operating is 40. The loss to the doctor from the noise is 60. The efficient outcome is for the confectioner to shut down, and this happens under both legal regimes.

Legal regime	Outcome	Net benefit		
		Doctor	Confectioner	Total
Liable	Confectioner shuts down to avoid liability payment	60	0	60
Not liable	Doctor pays confectioner P to shut down, $40 \leq P \leq 60$	$60 - P$	P	60

EXAMPLE 17-2

Same as Example 17-1, except now the benefit to the confectioner of operating is 60, the benefit to the doctor in a noise-free environment only 40. Assume that the doctor must shut down if the noise continues.

This time the efficient outcome is for the confectioner to continue operating, since his gain exceeds the cost he imposes on the doctor. If he is not liable for noise damages, the confectioner will stay open and the doctor's best option will be to shut down. Alternatively, if the confectioner is liable for noise damage, he will again continue to operate and pay the doctor 40 to compensate him for his losses. The net results for this example are summarized in Table 17-2. Note that, as in Example 17-1, both legal regimes lead to the most efficient outcome, but have very different distributional consequences.

TABLE 17-2

Outcome and Payoff Summary for Example 17-2
The gain to the confectioner from operating is 60. The loss to the doctor from the confectioner's noise is 40. The efficient outcome is for the confectioner to continue operating, and this happens under both legal regimes.

Legal regime	Outcome	Net benefit		
		Doctor	Confectioner	Total
Liable	Confectioner stays open and pays doctor 40	40	20	60
Not liable	Confectioner stays open; doctor shuts down	0	60	60

The preceding examples assumed that the only alternatives open to two parties were either to continue operations in the current form or to shut down entirely. In practice, however, one or both parties often face a broader range of alternatives. As the following examples will illustrate, here too the ability to negotiate costlessly leads to efficient outcomes.

EXAMPLE 17-3

Same as Example 17-1, except now the confectioner has access to a soundproofing device that will completely eliminate the noise from his machines. The cost of the device is 20, which means that if he installs it his net gain from operating will fall from 40 to 20. As in Example 17-1, the doctor will gain 60 if there is no noise, 0 if there is noise.

If the confectioner is liable for noise damage, his best option will be to install the soundproofing. His alternatives are either to shut down or to pay the doctor 60 in noise damages, and each of these is clearly worse. If the confectioner is not liable, it will be in the doctor's interest to pay the confectioner to install the soundproofing. His alternative, after all, is to shut down or to endure the noise damage. The minimum payment that would be acceptable to the confectioner to install the soundproofing is 20, its cost. The most the doctor would be willing to pay for him to install it is 60, the amount the doctor would lose if it weren't installed. Again letting P denote the payment from the doctor to the confectioner, the outcomes and payoffs for the two legal regimes are as summarized in Table 17-3.

Let us now consider what happens when the doctor too has some adjustment he can make to escape the damage caused by the confectioner's noise.

TABLE 17-3

Outcome and Payoff Summary for Example 17-3
The gain to the confectioner from operating without soundproofing is 40. Soundproofing costs 20. The loss to the doctor from the confectioner's noise is 60. The efficient outcome is for the confectioner to install soundproofing and to continue operating, and this happens under both legal regimes.

Legal regime	Outcome	Net benefit		
		Doctor	Confectioner	Total
Liable	Confectioner installs soundproofing at own expense	60	20	80
Not liable	Doctor pays confectioner P to install soundproofing, $20 \leq P \leq 60$	$60 - P$	$20 + P$	80

EXAMPLE 17-4

Same as Example 17-3, except now the doctor can escape the noise damage by moving his examination room to the other side of his office. The noisy room in which he now examines patients could then be used for storage. The cost to the doctor of this rearrangement is 18.

With this new option available, the doctor is the one who is able to eliminate the noise damage at the lowest possible cost. If the confectioner is liable for noise damage, he will offer the doctor a payment P to compensate him for rearranging his office. The payment must be at least 18, or else the doctor would not make the accommodation. (Recall that, with the confectioner liable, the doctor has the option of being fully compensated for any noise damage.) And the payment cannot exceed 20, or else the confectioner could install soundproofing and solve the problem on his own. If the confectioner is not liable for noise damage, the doctor will rearrange his office at his own expense. The outcomes and payoffs for this example are summarized in Table 17-4. Note that we again get the efficient outcome no matter which legal regime we choose. Note also that the choice of legal regime again affects the distribution of costs and benefits, only this time by a much smaller margin than in Example 17-3. The difference is that each party now has a relatively inexpensive method for solving the noise problem unilaterally. In Example 17-3, the doctor lacked such an alternative, making the confectioner's bargaining power very strong when he was not liable for noise damage. In this example, by contrast, the confectioner cannot extract a large payment from the doctor for keeping quiet because the doctor can solve the noise problem on his own.

TABLE 17-4

Outcome and Payoff Summary for Example 17-4
The gain to the confectioner from operating without soundproofing is 40. Soundproofing costs 20. The loss to the doctor from the confectioner's noise is 60. The doctor can rearrange his office to eliminate the noise problem at a cost of 18. The efficient outcome is for the doctor to rearrange his office, and this happens under both legal regimes.

Legal regime	Outcome	Net benefit		
		Doctor	Confectioner	Total
Liable	Confectioner pays doctor P to rearrange his office, $18 \leq P \leq 20$	$42 + P$	$40 - P$	82
Not liable	Doctor rearranges his office at his own expense	42	40	82

The patterns revealed in the preceding examples may be stated formally as:

The *Coase Theorem:* When the parties affected by externalities can negotiate costlessly with one another, an efficient outcome results no matter how the law assigns responsibility for damages.

In the wake of its publication, Coase's classic paper became a subject of great controversy. Many took him to be saying that there is no real role for government in solving problems related to pollution, noise, and other externalities. On this interpretation, Coase's message seemed to be that if government stays out of the way, people will always come up with efficient solutions on their own. And yet Coase stated clearly that this conclusion holds only for a world in which parties can negotiate with one another at relatively low cost. He recognized that there are many important externalities for which this assumption is not satisfied. At the simplest level, time and energy are required for negotiation, and when the potential benefits are small, it may simply not be worth it. Alternatively, there are situations in which a single polluter causes damage to a large number of people. Negotiating with large groups is inherently difficult and

Coase theorem When the parties affected by externalities can negotiate costlessly with one another, an efficient outcome results no matter how the law assigns responsibility for damages.

costly, and each person in the group faces strong incentives to escape these costs. Another serious barrier to negotiation is the problem of how to divide the surplus. Recall from Example 17-3 that the efficient outcome was for the doctor to pay the confectioner to install soundproofing. The minimum payment acceptable to the confectioner was 20, the cost of the soundproofing. The most the confectioner could hope to extract from the doctor was 60, the value to the doctor of eliminating the noise. The doctor would naturally like to pay only 20, and the confectioner would like to get 60. If each takes a hard line in the discussion, animosities may emerge and the possibility of a deal may break down altogether. For these and a host of other reasons, negotiations are often costly. When they are, it matters very much indeed which legal regime we choose, as the following examples will illustrate.

EXAMPLE 17-5	**As in Example 17-2, suppose that the gain to the doctor in a noise-free environment is 40, while the gain to the confectioner from unfettered operations is 60. Suppose also that the confectioner has access to a soundproofing device that eliminates all noise damage at a cost of 20. And suppose, finally, that it costs the doctor and confectioner 25 to negotiate a private agreement between themselves. For negotiation to be a worthwhile alternative, they must be able to share this cost in some way that makes each of them better off than if they did not negotiate.**

If the confectioner is made liable for noise damage, he will install the soundproofing. His next-best alternative, after all, is to pay the doctor 40 in noise damages,[4] and the installation of soundproofing costs him only 20. Because being liable gives the confectioner an incentive to install the soundproofing on his own, there is no need for him to negotiate an agreement with the doctor, and thus no need to incur the cost of negotiation.

But now suppose that the confectioner is not liable for noise damage. If there were no costs of negotiation, the doctor would pay the confectioner P, where $20 \leq P \leq 40$, to install soundproofing. If it costs 25 to negotiate an agreement, however, then it is no longer possible for the doctor to compensate the confectioner for installing soundproofing. The soundproofing makes it possible for the doctor to gain 40, which is insufficient to cover both the cost of the soundproofing (20) and the cost of negotiating the agreement (25), which total 45. When it is costly to negotiate, we no longer get the most efficient outcome irrespective of which legal regime we choose. In this example, for which the relevant data are summarized in Table 17-5, we get the most efficient result only if the confectioner is liable.

TABLE 17-5

Outcome and Payoff Summary for Example 17-5
The gain to the confectioner from operating without soundproofing is 60. Soundproofing costs 20. The loss to the doctor from the confectioner's noise is 40. The cost of negotiating a private agreement is 25. The efficient outcome is for the confectioner to install soundproofing, but this happens only when he is made liable for noise damage.

Legal regime	Outcome	Net benefit		
		Doctor	Confectioner	Total
Liable	Confectioner installs soundproofing at his own expense	40	40	80
Not liable	Confectioner does not install soundproofing; doctor shuts down	0	60	60

---

[4]For the confectioner to operate and pay noise damages to the doctor, it is not necessary for them to incur the cost of negotiating a private agreement.

In Example 17-5, the total gain for society as a whole is 80 if the confectioner is liable, only 60 if he is not liable. But as the following example will illustrate, the existence of barriers to negotiation does not guarantee that we will always get a more efficient outcome by making parties liable for the damage caused by external effects.

EXAMPLE 17-6 **Same as Example 17-5, except the confectioner no longer has a soundproofing option; instead, the doctor has the option of avoiding the noise by rearranging his office, which will cost him 18.**

If the confectioner is not liable for noise damage, this is exactly what the doctor will do. But if the confectioner is liable, the cost of negotiation now stands in the way of his paying the doctor to rearrange his office. The sum of negotiating costs (25) and rearrangement costs (18) comes to 43, which is 3 more than the 40 that will be saved by avoiding the noise. So if he is liable, the best option available to the confectioner is simply to continue operating and pay the doctor 40 for the noise damage.[5] Here, unlike Example 17-5, we get the most efficient outcome when the confectioner is not liable. The data for Example 17-6 are summarized in Table 17-6.

TABLE 17-6

Outcome and Payoff Summary for Example 17-6
The gain to the confectioner from operating is 60. The loss to the doctor from the confectioner's noise is 40. The doctor can escape the noise by rearranging his office at a cost of 18. The cost of negotiating a private agreement is 25. The efficient outcome is for the doctor to rearrange his office, but this happens only when the confectioner is not liable for noise damage.

Legal regime	Outcome	Net benefit		
		Doctor	Confectioner	Total
Liable	Confectioner operates and pays doctor 40 for noise damage	40	20	60
Not liable	Doctor rearranges his office at his own expense	22	60	82

EXERCISE 17-1

How would the entries in Table 17-6 be affected if the cost of negotiation were 20 instead of 25?

Coase's observation that people will reach the most efficient outcomes when they can negotiate costlessly has widespread application. In many situations, after all, the costs of negotiation are small relative to the benefits of reaching agreements about externalities. But the more far-reaching implications of Coase's work lie in the pattern illustrated in Examples 17-5 and 17-6, where we find the seeds of a very powerful theory of law and social institutions. Boiled down to its essence, the theory can be stated as the following rule:

> The most efficient laws and social institutions are the ones that place the burden of adjustment to externalities on those who can accomplish it at least cost.

---

[5]Again, making a liability payment does not require the parties to incur the costs of negotiation.

One of the immediate implications of this rule is that the best laws regarding harmful effects cannot be identified unless we know something about how much it costs different parties to avoid harmful effects. If, as in Example 17-5, the emitter of noise has lower costs, we get a more efficient outcome by making him liable for damages. But if the person adversely affected by the noise has a lower cost of avoidance, as in Example 17-6, we do better by not making the noisemaker liable.

The efficiency rule finds application in a rich variety of situations, several of which we examine in the sections that follow.

17.2 PROPERTY RIGHTS

Some Examples

The examples with which we began the chapter illustrate some applications of the Coasian efficiency rule. In the Canadian West, cattle imposed an externality on farmers, and the cost of negotiations between individual ranchers and farmers was prohibitive. In an area with 40 farms and 100 ranches, 4000 *individual* agreements would have been required. This fact alone helps to explain the rise of ranchers' and farmers' associations, and by extension the growth of government itself, as a means of economizing on negotiations costs. When there were comparatively few farmers, the total cost of fencing was much lower if the farmers did it. Yet even though the average ranch was larger—and therefore required more fencing—than the average farm, when the proportion of farmers came to exceed that of ranchers by a sufficient margin, the total cost of fencing was lower if ranchers were made responsible. The result was a shift in the structure of property rights.

As with the cattle, the loud 3 a.m. party also generates negative externalities, for all neighbours within hearing range. The cost to the perpetrators of eliminating the externality (the effort of turning down the volume knob) is negligible, while the noise pollution cost is substantial. Most municipalities have therefore passed police-enforced noise by-laws, which often specify times—particularly when most people are sleeping—during which excessive noise is not permitted.

In contrast, externalities notwithstanding, the economic benefits of the trucking and air transport industries are substantial, but the costs of negotiating with *all* affected parties would be prohibitive. Moreover, a person who purchases a house near a highway or an airport is assumed to know that there *will* be noise, and property values in such areas will typically be lower than for otherwise equivalent property elsewhere, reflecting the capitalized negative value of the externality. Even in these cases, there are often restrictions on times during which airplanes can take off and land, and some highways are constructed with high noise-buffering fences, in order to reduce the cost of the externality to those affected. Residents' associations often form when there is a proposal to build a new airport or highway in their area, because the proposal involves the *unanticipated* intrusion of an externality that will affect their lives and property values.

The Coasian perspective is also helpful in understanding other cases in which private property rights are constrained, rather than absolute, in the presence of externalities.

WHY DOES THE LAW OF TRESPASS OFTEN NOT APPLY ON LAKEFRONT PROPERTIES? AND WHY ARE PROPERTY LAWS OFTEN SUSPENDED DURING STORMS?

Most people would regard an uninvited stranger walking across their land as an intrusion. The trespasser, in economic parlance, confers a negative externality on the property owner, and normally the property owner is entitled to use reasonable means—excluding land mines and booby traps—to exclude trespassers. Yet on some lakefront properties, cottage owners do not have the right to exclude those walking along the beach from their property, even though in principle their property may extend to the water's edge. The reason is that requiring people to travel two kilometres out to the road and back, just to go 50 metres down the beach, would be unduly costly. Moreover, the cottage owners themselves benefit from the right to cross the property of others. Similarly, a cottage owner may have the right to prohibit others from using his dock under normal circumstances. In a major storm, however, the minor negative externality to the owner of having a stranger moor at the dock is outweighed by the substantial benefit of saving a boat or even lives, and this evaluation has been reflected in law.

Many municipal by-laws have been passed principally to deal with problems arising from externalities. Let us consider just three examples. If someone wants to build an addition onto her home, typically she requires a building permit. To receive it, she needs to establish that the addition will not be an eyesore, nor obstruct someone's view, nor constitute a fire or safety hazard. Similarly, most municipalities have sign by-laws to regulate the size and position of signs and billboards, even if the signs are on private property, reflecting the view that an excessive number of signs can be a form of visual pollution and a potential road safety hazard. Zoning by-laws perform a similar function. Most North American cities have established heavy industrial, light industrial, commercial, and residential areas, in order to reduce the effect of externalities. To obtain a variance of such a by-law often requires a public hearing process, where neighbourhood concerns can be addressed. Had the doctor and confectioner been subject to zoning by-laws, you might never have had to work through the examples at the start of the chapter!

These examples should suggest that the details of our various property laws have a great deal of economic structure. They embody sophisticated, if often implicit, calculations about how to reach the most efficient solutions to practical problems involving externalities. The following section shows how the absence of a structure of property rights can sometimes lead to drastic economic consequences.

17.3 THE TRAGEDY OF THE COMMONS

To explore the institution of private property, it is instructive to consider, as in the next example, what would happen in a society that lacked a well-developed institution of property rights.

A village has six residents, each of whom has wealth of $100. Each resident may either invest his money in a government bond, which pays 12 percent per year, or use it to buy a year-old steer, which will graze on the village commons (there being no individually owned grazing land in this village). Year-old steers and government bonds each cost exactly $100. Steers require no effort to tend and can be sold for a price that depends on the amount of weight they gain during the year. Yearly weight gain, in turn, depends on the number of steers that graze on the commons. The prices of 2-year-old steers are given in Table 17-7 as a function of the total number of steers. If village residents make their investment decisions independently, how many steers will graze on the commons?

As long as each villager cannot control access to the commons by cattle owned by others, the income-maximizing strategy will be to send an extra steer out onto the commons if and only if its price next year will be at least $112. (At that price, the gain from owning a steer is equal to the gain from buying a bond.) By this reckoning, there will be 3 steers sent onto the commons, and the rest of the villagers' money will be invested in government bonds. With this pattern of investment, village income from investment will be $14 from each of the 3 steers and $12 from each of the 3 bonds, for a total of $78.

Notice, however, that this is not the largest possible income the villagers could have earned. From the point of view of the village as a whole, the investment rule for steers should be: send an extra steer onto the commons if and only if its *marginal* contribution to the value of the total herd after 1 year is greater than or equal to $112. Sending the third steer onto the commons resulted in a total herd worth $3 \times 114 = \$342$, which is only $106 more than the value of a herd with only 2 steers ($2 \times 118 = \$236$). Total village income is maximized by buying 4 bonds and sending 2 steers onto the commons. This pattern results in an income of $48 from bonds and $36 from steers, for a total of $84.

The reason that the invisible hand failed to produce the best social result here is that individual villagers ignored an important externality. Their criterion for deciding to send another steer was based only on the increase over the year in the price of that particular steer. They took no account of the fact that sending an extra steer would cause existing cattle to gain less weight. Pastureland is a scarce resource in this example, and the villagers failed to allocate it efficiently because they were allowed to use it for free.

One solution to the problem would be if individual villagers could own pastureland and exclude others from using it. Suppose, for example, the village government decided to put the pastureland up for auction. In a competitive auction, what price would it fetch? Anyone who buys the pastureland has the right to restrict the number of steers to 2, which is the income-maximizing amount. We saw that, if used in this way, the land will generate an annual income of $36 from an annual investment of $200 (the price of two steers). Had the $200 instead been used to purchase government bonds, only $24

TABLE 17-7

Steer Prices as a Function of Grazing Density
As more steers graze on the commons, each steer gains less weight, resulting in a lower price per steer.

Number of steers	Price per 2-year-old steer ($/steer)
1	120
2	118
3	114
4	111
5	108
6	105

would have been earned. Having control over the commons thus yields a surplus of $12 per year over the income available to a person able to buy only government bonds. It follows that the price of the pastureland at auction will be $100 (the price of a bond that pays an income of $12 per year). If the price of pastureland were any less than $100, all investors would want to buy it instead of buying government bonds. If it sold for more than $100, every investor could do better by buying government bonds. The village government could take the $100 raised from the auction of its pastureland and distribute it among the 6 villagers, for an average payment of $16.67. Alternatively, of course, the government could retain public ownership of the land and charge an annual grazing fee, the proceeds of which could likewise be distributed among the villagers.

EXERCISE 17-2

What grazing fee would solve the commons problem discussed in Example 17-7?

In some early societies, it was the practice for important resources such as pastureland and fisheries to be owned in common. The difficulty with such ownership schemes is that they can lead to overexploitation of the resource. Figure 17-1 illustrates the problem of individual villagers who have the option of working in a factory at a wage of W per day, or of keeping all the fish they can catch from the village lake. The curve labelled AP shows how the average catch per fisherman varies with the number of fishermen, while MP shows the change in the total catch as a function of the number of fishermen. If fishermen get to keep whatever they catch, their decision rule will be to fish up to X', the point where AP = W. At X', the value of the total catch is exactly equal to the total income that the villagers who fished could have earned by working in the factory.

FIGURE 17-1

The Tragedy of the Commons
When a resource, such as a fishery or a pasture, is owned in common, each user gets to keep the average product of his own productive inputs he applies to the resource. Privately owned inputs will be applied to the resource until X', the point at which their average product equals their opportunity cost, W, resulting in an economic surplus of zero. The socially optimal allocation is X^*, the level of input for which W is equal to the marginal product of privately owned inputs, and results in an economic surplus of S^*.

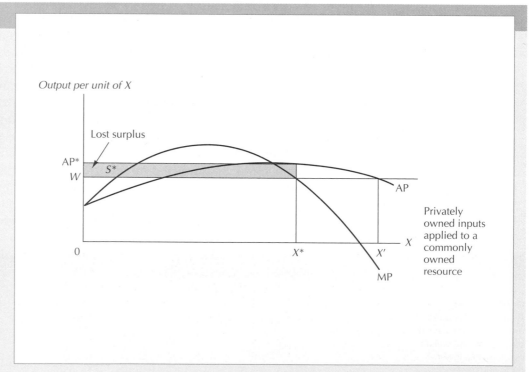

The socially optimal allocation is to fish only up to X^* in Figure 17-1, the point at which $W = $ MP, and for all remaining villagers to work in the factory. At this allocation, the villagers who fish will earn a total of S^* (the shaded area) more than they could have earned by working in the factory.

If villagers are given free access to fish in the lake, the allocation that sends X^* out to fish will not be stable. Because each fisherman will be earning more than the villagers who work in the factory, factory workers will have an incentive to switch to fishing. Switching will stop only when X' have gone out to fish, making earnings in the two alternatives the same. As in the earlier pastureland example, the additional fishermen ignore the externality they impose on the existing fishermen. Each looks only at the size of his own catch, ignoring the fact that his presence makes everyone else's catch smaller.

In order to sustain the efficient allocation, something must be done to limit access to the lake. The simplest approach is to charge people for the right to go fishing. If the fishing fee were set at $AP^* - W$ (see Figure 17-1), the optimal allocation would result automatically from the income-maximizing decisions of individual villagers. Here, as in the pasture example, the problem was that individuals overutilized a productive resource they were allowed to use for free. The invisible hand mechanism can function properly only when all resources sell for prices that reflect their true economic value.

Global Tragedies of the Commons

One of the continuing sources of inefficiency in modern economies involves the allocation of resources that no single nation's property laws can govern. For instance, several species of whales have been hunted to near extinction because no international laws of property exist to restrain individual incentives to kill whales. The moratorium on fishing on the Grand Banks was similarly a result not only of technological change in the international fishing industry represented by the increased use of "factory ships," but also of the ineffectiveness of Canadian government efforts to enforce limits on the annual catch. The collapse of the economic base of many Newfoundland outports is in large measure a maritime tragedy of the commons. The problem of pollution of the Mediterranean Sea, like that of acid rain in North America, has been difficult to resolve because it requires agreement and policy coordination among different national governments. As the world's population continues to grow and the human impact on the environment increases, the absence of an effective system of international property rights will become an economic problem of increasing significance.

An important case in point is the trend toward global warming. Some scientists have estimated that if carbon dioxide and other greenhouse gases continue to accumulate in the atmosphere at current rates, the earth's average temperature could rise by as much as 4° Celsius during the twenty-first century—enough to cause a significant acceleration in desertification, the melting of the polar ice caps, and a rise in ocean levels that would flood many thousand square kilometres of coastal land. If a single agency had the power to enact globally binding environmental legislation, it would be a straightforward matter to reduce the buildup of greenhouse gases. Yet even within Canada alone, the adoption and implementation of the 1997 Kyoto Protocol on the reduction of greenhouse gases has proved to be a difficult and contentious issue. In the United States, there has been active opposition at the highest levels of government to its adoption. At a global level, the political capacity to enforce such agreements is still in its infancy.

17.4 SMOKING RULES, PUBLIC AND PRIVATE

Research studies show that exposure to cigarette smoke exhaled by others can be harmful to one's health. Such findings have lent considerable support to the trend in Canada and elsewhere toward laws that ban or restrict smoking in public places. On the plausible assumptions that (1) negotiating with strangers in public places is generally impractical and (2) the harm to nonsmokers from undesired exposure to smoke is more important than the harm to smokers from not being able to smoke in public places, such laws make good sense in the Coasian framework.

So far, however, no law has been proposed that would disallow smoking in private dwellings. The result is that sometimes people are exposed to smoke from their roommates. On the assumption that the cost of negotiation with prospective roommates is relatively low, the following example illustrates that the lack of such laws does not necessarily lead to an undesirable outcome.

EXAMPLE 17-8

Smith and Jones are trying to decide whether to share a two-bedroom apartment or to live separately in one-bedroom apartments. The rental fees are $300 per month for one-bedroom and $420 per month—or $210 per month per person—for two-bedroom apartments. Smith is a smoker and would be willing to give up $250 per month rather than give up being able to smoke at home. Jones, however, is a nonsmoker and would sacrifice up to $150 per month rather than live with a smoker. Apart from the issues of smoking and rent, the two find joint living neither more nor less attractive than living alone. Neither has an alternative roommate available. Will they live together or separately?

If they live separately, each can have things the way he wants on the smoking issue. The downside is that it is more costly to live alone. If they live together, they will save on rent, but one of them will have to compromise. Either Smith will have to give up smoking, or Jones will have to tolerate Smith's smoke. If a compromise is to be made at all, it will be made by Jones, since he is willing to pay less than Smith is to have his way. By living together, each party saves $90 per month in rent. If we ignore the possibility of negotiation, they will not live together because this savings is less than the cost to Jones of having to live with a smoker.

But suppose they are able to negotiate costlessly. The practical question then becomes whether the *total* savings in rent justifies the cost of the compromise to Jones. The total savings in rent is $180 per month, which is the difference between the $600 per month total they would pay if they lived alone and the $420 they will pay living together. And since this savings exceeds the cost to Jones by $30 per month, it should be possible to negotiate an agreement whereby the two will prefer to live together. Smith will have to give some of his $90 per month savings to Jones.

Let X denote the amount Smith gives to Jones. Since the cost to Jones of living with a smoker is $150 per month, and his savings in rent is only $90 per month, X must be at least $60 per month. Because Smith gets to continue smoking in the shared living arrangement, his $90 per month rent savings is pure gain, which means that $90 per month is the largest possible value for X. The relevant details for this example are summarized in Table 17-8.

Example 17-8 drives home the point that external effects are completely reciprocal. Smith's smoking harms Jones, just as traditional discussions of the issue emphasize. But denying Smith the opportunity to smoke will harm him, at least as he sees it. When

TABLE 17-8

Payoff Summary for Example 17-8
The cost to Smith of not smoking is $250 per month. The cost to Jones of living with a smoker is $150 per month. The total savings in rent from living together is $600 per month −$420 per month = $180 per month, which is $30 per month more than the least costly compromise required by shared living quarters, which is the $150 per month it costs Jones to live with a smoker.

	Net rental payment ($ per month)		Net gain ($ per month)		
	Jones	Smith	Jones	Smith	Total
Live separately	300	300	—	—	—
Live together; Smith pays Jones X to compensate for smoke, $60 \leq X \leq 90$	$210 - X$	$210 + X$	$X - 60$	$90 - X$	30

it comes to the question of sharing living quarters, the smoke problem is a quintessentially shared problem. Because people are free to make whatever living arrangements they find mutually agreeable, Jones cannot be forced to endure smoke against his wishes. And by the same token, Smith cannot be forced to give up smoking. If they are to reap the savings from living together, one party must compromise on the smoke issue, and the other must compromise financially. Unless the terms of their agreement represent a clear improvement for both parties over the alternative of living alone, there will simply be no agreement.

EXERCISE 17-3

How would the entries in Table 17-8 be different if there were an exhaust system that completely eliminated the damage from smoke at a cost of $60 per month?

17.5 POSITIVE EXTERNALITIES

The Coase theorem applies not only to negative externalities but also to positive ones. Recall from Chapter 16 the example of the beekeeper and the owner of the apple orchard. The activities of each confer positive externalities on the other, which, if ignored, will result in suboptimally small levels of both apple and honey production. But if negotiation between them is costless, the beekeeper can offer to subsidize the orchard owner for planting more trees. The orchard owner, likewise, can offer payments to induce the beekeeper to enlarge his apiary. With either positive or negative externalities, inefficiencies result only if it is costly or otherwise impractical to negotiate agreements about how to correct them.

17.6 POSITIONAL EXTERNALITIES

In Chapter 5, we considered positional goods, and saw how the desire to acquire them could lead to costly *positional arms races*. In many areas of endeavour, rewards are determined not by our absolute performance, but by how we perform relative to others. Situations in which rewards are determined by relative performance are often called contests. In virtually every contest, each contestant will take a variety of actions in an attempt to enhance his or her probability of winning. Indeed, to take such actions is the essence of what it means to be in a contest.

Because the rewards in contests are distributed according to relative position, the laws of simple arithmetic tell us that any action that increases one contestant's chances of winning must necessarily reduce the chances of others. With this observation in mind, it is instructive to think of performance-enhancing actions as giving rise to *positional externalities.* If *A* and *B* are competing for a prize that only one of them can attain, anything that helps *A* will necessarily harm *B*. Political campaign expenditures, advertising expenditures that increase a firm's market share but do not increase overall market demand, and the use of anabolic steroids by athletes to enhance their size, strength, and performance, all involve positional externalities.

Given what is at stake, voluntary restraint is rarely an effective solution to positional arms races. And so governing bodies in many sports now require strict drug testing of all competing athletes. Similarly, restrictions are placed on the maximum amount that can be spent by an individual electoral candidate. There is no such limit on the amount that can be spent by a commercial advertiser, and in Chapter 13 we showed how restrictions on cigarette advertising may even have *increased* the profits of the tobacco companies, by placing limits on their advertising arms race.

Positional externalities are also present, as we saw in Chapter 5, in the decision to provide "the best" schooling for one's children, and thus in the tradeoff between spending now on their education or saving for retirement. In the Web Supplement for Chapter 14, we showed how the decision to work in an unsafe work environment (and by extension, the length of the standard workweek discussed in Chapter 14) could be explained in part in terms of concerns regarding relative income. These concerns involve positional externalities in an essential way. In such cases, social programs and policies, such as the Canada Pension Plan, and workweek and health and safety legislation, can put limits on the negative effects of positional externalities.

17.7 TAXING EXTERNALITIES

Before the appearance of Coase's 1960 paper, the economics profession was wedded to the view, pioneered by the British economist A. C. Pigou, that the best solution to negative externalities is to tax them. The idea is simple. If *A* carries out an activity that imposes a cost on *B*, then taxing *A* by the amount of that cost will provide him with the proper incentive to consider the externality in his production decisions. In some circumstances, which we consider below, taxing *A will* be the best policy. As the following example makes clear, however, such taxes sometimes make matters worse than if we did nothing at all.

EXAMPLE 17-9

Consider again the doctor and confectioner from Examples 17-1 to 17-6. Suppose that the doctor gains 60 by operating in a noise-free environment, and that the confectioner gains 40 by operating his noisy equipment. Suppose also that the doctor can eliminate the noise problem by rearranging his office at a cost of 18. And suppose, finally, that negotiation between the doctor and confectioner is prohibitively costly. The tax approach calls for a tax on the confectioner equal to the damage his activity would cause, which, in the absence of a response by the doctor, means a tax of 60. How will the outcome under such a tax compare with what would have happened in its absence?

If there were costless negotiation, the confectioner could pay the doctor to rearrange his office and then operate without paying the tax, since his operation would cause no noise damage. But since negotiation is impractical, the doctor has no reason to incur this cost on his own. He knows that by doing nothing, the confectioner will face a tax of 60 if he operates, which in turn means that the confectioner's best option is to shut down. After all, his operation generates a gain of only 40 to begin with. With the confectioner no longer in operation, the doctor will gain 60 and the confectioner 0.

With no tax, however, the confectioner would have continued operations, for a gain of 40. The doctor's best response would have been to rearrange his office at a cost of 18, leaving him with a net gain of 42. Without the tax, we thus get the most efficient outcome, whereas the total gain with the tax is considerably smaller. The relevant data for this example are summarized in Table 17-9.

TABLE 17-9

Outcome and Payoff Summary for Example 17-9
The gain to the confectioner from operating is 40. The loss to the doctor from the confectioner's noise is 60. The doctor can rearrange his office to eliminate the noise problem at a cost of 18. The efficient outcome is for the doctor to rearrange his office, and this happens only when there is no tax on the confectioner.

Legal regime	Outcome	Net benefit		
		Doctor	Confectioner	Total
Tax of 60 on confectioner	Confectioner shuts down	60	0	60
No tax or liability	Doctor rearranges his office at his own expense	42	40	82

As Example 17-9 demonstrates, a tax on pollution can leave us in a worse position than if there were no tax at all. This is not surprising once we recognize that a tax on pollution has essentially the same effect as making the polluter liable for pollution damages. But this same recognition implies that taxation will not *always* be inefficient. It happened to be inefficient in Example 17-9 because the doctor happened to be the party who was best able to deal with the noise problem and the tax removed all incentive for him to do so. Suppose, to the contrary, the doctor had not had some inexpensive means of escaping the noise damage. The tax still would have led the confectioner to shut down, but this would now be the most efficient outcome. (See Example 17-1.)

Alternatively, suppose the confectioner had had some inexpensive means of eliminating the noise problem. Suppose, for example, that he could have installed sound-proofing for a cost of 10. Here, too, the tax would have led to the most efficient outcome. The confectioner would have installed the soundproofing to escape the tax, and the doctor would have operated without disturbance.

Whether it is efficient to tax pollution thus depends on the particular circumstances at hand. If negotiation is costless, taxing will always lead to an efficient outcome. (But so, for that matter, will not taxing.) If negotiation is impractical, taxing pollution will still lead to an efficient outcome if the polluter has the least costly way of reducing pollution damage. Only if negotiation is impractical and the victim has the least costly means of avoiding damage will taxing pollution lead to an inefficient outcome. Taxing and not taxing will yield essentially the same outcomes if the costs of limiting pollution damage are roughly the same for both polluter and victim.

Suppose society has reached the judgment that the producers of pollution are in fact the ones who can mitigate its damages at the lowest cost. Society must then choose a policy that provides an incentive for the polluter to take action. One option is to set direct limits on the amount of pollution discharged. Alternatively, we could adopt a pollution tax, which means to charge polluters a fee for each unit of pollution they discharge. As the following example will demonstrate, the tax option offers a compelling advantage over the option of direct regulation.

EXAMPLE 17-10

Two firms, X and Y, have access to five different production processes, each one of which has a different cost and gives off a different amount of pollution. The daily costs of the processes and the corresponding number of tonnes of smoke are listed in Table 17-10. If pollution is unregulated, and negotiation between the firms and their victims is impossible, each firm will use A, the least costly of the five processes, and each will emit 4 tonnes of pollution per day, for a total pollution of 8 tonnes per day. The government wants to cut smoke emissions by half. To accomplish this, it is considering two options. The first is to require each firm to curtail its emissions by half. The alternative is to set a tax of T on each tonne of smoke emitted each day. How large would T have to be in order to curtail emissions by half? And how would the total costs to society compare under the two alternatives?

If each firm is required to cut pollution by half, each must switch from process A to process C. The result will be 2 tonnes per day of pollution for each firm. The cost of the switch for firm X will be 600 per day − 100 per day = 500 per day. The cost to Y will be 140 per day − 50 per day = 90 per day, which means a total cost for the two firms of 590 per day.

How will each firm respond to a tax of T per tonne of pollution? First it will ask itself whether switching from process A to B will increase its costs by more or less than T per day. If by less, it will pay to switch, because process B, which yields 1 tonne less smoke, will save the firm T per day in taxes. If process B's costs exceed A's by more than T, however, the firm will not switch. It will be cheaper to stick with A and pay the extra T in taxes. If the switch from A to B pays, the firm will then ask the same question about the switch from B to C. It will keep switching until the extra costs of the next process are no longer smaller than T.

To illustrate, suppose a tax of 50/tonne were levied. Firm X would stick with process A because it costs 90 per day less than process B and produces only 1 tonne per day of extra smoke, and thus 50 per day in extra taxes. Firm Y, in contrast, will switch to process B because it costs only 30 per day more and will save 50 per day in taxes. But firm Y will not continue on to C because it costs 60 per day more than B and will save only an additional 50 per day in taxes. With firm X staying with A and firm Y switching to B, we get a total pollution reduction of 1 tonne per day. A tax of 50/tonne thus does not produce the desired 50 percent reduction in pollution.

The solution is to keep increasing the tax until we get the desired result. Consider what happens with a tax of 91/tonne. This tax will lead firm X to adopt process B, firm Y to adopt process D. Total emissions will be the desired 4 tonnes per day. The cost to firm X will be 190 per day − 100 per day = 90 per day, and the cost to firm Y will be 230 per day − 50 per day = 180 per day. The total cost for both firms is thus only 270 per day, or 320 per day less than the cost of having each firm cut pollution by half. Note that the taxes paid by the firm are not included in our reckoning of the social costs of the tax alternative, because this money is not lost to society. It can be used to reduce whatever taxes would otherwise have to be levied on citizens.

The advantage of the tax approach is that it concentrates pollution reduction in the hands of the firms that can accomplish it in the least costly way. The direct regulatory approach of requiring each firm to cut by half took no account of the fact that firm Y can reduce pollution much more cheaply than firm X can. Under the tax approach, note that the cost of the last tonne of smoke removed is the same for each firm.

TABLE 17-10

Cost and Emissions for Five Production Processes
Each firm has access to five alternative production processes, A–E, which vary both in cost and in the amount of pollution they produce.

Process (smoke)	(4 tonnes per day)	(3 tonnes per day)	(2 tonnes per day)	(1 tonne per day)	(0 tonnes) per day)
Cost to firm X	100	190	600	1200	2000
Cost to firm Y	50	80	140	230	325

More generally, suppose that there are two producers, firm X and firm Y, whose marginal costs of smoke removal are shown by the curves labelled MC_X and MC_Y, respectively, in Figure 17-2. If the goal is to reduce total smoke emissions by $Q = Q_X^* + Q_Y^*$ tonnes per day, a tax of T^* will accomplish that goal in the least costly way. The characteristic feature of this solution is that the marginal cost of pollution reduction would be exactly the same for all firms. If that were not the case, it would always be possible to reallocate the pollution reduction in such a way as to reduce total costs.

The direct regulatory approach (telling each firm how much to reduce pollution) could also achieve any given total pollution reduction at minimum cost if regulators knew each firm's marginal cost of reduction curve. They could then simply assign reduction quotas in such a way as to equate marginal reduction costs across firms. The difficulty is that regulatory officials will often not have even the vaguest idea of what these curves look like. The compelling advantage of the tax approach is that it achieves efficiency without requiring any such knowledge on the part of regulators.

Recall from Chapter 16 our discussion of the efficiency losses potentially caused by taxation. Another important advantage of taxing negative externalities is that it provides a means of raising government revenue that does not entail such efficiency losses. On the contrary, we have seen that the taxation of negative externalities can actually *increase* efficiency. Whether taxing negative externalities would yield enough revenue for government to carry out all its activities is an empirical question. If it would, then concerns about inefficiencies from taxation would no longer be a subject of concern.

FIGURE 17-2

The Tax Approach to Pollution Reduction
MC_X and MC_Y represent the marginal cost of smoke reduction for firms X and Y, respectively. When pollution is taxed at a fixed rate, each firm reduces its emissions up to the point where the marginal cost of further reduction is exactly equal to the tax. The result is the least costly way of achieving the corresponding aggregate pollution reduction.

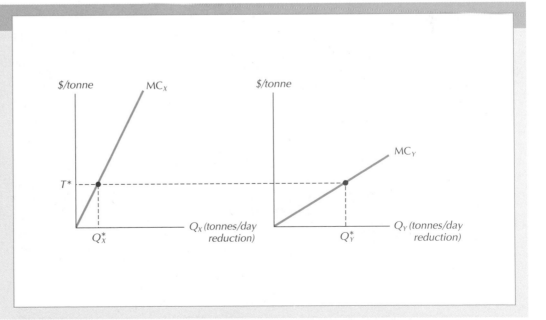

Taxing Positional Externalities

There is considerable evidence in support of the proposition that the utility that people get from consumption depends not only on absolute consumption levels, but also on relative consumption levels. If relative consumption is important, it follows logically that each person's consumption imposes negative externalities on others. When any one person increases his consumption, he raises, perhaps imperceptibly, the consumption standard for others.

The fact that many forms of consumption generate negative externalities has important implications for tax policy. The standards that define acceptable schools, houses, wardrobes, cars, vacations, and a host of other important budget items are inextricably linked to the amounts other people spend on them. Because individual consumers ignore positional externalities in their choices, the result is that such commodities have greater value for individuals than they do for society as a whole. For the same reasons that it is often efficient to tax pollution, it will often be efficient to tax many of these forms of consumption. On efficiency grounds, such taxes would be an attractive substitute for taxes that interfere with efficient resource allocation.

SUMMARY

- When an action by one party harms another and the parties are able to negotiate costlessly with one another, the negative externalities are dealt with efficiently regardless of whether the law makes people liable for the harmful effects of their actions. This result is known as the Coase theorem.

- When negotiation is costly, it does matter how liability is assigned. In general, the most efficient outcome occurs when the law places the burden of avoiding harmful effects on the party that can accomplish it at the lowest cost.

- This general principle sheds light on a variety of questions regarding the design of property rights. In many instances, the laws of property have been set up to generate the kinds of accommodations people would reach for themselves if they were free to negotiate costlessly with one another.

- Similar conclusions apply in situations that involve positive externalities. If negotiation is costless, people will forge agreements that result in efficient outcomes, even in cases where one party's activities create indirect benefits to the other. And where negotiation is costly, institutions tend to evolve that encourage activities with positive external effects.

- In contests for relative position, as in all other contests, the efforts by one contestant confer a negative externality on other contestants: anything that increases one party's odds of winning necessarily reduces the odds of others. The effect is almost always to induce some form of arms race among contestants, in which the efforts of each party serve largely to offset one another. The theory of externalities and property rights sheds a great deal of light on the laws by which citizens of modern societies restrict such arms races.

- Taxation is one solution to the problem of negative externalities. Although it is not always an ideal answer, it does offer several important advantages over direct regulation in many situations. Taxation of negative externalities provides a source of governmental revenue that can be exempt from the allocative inefficiencies we encountered in Chapter 16.

1. When negotiation costs are negligible, why is the assignment of liability for externalities irrelevant for efficiency?
2. Does the assignment of liability matter for distributional reasons?
3. Suppose you are the party who can avoid a particular external effect at the lowest cost. Why might you favour a general rule that assigns liability to whichever party can avoid damage at the lowest cost?
4. Why do we permit airplanes but not real estate developers to use the airspace over private homes without prior consent?

5. Why do some property laws limit private coastal property to the waterline at high tide?
6. Give three examples of the tragedy of the commons on your campus.
7. How does the widespread existence of negative externalities alter the argument (see Chapter 16) that taxing goods can lower economic efficiency?

PROBLEMS

1. Every November, Smith and Jones both face the choice between burning their leaves or stuffing them into garbage bags. Burning the leaves is much easier but produces noxious smoke. The utility values for each person, measured in utils, are listed in the table for each of the four possible combinations of actions:

		Smith	
		Burn	Bag
Jones	Burn	Jones: 4 Smith: 4	Jones: 8 Smith: 2
	Bag	Jones: 2 Smith: 8	Jones: 6 Smith: 6

a. If Smith and Jones are utility maximizers and make their decisions individually, what will they do?
b. How will your answer to 1a differ, if at all, if Smith and Jones can costlessly make binding agreements with each other?

Now suppose the payoff matrix is as follows:

		Smith	
		Burn	Bag
Jones	Burn	Jones: 6 Smith: 6	Jones: 8 Smith: 2
	Bag	Jones: 2 Smith: 8	Jones: 4 Smith: 4

c. What will they do this time if they can make costless binding agreements?

2. Smith can produce with or without a filter on his smokestack. Production without a filter results in greater smoke damage to Jones. The relevant gains and losses for the two individuals are listed in the table below:

	With filter	Without filter
Gains to Smith	$200 per week	$245 per week
Damage to Jones	$35 per week	$85 per week

   a. If Smith is not liable for smoke damage and there are no negotiation costs, will he install a filter? Explain carefully.
   b. How, if at all, would the outcome be different if Smith were liable for all smoke damage and the cost of the filter were $10 per week higher than indicated in the table? Explain carefully.

3. Smith can operate his sawmill with or without soundproofing. Operation without soundproofing results in noise damage to his neighbour Jones. The relevant gains and losses for Smith and Jones are listed in the table:

	Without soundproofing	With soundproofing
Gains to Smith	$150 per week	$34 per week
Damage to Jones	$125 per week	$6 per week

   a. If Smith is not liable for noise damage and there are no negotiation costs, will he install soundproofing? Explain.
   b. How, if at all, would your answer differ if the negotiation costs of maintaining an agreement were $4 per week? Explain.
   c. Now suppose Jones can escape the noise damage by moving to a new location, which will cost him $120 per week. With negotiation costs again assumed to be zero, how, if at all, will your answer to 3a differ? Explain.

4. Smith and Jones are trying to decide whether to share an apartment. To live separately, each would have to pay $300 per month in rent. An apartment large enough to share can be rented for $450 per month. Costs aside, they are indifferent between living together and living separately except for these two problems: Smith likes to play his stereo late at night, which disturbs Jones's sleep; and Jones likes to sing in the shower at 6 A.M., which awakens Smith. Jones would sacrifice up to $80 per month rather than stop singing in the shower, and Smith would sacrifice up to $155 per month rather than stop playing his stereo late at night. Smith would tolerate Jones's singing and Jones would tolerate Smith's stereo in return for compensation payments not less than $75 per month and $80 per month, respectively.
   a. Should they live together? If so, indicate how they can split the rent so that each does better than by living alone. If not, explain why no such arrangement is feasible.
   b. Now suppose Smith wins a free pair of stereo headphones. If he wears them late at night, Jones's sleep is not disturbed. Smith likes the headphones well enough, but would be willing to pay $40 per month to keep on listening to late-night music through his speakers. How, if at all, does the existence of this new option affect your answer to part (a)? Explain carefully.

5. *A* and *B* can live separately at a rent of $400 per month each, or together at a rent of $600. Each would be willing to give up $30 per month to avoid having to give up his privacy. In addition to the loss of privacy, joint living produces two other conflicts, namely, each has a particular behaviour the other finds offensive: *B* is a trumpet player, and *A* smokes cigarettes. *B* would be willing to pay $60 per month rather than tolerate smoking in his house and $120 per month to continue playing his trumpet. *A*, for his part, would pay up to $100 per month to continue smoking and up to $90 per month to avoid listening to trumpet music. Will they

live together? Explain carefully. Would your answer be different if *A* didn't mind giving up his privacy?

6. *A* and *B* live on adjacent plots of land. Each has two potential uses for her land, the present values of each of which depend on the use adopted by the other, as summarized in the table. All the values in the table are known to both parties.

		A	
		Apple growing	**Pig farming**
B	**Rental housing**	A: $200 B: $700	A: $450 B: $400
	Bee keeping	A: $400 B: $650	A: $450 B: $500

    a. If there are no negotiation costs, what activities will the two pursue on their land?
    b. If there are negotiation costs of $150, what activities will the two pursue on their land?
    c. What is the maximum net income *A* can earn in parts 6a and 6b above?

7. A village has six residents, each of whom has $1000. Each resident may either invest his money in a government bond, which pays 11 percent per year, or use it to buy a year-old steer, which will graze on the village commons. Year-old steers and government bonds each cost exactly $1000. Steers require no effort to tend and can be sold for a price that depends on the amount of weight they gain during the year. Yearly weight gain, in turn, depends on the number of steers that graze on the commons. The prices of 2-year-old steers are given in the table as a function of the total number of steers:

Number of steers	Price per 2-year-old steer
1	$1200
2	1175
3	1150
4	1125
5	1100
6	1075

    a. If village residents make their investment decisions independently, how many steers will graze on the commons?
    b. How many steers would graze on the commons if investment decisions were made collectively?
    c. What grazing fee per steer would result in the socially optimal number of steers?

8. A competitive fishing industry consists of five independently owned and operated fishing boats working on Needle Lake. Assume that no other fishermen fish Needle Lake, and that the MC of operating a boat for one day is equivalent to 70 kilograms of fish. (A boat left idle generates no costs.) The total catch per shoreline, in kilograms, is given in the following table as a function of the number of boats fishing the east and west shores of the lake:

	Total catch	
Number of boats per side	East shore	West shore
1	100	85
2	180	150
3	255	210
4	320	260
5	350	300

a. If each boat owner decides independently which side of the lake to fish and all boats are in plain view of each other, how many boats would you expect to find fishing each shore on any given day? What is the net catch (that is, the total catch from both shores, less operating costs)?

b. Is this distribution of fishing craft optimal from the social point of view? If so, explain why. If not, what is the socially optimal distribution and the corresponding net catch?

9. Two firms, X and Y, have access to five different production processes, each one of which gives off a different amount of pollution. The daily costs of the processes and the corresponding number of tonnes of smoke are listed in the table:

Process (smoke)	(4 tonnes per day)	(3 tonnes per day)	(2 tonnes per day)	(1 tonne per day)	(0 tonnes per day)
Cost to firm X	100	120	140	170	220
Cost to firm Y	60	100	150	255	375

a. If pollution is unregulated, which process will each firm use, and what will be the total daily smoke emissions?

b. The government wants to cut smoke emissions by half. To accomplish this, it requires a permit for each tonne of smoke emitted and limits the number of permits to the desired level of emissions. The permits are then auctioned off competitively to the highest bidders. If X and Y are the only polluters, how much will each permit cost? How many permits will X buy? How many will Y buy?

c. Compare the total cost to society of this permit auction procedure to the total cost of having each firm reduce emissions by half.

10. Two firms, firm 1 and firm 2, produce effluent that is polluting the Crystal River, now affectionately known as "Old Muddy." Their marginal costs of pollution reduction are given by the equations

$$MC_1 = 4Q_1 \quad \text{and} \quad MC_2 = 30 + Q_2,$$

respectively, where MC_1 and MC_2 are in dollars per tonne and Q_1 and Q_2 are in tonnes per day of effluent reduction.

a. If the regional hydrological authorities have determined that effluent into the Crystal River needs to be reduced by 15 tonnes per day, what tax per tonne on effluent will result in the required reduction, and by how much will each firm reduce its effluent?

b. If instead the authorities determine that effluent into the Crystal River needs to be reduced by 30 tonnes per day, what tax per tonne on effluent will result in the required reduction, and by how much will each firm reduce its effluent?

11. Suppose the government attempts to restrict pollution by mandating a maximum amount that each firm can pollute. In general, this will result in a higher cost for pollution control than is necessary. Explain why.

**12. A small village has ten people. Each can either fish in a nearby lagoon or work in a factory. Wages in the factory are $4 per day. Fish sell in competitive markets for $1 apiece. If L persons fish the lagoon, the total number of fish caught is given by $F = 16L - 2L^2$. People prefer to fish unless they expect to make more money working in the factory.

a. If people decide individually whether to fish or work in the factory, how many will fish? What will be the total earnings for the village?

b. What is the socially optimal number of fishermen? With that number, what will the total earnings of the village be?

c. Why is there a difference between the equilibrium and socially optimal numbers of fishermen?

13. Once a week Smith purchases a six-pack of cola and puts it in his refrigerator for his two children to drink later. He invariably discovers that all six cans get drunk the first day. Jones also purchases a six-pack of cola once a week for his two children, but unlike Smith, he tells them that each may drink no more than three cans. Explain why the cola lasts much longer at Jones's house than at Smith's.

**14. Suppose Smith owns and works in a bakery located next to an outdoor café owned by Jones. The patrons of the outdoor café like the smell that emanates from the bakery. When Smith leaves his windows open, the café faces the demand curve $P_C = 30 - .2Q_C$, while when the windows are closed, demand is given by $P_C = 25 - .2Q_C$. However, Smith doesn't like the street noise he hears when his windows are open, and in particular, the disutility he receives has a monetary value of 5. Assume that the café has a constant marginal cost of 10, and that integration (merger) is not a possibility because each owner greatly enjoys owning and operating his own establishment.

   a. In the absence of a contract between the parties, do the firms behave in an efficient fashion? If not, describe the range of contracts that might emerge in response to the externality problem present in the environment. In answering this question, assume Smith understands how the bakery aroma affects demand at the café, and Jones knows how much Smith dislikes street noise.

   b. Suppose now everything is the same as above, except that given the current seating arrangement in the café, the café does not face a higher demand when the bakery windows are open. To realize this higher demand, Jones needs to make a sunk investment of 50, which moves the tables closer to the bakery. Is it wise for Jones to make this investment before he and Smith sign a contract? Explain.

   c. Go back to the initial setup, but now assume that Smith's disutility from street noise equals 50 rather than 5. Further, suppose that prior to the parties' agreeing on a contract, Jones becomes the mayor and grants to himself the property rights concerning whether the bakery windows are left open or closed. Does this have an effect on whether the parties reach an efficient outcome? Explain.

15. Smith and Jones face the choice of driving to work early or late. If they both drive to work at the same time, each gets in the way of the other on the road, and so their daily commute takes longer and is more irritating. The monetary payoffs for each person are listed in the table below for each of the four possible combinations of actions:

		Smith	
		Early	Late
Jones	Early	Jones: 30 Smith: 30	Jones: 50 Smith: 20
	Late	Jones: 20 Smith: 50	Jones: 10 Smith: 10

   a. If Smith and Jones are payoff maximizers and make their decisions individually, what will they do?

   b. If Smith and Jones can make costless binding agreements with each other, what will they do?

16. Same as Problem 15, except now the payoff values of each person are

		Smith	
		Early	Late
Jones	Early	Jones: 30 Smith: 30	Jones: 50 Smith: 20
	Late	Jones: 20 Smith: 60	Jones: 10 Smith: 10

   a. If Smith and Jones are payoff maximizers and make their decisions individually, what will they do?
   b. If Smith and Jones can make costless binding agreements with each other, what will they do?
   c. How do your answers differ from Problem 15 and why?

17. Smith loves dogs and has a pair of West Highland terriers. Jones has an incredible fear of dogs and cannot stand to be within sight of them. Smith and Jones are deciding whether to live in Arlington or Bexley. If they end up living in the same part of town, Jones will run into Smith out walking the Westies and get frightened. Thus, Jones prefers to be physically separated from Smith. The payoffs for each person are listed in the table below for each of the four possible combinations of actions:

		Smith	
		Arlington	Bexley
Jones	Arlington	Jones: 0 Smith: 800	Jones: 500 Smith: 900
	Bexley	Jones: 800 Smith: 800	Jones: 0 Smith: 900

   a. If Smith and Jones are payoff maximizers and make their decisions individually, what will they do?
   b. If Smith and Jones can make costless binding agreements with each other, what will they do?

18. Same as Problem 17, except now payoff values of each person are

		Smith	
		Arlington	Bexley
Jones	Arlington	Jones: 0 Smith: 800	Jones: 500 Smith: 1000
	Bexley	Jones: 600 Smith: 800	Jones: 0 Smith: 1000

   a. If Smith and Jones are payoff maximizers and make their decisions individually, what will they do?
   b. If Smith and Jones can make costless binding agreements with each other, what will they do?
   c. How do your answers differ from Problem 17 and why?

17-1. With a negotiation cost of only 20, it is now practical for the confectioner to pay the doctor to rearrange his office when the confectioner is liable. But note in the table below that it is still more efficient for the confectioner not to be liable:

Legal regime	Outcome	Net benefit		
		Doctor	Confectioner	Total
Liable	Confectioner operates and pays doctor $18 \leq P \leq 20$ to rearrange office	$22 + P$	$40 - P$	62
Not liable	Doctor rearranges his office at his own expense	22	60	82

17-2. Recall that the optimal number of steers is two. The grazing fee must be more than $2 per steer to prevent a third steer from being sent out to graze. The fee cannot be more than $6 per steer without keeping the second steer from being sent out.

17-3. Now the cost of accommodating to the smoke problem is 60, which is again less than the joint savings in rent. Let X represent Jones's contribution to the cost of the exhaust system, which means that Smith's contribution is $60 - X$. X cannot exceed 90, or else Jones will live separately; and X cannot be less than -30, or else Smith will live separately. The total gain is $180 - 60 = 120$.

	Net rental payment ($ per month)		Net gain ($ per month)		
	Jones	Smith	Jones	Smith	Total
Live separately	300	300	—	—	—
Live together and install smoke exhaust system, $-30 \leq X \leq 90$	$210 + X$	$270 - X$	$90 - X$	$30 + X$	120

Chapter 18

GOVERNMENT

In the spring of 1997, southern Manitoba experienced one of the worst floods in its recorded history, second only to the flood of 1826, which converted most of southern Manitoba into a huge lake. Yet the amount of flood damage to Winnipeg was less in real terms than that from the disastrous 1950 flood. The main reason was the Red River Floodway. The Floodway, along with the Portage Diversion, diverted the water around Winnipeg and enabled the level of the Red River as it passed through Winnipeg to be kept more than three metres lower than it would have been in its absence. Without the Floodway, all of central Winnipeg would have been under more than a metre of water, and 85 percent of the city's population would have had to be evacuated.

The Floodway was completed in 1968, to prevent a new disaster like the 1950 flood. It came to be known as "Duff's Ditch," or by skeptics as "Roblin's Folly," after Premier Duff Roblin, whose government had initiated the project. Over 75 million cubic metres of earth were moved in its construction. Although it was used periodically in years of high water to control the level of the Red River, it didn't really fully pay for itself until almost thirty years after its completion. Yet eventually, in 1997, it paid for itself many times over. The Red River Floodway was a mammoth public works project. It is difficult to imagine how a private firm, or even a private consortium of firms, could have brought it into existence. The problem is not primarily the size of the project, although its financial scale and the amount of land it required were substantial. Rather, the problem is how to get the people who would benefit from the project to pay for it.

Suppose, for instance, that if every second household subscribed a certain amount, then the Floodway could be built, because the total amount subscribed would cover all of its costs, including a normal rate of return for the private consortium undertaking the project. Suppose further that *every* Winnipeg household valued the benefits of the Floodway to itself, in terms of life and property insurance and peace of mind, at more than this amount. Then if every second household subscribed, the Floodway *would* be built. But here a problem arises. Suppose that each household reasons as follows: "If we subscribe to the project, then when the big flood comes, our neighbours on either side will be just as dry as we are, even though they haven't paid for the project at all. Why should we pay for them? It's much better if they pay for us." Each household thus has an incentive to lie (or in economic parlance, "engage in a strategic misrepresentation of preferences") regarding its willingness to pay for the project. But if every household misrepresents its preferences, in order to have a "free ride" on its neighbours' contributions, then the Floodway is not built, and in 1997 most of Winnipeg is under a metre of water. How does society ensure that the optimum quantity of public goods like the Floodway is provided, and how does it fund their provision?

CHAPTER PREVIEW

Our task in this chapter is to explore two important functions of government: the provision of public goods and the direct redistribution of income. Concerns about both fairness and efficiency, we shall see, are inextricably linked in both of these areas.

We shall also see that the mere fact that a good has the characteristics of a public good does not mean that it must necessarily be provided by government. We shall examine a variety of ingenious schemes, ranging from commercial broadcast television to highly structured collective legal contracts, whereby public goods are provided with little direct government involvement.

We shall also see that problems similar to those that arise in connection with public goods are encountered whenever there are significant indivisibilities or economies of scale in the production of private consumption goods.

Next we take up the question of how societies make choices between competing public projects, with particular focus on cost-benefit analysis as an alternative to majority voting schemes.

Our next topic is a problem that plagues all mechanisms of public decision making, namely, that self-interested parties have an incentive to influence outcomes in their own favour. This problem goes by the name of rent seeking and has become an increasingly serious threat to our social welfare.

From the problems of public choice, which themselves have important distributional overtones, we next turn our attention to the topic of income redistribution itself, and the relationship between fairness and efficiency.

18.1 PUBLIC GOODS

As noted in Chapter 16, public goods are those goods or services that possess, in varying degrees, the properties of *nondiminishability* (sometimes referred to as *nonrivalry*) and *nonexcludability*. The nondiminishability property, again, says that any one person's consumption of a public good has no effect on the amount of it available for others. Nonexcludability means that it is either impossible or prohibitively costly to exclude nonpayers from consuming the good.

Pure public good
A good that has a high degree of non-diminishability and nonexcludability.

Collective good A good that is excludable but has a high degree of nondiminishability.

Goods that have high degrees of both of these properties are often called **pure public goods**, the classic example of which is national defence. Goods that have only the nondiminishability property are sometimes referred to as **collective goods**. We have met goods characterized by diminishability and nonexcludability before, in Chapter 17. The tragedy of the commons, as manifested in overgrazing and overfishing, is a result of the difficulty of excluding additional livestock or fishing boats after the point where their presence begins to confer negative externalities on those already utilizing a resource. An open access highway may be a pure public good for much of the day. During rush hour, however, as the capacity limits of the highway are neared, each additional vehicle on the highway diminishes the driving space and speed of all the others. When full, bumper-to-bumper gridlock is achieved, it is even difficult to get onto the highway to contribute to the traffic jam.

Located north of Toronto, Highway 407, which extends for about 108 kilometres, is one of the world's most technologically sophisticated toll roads. There are no tollbooths. Vehicles that travel the 407 regularly are equipped with transponders, which signal the length of each trip. Vehicles without transponders are photographed when they enter and leave the 407. Vehicle owners are billed on a monthly basis for the kilometres they have travelled. The toll system provides a form of high-tech excludability, and since it keeps the traffic volume down, the 407 is generally characterized by nondiminishability: at any time the marginal cost of an additional vehicle is effectively zero. As these examples suggest, nondiminishability and nonexcludability are not absolute and fixed characteristics of particular goods, but are often conditioned by social decisions as well as by organizational and technical capacities.

The Marginal and Total Benefit of a Public Good

Let's begin our analysis with the case of a government trying to decide what quantity to provide of some pure public good—say, public parks. For simplicity, imagine that there are only two citizens, *A* and *B*, and that each assigns a different value to any given quantity of the public good. In Figure 18-1, the horizontal axis measures the quantity of parkland, in hectares. The curve labelled *AA'* represents the amount *A* would be willing to pay for an additional hectare, and *BB'* represents the corresponding curve for *B*. Thus, at a level of 4 hectares, *A* would be willing to pay $9 for an additional hectare, while *B* would be willing to pay only $6. The fact that the two marginal willingness-to-pay curves are downward sloping reflects the fact that the more hectares there already are, the less valuable an additional hectare will be.

The central fact about any pure public good is that each person must consume the same amount of it, namely the amount provided. With private goods, in contrast, each person can consume whatever amount she chooses at the prevailing price. To obtain the market demand curve for a private good, we simply added the individual demand curves horizontally. In the case of public goods, the analogue to the market demand curve is the aggregate marginal willingness-to-pay (AMWP) curve. It is obtained by

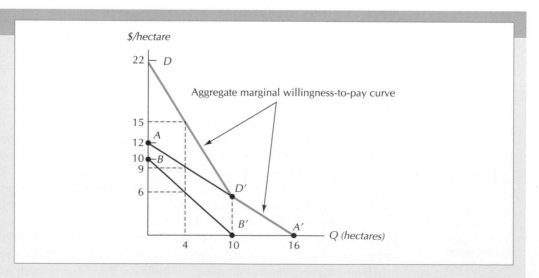

FIGURE 18-1

The Aggregate Marginal Willingness-to-Pay Curve for a Public Good

AA' and *BB'* represent the respective amounts that *A* and *B* are willing to pay for an additional unit of the public good. The aggregate marginal willingness-to-pay curve is the vertical summation of the individual marginal willingness-to-pay curves, the curve labelled *DD'A'*.

adding the individual marginal willingness-to-pay curves not horizontally but vertically. At $Q = 4$ hectares in Figure 18-1, for example, A and B together are willing to pay a total of $9 + 6 = \$15$ for an additional hectare. The curve labelled $DD'A'$ represents the vertical summation of the two individual willingness-to-pay curves.

It is important to keep in mind that the marginal willingness-to-pay curves are *marginal* benefit curves. At any level of provision of the public good, they measure the benefit derived from an *additional* unit of the public good, in terms of how much an individual is willing to pay for that additional unit. The *total* benefit that A receives from consuming 4 units of the public good is therefore the *sum* of all of the marginal benefits up to 4 units, which is given by the area under the AA' curve between the origin and 4, or $4[(12 + 9)/2] = \$42$. Similarly, the total benefit to B is the corresponding area under BB', or $4[(10 + 6)/2] = \$32$. The aggregate total benefit when $Q = 4$ units is thus $42 + 32 = \$74$, the corresponding area under $DD'A'$.

EXERCISE 18-1

Ten homogeneous consumers all have individual marginal willingness-to-pay curves $\text{MWP}_i = 12 - \frac{1}{5}Q$ for a public good—say, a concert in an open park (where MWP_i is measured in dollars per minute and Q is measured in minutes). Construct and graph the aggregate marginal willingness-to-pay (AMWP) curve. When $Q = 30$ minutes, what is the maximum each individual would be willing to pay for an additional minute? What is the total benefit each receives from the concert when $Q = 30$ minutes?

The Analogy to Joint Production

In passing, let's note the striking similarity between the procedure for generating the aggregate willingness-to-pay curve for a public good and the procedure whereby the demand curve for a product like chicken is generated from the demand curves for the various parts of a chicken. For simplicity, suppose chickens are composed of only two parts, wings and drumsticks, the demand curves for which are given by the curves labelled WW' and DD' in Figure 18-2. The horizontal axis in Figure 18-2 measures three things simultaneously: total pairs of drumsticks, total pairs of wings, and total number of chickens—because any given number of chickens will give rise to that same number of pairs of wings and drumsticks. On the simplifying assumption that wings and drumsticks are the only two chicken parts, we get the market demand curve for chickens by adding the demand curve for wings and the demand curve for drumsticks vertically. The curve labelled $CC'D'$ in Figure 18-2 represents this vertical summation.

The curve labelled SS' in Figure 18-2 is the supply curve for chickens. Assuming the chicken industry is competitive, it is the horizontal summation of the marginal cost curves of the individual chicken producers. As in any other competitive market, equilibrium in the market for chickens occurs at the intersection of the supply and demand curves. The equilibrium quantity of chickens will be Q^*, and that quantity will give rise to Q^* pairs of drumsticks and Q^* pairs of wings. The market-clearing prices for drumsticks and wings will be P_D^* and P_W^*, respectively. These two prices sum to the equilibrium price of chickens, P_C^*.

There are several important points to note about the equilibrium in the market for jointly produced goods. First note that the equilibrium quantities of wings, drumsticks, and chicken are efficient in the Pareto sense. At Q^* the cost to society of producing another chicken is P_C^*, and this is exactly the total value that consumers place on its

FIGURE 18-2

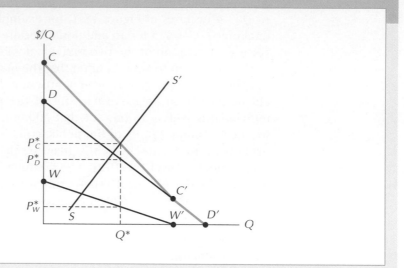

component parts. Any other quantity of chickens would leave open the possibility of mutual gains from exchange. Note also that the price of each chicken part cannot be determined from cost information alone, even if we know exactly the marginal cost of raising another chicken. There is simply no scientific basis for apportioning the cost of the entire bird among each of its constituent parts. Drumsticks and wings sell for their respective prices because those are the prices necessary to clear the markets for each. In a precisely analogous way, there is no correspondence between the amount that any one individual is willing to pay for a public good and its marginal cost of production.

The Optimal Quantity of a Public Good

Let's return again to our example of public parks. Given the aggregate marginal willingness-to-pay curve, what is the optimal area of parkland? The answer is determined in much the same way as in the market for chickens. In Figure 18-3, the curve labelled *DD'A'* again represents the aggregate marginal willingness-to-pay curve for public parkland. The curve labelled MC represents the marginal cost of parkland as a function of its quantity. The intersection of these two curves establishes $Q^* = 4$ ha, the optimal area of public parkland. At $Q^* = 4$ ha, the amounts that *A* and *B* would be willing to pay for another hectare add to exactly the cost ($15) of another hectare. If this equality did not hold, we could easily show that society would be better off by either expanding or contracting the amount of parkland.

EXERCISE 18-2

Consider the situation described in Exercise 18-1, but now suppose that the marginal cost of providing the concert is MC = $2Q$. Determine the optimal length of the concert. How will your answer change if MC = Q?

Paying for Q^*

We must make a slight qualification to the claim that Q^* is the optimal level of the public good in Figure 18-3. The statement is true subject to the provision that the *total* cost of

FIGURE 18-3

**Optimal Provision
of a Public Good**
The optimal level of the
public good is $Q^* = 4$ ha,
the level for which
aggregate marginal
willingness to pay for
the good is exactly equal
to its marginal cost.

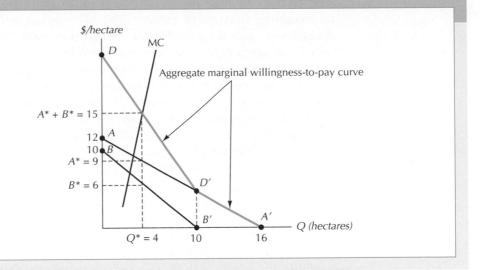

Q^* does not exceed the total amount that the public would be willing to pay for it. The total willingness to pay for Q^* is the area under the aggregate willingness-to-pay curve up to Q^*. The total cost is the area under the marginal cost curve up to Q^*, plus any fixed costs. Provided that the total cost is smaller than the total willingness to pay, Q^* is the optimal level of the public good. This qualification is similar to the requirement that a profit-maximizing firm produce where MR = MC, subject to the proviso that total revenues cover total costs (total variable costs in the short run, all costs in the long run).

If the government is to produce Q^* units of a public good, it must somehow raise sufficient tax revenue to cover the total production costs of that amount. Suppose, for the sake of discussion, that the government's tax structure requires the collection of equal tax payments from all citizens. In the example in Figure 18-3, B's willingness to pay for the public good is smaller than A's. It follows that B will vote for the provision of Q^* only if the total cost of Q^* is less than twice the area under BB' up to Q^*. For example, if the total cost of the good is $66, and each party must be taxed equally, B will vote for it only if his total willingness to pay exceeds $33. Since the amount B is willing to pay for 4 units of the public good is only $32, this condition will not be satisfied, and so the project will not win approval.

And yet we know that this public good is one whose benefits to all citizens ($74) add up to more than its costs ($66). Compared with the alternative in which the public good is not provided, both A and B can be made better off by providing Q^* of it and then taxing A more heavily than B in order to pay for it. It follows that a tax structure that levies the same tax on all citizens cannot in general be Pareto efficient.

The situation here is analogous to the case in which the incomes of two spouses differ substantially. Suppose Julie earns $100,000 per year while her husband, Bruce, earns only $15,000. Given her income, Julie as an individual would want to spend much more than Bruce would on housing, travel, entertainment, and the many other items they consume in common. But suppose the couple adopted a rule that each had to contribute an equal share toward the purchase of such items. The result would be to constrain the couple to live in a small house, to take only inexpensive vacations, to skimp on entertainment and dining out, and so on. And so it is easy to imagine that Julie would find it attractive to pay considerably more than 50 percent for jointly consumed goods, thereby enabling both of them to consume in the manner their combined income affords.

As in the case of private goods, the willingness to pay for public goods is generally an increasing function of income. The rich, on the average, assign greater value to public goods than the poor do, not because they have different tastes but because they have more money. A tax system that taxed the poor just as heavily as the rich would result in the rich getting smaller amounts of public goods than they want. Rather than see that happen, the rich might well agree to a tax system that assigns them a larger share of the tax burden. It would be missing the point to criticize such a system by saying that the system is unfair because it enables the poor to enjoy the services of public goods for a smaller price. It does have this property, to be sure; but from the viewpoint of the rich, its terms are still attractive because the tax payments of the poor, though small, mean the rich end up paying less than if they had to finance public goods all by themselves.

This analysis does not imply that the "free rider" problem that we noted at the beginning of the chapter has disappeared. Self-interested persons, rich or poor, could still have an incentive to misrepresent their preferences if they thought their tax burden would thereby be lessened. Moreover, there could in theory be individuals who derived no benefit from *any* public good, although it is hard to imagine that they would not derive at least some benefit from, for example, a peaceful and orderly social and economic environment. Note, however, that the provision of public goods through government, financed by taxation, can have some advantages to which the analysis points. The first is that if *everybody* pays for a particular public good, the cost per person is lower, and therefore the greater is the likelihood that most people will experience a net benefit. The second advantage of public provision of public goods occurs because a *bundle* of public goods is provided. It is possible that a person's proportional tax share of the total expenditure on a particular public good may exceed her estimate of its total benefit to her, but it is likely that her share of the cost of all public goods combined will be *less* than her perceived benefit from them. On balance, therefore, financing a *bundle* of public goods through taxes is more likely to result in provision of the socially efficient quantity of public goods and in higher general levels of satisfaction than if the level of provision of public goods is determined on an item-by-item basis.

Private Provision of Public Goods

Governments are not the exclusive providers of public goods in any society. Substantial quantities of such goods are routinely provided through a variety of private channels. If it is impractical to exclude people from consuming a public good, the pressing question is how can the good be paid for, if not by mandatory taxes?

Funding by Donation. One method for funding public goods is through voluntary donations. People donate great artworks to museums; they make contributions to listener-supported radio stations, to fund animal shelters, to research debilitating diseases, and so on. Motives for such donations are as varied as the projects they support. Some see charitable giving as a means to achieve respect and admiration in the community.[1] Others may feel pressure to give in order to avoid social ostracism. These motives are really two sides of the same coin—social reward in the first case and social penalty in the second. Where such social forces are effective, they are a practical way of excluding nonpayers from full enjoyment of the public good.

---

[1] To achieve the social benefit of charitable giving, the gift must become public knowledge. Most charitable organizations publicize their list of donors.

Alternatively, people may donate because the increment to the public good that their contribution will finance is simply worth that much money to them. This motive is most likely to be important in situations where one person's action can significantly affect the scale of the public good. Someone who lives at the end of a short dirt road in a rural area, for example, may find it worthwhile to pave the entire road at his own expense. He would naturally be happier if everyone who lived on the road chipped in. But rather than do without the road altogether, it may be worthwhile for him to pave it himself. Similarly, a person who plants a flower garden in front of her house provides a public good for neighbours to enjoy. If her own personal enjoyment from the garden exceeds its cost, pure self-interest is a sufficient motive for her to plant it.

But self-interested motives do not seem sufficient to explain why people make anonymous donations that will have no appreciable effect on the benefits they themselves receive. In the case of listener-supported radio stations, a single person's contribution will rarely make a perceptible difference in the nature or quality of programming. The station will either continue to operate in its current form, or else improve, or else get worse—irrespective of what any one person does.

Free riding Choosing not to donate to a cause but still benefiting from the donations of others.

In such situations, the logic of pure self-interest seems to dictate *free riding*—abstaining in the hope that others will contribute. And yet millions of people contribute to such enterprises each year. For many of these people, the satisfaction of giving—of having contributed to the common good—is an end in itself. And as we saw in Chapters 1 and 7, there may well be important material advantages in being such a person.

The fact that public goods are often supported through voluntary contributions does not necessarily mean, however, that they are supported at socially optimal levels. Residents might be perfectly willing to pay sufficient taxes to build the socially optimal road. And yet, in the absence of taxes, the road that actually gets built is likely to be considerably smaller. Similarly, many people might strongly want society to invest more in public television programming. But these same people might be reluctant to give voluntarily as much as they would be willing to pay in taxes.

Sale of By-Products. Free-rider problems are sometimes solved by devising novel means to finance the public good. One such way is the sale of an important by-product of the public good. In the case of commercial television, for example, financing comes from sponsors, generally private corporations, who pay for the right to beam advertising messages to the audience attracted by the broadcast. The captive viewing audience is a by-product of the broadcast, and sponsors are willing to pay a lot for access to it. As the following example makes clear, however, this system does not always assure an optimal allocation of broadcast resources.

EXAMPLE 18-1

In a given time slot, a television network faces the alternative of broadcasting either *Celebrity Mud Wrestling (CMW)* or a special documentary, *The Emerging Global Economy: A Crash Course.* If it chooses *CMW*, it will win 20 percent of the viewing audience, but only 18 percent if it chooses *Global Economy*. Suppose those who would choose *CMW* would collectively be willing to pay $1 million for the right to see that program, while those who choose *Global Economy* would be willing to pay $3 million. And suppose, finally, that the time slot is to be financed by a detergent company. Which program will the network choose? Which program would be socially optimal?

If we ignore demographic factors, then the sponsor cares primarily about the number of people who will see its advertisements, and will thus choose the program that will attract the largest audience—here, *Celebrity Mud Wrestling*. The fact that those who prefer *Global Economy* would be willing to pay a lot more to see it is of little concern to the sponsor. But this difference in willingness to pay is critical when it comes to determining the optimal result from society's point of view. Because the people who prefer *Global Economy* could more than compensate the *CMW* viewers for relinquishing the time slot, *Global Economy* is a Pareto-superior outcome. But unless its supporters happen to buy more soap in total than the *CMW* viewers, *CMW* will prevail. The difficulty with reliance on advertising and other indirect mechanisms for financing public goods is that there is no assurance that they will reflect the relevant benefits to society.

The same method is used in the sponsorship of various informational websites by commercial advertisers, with the added advantage to the advertiser that links on the site will take interested potential customers directly to the sponsor's homepage, with just a click of the mouse. In the early days of the Internet, individuals with certain demographic characteristics were given free access to the Internet, or were even paid to surf the Net, so that market researchers could monitor their surfing patterns and generate information that could be sold to marketers. Here, however, the development of software that mimicked the activity of someone randomly surfing the net even when nobody was operating the system, in order to increase web-surfing payments, killed the goose that laid the golden egg. Now such schemes have disappeared. The development of technology to eliminate pop-up ads similarly devalues this form of advertising.

Development of New Means to Exclude Nonpayers.   Another way to finance public goods privately is to devise cheap new ways of excluding people who do not pay for the good. In broadcast television, it was once impossible to prevent any household from tuning in to a program once it was sent out over the airwaves. With the advent of cable and satellite TV and advances in signal-scrambling technology, however, it is now easier to exclude households. With the ability to charge for specific programs using pay-per-view systems, it is no longer necessary to make all programming decisions on the basis of which program will garner the largest audience. In our *CMW* versus *Global Economy* example, a broadcasting company that can exclude nonpayers would have an incentive to show *Global Economy,* because its potential viewers now have a practical means of translating their greater willingness to pay into profits for the producer.

But note that whereas the outcome of pay-per-view TV is more efficient in the sense of selecting the programs the public most values, it is less efficient in one other important respect. By charging each household a fee for viewing, it discourages some households from tuning in. And since the marginal social cost of an additional household's watching a program is exactly zero, it is inefficient to limit the audience in this way. Which of the two inefficiencies is more important—free TV's inefficiency in choosing between programs or pay TV's inefficiency in excluding potential beneficiaries—is both an empirical and a philosophical question.[2]

---

[2]This issue is not confined to television. Indeed, it is one of the fundamental unresolved issues of the twenty-first century global economy. Information is inherently nondiminishable, and the marginal cost of reproducing and distributing information is often negligible. Partly for this reason, global "informational piracy"—considering only software and video piracy, and ignoring issues related to person-to-person (P2P) file sharing—is annually a multibillion dollar industry. Should information be treated as a pure public good or as digital private property? If its dissemination increases productivity, should it not be made available at its marginal cost; that is, for free? But if it is provided free, then what incentive exists to produce the information in the first place? See Lesley Ellen Harris, *Digital Property*, McGraw-Hill Ryerson, 1998.

Private Contracts. Legal contracts among private individuals offer yet another means for overcoming some of the difficulties associated with the free-rider problem. Consider, for example, the public good consisting of residential maintenance and beautification. As neighbourhoods are customarily organized, it is impractical to exclude your neighbours from the benefits they will reap if you keep your house well painted and your yard neatly trimmed. Nor would it be efficient to exclude them, because their consumption of these benefits does not diminish their value to you and others in any way. In this respect, home maintenance and beautification satisfy the definition of a pure public good and, for this reason, will generally be undersupplied by private individuals.

The organizers of condominiums, cooperatives, and other forms of legal residential associations have come up with an effective solution to this problem. The condominium contract requires each owner to contribute a specified sum each month toward maintenance and beautification. This payment functions much like a tax in the sense that it is mandatory for all parties to the contract. It is less coercive than a tax, however, in one important respect: people who wish to spend less on home maintenance are free to live elsewhere.

The Economics of Clubs. A pure public good has the property that an additional person's consumption of the good does not limit the amount of it available to others. Stated another way, the marginal cost of additional consumption of the public good is exactly zero. Many privately produced goods have the property that marginal cost, although not zero, declines sharply with the number of users accommodated. The swimming pool is a case in point. The number of swimmers it can accommodate rises in proportion to its surface area, but its cost rises much more slowly. The difference between such goods and goods that satisfy the nondiminishability criterion perfectly is thus one of degree rather than of kind.

When the marginal cost of expanding the capacity of a private good is low relative to its average cost, consumers face an economic incentive to share the purchase and use of the good. In the swimming pool example, the cost to each of 20 families of a pool large enough for all to share will be much smaller than the cost of a pool large enough to serve the needs of only a single family. Indeed, the same statement is true of virtually any good that is not kept in continuous use by a single user. For example, most homeowners use extension ladders only once or twice a year, making it possible for several families to cut costs by sharing a single ladder.

The disadvantage of sharing, besides the fact that it requires someone to take the initiative to organize the arrangement, is that it limits both privacy and flexibility of access to the good. Thus, a homeowner might want to use the ladder on a particular Saturday afternoon, only to find it already in use by one of its other co-owners. Sometimes such inconveniences are trivial in relation to the cost savings; other times they will not be.

Opportunities for shared ownership thus confront the consumer with a variant of the standard consumer choice problem. To illustrate, consider again the choice between a privately owned pool and a shared pool. If we measure privacy and flexibility in the use of a pool on a scale from 0 to 1.0, a private pool would take the value 1.0, representing maximal privacy and flexibility. The limiting case at the other extreme is a large pool shared by infinitely many other people; the flexibility index for such a pool takes the value 0, representing virtually no privacy or flexibility.

The vertical axis in Figure 18-4 measures the amount the consumer spends on all other goods besides pools. If she buys her own private pool, at a cost of $Y' - Y_0$, she will achieve a privacy and flexibility index of 1.0. The other extreme represents a completely crowded pool, at a cost of 0 and a flexibility index of 0. Pools of intermediate

FIGURE 18-4

The Tradeoff between Privacy and Cost
When the marginal cost of accommodating an extra user of a consumption good is less than the average cost, consumers can save money by forming clubs that share ownership of such goods. The optimal club for members with the same tastes is one for which the marginal rate of substitution between all other goods and privacy is exactly equal to the cost of additional privacy.

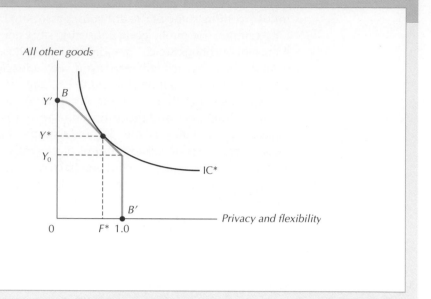

size and crowdedness are represented by intermediate points on the budget constraint BB' in Figure 18-4. The consumer's best option is (F^*, Y^*), the point for which this budget constraint is tangent to an indifference curve (IC*).

On the plausible assumption that the demand for privacy increases with income, we would predict that high-income consumers would be more likely to purchase their own pools than low-income consumers. But even consumers with very high incomes will find it attractive to participate in sharing arrangements for extremely costly consumption goods. Rather than maintain exclusive rights to operate an airplane that would sit idle on the tarmac most hours of the week, for example, even wealthy amateur pilots often choose to become members of flying clubs, the use of whose aircraft is shared with other members.

In the case of very inexpensive goods, in contrast, we would expect the demand for privacy to take precedence over the lure of cost savings even for consumers of relatively modest means. A privately owned toothbrush, like a privately owned airplane or swimming pool, is destined to remain idle for most hours of the day. Its cost per owner could be lowered substantially if it were shared by the members of a toothbrushing club. But the savings from such a transaction would be far too small to justify the sacrifice in privacy. Virtually everyone, even the poorest citizen, finds it worthwhile to maintain exclusive access to his personal toothbrush.

18.2 PUBLIC CHOICE

Whether public goods are provided by governments, charitable organizations, or private clubs, decisions must be made about the types and quantities to provide. The budget constraint confronting the group is often clear enough. The much more difficult aspect of the problem is to devise some means for translating the diverse preferences of the group's members into a single voice.

Majority Voting

One method of discerning group preferences is the majority vote. By this standard, projects favoured by a majority—in either a direct referendum or a vote taken by elected

TABLE 18-1

	Helen	Ralph	Eve
Best	Highway	Research	Education
Second	Research	Education	Highway
Third	Education	Highway	Research

representatives—are adopted and all others are abandoned. In recent years, much attention has been given to the fact that majority voting often leads to intransitivities in the ranking of alternatives. To illustrate, consider a group with three members—Helen, Ralph and Eve—each of whom has a well-ordered ranking of three alternative projects: a new highway, a medical research project, and more education. Their rankings are summarized in Table 18-1.

Given these rankings, note what happens when each of the three pairs of alternatives is put to a vote. In deciding which of any pair of alternatives to vote for, each voter will naturally choose the one he or she prefers to the other. Thus, in a vote between a new highway and medical research, the highway will get 2 votes (Helen and Eve); the research only 1 (Ralph). In a vote between research and education, research gets 2 votes (Ralph and Helen); education only 1 (Eve). And finally, in a vote between education and the highway, education gets 2 votes (Eve and Ralph); the highway only 1 (Helen). Thus the highway defeats the research program and the research program defeats education, and yet education defeats the highway! Such intransitivities were assumed not to occur in individual preference orderings, but can easily happen if social choice takes place by successive majority votes between pairs of alternatives.

Agenda Manipulation.   The possibility of intransitivities in majority voting makes the order in which alternatives are considered by the electorate critically important. Suppose, for example, that Helen is in charge of setting the agenda for voting. Her first priority will be to avoid a direct confrontation between the highway (her most favoured project) and education (which she knows will defeat the highway in a majority vote). She can ensure the highway's success by first conducting a vote between education and the research project, followed by a vote between the winner of that election and the highway. The research project will win the first vote and will then be defeated by the highway in the second. Given power to set the agenda, either Ralph or Eve could have taken similar steps to ensure victory for either the research project or education.

The Median Voter Theorem.   Intransitive rankings do not always result when alternatives are considered pairwise in a majority voting system. For example, we will get no intransitivities when the alternatives represent different quantities of a given public good and each voter ranks each alternative according to how close it is to what, for him or her, is the optimal amount of the good. To illustrate, suppose our three voters are now considering what percentage of the budget to devote to highways; and suppose that, as shown in Figure 18-5, the ideal percentages for Helen, Ralph, and Eve are 50, 6, and 10, respectively. Suppose, finally, that the percentages being considered for adoption are 5, 8, 11, 20, 40, and 60.

Does the power to set the order in which pairs of alternatives are considered confer the power to choose the ultimate outcome? This time the answer is no. In any pair of alternatives put to a vote, the winner will always be the one preferred by Eve. Suppose, for instance, that 5 and 8 are put to a vote. Helen and Eve will vote for 8 and Ralph for 5,

FIGURE 18-5

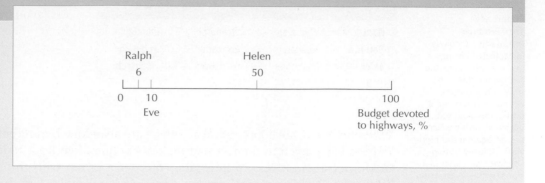

making Eve's choice the winner. If the alternatives are 20 and 60, Ralph and Eve will vote for 20 and Helen for 60, and Eve's choice again wins. Because Eve's most preferred outcome lies between the most preferred choices of the other two, she is the so-called ***median voter*** in this situation, and her vote will always prevail. The *median voter theorem* states that whenever alternatives can be ranked according to their closeness to each voter's ideal outcome, majority voting will always select the alternative most preferred by the median voter.

Median voter The voter whose ideal outcome lies at or just above the ideal outcomes of half the voters.

EXERCISE 18-3

Given that the percentages of the budget under consideration for spending on highways are again 5, 8, 11, 20, 40, and 60, which outcome will be chosen if the most preferred percentages of Ralph, Eve, and Helen are 11, 25, and 40, respectively?

Single-peaked preferences Preferences that exhibit a single most-preferred outcome, with other outcomes ranked lower as their distances from the most-preferred outcome increase.

The technical feature of preferences that eliminates intransitivities in the highway spending example is called ***single peakedness***. To have single-peaked preferences with respect to the share of the budget spent on highways means to have a uniquely most preferred outcome and to rank all other outcomes in terms of their distance from it. Such preferences rule out liking 10 percent most and then ranking 30 percent better than 20 percent.

In contexts like the highways example, it seems plausible to assume that preferences are indeed single peaked. But in other contexts, such as the highway-education-research example, preferences need not have this property. Numerous important examples occur in practice in which majority voting leads to intransitive rankings, making the power to set the agenda tantamount to the power to choose the final outcome.

18.3 COST-BENEFIT ANALYSIS

The difficulty of public choice by majority voting is not just that it sometimes leads to intransitivities. An even more serious problem is that it almost completely obscures important differences in the intensity with which different voters hold their preferences. Suppose, for example, that there are two alternatives put to a vote: (1) to allow smoking in public buildings and (2) to prohibit smoking in public buildings. If 51 percent of the voters prefer the first alternative and only 49 percent the second, the result will be to allow smoking in public buildings. But suppose the 49 percent who favour a prohibition feel very strongly about it and collectively would be willing to pay $100 million per year in order to have it. And suppose the opponents of the prohibition are only mildly opposed; they know it will cause them some short-term inconvenience, but most of them want to quit or cut down on their smoking anyway, and they realize the ordinance will help them to do that. Collectively, the most they would be willing to pay in order to continue smoking in public buildings is only $1 million per year. Under these circumstances, a simple transfer payment would make the outcome chosen by the majority clearly Pareto inferior to the prohibition on smoking in public buildings. If the prohibitionists give the smokers $10 million per year in exchange for agreeing to the ban, both groups will be better off than if smoking continues—the smokers by $9 million per year, the nonsmokers by $90 million per year.

Cost-benefit analysis is an alternative to majority voting that attempts to take explicit account of how strongly people feel about each of the alternatives under consideration. Its method for measuring intensity of preference is to estimate how much people would be willing to pay in order to have the various alternatives. In the smoking example, it would immediately rule in favour of the prohibition because its benefits to its supporters (as measured by what they would be willing to pay to have it) strongly outweigh its costs to its opponents (as measured by what they would be willing to pay to avoid it).

Cost-benefit analysis can avoid the intransitivities that often arise under majority voting. To illustrate, let's consider how it would deal with the highway-education-research decision we discussed earlier. Table 18-2 displays hypothetical valuations assigned by Helen, Ralph, and Eve to each of the three alternatives. Positive entries in the table represent the amounts each person would pay to have a program he or she likes. Negative entries represent what someone would pay to avoid a program he or she dislikes. The entries in the first column of the table, for instance, indicate that Helen would pay 100 to have the highway, 35 to have the medical research program, and 20 to avoid education. Note that each person's ranking of the alternatives is the same in Table 18-2 as it was in Table 18-1.

To keep the discussion simple, suppose that the cost of each program is 100, but that because of budgetary shortages, only one of the three programs can be undertaken. How will cost-benefit analysis choose among them? It will pick the one for which the surplus of total benefit over cost is greatest. Again for simplicity, assume that the amounts the three voters would pay for each program accurately capture all relevant benefits. The total benefit of each program will then be the sum of what each voter would pay to have (or avoid) it. These totals are listed in the last column of Table 18-2 and reveal that the research program is the clear winner.

Note also that the research program would not have won if Helen had been able to set the agenda for a majority voting session. She would first pit the research program against education, defeating it 2 to 1. And Helen's favoured highway project would then defeat the research program by the same margin. Eve, through similar agenda manipulation, could arrange for her favoured education program to emerge the winner in a majority voting sequence.

TABLE 18-2

Willingness to Pay for Three Projects
Cost-benefit analysis chooses the project with the largest surplus of benefits over costs. If each project costs 100, the surplus will be 20 for the highway, 65 for the research program, and 35 for education. The cost-benefit test will therefore choose the research program.

	Helen	Ralph	Eve	Total
Highway	100	−25	45	120
Research	35	90	40	165
Education	−20	60	95	135

Note, finally, that if the research program did *not* get adopted, it would always be possible to construct a Pareto-preferred switch to the research program. Suppose, for example, that Helen set the agenda in a majority voting sequence, with the result that the highway was chosen. This outcome yields a loss of 25 for Ralph. In contrast, had the research program been chosen, Ralph would have had a gain of 90, a net improvement of 115 for him. This improvement is big enough to enable Ralph to compensate both Helen and Eve for the losses they would suffer by switching from the highway to the research program. Suppose, for example, that Ralph gives Helen 70 and Eve 10 for switching. Then the net benefits to Helen and Eve will be 105 and 50, respectively, a gain of 5 each over their positions with the highway. A similar Pareto-improving move could be constructed if we had begun with the education program. Indeed, the cost-benefit test will in general lead to a Pareto-efficient outcome.

If cost-benefit analysis satisfies the Pareto criterion while majority voting doesn't always do so, why do we so often use majority voting for making collective choices? One objection to cost-benefit analysis is that because it measures benefits by what people are willing to pay, it gives insufficient weight to the interests of people with little money. On this view, the poor may feel very strongly about an issue, and yet their feelings will not count for much in cost-benefit analysis since they don't translate into large willingness-to-pay values. This sounds at first like a serious objection, but as the following example clearly demonstrates, it is possible to overcome the objection if the gainers can *(and do)* compensate the losers.

| EXAMPLE 18-2 | Suppose there are only two people, *R* (who is rich) and *P* (who is poor). And suppose that *R* favours a public project that *P* opposes. In purely psychological terms, their intensity of feeling is the same. But because *R* has much more money, he would be willing to pay 100 to have the project, while *P* would be willing to pay only 10 to avoid it. If each could choose which method to use for deciding on public projects, which would each favour, cost-benefit analysis or majority rule? |

At first glance, majority rule sounds attractive to *P* because it gives him veto power over any project he does not favour. But the first step *P* would take if he were given that veto power would be to yield it in exchange for a compensation payment. If *R* values the project at 100 and *P* would pay only 10 to avoid it, the most efficient outcome here is to go ahead with the project. If *R* gives *P* a compensation payment of *X*, where $10 \leq X \leq 100$, then each party will be better off than if *P* had insisted on exercising his veto. By *P*'s own reckoning, the inconvenience of the project is less than the value to him of the compensation payment. The fact that the cost-benefit test always leads to the greatest economic surplus means that it will always be in the interests of *R* and *P* alike to use it, provided that the compensation *X* is actually paid.

Critics of cost-benefit analysis sometimes concede that it would lead to Pareto-optimal outcomes in every case if it were practical to make the needed compensation payments. But they go on to argue that such compensation payments usually are not practical on a case-by-case basis. And so, they conclude, it is unfair to make decisions on the basis of cost-benefit analysis.

Yet it is also possible to address this objection. First, note that in most societies literally thousands of decisions are taken each year with respect to public goods and programs. Each one, if adopted, would help some people and hurt others. Generally the individual magnitudes of the gains and losses in any one decision are extremely small, much less than

1 percent of even a poor person's annual earnings. If projects are decided by the cost-benefit criterion, the amount that winners gain on any adopted project will necessarily outweigh the amount that losers lose. Where small projects are concerned, then, the cost-benefit test is like flipping a coin that is biased in your favour. On each flip of the coin you might either win or lose, but the probability of winning exceeds the probability of losing. If both the gains and losses are small and randomly distributed among individuals, and if the coin is to be flipped thousands of times, this makes for a very attractive gamble indeed. The law of large numbers (see Chapter 6) tells us that it is virtually certain that everyone will come out a winner in the end.

But suppose that the gains and losses from each outcome are not random; that, on the contrary, the poor usually come out on the losing side of the cost-benefit test because of their inability to back up their favoured programs with high willingness-to-pay values. Even if it is impractical to compensate the poor on an issue-by-issue basis, it is *still* possible to achieve a better outcome for everyone by relying on the cost-benefit criterion, provided that the poor can be compensated on an ongoing basis through the tax system. If the only alternative is to rely on majority voting, which would allow the poor to block projects whose benefits exceed their cost, the cost-benefit criterion, together with compensation through the tax system, can deliver a preferred outcome for every party.

The one telling argument in favour of majority voting is its simplicity. It is much easier to take a majority vote than to gather detailed information about what different individuals would be willing to pay for their preferred alternatives. Much progress has been made in recent years in the design of mechanisms that induce people to reveal truthfully what their valuations are. But these mechanisms remain cumbersome, and it is a lot easier to allow people to reveal their preferences by their votes. And in many situations, of course, majority voting and cost-benefit analysis will lead to the same outcome anyway.

18.4 RENT SEEKING

As a practical matter, the gains from public choices are often large and concentrated in the hands of a few, whereas the costs, while also large, are spread among many. The difficulty such situations create for the public is clear. The prospective beneficiaries of a public program have powerful incentives to lobby government in favour of it, while each of the prospective losers has too little at stake to bother about. The result, all too frequently, is that projects are approved even when their benefits do not exceed their costs.

A related difficulty arises in the case of similar projects whose benefits do exceed their costs. Because there are large gains to be had from the project, private parties are willing to spend large sums in order to enhance their odds of being chosen as its beneficiaries. Pursuit of these gains goes by the name of ***rent seeking***. One consequence of rent seeking is that the expected gains from government projects are often squandered by the competition among potential beneficiaries.

Rent seeking
Unproductive expenditure of resources made in an effort to gain control of a scarce resource or right.

Consider, for example, a local government faced with the task of awarding the city's food services contract. Assume that the franchisee can expect to earn substantial monopoly profits. The likelihood of any applicant being awarded the franchise is an increasing function of the amount of money it spends lobbying local councillors. The lure of the franchise's expected profits thus causes applicants to engage in a lobbying war to win the franchise. And as the following example illustrates, such lobbying wars tend to dissipate much of the gains made possible by the project.

EXAMPLE 18-3

Three firms have met the application deadline for the Melonville food services contract for the coming year. The annual fixed cost of operating the system is 25, and the marginal cost per meal is 10. The demand curve for its services is given by $P = 60 - Q$, where P is the price per meal and Q is the number of meals. The franchise lasts for exactly one year and permits the franchisee to charge whatever price it chooses. The city council will choose the applicant that spends the most money lobbying city council members. If the applicants cannot collude, how much will each spend on lobbying?

The winner will set the monopoly price for the service, which is the price that corresponds to the quantity at which marginal revenue equals marginal cost. Marginal revenue for food services is given by $MR = 60 - 2Q$, and marginal cost is 10. The profit-maximizing quantity will thus be 25, which gives rise to a price of 35. Total revenue will be 35(25) = 875, which makes for a profit of 875 − 275 = 600. If any applicant spends more on lobbying than the other two spend, it will win the franchise. If all three spend the same, each applicant will have a 1-in-3 chance of earning 600 in profit, which means an expected profit of 200. If the lobbyists could collude, each would agree to spend the same small, token amount on lobbying. But in the absence of a binding agreement, each will be strongly tempted to try to outspend the others. If each firm's spending reaches 200, each will have expected profits of zero (a one-third chance to earn 600, minus the 200 spent on lobbying). At this point, it might seem foolish to bid any further, because higher spending levels would mean an expected loss. And yet if any one of the three spent 201, while the other two stayed at 200, it would get the franchise for sure and earn a net profit of 399. The losers would each have losses of 200. Rather than face a sure loss of 200, the losers may well find it attractive to bid 201 themselves. Where this process will stop is anyone's guess.[3] The one thing that seems certain is that it will dissipate some or all of the gains that could have been had from the project. From the viewpoint of any individual firm, it is perfectly rational to lobby in this fashion for a chance to win government benefits. From the standpoint of society as a whole, however, such activity is almost completely wasteful. The efficient government is one that takes every feasible step to discourage rent seeking—for example, by selecting contractors on the basis of the price they promise to charge, not on the amount they lobby.

18.5 INCOME DISTRIBUTION

In market economies, the main means of earning income is by selling factors of production. Some people, by far the minority, earn a significant portion of their income from the ownership of stocks, bonds, and other financial instruments. Most people depend primarily on the proceeds from the sale of their own labour.

This system of distributing incomes is far from perfect, but it does have several attractive properties. First, under conditions of perfect competition and constant returns to scale, it leads to a determinate outcome: the theory of competitive factor markets tells us that each factor will be paid the value of its marginal product, and that in long-run

---

[3]The following experiment provides some relevant evidence. A $1 coin is auctioned off subject to the following rules. The dollar goes to the highest bidder, who must pay the auctioneer the amount he bid. The second-highest bidder gets nothing, but must also pay the auctioneer the amount he bid. In a typical trial of this auction, the bids slowly approach fifty cents, at which point there is a pause. Then the second bidder offers more than fifty cents and the bids quickly escalate to $1. There is another pause at $1, whereafter the second bidder bids more than $1, and the bids again quickly escalate. It is not uncommon for the winning bid to exceed several dollars.

competitive equilibrium, these payments will add up to exactly the total product available for distribution.[4] Given the obvious potential for claims to exceed available output in any system, the fact that the marginal productivity scheme clearly identifies a feasible payment for every party is no small advantage. A second attractive feature of the marginal productivity system is that it rewards initiative, effort, and risk taking. The harder, longer, and more effectively a person works, the more she will be paid. And if she risks her capital on a venture that happens to succeed, she will reap a handsome dividend.

The Rawlsian Criticism of the Marginal Productivity System

The marginal productivity system is not without flaws, however. The most common criticism is that it often generates a high degree of inequality. Those who do well in the marketplace end up with vastly more than they can spend, while those who fail often cannot meet even their basic needs. Such inequality might be easier to accept if it were strictly the result of differences in effort. But it is not. Talent plays an important role in most endeavours, and although it can be nurtured and developed if you have it, whether you have it in the first place is essentially a matter of luck.

Even having abundant talent is no guarantee of doing well. It is also necessary to have the *right* talent. Being able to hit a baseball out of the park regularly will earn you millions annually, while being the best fourth-grade teacher in the country will earn you little; and being the best handball player in the world will earn you virtually nothing. The baseball star earns so much more, not because he works harder or has more talent, but because he is lucky enough to be good at something people are willing to pay a lot for.

John Rawls, a Harvard moral philosopher, constructed a cogent ethical critique of the marginal productivity system, one based heavily on the microeconomic theory of choice itself.[5] The question he asked was "What constitutes a just distribution of income?" To answer it, he proposed the following thought experiment. Imagine that you and the other citizens of some country have been thrown together in a meeting to choose the rules for distributing income. This meeting takes place behind a "veil of ignorance," which conceals from each person any knowledge of what talents and abilities he and others have. No individual knows whether he is smart or dull, strong or weak, fast or slow, and so on—which means that no one knows which particular rules of distribution would work to his own advantage. Rawls argued that the rules people would choose in such a state of ignorance would necessarily be fair; and if the rules are fair, it follows that the distribution to which they give rise will also be fair.

What rules would people choose from behind a veil of ignorance? If the national income to be distributed were a fixed amount every year, it is likely that most would choose to give everyone an equal share. This is likely, Rawls argued, because most people are strongly risk averse. Since an unequal distribution would involve not only a chance of doing well, but also a chance of doing poorly, most people would prefer to eliminate the risk by choosing an equal distribution.

The difficulty, however, is that the total amount of income available for distribution is *not* a fixed amount every year. Rather, it depends on how hard people work, how much initiative and risk they take, and so on. If everyone were guaranteed an equal share of

---

[4]Recall that long-run competitive equilibrium occurs at the minimum point of every firm's long-run average cost curve; at that point there are constant returns in production. It is a property of production functions with constant returns that $F(K, L) = K\partial F/\partial K + L\partial F/\partial L$, which says that paying each factor its marginal product will exactly exhaust the total product available.

[5]John Rawls, *A Theory of Justice*, Cambridge MA: Harvard University Press, 1971.

the national income at the outset, why would anyone work hard or take risks? Without rewards for hard work and risk taking, national income would be dramatically smaller than if such rewards existed. Of course, material rewards for effort and risk taking necessarily lead to inequality. But Rawls argues that people would be willing to accept a certain degree of inequality as long as these rewards produced a sufficiently large increase in the total amount of output available for distribution.

How much inequality? Much less than the amount produced by purely competitive factor markets, Rawls argued. The idea is that each person behind the veil of ignorance would rationally fear being in a disadvantaged position, and so each would choose distributional rules that would maximize the income of the poorest citizen. That is, additional inequality would be considered justified as long as it had the effect of raising the income of each and every citizen. Rawls's own critics responded that his proposal was unrealistically conservative—that most people would allow additional inequality if the effect, say, were to increase *most* incomes. But Rawls's basic point was that people behind a veil of ignorance would choose rules that would produce a more equal distribution of income than we get under the marginal productivity system. And since these choices define what constitutes a just distribution of income, he argued, fairness requires at least some attempt to reduce the inequality produced by the marginal productivity system.

Practical Reasons for Redistribution

The moral argument Rawls outlined has obvious force. But there are also compelling practical reasons for limiting inequality. We saw, for example, that an equal tax levied on every citizen will in general result in an inefficient level of public goods. To the extent that willingness to pay for government-provided public goods increases with income, high-income citizens will have a self-interested reason to support a tax structure in which they carry a much larger share of the tax burden than the poor do. And to the extent that the public goods financed under such a tax system are equally available to persons of different income levels, the effect will be to reduce inequality.

There is another practical reason for income redistribution at the society-wide level. It is obviously advantageous to occupy a position in the upper portion of society's income distribution. Such positions exist, however, only if there are others willing to occupy positions in the lower portion of the income distribution. Society has a clear interest in forging terms on which all members will view it as in their interests to remain part of society. If experience is any guide, social cohesion may simply not be possible without some attempt to compensate people for the implicit burden of occupying low positions in the overall distribution of income.

Fairness and Efficiency

We saw that efforts to reduce inequality may be justified on the basis of both moral and practical arguments. Some mix of such arguments has apparently been found compelling, for no modern economy leaves income distribution entirely to the marketplace. This underlying commitment to norms of equality is strong and plays a pivotal role in almost every debate on public policy.

The economist's natural advantage lies in answering questions related to efficiency. For this reason, many economists are reluctant even to discuss issues related to equity. Yet virtually every policy change will affect not only efficiency, but also the distribution of income. And we know that most societies seem prepared to reject efficient allocations if they do not pass muster on grounds of fairness. The result is that unless economists are prepared to work within social constraints on inequality, there will be little or no audience for their policy recommendations.

During a supply interruption of some important commodity, for example, economists typically recommend letting the price rise to market-clearing levels. We know, after all, that this policy will normally lead to an efficient allocation of the scarce good. The social concern, however, is that sharply rising prices will impose an unacceptable burden on the poor. If inefficient methods of addressing this distributional concern are adopted, however, ironically the economic pie becomes smaller for everyone, rich and poor alike. The goals of fairness and efficiency need not be in conflict. Given a suitable choice of initial endowments, *any* Pareto-efficient allocation is sustainable as a competitive equilibrium. When economists recommend a policy on grounds of efficiency, they must *also* be prepared to explain how its distributional consequences can be altered to meet social constraints.

The methods by which society redistributes income are subject to the same kinds of analysis that economists bring to bear on other programs and institutions. Our principal concern must be that poorly designed redistributive programs can easily undo the very efficiency gains they were created to facilitate.

Independently of particular political convictions, society has a common interest—both moral and practical—in redistributing income in ways that do not undermine efficiency. Many current redistributive programs are costly and less than fully effective. Microeconomic analysis has as much to teach us about the reform of these programs as it does about the many other important policy issues we've examined throughout this text.

- Public goods are like other goods in that their value can be measured by what people would be willing to pay to have more of them. But whereas the aggregate demand curve for a private good is formed by adding the individual demand curves horizontally, the aggregate marginal willingness-to-pay curve for a public good is the vertical summation of the corresponding individual curves. This difference exists because the quantity of a public good must be the same for every consumer, and because public goods are characterized by nondiminishability. In the private case, in contrast, the price is the same for different buyers, who then select different quantities.

- There is a clear analogy between the demand for public goods and the demand for jointly produced private goods. To produce additional chicken wings, it is necessary to produce additional drumsticks. Just as the quantity of a public good must be the same for all consumers, so must the quantity of chicken wings consumed be exactly equal to the quantity of drumsticks consumed. And just as the price one person is willing to pay for a given quantity of a public good can differ from what another is willing to pay, so will the price of drumsticks generally be different from the price of wings.

- As with private goods, the supply curve of a public good is simply the marginal cost of producing it. The optimal quantity of a public good is the level for which the aggregate marginal willingness-to-pay curve intersects the supply curve. In order to pay for the optimal quantities of public goods, it will generally be necessary for individual tax payments to vary directly with the amounts that individuals are willing to pay for public goods. To the extent that people with higher incomes demand higher quantities of public goods and that these goods are provided through government, both rich and poor will favour a tax system that places a larger share of the total tax burden on the rich.

- The mere fact that a good has the characteristics of a public good does not mean that it must necessarily be provided by government. There are a number of schemes, ranging from free commercial television to highly structured collective legal contracts, whereby public goods are provided with little direct government involvement.

- Problems similar to those that arise in connection with public goods are encountered whenever there are significant indivisibilities or economies of scale in the production of private consumption goods. In such situations, we saw, clubs can form in which members share the costs of important consumption goods. The tradeoff confronting a potential member of such a club can be viewed as one between cost savings and reduced privacy in the use of the good.

- Majority voting sometimes produces intransitive rankings among projects. When it does, the power to choose the order in which different pairs of alternatives are considered is often tantamount to the power to determine the final outcome. There is a special class of issues in which majority voting is not vulnerable to agenda manipulation. With respect to single issues in which each voter ranks every alternative in terms of its distance from his ideal choice, the final outcome will be the one most preferred by the median voter, no matter what order the votes are taken in. This result is known as the median voter theorem.

- Cost-benefit analysis is a simple but very powerful alternative to majority voting. Applied in the proper way to a sufficiently large number of small decisions, it almost always satisfies the Pareto criterion.

- A problem that plagues all mechanisms of public decision making is that self-interested parties have an incentive to influence outcomes in their own favour. This problem goes by the name of rent seeking and has become an increasingly serious threat to our social welfare.

- The primary mechanism for distributing income in market economies is the factor market. People sell their labour in return for a payment equal to the value of its marginal product. And they invest their savings at interest rates that are similarly linked to the marginal productivity of capital. This method of income distribution has several desirable properties on efficiency grounds—in particular, it rewards effort and the willingness to incur risk. But critics, notably John Rawls, have argued that people would never voluntarily choose to live under a process that yields such highly unequal outcomes as we see in untempered factor markets.

- In addition to the moral argument Rawls offered, there are at least two practical reasons for income redistribution. First, the rich would favour paying more than an equal share of the total tax burden because otherwise they would end up with an inefficiently small provision of public goods. And second, redistribution may be necessary to maintain a voluntary sense of social cohesion, something as much in the interests of the rich as of the poor.

- Our current array of welfare programs is costly, not only because of bureaucratic duplication, but also because of its indirect effects on work incentives and on public policies with respect to private markets. The reform of redistributive programs requires attention to both fairness and efficiency.

QUESTIONS FOR REVIEW

1. Why are the individual marginal willingness-to-pay curves added vertically, not horizontally, to get the aggregate marginal willingness-to-pay curve for a public good?
2. How are jointly produced private goods analogous to public goods?
3. Why would even rich citizens be likely to oppose having equal tax payments by rich and poor alike?
4. In what way does a private good produced under conditions of increasing returns to scale resemble a public good? Describe the tradeoff between flexibility and cost that confronts users of such goods.
5. How can majority voting lead to intransitive social rankings?
6. Describe two forms of inefficiency associated with rent seeking.

PROBLEMS

1. A government is trying to decide how much of a public good (a park) to provide. The marginal willingness-to-pay curves for each of its two citizens are as given in the diagram. The marginal cost curve for the public good is given by $MC = Q/2$, where MC is in dollars per hectare and Q is the number of hectares. There is also a fixed cost of $10 associated with production of the good.
   a. What is the optimal size of the park?
   b. If both citizens must be taxed equally to provide the good, will it receive a majority vote?

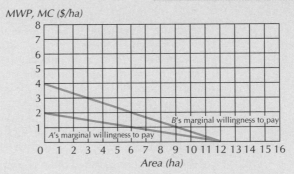

2. On the assumption that the park described in Problem 1 is provided at the optimal size, how much should the government charge each citizen each time he or she uses the public good?

3. Ten identical consumers all have individual marginal willingness-to-pay curves $MWP_i = 5 - .05Q$ for a public good, where MWP_i is measured in dollars per unit and Q is measured in units. Construct and graph the aggregate marginal willingness-to-pay curve. When $Q = 50$ units, what is the maximum each individual would be willing to pay for an additional unit? What is the total benefit to each individual when $Q = 50$ units?

4. Consider the situation described in Problem 3, but now assume that the marginal cost of providing the public good is $MC = .5Q$, where MC is in dollars per unit. Determine the optimal level of provision of the public good.

5. Chicken wings and chicken drumsticks are jointly produced private goods. The introduction of Wildfire Wings—the fast-food sensation—has led to a sharp increase in the demand for chicken wings. Show how this affects the equilibrium price and quantity of drumsticks.

6. Lumber and sawdust are joint products, whose demand functions are D_L and D_S, as shown in the diagram below. The quantity axis measures the number of trees. Points on the demand schedules indicate demands for the lumber or sawdust equivalents of a given quantity of trees.
   a. Provide an economic interpretation of the fact that the demand schedule for sawdust extends below the horizontal axis.
   b. If the supply schedule for trees is as given in the diagram, show the equilibrium prices and quantities of sawdust and lumber on a graph.

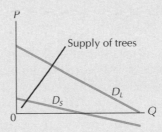

7. Viewer-supported television stations often give contributors "free" gifts for making contributions at various levels. ("Two handsome *'Television that matters'* coffee mugs for a donation of $120.") Based on what you know about the psychology of framing decisions (see Chapter 8), explain why this practice might help stations raise more money.

8. Colleges and universities sometimes name buildings and business or medical schools after substantial donors. Meanwhile, few donors care to earmark their gifts for routine maintenance of university buildings. How might the social benefits of charitable giving explain these observations?

9. The marginal willingness-to-pay (MWP) curve for a public good of each of 4 identical individuals is given by the equation $MWP_i = 10 - .1Q$, where MWP_i is in dollars per unit and Q is in units. It has been determined that the public good must be provided by the government. There are no fixed costs of providing the public good, and the marginal cost of providing it is $40 per unit. Each individual pays an equal share of the tax needed to pay for the public good.

a. Give the equation of the aggregate marginal willingness-to-pay (AMWP) curve, and calculate the optimal level of provision of the public good, the total benefit to each individual, the aggregate total benefit, the total cost of the public good, the tax per person to pay for it, the net benefit to each individual, and the aggregate net benefit.

b. Suppose that the situation is the same except that there are 5 identical individuals with the same MWP_i curve. Give the answers to part 9a on this assumption, and compare your results.

c. Suppose that the situation is the same except that there are *100* identical individuals with the same MWP_i curve. Give the answers to part 9a on this assumption, and compare your results.

10. Suppose that the taxes required to finance provision of the public good in the preceding question result in allocative inefficiencies amounting to $10 for every $40 raised in taxes, and that there are 100 identical individuals with $MWP_i = 10 - .1Q$. Does this mean that the public good should not be provided? If so, explain. If not, explain and indicate whether there should be any change in the amount of the public good that is provided, to address the inefficiency problem.

11. Three clubs with 20 members each are about to vote on the Clubs Representative to Student Council. Arnold, Bo, and Chuck are the three candidates. Members of each club have the ranking schemes given in the table:

Club	Best	Next best	Last
Archery	Arnold	Bo	Chuck
Bowling	Bo	Chuck	Arnold
Chess	Chuck	Arnold	Bo

The tradition is to pit two candidates against each other and then pit the winner of that contest against the third candidate. If you were in the Archery Club, whom would you pair off in the preliminary round? If you were in the Bowling Club?

ANSWERS TO IN-CHAPTER EXERCISES

18-1. The aggregate marginal willingness-to-pay curve would be AMWP $= 120 - 2Q$, the vertical summation of the individual marginal willingness-to-pay curves (see graph). At $Q =$ 30 minutes, each individual would be willing to pay up to $MWP_i = 12 - \frac{1}{5}Q = 12 - \frac{1}{5}(30)$ $= \$6$ for an additional minute, for a total of $60 per minute from 10 consumers. The total benefit each receives is $30[(12 + 6)/2] = \$270$, or $2700 for all 10 consumers.

18-2. To find the optimal duration of the concert, equate the aggregate marginal willingness-to-pay $P = 120 - 2Q$ and the marginal cost $MC = 2Q$ to find $Q = 30$ minutes.

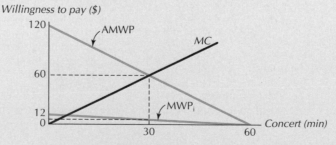

If $MC = Q$, then (setting $P = 120 - 2Q = Q = MC$) the optimal duration of the concert becomes 40 minutes. (As an exercise, graph this result.)

18-3. Again, Eve is the median voter. The alternative closest to her ideal percentage is 20, and this will win a majority in a vote on any pair of alternatives.

GLOSSARY

Accounting profit   Total revenue minus total explicit costs incurred.

Adverse selection   Process by which the less desirable potential trading partners volunteer to exchange.

Affordable set   Bundles on or below the budget constraint; bundles for which the required expenditure at given prices is less than or equal to the income available.

Allocative efficiency   A condition in which all possible gains from exchange are realized.

Allocative function of price The process whereby price acts as a signal that guides resources away from the production of goods whose prices lie below cost toward the production of goods whose prices exceed cost.

Arbitrage   The purchase of something for costless risk-free resale at a higher price.

Average benefit   The average benefit of undertaking *n* units of an activity is the total benefit of the activity divided by *n*.

Average cost   The average cost of undertaking *n* units of an activity is the total cost of the activity divided by *n*.

Average factor cost (AFC) Another name for the supply curve for an input.

Average fixed cost (AFC)   Fixed cost divided by the quantity of output.

Average product   Total output divided by the quantity of the variable input.

Average total cost (ATC) Total cost divided by the quantity of output.

Average variable cost (AVC) Variable cost divided by the quantity of output.

Bertrand duopoly model An industry in which two firms produce identical goods and each firm chooses its price taking its rival's price as given.

Best affordable bundle   The most preferred bundle of those that are affordable.

Black market   An illegal market, set up to facilitate transactions prohibited by law.

Budget constraint   The set of all bundles that can be purchased with given income and prices, if all income is spent.

Bundle   A particular combination of two or more goods.

Certainty equivalent value The certainty equivalent value of a gamble is the sum of money for which an individual would be indifferent between receiving that sum and taking the gamble.

Chain index   Single price index series created by splicing together two or more overlapping series based on different reference years with different quantity weights.

Coase theorem   When the parties affected by externalities can negotiate costlessly with one another, an efficient outcome results no matter how the law assigns responsibility for damages.

Collective good   A good that is excludable but has a high degree of nondiminishability.

Commitment device   A device that commits a person to behave in a certain way in the future, even though he may wish to behave otherwise when the time comes.

Compensating variation for a price change   The change in money income that would enable a consumer to attain the *original* level of utility at the *new* set of prices.

Composite good   A hypothetical construct representing all *other* goods on which income could be spent, with their prices relative to each other held constant.

Constant returns to scale   The property of a production process whereby a proportional increase in every input yields an equal proportional increase in output.

Consumer surplus   A dollar measure of the extent to which a consumer benefits from participating in a transaction.

Contract curve   A curve along which all final, voluntary contracts must lie.

Corner solution   In a choice between two goods, a case in which the consumer does not consume one of the goods.

Costly-to-fake principle   For a signal to an adversary to be credible, it must be costly to fake.

Cournot model   An industry in which firms produce identical goods and each firm determines its profit-maximizing output level, taking its rivals' current output levels as given.

Cross-price elasticity of demand The percentage change in the quantity of one good demanded that results from a 1 percent change in the price of another good.

Decreasing returns to scale   The property of a production process whereby a proportional increase in every input yields a less than proportional increase in output.

Diminishing marginal utility For a utility function defined by wealth, one in which the marginal utility declines as wealth rises.

Dominant strategy   A strategy in a game that (if it exists) produces the best outcome for a player regardless of the strategy chosen by the other player.

Economic efficiency   Producing a given level of output at minimum cost.

Economic profit   Total revenue minus total explicit and *implicit costs* incurred.

Economic rent   The difference between what a factor of production is paid and the minimum amount necessary to induce it to remain in its current use.

Edgeworth exchange box   A diagram used to analyze the general equilibrium of an exchange economy.

Edgeworth production box A diagram used to analyze feasible and efficient quantities of two outputs using fixed quantities of two inputs.

Engel curve A curve that plots the relationship between the quantity of a good consumed and income.

Equivalent variation for a price change The change in money income that would enable a consumer to attain the *new* level of utility at the *original* set of prices.

Excess demand The amount by which quantity demanded exceeds quantity supplied at a given price.

Excess supply The amount by which quantity supplied exceeds quantity demanded at a given price.

Expected utility The expected utility of a gamble is the expected value of utility over all possible outcomes.

Expected value The weighted sum of all possible outcomes, with each outcome weighted by its probability of occurrence.

External cost of an activity A cost that is generated by an activity and that falls on people who are not directly involved in the activity.

Externality Either a benefit or a cost of an action that accrues to someone other than the people directly involved in the action.

Fair gamble A gamble whose expected value is zero.

Fixed cost (FC) Cost that does not vary with the level of output in the short run.

Free riding Choosing not to donate to a cause but still benefiting from the donations of others.

Full-disclosure principle Individuals must disclose even unfavourable qualities about themselves, lest their silence be taken to mean that they have something even worse to hide.

General equilibrium analysis The study of how conditions in each market in a set of related markets affect equilibrium outcomes in other markets in that set.

Gross complement A good Y is a gross complement of good X if the

total effect of an increase (decrease) in the price of X is a decrease (increase) in the quantity of Y demanded.

Gross substitute A good Y is a gross substitute for good X if the *total* effect of an increase (decrease) in the price of X is an increase (decrease) in the quantity of Y demanded.

Hurdle model of price discrimination Price discrimination using an obstacle that must be surmounted to become eligible for a discount price.

Income effect That component of the total effect of a price change that results from the associated change in real purchasing power.

Income elasticity of demand The percentage change in the quantity of a good demanded that results from a 1 percent change in income.

Income-consumption curve (ICC) Holding the prices of all goods constant, the ICC is the set of optimal bundles traced on an indifference map as money income varies.

Increasing returns to scale The property of a production process whereby a proportional increase in every input yields a more than proportional increase in output.

Indifference curve A set of bundles among which the consumer is indifferent.

Indifference map A representative sample of the set of a consumer's indifference curves, used as a graphical summary of her preference ordering.

Insider trading Using privileged information that will affect the price of a company's stock before the information has been made public, to conduct personally advantageous transactions.

Interest The sum paid by a borrower to a lender in addition to repayment of the principal amount of a loan, to compensate the lender for the opportunity cost of not having the use of the principal during the loan period.

Intermediate products Products that are transformed by a production process into products of greater value.

Isoquant The set of all technically efficient input combinations that yield a given level of output.

Law of demand The empirical observation that when the price of a product falls, people demand larger quantities of it.

Law of diminishing returns If other inputs are fixed, the increase in output from an increase in the variable input must eventually decline.

Law of large numbers A statistical law that says that if an event happens independently with probability p in each of N instances, the proportion of cases in which the event occurs approaches p as N grows larger.

Law of supply The empirical observation that when the price of a product rises, firms offer more of it for sale.

Limit pricing/output strategy A strategy whereby an incumbent sets its output level so that the market price is just low enough to keep out a potential entrant with given fixed costs of entry.

Long run The shortest period of time required to alter the amounts of all inputs used in a production process.

Marginal benefit The increase in total benefit that results from carrying out one additional unit of an activity.

Marginal cost (MC) The increase in total cost that results from carrying out one additional unit of an activity.

Marginal factor cost (MFC) The amount by which total factor cost changes with the employment of an additional unit of input.

Marginal product Change in total product due to a one-unit change in the variable input.

Marginal rate of substitution (MRS) At any point on an indifference curve, the rate at which the consumer is willing to exchange the good measured along the vertical axis for the good measured along the horizontal axis; equal to the negative of the value of the slope of the indifference curve.

Marginal rate of technical substitution (MRTS) The rate at which one input can be exchanged for another without altering the total level of output.

Marginal rate of time preference (MRTP) The number of units of consumption in the future a consumer would exchange for one unit of consumption in the present.

Marginal rate of transformation (MRT) The rate at which one output can be transformed into another at a point along the production possibilities frontier.

Marginal revenue (MR) The change in total revenue that occurs as a result of a one-unit change in quantity sold.

Marginal revenue product (MRP) The amount by which total revenue changes with the employment of an additional unit of an input.

Market failure Situation in which the unaided operation of the market mechanism results in an inefficient allocation of resources.

Median voter The voter whose ideal outcome lies at or just above the ideal outcomes of half the voters.

Microeconomics The study of how people choose under conditions of scarcity.

Minimax strategy Choosing the option that minimizes the maximum loss (maximizes the minimum gain) one receives.

Monopolistic competition An industry in which each of a number of firms produces a product that is an imperfect substitute for the products of the other firms and where there is free entry and exit of firms.

Monopoly A market served by a single seller of a product with no close substitutes.

Moral hazard The incentive for people to change their behaviour in a situation where the behaviour cannot be costlessly observed and they do not bear all of the costs of the changed behaviour.

Nash equilibrium The combination of strategies in a game such that no player has an incentive to change strategies, given the strategy adopted by each of his opponents.

Natural monopoly An industry whose market output is produced at the lowest cost when production is concentrated in the hands of a single firm.

Net complement A good Y is a net complement of good X if the *substitution* effect of an increase (decrease) in the price of X is a decrease (increase) in the quantity of Y demanded.

Net substitute A good Y is a net substitute for good X if the *substitution* effect of an increase (decrease) in the price of X is an increase (decrease) in the quantity of Y demanded.

Normative question A question regarding the action that *should* be taken in a particular situation, in relation to given ethical criteria.

Oligopoly An industry in which there are only a few important sellers.

Opportunity cost The cost of taking an action, as measured by the benefit forgone by not taking the best alternative action.

Optimality condition for a monopolist A monopolist maximizes profit by choosing the level of output where marginal revenue equals marginal cost.

Output expansion path The locus of tangencies (minimum-cost input combinations) traced out by an isocost line of given slope as it shifts outward into the isoquant map for a production process.

Pareto optimal The term used to describe situations in which it is impossible to make one person better off without making at least one other worse off.

Pareto-superior allocation An allocation that at least one individual prefers and others like at least as well.

Peak-load pricing The practice whereby higher prices are charged for goods or services during which the periods in which they are consumed most intensively.

Pecuniary economy A decrease in production cost that occurs when an expansion of industry output causes a fall in the prices of inputs.

Pecuniary diseconomy A rise in production cost that occurs when an expansion of industry output causes a rise in the prices of inputs.

Permanent income The present value of lifetime income.

Positional good A good whose value depends strongly on how it compares with similar goods consumed by others; also called a *status good*.

Positive question A question regarding the probable consequences of taking a specific action in a particular situation.

Pre-emptive action An initial action, taken by one player in a sequential game, that restricts the strategic options available to other players.

Preference ordering A scheme whereby the consumer ranks all possible consumption bundles in order of preference.

Present-aim standard of rationality A theory that says rational people act efficiently in pursuit of whatever objectives they hold at the moment of choice.

Present value The present value of a payment of X dollars T years from now is $X/(1+r)^T$, where r is the annual rate of interest.

Price ceiling Government-fixed *maximum* price that can be charged for a good.

Price elasticity of demand The percentage change in the quantity of a good demanded that results from a 1 percent change in its price.

Price-consumption curve (PCC) Holding money income and the prices of all other goods constant, the PCC for a good X is the set of optimal bundles traced on an indifference map as the price of X varies.

Price support Program where the government sets a minimum (*floor*) price for a good and guarantees to purchase the good at that price.

Principal–agent situation A situation in which one economic actor (the principal) contracts with another (the agent) to act on the principal's behalf, and where the economic interests of the two parties may not coincide.

Producer surplus The difference between total revenue and variable cost at a given level of output; equivalently, the sum of fixed cost and economic profit.

Production function   A means of describing the technically efficient quantities of output corresponding to all possible combinations of inputs.

Production possibilities frontier   The set of output combinations such that (with a fixed endowment of factor inputs) the production of each good is maximized for any given level of efficient production of all other goods.

Pure public good   A good that has a high degree of nondiminishability and nonexcludability.

Rationing function of price   The process whereby price directs existing supplies of a product to the users who value it most highly.

Reaction function   A curve that tells the profit-maximizing level of output for one oligopolist for each amount supplied by another.

Real price of a product   Its price relative to the prices of other goods and services.

Rent seeking   Unproductive expenditure of resources made in an effort to gain control of a scarce resource or right.

Reservation price of activity *x*   The price at which a person would be indifferent between doing *x* and not doing *x*.

Risk averse   Preferences described by a utility function with diminishing marginal utility of wealth.

Risk neutral   Preferences described by a utility function with constant marginal utility of wealth.

Risk premium   A payment differential necessary to compensate the supplier of a good or service for having to endure risk.

Risk seeking   Preferences described by a utility function with increasing marginal utility of wealth.

Self-interest standard of rationality   A theory that says rational people consider only costs and benefits that accrue directly to themselves.

Short run   The longest period of time during which at least one of the inputs used in a production process cannot be varied.

Shutdown condition   If price falls below the minimum of average variable cost, the firm should shut down in the short run.

Signalling   Communication that conveys information.

Single-peaked preferences   Preferences that exhibit a single most-preferred outcome, with other outcomes ranked lower as their distances from the most-preferred outcome increase.

Stackelberg model   An industry in which one firm (the Stackelberg leader) sets its profit-maximizing level of output first, knowing that its rival (the Stackelberg follower) will behave as a Cournot duopolist.

Substitution effect   That component of the total effect of a change in the price of a good that results from the associated change in the relative attractiveness of other goods.

Sunk costs   Past expenditures that can no longer be recovered at the time of making a decision.

Technical efficiency   Attaining the maximum possible output from a given combination of inputs.

Technological obsolescence   The process by which a good loses value not because of physical depreciation, but because improvements in technology make substitute products more attractive.

Total cost (TC)   All costs of production: the sum of variable cost and fixed cost.

Total factor cost (TFC)   The product of the employment level of an input and its average factor cost.

Total product curve   A curve showing the amount of output as a function of the amount of a variable input.

Two-part pricing   Pricing system with a fixed access fee and a charge per unit of a good purchased.

Value of marginal product (VMP)   The value, at current market prices, of the extra output produced by an additional unit of input.

Variable cost (VC)   Cost that varies with the level of output in the short run.

Weber-Fechner law   The property of perception whereby the just noticeable difference in a stimulus tends to be proportional to the value of the stimulus.

X-inefficiency   A condition in which a firm fails to obtain maximum output from a given combination of inputs.

INDEX